world's first & only
am/fm shortwave tuner with xm satellite radio

E1XM

The E1 XM is the world's first radio that combines AM, FM, Shortwave, and XM Satellite radio into one ultra high-performance unit. In collaboration with RL Drake Company and XM Satellite Radio, the E1 is the finest full-sized portable in the world.

etón®
www.etoncorp.com

2005 Passport® to

TABLE OF CONTENTS

6 World of World Band Radio
Map pinpoints stations, time zones.

Radio on Buddha's Turf

10 Thailand—Radio Active!
Little tiger, big signal.

30 Laos: Radio Under Fire
Bygone flamethrower, caveman radio.

Compleat Idiot's Guide to Getting Started

52 Ramping Up: Three World Band "Musts"
Eight pages and you're ready.

53 PASSPORT's Three-Minute Start
No time? Try this.

54 Setting Your World Time Clock
One time, one planet.

58 Best Times and Frequencies for 2005
Where to tune, day and night.

66 First Tries: Ten Easy Catches
Stations heard everywhere in English.

78 Ten of the Best: 2005's Top Shows
Aboriginal blues, venerated virgins.

404 Worldly Words
PASSPORT's glossary explains all.

What to Choose: PASSPORT REPORTS—2005

90 How to Choose a World Band Radio
What counts, what doesn't. Savvy shopping.

96 Portable Radios
More bang, less buck.

149 World Band Cassette Recorders
Tape shows while you're away.

152 Radios for Emergencies
No batteries needed.

156 Portatop Receivers
Tabletop results, portable price.

World Band Radio

TABLE OF CONTENTS

162 **Tabletop Receivers**
Tough radios snare tough signals.

175 **Build Your Own**
Weekend radio project, family fun.

184 **Professional Receivers**
Pass the Grey Poupon.

192 **Receivers for PCs**
True wireless for computers.

199 **Index to Tested Radios**
A-Z, by make and model.

200 **Skywave Lassos**
Serious antennas for serious receivers.

206 **Compact Antennas**
Have loop, will travel. Home, too.

227 **Index to Tested Antennas**
Big and little, indoor and out.

When and Where: WORLDSCAN®

228 **HOUR-BY-HOUR**
What's On Tonight?
Hourly guide to shows in English.

362 **COUNTRY-BY-COUNTRY**
Worldwide Broadcasts in English
Albania to Yemen.

384 **Voices from Home**
News for diaspora. Music for all.

414 **CHANNEL-BY-CHANNEL**
The Blue Pages
Quick-access to world band schedules.

Making Contact

288 **Addresses PLUS**
Internet, mail, phone, fax, who's who. What's sold, what's free.
Local times for each country.

International Broadcasting Services, Ltd.

ISSN 0897-0157

OUR READER IS THE MOST IMPORTANT PERSON IN THE WORLD!

Editorial

Editor in Chief	Lawrence Magne
Editor	Tony Jones
Assistant Editor	Craig Tyson
Consulting Editor	John Campbell
Founder Emeritus	Don Jensen
PASSPORT REPORTS	George Heidelman, Lawrence Magne, Dave Zantow, George Zeller
WorldScan® Contributors	Gabriel Iván Barrera (Argentina), James Conrad (U.S.), David Crystal (Israel), Alok Dasgupta (India), Graeme Dixon (New Zealand), Nicolás Eramo (Argentina), Paulo Roberto e Souza (Brazil), Alokesh Gupta (India), Jose Jacob (India), *Jembatan DX*/Juichi Yamada (Japan), Anatoly Klepov (Russia), Marie Lamb (U.S.), Célio Romais (Brazil), Nikolai Rudnev (Russia), David Walcutt (U.S.)
WorldScan® Software	Richard Mayell
Laboratory	Robert Sherwood
Artwork	Gahan Wilson, cover
Graphic Arts	Bad Cat Design; Mike Wright, layout
Printing	Tri-Graphic Printing

Administration

Publisher	Lawrence Magne
Associate Publisher	Jane Brinker
Offices	IBS North America, Box 300, Penn's Park PA 18943, USA; www.passband.com; Phone +1 (215) 598-9018; Fax +1 (215) 598 3794; mktg@passband.com
Advertising & Media Contact	Jock Elliott, IBS Ltd., Box 300, Penn's Park PA 18943, USA; Phone +1 (215) 598-9018; Fax +1 (215) 598 3794; media@passband.com

Bureaus

IBS Latin America	Tony Jones, Casilla 1844, Asunción, Paraguay; schedules@passband.com; Fax +1 (215) 598 3794
IBS Australia	Craig Tyson, Box 2145, Malaga WA 6062; Fax +61 (8) 9342 9158; addresses@passband.com
IBS Japan	Toshimichi Ohtake, 5-31-6 Tamanawa, Kamakura 247-0071; Fax +81 (467) 43 2167; ibsjapan@passband.com

Library of Congress Cataloging-in-Publication Data

Passport to World Band Radio.
1. Radio Stations, Shortwave—Directories. I. Magne, Lawrence
TK9956.P27 2004 384.54'5 04-22739
ISBN 0-914941-85-2

PASSPORT, PASSPORT TO WORLD BAND RADIO, *WorldScan*, *Radio Database International*, *RDI White Papers* and *White Papers* are among the registered trademarks of International Broadcasting Services, Ltd., in the United States, Canada, United Kingdom and various other parts of the world.

Opener credits: M. Guha (pp. 2, 3, 10, 30, 384); M. Wright (pp. 52, 66, 90, 96, 152, 156, 162, 184, 192, 200, 228, 288, 362, 404); R. Sherwood (p. 206); Corbis (p. 78, 414)

IC-R20
Dual watch & audio record!

150 kHz – 3.3 GHz* • AM, FM, WFM, USB, LSB, CW • 1250 Alphanumeric Memories • CTCSS/DTCS Decode • Dual Watch • Audio Recorder • Weather Alert • Dynamic Memory Scan • Icoms Hot 100 Preprogrammed TV & Shortwave Channels • Lithium Ion Power

IC-R10
Advanced performance!

500 kHz – 1.3 GHz* • AM, FM, WFM, USB, LSB, CW • 1000 Alphanumeric Memories • Attenuator • Backlit Display & Key Pad • Voice Scan Control • 7 Different Scan Modes • Beginner Mode • Band Scope • AA Ni-Cds & Charger

IC-R3
See & hear all the action!

• 500 kHz – 2.45 GHz* • AM, FM, WFM, AM-TV, FM-TV • 450 Alphanumeric Memories • CTCSS with Tone Scan • 4 Level Attenuator • Antenna with BNC Connector • 2" Color TFT Display with Video and Audio Output Jacks • Lithium Ion Power

IC-R5
Compact performance!

150 kHz – 1.3 GHz* • AM, FM, WFM • 1250 Alphanumeric Memories • CTCSS/DTCS Decode • Weather Alert • Dynamic Memory Scan • Icoms Hot 100 Preprogrammed TV & Shortwave Channels • Weather Resistant • 2 AA Ni-Cd Batteries

Tune in the world with Icom!

IC-R75
Pull out the weak signals! **DSP included, US models only!**

• 30 kHz - 60.0 MHz* • AM, FM, S-AM, USB, LSB, CW, RTTY • 101 Alphanumeric Memory Channels • Twin Passband Tuning (PBT) • Synchronous AM Detection (S-AM) • Optional DSP with Noise Reduction Auto Notch Filter • Triple Conversion • Up to Two Optional Filters • Front Mounted Speaker • Large Display • Well Spaced Keys and Dials • PC Remote Control with Optional Icom RSR75 Software for Windows® • And Many Other Features

All Icom receivers are PC programmable. See your dealer for details.

AMATEUR | AVIONIC | LAND MOBILE | MARINE | RECEIVER | WWW.ICOMAMERICA.COM

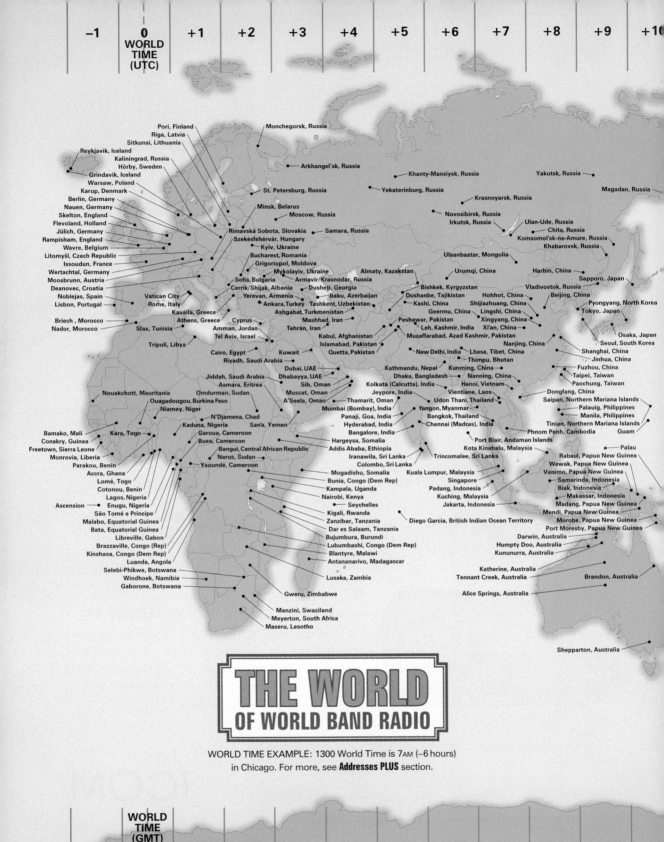

WORLD TIME EXAMPLE: 1300 World Time is 7AM (−6 hours) in Chicago. For more, see **Addresses PLUS** section.

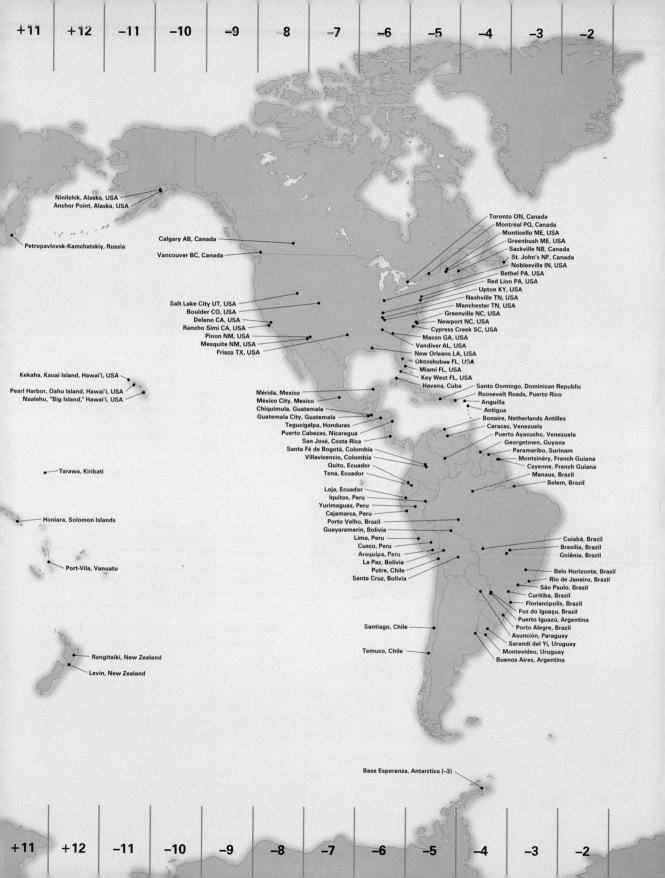

+11 +12 −11 −10 −9 −8 −7 −6 −5 −4 −3 −2

Ninilchik, Alaska, USA
Anchor Point, Alaska, USA

Petropavlovsk-Kamchatskiy, Russia

Calgary AB, Canada

Vancouver BC, Canada

Toronto ON, Canada
Montréal PQ, Canada
Monticello ME, USA
Greenbush ME, USA
Sackville NB, Canada
St. John's NF, Canada
Noblesville IN, USA
Bethel PA, USA
Red Lion PA, USA
Upton KY, USA
Nashville TN, USA
Manchester TN, USA
Greenville NC, USA
Newport NC, USA
Cypress Creek SC, USA
Macon GA, USA
Vandiver AL, USA
New Orleans LA, USA
Okeechobee FL, USA
Miami FL, USA
Key West FL, USA
Havana, Cuba

Salt Lake City UT, USA
Boulder CO, USA
Delano CA, USA
Rancho Simi CA, USA
Piñon NM, USA
Mesquite NM, USA
Frisco TX, USA

Kekaha, Kauai Island, Hawai'i, USA

Pearl Harbor, Oahu Island, Hawai'i, USA
Naalehu, "Big Island," Hawai'i, USA

Tarawa, Kiribati

Honiara, Solomon Islands

Port-Vila, Vanuatu

Santiago, Chile

Temuco, Chile

Rangitaiki, New Zealand

Levin, New Zealand

Mérida, Mexico
México City, Mexico
Chiquimula, Guatemala
Guatemala City, Guatemala
Tegucigalpa, Honduras
Puerto Cabezas, Nicaragua
San José, Costa Rica
Santa Fé de Bogotá, Colombia
Villavicencio, Colombia
Quito, Ecuador
Tena, Ecuador
Loja, Ecuador
Iquitos, Peru
Yurimaguas, Peru
Cajamarca, Peru
Porto Velho, Brazil
Guayaramerín, Bolivia
Lima, Peru
Cusco, Peru
Arequipa, Peru
La Paz, Bolivia
Putre, Chile
Santa Cruz, Bolivia

Santo Domingo, Dominican Republic
Roosevelt Roads, Puerto Rico
Anguilla
Antigua
Bonaire, Netherlands Antilles
Caracas, Venezuela
Puerto Ayacucho, Venezuela
Georgetown, Guyana
Paramaribo, Surinam
Montsinéry, French Guiana
Cayenne, French Guiana
Manaus, Brazil
Belem, Brazil

Cuiabá, Brazil
Brasília, Brazil
Goiânia, Brazil

Belo Horizonte, Brazil
Rio de Janeiro, Brazil
São Paulo, Brazil
Curitiba, Brazil
Florianópolis, Brazil
Foz do Iguaçu, Brazil
Puerto Iguazú, Argentina
Porto Alegre, Brazil
Asunción, Paraguay
Sarandí del Yí, Uruguay
Montevideo, Uruguay
Buenos Aires, Argentina

Base Esperanza, Antarctica (−3)

+11 +12 −11 −10 −9 −8 −7 −6 −5 −4 −3 −2

BE INFORMED
GLOBAL EVENTS DIRECT FROM THE SOURCE

E10
am/fm shortwave radio

Intelligent features that simplify. Performance that reaches out to the world. Imagine a radio that combines strong performance for fantastic reception and all of today's digital wizardry, bringing the world to your fingertips. The E10 is where intelligence meets performance.

- Shortwave range of 1711 – 29,999 KHz
- 550 programmable memories
- Memory page customization
- Manual & auto scan, tuning knob
- Direct keypad frequency entry, ATS
- IF shift (Intermediate Frequency)
- Shortwave antenna trimmer
- Sleep timer, snooze, and favorite station wake-up timers
- Includes AC adaptor/charger and 4 AA Ni-MH batteries
- Internally charges AA Ni-MH batteries
- Clean-design body with fine lines with metallic finish

Dimensions: 7.4"W x 4.5"H x 1.3"D **Weight:** 1lbs. 5oz.
Power Source: 4 AA batteries or included AC adaptor/charger

E100
am/fm shortwave radio

Fits into your palm or pocket, but fitted with full-sized features. Imagine a radio packed with all the bells and whistles: digital tuning AM, FM, Shortwave reception, and small enough to fit into your coat pocket. The E100 is a dream come true.

- Shortwave range of 1711 – 29,999 KHz
- 200 programmable memories with memory page customization
- Manual & auto scan, direct keypad frequency entry, tuning knob
- Programmable alarm & sleep functions with digital clock
- Clean-design body with fine lines & metallic finish

Dimensions: 4.9"W x 3"L x 1.2"D **Weight:** 7.4oz.
Power Source: 2 AA batteries (included) or AC adaptor (not included)

introducing etón elite series
high performance, feature packed, enthusiast savy

Thailand—
Radio
Active!

by Manosij Guha

Asia's "Land of Smiles" has stood serene for centuries. At the crossroads of the Indian Ocean and the South China Sea, it has been wooed by Dutch, British, Portuguese, French, Arab and Indian traders.

Historically, the unified kingdom of Siam was established in the mid-14th century. In 1930 the country was renamed Thailand, then a bloodless coup in 1932 led to a constitutional monarchy.

It is the only Southeast Asian nation never to have been colonized, thanks to a nimble foreign policy. During World War II, for example, it initially allied with Japan. But when Nippon's sun began to set, the kingdom did an about face. It became, and continues to be, friendly with the United States.

Temple Houses Early Radio

Like everything else in this monarchy, there is a royal twist to pioneering efforts. So it was with broadcasting.

Two experimental transmitters were inaugurated during the reign of King Chulalongkorn (Rama V) in the early 1900s. One, in Bangkok, was inside Wat Sa Ket, a Buddhist temple popularly known as the Golden Mount. The other was on Si Chang island in the Gulf of Siam, off the coast of Chonburi. Both were used by the Royal Thai Navy for ship-to-shore communication.

In 1919 the next monarch, King Vajiravudh (Rama VI) used these transmitters to proclaim the birth of broadcasting in Thailand. However, radio was perceived as a Western intrusion, so traditionalist resistance had to be overcome. It took nearly a decade before broadcasting became a reality.

The father of this glasnost was the ruler of Kamphaengphet, Prince Purachatra Jayagara, who in the early 1920s was also Minister of Commerce and Telecommunications. He had a natural technical bent, and was credited with introducing the telegraph and railroad to the kingdom. The prince installed a small transmitter in his palace and began experimental broadcasts using his voice accompanied by classical music. He was so pleased with the result that by 1927 he instructed his ministry to carry out further tests.

"The Radio Prince,"
Purachatra Jayagara.
PRD

Radio Thailand World Service uses powerful American transmitters.

Once home to Thailand's first public broadcaster, the Phyathai Palace is now a renowned hospital.
PRD

The Thailand-Burma Railway, immortalized in "Bridge on the River Kwai." About 16,000 British, Dutch, Australian and American POWs and 80,000 Asians died during construction in 1942-3. Edith Meier

However, the first regular transmission had to wait until May 31, 1929 when station 4PJ, carrying the prince's initials as part of its call sign, went on the air. Located near the Memorial Bridge in Bangkok, the transmitter used a mere 200 Watts on 37 meters. Later, a one kilowatt mediumwave AM transmitter supplemented this on 320 meters, call sign 11PJ.

"Broadcasting" originally was narrowcasting—not intended for general consumption but, rather, for royalty and its institutions. However, the Telegraph Act was amended in September, 1929 to allow the public to own radio receivers. To cater to this audience, the Post and Telegraph Department set up a new station, Radio Bangkok at Phyathai, within the palace of

the same name. It was inaugurated on February 25, 1930 to commemorate the coronation of King Prajadhipok (Rama VII).

From the regal Amarindravinitchai Throne Hall in the Grand Palace, His Majesty announced, "Radio broadcasting, which has been experimented for the past years, is meant to enhance education, trade and entertainment for members of the public." True broadcasting had finally arrived in this authoritarian but prosperous kingdom.

Starting in 1931, broadcasting became a state monopoly operated by the Royal Thai government. Following a coup in 1932 which changed the kingdom into a constitutional monarchy, the national radio station at Phyathai Palace was moved to suburban Bangkok. Renamed Radio Bangkok at Saladaeng, it had a new call sign, 7PJ, along with a beefier transmitter.

Thailand Pioneers World Band

Tests were also carried out on a shortwave transmitter, 8PJ, to reach an international audience. Its original antenna can still be seen at the Armed Forces Academics Preparatory School, near Lumphini Park, where the street continues to be called Withayu (Wireless) Road.

Initially, there were four stations. Besides Radio Bangkok, there were the experimental stations of the Post and Telegraph Department, the Military Signal Corps and the Territorial Army. In 1933, the Government Public Relations Department took over responsibility for broadcasting from Post and Telegraph.

War Boosts External Service

There was now a regular mediumwave AM service in Thai, an experimental mediumwave AM station, and a shortwave external service. On April 1, 1939 the 7PJ station's transmitter was upgraded to ten kilowatts and began service as the National Broadcasting Station of Thailand. It was financed by government grants and advertising revenues, with listener license fees being collected by the government until the fee system ended in 1952.

With World War II imminent, services were added in English and French to reach out to neighboring countries ruled by Britain and France. In keeping with the kingdom's neutrality, foreign dignitaries were invited to state their views over the air.

In 1942, as the war peaked, Burmese, Hindi, Japanese and Malay were added to the world band roster. These programs were simple and for only a few hours a day. Yet, they served as vital sources of information and entertainment throughout Asia.

The Public Relations Department's musical ensembles provided much-needed distraction during the dark years of war. The domestic services also aired an almost daily fare of drama and plays that reinforced Thai national feelings. This defiance was especially appreciated during the de facto Japanese occupation of the kingdom.

Broadcasting history scholar Adrian Peterson of the Ragusa Media Group witnessed much of what went on. He writes in "Japanese Occupation Radio—South East Asia":

"Although the original shortwave transmitters near Bangkok were quite low powered, just 2.5 kilowatts, a new international shortwave service in English was launched on October 20, 1938. This new programming from HSP5 & HS6PJ was beamed towards the United States, though there is no evidence that it was ever heard on the American mainland."

Peterson, back then based in Australia, adds, "Work began on the construction of a 100 kilowatt shortwave station at a new location, Nonthaburi, in 1941 and test broadcasts were noted early in the following year. Soon afterwards, the Japanese took over the operation of Radio Siam and a very

strong signal was noted in Australia. However it would seem that usage of the 100 kilowatt unit ended quite soon and the Japanese were then on the air from the two lower powered units.

"On one occasion Radio Bangkok was noted calling Osaka in Japan and Berlin in Germany with a programming relay. They were heard quite frequently in both Australia & New Zealand. This station was reactivated under Thai control at the end of 1945 with two new call signs, HSP2 & HS8PD." The Transmitter Documentation Project shows HSP2 as a 2.5 kilowatt Philips from the Netherlands.

Traditional boats still offer fresh produce at the floating market in Damneon Saduk. However, much of their former glory and purpose have been lost in the rush to cater to mass tourism. M. Guha

BE INFORMED

GLOBAL EVENTS DIRECT FROM THE SOURCE

G2000A

am/fm shortwave radio
by porsche

From its sleek sculpted lines to its soft leather case to its high performance, the G2000A designed by the legendary F.A. Porsche, is reminiscent of its fine automotive design heritage in every way.

- F.A. Porsche Design styling
- Autoscan and direct keypad tuning
- 20 customizable station presets
- Dual alarm and sleep timer functions
- Snap-on leather protective case that converts to stand

Dimensions: 5.5"W x 3.5"H x 1.3"D Weight: 7.4 oz.
Power Source: 3 AA batteries (not included) or AC adaptor (included)

high performance porsche design & family
choose style, power, or travel-size

G4000A
am/fm shortwave radio

The G4000A is an enthusiast-quality world receiver, packed with the power to scan and lock-on to even the weakest Shortwave signals with rock-solid precision. The G4000A is capable of receiving AM, FM, continuous Shortwave, and even SSB (Single Sideband) for two-way Shortwave communications such as amateur radio operators.

- Single Sideband (SSB) reception
- Wide and narrow bandwidth filter controls
- Autoscan and direct keypad tuning. 40 customizable station presets
- Alarm and sleep timer functions

Dimensions: 7.8"W x 4.6"H x 1.4"D **Weight:** 1lbs. 5oz.
Power Source: 6 AA batteries (not included) or AC adaptor (included)

G1000A
am/fm shortwave radio

Small enough to fit in a coat pocket, yet powerful enough to capture eight Shortwave bands and feature a digital frequency readout and alarm, the G1000A is a the perfect all-purpose radio for home or travel.

- Receives 8 International Shortwave bands
- Alarm and sleep timer functions with illuminated multi-function LCD screen
- Snap-on protective case and stand
- AC adaptor and earphone inputs

Dimensions: 4.5"W x 3"H x 1.1"D **Weight:** 7 oz.
Power Source: 2 AA batteries (included)

etón®
www.etoncorp.com

The Hindu bird god Garuda watches over the Buddhist temple inside Bangkok's Grand Palace. Ties have existed for centuries between these two influential Asian religions. M. Guha

After World War II, Thailand faced its own years of internal strife. Following a period of dalliance with constitutional monarchy, the country was beset with a series of coups and counter-coups by varying degrees of authoritarian and military regimes. Such was the impact of broadcasting that radio stations became the first buildings to be occupied, so takeovers could be announced to a national audience. State radio and eventually television deteriorated to the status of political footballs to promote whoever was in power at the time.

As the Kingdom of Siam morphed into Thailand, the official station's name was changed to Radio Thailand. Over the following years the development of radio increasingly took a backseat to televison, which had wider appeal. Yet, radio was found to have an unusual impact in the provinces. So, on July 21, 1955 Radio Thailand opened its first station outside the capital, in the southern city of Surat Thani. This paved the way in 1959 for a full blown plan to develop countrywide regional broadcasting.

Competing Agency Chops Funding

Unlike sluggish governments in some other Asian countries, Thailand has been quick to enact legislation to keep pace with media changes. Apart from the Telegraph Act of 1929, which governed early broadcasting, the Radio Communications Act was enacted in 1955 under the aegis of the Post and Telegraph Department. This act for the first time spelled out licensing regulations in detail.

The Radio Broadcasting Act of 1965 also covered television, legally defined objectives of broadcasting, and laid the groundwork for the establishment of similar ventures by other government agencies. To oversee this expanded regulatory role, a few years earlier, in 1962, the government had chosen to establish a national broadcasting board. This was the Committee of Radio Broadcasting and Communication of Thailand, which included representatives from every branch of government. This put the new Committee at counterpoint with the earlier regulatory authority, the Government Public Relations Department.

The entrance to the Radio Thailand World Service is watched over by a serene Buddhist shrine.   M. Guha

have done so, often to generate revenue. This includes the armed forces, universities, the police, and several government departments and ministries—together, they control over 500 frequencies. Some, such as the Ministry of Education, have even operated at one time or another on world band. More recently, nearly 200 National Community Radio Network stations have been set up. Although nominally independent, they are under the thumb of the government's Public Relations Department.

All stations are required to relay news and live coverage of major national events from Radio Thailand, as well as programs deemed supportive of government policy. Otherwise, they largely maintain their own editorial control, even during national emergencies.

Nevertheless, in keeping with Thai norms, there is an unwritten broadcasting code. This effectively prohibits coverage of events which might threaten national unity or security, or which question foreign policy.

Franchises Breed Commercialism

Even though radio ownership remains in the hands of government entities, there appears to be more commercialization than in any other Asian nation.

This seeming contradiction is because these stations are classified as "experimental," with no state budget or funding. To cover expenses these outlets have been franchised to private operators, who return the favor in cash and in kind to personnel at the parent agencies. Thus, programming is centered on generating the most revenue, politics be damned.

Little Tiger, Big Voice

Since the end of the Cold War, many Western nations have lost their sense of purpose with international broadcasting. While these operations continue to stumble

In the resulting turf struggle the Committee banned advertisements on all state run stations. Commercials were a major source of revenue, so their loss caused programming to be diminished and some stations to be closed down. Fortunately, the ban was lifted in 1969, which breathed new life into Thai radio. In 1970 an attempt was made to define broadcasting rules even more clearly, so the Regulation of Radio Broadcasting Law was enacted on September 4, 1974.

Unusual Ownership Allows Diversity

In Thailand, unlike elsewhere in the region, broadcasting is not controlled by just one arm of the government. Instead, any government agency or enterprise can acquire a broadcast license and several and withdraw, the rising nations of Asia are filling the void. The status of China and Thailand, in particular, has risen as they have expanded world band coverage and enhanced program quality.

The National Broadcasting Services of Thailand operates Radio Thailand's World Service, which offers news, current affairs and entertainment. This started under the call sign HSK-9 on October 28, 1938 after three years of experimentation and testing. It now broadcasts globally for over ten hours a day in a dozen languages.

Inside Radio Thailand

The Government Public Relations Department lies on the main road to the airport. Nestled amidst various high security government facilities, this not only houses the studios and administration of the Radio Thailand World Service, but also the domestic service. An ornate shrine at the entrance throws a celestial hand into the technological mix.

Suphachai Chantha tweaks signal processors at the Radio Thailand World Service, Bangkok.   M. Guha

Hall B of the radio building is dedicated to external broadcasting. Mrs. Porntip Utogapach, director of the external service, extends visitors a warm welcome despite

FRONTIER PROPAGANDA TARGETS NEIGHBORS

In the northern and northeastern provinces, Thais share a common history, language and culture with neighboring Laos. There, most of the Thai Government Public Relations Department outlets on FM and mediumwave AM serve in part as a "frontier broadcasters club." These transmissions propagate the dominant Thai viewpoint across the mighty Mekong that separates the two countries. One effect has been to increase dominance of the fragile Lao economy by Thai entrepreneurs of Lao origin.

The "club" consists of government outlets from the 11 provinces of north and northeast Thailand commonly called Isan and populated by ethnic Laotians. This area was once part of an early Lao kingdom, so Thai dominance is not viewed benignly by Laos.

The Thai Military's Supreme Command Headquarters also operates five mediumwave AM and six FM transmitters. These are in Bangkok and the sensitive provinces of Narathiwat in the south, Muang Phetchabun in the center, Uthai Thani in the north, and Muang Sakon Nakhon in the northeast. Powers range from five to ten kilowatts, although 50 kilowatts has been used during emergencies.

These military broadcasts originated during the Vietnam War to support Thai troops in South Vietnam. Now, suitably altered, they are directed at the sizable Burmese, Laotian and Khmer populations across Thailand's borders.

BE INFORMED

GLOBAL EVENTS DIRECT FROM THE SOURCE

- Separate bass, treble, and RF gain controls. Wide and narrow bandwidth filter controls
- Line-level audio outputs and external antenna input
- Alarm and sleep timer functions with illuminated multi-function LCD screen

Dimensions: 10.5"W x 6.5"H x 3.5"D **Weight:** 3lbs. 9oz.
Power Source: 4 D batteries (not included) or AC adaptor (included)

high performance field radio
powerful reception with rugged design

S350
am/fm shortwave radio

With the rugged look of a retro field radio and the latest in AM, FM, Shortwave radio technology, the S350 features the best of analog and digital. The S350 is the perfect addition to active lifestyles that demand high-performance portable audio capable of receiving news and information from across the globe.

Mrs. Porntip Utogapach, director of the Radio Thailand External Service.
M. Guha

her busy schedule. "What we broadcast is the framework of the foreign policy, to provide a good image of Thailand, to attract tourism and investment," she explains.

The station has succeeded, judging from the volume of letters it receives from listeners across the world. "It is very heartening to receive personal letters from listeners," enthuses Mrs. Utogapach. "It is very important that they write to us. But because of a reduced budget, we cannot always provide a souvenir or a detailed reply. This is what we would like to change."

Four news and talk studios and one large music studio with adjoining control rooms are used to produce programs in two language groups. In keeping with the ambitious National Broadcasting Master Plan of 2001, Radio Thailand has seven networks, with each catering to a select target audience or interest. Network One is the national channel, whereas Two is for special broadcasts. Three promotes a "developing society and quality of life," while Four targets educational development and Five is for the provinces.

The World Service of Radio Thailand comprises Networks Six and Seven, each with a distinct role in 12 languages. Network Six targets neighboring countries and foreigners in the kingdom in Thai, Lao, Khmer, Vietnamese, Bamar (Burmese), Malay and Bahasa Indonesia. Six also targets Europe, North America and the Far East in Thai.

Network Seven, like Six in Thai, is a true global service for Europe, North America and the Far East in English, French, German, Japanese and Mandarin. The English portion is aired over four hours a day, with newscasts relayed in Bangkok on 95.5 and 105.0 MHz FM, both ten kilowatts.

Programs are fed locally by landline and nationally by the Thaicom 1 satellite. The building also houses six FM transmitters and a technical staff of 61 to oversee domestic and external services.

Rangsit Si Goes Digital

About 40 miles or 65 km from Bangkok is the first stop along the "transmitter highway." Here, the village of Rangsit Si in Pathum Thani province is home to Radio Thailand's mediumwave AM facility, which uses a ten kilowatt Harris DX-10 transmitter.

During our visit this solid-state unit was being retrofitted to test DRM digital broadcasts for 150 minutes a day on 837 kHz. This showcase project was inaugurated with much fanfare in the presence of representatives of Digital Radio Mondiale, Deutsche Welle, VT Merlin, Harris Corporation, Asia-Pacific Broadcasting Union and the Thai government.

Weeds and Rotting Masts

The next stop along our road, the village of Si Bang Phun, lies amidst green rice fields.

THE MAJESTY OF RADIO

King Bhumibol Adulyadej (Rama IX) was born in 1927, about the time his family was pioneering broadcasting in the kingdom. So it was no surprise when as a child he began dabbling in radio. During his student days in Lausanne, Switzerland, he continued by constructing his own receiver.

After his return to Thailand in 1952, he established his own radio operation, The Amphone Sathan Throne Station, at the Dusit Palace. His aim was to get a direct line of contact with his people without the complicated procedures that dogged royal protocol in those days.

In the beginning the station was equipped with two 100 Watt communications transmitters from World War II donated by the Government Public Relations Department. Broadcasts were on shortwave and mediumwave AM, and were received as far afield as New Zealand, Japan, North America and Europe. The royal station was subsequently boosted to one kilowatt with the call sign HS1AS.

In 1967 power was further increased and an FM transmitter was added in 1982—all equipment funded by voluntary gifts from private and public organizations. In turn, the king donated the original 100 Watt duo to the engineering school at Chulalongkorn University, where there is a large electronic media department.

King Bhumibol Adulyadej (Rama IX). PRD

The royal station airs news and information, and has been especially helpful during emergencies. For example, it kept Thais updated on the polio epidemic in 1952 and a cholera outbreak in 1958. When in 1962 a storm wreaked havoc on southern Thailand, the king broadcast a personal appeal for relief supplies and donations. The response was overwhelming, and the king wound up personally supervising the distribution of supplies.

The Bureau of the Royal Household still has a daily presence on the airwaves. For about three hours daily, four times a week, the Amphone station radiates on 1332 kHz mediumwave AM with ten kilowatts and on 104.0 MHz FM at five kilowatts from the regal environs of the Chitralada Villa at Dusit Palace in northern Bangkok.

Alas, the modest world band transmitter is history. In the early 1970s it was a worldwide DX catch on 9732 kHz and the clear channel of 6405 kHz. When last heard a few years back, it was operating with a weak signal on 6149.5 kHz with severe interference from Singapore's MediaCorp Radio on 6150 kHz. Perhaps it was this interference combined with the transmitter's increasingly low power that accelerated its demise.

Hall "B" is the modern production center for Radio Thailand World Service's programs.
M. Guha

This is the designated transmitter farm, and it boasts more antenna masts than trees. Transmission facilities line the highway, and include station HSK9 which until recently was Radio Thailand's dedicated shortwave transmission facility. A guarded gate leads through a secluded half-mile drive to the station building and adjoining transmitter hall.

Sadly, scarcely a soul is in sight. The entire place has been abandoned in favor of the giant Udon Thani transmitting station. All we found was a lone gardener weeding overgrown grass, oblivious to our presence. Some shortwave dipole aerials and feeders appear to be in good shape, but the older antennas are simply rusting away. Even the little Buddhist shrine near the entrance is unkempt.

This facility was set up in late 1941 with three 10 kilowatt CCA transmitters from Fairburn, Georgia. It was upgraded in 1953 with an RCA 50 kilowatt BHF 50, followed later by a similar BHF 100 (100 kW) and in 1985 by a ten kilowatt NEC.

Until July 2004 the transmitters were fired up daily at 1100 to 1215 World Time. They aired Radio Thailand's external services to neighboring countries in Vietnamese, Khmer, Lao, Burmese and Malay on 4830,

6070 and 7115 kHz. Now silent, they await their ultimate disposition.

Udon Thani, Thailand's Mighty Mouth

On April 4, 1984 the Royal Thai and American governments signed a landmark 25 year renewable agreement. This established a joint super-powered shortwave facility to relay both the Voice of America and Radio Thailand World Service. The northeastern province of Udon Thani, which had hosted the U.S. Air Force during the Vietnam War, was the logical choice.

There is a large expat population in the region and even an American consulate to look after their interests. Fully 8,500 acres were selected in a deserted area outside Ban Dung, where a little sign in the center of the town unobtrusively says, "VOA."

But the huge complex—sometimes simply called IBB-Udon or even IBB-Udorn by American employees—is nowhere near the town. About three miles or five kilometers away there finally appear telltale signs: tall antenna masts, curtain dipole arrays and blinking safety lights shrouded by a thick layer of tall trees. Obviously, we had not stumbled across the local Shell station.

Alas, we had to content ourselves with poking around the periphery. "Due to the present situation, we would like to maintain a low profile," explained Richard Baltes, Transmission Supervisor, when approached by telephone. Given the vast size and visibility of the facility, this seems more wishful than thinking.

The mighty Udon Thani facility began testing in 1991 and was completed in 1993. It houses seven 500 kilowatt Marconi B 6128 transmitters, according to George Woodard, then vice president of engineering at RFE/RL and later director of engineering at IBB. Woodard adds that the Marconis were retrofitted with Continental solid-state modulators, and thus were identical to the ten transmitters at the IBB/VOA facility in Tangier, Morocco. Additionally, a 40 kilowatt PEP single sideband Continental transmitter may have been brought out of 25-year storage.

These powerful transmitters feed 25 high-gain antennas that use the latest fourth generation technology designed for IBB by TCI of Sunnyvale, California. A coaxial switching matrix feeds HR 4/6/Lambda curtain arrays which are electrically slewable in both azimuth and elevation. This fills gaps in VOA coverage in China, Southeast Asia and parts of the former USSR which were not adequately served by

IBB relay stations in Sri Lanka and the Philippines.

Thanks to its tremendous reach—it is audible throughout 40 percent of the world—Udon Thani also carries other IBB services, such as Radio Farda, Radio Free Afghanistan and Radio Liberty. A terrestrial two-way station receives IBB/VOA program feeds in multiple streams from the Network Control Center in Washington.

Radio Muscle Expands Audience

Since 1994 Udon Thani has also been relaying the entire program load of the Radio Thailand World Service, beginning a major new chapter in Thai external broadcasting. A separate agreement in 2004 resulted in Radio Thailand being relayed to North America two hours daily by IBB/VOA transmitters in Greenville, North Carolina and Delano, California.

Taken together, these facilities have helped Radio Thailand become a significant source of Asian news and culture for the planet's 600 million world band listeners.

Which "Free Asia"?

Another Thai-American agreement, signed on August 11, 1965, expired on March 27,

Udon Thani, tucked in the wilderness of northeastern Thailand. This is the largest American transmitter plant in Asia and dominates the airwaves with powerhouse signals.

M. Guha

The shallow Mekong river, once the lifeline of Laos, forms much of the border with Thailand. The Thai frontier town of Nong Khai is only short swim away from this Lao shoreline. M. Guha

1998. For 33 years, from studios in Bangkok, the Voice of Free Asia beamed official American programs to Southeast Asia in languages of the region. The spot on the AM dial was 1575 kHz, with a hair-curling one million Watts from Tambon Rasom village in neighboring Ayutthaya province.

The original 1,000 kilowatt transmitter was a Continental Doherty 105B installed in 1952, according to former IBB engineering chief George Woodard. It was replaced in 1996 by an efficient Harris DX-1000.

Woodard points out that the original weary transmitter could pump out no more than 600 kW by the time it was replaced. "When the Harris came online, voltage breakdown problems in the antenna tuning houses began to appear because it had been so long since they had seen a full Megawatt," Woodard recalls. But once these were fixed there was reduced electrical consumption, greater reach and better modulation.

On April 1, 1998, after the U.S.-Thai agreement ended, the facility became "Radio Saranrom," an official voice of the Thai Ministry of Foreign Affairs. New studios have been constructed at the ministry in Bangkok, although for now programs are being produced only in Thai.

The similarly named Radio Free Asia is another and very different IBB station. Its large studio and bureau in Bangkok produces programs for Southeast Asia in Burmese, Lao, Khmer and Vietnamese. The Thai government won't allow anti-establishment broadcasts to its neighbors, so transmitters are in faraway Armenia, Kazakhstan, Mongolia, Palau, Saipan, Sri Lanka, Taiwan, Tajikistan and Tinian Island.

BBC Erects Relay

In 1989 the BBC erected its Asia Relay Station in north-central Thailand to replace the former Hong Kong relay. It is tucked away from prying eyes, about 13 miles or 21 km from the town of Kao Lieo in the province of Nakhon Sawan. Hardware includes four Thomcast one-tube TSW-2250 250 kilowatt shortwave transmitters feeding several 6-11 MHz TCI curtain arrays. Future plans call for at least one more comparable transmitter.

Even though the station is owned by the BBC, like other British relay stations outside the United Kingdom it is operated by VT Merlin under a management contract. In 2003 one of the 250 kilowatt transmitters was modified for DRM digital broadcasting, after which extensive tests were conducted.

WHO'S ON?

Thailand has 524 local and national radio stations—211 mediumwave AM, the rest FM. The biggest operators are the Public Relations Department with 147, followed by the Royal Thai Army with 127 and the Mass Communication Organisation of Thailand with 62. Except for a small number of specialist stations, such as those dedicated to traffic reports, all link twice daily with Radio Thailand for official newscasts. Stations must also relay messages from the king and the prime minister, as well as daily Buddhist sermons. Otherwise, they enjoy a fair amount of freedom to produce independent newscasts.

Armed Forces and Police Networks

The Thai armed forces have long been active broadcasters, ostensibly to promote inter-agency cooperation and for national security. The largest has been the Royal Thai Army, today with 51 mediumwave AM and the same number of FM transmitters operating nationwide. Yet other army radio facilities have become weapons in the struggle against Islamist terrorism and for border propaganda (*see* sidebar).

The Royal Thai Navy operates seven mediumwave AM and 14 FM outlets scattered across the country, while the Royal Thai Air Force has 18 each on mediumwave AM and FM. The Supreme Command Headquarters does its share with five mediumwave AM and six FM stations. Even the police get in the act with seven mediumwave AM and 38 FM outlets dotting the landscape.

The present king is both a radio aficionado and a seasoned broadcaster. His Bureau of the Royal Household has participated greatly in advancing broadcasting in the kingdom (*see* sidebar).

Media Agencies Operate Nationwide

The Mass Communication Organization of Thailand (MCOT) was constituted by royal decree under the prime minister's office to operate commercial radio and television networks in the country. The organization operates two mediumwave AM and 60 FM transmitters scattered nationwide, and also runs the Thai News Agency.

However, change is in the wind. The Thai cabinet recently unveiled a plan to partially privatize this state enterprise and incorporate the remainder into a public limited company.

The Government Public Relations Department continues to run the influential National Broadcasting Services of Thailand. Domestically, it operates 60 mediumwave AM and 85 FM transmitters from 58 facilities located in five administrative regions. Of the 12 transmitters in Bangkok, six are on mediumwave AM, the rest on FM, while two include English programs. Sizable chunks of the BBC World Service are relayed on mediumwave AM and FM in Bangkok, Chiang Mai in the north and Hat Yai in the extreme south.

Bangkok's police use radio for more than this. They also operate their own commercial AM/FM stations.   M. Guha

BE INFORMED

GLOBAL EVENTS DIRECT FROM THE SOURCE

G4000A
am/fm shortwave radio

The G4000A is an enthusiast-quality world receiver, packed with the power to scan and lock-on to even the weakest Shortwave signals with rock-solid precision. The G4000A is capable of receiving AM, FM, continuous Shortwave, and even SSB (Single Sideband) for two-way Shortwave communications such as amateur radio operators.

- Single Sideband (SSB) Reception
- Wide & narrow bandwidth filter controls
- Autoscan and direct keypad Tuning; 40 customizable station presets
- Alarm and sleep timer functions

Dimensions: 7.8"W x 4.6"H x 1.4"D **Weight:** 1lbs. 5oz.
Power Source: 6 AA batteries (not included) or AC adaptor (included)

G2000A
am/fm shortwave radio by **porsche**

From its sleek sculpted lines to its soft leather case to its high performance, the G2000A designed by the legendary F.A. Porsche, is reminiscent of its fine automotive design heritage in every way.

- F.A. Porsche Design styling
- Autoscan and direct keypad tuning
- 20 customizable station presets
- Dual alarm and sleep timer functions
- Snap-on leather protective case that converts to stand

Dimensions: 5.5"W x 3.5"H x 1.3"D **Weight:** 7.4 oz.
Power Source: 3 AA batteries (not included) or AC adaptor (included)

high performance world band receivers
portable powerhouses for anyone

E10
am/fm shortwave radio

Intelligent features that simplify. Performance that reaches out to the world.
Imagine a radio that combines strong performance for fantastic reception and all of today's digital wizardry, bringing the world to your fingertips. The E10 is where intelligence meets performance.

- AM/FM Shortwave radio with Shortwave range of 1711 – 29,999 KHz
- 550 programmable memories with memory page customization
- Manual & auto scan, direct keypad frequency entry, ATS, tuning knob
- IF shift (Intermediate Frequency) and Shortwave antenna trimmer
- Sleep timer, snooze, and favorite station wake-up timers
- Includes AC adaptor/charger and 4 AA Ni-MH batteries
- Internally charges AA Ni-MH batteries
- Clean-design body with fine lines and metallic finish

Dimensions: 7.4"W x 4.5"H x 1.3"D **Weight:** 1lbs. 5oz.
Power Source: 4 AA batteries or included AC adaptor/charger

YB 550PE
am/fm shortwave radio

The YB line, manufactured since the 1960's, has always stood for performance and portability. The latest in this family, the YB 550PE carries on the tradition, capable of receiving AM/FM and continuous Shortwave across all 14 international bands. Palm-sized and only 10oz, the YB 550PE features five tuning methods, including 200 station presets and the handy scroll wheel.

- Continuous Shortwave of 1711-29.995 KHz
- Autoscan, direct keypad, and scroll wheel tuning with 200 customizable station presets
- Alarm and sleep timer functions; AC adaptor and supplementary antenna inputs

Dimensions: 3.5"W x 5.8"H x 1.4"D **Weight:** 10 oz.
Power Source: 4 D batteries (not included) or AC adaptor (included)

etón®
www.etoncorp.com

Laos: Radio Under Fire

by Manosij Guha

Once a backwater of the former French Indochina, Laos is still largely untouched by western influence. Its measured pace of life is as sluggish the muddy Mae Nam Mae Khong—the Mekong River.

For centuries, Laos has been a buffer between powerful kingdoms that played its gentle people against each other, like pawns in a devious chess game. The early history of Laos was especially dominated by migrating Shan, Siamese, Lao and Hmong, who depleted much of the forest cover through slash and burn agriculture.

There was infighting among the early Lao principalities, but they eventually banded together to repel the Mongol hordes of Kublai Khan. Laos was first unified in 1353 under the rule of Fa Ngum, a ferocious

Khmer protégé who consolidated principalities around Luang Prabang to form Lan Xang. The kingdom initially became prosperous, but by the 17th century internecine quarrels and interference from neighbors balkanized it into three smaller principalities.

By the end of the 18th century, most of Laos was under Siamese suzerainty, but the region was also coveted by Annam, part of today's Vietnam. In the 1820s, fed up with both oppressors, the country unwittingly went to war against powerful Siam. This proved so disastrous that both Laos and Annam fell under Siamese control, reducing Laos to a Siamese vassal state until the 1890s.

French Create Indochina

By the late 19th century, France had created French Indochina from the Vietnamese provinces of Tonkin and Annam. Unwilling to take on the might of the French empire, Siam eventually ceded all of Laos to France, which treated it as a protectorate within Indochina.

The French had no interest in developing Laos, so they relegated it to be governed by the Vietnamese civil service—a practice which continues to this day. The French then used the territory as a buffer to thwart the opportunistic designs of Siam, as well as potential British expansionism from Burma in the north and Malaya to the south.

With the advent of World War II, Japanese troops overran Indochina. In order not to return the territory to French rule, a Lao resistance group, Lao Issara, was formed, which ultimately led Laos to independence in 1953. But conflict soon erupted among royalist, neutralist and communist factions. The next few years saw bitter civil war, with foreign interference stoking hostilities.

Dy Sisombath, the "Father of Lao Radio," relies on hard-copy documents.
M. Guha

In the 1950s many countries donated broadcasting equipment.

Designated as a world heritage site by UNESCO, Luang Prabang was once a jewel in the crown of French Indochina. Now, with its idyllic vistas and a laid-back lifestyle, it is a paradise where time stands still.   M. Guha

Khmu newscaster at rough-and-ready Houa Phan Provincial Radio Station, Sam Neua.   M. Guha

War Devastates Region

By 1957, pro-communist Pathet Lao rebels had advanced into the north and were bidding for power. By the early 1960s, they had aligned themselves with the Soviet Bloc and were being actively aided by the USSR and North Vietnam.

Washington was concerned about communist advances, but was unwilling to become visibly involved. Instead, the Central Intelligence Agency was tapped to covertly aid the Royal Lao Government. The "secret war" that followed ran from 1964 to 1969.

With the Vietnam War in high gear, American bombing in eastern Laos targeted the Ho Chi Minh Trail, the major communist supply route. But in the process, it also obliterated nearby Lao towns, cities and villages, creating vast civilian casualties and flows of refugees. By the cease-fire of 1973, Laos had earned the sad distinction of being the most bombed country on Earth.

French Inaugurate Broadcasting

Laos was a tardy entrant to radio broadcasting, perhaps a result of its low standing within the French Indochina colonial administration. The first Lao station was set up, unofficially, in 1950 on 7215 kHz with a one kilowatt shortwave transmitter provided by the French. In April 1952, it was officially opened by Prince Souvanna Phouma in Vientiane, from where Lao National Radio still operates.

In reality, the building was ceremoniously inaugurated much later. An almost hidden inscription in concrete near the entrance reads, translated, "This stone was laid by His Highness Prince Souvanna Phouma, Prime Minister of Laos, on 27th January 1996."

Yanks, Brits, Aussies and Germans Pitch In

In 1954, the Eisenhower administration donated a second one kilowatt shortwave transmitter to Lao National Radio. This was followed in 1957 by a five kilowatt medium-wave AM transmitter on 1340 kHz to complement existing world band frequencies of 6130 and 7145 kHz.

The United States also loaned a ten kilowatt shortwave transmitter in 1960 for use on 6150 kHz. According to one recollection a second identical transmitter was also loaned, but no record of its operation has been found.

Not to be left behind, in 1964 the British government donated Marconi transmitters and provided scholarships for training engineers. The equipment was installed in Vientiane, Luang Prabang and Pakse, but the transmitter in Vientiane, and probably others, were destroyed in a coup in February 1965. To make up for these losses, USAID donated a 50 kilowatt transmitter, with more being provided by ally Australia in 1965.

By 1966, Lao National Radio was broadcasting over 13 hours a day in two separate transmissions. Programs were mostly in Lao, with music and features for the army and farmers, as well as educational programs. These were supplemented by programs in Vietnamese and French.

CAVEMAN RADIO

Remote northern Houa Phan province, dotted with verdant hills and limestone cliffs, is located along the Vietnamese border. The provincial capital is small and picturesque Sam Neua, with the gentle Nam Sam river flowing by. It occupies a world of its own, all but cut off from the rest of the country except for biweekly flights on Lao Airline's overgrown crop duster.

The other way to reach Sam Neua is from Vientiane by bus or *songthiaw*—a truck modified to carry people. This takes about three days, but meanders through bandit-ridden mountain terrain where even locals fear to tread.

Picturesque Sam Neua, with Lego-like huts clustered amidst verdant hills.   M. Guha

This is the setting for Laos' most important and intriguing chapter in radio broadcasting. Here, a clandestine station operated against impossible odds and finally became the beleaguered nation's official broadcaster.

Twenty nine kilometers from the provincial capital of Sam Neua on Route 5 is impregnable karst topography riddled with the caves of Vieng Xai. These are adjacent to a tiny town of the same name, and is literally the end of the road. These caverns were once home to clandestine "Radio Pathet Lao" of the Neo Lao Hak Sat (Lao Patriotic Front), the communist independence movement formed by "Red Prince" Souphanouvong in 1951. The caves also served as Pathet Lao headquarters and domicile for the Chinese ambassador.

The station was active until August 1960, but once the Front joined the coalition it was integrated with Lao National Radio. However, it was revived that December when the coalition broke up. It continued until December 2, 1975, when Pathet Lao forces overthrew the monarchy and created the Lao People's Democratic Republic.

Broadcasts Aided by Hanoi

Pathet Lao lore has it that after the start of American bombing, all broadcasts were heroically transmitted from the "radio cave" until the communist takeover. The less romantic reality is that at least some transmissions were from the Voice of Vietnam facility, as was underscored when it was damaged during a 1972 bombing of Hanoi. To this day the Pathet Lao and Vietnamese authorities have avoided addressing this awkward point.

Dense overgrowth makes the old broadcast cave virtually inaccessible; in any

Superb piloting allows Lao Airlines to provide regular service under fearsome conditions.
M. Guha

event, all artifacts were removed after the war. But in its heyday it is said to have secreted several one kilowatt Sino-Russian communications transmitters, which originally were for sending messages to Pathet Lao units across the country.

Later, in 1967-8, it took on the mantle of broadcaster and started transmitting on a regular schedule. Programs were initially in Lao, but Vietnamese and French were added later. The station staff was enthusiastic but untrained, consisting of eager intellectuals, teachers and monks.

Caves Provided Autonomy

The Pathet Lao leadership started using these caverns in 1964 because they are virtually unassailable by air. Wooden walls and floors, as well as natural rock formations, divided the caverns into bedrooms,

Pathet Lao toil within the protective cocoon of Vieng Xai's caves. These also sheltered "Radio Pathet Lao." LNR

meeting rooms, artillery and weapons storage areas, and various other spaces. Most had an airtight chamber which could be sealed during an air raid, with oxygen being artificially generated by a Russian device.

One of the deepest caves housed the hospital, while others held weaving mills, printing presses and other facilities so the Pathet Lao could be self-sufficient. Tunnels connected the caverns and even extended to elegant houses the leaders built in front of their respective caves. Electricity was provided by nearby Vietnam, just as it is today in this region.

There was considerable fear that Americans would use bunker-busting chemical bombs to demolish the Pathet Lao's hideout. However, what was dropped, instead, was a relatively benign mixture of detergent and herbicides to make the mountain roads slippery.

Visitors Face Grim Reminder

After the war, the deposed royal family suddenly disappeared during massive retaliations against Hmong and other former enemies of the Pathet Lao. They are presumed to have been sent to die in the area, where there is a surprising reminder of this grim period. A nearby "reeducation" camp, built by the Vietnamese in 1973, has been turned into what is surely one of the world's most grotesque hotels.

Among the various shortwave transmitters in the caves of Vieng Xai, at least two were sent to nearby Sam Neua and another to Luang Prabang. Of these, the unit in Luang Prabang has since been decommissioned. Only one in Sam Neua continues to soldier on, serving the remote region as its provincial radio service.

Pathet Lao tunnels were hewn using primitive tools.
M. Guha

BE INFORMED

GLOBAL EVENTS DIRECT FROM THE SOURCE

FM/SW ANTENNA

MINI 300 WORLD BAND RECEIVER

GRUNDIG

mini 300pe
am/fm shortwave radio

The Mini 300PE is a pocket-sized and power-packed wonder. Only 4.7 ounces, the Mini 300PE is not only an AM and FM-Stereo radio, but also a world band receiver capable of pulling in seven international Shortwave bands. With its large LCD screen and simple operation, the ability to tune-in world news and information has never been easier.

- Receives 7 international Shortwave bands with telescopic and internal ferrite bar antennas
- Built-in speaker, earphone input, ear buds (included), protective travel case (included)
- Multi-function LCD screen with clock, alarm, and sleep timer functions

Dimensions: 2.5"W x 4.3"H x 0.9"D **Weight:** 4.7oz.
Power Source: 2 AA batteries (included)

5 colors to choose from:
- Metallic Blue
- Gold
- Metallic Red
- Metallic Pearl
- Metallic Bronze

perfect for travelling the world
lightweight, strong reception, feature packed

E100
am/fm shortwave radio

Fits into your palm or pocket, but fitted with full-sized features. Imagine a radio packed with all the bells and whistles: digital tuning AM, FM, Shortwave reception, and small enough to fit into your coat pocket. The E100 is a dream come true.

- AM/FM Shortwave radio with Shortwave range of 1711 – 29,999 KHz
- 200 programmable memories with memory page customization
- Manual & auto scan, direct keypad frequency entry, tuning knob
- Programmable alarm & sleep functions with digital clock
- Clean-design body with fine lines & metallic silver finish

Dimensions: 4.9"W x 3"L x 1.2"D **Weight:** 7.4oz.
Power Source: 2 AA batteries (included) or AC adaptor (not included)

G1000A
am/fm shortwave radio

Receives 8 international Shortwave bands. Alarm and sleep timer functions. Illuminated multi-function LCD screen. Snap-on protective case and stand. AC adaptor and earphone Inputs

Dimensions: 4.5"W x 3"H x 1.1"D **Weight:** 7 oz.
Power Source: 2 AA batteries (included)

etón®
www.etoncorp.com

Sam Nuea's neat appearance and satellite dish belie the "flamethrower" transmitter inside. This artifact frequently conks out and wanders off frequency, frustrating reception. During breaks in transmission residents can stroll outdoors and listen instead to wired loudspeakers. M. Guha

Two years later, Lao National Radio, sometimes identifying as Radio Laos, operated from Vientiane using a 25 kilowatt Philips shortwave transmitter provided by German aid. This transmitter still exists in derelict condition at the KM6 transmitting station.

Three mediumwave AM transmitters aired the same content: Luang Prabang at 2.5 kilowatts, and Vientiane and Pakse at ten kilowatts each. Everything originated at the Vientiane studios, with the same programs carried on shortwave and mediumwave AM simultaneously in a rudimentary national grid.

This continued well into 1972 when a different, unnamed, station began operating from Luang Prabang. Yet another station began construction at Savannakhet in the south, close to the Thai border. In all, four different radio stations, each managed by a separate coalition partner, could be heard. As each relayed a bit of the other's programming, the mix resembled a joint operation.

All would broadcast about 12 hours daily, with extended hours on weekends. Programs were primarily in Lao tongues, but some were in French, usually prepared by the French foreign ministry in Vientiane. They included traditional and modern Lao

music, political talks, broadcasts from the National Assembly, news in French, children's stories, special programs for housewives, and several hours of in-school curricula and adult literacy courses.

The Laos Second System station, which seemingly broadcast from Luang Prabang, aired in Khmu and other dialects, as well as Cambodian, Vietnamese and French. The third station, Radio of the Lao Kingdom in Luang Prabang, relayed news from "Radio Pathet Lao" and Vientiane.

Sieng Santisouk (Voice of Peaceful Laos), probably from Pakse, was—until 1975—the fourth outlet. Like the third station, it included programs from Vientiane and "Radio Pathet Lao."

Lao Radio Today

Domestically, Lao National Radio transmits only from the capital, Vientiane. Provincial centers independently manage their own radio stations, albeit under the aegis of the Ministry of Information and Culture, with technical and material help from the federal Department of Mass Media.

"Unlike other socialist countries, the government of the Lao PDR operates a decentralized broadcasting infrastructure," points out Dy Sisombath, the genial network planning manager of the Department of Mass Media. Sisombath, who is a walking encyclopedia of Lao broadcasting, adds, "Provincial broadcasting is controlled by the Provincial Committee, which is headed by the Governor."

These broadcast centers exist in the provincial capitals of Luang Prabang, Sam Neua, Attapeu, Luang Namtha, Saiyabouli, Muang Khong, Thakek, Savannakhet and Pakse. They operate on mediumwave AM or FM or both but, either way, all must relay news from Vientiane.

Among provincial outlets, only Sam Neua has a presence on the world band airwaves. The shortwave transmitter in Luang Prabang has been phased out, while the one in Xeing Khoung was bombed.

Sam Neua: Flamethrower Radio

Today's Radio Station of Houa Phan Province is located on Transmitter Hill, looking down on Sam Neua. The arduous uphill hike is a challenge, but at least the language barrier is insurmountable—almost.

This where the language of love for radio kicks in. Phrase books, hand signs, stick figure diagrams, drawing on the sand and even telephone calls to an English translator in Vientiane were all effective tools to understand these people and their fascinating culture.

The radio station itself is an oblong two-building affair with a shack in between. The place could easily be mistaken for a village school, given the multitude of children playing ball, but dipole masts and a rusty dish antenna point to the true purpose.

CLANDESTINE BROADCASTING

By the late 1960s, Lao National Radio was the official voice of independent Laos, which was then governed by a diverse coalition of royalists, neutralists and communists. However, various Lao groups operated clandestine stations, such as "Radio of the Patriotic Neutralist Forces" on 4247v, 4575, 6273 and 8600v kHz. The CIA also participated actively, notably with "United Lao Races."

Later, black clandestine stations also appeared. These pretended to be operated by the enemy, so as to trick listeners and thus reduce the enemy's credibility or confuse. This concept reportedly fascinated then-Secretary of State Henry Kissinger, who is said to have ordered the CIA to create a number of black stations for audiences in Vietnam and Laos. Among these was "Radio Khana Pathet Lao," which from July 1973 to February 1974 pretended to be an outlet for the Pathet Lao on 5012 kHz.

Dissident Broadcasting Continues

This spirit of disestablishmentarianism continues even now. Since May 2002, United Lao Movement for Democracy, an American based pro-democracy group in St. Paul, Minnesota has been airing "Hmong Lao Radio" over powerful transmitters in such countries as Uzbekistan, Taiwan and the United Kingdom. Programs are in Hmong from 0100 to 0200 World Time Wednesdays and Fridays; frequencies change, but recently have been 6040 (formerly 9515, 11725) and 15260 kHz. According to their website, broadcasts are directed not only towards Southeast Asia, but also to North America where it has a sizeable diaspora.

Whether this is related to a similar station broadcasting from Thailand or the mountains of northern Laos remains to be proven.

The building for technical facilities is normally inactive during the day. But by evening it becomes a hotbed of activity as the weary lone working transmitter is fired up—literally, as flames are actually visible, their hot tongues licking inside the transmitter case.

Two very small rooms serve as a basic studio, with simple cassette decks, mixers and microphones. All news and commentary are taped, but during transmission the voice audio and music tapes are mixed live by a technician. Television and FM are next door.

Two Transmitters, One Works

There are two one kilowatt shortwave units of identical Sino-Russian vintage which were moved from the Vieng Xai cave in 1977. Plate markings state: "1 kilowatt SW CW + Phone Transmitter, Type 200A-1, Serial No. 64-082, Power Supply 380v 3 phase 50 c/s, Frequency Range 3-18 Mc/s. Power output 1kilowatt." One is silent and pitiful, existing only to provide parts for the transmitter that still works.

Sam Neua operates from 2300 to 0130 and 1000 to 1230 World Time on nominal 4640

kHz, which drifts plus or minus 5 kHz, and FM 102.75 MHz. While FM normally relays Lao National Radio from Vientiane, shortwave usually carries locally produced programs, along with news relayed from Vientiane.

Besides Lao, much programming is in the Hmong and Khmu tongues of this hill tribe region. Local content often consists of news or commentary interspersed with generous doses of music. There is no advertising, but public service announcements are read during and after local newscasts.

Signals Heard by Western DXers

Music requests are hugely popular at Sam Neua. "Each month over a thousand letters for requests are received, including from elsewhere in Laos and in neighboring Vietnam," beams Veeyang, a Hmong announcer and the only staffer who speaks good English, having once been a teacher.

World band DXers get into the act, too. Reception reports have come from as far afield as South America, Finland and Singapore, although most remain unanswered because of language difficulties and insufficient funds. However, a report translated into Lao or Hmong with suitable reply postage should eventually be verified.

The station has a staff of 17, including three Hmong, two Lao and two Khmu announcers. Also present are three engineers, including Khong Kham, an enigmatic character. At 52 he is probably the most senior transmitter engineer, having served since the days of cave broadcasts.

"I didn't really want to be a radio technician," he explains in Lao, using gestures to compensate for the language barrier. He was never formally trained in broadcast engineering, so everything he knows has been learned through bumps and scrapes.

He is a simple but dedicated man, with the onerous task of vandalizing a beloved

Engineer Khong Kham laments that his drifty transmitter lacks the keypad tuning of a Sony portable.   M. Guha

Sam Neua's family of vintage transmitters comprises two Russian-designed workhorses and a veteran from Mao's China. Engineering wizardry keeps all three from the scrap heap.

M. Guha

transmitter for parts to keep his remaining baby alive. Still, frequent breakdowns agonize this surrogate father as he struggles to keep the last of his electronic family from the boneyard.

Vientiane, Studio Central

Present-day Lao National Radio operates from a nondescript 1954 building on Phangkham Road in Vientiane's Chantabouli district. This quiet government quarter was once the village of Ban Si Saket, named after a local Buddhist monastery.

We are greeted by Inpanh Satchaphansy, who wears many hats: Deputy Head of the Foreign Desk, Head of External Relations and Head of the English Language Service. Other employees include 60 technicians and another 100 or so program staff and journalists.

One studio is for live on-air announcements and playouts; it doubles as master control. Other studios, for recording and editing, include digital audio workstations and servers which replaced analog tape systems in 2000. Two-channel Marti VHF links

connect to shortwave and mediumwave AM transmission facilities on the city's outskirts.

Studio modernization has been funded in part by the Japanese agency JICA, underscoring the crucial role foreign aid has played in the station's development. Sweden, for example, underwrote a pilot project from 2000 to 2003. And a number of producers have received Australian government scholarships.

Domestic Services Grow

From a mere 14 hours of programs a day in 1975, Lao National Radio has grown to over 40 hours. The domestic service of Lao National Radio airs regionally from 2200 to 0830 and 0930 to 1500 World Time on 6130 kHz from a 50 kilowatt shortwave transmitter, and locally on 576 kHz mediumwave AM and 103.7 MHz FM.

Programming is mainly in Lao, with Hmong and Khmu segments thrown in twice daily. English language lessons can be heard from 1300 to 1315 World Time, followed by French lessons to 1330. Commercials have been allowed only since 1995.

Cattle with loud bells sometimes to do a better job than paid guards in protecting Lao National Radio's KM6 facility.

M. Guha

Vientiane has a second station, Vientiane City Radio. This is operated by the municipality on 105.5 MHz FM and 640 kHz mediumwave AM using their own facilities.

International Service Loses Relay

The International Service broadcasts for five hours daily, with half-hour segments each in Vietnamese, Khmer, Thai, French and English—English is at 0600-0630 and 1330-1400 World Time. The regional audience is reached by a ten kilowatt shortwave transmitter on 7145 kHz, while 97.25 MHz is available for local listeners.

This is a plunge from the station's former grandeur, when the International Service put out powerful world band signals. From 1987 to 1991, before the collapse of the Soviet Union, it was relayed to Europe by a pair of beefy transmitters within the USSR.

Shortwave Site Feeds Cows

Transmitter sites in Laos are named after the distance in kilometers from its studio. Therefore, the shortwave transmitting

station for Vientiane is called "KM6," or six kilometers from the studios in downtown Vientiane. KM6 can be reached by rickety tuk-tuk—a motorcycle-fronted people carrier that jounces along winding village roads and dirt paths.

Engulfed by the village of Ban Chommany Neuk is the facility's fenced but unguarded compound. Its large antenna farm is shared with cattle which, like their BBC Monitoring counterparts at Caversham Park, keep the grass trim by grazing between masts.

Two Marti VHF link receivers, in a small rack, receive program feeds from the Vientiane studios on 243 and 245 MHz, respectively. Unused are vintage Australian STC rack receivers and measurement and patch panels. Adjacent to the control room is a large transmitter hall, now largely empty but which once held numerous mediumwave AM and shortwave transmitters.

Hardware Diaspora

The exodus of transmitters from KM6 has been worthy of a latter-day Leon Uris.

JRC NRD-545

Legendary Quality. Digital Signal Processing. Awesome Performance.

With the introduction of the NRD-545, Japan Radio raises the standard by which high performance receivers are judged.

Starting with JRC's legendary quality of construction, the NRD-545 offers superb ergonomics, virtually infinite filter band-width selection, steep filter shape factors, a large color liquid crystal display, 1,000 memory channels, scan and sweep functions, and both double sideband and sideband selectable synchronous detection. With high sensitivity, wide dynamic range, computer control capability, a built-in RTTY demodulator, tracking notch filter, and sophisticated DSP noise control circuitry, the NRD-545 redefines what a high-performance receiver should be.

- LSB, USB, CW, RTTY, FM, AM, AMS, and ECSS (Exalted Carrier Selectable Sideband) modes.
- Continuously adjustable bandwidth from 10 Hz to 9.99 kHz in 10 Hz steps.
- Pass-band shift adjustable in 50 Hz steps up or down within a ±2.3 kHz range.
- Noise reduction signal processing adjustable in 256 steps.
- Tracking notch filter, adjustable within ±2.5 kHz in 10 Hz steps, follows in a ±10 kHz range even when the tuning dial is rotated.
- Continuously adjustable AGC between 0.04 sec and 5.1 sec in LSB, USB, CW, RTTY, and ECSS modes.
- 1,000 memory channels that store frequency, mode, bandwidth, AGC, ATT, and (for channels 0–19) timer on/off.
- Built-in RTTY demodulator reads ITU-T No. 2 codes for 170, 425, and 850 Hz shifts at 37 to 75 baud rates. Demodulated output can be displayed on a PC monitor through the built-in RS-232C interface.
- High sensitivity and wide dynamic range achieved through four junction-type FETs with low noise and superior cross modulation characteristics.
- Computer control capability.
- Optional wideband converter unit enables reception of 30 MHz to 2,000 MHz frequencies (less cellular) in all modes.

JRC Japan Radio Co., Ltd.

Japan Radio Company, Ltd., New York Office —
2125 Center Ave., Suite 208, Fort Lee, NJ 07024
Voice: 201 242 1882   Fax: 201 242 1885

Japan Radio Company, Ltd. — Nittochi Nishi-Shinjuku Bldg.
10-1 Nishi-Shinjuku 6 chome, Shinjuku-ku, Tokyo 160-0023, Japan
Voice: 81 3 3348 3858   Fax: 81 3 3348 3938

A derelict Philips (left) stands mute alongside the new CEC transmitter at the KM6 facility. M. Guha

Sysamone Phommaxay, the facility's Soviet educated engineer, relates the history to PASSPORT.

First to go was a Soviet 175 kilowatt mediumwave AM unit, installed in 1959. That was sent to the scrap heap. Next, a five kilowatt shortwave transmitter, also

Russian, suffered the same fate in 1994. Then, in 2001, a Chinese ten kilowatt mediumwave AM rig was transferred to the new Thakek station.

A newer Marconi transmitter was moved down the road in 2003 to replace Vientiane City Radio's original kilowatter on 702 kHz. This came on the air in 2004 on the replacement frequency of 640 kHz to overcome mutual interference with Luang Prabang on 705 kHz. The replacement was described to us as ten kilowatts, but signal strength makes it seem more like one kilowatt. Possibly the new transmitter is not yet in operation.

Finally, laments engineer Phommaxay, an aged ten kilowatt mediumwave AM transmitter was plucked from its foundation. Made by STC of Australia, it was discarded in 2002.

Corner Reveals Old Workhorse

Only two functioning shortwave transmitters remain at KM6, so enough space is left for future expansion. However, at present the area is earmarked for recreation, as could be deduced from a ping-pong table.

What intrigues the nostalgic interloper is none of this, but rather something lurking in

With its motorcycle front and cattle-cart back, the "tuk-tuk" is named after the sound it makes. People share seats with pigs and chickens.
M. Guha

a damp, dark corner. Here lies a very large, very heavy and very derelict transmitter in three stages, each big enough to pass as a butcher's freezer.

This is Radio Laos' old 25 kilowatt Philips manufactured in Eindhoven, the Netherlands. As emblazoned on a plaque, it was part of a German aid program to the Royal Lao Government in 1968. Once the station's workhorse, this beefy sender was finally retired about 1993, because transmitter tubes had become too costly and scarce. This has also made redundant its three-tower helical antenna—once state-of-art—as its fixed beam heading was to the former priority targets of Vietnam and China.

The domestic program load has since been transferred to a newer 50 kilowatt shortwave transmitter, which is as large as the old Philips and occupies the space next to it. Though made by Continental Electronics Corporation of Dallas, it was procured in 1987 from Lao Telstra, a subsidiary of the Australian telecom giant Telstra. There were no direct trade relations between the United States and Laos, but the Australians cheerfully served as go-between.

The Continental transmitter operates from 2.3 to 16 MHz, and during our visit its counter showed 36,865.5 hours of operation. The core is a hybrid, with one large tube and the rest solid state. When running, it produces considerable heat, so it is cooled by an elaborate water system.

Also installed by Telstra were two shortwave antennas from TCI of Sunnyvale, California. These are omnidirectional, using an inverted cone centered around a single high tower. One is a TCI-613 fed by the 50 kilowatt shortwave transmitter for Laos National Radio's domestic service on 6130 kHz.

Unused antenna stands silent at station KM6.

M. Guha

The exodus from KM6 has been worthy of a latter-day Leon Uris.

Engineer Sysamone Phommaxay leads a twilight tour of the antenna farm at transmitting station KM6.

M. Guha

BE PREPARED
LET ETÓN EMPOWER YOU WITH NEWS & LIGHT

FR100
Blackout
Buddy

Emergency
Plug-In AM/FM Radio with Blackout Alert

Plug the Blackout Buddy into AC sockets around your home. When the power fails, Blackout Buddy automatically shines to the rescue, with a brilliant beam of light that illuminates the room and its AM/FM radio to give you breaking news. Blackout Buddy also makes a perfect AM/FM clock radio & LED flashlight for everyday listening around the home

- Automatically turns on radio/flashlight during power outages
- Super-bright LED flashlight
- Illuminated multi-function blue LCD screen and nightlight
- Patent-pending plug-in design recharges internal battery
- AM/FM radio with telescopic antenna
- Headphone jack and FM antenna input
- AC plug folds down for easy transportation

Dimensions: 3"W x 5"H x 1.4"D **Weight:** 10oz.
Power Source: AC power (direct plug-in)

all-in-one emergency radios

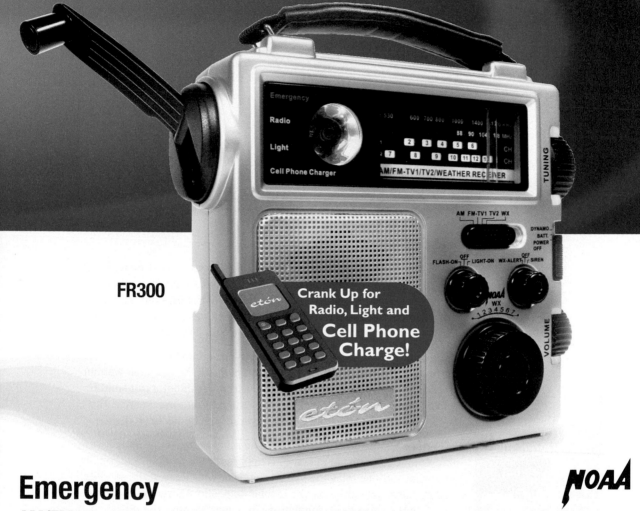

FR300

Crank Up for
Radio, Light and
**Cell Phone
Charge!**

Emergency

AM/FM Weather Alert Radio with NOAA, TV VHF, built-in Cell Phone Charger

This all-in-one unit offers functionality and versatility that makes it ideal for emergencies. The **FR300** provides you radio, light, and cell phone battery life when you need it most. The Hand-Crank Power Generator charges the internal rechargeable Ni-MH battery pack, making batteries unnecessary! Just 90 seconds of cranking provides up to an hour of radio play. With the NOAA Weather Channels and TV VHF channels, find forecasts or catch TV shows when you're away from the set.

- AM/FM with built-in antenna
- All 7 NOAA weather channels plus "Weather Alert"
- TV VHF channels 2-13
- Hand-Crank Power Generator
- Built-in Cell Phone Charger, flashlight, and emergency siren
- Rugged splash-proof ABS body
- Inputs for AC adaptor and earphones

Dimensions: 6.7"W x 6.5"H x 2.5"D **Weight:** 1.3lbs.
Power Source: Hand-Crank Power Generator with rechargeable battery pack, 3 AA batteries (not included) or AC adaptor (not included)

etón®
www.etoncorp.com

Japan Radio Transmitter

The second, TCI-615, is fed by a small ten kilowatt solid state transmitter from the same Japan Radio Company famous for tough world band receivers. Obtained in 2000, perhaps as part of the JICA aid that funded studio digitization in Vientiane, the unit is noiseless and energy efficient. Normally, it carries the International Service on 7145 kHz.

A key feature is that the transmitter is keypad-tuneable from 3.2 to 29 MHz with almost no warmup time, as compared to the half-hour warmup for the Continental. When the more powerful Continental transmitter acts up and the JRC isn't being used for the International Service, the Japanese unit instantaneously takes over for the domestic audience.

The nostalgic interloper finds pieces as big as a butcher's freezer.

At these times the domestic service is heard at reduced power and with different modulation, so the swap is apparent to listeners. Additionally, provincial stations relay the Vientiane news twice daily. If the satellite feed isn't available, they use the regular domestic shortwave frequency. So, when the shortwave signal drops in power because the JRC transmitter has replaced the Continental, the quality of relayed newscast audio from provincial stations sometimes also suffers.

Laid Back Operation

About ten people work at the station. This includes an engineer who lives in a red hut nearby, along with six assistants, a groundskeeper who seems to have delegated his work to cattle wandering in, and two conveniently absent security men deputized from the village police station.

Although there is plenty of room for more transmitters, future expansion at this site is unlikely as the surrounding village has almost engulfed it. Too, there are plans to build a road through the antenna farm. Even the mediumwave AM site of KM49 has no room to grow. "I think the likely place for expansion is the KM52 station, which has enough space," muses Dy Sisombath of the Mass Media Dept. "Incidentally, I was born in the village next to it. It is called Ban Labhasipsong, or Village 52, too," he chuckled.

A 100 kilowatt shortwave transmitter is planned, apparently for KM52, but with a big "if": They first have to locate a donor or receive a budget appropriation. No one is holding their breath.

Transmitter That Didn't Exist

A similar scene unfolds at the KM4 transmitting station in the village of Ban Tankhalok, just outside the picturesque royal capital of Luang Prabang. The control room has many receiving and monitoring racks in an odd mix that includes unused Eddystone receivers. Also on hand, from Amalgamated Wireless of Sydney, Australia, are HR21 single sideband telephone receivers probably once used to pick up program feeds; an HZ301 shortwave receiver for the Radio Telephone Terminal Unit; and an audio rack with a distortion/noise meter.

The only items that appear new and operational are the two Marti VHF link receivers that feed VHF link transmitters operating at the studio end on 155.5 and 150.5 MHz, respectively. These, in turn, feed the new ten kilowatt solid state Harris DX-10 mediumwave AM transmitter next door on 705 kHz.

The cavernous original transmitter hall is dark and empty except for the technicians' laundry drying on a clothesline. But lovers of cobwebs are rewarded when stepping into one of the anterooms. Here rests an old Chinese shortwave transmitter, still intact with its resplendent knobs and dials. This, of course, was once a big secret as it officially didn't exist—it was one of the two transmitters Mao's China surreptitiously furnished to "Radio Pathet Lao."

Metal from bombs that killed thousands of Laotians during the 1960's "secret war" are used to make artificial limbs for "bombies." UXO Lao via MCC

After the revolution ended in 1975, it was dispatched to Xeing Khoung in central Laos. However, it was then hastily moved to Luang Prabang because of heavy American bombardment. For a number of years it relayed the provincial service on the relatively clear frequency of 6970v kHz, but was finally taken off the air in 1999.

Since Laos' independence, the French connection has all but vanished. Nevertheless, French-made VHF transmitters and receivers work in tandem to provide studio-to-transmitter links. M. Guha

BE PREPARED
LET ETÓN EMPOWER YOU WITH NEWS & LIGHT

FR200

Emergency
AM/FM Shortwave Crank Radio

Requiring no batteries, the self-powered **FR200** keeps you informed and prepared for emergencies. The Hand-Crank Power Generator provides unlimited power for AM/FM radio use, access to 7 International Shortwave bands, and the built-in flashlight. Just 90 seconds of cranking provides up to an hour of radio play, making the FR200 perfect not only for emergencies, but also camping, hiking, or just relaxing in the backyard. Choose from 5 colors: Metallic Red, Metallic Blue, Metallic Pearl, Yellow, and Sand.

- AM/FM Shortwave with built-in antenna
- 7 international Shortwave bands
- Hand-Crank Power Generator
- Built-in flashlight
- Rugged splash-proof ABS body
- Inputs for AC adaptor and earphones
- 5 colors to choose from

Dimensions: 6.8"W x 5.8"H x 2.1"D **Weight:** 1.3lbs.
Power Source: Hand-Crank Power Generator with rechargeable battery pack, 3 AA batteries (not included) or AC adaptor (not included)

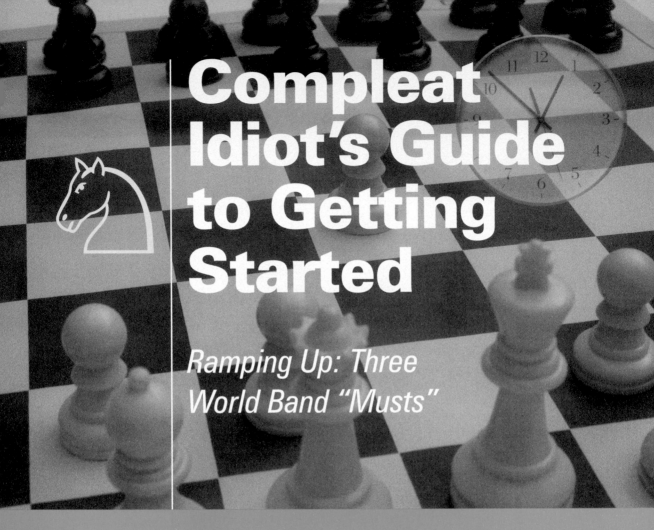

Compleat Idiot's Guide to Getting Started

Ramping Up: Three World Band "Musts"

World band isn't your everyday radio. It not only requires special receivers, it also operates differently. So here are three "musts" to tune in the world without fumbling around or wasting time.

"Must" #1: World Time and Day

World band schedules use a single time, *World Time*. World band radio is global, with stations beaming around-the-clock from nearly every time zone. Imagine the chaos if each station announced its local time to tell listeners worldwide when to tune in.

World Time to the rescue! It offers one time zone for one planet.

World Time, or Coordinated Universal Time (UTC), supercedes the almost-identical Greenwich Mean

Time (GMT) as the global standard. It uses the 24-hour format, so 2 PM is 14:00 ("fourteen hundred") hours, and strictly speaking leading zeroes are shown (e.g., "08:00," read as "oh-eight-hundred hours," not "8:00"). In the military, it is often called "Zulu."

Most major international broadcasters announce World Time at the hour. On the Internet, World Time is given at various sites, including http://time5.nrc.ca/webclock_e.shtml. Around North America, World Time is announced over standard time stations WWV in Colorado, WWVH in Hawaii and CHU in Ottawa. WWV and WWVH use world band on 5000, 10000 and 15000 kHz, with WWV also on 2500 and 20000 kHz. CHU ticks away on 3330, 7335 and 14670 kHz.

See the "Setting Your Clock" sidebar to adjust your 24-hour clock. For example, if you live on the east coast of the United States, *add* five hours winter (four hours summer) to your local time to get World Time. So, if it is 8 PM EST (the 20th hour of the day) in New York, it is 01:00 hours World Time.

Adjust your radio's 24-hour clock. No clock? Get one now unless you enjoy doing weird computations in your head (it's 6:00 PM here, so add five hours to make it 11:00 PM, which on a 24-hour clock converts to 23:00 World Time—but, whoops, it's summer so I should have added four hours instead of five . . .). The best money you'll ever spend.

Don't forget to "wind your calendar," because at midnight a new *World Day* arrives. This can trip up even experienced listeners—sometimes radio stations, too. So if it is 9:00 PM EST Wednesday in New York, it is 02:00 hours World Time *Thursday*.

"Must" #2: Finding Stations

PASSPORT **shows station schedules three ways: by country, time of day and frequency.** By-country is best for tuning to a given station. "What's On Tonight"—the time-of-day section—is like *TV Guide* and has program descriptions. Quick-access Blue Pages show what you might

Analog timepieces are *de rigueur* for fastidious traditionalists. This World Time chronograph is from Germany's Tutima, maker of official watches for NATO.

World Time offers one zone for one planet.

PASSPORT'S THREE-MINUTE START

Too swamped to read the owner's manual? Try this:

1. Night time is the right time, so wait until evening when signals are strongest. In a concrete-and-steel building put your radio by a window or balcony.

2. Make sure your radio is plugged in or has fresh batteries. Extend its telescopic antenna fully and vertically. Set the DX/local switch (if there is one) to "DX," but otherwise leave the controls the way they came from the factory.

3. Turn on your radio. Set it to 5900 kHz and begin tuning slowly toward 6200 kHz. You should hear stations from around the world.

Other times? Read "Best Times and Frequencies for 2005."

SETTING YOUR CLOCK TO WORLD TIME

PASSPORT's "Addresses PLUS" chapter lets you figure out local time in other countries by adding or subtracting from World Time. Use that section to ascertain time within a country you are hearing.

This sidebar does the opposite—it shows what to add or subtract from your local time to determine World Time. For example, if you live in Chicago and it's 7:00 AM, World Time is five hours later (noon, or 12:00 World Time) summer, or six hours later (13:00 World Time) winter. Use this to set your 24-hour clock permanently to World Time so you won't have to convert time again.

What about summer or saving time? No problem. Although your local clock may change by an hour each spring and fall, World Time stays the same year round.

Too confusing? In many parts of the world you can simply tune to stations that broadcast nothing but World Time, 24/7. In and around North America try WWV in Colorado on 2500, 5000, 10000, 15000 and 20000 kHz; also, Canada's CHU on 3330, 7335 and 14670 kHz. In the Pacific tune to WWVH in Hawaii on 2500, 5000, 10000 and 15000 kHz.

WHERE YOU ARE 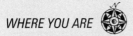   *TO DETERMINE WORLD TIME*

North America

Newfoundland St. John's NF, St. Anthony NF	Add 3 hours, 2 summer
Atlantic St. John NB, Battle Harbour NF	Add 4 hours, 3 summer
Eastern New York, Atlanta, Toronto	Add 5 hours, 4 summer
Central Chicago, Mexico City, Nashville, Winnipeg	Add 6 hours, 5 summer
Mountain Denver, Salt Lake City, Calgary	Add 7 hours, 6 summer
Pacific San Francisco, Vancouver	Add 8 hours, 7 summer
Alaska	Add 9 hours, 8 summer
Hawaii	Add 10 hours

Central America & Caribbean

Bermuda	Add 4 hours, 3 summer
Barbados, Puerto Rico, Virgin Islands	Add 4 hours
Bahamas, Cuba	Add 5 hours, 4 summer
Jamaica	Add 5 hours
Costa Rica	Add 6 hours

Europe

United Kingdom, Ireland, Portugal	Same time as World Time winter, subtract 1 hour summer
Continental Western Europe; parts of Central and Eastern Continental Europe	Subtract 1 hour, 2 hours summer
Elsewhere in Continental Europe: Belarus, Bulgaria, Cyprus, Estonia, Finland, Greece, Latvia, Lithuania, Moldova, Romania, Russia (Kaliningradskaya Oblast), Turkey, Ukraine	Subtract 2 hours, 3 summer
Moscow	Subtract 3 hours, 4 summer

Mideast & Africa

Côte d'Ivoire, Ghana, Guinea, Liberia, Mali, Morocco, Senegal, Sierra Leone	World Time exactly
Angola, Benin, Chad, Congo, Nigeria, Tunisia	Subtract 1 hour
Egypt, Israel, Jordan, Lebanon, Syria	Subtract 2 hours, 3 summer
South Africa, Zambia, Zimbabwe	Subtract 2 hours
Ethiopia, Kenya, Kuwait, Saudi Arabia, Tanzania, Uganda	Subtract 3 hours
Iran	Subtract 3½ hours, 4½ summer

Asia & Australasia

Pakistan	Subtract 5 hours
India	Subtract 5½ hours
Bangladesh, Sri Lanka	Subtract 6 hours
Laos, Thailand, Vietnam	Subtract 7 hours
China (including Taiwan), Malaysia, Philippines, Singapore	Subtract 8 hours
Japan, Korea	Subtract 9 hours
Australia: *Victoria, New South Wales, Tasmania*	Subtract 11 hours local summer, 10 local winter (midyear)
Australia: *South Australia*	Subtract 10½ hours local summer, 9½ hours local winter (midyear)
Australia: *Queensland*	Subtract 10 hours
Australia: *Northern Territory*	Subtract 9 1/2 hours
Australia: *Western Australia*	Subtract 8 hours
New Zealand	Subtract 13 hours local summer, 12 hours local winter (midyear)

porsche design
G2000A am/fm shortwave radio

From its sleek sculpted lines to its soft leather case to its high performance, the G2000A designed by the legendary F.A. Porsche, is reminiscent of its fine automotive design heritage in every way.

- F.A. Porsche Design styling
- Autoscan and direct keypad tuning
- 20 customizable station presets
- Dual alarm and sleep timer functions
- Snap-on leather protective case that converts to stand

Dimensions: 5.5"W x 3.5"H x 1.3"D **Weight:** 7.4 oz.
Power Source: 3 AA batteries (not included) or AC adaptor (included)

high performance portable
G4000A am/fm shortwave radio

The G4000A is an enthusiast-quality world receiver, packed with the power to scan and lock-on to even the weakest Shortwave signals with rock-solid precision. The G4000A is capable of receiving AM, FM, continuous Shortwave, and even SSB (Single Sideband) for two-way Shortwave communications such as amateur radio operators.

- Single Sideband (SSB) reception
- Wide and narrow bandwidth filter controls
- Autoscan and direct keypad tuning; 40 customizable station presets
- Alarm and sleep timer functions

Dimensions: 7.8"W x 4.6"H x 1.4"D **Weight:** 1lbs. 5oz.
Power Source: 6 AA batteries (not included) or AC adaptor (included)

high performance field radio
S350 am/fm shortwave radio

With the rugged look of a retro field radio and the latest in AM, FM, Shortwave radio technology, the S350 features the best of analog and digital. The S350 is the perfect addition to active lifestyles that demand high performance portable audio capable of receiving news and information from across the globe.

- Separate bass, treble, and RF gain controls
- Wide and narrow bandwidth filter controls
- Line-level audio outputs and external antenna input
- Alarm & sleep timer functions with illuminated multi-function LCD screen

Dimensions: 10.5"W x 6.5"H x 3.5"D Weight: 3lbs. 9oz.
Power Source: 4 D batteries (not included) or AC adaptor (included)

emergency crank radio

FR200 am/fm shortwave radio & flashlight

Requiring no batteries, the FR200's Hand-Crank Power Generator provides unlimited power for AM/FM radio use, access to 7 international Shortwave bands, and the built-in Flashlight. Just 90 seconds of cranking provides up to an hour of radio play.

- 7 International Shortwave bands
- Built-in antenna
- Hand-Crank Power Generator
- Built-in flashlight
- Rugged splash-proof ABS body
- Inputs for AC adaptor and earphones

Dimensions: 6.8"W x 5.8"H x 2.1"D **Weight:** 1.3lbs. **Power Source:** Hand-Crank Power Generator with rechargeable battery pack, 3 AA batteries (not included) or AC adaptor (not included)

emergency plug-in am/fm radio with blackout alert

FR100 Blackout Buddy

Plug the Blackout Buddy into AC sockets around your home. When the power fails, Blackout Buddy automatically shines to the rescue, with a brilliant beam of light that illuminates the room and its AM/FM radio to give you breaking news. Blackout Buddy also makes a perfect AM/FM clock radio & LED flashlight for everyday listening around the home.

- Automatically turns on radio/flashlight during power outages
- Super-bright LED flashlight
- Illuminated multi-function blue LCD screen and nightlight
- Patent-pending plug-in design recharges internal battery. AC plug folds down
- Telescopic antenna, headphone jack and FM antenna input

Dimensions: 3"W x 5"H x 1.4"D **Weight:** 10oz.
Power Source: AC power (direct plug-in)

With world band, if you dial randomly through the shortwave spectrum you're more likely to get dead air than a program. That's because world band stations transmit only on limited segments within the shortwave spectrum. Too, some of these segments are alive and kicking only by day, while others spring to life at night. The time of year also influences which segments hold promise.

Treat this guide like a good weather forecast—helpful but not holy writ, as Nature has a mind of its own. The guide is most accurate if you're north of the African and South American continents. Even then, what you hear will vary—depending upon your location, where the station transmits from, the time of year and your radio (*see* Propagation in PASSPORT's Glossary).

Although world band is active around the clock, signals are usually best from an hour or two before sunset until sometime after midnight. Too, try a couple of hours on either side of dawn. If your radio setup has good weak-signal sensitivity, also listen after lunch. Thanks to the scattering properties of shortwave, signals beamed elsewhere are increasingly likely to be audible at your location at these times.

Fine print: "Night" refers to your local hours of darkness, plus dawn and dusk. Also, a number of official frequency segments are allocated for broadcasting. Broadcasters additionally operate beyond these segments—"out-of-band"—as secondary users, provided they do not cause harmful interference to such primary users as fixed-service utility stations.

Night—Very Limited Reception
Day—Local Reception Only

2 MHz (120 meters) **2300-2495 kHz**—overwhelmingly domestic stations, plus 2496-2504 kHz for time stations only.

Night—Limited Reception
Day—Local Reception Only

3 MHz (90 meters) **3200-3400 kHz**—overwhelmingly domestic broadcasters, but also some international stations.

Day and Night—Good-to-Fair in Europe and Asia except Summer Nights
Elsewhere, Limited Reception Night

4 MHz (75 meters) **3900-4050 kHz**—international and domestic stations, primarily not in or beamed to the Americas; 3900-3950 kHz mainly Asian and Pacific transmitters; 3950-4000 kHz also includes European and African transmitters; 4001-4050 kHz currently out-of-band.

Night—Fair Reception
Day—Regional Reception Only

5 MHz (60 meters) **4750-4995 kHz** and **5005-5100 kHz**—mostly domestic stations, plus 4996-5004 kHz for time stations only; 5061-5100 kHz currently out-of-band.

be hearing when you're dialing around the bands.

World band frequencies are usually given in kilohertz (kHz), but some stations use Megahertz (MHz). The only difference is three decimal places, so 6170 kHz is the same as 6.17 MHz, 6175 kHz identical to 6.175 MHz, and so on.

FM and other stations keep the same spot on the dial, day and night—webcast URLs,

Night—Excellent Reception
Day—Regional Reception Only

6 MHz (49 meters) **5730-6300 kHz**—5730-5899 kHz and 6201-6300 kHz currently out-of-band.

Night—Good Reception
Day—Mainly Regional Reception

7 MHz (41 meters) **6890-6990 kHz** and **7100-7600 kHz**—6890-6990 kHz and 7351-7600 kHz currently out-of-band; 7100-7300 kHz no American-based transmitters and few transmissions targeted to the Americas. Some years hence, the 7100 kHz lower parameter may shift to 7200 kHz, with 7200-7300 kHz rather than 7100-7300 kHz being for outside the Americas.

Day—Fair Reception Winter; Regional Reception Summer
Night—Good Reception Summer

9 MHz (31 meters) **9250-9995 kHz**—9250-9399 kHz and 9901-9995 kHz currently out-of-band, plus 9996-10004 kHz for time stations only.

Day—Good Reception
Night—Variable Reception Summer

11 MHz (25 meters) **11500-12200 kHz**—11500-11599 kHz and 12101-12200 kHz currently out-of-band.

13 MHz (22 meters) **13570-13870 kHz**

15 MHz (19 meters) **15005-15825 kHz**—15005-15099 kHz and 15801-15825 kHz currently out-of-band, plus 14996-15004 kHz for time stations only.

Day—Good Reception
Night—Limited Reception Summer

17 MHz (16 meters) **17480-17900 kHz**

19 MHz (15 meters) **18900-19020 kHz**—few stations use this segment.

Day—Variable Reception
Night—Little Reception

21 MHz (13 meters) **21450-21850 kHz**

Day—Rare, if Any, Reception
Night—No Reception

25 MHz (11 meters) **25670-26100 kHz**

> Thanks to world band's scattering properties, even stations beamed elsewhere may be heard at your location.

Emergency Plug-In AM/FM Radio with Blackout Alert

Plug the Blackout Buddy into AC sockets around your home. When the power fails, Blackout Buddy automatically shines to the rescue, with a brilliant beam of light that illuminates the room and its AM/FM radio to give you breaking news. Blackout Buddy also makes a perfect AM/FM clock radio & LED flashlight for everyday listening around the home.

- Automatically turns on radio/flashlight during power outages
- Super-bright LED flashlight
- Illuminated multi-function blue LCD screen and nightlight
- Patent-pending plug-in design recharges internal battery
- Telescopic antenna, headphone jack and FM antenna input

FR100 Blackout Buddy

Dimensions: 3"W x 5"H x 1.4"D
Weight: 10oz. **Power Source:** AC power (direct plug-in)

FR200

Emergency
AM/FM Shortwave Crank Radio

Requiring no batteries, the FR200's Hand-Crank Power Generator provides unlimited power for AM/FM radio use, access to 7 International Shortwave bands, and the built-in flashlight. Just 90 seconds of cranking provides up to an hour of radio play.

- 7 International Shortwave bands. Built-in antenna
- Hand-Crank Power Generator with built-in flashlight
- Rugged splash-proof ABS body. Inputs for AC adaptor and earphones

Dimensions: 6.8"W x 5.8"H x 2.1"D **Weight:** 1.3lbs.
Power Source: Hand-Crank Power Generator with rechargeable battery pack, 3 AA batteries (not included) or AC adaptor (not included)

perfect for travelling the world

Mini 300PE am/fm shortwave radio

The Mini 300PE is a pocket-sized and power-packed wonder. Only 4.7 ounces, the Mini 300PE is not only an AM and FM stereo radio, but also a world band receiver capable of pulling in seven international Shortwave bands.

- 7 international Shortwave bands
- Telescopic and internal ferrite bar antennas
- Includes protective travel case, ear buds, earphone input
- Clock, alarm, and sleep timer functions
- Multi-function LCD screen

Dimensions: 2.5"W x 4.3"H x 0.9"D **Weight:** 4.7oz.
Power Source: 2 AA batteries (included)

FR300

Emergency AM/FM Weather Alert Radio with NOAA, TV VHF, built-in Cell Phone Charger

This all-in-one unit offers functionality and versatility that makes it ideal for emergencies. The FR300 provides you radio, light, and cell phone battery life when you need it most. The Hand-Crank Power Generator charges the internal rechargeable Ni-MH battery pack, making batteries unnecessary! Just 90 seconds of cranking provides up to an hour of radio play. With the NOAA Weather Channels and TV VHF channels, find forecasts or catch TV shows when you're away from the set.

- AM/FM radio with built-in antenna, TV VHF channels 2-13
- All 7 NOAA weather channels plus "Weather Alert"
- Hand-Crank Power Generator
- Built-in Cell Phone Charger, flashlight, and emergency siren
- Splash-proof ABS body, inputs for AC adaptor & earphones

Dimensions: 6.7"W x 6.5"H x 2.5"D **Weight:** 1.3lbs. **Power Source:** Hand-Crank Power Generator with rechargeable battery pack, 3 AA batteries (not included) or AC adaptor (not included)

too. But things are different on international airwaves.

World band radio is like a global bazaar where a variety of merchants come and go at various times of the day and night. Where you once tuned in, say, a French station, hours later you might find a Russian or Chinese broadcaster roosting on that same spot.

Or on a nearby perch. If you suddenly hear interference from a station on an adjacent channel, it doesn't mean something is wrong with your radio; another station has probably begun broadcasting on a nearby frequency. There are more stations on the air than available space, so sometimes they try to outshout each other.

To cope with this, purchase a radio with superior adjacent-channel rejection—selectivity—and lean towards radios with synchronous selectable sideband. PASSPORT REPORTS, a major section of this book, tells you which models stand out.

Because world band is full of surprises from one listening session to the next, experienced listeners like to surf the airwaves. Daytime, you'll find most stations above 11500 kHz; at night, below 10000 kHz.

If a station can't be found or fades out, there is probably nothing wrong with your radio.

World band stations are located on *terra firma*, but because of the earth's curvature their signals eventually run into the atmosphere's sky-high ionosphere. When the ionosphere is suitably energized, it deflects world band signals back down, after which they bounce off oceans or soil and sail once again back up to the ionosphere.

This process of bouncing up and down like a dribbled basketball continues until a signal finally arrives at your radio. However, if the ionosphere at any one "bounce point" isn't in a bouncing mood—this varies daily and seasonally, like the weather—the signal goes off into space instead of back down to earth. That's great for travelers to Uranus, but for the rest of us it's a major reason why a scheduled signal might be audible one hour, gone the next.

Nature's ionosphere is why world band radio is so unencumbered—its signals don't rely on cables or satellites or the Internet, just layers of ionized gases which have enveloped our planet for eons. World band is free from regulation, taxes and fees, too. And, like domestic public radio, it's largely free from ads.

But nature's ionosphere, like the weather, changes constantly. World band stations cope by operating within different frequency ranges, depending upon the time of day and

WORLD TIME CLOCKS

Some radios include a World Time clock displayed fulltime—this is best. Other radios may have World Time clocks, but to see time when the radio is on you have to press a button.

Because World Time uses the 24-hour format, digital clocks are easier to read than hands. MFJ Enterprises makes several 24-hour clocks—conventional or atomic-synchronized, some with seconds displayed numerically—from $9.95 to $79.95 at MFJ and radio dealers. Sharper Image also offers three clocks in the $39.95–49.95 range.

Other 24-hour clocks run up to $2,000, including models designed primarily for professionals.

David Zantow

When not at his PC, retiree Louis Magne, 91 years young, uses the Sony ICF-SW07 with "tennis racquet" antenna to hear the world from Barbados. The Sony AN-LP1 antenna, virtually identical, improves reception on most portables. J. Brinker

season of the year. This changeability can work in your favor, especially if you like to eavesdrop on signals not intended for your part of the world. Sometimes stations from exotic locales—places you would not ordinarily hear—become surprise arrivals at your radio, thanks to the ionosphere's shifting characteristics.

"Must" #3: The Right Radio

Choose carefully, but you don't need a costly set. If you just want to hear major stations, you'll do fine with a moderately priced portable. Beyond that, portatop models have a better chance of bringing in faint and difficult signals—they usually sound better, too. Tabletop receivers are aimed at experienced DX radio enthusiasts, so they tend to be unnecessarily costly and complex for most program listeners to operate.

Look for a radio with digital frequency display, which is far and away the easiest to tune—all radios tested for PASSPORT REPORTS have digital displays, but analog (slide-rule-tuning) models are still available. Also, get a radio that tunes at least 4750-21850 kHz with no significant frequency gaps or "holes." Otherwise, you may not be able to tune all stations.

You won't need an exotic outside antenna unless you're using a tabletop model. All portables, and to some extent portatops, are designed to work well off their built-in telescopic antennas. If you want to enhance weak-signal sensitivity, clip several yards or meters of insulated wire onto that antenna.

Finally, avoid cheap radios, as they suffer from one or more major defects. With one of the better-rated portables you'll be able to hear much more of what world band has to offer.

_____

Prepared by Jock Elliott, Tony Jones and Lawrence Magne.

porsche design
G2000A am/fm shortwave radio

From its sleek sculpted lines to its soft leather case to its high performance, the G2000A designed by the legendary F.A. Porsche, is reminiscent of its fine automotive design heritage in every way.

- F.A. Porsche Design styling
- Autoscan and direct keypad tuning
- 20 customizable station presets
- Dual alarm and sleep timer functions
- Snap-on leather protective case that converts to stand

Dimensions: 5.5"W x 3.5"H x 1.3"D **Weight:** 7.4 oz.
Power Source: 3 AA batteries (not included) or AC adaptor (included)

high performance
G4000A am/fm shortwave radio

The G4000A is an enthusiast-quality world receiver, packed with the power to scan and lock-on to even the weakest Shortwave signals with rock-solid precision. The G4000A is capable of receiving AM, FM, Continuous Shortwave, and even SSB (Single Sideband) for two-way Shortwave communications such as amateur radio operators.

Single Sideband (SSB) reception • Wide and narrow bandwidth filter controls • Autoscan and direct keypad tuning; 40 customizable station presets • Alarm and sleep timer functions • **Dimensions:** 7.8"W x 4.6"H x 1.4"D • **Weight:** 1lbs. 5oz. • **Power Source:** 6 AA batteries (not included) or AC adaptor (included)

high performance field radio
S350 am/fm shortwave radio

With the rugged look of a retro field radio and the latest in AM, FM, Shortwave radio technology, the S350 features the best of analog and digital. The S350 is the perfect addition to active lifestyles that demand high-performance portable audio capable of receiving news and information from across the globe.

Separate bass, treble, and RF gain controls • Wide and narrow bandwidth filter controls • Line-level audio outputs and external antenna input • Alarm & sleep timer functions with illuminated multi-function LCD screen • **Dimensions:** 10.5"W x 6.5"H x 3.5"D • **Weight:** 3lbs. 9oz. • **Power Source:** 4 D batteries (not included) or AC adaptor (included)

palm-size world band radio
G1000A am/fm shortwave radio

Small enough to fit in a coat pocket, yet powerful enough to capture eight Shortwave bands and feature a digital frequency readout and alarm, the G1000A is a the perfect all-purpose radio for home or travel.

Receives 8 International Shortwave bands • Alarm and sleep timer functions with illuminated multi-function • LCD screen • Snap-on protective case and stand • AC adaptor and earphone inputs • **Dimensions:** 4.5"W x 3"H x 1.1"D • **Weight:** 7 oz. • **Power Source:** 2 AA batteries (included)

fits into your palm or pocket

E100 Elite Series am/fm shortwave radio

Fits into your palm or pocket, but fitted with full-sized features. Imagine a radio packed with all the bells and whistles: digital tuning AM, FM, Shortwave reception, and small enough to fit into your coat pocket. The E100 is a dream come true.

Shortwave range of 1711 – 29,999 KHz • 200 programmable memories with memory page customization • Manual & auto scan, direct keypad frequency entry, tuning knob • Programmable alarm & sleep functions with digital clock • Clean-design body with fine lines & metallic finish • **Dimensions:** 4.9"W x 3"L x 1.2"D • **Weight:** 7.4oz. • **Power Source:** 2 AA batteries (included) or AC adaptor (not included)

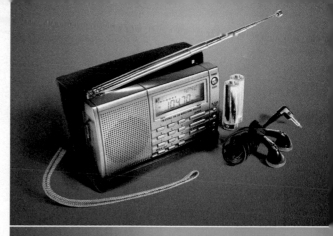

intelligent features that simplify

E10 Elite Series am/fm shortwave radio

Performance that reaches out to the world. Imagine a radio that combines strong performance for fantastic reception and all of today's digital wizardry, bringing the world to your fingertips. The E10 is where intelligence meets performance.

Shortwave range of 1711 – 29,999 KHz • 550 programmable memories with memory page customization • Manual & auto scan, direct keypad frequency entry, ATS, tuning knob • IF shift (Intermediate Frequency) and Shortwave antenna trimmer • Sleep timer, snooze, and favorite station wake-up timers • Includes AC adaptor/charger and 4 AA Ni-MH batteries • Internally charges AA Ni-MH batteries • Clean-design body with fine lines and metallic finish • **Dimensions:** 7.4"W x 4.5"H x 1.3"D • **Weight:** 1lbs. 5oz. • **Power Source:** 4 AA batteries or included AC adaptor/charger

world's first & only am/fm shortwave XM Satellite radio

E1XM Elite Series am/fm/sw/xm radio

The E1 XM is the world's first radio that combines AM, FM, Shortwave, and XM Satellite radio into one ultra high-performance unit. In collaboration with RL Drake Company and XM Satellite Radio, the E1 is the finest full-sized portable in the world.

- XM Satellite Radio or Digital Audio Broadcasting (DAB) ready
- Selectable Single Sideband (SSB) reception
- Digitally synthesized PLL tuner with synchronous detector
- Dual conversion superheterodyne circuit design
- Passband tuning, selectable bandwidth filters
- 1700 station presets, memory scan function
- 5.7" square illuminated multi-function dot-matrix LCD screen
- Stereo line-level audio inputs and outputs. External antenna connections
- Dual clocks and programmable timers

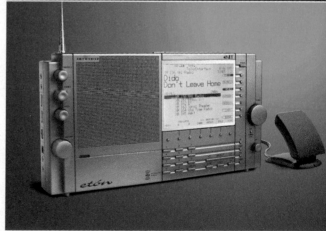

Dimensions: 13.1"W x 7.1"H x 2.3"D **Weight:** 4lbs. 3oz.
Power Source: 4 D batteries (not included) or AC adaptor (included)

SATELLiTE RADiO

RadioShack.®
You've got questions. We've got answers.®

etón®
www.etoncorp.com

First Tries: Ten Easy Catches

World band listeners usually focus on a manageable number of easily heard stations. So, in that spirit, here are ten powerhouses that can be enjoyed nearly anywhere. Several have first-rate programs, and all are in English.

Hours and days are in World Time. "Winter" and "summer" refer to seasons in the Northern Hemi-sphere, where summer takes place in the middle of the year.

EUROPE
France

Radio France Internationale is arguably more respected than its government. Although its output in English was never extensive—its central mission is *francophone*—its programs have always been popular. In recent years it has tailored its broadcasts to audiences in Africa, the Middle East and South Asia. Fortunately, its signals reach far beyond.

☞ RECOMMENDED PROGRAM: All are first-rate.

North America: Although RFI does not target English to North America, the station is still audible, albeit at inconvenient hours. Best by far is the 0700-0800 broadcast from the RFI relay in Gabon, intended for West Africa. It is widely heard in parts of North America—especially in the east. Winter on 11725 and 15605 kHz, and summer on 15605 kHz. Also, the 1600 transmission to Africa is often audible on higher frequencies, but at lesser strength.

Middle East: 1400-1500 on 17620 kHz winter, and 15615 or 17515 kHz summer; also 1600-1730 winter on 11615 kHz and summer on 15605 kHz.

South Asia: 1400-1500 on 7180 or 9580 kHz in winter, and 9580 or 11610 kHz in summer. This broadcast, via a transmitter in China, can also be well heard in western parts of *Southeast Asia* and *Australia.*

Africa: RFI's popular broadcasts to Africa are audible at 0400-0430 winter weekdays on 9555 or 11995 kHz, and summer on 7280 kHz (plus the irregular 11700 kHz); 0500-0530 weekdays on any two channels from 11685, 11850, 11995, 15155 and 15605 kHz; 0600-0630 weekdays on two or more frequencies from 11665, 11725, 15155, 17800 and 21620 kHz; 0700-0800 winter on 11725 kHz, and year-round on 15605 kHz; 1200-1230 on 17815 and 21620 or 25820 kHz; 1600-1700 on any four frequencies from 9590, 9730, 11615, 15160, 15365, 15605, 17605, 17850 and 21580 kHz; and 1700-1730 winter on 15605 kHz, and summer on 17605 kHz.

Radio France Internationale may be more respected than its government.

Most RFI programming is in French, but English also reaches worldwide. It focuses on regions and events that often get short shrift from other news sources. Corbis

The busy newsroom at Radio Netherlands, where "Newsline" is produced.   RNW

Germany

Arguably world band's most professional broadcaster, **Deutsche Welle** produces some excellent content. Though not officially broadcast to North America and Australasia, transmissions in English are still heard far and wide. Originally airing mostly news, DW now includes some excellent music programs.

☞ RECOMMENDED PROGRAMS: "Inside Germany" and "Money Talks."

North and Central America: Best for the eastern and southern United States and the Caribbean is the broadcast for West Africa at 2100-2200. Try 13780 and 15410 kHz in winter, and 11865 and 15205 kHz in summer. For night owls, 0600-0700 to the same region should also be audible, especially to the south. Best is 15410 kHz winter, 17860 kHz summer.

Europe: 0600-1000 and 1300-1600 year-round on 6140 kHz.

Middle East: 0400-0500 winter on 9545 kHz and summer on 9630 kHz. The 1900-2000 broadcast to East Africa can also be heard well in some areas. Try 11865 kHz winter, 13590 kHz summer.

Southern Africa: 0500-0600 winter—summer in the Southern Hemisphere—on 12035 kHz, and midyear on 12045 kHz. The evening transmission airs at 2000-2100 winter on 12025 kHz, and midyear on 7130 kHz.

East Asia: A 30-minute Asian edition of "NewsLink" can be heard at 1000-1030 winter on 6205 and 17820 kHz, and summer on 15350 and 17820 kHz. A one-hour broadcast airs at 2200-2300, winter on 6180 kHz and summer on 7115 and 9720 kHz.

Southeast Asia: 1100-1200 winter on 15410 kHz; summer on 15105, 17820 and 21820 kHz. Also at 2300-2400 winter on 7250, 9815 and 12035 kHz; replaced summer by 7115, 9890 and 15135 kHz.

Australasia: There's nothing beamed to Australasia, but some frequencies for Southeast Asia are audible when there's no interference from other stations.

Netherlands

Radio Netherlands—the English service of **Radio Nederland Wereldomroep**—succeeds by avoiding cookie-cutter production. Its strong commitment to social issues and willingness to tackle controversial topics has proved to be a winning formula. The station's on-air slogan gets it right: "Radio Netherlands—A Different Perspective."

☞ RECOMMENDED PROGRAMS: "Euroquest" and "Insight."

North America: (East) 1200-1300 (one hour earlier in summer) on 11675 kHz; 1900-2100 (weekends only) on 17725 kHz winter, and 17735 kHz summer; and 0000-0100 on 9845 kHz; *(Central)* 1900-2100 (weekends only) on 15315 kHz; and 0100-0200 winter on 6165 kHz, replaced summer by 9845 kHz; *(West):* 1900-2100 (weekends only) on 17875 kHz winter, and 17660 kHz summer; and 0400-0500 on 6165 and 9590 kHz.

Southern Africa: 1800-1900 on 6020 kHz, and 1900-2100 on 7120 kHz.

intelligent features that simplify
E10 Elite Series am/fm shortwave radio

Performance that reaches out to the world. Imagine a radio that combines strong performance for fantastic reception and all of today's digital wizardry, bringing the world to your fingertips. The E10 is where intelligence meets performance.

Shortwave range of 1711 – 29,999 KHz • 550 programmable memories with memory page customization • Manual & auto scan, direct keypad frequency entry, ATS, tuning knob • IF shift (Intermediate Frequency) • Shortwave antenna trimmer • Sleep timer, snooze, and favorite station wake-up timers • Includes AC adaptor/charger & 4 AA Ni-MH batteries • Internally charges AA Ni-MH batteries • **Dimensions:** 7.4"W x 4.5"H x 1.3"D • **Weight:** 1lbs. 5oz. • **Power Source:** 4 AA batteries or included AC adaptor/charger

fits into your palm or pocket
E100 Elite Series am/fm shortwave radio

Fits into your palm or pocket, but fitted with full-sized features. Imagine a radio packed with all the bells and whistles: digital tuning AM, FM, Shortwave reception, and small enough to fit into your coat pocket. The E100 is a dream come true.

Shortwave range of 1711 – 29,999 KHz • 200 programmable memories with memory page customization • Manual & auto scan, direct keypad frequency entry, tuning knob • Programmable alarm & sleep functions with digital clock • Clean-design body with fine lines & metallic finish • **Dimensions:** 4.9"W x 3"L x 1.2"D • **Weight:** 7.4oz. • **Power Source:** 2 AA batteries (included) or AC adaptor (not included)

high performance portable
G4000A am/fm shortwave radio

The G4000A is an enthusiast-quality world receiver, packed with the power to scan and lock-on to even the weakest Shortwave signals. The G4000A is capable of receiving AM, FM, continuous Shortwave, and even SSB (Single Sideband) for two-way Shortwave communications such as amateur radio operators. • Wide & narrow bandwidth filter controls • Autoscan & direct keypad tuning • 40 customizable station presets • Alarm & sleep timer • 7.8"W x 4.6"H x 1.4"D • 1lbs. 5oz. • **Power Source:** 6 AA batteries (not included) or AC adaptor (included)

high performance field radio
S350 am/fm shortwave radio

With the rugged look of a retro field radio and the latest in AM, FM, Shortwave radio technology, the S350 features the best of analog and digital. The S350 is the perfect addition to active lifestyles that demand high-performance portable audio capable of receiving news and information from across the globe.

Separate bass, treble, and RF gain controls • Wide and narrow bandwidth filter controls • Line-level audio outputs and external antenna input • Alarm & sleep timer functions with illuminated multi-function LCD screen • **Dimensions:** 10.5"W x 6.5"H x 3.5"D • **Weight:** 3lbs. 9oz. • **Power Source:** 4 D batteries (not included) or AC adaptor (included)

Voice of Russia staff (from left): Svetlana Yekimenko, Vitaly Glazunov, Estelle Winters, Carl Watts, Elena Baskakova.   VoR

East and Southeast Asia: 1000-1100 on 7315 (winter), 12065 kHz, 13710 (summer) and 13820 kHz. These frequencies are also well heard in parts of Australasia.

Australasia: 1000-1100 on 9785 kHz.

Russia

Despite a slim budget and a reduced number of transmitters, the **Voice of Russia** continues to be well heard worldwide. Its friendly announcers and culturally oriented programming make it a global favorite.

☞ RECOMMENDED PROGRAMS: "Christian Message from Moscow" and "Music and Musicians."

Eastern North America: Winter, 0200-0600 on 7180 kHz, 0300-0500 on 7350 kHz, and 0400-0600 on 7240 kHz; summer, 0100-0500 on 9665 kHz (7180 kHz in autumn), 0200-0400 on 9860 kHz, and 0300-0500 on 9880 kHz (7300 kHz in autumn). Winter afternoons, try frequencies beamed to Europe—some make it to eastern North America.

Western North America: Winter, 0200-0400 on 15445 and 15595 kHz, and 0400-0600 on 12010, 15445 and 15595 kHz; summer, 0100-0300 on 15595 and 17660 kHz, and 0300-0500 on 15455, 15595 and 17660 kHz.

Europe: Winter, 1800-1900 on 7290 kHz; 1900-2000 on 6175, 6235, 7290 and 7360 kHz; and 2000-2200 on 6145 (till 2100), 6175, 6235, 7290, 7300 (from 2100) and 7340 kHz. Summer, 1700-1800 on 9890 kHz; 1800-1900 on 9480, 9890 and 11630 (or 9820) kHz; and 1900-2100 on 7440 (till 2000), 9480, 9890 (till 2000), 12070 (or 7310) and (from 2000) 15455 (or 11980) kHz [5950 and 6175 kHz (winter), 9480 and 11675 (summer) and 7350 and 9820 kHz (autumn) are also available weekends during the first hour].

Middle East: Winter, 0200-0400 on 5995 kHz, 1600-1700 on 6005 and 9830 kHz, and 1700-1900 on 9830 kHz. Summer, 0100-0300 on 5945 kHz, 1500-1600 on 7325 and 11985 kHz, 1600-1700 on 11985 and 15540 kHz, and 1700-1800 on 11985 kHz.

Southern Africa: 1800-2000 (one hour earlier in summer) on 11510 kHz.

Southeast Asia: Winter, 0800-1000 on 17495, 17525 and 17850 kHz; and 1500-1600 on 6205 and 11500 kHz. Summer, 0700-0900 on 17495 and 17525 kHz; 1400-1500 on 7390 kHz; and 1500-1600 on 7390 and 11500 kHz.

Australasia: 0500-0900 on 21790 kHz; 0800-1000 winter on 17495, 17525 and 17665 kHz; and 0700-0900 midyear on 17495, 17525 and 17635 kHz.

United Kingdom

The **BBC World Service** shows no sign of turning around the decline of the past decade. Its credibility continues to be questioned, and the current quality of its programs offers little hope of improvement.

Thankfully, good programs still exist—even if they are no longer the norm. Mainly, the sheer depth of the Beeb's news reporting in times of international crisis continues to put it in a class apart.

☞ RECOMMENDED PROGRAMS: "Charlie Gillett" and "Everywoman."

North America: Nothing is officially beamed to the United States and Canada, but North America continues as a secondary target. As a result, and thanks to the scattering properties of shortwave, the BBC is well heard in most places.

Best for eastern North America is the powerful service for the Caribbean: 1000-1100 on 6195 kHz, 1100-1400 on 6195 and 15190 kHz, 1400-1700 on 15190 kHz, and 2100-0500 on 5975 kHz. The transmission for South America at 2100-0300 on 12095 kHz is also heard in parts of North America (especially at 0000-0300 summer), but tends to suffer from teletype interference unless your radio has synchronous select-able sideband (*see* PASSPORT REPORTS). Too, some daytime frequencies for Europe, Africa and the Mideast can be heard— particularly during summer—but times vary, depending on your location and the time of year.

For nighttime and early morning reception in western North America, tune to the BBC's East Asia stream on 9740 kHz (1000-1600); reception is especially good on the West Coast. Winter evenings, try 9525 kHz (0100-0400) and 6135 kHz (0400-0600), replaced summer by 11835 kHz at 0100-0500—these are targeted at nearby Mexico.

Europe: A powerhouse 0300-2300 on 6195, 9410, 12095, 15485, 15565 and 17640 kHz, with times varying for each channel. Not all frequencies carry the same programming.

Middle East: 0200-2000. Key frequencies— times for each vary seasonally—are 9410, 11760, 12095, 15310, 15565, 15575 and 17640 kHz. The 12095, 15565 and 17640 kHz frequencies are mainly intended for

Eastern Europe, but provide acceptable reception in northern parts of the Mideast.

Southern Africa: 0300-2200 on, among others, 3255, 6005, 6190, 11940, 12095 and 21470 kHz—times vary for each channel.

East and Southeast Asia: 0000-0300 on 6195 (till 0200), 15280 and 15360 kHz; 0300-0500 on 15280, 15360, 17760 and 21660 kHz; 0500-0900 on 11955, 15280 (till 0530), 15360, 17760 and 21660; 0900-1030 on 6195, 9605, 9740, 15360, 17760 and 21660 kHz; 1030-1400 on 6195, 9740 and 17760 kHz; 1400-1600 on 6195, 7160 (or 7105) and 9740 kHz; 1600-1700 on 3915, 6195 and 7160 kHz; and 1700-1800 (to Southeast Asia) on 3915 and 7160 kHz. Local mornings, it's 2100-2200 on 3915, 5965, 6110 and 6195 kHz; 2200-2300 on 5965, 6195, 7105, 9605 (summer), 9740 and 11955 kHz; and 2300-2400 on 3915, 5965, 6195, 7105, 9605 (summer), 9740, 11955 and 15280 kHz.

Australasia: Like North America, Australasia is not an official target for BBC broadcasts. However, some transmissions for Southeast Asia are easily heard in Australia and New Zealand. Best bets: 0500-0900 on 11955 and 15360 kHz and 0900-1600 on 9740 kHz. At 2200-2300, 12080 kHz is also available for the southwestern Pacific.

ASIA
China

China Radio International now has more shortwave transmitters at its disposal than any other station on the planet, and is one of the few stations to offer genuine world-wide reception. Its vast network of trans-mitting sites across China, plus overseas relays, ensure that this major nation's broadcasts are heard just about everywhere.

CRI is also actively increasing its output in several languages. Indeed, in 2004 it expanded English to a full 24 hours, moving it closer to the goal of "radio's CNN." This expansion is expected to continue in 2005, both in transmitting hours and geographical availability.

☞ RECOMMENDED PROGRAMS: "RealTime Beijing" and "Voices from Other Lands."

Eastern North America: 0100-0200 on 9580 kHz, 0300-0400 on 7190 (better in the South) and 9690 kHz, 0400-0500 on 9755 kHz, 1000-1200 summer on 6040 and 11750 kHz, 1100-1200 winter on 5960 kHz, 1200-1300 winter on 9560 kHz, 1300-1400 on 9570 and (summer) 9650 kHz, 1300-1500 winter on 15230 kHz, and 2300-2400 on 5990 (better in the South), 6040 (winter) and (summer) 6145 kHz.

Western North America: 0000-0100 on 9790 kHz, 0300-0400 on 9690 and 9790 kHz, 0400-0500 on 9755 kHz, 0400-0600 (0400-0500 in summer) on 9560 kHz, 0400-0600 on 6190 kHz,1300-1400 winter on 11885 kHz, 1400-1500 on 13675 kHz, 1400-1600 on 7405 (1300-1500 in summer), and 17730 (or 13740) kHz, and 2300-2400 on 11970 (or 13680) kHz.

Broadcasts for *Europe* are in a state of flux, but these tend to be workhorses: 0800-1300 (to 1700 summer) on 17490 kHz; 2000-2200 winter on 5965, 7190, 9600 and/or 9855 kHz, and summer on 7190, 9600 and 11790 kHz. A relay via Moscow can be

heard winter at 2200-2300 on 7170 kHz, and summer on 9880 kHz (replaced by 7175 kHz in autumn).

Middle East: 1900-2000 on 9585 kHz.

Southern Africa: 1600-1800 on 9570 and 11900 kHz, and 2000-2130 on 11640 and 13630 kHz.

Southeast Asia: 1200-1300 on 9730 and 11980 kHz; and 1300-1400 on 11980 and 15180 kHz.

Australasia: 0900-1100 on 15210 and 17690 kHz; 1200-1300 on 11760 and 15415 kHz; and 1300-1400 on 11760 and 11900 kHz.

China (Taiwan)

Ironically, **Radio Taiwan International** has had to rationalize its broadcasts just as China Radio International is aggressively expanding its world band operations. However, the two stations don't really compete. CRI is heavily geared to serious news reporting, while RTI's programming is more relaxed.

☞ RECOMMENDED PROGRAM: "Jade Bells and Bamboo Pipes."

North America: (East and Central) 0200-0300 on 5950 and 9680 kHz; *(West)* 0300-0400 and 0700-0800 on 5950 kHz.

Europe: 1800-1900 on 3955 kHz; and 2200-2300 winter on 9355 kHz, replaced summer by 15600 kHz.

Middle East: There is nothing specifically targeted at the Mideast, but try the 2200-2300 broadcast to Europe via RTI's North American relay.

Asia: (East) 0200-0300 on 15465 kHz, and 1200-1300 on 7130 kHz; *(Southeast)* 0200-0300 on 11875 kHz; 0300-0400 on 15320 kHz; 1100-1200 on 7105 kHz, and 1400-1500 on 15265 kHz; *(South)* 1600-1700 on 11815 kHz.

Carlson Wong presents "Taipei Magazine" over Radio Taiwan International. RTI

Australasia: 0800-0900 on 9610 kHz.

intelligent features that simplify
E10 Elite Series am/fm shortwave radio

Performance that reaches out to the world. Imagine a radio that combines strong performance for fantastic reception and all of today's digital wizardry, bringing the world to your fingertips. The E10 is where intelligence meets performance.

Shortwave range of 1711 – 29,999 KHz • 550 programmable memories with memory page customization • Manual & auto scan, direct keypad frequency entry, ATS, tuning knob • IF shift (Intermediate Frequency) • Shortwave antenna trimmer • Sleep timer, snooze, and favorite station wake-up timers • Includes AC adaptor/charger & 4 AA Ni-MH batteries • Internally charges AA Ni-MH batteries • **Dimensions:** 7.4"W x 4.5"H x 1.3"D • **Weight:** 1lbs. 5oz. • **Power Source:** 4 AA batteries or included AC adaptor/charger

standing tall
YB 550PE am/fm shortwave radio

The YB line, manufactured since the 1960's, has always stood for performance and portability. The latest in this family, the YB 550PE carries on the tradition, capable of receiving AM/FM and continuous Shortwave across all 14 international bands. Palm-sized and only 10oz, the YB 550PE features five tuning methods, including 200 station presets and the handy scroll wheel.

Continuous Shortwave of 1711-29.995 KHz • Autoscan, direct keypad, and scroll wheel tuning • 200 csustomizable station presets • Alarm and sleep timer functions • AC adaptor and supplementary antenna inputs • **Dimensions:** 3.5"W x 5.8"H x 1.4"D • **Weight:** 10 oz. • **Power Source:** 4 D batteries (not included) or AC adaptor (included)

high performance portable
G4000A am/fm shortwave radio

The G4000A is an enthusiast-quality world receiver, packed with the power to scan and lock-on to even the weakest Shortwave signals. The G4000A is capable of receiving AM, FM, continuous Shortwave, and even SSB (Single Sideband) for two-way Shortwave communications such as amateur radio operators. • Wide & narrow bandwidth filter controls • Autoscan & direct keypad tuning • 40 customizable station presets • Alarm & sleep timer • 7.8"W x 4.6"H x 1.4"D • 1lbs. 5oz. • **Power Source:** 6 AA batteries (not included) or AC adaptor (included)

high performance field radio
S350 am/fm shortwave radio

With the rugged look of a retro field radio and the latest in AM, FM, Shortwave radio technology, the S350 features the best of analog and digital. The S350 is the perfect addition to active lifestyles that demand high-performance portable audio capable of receiving news and information from across the globe.

Separate bass, treble, and RF gain controls • Wide and narrow bandwidth filter controls • Line-level audio outputs and external antenna input • Alarm & sleep timer functions with illuminated multi-function LCD screen • **Dimensions:** 10.5"W x 6.5"H x 3.5"D • **Weight:** 3lbs. 9oz. • **Power Source:** 4 D batteries (not included) or AC adaptor (included)

www.etoncorp.com

Radio Japan is among Asia's most respected sources for news, including technology updates. T. Ohtake

Japan

For a number of years, **Radio Japan** was the dominant voice of Asia on the world bands. Today, it has been overtaken by China Radio International, although both stations can be heard just about anywhere. Fortunately, the two broadcasters offer different styles of programming, with Radio Japan airing more music.

☞ RECOMMENDED PROGRAM: "Japan Music Travelogue."

Eastern North America: Best bets are 0000-0100 on 6145 kHz, and 1000-1200 on 6120 kHz, all via the Canadian relay at Sackville, New Brunswick.

Western North America: 0100-0200 on 17825 kHz; 0500-0600 on 6110 kHz; 0600-0700 winter on 11690 kHz, and summer on 13630 kHz; 1500-1600 on 9505 kHz; 1700-1800 on 9535 kHz; and 2100-2200 on 17825 kHz. Listeners in Hawaii can tune in at 0600-0700 on 17870 kHz, and 2100-2200 on 21670 kHz. For Central America there's 0300-0400 on 17825 kHz.

Europe: 0500-0600 on 5975 kHz; 0500-0700 on 7230 kHz; 1000-1100 on 17585; 1700-1800 on 11970 kHz; 2100-2200 on 6055 (summer), 6090 (winter) and 6180 kHz.

Middle East: 0100-0200 on 6025 (or 6030) and 17560 kHz; and 1000-1100 on 17720 kHz.

Southern Africa: 1700-1800 on 15355 kHz.

Asia: 0000-0015 on 13650 and 17810 kHz; 0100-0200 on 11860, 15325, 17810 and 17845 kHz; 0500-0600 on 15195 and 17810 kHz; 0600-0700 on 11715, 11740, 11760 and 15195 kHz; 1000-1200 on 9695 and 11730 kHz; 1400-1500 on 7200 and 9845 (or 11730) kHz; and 1500-1600 on 6190, 7200 and 9845 (or 11730) kHz. Transmissions to Asia are often heard in other parts of the world, as well.

Australasia: 0100-0200 on 17685 kHz; 0300-0400 on 21610 kHz; 0500-0700 and 1000-1100 on 21755 kHz; 1400-1500 on 11840 kHz; and 2100-2200 winter on 11920 kHz, replaced midyear by 6035 kHz.

NORTH AMERICA
Canada

Having survived years of near-extinction, **Radio Canada International** still seems unable to settle down. Frequent chopping and changing of times, frequencies and broadcasts has had a disconcerting effect on listeners. Part of the problem seems to be cultural, relating to the amount of airtime to be given to broadcasts in French vis-à-vis those in English.

Most of RCI's English programs continue to be produced by its parent organization, the domestic Canadian Broadcasting Corporation. Many are long-running listener favorites.

☞ RECOMMENDED PROGRAMS: "The Vinyl Café" and "Global Village."

North America: Morning reception is much better in eastern North America than farther west, but evening broadcasts propagate more widely. Winter, morning broadcasts air at 1300-1400 weekdays, 1400-1600 (daily) and 1600-1700 Saturday and Sunday, all on 9515, 13655 and 17820 kHz. In summer these transmissions are one hour earlier, on 9515, 13655 and 17800 kHz. During winter, evening broadcasts air at 0100-0300 on 6190 and 9755 kHz. Summer, one hour earlier, they're on 9755 and 13710 kHz.

Europe: 2100-2200 winter on 5850 and 9770 kHz; and 2000-2100 summer on 5850, 11690 and 13700 kHz.

Middle East: 2100-2200 winter on 7425 kHz; and 2000-2100 summer on 11690 kHz.

Asia: To East Asia at 1200-1300 winter on 9795 kHz, and summer on 9660 kHz; to Southeast Asia at 0000-0100 winter on 9755 and 9880 kHz, summer on 9640 and 15205 kHz; and 1200-1300 winter on 11730 kHz, summer on 15190 kHz; to South Asia at 1500-1600 winter on 9635 and 11730 kHz, replaced summer by 15455 and 17720 kHz.

United States

Once venerated by millions and a key reason the Cold War was won, the **Voice of America** is in danger of joining the dodo. The English service for the Americas has already disappeared, and broadcasts to the rest of the world have been slashed. Insiders say there are yet more cuts to come.

Don't blame the station. Less money for the VOA means more funds for non-VOA radio and TV operations like Radio Sawa, brainchildren of politicians and decision makers at the VOA's overseeing agency, the

Broadcasting Board of Governors, now led by a commercial mogul.

☞ RECOMMENDED PROGRAM: None.

North America: There is a widespread misconception that by law or because the VOA isn't beamed to North America, it can't be heard within the United States. Although the best opportunity used to be from now-extinct services to the Caribbean and South America, the African Service is still audible; try 0400-0500 weekdays on 9575 kHz, 0500-0630 weekdays on 6035 kHz, 1800-2200 winter on 15580 kHz, 1900-2200 summer on 15445 kHz, and 2000-2200 winter on 17895 kHz.

Middle East: 0400-0600 winter on 15205 kHz; 0300-0500 summer on 9695 and 11695 kHz; 1600-1800 summer on 9700 and 15255 kHz; 1700-2100 on 6040 and 9760 kHz; and 1800-2100 summer on 9770 kHz.

Southern Africa: 0300-0500 weekdays on 6080, 7340 (to 0330), 7415 (winter), 9575 (from 0400), 9885 (till 0430), and (midyear) 17895 kHz; 0500-0630 weekdays on 11835 and 12080 (or 13710) kHz; 1600-1700 on 15225, 15240 (or 15410) and 17895 kHz; 1700-1800 on 15240 (or 15410) kHz; and 1800-2200 on 7415 (from 1900, winter only), 15240 (or 15410), 15445 (from 1900, midyear only), 15580 (winter) and 17895 kHz.

East and Southeast Asia: 1200-1300 winter on 6110, 9760, 11705 and 15250 kHz; summer on 6160, 9645, 9760 and 15240 kHz; 1300-1500 winter on 6110, 9760 and 11705 kHz; summer on 6160, 9645 (till 1400) and (from 1400) 15160 and 15425 kHz; 1700-1800 on 9640 kHz; 2200-2400 on 7215, 15185, 15290, 15305, 17740 and 17820 kHz; and 0000-0100 on 7215, 15185, 15290 and 17820 kHz.

Australasia: 1200-1400 on 9645 kHz, 1400-1500 on 15425 kHz, and 2200-2400 on 11760 and 17740 kHz.

Prepared by Tony Jones and the staff of PASSPORT TO WORLD BAND RADIO.

fits into your palm or pocket

E100 Elite Series am/fm shortwave radio

Fits into your palm or pocket, but fitted with full-sized features. Imagine a radio packed with all the bells and whistles: digital tuning AM, FM, Shortwave reception, and small enough to fit into your coat pocket. The E100 is a dream come true.

Shortwave range of 1711 – 29,999 KHz • 200 programmable memories with memory page customization • Manual & auto scan, direct keypad frequency entry, tuning knob • Programmable alarm & sleep functions with digital clock • Clean-design body with fine lines & metallic finish • **Dimensions:** 4.9"W x 3"L x 1.2"D • **Weight:** 7.4oz. • **Power Source:** 2 AA batteries (included) or AC adaptor (not included)

intelligent features that simplify

E10 Elite Series am/fm shortwave radio

Performance that reaches out to the world. Imagine a radio that combines strong performance for fantastic reception and all of today's digital wizardry, bringing the world to your fingertips. The E10 is where intelligence meets performance.

Shortwave range of 1711 – 29,999 KHz • 550 programmable memories with memory page customization • Manual & auto scan, direct keypad frequency entry, ATS, tuning knob • IF shift (Intermediate Frequency) and Shortwave antenna trimmer • Sleep timer, snooze, and favorite station wake-up timers • Includes AC adaptor/charger and 4 AA Ni-MH batteries • Internally charges AA Ni-MH batteries • Clean-design body with fine lines and metallic finish • **Dimensions:** 7.4"W x 4.5"H x 1.3"D • **Weight:** 1lbs. 5oz. • **Power Source:** 4 AA batteries or included AC adaptor/charger

world's first & only am/fm shortwave XM Satellite radio

E1XM Elite Series am/fm/sw/xm radio

The E1 XM is the world's first radio that combines AM, FM, Shortwave, and XM Satellite radio into one ultra high-performance unit. In collaboration with RL Drake Company and XM Satellite Radio, the E1 is the finest full-sized portable in the world.

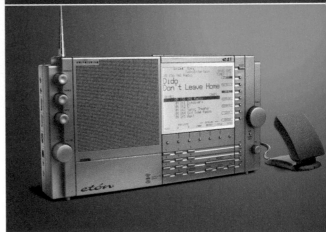

- XM Satellite Radio or Digital Audio Broadcasting (DAB) ready
- Selectable Single Sideband (SSB) reception
- Digitally synthesized PLL tuner with synchronous detector
- Dual conversion superheterodyne circuit design
- Passband tuning, selectable bandwidth filters
- 1700 station presets, memory scan function
- 5.7" square illuminated multi-function dot-matrix LCD screen
- Stereo line-level audio inputs and outputs. External antenna connections
- Dual clocks and programmable timers

Dimensions: 13.1"W x 7.1"H x 2.3"D   **Weight:** 4lbs. 3oz.
Power Source: 4 D batteries (not included) or AC adaptor (included)

SATELLITE RADIO

a shortwave legend
Satellit 800 am/fm shortwave radio

In the history of shortwave receivers, no other manufacturer has maintained a continuously evolving series of high-end portable radios, decade after decade.

Long wave, AM-broadcast and Shortwave, 100-30,000 KHz, continuous • VHF aircraft band, 118-137 MHz • Single Side Band (SSB) • Large, illuminated LCD at 6" x 6.5" • A real tuning knob, like on traditional radios, but with ultra-precise digital tuning, with absolutely no audio muting when used • 70 programmable memories • Built-in telescopic antenna for use on all bands • External antenna connections for the auxiliary antennas. • Dimensions: 20.5"L x 9"H x 8"W • Weight: 14.5lbs.

high performance portable
G4000A am/fm shortwave radio

The G4000A is an enthusiast-quality world receiver, packed with the power to scan and lock-on to even the weakest Shortwave signals with rock-solid precision. The G4000A is capable of receiving AM, FM, Continuous Shortwave, and even SSB (Single Sideband) for two-way Shortwave communications such as amateur radio operators.

Single Sideband (SSB) reception • Wide and narrow bandwidth filter controls • Autoscan and direct keypad tuning; 40 customizable station presets • Alarm and sleep timer functions • **Dimensions:** 7.8"W x 4.6"H x 1.4"D • **Weight:** 1lbs. 5oz. • **Power Source:** 6 AA batteries (not included) or AC adaptor (included)

high performance field radio
S350 am/fm shortwave radio

With the rugged look of a retro field radio and the latest in AM, FM, Shortwave radio technology, the S350 features the best of analog and digital. The S350 is the perfect addition to active lifestyles that demand high-performance portable audio capable of receiving news and information from across the globe.

Separate bass, treble, and RF gain controls • Wide and narrow bandwidth filter controls • Line-level audio outputs and external antenna input • Alarm & sleep timer functions with illuminated multi-function LCD screen • **Dimensions:** 10.5"W x 6.5"H x 3.5"D • **Weight:** 3lbs. 9oz. • **Power Source:** 4 D batteries (not included) or AC adaptor (included)

universal radio inc.

etón®
www.etoncorp.com

Ten of the Best: 2005's Top Shows

World band offers all kinds of unexpected finds, some better than others. Here are ten shows that our listening panel has found offer exceptional distinction.

Times and days are in World Time. "Winter" and "summer" refer to seasons in the Northern Hemisphere, where summer takes place in the middle of the year, so Aussies and Argies need to do a mental flip.

"The Vinyl Café"
CBC/Radio Canada International

As its name suggests, "The Vinyl Café" features music, both live and recorded, and much of it from down memory lane. It's also eclectic—where you can hear Hinge and Brackett's "Midnight Choo Choo" sharing airtime with the likes of Paul Simon and the Nitty Gritty Dirt Band.

Stirred in are snippets of Canadian history, yarns and the misadventures of Dave, owner of the "Vinyl Café." The best bring to mind Gerard Hoffnung's ubiquitous "Bricklayer Story."

"The Vinyl Café" is enjoyed each week by more than 700,000 listeners in Canada. However, RCI beams the show only to *North and Central America*—although shortwave's scattering properties carry it farther. Winter on Saturdays, it airs at 1406-1459 on 9515, 13655 and 17820 kHz; summer, it's one hour earlier, on 9515, 13655 and 17800 kHz.

"Report from Austria—The Week in Review"
Radio Austria International

In 2003, Radio Austria International almost disappeared. Broadcasts in several languages were terminated and the station's output in English was severely curtailed. The highly respected "Report from Austria" was reduced to a quarter hour, and weekend programming consisted of "Insight Central Europe," a joint production with other European stations.

Because of limited resources, Radio Austria International eventually withdrew from the collective "Insight Central Europe" exercise, and to the delight of listeners, this was replaced by "Report from Austria—The Week in Review." The best items from the weekday "Report from Austria" now form the bulk of this show, with the final six minutes being responses to listeners' queries and comments.

All transmissions, except to the Middle East, are aired Saturday and Sunday, local days in the target areas.

> Coverage includes shooting contests for the blind.

Stuart McLean's "Vinyl Café" entertains and amuses with finesse. Each week a vast audience tunes in from Saskatoon to Sarasota.
CBC

Jonathan Groubert hosts "Euroquest," Radio Netherlands' look at the quirkier side of life across Europe. RNW

Winter times for *eastern North America* are 0005 and 0035 (weekend evenings, local American date) on 7325 kHz. In summer, it's 0105 and 0135 on 9870 kHz. For *western North America* there's 1605 and 1635 on 13675 kHz in winter, and 1505 and 1535 on 13755 kHz in summer. *Central America* has the same year-round slots: 0005 and 0035 on 9870 (or 13730) kHz.

In *Europe*, tune in at 1305 or 1335 winter (one hour earlier in summer) on 6155 and 13730 kHz; and in the *Middle East*, Sunday only, at 0605 and 0635 winter (one hour earlier in summer) on 17870 kHz.

The transmission for *South* and *Southeast Asia* and *Australasia* can be heard winter at 1305 and 1335 on 17855 kHz, and summer an hour earlier on 17715 kHz.

"Euroquest"
Radio Netherlands

If you want a single source for what the past week has been like in Europe, "Euroquest" is a step above. It takes a wide-ranging look at politics, the arts, science, health and other issues around Europe, with correspondents' reports deftly blended by host Jonathan Groubert. Young Muslims in France, stepchild adoption by homosexual couples,

a shooting competition for the blind— whatever counts, it's covered.

The first airing for *eastern North America* is at 1230 Tuesday (one hour earlier in summer) on 11675 kHz, with a repeat later the same day at 0030 on 9845 kHz. For *central North America* it's one hour later, at 0130, on (winter) 6165 or (summer) 9845 kHz. *Western North America* gets the last slot, 0430 Wednesday (Tuesday evening local date) on 6165 and 9590 kHz.

There's nothing for *Europe* or the *Middle East*, but there are two Tuesday slots for *southern Africa*: 1830 on 6020 kHz, and 2000 on 7120 kHz; with a repeat at 1900 the following Monday on 7120 kHz.

In *East* and *Southeast Asia* it's 1030 Tuesday on 7315 (winter), 12065, 13710 (summer) and 13820 kHz. *Australasia* has the same slot, but on 9785 or 9790 kHz. Channels for Asia are also audible in parts of Australasia.

"Jade Bells and Bamboo Pipes"
Radio Taiwan International

An exotic title for an exotic program, if not altogether correct. More often than not, bells and pipes give way to stringed instruments.

Taiwanese traditional music is diverse. From gentle serenades to "aboriginal blues" of the central highlands, the music appeals to Western and Eastern ears, alike.

All broadcasts are aired Wednesday, World Time.

In *eastern and central North America*, tune in at 0220 (Tuesday evening, local date) on 5950 and 9680 kHz. For *western North America* there's a choice between 0320 and 0720, both on 5950 kHz. All are relayed by Family Radio in Okeechobee, Florida, so reception is usually good.

Europe is also served by relays: 1820 (via Issoudun, France) on 3965 kHz; and 2220 (via Okeechobee), winter on 9355 kHz and summer on 15600 kHz.

high performance portable

G4000A am/fm shortwave radio

The G4000A is an enthusiast-quality world receiver, packed with the power to scan and lock-on to even the weakest Shortwave signals. The G4000A is capable of receiving AM, FM, continuous Shortwave, and even SSB (Single Sideband) for two-way Shortwave communications such as amateur radio operators. • Wide & narrow bandwidth filter controls • Autoscan & direct keypad tuning • 40 customizable station presets • Alarm & sleep timer • 7.8"W x 4.6"H x 1.4"D • 1lbs. 5oz. • **Power Source:** 6 AA batteries (not included) or AC adaptor (included)

high performance field radio

S350 am/fm shortwave radio

With the rugged look of a retro field radio and the latest in AM, FM, Shortwave radio technology, the S350 features the best of analog and digital. The S350 is the perfect addition to active lifestyles that demand high-performance portable audio capable of receiving news and information from across the globe.

Separate bass, treble, and RF gain controls • Wide and narrow bandwidth filter controls • Line-level audio outputs and external antenna input • Alarm & sleep timer functions with illuminated multi-function LCD screen • **Dimensions:** 10.5"W x 6.5"H x 3.5"D • **Weight:** 3lbs. 9oz. • **Power Source:** 4 D batteries (not included) or AC adaptor (included)

standing tall

YB 550PE am/fm shortwave radio

The YB line, manufactured since the 1960's, has always stood for performance and portability. The latest in this family, the YB 550PE carries on the tradition, capable of receiving AM/FM and continuous Shortwave across all 14 international bands. Palm-sized and only 10oz, the YB 550PE features five tuning methods, including 200 station presets and the handy scroll wheel.

Continuous Shortwave of 1711-29.995 KHz • Autoscan, direct keypad, and scroll wheel tuning • 200 customizable station presets • Alarm and sleep timer functions • AC adaptor and supplementary antenna inputs • **Dimensions:** 3.5"W x 5.8"H x 1.4"D • **Weight:** 10 oz. • **Power Source:** 4 D batteries (not included) or AC adaptor (included)

intelligent features that simplify

E10 Elite Series am/fm shortwave radio

Performance that reaches out to the world. Imagine a radio that combines strong performance for fantastic reception and all of today's digital wizardry, bringing the world to your fingertips. The E10 is where intelligence meets performance.

Shortwave range of 1711 – 29,999 KHz • 550 programmable memories with memory page customization • Manual & auto scan, direct keypad frequency entry, ATS, tuning knob • IF shift (Intermediate Frequency) • Shortwave antenna trimmer • Sleep timer, snooze, and favorite station wake-up timers • Includes AC adaptor/charger & 4 AA Ni-MH batteries • Internally charges AA Ni-MH batteries • **Dimensions:** 7.4"W x 4.5"H x 1.3"D • **Weight:** 1lbs. 5oz. • **Power Source:** 4 AA batteries or included AC adaptor/charger

"Living in Germany's" Rajiv Sharma at Deutsche Welle studios in Bonn.
DW

The first broadcast for *East Asia* is at 0220 on 15465 kHz, repeated at 1220 on 7130 kHz. Listeners in southern China can also tune to the transmission for *South Asia* at 1620 on 11815 kHz. *Southeast Asia* gets four slots: 0220 on 11875 kHz, 0320 on 15320 kHz, 1120 on 7105 kHz, and 1420 on 15265 kHz. In *Australasia*, go for 0820 on 9610 kHz.

"Living in Germany"
Deutsche Welle

"Living in Germany" may not be much of a grabber as a program title. Yet, it is an informative and well produced 15-minute focus on Germans and how they live.

Each show hits a particular theme: anything from unemployment in eastern Germany, to Dortmund's Domicil jazz club, to the Rhine as a waterway. But don't let that bland title fool you—the program is interesting throughout.

Deutsche Welle doesn't specifically target *North America*, but listeners in the eastern and southern United States often have good reception of the 2100-2200 transmission to West Africa. Luckily, "Living in Germany" is part of the Wednesday broadcast at this

time, so try 2130 on 13780 and 15410 kHz in winter, and 11865 and 15205 kHz in summer.

Listeners in *Europe* have three opportunities, all on Thursday: 0730, 0930 and 1430 on 6140 kHz.

There's no official slot for the *Middle East*, but the 1930 Wednesday broadcast for East Africa should provide reasonable reception. Try 11865 kHz in winter and 13590 kHz in summer.

Southern Africa: 0530 Thursday, winter on 12035 kHz and midyear on 12045 kHz.

There's zip for *East Asia*, but *Southeast Asia* gets its chance at 2330 Wednesday (Thursday morning local date). Winter frequencies are 7250, 9815 and 12035 kHz; replaced summer by 7115, 9890 and 15135 kHz.

Listeners in *Australasia* can bend an ear for the Southeast Asia broadcast.

"RealTime Beijing"
China Radio International

"RealTime Beijing" started life as a drive-time magazine show targeted at English-speaking residents in China. It gained an international presence when CRI moved to a 24-hour English schedule on the world bands.

Coverage includes business, sports, technology and entertainment, with presentation that is livelier and more relaxed than standard CRI programming

As we go to press, there are four broadcasts daily. However, this may change during the coming year as CRI continues to increase its presence on the world's airwaves. Although nominally 45 minutes, "RealTime Beijing" has been observed to broadcast 50 minute editions.

All transmissions are Monday through Friday.

Eastern North America is the only part of the continent to get a shot at "RealTime Beijing": 1105 winter on 5960 kHz, summer on 6040 and 11750 kHz—all via transmitters of Radio Canada International.

Best for *Europe* are 1005 and 1105 on 17490 kHz.

There's nothing for the *Middle East*, but listeners in *southern Africa* can try at 1705 on 9570 and 11900 kHz.

Asia, ironically, gets a bad deal, but *Australasia* is targeted at 1005 on 15210 and 17690 kHz.

Short features about the Russian Orthodox Church, stories about Russian saints and religious experiences—these and more are interwoven with Russian church music to create a unique and emotive atmosphere. Even a nonbeliever can enjoy the program.

Winter in *North America*, listen at 0231 Saturday (Friday evening local American date) on 7180, 15445 and 15595 kHz. In summer, one hour earlier, it's 0131 Saturday on 9665 (7180 in autumn), 15595 and 17660 kHz.

Europe's winter slots are 2031 Saturday on 6145, 6175, 6235, 7290 and 7340 kHz; and 1931 Sunday on 6175, 6235, 7290 and 7360 kHz. Summer, it's 1931 Saturday on 7440, 9890 and 12070 (or 7310) kHz; and 1831 Sunday on 9480, 9820 (or 11630) and 9890 kHz.

Winter in the *Middle East* there's 0231 Saturday on 5995 kHz, and 1631 Saturday on 6005 and 9830 kHz. For summer, try 0131 Saturday on 5945 kHz, and 1531 Saturday on 7325 and 11985 kHz.

In *Southeast Asia* winter, tune in at 0931 Saturday on 17495, 17525 and 17850 kHz. Summer options are 0831 Saturday on 17495 and 17525 kHz, and 1531 Saturday on 7390 and 11500 kHz.

"Christian Message from Moscow"
Voice of Russia

There's no shortage of Christian programs on world band. You name it, they offer it: old-time preaching, mainstream homilies, evangelical inspiration, bible reading, shameless huckstering, Christian rock—even hip hop. Yet, although there's lots of religion, these programs frequently offer little in the way of spirituality.

Not so, "Christian Message from Moscow," from a land where religion has only recently been rediscovered. This weekly look at Russian Orthodoxy overflows with spirituality while avoiding preaching and the open palm.

"Christian Message from Moscow" features Russian Orthodox music and tales. VoR

porsche design
G2000A am/fm shortwave radio

From its sleek sculpted lines to its soft leather case to its high performance, the G2000A designed by the legendary F.A. Porsche, is
reminiscent of its fine automotive design heritage in every way.

- F.A. Porsche Design styling
- Autoscan and direct keypad tuning
- 20 customizable station presets
- Dual alarm and sleep timer functions
- Snap-on leather protective case
  that converts to stand

Dimensions: 5.5"W x 3.5"H x
1.3"D **Weight:** 7.4 oz.
Power Source: 3 AA batteries (not
included) or AC adaptor (included)

high performance portable
G4000A am/fm shortwave radio

The G4000A is an enthusiast-quality world receiver, packed
with the power to scan and lock-on to even the weakest
Shortwave signals with rock-solid precision. The G4000A
is capable of receiving AM, FM, Continuous Shortwave,
and even SSB (Single Sideband) for two-way Shortwave
communications such as amateur radio operators.

- Single Sideband (SSB) reception
- Wide and narrow bandwidth filter controls
- Autoscan and direct keypad tuning; 40 customizable station presets
- Alarm and sleep timer functions

Dimensions: 7.8"W x 4.6"H x 1.4"D **Weight:** 1lbs. 5oz.
Power Source: 6 AA batteries (not included) or AC adaptor (included)

palm-size
G1000A am/fm shortwave radio

Small enough to fit in a coat pocket, yet powerful enough to capture
eight Shortwave bands and feature a digital frequency readout and
alarm, the G1000A is the perfect all-purpose radio for home or travel.

- Receives 8 international Shortwave bands
- Alarm and sleep timer functions with illuminated multi-function
  LCD screen
- Snap-on protective case and stand
- AC adaptor and earphone inputs

Dimensions: 4.5"W x 3"H x 1.1"D **Weight:** 7 oz.
Power Source: 2 AA batteries (included)

emergency crank radio

FR200 am/fm shortwave radio & flashlight

Requiring no batteries, the self-powered FR200 keeps you informed and prepared for emergencies. The Hand-Crank Power Generator provides unlimited power for AM/FM Radio use, access to 7 international Shortwave bands, and the built-in flashlight. Just 90 seconds of cranking provides up to an hour of radio play, making the FR200 perfect not only for emergencies, but also camping, hiking, or just relaxing in the backyard. Choose from 5 colors: Metallic Red, Metallic Blue, Metallic Pearl, Yellow, and Sand.

- 7 international Shortwave bands and built-in antenna
- Hand-Crank Power Generator
- Built-in flashlight
- Rugged splash-proof ABS body
- Inputs for AC adaptor and earphones

Dimensions: 6.8"W x 5.8"H x 2.1"D **Weight:** 1.3lbs.
Power Source: Hand-Crank Power Generator with rechargeable battery pack, 3 AA batteries (not included) or AC adaptor (not included)

high performance field radio

S350 am/fm shortwave radio

With the rugged look of a retro field radio and the latest in AM, FM, Shortwave radio technology, the S350 features the best of analog and digital. The S350 is the perfect addition to active lifestyles that demand high-performance portable audio capable of receiving news and information from across the globe.

- Separate bass, treble, and RF gain controls
- Wide and narrow bandwidth filter controls
- Line-level audio outputs and external antenna input
- Alarm & sleep timer functions with illuminated multi-function LCD screen

Dimensions: 10.5"W x 6.5"H x 3.5"D Weight: 3lbs. 9oz.
Power Source: 4 D batteries (not included) or AC adaptor (included)

amazon.com. etón®
www.etoncorp.com

Australasia has two winter slots: 0631 Saturday on 21790 kHz, and 0931 the same day on 17495, 17525 and 17665 kHz. Midyear, the times are one hour earlier, 0531 on 21790 kHz, and 0831 on 17495, 17525, 17635 and 21790 kHz.

"Money Talks"
Deutsche Welle

Financial programs are usually for specialized audiences, but Deutsche Welle's "Money Talks" is for all. It contains the obligatory summary of the week's international financial news, but after that it takes off on its own path. It covers stories like compensation for victims of terrorism, reform of unemployment payments, funding of political campaigns and environmental economics. It is worthwhile, even for the financially challenged.

Deutsche Welle doesn't beam English to *North America*, but is still audible at certain hours. The best chance to hear "Money Talks" is at 0630 Thursday during the broadcast to West Africa. Try 15410 kHz in winter, and 17860 kHz in summer.

Listeners in *Europe* can choose from 0630, 0830, 1330 and 1530 Thursday on 6140 kHz.

For the *Middle East* it's 0430 Thursday, winter on 9545 kHz and summer on 9630 kHz. *Southern Africa* gets its chance a day earlier, at 2030 Wednesday, winter on 12025 kHz and midyear on 7130 kHz.

In *East Asia*, tune in at 2230 Wednesday (Thursday morning in the target area), winter on 6180 kHz and summer on 7115 and 9720 kHz. For *Southeast Asia* there's 1130 Thursday, winter on 15410 kHz; and summer on 15105, 17820 and 21820 kHz.

Listeners in *Australasia* should try the broadcast for Southeast Asia.

"The Folk Music Box"
Radio Romania International

Gone are the days when eastern European stations showcased their country's folk music. A few remnants persist, but with pitifully reduced airtime.

One long-running show and listener favorite, Radio Romania International's "Skylark," shriveled to just a few minutes some years back. It is still on, albeit only during the final minutes of RRI's Thursday broadcasts, but something else has come to the rescue: the new 12-minute "Folk Music Box." It is a first-rate focus on Romanian folk music, and fits in with the resurgence of interest in traditional music elsewhere in the region, such as in neighboring Hungary.

Start times sometimes vary slightly.

In *eastern North America*, try 2340 Friday on 6180 and 9610 kHz winter, and 9645 and 11940 kHz summer; and 0140 Saturday (Friday evening local American date) on 6140 and 9690 kHz winter, and 9690 and 11940 kHz summer. For *western North America* there's 0440 Saturday, winter on 6125 and 9515 kHz, and summer on 11820 and 15235 kHz.

Europe's slots are 1840 Friday on 5965 and 7130 kHz winter, and 11940 and 15380 kHz summer; and 2340 Friday on 6135 and 7105 kHz winter, and 7280 and 9590 kHz summer.

In *Australasia*, tune in at 0140 Saturday, winter on 9510 and 11740 kHz, and summer on 15430 and 17760 kHz.

> **Traditional music is again popular in Eastern Europe.**

"Insight"
Radio Netherlands

Our final choice may be one of the shortest programs on the air, but what it lacks in length it makes up in punch.

With political correctness having taken the bite out of much of what is on radio and television, Radio Netherlands' "Insight" is commentary at its refreshing best. "Thou shalt not offend" is given short shrift, being replaced by a combination of irreverence and common sense. Nothing is sacred—not even the Catholic Church's most venerated virgins—although politicians and bureaucrats tend to get the most flak.

All editions are heard Saturday, local date in the target areas.

Eastern North America gets three offerings: 1225 (one hour earlier in summer) on 11675 kHz, with repeats at 1955 winter on 17725 kHz and summer on 17735 kHz, and 0025 on 9845 kHz. The 1955 slot is also available for *central North America* on 15315 kHz, and is repeated at 0125 on (winter) 6165 or (summer) 9845 kHz. In *western North America* the 1955 broadcast is heard winter on 17875 kHz and summer on 17660 kHz, and is repeated at 0425 on 6165 and 9590 kHz.

There's nothing for *Europe* or the *Middle East*, but there are three slots for *southern Africa*: 1825 on 6020 kHz, and 1955 and 2053 on 7120 kHz.

East and *Southeast Asia* are targeted at 1025 on 7315 (winter), 12065, 13710 (summer) and 13820 kHz. Listeners in *Australasia* can tune in at the same time on 9785 and 9790 kHz, although the channels for Asia can also provide good reception.

"Insight's" Rob Greene targets bumbling bureaucrats and venerated virgins.
RNW

Prepared by the staff of PASSPORT TO WORLD BAND RADIO.

porsche design

G2000A am/fm shortwave radio

From its sleek sculpted lines to its soft leather case to its high performance, the G2000A designed by the legendary F.A. Porsche, is reminiscent of its fine automotive design heritage in every way.

- F.A. Porsche Design styling
- Autoscan and direct keypad tuning
- 20 customizable station presets
- Dual alarm and sleep timer functions
- Snap-on leather protective case that converts to stand

Dimensions: 5.5"W x 3.5"H x 1.3"D **Weight:** 7.4 oz. **Power Source:** 3 AA batteries (not included) or AC adaptor (included)

emergency crank radio and cell phone charger

FR300 am/fm radio with NOAA and TV VHF

This all-in-one unit offers functionality and versatility that makes it ideal for emergencies. The FR300 provides you radio, light, and cell phone battery life when you need it most. The Hand-Crank Power Generator charges the internal rechargeable Ni-MH battery pack and just 90 seconds of cranking provides up to an hour of radio play. With the NOAA Weather Channels and TV VHF channels, find forecasts or catch TV shows when you're away from the set.

- AM/FM with built-in antenna. TV VHF channels 2-13
- All 7 NOAA weather channels plus "Weather Alert"
- Hand-Crank Power Generator. Inputs for AC adaptor and earphones
- Built-in Cell Phone Charger, flashlight, and emergency siren

NOAA

Dimensions: 6.7"W x 6.5"H x 2.5"D **Weight:** 1.3lbs. **Power Source:** Hand-Crank Power Generator with rechargeable battery pack, 3 AA batteries (not included) or AC adaptor (not included)

emergency plug-in am/fm radio with blackout alert

FR100 Blackout Buddy

Plug the Blackout Buddy into AC sockets around your home. When the power fails, Blackout Buddy automatically shines to the rescue, with a brilliant beam of light that illuminates the room and its AM/FM radio to give you breaking news. Blackout Buddy also makes a perfect AM/FM clock radio & LED flashlight for everyday listening around the home.

- Automatically turns on radio/flashlight during power outages
- Super-bright LED flashlight
- Illuminated multi-function blue LCD screen and nightlight
- Patent-pending plug-in design recharges internal battery
- AM/FM radio with telescopic antenna
- Headphone jack and FM antenna input

Dimensions: 3"W x 5"H x 1.4"D **Weight:** 10oz. **Power Source:** AC power (direct plug-in)

high performance field radio
S350 am/fm shortwave radio

With the rugged look of a retro field radio and the latest in AM, FM, Shortwave radio technology, the S350 features the best of analog and digital. The S350 is the perfect addition to active lifestyles that demand high-performance portable audio capable of receiving news and information from across the globe.

- Separate bass, treble, and RF gain controls
- Wide and narrow bandwidth filter controls
- Line-level audio outputs and external antenna input
- Alarm & sleep timer functions with illuminated multi-function LCD screen

Dimensions: 10.5"W x 6.5"H x 3.5"D Weight: 3lbs. 9oz.
Power Source: 4 D batteries (not included) or AC adaptor (included)

emergency crank radio
FR200 am/fm shortwave radio & flashlight

Requiring no batteries, the FR200's Hand-Crank Power Generator provides unlimited power for AM/FM radio use, access to 7 International Shortwave bands, and the built-in Flashlight. Just 90 seconds of cranking provides up to an hour of radio play.

- 7 International Shortwave bands. Built-in antenna
- Hand-Crank Power Generator with built-in flashlight
- Rugged splash-proof ABS body. Inputs for AC adaptor and earphones

Dimensions: 6.8"W x 5.8"H x 2.5"D Weight: 1.3lbs. Power Source: Hand-Crank Power Generator with rechargeable battery pack, 3 AA batteries (not included) or AC adaptor (not included)

www.etoncorp.com

How to Choose a World Band Radio

Some electronic products are commodities. Use a little horse sense and you can find just what you want.

Not so world band receivers, which can vary greatly from model to model. As usual money talks, but even that's a fickle barometer.

Fortunately, many perform well and we rate them accordingly. Yet, even among models with comparable star ratings it helps to read the fine print. If you are in Arizona you probably don't want fur-lined boots—even the best fur-lined boots. So, read carefully and choose a radio that satisfies your requirements.

So Many Stations, So Little Room

World band radio is packed tighter than a Saturday night mosh pit:

1,100 channels, with stations rump-to-thigh. It's more crowded than FM or mediumwave AM, and it gets worse: Global voyaging wears down signals, making them weak and quavery.

To cope with this Iron Man environment, a world band radio has to perform exceptional electronic gymnastics. Some succeed, others don't.

This is why PASSPORT REPORTS was created. At International Broadcasting Services we've tested hundreds of world band radios and accessories since 1977. These evaluations include rigorous hands-on use by listeners, plus specialized lab tests developed over the years. These form the basis of PASSPORT REPORTS, and for some popular premium receivers and antennas there are also soup-to-nuts Radio Database International White Papers®.

Numbers game: Grundig's Yacht Boy 550PE is also sold as the Etón YB 550PE. It is similar to the Tecsun PL-230 and even the Tecsun PL-200, but don't confuse it with the new and different Tecsun PL-550.

Four-Point Checklist

✔ **Price.** Do you want to hear big stations? Or would you rather flush out gentle voices from exotic lands? Powerful evening signals, or weaker stations by day? Decide, then choose a radio that surpasses your needs by a good notch or so—this helps ensure against disappointment without wasting money.

Once the novelty wears thin, most people give up on cheap radios—they're clumsy to tune, often receive poorly and can sound terrible. That's why we don't cover analog-readout models. Yet, even some models with digital frequency readout can disappoint.

Most find satisfaction with digital-readout portables selling for $65–200 in the United States or £60–130 in the United Kingdom with a rating of ✪✪¾ or more. If you're looking for elite performance, shoot for a portable or portatop rated ✪✪✪¾ or better—at least $350 or £300—or consider a five star tabletop model.

Dentist Ronald Birnbaum uses PASSPORT's Blue Pages while pondering the Da Vinci Code from his Manhattan apartment. He is kept informed, no matter what, by Tecsun BCL-2000 and Degen DE1103 portables.

R. Birnbaum via Ulis Fleming

PERFORMANCE FEATURES TO LOOK FOR

A signal should not just be audible, but actually sound pleasant. To help, some radios incorporate features to ward off unwanted sounds or enhance audio quality. Of course, just because a feature exists doesn't mean it functions properly, but we check for this in PASSPORT REPORTS.

"Musts" for Top Reception

Full world band coverage from 2300-26100 kHz is best, although 3200-21850 kHz or even 4750-21850 kHz is usually adequate. Less coverage? Look over "Best Times and Frequencies for 2005" elsewhere in PASSPORT to ensure that important world band segments are fully covered.

Synchronous selectable sideband greatly enhances rejection of adjacent-channel interference while reducing fading distortion. This advanced feature is found on some models selling for $150 or £110 and up. PASSPORT REPORTS indicates which work well.

Especially if a receiver doesn't have synchronous selectable sideband, it helps to have two or more *bandwidths* for superior adjacent-channel rejection. Some premium models incorporate this *and* synchronous selectable sideband—a killer combo. Multiple bandwidths are found on a number of models over $70 or £65.

Multiple conversion or *double conversion* helps reject spurious "image" signals— unwanted growls, whistles, dih-dah sounds and the like. Few models under $100 or £70 have it, although the number is growing; nearly all over $150 or £100 do.

Niceties

High-quality speakers are an aural plus, as are *tone controls*—preferably continuously tunable with separate bass and treble adjustments. For world band reception, *single-sideband* (SSB) reception capability is only slightly relevant, but it is essential for utility or

Marthamaria Morales, program producer and editor of EWTN's Spanish service, Radio Católica Mundial. EWTN

"ham" signals. For world band the main use of SSB is to hear the popular American Forces Radio and Television Service.

Not satisfied with available speaker quality? Try feeding your receiver's audio line output, if it has one, through an outboard amplified speaker.

Heavy-hitting tabletop models are designed to flush out all but the most stubborn signal, but they usually require experience to operate and are overkill for casual listening. Among these, look for a tunable *notch filter* to zap howls; *passband offset* (a/k/a *passband tuning* and *IF shift*) for superior adjacent-channel rejection and audio contouring, especially in conjunction with synchronous selectable sideband; and multiple *AGC* decay rates. At electrically noisy locations a *noise blanker* is essential, although some work much better than others.

Digital signal processing (DSP) is the latest attempt to enhance mediocre signal quality. Until recently it has been much smoke, little fire, but the technology has improved. Watch for more DSP receivers to appear, but don't worship at their altar.

With portables and portatops an *AC adaptor* reduces operating costs and may improve weak-signal performance—usually the best performers and values are those that come with a radio. Some are poorly made and cause hum or buzzing, but most are quite good. With tabletop models an *inboard AC power supply* is preferable but not essential.

Looking ahead, *digital shortwave transmission* from Digital Radio Mondiale (www.drm.org) is being actively implemented, although as a practical matter ready-to-use receivers are not yet available. The only existing DRM portable, sold in Europe for €860 (about $1,000) with shipping and VAT, performs abominably.

Early DRM adopters with a technical bent should consider the WiNRADiO G-303i, Ten-Tec RX-320 or AOR AR-7030/DRM reviewed in this PASSPORT REPORTS. Whatever the fate of world band DRM, it will be years, if then, before existing analog transmissions are phased out in favor of digital. Aside from DRM's persistent shortcomings, there are currently 600 million people using roughly a billion analog radios to listen to world band.

✔ **Location**. Signals tend to be strongest in and around Europe, North Africa and the Near East, next-strongest in eastern North America. Elsewhere in the Americas, or in Hawaii or Australasia or the Middle East, you'll need a receiver with superior sensitivity to weak signals—some sort of accessory antenna helps, too.

✔ **Which features?** Divide features between those which affect performance and those that impact operation (see sidebars), but be wary of judging a radio mainly by its features. Indeed, among lower-cost models, radios with relatively few features often significantly outperform those laden with seductive goodies.

✔ **Where to buy?** Whether you buy in a store, by phone or on the Internet makes little difference. That's because world band receivers don't test well in stores except in the handful of world band showrooms with outdoor antennas. Even then, long-term satisfaction is hard to gauge from a spot test, so tests at different times are advisable.

One thing you can get a feel for in a store is ergonomics—how intuitive a radio is to operate. You can also get a thumbnail idea of world band fidelity by listening to mediumwave AM stations or a muscular world band station.

www.passband.com

HANDY THINGIES

To operate enjoyably a radio needs helpful operating features. For example, a "must" to find stations quickly is *digital frequency readout*, found on virtually all models tested by PASSPORT. A *24-hour clock* for World Time simplifies knowing when to tune in; many receivers include them. Best is if time can be read while the frequency is being displayed.

If your favorite radio doesn't include a World Time clock, then spring for a standalone 24-hour clock or watch. Seconds displayed numerically are a nice touch so you can be alert for station IDs.

Other important features: direct-access tuning via *keypad* and *station presets* ("memories"); and any combination of a *tuning knob*, up/down *slewing controls* or *"signal-seek"* scanning to search for stations. A few models have handy *one-touch presets* buttons, like a car radio. Quick access to *world band segments* (meter bands) is another ergonomic bonus.

Presets are important because world band stations, unlike locals, don't stay on the same frequency throughout the day. Being able to store all of a station's frequencies makes it easier to hear whenever you want. With sophisticated receivers, presets should be able to store not only frequency, but also such other parameters as bandwidth, mode and AGC.

Useful but less important is an *on/off timer*—a couple of timer-controlled models even come with built-in cassette recorders. Also, look for an *illuminated display* and a good *signal-strength indicator*, either as an analog meter or digital display.

Travelers prefer portables with *power-lock switches* or *recessed power buttons*. These keep the radio from going on accidentally, although the lock on some Chinese portables doesn't work on display illumination.

If ergonomics stand out, bad or good, this is cited in PASSPORT REPORTS. Counterintuitive, perhaps, but similar-caliber receivers with many controls tend to be easier to operate than comparable receivers with few controls—especially if the latter's operation involves complex tree-type software menus.

Listening is only half the fun...
POPULAR
COMMUNICATIONS
is the other half

If you enjoy radio communications, you'll love

POPULAR COMMUNICATIONS
— the largest, most authoritative monthly magazine for Shortwave Listening and Scanner Monitoring.
Get fast home delivery and find out why

POPULAR COMMUNICATIONS
is read by more active listeners than all other communications publications combined!
Subscribe today and SAVE over 58% off the newsstand price
(Save even more off 2- and 3-year subscriptions).

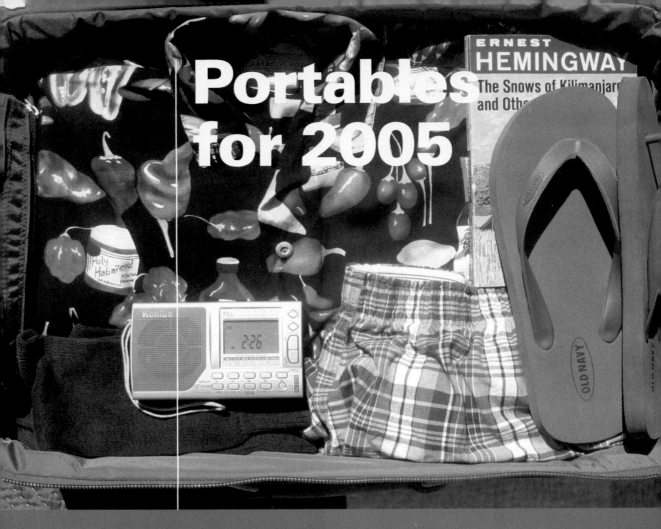

Portables for 2005

Portables are what most of us get, even if we already have something fancier. They are handy, affordable and usually do the trick at home and away.

In Europe and along the east coast of North America, evening signals come in so well that virtually any well-rated portable should be all you'll need. Even if you live elsewhere or listen during the day, when broadcasts are interesting but weaker, a top-ranked portable can be boosted by a simple outdoor wire antenna.

Keep In Touch When Away

World band makes for unbeatable outdoor entertainment, as well as a global link when you're traveling. For these and emergency situations (see separate article), only a portable will do.

Pocket portables are similar to cell phones, compacts are like Palm-type handhelds, and larger portables are akin to smaller laptop computers. You can't go wrong with a $150 compact rated at three or more stars, while models rated slightly lower can cut that price in half.

Friendly skies? Pocket models are ideal, and their limited speaker audio can be overcome with earbuds. Yet, slightly larger "compact-compacts" sometimes sell for much less and are handy enough for most.

More Value for 2005

The shift continues towards better choice and performance among low-cost portables. That's because there is a lively world band market within China, where inexpensive portables are being manufactured in vast quantities. Having created radios for the domestic market, manufacturers are now starting to export.

DRM Digital Broadcasts

Thus far only one portable has been designed to receive DRM digital broadcasts. Unfortunately, it borders on the nonfunctional, not even meeting minimum standards for inclusion in PASSPORT REPORTS. Given this, it is arguably beside the point that in Germany it sells for over €800, and it is not available within the United States and nearly all other countries. A German tabletop model is about to be offered, but the rub is that it will go for €2,003. Neither the portable nor the tabletop is from a known consumer electronics firm.

Nor is any portable yet DRM ready—equipped to receive digital world band broadcasts after being connected to a PC. However, modification instructions for some models are at www.drmrx.org/receiver_mods.html. After modification, DRM software—€60 from www.drmrx.org/purchase.php—needs to be loaded into the host PC.

This is a clunky solution, but self-contained DRM portables from familiar manufacturers may start to appear by late 2005. This choice should grow, thanks to the Chinese government's commitment to DRM for both domestic and world band broadcasting.

Is Longwave Useful?

The longwave band is still used for domestic broadcasts in Europe, North Africa and Russia. If you live or travel in rural areas there, longwave coverage may be a plus. Otherwise, forget it.

Fix or Toss?

Portables aren't meant to be friends for life, and are priced accordingly. The most robust models are usually not ready for the landfill until a decade or more of use, whereas pedestrian portables may give only a

Find major updates to the 2005 PASSPORT REPORTS at www.passband.com.

WHAT TO LOOK FOR

• **AC adaptor.** Those provided by the manufacturer are usually best and should be free from hum and noise—those that aren't are cited under "Con." Some are multivoltage and operate almost anywhere in the world. ☞ Beware of "switching" type power supplies, as these disrupt radio signals. In principle no radio manufacturer should be offering switching power supplies for use with radios, but it sometimes happens. PASSPORT REPORTS points these out.

• **Adjacent-channel rejection—I:** *selectivity, bandwidth.* World band stations are about twice as tightly packed as ordinary mediumwave AM stations. So, they tend to slop over and interfere with each other—DRM digital broadcasts are even worse. Radios with superior selectivity are better at rejecting interference, but at a price: better selectivity also means less high-end ("treble") audio response and muddier sound. So, having more than one bandwidth allows you to choose between tighter selectivity (narrow bandwidth) when it is warranted, and more realistic audio (wide bandwidth) when it is not.

• **Adjacent-channel rejection—II:** *synchronous selectable sideband.* With powerful stations "out in the clear," this has little audible impact. However, for tough catches it improves listening quality by minimizing selective-fading distortion and adjacent-channel interference. *Bonus:* it also helps reduce distortion with fringe mediumwave AM stations at twilight and even at night.

• **Ergonomics.** Some radios are a snap to use because they don't have complicated features. Yet, even sophisticated models can be designed to operate intuitively. Choose accordingly—there's no reason to take the square root and cube it just to hear a radio station.

• **Single-sideband demodulation.** If you are interested in hearing non-broadcast short-wave signals—"hams" and utility stations—single-sideband circuitry is *de rigueur*. Too, the popular low-powered American Forces Radio-Television Service requires this.

• **Speaker audio quality.** Unlike many portatop and tabletop models, few portables have rich, full audio through their speakers. However, some are much better than others, and with a model having line output you can connect amplified PC speakers for pleasant home listening.

• **Tuning features.** Models with digital frequency readout are so superior to analog that these are now the only radios normally tested by PASSPORT. Look for such handy tuning aids as direct-frequency access via keypad, station presets (programmable channel memories), up-down tuning via tuning knob and/or slew keys, band/segment selection, and signal-seek or other (e.g., presets) scanning. These make the radio easier to tune—no small point, given that a hundred or more channels may be audible at a time.

• **Weak-signal sensitivity.** Sensitivity is important if you live in a weak-signal location or tune exotic or daytime stations. Most portables have enough sensitivity to pull in major stations during prime time if you're in such places as Europe, North Africa or eastern North America.

• **World Time clock.** In 24-hour format, this is a "must." You can obtain these separately, but many radios have them built in; the best provide time whether the radio is on or off. However, many portable radios' clocks tend to gain or lose time if not reset periodically. In North America and beyond, the official shortwave time stations WWV on 2500, 5000, 10000, 15000 and 20000 kHz and CHU on 3330, 7335 and 14670 kHz are ideal for this; the Pacific is also served by WWVH in Hawaii on 2500, 5000, 10000 and 15000 kHz.

few years of regular service. Rarely are they worth fixing unless they are fairly new.

If you purchase a new portable that is defective, insist upon an immediate exchange without a restocking fee—manufacturers' repair facilities tend to have a disappointing record. But if quality of service is a priority, consider a tabletop model instead of a portable.

Shelling Out

Street prices are cited, including European and Australian VAT/GST where applicable. These vary plus or minus, so take them as the general guide they are meant to be. Shortwave specialty outlets and some other retailers usually have attractive prices, but duty-free shopping is not always the bargain you might expect.

David Heim, electronics deputy editor at *Consumer Reports* and quoted in *Reader's Digest*, suggests, "Look for stuff that's been factory refurbished." In North America refurbished Grundig and Etón portables are occasionally available—these are cited in PASSPORT REPORTS—and try pot luck if you are near a Sony outlet store.

We try to stick to plain English, but specialized terms can be useful. If you come across something that's not clear, flip to PASSPORT's glossary.

What PASSPORT's Ratings Mean

Star ratings: ✪✪✪✪✪ is best. Stars reflect overall performance and meaningful features, plus to some extent ergonomics and perceived build quality. Price, appearance, country of manufacture and the like are not taken into account. To facilitate comparison, portable rating standards are quite similar to those used for the portatop, tabletop and professional models reviewed elsewhere in this PASSPORT.

A rating of at least ✪✪½ should please most who listen to major stations regularly

during the evening. However, for casual use on trips virtually any small portable may suffice.

Passport's Choice. La crème de la crème. Our test team's personal picks of the litter—models we would buy or have bought for our personal use. Unlike star ratings, these choices are unapologetically subjective.

✪: A relative bargain, with decidedly more performance than the price would suggest.

Tips for Using This Section

Models are listed by size; and, within size, in order of world band listening suitability. Street selling prices are cited, including VAT/GST where applicable.

Unless otherwise indicated, each model has:

- Keypad tuning, up/down slew keys, station presets and signal-seek tuning/scanning.
- Digital frequency readout to the nearest kilohertz or five kilohertz.
- Coverage of the world band shortwave spectrum from at least 3200–26100 kHz.
- Coverage of the usual 87.5–108 MHz FM band, but not the Japanese and other FM bands below 87 MHz.
- Coverage of the AM (mediumwave) band in selectable 9 and 10 kHz channel increments from about 530–1705 kHz. No coverage of the 153–279 kHz longwave band.
- Adequate image rejection, almost invariably resulting from double-conversion circuitry.

Unless otherwise indicated, each model lacks:

- Single-sideband demodulation.
- Synchronous selectable sideband. However, when it is present the unwanted sideband is rejected approximately 25 dB via phase cancellation, not IF filtering.
- If 24-hour clock included, lacks tens-of-hours leading zero that properly should be displayed with World Time (UTC).

HAVE RADIO, WILL TRAVEL

Getting Past Airport Annie

Even in times of high alert, air travel with a world band radio is almost always trouble-free if common-sense steps are taken. To minimize the odds of delay at airport security, remember that their job is to be paranoid about you, so it's prudent to be paranoid about them.

• Answer all questions honestly, but don't volunteer information or joke around. Friendly banter can get you into the Dreaded Search corner.

• The nail that sticks out gets hammered first. Good security focuses on the unfamiliar or unusual, no matter how innocuous it may seem to you. Be gray.

• Bring a portable, not a portatop or tabletop—terrorists like big radios (they don't call them boom boxes for nothing). Best by far is a pocket or compact model.

• Stow your radio in a carry-on bag, not in checked luggage or on your person. Don't stuff it at the bottom, wrapped in clothing, like you're trying to hide something. Equally, it's usually best not to place it out in the open where it can be seen. However, if you decide to put a small radio into the manual inspection basket at the security portal, have it playing softly with earbuds or earphones attached, as though it were a Walkman you're listening to. Place any world band accessories, extra batteries, guides and instruction books in your checked luggage, or at least in a separate carry-on bag.

• Before entering the terminal, or at least before entering the security area, preset the radio to any popular FM music station, then keep batteries inside the radio so you can demonstrate that it actually works. Don't mention world band or shortwave unless queried.

• If asked what the radio is for, say for your own listening. If they persist, reply that you like to keep up with news and sports while away, and leave it at that. Don't volunteer information about alarm, snooze or other timer facilities, as timers can be components in bombs.

• If traveling in zones of war or civil unrest, or off the beaten path in parts of Africa or South America, take a radio you can afford to lose and which fits inconspicuously inside a pocket.

• If traveling to Bahrain, avoid taking a radio which has "receiver" visible on its cabinet. Security personnel may think you're a spy.

• If traveling to Malaysia, Bahrain or Saudi Arabia, don't take a model with single-sideband capability—or at the very least take steps to disguise this capability so it is not visually apparent. If things get dicey, point out that you listen to news and sports from the popular American AFRTS station, which transmits only in the single-sideband mode. (PASSPORT can be used to authenticate this.)

Theft? Radios, cameras, binoculars, laptops and other glitzy goodies are almost always stolen to be resold. The more worn the item looks—affixing scuffed stickers helps—the less likely it is to be confiscated by corrupt inspectors or stolen by thieves.

Tuning Local Stations Overseas

Mediumwave AM channel separation in the Americas is 10 kHz, elsewhere 9 kHz. When choosing a radio for traveling between these zones, try to select a model that tunes both norms. FM differs too, so Americans should select a model which can tune FM in increments of 0.1 MHz or less.

| STORE: 0211 | REG: 02/56 | TRAN#: 0506 |
| SALE | 12/30/2004 | EMP: 00732 |

****

st be accompanied by the original Borders store receipt. Returns must completed within 30 days of purchase. The purchase price will be ofunded in the medium of purchase (cash, credit card or gift card). Items purchased by check may be returned for cash after 10 business days.

Merchandise unaccompanied by the original Borders store receipt, or presented for return beyond 30 days from date of purchase, must be carried by Borders at the time of the return. The lowest price offered for the item during the 12 month period prior to the return will be refunded via a gift card.

Opened videos, discs, and cassettes may only be exchanged for replacement copies of the original item.
Periodicals, newspapers, out-of-print, collectible and pre-owned items may not be returned.
Returned merchandise must be in saleable condition.

BORDERS®

Merchandise presented for return, including sale or marked-down items, must be accompanied by the original Borders store receipt. Returns must be completed within 30 days of purchase. The purchase price will be refunded in the medium of purchase (cash, credit card or gift card). Items purchased by check may be returned for cash after 10 business days.

Merchandise unaccompanied by the original Borders store receipt, or presented for return beyond 30 days from date of purchase, must be carried by Borders at the time of the return. The lowest price offered for the item during the 12 month period prior to the return will be refunded via a gift card.

Opened videos, discs, and cassettes may only be exchanged for replacement copies of the original item.
Periodicals, newspapers, out-of-print, collectible and pre-owned items may not be returned.
Returned merchandise must be in saleable condition.

BORDERS®

Merchandise presented for return, including sale or marked-down items, must be accompanied by the original Borders store receipt. Returns must be completed within 30 days of purchase. The purchase price will be refunded in the medium of purchase (cash, credit card or gift card). Items purchased by check may be returned for cash after 10 business days.

BORDERS

BORDERS
BOOKS AND MUSIC
500 FIRST STREET #1
DAVIS CA 95616
(530) 750-3723

STORE: 0211   REG: 02/56   TRAN#: 0506
SALE   12/30/2004   EMP: 00732

PASSPORT TO WORLD BAND RADIO 2
    7596132   QP T   22.95

              Subtotal   22.95
              CALIFORNIA 7.75% 1.78
    Item   Total   24.73
              CASH   25.00
              Cash Change Due   .27

         12/30/2004 01:13PM

Check our store inventory online
   at www.bordersstores.com

Shop online at www.borders.com

POCKET PORTABLES

Perfect for Travel, Marginal for Home

Pocket portables weigh around half pound, or 0.2 kg, and are between the size of an audio cassette jewel box and a handheld calculator. They operate off two to four "AA" (UM-3 penlite) batteries. These diminutive models are ideal to carry on your person, but listening to tiny speakers can be tiring. If you plan to listen for long periods or to music, opt for using headphones or earpieces, or look into one of the better compact models.

Sony's high-tech ICF-SW100 is cell-phone small.

★★★ (see ☞) *Passport's Choice*
Sony ICF-SW100S

Price: $359.95 in the United States. ¥46,000 in Japan.

Pro: Tiny, easily the smallest tested, but with larger-radio performance and features. High-tech synchronous selectable sideband generally performs well, reducing adjacent-channel interference and selective-fading distortion on world band, longwave and mediumwave AM signals, while adding slightly to weak-signal sensitivity and audio crispness (*see* Con). Single bandwidth, especially when synchronous selectable sideband is used, exceptionally effective at adjacent-channel rejection. Relatively good audio, provided supplied earbuds or outboard audio are used (*see* Con). FM stereo through earbuds. Numerous helpful tuning features, including keypad, two-speed slew, signal-seek-then-resume scanning (*see* Con), five handy "pages" with ten station presets each. Station presets can display station name. Tunes in relatively precise 0.1 kHz increments. Good single-sideband performance (*see* Con). Good dynamic range. Worthy ergonomics for size and features. Illuminated display. Clock for many world cities, which can be made to work as a *de facto* World Time 24-hour clock (*see* Con). Timer and sleep delay. Travel power lock. Japanese FM (most versions) and longwave bands. Amplified outboard antenna, included, in addition to usual built-in antenna, enhances weak-signal reception (*see* Con). Weak-battery indicator; about 16 hours from a set of batteries (*see* Con). High-quality travel case for radio. *Except for North America:* AC adaptor comes with American and European plugs and adjusts automatically to local voltages worldwide.

Con: Tiny speaker, although innovative, has mediocre sound, limited loudness and little tone shaping. Closing clamshell reduces speaker loudness and high-frequency response. Weak-signal sensitivity could be better, although included outboard active antenna helps. Expensive. No tuning knob. Clock not readable when station frequency displayed. As "London Time" is used by the clock for World Time, the summertime clock adjustment cannot be used if World Time is to be displayed accurately. Rejection of images, and 10 kHz "repeats" when synchronous selectable sideband off, could be better. In some urban locations, FM signals from 87.5 to 108 MHz can break through into world band segments with distorted sound, e.g. between 3200 and 3300 kHz. Synchronous selectable sideband tends to lose lock if batteries weak, or if NiCd cells are used. Synchronous selectable sideband alignment can vary with temperature, factory alignment and battery voltage, causing synchronous selectable sideband reception to be slightly more muffled in one sideband than the other. Some readers report BFO pulling causes audio quavering, not found in our test units. Batteries run down faster than usual when radio off. Tuning in 0.1 kHz increments means that non-synchronous single-sideband reception can be mis-tuned by up to 50 Hz, so audio quality varies. Signal-seek scanner sometimes stops 5 kHz before a strong "real" signal. No meaningful signal-strength indicator. Included accessory antenna performs less well than another Sony accessory antenna, the AN-LP1. Mediumwave AM reception only fair. Mediumwave AM channel spacing adjusts peculiarly. Flimsy battery cover. No batteries (two "AA" required). *North America:* AC adaptor only 120 Volts.

☞ The above star rating reflects mediocre speaker audio quality. Through earpieces, the rating rises to ✪✪✪⅛.

☞ In early production samples, the cable connecting the two halves of the "clamshell" case tended to lose continuity with extended use because of a very tight radius and an unfinished edge; this was successfully resolved with a design change in 1997. eBay buyers and owners of early units who encounter this problem should go to www.tesp.com/sw100faq.htm for repair tips.

Verdict: This jewel among world band radios is a shoehorning *tour de force*—don't leave Langley without it. Its synchronous selectable sideband and effective bandwidth filter provide superior adjacent-channel rejection. Speaker and, to a lesser extent, weak-signal sensitivity keep it from being all it could have been, and the accessory antenna isn't Sony's latest or best. Yet, this Japanese-made gem rules the pocket category, and even outperforms most compact models.

✪✪✪   *Passport's Choice*
Sony ICF-SW100E

Price: *ICF-SW100E:* £159.95 in the United Kingdom. €265.00 in Germany. *ACE-30 220V AC adaptor:* £24.95 in the United Kingdom. €25.50 in Germany.

Verdict: This version, not available in North America, includes only a case, outboard reel passive antenna and earbuds. Otherwise, it is identical to the Sony ICF-SW100S, above.

New for 2005
✪✪
Degen DE105, Kaito KA105

Price: *KA105:* $54.95 in the United States.

Pro: Reasonably good selectivity from single bandwidth. Good voice-audio quality, with ample volume, for a small speaker (*see* Con). A number of helpful tuning features, including keypad (*see* Con), up/down slew (*see* Con) and "signal seek" frequency scanning; also, 30 station presets, of which ten are for world band with others divided between FM and mediumwave AM. Above-average weak-signal sensitivity. Dual-zone 24-hour clock (*see* Con) with clock radio/alarm and sleep delay. Illuminated display via non-timed pushbutton. Clicky keys have superior tactile feel. LCD has excellent contrast. Low battery consumption. Weak-battery indicator. Battery cover hinged to avoid loss. Travel power lock (*see* Con). FM in stereo through earbuds, included (*see* Con). Build quality appears superior for price class, and manufacturer has solid if relatively brief construction history. Telescopic antenna swivels and rotates (*see* Con). Reset control for microprocessor and memory. Insertable elevation tab, attached to carrying strap, tilts radio to handier operating angle. Includes short external wire antenna accessory. *Kaito:* Tough, attractive matte aluminum alloy face plate. 120V AC adaptor (*see* Con). Mediumwave AM 9/10 channel steps user-selectable, tunes up to 1710 kHz. *Degen:* Available in either slate blue or silver.

Con: World band coverage of 5950–15600 kHz misses 17 and 21 MHz segments, skips chunks of 6 and 15 MHz, and omits lesser 25, 19, 5, 4, 3 and 2 MHz segments. Single-conversion IF circuitry results in poor image rejection. Speaker audio bereft of low-frequency ("bass") response. Audio through earbuds may be stronger in one channel at lower volume. No tuning knob. Keypad not in standard telephone format. Tunes world band only in 5 kHz steps and displays in nonstandard XX.XX/XX.XX5 MHz format. Slow microprocessor lock time while slew tuning degrades bandscanning. No signal-strength indicator. Clock doesn't display when frequency is shown. Mediumwave AM coverage of 520–1620 kHz omits 1625–1705 kHz. Mediumwave AM suffers slightly from LCD digital hash. FM has so-so sensitivity, mediocre capture ratio and some tendency to overload. FM audio distorted through earbuds. Because telescopic antenna exits from cabinet's side, it can't tilt to the right for optimum FM reception. Travel power lock does not disable LCD illumination. Two "AA" batteries not supplied. *Kaito:* Minor hum with AC adaptor.

Verdict: This new Chinese travel portable is as tough and well built as anything near its price. Except for the lack of single-sideband to hear the American Forces Radio and Television Service, it makes a rugged choice for areas of turmoil. Otherwise, the larger Degen/Kaito siblings DE1101/KA1101 and DE1102/KA1102 cover more frequencies, perform significantly better and cost little more.

Evaluation of New Model: Degen's new DE105 travel portable, sold in North America as the Kaito KA105, includes keypad tuning, up/down frequency slewing, "signal-seek" frequency scanning, and ten world band presets (20 more for FM and mediumwave AM)—but no tuning knob. The slew cycle when going from one frequency to the next is just long enough to discourage bandscanning.

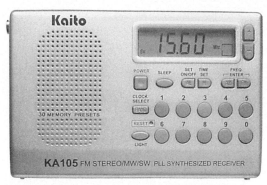

The Kaito KA105 sports a tank-tough aluminum alloy front panel, yet is small enough for personal use. Otherwise, the kindred DE1101/KA1101 is better and costs little more. D. Zantow

Other features include a weak-battery indicator and a hinge to keep the battery cover from being misplaced. Interestingly, the front panel, at least in the Kaito incarnation, is made not from the customary plastic, but of rugged aluminum alloy (the back and sides are the usual silver-colored plastic). The Kaito version also comes with a 120V AC adaptor that causes minor hum but otherwise works acceptably. Battery consumption is low, so it's hardly needed, anyway.

Tuning is in 5 kHz increments, and the readout displays in nonstandard XX.XX/XX.XX5 MHz format that is an earmark of many Chinese cheaps. The LCD has good contrast, but is small; it remains illuminated so long as a button is held down. The radio offers only one bandwidth and single conversion, but includes a travel power lock that doesn't disable LCD illumination.

A two-zone 24-hour clock reads out only when the radio is off, and controls a clock radio timer with sleep function. A stick-in elevation tab is attached to the carrying strap.

World band coverage is limited to 5950–15600 kHz. AWOL are the important 17 and 21 MHz (16 and 13 meter) world band segments, along with the lesser 25, 19, 5, 4,

3 and 2 MHz (11, 15, 60, 75, 90 and 120 meter) segments. Also omitted are the 5730–5945 and 15605–15825 kHz portions of the vital 6 and 15 MHz (49 and 19 meter) segments.

Mediumwave AM coverage is 520–1620 kHz, which orphans the 1625–1705 kHz portion of the X-band used in many parts of the world—another pointless omission.

Passable Performance

Speaker audio has virtually no bass reproduction, but overall is quite acceptable for the radio's small size. What is unexpected are audio lapses with earpieces: distortion on FM (although, ironically, not on other bands), and one side annoyingly louder than the other except at high volume in either to mono or stereo. Perhaps these will improve in later production runs.

World band performance is predictable. Image rejection is poor, but selectivity and dynamic range are reasonable. Sensitivity is superior and aided by the short wire antenna included with the radio.

Mini size, mini price, mini performance. For casual use on trips.

Mediumwave AM has 9/10 kHz tuning steps and performs acceptably, although there is some digital hash. Included for globetrotters are selectable 9/10 kHz tuning steps.

FM is in stereo through included earpieces. It has a reasonable capture ratio and sensitivity, and there is only a slight tendency to overload when there are nearby FM transmitters. The telescopic antenna swivels and rotates, but exits from the radio's left side so it can't be tilted to the right for optimum FM reception.

As we have come to expect from Degen-manufactured portables, the '105 appears to be constructed to a higher standard than most other under-$100 models. The Kaito version adds to this with a tank-tough front panel and includes a one-year warranty.

✪⅝ 🖋

Etón Mini 300PE, Grundig Mini 300PE, Tecsun R-919

Price: *Mini 300PE:* $39.95 in the United States. $49.95CAD in Canada. Price not yet established in the United Kingdom.

Pro: Weak-signal sensitivity quite reasonable. Pleasant room-filling audio for such a small package (*see* Con). Clock/alarm-timer with sleep delay (*see* Con). FM in stereo with earbuds, included. Low battery consumption. Soft carry case affixes to belt or purse strap. Two "AA" batteries included.

Con: Analog-tuned with digital frequency counter, so tunes only by thumbwheel, which is somewhat touchy. Does not tune 120, 75, 90, 60, 15, 13 and 11 meter segments; misses small bits of tuned world band segments. Single-conversion IF circuitry results in poor image rejection. Audio lacks bass response. Frequency drift with changes in temperature. Telescopic antenna does not rotate or swivel. Antenna's plastic base protrudes even when antenna collapsed. Displays in nonstandard XX.XX/XX.XX5 MHz format. Display not illuminated. Minor drift when hand grasps back of cabinet. Frequency counter noise slightly audible when finger placed over LCD during mediumwave AM reception. Some FM overloading in strong-signal environments. Clock in 12-hour format, displays only when radio off. No port for AC adaptor, much less an adaptor. *North America:* Toll-free tech support.

Verdict: Best of the really inexpensive portables, even though it comes up short on daytime frequency coverage, lacks display illumination and its clock isn't in World Time format. But thanks to true pocket size, nice weak-signal sensitivity and decent audio quality it is hard to resist for casual use on trips.

New for 2005
✪½ ⓔ
Degen DE205

Price: ¥76 (under $10) in China, but currently not available elsewhere. If it is introduced in the U.S. as the Kaito KA205, the price will higher.

Pro: Build quality appears superior for price class, and manufacturer has solid if relatively brief construction history. Reasonably good dynamic range for class. Ample volume (*see* Con). Clock with clock-radio (*see* Con). LCD has good contrast when viewed from below or head-on. Illuminated display (*see* Con). Low battery consumption. Battery cover hinged to avoid loss. FM 70–109 MHz coverage includes 76–90 MHz Japanese FM band and 70–74 MHz portion of 66–74 MHz low band still used within some former Warsaw Pact countries. Telescopic antenna swivels and rotates (*see* Con). Insertable elevation tab, attached to carrying strap, tilts radio to handier operating angle.

Con: Try finding one! Analog-tuned with digital frequency counter, so tunes only by thumbwheel, which operates smoothly. Unhandy and archaic "FM/MW/SW1/SW2" switch required for tuning within ranges

Degen's DE205 is well built, yet popcorn priced.

5450–10200 kHz *vs.* 11350–18180 kHz or *vice versa*. Does not tune 120, 75, 90, 60, 15, 13 or 11 meter segments. Mediocre speaker audio, although reasonable for size. Single-conversion IF circuitry results in poor image rejection. Poor selectivity. Mediocre weak-signal sensitivity; improves greatly if ten feet or three meters of wire are clipped to telescopic antenna. Frequency drift with changes in temperature. Frequency counter omits last digit so, say, 5995 kHz appears as either 5.99 or 6.00 MHz. Readout at least 1 kHz high on world band, 2 kHz high on mediumwave AM on our unit. Clock in 12-hour format only, doesn't display when radio is on. No signal-strength indicator. Display illumination dim. Slight digital hash at times on shortwave. Digital hash degrades mediumwave AM weak-signal reception. Mediumwave AM 525–1620 kHz coverage omits 1625–1705 kHz portion of the X-band; mediocre selectivity; mediocre sensitivity; and inferior spurious-signal rejection on mediumwave AM. Pedestrian FM in mono only, with mediocre sensitivity, dynamic range and capture ratio. Because telescopic antenna exits from cabinet's side, it can't tilt to the right for optimum FM reception. Two "AA" batteries not included. No AC adaptor, carrying pouch or earbuds; aftermarket AC adaptor would require uncommon 5V DC output (4.5V DC with correct pin type and center-pin negative, such as Kaito provides for the KA105, suffices).

☞ Shortwave tuning ranges (5.95–9.95 and 11.65–17.90 MHz) marked on back of panel are pessimistic; actual tuning ranges are significantly better: 5.45–10.20 and 11.35–18.18 MHz.

☞ Don't confuse the Degen DE205 (or potential Kaito KA205) with the analog-readout Grundig YB205 distributed in North America by Kaito (but not, ironically, by Grundig's North American distributor, Etón).

Verdict: Degen's new DE205 is the cheapest world band radio tested that has digital frequency readout, and it outperforms a number of models that cost more. Equally encouraging, visual inspection suggests its build quality is superior to that of other tested cheaps.

Evaluation of New Model: Degen's new DE205, manufactured and sold only in China, is the cheapest radio tested with digital frequency readout. It uses two "AA" batteries with miserly battery consumption, and a hinge prevents battery cover loss.

Still, something this inexpensive has serious limits: no batteries, no carrying pouch, no earbuds and no AC adaptor (although there are jacks for earphones and an adaptor). And while it features digital frequency readout, it is analog-tuned. There are no presets or keypad—tuning is solely by a thumbwheel that, thankfully, turns smoothly.

Also, the frequency readout doesn't display the kilohertz digit; so, say, 11995 kHz shows as either 11.99 or 12.00 MHz. Like other cheap models, there's only one bandwidth and a clunky "SW1/SW2" bandswitch.

But the '205 offers pleasant surprises: an illuminated display and broad FM coverage. There's also a 12-hour (only, alas) clock/clock radio and an insertable elevation tab. However, the clock shows only when the radio is off, and pushbutton illumination is faint.

World band coverage is 5450–10200 kHz ("SW1") and 11350–18180 kHz ("SW2"); omitted are the 120, 90, 75, 60, 15, 13 and 11 meter world band segments. Mediumwave AM is 525–1620 kHz, excluding 1625–1705 kHz. FM tunes a whopping 70–109 MHz FM, which includes the Japanese 76–90 MHz FM band and much of the 66–74 MHz "Warsaw Pact" FM band.

Mediocre Performer

Speaker audio is decent with volume aplenty, but lacks bass. There is no perceptible drift except with temperature change, but world band frequencies tend to read out a kilohertz or so high. World band image rejection and selectivity are both poor. Sensitivity to weak signals is mediocre, but profits from ten feet or three meters of wire clipped to the telescopic antenna.

Reception of weak mediumwave AM stations is limited, as sensitivity is only fair and there is digital hash; also, selectivity is mediocre, image-type spurious signals intrude, and the frequency readout can be off slightly. FM is only in mono, with mediocre capture ratio, fair sensitivity and a tendency to overload.

The '205 appears to be constructed to a high standard for its price class. It calls for an unusual 5V DC (center-pin negative) AC adaptor, but a 4.5V DC adaptor works fine. Given its thriftiness with batteries, you don't really need one, though.

The '205 is not yet available outside China, but Chinese speakers can try degen.mall.sz.net.cn.

✪½
Kaiwa KA-818, Tecsun R-818

Price: $34.95 or less in the United States. $46.95CAD in Canada.

Pro: Reasonable weak-signal sensitivity for low-cost pocket model. Clock with timer/alarm (*see* Con).

Con: Analog-tuned with digital frequency counter, so tunes only by thumbwheel, which is somewhat touchy. Does not tune 120, 75, 90, 60, 22, 15, 13 or 11 meter segments; misses some expanded coverage of other world band segments. Single-conversion IF circuitry results in poor image rejection. Frequency drift with changes in temperature. Frequency counter completely omits last digit so, say, 9575 kHz appears as either 9.57 or 9.58 MHz. Clock in 12-hour format only, displays only when radio off. Display not illuminated. Mediocre speaker audio quality. Telescopic antenna does not rotate or swivel. Mediumwave AM lacks weak-signal sensitivity. Pedestrian FM, with spurious signals. On one of our new units the telescopic antenna immediately fell apart. Two "AA" batteries not included. Few vendors in America and Europe. Warranty only 90 days in United States and various other countries.

Verdict: Performance brings up the rear, but price, size and alarm make this Chinese-made model worth consideration for casual use on trips.

New for 2005

✪¼

Kchibo KK-C300, Sharper Image SN400

Sharper Image: $39.95 in the United States. *Kchibo:* About the equivalent of $20 in East Asia.

Pro: Helpful tuning features include up/down slew and "signal seek" frequency scanning; also, world band segment selection and 30 station presets (*see* Con), of which ten are for world band with others divided between FM and mediumwave AM. Clicky keys have superior tactile feel. Timed LCD illumination (*see* Con). Travel power lock (*see* Con). Dual-zone clock (*see* Con) with sleep delay. FM stereo through earbuds (see *Con*), included. Mediumwave AM 9/10 kHz switch. Telescopic antenna rotates and swivels. Elevation panel. Superior carrying pouch (*see* Con).

Tecsun's tiny R-818 brings up the rear.

Con: Digital buzz often degrades, and sometimes obliterates, world band reception. World band coverage of 5950–15600 kHz misses 17 and 21 MHz segments, skips chunks of 6 and 15 MHz, and omits lesser 25, 19, 5, 4, 3 and 2 MHz segments. No keypad or tuning knob. Slow microprocessor lock time while slew tuning degrades bandscanning. Single-conversion IF circuitry results in poor image rejection. Speaker audio bereft of low-frequency ("bass") response. Peculiar battery replacement/AC adapter procedure to retain memory data. Tunes world band only in 5 kHz steps and displays in nonstandard XX.XX/XX.XX5 MHz format. Presets accessible only serially via up/down carousel. Mediumwave AM coverage of 520–1620 kHz omits 1625–1705 kHz. FM has so-so sensitivity, mediocre capture ratio and some tendency to overload. FM audio distorted through earbuds. Audio through earbuds may be a skosh stronger in one channel. Both clocks only in 12-hour format and neither displays when frequency is shown. No signal-strength indicator. Travel power lock does not deactivate LCD illumination button. No AC adaptor, and no indication of required polarity for an aftermarket adaptor. Two "AA" batteries not included. Carrying pouch has slight tire odor. *Sharper Image:* Warranty only 90 days.

The new Sharper Image SN400 isn't sharp, but it has images aplenty. Buzzing, too. Also sold as the Kchibo KK-C300.   D. Zantow

Verdict: Sharp, this isn't. No low price can't justify the digital buzz that plagues world band reception, and important world band frequencies can't be tuned. Made in China.

Evaluation of New Model: Kchibo's new KK-C300 travel portable, sold in North America as the Sharper Image SN400, includes up/down frequency slewing, "signal seek" frequency scanning, world band segment selection and ten one-push world band presets (20 more are for FM and mediumwave AM)—but no keypad or tuning knob. The poky slew cycle when going from one frequency to the next makes bandscanning an exercise in frustration.

Tuning, only in 5 kHz increments, reads out in nonstandard XX.XX/XX.XX5 MHz format. There is a travel power lock that doesn't disable LCD illumination. A two-zone 12-hour clock shows only when the radio is off and includes a sleep function. An elevation panel tilts the radio to a comfortable operating angle.

World band coverage is 5950–15600 kHz. This omits the 5730–5945 and 15605–15825 kHz portions of the vital 6 and 15 MHz (49 and 19 meter) segments. Also absent are the important 17 and 21 MHz (16 and 13 meter) world band segments, along with the lesser 25, 19, 5, 4, 3 and 2 MHz (11, 15, 60,

75, 90 and 120 meter) segments. Another design flop is that mediumwave AM tunes only 520–1620 kHz, so 1625–1705 kHz can't be heard.

Dismal Performer

The speaker reproduces virtually no bass and there is distortion on FM through earpieces. World band image rejection is poor, but selectivity and dynamic range are reasonable.

World band sensitivity is another matter. There is so much digital circuit buzz mixing in with signals that weaker signals are often useless, even though the radio is otherwise sensitive enough to bring them in. Moderate signals fare better, but the tireless buzzing still annoys. Strong signals are okay.

Mediumwave AM performance is acceptable, albeit with a bit of digital buzz. Selectable 9/10 kHz tuning steps are included for globetrotting.

FM is in stereo through included earpieces. It has a reasonable capture ratio and sensitivity, but can overload when there are nearby FM transmitters. The telescopic antenna swivels and rotates to aid FM reception.

Battery replacement or switching over to an AC adaptor is convoluted: 1) turn off radio, 2) wait 30 seconds, then 3) replace batteries within ten seconds (or plug in adaptor). Otherwise, all memories will be wiped out. Fortunately, there isn't a whole lot to reprogram if you fail this memory mambo.

The radio doesn't come with an AC adaptor, so the only alternative is an aftermarket model. Alas, Kchibo failed to indicate the required polarity either on the radio's case or in the SN400's owner's manual.

★¼
Kaide KK-989

Price: $24.95 in the United States.

Pro: Very small, ideally sized for air travel and has handy built-in belt clip. Clock with timer/alarm (*see* Con).

Con: Mediocre weak-signal sensitivity; helps considerably to clip a few yards of wire to the built-in antenna. Tinny audio. Analog-tuned with digital frequency counter, so tunes only by thumbwheel, which is very touchy. Does not tune 120, 75, 90, 60, 15, 13 or 11 meter segments; omits coverage of nearly all the 1605–1705 kHz mediumwave AM X-band; which frequencies are missed varies with battery voltage and from sample to sample. Single-conversion IF circuitry results in poor image rejection. Frequency counter completely omits last digit so, say, 9575 kHz appears as either 9.57 or 9.58 MHz. Clock in 12-hour format only, displays only when radio off. Display not illuminated. Telescopic antenna does not rotate or swivel. If hand is placed on rear of cabinet, world band drifts considerably; mediumwave AM drifts, too, but less badly. Frequency counter buzzes faintly on mediumwave AM; if finger placed over LCD display, buzz becomes strong and is also audible on lower world band frequencies. FM overloads in presence of strong signals, remediable by shorting antenna (which also reduces weak-signal sensitivity). Mediocre FM weak-signal sensitivity. Poor mediumwave AM weak-signal sensitivity. When first turned on, radio always reverts to FM band. FM in mono only. Three "AAA" batteries not included; "AAA" cells require more frequent replacement than standard "AA" cells, raising the cost of operation. No port for AC adaptor. In the United States, no warranty information comes with radio; best purchased from dealer who will swap if DOA. Although radio purchased from U.S. dealer, operating instructions only in Chinese. Country of manufacture not indicated on radio or box, but almost certainly is China.

Verdict: Nicely sized, and priced for every budget. Yet, with a long roster of significant drawbacks the Kaide KK-989 is a dud.

Even by el cheapo standards, the Kaide KK-989 is overpriced for what it does.

COMPACT PORTABLES
Nice for Travel, Okay for Home

Compacts are hugely popular, and no wonder. They offer a value mix of affordable price, worthy performance, manageable size and acceptable speaker audio. They tip in at one to two pounds, under a kilogram, and are typically sized less than 8 × 5 × 1.5 inches, or 20 × 13 × 4 cm. Like pocket models, they feed off "AA" (UM-3 penlite) batteries—but, usually, more of them. They travel almost as well as pocket models, but sound better through their larger speakers. They can also suffice for home use.

Retested for 2005
✪✪✪¼ *Passport's Choice*
Sony ICF-SW07

Price: $399.95 as available in the United States. £229.95 in the United Kingdom. ¥51,000 in Japan.

Pro: Best non-audio performance among travel-worthy compact portables. Attractive and unusual styling. High-tech synchronous selectable sideband generally performs well

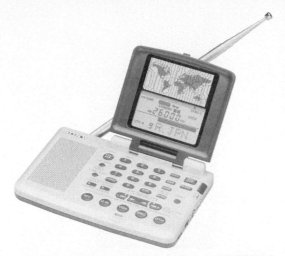

The best travel-sized portable is Sony's ICF-SW07. It includes an excellent outboard antenna.

and is straightforward to operate; reduces adjacent-channel interference and selective-fading distortion on world band, longwave and mediumwave AM signals while adding slightly to weak-signal sensitivity. Unusually small and light for a compact model when used without accessory antenna. Numerous tuning aids, including pushbutton access of frequencies for four stations stored on a replaceable ROM, keypad, two-speed up/down slew, 20 station presets (ten for world band) and "signal-seek, then resume" tuning. Clamshell design aids in handiness of operation, and is further helped by illuminated LCD readable from a wide variety of angles. Hump on the rear panel places the keypad at a convenient operating angle. Comes with AN-LP2 outboard "tennis racquet" antenna, commendably effective in raising the 'SW07's weak-signal sensitivity to excellent on world band; this antenna, unlike the Sony AN-LP1 optional accessory antenna for other receivers, has automatic preselector tuning, simplifying operation. Good single sideband performance (*see* Con). Clock covers most international time zones, as well as UTC (*see* Con). Outstanding reception of weak and crowded FM stations, with limited urban FM overloading resolved by variable-level attenuator. FM

stereo through earbuds, included. Japanese FM (most versions) and longwave bands. Above-average reception of mediumwave AM band. Travel power lock. Closing the clamshell does not interfere with speaker performance. Low-battery indicator. Presets information is non-volatile, can't be erased when batteries changed. Presets and time zone readout can be user-programmed to display six-character alphanumeric readout on LCD. Two turn-on times for alarm/clock radio. Sleep delay. Battery cover hinged to avoid loss, although AN-LP1 antenna battery cover not hinged. AC adaptor, albeit only single-voltage (e.g., 120V in version for North America).

Con: Only one bandwidth, surprising at this price—even some under-$100 models now provide two bandwidths. Pedestrian audio quality through small speaker, with relatively narrow audio-frequency response and above-average "hiss." Audio fidelity diminished, even with earbuds, in part because of the lack of a second, wider, bandwidth and meaningful tone control. No tuning knob. On our latest sample, the telescopic antenna would break its internal case mounting. Display shows time and tuned frequency, but not both simultaneously. Tuning resolution of 0.1 kHz above 1620 kHz means that non-synchronous single-sideband reception can be mis-tuned by up to 50 Hz, allowing audio fidelity to suffer. Synchronous selectable sideband tends to lose lock if batteries weak or if NiCd cells used. Synchronous selectable sideband alignment can vary with temperature, factory alignment and battery voltage, causing synchronous selectable sideband reception to be slightly more muffled in one sideband than the other. No meaningful signal-strength indicator, an unusual shortcoming at this model's price. LCD frequency/time numbers relatively small for size of display. AN-LP2 accessory antenna has to be physically disconnected for proper mediumwave AM reception. 1621–1705 kHz portion of American AM band and 1705–

1735 kHz potential public service segment are erroneously treated as shortwave, although this does not harm reception quality. Low battery indicator misleadingly shows batteries as dead immediately after fresh batteries are installed; clears up when radio is turned on. No batteries (two "AA" required for radio, two more for antenna). UTC displays as "London" time even summer during DST, when London is an hour ahead of UTC; best is to re-label "London" as "UTC" and not display that zone at DST; however, the DST key can change UTC to UTC +1 in error if user is not careful.

☞ The ICF-SW07 is no longer listed on Sony of America's Website, nor that of Sony Canada or Sony Deutschland. However, U.S. radio dealers report that they continue to obtain stock on a regular basis. This model is listed as Sony's "Flagship World Band Receiver" on the Website of Sony United Kingdom.

Verdict: Our latest unit is unchanged from earlier production. Speaker audio and sticker shock aside, this Japanese-made model is still the best compact portable for travel. Unbeatable for Father's Day.

It also passes the Caribbean Palm Frond Test as an effective prop for attracting friendly strangers. Clamshell open and antenna unfurled, the Sony ICF-SW07 is a great conversation-starter, especially among the intellectually curious . . . or, sometimes, the curiously intellectual.

DRM Modifiable
★★★⅛ ℮ *Passport's Choice*
Sony ICF-SW7600GR

Price: *ICF-SW7600GR:* $169.95 in the United States. $299.00CAD in Canada. £129.95 in the United Kingdom. €169.00 in Germany. $509.00AUD in Australia. ¥33,000 in Japan. *MW 41-680 120V regulated AC adaptor (aftermarket, see below):* $19.95 in the United States.

Pro: One of the great values in a meaningful world band radio. Far and away the least-costly model available with high-tech synchronous selectable sideband; this generally performs well, reducing adjacent-channel interference and selective-fading distortion on world band, longwave and mediumwave AM signals (*see* Con). Single bandwidth, especially when synchronous selectable sideband is used, exceptionally effective at adjacent-channel rejection. Seemingly robust—similar predecessor had superior quality of components and assembly for price class, and held up unusually well. Numerous helpful tuning features, including keypad, two-speed up/down slew, 100 station presets and "signal-seek, then resume" tuning. For those with limited hearing of high-frequency sounds, such as some men over the half-century mark, speaker audio quality may be preferable to that of Grundig G4000A/Yacht Boy 400PE (*see* Con). Single-sideband performance arguably the best of any portable; analog clarifier, combined with LSB/USB switch, allow single-sideband signals (e.g., AFRTS, utility, amateur) to be tuned with uncommon precision, and thus with superior

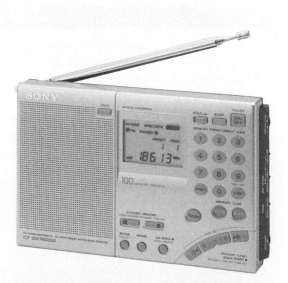

Favorite starter radio: Sony's ICF-SW7600GR. High tech, it does nicely both at home and on trips.

carrier phasing and the resulting natural-sounding audio. DRM modifiable (see www.drmrx.org/receiver_mods.html). Dual-zone 24-hour clock with single-zone readout, easy to set. Slightly smaller and lighter than most other compact models. Outboard reel passive wire antenna accessory aids slightly with weak-signal reception. Simple timer with sleep delay. Illuminated LCD has high contrast when read head-on or from below. Travel power lock. Superior reception of difficult mediumwave AM stations. Superior FM capture ratio aids reception when band congested, including helping separate co-channel stations. FM stereo through earpieces or headphones. Japanese FM (most versions) and longwave bands. Superior battery life. Weak-battery indicator. Stereo line output for recording, FM home transmitters and outboard audio systems. Battery cover hinged to avoid loss. Automatically provides power for optional AN-LP1 active antenna.

Con: Audio lacks tonal quality for pleasant world band or mediumwave AM music reproduction, and speaker audio tiring for any type of FM program. Weak-signal sensitivity, although respectable, not equal to that of the top handful of top-rated portables; helped considerably by extra-cost Sony AN-LP1 active antenna reviewed elsewhere in this edition. Image rejection adequate, but not excellent. Three switches, including those for synchronous selectable sideband, located unhandily at the side of the cabinet. No tuning knob. Slow microprocessor lock time while slew tuning degrades bandscanning. No meaningful signal-strength indicator. Synchronous selectable sideband holds lock decently, but less well on weak signals than in Sony's larger models; too, it tends to lose lock even more if batteries weak or if NiCd cells used. Synchronous selectable sideband alignment can vary with temperature, factory alignment and battery voltage, causing synchronous selectable sideband reception to be slightly more muffled in one sideband than the other. No AC adaptor included, while in North America the new optional Sony AC-E60A "switching" adaptor causes serious interference to radio signals and, incredibly, is labeled "Not for use with radios"; Universal Radio offers its own MW 41-680 to remedy

CAR RADIOS

Over the years we have tested car radios with significant shortwave coverage, and found they have two things in common: At any given time only one model is readily available; and performance differences are not great.

In recent years Sony has been offering an ever-changing line of car radios, usually with cassette players, that cover most world band segments. They differ in various ways, but their world band circuitry thus far has been shared. These are available in the United States and Canada from Durham Radio in Ontario (www.durhamradio.com), worldwide from Jacky's in Dubai (www.jackys.com). Sometimes in Australia and South Asia, too.

The robust Becker Mexico 2340 has been discontinued, but may still be available from Continental Imports in Miami (http://www.continentalimports.com/2340.html). Other Becker models with world band cover only the 49 meter segment.

On the road: Becker Mexico 2340.

this, and presumably other firms will be offering something similar in due course. Radio's adaptor socket is of an unusual size, making it difficult to find a suitable third-party AC adaptor. 1621-1705 kHz portion of American AM band and 1705-1735 kHz potential public-service segment are erroneously treated as shortwave, although this does not harm reception quality. Even though it has a relatively large LCD, same portion of display is used for clock and frequency digits; thus, clock doesn't display when frequency is shown, although pressing the EXE key allows time to replace frequency for nine seconds. No earphones or earpieces. No batteries (four "AA" needed).

Verdict: The robust Sony ICF-SW7600GR provides excellent bang for the buck, even though it is manufactured in high-cost Japan. Its advanced-tech synchronous selectable sideband is a valuable feature that other portable manufacturers have yet to engineer properly—even some professional models costing thousands of dollars still haven't got it right. To find this useful operating feature at this price is without parallel.

Top drawer single-sideband reception for a portable, too, along with superior tough-signal FM and mediumwave AM reception. But it has warts: Musical audio quality through the speaker is only *ordinaire* and Sony of America's horrible new optional 117V AC adaptor should be avoided.

★★★ @ *Passport's Choice*
Degen DE1102, Kaito KA1102

Price: *Kaito:* $99.99 in the United States.

Pro: Unusually small and light for a sophisticated compact model; only a skosh larger and one ounce (28 grams) heavier than its simpler sibling '1101. Two bandwidths, both well chosen. A number of helpful tuning features, including keypad, up/down slew (1 or 5 kHz steps for world band, 1 or 9/10 kHz for mediumwave AM), carousel selector

Best under $100 is Degen's DE1102, sold in North America as the Kaito KA1102. Small size makes it handy for travel. D. Zantow

for 49-16 meter segments, and "signal seek" frequency scanning (*see* Con) and memory scanning; also, ten 19-preset "pages" provide a total of 190 station presets, of which 133 can be used for shortwave (*see* Con). Auto-store function automatically stores presets; works on all bands. Tunable BFO allows for precise signal phasing during single-sideband reception (*see* Con). No muting during manual shortwave bandscanning in 1 or 5 kHz steps, or mediumwave AM bandscanning in 1 kHz steps. PLL and BFO relatively free from drift during single-sideband operation (*see* Con). Above-average weak-signal sensitivity and image rejection. Little circuit "hiss." Superior speaker audio quality, intelligibility and loudness for size. Build quality appears superior for price class, and manufacturer has solid if relatively brief construction history. Four-LED signal-strength indicator for mediumwave AM and shortwave (*see* Con); three-level signal-strength indicator for FM (fourth LED becomes stereo indicator). World Time 24-hour clock displays seconds numerically when radio is off; when on, time (sans seconds) flashes on briefly when key is held down; user may choose 12-hour format, instead. Unusually appropriate for use in the dark, as display and keypad illuminated by pleasant blue light which works only in dark (*see* Con). Clicky keys have superior tactile feel. LCD has excellent contrast when viewed from sides or below. Alarm with sleep delay (*see* Con). Travel power lock. Rechargeable NiMH batteries (3 × "AA"), included, can be charged within the radio; station presets and time not erased during charging. Switchable bass boost supplements high-low tone switch, significantly improves FM audio (*see* Con). Low battery consumption except with FM bass boost. Battery-level indicator. Battery cover hinged to avoid loss. Superior FM weak-signal sensitivity. Excellent FM capture ratio aids reception when band congested, including helping separate co-channel stations. FM in stereo through earbuds, included (*see* Con). FM 70–108 MHz coverage includes 76–90 MHz Japanese FM band and 70–74 MHz portion of 66–74 MHz low band still used within some former Warsaw Pact countries (*see* Con). Full coverage of mediumwave AM band. Includes short external wire antenna accessory, which in many locations is about the most that can be used without generating overloading. Available in black or aluminum colors. *Degen:* AC adaptor (220V). *Kaito:* AC adaptor (120V).

Con: Speaker audio, except FM, lacks low-frequency ("bass") response as compared to larger models. Bass-boost circuit, which could relieve this on world band, works only on FM. Dynamic range, although roughly average for a compact portable, not anywhere equal to that of the sibling '1101; overloads easily with a significant outdoor antenna, although much less often with the built-in antenna or a short outboard antenna. Not so straightforward to operate as some other portables; for example, single-sideband mode works only when presets "page 9" is selected (or SSB button is held in manually), even if no presets are to be chosen (in any event, presets don't store mode); otherwise, "ERR" is displayed; manufacturer says this is to prevent its Chinese consumers, who are unfamiliar with single sideband, from turning on the BFO accidentally and thus becoming confused. Slight warble in audio with ECSS reception, varies with how many signal-strength LEDs are being illuminated; LEDs can't be turned off. Volume at earphone jack sometimes inadequate with weak or undermodulated signals; variable-level earphone jack misleadingly described as "line out." Power button activates a 99-minute sleep delay; to turn the radio on fulltime, a second key must be pressed immediately afterwards. No tuning knob. No LSB/USB switch. Displays in nonstandard XX.XX/XX.XXx MHz format. Signal-strength indicator overreads. Little-used 2 MHz (120 meter) world band segment not covered. Clock doesn't display when frequency is shown, although pushbutton allows time to replace frequency briefly. Always-on LCD/keypad illumination with AC adaptor, as described in owner's manual, did not function on test sample. LCD/keypad illumination dim and uneven. FM IF produces images 21+ MHz down.

Verdict: An exceptional price and performance winner from Degen, with superior build. Just don't expect much in the way of low-end audio.

Changed for 2005
DRM Modifiable

✪✪✪ ⓔ *Passport's Choice*
Grundig G4000A, Grundig Yacht Boy 400PE

Price: $149.95 in the United States. $199.95CAD in Canada. £99.95 in the United Kingdom. $279.00AUD in Australia. *Refurbished units, as available:* $99.95 in the United States. $169.00CAD in Canada.

Pro: Speaker audio quality tops in size category for those with sharp hearing. Two bandwidths, both well-chosen. Ergonomically superior, a pleasure to operate. A number of helpful tuning features, including keypad, up/down slew, 40 station presets, "signal seek" frequency scanning and scanning of station presets. Signal-strength indicator. Dual-zone 24-hour clock, with one zone shown at all times; however, clock displays seconds only when radio is off. Illuminated display. Alarm with simple sleep delay. Tunable BFO allows for superior signal phasing during single-sideband reception (*see* Con). DRM modifiable (see www.drmrx.org/receiver_mods.html). Outboard reel passive wire antenna accessory aids slightly with weak-signal reception. Generally superior FM perfor-mance, especially in weak-signal locations. FM in stereo through headphones. Longwave. AC adaptor. *G4000A:* Excellent hardside leather travel case. *North America:* Toll-free tech support.

Con: Circuit noise ("hiss") can be slightly intrusive with weak signals. No tuning knob. At many locations there can be break-through of powerful AM or FM stations into the world band spectrum. Keypad not in telephone format. No LSB/USB switch, and single-sideband reception is below par. Battery consumption slightly above norm. No batteries (six "AA" needed).

☞ Refurbished units reportedly include gift and similar returns from department stores and other outlets where customers tend to be unfamiliar with world band radio. Everything but the radio itself is supposed to be replaced. Limited availability.

Verdict: This most popular of Grundig's digital-readout portables offers superior audio quality, ease of use and a roster of other virtues. So it's hardly surprising that this Chinese-made receiver is unusually popular for enjoying world band programs, including music. Tough FM catches, too, although single-sideband isn't all it could be.

Changes for 2005: Apparently on the principle that you never tamper with success, the Yacht Boy 400PE is undergoing only the most superficial of changes as it morphs into the G4000A. Etón's established portable is being visually freshened with a

Grundig's popular Yacht Boy 400PE has morphed into the Grundig G4000A. Same pleasant "Grundig sound" and ease of use.

hardside leather travel case and similar tweaks, but otherwise is as before. These changes allow it to be marketed as part of Grundig's family of Porsche models.

New for 2005

✪✪⅞ (*see* ☞) ♻
Degen DE1103, Kaito KA1103

Price: *Kaito:* $99.95 in the United States.

Pro: Two bandwidths, both well chosen (*see* Con). Helpful tuning features include tuning knob (*see* Con), keypad (*see* Con), world band segment up/down carousel, "signal seek" (pause, resume) frequency scanning and presets scanning; also, sixteen "pages" holding 16 presets each provide 256 station presets, plus another dozen to select among world band segments (alternatively, "pages" may be bypassed for quick-access tuning, reducing available presets to 100). Presets store mode (*see* Con). Tuning knob not muted when tuned, facilitating bandscanning (*see* Con). Scanner works better than most. Radio can return to last-tuned frequency within ten world band segments, as well as FM and mediumwave AM. Superior dynamic range for a compact portable—better than that of DE1102/KA1102, and even ap-proaching that of DE1101/KA1102 (*see*

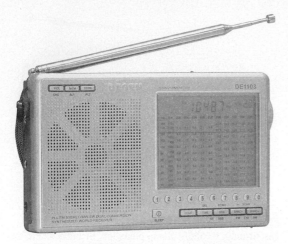

The new DE1103 is Degen's best performer, but its worst ergonomically. The "dial" is fake and there's not even a dedicated volume control.

Con). Tunable BFO (*see* Con) allows for precise signal phasing during single-sideband reception. Relatively free from drift during single-sideband operation. Above-average sensitivity aided by quiet circuitry. Using dual conversion, image rejection is above average (*see* Con). Speaker audio quality, although limited, fairly good except during single-sideband reception (*see* Con). Four-level signal-strength indicator (*see* Con). World Time 24-hour clock (*see* Con). Display and keypad illumination is about as good as it gets: During battery operation, it can be switched not to go on; otherwise, it is automatically activated by any of various controls, including those for tuning, and stays on for a full 15 seconds. Clicky keys with superior tactile feel (*see* Con). Sleep delay. Two-event timer. NiMH batteries (4 × "AA"), included, slowly rechargeable within radio. Travel power lock. Station presets and time not erased during battery charging or replacement. Battery-level indicator. Battery cover hinged to avoid loss. Superior FM sensitivity. Excellent FM capture ratio aids reception when band congested, including helping separate co-channel stations. FM in stereo through earbuds, included (*see* Con). Stereo

audio line output, has appropriate level. Coverage of 76–108 MHz includes Japanese FM band. Longwave (*see* Con) tunes down to 100 kHz. Elevation panel. Includes short external wire antenna accessory. *Degen:* AC adaptor (220V). *Kaito:* AC adaptor (120V).

Con: Hostile ergonomics include having to operate two controls to change volume; nonstandard single-row keypad; small keys; stiff slider controls; only one knob tuning rate (1 kHz, slow) for world band and mediumwave AM; and no center detent for fine-tuning (tunable BFO) thumbwheel. Pseudo-analog LCD "dial," a pointless gimmick that takes up space which could have been used to display useful information and provide proper keypad layout. No up/down slew controls. No tone control except "news-music" switch that works only on FM. No LSB/USB switch. Single-sideband has audible distortion, seemingly from AGC. Image rejection, although fairly good, not all that it could be for a model with enough dynamic range to handle some outboard antennas. Slight microprocessor noise when tuning knob turned—a small price to pay to avoid bandscan limitations brought about by muting. Even though dynamic range superior, AGC seemingly swamped by exceptionally powerful signals, causing lowered volume; switching attenuator to "LO" allows volume to return to normal level. Signal-strength indicator overreads and does not operate on FM. Clock doesn't display when frequency is shown, although pushbutton allows time to replace frequency briefly. Presets do not store bandwidth. Longwave less convenient to access than other bands.

☞ The '1103 merits three stars for performance, but only two for ergonomics (*see* Evaluation).

☞ Unlike the sibling DE1101/KA1101 and DE1102/KA1102, the '1103's AC adaptor jack uses standard center-pin-positive polarity.

Verdict: Dreadful ergonomics and a wasted LCD make this a model to approach with caution. Yet, the Degen DE1103/Kaito KA1103 is a solid and versatile performer at a surprisingly low price. If you can endure its ergonomic shortcomings, the '1103 offers excellent performance value.

Evaluation of New Model: The '1103 is Degen's third serious world band offering. Like the '1101 and '1102 it provides more than its price suggests and is sold in North America as the Kaito KA1103. But the '1103 is larger than the other two models, more along the lines of the Sony ICF-SW7600GR and Grundig Yacht Boy 400. This makes it a popular size for use both at home and on trips.

Useful Features

With the '1103, buying batteries becomes a thing of the past. The radio comes complete with an AC adaptor and four NiMH "AA" cells that recharge where they should, inside the radio; these should last a good five years. There's also an accurate battery-level indicator, and the battery cover is hinged to prevent loss.

Included are two bandwidths, no small achievement in this price class. Both are well-chosen for world band listening and are selectable independent of mode. There is no ear-pleasing synchronous selectable sideband, but the '1103 demodulates conventional single-sideband (SSB) signals using fine tuning rather than LSB/USB switching.

Although the usual up/down slew buttons are absent, on the side is a tuning knob ("jog dial" in electronics newspeak); it turns from the knurled edge or the side with concentric nubs—a thoughtful touch. Even nicer for bandscanning is that the receiver does not mute when the knob is spun. This allows for a skosh of chuffing buzz, but that is picayune compared to having the sound disappear while tuning.

Other tuning options include a keypad, along with "signal seek" scanning and presets scanning that work unusually well. Also offered is an up/down carousel to select among world band segments. Sensibly, it returns to the last-tuned frequency within each of those segments, as well as within the FM and mediumwave AM bands.

Presets? Fully 256, residing within sixteen pages holding 16 presets apiece. That's awesome at any price, but not everybody wants presets buried in pages. For them, the keypad can be used to access 100 presets directly—no frills, no fads, no fancy stuff. Either way presets store mode, but not bandwidth.

Dialing for Dummies

But one look at the '1103 reveals something odd: an up-to-date digital frequency readout, yet what also appears to be an analog needle-and-dial frequency readout. What gives?

Actually, the "dial" is a large LCD that's digitalized to look analog. If this sounds familiar, flip to the photo of the Sony ICF-SW40. Sony went this route years ago so it could offer a digital portable that wouldn't scare off traditionalists. Trouble is, the 'SW40 has been a limp seller—hardly surprising, as even in Kathmandu people are familiar with digital readouts.

Like the 'SW40, the '1103's LCD includes a precise five-digit frequency readout. That's great, but it makes the vague, jerky "analog" display as pointless as a purple blazer on St. Patrick's Day. Worse, it chews up front-panel acreage that could have been used to better effect. For example, the big LCD leaves no room for a keypad in customary telephone format. Instead, bantam keys have been shoehorned into a single row, making keying a squint-and-peck exercise. And with a fake analog "dial" hogging the LCD, there's also no room for a separate display of World Time or much other useful information.

Illumination is first rate—not only does the LCD light up, but so, too, does the keypad. Given the oddball key layout, this illumination is unusually helpful. Also, during battery operation lighting can be switched to stay off to conserve power. Otherwise, it is automatically activated by any of various controls, including those for tuning, after which it stays on for a full 15 seconds. For bandscanning under the stars this is about as good as it gets.

Frankenvolume

Not only the keypad and weird LCD compromise ergonomics. Incredibly, there is also no separate volume control. No knob, no up/down buttons—not even a little stick. Instead, to adjust volume you first press a key, then quickly start turning the tuning knob until the desired level is reached, then wait about three seconds; alternatively, you can enter the desired volume level (0–63) on the keypad, then press the volume key.

In time you'll probably come across somebody who proclaims, "Hey, that doesn't bother me!" He's probably the same guy who likes bee stings.

Lesser ergonomic lapses include stiff slider controls; also, a lone 1 kHz tuning rate for the tuning knob within the shortwave and mediumwave AM spectra. A second tuning rate of, say, 5 kHz for shortwave and selectable 9/10 kHz for mediumwave AM would have made operation more flexible and convenient.

Although diminutive keys are a disappointment, they are clicky and have superior tactile response. Degen models have thus far been well built and robust, and we have yet to hear of any with failing or intermittent keys.

World Band Performer

Ergonomics may bring up the rear, but Degen's latest offering makes amends by performing nicely.

Weak-signal sensitivity is superior, being aided by circuitry that is quieter than most. It also has unusually worthy dynamic range for a portable. Adjacent-channel rejection—selectivity—is above average and flexible, thanks to a choice between two excellent bandwidths. Image rejection is superior, thanks to double conversion that's rarely found around this price.

The '1103 provides single sideband demodulation to eavesdrop on utility and ham signals or the American Forces Radio and Television Service. For this, a variable-pitch thumbwheel fine tunes between 1 kHz tuning increments, but it lacks a center detent. The '1103 also has the stability and narrow selectivity needed for all but serious utility/ham DXing.

The '1103 uses its LCD instead of power hungry LEDs to indicate four levels of signal strength. So, unlike the '1102, which uses LEDs, the analog BFO's pitch doesn't warble in concert with the number of LEDs going on and off as signal modulation and strength changes. This makes not only for slightly improved single sideband reception, but also audibly better manual ("exalted-carrier") selectable sideband (ECSS) operation.

AGC timing appears to be the cause of some distortion during single sideband reception. Otherwise, speaker audio is pleasant—a bit more crispness and bass response would have been nice, but it is an improvement over siblings '1101 and '1102.

Superior FM, Mediumwave AM

Worthy performance isn't limited to world band—FM and mediumwave AM come across commendably, as well, even if the signal-strength indicator doesn't function on FM. FM tunes not only the usual 87–108 MHz FM band, but also the 76–90 MHz Japanese band. It has a superior capture ratio and weak-signal sensitivity, along with stereo audio through earbuds, included, and

MAKE YOUR PORTABLE "HEAR" BETTER

Regardless of which portable you own, you can boost weak-signal sensitivity on the cheap. How cheap? Nothing, for starters.

Look for "sweet spots" to place your radio: near windows, appliances, telephones, building I-beams and the like. If your portable has an AC adaptor, try that, then batteries; sometimes the adaptor works better, sometimes batteries. Places to avoid are near computers and appliances with microprocessors; also, light dimmers, non-incandescent lighting and cable TV or telephone lines. Sometimes power lines and cords can be noisy, too.

Outdoor Antenna Optional

An outdoor antenna shouldn't be needed with a portable. But it can help, especially with models lacking in weak-signal sensitivity with their built-in telescopic antennas. With compact and pocket models, simplest is often best—sophisticated or big antennas can cause "overloading." Run several meters or yards of ordinary insulated wire to a tree, then clip one end to your set's telescopic antenna with an alligator or claw clip available from RadioShack and such. It's fast and cheap, yet effective.

If you are in a weak-signal location, such as central or western North America or Australia, and want signals to be more audible, even better is to erect an inverted-L (so-called "longwire") antenna. Also sometimes called random-length antennas, they are available in the United States at RadioShack (278-758, $9.99) and worldwide at radio specialty outlets. Powerful versions can be constructed from detailed instructions in the RDI White Paper, *PASSPORT Evaluation of Popular Outdoor Antennas.* Antenna length is not critical, but keep the lead-in wire reasonably short.

Use an outdoor antenna only when required—disconnect during thunder, snow or sand storms, and when the radio is off. And don't touch any connected antenna during dry weather, as discharged static electricity might damage the radio.

Creative Indoor Solutions

All antennas work best outdoors, away from electrical noises inside the home. If your supplementary antenna has to be indoors, run it along the middle of a window with Velcro, tape or suction cups. In a reinforced-concrete building which absorbs radio signals, you can affix a telescopic car antenna so it sticks outdoors, like a wall flagpole. These are all but invisible, but work because they reach away from the building.

Compact amplified ("active") antennas, reviewed in this PASSPORT REPORTS, are small and handy but cost more. Many are for tabletop models, but some are for portables.

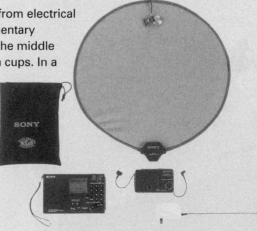

Sony's AN-LP1, for home and travel.

J. Brinker

a line output jack that provides a well-chosen level of audio.

As a result, the '1103 performs nicely on FM in rural fringe areas, as well as in suburban locations with band congestion. There is also slightly less than the usual level of overloading near FM transmitters, making it a sensible choice for urban locations.

Mediumwave AM provides yeoman service, and long-distance reception is aided by dual bandwidths. But the knob's lone 1 kHz tuning rate makes bandscanning painstakingly poky.

In all, the new Degen DE1103/Kaito KA1103 is an ergonomic dud. After that it's completely uphill, thanks to the radio's outstanding price-to-performance ratio on all bands.

✪✪⅛
Sony ICF-SW55, Sony ICF-SW55E (as available)

Price: £224.95 in the United Kingdom. €398.00 in Germany. ¥45,000 in Japan.

Pro: Audio quality. Dual bandwidths. Logical controls. Innovative tuning, with alphabetic identifiers for groups ("pages") of stations; some like this approach. Weak-

The Sony ICF-SW55 has long been out of production, but can still be found.

signal sensitivity a bit better than most. Demodulates single-sideband signals (*see* Con). Reel-in antenna, AC adaptor, earbuds and cord for external DC power. Signal/battery strength indicator. Local and World Time clocks, one displayed separately from frequency. Snooze/alarm. Five-event (daily only) timer. Illuminated display. Longwave and Japanese FM.

Con: Page tuning system cumbersome for some. Spurious-signal rejection in higher segments not commensurate with price. Wide bandwidth rather broad for receiver lacking synchronous selectable sideband. Tuning increments of 0.1 kHz and frequency readout of 1 kHz compromise single-sideband reception. BFO pulling reportedly causes audio quavering; not found in our test units. Display illumination dim and uneven. High battery consumption.

Verdict: Overpriced, but if you like the Sony ICF-SW55's operating scheme and want a small portable with good audio quality, this veteran model is a respectable performer in its size class. But this Japanese-made unit, now discontinued but still available in some markets, lacks synchronous selectable sideband—a major plus found on newer Sony models.

✪✪⅞
Sangean ATS 909, Sangean ATS 909 "Deluxe," Roberts R861

Price: *ATS 909:* $259.95 in the United States. $369.00CAD in Canada. £139.95 in the United Kingdom. €168.00 in Germany. *ATS 909 "Deluxe":* $289.90 in the United States. *Multivoltage AC adaptor:* £16.95 in the United Kingdom. *R861:* £179.00 in United Kingdom.

Pro: Exceptionally wide range of tuning facilities, including hundreds of world band station presets (one works with a single touch) and tuning knob. Tuning system uses 29 "pages" and alphanumeric station descriptors for world band. Two voice bandwidths. Tunes single-sideband signals in unusually precise 0.04 kHz increments without having to use a fine-tuning control, making this one of the handiest and most effective portables for listening to these signals (*see* Con). Shortwave dynamic range slightly above average for portable, allowing it to perform unusually well with an outboard antenna (*see* Con). Travel power lock. 24-hour clock shows at all times, and can display local time in various cities of the world (*see* Con). Excellent 1–10 digital signal-strength indicator. Low-battery indicator. Clock radio feature offers three "on" times for three discrete frequencies. Sleep delay. FM sensitive to weak signals (see Con) and performs well overall, has RDS feature, and is in stereo through earpieces, included. Illuminated display. Superior ergonomics, including tuning knob with tactile detents. Longwave. *ATS 909 (North American units), ATS 909 "Deluxe" and Roberts:* Superb, but relatively heavy, multivoltage AC adaptor with North American and European plugs. ANT-60 outboard reel passive wire antenna accessory aids slightly with weak-signal reception. Sangean service provided by Sangean America on models sold under its name. *ATS 909 "Deluxe," available only from C. Crane Company):* Enhanced tuning knob operation and elimination of muting between stations.

Con: Weak-signal sensitivity with built-in telescopic antenna not equal to that of comparable models; usually remediable with ANT-60 accessory antenna (provided) or other suitable external antenna. Tuning knob tends to mute stations during bandscanning; C. Crane Company offers a "Deluxe" modification to remedy this. Larger and heavier than most compact models. Signal-seek tuning, although flexible and relatively sophisticated, tends to stop on few active shortwave signals. Although scanner can operate out-of-band, reverts to default (in-band) parameters after one pass. When entering a new page, there is an initial two-second wait between when preset is

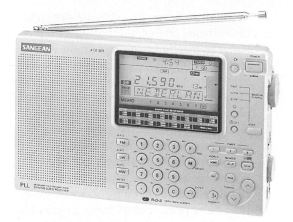

The Sangean ATS 909 works best with an outboard antenna, which it handles well.

keyed and station becomes audible. Although synthesizer tunes in 0.04 kHz increments, frequency readout only in 1 kHz increments. Software oddities; e.g., under certain conditions, alphanumeric station descriptor may stay on full time. Page tuning system enjoyed by some users, but cumbersome for others. Speaker audio quality only so-so, not aided by three-level treble-cut tone control. No carrying handle or strap. The 24-hour clock set up to display home time, not World Time, although this is easily overcome by not using world-cities-time feature or by creative setup of World/ Home display to London/Home. Clock does not compensate for daylight (summer) time in each displayed city. FM can overload in high-signal-strength environments, causing false "repeat" signals to appear; capture ratio average. Heterodyne interference, possibly related to the digital display, sometimes interferes with reception of strong mediumwave AM signals. Battery consumption well above average. No batteries (four "AA" required). Elevation panel flimsy.

☞ Frequencies pre-programmed into "pages" vary by country of sale. It helps to keep a couple of empty pages to aid in editing, deleting or changing pre-programmed page information.

Verdict: While many models are similar to others being offered, this compact from Sangean marches to its own drummer. Relatively high battery consumption and insufficient weak-signal sensitivity lower its standing as a portable, and our star rating reflects this. Yet, when it is used as a *de facto* tabletop connected to household current and an outboard antenna, it becomes worthy of a three-star rating— even if not as a genuine portable. In part, this is because its circuitry is more capable than those of most other compact portables in handling the increased signal load from an outboard antenna.

As a result, this feature-laden model has a visible and enthusiastic following among radio aficionados for whom portability is not *de rigueur*. Like the tabletop Icom IC-R75, it is a favorite for tuning utility and ham signals, as it offers superior single-sideband performance at an attractive price. The '909 is also the only Sangean model still made exclusively in Taiwan.

New for 2005
✪✪⅞
Sangean PT-80, Grundig Yacht Boy 80

Price: *Sangean:* $159.95 in the United States. *Grundig:* €129.00 in Germany.

Pro: Excellent world band selectivity (*see* Con). Worthy sensitivity and image rejection. Numerous helpful tuning features, including tuning disc-type knob with raised dots (*see* Con); nicely located up/down slew-scan keys; 18 world band presets; 9 additional presets each for longwave, FM and mediumwave AM; "auto arrange" scanning of presets from low-to-high frequency; auto entry of presets (*see* Con); meter-segment selector; and selectable 5 kHz/1 kHz tuning steps on shortwave. For size, generally pleasant speaker audio in all bands (*see* Con). Single-sideband demodulation (*see* Con), with precise analog +/– 1.5 kHz fine-tuning thumbwheel. No muting

with tuning disc, aids bandscanning. Unusually attractive, sheathed in tan leather. Flip-open leather case excellent at protecting front, top and rear of the receiver (*see* Con). Leather case affixed to receiver with snaps and magnetic catches, so nearly impossible to misplace. Frequency easy to read, with decent-sized digits and good contrast. Illuminated LCD (*see* Con). Travel power lock (*see* Con). Tuning-disc lock. Superior mediumwave AM performance. On FM, superior capture ratio and worthy sensitivity. Dual-zone clock in 12 or 24 hour format (*see* Con). Alarm/clock radio with sleep delay. Rubber feet on bottom to prevent slipping. Stereo indicator (*see* Con). Battery cover hinged to avoid loss. Keys have good feel (*see* Con). Low battery indicator. Reset control for microprocessor and memory. Outboard reel passive wire antenna accessory aids slightly with weak-signal reception. Longwave. Earbuds. *Sangean (North America):* 120V AC adaptor (*see* Con).

Con: During single-sideband reception, circuit "pulling" during strong modulation peaks causes annoying warbling in audio. Just enough drift at times to prompt occasional tweaking during single-sideband reception. World band and mediumwave AM audio slightly muffled; becomes clearer if station off-tuned by 1 kHz or so, which also can reduce adjacent-channel interference. Limited dynamic range; tends to overload with significant external antenna; attenuator helps, but also reduces signal considerably. (Better to skip attenuation and use the outboard reel antenna, letting out just enough wire to give good reception.) Attenuator doesn't work on mediumwave AM or longwave; however, in unusual circumstances this can be a convenience. Birdies. Tuning disc has some "play," and raised dots can irritate finger during lengthy bandscanning sessions. Long-stroke keys need to be depressed fully to make contact. No meaningful signal-strength indicator. Spurious signal rejection wanting; at one test location, and alone among several radios there, the PT-80 occasionally had a point-to-point voice transmission puffing away in the background throughout the entire shortwave spectrum. When radio on, displays either frequency or time, but not both at the same time. FM stereo indicator worked at some test locations, but not all. External antenna jack functions only on shortwave; however, this can also be a convenience. No audio line output. Auto entry of presets does not function on world band. Leather case: 1) sags when used as an elevation panel; 2) has no holes for speaker on front, just on back, so audio is muffled when case closed; and 3) does not protect receiver's sides or bottom. Travel power lock does not deactivate LCD illumination key. No batteries (four "AA" required). *Sangean:* Country of origin, China, not shown on radio, manual or box. Instructions for setting clocks may confuse newcomers, as both clocks are referred to as being for "local time," not UTC, and the manual's mention of UTC mis-states it as "Universal Time Coordinated" instead of Coordinated Universal Time (however, the PT-50's manual gets it right). *Sangean (North America):* 120V AC adaptor generates minor hum.

Verdict: This welcome new entry from Sangean is pleasant performer on world band and superior on mediumwave AM and FM. Its main drawbacks: single-sideband reception with "warbling" audio, and no meaningful signal-strength indicator.

With an external antenna, the sibling Sangean ATS 909 gets the nod, mainly for superior single-sideband performance, dual bandwidths, signal-strength indicator and sophisticated presets. However, as a true portable for only occasional single-sideband listening the new PT-80 holds its own, plus it doesn't mute during bandscanning and costs much less.

Evaluation of New Model: For 2005, Sangean has introduced the new ProTravel

Sangean's PT-80 is a pleasant new offering, but lacks value. In its price range there are better performers, while in its performance class there are cheaper models.

series of leather-sheathed travel portables, two with digital frequency readout.

Top of the line is the great-looking PT-80, which although a compact is almost large enough to weigh in as a lap portable. Grundig also sells it in Europe and beyond as the Yacht Boy 80. However, unlike its smaller '50 cousin, the '80 is a radio with a clock, rather than the other way around.

On the '80's front is what looks like the time-selector disc on the '50. Instead, it is a tuning knob, or what's really more like a tuning disc. It does what it is supposed to, and there's even a switch to keep it from functioning while the radio is being carried around. However, the disc has some "play," and its raised dots can irritate the finger after enough use. Thankfully, there is no muting with the tuning disc—just some chugging—which aids considerably in bandscanning.

Like the '50, the '80 has two clocks in either 24 or 12 hour format, with the format choice applying to both clocks. However, unlike the '50 only one clock is displayed at a time; when the radio is on, only time or frequency can be displayed—not both at the same time. Both clocks are adjusted independently of each other, so you can set summer "savings" time on the local clock and not impact the World Time/UTC setting. Rounding out the time features is an alarm/clock-radio with sleep delay.

The LCD is illuminated, with decent-sized characters and good contrast. There's also a travel power lock to help prevent batteries from draining accidentally on trips. However, that lock allows the LCD illumination to function, partially defeating its purpose.

Another boon for travelers is the radio's snap-on leather case. Its handy flip-open design does a great job of protecting the front, back and top of the radio, and because it's attached there is no separate carrying case to misplace. The rub: There are no perforations over the face of the speaker, just the back, so the audio is seriously muffled with the case's front flipped down. Even when it is flipped open it blocks the folded telescopic antenna, frustrating its use. Best is not to push the antenna into the cabinet's snap-in antenna catch.

The leather case sags if adjusted to angle the radio to a comfortable operating position. However, there are four rubber feet to keep the radio from sliding around when vertical.

Numerous helpful tuning features, besides the tuning disc, include up/down slew-scan keys that are sensibly located along the periphery of the disc; 18 world band presets, along with nine more each for longwave, FM and mediumwave AM; "auto arrange" scanning of presets from low-to-high frequency; a meter-segment selector; and selectable 5 kHz/1 kHz shortwave tuning steps.

Single-sideband signals are demodulated sans frills. Precise phasing is accomplished by an analog +/- 1.5 kHz fine-tuning thumbwheel, and stability is good for the radio's class. However, at times audio quality profits from tweaking of the thumbwheel to offset very minor drifting.

Not so easy to overcome is the tendency for powerful single-sideband modulation peaks to cause circuit "pulling," which creates audio warbling. Shortening the telescopic antenna sometimes helps, but those with fussy ears are unlikely to be delighted by the '80's single-sideband performance—particularly with broadcast signals, such as the popular AFRTS.

Ergonomic pluses include clicky keys, although these have a relatively long throw and need to be pushed in fully to make proper contact. The battery cover is hinged to prevent loss, and there's a low-battery indicator. Within North America, Sangean includes a 120V AC adaptor, although it introduces slight hum. No batteries, though.

The FM-stereo indicator worked at some test locations, but not all. The single-LED signal-strength indicator is all but useless.

Mediumwave AM is tuned in 1, 9 and 10 kHz increments throughout the entire 520–1710 kHz range. The shortwave band is covered from 1711 to 29999 kHz, so all world band segments are included.

Commendable Reception

World band reception is commendable, overall, with worthy sensitivity and image rejection. Selectivity is excellent, but either a second bandwidth or synchronous selectable sideband would not be unreasonable to expect at this price.

Dynamic range is typical for a compact portable, so it's fine with the built-in telescopic antenna and, usually, the outboard reel wire antenna included with the radio. However, limited spurious-signal rejection can allow for background interference at some locations. For example, at one of our test sites a voice utility signal was puffing away in the background much of the daytime throughout the entire shortwave spectrum. No other receivers at that site had this problem, nor did it materialize at other locations.

The last time we encountered this during testing was over 30 years ago with an otherwise superior portable having poor first-IF rejection. It wasn't a major drawback then, and with some exceptions shouldn't be now.

Mediumwave AM performance is delightful, making the '80 a solid choice for long-distance listening. With synchronous selectable sideband and/or a second bandwidth it would have been even better, but even "as is" this is a superior AM-band performer.

The '80 tunes the usual FM band in mono through the speaker and in stereo through the supplied or other earpieces. Reception is superior, thanks in part to the excellent capture ratio. Other FM performance variables are commendable, as well.

Speaker audio is reasonably pleasant, even if a skosh muffled, so the '80 is suitable for listening over chunks of time. Except on FM, audio becomes clearer if the station off-tuned by 1 kHz or so, which has the added virtue of helping reduce adjacent-channel interference. Given the decent audio, you'd think there would be a fixed-level line output for recorders or outboard amplifiers, but there isn't.

The PT-80 has no indication of the country of origin, which we confirmed is China. Legal issues aside, this omission is unworthy of a reputable firm like Sangean.

Bargain: Degen's DE1101/Kaito KA1101 offers superior performance, rechargeable batteries and handy travel size. No single or selectable sideband, though. Prices vary, so shop around. D. Zantow.

❶❷⅛ ⓒ *Passport's Choice*
Degen DE1101, Kaito KA1101

Price: *Kaito:* $74.95 in the United States.

Pro: Exceptional dynamic range for a compact portable. Unusually small and light for a compact model. Two bandwidths, both well chosen. A number of helpful tuning features, including keypad, up/down slew and "signal seek" frequency scanning (*see* Con); also, 50 station presets of which ten are for 3,000–10,000 kHz and ten for 10,000–26,100 kHz; others are for FM, FML and mediumwave AM. Above-average weak-signal sensitivity and image rejection. Little circuit "hiss." Superior intelligibility and loudness for size. World Time 24-hour clock displays seconds numerically when radio is off; when on, time (sans seconds) flashes on briefly when key is held down. Illuminated display, works only in dark. Clicky keys have superior tactile feel. LCD has excellent contrast when viewed from sides or below. Alarm with sleep delay (*see* Con). AC adaptor (120V Kaito, 220V Degen). Rechargeable NiMH batteries (3 × "AA"), included, can be charged within the radio; station presets and time not erased during charging. Low battery consumption. Battery-level indicator. Battery cover hinged to avoid loss. Travel power lock. Superior FM weak-signal sensitivity. Excellent FM capture ratio aids reception when band congested, including helping separate co-channel stations. FM in stereo through earbuds, included. "FML" covers 76–90 MHz Japanese FM band and 70–74 MHz portion of 66–74 MHz low band still used within some former Warsaw Pact countries. Line output socket (separate from earphone socket) for recording, FM home transmitters and outboard audio systems. *Kaito:*

Mediumwave AM 9/10 channel steps user-selectable, tunes up to 1710 kHz.

Con: Speaker audio quality lacks low-frequency ("bass") response as compared to larger models. Power button activates a 99-minute sleep delay; to turn the radio on fulltime, a second key must be pressed immediately afterwards. Station presets, slew and scanning require pressing bandswitch carousel button up to four times when tuning from below 10 MHz to above 10 MHz and *vice versa*. No tuning knob. Tunes world band only in 5 kHz steps and displays in nonstandard XX.XX/XX.XX5 MHz format. Digital buzz under some circumstances, such as when antenna is touched. Spurious signals can appear when user's hand is pressed over back cover. With our unit, microprocessor locked up when batteries removed for over a day; resolved by pressing tiny reset button. No signal-strength indicator (what appears to be an LED tuning indicator is actually an ambient-light sensor to disable LCD illumination except when it's dark). Clock doesn't display when frequency is shown, although pushbutton allows time to replace frequency briefly. Little-used 2 MHz (120 meter) world band segment not covered. On Degen unit tested, FM sounded best when tuned 50 kHz above nominal frequency on LCD; this would appear to be a sample-to-sample issue. *Degen:* Upper limit of mediumwave AM tuning is 1620 kHz, rather than the 1705 kHz band upper limit in the Americas, Australia and certain other areas. Mediumwave AM tunes only in 9 kHz steps, making it ill-suited for use in the Americas.

☞ The Kaito version comes with the proper 120V AC adaptor for North America, whereas the Degen version comes with a 220V AC adaptor suitable for most other parts of the world. Both are safe when used "as is," or with a Franzus or other recognized 120V-to-220V or 220V-to-120V AC converter. However, according to unconfirmed reports, the Degen version ordered by Americans from an unofficial eBay vendor in Hong Kong comes with a 220-to-120V AC converter that appears to pose a fire hazard.

☞ The Kaito version comes with the proper 120V AC adaptor for North America, whereas the Degen version comes with a 220V AC adaptor suitable for most other parts of the world. Both are safe when used "as is," or with a Franzus or other recognized 120V-to-220V or 220V-to-120V AC converter. However, according to unconfirmed reports, the Degen version ordered by Americans from an unofficial eBay vendor in Hong Kong comes with a 220-to-120V AC converter that appears to pose a fire hazard.

Verdict: The gray-painted Degen DE1101, sold in North America as the aluminum-colored Kaito KA1101, is a knockout bargain. Engineered and manufactured in China, it is one of the smallest compact models tested, and has exceptional dynamic range. It comes with an enviable grab-bag of features and accessories, right down to inboard rechargeable batteries. But if you want music-quality audio, be prepared to use earpieces.

New for 2005

✪✪¾
Etón E10, Tecsun PL-550

Price: *Etón:* $129.95 in the United States.

Pro: Superior audio quality for size. Numerous helpful tuning features include 1/5 kHz knob, 5/100 kHz up/down slew, world band segment selector (covers all 14 segments), signal-seek scanning, keypad and 550 station presets clustered within pages. Fully 500 presets are for general use (*see* Con), including world band; the other 50 are for the "Automatic Tuning System" (ATS), which installs strong FM and mediumwave AM stations (not world band) into presets, like when setting up a VCR.

Presets pages programmable to hold 10, 20, 25 or 50 presets per page. Audio muting scarcely noticeable when tuning by knob. Respectable world band and mediumwave AM sensitivity, with low circuit noise. Overloading, which can appear with a substantial external antenna, controllable by two levels of attenuation via a three-position switch. Two well-chosen band-widths for program listening (*see* Con). Generally worthy ergonomics, including keys with positive-action feel (*see* Con). World Time clock (*see* Con) with alarm, clock radio (two on/off 30-minute timers), snooze and sleep delay (*see* Con); may also be set to 12-hour format. Clock reads out separately from frequency. Clock operates after batteries removed. LCD large and easy to read. Display illumination can either fade out in five seconds, be switched off before the five seconds have expired, or stay on fulltime when button held down more than five seconds. Five-level signal-strength indicator (*see* Con). External antenna jack for world band and FM. Novel 455/450 kHz IF control shifts images by 10 kHz (*see* Con). Rubber pads on bottom reduce sliding when elevation panel in use. Worthy FM sensitivity for superior fringe reception. Japanese FM band. Weak-battery indicator. Includes worthy travel pouch, stereo earbuds and outboard reel passive wire antenna. Numerous user-defined software functions, including page definitions for presets, FM frequency coverage and battery type (1.6V normal *vs.* 1.3V rechargeable). Travel power lock (*see* Con). Elevation panel. *Etón:* Two "AA" alkaline batteries included. Stylish curved front panel, silver colored. Toll-free tech support. *Tecsun:* Regulated 220V AC adaptor and four "AA" nickel metal hydride cells that recharge inside the radio.

Con: Single-conversion circuitry allows for images, although these are weaker than usual even without the novel image-shifting control. Image-shifting control eliminates most image interference, but complicates operation. When image-shifting control

Etón's new E10 evolved from the Tecsun PL-550. Both have pleasant audio and a first-ever selectable-IF circuit. D. Zantow.

adjusted from 455 kHz IF with wide band-width to the 450 kHz alternative to escape image interference, only the narrow bandwidth functions; too, when returning to the 455 kHz IF, the narrow bandwidth appears even if the wide bandwidth had originally been in use. Narrow bandwidth too broad for many DX situations. Signal-strength indicator overreads somewhat. Antenna-tuning control seems pointless: does not work with external antenna; yet, with telescopic antenna appears to require only initial tweaking—no adjusting thereafter. No audio line output for tape recording. Signal-seek scan rate is slow, and scanner stops only at strongest stations. Entering presets data unnecessarily complicated. Some keys relatively small for large fingers. Telescopic antenna, with fixed-height base, does not allow for full vertical positioning when radio laid flat; partially remedied by elevation panel. Travel power lock does not deactivate timers or LCD illumination key. Clock when in 24-hour format does not show leading tens-of-hours zero. Power switch needs to be held down for a second for radio to stay on fulltime; otherwise, sleep-delay function eventually turns off radio. FM frequency readout slightly off on one sample. *Etón:* Recessed keys not as easy as most to engage. On our unit from the brief initial production run, there were three issues that may not appear in later production: at one spot on tuning knob rotation an increment (1/5 kHz) was consistently skipped; tuning knob slid off shaft easily; silver paint wore through near antenna base.

☞ With early Tecsun units, the travel pouch emitted a powerful odor of old tires. This was not found with early samples of the newer Etón version, and thus presumably is being remedied with the Tecsun version, as well.

Verdict: This new model offers unusually pleasant program listening and is loaded with useful goodies, even if it does not demodulate single-sideband signals. There are some questionable features, but the good points are significant while negatives are mainly small potatoes.

Evaluation of New Model: With manufacturers trying for the radio equivalent of a good five-cent cigar, Tecsun and Grundig/Etón have been scrapping it out with newcomers Degen and Kaito. The Degen/Kaito offerings have performed exceptionally well for the price, but have had pedestrian audio quality. Tecsun's BCL-2000, also sold as the Grundig/Etón S350, features great audio but otherwise is only a so-so performer.

Pleasant Audio

Enter the affordable new Tecsun PL-550, which with changes became available in late 2004 as the Etón E10. Its agreeable audio quality is evident right off. Although the sound is not equal to that of the BCL-2000/S350 and uses only a hi-lo tone switch, it is very pleasant for a compact portable. And, unlike the '2000/'350, it has synthesized tuning and all the positives that go with it.

Tuning Options Aplenty

For starters, there is a cornucopia of tuning options. These include fully 550 presets—enough for even the most dedicated listener

and presumably what accounts for the PL-550's name (which, unfortunately, is easily confused with Etón/Grundig's YB 550PE). Fifty are reserved for the Automatic Tuning System, which loads powerful local (FM and mediumwave AM) stations into presets, just as does a VCR when it is first set up. But that leaves 500 presets for all other uses, including world band. These roost within pages, which can be programmed to hold 10, 20, 25 or 50 presets per page.

Another unexpected plus is a tuning knob, which works in user-selectable increments of 5 kHz or 1 kHz. There's nothing finer than 1 kHz because it's not needed: The '550 doesn't demodulate single-sideband signals. Thankfully, there is nearly no muting when turning the tuning knob, so bandscanning is better on this model than on the vast majority of other portables.

There are also the usual up/down slew buttons, with user-selectable 5 kHz and 100 kHz increments. These second as "signal-seek" scanner controls, although the scanner is poky and stops only for strong signals. There is also a world band segment selector that even includes the new 19 MHz (15 meter) segment.

Clock Nearly Always Displays

The 24/12 hour clock shows time separate from frequency except when flipping through the memory channels; then, the clock display indicates the presets' pages. Time and frequency both show up clearly on the large LCD, which has user-selectable auto-fade or fulltime illumination. Anyone who bandscans in the dark will be delighted with the latter.

The clock's circuitry is used to provide two 30-minute timers, sleep delay and snooze. Indeed, turning the radio's power on activates the sleep timer, but the radio stays on fulltime if the power button is held down for more than a second. There is a travel power lock, but it doesn't turn off the battery-gobbling display illumination or either timer.

Worthy Performance, Unusual Controls

World band performance is far from shabby, even if it's not in the same near-tabletop category as the tuning system.

Sensitivity to weak signals is above average on all bands—world, FM and mediumwave AM—with little circuit noise. To help make this even better, there is a jack for an external FM or world band antenna, although not for mediumwave AM. There is also a shortwave antenna trimmer knob on the side which, in principle, should allow the user to enhance world band sensitivity by peaking the control for the antenna in use and the received station. Alas, it works only with the built-in telescopic antenna, not an external antenna where it might really come in handy. It appears that once it's been adjusted for optimum performance, you can thereafter remove the knob or leave it untouched regardless of which world band frequency is being tuned.

Sensitivity improves slightly with the supplied outboard reel passive wire antenna. Fortunately, with the built-in and reel antennas overloading is usually not an issue. However, should you go the whole hog with a more substantial external antenna, there is a two-level attenuator that works unusually well to control overloading.

Station monitors and others will appreciate that the E10/PL550 has a five-level signal-strength indicator. Although it tends to overread, it runs circles around the "glow light" found on many other portables.

Selectivity is appropriate for listening to world band and mediumwave AM programs, whether music or speech. Two bandwidths are offered and work well. However, for many DX situations even the narrow setting is too broad.

This is probably just as well, as few DXers will gravitate to a radio with single-conver-sion IF circuitry. But here, there is a surprise: There are bandwidth filters having *two* IFs—455 kHz and 450 kHz—which the user can select. The 455 kHz setting includes both bandwidths, while the 450 kHz position allows for only a single bandwidth (narrow) in order to save cost.

Here's how it works. Say, you're tuning the 60 meter (5 MHz) tropical segment, and come across a signal on 5010 kHz, and that same signal appears at much greater strength where it belongs: 910 kHz (2x455 kHz) higher, on 5920 kHz. This means you have been listening to the receiver image, a phony internally generated signal which probably would be inaudible on a double-conversion model. Switch in this IF selector, and—poof!—the image disappears from 5010 kHz (2x455 kHz), as it has been shifted to 5020 kHz (2x450 kHz).

Fortunately, by the standards of single-conversion the '550's image rejection is superior even without this weird feature. But even the best single conversion circuit has audible image-rejection limits, so being able to shift images by 10 kHz is helpful, although not without some downside. To begin with, you may be robbing Peter to pay Paul by eliminating one image only to replace it with another. Too, if you hear an unidentified weak station within the 60 meter segment, which is prone to image intrusion from the 49 meter (6 MHz) segment, you need to briefly select the 450 kHz IF to ensure you're not hearing an image.

FM is in stereo through headphones and excels in fringe-area reception. The tuning range can be set by software command to cover either the conventional 87–108 MHz band or the full 76–108 MHz range that includes the Japanese FM band. Alas, there is no fixed-level "line output" audio jack.

In all, this new portable is a surprisingly strong offering. It boasts a near-tabletop caliber of tuning features, while offering superior aural pleasure.

The classic Sangean ATS 606AP is also available as the Panasonic RF-B55, Sanyo MB-60A and Roberts R876. This proven performer has no real flaws and is nicely sized for travel.

✪✪¾ ✐

Sangean ATS 606AP, Sangean ATS 606A, Panasonic RF-B55, Roberts R876, Sanyo MB-60A

Price: *ATS 606AP:* $139.95 in the United States. $199.00CAD in Canada. £109.95 in the United Kingdom. €105.00 in Germany. *ATS 606A:* €95.00 in Germany. *RF-B55:* £109.95 in the United Kingdom. €149.00 in Germany. *R876:* £129.95 in the United Kingdom. *MB-60A:* R1,000.00 in South Africa.

Pro: Relatively diminutive for a compact model. Single bandwidth reasonably effective at adjacent-channel rejection, while providing reasonable audio bandwidth. Speaker audio quality better than most for size (*see* Con). Weak-signal sensitivity at least average. Various helpful tuning features, including keypad, 54 station presets, slew, signal-seek tuning and meter band selection. Keypad has superior feel and tactile response. Easy to operate. Longwave. Dual-zone 24-hour clock. Illuminated LCD. Alarm. Sleep delay. Travel power lock (*see* Con). Multi-level battery strength indicator; also, weak-battery warning. Stereo FM through earphones or earbuds. Above-average FM weak-signal sensitivity and selectivity. Above-average capture ratio aids reception when band congested, including helping separate co-channel stations. Memory scan. Rubber feet reduce sliding while elevation panel in use. *R876 and ATS 606AP:* UL-approved 120/230V AC adaptor, with American and European plugs, adjusts to proper AC voltage automatically. *ATS 606AP:* ANT-60 outboard reel passive wire antenna accessory aids slightly with weak-signal reception. In North America, service provided by Sangean America to models sold under its name. *RF-B55:* Cabinet and controls not painted, so should maintain their appearance unusually well. Country of manufacture (Taiwan) specified on radio and box.

Con: No tuning knob. Speaker audio quality lacks low-frequency ("bass") response as compared to larger models. Clock not readable while frequency displayed. No meaningful signal-strength indicator. Keypad not in telephone format. Travel power lock doesn't disable LCD illumination button. No carrying strap or handle. No batteries (three "AA" needed). *ATS 606AP:* Country of manufacture (China) not specified on radio or box. *RF-B55:* No AC adaptor or outboard reel antenna included, although the owner's manual says that the radio is supposed to come with an "external antenna." Not available within the Americas.

Verdict: This classic continues to hold its own among travel-friendly compact models. Now, it is available in separate Chinese-made and Taiwanese-made versions.

✪✪⅝

Sangean ATS 505P, Sangean ATS 505, Roberts R9914

Price: *ATS 505P:* $129.95 in the United States. $179.00CAD in Canada. £79.95 in the United Kingdom. €119.00 in Germany. $199.00AUD in Australia. *ATS 505:* €95.00 in

Germany. *R9914:* £99.95 in the United Kingdom. IAC adaptor: £16.95 in the United Kingdom.

Pro: Numerous helpful tuning features, including two-speed tuning knob, keypad, station presets (*see* Con), up/down slew, meter-band carousel selection, signal-seek tuning and scanning of presets (*see* Con). Automatic-sorting feature arranges station presets in frequency order. Analog clarifier with center detent and stable circuitry allows single-sideband signals to be tuned with uncommon precision and to stay properly tuned, thus allowing for superior audio phasing for a portable (*see* Con). Illuminated LCD. Dual-zone 24/12-hour clock. Alarm with sleep delay. Modest battery consumption. Nine-level battery-reserve indicator. Travel power lock (*see* Con). FM stereo through earbuds, included. Longwave. AC adaptor. *ATS 505P:* Tape measure antenna.

Con: Bandwidth slightly wider than appropriate for a single-bandwidth receiver. Large for a compact. Only 18 world band station presets, divided up between two "pages" with nine presets apiece. Tuning knob tends to mute stations during bandscanning by knob, especially when tuning rate is set to fine (1 kHz); muting with coarse (5 kHz) tuning is much less objectionable. Keys respond slowly, needing to be held down momentarily rather than simply tapped. Stop-listen-resume scanning of station presets wastes time. Pedestrian overall single-sideband reception because of excessively wide bandwidth and occasional distortion caused by AGC timing. Clock does not display independent of frequency. No meaningful signal-strength indicator. No carrying handle or strap. Country of manufacture (China) not specified on radio or box. Travel power lock does not deactivate LCD illumination key. No batteries (four "AA" needed).

Verdict: An okay portable that demodulates single-sideband signals.

Sangean's ATS 505P is also sold in the United Kingdom as the Roberts R9914.

★★⅝ *ⓒ*
Sony ICF-SW35

Price: $89.95 in the United States. $149.99CAD in Canada. £79.95 in the United Kingdom. €105.00 in Germany. $269.00AUD in Australia. ¥17,000 in Japan. *AC-E45HG 120V AC adaptor:* $19.95 in the United States.

Pro: Superior reception quality, with excellent adjacent-channel rejection (selectivity) and image rejection. Fifty world band station presets, which can be scanned

Sony's ICF-SW35 is pleasant for listening to a preset roster of stations.

within five "pages." Signal-seek-then-resume scanning works unusually well. Two-speed slew. Illuminated display. Dual-zone 24-hour clock. Dual-time alarm. Sleep delay. Travel power lock. FM stereo through headphones, not included. Weak-battery indicator. Japanese FM (most versions) and longwave bands.

Con: No keypad or tuning knob. Synthesizer muting and poky slew degrade bandscanning. Speaker audio quality clear, but lacks low-frequency response ("bass"). Clock not displayed independent of frequency. LCD lacks contrast when viewed from above. No jacks for recording or outboard antenna. AC adaptor is extra and pricey. No batteries (three "AA" required).

Verdict: The Sony ICF-SW35 has superior rejection of images, which are the bane of most other under-$100 models. This Chinese-made compact lacks a keypad, which is partially overcome by a large number of station presets and effective scanning. Overall, a decent choice only if you listen to a predictable roster of stations.

New for 2005
✪✪½
Etón E100, Tecsun PL-200

Price: *Etón:* $99.95 in the United States.

Pro: Handy size for travel. Very good weak-signal sensitivity. Above-average dynamic range. Superior audio for size, aided by hi/lo tone switch. Several handy tuning aids, including keypad; tuning knob in 1 kHz segments for world band/MW AM (*see* Con); 200 station presets, with eight pages where user selects how many presets per page; world band segment selector; and slew buttons (5 kHz world band increments, 9/10 kHz MW AM increments). Illuminated LCD, easy to read. World Time clock (*see* Con) with alarm, clock radio, snooze and sleep delay; may also be set to 12-hour format. Clock reads out separately from frequency.

Signal-seek scanner searches world band segments or preset channels (*see* Con). Five-level signal/battery strength indicator, works well. Keys have positive-action feel (*see* Con). FM stereo with earbuds, included. Japanese FM. Travel power lock. Telescopic antenna swivels and rotates. Setting to allow for optimum performance from either regular or rechargeable batteries. Elevation panel. Microprocessor reset control. *Etón:* Excellent hardside leather travel case. Two "AA" alkaline batteries included. Stylish curved front panel, silver colored. Toll-free tech support. Owner's manual unusually helpful for newcomers. *Tecsun:* 220V AC adaptor/battery charger and rechargeable "AA" batteries included. Softside travel case protects better than most. Choice among three colors (red, gray, silver).

Con: Single-conversion IF circuitry results in mediocre image rejection. Signal-seek scanner progresses slowly. Some muting when tuning by knob or slewing, slows down bandscanning. Tuning knob has no selectable 5 kHz step option. Power button activates 90-minute sleep delay; works as full-time "on" control only if held down for two seconds, a minor inconvenience; there is an additional three seconds to boot up, so basically it takes five seconds to turn on. World band frequencies on all Etón and Tecsun samples displayed 1 kHz high. Small, cramped keys. No jacks for line output or external antenna. *Etón:* No AC adaptor included. On our early sample the tuning knob rubbed the cabinet slightly.

Verdict: A spit-and-polish offering for tuning major stations at home or away.

Evaluation of New Model: The travel-sized Etón E100, which builds on the original Tecsun PL-200, is a solid performer with superior software and other touches. Among these, you can define the number of presets per page, then scan a chosen page to find the strongest frequency. Too, while most radios simply limp along when using rechargeable batteries, which produce about a third of a Volt less per cell, this model has a software adjustment to compensate.

Other touches include an illuminated, easy-to-read LCD that offers useful information. It includes a 24/12 hour clock which thankfully displays independent of the tuned frequency, a rarity at any price. That clock circuit also operates clock-radio, sleep and snooze functions. Also welcome is an accurate five-level signal strength and battery indicator.

Although all keys are small, they have decisive feel and engagement. Nevertheless, the power key must be held down for two seconds or else the radio goes off after 90 minutes. Add to this a boot-up time of three seconds, and it takes fully five seconds just to turn the radio on.

Like a number of other Etón models, the silver-colored E100 offers eye appeal usually absent on world band radios. While the plainer PL-200 has the customary flat front panel and flat keys, the E100 struts a curved panel with rounded and recessed keys. It doesn't sound like much, and it really isn't. Yet, to the eye it makes enough difference to convert the utilitarian '200 into something to be shown off.

Etón includes a hardside leather travel case that protects as nicely as it looks. The Tecsun softside case is also superior, although it's not in the E100's league.

Tuning options abound. There's a keypad, properly configured, along with a genuine tuning knob, slew tuning/"signal-seek" scanning and world band segment selection. There are fully 200 presets which can be stored in pages in any of a number of ways, and the scanner can select channels within any page. The tuning knob is handy and a rarity among digitally tuned models at this price level. Still, it would have been better with less muting between frequencies and a second tuning step of 5 kHz.

Performance is better than with pre-Etón samples of the PL-200. Although it is too

Etón/Grundig has long serviced the travel market with small, affordable portables. Its latest offering, the E100, continues this tradition.

early to be certain, history strongly suggests that future Tecsun units will incorporate the improved innards. Otherwise, the findings in last year's PASSPORT will continue to apply for the '200.

Performance Generally Good

The E100's sensitivity to weak signals is very good, and dynamic range is superior for the price class. Audio is no barnburner, but is surprisingly pleasant for a set so small. Unfortunately, cost-cutting single conversion results in poor image rejection, and the lone bandwidth, while fine for general listening, is broad for coping with moderate adjacent-channel interference. Too, there is no demodulation of single-sideband signals.

The owner's manual is helpfully written for the newcomer, even if it has its share of typos (e.g., stating the radio uses three batteries instead of two and giving the wrong band where the attenuator doesn't function).

✪✪½ ✪
Grundig eTraveller VII (as available)

Price: $99.95 in the United States. CAN$99.00 in Canada.

Grundig's discontinued eTraveller VII is still occasionally found on dealer shelves.

Pro: Good rejection of spurious "image" signals, unusual at this price. Single bandwidth reasonably effective at adjacent-channel rejection, while providing adequate audio bandwidth. Audio quality above average for size class (*see* Con). Auto scan/slew-tuning works better than most—thankfully, as there are almost no other tuning features (*see* Con). Hinged protective travel cover, like on a Flip Phone, protects front of radio (*see* Con). World Time clock, with snooze and two-event timer that activates last-tuned frequency. Power/

The YB 550PE/PL-230 is not equal to similarly priced models from the same companies.

standby switch not easy to turn on accidentally while packed away in luggage (*see* Con). FM stereo through earbuds, included. Also comes with 117V AC adapter, desk stand, soft travel case and two "AA" alkaline batteries. *North America:* Toll-free tech support.

Con: Paucity of helpful tuning facilities, including no keypad or tuning knob and only ten world band presets (20 more are for FM and mediumwave AM). Audio quality, although decent for size class, lacks low-frequency ("bass") response. Antenna does not rotate or swivel. Almost large and heavy enough to qualify as a compact model. Tunes world band only in 5 kHz steps and displays in nonstandard XX.XX/XX.XX5 MHz format. No signal-strength indicator. Hinged front cover can get in the way, although it may be removed. Clock not readable while frequency displayed, although time replaces frequency briefly if button is pushed. No travel power lock, although power/standby function provides considerable protection. Turning radio on for the first time is thoroughly counterintuitive. No LCD illumination. No carrying strap or handle.

Verdict: A handsome, affordable package with pleasant performance. Yet, the discontinued eTraveller's hinged front cover and paucity of tuning features make it more appropriate for traveling than for routine daily use—hardly surprising, given its name. Like all Grundig radios of recent times, it is made in China.

✪✪⅜
Etón YB 550PE, Grundig YB 550PE, Tecsun PL-230

Price: *Grundig:* $99.95 in the United States. $129.95CAD in Canada. *Etón:* €99.95 in Germany.

Pro: Very good selectivity. Above-average dynamic range. Several handy tuning aids, including 200 station presets with eight pages where user selects how many presets per page; also, world band segment selector. For world band, slew buttons tune in 5 kHz increments, while a fine-tuning (encoder) thumbwheel tunes shortwave and mediumwave AM in 1 kHz increments. Illuminated LCD (*see* Con). World Time clock (*see* Con) with alarm, clock radio and sleep delay; may also be set to 12-hour format. Clock readout separate from frequency display, shows whether radio on or off. Signal-seek scanner searches world band segments or preset channels (*see* Con). Five-level signal/battery strength indicator, works well. FM stereo with earbuds, included. Japanese FM. Travel power lock. Telescopic antenna swivels and rotates (*see* Con). Setting to allow for optimum performance from either regular or rechargeable batteries. *YB 550PE and PL-230:* Generally pleasant audio (*see* Con). Stylish. Removable elevation panel (*see* Con). LCD easy to read. *PL-230:* AC adaptor/battery charger and rechargeable "AA" batteries included. *YB 550PE:* Three "AA" alkaline batteries included. *North America (Grundig YB 550PE):* Toll-free tech support.

Con: Weak-signal sensitivity only fair. Single-conversion IF circuitry results in mediocre image rejection. Signal-seek scanner stops only on very strong signals. Power button activates 90-minute sleep delay; works as full-time "on" control only if held down for two seconds, a minor inconvenience. Takes an additional five seconds to fully turn on (or boot up). Small, cramped keys. *YB 550PE:* No AC adaptor included. *YB 550PE and PL-230:* Audio crispness on FM through headphones not fully up to Grundig standard. Keypad has oddly placed zero key. Telescopic antenna placement on right side disallows tilting to left. Illumination dim. Snap-on elevation panel must be removed to replace batteries. Battery cover comes loose easily if elevation panel not attached. One of our two units displayed FM 50 Hz high, whereas world band frequencies on both samples were 1 kHz high.

☞ The Tecsun PL-230 is essentially identical to the YB 550PE except for color and the inclusion of rechargeable batteries and an AC adaptor/charger.

Verdict: Under-$100 radios used to look blah and often sounded that way, but no more. These stylish portables are straightforward to use and full of software conveniences. However, images and weak-signal sensitivity keep them from reaching their full potential.

✪✪⅜
Sony ICF-SW40

Price: $119.95 in the United States. £89.95 in the United Kingdom. *AC-E45HG 120V AC adaptor:* $19.95.

Pro: Technologically unintimidating for analog traditionalists, as its advanced digital tuning circuitry is disguised to look like slide-rule, or analog, tuning. World Time 24-hour clock. Two "on" timers and sleep delay. Travel power lock. Illuminated LCD. Japanese FM band (most versions).

Con: Single bandwidth is relatively wide, reducing adjacent-channel rejection. No keypad. Lacks coverage of 1625–1705 kHz portion of North American and Australian

Sony's ICF-SW40: digital radio for digiphobes, and inspiration for the Degen DE1103/Kaito KA1103.

mediumwave AM band and 1705–1735 kHz potential public service segment. AC adaptor, much-needed, is extra and over-priced. No batteries (three "AA" required).

Verdict: If you're turned off by things digital and complex, Sony's Japanese-made ICF-SW40 will feel like an old friend. Otherwise, forget it.

✪✪⅜
Sangean ATS 404, Roberts R881

Price: *Sangean:* $79.95 in the United States. $129.00CAD in Canada. £64.95 in the United Kingdom. €68.00 in Germany. *ADP-808 120V AC adaptor:* $10.95 in the United States. *Roberts:* £79.95 in the United Kingdom.

Pro: Superior weak-signal sensitivity. Several handy tuning features. Stereo FM through earpieces, included. Dual-zone 24/12-hour clock displays seconds numerically. Alarm with sleep delay. Travel power lock. Illuminated LCD. Battery indicator.

Con: Single-conversion IF circuitry results in poor image rejection. No tuning knob. Overloading, controllable by shortening telescopic antenna on world band and collapsing it on mediumwave AM band. Picks up some internal digital "buzz." Tunes only in 5 kHz increments. No signal-strength

Nice sound, decent price. Otherwise, the Sangean ATS 404 doesn't have a great deal to offer.

indicator. Frequency and time cannot be displayed simultaneously. Travel power lock does not disable LCD illumination. No handle or carrying strap. AC adaptor extra. Country of manufacture (China) not specified on radio or box. No batteries (four "AA" needed).

Verdict: Look elsewhere.

✪⅞ ✐
Kchibo KK-E200

Price: $64.95 in the United States. $89.95CAD in Canada.

Pro: Pleasant audio for size and price. Various helpful tuning features, including keypad (*see* Con), 12 world band station presets (*see* Con), up/down slew, meter-band carousel selection and signal-seek tuning. High-contrast illuminated LCD (*see* Con) indicates which preset is in use. Agreeable selectivity and weak-signal sensitivity for price class. World Time clock with sleep delay. Travel power lock (*see* Con). AC adaptor (*see* Con). FM stereo through earbuds, included. Pleasant FM performance for price and size class. Control to reset microprocessor and memory. Battery cover hinged to avoid loss (*see* Con).

Con: Single-conversion IF circuitry results in mediocre image rejection. Dynamic range mediocre, sometimes overloads even with built-in antenna. Does not receive important 7305–9495 kHz chunk of world band spectrum. Does not receive 1621–1705 kHz portion of expanded AM band in the Americas and Australia and the 1705–1735 kHz potential public service segment. No tuning knob. Tunes world band only in 5 kHz steps and displays in nonstandard XX.XX/XX.XX5 MHz format. Unhandy carouseling "MW/SW1/SW2/FM" control required when shifting from tuning within 2300–7300 kHz *vs.* 9500–26100 kHz range or *vice versa*. No signal-strength indicator. Annoying one-second pause when tuning from one channel to the next. Only six station presets for each of the four "bands" (FM/MW-AM/SW1/SW2). Dreadful mediumwave AM performance, with circuit noise drowning out weak stations and degrading stronger ones. AC adaptor sometimes produces slight hum. Elevation panel flimsy; also, hard to open with short fingernails. Clock doesn't display when frequency is shown, although pushbutton allows time to replace frequency. No alarm or other awakening function. Keypad not in telephone format. Fragile battery-cover hinge pins snap off easily. LCD illumination only fair. Travel power lock doesn't disable LCD light button. Using 9/10 kHz mediumwave AM channel switch erases station presets and clock setting. No weak-battery indicator; radio goes abruptly silent when batteries weaken. No batteries (three "AA" needed). Box claims "fancy leather cover," but it is ordinary vinyl. No indication of county of manufacture (China) on product, box or manual. "Chinglish" owner's manual occasionally puzzles. Warranty only 90 days in North America.

Verdict: The stylish Kchibo KK-E200 comes with useful accessories omitted on models costing much more. Its speaker audio quality is pleasant for its size and price, too. Although it lacks full frequency coverage, has no alarm and is overly muted for bandscanning, the 'E200 is cheap and an eyeful.

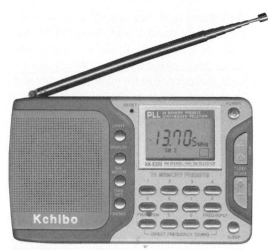

Kchibo's KK-E200 features pleasant audio and a snappy design. Modest price, too.   J. Brinker

superior ergonomics include a handy flip-open leather protective case that seconds as an elevation panel. Leather case excellent at protecting front, top and rear of the receiver (*see* Con). Leather case affixed to receiver with snaps and magnetic catches, so nearly impossible to misplace. Superior adjacent-channel rejection—selectivity—for price and size class. Keypad (in proper telephone format), handy meter-band carousel control, signal-seek and up/down slew tuning. Twenty station presets, of which ten are for world band and the rest

★⅞
Grundig G2000A/B "Porsche Design," Grundig Porsche P2000, Grundig Yacht Boy P2000

Price: *G2000A/B:* $79.95 in the United States. $99.95CAD in Canada. £89.95 in the United Kingdom. *P2000:* £84.95 in the United Kingdom. $199.00AUD in Australia. *G2ACA 120V AC adaptor:* $12.95 in the United States.

Pro: One of the most functionally attractive world band radios on the market. Generally

Grundig's G2000A/B has great looks and a hard leather case, but performance is *ordinaire*.

for FM and mediumwave AM stations. FM stereo through earpieces, included. World Time 24-hour clock. Timer/alarm with sleep delay. Illuminated display. Travel power lock. Reset control for microprocessor and memory. *North America:* Toll-free tech support.

Con: Pedestrian audio. Weak-signal sensitivity mediocre between 9400–26100 kHz, improving slightly between 2300–7400 kHz. Single-conversion IF circuitry results in poor image rejection. Does not tune such important world band ranges as 7405–7550 and 9350–9395 kHz. Tunes world band only in 5 kHz steps and displays in nonstandard XX.XX/XX.XX5 MHz format. No tuning knob. Annoying one-second pause when tuning from one channel to the next. Old-technology SW1/SW2 switch complicates tuning. Protruding power button can get in the way of nearby slew-tuning and meter-carousel keys. Using 9/10 kHz mediumwave AM channel switch erases station presets and clock setting. Leather case makes it difficult to retrieve folded telescopic antenna. Leather case does not protect bottom or sides of radio. Magnetic catches weak on leather case. No carrying strap. Signal-strength indicator nigh useless. Clock not displayed separately from frequency. No batteries (three "AA" required).

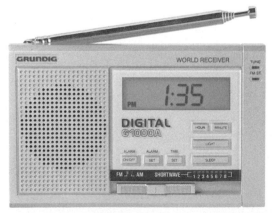

The low-cost Grundig/Etón G1000A is also available in China as the Tecsun DR-910.

☞ At present there are no plans to sell this model under the Etón name.

Verdict: This German-styled, Chinese-manufactured portable is the ultimate in tasteful design, but performance is another story.

✪¾ ✇
Etón G1000A, Grundig G1000A, Tecsun DR-910

Price: *Grundig:* $49.95 in the United States. $69.95CAD in Canada. *Etón:* Price not yet established in the United Kingdom.

Pro: Clock/timer with sleep delay (*see* Con). Illuminated LCD has bigger digits than most models of this size. Elevation panel. FM in stereo with earbuds, included. Two "AA" batteries included. Superior carrying case. *North America:* Toll-free tech support.

Con: Analog-tuned with digital frequency counter, so tunes only by thumbwheel, which is slightly touchy. Does not tune 120, 75, 90, 60, 15 and 11 meter segments; misses a small amount of expanded coverage of 41 and 31 meter segments. Single-conversion IF circuitry results in poor image rejection. Audio lacks bass response. Frequency drift with changes in temperature. Clock in 12-hour format, displays only when radio off. Displays in nonstandard XX.XX/XX.XX5 MHz format. "Play" in bandswitch allows wiggling to slightly alter frequency readout. FM overloads in presence of strong signals, remediable by shorting antenna (which also reduces weak-signal sensitivity). On our units, FM frequency misread by 100 kHz (half a channel). If finger placed over LCD display, buzzing audible on mediumwave AM and lower world band frequencies.

Verdict: More spit and polish, and better daytime frequency coverage, than truly cheaper alternatives. It's also backed up by a solid warranty from a reputable company. The G1000A occupies a spot between "throwaway" models that are passable performers, and more highly rated models that cost more.

New for 2005

★¾
Sangean PT-50, Grundig Yacht Boy 50

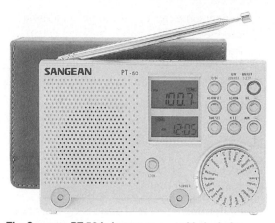

The Sangean PT-50 is better as a world clock than a world band radio.

Price: *Sangean:* $79.95 in the United States. *Grundig:* €78.00 in Germany.

Pro: Unusually attractive, sheathed in tan leather. Flip-open leather case excellent at protecting front, top and rear of the receiver (*see* Con). Leather case affixed to receiver with snaps and magnetic catches, so nearly impossible to misplace. Two clocks, with separate display windows for home time and World Time. Changing home time to summer (savings) setting does not alter World Time. Handy disc to select time in any of 24 world zones (*see* Con). 24 or 12 hour clock format (*see* Con). Illuminated display. Reasonably clean, pleasant speaker audio for size (*see* Con). Travel power lock (*see* Con). FM in stereo through earpieces (*see* Con). Generally good mediumwave AM performance (*see* Con). Low-battery indicator. Stereo indicator (*see* Con). Battery cover hinged to avoid loss. Keys "clicky," with excellent feel. Alarm/clock radio with sleep delay and snooze. Rubber feet on bottom to prevent slipping. Reset control for microprocessor and memory.

Con: Analog-tuned with digital frequency counter, so tunes only by thumbwheel, which is slightly touchy. Bandswitch must be adjusted when going from one world band segment to another, complicating operation. World band coverage omits 5730–5795 kHz portion of 49 meters; 6890–6990 and 7535–7600 kHz portions of 41 meters; 9250–9305 kHz portion of 31 meters; and all of 120, 90, 75, 60, 15, 13 and 11 meters. Frequency display nonstandard, being in Megahertz and reading out only to the nearest 10 kHz; thus, 6155 kHz shows as 6.15 and/or 6.16 MHz. Single-

conversion IF circuitry results in poor image rejection. World band sensitivity and selectivity only fair. No external antenna socket. Speaker audio weak in bass. Audio amplifier lacks punch; stations with weak audio hard to hear, or break into distortion. Frequency drift with changes in temperature. Time-format selection applies to World and home displays alike, so 24 hours can't be used for World Time and 12 hours for home. Small LCDs with thin characters for size of radio. FM performance ordinaire, with mediocre capture ratio; in strong-signal situations there can be overloading. FM stereo indicator worked at some test locations, but not all. Pedestrian spurious-signal rejection on mediumwave AM. No meaningful signal-strength indicator. Bandswitch designates world band segments as 1-7 rather than as MHz. No AC adaptor (needs 3–6V DC, center negative), batteries (two "AA" required) or earpieces. No audio line output. Leather case: 1) collapses when used as elevation panel; 2) no perforations over speaker, so case has to be opened for listening; 3) does not protect receiver's sides or bottom; 4) when case closed, telescopic antenna can only be extended roughly horizontally, to the left; and 5) even when open, case blocks folded telescopic antenna and there is no cabinet detent for finger, so unfolding antenna is cumbersome (best is not to push antenna into the cabinet's snap-in antenna catch). Travel power lock does not deactivate LCD illumination key. *Sangean:* Country of origin, China, not shown on radio, manual or box.

Verdict: Great clock, so-so radio. Unusually handy as a multi-zone timepiece and a class-act eyeful. Yet, by today's yardstick the '50's radio performance and features are inferior to various other models priced comparably or lower.

Evaluation of New Model: Sangean, once arguably the world's largest manufacturer of world band portables, has not introduced a new model for some time. That's changed for 2005 with the new ProTravel series of eye-catching travel portables, two of which—PT-50 and PT-80—feature digital frequency readout.

The more affordable is the '50, also sold in Europe (but not the Americas) as the Grundig Yacht Boy 50. This handsome compact model is clearly aimed at the globetrotting traveler, what with its small size and sophisticated clock configuration. Included are fully two clocks, with each appearing in a separate LCD window. As the upper window is also used for the frequency readout, time is displayed fulltime only in the other. However, you can choose what clock shows in which window.

That's just for starters. On the radio's front is what appears to a large tuning disc, but don't be fooled. It's actually a handy selector to choose among the world's 24 time zones. Dial it, and—*voilà!*—time appears for wherever you choose—Berlin, Moscow, Tokyo, Sydney and so on as marked on the disc. Otherwise, you can leave it set to London for World Time (UTC).

Sangean is hardly the first to do this, but they have gone most others one better. When you choose summer (savings) time for your home zone, it doesn't change the World Time/UTC setting as do some others. Too, time can be displayed in 12 or 24 hour

format. Unfortunately this applies to both clocks, so you can't have 24 hours for World Time and 12 hours (AM/PM) for home.

There is also an alarm/clock-radio with sleep delay, as well as snooze for poky risers. Both LCDs are illuminated, although characters are relatively small and thin for the radio's size.

Another boon for travelers is the radio's attractive snap-on leather case. Its handy flip-open design does a great job of protecting the front, back and top of the radio, and because it's attached there is no separate carrying case to misplace. Appropriately for a travel portable, there is also a travel power lock to help prevent batteries from draining accidentally on trips; however, it allows LCD illumination to function, partially defeating the lock's purpose.

Grundig introduced the attached-leather-case concept some years back with its Platinum Traveller—a great idea, even if leaves unprotected the radio's sides and bottom. That model has been discontinued, but the same case is now found on the Grundig G2000A and Grundig Yacht Boy P2000. These look similar to the new '50, but the '50's case has disadvantages: no perforations over the speaker, so the case has to be opened for listening; too, when the case is closed, the telescopic antenna can only be extended more or less horizontally, to the left. Indeed, even when open the case blocks the folded telescopic antenna. Added to this is no cabinet finger detent, so unfolding the antenna can be cumbersome. Best is not to push the antenna into the cabinet's snap-in antenna catch

Unlike the case on the Platinum Traveller, that on the '50 collapses if you try to use it to angle the radio to a comfortable operating position. However, there are four rubber feet to keep the radio from sliding around in the vertical position.

So, no question, the new '50 gets high fives as a global clock, and its looks are about as good as it gets. Included are nice ergonomic touches, too, such as clicky, positive-action keys and a hinged battery cover to prevent loss. There's also a low-battery indicator, even if the radio comes with no batteries or AC adaptor. There's an FM-stereo indicator, too; it worked at some of our test locations, but not all.

Performance Uninspiring

The '50 tunes the usual FM band in stereo through earpieces. FM reception is little more than acceptable, with mediocre capture ratio and a tendency to overload in the presence of nearby powerful signals.

The mediumwave AM band tunes from 520–1710 kHz, so all frequencies are included. Performance is quite decent, but spurious-signal rejection is pedestrian and selectivity doesn't rise above ordinaire.

The shortwave spectrum isn't fully covered, so some world band frequencies are missed: the 5730–5795 kHz portion of 49 meters; the 6890–6990 and 7535–7600 kHz portions of 41 meters; the 9250–9305 kHz portion of 31 meters; and all of 120, 90, 75, 60, 15, 13 and 11 meters. For casual listening this is adequate, but these limits are characteristic of models normally costing less.

Also disappointing at this price point is that tuning is not digitally synthesized. Instead, the '50 is analog-tuned with digital frequency readout. It lacks any tuning features whatsoever except a thumbwheel, and even this is a bit touchy to operate. Also, an old-technology bandswitch must be used when going from one world band segment to another. Adding to the confusion, that switch designates world band segments as 1-7 rather than as, say, Megahertz—6, 7, 9, 11 and so on.

The frequency display is another shortcoming. Not only does it fail to read in the customary kilohertz, it lacks the kilohertz units digit. Thus, 9635 kHz displays as 9.63

or 9.64 MHz, so there is no valid visual indication as to whether the radio is tuned to 9630, 9635 or 9640 kHz. This unnecessarily complicates figuring out what's being heard, and is a limitation normally found only in the cheapest of models.

World band reception is typical of many under-$100 portables, even if it is not equal to what's found on some other recently introduced compact portables at or below the '50's price. Weak-signal sensitivity, for example, is just passable, as is selectivity (adjacent-channel rejection). Being single conversion, the radio allows internally generated images to interfere with received signals—again, the norm for inexpensive portables introduced in years past, but not up to the best of the newest.

Speaker audio is clean and pleasant for a radio of this size, which helps make the '50 enjoyable for listening over chunks of time. It could use more oomph with weak signals and more bass response, but overall it sounds a cut above the competition.

The Sangean version of the '50 continues that Taiwanese company's unfortunate practice of not indicating the country of origin for its China-made models—not on the radio, not in the owner's manual, not on the box. Motorola's cell phones and any number of other sophisticated electronic products are now manufactured to a high standard in China, and avoid consumer deception by making this clear. It's high time Sangean did the same.

✪½
jWIN JX-M14

Price: $29.95 or less in the United States.

Pro: Handy small size for travel. Clock with timer/alarm (*see* Con). Elevation panel. Earbuds included (in separate bubble pack).

Con: Mediocre weak-signal sensitivity; helps considerably to clip a few yards of wire to the built-in antenna. Mediocre

The jWIN JX-M14's low price makes it hard to resist for casual use on trips.   D. Zantow

selectivity. Analog-tuned with digital frequency counter, so tunes only by thumbwheel, which is stiff. Does not tune 120, 75, 90, 60, 15, 13 or 11 meter segments; misses a small amount of expanded coverage of 49 and 41 meter segments. Single-conversion IF circuitry results in poor image rejection. Audio lacks bass response. Frequency counter completely omits last digit so, say, 9575 kHz appears as either 9.57 or 9.58 MHz. Clock in 12-hour format

only, displays only when radio off. Display not illuminated. If hand is placed on rear of cabinet, world band drifts up to 10 kHz. Frequency drift with changes in temperature. LCD buzzes on mediumwave AM; if finger placed over LCD, buzz also audible on lower world band frequencies. Mediumwave weak-signal sensitivity uninspiring. FM overloads in strong-signal environments, remediable by shorting antenna (which also reduces weak-signal sensitivity). When first turned on, radio always reverts to FM band. FM in mono only. Two "AA" batteries not included. Warranty in the United States only 90 days and requires $12 advance payment for "return shipping"; add to that the owner's cost to ship, and warranty is of dubious value; best purchased from dealer who will swap if DOA.

Verdict: At almost a throwaway price, the Chinese-made jWIN JX-M14 is a passable portable for casual use on trips or as a stocking stuffer, provided a hank of wire is clipped on to give world band signals a boost.

✪½
Kchibo KK-S320

Price: $ 54.99 plus shipping in the United States.

Pro: Even more compact than its costlier KK-E200 cousin, with better mediumwave AM performance and greater audio crispness. Agreeable weak-signal sensitivity. Sleep delay (*see* Con) and single-event on/ off timer. High contrast LCD indicates which preset is in use. AC adaptor. FM stereo via earbuds, included.

Con: No coverage of 120, 90, 75, 60, 16, 15, 13 and 11 meter (2, 3, 4, 5, 17, 19, 21 and 25 MHz) segments, with only partial coverage of 49 and 19 meters (6 and 15 MHz). No keypad or tuning knob; other tuning alternatives cumbersome, especially with "out-of-band" frequencies. Only five station presets for each of the three "bands"

The Kchibo KK-S320 is overpriced for the mediocre tuning, performance and frequency coverage it offers.

(FM/MW-AM/SW). "Signal seek" scanning works only within limited frequency segments. Radio cannot be turned on permanently; rather, the power button activates the 90-minute-or-less sleep-delay timer, forcing the radio to turn itself off after no more than an hour and a half. After radio powers up, slew buttons cannot be used nor the frequency displayed, until the user presses a preset or band key once, or presses the display key three times. Poor dynamic range, with overloading a major problem at night. Poor adjacent-channel selectivity. "Floating birdie" sometimes appears in various world band segments. Single-conversion IF circuitry results in mediocre image rejection. Poor dynamic range for nighttime listening in many parts of the world. Does not receive 1621–1710 kHz portion of expanded mediumwave AM band in the Americas. Tunes world band only in 5 kHz steps. Displays only in nonstandard XX.XX/XX.XX5 MHz format. Display not illuminated. Clock uses 12-hour format, not suitable for World Time. Elevation panel hard to open. Clock doesn't display when frequency is shown, although pushbutton allows time to replace frequency. No travel power lock. No signal-strength indicator. No weak-battery indicator; radio goes abruptly silent when batteries start to flag. No batteries included (three "AA" needed). Microprocessor sometimes freezes up, requiring activation of reset button; this also erases the station presets and clock setting stored in memory. No indication of county of manufacture (China) on product, box or manual. "Chinglish" owner's manual occasionally puzzles. FM performance pedestrian. Not easily purchased in the Americas or most other parts of the world. Warranty period not yet apparent.

Verdict: Conveniently smaller than its KK-E200 cousin, and priced to move. Yet, the KK-S320's cumbersome tuning, inadequate shortwave coverage and rudimentary world band performance make it a dubious choice.

The Coby CX-CB91 is not only an abomination to tune and poorly made, inadequate earpiece attenuation also allows for excessive volume.

New for 2005
Not Acceptable
Coby CX-CB91

Price: $19.95 in the United States. $7-20 or equivalent worldwide.

Pro: Clock (*see* Con) with clock radio function (*see* Con). Antenna swivels and rotates. Battery cover hinged to prevent loss (*see* Con). Earbuds (*see* ☞).

Con: Analog-tuned with digital frequency counter, so tunes only by knob. Tuning knob feels as if it were connected to a rubber band, makes finding stations a hit-and-miss frustration. Does not tune most of the crucial 6 MHz segment and some 7 MHz channels; also misses 2, 3, 4, 5 and 25 MHz segments. Mediocre weak-signal sensitivity. Fair-to-poor selectivity. Poor dynamic range and image rejection. Frequency counter omits last digit so, say, 9995 kHz appears as either 9.99 or 10.00 MHz. Clock only in 12-hour format. Clock radio allows only FM stations to heard. FM distorted and overloads, with poor sensitivity, mediocre capture radio and inaccurate frequency readout. FM not in stereo via earbuds (*see* ☞). LCD emits digital buzz that diminishes reception. DX/local switch has little expected effect. Display not illuminated. Construction quality poor.

Batteries difficult to insert and remove. No batteries (two "AA" required).

☞ **Warning:** *Minor increase in volume causes audio to suddenly become extremely loud. Exercise great care when inserting and using earbuds or headphones.*

Verdict: Worst of the cheaps. Not acceptable when used with earpieces.

Evaluation of New Model: With tuning so hopeless and earpiece audio that can be unexpectedly painful, this Chinese model is unfit for human consumption.

LAP PORTABLES

Pleasant for Home, Acceptable for Travel

A lap portable is for use primarily around the home and yard, plus on occasional trips. They are large enough to perform well, usually sound better than compact models, yet are not too big to fit into a carry-on or briefcase. Most take 3-4 "D" (UM-1) or "C" (UM-2) cells, plus sometimes a couple of "AA" (UM-3) cells for memory backup.

These are typically just under a foot wide—that's 30 cm—and weigh in around 3-5 pounds, or 1.4-2.3 kg. For air travel, that's okay if you are a dedicated listener, but a bit much otherwise.

Sony's ICF-SW77 is tough to find, but the forthcoming Etón E1 holds promise as a replacement.

Major Developments for 2005

Sony of America continues to fade from the market, so its top-ranked ICF-2010 is gone and the ICF-SW77 is no longer distributed in the Western Hemisphere. However, while Sony saws logs, Grundig/Etón makes hay.

Watch for the Etón E1 lap portable due out around early 2005. We haven't as yet tested a production version, but first looks are promising. When it comes out and we've put it through our chamber of horrors, a report will be posted at www.passband.com.

DRM Modifiable
✪✪✪¾
Sony ICF-SW77

Price: €499.00 in Germany. ¥65,000 in Japan.

Pro: A rich variety of tuning and other features, including sophisticated "page" tuning that some enjoy but others dislike; includes 162 station presets, two-speed tuning knob, signal-seek tuning (*see* Con), keypad tuning and meter-band access. Synchronous selectable sideband is exceptionally handy to operate; it significantly reduces selective-fading distortion and adjacent-channel interference on world band, longwave and mediumwave AM signals; although the sync chip part number was changed not long back, its performance is virtually unchanged (*see* Con). Two well-chosen bandwidths (6.0 kHz and 3.3 kHz) provide superior adjacent-channel rejection. Excellent image rejection and first-IF rejection, both 80 dB. Excellent-to-superb weak-signal sensitivity (noise floor –133 dBm, sensitivity 0.16 microvolts) in and around lower-middle portion of shortwave spectrum where most listening is done (*see* Con). Superb overall distortion, almost always under one percent. Dynamic range (82 dB) and third-order intercept point (–10 dBm) fairly good at 20 kHz separation (*see* Con). Tunes in very precise 0.05 kHz increments; displays in 0.1 kHz increments; these and other factors make this model superior to any other portable for single-sideband reception, although portatop and tabletop models usually fare better yet. Continuous separate bass and treble tone controls, a rarity. DRM modifiable (see www.drmrx.org/receiver_mods.html). Two illuminated multi-function liquid crystal displays. Dual-zone clock, displays separately from frequency. Station name appears on LCD when station presets used. 10-level signal-strength indicator (*see* Con). Excellent stability, less than 20 Hz drift after ten-second warmup. Excellent weak-signal sensitivity (noise floor –130 dBm, sensitivity 0.21 microvolts) within little-used 120 meter segment (*see* Con). Flip-up chart for calculating time differences. VCR-type five-

event timer controls radio and optional outboard recorder alike. Superior FM audio quality. Stereo FM through earpieces, included. Travel power lock. Japanese FM (most versions) and longwave bands. AC adaptor, hum-free. Outboard reel passive wire antenna accessory aids slightly with weak-signal reception. Rubber strip helps prevent sliding.

Con: No longer distributed by Sony outside Japan and Germany. "Page" tuning system relatively complex to operate; many find that station presets can't be accessed simply. World band and mediumwave AM audio slightly muffled even when wide bandwidth in use. Synthesizer chuffing degrades reception quality during bandscanning by knob. Dynamic range

NUMBERS: SONY ICF-SW77

Max. WB Sensitivity/Noise Floor	0.16 μV, **S**/–133 dBm, **E** [1]
Blocking	121 dB, **G**
Bandwidths *(Shape Factors)*	6.0 *(1:1.9,* **E***)*, 3.3 *(1:2.0,* **G***)* kHz
Ultimate Rejection	70 dB, **G**
Front-End Selectivity	— [2]
Image Rejection	80 dB, **E**
First IF Rejection	80 dB, **E**
Dynamic Range/IP3 (5 kHz)	64 dB, **F**/–37 dBm, **F**
Dynamic Range/IP3 (20 kHz)	82 dB, **F**/–10 dBm, **G**
Phase Noise	122 dBc, **E**
AGC Threshold	2.0 μV, **G**
Overall Distortion, sync	2.3%, **E**/3.3%, **G** [3]

IBS Lab Ratings: **S** Superb **E** Excellent **G** Good **F** Fair **P** Poor

(1) Sensitivity varies considerably by frequency at 2 MHz and between 10-29.9 MHz; *viz.*, from 0.16 μV to 1.40 μV, **S** - **F**. Noise floor varies by frequency from –133 dBm to –117 dBm, **E** - **G**. Neither measurement could be made at 5 MHz because of spurious responses, noise and leakage.

(2) Cannot be determined.

(3) Wide/narrow bandwidths.

(64 dB) and third-order intercept point (–37 dBm) only fair at 5 kHz separation. Weak-signal sensitivity varies from fair to superb, depending on where between 2 and 30 MHz receiver is being tuned. Synchronous selectable sideband holds lock reasonably. Synchronous selectable sideband tends to lose lock if batteries weak, or if NiCd cells are used. Synchronous selectable sideband alignment can vary with temperature, factory alignment and battery voltage, causing synchronous selectable sideband reception to be slightly more muffled in one sideband than the other. Signal-seek tuning skips over weaker signals. Flimsy 11-element telescopic antenna (the older version of the 'SW77 had nine elements). LCD characters small for size of receiver. Display illumination does not stay on with AC power. Unusual tuning knob design disliked by some. On mediumwave AM band, relatively insensitive, sometimes with spurious sounds during single-sideband reception; this doesn't apply to world band reception, however. Mundane reception of difficult FM signals. Signal-strength indicator grossly overreads, covering only a 20 dB range with maximum reading at only 3 microvolts. AGC threshold, 2 microvolts

The Roberts R827, available in the U.K., offers pleasant performance in a home-sized package.

(good). Painted surfaces can wear off with heavy use. No batteries (four "C" required).

Verdict: The Japanese-made Sony ICF-SW77 has been a strong contender among portables since it was improved some time back. After the Sony ICF-2010 was discontinued a few years back, the '77 became uncontested as the top portable.

The '77 has always been tops among portables for single-sideband reception, beating out even the legendary '2010. It's also one of the very few models with continuously tuned bass and treble controls. Ergonomics, however, are a mixed bag, so if you're interested consider trying it out first.

The rub in the Western Hemisphere is that it ceased being distributed by Sony of America, and virtually all units appear to have been sold by autumn of 2004. Americans either have to order by mail or web from sources in Germany or Japan, or wait to see how the forthcoming Etón E1 works out.

✪✪½
Roberts R827

Price: *Roberts:* £159.95 in the United Kingdom.

Pro: Superior overall world band performance. Numerous tuning features, including 18 world band station presets. Two bandwidths for good fidelity/interference tradeoff. Analog clarifier with center detent and stable circuitry allows single-sideband signals to be tuned with uncommon precision, thus allowing for superior audio phasing for a portable (*see* Con). Illuminated display. Signal-strength indicator. Dual-zone 24-hour clock, with one zone displayed separately from frequency. Alarm/timer with sleep delay. Travel power lock. FM stereo through headphones. AC adaptor. Longwave.

Con: Tends to mute when tuning knob turned quickly, making bandscanning difficult. Keypad not in telephone format.

Touchy variable control for single-sideband fine tuning. Does not come with tape-recorder jack. No batteries (four "D" and three "AA" needed). Country of manufacture (now China) not specified on radio or box.

Verdict: This is a decent, predictable radio—performance and features, alike—and reasonably priced. Sangean no longer makes this model under its own name, and we were unable to find out whether they will continue to manufacture it for Roberts once the existing inventory is exhausted.

★★¼ ☉ *Passport's Choice*
Etón S350, Grundig S350, Tecsun BCL-2000

Price: *Grundig:* $99.95 in the United States. $149.95CAD in Canada. £99.99 in the United Kingdom. *Etón:* €99.95 in Germany. *S350 refurbished units, as available:* $129.00CAD in Canada. *Franzus FR-22 120>220V AC transformer for BCL-2000:* $15-18 in the United States.

No other portable provides the audio quality of the Grundig S350/Tecsun BCL-2000.

Pro: Speaker audio quality substantially above the norm for world band portables, regardless of price. Separate bass and treble tone controls, a rarity at any price, help shape audio frequency response. Unusually powerful audio, suitable for relatively noisy ambient listening environments. Two bandwidths, well-chosen, are a real and

COMING UP

By early 2005 Etón plans to release its exotic new E1 lap portable, originally called the Satellit 900, as updated heir to the discontinued Sony ICF-2010. The American version is also to receive XM satellite broadcasts. Laden with sophisticated features and Drake-engineered performance, it's to be priced accordingly.

Degen's line of affordable compact portables is shortly to welcome another sibling, the DE1105. On paper it seems similar to the existing DE1102, but may use a cockamamie volume control scheme similar to that found on the new DE1103. It should eventually be sold in North America as the Kaito KA1105.

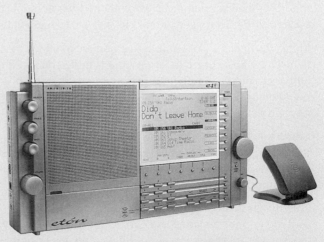

Etón's E1 is to include XM satellite reception.

pleasant surprise at this price; they provide effective and flexible adjacent-channel rejection *vis-à-vis* fidelity. Sensitive to weak signals, and exceptionally free from circuit noise ("hiss"). No chuffing while tuning. Relatively intuitive to operate, even for newcomers. World Time clock (*see* Con) with alarm, clock radio and sleep delay; may also be set to 12-hour format. Four-level (eight bar) signal-strength indicator. Battery-level indicator (*see* Con). Low battery consumption, combined with four "D" cells, reduces need for battery replacement. Most comfortable carrying handle of any world band radio tested; also seconds as a shoulder strap. Brightly illuminated LCD has high contrast, is visible from a variety of angles. LCD illumination may be left on fulltime or timed to turn off. Attractive. FM reception quality slightly above average. FM in stereo through headphones. RCA phono sockets provide stereo line

IS ANALOG KAPUT?

Does DRM signify the end for traditional analog broadcasts?

It depends on how larger events unfold. News and perspectives are the traditional workhorses of international broadcasting. For these, analog world band has such advantages as resistance to jamming—DRM doesn't, and local FM placement is similarly at the mercy of censors.

However, a post-cold war generation of managers has been reorienting global broadcasting away from news and ideas and towards music. This shifts the focus from assuring intelligible reception to enhancing audio fidelity. Indeed, the venerable news-oriented Voice of America is already dying as its funding is diverted to entertainment-oriented substitutes.

California Dreaming

Nevertheless, over half a billion people listen to traditional world band signals, and they are not the ones clamoring for replacement. Instead, put downs of analog shortwave broadcasting nearly always originate from those with little or no knowledge of the medium—newer executives who rely on their personal or commercial broadcasting backgrounds. Trouble is, the world isn't California writ large.

Music formats do yield impressive audience ratings, especially among the youth market favored by advertisers selling products and services. But "programming lite" doesn't influence minds among core decision-makers or other influentials. Instead, it raises the question of why taxpayers should be funding something with little foreign policy impact beyond what could be obtained for free through commercial stations.

Could this lead to international broadcasting operations being privatized, divorced from the very governments which created them? Perhaps, but in the final analysis analog world band radio has a proven ability to reach and influence global audiences with meaty programs. And nothing else is as difficult to censor.

This makes analog world band radio as much of a foreign policy tool for today's conflicts as it did in prior decades and conflicts. Add to that the wave of truly cheap digitally tuned analog portables coming out of China, and it is unlikely that the analog world band radio audience will be fading away anytime soon.

output for recording, FM home transmitters and outboard audio systems. Mediumwave AM reception better than most. *North America:* Toll-free tech support. *BCL-2000:* Built-in 220V AC power supply eliminates need for outboard AC adaptor. *S350:* Outboard 120V AC adaptor, included, can be left behind on trips, making the S350 lighter than the BCL-2000.

Con: Analog-tuned with digital frequency counter, so tunes only by pair of concentric (fast/slow) tuning knobs. This results in an unusually high degree of frequency drift, typically 1-4 kHz in the first half-hour, but greater with some samples in certain frequency ranges. Single-conversion IF circuitry results in poor image rejection. Power button activates 90-minute sleep-delay timer; works as full-time "on" control only if held down for three seconds, a minor inconvenience (*see* second ☞, below). Lacks such helpful tuning aids as station presets, keypad and scanning. Unhandy "MW/SW1/SW2/SW3" switch must often be used to tune mediumwave AM and short-wave spectra. Some user-correctable nighttime overloading in high-signal-strength parts of the world. Does not tune relatively unused 2 MHz (120 meter) tropical world band segment. Mediumwave AM frequency readout can be off by up to 2 kHz. Clock not displayed independent of frequency; button allows time to replace frequency for three seconds. Clock tends to be off slightly over time. Nominal 30 MHz low-pass filter has such high apparent insertion loss as to be useless except as a de facto attenuator. Poor visual indication of adjustment position of volume, tone and RF gain controls (user-remediable with paint or Wite-Out). Battery-level indicator gives little warning before radio becomes inoperative. Batteries (4 × "D") not included. *S350:* AC adaptor less handy than built-in power supply. *BCL-2000:* Mediumwave AM misses the 1650–1705 kHz portion of the X-band and 1705–1735 kHz potential public-service segment.

☞ Beware of a quasi-counterfeit clone labeled "ECB 2000," also produced in China.

☞ Initial BCL-2000 production samples, from early 2003, would always turn off after 90 minutes or less. This was remedied in subsequent production (*see* Con), but there's a roundabout solution for early units: have the radio turn off during the 30 minutes the clock radio stays on. For example, 60-85 minutes before the clock radio is programmed to go on, press the power button once so the radio will go off in 90 minutes. The radio will then stay on indefinitely until the power button is pressed again.

Verdict: Tecsun's BCL-2000—sold in North America as the Grundig S350 and in Europe as the Etón S350—is full of welcome surprises, as well as the other variety. Its flaws are obvious and real: drift, images and a paucity of tuning aids, so it receives a modest star rating.

Why, then, is something like this cited as a "Passport's Choice"? Because for pleasant listening to news, music and entertainment over the world band airwaves, it is hard to beat—its audio quality just isn't equaled by any other portable. If you want something that sounds as good but performs better, dig deep and spring for a Grundig Satellit 800 portatop.

WORLD BAND CASSETTE RECORDERS

What happens if your favorite show comes on at an inconvenient time? Why, tape it, of course, with a world band cassette recorder—just like on your VCR.

Two models are offered, and there's no question which is better: the Sony. Smaller, too, so it is less likely to raise eyebrows among airport security personnel. But there's a whopping price difference over the Sangean, and the Sony is getting hard to find.

Tops for automated recording of world band shows is the Sony ICF-SW1000T/TS, with two on/off timed events. If you want one, get it soon.

✪✪✪⅛ *Passport's Choice*
Sony ICF-SW1000T (as available), **Sony ICF-SW1000TS**

Price: *ICF-SW1000T:* $449.95 in the United States. €439.00 in Germany. *AC-E30HG 120V AC adaptor:* $19.95. *ICF-SW1000TS:* ¥46,000 in Japan.

Pro: Built-in recorder in rear of cabinet, with two events of up to 90 minutes each, selectable in ten-minute increments. Relatively compact for travel, also helpful to avoid airport security hassles. High-tech synchronous selectable sideband; this generally performs well, reducing adjacent-channel interference and selective-fading distortion on world band, longwave and mediumwave AM signals while adding slightly to weak-signal sensitivity (*see* Con). Single bandwidth, especially when synchronous selectable sideband is used, exceptionally effective at adjacent-channel rejection. Numerous helpful tuning features, including keypad, two-speed up/down slew, 32 station presets and signal-seek scanning. Thirty of the 32 station presets are within three easy-to-use "pages" so stations can be clustered. Weak-signal sensitivity above average up to about 16 MHz. Demodulates single-sideband signals (*see* Con). World Time 24-hour clock, easy to set (*see* Con). Sleep delay. Illuminated LCD readable from

a wide variety of angles. Travel power lock, also useful to keep recorder from being inadvertently switched on while cabinet being grasped (*see* Con). Easy on batteries. Records on both sides of tape without having to flip cassette (provided FWD is selected along with the "turning-around arrow"). Auto record level (*see* Con). "ISS" switch helps radio avoid interference from recorder's bias circuitry. FM stereo through earphones; earbuds included. Japanese FM (most versions) and longwave bands. Outboard reel passive wire antenna accessory aids slightly with weak-signal reception. Dead-battery indicator. Lapel mic (*see* Con). *ICF-SW1000TS:* AC adaptor (100V AC only). AN-LP1 active antenna.

Con: No longer distributed by Sony outside Japan, although some stocks remain. Pedestrian speaker audio quality. Synchronous selectable sideband tends to lose lock if batteries not fresh, or if NiCd cells are used. Synchronous selectable sideband alignment can vary with temperature, factory alignment and battery voltage, causing synchronous selectable sideband reception to be slightly more muffled in one sideband than the other. No tuning knob. Clock not readable when radio switched on except for ten seconds when key is pushed. No meaningful signal-strength indicator, which negates its otherwise obvious role for traveling technical monitors. No recording-level indicator or tape counter. Slow rewind. Fast forward and reverse use buttons that have to be held down. No built-in mic; outboard (lapel) mic is mono. Reception is interrupted for a good two seconds when recording first commences. No pause control. Single lock deactivates controls for radio and recorder alike; separate locks would have been preferable. Tuning resolution of 0.1 kHz allows single-sideband signals to be mis-tuned by up to 50 Hz. Frequency readout to 1 kHz, rather than 0.1 kHz tuning increment. Lacks flip-out elevation panel; instead, uses less handy plug-in tab. FM sometimes overloads.

Telescopic antenna exits from the side, which limits tilting choices for FM. Misleading location of battery springs makes it easy to insert one of the two "AA" radio batteries in the wrong direction, albeit to no ill effect. No batteries (three "AA" required, two for radio and one for recorder). *ICF-SW1000T:* 120V AC or other adaptor costs extra (avoid Sony multivoltage adaptors, as they don't provide enough torque for starting tape drive).

Verdict: Strictly speaking, Sony's pricey ICF-SW1000T/ICF-SW1000TS is the world's only true world band cassette recorder. Made in Japan, it is an innovative little package with surprisingly good battery life and build quality. The rub is that as of 2004 it is no longer being offered by Sony outside Japan.

Best buy in a world band recording radio is the Sangean ATS-818ACS, sold in the United Kingdom as the Roberts RC828. However, there is no timed "off."

★★½ ℗
Sangean ATS-818ACS, Roberts RC828

Price: *Sangean:* $224.95 in the United States. $289.00CAD in Canada. £199.95 in the United Kingdom. €169.00 in Germany. *AC adaptor:* £16.95 in the United Kingdom. *Roberts:* £219.95 in the United Kingdom.

Pro: Built-in cassette recorder. Price low relative to competition. Superior overall world band performance. Numerous tuning features, including 18 world band station presets. Two bandwidths for good fidelity/interference tradeoff. Analog clarifier with center detent and stable circuitry allows single-sideband signals to be tuned with uncommon precision, thus allowing for superior audio phasing for a portable (*see* Con). Illuminated display. Signal-strength indicator. Dual-zone 24-hour clock, with one zone displayed separately from frequency. Alarm/timer with sleep delay. Travel power lock. Stereo through headphones. Longwave. Built-in condenser mic. *Most versions:* AC adaptor.

Con: Recorder has no multiple recording events, just one "on" time (quits when tape runs out). Tends to mute when tuning knob turned quickly, making bandscanning difficult (the C. Crane Company offers a $20.00/$29.95 modification to remedy this). Wide bandwidth a bit broad for world band reception without synchronous selectable sideband. Keypad not in telephone format. Touchy single-sideband clarifier. Recorder has no level indicator and no counter. Fast-forward and rewind controls installed facing backwards. No batteries (four "D" and three "AA" needed). Country of manufacture (now China) not specified on radio or box.

Verdict: A great buy, although recording is only single-event with no timed "off."

The PASSPORT *portable-radio review team: Lawrence Magne and David Zantow; also, Tony Jones, with laboratory measurements performed independently by Rob Sherwood. Additional feedback from Toshimichi Ohtake, Craig Tyson and George Zeller.*

www.passband.com

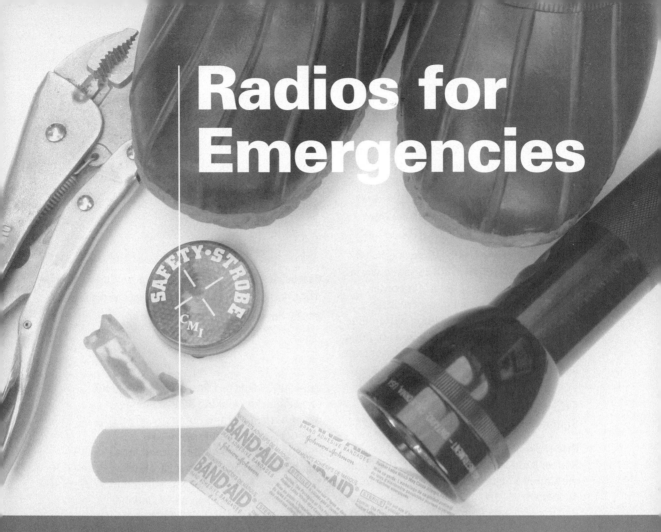

Radios for Emergencies

The thread of civilization periodically snaps. Whether it be blackout, civil unrest, pestilence or nature run amok, you need access to trusted information.

When all else fails, world band radio is there—it's the one medium that gets through freely, no matter what. Like an emergency room, the worse things get the more important it becomes.

World band soars direct to you, without wires and without censorship. Its far-reaching signals bounce off layers in the atmosphere that are invulnerable to human manipulation—no satellites, no cables, no cell towers. Even if attackers or officials try to disrupt world band, you still have a good chance of hearing what is being said. That's why world band radios are outlawed in gulags like North Korea; indeed, even some democratic societies display ambivalence.

What to Look for

If you already have a world band portable or portatop, look no further. Keeping extra batteries on hand allows your existing radio to serve nicely in a crisis.

If you don't already own a world band radio, consider getting one now—not after a crisis, when anything decent is sold out. Best is a three-star portable that works for both routine listening and emergency use.

Favor models that can process single-sideband signals, explained in PASSPORT's glossary. These allow for eavesdropping on aeronautical and other "utility" communications, as well as the important American Forces Radio and Television Service. Also, avoid battery hogs and look for illuminated LCDs, *de rigeur* for tuning in the dark—illuminated keypads are great, too.

What to avoid? Cheap radios lacking digital frequency readout—their imprecise dials make stations hard to find, they don't demodulate single-sideband signals and most are marginal performers. Also, think twice about wind-up radios. They seem promising on paper and have advantages, but are rudimentary performers. Best is to treat them as backup to your regular world band equipment.

Only one wind-up model, the Freeplay Summit, meets PASSPORT's minimum requirements for being tested. The Summit is heir to the esteemed BayGen "Clockwork Radio" experiment initiated a decade ago in South Africa. BayGen became known for hiring poor and handicapped black Africans, and founder Trevor Bayliss was honored by the iconic Nelson Mandela.

Media folk ate it up. Bayliss' adaption of long-existing technology became touted as an Edisonian nostrum for the global information divide. One Polish report even claimed that his

wind-up radio "could save the lives of millions of Africans." None of these enthusiastic projections came to pass, but they live on as legendary testimony to Bayliss' talent as pitchman.

The South African facility folded and corporate identities changed. But although the current Summit radio is made without fanfare in China and Bayliss (now OBE) is active in other arenas, the cultural afterglow continues. For example, Greenpeace distributes Freeplay products within the Benelux countries, and buyers continue to be attracted to the radio for reasons of conscience.

What to Do

An emergency radio has to work wherever you stay during a crisis. To check, go outdoors and tune to foreign stations that are weak but intelligible. Jot down their frequencies or load them into presets, then head to your safe room.

There, tune to those same frequencies and compare how well they come in. If reception is similar, you're all set. If not, put up a simple outdoor wire antenna, such as Radio Shack's cheap "Outdoor Antenna Kit" (278-758). Cut it to a convenient length, then run the feedline into your room without damaging the insulation. Also check out passive and other compact antennas reviewed in PASSPORT REPORTS.

Either way, keep PASSPORT nearby so you'll know what's on. A flashlight is another "must," along with a CB or FRS walkie-talkie and batteries.

Revised Version for 2005
✪¼
Freeplay Summit (International), Freeplay Summit (USA)

Price: *Summit (International):* $119.95 as available in the United States. $159.99CAD in Canada. £59.99 in the United Kingdom. €119.95 in Germany. *Summit (USA):* $99.95 in the United States.

Pro: Relatively technologically advanced for an emergency radio, including five world band

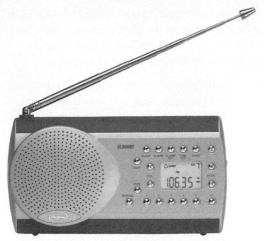

Freeplay's Summit stands out with synthesized tuning and digital frequency readout.

5.95–15.6 MHz omits 120, 75, 90, 60, 16, 15, 13 and 11 meter world band segments, along with lower end of 49 meters and upper end of 19 meters. Inconvenient to tune, what with no keypad, no tuning knob and "signal-seek" scanning that stops only at very powerful world band signals; this essentially leaves only single-speed (slow) up/down slewing and five world band presets to navigate the airwaves. No volume knob; level adjustable only through up/down slew controls. Mutes for a second whenever slew button pressed, an annoyance when band-scanning. Does not continuously display frequency—reverts back to clock after ten seconds. Tunes world band only in 5 kHz steps and displays in nonstandard XX.XX MHz/XX.XX5 MHz format. LCD hard to read in low light without turning on illumination, which fades away after only four seconds. FM overloads in strong-signal environments. No handle or carrying strap. *Summit (International):* Multivoltage AC adaptor disturbs reception with vigorous noise and hum; best is to limit adaptor use to charging battery pack, then disconnect from wall.

☞ The designations "International" and "USA" are informal terms used to differenti-ate between the two. Freeplay materials refer only to "Summit."

Verdict: Yes, world band performance is mediocre. And, yes, it is bereft of most tuning aids. Still, the Chinese-made Freeplay Summit is the most acceptable emergency radio we have come across, and it performs reasonably on FM and medium-wave AM. Were the facade of civilization to be stripped away for days or weeks, it could be invaluable.

Changes in New Version: Americans, rejoice! The Summit version now sold in the United States costs less, and its AC adaptor doesn't drown out radio signals.

presets and 25 more for other bands. Powered by a rechargeable battery pack which, in turn, is juiced three ways: a foolproof cranked alternator, solar energy and an AC adaptor. NiMH battery pack replaceable, although nominally the radio runs even if the pack no longer takes a charge. Reasonably pleasant audio quality. Timed LCD illumination. Low-battery and crank-charge indicators. World Time clock with alarm and sleep functions can also display in 12-hour format. Includes reel antenna and AC adaptor. Travel power lock. Mediumwave AM includes 9/10 kHz tuning steps. FM includes NTSC channel 6 audio. Longwave. More stylish than most. Two-year warranty. *Summit (International):* AC adaptor adjusts to line voltage (110–240V AC) anywhere in the world (*see* Con). Includes three types of power plugs for different countries; also, a carrying pouch. *Summit (USA):* 120V AC adaptor, works well.

Con: Slow battery recharge; full replenish-ment requires 24 hours with AC adaptor, 40 hours using sunlight, or 40 minutes of carpal crunching cranking. Poor sensitivity on world band using built-in but undersized telescopic antenna; reel-in accessory antenna, included, helps to a degree. Poor selectivity. Poor image rejection. Shortwave coverage of

---

The PASSPORT *emergency-radio review team: Lawrence Magne and David Zantow.*

POPULAR WIND-UP RADIO

Grundig FR-200, Grundig FR200G, Etón FR-200, Etón FR200G, Tecsun Green-88

Wind-up world band radios are major sellers, but one model leaps out: over a million Grundig FR-200 radios are claimed to be sold each year in North America alone. In addition, Etón and Tecsun versions are being offered in other parts of the world.

The '200 succeeds thanks to ubiquitous advertising, widespread availability and bargain pricing: under $40 Stateside, $10 or so more in Canada and around €30 in Germany. Its replaceable NiMH battery pack is charged not only by crank-driven dynamo, but in the costlier "G" (yellow) version there's also an AC adaptor. Even better, should the battery pack go dead the dynamo is designed to power the radio by itself. The only rub is that the battery cover opens too easily, allowing the pack to flop out. The front panel also sports a bright flashlight to keep the boogie man at bay—in a blackout this could be as important as the radio.

The '200 tunes mediumwave AM well beyond the upper band limit of 1705 kHz, as well as FM (including NTSC channel 6 audio) and two shortwave "bands": 3.2–7.6 MHz and 9.2–22 MHz. That includes nearly all world band segments, but the analog frequency readout crams hundreds of world band stations into a couple of inches (five centimeters) of dial space. Global signals can be hunted down only by ear, but even then you can't be sure whether you're hearing the station's real signal or its image 900 kHz or so down.

Audio quality is pleasant on all bands. However, reception quality otherwise is elemental. For starters, sensitivity to weak world band signals is marginal. Adjacent-channel rejection (selectivity) is equally dismal—image rejection, too. As to single-sideband signals, forget it.

Grundig/Etón's FR-200/Green-88 emergency radio comes with hand-cranked dynamo, multiband radio, carrying case and flashlight. Widely available and inexpensive, millions have been sold.

Local signals are important, even in a crisis. Although the '200's FM overloads in strong-signal environments, both it and mediumwave AM perform reasonably well.

The FR-200 doesn't send radio hearts aflutter, but it suffices for emergencies, is widely available and is eminently affordable. Performance and operation are bare-bones, but for $40 it offers versatile portable power, a flashlight, a travel-grade carrying case, earbuds and a one-year warranty.

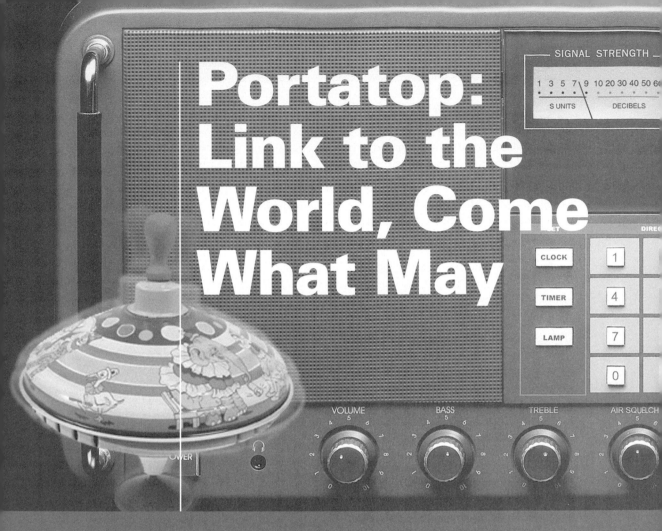

Portatop: Link to the World, Come What May

Most buy a world band radio not just for a room, but for the entire house. For this, portables are an obvious choice, and they can also be taken on trips.

Yet, portables rarely sound as pleasant as tabletop models. Nor do most cut the mustard with really tough signals. Solution: Combine various characteristics of portables and tabletops into one high-performance package—a portatop—which can be serviced, like tabletops, for years to come.

Drawbacks? A portatop is larger and usually costlier than a portable. It also goes through batteries with abandon, and it's not as well constructed as a tabletop model. But if you're comfortable with this, you'll find performance and fidelity approaching that of a good tabletop receiver—without the tabletop's sticker shock.

If you want top-notch reception, come what may—even during electrical outages, earthquakes and terrorist attacks—a portatop can't be beat. Yet, large radios of all types are slowly fading from the market. Expect portatops to give way to sophisticated lap portables before long.

What PASSPORT's Rating Symbols Mean

Star ratings: ✪✪✪✪✪ is best. Stars reflect overall performance and meaningful features, plus to some extent ergonomics and build quality. Price, appearance, country of manufacture and the like are not taken into account. With portatop models there is a balanced emphasis on listening quality, on one hand, and the ability to flush out tough, hard-to-hear signals on the other. Nevertheless, to facilitate comparison the portatop rating standards are very similar to those used for the professional, tabletop and portable models reviewed elsewhere in this PASSPORT.

Passport's Choice. La crème de la crème. Our test team's personal picks of the litter—models we would buy or have bought for our personal use.

🅒: A relative bargain, with decidedly more performance than the price would suggest.

> A portatop is larger and usually costlier than a portable.

✪✪✪✪⅜ 🅒 📄 *Passport's Choice*
Grundig Satellit 800, Tecsun HAM-2000

Price: *S800:* $499.95 including 120V AC adaptor and headphones in the United States. $599.99CAD including 120V AC adaptor and headphones in Canada. £549.00 including dual-voltage AC adaptor and headphones in the United Kingdom. €849.00 including dual-voltage AC adaptor and headphones in Germany. *S800 refurbished units, as available:* $399.95 in the United States. £399.00 in the United Kingdom.

Pro: Superior, room-filling tonal quality by world band, even if not audiophile, standards—whether with the internal speaker, outboard speakers or headphones. Only receiver tested that comes with full-size audiophile-style padded headphones. Tonal shaping aided by continuous separate bass and treble tone controls, a rarity among world band receivers at any price. Excellent-performing synchronous selectable sideband, with 27 dB of unwanted-sideband rejection; this reduces adjacent-channel interference and selective-fading distortion with world band, longwave and mediumwave AM signals. Synchronous selectable sideband also boosts recoverable audio from some of the weakest of signals, and halves overall distortion from 5.3% in the ordinary AM mode to 2.4% on audio frequencies from 100-3,000 Hz. Three voice/music bandwidths; wide measures around 7 kHz, while medium and narrow measure in the vicinity of 5.8 kHz and 2.6 kHz.

Bandwidths generally have excellent shape factors and excellent ultimate rejection; all bandwidths are selectable independent of mode (or dependent, if the user prefers), and work in concert with the synchronous selectable sideband feature to provide superior adjacent-channel rejection. Slow/fast AGC decay (*see* Con). Numerous helpful tuning aids, including 70 tunable station presets that store many variables (*see* Con); also, presets may be scanned (*see* Con). Excellent ergonomics, including many dedicated, widely spaced controls; exceptionally smooth knob tuning aided by ball bearings (*see* Con); and foolproof frequency entry. Superb LCD with huge, bold characters has high contrast and can be viewed clearly from virtually any angle; it is even readable by many with faltering eyesight (*see* Con). Analog signal-strength indicator, a rarity at this price, has gradations in useful S1-9/+60 dB standard (*see* Con). Single-sideband

reception above the portable norm (*see* Con), with rock-solid frequency stability and 50 Hz tuning increments. High- and low-impedance inputs for 0.1-30 MHz external antennas. Weak-signal shortwave sensitivity with built-in telescopic antenna equal to or better than that of top-rated portables; it works so well that such accessory antennas as the Sony AN-LP1 rarely improve performance substantially. Weak-signal shortwave sensitivity with an external antenna can be boosted by setting antenna switch to "whip," thus adding preamplification (and, in such locations as Europe evenings, sometimes generating overloading as well). Superior blocking performance aids consistency of weak-signal sensitivity. Generally superior dynamic range and third-order intercept point to the extent they can be measured amidst receiver phase noise and such. Two-event on/off timer and two 24-hour clocks (*see* Con). Large, tough telescopic antenna

NUMBERS: GRUNDIG SATELLIT 800/TECSUN HAM-2000

Max. Sensitivity/Noise Floor	0.43 μV, **G**/−124 dBm, **G** [1]
Blocking	132 dB, **E**
Bandwidths *(Shape Factors)*	7.1 *(1:1.6,* **E***)*, 5.8 *(1:1.6,* **E***)*, 2.6 *(1:2.2,* **G***)* kHz
Ultimate Rejection	75 dB, **E**
Front-End Selectivity	**F**
Image Rejection	65 dB, **G**
First IF Rejection	83 dB, **E**
Dynamic Range/IP3 (5 kHz)	67 dB, **F**/−26 dBm, **G** [2]
Dynamic Range/IP3 (20 kHz)	92 dB, **E**/+11 dBm, **S** [2]
Phase Noise	111 dBc, **G**
AGC Threshold	0.8 μV, **S**
Overall Distortion, sync	2.4%, **E**
Stability	10 Hz, **E**

IBS Lab Ratings: **S** Superb   **E** Excellent   **G** Good   **F** Fair   **P** Poor

(1) Sample-to-sample variation from 0.23 to 0.43 μV, −129 to −124 dBm.

(2) Estimated, as ability to measure limited by birdies, phase noise and other mixing products.

Grundig's Satellit 800 performs like a tabletop model—hardly surprising, as it was engineered by the American firm of R.L. Drake. However, it may not be available after 2005.

includes spring-loaded detents for vertical, 45-degree and 90-degree swiveling; also rotates freely 360 degrees (*see* Con). Clever display and signal strength meter illumination—with batteries in use, light automatically comes on for 15 seconds either at the touch of any button or when receiver is knob or slew tuned; 15-second illumination cycle can be aborted by pushing the light button a second time. FM—mono through built-in speaker, stereo through outboard speakers, headphones and line output—performs well, although capture ratio only average and nearby FM transmitters may cause some overloading. Covers longwave down to 100 kHz. Built-in ferrite rod antenna may be used for 0.1-1.8 MHz. Covers the 118-137 MHz aeronautical band, but only in the AM mode without synchronous selectable sideband; performs about as well as a simple handheld scanner. Excellent, long carrying handle. Comes with AC adaptor—120V AC or 220V AC, depending upon where radio is sold, otherwise, alkaline batteries need changing every 35 hours or so, about 25 cents per hour. Battery-strength indicator (*see* Con). Rack-type handles protect front panel should radio fall over. *North America:* Repairs in and out of one-year warranty are performed by the R.L. Drake Company, long known for superior service. Excellent toll-free tech support.

Con: Huge (20 3/8 inches—517 mm—wide) and weighty (15 pounds or 6.8 kg with batteries). Plastic cabinet and other components are of portable-radio quality, not in the same radiophile-hardware league as found on tabletop models. Synthesizer phase noise, only fair, slightly impacts reception of weak-signals adjacent to powerful signals and in other circumstances; also, limits ability to make certain laboratory measurements accurately. Lacks notch filter, noise blanker, passband tuning and digital signal processing (DSP) found on some tabletop models. When ungrounded (e.g., AC adaptor is not connected to a grounded AC socket) and powered by batteries, there is vigorous "hash" while the tuning knob is being handled within some portions of the mediumwave AM band; this ceases when the tuning knob is

Analog signal-strength indicators are costlier than digitals to make, but are ideal for fade-prone shortwave.

released, and reception quality of the received station is not affected. Each key push must each be done within three seconds, lest receiver wind up being mistuned or placed into an unwanted operating mode. No signal-seek frequency scanning. Signal-strength indicator greatly underreads, although arguably this is preferable to the overreading often found with other models. Outboard AC adaptor in lieu of inboard power supply. Single sideband's 50 Hz synthesizer increments allow tuning to be out of phase by up to 25 Hz, diminishing audio fidelity. Fast AGC decay setting is handy for bandscanning, but sometimes causes distortion with powerful signals; remedied by going to slow AGC when no longer actively bandscanning. Numerous modest birdies on longwave, mediumwave AM, shortwave and FM bands; these rarely cause heterodyne interference to world band signals, approximately one time in 250 they might heterodyne utility, ham and Eastern Hemisphere mediumwave signals. Spurious signal on 20,000 kHz obscures WWV reception. Ergonomics, although excellent, are not ideal; e.g., no rows and columns of dedicated buttons for station presets. Sharp bevel on tuning knob. Neither clock displays when frequency is shown; however, pushbutton allows time to replace frequency on the display for three seconds. Both clocks in 24-hour format and neither displays seconds numerically; 12-hour format not selectable for local time. For faint-signal DXing, recoverable audio with an outboard antenna, although good, not fully equal to that of most tabletop and professional models. Using the built-in antenna, sensitivity to weak signals is not of DX caliber in the mediumwave AM band; remedied by using Terk AM Advantage or similar accessory antenna. Some frontal (only) radiation of digital noise from LCD, rarely causes problem in actual use. No adjustable feet or elevation rod to angle receiver upwards for handy operation. When receiver leaned backward, the telescopic antenna, if angled, spins to the rear. Battery-strength indicator doesn't come on until immediately before radio mutes from low battery voltage. Misleading location of battery spring clips makes it easy to insert half the batteries in the wrong direction, albeit to no permanent ill effect. Battery cover may come loose if receiver bumped in a specific and unusual manner. Antenna switches located unhandily on rear panel. "USB" on LCD displays as "LISB." No schematic or repair manual available, making service difficult except at authorized repair facilities. No batteries (6 "D" needed). *Tecsun:* "HAM" a confusing name, as world band radio has nothing to do with hams, who are licensed to transmit to each other.

☞ Prior to 2003 there were a number of batches manufactured with an above-average defect rate. Since then production quality has improved.

☞ Refurbished Grundig units reportedly include gift and similar types of returns from department stores and other outlets where customers tend to be unfamiliar with world band radio. Refurbishing is done at Drake's facility in Ohio (see introduction to article).

☞ There appear to be no plans to sell the Satellit 800 under the Etón name.

Verdict: Big Bertha.

The beefy Grundig Satellit 800/Tecsun HAM-2000 offers near-tabletop performance at a near-portable price. Great audio quality and ergonomics, and it receives well with just its telescopic antenna. With pricing down and quality up, this receiver commands unusual attention.

▤ An *RDI WHITE PAPER* is available for this model.

The PASSPORT portatop review team includes Lawrence Magne, Tony Jones, Craig Tyson and George Zeller, with Avery Comarow, George Heidelman and John Wagner. Laboratory measurements by Robert Sherwood.

Tabletop Receivers for 2005

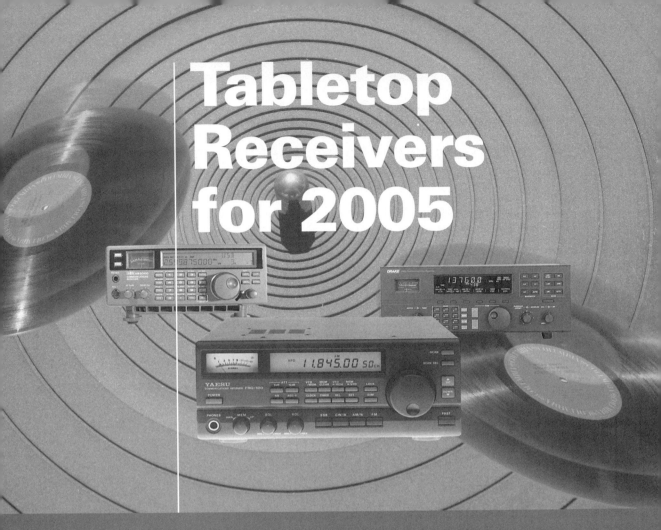

Tabletop receivers flush out the tough game—faint stations swamped by competing signals. That's why they are prized by radio aficionados known as "DXers," an old telegraph term meaning long distance. But tabletop models aren't for everybody, and it shows. Even in palmy North America and Europe, tabletop unit sales are uninspiring even while the roster of choices is as great as ever.

Virtually all models are pricier than portables or portatops, yet less expensive than the professional receivers reviewed in PASSPORT REPORTS. For the cost of a tabletop you tend to get not only excellent performance, but also superior construction and ruggedness. They are also relatively easy to service and are backed up by knowledgeable repair facilities.

What you rarely find in a tabletop is reception of the everyday 87.5-108 MHz FM band. For this, look to a portatop or portable.

Tabletop sets, like portatop and professional models, are heavy artillery for where signals are routinely weak—places like western and midwestern North American, or Australia and New Zealand. Even elsewhere there can be a problem when signals pass over or near the geomagnetic North Pole. To check, place a string on a globe—a conventional map won't do—between your location and the station's transmitter as given in the Blue Pages. If the string passes near or above latitude 60° north, beware.

Daytime Signals Interesting

Some programs formerly aired during prime time may now heard, instead, by day. These signals tend to be weaker, especially when not beamed to your part of the world, but they are also among the most interesting.

Thanks to the scattering properties of shortwave you can eavesdrop on many of these "off-beam" signals, but it's harder. That is where a superior receiver's longer reach comes in.

But not always. Say, you have a portable with an outdoor antenna and reception is being disrupted by electrical noise—nearby dimmers and such. Reception may not benefit from a tabletop model, as its superior circuitry boosts noise as much as signals.

An active loop antenna, evaluated elsewhere in PASSPORT REPORTS, might improve the signal-to-noise ratio. If so, you may profit from a good tabletop model even in the face of some local electrical noise.

Relief for Cliff Dwellers

In high-rise buildings, portables can disappoint. Reinforced concrete soaks up signals, while nearby broadcast and cellular transmitters can interfere.

Here, a good bet for reception of tough world band stations is a well-rated tabletop or portatop model fed by a suitable antenna. Experiment with something like a homebrew insulated-wire antenna along, or just outside, a window or balcony. Or try an everyday telescopic car antenna that angles, like a wall flag mast, out a window or balcony ledge.

Even better is to amplify your homebrew antenna with a good active preselector. You can also try factory-made amplified ("active") antennas that have reception elements and amplifiers in separate modules. These are reviewed in another section of PASSPORT REPORTS.

If you don't live in an apartment, consider a first-rate passive (unamplified) outdoor wire antenna, usually under $100. Performance findings and installation tips are detailed in the Radio Database International White Paper, *Popular Outdoor Antennas*, and summarized in this PASSPORT REPORTS.

DRM Digital Broadcasts

Some models come equipped to receive DRM digital world band broadcasts that are currently being tested. These receivers are designated as "DRM Ready," but that's just the first step. To reproduce DRM transmissions, a receiver also needs to be connected to a PC using separately purchased DRM software—€60 from www.drmrx.org/purchase.php. Finally, an outboard antenna has to be chosen and situated to minimize pickup of digital "hash" from the computer, ancillary hardware and cables.

A number of other tabletop models can be modified to receive DRM— see www.drmrx.org/receiver_mods.html. This is one step removed from "DRM ready," but helps ensure the radio will not become technologically limited.

Shortwave's Other Offerings

Although virtually all shortwave listeners are interested in world band, some also seek out "utility" and "ham" signals. These have reception challenges of their own and, unlike world band, don't require much in the way of receiver audio quality. This allows some receivers to stand out even when their world band audio isn't inspiring. The Icom IC-R75 and Japan Radio NRD-545 are two popular examples.

Other top-rated tabletop models perform solidly with all kinds of signals. These receivers allow those primarily concerned with world band to also enjoy chasing after utilities and hams.

Price *vs.* Performance

Top-rated tabletop models cost over the equivalent of $1,000, but they really cut the mustard. Five-star Drake and AOR models, in particular, are especially effective for world band reception.

While the Icom IC-R75 isn't quite is that exalted league, it comes close for world band and is rock solid for utility and "ham" reception. Icom periodically tacks on a free $140 DSP accessory and $50 rebate coupon, making the 'R75 an astonishingly good buy.

Complete Findings Now Available

Our unabridged laboratory and hands-on test results for each receiver are too exhaustive to reproduce here. However, they are available for selected current and classic models as PASSPORT's Radio Database International White Papers—details are elsewhere in this book.

Tips for Using this Section

Receivers are listed in order of suitability for listening to difficult-to-hear world band stations; important secondary consideration is given to audio fidelity, ergonomics and perceived build quality. Street selling prices are cited, including British and Australian VAT/GST where applicable. Prices vary, so take them as the general guide they are meant to be.

Unless otherwise stated, all tabletop models have the following characteristics. See PASSPORT's glossary to understand terms used.

- Digital frequency synthesis and display.
- Full coverage of at least the 155-29999 kHz longwave, mediumwave AM and short-wave spectra—including all world band frequencies—but no coverage of the FM broadcast band (87.5-108 MHz). Models designed for sale in certain countries have reduced shortwave tuning ranges.
- A wide variety of helpful tuning features.
- Synchronous selectable sideband via high-rejection IF filtering (not lower-rejection phase cancellation), which greatly reduces adjacent-channel interference and selective-fading distortion.

☞ ECSS: Many tabletop models can tune to the nearest 10 Hz or even 1 Hz, allowing the operator to use the receiver's single-sideband circuitry to manually phase its BFO (internally generated carrier) with the station's transmitted carrier. Called "ECSS" (exalted-carrier, selectable-sideband) tuning, this can be used in lieu of synchronous selectable sideband. However, in addition to the relative inconvenience of this technique, unlike synchronous selectable sideband, which re-phases continually and perfectly, ECSS is always slightly out of phase. This causes at least some degree of harmonic distortion to music and speech, while tuning to the nearest Hertz can generate slow-sweep fading (for this reason, mis-phasing by two or three Hertz may provide better results).

- Proper demodulation of modes used by non-world-band shortwave signals, except for models designed to be sold in certain countries. These modes include single sideband (LSB/USB) and CW ("Morse code"); also, with suitable ancillary devices, radioteletype (RTTY), frequency shift key (FSK) and radiofax (FAX).

- Meaningful signal-strength indication.
- Illuminated display.

What PASSPORT's Rating Symbols Mean

Star ratings: ✪✪✪✪✪ is best. Stars reflect overall performance and meaningful features, plus to some extent ergonomics and perceived build quality. Price, appearance, country of manufacture and the like are not taken into account. With tabletop models there is a slightly greater emphasis on the ability to flush out tough, hard-to-hear signals, as this is one of the main reasons these sets are chosen. Nevertheless, to facilitate comparison the tabletop rating standards are very similar to those used for the professional, portatop and portable models reviewed elsewhere in this PASSPORT.

Passport's Choice. La crème de la crème. Our test team's personal picks of the litter—models we would buy or have bought for our personal use. Unlike star ratings, these choices are unapologetically subjective.

🅒: A relative bargain, with decidedly more performance than the price would suggest. However, none of these receivers is cheap.

✪✪✪✪✪ 🗐 *Passport's Choice*
Drake R8B

Price: *R8B:* $1,499.00 in the United States. $2,275.00CAD in Canada. *MS8 Speaker:* US$59.00 in the United States. $89.00CAD in Canada. *VHF Converter:* US$269.00 plus $20 installation in the United States. $409.00CAD plus installation in Canada. *R8B Technical Manual:* $39.95 in the United States.

Pro: Superior all-round performance for listening to world band programs and hunting DX catches, as well as utility, amateur and mediumwave AM signals. Mellow, above-average audio quality,

Drake R8B: superb world band performance, proven technology.

especially with suitable outboard speaker or headphones (*see* Con). Synchronous selectable sideband excels at reducing distortion caused by selective fading, as well as at diminishing or eliminating adjacent-channel interference; also has synchronous double sideband. Five well-chosen bandwidths, four suitable for world band. Highly flexible operating controls, including a powerful tunable AF notch filter (tunes to 5,300 Hz AF, but *see* Con) and an excellent passband offset control. Established model, relatively free from production glitches and showing minor performance improvement over the years. Most-acceptable ergonomics of any five-star model (*see* Con). Tunes and displays in precise 10 Hz increments. Slow/fast/off AGC with superior performance characteristics. Exceptionally effective noise blanker. Helpful tuning features include 1,000 station presets and sophisticated scanning functions; presets can be quickly accessed via the tuning knob and slew buttons. Built-in switchable preamplifier. Accepts two antennas, selectable via front panel. Two 24-hour clocks, with seconds displayed numerically and two-event timer (*see* Con). Helpful operating manual. Power cord detaches handily from receiver, making it easy to replace. Fifteen-day money-back trial period if ordered from factory. Superior factory service.

Con: To exhibit its fidelity potential, the R8B needs a good outboard speaker for non-headphone listening; the optional Drake MS8 outboard speaker is not equal to this task, so instead try a good amplified computer speaker or high-efficiency passive speaker. Slight bassiness in audio, remediable through careful choice of the right outboard speaker. Neither clock shows when frequency displayed. Lightweight plastic tuning knob lacks any trace of flywheel effect (it helps noticeably if BBs are glued into the back of the knob); this, along with thin cabinet metal and mechanical frequency encoder in lieu of optical encoder used in original R8, exude an aura of cheesiness; nevertheless, years-long track record indicates that reliability is at least average. No IF output. Otherwise-excellent tilt bail difficult to open. Notch filter does not tune below 500 Hz (AF). Not available from dealers outside North America. When changing from 90-132V to 180-264V AC, a resistor must be removed from receiver, which for some users will require a technician. Optional VHF converter difficult to install; best is to have this done when receiver is purchased.

Verdict: There are models that are superior to the American-made Drake R8B in certain respects. And some other receivers are more technologically advanced in ways that may not always be relevant.

The R8B is priced below other top-end tabletop and professional models. Yet, although some other manufacturers have been lowering prices, Drake's R8B has become costlier even as the receiver's technology keeps getting longer in the tooth.

Nevertheless, the R8B is the only non-professional receiver tested that gets everything right—where something important isn't missing or sputtering, and ergonomics are worthy. This means there's little point spending money on such performance-enhancing accessories as the Sherwood SE-3 Mk III D, although a good outboard speaker enhances audio fidelity.

📋 An *RDI WHITE PAPER* is available for this model.

Enhanced for 2005
DRM Ready

✪✪✪✪✪

AOR AR7030, AOR AR7030/DRM, AOR AR7030+3, AOR AR7030+3/DRM

Price: *AR7030:* £749.00 in the United Kingdom. €1,140.00 in Germany. *AR7030/DRM:* £949.00 in the United Kingdom. *AR7030+3:* £899.00 in the United Kingdom. €1,298.00 in Germany. *AR7030+3/DRM:* £1,099.00 in the United Kingdom. €1,579.00 in Germany. *UPNB7030 Noise Blanker & Notch Upgrade:* €280.70 in Germany. *DRM software:* €60.00 worldwide from www.drmrx.org/purchase.php.

Pro: In terms of sheer performance for program listening, as good a radio as we've ever tested. Except for sensitivity to weak signals (*see* Con), easily overcome, the same comment applies to DX reception. Exceptionally quiet circuitry. Superior audio quality when used with a first-rate outboard speaker or audio system. Synchronous selectable sideband performs exceptionally well at reducing distortion caused by selective fading, as well as at diminishing or eliminating adjacent-channel interference; also has synchronous double sideband. Best dynamic range of any consumer-grade radio tested. Nearly all other lab measurements are top-drawer. Four voice bandwidths (2.3, 7.0, 8.2 and 10.3 kHz), with cascaded ceramic filters, come standard; up to six, either ceramic or mechanical, upon request (*see* Con). Advanced tuning and operating features aplenty, including passband tuning. Tunable audio (AF) notch and noise blanker now available, albeit as an option; notch filter extremely effective, with little loss of audio fidelity. Built-in preamplifier (*see* Con). Automatically self-aligns and centers all bandwidth filters for optimum performance, then displays the actual measured bandwidth of each. Remote keypad (*see* Con). Accepts two antennas. IF output. Optional improved processor unit now has 400 memories, including 14-character alphanumeric readout for station names. World Time 24-hour clock, which displays seconds, calendar and timer/sleep-delay features. Superior mediumwave AM performance. Variety of bandwidth, on-site diagnostic and field (battery) operation options. Superior service at the factory in England. *AR7030/DRM and AR7030+3/DRM:* Receives digital (DRM) world band broadcasts by connecting it to a PC using DRM software purchased separately.

Con: Unusually convoluted ergonomics, including tree-logic operating scheme, especially in +3 version; once the initial glow of ownership has passed, this may become tiresome. Remote control unit, which has to be aimed carefully at either the front or the back of the receiver, is required to use certain features, such as direct frequency entry; not all panelists were enthusiastic about this arrangement, wishing that a mouse-type umbilical cable had been used instead. Although the remote keypad can operate from across a room, the LCD characters are too small to be seen from such a distance. LCD omits certain important information, such as signal strength, when radio in various status modes. Sensitivity to weak signals good, as are related noise-floor measurements, but could be a bit better; a first-rate antenna, as indicated elsewhere in this PASSPORT, overcomes this. Because of peculiar built-in preamplifier/attenuator design in which the two are linked, receiver noise rises slightly when preamplifier used in +10 dB position, or attenuator used in –10 dB setting; however, +3 version remedies this. When six bandwidths used (four standard ceramics, two optional mechanicals), ultimate rejection, although superb with widest three bandwidths, cannot be measured beyond -80/-85 dB on narrowest three bandwidths because of phase noise; still, ultimate rejection is excellent or better with these narrow bandwidths. Lacks, and would profit from, a bandwidth of around 4 or 5 kHz; a Collins mechanical bandwidth filter of 3.5

kHz (nominal at –3 dB, measures 4.17 kHz at –6 dB) is an option worth considering. Such Collins filters, in the two optional bandwidth slots, measure as having poorer shape factors (1:1.8 to 1:2) than the standard-slot ceramic filters (1:1.5 to 1:1.6). LCD emits some digital electrical noise, potentially a problem only if an amplified (active) antenna is used with its pickup element (e.g. telescopic rod) placed near the receiver. Minor microphonics (audio feedback), typically when internal speaker is used, noted in laboratory; in actual listening, however, this is not noticeable; in any event, this is moot when an outboard speaker is used. Uses outboard AC adaptor instead of built-in power supply. No longer sold within North America, although available worldwide via export from England.

☞ Mechanical encoders on the '7030 used to have an above-average failure rate, seemingly because of corrosion on contacts. Starting from serial number 102050, with production as of late July, 1999, AOR has replaced the original Bourns mechanical encoder with a metal-encased version from Alps—the AR7030 now uses only Alps mechanical encoders, whereas the AR7030+3 uses Alps mechanical and Bourns optical encoders. A conversion kit for earlier units is available for £20 plus shipping, although it requires skill to install. Similarly, features of the +3 version can be

AOR's AR7030 series is no longer sold in North America, but has exceptional performance.

incorporated into existing regular models by skilled technicians.

Verdict: If you enjoy the BMW 745i, you'll be right at home with the AOR AR7030. Like the 745i, it not only has Star Trek ergonomics, but also performs right up there with the very best. It is said that the 745i makes you a better driver than you really are, so it just may be that the AR7030 will make you a better DXer than you really are.

Designed by John Thorpe and manufactured in England, the '7030 is an even better performer, and more robust, in its +3 incarnation. But those Bimmer iDrive-type ergonomics, already peculiar and cumbersome in the "barefoot" version, are even more challenging in the +3. For some, this is not a problem—indeed, it can provide an avant-garde cachet, like a Prius. But for a number of others it's just not worth the bother, and that includes our panelists. As a result the '7030 is reportedly a slow seller, but among its community of owners it is usually praised as the *ne plus ultra*.

Ergonomics and slightly limited sensitivity to weak signals aside, the '7030 is arguably the best choice—certainly among the best of choices—for serious DXing available on the scotch side of a professional-grade model. This is a receiver you'll really need to lay your hands on before you'll know whether it's love or hate—or something between.

Enhancement for 2005: For 2005 the '7030 and '7030+3 is also being offered "DRM ready." When mated to a PC and DRM software, these can receive DRM world band broadcasts. Earlier units can be retrofitted to be DRM ready, but only at the factory in England.

NUMBERS: TOP TWO TABLETOPS

	Drake R8B	AOR AR7030
Max. Sensitivity/Noise Floor	0.21 μV, $\mathbf{E}$[(1)]/–130 dBm, $\mathbf{E}$[(1)]	0.2 μV, $\mathbf{E}$/–128 dBm, $\mathbf{G}$
Blocking	136 dB, $\mathbf{S}$	>130 dB, $\mathbf{E}$
Shape Factors, voice BWs	1:1.96–1:2.70, $\mathbf{G}$	1:1.52–1:1.96, $\mathbf{E}$
Ultimate Rejection	75 dB, $\mathbf{E}$	90 dB, $\mathbf{S}$
Front-End Selectivity	$\mathbf{E}$	$\mathbf{F}$
Image Rejection	>90 dB, $\mathbf{S}$	>100 dB, $\mathbf{S}$
First IF Rejection	>90 dB, $\mathbf{S}$	95 dB, $\mathbf{S}$
Dynamic Range/IP3 (5 kHz)	77 dB, $\mathbf{E}$/–17 dBm, $\mathbf{E}$	82 dB, $\mathbf{E}$/+1 dBm, $\mathbf{S}$
Dynamic Range/IP3 (20 kHz)	93 dB, $\mathbf{E}$/+8 dBm, $\mathbf{E}$	100 dB, $\mathbf{S}$/+28 dBm, $\mathbf{S}$
Phase Noise	113 dBc, $\mathbf{G}$	130 dBc, $\mathbf{S}$
AGC Threshold	0.55 μV, $\mathbf{E}$	2.25 μV, $\mathbf{G}$
Overall Distortion, sync	0.6%, $\mathbf{S}$	2.0%, $\mathbf{E}$
Stability	25 Hz, $\mathbf{E}$	30 Hz, $\mathbf{E}$
Notch filter depth	55 dB, $\mathbf{S}$	55 dB, $\mathbf{S}$

IBS Lab Ratings: $\mathbf{S}$ Superb $\mathbf{E}$ Excellent $\mathbf{G}$ Good $\mathbf{F}$ Fair $\mathbf{P}$ Poor

(1) Preamp on; 0.45 μV $\mathbf{G}$/–124 dBm $\mathbf{G}$ with preamp off.

✪✪✪✪½
Japan Radio NRD-545

Price: $1,799.95 in the United States. $3,700.00CAD as available in Canada. £1,299.00 in the United Kingdom. €1,798.00 in Germany. $3,589.00AUD in Australia. *NVA-319 external speaker:* $199.95 in the United States. £199 in the United Kingdom. €259.00 in Germany. *CHE-199 VHF-UHF converter:* $369.95 in the United States. £289 in the United Kingdom. €398.00 in Germany. *CGD-197 frequency stabilizer:* $99.95 in the United States. E149.00 in Germany.

The Japan Radio NRD-545 offers digital signal processing at an attractive price.

Pro: Superior build quality, right down to the steel cabinet with machined screws. Easily upgraded by changing software ROMs. Fully 998 bandwidths provide unprecedented flexibility. Razor-sharp skirt selectivity, especially with voice bandwidths. Outstanding array of tuning aids, including 1,000 station presets (*see* Con). Wide array of reception aids, including passband offset, excellent manual/automatic tunable notch, and synchronous selectable sideband having good lock. Superb reception of single-sideband and other "utility" signals. Demodulates C-Quam AM stereo signals, which then need to be fed through an external audio amplifier, not provided (the headphone jack can't be used for this, as it is monaural). Highly adjustable AGC in all modes requiring BFO (*see* Con). Tunes in ultra-precise 1 Hz increments, although displays only in 10 Hz increments. Ergonomics, including the physical quality of tuning knob and other controls, among the very best. Some useful audio shaping. Computer interface with free NRDWIN software (*see* Con); among other things, is effective at processing RTTY signals. Virtually no spurious radiation of digital "buzz." Hiss-free audio-out port for recording or feeding low-power FM transmitter to hear world band around the house. Internal AC power supply is quiet and generates little heat. Power cord detaches handily from receiver, like on a PC, making it easy to replace. Includes a "CARE package" of all needed metric plugs and connectors, along with a 12V DC power cord.

Con: Ultimate rejection only fair, although average ultimate rejection equivalent is 10–15 dB better; this unusual gap comes about from intermodulation (IMD) inside the digital signal processor, and results in audible "monkey chatter" under certain specific reception conditions. Audio quality sometimes tough sledding in the unvarnished AM mode—using synchronous selectable sideband helps greatly. No AGC adjustment in AM mode or with synchronous selectable sideband, and lone AGC decay rate too fast. Dynamic range only fair. Synchronous selectable sideband sometimes slow to kick in. Notch filter won't attenuate heterodynes (whistles) any higher in pitch than 2,500 Hz AF. Noise reduction circuit only marginally useful. Signal-strength indicator overreads at higher levels. Frequency display misreads by up to 30 Hz, especially at higher tuned frequencies, and gets worse as the months pass by. Station presets don't store synchronous-AM settings. Audio amplifier lacks oomph with some poorly modulated signals. No IF output, nor can one be retrofitted. NRD Win software, at least the current v1.00, handles only uploads, not downloads, and works only on com port 1 that is usually already in use. World Time 24-hour clock doesn't show when frequency displayed. No tilt bail or feet. Anti-reflective paint on buttons and knobs becomes shiny with wear.

Verdict: In many ways Japan Radio's NRD-545 is a remarkable performer, especially for utility and tropical-bands DXing. With its first-class ergonomics and the fine feel of superior construction quality, it is always a pleasure to operate. Yet, more is needed to make this the ultimate receiver it could be. By now Japan Radio should have issued a ROM upgrade to remedy at least some of these long-standing issues, but contrary to urban legend *nada* as yet.

Whether "monkey chatter" and other manifestations of DSP overload are an issue varies markedly from one listening situation to another—some hear it, others don't. It depends on the specifics of the signal being received, what part of the world you are in and your own aural perceptions. Among our panelists, all noticed it eventually, but reaction varied from "no big deal" to howls of derision.

✪✪✪✪⅜
Japan Radio "NRD-545SE"

Price: *NRD-545SE:* $1,899.00 in the United States. *Retrofit to change an existing receiver to "SE":* $104.00 plus receiver shipping both ways.

Pro: Dynamic range, 5 kHz, improves from 66 dB to 73 dB.

Con: Not available outside North America. *With 8 kHz replacement filter:* Audio bandwidth reduced by 20 percent at the high end. *With 6 kHz replacement filter (not tested):* Audio bandwidth reduced by about 40 percent at the high end.

☞ For all except those who largely confine their listening to tough DX or utility catches, the 8 kHz filter is a preferable choice over the 6 kHz option.

Verdict: Sherwood Engineering, an American firm, replaces the stock DSP protection filter with one of two narrower filters of comparable quality. In principle, this should provide beaucoup decibels of audible improvement in the "monkey chatter" encountered on the

'545 from adjacent-channel signals. Perhaps, but we couldn't hear the difference. What was noticed, instead, was an unwelcome reduction in audio crispness with world band signals—as well as, of course, with mediumwave AM reception.

Some readers have tried this modification and take exception to our comments—they are pleased with the result. Given that the '545 is best suited to non-broadcast-listening applications, anyway, this makes sense. For these uses the aural drawback of the Sherwood modification can be less important than its 7 dB improvement in dynamic range.

But if your main interest is in listening to world band programs, this modification is not the way to go.

✪✪✪✪½ 🅒
Icom IC-R75/Icom IC-R75E (Kiwa version)

Price (Kiwa modifications): *Synchronous detector upgrade:* $45.00 in the United States. *Audio upgrade:* $35.00 in the United States.

Pro: Synchronous detection performance improved slightly, with synchronous selectable sideband actually being somewhat functional with a narrow-bandwidth setting. Added crispness marginally improves audio quality with wide IF bandwidth settings. Generally high-quality parts and installation. Exceptionally fast turnaround from Kiwa.

Con: When sync loses lock during deep fades, there is a heterodyne squeal or warble not evident before modification; slow AGC setting occasionally helps ameliorate this. Audio muffled when selectable synchronous sideband in upper-sideband setting, although lower sideband sounds appropriate. Slight increase in audible hiss with narrow bandwidth settings. In principle, modifications may invalidate Icom's warranty although in practice this may not be enforced, and they are not readily undone.

☞ Since our testing, another Kiwa modification, the $35 High Fidelity Audio Filter, has appeared. It extends audio response to just over 4 kHz and appears to be a worthwhile change.

Verdict: The two tested Kiwa modifications, particularly that for the synchronous detector, provide a slight improvement in the popular Icom IC-R75's performance. They are reasonably priced, but are best deferred until the factory warranty has expired.

Observations with Modified Receiver:
Over the years Icom's IC-R75 has come down in price to the point where it has become one of the best-selling tabletops on the market. Its performance with utility and ham signals is top-notch, making it a true bargain for monitoring non-broadcast transmissions. Alas, its synchronous selectable sideband performance is as bad as we've ever encountered, and this limits the 'R75's attractiveness for listening to world band broadcasters.

Enter the small American firm of Kiwa Electronics, which offers two modifications to help overcome the 'R75's world band performance deficiencies. The synchronous detector upgrade is achieved via the installation of a small "potted" cube affixed to the back microprocessor shield. As two pins of the sync chip are lifted and wired to the module, undoing the modification is no simple task.

The audio upgrade is achieved by changing a few capacitors. This is less difficult to undo than the sync mod, but requires yeoman soldering skills. Consequently, either modification is best put off until after the manufacturer's warranty expires. Unless the tech at Icom is in a magnanimous mood, either Kiwa modification may invalidate the receiver's warranty.

Just as the 'R75 has become popular because of its price, so, too, have the Kiwa modifications. The Sherwood SE-3 Mk III D device works wonders, but costs nearly as

With twofer offers, Icom's IC-R75 is one of world band radio's great values. Kiwa modifications improve listenability, too.

much as the receiver, making it a non-starter. Viewed in that context, the modest improvements provided by the upgrades become relatively interesting.

The stock 'R75's synchronous selectable sideband performance is pitiful. While the Kiwa upgrade doesn't turn this sow's ear into a silk purse or even a cotton tote bag, there is a degree of audible improvement and the price is right.

We ordered the modifications to our 'R75 "blind" so, we hoped, results wouldn't be tainted by our status as reviewers. Kiwa's workmanship and turnaround were both excellent.

✪✪✪✪⅜ ✐
Icom IC-R75/Icom IC-R75E

Price: *Receiver only:* $549.95 in the United States, sometimes lower depending on factory rebates and twofer offers. $899.00CAD in Canada. £649.00 in the United Kingdom. €749.00 in Germany. $1,610.00AUD in Australia. *UT-106 DSP unit:* $139.95 in the United States, although periodically it is bundled for free with the 'R75. $250.00CAD in Canada. £79.95 in the United Kingdom. €99.00 in Germany. $172.00AUD in Australia. *Icom Replacement Bandwidth Filters (e.g., FL-257 3.3 kHz):* $159.95 in the United States. €159.00 in Germany. *SP-23 amplified audio-shaping speaker:* $169.95 in the United States.

Pro: Dual passband offset acts as variable bandwidth and a form of IF shift (*see* Con). Reception of faint signals alongside powerful competing ones aided by excellent ultimate selectivity and good blocking. Excellent front-end selectivity, with seven filters for the shortwave range and more for elsewhere. Two levels of preamplification, 10 dB and 20 dB, can be switched off. Excellent weak-signal sensitivity and good AGC threshold with +20 dB preamplification. Superior rejection of spurious signals, including images. Excellent stability, essential for unattended reception of RTTY and certain other types of utility transmissions. Excels in reception of utility and ham signals, as well as world band signals tuned via "ECSS" technique. Ten tuning steps. Can tune and display in exacting 1 Hz increments (*see* Con). Adjustable UT-106 DSP audio accessory with automatic variable notch filter, normally an extra-cost option, helps to a degree in improving intelligibility, but not pleasantness, of some tough signals; also, it reduces heterodyne ("whistle") interference. Fairly good ergonomics, including smooth-turning weighted tuning knob; nice touch is spinning finger dimple, even if it doesn't spin very well. "Control Central" LCD easy to read and evenly illuminated by 24 LEDs with dimmer. Adjustable AGC—fast, slow, off. Tuning knob uses reliable optical encoder normally found only on professional receivers, rather than everyday mechanical variety. Low overall distortion. Pleasant and hiss-free audio with suitable outboard speaker; audio-shaping amplified Icom SP-20, although pricey, works well for a number of applications. 101 station presets. Two antenna inputs, switchable. Digital bar graph signal-strength indicator, although not as desirable as an analog meter, is unusually linear above S-9 and can be set to hold a peak reading briefly. Audio-out port for recording or feeding low-power FM transmitter to hear world band around the house. World Time 24-hour clock, timer and sleep delay (*see* Con). Tunes to 60 MHz, including 6 meter VHF ham band. Tilt bail (*see* Con).

Con: Synchronous detector virtually nonfunctional; operates reasonably only with modification by user or specialty firm, or by addition of a specialized auxiliary device. Dual passband offset usually has little impact on received world band signals and is inoperative when synchronous detection is in use. DSP's automatic variable notch tends not to work with AM-mode signals not received via "ECSS" technique (tuning AM-mode signals as though they were single sideband). Mediocre audio through internal speaker, and no tone control to offset slightly bassy reproduction that originates prior to the audio stage; audio improves to pleasant with an appropriate external speaker, especially one that offsets the receiver's slight bassiness. Suboptimal audio recovery with weak AM-mode signals having heavy fading; largely remediable by "ECSS" tuning and switching off AGC. Display misreads up to 20 Hz, somewhat negating the precise 1 Hz tuning. Keypad requires frequencies to be entered in MHz format with decimal or trailing zeroes, a pointless inconvenience. Some knobs small. Uses outboard "floor brick" AC adaptor in lieu of internal power supply; adaptor's emission field may be picked up by nearby indoor antennas or unshielded antenna lead-in wiring, which can cause minor hum on received signals (remediable by moving antenna or using shielded lead-in cable). Can read clock or presets IDs or frequency, but no more than one at the same time. RF/AGC control operates peculiarly. Tilt bail lacks rubber protection for furniture surface. Keyboard beep appears at audio line output. No schematic provided.

Verdict: The Japanese-made Icom IC-R75, formerly $800 in the United States, is now an excellent value. It is a first-rate receiver for unearthing tough utility and ham signals, as well as world band signals received via manual "ECSS" tuning—the receiver's exacting frequency steps facilitate tuning world band signals as though they were single sideband. For these applications nothing else equals it on the sunny side of a kilobuck.

It is less of an unqualified success for listening to world band broadcasts. Its hopeless synchronous detector performance is only very slightly improved by modifications from specialty firms like Kiwa (see preceding review). Sherwood's SE-3 Mk III D accessory brings the 'R75's fidelity to life by entirely replacing the synchronous and audio circuits, but it costs as much as the receiver and complicates operation.

If you're not in a hurry, consider waiting for the next time Icom offers the UT-106 DSP Unit, normally $140, free with the purchase of a new 'R75. Look for factory coupons, too—when added to a free UT-106 they make the 'R75 an incredible value.

Enhanced for 2005
DRM Ready
✪✪✪✪⅛
Ten-Tec RX-350D

Price: *RX-350D:* $1,199.00 in the United States. £999.00 in the United Kingdom. $2,175.00AUD in Australia. *302R external keypad/tuning knob:* $139.00 in the United States. £129.00 in the United Kingdom. *307B external speaker:* $98.00 in the United States. £89.00 in the United Kingdom.

Pro: DRM ready (a modification, not tested by us, for pre-"D" versions of the RX-350 is described at http://home.satx.rr.com/ ka5jgv/RX-350Mod.htm). Receiver is unlikely to become dated for some time, as many aspects of performance and operation can be readily updated, thus far and presumably always for free, by downloading revised firmware from the manufacturer's website (*see* Con); except for clock, all memory, including for firmware, is non-volatile and thus not dependent on battery backup.

Ten-Tec emphasizes DRM digital reception, so the RX-350D comes digital ready.

Lowest-cost tabletop model available with genuine DSP bandwidth filtering. A superb choice of no less than 34 bandwidths, including at least a dozen suitable for world band reception. Numerous helpful tuning features—front-panel tuning knob; up/down frequency and band slew; 1024 station presets divided into eight banks with alphanumeric station indicators; sophisticated scanning; optional keypad/tuning knob; and two VFOs. Optional external keypad/tuning knob is handy, comfortable and works well (*see* Con); it allows for frequency entry not only in Megahertz, but also in kilohertz via the enter key if the leading zero is entered first for frequencies under 10000 kHz. Tuning knobs on receiver and outboard keypad both use a reliable optical encoder normally found only on professional receivers, rather than the everyday mechanical variety. Tunes and displays in ultra-precise 1 Hz increments (*see* Con). Superior close-in (5 kHz separation) dynamic range/IP3. Excellent passband offset works in all non-FM modes, providing (in addition to the handy AML/AMU settings) selectable sideband for the synchronous detector (*see* Con). Generally worthy ergonomics with large display and seven useful tuning steps; also, bandwidths and station presets conveniently selectable by knob (*see* Con), and controls have good tactile feel—especially the large, weighted metal tuning knob with rubber edging (*see* Con). Punchy, above-average audio with low overall distortion adds to enjoyment of music and enhances intelligibility, especially with suitable external speaker (*see* Con). Audio-out port for recording or feeding low-power FM transmitter to hear world band around the house. Unlike a number of other DSP receivers, does not make static crashes sound harsh; additionally, DSP noise reduction feature can moderate static noise a bit more. DSP noise reduction also of some use in improving aural quality of certain received signals (*see* Con). Receiver emits very little radiated digital "buzz," so inverted-L antennas with single-wire feedlines and proximate loop antennas don't suffer from noise pickup. Rock stable, essential for unattended reception of RTTY and certain other types of utility transmissions. Notch filter automatic, effective over a wide range (0.1 to over 8.0 kHz AF), and can attenuate more than one heterodyne at a time (*see* Con). AGC threshold, originally poor, improved to excellent in latest version. Signal-strength indicator unusually accurate (*see* Con). More likely than most other models to be adaptable to possible future digital world band transmissions. Soft and hard microprocessor resets provide useful flexibility in case receiver's "computer" gets its knickers in a twist. AC power supply is inboard, where it belongs, and does not run hot. Tilt bail places receiver at handy angle for operation (*see* Con). Timer.

Con: Poor front-end selectivity; so, for example, local mediumwave AM stations can cross-modulate with other local stations and even world band stations 4 MHz and below. RF preamplifier cannot be switched off to help prevent overloading. Our receiver froze up periodically; also, when going from memory channels back to a VFO, display showed invalid frequencies in the 45 to 94 MHz range (*see* ☞). Significant phase noise kept us from meaningfully measuring dynamic range/IP3 at 20 kHz separation; it also precluded plausible skirt-selectivity and ultimate rejection measurements. Synchronous selectable sideband loses lock easily during fades, albeit without causing whistling.

Circuit hiss with widest bandwidths, a common syndrome with DSP receivers, although the noise reduction feature helps. Spectrum display of marginal utility—limited visual indication, poor contrast, significant time lag and it mutes the receiver during sweep; potentially the most useful range shown in the owner's manual is 120 kHz, but this does not appear in the receiver's menu. Keypad costs extra, even though it is virtually a necessity; it also comes with a remote tuning knob that some may find redundant and which adds to size and cost. Optional outboard keypad has intermittent frequency-entry hesitation. On one unit the display misread up to 30 Hz, somewhat negating the precise 1 Hz tuning; other samples did better. Ineffective noise blanker—DSP, not IF—unnecessarily complicated to turn on as instructed via menu (not indicated in the owner's manual, but the key combination of Alt NR can turn it on more simply), and its 1–7 adjustment needs to be at 5 or above to really work. AM-mode signals, whether received in the conventional AM mode or synchronous, sound harsh with fast AGC. No AGC off. Friction when turning knobs, at least with samples tested; remediable by easing knobs slightly away from front panel (with tuning knob, remove rubber edging to access hex screw). Passband offset requires many turns of the knob to shift the setting significantly with AM-mode or synchronous (SAM) reception, although not in other modes. Automatic notch filter can't be tuned manually in CW and RTTY reception modes, so the notch automatically impacts the desired signal along with any heterodyne(s). Signal-strength indicator's format, using numeric decibels and a short displayed scale, generally disliked by panelists. Noise reduction not adjustable, and solitary setting sometimes reduces intelligibility. Audio control in original version required more than three turns from soft to loud, although revised version uses the traditional single turn; however, as a result the audio scale display now shows 25 percent when the control is set to 100 percent. Unusual 9-pin-to-9-pin serial cable needed to download software not included with receiver. A number of commonly used controls are on the left, inconvenient for northpaws. No IF output. User reports in the past have told of display illumination flickering, then failing, necessitating a $55 factory repair; display board is made in China. Tilt bail lacks protective rubber sheathing. Neither speaker wire can connect to ground, so an external speaker should not have a grounded cabinet (the 307B is appropriate in this regard).

☞ Two of our three units tested suffered from periodic freezing, or lockup, and occasional peculiar display readings. All were resolved by turning the receiver off, then back on again after no more than ten minutes, but re-downloading the firmware made no difference. The manufacturer insists these are sample defects, although to us it appears to have the earmarks of an inherent, but remediable, firmware cause.

Verdict: Ten-Tec indicated *years* back that it would shortly resolve the RX-350's poor front-end with a hardware fix, and even retrofitted our original receiver with an advance version of a front-end selectivity enhancement. Software fixes for various other problems were expected, as well.

None of these upgrades have materialized.

Enhancement for 2005: Although the '350's debugging seems to have been lost in Ten-Tec's Department of High Intentions, a useful new feature has appeared: a 12 kHz IF output to allow the receiver to interface with a suitably equipped PC and DRM software to receive DRM digital world band radio transmissions.

✪✪✪✪
Icom IC-R8500A

Price: *IC-R8500A-02 (no cellular reception):* $1,499.95 in the United States, the exact price depending on factory rebates, if any,

available at the time. *IC-R8500A:* $1,749.95 for government use or export in the United States. $2,599.00CAD in Canada. £1,149.00 in the United Kingdom. €1,398.00 in Germany. $3,480.00AUD in Australia. *CR-293 frequency stabilizer:* $269.95 in the United States. £89.99 in the United Kingdom. €109.00 in Germany. *External speakers:* Up to three Icom speakers available worldwide, with prices ranging from under $65 to $220 or equivalent. *Aftermarket Sherwood SE-3 Mk III D:* $549.00 in the United States. *Aftermarket BHT DSP noise canceller (www.radio.bhinstrumentation.co.uk/index.html):* under £90 in the United Kingdom.

Pro: Wide-spectrum multimode coverage from 0.1-2000 MHz includes longwave, mediumwave AM, shortwave and scanner frequencies. Physically very rugged, with professional-grade cast-aluminum chassis and impressive computer-type innards. Generally superior ergonomics, with generous-sized front panel having large and well-spaced controls, plus outstanding tuning knob with numerous tuning steps. 1,000 station presets and 100 auto-write presets have handy naming function. Superb weak-signal sensitivity. Pleasant, low-distortion audio aided by audio peak filter. Passband tuning ("IF shift"). Unusually readable LCD. Tunes and displays in precise 10 Hz increments. Three antenna connections. Clock-timer, combined with record output and recorder-activation jack, make for superior hands-off recording of favorite programs, as well as for feeding a low-

Icom offers superior broadband receivers, including this IC-R8500A tabletop.

power FM transmitter to hear world band around the house.

Con: No synchronous selectable sideband. Bandwidth choices for world band and other AM-mode signals leap from a very narrow 2.7 kHz to a broad 7.1 kHz with nothing between, where something is most needed; third bandwidth is 13.7 kHz, too wide for world band, and no provision is made for a fourth bandwidth filter. Only one single-sideband bandwidth. Unhandy carousel-style bandwidth selection with no permanent indication of which bandwidth is in use. Poor dynamic range, surprising at this price point. Passband tuning ("IF shift") does not work in the AM mode, used by world band and mediumwave AM-band stations. No tunable notch filter. Built-in speaker mediocre. Uses outboard AC adaptor instead of inboard power supply.

☞ The Icom IC-R8500 is available in two similarly priced versions. That sold to the public in the United States is blocked so it cannot receive the 824-849 and 869-894 MHz cellular bands. In the U.S., the un-blocked version is sold only to government-approved organizations, although Canadian mail-order firms will ship this version to customers in the United States

☞ Also tested with Sherwood SE-3 Mk III D aftermarket accessory, which proved to be outstanding at adding selectable synchro-nous sideband. It also provides passband tuning in the AM mode used by nearly all world band stations. Adding the SE-3 and

replacing the widest bandwidth with a 4 to 5 kHz bandwidth filter dramatically improve performance on shortwave, mediumwave AM and longwave.

Verdict: The large Icom IC-R8500 is a scanner that happens to cover world band, rather than *vice versa*.

As a standalone world band radio, this Japanese-made wideband receiver makes little sense. Yet, it is well worth considering if you want an all-in-one scanner that also serves as a shortwave receiver.

DRM Modifiable
✪✪✪✪
AOR AR5000A+3

Price: *AR5000A+3 (cellular-blocked version) receiver:* about $2,100.00 in the United States. *AR5000A+3 (full-coverage version) receiver:* $2,469.95 in the United States. $3,799.00CAD in Canada. £1,799.00 in the United Kingdom. €2,298.00 as available in Germany. *Collins 6 kHz mechanical filter (recommended):* $99.95 in the United States. £76.00 in the United Kingdom. *SDU-5600 spectrum display unit:* $1,499.95 in the United States. $2,099CAD in Canada. €1,155.00 in Germany.

Pro: Ultra-wide-spectrum multimode coverage from 0.01-3,000 MHz includes longwave, mediumwave AM, shortwave and scanner frequencies. Helpful tuning features include 2,000 station presets in 20 banks of 100 presets each. Narrow bandwidth filter and optional Collins wide filter both have superb skirt selectivity (standard wide filter's skirt selectivity unmeasurable because of limited ultimate rejection). Synchronous selectable and double sideband (*see* Con). Front-end selectivity, image rejection, IF rejection, weak-signal sensitivity, AGC threshold and frequency stability all superior. Exceptionally precise frequency readout to nearest Hertz. Most accurate displayed frequency measurement of any receiver

The broadband AOR AR5000A+3 can be modified to receive DRM digital broadcasts.

tested to date. Superb circuit shielding results in virtually zero radiated digital "buzz." IF output (*see* Con). DRM modifiable; see www.aoruk.com/drm.htm#ar5000_drm or www.drmrx.org/receiver_mods.html. Automatic Frequency Control (AFC) works on AM-mode, as well as FM, signals. Owner's manual, important because of operating system, unusually helpful.

Con: Synchronous detector loses lock easily, especially if selectable sideband feature in use, greatly detracting from the utility of this high-tech feature. Substandard rejection of unwanted sideband with selectable synchronous sideband. Overall distortion rises when synchronous detector used. Ultimate rejection of "narrow" 2.7 kHz bandwidth filter only 60 dB. Ultimate rejection mediocre (50 dB) with standard 7.6 kHz "wide" bandwidth filter, improves to an uninspiring 60 dB when replaced by optional 6 kHz "wide" Collins mechanical filter. Installation of optional Collins filter requires expertise, patience and special equipment. Poor dynamic range. Cumbersome ergonomics. No passband offset. No tunable notch filter. Needs good external speaker for good audio quality. World Time 24-hour clock does not show when frequency displayed. IF output frequency 10.7 MHz instead of standard 455 kHz.

Verdict: Unbeatable in some respects, inferior in others—it comes down to what use you will be putting the radio. The optional 6 kHz Collins filter is strongly recommended, but it should be installed by your dealer at the time of purchase. Although some AOR receivers are engineered and made in the United Kingdom, this model is designed and manufactured in Japan.

✪✪✪✪
Palstar R30C/CC/Sherwood

Price: *Sherwood SE-3 Mk III D:* $549.00 in the United States. *Palstar R30C/CC:* See below.

Pro: SE-3 provides nearly flawless synchronous selectable sideband, reducing adjacent-channel interference while enhancing audio fidelity. Foolproof installation; plugs right into the Palstar's existing IF output.

Con: Buzz occasionally heard during weak-signal reception. SE-3 costs roughly as much as a regular Palstar receiver.

Verdict: If you're going to spend $550 to upgrade a $575-650 receiver, you may as well spring for a Drake R8B.

Discontinued Version for 2005
✪✪✪⅛ *@*
Palstar R30C, Palstar R30CC

Price: *R30C:* $575.00 in the United States. $799.00CAD in Canada. *R30CC:* $650.00 in the United States. $869CAD in Canada. *SP30 speaker:* $59.95 in the United States. $89.00CAD in Canada. £59.95 in the U.K.

☞ We tested the basic version with two MuRata bandwidth filters; this was discontinued abruptly just before we went to press. We also tested the CC version, but not the C version. The C version is identical to the discontinued version, but uses a MuRata filter only in the wide position, with a Collins mechanical filter in the narrow setting. That same narrow Collins filter is used in the CC version, but there's a Collins filter in the wide position.

Pro: Generally good dynamic range. Overall distortion averages 0.5 percent, superb, in single-sideband mode (in AM mode, averages 2.9 percent, good, at 60% modulation and

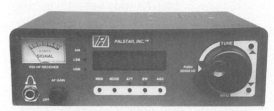

Features are scant on the Palstar R30C/CC, but what it does is done well.

4.4 percent, fair, at 95% modulation) (see Con, R30CC). Every other performance variable measures either good or excellent in PASSPORT's lab; four variables measure slightly better, two slightly worse than in our tests for PASSPORT 2001; also, former "birdies" now nearly all gone. Excellent AGC performance with AM-mode and single-sideband signals. Robust physical construction of cabinet and related hardware. Microprocessor section well shielded to minimize radiation of digital "buzz." Features include selectable slow/fast AGC decay (see Con), 20–100 Hz/100–500 Hz VRIT (slow/fast variable-rate incremental tuning) knob, 0.5 MHz slew and 455 kHz IF output. One hundred non-volatile station presets, using a generally well-thought-out scheme (see Con); they store frequency, bandwidth, mode, AGC setting and attenuator setting; also, presets displayed by channel number or frequency. Excellent illuminated analog signal-strength meter reads in useful S1-9/+60 dB standard and is reasonably accurate (see Con). LCD and signal-strength indicator illumination can be switched off. Also operates from ten firmly secured "AA" internal batteries (see Con). Lightweight and small (see Con). Good AM-mode sensitivity within longwave and mediumwave AM bands. Audio line output has suitable level and is properly located on back panel. Self-resetting circuit breaker for outboard power (e.g., AC adaptor); fuse used with internal batteries and comes with spare fuses. Tilt bail quite useful (see Con). Optional AA30A and AM-30 active antennas, evaluated elsewhere in this PASSPORT REPORTS. R30C: Pleasant audio quality with wide (7.7 kHz) bandwidth (see Con). R30CC: Virtually superb skirt selectivity (1:1.4 wide and 1:1.5 narrow) and ultimate rejection (90 dB); bandwidths measure 6.3 kHz and 2.6 kHz, using Collins mechanical filters. Adjacent-channel 5 kHz heterodyne whistles largely absent with wide bandwidth (see Con, R30CC).

Con: No keypad for direct frequency entry, not even as an outboard mouse-type option; only some of the very cheapest of portables now don't come with or offer a keypad. No 5 kHz tuning step choice to aid in bandscanning. Lacks control to hop from one world band segment to another; instead, uses 0.5 MHz fast-slew increments. No synchronous selectable sideband without pricey Sherwood SE-3 Mk III D aftermarket accessory (see preceding review). ECSS tuning can be up to 10 Hz out of phase because of 20 Hz minimum tuning increment. Mechanical tuning encoder play gives tuning knob sloppy feel, making precise ECSS tuning difficult; an optical encoder could have helped avoided this while adding to reliability. Lacks features found in top-gun receivers, such as tunable notch filter, noise blanker, passband tuning and adjustable RF gain. Recovered audio fine with most signals, but with truly weak signals is not of the DX caliber found with top-gun receivers. No visual indication of which bandwidth is being used. No tone controls. Small identical front-panel buttons, including the MEM button which if accidentally pressed can erase a preset. Station presets not as intuitive or easy to select as with various other models; lacks frequency information on existing presets during memory storage. Lightweight plastic tuning knob lacks mass to provide good tuning feel. No AGC off. No RF gain control. Uses AC adaptor instead of built-in power supply. High battery consumption. Batteries frustratingly difficult to install, requiring partial disassembly of the receiver and care not to damage speaker connections or confuse polarities. Receiver's lightness and tilt bail's lack of rubber sheathing allow it to slide around, especially when tuning knob pushed to change VRIT increments; the added weight of batteries helps slightly. Unsheathed tilt bail digs into some surfaces. Mono headphone jack produces output in only one ear of stereo 'phones (remedied by user-purchased mono-to-stereo adaptor). Signal-strength meter illumination dims when volume turned high with AM-mode signals; LCD illumination unaffected. Three bulbs used for illumination are soldered into place, making replacement difficult, although they should last a very long time. *R30C:* Wide bandwidth slightly broad for a model lacking synchronous selectable sideband, often allowing adjacent-channel (5 kHz) heterodyne whistles to be heard; largely remedied by detuning 1–2 kHz, which unlike with some receivers doesn't significantly increase distortion. *R30CC:* Intermittent microphonics in AM mode when using narrow bandwidth and internal speaker. Audio frequency response with wide filter makes for slightly muffled audio as compared with R30C; largely remedied by detuning 1–2 kHz, which unlike with some receivers doesn't significantly increase distortion.

☞ Works best when grounded.

Verdict: Although the Ohio-made Palstar R30C/CC receivers are conspicuously lacking in tuning and performance features, what they set out to do, they tends to do to a high standard. If you can abide the convoluted battery installation procedure and don't mind having to add an outboard antenna, either version can work as a field portable.

Nevertheless, these receivers lack a distinct identity. Although audio is fairly pleasant, especially in the original and discontinued basic version, there isn't synchronous selectable sideband that's needed to make it a premium listener's radio.

The lack of operating features is especially disappointing—not even a keypad, something routinely found on portables costing a fraction as much. And the lack of signal-tweaking features, along with pedestrian weak-signal recovered audio, preclude serious DX use.

Yet, not everybody fits neatly into routine categories. One size doesn't fit all, and to that end the straightforward concept and physical robustness arguably make it a better heir to the legendary Yaesu FRG-7 tradition than even the Yaesu FRG-100 *(see)*.

Yaesu's FRG-100 is discontinued, but units should be available for months.

✪✪✪¼ ◶ 📄
Yaesu FRG-100 (as available)

Price: *FRG-100:* $599.95 in the United States. $899.00CAD in Canada. £449.00 in the United Kingdom. *TCXO-4 frequency stabilizer:* $99.00 in the United States. £45.00 in the United Kingdom. *Universal Radio remote-control module and controller:* $94.90 in the United States.

Pro: Excellent performance in many respects. Includes three bandwidths, a noise blanker, selectable AGC, two attenuators, the ability to select 16 pre-programmed world band segments, two clocks, on-off timers, 52 tunable station presets that store frequency and mode data, a variety of scanning schemes and an all-mode squelch.

Con: No factory-provided keypad for direct frequency entry, although a two-part user-installable aftermarket infrared keypad system is available by post from at least one American source (Universal Radio); it also allows for remote control of a variety of receiver functions, although not volume. No synchronous selectable sideband. Lacks features found in "top-gun" receivers: passband tuning, notch filter, adjustable RF gain. Simple controls and display, combined with complex functions, can make certain operations confusing. Dynamic range only fair. Uses AC adaptor instead of built-in power supply.

☞ In 1999 the FRG-100 was discontinued, only to continue to be sold to dealers. In

2001 it was again "discontinued," but kept being sold anyway. In mid-2004 it was yet again officially proclaimed as discontinued.

This third strike appears to have finally put it out. According to a reliable source, in the latter half of 2004 the only units left worldwide were whatever remained in dealer inventories plus a few dozen stored in a Yaesu warehouse.

Verdict: Last call! The receiver that wouldn't die finally appears to be headed to world band Valhalla.

In the tradition of the Yaesu FRG-7 that started it all, this minimalist model is sparse on factory-provided features. Yet, the FRG-100 succeeds in delivering worthy performance within an attractive price class.

Too late? Check out the Palstar R30C/CC, above.

An *RDI WHITE PAPER* is available for this model.

✪✪✪ ✇
Yaesu VR-5000

Price: *VR-5000 Receiver, including single-voltage AC adaptor:* $599.95 in the United States. $899.00CAD or more in Canada. £579.00 in the United Kingdom. €649.00 in Germany. $1,399.00AUD in Australia. *DSP-1 digital notch, bandpass and noise reduction unit:* $119.95 in the United States. $199.00CAD in Canada. £94.95 in the United Kingdom. €98.00 in Germany. *DVS-4*

The Yaesu VR-5000 provides broadband reception at relatively low cost.

16-second digital audio recorder: $47.00 in the United States. $80.00CAD in Canada. £29.95 in the United Kingdom. €39.00 in Germany. *FVS-1A voice synthesizer (as available):* $75.00CAD in Canada. £39.95 in the United Kingdom. €55.00 in Germany. *RadioShack 22-504 aftermarket 120V AC>13.8V DC power supply:* $39.99 in the United States.

Pro: Unusually wide frequency coverage, 100 kHz through 2.6 GHz (U.S. version omits cellular frequencies 869–894 MHz). Two thousand alphanumeric-displayed station presets, which can be linked to any of up to 100 groupings of presets. Up to 50 programmable start/stop search ranges. Large and potentially useful "band scope" spectrum display (*see* Con). Bandwidths have superb skirt selectivity, with shape factors between 1:1.3 and 1:1.4. Wide AM bandwidth (17.2 kHz) allows local mediumwave AM stations to be received with superior fidelity (*see* Con). Flexible software settings provide a high degree of control over selected parameters. Sophisticated scanning choices, although they are of limited use because of false signals generated by receiver's inadequate dynamic range (*see* Con). Dual-receive function, with sub-receiver circuitry feeding "band scope" spectrum display; when display not in use, two signals may be monitored simultaneously, provided they are within 20 MHz of each other. Sensitivity to weak signals excellent-to-superb within shortwave spectrum, although combined with receiver's inadequate dynamic range this tends to cause overloading when a worthy antenna is used (*see* Con). Appears to be robustly constructed. External spectrum display, fed by receiver's 10.7 MHz IF output, can perform very well for narrow-parameter scans (*see* Con). Two 24-hour clocks, both of which are shown except when spectrum display mode is in use; one clock tied into an elementary map display and database of time in a wide choice of world cities. On-off timer allows for up to 48 automatic events. Sleep-delay/alarm timers. Lightweight and compact. Multi-level display dimmer. Optional DSP unit includes adjustable notch filtering, a bandpass feature and noise reduction (*see* Con). Tone control. Built-in "CAT" computer control interface (*see* Con). Control and memory backup/management software available from www.g4hfq.co.uk.

Con: Exceptionally poor dynamic range (49 dB at 5 kHz separation, 64 dB at 20 kHz) and IF/image rejection (as low as 30 dB) for a tabletop model; for listeners in such high-signal parts of the world as Europe, North Africa and eastern North America, this shortcoming all but cripples reception of shortwave signals unless a very modest antenna is used; the degree to which VHF-UHF is degraded depends *inter alia* upon the extent of powerful transmissions in the vicinity of the receiver. No synchronous selectable sideband, a major drawback for world band and mediumwave AM listening, but not for shortwave utility/ham, VHF or UHF reception. Has only one single-

sideband bandwidth, a relatively broad 4.0 kHz. Wide AM bandwidth (17.2 kHz) of no use for shortwave reception. For world band listening, the middle (8.7 kHz) AM bandwidth lets through adjacent-channel 5 kHz heterodyne, while narrow bandwidth (consistently 3.9 kHz, not the 4.0 kHz of the SSB bandwidth) produces muffled audio. Line output level low. Audio distorts at higher volume settings. Limited bass response. Audio hissy, especially noticeable with a good outboard speaker. DSP-1 option a mediocre overall performer and adds distortion. Phase noise measures 94 dBc, poor. AGC threshold measures 11 microvolts, poor. No adjustment of AGC decay. Single-sideband AGC decay too slow. Most recent sample's (firmware v1u.17) tuning encoder sometimes has rotational delay that requires three clicks instead of one to commence down-frequency tuning when reversing direction from clockwise to counterclockwise. Mediocre tuning-knob feel. Signal-strength indicator has only five levels and overreads; an alternative soft-

BUILD YOUR OWN

Most shortwave kits are novelties or regenerative radios. But there is one exception: Ten-Tec's small 1254 world band radio, $195. Parts quality for this superheterodyne appears to be excellent, while assembly runs at least 24 hours. It has 15 station presets, but lacks keypad, signal-strength indicator, synchronous selectable sideband, tilt bail, LSB/USB settings and adjustable AGC. Tuning increments are 500 Hz for single sideband and 5 kHz for AM-mode, plus there is an analog clarifier for tweaking between increments.

Phase noise, front-end selectivity, and longwave and mediumwave AM sensitivity are poor. Bandwidth is a respectable 5.6 kHz, and there is worthy ultimate rejection, image rejection, world band sensitivity, blocking, AGC threshold and frequency stability. Dynamic range and first IF rejection are fair, while overall distortion is good—with an external speaker, audio is pleasant.

The Ten-Tec 1254 is a fun weekend project, and the manufacturer's track record for hand-holding means that when you're through the radio should really work.

Ten-Tec's 1254 is the best kit available.

ware-selectable signal-strength indicator—not easy to get in and out of—has no markings other than a single reference level. Built-in spectrum display's dynamic range only 20 dB (–80 to –100 dBm), with a very slow scan rate. Single-sideband frequency readout of latest sample more accurate, but after warmup LSB is still 70 Hz and USB 100 Hz off. Long learning curve: Thirty buttons (often densely spaced, lilliputian and multifunction)—along with carouseling mode/tune-step selection and a menu-driven command scheme—combine to produce ergonomics that are not intuitive. Only one low-impedance antenna connector, inadequate for a wideband device that calls for multiple antennas. Longwave sensitivity mediocre. Clocks don't display seconds numerically. Marginal display contrast. Although four LEDs used for backlighting, the result is unevenly distributed. Uses AC adaptor instead of built-in power supply; adaptor and receiver both tend to run warm. Repeated microprocessor lockups, sometimes displayed as "ERROR LOW VOLTAGE," even though the receiver now comes with a 7.2V NiCd battery pack to help prevent this; unplugging set for ten minutes resolves problem until it occurs again, but the only permanent solution appears to be replacing the receiver's AC adaptor with a properly bypassed and regulated non-switching AC adaptor/DC power supply of at least one ampere that produces no less than 13.5V DC—certainly no less than 13.2V DC—and no more than

13.8V DC (we use a lab power supply, but in North America the RadioShack 22-504 appears promising). Even with aforementioned battery, clock has to be reset if power fails. Squelch doesn't function through audio line output (for recording, etc.). Line output gain is somewhat low. Sub-receiver doesn't feed line output. Computer interface lacks viable command structure, limiting usefulness. Tilt feet have inadequate rise. Owner's manual (0104q-DY) doesn't cover all receiver functions, so user has to learn much by trial and error. *United States:* Based on our recent experiences, customer support appears to be indifferent.

Verdict: With existing technology, DC-to-daylight receivers which provide excellent shortwave performance are costly to produce, and thus expensive.

The relatively affordable wideband Yaesu VR-5000 tries to overcome this. This Japanese-made model acts as a VHF/UHF scanner as well as a shortwave receiver, but falls woefully shy for world band reception in strong-signal parts of the world. Elsewhere, it fares better on shortwave, especially if a modest antenna is used. VHF/UHF performance depends on the number and strength of local transmitters.

DRM Modifiable

✪✪✪   ✐

AKD Target HF-3M, NASA HF-4/HF-4E/S, SI-TEX NAV-FAX 200

Price: *HF-3M/HF-4/HF-4E:* £149.95 in the United Kingdom. *HF-4E/S:* £159.95 in the United Kingdom. €298.00 in Germany. *PA30 antenna:* €45.50 in Germany. *NAV-FAX 200 (www.si-tex.com):* $399.00 in the United States. *SI-TEX ACNF 120V AC adaptor:* $19.95 in the United States.

Pro: Superior rejection of images. High third-order intercept point for superior strong-signal handling capability. Bandwidths have superb ultimate rejection. *HF-4/HF-4E/*

Target's HF-3M has few features, but can be modified for digital reception.

HF-4E/S: Two AM-mode bandwidths. DRM modifiable (www.drmrx.org/ receiver_mods.html). Illuminated LCD. *Except NAV-FAX 200:* Comes with DOS software for weatherfax ("WEFAX") reception using a PC; software upgrade may be in the offing. *NAV-FAX 200:* Comes with Mscan Meteo Pro Lite software (www.mscan.com) for WEFAX, RTTY and NAVTEX reception using a PC with Windows XP or earlier. Comes with wire antenna and audio patch cable. Two-year warranty, with repair facility in Florida.

Con: No keypad, and variable-rate tuning knob is difficult to control. Broad skirt selectivity. Single-sideband bandwidth relatively wide. Volume control fussy to adjust. Synthesizer tunes in relatively coarse 1 kHz increments, supplemented by an analog fine-tuning "clarifier" control. Only ten station presets. Single sideband requires both tuning controls to be adjusted. No synchronous selectable sideband, notch filter or passband tuning. Frequency readout off by 2 kHz in single-sideband mode. Uses AC adaptor instead of built-in power supply. No clock, timer or sleep-delay feature. *HF3M:* Bandwidths not selectable independent of mode. Only AM-mode bandwidth functions for world band reception. LCD not illuminated. *Except NAV-FAX 200:* Apparently not available outside United Kingdom.

Verdict: Pleasant world band performance at an affordable price, although numerous features are absent and operation is more frustrating than on many other models. Logical for yachting.

✪✪
Realistic DX-394 (as available)

Price: £199.95 in the United Kingdom.

Pro: Helpful tuning features include 160 tunable presets (*see* Con). Tunes in precise 10 Hz increments. Modest size, light weight and built-in telescopic antenna provide some portable capability. Bandwidths have superior shape factors and ultimate rejec-

The Realistic DX-394 is long gone from Radio Shack, but sells in the U.K.

tion. Two 24-hour clocks, one of which shows independent of frequency display. Five programmable timers. 30/60 minute snooze feature. Noise blanker.

Con: What appear to be four bandwidths turn out to be virtually one bandwidth, and it is too wide for optimum reception of many signals. Bandwidths, such as they are, not selectable independent of mode. No synchronous selectable sideband. Presets cumbersome to use. Poor dynamic range for a tabletop, a potential problem in Europe and other strong-signal parts of the world if an external antenna is used. Overall distortion, although acceptable, higher than desirable.

Verdict: Nominally discontinued, but still sometimes available in the United Kingdom. Modest dimensions, equally modest performance.

_____

The PASSPORT *tabletop-model review team consists of Lawrence Magne, David Zantow and George Zeller; also, George Heidelman, Tony Jones, Chuck Rippel and David Walcutt, with Craig Tyson. Laboratory measurements by J. Robert Sherwood.*

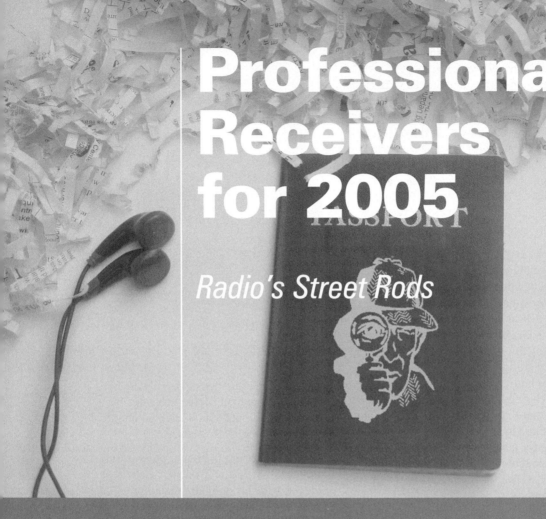

Professional Receivers for 2005

Radio's Street Rods

Professional-grade receivers are designed for commercial, maritime, surveillance and military uses. Requirements for these applications have much in common with the needs of world band listening. Yet, there are enough differences that these models are not always as suitable for world band use as consumer-grade offerings.

Some variants make for better results, others worse. But when it all comes together, as it does with the models tested for PASSPORT, professional hardware excels in snaring DX rarities.

Three Little Piggies

There are three key categories of professional receivers: easy for human operation, complex for human operation and no human operation.

The first are designed so personnel can tune "utility" signals with minimal training. After all, if an AWACS plane takes shrapnel and the radioman is unable to function, the more straightforward a radio is to operate, the more likely it is that other crew members will be able to carry on. Trouble is, simplicity of operation can also result in performance compromises.

The second category goes to the other extreme, offering "no holds barred" features and performance. These assume a high degree of operator skill, and are the type we analyze in this portion of PASSPORT REPORTS. If only the very best will do, they are worth considering if you aren't put off by their complexity of operation and sticker shock.

Simplest are "black box" professional receivers, with virtually no controls. These are operated remotely or by computers, often at hush-hush surveillance facilities. We don't cover this category, as some of the best models are available only at U.S. Federal agencies or NATO organizations. However, consumer-grade versions are evaluated elsewhere within PASSPORT REPORTS.

Shared Characteristics

All professional receivers should be physically and electrically robust, with resistance to hostile environments and rough handling, as well as having superior reliability (mean time between failures, MTBF). Additionally, their components need to be consistent so board swapping and other field repairs can be accomplished easily and without compromising performance.

The two professional models reviewed in this PASSPORT REPORTS were developed to replace the erstwhile consumer-grade Icom IC-R71A reviewed in a Radio Database International White Paper that's still available. Years ago, the tabletop 'R71A was used by the U.S. National Security Agency for offshore surveillance, but it was not made to NATO spec and had certain other limitations. Thankfully, the two models designed to replace it are as good as it gets for shortwave DXing by normal people.

Even with heightened security considerations, professional receivers tested by PASSPORT are officially classified as "NLR"— no license required, and thus not subject to U.S. Government export controls.

One Ready for Digital Broadcasts

One tested model, from Ten-Tec, is factory-equipped to receive DRM digital world band broadcasts. While the Watkins-Johnson equivalent isn't DRM ready, this appears to be only because nobody has yet bothered to devise a modification procedure.

Either way, DRM requires that the receiver interface with a PC and separately purchased DRM software (€60 at www.drmrx.org/purchase.php).

Good Antenna and Low Noise Essential

Top-rated, properly erected antennas are an absolute "must" for professional receivers to reach their potential. For test results and installation information, peruse the Radio Database International White Paper, *Evaluation of Popular Outdoor Antennas*, as well as reviews of antennas found elsewhere in this PASSPORT REPORTS.

If reception at your location is already disrupted by electrical noise even when a suitable antenna is in use, a better receiver would be a waste of money. Before buying, try eliminating the source of noise, or repositioning or replacing your antenna.

Volts with Jolts

Professional receivers tend to be unusually rugged, and often include MOV surge protection. Nevertheless, it helps to plug your pricey prize into a non-MOV surge arrestor, such as those manufactured by Zero-Surge (www.zerosurge.com) and Brick Wall (www.brickwall.com).

Any receiver's outdoor antenna always should be fed through a top-caliber static protection device, but this is especially important with the Watkins-Johnson WJ-8711A when it's not equipped with the 8711/PRE option. Even then, it's also a good idea to disconnect outdoor antennas whenever a thunderstorm threatens.

DSP Audio Qualities

In principle, there is no reason DSP (digital signal processing) receivers can't produce audio quality equal to, and in some respects better than, conventional models. Witness the audio quality of digital CDs, for example.

But a multi-stage receiver is much more complex than a CD, so it requires gobs of processing horsepower. Today's DSP receivers still fall short in this regard, one result being that audio quality is not all it could be. In particular, static crashes tend to sound harsher.

Helping offset this is that hard-core DXers often find recoverable audio to be slightly better with professional-grade DSP receivers. This is why these receivers are not strangers to "DXpeditions," where the rarest and most difficult of radio signals are sought out.

For tuning world band the Sherwood SE-3 accessory is nearly a "must" for most current and recently discontinued professional receivers. While the Sherwood device doesn't fundamentally resolve the DSP audio issue, it really helps. It also provides high-quality synchronous selectable sideband, a major plus. But there are downsides, too: extra cost, added operating complexity and a BFO that is not as stable as those on professional receivers.

Tips for Using this Section

Professional receivers are listed in order of suitability for listening to difficult-to-hear world band stations. Important secondary consideration is given to audio fidelity, ergonomics and reception of utility signals. Build quality is superior unless otherwise indicated. Selling prices, street, are as of when we go to press, and include European VAT and Australian GST where applicable.

Unless otherwise stated, all professional models have the following characteristics. Refer to PASSPORT's glossary to understand specialized terms.

- Digital signal processing, including digital frequency synthesis and display.
- Full coverage of at least the 5-29999 kHz VLF/LF/MF/HF portions of the radio spectrum, encompassing all the longwave, mediumwave AM and shortwave portions—including all world band frequencies—but no coverage of the standard FM broadcast band (87.5-108 MHz).
- A wide variety of helpful tuning features, including tuning and frequency display in 1 Hz increments.
- Synchronous selectable sideband via high-rejection IF filtering (not lower-rejection phasing), which greatly reduces adjacent-channel interference and fading distortion. On some models this is referred to as "SAM" (synchronous AM).

☞ **ECSS:** Professional models tune to the nearest 1 Hz, allowing the user to use the receiver's single-sideband circuitry to manually phase its BFO (internally generated carrier) with the station's transmitted carrier. Called "ECSS" (exalted-carrier, selectable-sideband) tuning, this can be used with AM-mode signals in lieu of synchronous selectable sideband. However, in addition to the relative inconvenience of this technique, unlike synchronous detection, which rephases continually and essentially perfectly, ECSS is always slightly out of phase. This causes at least some degree of harmonic distortion to music and speech, while tuning to the nearest Hertz can generate slow-sweep fading (for this reason, high-pass audio filtering or mis-phasing by two or three Hertz may provide better results).

- Proper demodulation of modes used by non-world-band—utility and amateur—shortwave signals. These modes include single sideband (LSB/USB and sometimes ISB) and CW ("Morse code"); also, with suitable ancillary devices, radioteletype (RTTY), frequency shift key (FSK) and radiofax (FAX).
- Meaningful signal-strength indication.
- Illuminated display.
- Superior build quality, robustness and sample-to-sample consistency as compared to consumer-grade tabletop receivers.
- Audio output for recording or low-power FM retransmission to hear world band around your domicile.

What PASSPORT's Rating Symbols Mean

Star ratings: ✪✪✪✪✪ is best. Stars reflect overall performance and meaningful features, plus to some extent ergonomics and perceived build quality. Price, appearance, country of manufacture and the like are not taken into account. With professional models there is a strong emphasis on the ability to flush out tough, hard-to-hear signals, as this is usually the main reason these sets are chosen by world band enthusiasts. Nevertheless, to facilitate comparison professional receiver rating standards are very similar to those used for the tabletop, portatop and portable models reviewed elsewhere in this PASSPORT.

Passport's Choice. La crème de la crème. Our test team's personal picks of the

litter—models we would buy or have bought for our personal use. Unlike star ratings, these choices are unapologetically subjective.

✪✪✪✪✪ *Passport's Choice*
Watkins-Johnson WJ-8711A

Price (receiver, factory options; single-quantity prices change often): *WJ-8711A:* $5,500.00 plus shipping worldwide. *871Y/ SEU DSP Speech Enhancement Unit:* $1,200.00. *8711/PRE Sub-Octave Preselector:* $1,100.00. *871Y/DSO1 Digital Signal Output Unit:* $1,150.00.

Price (aftermarket options): *Hammond RCBS1900517BK1 steel cabinet and 1421A mounting screws and cup washers:* $120-140 in the United States from manufacturer (www.hammondmfg.com/rackrcbs.htm) or Newark Electronics (www.newark.com). *Sherwood SE-3 MK III accessory:* $549.00 plus shipping worldwide.

Pro: Proven robust. BITE diagnostics and physical layout allows technically qualified users to make most repairs on-site. Users can upgrade receiver performance over time by EPROM replacement. Exceptional overall performance. Unsurpassed reception of feeble world band DX signals, especially when mated to the Sherwood SE-3 synchronous selectable sideband device and the WJ-871Y/SEU noise-reduction unit (*see* Con). Unusually effective "ECSS" reception, tuning AM-mode signals as though they were single sideband. Superb reception of non-

By a hair, the Watkins-Johnson WJ-8711A is the best tough-signal receiver tested.

AM mode "utility" stations. Generally superior audio quality when coupled to the Sherwood SE-3 fidelity-enhancing accessory, the W-J speech enhancement unit and a worthy external speaker (*see* Con). Unparalleled bandwidth flexibility, with no less than 66 outstandingly high-quality bandwidths. Trimmer on back panel allows frequency readout to be user-aligned against a known frequency standard, such as WWV/WWVH or a laboratory device. Extraordinary operational flexibility—virtually every receiver parameter is adjustable. One hundred station presets. Synchronous detection, called "SAM" (synchronous AM), reduces selective-fading distortion with world band, mediumwave AM and longwave signals, and works even on very narrow voice bandwidths (*see* Con). Rock stable. Built-in preamplifier. Tunable notch filter. Effective noise blanking. Highly adjustable scanning of both frequency ranges and station presets. Easy-to-read displays. Large tuning knob. Unusually effective mediumwave AM performance. Can be fully and effectively computer and remotely controlled. Passband shift (*see* Con). Numerous outputs for data collection and ancillary hardware, including 455 kHz IF output which makes for instant installation of Sherwood SE-3 accessory and balanced line outputs (connect to balanced hookup to minimize radiation of digital "buzz"). Remote control and dial-up data collection; Windows control software available from manufacturer. Among the most likely of all world band receivers tested to be able to be retrofitted for eventual reception of digital world band broadcasts. Inboard AC power supply, which runs unusually cool, senses incoming current and automatically adjusts to anything from 90–264 VAC, 47–440 Hz—a plus during brownouts or with line voltage or frequency swings. Superior-quality factory service (*see* Con). Comprehensive and well-written operating manual, packed with technical information and schematic

diagrams. Hammond aftermarket cabinet is exceptionally robust.

Con: Static crashes and modulation-splash interference sound noticeably harsher than on analog receivers, although this has been improved in latest operating software. Synchronous detection not sideband-selectable, so it can't reduce adjacent-channel interference (remediable by Sherwood SE-3). Basic receiver has mediocre audio in AM mode; "ECSS" tuning or synchronous detection, along with the speech enhancement unit (W1 noise-reduction setting), required to alleviate this. Some clipping distortion in the single-sideband mode. Complex to operate to full advantage. Circuitry puts out a high degree of digital "buzz", relying for the most part on the panels for electrical shielding; one consequence is that various versions emanate digital "buzz" through the non-standard rear-panel audio terminals, as well as through the signal-strength meter and front-panel headphone jack—this problem is lessened when the Sherwood SE-3 is used. Antennas with shielded (e.g., coaxial) feedlines are less likely to pick up receiver-generated digital "buzz." Passband shift operates only in CW mode. Jekyll-and-Hyde ergonomics: sometimes wonderful, sometimes awful. Front-panel rack "ears" protrude, with the right "ear" getting in the way of the tuning knob; fortunately, these are easily removed. Mediocre front-end selectivity, remediable by 8711/PRE option (with minor 2.5 dB insertion loss); e.g. for those living near mediumwave AM transmitters. 871Y/SEU option reduces audio gain and is extremely difficult to install; best to have all options factory-installed. Signal-strength indicator's gradations in dBm only. No DC power input. Keypad lettering wears off with use; replacement keys available at under $8 each. Each receiver is built on order (David Shane at 1-800/954-3577), so it can take up to four months for delivery. Factory service can take as much as two months. Cabinet extra, available from Hammond and Premiere. Plastic feet have no front elevation and allow receiver to slide around. Available only through U.S. manufacturer, DRS Technologies (www.drs.com); receiver and factory options have been subjected to a number of price increases since 2000.

Verdict: The American-made WJ-8711A is, by a skosh, the ultimate machine for down-and-dirty world band DXing when money is no object.

Had there not been digital "buzz," inexcusable at this price—and had there been better audio quality, a tone control, passband shift and synchronous selectable sideband—the '8711A would have been even better, especially for program listening. Fortunately, the Sherwood SE-3 accessory remedies virtually all these problems and improves DX reception, to boot; W-J's optional 871Y/SEU complements, rather than competes with, the SE-3 for improving recovered audio.

Overall, the WJ-8711A DSP receiver, properly configured, is as good as it gets. It is exceptionally well-suited to demanding connoisseurs with the appropriate financial wherewithal—provided they seek an extreme degree of manual receiver control.

DRM Ready
✪✪✪✪✪ *Passport's Choice*
Ten-Tec RX-340

Price: $3,950.00 in the United States. £3,299.00 in the United Kingdom. $7,650.00AUD in Australia. *Hammond RCBS1900513GY2 or RCBS1900513BK1 13" deep cabinet (www.hammondmfg.com/rackrcbs.htm):* $99.95 in the United States. *Ten-Tec #307G (gray) external speaker:* $98.00 in the United States. *Ten-Tec #307B (black) external speaker:* £89.00 in the United Kingdom. *Sherwood SE-3 MK III accessory:* $549.00 plus shipping worldwide.

Even at four large, Ten-Tec's RX-340 is the best buy among professional receivers. DRM ready, too.

Pro: Appears to be robust (*see* Con). BITE diagnostics and physical layout allows technically qualified users to make most repairs on-site. Users can upgrade receiver performance over time by replacing one or another of three socketed EPROM chips (currently v1.10A). Superb overall performance, including unsurpassed readability of feeble world band DX signals, especially when mated to the Sherwood SE-3 device; in particular, superlative image and IF rejection, both >100 dB. Few birdies. Audio quality usually worthy when receiver coupled to the Sherwood SE-3 accessory and a good external speaker. Average overall distortion in single-sideband mode a breathtakingly low 0.2 percent; in other modes, under 2.7 percent. Exceptional bandwidth flexibility, with no less than 57 outstandingly high-quality bandwidths having shape factors of 1:1.33 or better; bandwidth distribution exceptionally good for world band listening and DXing, along with other activities (*see* Con). Receives digital (DRM) world band broadcasts by connecting it to a PC using DRM software purchased separately; *see* www.tentec.com/TT340DRM.htm. Tunes and displays accurately in ultra-precise 1 Hz increments. Extraordinary operational flexibility—virtually every receiver parameter is adjustable; for example, the AGC's various time constants have 118 million possible combinations, plus pushbutton AGC "DUMP" to temporarily deactivate AGC (*see* Con). Worthy front-panel ergonomics, valuable given the exceptional degree of manual operation; includes easy-to-read displays (*see* Con). Also, large, properly weighted rubber-track tuning knob with fixed dimple and Oak Grigsby optical encoder provide superior tuning "feel" and reliability. Attractive front panel. Two hundred station presets, 201 including the scratchpad. Synchronous selectable sideband, called "SAM" (synchronous AM), reduces selective-fading distortion, as well as at diminishing or eliminating adjacent-channel interference, with world band, mediumwave AM and longwave signals; with earlier software lock was easily lost, but from v1.10A it now holds lock accept-

ably (*see* Con). Built-in half-octave preselector comes standard. Built-in preamplifier (*see* Con). Adjustable noise blanker, works well in most situations (*see* Con). Stable as Gibraltar, as good as it gets. Tunable DSP notch filter with exceptional depth of 58 dB (*see* Con). Passband shift (passband tuning) works unusually well (*see* Con). Unusually effective "ECSS" reception by tuning AM-mode signals as though they were single sideband. Superb reception of "utility" (non-AM mode) stations using a wide variety of modes and including fast filters for delay-critical digital modes. Highly adjustable scanning of both frequency ranges and station presets. Can be fully and

NUMBERS: TOP TWO PROFESSIONAL RECEIVERS

	Watkins-Johnson WJ-8711A	Ten-Tec RX-340
Max. WB Sensitivity/Noise Floor	0.13 μV, **S**/−136 dBm, **E**	0.17 μV, **S**/−132 dBm, **E**[1]
Blocking	123 dB, **G**	109 dB, **F**
Shape Factors, voice BWs	1:1.21-1:1.26, **S**	1:1.15-1:1.33, **S**
Ultimate Rejection	>80 dB, **E**	70 dB, **G**
Front-End Selectivity	**F**/**E**[2]	**E**
Image Rejection	80 dB, **E**	>100 dB, **S**
First IF Rejection	—[3]	>100 dB, **S**
Dynamic Range/IP3 (5 kHz)	74 dB, **G**/−18 dBm, **E**	46 dB, **P**/−53 dBm, **P**
Dynamic Range/IP3 (20 kHz)	99 dB, **S**/+20 dBm, **S**	84 dB, **G**/+4 dBm, **E**
Phase Noise	115 dBc, **G**	113 dBc, **G**
AGC Threshold	0.1 μV, **P**	0.3 μV, **G**[4]
Overall Distortion, sync	8.2%, **P**	2.6%, **G**
Stability	5 Hz, **S**	5 Hz, **S**
Notch filter depth	58 dB, **S**	58 dB, **S**

IBS Lab Ratings: **S** Superb   **E** Excellent   **G** Good   **F** Fair   **P** Poor

(1) Preamp on. With preamp off, 0.55 μV, **G**/−122 dBm, **G**.
(2) **F** standard/**E** with optional preselector.
(3) Adequate, but could not measure precisely.
(4) Preamp on. With preamp off, 1.3 μV, **G**.

effectively computer and remotely controlled. Numerous outputs for data collection and ancillary hardware, including 455 kHz IF-out for instant hookup of Sherwood SE-3 accessory. Remote control and dial-up data collection. Superb analog signal-strength indicator (*see* Con). Among the most likely of all world band receivers tested to be able to be retrofitted for eventual reception of digital world band broadcasts. Inboard AC power supply senses incoming current and automatically adjusts to anything from 90–264 VAC, 48–440 Hz—a plus during brownouts or with line voltage or frequency swings. Superior control of fluorescent display dimming (*see* Con). Factory repair service is reasonably priced by professional standards, with relatively prompt turnaround. Comprehensive and well-written operating manual, packed with technical information and schematic diagrams.

Con: Synchronous selectable sideband loses lock relatively easily; e.g., if listening to one sideband and there is a strong signal impacting the other sideband, lock can be momentarily lost; resolved by Sherwood SE-3 fidelity device. DSP microprocessor limitations result in poor dynamic range/IP3 at 5 kHz signal spacing. Blocking, phase noise and ultimate rejection all pretty good, but not of professional caliber. Complex to operate to full advantage. Static crashes sound harsher than on analog receivers. Not all bandwidths available in all modes. Spurious signals noted around 6 MHz segment (49 meters) at night at one test location having superb antennas. Synchronous selectable sideband, although recently improved, doesn't hold lock quite as well as some other models. When 9–10 dB preamplifier turned on, AGC acts on noise unless IF gain reduced by 10 dB. Notch filter does not work in AM, synchronous selectable sideband or ISB modes. Passband shift tunes only plus or minus 2 kHz and does not work in the ISB or synchronous selectable sideband modes; remediable with Sherwood SE-3. Audio quality and synchronous

selectable sideband's lock both profit from Sherwood SE-3 accessory and good outboard speaker. Occasional "popping" sound, notably when synchronous selectable sideband or ISB in use—DSP overload? No AGC off except by holding down DUMP button. Noise blanker not effective at some test locations; for example, other receivers work better in reducing noise from electric fences. Audio power, especially through headphones, could be greater. On our unit, right-channel headphone audio cuts out at full volume. On our unit, occasional minor buzz from internal speaker. Keypad not in telephone format; rather, uses computer keyboard numeric-keypad layout. Some ergonomic clumsiness when going back and forth between the station presets and VFO tuning; too, "Aux Parameter" and "Memory Scan" knobs touchy to adjust. Signal-strength indicator illuminated less than display. Digital "buzz" from fluorescent display emits from front of receiver, although not elsewhere. On our latest unit, stick-on decal with front-panel markings has peeled loose above the main display, and pushing it back into place hasn't helped; this has not been a problem on other units. No DC power input. Cabinet extra.

Verdict: With an exceptional degree of manual control, the Ten-Tec RX-340, when coupled to fidelity-enhancing hardware, is a superb DSP receiver for those who want no-compromise performance for years to come.

It is technologically advanced, including being able to interface with a PC to receive digital (DRM) world band broadcasts. The '340 is a sensible value, too—with bells and whistles, it costs considerably less than a fully equipped WJ-8711A.

The PASSPORT *professional-model review team consists of Tony Jones, Lawrence Magne, Chuck Rippel, David Walcutt, David Zantow and George Zeller. Laboratory measurements by J. Robert Sherwood.*

Receivers for PCs

Affordable Reception of Digital Broadcasts

It helps to have knobs and buttons to find stations and boost reception, but not always. A dedicated core of radio enthusiasts prefers knob-free receivers controlled by a PC. Professional surveillance organizations, too, as their receivers rarely interact with real, live people.

Mating a shortwave receiver with a PC allows each to enhance the other. Yet, this synergy can be offset by drawbacks, such as hardware complication and instability. There can also be radio interference from PC stuff—monitors, cables and so on. Professional receiving facilities are designed to overcome these challenges, but at home it's a lot tougher.

DRM Digital Reception

Some models, shown as "DRM Ready," process Digital Radio

Mondiale (DRM) world band broadcasts. These require DRM application software, not included but available for €60 at www.drmrx.org/purchase.php. Limited experience so far suggests that to hear DRM over time you may also need to obtain software revisions as they come out.

The Icom IC-PCR1000 can be modified to receive DRM—see www.drmrx.org/receiver_mods.html. This is one step removed from "DRM ready," but helps ensure that the '1000 won't fall behind the technological curve should DRM succeed in the years to come.

A major advantage of a PC controlled receiver for DRM is that it is already within or connected to a computer. Existing tabletop and professional receivers, which ordinarily are standalone, have to be tethered to a separate PC to process DRM signals.

Our tests take place in a Windows environment. If you're using Mac or Linux, check manufacturers' websites for the latest on non-Windows operating software. For long-term ownership remember that once a receiver becomes discontinued it eventually may not work to full advantage with new or revised computer operating systems. This can be overcome by retaining the ability to use legacy OS.

No matter how carefully a PC controlled receiver is tested, its performance depends partly on the individual computer configuration. This increases the odds that you'll encounter an unwelcome surprise, so it's always best to purchase on a returnable basis.

Tip: A PC controlled receiver's clock works off the host computer's clock. These are notoriously inaccurate, but About Time, free from www.arachnoid.com/abouttime/index.html, is accurate and stable with Windows.

DRM Ready

❂❂❂❂⅜ *Passport's Choice*

WiNRADiO G303i, WiNRADiO G303i-PD/P

Price: *G303:* $499.95 in the United States. $699.00CAD in Canada. £440.00 in the United Kingdom. $995.50AUD in Australia. *G303i-PD/P:* $599.95 in the United States. $799.00CAD in Canada. £439.95 in the United Kingdom. €619.00 in Germany. $1,199.50AUD in Australia. *WiNRADiO DRM plug-in (special version of DRM software):* €60.00 worldwide from www.drmrx.org/purchase.php.

Pro: Plug and play aids setup. Once receiver is installed, the included software loads without problem; software updates available for free from manufacturer's Website, and open source code allows third-party software to be developed. With optional

The WiNRADiO G303i is tops among affordable PC receivers. The G313i goes further by not needing a sound card, but costs much more.

plug-in (software), receives digital (DRM) world band broadcasts. Superb stability, almost unexcelled. Tunes and displays in ultra-precise 1 Hz increments. A thousand station presets which can be clustered into any of 16 groups (*see* Con—Other). Excellent shape factors (1:1.6, 1:1.8) for 5.0 kHz and 3.2 kHz bandwidths aid selectivity/adjacent-channel rejection; 1.8 kHz bandwidth measures with good shape factor (1:2.3); additional bandwidths available in the PD/P version perform similarly. Excellent short-wave sensitivity (0.21 µV)/noise floor (–130 dBm), good mediumwave AM and longwave sensitivity (0.4 µV)/noise floor (–125 dBm). Potentially excellent audio quality (see below). Excellent dynamic range (90 dB) and third-order intercept point (+5 dBm) at 20 kHz signal separation points (*see* Con—AGC/AVC). Phase noise excellent (*see* Con—AGC/AVC). Image rejection excellent. Spurious signals essentially absent. Screen, and operation in general, unusually pleasant and intuitive. Single-sideband performance generally excellent (*see* Con—AGC/AVC). AGC fast, medium, slow and off. Spectrum display shows real-time signal activity, performs commendably and in particular provides signal strength readings to within plus or minus 3 dB. Spectrum scope sweeps between two user-chosen frequencies, displays the output while receiver mutes, then a mouse click can select a desired "peak"; it works quickly and well, and when the step size is set to small (e.g., 1 kHz),

resolution is excellent and quite useful. Large signal-strength indicator highly accurate, as good as we've ever tested; display is both numeric and a digitized "analog meter"; reads out as "S" meter, in dBm or in microvolts. Two easy-to-read on-screen clocks for World Time and local time, display seconds numerically, as well as date (*see* Con—Other). Superior and timely free factory assistance via email, seemingly seven days a week. *G303i-PD/P:* Continuously adjustable bandwidths from 1Hz to 15 kHz (single sideband/ECSS 1 Hz to 7.5 kHz), with bandwidth presets, aid greatly in providing optimum tradeoff between audio fidelity and adjacent-channel interference rejection. AVC settings, limited to "on-off" in standard version, allow for control over decay and attack times. Improved audio quality in some test configurations. Demodulates ISB signals used by a small proportion of utility stations. SINAD and THD indicators. AF squelch for FM mode.

Pro/Con—Sound: Outstanding freedom from distortion aids in providing good audio quality with appropriate sound cards/chips and speakers; sound quality and level can run the gamut from excellent to awful, depending on the PC's sound card or chipset, which needs to be full duplex. Sound Blaster 16 cards are recommended by manufacturer, but not all models work. During our tests the $130 Sound Blaster Audigy 2 performed with considerable distortion—it doesn't offer full duplex operation for the line input—whereas the $43 Sound Blaster PCI 512 worked splendidly. (ISA sound cards perform terribly; quite sensibly, these are not recommended by the manufacturer.) All input settings for the audio card need to be carefully set to match the settings within the receiver's software. If wrong, there may be no audio or it may be grossly distorted. Indeed, a sound card isn't always necessary, as some sound chipsets commonly found within PCs produce excellent audio with the G303i. Another reason the chipset may be prefer-

The G303i slips easily into a PC card slot.

able is that Sound Blaster manuals recommend that if there is an audio chipset on the motherboard, it first be disabled in the BIOS and all related software uninstalled—potentially a Maalox Moment. However, even with a suitable board or chipset installed, the user must carefully set the AGC and AVC (automatic volume control, termed "Audio AGC" on the G303i) for distortion-free audio. Powerful amplified speakers provide room-filling sound and allow the AVC to be kept off, thus reducing band noise that can be intrusive when it is on.

Con—AGC/AVC: Weak-signal reception can be compromised by the AGC, which "sees"

10–15 kHz of spectrum within the IF upon which to act. So, if an adjacent world band channel signal is 20 dB or more stronger than a desired weak signal, the AGC's action tends to cause the adjacent signal to mask the desired signal. Inadequate gain with the AVC ("Audio AGC") off, but the aggressive AVC adds listening strain with single-sideband signals, as it tends to increase band noise between words or other modulation peaks. Powerful outboard amplified speakers help reduce the need for the additional audio gain brought about by the AVC and thus are desirable, but be prepared for jumps in volume when you tune to strong stations. Reception sometimes

NUMBERS: TOP PC RECEIVERS

	WiNRADiO G303i	Ten-Tec RX-320D
Max. WB Sensitivity	0.21 μV **E**	0.31 to 0.7 μV **E**-**F**[1]
Noise Floor, WB	–130 dBm **E**	–126 to –119 dBm **G**-**F**[2]
Blocking	120 dB **G**	>146 dB **S**
Shape Factors, voice BWs	1:1.6 **E**–1:2.4 **G**	n/a[3]
Ultimate Rejection	70 dB **G**	60 dB **G**
Front-End Selectivity	**G**	**F**
Image Rejection	85 dB **E**	60 dB **G**
First IF Rejection	52 dB **F**	60 dB **G**
Dynamic Range/IP3 (5 kHz)	45 dB **P**/–62 dBm **P**	n/a[3]
Dynamic Range/IP3 (20 kHz)	90 dB **E**/+5 dBm **E**	n/a[3]
Phase Noise	124 dBc **E**[4]	106 dBc **F**
AGC Threshold	2.7 to 8.0 μV **G**-**P**	4.0 μV **F**
Overall Distortion, voice	<1.0% **S**	<1% **S**
Stability	5 Hz **S**	80 Hz **G**
Notch filter depth	n/a	n/a

IBS Lab Ratings: **S** Superb   **E** Excellent   **G** Good   **F** Fair   **P** Poor

(1) Excellent 60 meters and up.
(2) Good 60 meters and up.
(3) Could not be measured accurately because of synthesizer noise and spurious signals, but appears to be very good.
(4) Worse at close-in measurement.

further improves if the AGC is switched off and IF gain is manually decreased, but the operator then has to "ride" the volume control to smooth out major fluctuations. Manual ECSS tuning frequently helps, too. During moments of transient overload, the AVC can contribute to the creation of leading-edge "pops" with powerful signals (slightly more noticeable in the PD/P version). Single-sideband performance, particularly within crowded amateur bands, can be even more audibly compromised by the aforementioned out-of-passband AGC action. Dynamic range/IP3 at 5 kHz signal separation points couldn't be measured with AGC on, as test signals trigger the AGC and keep the receiver from going into overload; measurement with the AGC off resulted in exceptionally poor numbers (45 db/–62 dBm). Phase noise poor when measured close-in for the same reason.

Con—Other: No outboard version available; requires installation within a vacant PCI card slot inside computer. No synchronous selectable sideband, and double-sideband "AMS" mode loses lock easily. First IF rejection only fair. Front-end selectivity, although adequate for most uses, could be better. Station presets ("memory channels") store only frequency and mode, not band-width, AGC or attenuation settings. No passband offset or tunable notch filter. Emits a pop-screech sound when first brought up or when switching from standard to professional demodulator. Uses only SMA antenna connection, typically found on handheld devices rather than tabletop receivers; an SMA-to-BNC adapter is included, but for the many shortwave antennas with neither type of plug a second adaptor or changed plug is needed. World Time clock tied into computer's clock, which may not be accurate without periodic adjustment. On our sample, country of manufacture not found on receiver, box or enclosed printed matter. Erratum sheet suggests that a discone antenna be used; this is fine for reception above roughly 25 MHz; however, in our

tests we confirmed that conventional shortwave antennas provide much broader frequency coverage with the G303i, just as they do with other shortwave receivers.

☞ Minimum of 1 GHz Pentium recommended by manufacturer, although in the process of checking this out we obtained acceptable results using vintage 400 MHz and 500 MHz Pentium II processors with Windows 2000. However, if your PC is multitasking, then 2 GHz or more helps keep the PC from bogging down. Primary testing was done using various desktop Pentium IV PCs at 1.5–2.4 GHz, 256–512 MHz RAM and Windows 2000, XP-Home and XP-Pro operating systems. WiNRADiO operating software used during tests were v1.07, v1.14, v1.25 and v1.26.

Verdict: The G303i is a vast improvement in shortwave performance over WiNRADiO wide-spectrum models we have tested to date. Overall, it is the best among PC receivers tested, especially in the highly desirable Professional Demodulator version. It can also be configured for reception of DRM digital broadcast signals, and is a pleasure to operate.

The G303i provides laboratory-quality spectrum displays and signal-strength indication. These spectrum-data functions are top drawer, regardless of price or type of receiver, and that's just the beginning of things done well. The few significant warts: AGC/AVC behavior, possible audio hassles during installation, and the absence of synchronous selectable sideband.

Nevertheless, WiNRADiO's G303i is the *ne plus ultra* among tested PC controlled receivers for world band reception.

DRM Ready
✪✪✪✪ ❷ *Passport's Choice*
Ten-Tec RX-320D

Price: *RX-320D:* $329.00 plus shipping worldwide. £239.00 in the United Kingdom.

€449.00 in Germany. $575.00AUD in Australia. *DRM software:* €60.00 worldwide from www.drmrx.org/purchase.php. *Third-party control software:* Free–$99 worldwide.

Pro: The "D" version's 12 kHz IF output allows the receiver to receive digital (DRM) world band broadcasts by using DRM software purchased separately. Superior dynamic range. Apparently superb bandwidth shape factors (*see* Con). In addition to the supplied factory control software, third-party software is available, often for free, and may improve operation. Up to 34 bandwidths with third-party software. Tunes in extremely precise 1 Hz increments (10 Hz with tested factory software); displays to the nearest Hertz, and frequency readout is easily user-aligned. Large, easy-to-read digital frequency display and faux-analog frequency bar. For PCs with sound cards, outstanding freedom from distortion aids in providing good audio quality with most but not all cards and speakers. Fairly good audio, but with limited treble, also available through radio for PCs without sound cards. Superb blocking performance helps maintain consistently good world band sensitivity. Passband offset (*see* Con). Spectrum display with wide variety of useful sweep widths (*see* Con). World Time on-screen clock (*see* Con). Adjustable AGC decay. Thousands of station presets, with first-rate memory configuration, access and sorting—including by station name and frequency. Only PC-controlled model tested which returns to last tuned frequency when PC turned off. Superior owner's manual. Outstanding factory help and repair support.

Con: No synchronous selectable sideband, although George Privalov's Control Panel Program now automates retuning of drifty AM-mode signals received as "ECSS." Some characteristic "DSP roughness" in the audio under certain reception conditions. Synthesizer phase noise measures only fair; among the consequences are that bandwidth shape factors cannot be measured exactly. Some

Ten-Tec's RX-320D is attractively priced for the high level of performance it offers.

tuning ergonomics only fair as compared with certain standalone receivers. No tunable notch filter. Passband offset doesn't function in AM mode. Signal-strength indicator, calibrated 0–80, too sensitive, reading 20 with no antenna connected and 30 with only band noise being received. Mediocre front-end selectivity can allow powerful mediumwave AM stations to "ghost" into the shortwave spectrum, thus degrading reception of world band stations. Uses AC adaptor instead of built-in power supply. Spectrum display does not function with some third-party software and is only a so-so performer. Mediumwave AM reception below 1 MHz suffers from reduced sensitivity, and longwave sensitivity is atrocious. No internal speaker on outboard receiver module. World Time clock tied into computer's clock, which may not be accurate without periodic adjustment. Almost no retail sources outside the United States.

☞ PASSPORT's four-star rating is for the RX-320D with third-party control software. With factory software the rating is marginally lower.

Verdict: The American-made Ten-Tec RX-320D is one of the best PC controlled receivers tested. Yet, even with DRM software it is value priced. It is also less chancy to install to full operating advantage than the WiNRADiO G303i.

DRM Modifiable

✪✪✪ *C*
Icom IC-PCR1000

Price: *IC-PCR1000:* $399.95 in the United States. $699.00CAD in Canada. £319.99 in the United Kingdom. €479.00 in Germany. $977.00AUD in Australia. *UT-106 DSP Unit:* $139.95 in the United States. £82.00 in the United Kingdom. €99.00 in Germany. $172.00AUD in Australia.

Pro: Wideband frequency coverage. Spectrum display with many useful sweep widths for shortwave, as well as good real-time performance. Tunes and displays in extremely precise 1 Hz increments. Comes with reasonably performing control software (*see* Con). Excellent sensitivity to weak signals. AGC, adjustable, performs well in AM and single-sideband modes. Nineteen banks of 50 memories each, with potential for virtually unlimited number of memories. Passband offset (*see* Con). Powerful audio with good weak-signal readability and little distortion (*see* Con). DRM modifiable (http://www.drmrx.org/receiver_mods.html).

Con: Poor dynamic range. Audio quality, not pleasant, made worse by presence of circuit hiss. No line output to feed PC sound card and speakers, so no alternative to using receiver's audio. No synchronous selectable sideband. Only two AM-mode bandwidths— 8.7 kHz (nominal 6 kHz) and 2.4 kHz (nominal 3 kHz)—both with uninspiring shape factors. Synthesizer phase noise, although not measurable, appears to be only fair; among the effects of this are that bandwidth shape factors cannot be exactly measured. Mediocre blocking slightly limits weak-signal sensitivity when frequency segment contains powerful signals. Tuning ergonomics only fair as compared with some standalone receivers. Automatic tunable notch filter with DSP audio processing (UT-106, not tested) an extra-cost option. Lacks passband offset in AM mode. Uses AC adaptor instead of built-in power supply. Spectrum display mutes audio when single-sideband or CW signal being received. No clock. Mediocre inboard speaker, remediable by using outboard speaker. Sparse owner's manual.

☞ The 'PCR1000 sometimes comes with a seasoned version of Bonito RadioCom software as a free bonus. RadioCom provides more-flexible audio shaping and the ability to record programs onto hard drives, but its improved current version costs extra.

Verdict: Among tested PC-controlled receivers, the Japanese-made Icom IC-PCR1000 is not the strongest world band performer. However, it is the most appropriate for wideband frequency coverage. Its spectrum display is a solid performer, as well. For all that, it is attractively priced.

Robert Sherwood and David Zantow, with Lawrence Magne and Chuck Rippel; also, Craig Tyson.

Icom's IC-PCR1000 offers wideband coverage at a value price. Superior spectrum display, too.

WHERE TO FIND THE INDEX TO TESTED RADIOS

PASSPORT REPORTS evaluates nearly every digitally tuned receiver on the market. Here's where each is found, with those that are new, forthcoming, revised, rebranded or retested in **bold**. Those which can be equipped for digital (Digital Radio Mondiale) broadcast reception are in *italics*.

Comprehensive PASSPORT® Radio Database International White Papers® are available for the many popular premium receivers. Each RDI White Paper®—$6.95 in North America, $9.95 airmail elsewhere, including shipping—contains virtually all our panel's findings and comments during hands-on testing, as well as laboratory measurements and what these mean to you. These unabridged reports are available from key world band dealers, or contact our 24-hour VISA/MC order channels for immediate shipment (www.passband.com, autovoice +1 215/598-9018, fax +1 215/598 3794), or write PASSPORT RDI White Papers, Box 300, Penn's Park, PA 18943 USA.

Receiver	Page	Receiver	Page	Receiver	Page
AKD Target HF3M	*182*	**Grundig Yacht Boy 80**	**122**	Sangean ATS-818ACS	151
AOR AR5000A+3	*176*	*Grundig Yacht Boy 400PE*	*114*	Sangean ATS 909/	
AOR AR7030	166	Grundig Yacht Boy P2000	137	ATS 909 "Deluxe"	120
AOR AR7030/DRM	***166***	Grundig YB-550PE	134	**Sangean PT-50**	**139**
AR7030+3	166	*Icom IC-PCR1000 (PC)*	*198*	**Sangean PT-80**	**122**
AOR AR7030+3/DRM	***166***	Icom IC-R75/R75E	171	Sanyo MB-60A	130
Coby CX-CB91	**143**	Icom IC-R75/R75E (Kiwa)	170	**Sharper Image SN400**	**107**
Degen DE105	**102**	Icom IC-R8500A	175	*Si-Tex Nav-Fax 200*	*182*
Degen DE205	**105**	Japan Radio NRD-545	169	**Sony ICF-SW07**	**109**
Degen DE1101	125	Japan Radio "NRD-545SE"	170	Sony ICF-SW35	131
Degen DE1102	113	jWIN JX-M14	141	Sony ICF-SW40	135
Degen DE1103	**115**	Kaide KK-989	108	Sony ICF-SW55/SW55E	120
Degen DE1105 (info)	**147**	**Kaito KA105**	**102**	*Sony ICF-SW77/SW77E*	*144*
Drake R8B 📖	165	Kaito KA1101	125	Sony ICF-SW100E	102
Etón E1 (info)	**147**	Kaito KA1102	113	Sony ICF-SW100S	101
Etón E10	**126**	**Kaito KA1103**	**115**	Sony ICF-SW1000T/	
Etón E100	**132**	**Kaito KA1105 (info)**	**147**	SW1000TS	150
Etón FR-200/FR-200G	155	Kaiwa KA-818	106	*Sony ICF-SW7600GR*	*111*
Etón G1000A	138	**Kchibo KK-C300**	**107**	Tecsun BCL-2000	147
Etón Mini 300	104	Kchibo KK-E200	136	Tecsun DR-910	138
Etón S350	147	Kchibo KK-S320	142	Tecsun Green-88	155
Etón YB-550PE	134	*NASA HF-4/HF-4E/S*	*182*	Tecsun HAM-2000	157
Freeplay Summit		**Palstar R30C/CC/**		Tecsun PL-200	132
(International)	153	**Sherwood**	**177**	Tecsun PL-230	134
Freeplay Summit (USA)	**153**	**Palstar R30C/R30CC**	**177**	**Tecsun PL-550**	**126**
Grundig eTraveller VII	133	Panasonic RF-B55	130	Tecsun R-818	106
Grundig FR-200/FR200G	155	Realistic DX-394	183	Tecsun R919	104
Grundig G1000A	138	Roberts R827	146	Ten-Tec 1254 Kit	181
Grundig G2000A/B		Roberts R861	120	*Ten-Tec RX-320D (PC)*	*196*
"Porsche Design"	137	Roberts R876	130	*Ten-Tec RX-340*	*189*
Grundig G4000A	***114***	Roberts R881	136	***Ten-Tec RX-350D***	***173***
Grundig Mini 300PE	104	Roberts R9914	130	Watkins-Johnson	
Grundig Porsche P2000	137	Roberts RC828	151	WJ-8711A	187
Grundig S350	147	Sangean ATS 404	136	*WiNRADiO G303i/*	
Grundig Satellit 800 📖	157	Sangean ATS 505/505P	130	*G303i-PD/P (PC)*	*193*
Grundig Yacht Boy 50	**139**	Sangean ATS 606A/606AP	130	Yaesu FRG-100 📖	179
				Yaesu VR-5000	180

📖 *Radio Database International White Paper® available.*

Skywave Lassos

World band radio's appeal includes unfettered reception with no wires. War or peace, censorship or freedom—it's always there. Yet, for top world band performance an outdoor antenna helps, and most are made from . . . wires.

Not just any old wire will lasso radio's tough catches, so:

• Match antenna to radio—simple antennas for simple portables, sophisticated antennas for sophisticated tabletops.

• Purchase the best within the type you want. Price differences are rarely great among similar antennas.

• Erect the antenna safely and for best performance. If you can't mount it outdoors, consider a compact antenna (see next article).

Goal: Improve Signal-to-Noise

A properly located antenna provides more signal and relatively less electrical and receiver noise. The result—more signal, proportionately less noise—improves the signal-to-noise ratio.

This is essential, as signal boosting means little if background noise goes up correspondingly. Noise can be from nearby sources—cable and power lines, fluorescent and low-energy lights, appliances, computers, dimmers and the like. It can also be from "hiss" and other noise generated within your receiver.

When Antennas Help

No surprise—stations already booming in aren't going to do much better with an improved antenna. Your receiver's signal-strength indicator may read higher, but its automatic-gain control (AGC) ensures that what you hear isn't going to sound much different than before.

With an everyday portable, forget sophisticated antennas—outdoor or in, passive or active. Make do with the radio's built-in telescopic antenna, or for more oomph use a simple inverted-L antenna (see below) or the compact Sony AN-LP1 evaluated in the next article.

At the other extreme, tabletop and professional receivers usually don't have built-in antennas, as proximate antennas—those on or near the receiver—can't cut the mustard. A first-rate remote antenna is as essential to elite receivers as high-octane fuel is to a Maserati.

Volksantenna

Inverted-L antennas are simple, flexible and inexpensive. Inconspicuous, too, as they have no unsightly traps and, being end-fed, their feedlines are usually next to the house rather than dangling out in the open. For most radios they provide excellent results, and are even reasonable for mediumwave AM.

Rough-and-ready inverted-Ls are cheap and usually rate three stars, sometimes four. Among those available in the United States is

Radio Shack's $10 Outdoor Antenna Kit (278-758) with wire, insulators and other bits. Add loose change for a claw/alligator clip or other connector.

World band and antenna specialty outlets often stock inverted-L antennas, as well as such add-ons as baluns and antenna tuners. These are made from higher-quality materials and priced accordingly; for example, £26 for the Watson SWL-DX1 and £40 for the Moonraker Skywire. Others are creative end-fed variants of the classic inverted-L.

At full length, a typical inverted-L antenna can be too long for many portables, causing overloading from hefty incoming signals. Experiment, but usually the less costly the portable, the shorter an inverted-L antenna should be. But unlike other antenna types the inverted-L can be readily shortened to avoid overloading or to fit into a yard.

Longwires Reduce Fading

Acres aplenty?

Lengthy inverted-L antennas, detailed in the RDI White Paper on outdoor antennas, can run over 200 feet, or 60 meters. These homebrew skyhooks are readily assembled from parts found at world band and amateur radio outlets.

They qualify as genuine longwire antennas, thanks to their wavelength-plus design. This helps reduce fading—something shorter antennas can't do—while improving the signal-to-noise ratio.

Pitfalls

A good antenna static protector is essential during nearby thunderstorms, windy snowfalls and sandstorms. These generate electrical charges that can seriously damage your radio.

Some of the best are made by Alpha Delta Communications. It's also a good idea to have a surge arrestor or UPS on the power line, too—just like with a PC.

Most Americans don't encounter legal prohibitions on erecting world band antennas. However, covenants and deed restrictions, increasingly common in gated communities, can limit choices. Regardless, the Golden Rule of Aerials applies: Outdoor antennas should be neither unsightly nor particularly visible. If you want to annoy neighbors, put out plastic flamingos.

Most wire antennas are robustly constructed to withstand ice buildup during storms, but wire sometimes stretches. Bungee straps and pulley counterweights help prevent this.

Performance Freebie

You wouldn't bathe in dirty water, so why place your antenna where it is electrically "dirty"?

Antenna location is one of the neat little secrets of world band radio. An antenna hung out in the fresh air—high and away from electrical lines, cables and other sources of noise—reduces the "noise" portion of the signal-to-noise ratio. And it's free.

Emerging digital technologies are creating so much RF pollution that antenna location is becoming a key performance variable. One noise, broadband over power lines (BPL), is particularly odious because it acts, in effect, as a world band jammer. Fortunately, BPL is not yet widespread and hopefully never will be, but it can be fought with antenna placement.

Safe Installation

Safety is rule one during installation. Avoid falls or making contact with potentially lethal electrical utility and other lines.

There's much more to this than can be covered here, but it's detailed in the RADIO DATABASE INTERNATIONAL report, *Evaluation of Popular Outdoor Antennas*. Also, check out www.universal-radio.com/catalog/sw_ant/safeswl.html.

GO STRAIGHT?

Accessory antennas come in two flavors: unamplified or "passive" (typically outdoor), and amplified or "active" (indoor, outdoor or both). An unamplified antenna uses a wire or rod receiving element which sends radio signals straight to the receiver. All antennas in this article are unamplified.

An amplified or active antenna has a receiving element that's shorter but enhanced by an electronic boost. Certain models even outperform big outdoor antennas, at least with staticky signals below 5 MHz.

Amplified antennas are popular because they are compact, making them especially handy for apartments. Even homeowners sometimes prefer them because they are so inconspicuous and easy to erect.

But amplified antennas have potential drawbacks. First, their short receiving elements usually don't provide the signal-to-noise enhancement of lengthy elements. Second, the antenna's amplifier can generate noise of its own. Third, the antenna's amplifier can overload, with results comparable to those found when a receiver overloads . . . a mumbling mishmash of stations up and down the dial. Indeed, if antenna amplification is excessive it can overload the receiver, too.

Finally, many amplified antennas have mediocre front-end selectivity. This sometimes allows local mediumwave AM signals to get jumbled in with world band signals.

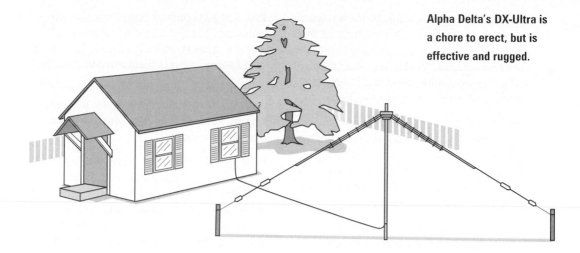

Alpha Delta's DX-Ultra is a chore to erect, but is effective and rugged.

What's Best?

For that RDI White Paper we also tested a number of popular outdoor wire antennas, three which are summarized here. All are dipoles which rely on traps for frequency resonance, but a variety of mounting layouts are used:

- End-fed sloper, with the antenna about 30 degrees from horizontal.
- Center-fed tapered wing, with a tall (about 20 feet or 6 meters) mounting amidships, plus two lower mountings.
- Center-fed horizontal, hung between two points of comparable height.

Passive antennas are tricky to evaluate properly. Reception varies by tuned frequency, so an overall rating is only a generalization. Performance even depends on such local imponderables as type of soil, moisture and bedrock.

So, don't hold back from "rolling your own" or buying something that, tests be damned, you think might do well at your location. There are countless designs on the market, and most wire antennas are eminently affordable.

Indeed, in the real world of tradeoffs and compromises the clincher may be yard space. Too, some wire antennas are almost

kits, while others arrive ready to put up. Do you have time or patience for the former?

Ratings

PASSPORT's star ratings mean the same thing regardless of whether an antenna is active or passive, big or little, indoor or out. This helps when you're trying to compare one type of antenna with another.

✪✪✪✪¼ *Passport's Choice*
Alpha Delta DX-Ultra

Price: $129.95 in the United States. $179.00CAD in Canada. Coaxial cable extra.

Pro: Best overall performer of any antenna tested, passive or active. Little variation in performance from one world band segment to another. Rugged construction. Comes with built-in static protection. Wing design appropriate for certain yard layouts. Covers mediumwave AM band.

Con: Assembly a major undertaking, with stiff wire having to be bent and fed through spacer holes, then affixed. Unusually lengthy, 80 feet or 25 meters. Coaxial cable lead-in not included. Relatively heavy, adding to erection effort. Warranty only six months.

Verdict: The Alpha Delta DX-Ultra rewards sweat equity—it is really more of a kit than a finished product. First, you have to purchase the needed lead-in cable and other hardware bits, then assemble, bend and stretch the many stiff wires, section-by-section.

Because the wire used should outlast the Pyramids, assembly is a trying and unforgiving exercise. Each wire needs to be rigorously and properly affixed, lest it slip loose and the erected antenna comes tumbling down, as it did at one of our test sites.

While all outdoor antennas require yard space, the Ultra is the longest manufactured antenna tested. It is also relatively heavy, making installation an even more tiresome chore than it already is. In ice-prone climates, be sure any trees or poles attached to the antenna are sturdy. Don't even think about using a chimney.

But if you have the yard space and don't object to assembly and erection hurdles, you are rewarded with a robust antenna that is outperformed only by hugely long inverted-L antennas and professional-grade antennas beyond the financial reach of even the most enthusiastic listener.

✪✪✪½ *Passport's Choice*
Alpha Delta DX-SWL Sloper

Price: $89.95 in the United States. $149.00CAD in Canada. Coaxial cable and static protector extra.

Pro: Rugged construction. Sloper design uses traps to keep the length down to 60 feet (18 meters), make it suitable for certain yard layouts. Covers mediumwave AM band.

Con: Requires assembly, a significant exercise. Does not include static protection. Coaxial cable lead-in not included. Warranty only six months.

☞ A greatly shortened version, the 40-foot (12 meter) DX-SWL-S (not tested), is available for $69.95, with coaxial cable and static protector extra. Its nominal coverage is 3.2–22 MHz, omitting the little-used 2 MHz (120 meter) world band segment. Although both Sloper versions nominally don't cover the 25 MHz (11 meter) world band segment, our measurements of the full-length Sloper show excellent results there (25650-26100 kHz).

Verdict: An excellent choice where space is limited, but a chore to assemble.

✪✪✪⅛ *Passport's Choice*
Eavesdropper Model T, Eavesdropper Model C

Price: *Model T:* $89.95, complete, in the United States. *Model C:* $89.95 in the United States. Coaxial cable extra.

The Alpha Delta DX-SWL
Sloper's layout works
nicely at some locations.

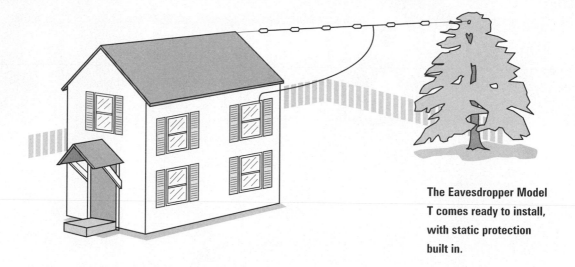

The Eavesdropper Model T comes ready to install, with static protection built in.

Pro: Unusually compact at 43 feet or 13 meters, it fits into many yards. Comes with built-in static protection. One-year warranty, after which repairs made "at nominal cost." *Model T:* Easiest to install of any Passport's Choice antenna—unpack, and it's ready to hang. Comes with ribbon lead-in wire, which tends to have less signal loss than coaxial cable. *Model C:* Easier than most to install, with virtually everything included and assembled but the coaxial cable lead-in.

Con: Some performance drop within the 2 MHz (120 meter) and 3 MHz (90 meter) tropical world band segments. *Model C:* Coaxial cable lead-in not included.

☞ Eavesdropper also makes the $89.95 sloper antenna, not tested by us, similar to the Alpha Delta DX-SWL Sloper. It comes with a static arrestor, but no coaxial cable lead-in.

Verdict: If your teeth gnash when you see packages saying, "Some Assembly Required," take heart. The Eavesdropper T, unlike the Alpha Delta alternatives, comes "ready to go" and is straightforward to erect. At most, you might want to get a pair of bungee straps to provide flexibility at the ends.

The size is user-friendly, too. There's no getting around the rule that the longer the antenna, the more likely it is to do well at low frequencies. The Eavesdropper's designer, the late Jim Meadow, once told PASSPORT that they found nearly no listener interest below 4.7 MHz. On the other hand, many folks had problems with yard space or wanted a shorter antenna less likely to come down in an ice storm. So, he designed the Eavesdropper to be relatively compact, yet perform optimally above 4.7 MHz while still working decently lower down.

Our tests confirm this. The Eavesdropper horizontal trap dipoles perform quite nicely above 4.7 MHz, with a notch less gain than Alpha-Delta models in the 2 MHz and 3 MHz tropical world band segments.

In practice the ribbon lead-in wire used by the T version works very well, using phasing to cancel out much electrical noise. Too, it stands up to the weather and usually has less signal loss than the coaxial cable used by its C sibling, which is preferable only when significant electrical noise is near the feedline.

Otherwise, the T version should get the nod.

Prepared by Stephen Bohac, Jock Elliott, Tony Jones, Lawrence Magne and David Walcutt.

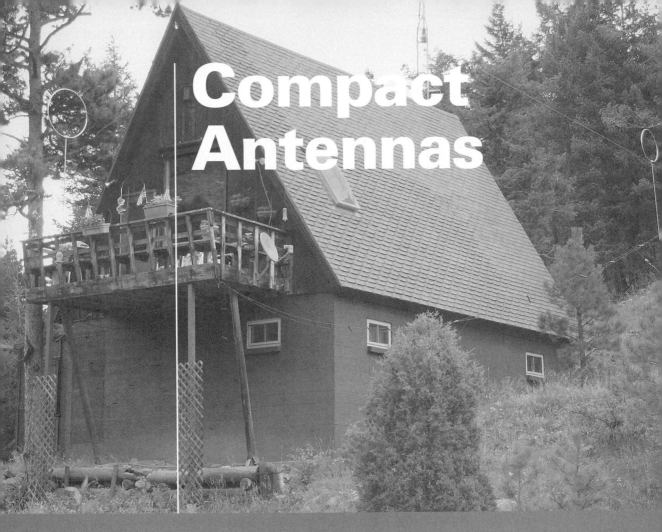

Compact Antennas

Do you surf world band by day, when signals are weaker? Or enjoy flushing out elusive stations, day or night? If so, a good accessory antenna should be on your wish list.

The best antennas consist of outdoor wires that are unamplified—*passive* in electrospeak. Trouble is, they are lengthy, inconvenient to erect (think, "big trees") and require beaucoup yard space. But if you don't have ample acreage or are allergic to high-wire gymnastics, there is something else: a compact antenna.

Compacts feature a small rod, loop or wire receiving element to snatch signals from the airwaves. Each has a little element that normally would provide weak signals to a receiver.

However, *active* compact antennas amplify those signals so they are about as strong as if they came from a lengthy wire antenna.

New Generation Improves Reception

Compact antennas are ideal for townhouses, apartments and hotels. Trouble is, early models were noisy, overloaded easily, generated harmonic "false" signals and suffered from the ravages of outdoor use. They quickly earned a reputation for failing to deliver what serious listeners demanded, and that reputation has tended to stick.

In recent years, however, a new generation of robust, well-engineered models have appeared. While no compact antenna fully equals a well-rated outdoor wire antenna, the gap has closed considerably. Indeed, some occasionally outperform passive wire antennas in lower frequencies during high-static months.

PASSPORT's tests have been limited to antennas likely to be satisfactorily under a wide range of circumstances. In addition to these tested models, there are elementary amplified antennas for everyday portables available at low cost from a variety of firms. In general, the weaker the overall signal strengths at your location, the greater the chances these rudimentary offerings may meet your needs.

> **Active compact antennas amplify signals, making them stronger.**

Proximate *vs.* Remote

Compact antennas come in two flavors: proximate and remote. With a proximate model the receiving element is affixed to an amplifier box beside the receiver. Remote models, whether active or passive, allow the receiving element to be mounted farther away—either indoors or, with some models, outdoors where reception is superior.

Remote units are the better way to go, as the receiving element can be placed where electrical noise seems least and incoming signals are strongest. Proximate models give you no such choice unless you are willing to move the entire receiver to where reception happens to be optimum.

The Yaesu G-5500 rotor not only turns, but tilts. With it, the Wellbrook ALA 1530 provides great reception from 0.15–5.1 MHz.

Too, many radios put out some degree of electrical "hash," or noise. Typically, this racket radiates forward from the receiver's digital display. So, if you must use a proximate antenna, put it behind or alongside the radio.

Loops Reduce Local Noise

Proximate loop antennas, such as the AOR LA-350, and indoor-remote loops, such as the AOR WL500 and Sony AN-LP1, are less prone than many other antennas to pick up local electrical noise. They can sometimes be aimed away from the source of disruptive electrical noise, and are less likely to pick up thunderstorm static. This can be a real plus, improving the signal-to-noise ratio—especially within lower frequency segments during warmer months.

Outdoors, Wellbrook loops are particularly effective in this regard. In part that's because, unlike the unbalanced LA-350 loop, they are balanced. During high-static summer months their superior signal-to-noise ratios can make the difference between hearing a pileup of static crashes and understanding what's being said.

Wellbrook models have been tweaked for 2005, but differences from earlier versions are not great. Both remain as top performers.

INSTALLATION TIPS

The good news is that if a top-rated compact antenna is installed properly, it can perform very well. The bad news is that if you have room outdoors to mount it optimally, you may also have room for a passive wire antenna that will perform better, yet. Probably cheaper, too.

Here are tips on placement of weather-resistant remote models, but creativity rules— don't be afraid to experiment.

- If you can mount the receiving element outdoors, put it out in the clear and away from anything metal. Use a nonconductive mast or capped PVC pipe, as metal masts or pipes may degrade performance. Optimum height from ground is usually around 10-25 feet or 3-8 meters. However, "ground" refers not to soil but to the electrical ground. This includes non-wooden roofs and the like.

  Not feasible? Try a nearby tree. Although tree sap is electrically conductive, this is a reasonable fallback, especially with hardwood deciduous varieties. Keep leaves from brushing up against the receiving element.

- If outdoor mounting is impractical, then at least place the receiving element out in the fresh air as far as possible. Even if you are in a high-rise building, this can work so long as a window opens or there is a balcony. For example, if the receiving element is a rod, you can point it away from the building 45 degrees or so, like a wall flagpole. If that is too unsubtle, try using a string or rope to pull it up, out of view, by day.

  If you are in a house with an attic, especially with no foil-lined insulation under the shingles and assuming the roof is not metal, that room can pretty much suffice if outdoor placement is not feasible. Indeed, with large Wellbrook models this is a tempting alternative to having it hog a regular room, especially if a rotor is used.

- If all these choices are impractical, then at least place the receiving element alongside a large window. Glass absorbs signals much less than most other materials.

Travel Loops Best for Portables

Most active antennas are designed for tabletop models, but not all. The Sony AN-LP1, great for home and on trips, is an exceptional value for use with nearly any portable. A second choice is the AOR WL500—pricier and less handy for trips, but an impressive performer.

Tough Model for Emergencies

Often the first thing to go in an emergency is electricity. Batteries sometimes fill in, but nothing beats not needing electricity in the first place.

The R.F. Systems GMDSS-1 is that most unusual of antennas: short, yet with no electronic amplification. And it is tough enough to withstand serious abuse without flinching.

Preselection *vs.* Broadband

Broadband electronic amplifiers can cause all sorts of mischief. Some add noise and spurious signals, especially from the mediumwave AM band; others overload a receiver with too much gain.

A partial fix is to have effective tunable or switchable preselection. Preselection limits the band of frequencies which get full amplification, reducing the odds of spurious signals being created by the antenna or the receiver. Preselectors with high "Q" also improve image rejection in some receivers. Problem is, preselectors almost always have controls that need tweaking, complicating the listening experience.

Also, a high-pass filter can reduce gain at frequencies below around two Megahertz. Or a band rejection filter, such as is offered by Kiwa Electronics and Par Electronics, can attenuate mediumwave AM frequencies. Either approach helps to keep powerful mediumwave AM stations from sneaking in to disrupt world band reception.

How Much Oomph?

One way to judge an active antenna is by how much gain it provides. Bad idea.

A good active antenna should provide about the same natural signal strengths as obtained from a worthy passive wire antenna. Less gain, then circuit noise might appear. Too much more gain and the receiver's dynamic range—and maybe the antenna's amplifier—might falter under the strain.

When Your Antenna Arrives

Active antennas work best when powered by battery, and some models permit this. Rechargeable batteries eliminate all possibility of hum and buzz caused, directly or indirectly, by an AC-to-DC power supply or adaptor.

Otherwise, keep AC adaptors and cords away from the antenna's receiving element and feedline. However, if hum results from the adaptor's power supply diodes not being properly bypassed, this probably won't help. Instead, try substituting a higher-end AC adaptor from Radio Shack or other vendor.

Antenna performance is one part technology, another part geography-geology, and a third part installation. Here, we report on the first, with tips on the third. But so much depends on the second—local conditions—that our analysis can only boost your odds of success.

You can up those odds by experimenting with different locations before the final setup. Too, if your radio has multiple antenna inputs, try each to see which works best.

What PASSPORT's Ratings Mean

Star ratings: ✪✪✪✪✪ is best for any type of antenna, but in reality even the best of compact antennas don't yet merit more than four stars when compared against long passive antennas. To help in deciding, star ratings for compact antennas can be compared directly against those for "lasso" antennas found elsewhere in this PASSPORT REPORTS. Stars reflect overall world band performance and meaningful features, plus to some extent ergonomics and build quality. Price, appearance, country of manufacture and the like are not taken into account.

Passport's Choice. La crème de la crème. Our test team's personal picks of the litter—models we would buy or have bought for our personal use. Unlike star ratings, these choices are unapologetically subjective.

☺: A relative bargain, with decidedly more performance than the price would suggest.

Active antennas are listed in descending order of merit. Unless otherwise indicated each has a one-year warranty.

Revised for 2005

✪✪✪✪   *Passport's Choice*
Wellbrook ALA 330S

Outdoor-indoor. Active, remote, broad-band, 2.3–30 MHz

Price: *ALA 330S:* £169.00 plus £10.00 shipping in the United Kingdom and Eire. £169.00 plus £30.00 shipping elsewhere. *Upgrade kit '330 to '330S:* £80.00 plus £10.00 shipping in the United Kingdom and Eire. £80.00 plus £15.00 shipping elsewhere.

Pro: Best signal-to-noise ratio, including at times reduced pickup of thunderstorm static, on all shortwave frequencies, of any active model tested; low-noise/low-static pickup characteristics most noticeable below 8 MHz, especially during local summer, when it sometimes outperforms sophisticated outdoor wire antennas. Balanced loop design inherently helps reduce pickup of local electrical noise; additionally, aluminum loop receiving element can be affixed to a low-cost TV rotor to improve reception by directionally nulling local electrical noise and, to a lesser degree, static. Sometimes, rotatability also can slightly reduce co-channel shortwave interference below about

5 MHz. Superior build quality, including rigorous weatherproofing (*see* Con). Supplied AC adaptor, properly bypassed and regulated, is among the best tested for not causing hum or buzzing. Although any large loop is inherently susceptible to inductive pickup of local thunderstorm static, during our tests of the prior and new versions the antenna's amplifier has never suffered static damage during storms; indeed, even nearby one kilowatt shortwave transmissions have not damaged the antenna amplifier. Protected circuitry, using an easily replaced 315 mA slow-blow fuse. Threaded flange on "S" version improves mounting of loop receiving element (*see* Con). Superior factory support.

Con: Only moderate gain for reception within such modest-signal areas as Western Hemisphere, Asia and Australasia—a drawback only with receivers having relatively noisy circuitry. Slightly less gain than ALA 1530 within little-used 2.3– 2.5 MHz (120 meter) tropical world band segment, a drawback only with receivers having relatively noisy circuitry. Medium-wave AM coverage, although improved in the new version, is inferior to that of the '1530. Flange for loop receiving element has metric pipe threading; most U.S. users will need to re-thread. Loop receiving element, about one meter across, is large and cumbersome to ship, although loop is slightly smaller than in the prior version. Mounting mast and optional rotor add to cost and complexity. BNC connector at the receiving element's base is open to the weather and thus needs to be user-sealed with Coax Seal, electrical putty or similar. Encapsulated amplifier makes repair impossible. Manufacturer cautions against allowing high winds to stress mounting flange, or sunlight to damage head amplifier; however, one of our units survived 90+ mph Rocky Mountain winds until the locally procured pipe coupling to which we had attached the antenna snapped. Adaptor supplied for 117V AC runs hot after being plugged in for a few hours, while amplifier tends to run slightly warm. No coaxial cable supplied. Available for purchase or export only two cumbersome ways: via Sterling cheque or International Money Order through the English manufacturer (www.wellbrook.uk.com), or with credit card via an English dealer's unsecured email address (sales@shortwave.co.uk).

☞ The manufacturer offers a kit to convert the earlier ALA 330 to the improved "S" version. Recommended.

☞ The '330S amplification that's new for 2005 allows two loops to be operated from one control box, saving money and space. For example, existing ALA1530 owners can purchase a '330S loop receiving element and feed both loops via a good A/B switch to the one control box and power supply. (Make sure that no switch setting shorts the loop's DC to ground.)

Verdict: The more we use this antenna, the more we like it, especially for its ability to reduce the impact of static and noise on weak signals below 8 MHz. If its dimensions and purchase hurdles don't deter you, you will not find a better active model than the Welsh-made Wellbrook ALA 330S.

For limited-space situations, and even to complement passive wire antennas on large properties, the '330S is hard to equal. However, if your receiver tends to sound "hissy" with weak signals, then it probably needs an antenna which gives even more gain than the '330S provides so it can help overcome internal receiver noise. Of course, with top-rated tabletop models this is not an issue.

For best reception the antenna should be mounted outdoors, away from the house and atop a rotor. However, this is more important with the ALA 1530 model (*see* below) when used for longwave and mediumwave AM reception. In the real world of limited options, reasonable results on shortwave are sometimes obtained even

The Wellbrook ALA 330S, revised for 2005, works best when high and in the clear.   R. Sherwood

indoors sans rotor or with manual rotation, provided the usual caveats are followed for placement of the reception element. But there's no getting around the laws of physics: The Wellbrook loop is an antenna, and all antennas work much better when not shielded by absorptive materials or placed near sources of electrical interference.

What's not to like? An ordering procedure that's inconvenient and démodé. There are no dealers outside the United Kingdom, and as there is still no secure way for those beyond U.K. borders to order by credit card on the Internet. Presumably this won't change anytime soon, as it limits ordering to those who emphatically want an antenna. In turn, this avoids straining the manufacturer's finite production capacity.

Even Wellbrook's latest tweak doesn't put the '330S into the same league as worthy outdoor wire antennas, such as those evaluated in PASSPORT REPORTS. However, the '330S can outperform even those antennas with some static-prone signals or when local electrical noise is a problem—provided it is erected properly.

Evaluation of Revised Version: One Wellbrook loop, the ALA1530, performs superbly with mediumwave AM stations and has been available for years. However, depending on how awash your location is in local radio signals, you might find the '1530 allowing mediumwave AM stations to "ghost" and cause audible disturbance to world band stations.

Alternatively, you could obtain a Wellbrook ALA330S designed to target shortwave reception. This model didn't have the "ghosting" problem, but reception was nigh deaf in the lower reaches of the AM band.

Enter Goldilocks. From the autumn of 2004 onwards, the manufacturer has tried to make the '330S "just right" by offering better pickup of mediumwave AM signals. The new version has the same gain as before at the top end of the mediumwave AM band, but much more at the lower end—only about 10 dB less than the ALA1530. Simultaneously, the amplification layout has been simplified, presumably to reduce cost. This was done by moving all gain to the loop receiving element instead of divvying it between that and the control box next to the receiver.

Except in settings very close to local medium-wave AM transmitters, there continues to be an almost complete absence of "ghosting" within the shortwave spectrum—including all world band segments. Yet, mediumwave AM reception, formerly poor below 1 MHz and hopeless around 540 kHz, is now reasonable even if not the stuff of DX dreams.

As before, the '330S performs best between 2 and 12 MHz, while at 7–14 MHz gain is virtually identical to last year's version. The 3–5 dB gain blip between 3 and 5 MHz in the earlier version is gone, with the level now more consistent from 2 through 12 MHz. This is consistent with good engineering practice, although some tropical band DXers might disagree.

As we were testing a late pre-production unit, we informed the manufacturer that we had encountered excessive gain above 15 MHz. This rise did nothing to improve the signal-to-noise ratio, but added to receiver burden and departed from the ideal of comparable gain throughout the shortwave spectrum. Wellbrook indicated it would remedy this in regular production by improving termination of the amplifier, so we made this change to our unit as indi-

SNEAKY ANTENNAS

Listeners facing antenna restrictions have concocted a dog's breakfast of hidden and camouflaged outdoor wire antennas. Some look like a clothesline or part of a badminton net, while others may be tucked underneath awnings or canopies.

Some folks play to urban apathy by erecting thin-wire antennas out in the open, then wait to see what happens. One creative Australian simply told a curious neighbor that his loop antenna was an art "sculpture"—it worked!

Trompe d'oeil antennas can perform surprisingly well when mated to an MFJ-1020C, around $80. Just unscrew its built-in antenna and use it as a tunable active preselector.

Deep pockets? If you want something James Bondish but ready to go, the SGC Stealth Antenna Kit (not tested) is £349.95 in the United Kingdom during sales, £489.00 otherwise.

cated. It reduced but didn't fully eliminate the problem, although this might be further tweaked by the time you read this.

Is the new version an improvement? For world band and other shortwave use, differences either way, cited above, are small potatoes. Yes, mediumwave AM reception is vastly improved below the top end of the band, but our overall rating for world band remains unchanged.

Wellbrook is retaining the ALA 330S model designation from the earlier version—normally not the best practice. But the lack of any real dealer network ensures that every model purchased new is the latest version.

Enhanced for 2005
❶❶❶⅛ *Passport's Choice*
Wellbrook ALA 1530, Wellbrook ALA 1530P

Outdoor-indoor. Active, remote, broadband, 0.15–30 MHz

Price: *ALA 1530:* £129.95 plus £10.00 shipping in the United Kingdom and Eire. £129.95 plus £30.00 shipping elsewhere. *ALA 1530P (not tested):* £129.95 plus £10.00 shipping in the United Kingdom and Eire. £129.95 plus £30.00 shipping elsewhere. *Yaesu G-5500/G-5500B twin-axis rotor:* $639.95 in the United States. $1,060.00CAD in Canada. £559.00 in the United Kingdom. €659.00 in Germany.

Pro: Covers at comparable levels of performance not only shortwave, but also mediumwave AM and longwave nominally down to 150 kHz—but actually down to 30 kHz with reduced sensitivity (*see* Con); other Wellbrook models offer longwave coverage down to 50 kHz (LA 5030, 50 kHz–30 MHz indoor model) or 10 kHz (LFL 1010, 10 kHz–10 MHz outdoor model). Mediumwave AM and longwave performance superb when '1530 coupled to a Yaesu G-5500/G-5550B rotor, which has twin-axis directionality; rotor can also slightly reduce co-channel

Wellbrook's ALA 1530 can be rotated by hand from a balcony or other convenient spot.   R. Sherwood

shortwave interference below about 5 MHz. Very nearly the best signal-to-noise ratio among active models tested, including reduced pickup of thunderstorm static. Balanced loop design inherently helps reduce pickup of local electrical noise. Low-noise/low-static pickup characteristic most noticeable below 8 MHz during summer, when it sometimes outperforms sophisticated outdoor wire antennas. Slightly more gain than sibling ALA 330S within little-used 2.3–2.5 MHz (120 meter) tropical world band segment. Superior build quality, including rigorous weatherproofing (*see* Con). Supplied AC adaptor, properly bypassed and regulated, is among the best tested for not causing hum or buzzing. Although any large loop's amplifier is inherently susceptible to inductive pickup of local thunderstorm static, during our tests the antenna's amp never suffered static damage during storms; indeed, even nearby one kilowatt shortwave transmissions did no damage to the antenna amplifier. Protected circuitry, using an easily replaced

315 mA slow-blow fuse. Superior factory support.

Con: Extended frequency range can result in mediumwave AM signals surfacing within the shortwave spectrum, degrading reception—usually a more significant issue in urban and suburban North America than elsewhere (even an unsophisticated rotor can help by turning the antenna perpendicular to an offending mediumwave AM signal's axis); this tends to be less of a problem at night because of reduced local transmitting powers, and is less of a problem in our latest unit. Prone to overloading some receivers in locations rich with strong mediumwave AM signals; this also tends to be less of a problem at night because of reduced local transmitting powers. Only moderate gain, slightly less than sibling ALA 330S, for reception within such modest-signal areas as Western Hemisphere, Asia and Australasia. Balanced loop receiving element, about one meter across, not easy to mount and is large and cumbersome to ship. Mounting mast and optional rotor add to cost and complexity of erection. BNC connector at the receiving element's base is open to the weather and thus needs to be user-sealed with Coax Seal, electrical putty or similar. Encapsulated amplifier makes repair impossible. Manufacturer cautions against allowing high winds to stress mounting flange or sunlight to damage head amplifier; however, after a summer of wind and sun at one outdoor test location, nothing untoward has materialized. Adaptor supplied for 117V AC runs hot after being plugged in for a few hours, while amplifier tends to run slightly warm. No coaxial cable supplied. Available for purchase or export only two cumbersome ways: via Sterling cheque or International Money Order through the English manufacturer (www.wellbrook.uk.com), or with credit card via an English dealer's unsecured email address (sales@shortwave.co.uk).

☞ If your receiver has antenna inputs with varying impedances, experiment to see which provides the greatest signal strength. Also, at times an antenna tuner can improve signal level as much as 6 dB.

☞ Mediumwave AM and longwave performance directionality may suffer if the '1530 is not mounted well away from other antennas.

☞ The "P" version, not tested uses a semi-rigid plastic loop rather than aluminum. It is intended for indoor use only.

Verdict: Interested in distant broadcast goodies below the shortwave spectrum, as well as world band? If so, the Wellbrook ALA 1530 is hard to beat—so long as you don't live near local mediumwave AM transmission facilities. A rotor is *de rigeur* for nulling co-channel interference below 1.7 MHz, and also can help with tropical world band stations. As with all Wellbrook loop antennas, the '1530 excels at rejecting noise and static, particularly below 8 MHz.

Keep in mind that the '1530 is the sibling of the former ALA 330, not the newer ALA 330S.

Evaluation of Revised Version: The ALA1530 loop has been going through a gentle evolution rather than a redo over the past few years. According to Wellbrook, the third-order intercept point of the head amplifier has been improved by about 6 dB in the mediumwave AM band, resulting is less overload from mediumwave AM stations. This could not be verified quantitatively, as we no longer have on hand the earlier version of the '1530. The loop itself is also slightly smaller.

For reception below 1.7 MHz the '1530, mounted well outdoors atop a proper rotor, is as good as we've come across among commercial antennas. For 2005 there's just enough noticeable improvement for those DXing longwave, mediumwave AM and shortwave to give the '1530 a fresh look. Although it is still susceptible to "ghosting" local mediumwave AM signals into the shortwave spectrum, for most locations this is now less likely to materialize.

Like its ALA330S sibling, for world band the '1530 doesn't provide the signal-to-noise ratio of a well-rated outdoor wire antenna. However, it can sometimes outperform even those antennas with staticky signals below 8 MHz.

✪✪✪½ *Passport's Choice*
RF Systems DX-One Professional Mark II

Outdoor-indoor "eggbeater." Active, remote, broadband, 0.02-60 MHz.

Price: *DX-One Pro antenna:* $669.95 in the United States. £359.95 in the United Kingdom. €498.00 in Germany. $1,170.00AUD in Australia.

Pro: Outstanding dynamic range. Very low noise. Outputs for two receivers. Comes standard with switchable band rejection filter to reduce the chances of mediumwave AM signals ghosting into the shortwave spectrum. Receiving element has outstanding build quality. Coaxial connector at head amplifier is completely shielded from the weather by a clever mechanical design. Superior low noise, high gain performance on mediumwave AM.

Con: Unbalanced design makes antenna susceptible to importing buzz at some locations; this is especially noticeable because of otherwise-excellent performance. AC power supply not bypassed as well as it could be, causing slight hum on some signals. More likely than most antennas to exacerbate fading, even though design nominally reduces fading effects. No coaxial cable supplied. Output position for 10 dB gain measures +6 dB. Warranty only six months.

Verdict: Substantially improved over the discontinued original version, the pricey new RF Systems DX-One Professional Mark II is now a superior performer. As with any antenna with a small capture area that has an unbalanced design, at some locations it will be prone to pick up local electrical noise. Made in the Netherlands.

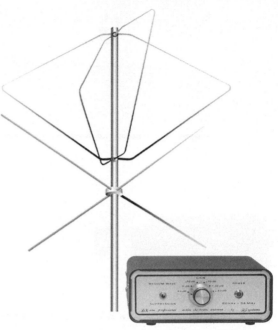

The RF Systems DX-One Professional Mark II is used by embassies and intelligence eavesdroppers. R. Sherwood

✪✪✪¼ *Passport's Choice*
AOR WL500

Indoor-portable loop. Active, remote, manual preselection, 0.155–1.71 MHz + 3.1–30 MHz.

Price: *WL500, 3.1-30 MHz:* $198.95 in the United States. *Optional 500LM, 0.155-1.71 MHz:* $74.95 in the United States.

Pro: Very good for use with portable receivers; also works well with portatop and tabletop models. Can be easily assembled and disassembled during airline and other travel, although its transportability is not so clever as that of the Sony AN-LP1 (the '500 uses zip cord held in place by a two-piece wooden rod with wing nuts on the ends); except for the two rod parts, which could be sharpened and used as weapons, it is handy for hospital, prison or other institutional use where an antenna must be stashed away periodically. Excellent gain. As compared to proximate antennas and most other indoor-remote antennas, somewhat lower pickup of local

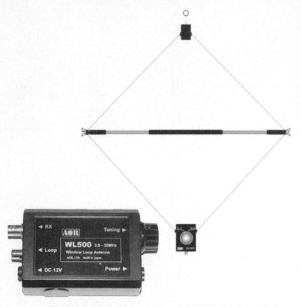

Best travel antenna is the AOR WL500 loop. It has excellent gain, and works with tabletop and portatop receivers, alike. Many better-rated portables, too. However, it costs more than the Sony AN-LP1 travel loop and is harder to set up.

electrical noise. Modest battery consumption (16 mA) allows for use without an AC adaptor; this prevents added hum and noise (*see* Con). Screw configuration to access battery cavity unlikely to be stripped with use (*see* Con).

Con: One of only two remote models tested which can't be mounted outdoors during inclement weather. Possible sensitivity to static charges (*see first* ☞, below). Some birdies and tweets, possibly from incipient spurious oscillation. Two rod parts could be thought of by airport security as potential weapons, so should be stowed as checked luggage. Performs only marginally within little-used 2 MHz (120 meter) tropical world band segment. Requires manual peaking when significantly changing received frequency, although not as often as some other models thanks to fairly low circuit "Q." Changing 9V battery calls for unscrewing six annoyingly tiny screws to remove protective plate. AC adaptor not available

from AOR for continuous-use applications, although manufacturer states that one eventually will be offered in certain as-yet-unspecified markets (alternatively, an outboard rechargeable battery can be used). Comes with only a BNC connector for the receiver; user has to modify the antenna-to-receiver cable or obtain adaptors for other types of receiver inputs. Comes with two wing nuts that are easily lost on trips; frequent travelers should obtain spares in advance. Optional longwave/mediumwave receiving element performs poorly, not recommended.

☞ Our first sample ceased functioning in a low-humidity environment when the operator's hand apparently discharged static electricity onto the connector to the antenna range switch. This happened as he reached to adjust it from high to low range, damaging circuitry within the control box at the opposite end of the cable. However, those who sell the antenna indicate that there have been no other known failures of this sort, but this is a new model so it's not yet certain whether the '500's interface unit is genuinely sensitive to static charges.

☞ Although the lower tuning parameter of the WL500 is nominally 3.5 MHz, tests show that performance remains equally good down to just below 3.1 MHz.

Verdict: For the traveling listener or DXer focused on reception quality, the new AOR WL500 is a welcome but pricey alternative to the Sony AN-LP1. Overall, it slightly outperforms the Sony, but it lacks the Sony's spit and polish for mounting and packing on trips. Both are made in Japan.

✪✪✪
Dressler ARA 100 HDX

Outdoor-indoor rod. Active, remote, broadband, 0.04-40 MHz.

Price: $529.95 in the United States. £349.95 in the United Kingdom.

Pro: Superior build quality, with fiberglass whip and foam-encapsulated head amplifier to resist the weather (*see* Con). Very good gain below 20 MHz (*see* Con). Superior signal-to-noise ratio. Handy detachable "N" connector on bottom. AC adaptor with properly bypassed and regulated DC output is better than most.

Con: Even though it has an amplifier with superior dynamic range, tends to overload in urban/suburban environments awash in powerful mediumwave AM signals unless antenna element mounted close to the ground; this tends to be less of a problem at night because of reduced local transmitting powers. Encapsulated design makes most repairs impossible. Above 20 MHz gain begins to fall off slightly. Body of antenna runs slightly warm. "N" connector at the head amplifier/receiving element exposed to weather, needs to be sealed with Coax Seal, electrical putty or similar by user. Gain control cumbersome to adjust; fortunately, in practice it is rarely needed. Reader reports suggest that ordering direct from the factory can be a frustrating experience.

☞ Star rating applies only when used where there is not significant ambient mediumwave RF, as the Dressler ARA 100 HDX, unless mounted close to the ground, is prone to overloading at locations rich with strong mediumwave AM signals or low-band VHF-TV stations. At some locations, even mounting the antenna on the ground does not eliminate overloading.

Verdict: The robust Dressler ARA 100 HDX, made in Germany, is an excellent but costly low-noise antenna so long as you are not located near one or more powerful mediumwave AM or low-band VHF-TV transmitters.

✪✪✪ ✐ *Passport's Choice*
MFJ-1020C (with short wire element)

Outdoor-indoor wire. Active, remote, manual preselection, 0.3-40 MHz.

Price: *MFJ-1020C (without antenna wire or insulators):* $79.95 in the United States.

Dressler's **ARA 100 HDX** and **ARA 60** are steeply priced for the performance offered. R. Sherwood

$125.00CAD in Canada. £89.95 in the United Kingdom. $229.00AUD in Australia. *MFJ-1312D 120V AC adaptor:* $14.95 in the United States. *Radio Shack 278-758 "Outdoor Antenna Kit":* $9.99 in the United States.

Pro: Superior dynamic range, so functions effectively with an outboard wire receiving element, preferably mounted outdoors, in lieu of built-in telescopic antenna element. Sharp preselector peak unusually effective in preventing overloading. Works best off battery (*see* Con). Choice of PL-259 or RCA connections. 30-day money-back guarantee if purchased from manufacturer.

Con: Preselector complicates operation; tune control needs adjustment even with modest frequency changes, especially within the mediumwave AM band. Knobs small and touchy to adjust. High current draw (measures 30 mA), so battery runs down quickly. Removing sheet-metal screws often to change battery should eventually result in stripping unless great care is taken. AC adaptor, optional, causes significant hum on many received signals.

**The MFJ-1020C antenna works nicely with a short
length of outdoor wire. Forget its built-in rod.**

R. Sherwood

☞ The '1020C serves little or no useful
purpose as a tunable preselector for *long*
inverted-L or other normally passive wire
antennas. It cannot be used as an unamplified
preselector; e.g., to improve front-end
selectivity with significant wire antennas.
Trying to do something similar by using the
amplified unit at reduced gain does not
improve the signal-to-noise ratio, nor does it
improve dynamic range (reduce potential to
overload), as the gain potentiometer is only
an output pad (with a measured 40 dB range).

☞ Two manufacturing flaws found on one
of our "B" version units tested in the past,
but this year's "C" unit had no defects. The
owner's manual warns of possible "taking
off" if the gain is set too high, but during our
tests using a variety of receivers we
encountered oscillation with only one model.

Verdict: The '1020C has a little secret: It's
only okay the way the manufacturer sells it
as a proximate active antenna, but as a
preselector with an outdoor random-length
wire antenna it is a worthy low-cost
performer. Simply collapse (or, better,
remove) the built-in telescopic antenna,
then connect the outboard wire antenna to
the '1020C's external antenna input. For
this, Radio Shack's "Outdoor Antenna Kit"
or equivalent works fine, with the receiving
element cut down to a convenient length.

Alas, the optional AC adaptor introduces
hum much of the time, battery drain is
considerable, and changing the built-in
battery is inconvenient and relies on wear-
prone sheet-metal screws. Best bet, unless
you're into experimenting with power
supplies: Skip the adaptor and use a large
outboard rechargeable battery.

Peso for peso, the MFJ-1020C fed by a
remote wire receiving element is the best
buy among active antennas. The rub is the
use of several yards or meters of wire,
preferably outdoors, makes it something of
a hybrid requiring more space than usual.
But for many row houses, townhouses,
ground-floor and rooftop apartments with a
patch of space outdoors it can be a god-
send. If visibility is an issue, use ultra-thin
wire for the receiving element, or consider it
as an environmentally friendly alternative to
power lines as a resting spot for birds.

✪✪✪
Dressler ARA 60 S

**Outdoor-indoor rod. Active, remote,
broadband, 0.04–60/100 MHz.**

Price: $299.95 in the United States. £189.95
in the United Kingdom. €219.00 in Germany.

Pro: Superior build quality, with fiberglass
whip and foam-encapsulated head amplifier
to resist weather (*see* Con). Very good and
consistent gain, even above 20 MHz. AC
adaptor with properly bypassed and
regulated DC output is better than most.

Con: Encapsulated design makes most
repairs impossible. RG-58 coaxial cable
permanently attached on antenna end,
making user replacement impossible. Gain
control cumbersome to adjust; fortunately,
in practice it is rarely needed. Reader
reports suggest that ordering direct from
the factory can be a frustrating experience.

☞ Comments about overloading in the above
review of the ARA 100 HDX likely apply to
the '60 S, as well.

Verdict: Very similar to the ARA 100 HDX—even its dynamic range and overloading performance are virtually identical. This makes the German-made ARA 60 S an excellent lower-cost alternative to the ARA 100 HDX.

New for 2005
✪✪⅞
RF Systems GMDSS-1

Outdoor vertical rod. Passive, remote, broadband, 0.1–25 MHz.

Price: *Antenna:* $204.95 in the United States. €158.00 in the Netherlands. *AK-1 mounting bracket kit:* $22.95 in the United States. *AK-2 mounting bracket kit:* $34.95 in the United States. €35.00 in the Netherlands.

Pro: Superior signal-to-noise ratio for a compact antenna except within 21 MHz segment. Superior rejection of local electrical noise. Passive (unamplified) design avoids hum, buzz and other shortcomings often inherent with active antennas (*see* Con). No amplification required; yet, from about 9–12 MHz this short antenna (6.5 feet, two meters) produces signals almost comparable to those from a lengthy outdoor wire antenna (*see* Con). Passive design allows it to function in emergency situations where electricity is not assured. Vertical configuration unusually appropriate for certain locations; can be further camouflaged with non-metallic paint. Superior build quality, using stainless steel and heavy UV resistant PVC; also, internal helical receiving element is rigorously sealed (*see* Con). No radials required, unusual for a vertical antenna. Worthy mediumwave AM reception for a nondirectional antenna.

Con: Except for approximately 9–12 MHz, weak-signal performance varies from fair to poor, depending on the tuned frequency. Required AK-1 mounting bracket kit, sold in North America, not stainless. Mounting bracket kit extra. Connecting cable between antenna and radio not included.

☞ A slightly less costly variant of the GMDSS-1 is the RF Systems MTA-1, which nominally operates to full specification from 0.5–30 MHz.

Verdict: Although unamplified and scarcely taller than most men, the RF Systems GMDSS-1 vertical performs surprisingly well. However, pedestrian signal oomph in many world band segments limits its attraction except with a high-sensitivity receiver or an active preselector. Some portables can also benefit from the modest signal input.

Made in the Netherlands, it is constructed like a tank. Between this and its complete independence from electricity, it is unusually appropriate for emergencies, civil disorders and hostile climates.

Evaluation of New Model: At first glance, you would think that at this height—6.5 feet, or two meters—the RF Systems GMDSS-1 would need electronic amplification to provide even modest results.

Not so. Lacking electronics, which can add a cluster of reception problems, reception is refreshingly clean, providing an excellent signal-to-noise ratio not only because it lacks electronics, but also with respect to local electrical noises. This is accomplished in part by a totally grounded element and a Magnetic Transfer Balun to diminish background noise. Signal strength is generally quite good from roughly 9–12 MHz—this varies by location and other factors—but otherwise is not enough to do justice to weak signals. Indeed, the 21 MHz

RF Systems tank-tough GMDDS-1 vertical has no amplifier, so gain is limited. However, this also makes it an atom-quiet performer that never needs batteries or other juice.

segment not only had disappointing signal strength, but also relatively higher noise.

Nevertheless, as with all antennas, the farther the antenna is mounted from sources of electrical noise, the better the signal-to-noise ratio. Higher is almost always better, too.

The GMDSS-1 counts on receiver sensitivity to make up for the weak signals provided on most frequencies by the short element. Alternatively, an active preselector or even preamplifier can be added, although this somewhat defeats the purpose of using a passive antenna.

This is arguably the easiest of vertical antennas to erect, as it requires no radials. Construction is tank-like, with stainless steel, heavy UV resistant PVC and a rigorously sealed internal helical receiving element. Add to that a lack of electronics, and this is an antenna for the Ages. However, the required mounting hardware is not provided and, at least in the AK-1 offering, is not stainless (sticky goo is included to keep threads from rusting). Also not provided is the necessary coaxial cable and fittings to connect the antenna to a receiver. Most users will want to obtain cable with fittings already attached.

Handy, portable and affordable, the Sony AN-LP1 is a worldwide favorite for travel. R. Sherwood

★★¾ ● ✍ Passport's Choice
Sony AN-LP1

Indoor-portable loop. Active, remote, manual preselection, 3.9–4.3/4.7–25 MHz.

Price: $94.95 in the United States. €99.95 in Germany.

Pro: Excellent for use with portable receivers. Very good overall performance, including generally superior gain (see Con), especially within world band segments—yet surprisingly free from side effects. Battery operation, so no internally caused hum or noise (see Con). Clever compact folding design for airline and other travel; also handy for hospital, prison or other institutional use where an antenna must be stashed away periodically. Can be used even with portables that have no antenna input jack (see Con). Plug-in filter to reduce local electrical noise (see Con). Low battery consumption (see Con). Powered by the radio when used with Sony ICF-SW7600GR, ICF-SW7600G or ICF-SW1000T portables.

Con: One of only two remote models tested which can't be mounted outdoors during inclement weather. Functions acceptably on shortwave only between 3.9–4.3 MHz and 4.7–25 MHz, with no mediumwave AM coverage. Gain varies markedly throughout the shortwave spectrum, in large part because the preselector's step-tuned resonances lack variable peaking. Preselector bandswitching complicates operation slightly. Battery operation only (two "AA," not included)—no AC power supply, not even a socket for an AC adaptor—although battery drain is minimal. Consumer-grade plastic construction with no shielding. When clipped onto a telescopic antenna instead of fed through an antenna jack, the lack of a ground connection reduces performance. Plug-in noise filter unit reduces signal strength by several decibels.

☞ Sony recommends that the AN-LP1 not be used with the Sony ICF-SW77 receiver.

However, our tests indicate that so long as the control box and loop receiving element are kept reasonably away from the radio, the antenna performs well.

☞ The Sony ICF-SW07 compact portable comes with an AN-LP2 antenna. This is virtually identical in concept and performance to the AN-LP1, except that because it is designed solely for use with the 'SW07 it has automatic preselection to simplify operation. At present the AN-LP2 cannot be used with other radios, even those from Sony.

Verdict: A real winner if the shoe fits. This is the handiest model for travelers wanting superior world band reception on portables—and it is truly portable. It is often a worthy choice for portatop and tabletop models, as well, provided you don't mind battery-only operation. This Japanese-made device has generally excellent gain, low noise and few side effects. Priced right, too.

There is limited frequency coverage—90/ 120 meter DXers should look elsewhere— and the loop receiving element cannot be mounted permanently outdoors. Too, the lack of variable preselector peaking causes gain to vary greatly by frequency; this especially limits utility DX performance. Otherwise, the Sony AN-LP1 is nothing short of a bargain.

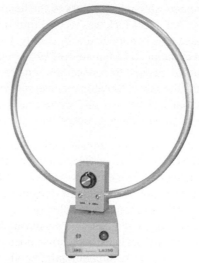

The AOR LA-350 rotatable indoor loop antenna is handy for locations with low signal absorption. R. Sherwood

⊗⊗¾
AOR LA-350

Indoor loop. Active, proximate, manual preselection, 0.2-1.6 MHz/2.5-33 MHz.

Price: *LA-350 antenna, with two shortwave elements:* $339.95 in the United States. £199.00 in the United Kingdom. €349.00 in Germany. *350L longwave element, 350M mediumwave AM element:* $72.95 each in the United States. £49.00 in the United Kingdom. €79.95 in Germany.

Pro: Above-average gain. Some directivity below 10 MHz, directionally nulling local electrical noise and static. Sometimes, rotatability can also slightly reduce co-channel shortwave interference; as is the norm with loop antennas, this modest nulling of co-channel skywave interference is best at frequencies below 5 MHz. Rotatability can also improve reception by directionally nulling local electrical noise. Small, easy to rotate. Antenna elements easy to swap (*see* Con). Relatively easy to peak by ear or signal-strength indicator (*see* Con).

Con: Proximate model, so receiving element has to be placed near receiver. Unbalanced design results in local electrical noise being passed into receiver at some locations; owner's manual says a better AC adaptor can reduce this, but a $300 product should come equipped with the proper adaptor. Requires change of antenna elements when going from 3–9 MHz range to 9–33 MHz range or *vice versa*; separate (optional) elements for mediumwave AM and longwave also require shuffling. Reduced performance within 2 MHz (120 meter) world band segment. Requires manual peaking when significantly changing received frequency. Phone plug, which connects antenna elements to the head amplifier, lacks lock washer and thus may loosen; easily remedied with Loctite. User has to supply BNC female-to-PL239 male adaptor, needed to connect antenna to many models of tabletop receivers. Owner's manual says BNC-to-BNC cable comes with antenna, but was not packed with our unit.

Verdict: The '350's unbalanced design makes it more susceptible to local electrical noise pickup than either Wellbrook model, and the supplied AC adaptor doesn't help. It also requires manual swapping of loop heads and circuit peaking. This having been said, where local electrical noise doesn't intrude the '350's superior gain, handy size and ease of rotation make it an effective choice for indoor use.

✪✪½ ✐
Ameco TPA

Indoor rod. Active, proximate, manual preselection, 0.22–30 MHz.

Price: $76.95 in the United States.

Pro: Highest recovered signal with the longest supplied whip of the four proximate models tested. Most pleasant unit to tune to proper frequency. Superior ergonomics, including easy-to-read front panel with good-sized metal knobs (*see* Con). Superior gain below 10 MHz.

Con: Proximate model, so receiving element has to be placed near receiver. Above 15 MHz gain slips to slightly below

The Ameco TPA works agreeably with its built-in rod, but nothing more.   R. Sherwood

average. Overloads with external antenna; because gain potentiometer is in the first stage, decreasing gain may increase overloading as current drops through the FET. Preselector complicates operation, compromising otherwise-superior ergonomics. No rubber feet, slides around in use; user-remediable. No AC adaptor. Consumer-grade plastic construction with no shielding. Comes with no printed information on warranty; however, manufacturer states by telephone that it is the customary one year.

Verdict: Since 2004 the venerable Ameco TPA has been associated with a new firm, Milestone Technologies of Colorado. It remains one of the best proximate models tested for bringing in usable signals with the factory-supplied whip—signal recovery is excellent. However, when connected to an external antenna it overloads badly, and reducing gain doesn't help.

✪✪½
McKay Dymek DA100E, McKay Dymek DA100EM, Stoner Dymek DA100E, Stoner Dymek DA100EM

Indoor-outdoor-marine rod. Active, remote, broadband, 0.05–30 MHz.

Price: *DA100E:* $179.95 in the United States. *DA100EM (marine version, not tested):* $199.95 in the United States.

Pro: Respectable gain and noise. Generally good build quality, with worthy coaxial cable and an effectively sealed receiving element; marine version (not tested) appears to be even better yet for resisting weather. Jack for second antenna when turned off. Minor gain rolloff at higher shortwave frequencies. *DA100EM (not tested):* Weather-resistant fiberglass whip and brass fittings help ensure continued optimum performance.

Con: Slightly higher noise floor compared to other models. Some controls may confuse initially. Dynamic range among the lowest of any model tested; for many applications in the Americas this is adequate, but for use near local transmitters, or in Europe and other strong-signal parts of the world, the antenna is best purchased on a returnable basis. *DA100E:* Telescopic antenna allows moisture and avian waste penetration between segments, and thus potential resistance and/or spurious signals; user should seal these gaps with Coax Seal, electrical putty or similar. Telescopic antenna could, in principle, be de-telescoped by birds, ice and the like, although we did not actually encounter this. Warranty only 30 days.

Verdict: The DA100E is a proven "out of the box" choice, with generally excellent weatherproofing and coaxial cable. Because its dynamic range is relatively modest, it is more prone than some other models to overload, especially in an urban environment or other high-signal-strength location. In principle the extra twenty bucks for the marine version should be a good investment, provided its fiberglass whip is not too visible for your location.

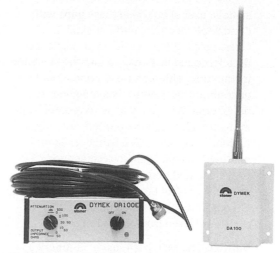

The Dymek DA100E uses a proven design that's been tweaked over many years. R. Sherwood

beforehand. Dynamic range among the lowest of any model tested; for many applications in the Americas it is adequate, but for use near local transmitters, or in Europe and other strong-signal parts of the world, antenna is best purchased on a returnable basis. Slightly increased noise floor compared to other models. Telescopic antenna allows moisture and avian waste penetration between segments, and thus potential resistance and/or spurious

✪✪¼
MFJ-1024

Indoor-outdoor rod. Active, remote, broadband, 0.05–30 MHz.

Price: $139.95 in the United States. $220.00CAD in Canada. £149.95 in the United Kingdom. $349.00AUD in Australia.

Pro: Overall good gain and low noise. A/B selector for quick connection to another receiver. "Aux" input for passive antenna. 30-day money-back guarantee if purchased from manufacturer.

Con: Significant hum with supplied AC adaptor; remedied when we substituted a suitable aftermarket adaptor. Non-standard power socket complicates substitution of AC adaptor; also, adaptor's sub-mini plug can spark when inserted while the adaptor is plugged in; adaptor should be unplugged

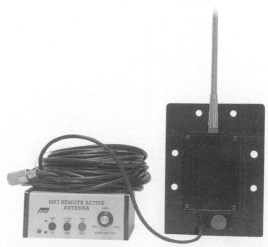

MFJ offers a remote compact antenna, the 1024. Handy, but a pedestrian performer. R. Sherwood

signals; user should seal these gaps with Coax Seal, electrical putty or similar. Telescopic antenna could, in principle, be de-telescoped by birds, ice and the like after installation, although we did not actually encounter this. Control box/amplifier has no external weather sealing to protect from moisture, although the printed circuit board nominally comes with a water-resistant coating. Coaxial cable to receiver not provided. Mediocre coaxial cable provided between control box and receiving element. On our unit, a coaxial connector came poorly soldered from the factory.

Verdict: The MFJ-1024, made in America, performs almost identically to the Stoner Dymek DA100E, but sells for $40 less. However, that gap lessens if you factor in the cost of a worthy AC adaptor—assuming you can find or alter one to fit the unusual power jack—and the quality of the 1024's coaxial cable is not in the same league.

✪✪¼
MFJ-1020C

Indoor rod. Active, proximate, manual preselection, 0.3–40 MHz.

Price: *MFJ-1020C:* $79.95 in the United States. $125.00CAD in Canada. £89.95 in the United Kingdom. $229.00AUD in Australia. *MFJ-1312D 120V AC adaptor:* $14.95 in the United States.

Pro: Rating rises to three stars if converted from a proximate to a remote model by connecting a wire to the external antenna input; see separate review, above. Superior dynamic range, and sharp preselector peak unusually effective in preventing overloading. Works best off battery (*see* Con). Choice of PL-259 or RCA connections. 30-day money-back guarantee if purchased from manufacturer.

Con: Proximate model, so receiving element has to be placed near receiver (can be converted, *see* Pro). Preselector complicates operation; tune control needs adjustment even with modest frequency changes, especially within the mediumwave AM band. Knobs small and touchy to adjust. High current draw (measures 30 mA), so battery runs down quickly. Removing sheet-metal screws often to change battery should eventually result in stripping unless great care is taken. AC adaptor, optional, causes significant hum on many received signals.

☞ Two manufacturing flaws found on one of our "B" version units tested in the past, but this year's "C" unit had no defects. The owner's manual warns of possible "taking off" if the gain is set too high, but during our tests using a variety of receivers we encountered oscillation with only one model.

Verdict: The MFJ-1020C, made in the United States, is okay as a proximate antenna with its own telescopic antenna. However, it works very well when coupled to a random-length wire in lieu of the built-in telescopic antenna; see the separate review earlier in this article.

Alas, the optional AC adaptor introduces hum much of the time, battery drain is considerable, and changing the built-in battery is inconvenient and relies on wear-prone sheet-metal screws. Best bet, unless you're into experimenting with power

Nicely priced, the MFJ-1020C can be either proximate or remote.   R. Sherwood

supplies: Skip the adaptor and use a large outboard rechargeable battery.

✪✪
Vectronics AT-100

Indoor rod. Active, proximate, manual preselection, 0.3–30 MHz.

Price: $79.95 in the United States. $109.00CAD in Canada. £79.95 in the United Kingdom.

Pro: Good—sometimes excellent—gain (*see* Con), especially in the mediumwave AM band. Good dynamic range. Most knobs are commendably large.

Con: Proximate model, so receiving element has to be placed near receiver. No AC power; although it accepts an AC adaptor, the lack of polarity markings complicates adaptor choice (it is center-pin positive). Preselector complicates operation, especially as it is stiff to tune and thus awkward to peak. Our unit oscillated badly with some receivers, limiting usable gain—although it was more stable with other receivers, and thus appears to be a function of the load presented by a given receiver.

Verdict: If ever there were a product that needs to be purchased on a returnable basis, this is it. With one receiver, this American-made model gives welcome gain and worthy performance; with another, it goes into oscillation nearly at the drop of a hat.

✪¾
Sony AN-1

Indoor-outdoor rod. Remote, broadband, 0.15–30 MHz.

Price: *AN-1:* $89.95 in the United States. €119.00 in Germany. *Aftermarket AC adaptor:* $14.95 in the United States.

Pro: Connects easily to any portable or other receiver, using supplied cables and inductive coupler. Unusually appropriate for low-cost portables lacking an outboard

The Vectronics AT-100 sometimes works well, sometimes not. Purchase on a returnable basis.
R. Sherwood

antenna input. Only portable-oriented model tested with weather resistant remote receiving element. Unlike Sony AN-LP1, it covers entire shortwave spectrum, plus mediumwave AM and longwave. AC adaptor jack, although antenna designed to run on six "AA" batteries. Good quality coaxial cable. Coaxial cable user replaceable once head unit is disassembled. Switchable high-pass filter helps reduce intrusion of mediumwave AM signals into shortwave spectrum; rolloff begins at 3 MHz. Receiving element's bracket allows for nearly any mounting configuration (*see* Con).

Con: Poor gain, with pronounced reduction as frequency increases. Mediocre

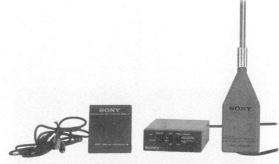

The Sony AN-1's plain appearance and broad coverage have won it favor among traveling intelligence operatives. R. Sherwood

mediumwave AM performance. Clumsy but versatile mounting bracket makes installation tedious. No AC adaptor included, although works off aftermarket adaptors.

☞ Sony offers a number of active antennas in various world markets. All appear to be similar to the AN-1, except for the very different AN-LP1.

Verdict: The Japanese-made Sony AN-1 has feeble gain, rendering it practically useless on higher frequencies and little better below. It is also can be hard to find; indeed, in the recent past it has been discontinued, only to later become un-discontinued. However, for outdoor mounting and reception on lower frequencies it provides passable performance.

✪¾
Palstar AA30/AA30A/AA30P/AM-30

Indoor rod. Active, proximate, manual preselection, 0.3–30 MHz.

Price: *AA30/AA30A:* $99.95 in the United States. £69.95 in the United Kingdom. *AA30P (not tested):* €96.50 in Germany. *AM-30 (not tested):* £69.95 in the United Kingdom.

Pro: Moderate-to-good gain. Tuning control easily peaked. Can be powered directly by the Palstar R30/R30C and Lowe HF-350 tabletop receivers, an internal battery or an AC adaptor.

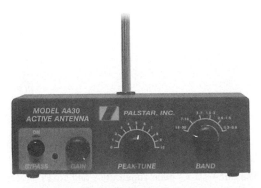

The Palstar AA30 suffers from oscillation but has good gain.   R. Sherwood

Con: Spurious oscillation throughout 14-30 MHz range. Overloads with external antenna. Proximate model, so receiving element has to be placed near receiver. Preselector complicates operation. No AC adaptor.

☞ At present, the AA30A's cabinets are silk screened simply as "AA30," although the accompanying owner's manual refers to the "AA30A."

☞ The Palstar AM-30, not tested, is sometimes sold in Europe. It appears to be comparable to the AA30A.

Verdict: Oscillation makes this a dubious choice except for reception below 14 MHz. Manufactured in the United States.

✪¾ ⓒ
MFJ-1022

Indoor rod. Active, proximate, broadband, 0.3–200 MHz.

Price: *MFJ-1022:* $49.95 in the United States. £55.95 in the United Kingdom. $119.00AUD in Australia. *MFJ-1312D 120V AC adaptor:* $14.95 in the United States.

Pro: Unusually broadband coverage reaches well into VHF spectrum. Considerable gain, peaking at 22.5 MHz, audibly helps signals that do not suffer from intermodulation. Idiot-proof to operate. Works best off battery (*see* Con). 30-day money-back guarantee if purchased from manufacturer.

Con: Proximate model, so receiving element has to be placed near receiver. Broadband design results in local mediumwave AM stations ghosting up to 2.7 MHz, and to a lesser degree up through the 3 MHz (90 meter) tropical world band segment at many locations; this often drops at night because of reduced local transmitting powers. Broadband design and high gain not infrequently results in intermodulation products/spurious signals and hiss between reasonable-level signals, and sometimes mixing with weaker signals. Within tropical world band segments, modest-level static from nearby thunderstorms, when coupled with overloading from local mediumwave AM signals, sometimes cause odd background sounds that are not heard with other antennas. High current draw (measures 35 mA), so battery runs down quickly. Removing sheet-metal screws often to change battery should eventually result in stripping unless great care is taken. AC adaptor, optional, causes significant hum on many received signals.

Verdict: Priced to move and offering broadband coverage, this compact antenna from MFJ couldn't be simpler to operate— one button, that's it. For helping to improve the listening quality of modest-strength international broadcasting signals, it works quite nicely. But don't expect to do much DXing, especially of the tropical world band segments unless you live well away from

The MFJ-1022 is inexpensive and easy to use, with modest performance. R. Sherwood

any mediumwave AM stations, and maybe not even then. Forget the AC adaptor and stick to batteries.

_____

Prepared by Robert Sherwood, with George Heidelman, Chuck Rippel and David Zantow; also, Lawrence Magne, with Carl Silberman.

WHERE TO FIND IT: INDEX TO TESTED ANTENNAS

PASSPORT REPORTS evaluates many antennas on the market. Here's where they are found, with those that are new, revised or retested shown in **bold**.

A comprehensive PASSPORT® Radio Database International White Paper®, *Passport Evaluation of Popular Outdoor Antennas*, is available for $6.95 in North America, $9.95 airmail elsewhere, including shipping. It contains virtually all our panel's findings and comments during testing, along with details for proper installation and instructions for inverted-L construction. This unabridged report is available from key world band dealers, or you can contact our 24-hour VISA/MC order channels (www.passband.com, autovoice +1 215/598-9018, fax +1 215/598 3794), or write us at PASSPORT RDI White Papers, Box 300, Penn's Park, PA 18943 USA.

Antenna	Page	Antenna	Page
Alpha Delta DX-SWL Sloper 🗏	204	MFJ-1022	226
Alpha Delta DX-Ultra 🗏	203	MFJ-1024	223
Ameco TPA	222	Palstar AA30/AA30A/AA30P/AM-30	226
AOR LA-350	221	RF Systems DX-One Pro Mk II	215
AOR WL500	215	**RF Systems GMDSS-1**	**219**
Dressler ARA 60 S	218	Sony AN-1	225
Dressler ARA 100 HDX	216	Sony AN-LP1	220
Eavesdropper Models T/C 🗏	204	Stoner Dymek DA100E/EM	000
McKay Dymek DX100E/EM	222	Vectronics AT-100	225
MFJ-1020C/Proximate	224	**Wellbrook ALA 330S**	**210**
MFJ-1020C/Remote	217	**Wellbrook ALA 1530/1530P**	**213**

🗏*Radio Database International White Paper*® available.

What's On Tonight?

PASSPORT's Hour-by-Hour Guide to World Band Shows

World band's voluminous variety of voices includes shows you rarely find anywhere else. Still, not all are worth your time, so here is an hour-by-hour selection of the main English-language programs, dross-free for quick reference. The best are tagged:

■ Station superior, with several excellent shows

● Show worth hearing

Some stations offer schedules, others don't. Yet, even among those that do, data isn't always credible or complete. To resolve this, PASSPORT monitors, firsthand, various stations around the world to detail actual schedule activity throughout the year—winter and summer.

Also to help the book be as useful as possible over the months to come, PASSPORT's schedules consist not just of observed activity, but also those which we have creatively opined will appear well into the year ahead. This predictive material is based on decades of experience and is original from us. Although this is inherently less exact than real-time data, it has proven to be very helpful.

Primary frequencies are given for North America, Western Europe, East Asia and Australasia, plus the Middle East, Southern Africa and Southeast Asia. For secondary and seasonal channels, or frequencies for other parts of the world, flip to "Worldwide Broadcasts in English" and the Blue Pages.

To eliminate confusion, World Time and World Day are used—both are explained in "Compleat Idiot's Guide to Getting Started" and "Worldly Words." Seasons are those in the Northern Hemisphere ("summer" July, etc.; "winter" January, etc.).

Rong-Liu Chao (left) and Hsien-Zhang Lin host the Mandarin service of Radio Taiwan International. RTI puts out powerful signals, including from relay transmitters in Florida.   RTI

00:00–05:59
North America—Evening Prime Time
Europe & Mideast—Early Morning
Australasia & East Asia—Midday and Afternoon

00:00

■BBC World Service for the Americas. Tuesday through Saturday winter (weekday evenings in the Americas), opens with five minutes of *news*. This is followed by the long-running *Outlook* and the 15-minute ●*Off the Shelf* (readings from world literature). Best of the weekend entertainment (a quiz or its alternative) can be found at 00:32 Monday. Summer programming starts with *News*, then it's a mixed bag of features. Recommended are ●*Everywoman* (00:06 Monday), ●*Charlie Gillett* (world music, 00:32 Thursday) and the eclectic ●*John Peel* (00:32 Saturday). Continuous programming to North America and the Caribbean on 5975 kHz. Listeners in eastern North America can also try 12095 kHz, targeted at South America; a radio with synchronous selectable sideband helps reduce teletype interference. Farther west, try 11835 kHz in summer.

■Radio Netherlands. Tuesday through Saturday (weekday evenings in North America) there's ●*Newsline* (current events) followed by a feature on the half-hour: ●*Research File* (Tuesday), ●*EuroQuest* (Wednesday), ●*Documentary* (Thursday), *Dutch Horizons* (Friday), and *A Good Life* (Saturday). On the remaining days, a six-minute *news* bulletin is followed Sunday by *Europe Unzipped*, ●*Insight* and *Amsterdam Forum*; and Monday by *Wide Angle*, *The Week Ahead* and *Vox Humana*. One hour to eastern North America on 9845 kHz.

Radio Bulgaria. Winter only at this time. Tuesday through Saturday (weekday evenings in North America), *News* is followed by *Events and Developments*, replaced Sunday and Monday by *Views Behind the News*. The remaining time is taken up by regular programs such as *Keyword Bulgaria* and *Time Out for Music*, and weekly features like ●*Folk*

00:00–00:00

Among traditional instruments featured on Radio Taiwan International's "Jade Bells and Bamboo Pipes" are the pipa (left) and erhu.
RTI

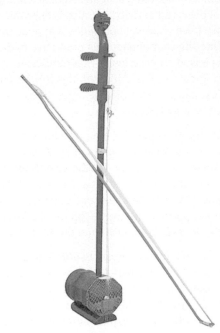

Studio (Monday), *Sports* (Tuesday), *Magazine Economy* (Wednesday), *The Way We Live* (Thursday), *History Club* (Friday), *DX Programme* (Saturday) and *Answering Your Letters*, a listener-response show, on Sunday. Sixty minutes to eastern North America and Central America on 7400 and 9400 kHz. One hour earlier in summer.

Radio Canada International. Summer only at this time, and the start of a two-hour broadcast. Tuesday through Saturday (weekday evenings in North America), opens with ●*The World at Six* and continues with ●*As It Happens*, a combination of international stories, Canadian news and general human interest features. On the remaining days it's ●*The World This Weekend* and either Sunday's comedy show or Monday's *Maple Leaf Mailbag*. To North America and the Caribbean on 9755 and 13710 kHz, and one hour later in winter. For a separate year-round broadcast to Asia, see the next item.

Radio Canada International. Tuesday through Saturday, it's ●*The World At Six*; and a shortened version of ●*As It Happens*, both news-oriented programs. These are replaced Sunday by *Business Sense* and *Sci-Tech File*,

and Monday by *The Maple Leaf Mailbag* and *Spotlight*. One hour to Southeast Asia winter on 9680 and 9755 kHz, and summer on 9640 and 15205 kHz. Also heard in parts of East Asia, especially during summer.

Radio Japan. *News*, then Tuesday through Saturday (weekday evenings local American date) it's *A Song for Everyone* followed by *Japan and the World 44 Minutes* (an in-depth look at current trends and events in Japan and elsewhere). This is replaced Sunday by *Hello from Tokyo*, and Monday by *Weekend Japanology* and *Japan Music Scene*. One hour to eastern North America on 6145 kHz via the powerful relay facilities of Radio Canada International in Sackville, New Brunswick. A separate 15-minute news bulletin for Southeast Asia is aired on 13650 and 17810 kHz.

Radio Exterior de España ("Spanish National Radio"). Tuesday through Saturday (local weekday evenings in the Americas), there's Spanish and international *news*, commentary, Spanish pop music, a review of the Spanish press, and a general interest feature. Weekends, it's all features, including rebroadcasts of some of the weekday programs. Sixty minutes to eastern North

America winter on 6055 kHz, and summer on 15385 kHz. Popular with many listeners.

Radio Ukraine International. Summer only at this time. Ample coverage of local issues, including news, sports, politics and culture. Worth hearing is ●*Music from Ukraine*, which fills most of the Monday (Sunday evening in the Americas) broadcast. Sixty minutes to eastern North America on 7545 kHz. One hour later in winter. Budget and technical limitations have reduced audibility of this station to only a fraction of what it used to be.

Radio Australia. *World News*, then a feature. Monday's offering—unusual, to say the least—is *Awaye*, a program dealing with indigenous affairs. This is replaced Tuesday by *Science Show* and Wednesday by *The National Interest* (topical events). Thursday's *Background Briefing* (investigative journalism) and Friday's historical *Hindsight* complete the weekday lineup. *Pacific Review*, ●*Ockham's Razor* and *Lingua Franca* fill the Saturday slots, and Sunday's feature is *Keys to Music*. Targeted at Asia and the Pacific on 9660, 12080, 13630, 15240, 15415 (from 00:30), 17580, 17750 (from 00:30), 17775, 17795 and 21725 kHz. In North America (best during summer) try 17795 kHz; and in East Asia go for 13630 and 21725 kHz. For Southeast Asia there's 15415, 17750 and 17775 kHz.

Radio Prague, Czech Republic. Summer only at this time. *News*, then Tuesday through Saturday (weekday evenings in the Americas) there's *Current Affairs* and one or more features: *Talking Point* (Tuesday); *Czech Science* and *One on One* (Wednesday); *Czechs in History*, *Czechs Today* or *Spotlight* (Thursday); *Business Report* (Friday); and *The Arts* on Saturday. The Sunday lineup is *Magazine*, *Letter from Prague* and *One on One*; replaced Monday by *Mailbox* and *ABC of Czech* followed by *Encore* (classical music), *Magic Carpet* (Czech world music) or *Czech Books*. Thirty minutes to North America and the Caribbean on 7345 and 9440 kHz. One hour later in winter.

Radio Austria International. Winter only at this time. Tuesday through Saturday (weekday evenings in the Americas), the 15-minute *Report from Austria* is aired at 0115, then

repeated at 01:45. Sunday and Monday, it's a similar arrangement, with ●*The Week in Review* airing at 01:05 and 01:35. The remainder of the one-hour broadcast is in German. To eastern North America on 7325 kHz. One hour later in summer.

Radio Thailand. *Newshour*. Thirty minutes to eastern and southern Africa, winter on 9680 kHz and summer on 9570 kHz.

All India Radio. The final 45 minutes of a much larger block of programming targeted at East and Southeast Asia, and heard well beyond. To East Asia on 9950, 11620 and 13605 kHz; and to Southeast Asia on 9705, 11620 and 13605 kHz.

■**Deutsche Welle,** Germany. *News*, then Tuesday through Saturday it's the comprehensive ●*NewsLink*—commentary, interviews, background reports and analysis. This is followed by *Insight* and *Business German* (Tuesday), *World in Progress* (Wednesday), ●*Money Talks* (Thursday), *Living Planet* (Friday), and *Spectrum* (Saturday). Sunday fare is *Religion and Society*, *German by Radio*, and *Asia This Week*; replaced Monday by *Mailbag*. Sixty minutes to South Asia winter on 6030 and 7290 kHz; and summer on 7130, 9505 and 9825 kHz. Also audible in parts of North America, interference permitting.

Radio Cairo, Egypt. The final half hour of a 90-minute broadcast to eastern North America. *Arabic by Radio* can be heard on the hour, and there's a daily *news* bulletin at 00:15. See 23:00 for more specifics. On 7115 kHz.

Radio New Zealand International. A friendly package of *news* and features sometimes replaced by live sports commentary. Part of a 24-hour broadcast for the South Pacific, but also heard in parts of North America (especially during summer) on 15720 or 17675 kHz.

AFRTS Shortwave, USA. Network news, live sports, music and features in the upper-sideband mode from the Armed Forces Radio & Television Service. Transmitted from modestly powered U.S. Navy stations around the globe. Try 4319, 5446.5, 5765, 6350, 7590, 9980, 10320, 12133.5, 12579 and 13362 kHz.

00:30–01:00

00:30

Radio Vilnius, Lithuania. A half hour that's heavily geared to news and background reports about events in Lithuania. Of broader appeal is *Mailbag*, aired every other Sunday (Saturday evenings local American date). For some Lithuanian music, try the next evening, towards the end of the broadcast. To eastern North America winter on 7325 kHz and summer on 11690 kHz.

Radio Thailand. *Newshour.* Thirty minutes to central and eastern North America on 5890 kHz, via a relay in Greenville, North Carolina.

01:00

■**BBC World Service for the Americas.** Winter, starts with *News*, then it's a mixed bag of features. Top choices are ●*Everywoman* (01:06 Monday), ●*Charlie Gillett* (world music, 01:32 Thursday) and the eclectic ●*John Peel* (01:32 Saturday). Pick of the summer shows is Sunday's ●*Play of the Week* (world theater at its best). Other interesting programs include ●*Health Matters* (0106 Tuesday) and ●*One Planet* (same time Friday). Continuous programming to North America and the Caribbean on 5975 kHz, and to western North America and Central America winter on 9525 kHz, and summer on 11835 kHz. In parts of eastern North America, 12095 kHz (nominally to South America) is also audible; a radio with synchronous selectable sideband helps reduce teletype interference.

Radio Canada International. Winter, the first of two hours to North America and the Caribbean; summer, the final 60 minutes. Tuesday through Saturday winter (weekday evenings in North America), opens with ●*The World at Six* and continues with ●*As It Happens*, both news-oriented programs. Summer, it's the final hour of ●*As It Happens*. On the remaining days, the winter lineup is ●*The World This Weekend* and either Sunday's comedy show or Monday's *Maple Leaf Mailbag*. These are replaced in summer by Sunday's ●*Global Village* (world music) and Monday's *Writers and Company*. Winter on 6190, 9755 and 9810 kHz; and summer on 9755 and 13710 kHz.

■**Radio Netherlands.** Repeat of the 00:00 broadcast; see there for specifics. One hour to central North America on 6165 kHz winter, and 9845 kHz summer.

Radio Slovakia International. Wednesday through Saturday (Tuesday through Friday evenings in the Americas), starts with *News* and *Topical Issue.* These are followed by features. Regulars include *Tourism News* (Wednesday), *Business News* and *Currency Update* (Thursday), *Culture News* (Friday) and *Regional News* (Saturday). Tuesday's news is followed by *Insight Central Europe.* Sunday's lineup includes *Front Page* and *Sports News*; and Monday there's *Sunday Newsreel* and *Listeners' Tribune.* A friendly half hour to eastern North America on 5930 kHz, and to South America on 9440 kHz.

Radio Austria International. Summer only at this time. Tuesday through Saturday (weekday evenings in the Americas), the 15-minute *Report from Austria* is aired at 01:15, then repeated at 01:45. Sunday and Monday, it's a similar arrangement, with ●*The Week in Review* airing at 01:05 and 01:35. The remainder of the one-hour broadcast is in German. To eastern North America on 9870 kHz. One hour earlier in winter.

Radio Budapest, Hungary. Summer only at this time. *News* and features, most of which are broadcast on a non-regular basis. Thirty minutes to North America on 9590 kHz. One hour later in winter.

Radio Prague, Czech Republic. *News*, then Tuesday through Saturday (weekday evenings in the Americas) there's the in-depth *Current Affairs* and a feature or two: *Talking Point* (Tuesday), *Czech Science* and *One on One* (Wednesday), *Czechs in History*, *Czechs Today* or *Spotlight* (Thursday), *Business Report* (Friday) and *The Arts* on Saturday. The Sunday news is followed by *Magazine*, *Letter from Prague* and a repeat of Wednesday's *One on One*; and Monday's lineup is *Mailbox* and *ABC of Czech* followed by *Encore* (classical music), *Magic Carpet* (Czech world music) or *Czech Books*. Thirty minutes to eastern and central North America and the Caribbean on 6200 and 7345 kHz.

A World of Listening from Sangean and Universal!

SANGEAN

ATS-909

The **ATS-909** is the flagship of the Sangean line. It packs features and performance into a very compact and stylish package. Coverage includes all long wave, medium wave and shortwave frequencies. FM and FM stereo to the headphone jack is also available. Shortwave performance is enhanced with a wide-narrow bandwidth switch and excellent single side band performance. Five tuning methods are featured: keypad, auto scan, manual up-down, memory recall or tuning knob. The alphanumeric memory lets you store 306 presets. The three event clock-timer displays even when the radio is tuning and has 42 world city zones. The large backlit LCD also features a signal strength and battery bar graph. The ATS-909 will display RDS on PL, PS and CT for station name and clock time in areas where this service is available. Also features a record jack and tone switch. Includes AC adapter, carry case, stereo ear buds and Sangean ANT-60 roll-up antenna. 8"' x 5"' x 1"'. Requires four AA cells (not supplied). *#1909*

ATS-505P

The **Sangean ATS-505P** covers long wave, AM, FM and all shortwave frequencies. The backlit display can show either the frequency or the time (12/24 format). Tune (normal or fine) via the tuning knob, Up-Down buttons, automatic tuning, keypad or from the 45 memories. The ATS-505P even has a Clarify knob on the side of the radio to smoothly tune SSB. Other features include: FM stereo to headphone jack, 9/10 kHz AM step, beep on/off, dial lock, stereo-mono switch, alarm by radio or buzzer, auto-scan, auto memory, sleep-timer, tune LED, stereo-mono switch, tilt-stand, external antenna input and 6 VDC jack. With: AC adapter, ANT-60 wind-up antenna, carry case and earphones. Titanium matte finish. 8.5"x5.3"x1.6" Requires four AA cells. *#3505*

ATS-818ACS

Have you been waiting for a quality digital world band radio with a built-in cassette recorder? Now you have it in the exciting **Sangean ATS-818ACS**. This no-compromise receiver has full dual-conversion shortwave coverage (1.6 - 30 MHz) plus long wave, AM and FM (stereo to headphone jack). A BFO control is included for smooth SSB/CW reception. A big LCD display with dial lamp shows: frequency (1 kHz on SW), 24 hour time, battery indicator and signal strength. The receiver features an RF gain, tone control, wide-narrow selectivity, keypad entry, external antenna jack, manual tuning knob, plus 54 memories (18 for shortwave). The monoral recorder has a built-in mic and auto-shutoff. This radio comes with an AC power adapter. Requires four D cells and three AA cells (not supplied). 11"' x 7" x 2"'. *#1069*

TP-633

The new **TP-633** *Traveler Pro* is a compact analog AM, FM radio with 9 shortwave bands. It features a built-in dual time zone LCD 12/24 hour digital clock. Also has: LED tune and battery indicator, stereo-mono switch and power lock button. Requires 4.5 VDC or 3 AA cells (not supplied). With carry pouch and stereo ear buds. *#3633*

PT-80

The Sangean PT-80 *Pro-Travel* is a compact digital radio with LW, AM, FM and continuous shortwave coverage. This dual conversion receiver features: 45 memories, single sideband, backlit LCD, dial lock plus dual world time clock with alarm, snooze and sleep. Tune by: keypad, autoscan, memory recall or rotary knob. Switches are provided for: Local-DX, dial lock and stereo-mono. With external antenna jack. Includes: AC adapter, earphones, wind-up antenna and butter-soft leather pouch. Requires four AA cells. *#1080*

Sangean makes more than world class shortwave radios! Please visit the Universal Radio website to learn about Sangean specialty receivers.

01:00–01:30

News pro Uta Thofern-Dieste heads Deutsche Welle's English Service. She focuses not only on programs, but also on enhancing DW's audience in the United States and beyond. DW higher-ups disdain world band, so Ms. Thofern has been cultivating alternatives. DW

RAI International—Radio Roma, Italy. Actually starts at 00:55. *News* and Italian music make up this 20-minute broadcast to North America on 11800 kHz.

Radio Japan. *News*, then Tuesday through Saturday it's *A Song for Everyone* and *Japan and the World 44 Minutes* (an in-depth look at trends and events in Japan and beyond). This is replaced Sunday by *Pop Joins the World*, and Monday by *Hello from Tokyo*. One hour to East Asia on 17845 kHz; to South Asia on 15325 kHz; to Southeast Asia on 11860 and 17810 kHz; to Australasia on 17685 kHz; to South America on 17835 kHz; to western North America and Central America on 17825 kHz; and to the Mideast on 6025 (summer), 6030 (winter) and 17560 kHz. The broadcast on 17685 kHz has different programming after 01:15.

China Radio International. Starts with *News*, followed Monday through Friday (Sunday through Thursday evenings in the Americas) by special reports—current events, sports, business, culture, science and technology and press clippings. The rest of the broadcast is devoted to features. Regulars include ●*People in the Know* (Monday), *Biz China* (Tuesday), *China Horizons* (Wednesday), ●*Voices from Other Lands* (Thursday), and *Life in China* on

Friday. Weekends, the news is followed by a shorter series of reports (current events and sport) and two features. Saturday there's *Cutting Edge*, and *Listeners' Garden* (listener mail, Chinese folk music, a preview of the next week's programs, and a Chinese language lesson); replaced Sunday by *Reports on Developing Countries* and *In the Spotlight*, a series of mini-features: *Cultural Carousel, In Vogue, Writings from China, China Melody* and *Talking Point*. One hour to North America on 9580 and 9790 kHz, via CRI's Cuban and Canadian relays.

Voice of Vietnam. A relay via the facilities of Radio Canada International. Begins with *news*, then there's *Commentary* or *Weekly Review*, followed by short features and some pleasant Vietnamese music (especially at weekends). Thirty minutes to eastern North America, with reception better to the south. On 6175 kHz. Repeated at 02:30 and 03:30 on the same channel.

Voice of Russia World Service. Summer only at this hour, and the start of a four-hour block of programming for North America. *News*, then Tuesday through Saturday (weekday evenings in North America), there's *Commonwealth Update*. This is replaced Sunday and Monday by *Moscow Mailbag*. The second half-hour contains some interesting fare, with just about everyone's favorite being Tuesday's ●*Folk Box*. Other shows include Friday's ●*Music at Your Request* (or ●*Music Around Us*), ●*Moscow Yesterday and Today* (Sunday), Wednesday's ●*Jazz Show*, and Saturday's evocative ●*Christian Message from Moscow*. Best for eastern North America is 9665 kHz, replaced by 7180 kHz in autumn. Farther west, use 15595 and 17660 kHz.

Radio Habana Cuba. The start of a two-hour cyclical broadcast to North America. Tuesday through Sunday (Monday through Saturday evenings in North America), the first half hour consists of international and Cuban *news* followed by *RHC's Viewpoint*. The next 30 minutes consist of a *news* bulletin and the sports-oriented *Time Out* (five minutes each) plus a feature: *Caribbean Outlook* (Tuesday and Friday), *DXers Unlimited* (Wednesday and Sunday), the *Mailbag Show* (Thursday) and

01:00–01:30

Weekly Review (Saturday). Monday, the hour is split between *Weekly Review* and *Mailbag Show*. To eastern and central North America on 6000 and 9820 kHz.

Voice of Korea, North Korea. Not quite the Radio Pyongyang of old, but the Voice of Korea is still a broadcasting dinosaur. Just about the only survivor from the former Communist Bloc. One hour to East Asia on 3560, 6195 (or 9720), 7140 and 9345 kHz; and to Central and South America on any three channels from 6520, 7580, 11735, 13760 and 15180 kHz.

Radio Australia. Part of a 24-hour service to Asia and the Pacific, but which can also be heard at this time in parts of North America (better to the west). Begins with world *news*, then Tuesday through Saturday there's *Asia Pacific* (regional current events), replaced Sunday by *Correspondents Report*. Weekdays on the half-hour, there's yet more reporting: *Health Report* (Monday), *Law Report* (Tuesday), *Religion Report* (Wednesday) and *Media Report* (Thursday). Friday brings some relief, with *Sports Factor*. Weekend fare consists of Saturday's *Jazz Notes* and Sunday's *The Chat Room*. Targeted at Asia and the Pacific on 9660, 12080, 13630, 15240, 15415, 17750, 17775 (till 01:30), 17795 and 21725 kHz. In North America (best during summer) try 17795 kHz; in East Asia go for 13630 and 21725 kHz; and best for Southeast Asia are 15415, 17750 and 17775 kHz. Some channels may carry a separate sports service on winter Saturdays.

Radio Ukraine International. Winter only at this time; see 00:00 for specifics. Sixty minutes of informative programming targeted at eastern North America. On 5910 kHz. One hour earlier in summer.

Radio Romania International. Starts with *Radio Newsreel*, a combination of news, commentary and press review. Features on Romania complete the broadcast. Regular spots include Tuesday's *Pro Memoria* (Romanian history) and *Pages of Romanian Literature* (Monday evening, local American date), Wednesday's *Business Club* and *Visual Arts*, Thursday's *Stage and Screen* and *Romanian Musicians*, and Friday's *Listeners Letterbox* and

●*Skylark* (Romanian folk music). Saturday fare includes *Cultural Survey* and ●*The Folk Music Box*, and Sunday there's *World of Culture*, *Roots*, *Radio Pictures* and *DX Mailbag*. Monday's broadcast has *Sunday Studio* and repeats of programs aired earlier in the week. Fifty-five minutes to eastern North America winter on 6140 and 9690 kHz, and summer on 9690 and 11940 kHz; and to Australasia winter on 9510 and 11740 kHz, and midyear on 15430 and 17760 kHz.

Radio New Zealand International. Continues with *news* and features sometimes replaced by live sports commentary. Continuous to the South Pacific, and also heard in parts of North America (especially during summer). On 15720 or 17675 kHz.

Radio Tashkent, Uzbekistan. Monday through Saturday, opens with *News*, replaced Sunday by *Significant Events of the Week*. The remaining fare consists mainly of features, with Monday's broadcast largely devoted to exotic Uzbek music. On the remaining days there's *Economic Commentary* (Tuesday), a program for women (Wednesday and Sunday), *Echo of History* (Wednesday), *Uzbekistan and the World* and *Man and Society* (Thursday) and a program for shortwave listeners on Friday. The week ends with a Saturday sports program followed by *In the World of Literature*. A half hour to West and South Asia, and occasionally heard in North America. Aired winter on two or more frequencies from 5975, 6165, 7135 and 7160 kHz; and summer on 7190 and 9715 kHz.

AFRTS Shortwave, USA. Network news, live sports, music and features in the upper-sideband mode from the Armed Forces Radio & Television Service. Transmitted from modestly powered U.S. Navy stations around the globe. Try 4319, 5446.5, 5765, 6350, 7590, 9980, 10320, 12133.5, 12579 and 13362 kHz.

01:30

Radio Sweden. Tuesday through Saturday (weekday evenings in North America), it's *news* and features in *Sixty Degrees North*, concentrating heavily on Scandinavian topics.

01:30–02:00

Bangkok's nightlife is a
notorious magnet for
tourists. A more edifying
view is offered by
powerful Radio Thailand.
M. Guha

Several of the features rotate from week to week, but a few are fixtures. Tuesday's *Sportsman* is replaced Wednesday by *Close Up* or an alternative feature, and Thursday by special features. Friday's carousel is *Nordic Lights*, *GreenScan* (the environment), *Heart Beat* (health), and *S-Files*, with *Weekly Review* filling the Saturday slot. The Sunday rotation is *Network Europe*, *Spectrum*, *Sweden Today* and *Studio 49*; while Monday's offering is *In Touch with Stockholm* (a listener-response program) or the musical *Sounds Nordic*. Thirty minutes to South Asia on 9435 kHz (may use 12060 kHz in winter). Also to North America, summer only, on 6010 kHz. The broadcast to North America is one hour later during winter.

01:45

Radio Tirana, Albania. Tuesday through Sunday (Monday through Saturday evenings in North America) and summer only at this time. Approximately 15 minutes of *news* and commentary from this small Balkan country. To North America on 6115 and 7160 kHz. One hour later in winter.

02:00

■**BBC World Service for the Americas.** Starts with *News*, then it's a mixed bag of features. Pick of the winter shows is Sunday's

●*Play of the Week* (world theater at its best). Other interesting programs include ●*Health Matters* (0206 Tuesday) and ●*One Planet* (same time Friday). Summer, opens with 30 minutes of *The World Today*, then Monday through Saturday (Sunday through Friday evenings in the Americas) there's 13 minutes of ●*World Business Report* followed most days by *Analysis* (current events). The exceptions are Thursday's ●*From Our Own Correspondent* and Monday's *Instant Guide*. Sunday programming consists of either an extra 30 minutes of ●*Play of the Week* or news coverage in *The World Today*. Continues to North America and the Caribbean on 5975 kHz. Also to western North America and Central America winter on 9525 kHz, and summer on 11835 kHz. In parts of eastern North America, 12095 kHz (nominally to South America) is also audible; a radio with synchronous selectable sideband helps reduce teletype interference.

Radio Cairo, Egypt. Repeat of the 23:00 broadcast, and the first hour of a 90-minute potpourri of *news* and features about Egypt and the Arab world. To North America on 11855 kHz (may use 7260 kHz in winter).

Radio Argentina al Exterior—RAE Tuesday through Saturday only (local weekday evenings in the Americas). A freewheeling presentation of news, press review, short features and local Argentinian music. Not the easiest station to tune, but popular with many of those who can hear it. Fifty-five minutes nominally to North America on 11710 kHz, but tends to be best heard in the southern U.S. and the Caribbean. Sometimes pre-empted by live soccer commentary in Spanish.

Radio Budapest, Hungary. Winter only at this time. *News* and features, most of which are broadcast on a non-regular basis. Thirty minutes to North America on 9775 kHz. One hour earlier in summer.

Wales Radio International. This time summer Saturdays only (Friday evenings American date). News, reports and music from the Welsh principality. Thirty minutes to North America on 9795 kHz, and one hour later in winter.

Radio Canada International. Winter only at this time. Tuesday through Saturday (weekday evenings in North America), it's the final hour of ●*As It Happens*—international stories, Canadian news and general human interest features. Sunday's show is ●*Global Village* (world music), replaced Monday by *Writers and Company*. To North America and the Caribbean on 6190, 9755 and 9810 kHz; and one hour earlier in summer.

Radio Bulgaria. Summer only at this time. Starts with *News*, then Tuesday through Saturday (weekday evenings in North America) there's *Events and Developments*, replaced Sunday and Monday by *Views Behind the News*. The remaining time is split between regular programs like *Keyword Bulgaria* and *Time Out for Music*, and weekly features like ●*Folk Studio* (Monday), *Sports* (Tuesday), *Magazine Economy* (Wednesday), *The Way We Live* (Thursday), *History Club* (Friday), *DX Programme* (for radio enthusiasts, Saturday) and *Answering Your Letters*, a listener-response show, on Sunday. Sixty minutes to eastern North America and Central America on 9400 and 11700 kHz. One hour later in winter.

Radio Prague, Czech Republic. Winter only at this time. *News*, then Tuesday through Saturday (weekday evenings in the Americas) it's a combination of *Current Affairs* and one or more features: *Talking Point* (Tuesday), *Czech Science* and *One on One* (Wednesday), *Czechs in History, Czechs Today* or *Spotlight* (Thursday), *Business Report* (Friday), and *The Arts* on

Saturday. The Sunday lineup is *Magazine, Letter from Prague* and *One on One*; replaced Monday by *Mailbox* and *ABC of Czech* followed by *Encore* (classical music), *Magic Carpet* (Czech world music) or *Czech Books*. A half hour to North America on 6200 and 7345 kHz. One hour earlier in summer.

Radio Taiwan International. Ten minutes of *News*, followed by features. Monday (Sunday evening in North America) there's *Taiwan Economic Journal, Discover Taiwan*, and *Asia Pacific* (produced by Radio Australia). These are replaced on successive days by *Kaleidoscope, Mailbag Time, Sound Postcard* and *Let's Learn Chinese* (Tuesday); *On the Job,* ●*Jade Bells and Bamboo Pipes* and *Life Unusual* (Wednesday); *Trends, People, Wisdom.com* and *Instant Noodles* (Thursday); *Politics Today; Culture Express* and *New Music Lounge* (Friday); *Bookworm,* then *Stage, Screen and Studio* and *Groove Zone* (Saturday); and *News Talk, Taipei Magazine, Sound Postcard* and *Hakka World* (Sunday). One hour to eastern and central North America on 5950 and 9680 kHz, to East Asia on 15465 kHz, and to Southeast Asia on 11875 kHz.

Voice of Russia World Service. Winter, the start of a four-hour block of programming to North America; summer, it's the beginning of the second hour. *News*, features and music to suit all tastes. Winter fare includes *Commonwealth Update* (02:11 Tuesday through Saturday), replaced Sunday and Monday by *Moscow Mailbag*. The second half-hour includes ●*Folk Box* (Tuesday), ●*Jazz Show* (Wednesday),●*Music at Your Request* or ●*Music Around Us* (Friday), ●*Christian Message from Moscow* (Saturday), ●*Moscow Yesterday and Today* (Sunday) and *Timelines* (Monday). In summer, *News and Views* replaces *Commonwealth Update* and Sunday's *Moscow Mailbag*, with *Sunday Panorama* and *Russia: People and Events* filling the Monday spots. There's a news summary on the half-hour, then ●*Audio Book Club* (Saturday), *Songs from Russia* (Sunday), *This is Russia* (Monday), *Kaleidoscope* (Tuesday), *Musical Tales of St. Petersburg* and *Russia: People and Events* (Wednesday), ●*Moscow Yesterday and Today* (Thursday) or Friday's *Russian by Radio*. Note that these days are World Time; locally in North America it will be

02:00–02:30

the previous evening. For eastern North America winter, tune to 7180 kHz; summer, it's 9665 and 9860 kHz. Listeners in western states should go for 15445 and 15595 kHz in winter; and 15595 and 17660 kHz in summer.

Radio Habana Cuba. The second half of a two-hour broadcast to eastern and central North America. Tuesday through Sunday (Monday through Saturday evenings in North America), opens with 10 minutes of international *news*. Next comes *Spotlight on the Americas* (Tuesday through Saturday) or Sunday's *The World of Stamps*. The final 30 minutes consists of news-oriented programming. The Monday slots are *From Havana* and ●*The Jazz Place* or *Breakthrough* (science). On 6000 and 9820 kHz.

Radio Station Belarus/Radio Minsk. Monday, Wednesday and Friday through Sunday, summer only at this time. See 03:00 for details. Thirty minutes to Europe on 5970 and 7210kHz. One hour later in winter. Sometimes audible in eastern North America.

Radio Australia. Continuous programming to Asia and the Pacific, but well heard in parts of North America (especially to the west). Begins with *World News*, then Monday through Friday it's *The World Today* (comprehensive coverage of world events). Weekends, there's Saturday's *Background Briefing* and *Correspondent's Notebook,* replaced Sunday by *Margaret Throsby* (interviews and music). Targeted at Asia and the Pacific on 9660, 12080, 13630, 15240, 15415, 15515, 17750 and 21725 kHz. Best heard in North America (especially during summer) on 15515 kHz; in East Asia on 13630 and 21725 kHz; and in Southeast Asia on 15415 and 17750 kHz. Some of these channels carry a separate sports service on summer (midyear) weekends and winter Saturdays.

Radio Korea International, South Korea. Opens with 10 minutes of *news*, then Tuesday through Saturday (weekday evenings in the Americas), a commentary. This is followed by 30 minutes (45 on Saturday) of *Seoul Calling*. Tuesday through Friday, the broadcast closes with a 15-minute feature: *Korea, Today and Tomorrow, Korean Kaleidoscope, Wonderful Korea* and *Seoul Report*, respectively. Sunday,

the news is followed by *Worldwide Friendship* (a listener-response program), and Monday by *Korean Pop Interactive*. Sixty minutes to North America on 9560 and 15575 kHz, and to East Asia on 11810 kHz.

Voice of Korea, North Korea. Repeat of the 0100 broadcast. One hour to South East Asia on 9325 (or 11845) and 11335 (or 15230) kHz. Also audible in parts of East Asia on 4405 kHz.

AFRTS Shortwave, USA. Network news, live sports, music and features in the upper-sideband mode from the Armed Forces Radio & Television Service. Transmitted from modestly powered U.S. Navy stations around the globe. Try 4319, 5446.5, 5765, 6350, 7590, 9980, 10320, 12133.5, 12579 and 13362 kHz.

02:15

Voice of Croatia. Summer only at this time. Nominally 15 minutes of news, reports and interviews. Actual length varies. To North America and South America on 9925 kHz. One hour later in winter.

02:30

Radio Sweden. Tuesday through Saturday (weekday evenings in North America), it's *news* and features in *Sixty Degrees North*, with the accent heavily on Scandinavian topics. See 0330 for full program details. Sunday there's *Network Europe, Spectrum* (the arts), *Sweden Today* or *Studio 49*. A listener-response program, *In Touch with Stockholm*, is aired on the first Monday of each month, and replaced by *Sounds Nordic* on the remaining weeks. Thirty minutes to North America winter on 9495 kHz and summer on 6010 kHz.

Radio Tirana, Albania. Tuesday through Sunday (Monday through Saturday evenings in North America) and summer only at this time. Thirty minutes of Balkan news and music to North America on 6115 and 7160 kHz. One hour later during winter.

Radio Budapest, Hungary. Summer only at this time. *News* and features, not many of which are broadcast on a regular basis. Thirty

02:30–03:00

minutes to North America on 9570 kHz. One hour later in winter.

Voice of Vietnam. Repeat of the 0100 broadcast; see there for specifics. A relay to eastern North America via the facilities of Radio Canada International on 6175 kHz. Reception is better to the south.

02:45

Radio Tirana, Albania. Tuesday through Sunday (Monday through Saturday local American date) and winter only at this time. Approximately 15 minutes of *news* and commentary from one of Europe's least known countries. To North America on 6115 and 7160 kHz. One hour earlier in summer.

Vatican Radio. Actually starts at 02:50. Concentrates heavily, but not exclusively, on issues affecting Catholics around the world. Twenty minutes to eastern North America on 7305 and 9605 kHz.

03:00

■**BBC World Service for the Americas.** Winter, opens with 30 minutes of *The World Today*, then Monday through Saturday (Sunday through Friday evenings in the Americas) there's 13 minutes of ●*World Business Report* followed most days by *Analysis* (current events). The exceptions are Thursday's ●*From Our Own Correspondent* and Monday's *Instant Guide.* Sunday programming consists of either an extra 30 minutes of ●*Play of the Week* or news coverage in *The World Today.* Summer programming starts with *News*, then Tuesday through Friday (Monday through Thursday evenings in the Americas) is followed by *Outlook* and the 15-minute ●*Off the Shelf* (also aired Monday). Best of the weekend programs is ●*From Our Own Correspondent* at 03:06 Sunday. Continues to North America and the Caribbean on 5975 kHz; also to western North America and Central America winter on 9525 kHz, and summer on 11835 kHz.

Wales Radio International. This time winter Saturdays only (Friday evenings American date). News, interviews and music from the land of the bards. Thirty minutes to North America on 9735 kHz, and one hour earlier in summer.

Radio Taiwan International. Repeat of the 02:00 broadcast; see there for specifics. One hour to western North America on 5950 kHz, to South America on 15215 kHz, and to Southeast Asia on 15320 kHz.

China Radio International. Starts with *News*, followed Monday through Friday (Sunday through Thursday evenings in the Americas) by special reports—current events, sports, business, culture, science and technology and press clippings. The rest of the broadcast is devoted to features. Regulars include ●*People in the Know* (Monday), *Biz China* (Tuesday), *China Horizons* (Wednesday), ●*Voices from Other Lands* (Thursday), and *Life in China* on Friday. Weekends, the news is followed by a shorter series of reports (current events and sport) and two features. Saturday there's *Cutting Edge*, and *Listeners' Garden* (listener mail, Chinese folk music, a preview of the next week's programs, and a Chinese language lesson); replaced Sunday by *Reports on Developing Countries* and *In the Spotlight*, a series of mini-features: *Cultural Carousel*, *In Vogue*, *Writings from China*, *China Melody* and *Talking Point*. One hour to North America on 9690 and 9790 kHz.

Radio Ukraine International. Summer only at this time, and a repeat of the 00:00 broadcast; see there for specifics. Sixty minutes to eastern North America on 7545 kHz. One hour later in winter.

Voice of Russia World Service. Continuous programming to North America at this hour. *News*, then winter it's *News and Views*—except Monday (Sunday evening in North America) when *Sunday Panorama* and *Russia: People and Events* are aired instead. At 03:31, there's ●*Audio Book Club* (Saturday), *Songs from Russia* and *You Write to Moscow* (Sunday), *This is Russia* (Monday), *Kaleidoscope* (Tuesday), *Musical Tales of St. Petersburg* and *Russia: People and Events* (Wednesday), ●*Moscow Yesterday and Today* (Thursday) and *Russian by Radio* on Friday. In summer, the news is followed by a feature: *Science and Engineering*

(Monday and Thursday), *Musical Tales of St. Petersburg* (Tuesday), *Moscow Mailbag* (Wednesday and Saturday) and *Newmarket* (business) on Friday. More features follow a brief news summary on the half-hour: ●*Audio Book Club* (Monday), *XX Century: Footprints in History* (Tuesday, Thursday and Saturday), and unscheduled features on Wednesday and Friday. Pride of place at this hour goes to Sunday's 45-minute ●*Music and Musicians*. In eastern North America, choose between 7180 and 7350 kHz in winter, and 9665, 9860 and 9880 kHz in summer. In western North America, the situation is a little better—for winter, try 15445 and 15595 kHz; in summer, pick from 15455, 15595 and 17660 kHz.

Radio Station Belarus/Radio Minsk. Monday, Wednesday and Friday through Sunday, winter only at this time. Thirty minutes of local *news* and interviews, plus a little Belarusian music. All transmissions at this hour are repeats of broadcasts originally aired Tuesday or Thursday evenings. To Europe on 5970 and 7210 kHz, and one hour earlier in summer. Sometimes heard in eastern North America.

Radio Australia. *World News*, then Monday through Friday there's *Sport* and *Life Matters*. Saturday, the out-of-town *Rural Reporter* is paired with *Australian Country Style*, and Sunday's *Australian Express* is followed by *Music Deli*. Continuous to Asia and the Pacific on 9660, 12080, 13630, 15240, 15415, 15515, 17750 and 21725 kHz. Also heard in North America (best in summer) on 15515 kHz. In East Asia, tune to 13630 kHz; for Southeast Asia, there's 15415, 17750 and 21725 kHz. Some of these channels carry a separate sports service at weekends.

Radio Habana Cuba. Repeat of the 01:00 broadcast. To eastern and central North America on 6000 and 9820 kHz.

Radio Thailand. *News Magazine*. Thirty minutes to western North America on 5890 kHz, via a relay in Delano, California.

Radio Prague, Czech Republic. Summer only at this hour; see 04:00 for program specifics. A half hour to North America on 7345 and 9870 kHz. This is by far the best opportunity for

Financial whiz Graeme Barclay has been managing director of Broadcast Australia since 2002. He chats with Nigel Holmes (right), Radio Australia's Transmission Manager.   M. Hemetsberger

listeners in western states. One hour later in winter.

Radio Cairo, Egypt. The final half-hour of a 90-minute broadcast to North America on 11855 kHz (may use 7260 kHz in winter).

Radio Bulgaria. Winter only at this time, and a repeat of the 00:00 broadcast; see there for specifics. A distinctly Bulgarian potpourri of news, commentary, features and music. Not to be missed is Monday's ●*Folk Studio* (Sunday evening local American date). Sixty minutes to eastern North America and Central America on 7400 and 9400 kHz. One hour earlier in summer.

Radio Japan. *News*, then weekdays it's *A Song for Everyone* and *Asian Top News*. These are followed by a 35-minute feature: *Japan Musicscape* (Monday), Japanese language lessons (Tuesday and Thursday), *Japan Music Travelogue* (Wednesday), and *Music Beat* (Japanese popular music) on Friday. *Weekend Japanology* and *Japan Music Scene* fill the Saturday slots, and *Hello from Tokyo* is aired Sunday. Sixty minutes to Australasia on 21610 kHz.

03:00–04:00

Radio New Zealand International. Continues with *news* and features targeted at a regional audience. Part of a 24-hour transmission for the South Pacific, but also heard in parts of North America (especially during summer). On 15720 or 17675 kHz. Often carries commentaries of local sporting events. Popular with many listeners.

Voice of Korea, North Korea. The rhetoric has been toned down over the years, but the programs are still abysmal. Of curiosity value only. One hour to East Asia on 3560, 6195 (or 9720), 7140 and 9345 kHz.

Voice of Turkey. Summer only at this time. *News*, followed by *Review of the Turkish Press* and features (some of them unusual). Selections of Turkish popular and classical music complete the program. Fifty minutes to Europe and North America on 6140 kHz, and to the Mideast on 7270 kHz. One hour later during winter.

AFRTS Shortwave, USA. Network news, live sports, music and features in the upper-sideband mode from the Armed Forces Radio & Television Service. Transmitted from modestly powered U.S. Navy stations around the globe. Try 4319, 5446.5, 5765, 6350, 7590, 9980, 10320, 12133.5, 12579 and 13362 kHz.

03:15

Voice of Croatia. Winter only at this time. Nominally 15 minutes of news, reports and interviews. Actual length varies. To North America and South America on 7280 kHz. One hour earlier in summer.

03:30

Radio Sweden. Winter only at this time. Tuesday through Saturday (weekday evenings local American date), it's *news* and features in *Sixty Degrees North*, concentrating heavily on Scandinavian topics. Several of the features rotate from week to week, but a few are fixtures. Tuesday's *Sportsman* is replaced Wednesday by *Close Up* or an alternative feature, and Thursday by a special feature. Friday's rotating lineup is *Nordic Lights*, *GreenScan* (the environment), *Heart Beat* (health), and *S-Files*, and *Weekly Review* fills

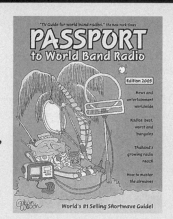

the Saturday slot. The Sunday rotation is *Network Europe*, *Spectrum*, *Sweden Today* and *Studio 49*; while Monday's offering is *In Touch with Stockholm* (a listener-response program) or the musical *Sounds Nordic*. Thirty minutes to western North America on 9495 kHz, and one hour earlier in summer.

Radio Prague, Czech Republic. Summer only at this time. See the 04:00 winter broadcast for North America for program specifics. Thirty minutes to the Mideast and South Asia on 11600 and 15600 kHz. One hour later in winter.

Kol Israel. Summer only at this time. *News* for 15 minutes from Israel Radio's domestic network. To Europe and eastern North America on 9435 and 11590 kHz, and to Central America and Australasia on 17600 kHz. One hour later in winter.

Radio Budapest, Hungary. This time winter only. *News* and features, most of which are broadcast on a non-regular basis. Thirty minutes to North America on 9775 kHz. One hour earlier in summer.

Voice of Vietnam. A relay via the facilities of Radio Canada International. Begins with *news*, then there's *Commentary* or *Weekly Review*, followed by short features and some pleasant Vietnamese music (particularly at weekends). A half hour to eastern North America on 6175 kHz.

Radio Tirana, Albania. Tuesday through Monday (Monday through Saturday evenings local American date) and winter only at this time. *News*, features and lively Albanian music. Thirty minutes to North America on 6115 and 7160 kHz. One hour earlier in summer.

04:00

■BBC World Service for the Americas. Winter, starts with *News*, then Tuesday through Friday (Monday through Thursday evenings in the Americas) is followed by *Outlook* and the 15-minute ●*Off the Shelf* (also aired Monday). Best of the weekend programs is ●*From Our Own Correspondent* at 04:06 Sunday. The summer opener is *World Briefing*, with *The World Today* completing the hour

Monday through Friday (Sunday through Thursday evenings in North America). This is replaced Saturday by ●*Reporting Religion*, and Sunday by *Letter* and *The Instant Guide*. Continuous programming to western North America and Central America on 5975, (winter) 6135 and (summer) 11835 kHz.

■Radio Netherlands. Tuesday through Saturday (weekday evenings in North America), opens with ●*Newsline* (current events). A feature follows on the half-hour: ●*Research File* (Tuesday), ●*EuroQuest* (Wednesday), ●*Documentary* (Thursday), *Dutch Horizons* (Friday), and *A Good Life* (Saturday). On the remaining days, a six-minute news bulletin is followed Sunday by *Europe Unzipped*, ●*Insight* and *Amsterdam Forum*; and Monday by *Wide Angle*, *The Week Ahead* and *Vox Humana*. One hour to western North America on 6165 and 9590 kHz.

Radio Habana Cuba. Repeat of the 02:00 broadcast. To east and central North America on 6000 and 9820 kHz.

Flanders Radio International, Belgium. Summer only at this time. See 05:00 for program specifics. Thirty minutes to western North America on 116355 kHz. One hour later in winter.

Radio Prague, Czech Republic. Winter only at this time. *News*, then Tuesday through Saturday (weekday evenings in the Americas) there's the in-depth *Current Affairs* and a feature or two: *Talking Point* (Tuesday), *Czech Science* and *One on One* (Wednesday), *Czechs in History*, *Czechs Today* or *Spotlight* (Thursday), *Business Report* (Friday) and *The Arts* on Saturday. The Sunday news is followed by *Magazine*, *Letter from Prague* and a repeat of Wednesday's *One on One*; and Monday's lineup is *Mailbox* and *ABC of Czech* followed by *Encore* (classical music), *Magic Carpet* (Czech world music) or *Czech Books*. Thirty minutes to North America on 6200 and 7345 kHz. By far the best opportunity for western states. One hour earlier in summer.

■Radio France Internationale. Weekdays only at this time. Starts with a bulletin of African *news* and an international newsflash. Next, there's a review of the French dailies, an

04:00–05:00

in-depth look at events in Africa, the main news event of the day in France, and sports. Thirty information-packed minutes to East Africa winter on 9555 or 11995 kHz, and summer on 7280 kHz (11700 kHz is also available in autumn). Heard well beyond the intended target area.

Radio Ukraine International. Winter only at this time, and a repeat of the 0100 broadcast. Ample coverage of local issues, including news, sports, politics and culture. Well worth a listen is ●*Music from Ukraine*, which fills most of the Monday (Sunday evening in the Americas) broadcast. Sixty minutes to eastern North America on 5910 kHz. One hour earlier in summer.

Radio Australia. *World News*, then Monday through Friday it's music and interviews with *Margaret Throsby*. Weekend fare consists of Saturday's *Books and Writing* and *Book Talk*, replaced Sunday by *The Europeans* and *The Chat Room*. Continuous to Asia and the Pacific on 9660, 12080, 13630, 15240, 15415 (from 04:30), 15515, 17750 and 21725 kHz. Should also be audible in parts of North America (best during summer) on 15515 kHz. In East Asia, go for 13630 kHz; for Southeast Asia, there's 15415, 17750 and 21725 kHz. Some channels carry separate sports programming at weekends.

■**Deutsche Welle,** Germany. *News*, followed Tuesday through Saturday by the comprehensive and well produced ●*NewsLink*—commentary, interviews, background reports and analysis. On the half-hour there's *Insight* and *Business German* (Tuesday), *World in Progress* (Wednesday), ●*Money Talks* (Thursday), *Living Planet* (Friday) and *Spectrum* (Saturday). Sunday brings ●*Inside Europe*, replaced Monday by *Mailbag*. Sixty minutes to East and Central Africa winter on 6180, 9545 and 9710 kHz; and summer on 7225, 9630 and 11945 kHz. Good winter reception in the Mideast on 9545 kHz, and summer on 9630 kHz.

Radio Romania International. Starts with *Radio Newsreel*, a combination of news, commentary and press review. Features on Romania complete the broadcast. Tuesday (Monday evening, local American date), the lineup includes *Pro Memoria* (Romanian

history), *Pages of Romanian Literature*, *Romanian Hits* and *Sports Roundup*. Regular features on other days include Wednesday's *Business Club* and *Visual Arts*, Thursday's *Stage and Screen* and *Romanian Musicians*, and Friday's *Listeners Letterbox* and ●*Skylark* (Romanian folk music). Saturday fare includes *Cultural Survey* and ●*The Folk Music Box*, and Sunday there's *World of Culture*, *Roots*, *Radio Pictures* and *DX Mailbag*. Monday's broadcast airs *Sunday Studio* and repeats of programs from earlier in the week. Fifty-five minutes to western North America winter on 6125 and 9515 kHz, and summer on 11820 and 15235; and to South Asia winter on 11870 and 15250 kHz, and summer on 15140 and 17860 kHz.

Voice of Turkey. Winter only at this time. See 03:00 for specifics. Fifty minutes to Europe and North America on 6020 kHz, and to the Mideast on 7240 kHz. One hour earlier in summer.

China Radio International. Repeat of the 03:00 broadcast (see there for specifics); one hour to North America on 6190 and 9755 kHz.

Radio New Zealand International. Continuous programming for the South Pacific. Part of a much longer broadcast, which is also heard in parts of North America (especially during summer). On 15340, 15720 or 17675 kHz. Sometimes carries commentaries of local sports events.

Voice of Russia World Service. Continues to North America at this hour. *News*, then a feature. Winter, there's *Science and Engineering* (Monday and Thursday), *Musical Tales of St. Petersburg* (Tuesday), *Moscow Mailbag* (Wednesday and Saturday) and *Newmarket* (business) on Friday. More features follow a brief news summary on the half-hour: ●*Audio Book Club* (Monday), *XX Century: Footprints in History* (Tuesday, Thursday and Saturday), and unscheduled features on Wednesday and Friday. Not to be missed at this hour is Sunday's 45-minute ●*Music and Musicians*. The summer schedule has plenty of variety, and includes ●*Jazz Show* (04:31 Monday), ●*Music at Your Request* and ●*Music Around Us* (same time Tuesday), the business-oriented *Newmarket* (04:11 Thursday), *Science and Engineering* (same time Wednesday and

Saturday), ●*Folk Box* (04:31 Thursday), ●*Audio Book Club* (04:31 Friday), *Moscow Mailbag* (04:11 Tuesday and Friday), the retrospective ●*Moscow Yesterday and Today* (04:31 Wednesday) and *Kaleidoscope* (04:31 Sunday). Note that these days are World Time; locally in North America it will be the previous evening. In eastern North America, tune to 7180, 7240 and 7350 kHz in winter, and 9665 and 9880 kHz in summer. Best winter bets for the West Coast are 12010, 15445 and 15595 kHz; in summer, choose from 15455, 15595 and 17660 kHz.

AFRTS Shortwave, USA. Network news, live sports, music and features in the upper-sideband mode from the Armed Forces Radio & Television Service. Transmitted from modestly powered U.S. Navy stations around the globe. Try 4319, 5446.5, 5765, 6350, 7590, 9980, 10320, 12133.5, 12579 and 13362 kHz.

04:30

Radio Prague, Czech Republic. Winter only at this time. See the 04:00 broadcast to North America for program specifics. Thirty minutes to the Mideast and South Asia on 9865 and 11600 kHz. One hour earlier in summer.

Kol Israel. Winter only at this time. *News* for 15 minutes from Israel Radio's domestic network. To Europe and eastern North America on 6280 kHz, and to Central America and Australasia on 15640 or 17600 kHz. One hour earlier in summer.

04:45

RAI International—Radio Roma, Italy. *News* and Italian music make up this 15-minute broadcast to southern Europe and North Africa. Winter on 5965, 6100 and 7230 kHz; and summer on 6110, 7235 and 9675 kHz.

05:00

■**BBC World Service for the Americas.** Winter only at this time. Starts with the daily *World Briefing*, then Monday through Friday

(Sunday through Thursday evenings in North America), *The World Today* completes the hour. This is replaced Saturday by ●*Reporting Religion*, and Sunday by *Letter* and *The Instant Guide*. The final hour to western North America and Central America on 6135 kHz.

Flanders Radio International, Belgium. Winter only at this time. Tuesday through Saturday (weekday evenings in North America), starts with *News*. The rest of the broadcast is a mix of current events, reports and Belgian music. Sunday, these are replaced by the entertaining ●*Music from Flanders*, and Monday by *Radio World*, *Tourism* and *Brussels 1043* (a listener-response program). A half hour to western North America on 9590 kHz. One hour earlier in summer.

■**Deutsche Welle,** Germany. *News*, then Tuesday through Saturday it's ●*NewsLink*—commentary, interviews, background reports and analysis. The second half-hour features ●*A World of Music* (Tuesday), *Arts on the Air* (Wednesday), ●*Living in Germany* and *Europe in Capitals* (Thursday), *Cool* (a well produced youth show, Friday) and ●*Focus on Folk* (Saturday). On Sunday there's *Religion and Society*, *German by Radio* and *Africa This Week*; and Monday's fare is *Hard to Beat* (sport), *Inspired Minds* and either *Hits in Germany* or *Melody Time*. Sixty minutes to East, Central and southern Africa, winter on 7285, 9565, 12035 and 15410 kHz; and summer on 9630, 9700, 12045, 15410 and 17860 kHz. Best winter channels for southern Africa are 7285 and 12035 kHz; in summer (winter in the Southern Hemisphere) choose from 9630, 12045 and 17860 kHz.

■**Radio France Internationale.** Monday through Friday only at this time. Similar to the 04:00 broadcast, but without the international newsflash. A half hour to East Africa (and heard well beyond) on any two channels from 11685, 11850, 11995, 15155 and 15605 kHz. Audible in southern Africa winter on 11850 kHz, and midyear on 11685 or 15605 kHz.

Vatican Radio. Summer only at this time. Twenty minutes of programming oriented to Catholics. To Europe on 4005, 5890 and 7250 kHz. One hour later in winter.

05:00–06:00

Radio Japan. *News*, then Monday through Friday there's *Japan and the World 44 Minutes* (an in-depth look at current trends and events). This is replaced Saturday by *Hello from Tokyo* and Sunday by *Pop Joins the World*. One hour to Europe on 5975 and 7230 kHz; to East Asia on 15195 kHz; to Southeast Asia on 17810 kHz; to Australasia on 21755 kHz; and to western North America on 6110 kHz.

China Radio International. Repeat of the 03:00 broadcast (see there for specifics); one hour to North America (better to the west) on 6190 and 9560 kHz via a Canadian relay.

Radio Habana Cuba. The start of a two-hour broadcast for western North America and Central America. Tuesday through Sunday (Monday through Saturday evenings in North America), the first half hour consists of international and Cuban news followed by *RHC's Viewpoint*. The next 30 minutes consist of a news bulletin and the sports-oriented *Time Out* (five minutes each) plus a feature: *Caribbean Outlook* (Tuesday and Friday), *DXers Unlimited* (Wednesday and Sunday), the *Mailbag Show* (Thursday) and *Weekly Review* (Saturday). Monday, the hour is split between *Weekly Review* and *Mailbag Show*. To Central America on 9550 kHz; and to western North America on 9820 kHz (also audible in parts of Australasia).

Radio Austria International. Summer Sundays only, and actually starts at 05:05. See 06:00 for details. To the Mideast on 17870 kHz, and one hour later in winter.

Radio New Zealand International. Continues with regional programming for the South Pacific. Part of a 24-hour broadcast, which is also heard in parts of North America (especially during summer). On 9615, 11820 or 15340 kHz.

Radio Australia. *World News*, then Monday through Friday there's *Pacific Beat* (background reporting on events in the Pacific)—look for a sports bulletin at 05:30, followed by *On the Mat*. Weekends, the news is followed Saturday by *Australian Express* and *All in the Mind*, and Sunday by *Arts on RA* and *The Ark*. Continuous to Asia and the Pacific on 9660, 12080, 13630, 15160, 15240, 15415 (from 0530), 15515 and 17750 kHz. In North America (best during summer) try 15160 and 15515 kHz. Best for East Asia is 13630 kHz; in Southeast Asia use 15415 or 17750 kHz. Some channels carry alternative sports programming at weekends.

Voice of Russia World Service. Winter, the final 60 minutes of a four-hour block of programming to North America; summer, the first of four hours to Australasia. Opens with *News*, followed winter by features. These includes ●*Jazz Show* (04:31 Monday), ●*Music at Your Request* and ●*Music Around Us* (same time Tuesday), the business-oriented *Newmarket* (04:11 Thursday), *Science and Engineering* (same time Wednesday and Saturday), ●*Folk Box* (04:31 Thursday), ●*Audio Book Club* (04:31 Friday), *Moscow Mailbag* (04:11 Tuesday and Friday), the retrospective ●*Moscow Yesterday and Today* (0431 Wednesday) and *Kaleidoscope* (0431 Sunday). Note that these days are World Time; locally in North America it will be the previous evening. Tuesday through Saturday summer, there's *Focus on Asia and the Pacific*, replaced Sunday by *Science and Engineering* and Monday by *Moscow Mailbag*. On the half-hour, look for *This is Russia* (Friday), ●*Audio Book Club* (Sunday), ●*Moscow Yesterday and Today* (Thursday), ●*Christian Message from Moscow* (Saturday), *Russian by Radio* (Monday and Wednesday) and *Kaleidoscope* on Tuesday. Winter only to eastern North America on 7180 and 7240 kHz, and to western parts on 12010, 15445 and 15595 kHz. Available year round to Australasia on 21790 kHz.

AFRTS Shortwave, USA. Network news, live sports, music and features in the upper-sideband mode from the Armed Forces Radio & Television Service. Transmitted from modestly powered U.S. Navy stations around the globe. Try 4319, 5446.5, 5765, 6350, 7590, 9980, 10320, 12133.5, 12579 and 13362 kHz.

05:30

Radio Thailand. Thirty minutes of *news* and short features relayed from one of the station's domestic services. To Europe winter on 13780 kHz, and summer on 21795 kHz.

06:00–11:59
Australasia & East Asia—Evening Prime Time
Western North America—Late Evening
Europe & Mideast—Morning and Midday

06:00

■**Deutsche Welle,** Germany. *News*, then Tuesday through Saturday it's ●*NewsLink*—commentary, interviews, background reports and analysis. This is followed by *Insight* and *Business German* (Tuesday), *World in Progress* (Wednesday), ●*Money Talks* (Thursday), *Living Planet* (Friday), and *Spectrum* (Saturday). Sunday fare is ●*Inside Europe*, replaced Monday by *Mailbag*. Sixty minutes to West Africa winter on 7225, 11785 and 15410 kHz; and summer on 7170, 15275 and 17860 kHz. Also year round to Europe on 6140 kHz.

Radio Habana Cuba. The second half of a two-hour broadcast. Tuesday through Sunday (Monday through Saturday evenings in North America), opens with 10 minutes of international news. Next comes *Spotlight on the Americas* (Tuesday through Saturday) or Sunday's *The World of Stamps*. The final 30 minutes consists of news-oriented programming. The Monday slots are *From Havana* and ●*The Jazz Place* or *Breakthrough* (science). To Central America to 9550 kHz; and to western North America 9820 kHz. Listeners in Australasia can try 9820 kHz, as it's also beamed their way.

Radio Japan. *News*, then weekdays it's *A Song for Everyone* and *Asian Top News*. This is followed by a 35-minute feature: *Japan Musicscape* (Monday), Japanese language lessons (Tuesday and Thursday), *Japan Music Travelogue* (Wednesday), and *Music Beat* (Japanese popular music) on Friday. On the remaining days, *Pop Joins the World* fills the Saturday slot and *Weekend Japanology* and *Japan Music Scene* are aired on Sunday. One hour to Europe on 7230 kHz; to East Asia on 11715, 11760 and 15195 kHz; to Southeast Asia on 11740 kHz; to Australasia on 21755 kHz; and to Hawaii on 17870 kHz (this channel has different programming after

06:15). Also to western North America winter on 11690 kHz, and summer on 13630 kHz.

Radio Austria International. Winter Sundays only. The 25-minute ●*Report from Austria-The Week in Review* is aired at 06:05, then repeated at 06:35. The remainder of the one-hour broadcast is in German. To the Mideast on 17870 kHz, and one hour earlier in summer.

■**Radio France Internationale.** Weekdays only at this time. Similar to the 04:00 broadcast (see there for specifics), but includes a report on the day's main international story. A half hour to East and West Africa winter on 11725, 15155 and 17800 kHz; and summer on 11665, 17800 and 21620 kHz. Heard well beyond.

Radio Australia. Opens with *News*, then the weekday lineup is *Regional Sports* and two features: ●*Ockham's Razor* and *Hit Mix* (Monday), *In Conversation* and *Music Deli* (Tuesday), *Lingua Franca* and *Jazz Notes* (Wednesday), *The Ark* and *Australian Country Style* (Thursday), and *The Makers* and *The Chat Room* (Friday). Saturday's pairing is *Verbatim* and *Jazz Notes*, replaced Sunday by *The Buzz* and *Hit Mix*. Continuous to Asia and the Pacific on 9660, 11880, 12080, 15160, 15240, 15415, 15515 and 17750 kHz. Listeners in North America should try 15160 and 15515 kHz. In East Asia, tune to 11880 kHz; for Southeast Asia, use 15415 or 17750 kHz. Some channels carry an alternative sports program until 07:00 on weekends (08:00 midyear).

Radio New Zealand International. Continues with regional programming for the South Pacific, which is also heard in parts of North America (especially during summer). On 9615, 11820 or 15340 kHz.

Voice of Russia World Service. *News*, then winter it's *Focus on Asia and the Pacific* (Tuesday through Saturday), *Science and*

06:00–07:00

Voice of America analyst Kim Andrew Elliott tries out a PC controlled receiver at the 2004 Shortwave Listeners' Fest in Kulpsville, Pennsylvania.   L. Magne

Engineering (Sunday), and *Moscow Mailbag* (Monday). On the half-hour, look for *This is Russia* (Friday), ●*Audio Book Club* (Sunday), ●*Moscow Yesterday and Today* (Thursday), ●*Christian Message from Moscow* (Saturday) and *Russian by Radio* on Monday and Wednesday. In summer, the news is followed by *Science and Engineering* (Monday and Friday), the business-oriented *Newmarket* (Wednesday and Saturday), and a listener-response program, *Moscow Mailbag*, on the remaining days. The second half hour is mostly a combination of *Russia: People and Events*, ●*Russian Treasures* (a gem of a classical music program) and the religious *Daily Reflections*. Continuous programming to Australasia on 21790 kHz.

Vatican Radio. Winter only at this time. Twenty minutes with a heavy Catholic slant. To Europe on 4005, 5890 and 7250 kHz. One hour earlier in summer.

Voice of Malaysia. *News*, followed Monday, Wednesday, Friday and Sunday by a two-minute Malayan language lesson (replaced by a local pop hit on Tuesday). The next 33 minutes are given over to *Hits All the Way*. Saturday, it's the 35-minute *Mailbag*. The hour is rounded off with a feature: *New Horizon*

(Monday), *ASEAN Focus* (Tuesday), *Malaysia in Perspective* (Wednesday), *Personality* (Thursday), *News and Views* (Friday), and *Weekly Roundup* and *Current Affairs* on the weekend. The first hour of a 150-minute broadcast to Southeast Asia and Australasia on 6175, 9750 and 15295 kHz.

AFRTS Shortwave, USA. Network news, live sports, music and features in the upper-sideband mode from the Armed Forces Radio & Television Service. Transmitted from modestly powered U.S. Navy stations around the globe. Try 4319, 5446.5, 5765, 6350, 7590, 9980, 10320, 12133.5, 12579 and 13362 kHz.

06:30

Radio Bulgaria. Summer only at this time. *News*, followed by *Answering Your Letters* (Monday), ●*Folk Studio* (Tuesday) and *Keyword Bulgaria* on the remaining days. Thirty minutes to Europe on 11600 and 13600 kHz. One hour later in winter.

Radio Romania International. Winter only at this time. *News* and commentary followed by features on Romania. Twenty-five minutes to western Europe on 9565 and 11710 kHz. Thirty minutes later in summer.

07:00

■**Deutsche Welle, Germany.** *News*, followed weekdays by the excellent ●*NewsLink* — commentary, interviews, background reports and analysis. The second half-hour features *Spectrum* (Monday), ●*A World of Music* (Tuesday), *Arts on the Air* (Wednesday), ●*Living in Germany* and *Europe in Capitals* (Thursday) and *Cool* (a youth show, Friday). Weekend fare consists of Saturday's ●*Inside Europe* and Sunday's *Hard to Beat* (sport), *Inspired Minds* and either *Hits in Germany* or *Melody Time*. Sixty minutes to Europe on 6140 kHz.

■**Radio France Internationale.** Starts with a bulletin of African *news*. Next, there's a review of the French dailies, an in-depth look at events in Africa, the main news event of the day in France, and sports. The broadcast ends with a 25-minute feature— *French Lesson*, *Crossroads*, *Voices*, *Rendez-Vous*, *World Tracks*, *Weekend* or *Club 9516* (a listener-response program). One hour to West Africa on 11725 (winter) and 15605 kHz. The latter frequency is via RFI's Gabon relay, and is also audible in parts of North America.

Flanders Radio International, Belgium. Summer only at this time; see 08:00 for specifics. Thirty minutes to western Europe on 5985 kHz, and one hour later in winter.

Radio Prague, Czech Republic. Summer only at this time. See 08:00 for specifics. Thirty minutes to Europe on 9880 and 11600 kHz. One hour later in winter.

Radio Romania International. Summer only at this time; see 06:30 for specifics. Twenty-five minutes to western Europe on 11830 and 15150 kHz. Thirty minutes earlier in winter.

Radio Slovakia International. Tuesday through Friday, starts with *News* and *Topical Issue*, then features. Regulars include *Tourism News* (Tuesday), *Business News* and *Currency Update* (Wednesday), *Culture News* (Thursday) and *Regional News* (Friday). Monday's news is followed by *Insight Central Europe*. The Saturday lineup includes *Front Page* and *Sports News*; and Sunday's features are *Sunday Newsreel* and *Listeners' Tribune*. Thirty minutes to Australasia on 9440 (midyear), 13715 (winter) and 15460 kHz.

Radio Australia. *World News*, then Monday through Friday it's *Pacific Beat* (background reporting on events in the Pacific)—look for the latest sports news at 0730, then *On the Mat*. Weekends, there's Saturday's *Asia Pacific* and *The Buzz*, and Sunday's *Correspondents' Report* and *Innovations*. Continuous to Asia and the Pacific on 9660, 11880 12080, 13630, 15160, 15240, 15415 and 17750 kHz. Listeners in North America can try 13630 (West Coast) and 15160 kHz (best during summer), while East Asia is served by 11880 kHz. For Southeast Asia, take your pick from 15415 and 17750 kHz.

Voice of Malaysia. Starts weekdays with 45 minutes of *Fascinating Malaysia*, replaced Saturday by *Malaysia Rama* and *Malaysia in*

Perspective, and Sunday by *ASEAN Melody* and *Destination Malaysia*. Not much doubt about where the broadcast originates! The hour ends with a 15-minute feature. Continuous to Southeast Asia and Australasia on 6175, 9750 and 15295 kHz.

Voice of Russia World Service. Continuous programming to Southeast Asia and Australasia. *News*, then a variety of features. The winter lineup includes *Science and Engineering* (Monday and Friday), the business-oriented *Newmarket* (Wednesday and Saturday), and a listener-response program, *Moscow Mailbag*, on the remaining days. The second half hour is mostly a combination of *Russia: People and Events*, ●*Russian Treasures* and the religious *Daily Reflections*. Summer, the news is followed by the informative ●*Update* on Tuesday, Thursday and Saturday. Other offerings include *Science and Engineering* (Wednesday), *Moscow Mailbag* (Friday) and Monday's masterpiece, ●*Music and Musicians*. On the half-hour, there's some of the Voice of Russia's best—●*Audio Book Club* (Wednesday), ●*Moscow Yesterday and Today* (Friday), *Songs from Russia* (Sunday), ●*Folk Box* (Tuesday) and *This is Russia* on Thursday. Mondays, it's a continuation of ●*Music and Musicians*. Well heard in Australasia winter (local summer) on 21790 kHz; and midyear on 17495, 17525, 17635 and 21790 kHz. Some of these frequencies also provide good reception in Southeast Asia.

Radio New Zealand International. Continues with regional programming for the South Pacific, which is also heard in parts of North America (especially during summer). On 9885 or 15340 kHz.

Radio Taiwan International. Ten minutes of *News*, followed by features. Monday (Sunday evening in North America) there's *Taiwan Economic Journal*, *Discover Taiwan*, and *Asia Pacific* (produced by Radio Australia). These are replaced on other days by *Kaleidoscope*, *Mailbag Time*, *Sound Postcard* and *Let's Learn Chinese* (Tuesday); *On the Job*, ●*Jade Bells and Bamboo Pipes* and *Life Unusual* (Wednesday); *Trends*, *People*, *Wisdom.com* and *Instant Noodles* (Thursday); *Politics Today*; *Culture Express* and *New Music Lounge* (Friday);

07:00–08:00

Bookworm, then *Stage, Screen and Studio* and *Groove Zone* (Saturday); and *News Talk, Taipei Magazine, Sound Postcard* and *Hakka World* (Sunday). One hour to western North America on 5950 kHz.

AFRTS Shortwave, USA. Network news, live sports, music and features in the upper-sideband mode from the Armed Forces Radio & Television Service. Transmitted from modestly powered U.S. Navy stations around the globe. Try 4319, 5446.5, 5765, 6350, 7590, 9980, 10320, 12133.5, 12579 and 13362 kHz.

07:30

Radio Bulgaria. This time winter only. *News,* followed by *Answering Your Letters* (Monday), ●*Folk Studio* (Tuesday) and *Keyword Bulgaria* on the remaining days. Thirty minutes to Europe on 11600 and 13600 kHz, and hour earlier in summer.

08:00

■**Deutsche Welle,** Germany. *News,* then Monday through Friday there's commentary, interviews, background reports and analysis in ●*NewsLink.* On the half-hour, look for ●*Focus on Folk* (Monday), *Insight* and *Business German* (Tuesday), *World in Progress* (Wednesday), ●*Money Talks* (Thursday) and *Living Planet* (Friday). Saturday's lineup is *Religion and Society, German by Radio* and ●*Network Europe,* replaced Sunday by *Mailbag.* Sixty minutes to Europe on 6140 kHz.

Flanders Radio International, Belgium. Winter only at this time. Monday through Friday, starts with *News.* The rest of the broadcast is a mix of current events, reports and Belgian music. Saturday, these are replaced by *Network Europe,* and Sunday by *Radio World, Tourism* and *Brussels 1043* (a listener-response program). Thirty minutes to Europe on 5985 kHz. One hour earlier in summer.

Voice of Malaysia. *News* and commentary, then *Golden Oldies.* The final half hour of a much longer transmission targeted at Southeast Asia and Australasia on 6175, 9750 and 15295 kHz.

Radio Prague, Czech Republic. Winter only at this time. *News,* then Monday through Friday it's the in-depth *Current Affairs* and one or more features: *Talking Point* (Monday), *Czech Science* and *One on One* (Tuesday), *Czechs in History Czechs Today* or *Spotlight* (Wednesday), *Business Report* (Thursday), and *The Arts* (Friday). Weekends, the news is followed by Saturday's *Insight Central Europe* or Sunday's *Mailbox* and *ABC of Czech* followed by *Encore* (classical music), *Magic Carpet* (Czech world music) or *Czech Books.* Thirty minutes to Europe on 7345 and 9880 kHz. One hour earlier in summer.

Radio Australia. Part of a 24-hour service to Asia and the Pacific, but which can also be heard at this time throughout much of North America. Begins with a bulletin of *World News,* then Monday through Friday there's an in-depth look at current events in *PM.* Weekends, the news is followed by *Grandstand Wrap,* a roundup of the latest Australian sports action, with Saturday's *Earthiest* or Sunday's *In the Pipeline* filling the second half hour. On 5995, 9580, 9590, 9710, 12080, 13630, 15240, 15415 (the first half hour weekends only) and 17750 kHz. Audible in parts of North America on 9580, 9590 and 13630 kHz. Best for East Asia is 15240 kHz, with 15415 and 17750 kHz the channels for Southeast Asia.

Voice of Russia World Service. Continuous programming to Southeast Asia and Australasia. Winter, *News* is followed by ●*Update* on Tuesday, Thursday and Saturday. Other features include *Science and Engineering* (Wednesday), *Moscow Mailbag* (Friday) and Monday's outstanding ●*Music and Musicians* (classical music). On the half-hour, there's some of the Voice of Russia's best—●*Audio Book Club* (Wednesday), ●*Moscow Yesterday and Today* (Friday), ●*Folk Box* (Tuesday), *Songs from Russia* (Sunday), *Kaleidoscope* (Saturday), and Thursday's *This is Russia.* In summer, ●*Update* is only available on Wednesday and Friday. It is replaced Monday by *Science and Engineering,* Tuesday by *Focus on Asia,* Thursday by *Newmarket* and Saturday by *Moscow Mailbag.* Sunday's offering is the 45-minute ●*Music and Musicians*—a jewel among classical music shows. Choice pickings from the second half hour include ●*Moscow Yesterday and Today* (Monday), ●*Folk Box* (Thursday), ●*Jazz Show* (Friday) and Saturday's ●*Christian Message from Moscow*. For Australasia winter (local Oz summer), use 17495, 17525, 17665 and 21790 kHz; midyear, the frequencies are the same, except that 17635 kHz replaces 17665 kHz. Some of these channels are also well heard in Southeast Asia.

Radio Taiwan International. Ten minutes of *News*, followed by features. Monday, there's *Taiwan Economic Journal*, *Discover Taiwan*, and Radio Australia's *Asia Pacific*. These are replaced on the following days by *Kaleidoscope*, *Mailbag Time*, *Sound Postcard* and *Let's Learn Chinese* (Tuesday); *On the Job*, ●*Jade Bells and Bamboo Pipes* and *Life Unusual* (Wednesday); *Trends*, *People*, *Wisdom.com* and *Instant Noodles* (Thursday); *Politics Today*; *Culture Express* and *New Music Lounge* (Friday); *Bookworm*, then *Stage, Screen and Studio* and

Groove Zone (Saturday); and *News Talk*, *Taipei Magazine*, *Sound Postcard* and *Hakka World* (Sunday). One hour to Australasia on 9610 kHz.

Radio New Zealand International. Continues with regional programming for the South Pacific. Part of a 24-hour broadcast which is also heard in parts of North America (especially during summer). On 9885 kHz.

Radio Korea International, South Korea. Opens with 10 minutes of *news*, then Monday through Friday, a commentary. This is followed by 30 minutes (45 on Friday) of *Seoul Calling*. Monday through Thursday, the broadcast closes with a 15-minute feature: *Korea, Today and Tomorrow*, *Korean Kaleidoscope*, *Wonderful Korea* and *Seoul Report*, respectively. Saturday's news is followed by *Worldwide Friendship* (a listener-response show), and Sunday by *Korean Pop Interactive*. Sixty minutes to Europe on 13670 kHz, and to Southeast Asia on 9570 kHz.

08:00–10:00

The Mekong begins in China's Qinghai province, near the Tibet border. It then winds through Yunnan province before emerging as the longest waterway in Southeast Asia. Some 60 million people live near its banks and floodplains.

M. Guha

AFRTS Shortwave, USA. Network news, live sports, music and features in the upper-sideband mode from the Armed Forces Radio & Television Service. Transmitted from modestly powered U.S. Navy stations around the globe. Try 4319, 5446.5, 5765, 6350, 7590, 9980, 10320, 12133.5, 12579 and 13362 kHz.

08:10

Voice of Armenia. Summer Sundays only. Twenty minutes of Armenian *news* and culture. To Europe on 15270 kHz, and to the Mideast on 4810 kHz. One hour later in winter.

09:00

■**Deutsche Welle,** Germany. *News*, then Monday through Friday it's the excellent ●*NewsLink* —commentary, interviews, background reports and analysis. The second half-hour features *Spectrum* (Monday), ●*A World of Music* (Tuesday), *Arts on the Air* (Wednesday), ●*Living in Germany* and *Europe in Capitals* (Thursday) and *Cool* (a well produced youth show, Friday). Weekend features are Saturday's ●*Inside Europe* and Sunday's *Religion and Society*, *Inspired Minds* and either *Hits in Germany* or *Melody Time*. Sixty minutes to Europe on 6140 kHz.

China Radio International. Starts with *News*, followed Monday through Friday by special reports—current events, sports, business, culture, science and technology and press clippings. The rest of the broadcast is devoted to features. Regulars include ●*People in the Know* (Monday), *Biz China* (Tuesday), *China Horizons* (Wednesday), ●*Voices from Other Lands* (Thursday), and *Life in China* on Friday. Weekends, the news is followed by a shorter series of reports (current events and sport) and two features. Saturday there's *Cutting Edge*, and *Listeners' Garden* (listener mail, Chinese folk music, a preview of the next week's programs, and a Chinese language lesson); replaced Sunday by *Reports on Developing Countries* and *In the Spotlight*, a series of mini-features: *Cultural Carousel*, *In Vogue*, *Writings from China*, *China Melody* and *Talking Point*. One hour to Europe on 17490 kHz, and to Australasia on 15210 and 17690 kHz.

Radio New Zealand International. Continuous programming for the islands of the South Pacific, on 9885 kHz. Audible in much of North America, especially in summer.

Voice of Russia World Service. Winter only at this time. *News*, followed by ●*Update* on Wednesday and Friday. This is replaced Monday by *Science and Engineering*, Tuesday by *Focus on Asia*, Thursday by *Newmarket* and Saturday by *Moscow Mailbag*. Sunday's offering is the 45-minute ●*Music and Musicians*—not to be missed if you are an aficionado of classical music. Choice pickings from the second half hour include ●*Moscow Yesterday and Today* (Monday), ●*Folk Box* (Thursday) ●*Jazz Show* (Friday) and Saturday's ●*Christian Message from Moscow*. The Tuesday and Wednesday slots are also worth a listen. To Australasia on 17495, 17525 and 17665 kHz; and to Southeast Asia on 17495, 17525 and 17850 kHz.

Radio Prague, Czech Republic. Summer only at this time. See 10:00 for specifics. Thirty minutes to South Asia and West Africa on 21745 kHz, and heard well beyond. One hour later in winter.

Radio Australia. *World News*, then weekdays it's a call-in show, *Australia Talks Back*. This is replaced Saturday by *The Science Show*, and Sunday by *The National Interest* (topical events). Continuous to Asia and the Pacific on 9580, 9590, 11880, 15240 and 15415 kHz; and heard in North America on 9580 and 9590 kHz. Best for East Asia is 15240 kHz; and for Southeast Asia, 11880 and 15415 kHz.

AFRTS Shortwave, USA. Network news, live sports, music and features in the upper-sideband mode from the Armed Forces Radio & Television Service. Transmitted from modestly powered U.S. Navy stations around the globe. Try 4319, 5446.5, 5765, 6350, 7590, 9980, 10320, 12133.5, 12579 and 13362 kHz.

09:10

Voice of Armenia. Winter Sundays only. Twenty minutes of Armenian *news* and culture. To Europe on 15270 kHz, and to the Mideast on 4910 kHz. One hour earlier in summer.

09:30

Radio Vilnius, Lithuania. A half hour that's mostly *news* and background reports about events in Lithuania. Of broader appeal is *Mailbag*, aired every other Sunday. For a little Lithuanian music, try the second half of Monday's broadcast. To western Europe on 9710 kHz.

10:00

■**BBC World Service for the Americas.** Monday through Friday, opens with a half hour of news and current events, followed by summer's ●*World Business Report* or winter's *Analysis* (except Thursday, when there's ●*From Our Own Correspondent*). Best of the weekend fare is Saturday's *Assignment* (10:06). *Sports Roundup* or *Football Extra* completes the hour. To the Caribbean on 6195 kHz, and audible in much of the southern and eastern United States. Listeners farther west can tune to the Asian stream on 9740 kHz.

■**Deutsche Welle,** Germany. *News*, then Monday through Friday, ●*NewsLink*. This is replaced Saturday by *Religion and Society* and *German by Radio*, and Sunday by *Hard to Beat* (sport) and *Inspired Minds*. Thirty minutes to East Asia on 6205 and 17820 kHz in winter, and 15350 and 17820 kHz in summer.

■**Radio Netherlands.** Monday through Friday it's ●*Newsline*, then a feature: ●*Research File* (Monday), ●*EuroQuest* (Tuesday), ●*Documentary* (Wednesday), *Dutch Horizons* (Thursday) and *A Good Life* (Friday). Weekend fare consists of a six-minute *news* bulletin followed by Saturday's *Europe Unzipped*, ●*Insight* and *Amsterdam Forum*; or Sunday's *Wide Angle*, *The Week Ahead* and *Vox Humana*. One hour to East and Southeast Asia and Australasia on 7315 (winter), 9785 (summer), 9790 (winter), 12065, 13710 (summer) and 13820 kHz. Recommended listening.

Radio Australia. Monday through Friday, there's *World News*, *Asia Pacific* and a feature: *Health Report* (Monday), *Law Report* (Tuesday), *Religious Report* (Wednesday), *Media Report* (Thursday) and *Sports Factor* (Friday). Weekends, it's Saturday's *Background Briefing* and *Correspondent's Notebook*, and Sunday's *Keys to Music*. Continuous to Asia and the Pacific on 9580, 9590, 11880, 15240 and 15415 kHz; and heard in North America on 9580 and 9590 kHz. Listeners in East Asia should tune to 15240 kHz; and Southeast Asia has 11880 and 15415 kHz.

Radio Prague, Czech Republic. Winter only at this time. *News*, then Monday through Friday there's *Current Affairs* and a feature or two:

10:00–11:00

Talking Point (Monday), *Czech Science* and *One on One* (Tuesday), *Czechs in History*, *Czechs Today* or *Spotlight* (Wednesday), *Business Report* (Thursday) and *The Arts* (Friday). On Saturday the news is followed by *Magazine*, *Letter from Prague* and a repeat of Tuesday's *One on One*. Sunday's lineup is *Mailbox* and *ABC of Czech* followed by *Encore* (classical music), *Magic Carpet* (Czech world music) or *Czech Books*. Thirty minutes to South Asia and West Africa on 21745 kHz, but audible well beyond. One hour earlier in summer.

Radio Japan. *News*, then Monday through Friday it's *A Song for Everyone* and *Japan and the World 44 Minutes* (an in-depth look at current trends and events). This is replaced Saturday by *Hello from Tokyo*, and Sunday by *Weekend Japanology* and *Japan Music Scene*. One hour to Asia on 11730 kHz, to Southeast Asia on 9695 kHz, to Europe on 17585 kHz, to the Mideast on 17720 kHz, to eastern North America on 6120 kHz, and to Australasia on 21755 kHz.

Voice of Mongolia. Original programming is aired on Monday, Wednesday and Friday, and is repeated on the following day. Starts with *News*, then it's either a listener-response program (Monday) or reports and interviews. The entire Sunday broadcast is devoted to exotic Mongolian music. Thirty minutes to Southeast Asia and Australasia on 12085 (or 12015) kHz. Often well heard in parts of the United States during March and September.

China Radio International. News, commentary, reports and interviews in the weekday ●*RealTime Beijing*. Weekends, there's Saturday's *China Roots* (folk music) and Sunday's *China Beat* (popular music). One hour to Europe on 17490 kHz, and to Australasia on 15210 and 17690 kHz.

All India Radio. *News*, then a composite program of commentary, press review and features, interspersed with exotic Indian music. One hour to East Asia on 13710, 15235 (or 15020) and 17800 kHz, and to Australasia on 13710, 17510 and 17895 kHz. Also beamed to Sri Lanka on 15260 kHz.

Voice of Korea, North Korea. Mind-numbing programs on themes such as the application of socialist thinking to industrial production are basic fare for this world band curiosity. Worth the occasional listen just to hear how bad it is. One hour to Central America on 9335 (or 15180) and 11710 kHz; and to Southeast Asia on 9850 (or 13650) and 11735 kHz. Also audible in parts of East Asia on 3560 kHz.

AFRTS Shortwave, USA. Network news, live sports, music and features in the upper-sideband mode from the Armed Forces Radio & Television Service. Transmitted from modestly powered U.S. Navy stations around the globe. Try 4319, 5446.5, 5765, 6350, 7590, 9980, 10320, 12133.5, 12579 and 13362 kHz.

10:30

Radio Prague, Czech Republic. This time summer only. Repeat of the 0700 broadcast but with different programming on Saturday; see 11:30 for program specifics. A half hour to northern Europe on 9880 and 11615 kHz. One hour later during winter.

Voice of the Islamic Republic of Iran. News, commentary and features, and a little Iranian music. Strongly reflects an Islamic point of view. One hour to South Asia, and widely heard elsewhere. Winter on 15480 and 15550 kHz, and summer on 15600 and 17660 kHz.

11:00

■**BBC World Service for the Americas.** Saturday and Sunday, opens with *news*, then backup reports. These are replaced weekdays by special programming for the Caribbean. Ends most days with the 15-minute *Sports Roundup*. The remaining programs change according to season. Continuous programming to eastern North America and the Caribbean on 6195 and 15190 kHz. Listeners farther west should tune to the Asian stream on 9740 kHz.

■**Radio Netherlands.** Summer only at this time; see 12:00 for specifics. Sixty minutes to eastern North America on 11675 kHz, and one hour later in winter.

■**Deutsche Welle,** Germany. *News,* then weekdays it's the comprehensive ●*NewsLink*—commentary, interviews, background reports and analysis. This is followed by *Spectrum* (Monday), *Insight* and *Business German* (Tuesday), *World in Progress* (Wednesday), ●*Money Talks* (Thursday) and *Living Planet* (Friday). Saturday's feature is the 55-minute ●*Inside Europe,* replaced Sunday by *Mailbag.* Sixty minutes to Southeast Asia winter on 15410 kHz, and summer on 15105, 17820 and 21820 kHz.

China Radio International. News, commentary, reports and interviews in the weekday ●*RealTime Beijing.* Weekends, there's Saturday's *China Roots* (folk music) and Sunday's *China Beat* (popular music). One hour to Europe on 17490 kHz; and to eastern North America winter on 5960 kHz, and summer on 6040 kHz.

Radio Taiwan International. Ten minutes of *News,* followed by features. Monday, there's *Kaleidoscope, Discover Taiwan,* and Radio Australia's *Asia Pacific.* These are replaced on successive days by *On the Job, Mailbag Time, Sound Postcard* and *Let's Learn Chinese* (Tuesday); *Trends,* ●*Jade Bells and Bamboo Pipes* and *Life Unusual* (Wednesday); *Politics Today, People, Wisdom.com* and *Instant Noodles* (Thursday); *Bookworm, Culture Express* and *New Music Lounge* (Friday); *News Talk,* then *Stage, Screen and Studio* and *Groove Zone* (Saturday); and *Taiwan Economic Journal, Taipei Magazine, Sound Postcard* and *Hakka World* (Sunday). Sixty minutes to Southeast Asia on 7105 kHz.

Radio Australia. Monday through Friday, there's *World News, Asia Pacific* and *Bush Telegraph* (rural and regional Australia). These are replaced Saturday by *Asia Pacific* and *All in the Mind,* and Sunday by *Sunday People* and *Speaking Out.* Continuous to East Asia and the Pacific on 5995, 6020, 6035, 9475, 9580, 9590, 11880, 12080 and (till 1130) 15240 kHz; and heard in much of North America on 6020, 9580 and 9590 kHz. Listeners in Southeast Asia should tune to 9475 and 11880 kHz. For East Asia, there's 15240 kHz till 11:30.

Radio Ukraine International. Summer only at this time. An hour's ample coverage of just about all things Ukrainian, including news, sports, politics and culture. A popular feature is ●*Music from Ukraine,* which fills most of the Sunday broadcast. Sixty minutes to western Europe on 15415 kHz. One hour later in winter.

HCJB—Voice of the Andes, Ecuador. The first hour of a religious broadcast to the Americas on 12005 and 15115 kHz.

Radio Japan. *News,* then weekdays it's *A Song for Everyone* and *Asian Top News.* These are followed by a 35-minute feature: *Japan Musicscape* (Monday), Japanese language lessons (Tuesday and Thursday), *Japan Music Travelogue* (Wednesday), and *Music Beat* (Japanese popular music) on Friday. *Pop Joins the World* fills the Saturday slot, and is replaced Sunday by *Hello from Tokyo.* One hour to eastern North America on 6120 kHz; to Asia on 11730 kHz; and to Southeast Asia on 9695 kHz.

Radio Singapore International. A three-hour package for Southeast Asia, and widely heard in Australasia. Starts with ten minutes of *news* (five at weekends), then Monday through Friday there's *Business and Market Report,* replaced Saturday by *Business Ideas,* and Sunday by *Connections.* These are followed by several mini-features, including a daily news and weather bulletin on the half-hour. Monday's lineup is *Undertones, Discovering Singapore, The Write Stuff* and *E-Z Beat;* and is replaced Tuesday by *A World of Our Own, Young Expressions, The Business Feature, Assignment* and a shorter edition of *E-Z Beat;* Wednesday offers *Perspective, Traveller's Tales, Eco-Watch, The Business Feature* and *Classic Gold;* Thursday has *Frontiers, Eco-Watch, The Business Feature, Potluck* and *Love Songs;* and Friday brings *Asian Journal, Arts Arena, The Business Feature, Indonesian Media Watch* and *Classic Gold.* Saturday's list includes *Regional Press Review* and *Frontiers* and Sunday there's *Comment, Discovering Singapore* and *Science and Technology.* On 6080 and 6150 kHz.

Voice of Vietnam. Begins with *news,* then there's *Commentary* or *Weekly Review* followed by short features and pleasant Vietnamese music (especially at weekends). A half hour to Southeast Asia on 7285 kHz.

11:00–12:00

Deutsche Welle, once the voice of West Germany, now symbolizes a united and proud Germany. The national break with the past is underscored by the station's universalist modern architecture.

DW

AFRTS Shortwave, USA. Network news, live sports, music and features in the upper-sideband mode from the Armed Forces Radio & Television Service. Transmitted from modestly powered U.S. Navy stations around the globe. Try 4319, 5446.5, 5765, 6350, 7590, 9980, 10320, 12133.5, 12579 and 13362 kHz.

11:30

Radio Korea International, South Korea. Opens with 10 minutes of *news*, then Monday through Friday, a commentary. This is followed by 30 minutes (45 on Friday) of *Seoul Calling*. Monday through Thursday, the broadcast closes with a 15-minute feature: *Korea, Today and Tomorrow*, *Korean Kaleidoscope*, *Wonderful Korea* and *Seoul Report*, respectively. On Saturday, the news is followed by *Worldwide Friendship* (a listener-response program), and Sunday by *Korean Pop Interactive*. Sixty minutes to eastern North America on 9650 kHz via their Canadian relay.

Radio Bulgaria. Summer only at this time. *News*, followed by *DX Programme* (for radio enthusiasts, Sunday), *Answering Your Letters* (a listener-response show, Monday), ●*Folk Studio* (Bulgarian folk music, Tuesday), and *Keyword Bulgaria* on the remaining days. Thirty minutes to Europe on 11700 and 15700 kHz, and one hour later in winter.

Flanders Radio International, Belgium. Monday through Friday, starts with *News*. The rest of the broadcast is a mix of current events, reports and Belgian music. Saturday, these are replaced by the entertaining ●*Music from Flanders*, and Sunday by *Radio World*, *Tourism* and *Brussels 1043* (a listener-response program). Thirty minutes to East Asia and Australasia on 9940 or 9945 kHz.

Radio Prague, Czech Republic. Winter only at this time. *News*, then Monday through Friday it's *Current Affairs* plus one or more features: *Talking Point* (Monday), *Czech Science* and *One on One* (Tuesday), *Czechs in History*, *Czechs Today* or *Spotlight* (Wednesday), *Business Report* (Thursday) and *The Arts* (Friday). The Saturday news is followed by *Magazine*, *Letter from Prague* and a repeat of Tuesday's *One on One*. Sunday's lineup is *Mailbox* and *ABC of Czech* followed by *Encore* (classical music), *Magic Carpet* (Czech world music) or *Czech Books*. Thirty minutes to northwestern Europe on 11640 kHz, and to East Africa on 21745 kHz. The latter channel is also audible in parts of the Mideast. The European broadcast is one hour earlier in summer, but there is no corresponding transmission for East Africa.

Wales Radio International. Winter Saturdays only at this time. Thirty minutes of news, interviews and music for Australasia on 17625 kHz. One hour later in summer (Oz winter).

12:00–17:59
Western Australia & East Asia—Evening Prime Time
North America—Morning and Lunchtime
Europe & Mideast—Afternoon and Early Evening

12:00

■**BBC World Service for the Americas.** A full hour of news and current events in *Newshour*, except for the first 30 minutes Monday through Friday, when there's alternative programming for the Caribbean. Continuous to North America and the Caribbean on 6195 and 15190 kHz. Listeners in western states may get a better signal from the Asian stream on 9740 kHz.

Radio Canada International. Summer weekdays only at this time. The Canadian Broadcasting Corporation's *The Current*. To eastern North America and the Caribbean on 9515, 13655 and 17800 kHz. For a separate year-round service to Asia, see the next item.

Radio Canada International. *News*, then Monday it's *Writers and Company*. This is replaced Tuesday, Wednesday, Friday and Saturday by *The Nighttime Review*, and Thursday by ●*Global Village* (world music). Sunday's slot goes to ●*Quirks and Quarks* (an irreverent look at science). One hour to East and Southeast Asia winter on 9660 (or 9670) and 11730 kHz, and summer on 9660 and 15190 kHz.

■**Radio Netherlands.** Winter only at this time. Monday through Friday, opens with ●*Newsline* (current events) which is replaced weekends by a *news* bulletin. The final 25 minutes (more at weekends) is devoted to features. The lineup includes ●*Research File* (science, Monday), ●*EuroQuest* (Tuesday), the award-winning ●*Documentary* (Wednesday), *Dutch Horizons* (Thursday) and *A Good Life* on Friday. Weekends, there's Saturday's *Europe Unzipped*, ●*Insight* and *Amsterdam Forum*; replaced Sunday by *Wide Angle*, *The Week Ahead* and *Vox Humana*. Sixty minutes to eastern North America on 11675 kHz, and one hour earlier in summer.

Radio Tashkent, Uzbekistan. Monday through Saturday, opens with *News*, replaced Sunday by *Significant Events of the Week*. Other programs include *Uzbekistan and the World* (Monday), *Life in the Village* and *Political Commentary* (Thursday), a listener-response show (Saturday) and *Traditions and Values* on Sunday. Programs of Uzbek music are aired on Tuesday, Wednesday and Friday. To South and Southeast Asia, and also heard in parts of Europe and Australasia. Thirty minutes winter on 5060, 5975, 6025 and 9715 kHz; and summer on 7285, 9715, 15295 and 17775 kHz. Best for Southeast Asia is 9715 kHz in winter, and 17775 kHz in summer.

■**Radio France Internationale.** Opens with a *news* bulletin, then there's a 25-minute feature— *French Lesson*, *Crossroads*, *Voices*, *Rendez-Vous*, *World Tracks*, *Weekend* or *Club 9516* (a listener-response program). A half hour to West Africa on 17815 kHz, and to East Africa on 21620 or 25820 kHz.

Radio Polonia, Poland. This time summer only. Sixty minutes of news, commentary, features and music—all with a Polish accent. Weekdays, starts with *News from Poland*—a potpourri of news, reports, interviews and press review. This is followed Monday by *Focus* (an arts program) and *Chart Show* (a look at Polish pop music); Tuesday by *A Day in the Life* (interviews) and *Request Show*; Wednesday by *Around Poland* and *The Best of Polish Radio* (or *Bookworm*); Thursday by *Letter from Poland* and *Multimedia Show*; and Friday by *Business Week* and *High Note* (or an alternative classical music feature). The Saturday broadcast begins with *From the Weeklies*, and is followed by *Insight Central Europe* (a joint-production with other stations of the region) and *Soundcheck* (new Polish music releases). The Sunday lineup includes *Europe East* (correspondents' reports) and *In Touch*, a listener-response program. To

12:00–12:30

western Europe on 9525 and 11820 kHz. One hour later in winter.

Radio Austria International. Summer only at this time. Weekdays, the 15-minute *Report from Austria* is aired at 12:15, then repeated at 12:45. Saturday and Sunday, it's a similar arrangement, with ●*Report from Austria-The Week in Review* airing at 12:05 and 12:35. The remainder of the one-hour broadcast is in German. To Asia and Australasia on 17715 kHz, and one hour later in winter. For a separate broadcast to Europe, see next item.

Radio Austria International. Summer only at this time. Similar to the broadcast for Asia and Australasia, but with no weekday ●*Report from Austria* at 12:15 (only at 12:45). To Europe on 6155 and 13730 kHz, and one hour later in winter.

Radio Australia. *World News*, then Monday through Thursday it's *Late Night Live* (round-table discussion). On the remaining days, there's Friday's *Sound Quality* (music), Saturday's *The Music Show*, and Sunday's *The Spirit of Things*. Continuous to Asia and the Pacific on 5995, 6020, 6035, 9475, 9580, 9590 and 11880 kHz; and well heard in much of North America on 6020, 9580 and 9590 kHz. Listeners in Southeast Asia can tune to 9475 and 11880 kHz.

Radio Ukraine International. Winter only at this time. See 11:00 for specifics. Sixty minutes to Europe on 13585 kHz. One hour earlier in summer.

HCJB—Voice of the Andes, Ecuador. The second hour of a religious broadcast to the Americas on 12005 or 15115 kHz.

Radio Singapore International. The second of three hours of continuous programming to Southeast Asia and beyond. Starts with five minutes of *news*, followed weekdays by *Newsline*. Most of the remaining time is devoted to short features. There's a weekday *Business and Market Report* on the half-hour, replaced weekends by a *news* bulletin. Monday's lineup includes *Perspective*, *Indonesian Media Watch*, *Frontiers*, *Eco-Watch* and *Young Expressions*; Tuesday, there's *Asian Journal*, *Undertones*, *Discovering Singapore* and

Film Talk; replaced Wednesday by *Call from America*, *The Write Stuff*, *Snapshots* and *A World of Our Own*; Thursday offers, among others, *Connections*, *Comment*, *Assignment* and *Arts Arena*; and Friday has *Regional Press Review*, *Business Ideas* and *Limelight*. Saturday's *Connections*, *Perspective*, *Indonesian Media Watch*, *Young Expressions* and *Comment* are replaced Sunday by *Regional Press Review*, *Business Ideas*, *Call from America*, *Undertones* and *Potluck*. On 6080 and 6150 kHz.

Radio Taiwan International. Repeat of the 11:00 broadcast; see there for specifics. One hour to East Asia on 7130 kHz.

Voice of America. A mixed bag of current events, sports, science, business and other news and features. Continuous to East and Southeast Asia winter on 6110, 9760, 11705, 15250 and 15425 kHz; and summer on 6160, 9760, 13610, 15160, 15240 and 15425 kHz. For Australasia there's 9645, 11715 (winter) and 15425 kHz.

China Radio International. Starts with *News*, followed Monday through Friday by special reports—current events, sports, business, culture, science and technology and press clippings. The rest of the broadcast is devoted to features. Regulars include ●*People in the Know* (Monday), *Biz China* (Tuesday), *China Horizons* (Wednesday), ●*Voices from Other Lands* (Thursday), and *Life in China* on Friday. Weekends, the news is followed by a shorter series of reports (current events and sport) and two features. Saturday there's *Cutting Edge*, and *Listeners' Garden* (listener mail, Chinese folk music, a preview of the next week's programs, and a Chinese language lesson); replaced Sunday by *Reports on Developing Countries* and *In the Spotlight*, a series of mini-features: *Cultural Carousel*, *In Vogue*, *Writings from China*, *China Melody* and *Talking Point*. One hour to Europe on 17490 kHz; to Southeast Asia on 9730 and 11980 kHz, to Australasia on 11760 and 15415 kHz; and to eastern North America winter on 9560 kHz.

AFRTS Shortwave, USA. Network news, live sports, music and features in the upper-sideband mode from the Armed Forces Radio & Television Service. Transmitted from modestly powered U.S. Navy stations around the globe. Try 4319, 5446.5, 5765, 6350, 7590, 9980, 10320, 12133.5, 12579 and 13362 kHz.

12:15

Radio Cairo, Egypt. The start of a 75-minute package of news, religion, culture and entertainment, much of it devoted to Arab and Islamic themes. The initial quarter hour consists of virtually anything, from quizzes to Islamic religious talks, then there's *news* and commentary, followed by political and cultural items. To South and Southeast Asia on 17670 kHz.

12:30

Radio Bulgaria. Winter only at this time. *News*, then *DX Programme* (for radio enthusiasts, Sunday), *Answering Your Letters* (a listener-response show, Monday), ●*Folk Studio* (Bulgarian folk music, Tuesday), and *Keyword Bulgaria* on the remaining days. Thirty minutes to Europe on 11700 and 15700 kHz and one hour earlier in summer.

Radio Bangladesh. *News*, followed by Islamic and general interest features and pleasant Bengali music. Thirty minutes to Southeast Asia, also heard in Europe, on 7185 and 9550 kHz. Frequencies may vary slightly, and one transmitter is often off the air.

Voice of Vietnam. Repeat of the 11:00 transmission; see there for specifics. A half hour to Southeast Asia on 9840 and 12020 kHz. Frequencies may vary slightly.

Radio Thailand. Thirty minutes of *news* and short features to Southeast Asia and Australasia, winter on 9810 kHz and summer on 9855 kHz.

12:30–13:00

Voice of Turkey. This time summer only. Fifty-five minutes of *news*, features and Turkish music. To Europe on 15225 kHz, and to Southeast Asia and Australasia on 15535 kHz. One hour later in winter.

Radio Sweden. Summer only at this time. Monday through Friday, it's *news* and features in *Sixty Degrees North*, concentrating heavily on Scandinavian topics. The Monday slot goes to *SportScan*, replaced Tuesday by *Close Up* or an alternative feature, and Wednesday by special features. Thursday's shows rotate from week to week—*Nordic Lights*, *GreenScan*, *Heart Beat* or *S-Files*, while Friday offers a review of the week's news. Saturday's slot is filled by *Network Europe*, *Spectrum* (the arts), *Sweden Today* or *Studio 49*; and Sunday there's *In Touch with Stockholm* (a listener-response program) or the musical *Sounds Nordic*. Thirty minutes to North America on 15240 kHz; and to Asia and Australasia on 13580 and 15735 kHz. One hour later in winter.

Wales Radio International. Summer Saturdays only at this time. News, interviews and local music from Britain's westernmost region. Thirty minutes to Australasia on 17745 kHz, and one hour earlier in winter.

13:00

■BBC World Service for the Americas. Weekdays, a five-minute *news* bulletin is followed by the long-running *Outlook* and ●*Off the Shelf* (readings from world literature), or *Newshour*, depending on the season. Best of the weekend fare can be found on Sunday. Continuous programming to North America and the Caribbean on 6195 and 15190 kHz. The Asian stream on 9740 kHz is likely to provide better reception in western North America.

Radio Canada International. Monday through Friday winter, and daily in summer. Winter, it's the Canadian Broadcasting Corporation's *The Current*. Summer weekdays there's *Sounds Like Canada*, replaced Saturday by *The House* (a look at Canadian politics) and Sunday by the first 60 minutes of *The Sunday Edition*. To eastern North America and the Caribbean winter weekdays on 9515, 13655 and 17820 kHz; and summer on 9515, 13655 and 17800 kHz.

China Radio International. Repeat of the 12:00 broadcast; see there for specifics. One hour to Southeast Asia on 11980 and 15180 kHz; and to Australasia on 11760 and 11900 kHz. Also available to eastern North America on 9570 kHz; and summer only to western North America on 7405 kHz.

■Deutsche Welle, Germany. *News*, then weekdays it's ●*NewsLink* —commentary, interviews, background reports and analysis. Next, on the half-hour, there's *Spectrum* (Monday), *Insight* and *Business German* (Tuesday), *World in Progress* (Wednesday), ●*Money Talks* (Thursday) and *Living Planet* (Friday). Saturday's feature is the 55-minute ●*Concert Hour*, replaced Sunday by *Mailbag*. Sixty minutes to Europe on 6140 kHz.

Radio Polonia, Poland. This time winter only. *News*, commentary, music and a variety of features. See 12:00 for specifics. Sixty minutes to Europe on 9525 and 11820 kHz. One hour earlier in summer.

Radio Prague, Czech Republic. Summer only at this hour. *News*, then Monday through Friday there's *Current Affairs* and one or more features: *Talking Point* (Monday), *Czech Science* and *One on One* (Tuesday), *Czechs in History*, *Czechs Today* or *Spotlight* (Wednesday), *Business Report* (Thursday) and *The Arts* (Friday). On Saturday the news is followed by *Magazine*, *Letter from Prague* and a repeat of Tuesday's *One on One*. Sunday's lineup is *Mailbox* and *ABC of Czech* followed by *Encore* (classical music), *Magic Carpet* (Czech world music) or *Czech Books* Thirty minutes to northern Europe on 13580 kHz, and to South Asia (audible in parts of the Mideast) on 21745 kHz. There is no corresponding broadcast in winter.

Radio Romania International. Starts with *Radio Newsreel*, a combination of news, commentary and press review. Features on Romania complete the broadcast. Monday, the lineup includes *Pro Memoria* (Romanian history), *Pages of Romanian Literature*, *Romanian Hits* and *Sports Roundup*. Regular

12:30–13:00

features on other days include Tuesday's *Business Club* and *Visual Arts*, Wednesday's *Stage and Screen* and *Romanian Musicians*, Thursday's *Listeners Letterbox* and ●*Skylark* (Romanian folk music), and Friday's *Cultural Survey* and ●*The Folk Music Box*. Saturday fare includes *World of Culture*, *Roots*, *Radio Pictures* and *DX Mailbag*; and Sunday's broadcast has *Sunday Studio* and repeats of programs aired earlier in the week. Fifty-five minutes to Europe winter on 15105 and 17745 kHz; and summer on 11830 and 15105 kHz.

Radio Jordan. Summer only at this time. The first hour of a partial relay of the station's domestic broadcasts, beamed to Europe on 11690 kHz. Continuous till 16:30 (17:30 in winter).

Radio Korea International, South Korea. Opens with 10 minutes of *news*, then Monday through Friday, a commentary. This is followed by 30 minutes (45 on Friday) of *Seoul Calling*. Monday through Thursday, the broadcast closes with a 15-minute feature: *Korea, Today and Tomorrow*, *Korean Kaleidoscope*, *Wonderful Korea* and *Seoul Report*, respectively. On Saturday, the news is followed by *Worldwide Friendship* (a listener-response program), and Sunday by *Korean Pop Interactive*. Sixty minutes to Southeast Asia on 9570 and 13670 kHz.

Radio Austria International. Winter only at this time. Starts weekdays at 13:15, and weekends at 13:05. See 12:00 for details. To Asia and Australasia on 17855 kHz, and one hour earlier in summer. For a separate broadcast to Europe, see the next item.

Radio Austria International. Winter only at this time. Similar to the broadcast for Asia and Australasia, but the weekday start is 13:45. See 12:00 for details. To Europe on 6155 and 13730 kHz, and one hour earlier in summer.

HCJB—Voice of the Andes, Ecuador. The final half hour of a 150-minute religious broadcast to the Americas on 12005 and 15115 kHz.

Radio Cairo, Egypt. The final half-hour of the 12:15 broadcast, consisting of listener participation programs, Arabic language

lessons and a summary of the latest news. To South and Southeast Asia on 17670 kHz.

Radio Australia. Monday through Friday, *News* is followed by world music in ●*The Planet*. Saturday, it's the second hour of *The Music Show*, and Sunday there's *Encounter*. Continuous programming to Asia and the Pacific on 5995, 6020, 6035, 9580 and 9590 kHz; and easily audible in much of North America on 6020, 9580 and 9590 kHz.

Radio Singapore International. The third and final hour of a daily broadcast to Southeast Asia and beyond. Starts with a five-minute bulletin of the latest *news*, then most days it's music: *Singapop* (local talent, Monday and Thursday); *Rhythm in the Sun* (Latin sounds, Tuesday and Sunday); *Spin the Globe* (world music, Wednesday and Saturday); and *Hot Trax* (new releases, Friday). There's another news bulletin on the half-hour, then a short feature. Monday's offering is *Traveller's*

This Victorian-era Thai edifice is the perfect backdrop for pith helmets and ladies' parasols. M. Guha

13:00–14:00

Tales, replaced Tuesday by *The Write Stuff*. Wednesday's feature is *Potluck*; Thursday has *Call from America*; and Friday it's *Snapshots*. These are followed by the 15-minute *Newsline*. Weekend fare is made up of Saturday's *Assignment*, *Film Talk* and *Arts Arena*; and Sunday's *A World of Our Own* and *Limelight*. The broadcast ends with yet another five-minute news update. On 6080 and 6150 kHz.

Voice of Korea, North Korea. The last of the old-time communist stations. One hour to Europe on 9325 (or 13760) and 11335 (or 15245) kHz; and to North America on 9335 and 11710 kHz. Also heard in parts of East Asia on 4405 kHz.

Voice of America. Opens with *news*, then it's music: *American Gold* (Monday), *Roots and Branches* (Tuesday), *Classic Rock* (Wednesday), *Top Twenty* (Thursday), *Country Hits* (Friday) and jazz at the weekend. Continuous programming to East and Southeast Asia winter on 6110, 9760, 11705 and 15425 kHz; and summer on 5955, 6160, 15160 and 15425 kHz. For Australasia there's 9645 and 15425 kHz.

AFRTS Shortwave, USA. Network news, live sports, music and features in the upper-sideband mode from the Armed Forces Radio & Television Service. Transmitted from modestly powered U.S. Navy stations around the globe. Try 4319, 5446.5, 5765, 6350, 7590, 9980, 10320, 12133.5, 12579 and 13362 kHz.

13:30

Voice of Turkey. This time winter only. *News*, then *Review of the Turkish Press* and some unusual features with a strong local flavor. Selections of Turkish popular and classical music complete the program. Fifty-five minutes to Europe on 15155 kHz, and to Southeast Asia and Australasia on 15195 kHz. One hour earlier in summer.

Radio Sweden. See 12:30 for program details. Thirty minutes to North America winter on 18960 kHz, and summer on 15240 kHz; and to Asia and Australasia winter on 9430 and 17505 kHz, and summer on 15735 and 17505 kHz.

All India Radio. The first half hour of a 90-minute block of regional and international *news*, commentary, exotic Indian music, and a variety of talks and features of general interest. To Southeast Asia and beyond on 9690, 11620 and 13710 kHz.

Radio Tashkent, Uzbekistan. Monday through Saturday, opens with *News*, replaced Sunday by *Significant Events of the Week*. Other programs include *Nature and Us* and *Cooperation* (Monday), *Political Commentary* and *Youth Program* (Wednesday), a feature for women (Thursday), *Parliamentary Herald* (Friday) a show for shortwave listeners (Saturday) and *Interesting Meetings* on Sunday. Programs of Uzbek music are aired on Tuesday, Friday and Saturday, and a competition with prizes on Thursday and Saturday. To South and Southeast Asia, and also heard in parts of Europe and Australasia. Thirty minutes winter on 5060, 5975, 6025 and 9715 kHz; and summer on 7285, 9715, 15295 and 17775 kHz. Best for Southeast Asia is 9715 kHz in winter, and 17775 kHz in summer.

14:00

■**BBC World Service for the Americas.** *News*, then weekdays it's a series of 25-minute arts programs. The second half hour is much more lowbrow—popular music. Best are Wednesday's ●*Charlie Gillett* (world music) and Friday's ●*John Peel* (alternative and indie rock). Weekend programming consists of a five-minute *news* bulletin followed by Saturday's live *Sportsworld* or a Sunday call-in show, *Talking Point*. Continuous to North America and the Caribbean on 15190 kHz. Listeners in the western United States may get better reception from the Asian stream on 9740 kHz.

Radio Japan. *News*, then Monday through Friday it's *Japan and the World 44 Minutes* (an in-depth look at current trends and events). Weekends, there's Saturday's *Weekend Japanology* and *Japan Music Scene*, and Sunday's *Pop Joins the World*. One hour to Southeast Asia on 7200 kHz; to Australasia on 11840 kHz; and to South Asia winter on 9845 kHz, and summer on 11730 kHz.

■**Radio France Internationale.** Weekdays, opens with international and Asian *news*, then in-depth reports, a look at the main news event of the day in France, and sports. *Asia-Pacific*, replaces the international report on Saturday, and Sunday fare includes a weekly report on cultural events in France and a phone-in feature. These are followed on the half-hour by a 25-minute feature— *French Lesson, Crossroads, Voices, Rendez-Vous, World Tracks, Weekend* or *Club 9516* (a listener-response program). An hour of interesting and well-produced programming to the Mideast and beyond, winter on 17620 kHz and summer on 15615 or 17515 kHz. Also to South Asia winter on 7180 or 9580 kHz, and summer on 9580 or 11610 kHz.

■**Deutsche Welle,** Germany. *News,* then Monday through Friday there's ●*NewsLink.* This is followed on the half-hour by ●*Focus on Folk* (Monday), ●*A World of Music* (Tuesday), *Arts on the Air* (Wednesday), ●*Living in Germany* and *Europe in Capitals* (Thursday) and the youth-oriented *Cool* (Friday). Weekends, the Saturday news is followed by ●*Inside Europe;* and Sunday by *Religion and Society, Inspired Minds* and either *Hits in Germany* or *Melody Time.* Sixty minutes to Europe on 6140 kHz.

Voice of Russia World Service. Summer only at this time. Eleven minutes of *News,* followed Monday through Saturday by much of the same in *News and Views.* Completing the lineup is *Sunday Panorama* and *Russia: People and Events.* On the half-hour, the lineup includes some of the station's better entertainment features. Try ●*Folk Box* (Monday), ●*Music at Your Request* or an alternative (Tuesday and Thursday), ●*Jazz Show* (Wednesday) and Friday's retrospective ●*Moscow Yesterday and Today,* all of which should please. Making up the roster are Saturday's *Timelines* and Sunday's *Kaleidoscope.* To Southeast Asia on 7390, 12055 and 17645 kHz.

■**Radio Netherlands.** The first 60 minutes of an approximately two-hour block of programming. Monday through Friday there's ●*Newsline* (current events) and a feature on the half-hour: ●*Research File* (Monday), ●*EuroQuest* (Tuesday), ●*Documentary* (Wednesday), *Dutch Horizons* (Thursday) and

A Good Life (Friday). Weekend programming opens with a *news* bulletin, then it's either Saturday's *Europe Unzipped,* ●*Insight* and *Amsterdam Forum;* or Sunday's *Wide Angle, The Week Ahead* and *Vox Humana.* To South Asia winter on 12070 (and/or 9345), 12080 and 15595 kHz; and summer on 9890, 11835 and 12075 kHz. Heard well beyond the target area.

Radio Australia. *World News* is followed Monday through Friday by *PM* and *Perspective.* These are replaced weekends by Saturday's *Background Briefing* and *Correspondent's Notebook,* and Sunday's *The Science Show* and *Business Weekend.* Continuous to Asia and the Pacific on 5995, 6080, 7240, 9475 (from 1430), 9590, 11660 (from 1430) and 11750 kHz (5995, 7240 and 9590 kHz are audible in North America, especially to the west). In Southeast Asia, use 6080, 9475, 11660 and 11750 kHz.

Radio Prague, Czech Republic. Winter only at this time. *News,* then weekdays it's *Current Affairs* plus features:. *Talking Point* (Monday), *Czech Science* and *One on One* (Tuesday), *Czechs in History Czechs Today* or *Spotlight* (Wednesday), *Business Report* (Thursday), and *The Arts* (Friday). Weekends, the news is followed by Saturday's *Insight Central Europe* or Sunday's *Mailbox* and *ABC of Czech* followed by *Encore* (classical music), *Magic Carpet* (Czech world music) or *Czech Books.* A friendly half hour to eastern North America and East Africa on 21745 kHz. There is no corresponding summer broadcast.

Radio Taiwan International. Ten minutes of *News,* followed by features. Monday, there's *Kaleidoscope, Discover Taiwan,* and *Asia Pacific* (produced by Radio Australia). These are replaced on other days by *On the Job, Mailbag Time, Sound Postcard* and *Let's Learn Chinese* (Tuesday); *Trends,* ●*Jade Bells and Bamboo Pipes* and *Life Unusual* (Wednesday); *Politics Today, People, Wisdom.com* and *Instant Noodles* (Thursday); *Bookworm, Culture Express* and *New Music Lounge* (Friday); *News Talk,* then *Stage, Screen and Studio* and *Groove Zone* (Saturday); and *Taiwan Economic Journal, Taipei Magazine, Sound Postcard* and *Hakka World* (Sunday). Sixty minutes to Southeast Asia on 15265 kHz.

14:00–15:00

Radio Thailand's listening quality is aided by tireless vigilance over rows of controls. M. Guha

China Radio International. Starts with *News,* followed Monday through Friday by special reports—current events, sports, business, culture, science and technology and press clippings. The rest of the broadcast is devoted to features. Regulars include ●*People in the Know* (Monday), *Biz China* (Tuesday), *China Horizons* (Wednesday), ●*Voices from Other Lands* (Thursday), and *Life in China* on Friday. Weekends, the news is followed by a shorter series of reports (current events and sport) and two features. Saturday there's *Cutting Edge*, and *Listeners' Garden* (listener mail, Chinese folk music, a preview of the next week's programs, and a Chinese language lesson); replaced Sunday by *Reports on Developing Countries* and *In the Spotlight*, a series of mini-features: *Cultural Carousel*, *In Vogue*, *Writings from China*, *China Melody* and *Talking Point*. One hour to western North America on 7405 and 13740 or 17730 kHz; to South Asia on 9700, 11675 and 11765 kHz; and to East Africa on 13685 and 15125 kHz.

All India Radio. The final hour of a 90-minute composite program of commentary, press review, features and exotic Indian music. To Southeast Asia and beyond on 9690, 11620 and 13710 kHz.

Radio Canada International. Winter weekdays it's *Sounds Like Canada*, replaced summer by *Outfront* (except for Friday's *C'est la Vie*). Winter Saturdays, there's a look at Canadian politics in *The House*; and summer it's the entertaining ●*Vinyl Café*. On Sunday there's 60 minutes of the three-hour show, *The Sunday Edition*. To eastern North America and the Caribbean winter on 9515, 13655 and 17820 kHz; and summer on 9515, 13655 and 17800 kHz.

Radio Jordan. Winter, starts at this time; summer, it's the second hour of a partial relay of the station's domestic broadcasts, and continuous till 16:30 (17:30 in winter). Aimed at European listeners but also audible in parts of eastern North America, especially during winter. On 11690 kHz.

Voice of America. The first of several hours of continuous programming to the Mideast. *News*, current events and short features covering sports, science, business, entertainment and other topics. Winter on 15205 kHz, and summer on 15255 kHz. Also the final hour to East and Southeast Asia winter on 6110, 9760, 11705 and 15425 kHz; and summer on 5955, 6160, 15160 and 15425 kHz. The 15425 kHz channel is also available to Australasia.

Radio Thailand. Thirty minutes of tourist features for Southeast Asia and Australasia. Winter on 9560 kHz, and summer on 9830 kHz.

AFRTS Shortwave, USA. Network news, live sports, music and features in the upper-sideband mode from the Armed Forces Radio & Television Service. Transmitted from modestly powered U.S. Navy stations around the globe. Try 4319, 5446.5, 5765, 6350, 7590, 9980, 10320, 12133.5, 12579 and 13362 kHz.

14:30

Radio Sweden. Winter only at this time. Monday through Friday, it's *news* and features in *Sixty Degrees North*, concentrating heavily on Scandinavian topics. Several of the features rotate from week to week, but a few are fixtures. Monday's *SportScan* is replaced Tuesday by *Close Up* or an alternative feature, and Wednesday by special features. Thursday's carousel is *Nordic Lights*, *GreenScan* (the environment), *Heart Beat* (health), and *S-Files*; with *Weekly Review* filling the Saturday slot. The Sunday rotation is *Network Europe*, *Spectrum*, *Sweden Today* and *Studio 49*; while Monday's offering is *In Touch with Stockholm* (a listener-response program) or the musical *Sounds Nordic*. Thirty minutes to North America on 18960 kHz, and to Asia and Australasia on 17505 kHz.

15:00

■BBC World Service for the Americas. Starts with five minutes of *news*, then features, including some of the BBC's better offerings (starting at 15:06): ●*Health Matters* (Monday), *Go Digital* (Tuesday), *Discovery* (science, Wednesday), ●*One Planet* (Thursday) and *Science in Action* (Friday). On the half-hour, a short news summary is followed by a mixed bag of programs. Best is Monday's light entertainment; worst is *Westway* (a soap, Wednesday and Friday). Saturday has live action in *Sportsworld*, and Sunday programming is either more sport or classical music. Continuous programming to the Caribbean

and North America on 15190 kHz. In western states, try the Asian stream on 9740 kHz—you may well get better reception, albeit of different programs.

China Radio International. See 14:00 for program details. Sixty minutes to western North America on 7405 (winter) and 13740 or 17730 kHz. Also available year round to South Asia on 7160 and 9785 kHz; and to East Africa on 13685 and 15125 kHz.

Radio Austria International. Summer only at this time. Weekdays, starts at 15:10; Saturday and Sunday at 15:05. See 16:00 for details. To western North America on 13755 kHz, and one hour later in winter.

■Radio Netherlands. The final 57 minutes of an approximately two-hour broadcast targeted at South Asia. Monday through Friday, starts with a feature and ends with ●*Newsline* (current events). The features are repeats of programs aired during the previous six days, and are all worthy of a second hearing: ●*EuroQuest* (Monday), *A Good Life* (Tuesday), *Dutch Horizons* (Wednesday) ●*Research File* (science, Thursday) and ●*Documentary* (winner of several prestigious awards) on Friday. The weekend format is feature-news-feature, with *Vox Humana* and *Europe Unzipped* on Saturday, and ●*Documentary* and *Wide Angle* on Sunday. To South Asia winter on 12070 (and/or 9345), 12080 and 15595 kHz; and summer on 9890, 11835 and 12075 kHz. Heard well beyond the target area.

Radio Australia. *World News*, then weekdays there's *Asia Pacific* and a feature on the half-hour. Monday, it's health; Tuesday, law; Wednesday, religion; Thursday, media; and Friday, sport. These are replaced Saturday by *In the Pipeline* and *Australian Express*, and Sunday by *National Interest* and *Perspective*. Continuous programming to the Pacific (and well heard in western North America) on 5995, 7240 and 9590 kHz. Additionally available to Southeast Asia on 6080, 9475, 11660 and 11750 kHz.

■Deutsche Welle, Germany. *News*, then weekdays it's ●*NewsLink* —commentary, interviews, background reports and analysis.

15:00–16:00

Next, on the half-hour, there's *Spectrum* (Monday), *Insight* and *Business German* (Tuesday), *World in Progress* (Wednesday), ●*Money Talks* (Thursday) and *Living Planet* (Friday). Saturday's features are *Religion and Society*, *German by Radio* and ●*Network Europe*; and the 55-minute ●*Concert Hour* fills the Sunday slot. Sixty minutes to Europe on 6140 kHz.

Voice of America. Continues with programming to the Mideast. A mixed bag of current events, sports, science, business and other news and features. Winter on 9575 and 15205 kHz, and summer on 9700 and 15205 kHz. Also heard in much of Europe.

Radio Canada International. Daily in winter, but weekends only in summer. Winter weekdays there's *Outfront* (except for Friday's *C'est la Vie*), replaced Saturday by the unique ●*Vinyl Café* (readings and music). Summer, the Saturday slot goes to ●*Quirks and Quarks* (a science show with a difference). On the remaining day it's *The Sunday Edition* both winter and summer. To North America and the Caribbean, winter on 9515, 13655 and 17820 kHz; and summer on 9515, 13655 and 17800 kHz. For a separate broadcast to South Asia, see the next item.

Radio Canada International. *News*; then Monday through Friday it's *Canada Today*, replaced Saturday by *Business Sense* and Sunday by *Maple Leaf Mailbag* (a listener-response show). On the half-hour there's *Spotlight* (Wednesday and Sunday), *Media Zone* (Monday), *The Mailbag* (Tuesday), *Business Sense* (Thursday) and *Sci-Tech File* on Friday and Saturday. Sixty minutes to South Asia winter on 9635 and 11730 kHz, and summer on 15455 and 17720 kHz. Heard well beyond the intended target area, especially to the west.

Radio Japan. *News*, then weekdays it's *A Song for Everyone* and *Asian Top News*. A 35-minute feature completes the broadcast: *Japan Musicscape* (Monday), Japanese language lessons (Tuesday and Thursday), *Japan Music Travelogue* (Wednesday), and *Music Beat* (Japanese popular music) on Friday. *Pop Joins the World* is aired Saturday, and *Hello from Tokyo* fills the Sunday slot. One hour to East Asia on 6190 kHz; to South Asia winter on 9845 kHz, and summer on 11730 kHz; to Southeast Asia on 7200 kHz; and to western North America and Central America on 9505 kHz.

Voice of Russia World Service. Predominantly news-related fare for the first half-hour, then a mixed bag, depending on the day and season. At 15:31 winter, look for ●*Folk Box* (Monday), ●*Jazz Show* (Wednesday), ●*Music at Your Request* or an alternative (Tuesday and Thursday), *Kaleidoscope* (Sunday) and Friday's retrospective ●*Moscow Yesterday and Today*. Summer at this time, look for some listener favorites. The lineup includes *This is Russia* (Monday), ●*Moscow Yesterday and Today* (Tuesday), ●*Audio Book Club* (dramatized reading, Wednesday), the incomparable ●*Folk Box* (Thursday), and *Songs from Russia* on Friday. Weekend fare is split between Saturday's *Kaleidoscope* and Sunday's *Russian by Radio*. To the Mideast summer on 7325 and 11985 kHz; and to Southeast Asia winter on 6205 an 11500 kHz, and summer on 7390 and 11500 kHz.

Voice of Mongolia. Original programming is aired on Monday, Wednesday and Friday, and is repeated on the following day. Starts with *News*, then it's either a listener-response program (Monday) or reports and interviews. The entire Sunday broadcast is devoted to exotic Mongolian music. Thirty minutes to West and Central Asia on 9720 kHz, and sometimes heard in Europe.

Radio Jordan. A partial relay of the station's domestic broadcasts, beamed to Europe on 11690 kHz. Continuous till 16:30 (17:30 in winter). Audible in parts of eastern North America, especially during winter.

Voice of Korea, North Korea. Repeat of the 13:00 broadcast. One hour to Europe on 9325 (or 13760) and 11335 (or 15245) kHz; and to North America on 9335 and 11710 kHz. Also heard in parts of East Asia on 4405 kHz.

Voice of Vietnam. Repeat of the 11:00 transmission; see there for specifics. A half hour to Southeast Asia on 7285, 9840 and 12020 kHz. Frequencies may vary slightly.

AFRTS Shortwave, USA. Network news, live sports, music and features in the upper-sideband mode from the Armed Forces Radio & Television Service. Transmitted from modestly powered U.S. Navy stations around the globe. Try 4319, 5446.5, 5765, 6350, 7590, 9980, 10320, 12133.5, 12579 and 13362 kHz.

15:30

Voice of the Islamic Republic of Iran. News, commentary and features, strongly reflecting an Islamic point of view. One hour to South and Southeast Asia (also heard in parts of Australasia), winter on 7190 and 9610 kHz, and summer on 9635 and 11650 kHz.

16:00

■BBC World Service for the Americas. Monday through Friday winter, it's mostly news, reports and analysis; summer, there's ●*Europe Today*. Weekends, year round, there's a short *news* bulletin followed by live sports. The final hour to the Caribbean and North America on 15190 kHz.

■Radio France Internationale. The first half hour includes *news* and reports from across Africa, international newsflashes and news about France. Next is a 25-minute feature—*French Lesson, Crossroads, Voices, Rendez-Vous, World Tracks, Weekend* or *Club 9516* (a listener-response program). A fast-moving hour to Africa and the Mideast on any four frequencies from 9590, 9730, 11615, 15160, 15365, 15605, 17605, 17850 and 21580 kHz. Best for the Mideast is 11615 kHz in winter, and 15605 kHz in summer. In southern Africa, tune to 9730 or 17850 kHz.

Radio Austria International. Winter only at this time. Weekdays, the 15-minute *Report from Austria* is aired at 16:10, then repeated at 16:40. Saturday and Sunday, it's a similar arrangement, with ●*Report from Austria-The Week in Review* airing at 16:05 and 16:35. The remainder of the one-hour broadcast is in German. To western North America on 13765 kHz, and one hour earlier in summer.

■Deutsche Welle, Germany. *News*, then Monday through Friday, ●*NewsLink*. The final 30 minutes consist of *Insight* and *Europe in Capitals* (Monday), *World in Progress* (Tuesday), ●*Money Talks* (Wednesday), *Living Planet* (Thursday) and *Asia This Week* (Friday). Weekends, the Saturday news is followed by *Hard to Beat* (sport), *German by Radio* and the youth-oriented *Cool*; and Sunday, by *Mailbag*. Sixty minutes to Europe on 6140 kHz. Also to South Asia on 6170 (or 6180), 7225 and (winter) 11695 or (summer) 17595 kHz.

Radio Korea International, South Korea. Opens with 10 minutes of *news*, then Monday through Friday, a commentary. This is followed by 30 minutes (45 on Friday) of *Seoul Calling*. Monday through Thursday, the broadcast closes with a 15-minute feature: *Korea, Today and Tomorrow, Korean Kaleido-scope, Wonderful Korea* and *Seoul Report*, respectively. On Saturday, the news is followed by *Worldwide Friendship* (a listener-response program), and Sunday by *Korean Pop Interactive*. One hour to East Asia on 5975 kHz, and to the Mideast and much of Africa on 9515 and 9870 kHz.

Radio Taiwan International. Ten minutes of *News*, then features. Monday, there's *Kaleido-scope, Discover Taiwan,* and Radio Australia's *Asia Pacific*. These are replaced on successive days by *On the Job, Mailbag Time, Sound Postcard* and *Let's Learn Chinese* (Tuesday); *Trends,* ●*Jade Bells and Bamboo Pipes* and *Life Unusual* (Wednesday); *Politics Today, People, Wisdom.com* and *Instant Noodles* (Thursday); *Bookworm, Culture Express* and *New Music Lounge* (Friday); *News Talk,* then *Stage, Screen and Studio* and *Groove Zone* (Saturday); and *Taiwan Economic Journal, Taipei Magazine, Sound Postcard* and *Hakka World* (Sunday). Sixty minutes to South Asia and southern China on 11815 kHz, and heard well beyond.

Voice of Korea, North Korea. Not quite the old-time communist station it was, but the "Beloved Leader" and "Unrivaled Great Man" continue to feature prominently. The Voice of Korea still has a long way to go before being accepted as a serious broadcaster. In the meantime, the uninspiring programs continue. One hour to the Mideast and Africa on 9975

16:00–17:00

and 11735 kHz. Also audible in parts of East Asia on 3560 kHz.

Radio Prague, Czech Republic. Summer only at this time. *News,* then Monday through Friday it's the in-depth *Current Affairs* and one or more features: *Talking Point* (Monday), *Czech Science* and *One on One* (Tuesday), *Czechs in History Czechs Today* or *Spotlight* (Wednesday), *Business Report* (Thursday), and *The Arts* (Friday). Weekends, the news is followed by Saturday's *Insight Central Europe* or Sunday's *Mailbox* and *ABC of Czech* followed by *Encore* (classical music), *Magic Carpet* (Czech world music) or *Czech Books.* A half hour to Europe on 5930 kHz, and to East Africa on 17485 kHz. The transmission for Europe is one hour later in winter, but there is no corresponding broadcast for East Africa.

Voice of Vietnam. *News,* then *Commentary* or *Weekly Review* followed by short features and pleasant Vietnamese music (especially at weekends). A half hour to Europe winter on 7280 and 9730 kHz, and summer on 9730 and 13740 kHz. Also available to West and Central Africa on 7220 and 9550 kHz.

Radio Australia. Continuous programming to Asia and the Pacific. Monday through Friday, *World News* is followed by *Bush Telegraph* (rural and regional Australia). Saturday's lineup is *Hindsight* (a look back into history) and *Perspective;* and *Books and Writing* and *Book Talk* fill the Sunday slots. Beamed to the Pacific on 5995 and 7240 (and well heard in western North America); and to Southeast Asia on 6080, 9475 and 11660 kHz.

Radio Ethiopia. An hour-long broadcast divided into two parts by the 16:30 *news* bulletin. Regular weekday features include *Kaleidoscope* and *Women's Forum* (Monday), *Press Review* and *Africa in Focus* (Tuesday), *Guest of the Week* and *Ethiopia Today* (Wednesday), *Ethiopian Music* and *Spotlight* (Thursday) and *Press Review* and *Introducing Ethiopia* on Friday. For weekend listening, there's *Contact* and *Ethiopia This Week* (Saturday), or Sunday's *Listeners' Choice* and *Commentary.* Best heard in parts of Africa and the Mideast, but sometimes audible in Europe. On 7165, 9560 and 11800 kHz.

Radio Jordan. A partial relay of the station's domestic broadcasts, beamed to Europe on 11690 kHz. The final half hour in summer, but a full 60 minutes in winter. Sometimes audible in parts of eastern North America, especially during winter.

Voice of Russia World Service. Continuous programming to the Mideast and West Asia at this hour. *News,* then very much a mixed bag, depending on the day and season. Winter weekdays, there's *Focus on Asia and the Pacific,* with Saturday's *Newmarket* and Sunday's *Moscow Mailbag* making up the week. On the half-hour, choose from *This is Russia* (Monday), ●*Moscow Yesterday and Today* (Tuesday), ●*Audio Book Club* (dramatized reading, Wednesday), the exotic and eclectic ●*Folk Box* (Thursday), and Friday's *Songs from Russia.* Weekend fare is split between Saturday's *Kaleidoscope* and Sunday's *Russian by Radio.*

Summer, the news is followed by the business-oriented *Newmarket* (Monday and Thursday), *Science and Engineering* (Tuesday and Sunday), *Moscow Mailbag* (Wednesday and Friday), and Saturday's showpiece, ●*Music and Musicians*. The features after the half-hour tend to be variable. Audible in the Mideast winter on 6005 and 9830 kHz, and summer on 11985 and 15540 kHz.

Radio Canada International. Winter weekends only at this hour. Saturday there's ●*Quirks and Quarks* (science), and Sunday it's the final hour of *The Sunday Edition*. To North America and the Caribbean on 9515, 13655 and 17820 kHz.

China Radio International. Starts with *News,* followed Monday through Friday by special reports—current events, sports, business, culture, science and technology and press clippings. The rest of the broadcast is devoted to features. Regulars include ●*People in the Know* (Monday), *Biz China* (Tuesday), *China Horizons* (Wednesday), ●*Voices from Other Lands* (Thursday), and *Life in China* (Friday). Weekends, the news is followed by a shorter series of reports (current events and sport) and two features. Saturday there's *Cutting Edge*, and *Listeners' Garden* (listener mail, Chinese folk music, a preview of the next week's programs, and a Chinese language lesson); replaced Sunday by *Reports on Developing Countries* and *In the Spotlight*, a series of mini-features: *Cultural Carousel, In Vogue, Writings from China, China Melody* and *Talking Point*. One hour to eastern and southern Africa on 9570 and 11900 kHz.

Voice of America. *News Now*—a mixed bag of news and reports on current events, sports, science, business and more. To the Mideast on 9575 (winter), 9700 (summer) and 15205 kHz summer on 9700 and 15205 kHz.

AFRTS Shortwave, USA. Network news, live sports, music and features in the upper-sideband mode from the Armed Forces Radio & Television Service. Transmitted from modestly powered U.S. Navy stations around the globe. Try 4319, 5446.5, 5765, 6350, 7590, 9980, 10320, 12133.5, 12579 and 13362 kHz.

16:30

Radio Slovakia International. Summer only at this time; see 17:30 for specifics. Thirty minutes of friendly programming to western Europe on 5920 and 7345 kHz. One hour later in winter.

Xizang [Tibet] People's Broadcasting Station, China. *Holy Tibet*, which describes itself as "a window to life in Tibet," is a 20-minute package of information and local music—mountains, monasteries, local customs, and (mostly) Tibetan popular music. Sometimes acknowledges listeners' reception reports at the end of the program. Well heard in East Asia, and sometimes provides fair reception in Europe. On 4905, 4920, 5240, 6110, 6130, 6200, 7385 and 9490 kHz.

Radio Cairo, Egypt. The first 30 minutes of a two-hour mix of Arab music and features on Egyptian and Islamic themes, with *news,* commentary, quizzes, mailbag shows, and answers to listeners' questions. To southern Africa on 9855 kHz.

17:00

Radio Prague, Czech Republic. See 17:00 for program specifics. A half hour winter to West Africa on 15710 kHz, and summer to Central Africa on 17485 kHz. Also year round to Europe on 5930 kHz.

Radio Australia. Continuous programming to Asia and the Pacific. Starts with *World News*, then Monday through Friday there's *Australia Talks Back*, replaced Saturday by *The Spirit of Things*, and Sunday by *Sound Quality*. Beamed to the Pacific on 5995, 7240, 9710 and 11880 kHz; to East Asia on 9710 kHz; and to Southeast Asia on 6080 and 9475 kHz. Also audible in parts of western North America on 5995, 7240 and 11880 kHz.

Radio Polonia, Poland. This time summer only. Monday through Friday, opens with *News from Poland*—a compendium of news, reports and interviews. A couple of features complete the broadcast. Monday's combo is *Around Poland* and *The Best of Polish Radio* (or

17:00–17:45

Bookworm); Tuesday, it's *Letter from Poland* and *Multimedia Show*; Wednesday, *A Day in the Life* (interviews) and *High Note* (or an alternative classical music program); Thursday, *Focus* (the arts in Poland) and *Soundcheck* (new Polish music releases); and Friday, *Business Week* and *In Touch*, a listener-response show. The Saturday broadcast begins with *Europe East* (correspondents' reports), and is followed by *From The Weeklies* and *Chart Show*. Sundays, it's five minutes of *news* followed by *Insight Central Europe* (a joint-production with other stations of the region) and *Request Show*. Sixty minutes to western Europe on 5995 and 7285 kHz. One hour later during winter.

Radio Jordan. Winter only at this time. The final 30 minutes of a partial relay of the station's domestic broadcasts. To Europe on 11690 kHz.

Voice of Russia World Service. *News*, then it's a mixed bag, depending on the day and season. Winter, the news is followed by the business-oriented *Newmarket* (Monday and Thursday), *Science and Engineering* (Tuesday and Sunday), and *Moscow Mailbag* (Wednesday and Friday). The choice of features for the second half hour is somewhat variable. In summer, the news is followed by a series of features: *Moscow Mailbag* (Monday, Thursday and Saturday), *Newmarket* (Tuesday and Friday), *Science and Engineering* (Wednesday) and Sunday's jewel, *Music and Musicians* On the half-hour, the lineup includes *Kaleidoscope* (Monday), ●*Music at Your Request* or an alternative (Tuesday), ●*Moscow Yesterday and Today* (Wednesday), Friday's ●*Folk Box* and Saturday's *Songs from Russia*. Summer only to Europe on 9890 kHz, plus weekends on 9480 and 11675 kHz. For the Mideast, tune to 9830 kHz in winter, and 11985 kHz in summer. In Southern Africa, try 11510 kHz midyear.

Radio Japan. *News*, then weekdays it's *A Song for Everyone* and *Japan and the World 44 Minutes* (in-depth reporting). Saturday's feature is *Hello From Tokyo*, replaced Sunday by *Pop Joins the World*. One hour to Europe on 11970 kHz; to southern Africa on 15355 kHz; and to western North America and Central America on 9535 kHz.

China Radio International. News, commentary, reports and interviews in the weekday ●*RealTime Beijing*. Weekends, there's Saturday's *China Roots* (folk music) and Sunday's *China Beat* (popular music). One hour to eastern and southern Africa on 9570 and 11900 kHz.

Voice of Vietnam. Summer only at this time. Thirty minutes to western Europe via an Austrian relay on 9725 kHz. See 18:00 for specifics. One hour later in winter.

Voice of America. Continuous programming to the Mideast and North Africa. *News*, then Monday through Friday it's the interactive *Talk to America*. Weekends, there's the ubiquitous *News Now*. Winter on 6040, 9760 and 15205 kHz; and summer on 9700 and 9760 kHz. For a separate service to Africa, see the next item.

Voice of America. Programs for Africa. Monday through Saturday, identical to the service for Europe and the Mideast (see previous item). Sunday, there's *Reporters Roundtable* and the entertaining ●*Music Time in Africa*. Audible well beyond where it is targeted. Winter on 13710, 15240, 15445 and 17895 kHz; and summer on 9850, 15410 and 15580 kHz. For yet another service (to East Asia and the Pacific), see the next item.

Voice of America. Monday through Friday only. *News*, followed by the interactive *Talk to America*. Sixty minutes to Asia on 5990, 6045, 6110, 6160, 7170, 7215, 9525, 9645, 9670, 9770, 9785, 9795, 11955, 12005 and 15255 kHz, some of which are seasonal. For Australasia, try 9525 and 15255 kHz in winter, and 7170 and 11770 kHz midyear.

■**Radio France Internationale.** An additional half-hour (see 1600) of predominantly African fare. Monday through Friday, focuses on *news* from the eastern part of Africa. Weekends, there's *Spotlight on Africa*, health issues, features on French culture, sports, media in Africa, and a phone-in feature, *On-Line*. To the Mideast winter on 11615 kHz, and summer on 15605 kHz; and to East Africa winter on 15605 kHz, and summer on 17605 kHz.

Radio Cairo, Egypt. See 16:30 for specifics. Continues with a broadcast to southern Africa on 9855 kHz.

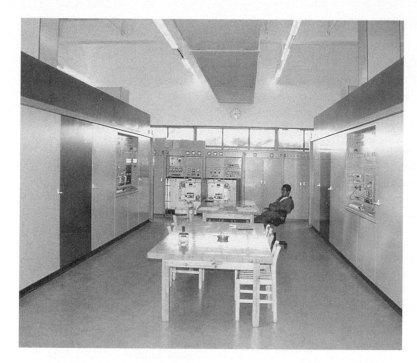

Inside the transmitter hall
at the Radio Netherlands
Madagascar relay station.
RNW

AFRTS Shortwave, USA. Network news, live sports, music and features in the upper-sideband mode from the Armed Forces Radio & Television Service. Transmitted from modestly powered U.S. Navy stations around the globe. Try 4319, 5446.5, 5765, 6350, 7590, 9980, 10320, 12133.5, 12579 and 13362 kHz.

17:30

Radio Slovakia International. Tuesday through Friday, starts with *News* and *Topical Issue*, then features. Regulars include *Tourism News* (Tuesday), *Business News* and *Currency Update* (Wednesday), *Culture News* (Thursday) and *Regional News* (Friday). Monday's news is followed by *Insight Central Europe*. The Saturday lineup includes *Front Page* and *Sports News*; and Sunday's features are *Sunday Newsreel* and *Listeners' Tribune*. A friendly half hour to western Europe on 5915 and 7345 kHz. One hour earlier in summer.

Radio Bulgaria. Summer only at this time. *News*, followed weekdays by *Events and Developments*, and Saturday and Sunday by

Views Behind the News. Thirty minutes to Europe on 9500 and 11500 kHz, and one hour later in winter.

Radio Sweden. Summer only at this hour; see 18:30 for program details. Thirty minutes of Scandinavian fare for Europe, Monday through Saturday, on 6065 kHz. One hour later in winter.

Flanders Radio International, Belgium. Summer only at this time. See 18:30 for program specifics. Thirty minutes to Europe on 9925, 11640 and 13690 kHz; and to the Mideast on 11640 kHz. One hour later in winter.

17:45

All India Radio. The first 15 minutes of a two-hour broadcast to Europe, Africa and the Mideast, consisting of regional and international *news*, commentary, a variety of talks and features, press review and exotic Indian music. Continuous till 19:45. To Europe on 7410, 9950 and 11620 kHz; to West Africa on 9445, 13605 and 15155 kHz; and to East Africa on 11935, 15075 and 17670 kHz.

18:00–23:59
Europe & Mideast—Evening Prime Time
East Asia—Early Morning
Australasia—Morning
Eastern North America—Afternoon and Suppertime
Western North America—Midday

18:00

■**Radio Netherlands.** The first 60 minutes of an approximately three-hour broadcast targeted at Africa, and heard well beyond. Monday through Friday, the initial 30 minutes are taken up by ●*Newsline* (current events), with a feature occupying the second half-hour: ●*Research File* (Monday), ●*EuroQuest* (Tuesday), ●*Documentary* (Wednesday), *Dutch Horizons* (Thursday) and *A Good Life* on Friday. Weekend fare consists of *News* followed by Saturday's *Europe Unzipped*, ●*Insight* and *Amsterdam Forum*; or Sunday's *Wide Angle*, *The Week Ahead* and *Vox Humana*. To West, Central and East Africa on 9895 and 11655 kHz; and to southern Africa on 6020 kHz.

Voice of Vietnam. Begins with *news*, which is followed by *Commentary* or *Weekly Review*, short features and some pleasant Vietnamese music (especially at weekends). A half hour to Europe winter on 5955, 7280 and 9730 kHz; and summer on 9730 and 13740 kHz. The 5955 kHz channel is via an Austrian relay, and should provide good reception.

All India Radio. Continuation of the transmission to Europe, Africa and the Mideast (see 17:45). *News* and commentary, followed by programming of a more general nature. To Europe on 7410, 9950 and 11620 kHz; to West Africa on 9445, 13605 and 15155 kHz; and to East Africa on 11935, 15075 and 17670 kHz.

Radio Prague, Czech Republic. Winter only at this time. *News*, then Monday through Friday there's *Current Affairs* and one or more features: *Talking Point* (Monday), *Czech Science* and *One on One* (Tuesday), *Czechs in History*, *Czechs Today* or *Spotlight* (Wednesday), *Business Report* (Thursday) and *The Arts* (Friday). On Saturday the news is followed by *Insight Central Europe*, and Sunday by *Mailbox*

and *ABC of Czech* followed by *Encore* (classical music), *Magic Carpet* (Czech world music) or *Czech Books*. A half hour to Europe on 5930 kHz, and to Australasia on 9415 kHz. Europe's broadcast is one hour earlier in summer, but for Australasia it's two hours later.

Radio Romania International. Starts with *Radio Newsreel*, a combination of news, commentary and press review. Features on Romania make up the remainder of the broadcast. Monday, the lineup includes *Pro Memoria* (Romanian history), *Pages of Romanian Literature*, *Romanian Hits* and *Sports Roundup*. Regular features on other days include Tuesday's *Business Club* and *Visual Arts*, Wednesday's *Stage and Screen* and *Romanian Musicians*, Thursday's *Listeners Letterbox* and ●*Skylark* (Romanian folk music), and Friday's *Cultural Survey* and ●*The Folk Music Box*. Saturday fare includes *World of Culture*, *Roots*, *Radio Pictures* and *DX Mailbag*; and Sunday's broadcast has *Sunday Studio* and repeats of programs aired earlier in the week. Fifty-five minutes to Europe winter on 5965 and 7130 kHz; and summer on 11940 and 15380 kHz.

Radio Australia. Sunday through Thursday, *World News* is followed by *Pacific Beat* (news and current events) and *On the Mat* (replaced Sunday by *Australian Express*). The Friday slots are *Pacific Review* and *Country Breakfast*, replaced Saturday by *Best of Late Night Live*. Part of a continuous 24-hour service, and at this hour beamed to the Pacific on 6080, 7240, 9580, 9710 and 11880 kHz; to East Asia on 6080 and 9710 kHz; and to Southeast Asia on 9475 kHz. In western North America, try 11880 kHz.

Radio Polonia, Poland. This time winter only. See 17:00 for program specifics. *News*, features and music reflecting Polish life and culture. Sixty minutes to Europe on 5995 and 7170 kHz. One hour earlier in summer.

Voice of Russia World Service. Continuous programming to Europe and beyond. Predominantly news-related fare during the initial half hour in summer, but the winter schedule offers a more varied diet. Winter, the *news* is followed by a series of features: *Moscow Mailbag* (Monday, Thursday and Saturday), *Newmarket* (Tuesday and Friday), *Science and Engineering* (Wednesday) and the outstanding ●*Music and Musicians* on Sunday. On the half-hour, the lineup includes *Kaleidoscope* (Monday), ●*Music at Your Request* or an alternative (Tuesday), ●*Moscow Yesterday and Today* (Wednesday), *Folk Box* (Friday) and Saturday's *Songs from Russia*. Summer weekdays, the first half hour consists of news followed by *Commonwealth Update*, while the features that follow tend to be somewhat variable. The Saturday slots are filled by *Science and Engineering* and *This is Russia*, replaced Sunday by *Musical Portraits of the Twentieth Century* and ●*Christian Message from Moscow* (an insight into Russian Orthodoxy). Best winter bets are 5950 and 6175 (weekends), and 7290 kHz; likely summer channels include 9480, 9890 and 11630 kHz. Also available winter only to the Mideast on 9830 kHz. In Southern Africa, try 11510 kHz.

Radio Argentina al Exterior—R.A.E. Monday through Friday only. *News* and short features on Argentina and its people. One of only a handful of stations which still give prominence to folk music. Tangos, too, if you're nostalgic. Fifty-five minutes to Europe on 9690 and 15345 kHz.

Voice of America. Continuous programming to the Mideast and North Africa. *News Now*—reports and features on a variety of topics. On 6040 (winter) and 9760 kHz. For a separate service to Africa, see the next item.

Voice of America. Monday through Friday, it's *News Now* and *Africa World Tonight*. Weekends, there's a full hour of the former. To Africa—but heard well beyond—on 7275, 11920, 11975, 12040, 13710, 15410, 15580 and 17895 kHz, some of which are seasonal.

Radio Cairo, Egypt. See 16:30 for specifics. The final 30 minutes of a two-hour broadcast to southern Africa on 9855 kHz.

Radio Taiwan International. Ten minutes of *News*, followed by features. Monday's *Kaleidoscope*, *Discover Taiwan*, and *Asia Pacific* (produced by Radio Australia) are replaced on other days by *On the Job*, *Mailbag Time*, *Sound Postcard* and *Let's Learn Chinese* (Tuesday); *Trends*, ●*Jade Bells and Bamboo Pipes* and *Life*

Voice of Russia Translation Department includes (seated from left) Alice Romanova, Tamara Murzina, Clara Belousova; middle row Eugene Prytov, Tanya Stukova, Olga Vinarskaya, Emil Akopov; back row Elena Golovkina, Julius Ileaboya, Andrei Zhamkin and Anton Kholodenko.

VoR

18:00–19:00

Dane Pavlic heads Croatian Radio-Television's "Transmitting Station Deanovec." Legendary pro Milan Prezelj (glasses) is Electronic Media Liaison for the Hrvatski Informativni Centar. M. Prezelj

Unusual (Wednesday); *Politics Today, People, Wisdom.com* and *Instant Noodles* (Thursday); *Bookworm, Culture Express* and *New Music Lounge* (Friday); *News Talk*, then *Stage, Screen and Studio* and *Groove Zone* (Saturday); and *Taiwan Economic Journal, Taipei Magazine, Sound Postcard* and *Hakka World* (Sunday). One hour to western Europe on 3965 kHz.

AFRTS Shortwave, USA. Network news, live sports, music and features in the upper-sideband mode from the Armed Forces Radio & Television Service. Transmitted from modestly powered U.S. Navy stations around the globe. Try 4319, 5446.5, 5765, 6350, 7590, 9980, 10320, 12133.5, 12579 and 13362 kHz.

18:15

Radio Bangladesh. *News*, followed by Islamic and general interest features; some nice Bengali music, too. Thirty minutes to Europe on 7185 and 9550 kHz. Frequencies may be slightly variable.

18:30

Radio Bulgaria. This time winter only. *News*, then *Events and Developments* (weekdays) or *Views Behind the News* (Saturday and Sunday). Thirty minutes to Europe on 5800 and 7500 kHz, and one hour earlier in summer.

Radio Slovakia International. Summer only at this time; see 19:30 for program specifics. Thirty minutes of *news* and features with a strong Slovak flavor. To western Europe on 5920 and 6055 kHz. One hour later in winter.

Flanders Radio International, Belgium. Winter only at this time. Monday through Friday, starts with *News*. The rest of the broadcast is a mix of current events, reports and Belgian music. Saturday, these are replaced by the highly enjoyable ●*Music from Flanders*, and Sunday by *Radio World, Tourism* and *Brussels 1043* (a listener-response program). Thirty minutes to Europe on 5910 and 7330 kHz; and to the Mideast on 5910 kHz. One hour earlier in summer.

Voice of Turkey. This time summer only. *News*, followed by *Review of the Turkish Press*, then features on Turkish history, culture and international relations, interspersed with enjoyable selections of the country's popular and classical music. Fifty minutes to Western Europe on 9785 kHz. One hour later in winter.

Radio Sweden. Winter only at this time. Monday through Friday, it's *news* and features in *Sixty Degrees North*, concentrating heavily on Scandinavian topics. The Monday slot goes to *SportScan*, replaced Tuesday by *Close Up* or an alternative feature, and Wednesday by special features. Thursday's shows rotate from week to week—*Nordic Lights, GreenScan, Heart Beat* or *S-Files*, while Friday offers a review of the week's news. Saturday's slot is filled by *Network Europe, Spectrum* (the arts), *Sweden Today* or *Studio 49*; and Sunday fare consists of *In Touch with Stockholm* (a listener-response program) or the musical *Sounds Nordic*. Thirty minutes to Europe, Monday through Saturday on 6065 kHz. One hour earlier in summer.

18:45

Radio Tirana, Albania. Monday through Saturday, and summer only at this time. Approximately 15 minutes of *news* and commentary from this small Balkan country. To Europe on 7210 and 9620 kHz. One hour later in winter.

19:00

■**Radio Netherlands.** The second hour of an approximately three-hour block of programming for Africa. Monday through Friday, starts with a feature and ends with ●*Newsline* (current events). The features are repeats of programs aired during the previous six days, and are worth a second hearing: ●*EuroQuest* (Monday), *A Good Life* (Tuesday), *Dutch Horizons* (Wednesday) ●*Research File* (science, Thursday) and the award-winning ●*Documentary* on Friday. The weekend format is feature-news-features, with *Vox Humana*, *Europe Unzipped* and ●*Insight* on Saturday, and ●*Documentary*, *Wide Angle* and a program preview on Sunday. Continuous programming on 7120, 9895, 11655 and 17810 kHz. In southern Africa, tune to 7120 kHz. The weekend broadcasts are also available to North America winter on 15315, 17725 and 17875 kHz; and summer on 15315, 17660 and 17735 kHz. Weekdays, listeners in the United States should try 17810 kHz, which is via a relay in the Netherlands Antilles.

Radio Australia. Begins with *World News*, then Sunday through Thursday it's *Pacific Beat* (in-depth reporting on the region) and *The Best of Breakfast*. Friday's slots go to *Rural Reporter* and *Australian Country Style*, and Saturday there's *Earthiest* (the environment), *The Makers* and *Health Bites*. Continuous to Asia and the Pacific on 6080, 7240, 9500, 9580, 9710 and 11880 kHz. Listeners in western North America should try 11880 kHz, and best for East Asia are 6080 and 9710 kHz. Listeners in Southeast Asia should tune to 9500 kHz.

Kol Israel. Summer only at this time. Twenty-five minutes of even-handed and comprehensive news reporting from and about Israel. To Europe and North America on 11605 and 17535 kHz; and to Africa and South America on 15615 kHz. One hour later in winter.

All India Radio. The final 45 minutes of a two-hour broadcast to Europe, Africa and the Mideast (see 17:45). Starts off with *news*, then continues with a mixed bag of features and Indian music. To Europe on 7410, 9950 and 11620 kHz; to West Africa on 9445, 13605

and 15155 kHz; and to East Africa on 11935, 15075 and 17670 kHz.

Radio Budapest, Hungary. Summer only at this time. *News* and features, few of which are broadcast on a regular basis. Thirty minutes to Europe on 3975, 6025 and 11720 kHz. One hour later in winter.

■**Deutsche Welle,** Germany. *News*, then Monday through Friday there's ●*NewsLink*. The second half-hour consists of ●*A World Music* (Monday), *Arts on the Air* (Tuesday), ●*Living in Germany* and *Europe in Capitals* (Wednesday), the youth-oriented *Cool* (Thursday) and ●*Focus on Folk* (Friday). Weekends, the Saturday news is followed by *Hard to Beat* (sport), *German by Radio* and *Africa This Week*; and Sunday by *Religion and Society*, *Inspired Minds* and either *Hits in Germany* or *Melody Time*. One hour to Central and East Africa winter on 6180, 11865, 13780 and 17800 kHz; and summer on 7225, 13590, 15545 and 17770 kHz. Heard well in parts of the Mideast on 11865 kHz in winter, and 13590 kHz in summer.

Voice of Russia World Service. Continuous programming to Europe at this hour. *News*, then winter weekdays there's *Commonwealth Update* (news and reports from and about the CIS), replaced Saturday by *Science and Engineering*, and Sunday by *Musical Portraits of the Twentieth Century*. Monday through Saturday summer, it's *News and Views*, with *Sunday Panorama* and *Russia: People and Events* filling the Sunday slots. Winter weekends at 19:31, there's Saturday's *This is Russia*, and Sunday's emotive ●*Christian Message from Moscow*. During the week, the feature lineup is somewhat variable. Summer offerings at this time are mostly a combination of *Russia: People and Events*, the aptly-titled ●*Russian Treasures* and the religious *Daily Reflections*. Winter choices are 6175, 6235, 7290 and 7360 kHz; replaced summer by 7440, 9480, 9890 and 12070 kHz.

China Radio International. Repeat of the 16:00 transmission; see there for specifics. One hour to the Mideast on 9585 kHz; and to North Africa on 9440 kHz.

19:00–20:00

PASSPORT editor Lawrence Magne (left) admires a professional receiver from the collection of the VOA's Dan Robinson, whose reporting has earned the quiet respect of news colleagues and students of African affairs.

J. Brinker

Radio Thailand. A 60-minute package of *news*, features and (if you're lucky) enjoyable Thai music. To Northern Europe winter on 9840 kHz, and summer on 7155 kHz.

Voice of Korea, North Korea. For now, of curiosity value only. An hour of old-style communist tub-thumping to Europe on 9325 (or 13760) and 11335 (or 15245) kHz; and to Africa on 9660 (or 11710) kHz. Also heard in parts of East Asia on 4405 kHz.

Voice of Vietnam. Repeat of the 18:00 transmission (see there for specifics). A half hour to Europe winter on 7280 and 9730 kHz, and summer on 9730 and 13740 kHz.

Voice of America. Continuous programming to the Mideast and North Africa. *News Now*—news and reports on a wide variety of topics. On 9760 and (summer) 9770 kHz. Also heard in Europe. For a separate service to Africa, see the next item.

Voice of America. *News Now*, then Monday through Friday it's *World of Music*. Best of the weekend programs is ●*Music Time in Africa* at 19:30 Sunday. Continuous to most of Africa on 6035, 7375, 7415, 11920, 11975, 12040, 15410, 15445 and 15580 kHz, some of which are seasonal.

Radio Korea International, South Korea. Opens with 10 minutes of *news*, then Monday

through Friday, a commentary. This is followed by 30 minutes (45 on Friday) of *Seoul Calling*. Monday through Thursday, the broadcast closes with a 15-minute feature: *Korea, Today and Tomorrow*, *Korean Kaleidoscope*, *Wonderful Korea* and *Seoul Report*, respectively. On Saturday, the news is followed by *Worldwide Friendship* (a listener-response program), and Sunday by *Korean Pop Interactive*. Sixty minutes to East Asia on 5975 kHz, and to Europe on 7275 kHz.

AFRTS Shortwave, USA. Network news, live sports, music and features in the upper-sideband mode from the Armed Forces Radio & Television Service. Transmitted from modestly powered U.S. Navy stations around the globe. Try 4319, 5446.5, 5765, 6350, 7590, 9980, 10320, 12133.5, 12579 and 13362 kHz.

19:30

Radio Slovakia International. Tuesday through Friday, starts with *News* and *Topical Issue*, then features. Regulars include *Tourism News* (Tuesday), *Business News* and *Currency Update* (Wednesday), *Culture News* (Thursday) and *Regional News* (Friday). Monday's news is followed by *Insight Central Europe*. The Saturday lineup includes *Front Page* and *Sports News*; and Sunday's features are *Sunday*

Newsreel and *Listeners' Tribune*. Thirty minutes to western Europe on 5915 and 7345 kHz. One hour earlier in summer.

Voice of Turkey. Winter only at this time. See 18:30 for program details. Some unusual programs and friendly presentation make for entertaining listening. Fifty minutes to Europe on 6055 kHz. One hour earlier in summer.

Voice of the Islamic Republic of Iran. A one-hour broadcast of news, commentary and features strong reflecting Islamic values. To southern Africa winter on 9800 and 11695 kHz, and midyear on 9800 and 11750 kHz.

Flanders Radio International, Belgium. Summer only at this time; see 20:30 for program specifics. Thirty minutes to Europe on 9925 kHz, and one hour later in winter.

Radio Sweden. Summer only at this time, and a repeat of the 17:30 broadcast. See 18:30 for program details. Thirty minutes to Europe on 6065 kHz, and one hour later in winter.

RAI International—Radio Roma, Italy. Actually starts at 19:35. Approximately 12 minutes of *news*, then some Italian music. Twenty minutes to western Europe winter on 5965 and 9755 kHz, and summer on 5970 and 9605 kHz.

Radio Station Belarus/Radio Minsk. Tuesday and Thursday, summer only at this time. See 20:30 for specifics. Thirty minutes to Europe on 7105 and 7210 kHz. One hour later in winter.

19:45

Voice of Armenia. Actually starts at 19:40. Monday through Saturday, summer only at this time. Twenty minutes of Armenian *news* and culture. To Europe on 9960 kHz, and to the Mideast on 4810 kHz. One hour later in winter.

Radio Tirana, Albania. Monday through Saturday, and winter only at this time. Approximately 15 minutes of *news* and commentary from this small Balkan country. To Europe on 6115 and 7210 kHz. One hour earlier in summer.

Vatican Radio. Summer only at this time, and actually starts at 19:50. Twenty minutes of programming oriented to Catholics. To Europe on 4005, 5890 and 7250 kHz. One hour later in winter.

20:00

■**Deutsche Welle,** Germany. *News*, then Monday through Friday there's the in-depth ●*NewsLink*. The second half-hour consists of features: *Insight* and *Business German* (Monday), *World in Progress* (Tuesday), ●*Money Talks* (Wednesday), *Living Planet* (Thursday) and *Spectrum* (Friday). Weekends, there's Saturday's ●*Inside Europe* and Sunday's *Mailbag*. One hour to East, Central and southern Africa, winter on 12025, 13780, 15205 and 15410 kHz; and summer on 7130, 13820 and 15205 kHz. Prime winter frequency for southern Africa is 12025 kHz, with 7130 kHz best midyear.

Radio Canada International. Summer only at this time. *News*, then Monday through Friday it's *Canada Today*, replaced Saturday by *Business Sense* and Sunday by *Maple Leaf Mailbag* (a listener-response show). On the half-hour there's *Spotlight* (Wednesday and Sunday), *Media Zone* (Monday), *The Mailbag* (Tuesday), *Business Sense* (Thursday) and *Sci-Tech File* on Friday and Saturday. Sixty minutes to Europe, North Africa and the Mideast on 5850, 7235, 11690 and 13700 kHz. One hour later during winter.

■**Radio Netherlands.** The final 57 minutes of an approximately three-hour broadcast targeted at Africa. Monday through Friday, opens with a feature: ●*Research File* (Monday), ●*EuroQuest* (Tuesday), ●*Documentary* (Wednesday), *Dutch Horizons* (Thursday) and *A Good Life* (Friday). ●*Newsline* (current events) completes the broadcast. The weekend format is feature-news-features, with *Amsterdam Forum*, *Europe Unzipped* and ●*Insight* on Saturday, and *Vox Humana*, *Wide Angle* and a program preview on Sunday. To southern Africa on 7120 kHz; and to West and Central Africa on 9895, 11655 and 17810 kHz. The weekend broadcasts are also available to North America winter on 15315, 17725 and

20:00–20:30

17875 kHz; and summer on 15315, 17660 and 17735 kHz. On other days, listeners in the United States can try 17810 kHz, which is via a relay in the Netherlands Antilles.

Radio Damascus, Syria. Actually starts at 20:05. *News*, a daily press review, and different features for each day of the week. These can be heard at approximately 20:30 and 20:45, and include a mix of political commentary, Islamic philosophy and Arab and Syrian culture. Most of the transmission, however, is given over to Syrian and some western popular music. One hour to Europe, occasionally audible in eastern North America, on 13610 kHz (and sometimes on 12085 kHz). Low audio level is often a problem.

Radio Australia. Starts with *World News*, then Sunday through Thursday there's a continuation of *Pacific Beat* (in-depth reporting). Friday fare consists of *Pacific Review* and *The Buzz*, and Saturday, *Australia All Over* (a popular show from the Radio National domestic service). Continuous programming to the Pacific on 6080 and 7240 (Friday and Saturday only), 9580, 9710, 11650, 11880 and 12080 kHz; to East Asia on 9710 kHz; and to Southeast Asia on 9500 kHz. In western North America, try 11880 kHz.

Voice of Russia World Service. Continuous programming to Europe at this hour. *News*, then Monday through Saturday winter it's *News and Views*, with *Sunday Panorama* and *Russia: People and Events* completing the lineup. In summer, these are replaced by a variety of features. Pick from *Science and Engineering* (Monday and Thursday), *Newmarket* (Wednesday and Saturday), *Moscow Mailbag* (Tuesday and Friday), and the 47-minute ●*Music and Musicians* on Sunday. Winter on the half-hour, it's mostly a combination of *Russia: People and Events*, ●*Russian Treasures* (gems of classical music) and the religious *Daily Reflections*. Best of the summer offerings at this time are Thursday's ●*Folk Box*, Friday's ●*Jazz Show* and Tuesday's ●*Music at Your Request* or its alternative. Other features include *Songs from Russia* (Monday), *Musical Portraits of the Twentieth Century* (Wednesday) and Saturday's *Russian by Radio*. Winter on 6145, 6175, 6235, 7290

and 7340 kHz; and summer on 9480, 12070 and 15455 kHz. Some channels are audible in eastern North America.

Radio Exterior de España ("Spanish National Radio"). Weekdays only at this time. Spanish and international *news*, commentary, Spanish pop music, a review of the Spanish press, and a general interest feature. Sixty minutes to Europe winter on 9690 kHz, and summer on 15290 kHz; and to North and West Africa winter on 9595 kHz, and summer on 9570 kHz.

Radio Budapest, Hungary. Winter only at this time. *News* and features, most of which are broadcast on a non-regular basis. Thirty minutes to Europe on 3975 and 6025 kHz. One hour earlier in summer.

China Radio International. Starts with *News*, followed Monday through Friday by special reports—current events, sports, business, culture, science and technology and press clippings. The rest of the broadcast is devoted to features. Regulars include ●*People in the Know* (Monday), *Biz China* (Tuesday), *China Horizons* (Wednesday), ●*Voices from Other Lands* (Thursday), and *Life in China* (Friday). Weekends, the news is followed by a shorter series of reports (current events and sport) and two features. Saturday there's *Cutting Edge*, and *Listeners' Garden* (listener mail, Chinese folk music, a preview of the next week's programs, and a Chinese language lesson); replaced Sunday by *Reports on Developing Countries* and *In the Spotlight*, a series of mini-features: *Cultural Carousel*, *In Vogue*, *Writings from China*, *China Melody* and *Talking Point*. One hour to Europe winter on 5965, 7190, 9600 and/or 9855 kHz, and summer on 7190, 9600 and 11790 kHz. Also available to eastern and southern Africa on 11640 and 13630 kHz; and to North and West Africa on 9440 kHz.

Kol Israel. Winter only at this time. Twenty-five minutes of *news* and in-depth reporting from and about Israel. To Europe and North America on any three channels from 6280, 7520, 9435 and 11605 kHz; and to Southern Africa and South America on 15640 kHz. One hour earlier in summer.

20:00–20:30

Voice of Vietnam. *News*, then it's either *Commentary* or *Weekly Review*, which in turn is followed by short features. Look for some pleasant Vietnamese music towards the end of the broadcast (more at weekends). A half hour to Europe winter on 7280 and 9730 kHz, and summer on 9730 and 13740 kHz.

Radio Prague, Czech Republic. Summer only at this time. *News*, then Monday through Friday there's *Current Affairs* plus features: *Talking Point* (Monday), *Czech Science* and *One on One* (Tuesday), *Czechs in History*, *Czechs Today* or *Spotlight* (Wednesday), *Business Report* (Thursday) and *The Arts* (Friday). Saturday's news is followed by *Magazine*, *Letter from Prague* and a repeat of Tuesday's *One on One*. The Sunday lineup is *Mailbox* and *ABC of Czech* followed by *Encore* (classical music), *Magic Carpet* (Czech world music) or *Czech Books*. Thirty minutes to western Europe on 5930 kHz, and to Southeast Asia and Australasia on 11600 kHz. One hour later in winter.

Voice of America. Continuous programming to the Mideast and North Africa. *News*, reports and capsulated features covering everything from politics to entertainment. On 6095 (winter), 9760, and (summer) 9770 kHz. For African listeners there's the weekday *Africa World Tonight*, replaced weekends by *Nightline Africa*, on 6035, 7275, 7375, 7415, 11715, 11855, 15410, 15445, 15580, 17725 and 17755 kHz, some of which are seasonal. Both transmissions are heard well beyond their target areas, including parts of North America.

AFRTS Shortwave, USA. Network news, live sports, music and features in the upper-sideband mode from the Armed Forces Radio & Television Service. Transmitted from modestly powered U.S. Navy stations around the globe. Try 4319, 5446.5, 5765, 6350, 7590, 9980, 10320, 12133.5, 12579 and 13362 kHz.

20:30

Radio Sweden. Winter only at this time. Monday through Friday, it's *news* and features in *Sixty Degrees North*, concentrating heavily

Electronics on the hoof. World band relieves monotony while riding through Araby sands, while global positioning satellites keep dromedaries on course.

M. Prezelj

on Scandinavian topics. Monday there's *SportScan*, replaced Tuesday by *Close Up* or an alternative feature, and Wednesday by special features. Thursday's shows rotate from week to week—*Nordic Lights*, *GreenScan*, *Heart Beat* or *S-Files*, while Friday offers a review of the week's news. Saturday's slot is filled by *Network Europe*, *Spectrum* (the arts), *Sweden Today* or *Studio 49*; and the Sunday lineup is *In Touch with Stockholm* (a listener-response program) or the musical *Sounds Nordic*. Thirty minutes to Europe (one hour earlier in summer) on 6065 kHz, and to Asia and Australasia (one hour later in summer) on 9400 or 9415 kHz.

Radio Thailand. Fifteen minutes of *news* targeted at Europe. Winter on 9535 kHz, and summer on 9680 kHz.

Flanders Radio International, Belgium. Winter only at this time. Monday through Friday, starts with *News*. The rest of the broadcast is a mix of current events, reports and Belgian music. Saturday, these are replaced by the entertaining ●*Music from Flanders*, and Sunday by *Radio World*, *Tourism* and *Brussels 1043* (a listener-response program). Thirty minutes to Europe on 7330 kHz, and one hour earlier in summer.

20:30–21:00

Voice of Turkey. This time summer only. *News*, followed by *Review of the Turkish Press* and features with a strong local flavor. Selections of Turkish popular and classical music complete the program. Fifty minutes to Southeast Asia and Australasia on 7170 kHz. One hour later during winter.

Radio Station Belarus/Radio Minsk. Tuesday and Thursday only at this time. Thirty minutes of local *news* and interviews, plus a little Belarusian music. To Europe on 7105 and 7210 kHz. Occasionally heard in eastern North America during winter.

Wales Radio International. Summer Fridays only at this time. News, interviews and music from the Welsh hills and valleys. Thirty minutes to Europe on 7150 and 7325 kHz, and one hour later in winter.

Radio Habana Cuba. The first half of a 60-minute broadcast. Monday through Saturday, there's international and Cuban news followed by *RHC's Viewpoint*. This is replaced Sunday by *Weekly Review*. To eastern North America on 11760 kHz, and heard in parts of Europe.

Radio Tashkent, Uzbekistan. Monday through Saturday, opens with *News*, replaced Sunday by *Significant Events of the Week*. Other programs include *Uzbekistan and the World* (Monday), *Life in the Village* and *Political Commentary* (Thursday), a listener-response show (Saturday) and *Traditions and Values* on Sunday. Programs of Uzbek music are aired on Tuesday, Wednesday and Friday. To Europe winter on two or more frequencies from 5025, 7105, 7185 and 11905 kHz; and summer on 5025 and 11905 kHz.

Voice of Vietnam. *News*, then it's either *Commentary* or *Weekly Review*, which in turn is followed by short features. Look for some pleasant Vietnamese music, especially at weekends. A half hour to West and Central Africa on 7220 and 9550 kHz, and heard far beyond.

RAI International—Radio Roma, Italy. Actually starts at 20:25. Twenty minutes of *news* and Italian music to the Mideast. Winter on 5985 and 11880 kHz; and summer on 6185 and 11880 kHz.

20:45

Voice of Armenia. Monday through Saturday, winter only at this time. Actually starts at 20:40. Twenty minutes of Armenian *news* and culture. To Europe on 9960 kHz, and to the Mideast on 4910 kHz. The channel for Europe sometimes produces fair reception in parts of eastern North America. One hour earlier in summer.

All India Radio. The first 15 minutes of a much longer broadcast, consisting of a press review, Indian music, regional and international *news*, commentary, and a variety of talks and features of general interest. Continuous till 22:30. To Western Europe on 7410, 9445, 9950 and 11620 kHz; and to Australasia on 9575, 9910, 11620 and 11715 kHz. Early risers in Southeast Asia can try the channels for Australasia.

Vatican Radio. Winter only at this time, and actually starts at 20:50. Twenty minutes of predominantly Catholic fare. To Europe on 4005, 5890 and 7250 kHz. One hour earlier in summer.

21:00

■**BBC World Service for the Americas.** Starts with five minutes of *news*, then features, including some of the BBC's better offerings (starting at 2106): ●*Health Matters* (Monday), *Go Digital* (Tuesday), *Discovery* (science, Wednesday), ●*One Planet* (Thursday) and *Science in Action* (Friday). On the half-hour, a short news summary is followed by a mixed bag of programs. Best is Monday's light entertainment; worst is *Westway* (a soap, Wednesday and Friday). Best of the weekend fare is ●*Everywoman* (2106 Sunday).To the Caribbean and eastern and southern parts of the United States on 5975 kHz. 12095 kHz, targeted at South America, is also audible in some areas; a radio with synchronous selectable sideband helps reduce teletype interference.

Radio Exterior de España ("Spanish National Radio"). Summer weekends only at this time. Features, including rebroadcasts of programs aired earlier in the week. One hour

20:30–21:00

Antenna mast and wire elements at Croatian Radio-Television's Deanovec transmission facility. M. Prezelj

to Europe on 9840 kHz, and to North and West Africa on 9570 kHz. One hour later in winter.

Radio Ukraine International. Summer only at this time. *News*, commentary, reports and interviews, providing ample coverage of Ukrainian life. A listener-response program is aired Saturday, and most of Sunday's broadcast is a showpiece for Ukrainian music. Sixty minutes to western Europe on 7420 kHz. One hour later in winter. Should be easily heard despite the station's technical limitations.

Radio Canada International. Winter only at his time. See 20:00 for program specifics. Sixty minutes to western Europe and North Africa on 5850 and 9770 kHz; and to the Mideast on 7425 kHz. One hour earlier in summer.

Radio Prague, Czech Republic. Winter only at this time. See 2000 for program details. *News* and features on Czech life and culture. A half hour to western Europe (and easily audible in parts of eastern North America) on 5930 kHz, and to Southeast Asia and Australasia on 9430 kHz. One hour earlier in summer.

Radio Bulgaria. This time summer only. Starts with *News*, then Monday through Friday there's *Events and Developments*, replaced weekends by *Views Behind the News*. The remaining time is taken up by regular programs such as *Keyword Bulgaria* and *Time Out for Music*, and weekly features like *Sports* (Monday), *Magazine Economy* (Tuesday), *The Way We Live* (Wednesday), *History Club* (Thursday), *DX Programme* (for radio enthusiasts, Friday) and *Answering Your Letters* (a listener-response show, Saturday). The week's highlight is Sunday's ●*Folk Studio* (Bulgarian folk music). Sixty minutes to Europe on 5800 and 7500 kHz. One hour later during winter.

China Radio International. Repeat of the 20:00 transmission; see there for specifics. One hour to Europe winter on 5965, 7190, 9600 and/or 9855 kHz, and summer on 7190, 9600 and 11790 kHz. A 30-minute shortened version is also available for eastern and southern Africa on 11640 and 13630 kHz.

Voice of Russia World Service. Winter only at this time. *News*, then *Science and Engineering* (Monday and Thursday), the business-oriented *Newmarket* (Wednesday and Saturday), *Moscow Mailbag* (Tuesday and Friday) or Sunday's excellent ●*Music and Musicians*. Best of the second half hour are

21:00–21:30

Thursday's ●*Folk Box*, Friday's ●*Jazz Show* and Tuesday's ●*Music at Your Request* or its alternative. Other features include *Songs from Russia* (Monday) and Saturday's *Russian by Radio*. The final 60 minutes for Europe on 6175, 6235, 7290, 7300 and 7340 kHz. One hour earlier in summer. Some channels are audible in eastern North America.

Radio Budapest, Hungary. Summer only at this time. *News* and features, few of which are broadcast on a regular basis. Thirty minutes to Europe on 6025 kHz, and to southern Africa on 11830 kHz. One hour later in winter.

Radio Japan. *News*, then Monday through Friday (Tuesday through Saturday local date in Australasia) it's *A Song for Everyone* and *Asian Top News*. A 35-minute feature completes the hour: *Japan Musicscape* (Monday), Japanese language lessons (Tuesday and Thursday), *Japan Music Travelogue* (Wednesday), and *Music Beat* (Japanese popular music) on Friday. *Weekend Japanology* and *Japan Music Scene* fill the Saturday slots, and *Pop Joins the World* is aired Sunday. Sixty minutes to Europe on 6055 (summer), 6090 (winter) and 6180 kHz; to Australasia winter on 11920 kHz, and midyear on 6035 kHz; to western North America on 17825 kHz; to Hawaii on 21670 kHz; and to Central Africa on 11855 kHz. The broadcast on 17825 kHz has different programming after 21:15.

Radio Australia. *World News*, then Sunday through Thursday there's a look at current events in *AM* (replaced Friday by a listener-response program, *Feedback*). Next, on the half-hour, there's a daily feature—*Country Breakfast* (Sunday and Monday), *Earthiest* (the environment, Tuesday), *Innovations* (Wednesday), and *In the Pipeline* (Thursday). Friday's slots are *Verbatim* and *In Conversation*; and Saturday there's the five-minute *Business Weekend*, the final part of *Australia All Over* and *Asia Sunday*. Continuous to the Pacific on 9660, 11650, 11880, 12080, 13630 and 21740 kHz; and to Southeast Asia (till 21:30) on 9500 kHz. Listeners in North America should try 21740 kHz.

■**Deutsche Welle,** Germany. *News*, then weekdays there's ●*NewsLink*. On the half-hour

you can listen to ●*A World of Music* (Monday), *Arts on the Air* (Tuesday), ●*Living in Germany* and *Europe in Capitals* (Wednesday), the youth-oriented *Cool* (Thursday) and ●*Focus on Folk* (Friday). Weekends, the Saturday news is followed by *Hard to Beat* (sport), *German by Radio* and *Africa This Week*; and Sunday by *Religion and Society*, *Inspired Minds* and either *Hits in Germany* or *Melody Time*. One hour to West Africa, and audible in much of eastern and southern North America. Winter on 9615, 13780 and 15410 kHz; and summer on 9440, 11865 and 15205 kHz. In North America, try 15410 kHz in winter, and 11865 and 15205 kHz in summer.

Radio Korea International, South Korea. Summer only at this time. Opens with 10 minutes of *news*, then Monday through Friday, a commentary and 15-minute feature: *Korea, Today and Tomorrow* (Monday), *Korean Kaleidoscope* (Tuesday), *Wonderful Korea* (Wednesday), *Seoul Report* (Thursday) and *Seoul Calling* (Friday). On Saturday, the news is followed by *Worldwide Friendship* (a listener-response program), and Sunday by *Korean Pop Interactive*. Thirty minutes to Europe on 3955 kHz, and one hour later in winter.

Voice of Korea, North Korea. Repeat of the 19:00 broadcast. The last of the old-time communist stations. One hour to Europe on 9325 (or 13760) and 11335 (or 15245) kHz. Also heard in parts of East Asia on 4405 kHz.

Radio Habana Cuba. The final 30 minutes of a one-hour broadcast. Monday through Saturday, there's a *news* bulletin and the sports-oriented *Time Out* (five minutes each), then a feature: *Caribbean Outlook* (Monday and Thursday), *DXers Unlimited* (Tuesday and Saturday), the *Mailbag Show* (Wednesday) and *Weekly Review* (Friday). These are replaced Sunday by a longer edition of *Mailbag Show*. To eastern North America on 11760 kHz, and also heard in parts of Europe.

Voice of America. Opens with *news*, then it's music: *American Gold* (Monday), *Roots and Branches* (Tuesday), *Classic Rock* (Wednesday), *Top Twenty* (Thursday), *Country Hits* (Friday) and jazz at the weekend. To Africa on (among others) 6035, 7375, 7415, 11715, 11975,

13670, 13710, 15410, 15445, 15580, 17725 and 17895 kHz (some of which are seasonal). In the United States, try 15580 and 17895 kHz in winter, and 15445 kHz in summer.

All India Radio. Continues to Western Europe on 7410, 9445, 9950 and 11620 kHz; and to Australasia on 9575, 9910, 11620 and 11715 kHz. Look for some authentic Indian music from 21:15 onwards. The European frequencies are audible in parts of eastern North America, while those for Australasia are also heard in Southeast Asia.

21:15

Radio Damascus, Syria. Actually starts at 21:10. *News*, a daily press review, and different features for each day of the week. These include a mix of political commentary, Islamic themes and Arab and Syrian culture. The transmission also contains Syrian and some western popular music. Sixty minutes to North America and Australasia on 12085 (frequently off the air) and 13610 kHz. Audio level is often very low.

BBC World Service for the Caribbean. *Caribbean Report*, although intended for listeners in the area, can also be clearly heard throughout much of eastern North America. This brief, 15-minute program provides comprehensive coverage of Caribbean economic and political affairs, both within and outside the region. Monday through Friday only, on 11675 and 15390 kHz.

Radio Cairo, Egypt. The start of a 90-minute broadcast highlighting Arab and Egyptian themes. The initial quarter-hour of general programming is followed by *news*, commentary and political items. This in turn is followed by a cultural program until 22:15, when the station again reverts to more general fare. A big signal to Europe on 9990 kHz.

AFRTS Shortwave, USA. Network news, live sports, music and features in the upper-sideband mode from the Armed Forces Radio & Television Service. Transmitted from modestly powered U.S. Navy stations around the globe. Try 4319, 5446.5, 5765, 6350, 7590, 9980, 10320, 12133.5, 12579 and 13362 kHz.

21:30

Radio Station Belarus/Radio Minsk. Tuesday and Thursday, winter only, at this time. See 20:30 for specifics. Thirty minutes to Europe on 7105 and 7210 kHz. One hour earlier in summer.

Wales Radio International. Winter Fridays only at this time. News, interviews and music from the Welsh principality. Thirty minutes to Europe on 5970 and 5995 (or 7110) kHz, and one hour earlier in summer.

Radio Romania International. *News* and commentary followed by features on Romania. Twenty-five minutes to Europe winter on 6055 and 7145 kHz, and summer on 7130 (or 7230), 7285 and 9725 kHz; and to eastern North America winter on 6015 and 9540 kHz, and summer on 11750 and 15285 kHz.

Radio Tashkent, Uzbekistan. Monday through Saturday, opens with *News*, replaced Sunday by *Significant Events of the Week*. Other programs include *Nature and Us* and *Cooperation* (Monday), *Political Commentary* and *Youth Program* (Wednesday), a feature for women (Thursday), *Parliamentary Herald* (Friday) a show for shortwave listeners (Saturday) and *Interesting Meetings* on Sunday. Programs of Uzbek music are aired on Tuesday, Friday and Saturday, and a competition with prizes on Thursday and Saturday. To Europe winter on two or more frequencies from 5025, 7105, 7185 and 11905 kHz; and summer on 5025 and 11905 kHz.

Radio Tirana, Albania. Monday through Saturday, summer only at this time. *News*, short features and some lively Albanian music. Thirty minutes to Europe on 7130 kHz. One hour later in winter.

Voice of Turkey. This time winter only. *News*, followed by *Review of the Turkish Press* and features, some of them unusual. Exotic Turkish music, too. Fifty minutes to Southeast Asia and Australasia on 9525 kHz. One hour earlier in summer.

Radio Sweden. Summer only at this time. Thirty minutes of predominantly Scandinavian fare (see 22:30 for specifics). To Europe on 6065 kHz, and to Australasia on 9880 kHz.

22:00–22:30

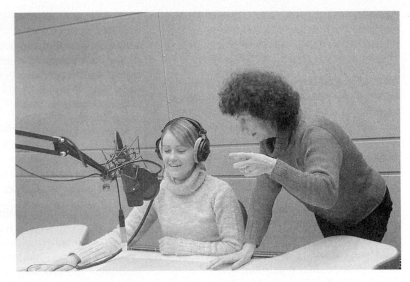

Irene Quaile, Deutsche Welle features editor, helps Nikki Karpeles prepare for her upcoming show. DW

22:00

■**BBC World Service for the Americas.** *The World Today*, with the exception of Friday, when the final 30 minutes are taken up by *People and Politics*. Weekends, it's more of *The World Today* except for *The Interview* (2232 Saturday).Continuous programming to the Caribbean and eastern North America on 5975 kHz. Also audible in some areas on 12095 kHz, beamed to South America; a radio with synchronous selectable sideband helps reduce teletype interference.

■**Deutsche Welle,** Germany. *News*, then Monday through Friday (Tuesday through Saturday local date in the target area) it's ●*NewsLink*—commentary, interviews, background reports and analysis. The second half-hour consists of features: *Insight* and *Business German* (Monday), *World in Progress* (Tuesday), ●*Money Talks* (Wednesday), *Living Planet* (Thursday) and *Spectrum* (Friday). Weekends, there's Saturday's ●*Inside Europe* and Sunday's *Mailbag*. One hour to East Asia winter on 6180 kHz, and summer on 7115 and 9720 kHz.

Radio Bulgaria. This time winter only. See 21:00 for specifics. News and features from the Balkans—don't miss Sunday's ●*Folk Studio* (Bulgarian folk music). Sixty minutes to Europe, also heard in parts of eastern North

America, on 5800 and 7500 kHz. One hour earlier in summer.

Radio Cairo, Egypt. The second half of a 90-minute broadcast to Europe on 9990 kHz; see 21:15 for program details.

Radio Exterior de España ("Spanish National Radio"). Winter weekends only at this time. Features, including repeats of programs aired earlier in the week. One hour to Europe on 9680 kHz, and to North and West Africa on 9595 kHz. One hour earlier in summer.

Flanders Radio International, Belgium. Monday through Friday, starts with *News*. The rest of the broadcast is a mix of current events, reports and Belgian music. Saturday, these are replaced by the entertaining ●*Music from Flanders*, and Sunday by *Radio World*, *Tourism* and *Brussels 1043* (a listener-response program). Thirty minutes to North America winter on 11730 kHz, and summer on 11635 kHz.

China Radio International. Repeat of the 20:00 transmission (see there for specifics), but with news updates. One hour to Europe winter on 7170 kHz, summer on 9880 kHz, and autumn on 7175 kHz.

Voice of America. The beginning of a three-hour block of programs to East and Southeast Asia and the Pacific. The ubiquitous *News*

Now—news and reports on current events, sports, science, business, entertainment and more. To East and Southeast Asia on 7215, 9705, 9770, 11760, 15185, 15290, 15305, 17735 (or 17740) and 17820 kHz; and to Australasia on 15185, 15305 and 17735 kHz. The first half hour is also available weekday evenings to Africa on 7340, 7375 and 7415 kHz.

RAI International—Radio Roma, Italy. Actually starts at 22:05. Twenty-five minutes of *news* and Italian music to East Asia on 11895 kHz.

Radio Australia. *News*, followed Sunday through Thursday by *AM* (current events) and at 22:40, *Australia Wide*. Friday's features are *Asia Pacific* and *Saturday AM*; and Saturday's pairing is *Correspondents' Report* and *Music Deli*. Continuous programming to the Pacific on 11880, 13630, 15230 and 21740 kHz; to East Asia on 15240 kHz; and to Southeast Asia on 13620 kHz. In North America, try 21740 kHz, especially during summer.

Radio Taiwan International. Ten minutes of *News*, followed by features. Monday, there's *Kaleidoscope*, *Discover Taiwan*, and Radio Australia's *Asia Pacific*. These are replaced on successive days by *On the Job*, *Mailbag Time*, *Sound Postcard* and *Let's Learn Chinese* (Tuesday); *Trends*, ●*Jade Bells and Bamboo Pipes* and *Life Unusual* (Wednesday); *Politics Today*, *People*, *Wisdom.com* and *Instant Noodles* (Thursday); *Bookworm*, *Culture Express* and *New Music Lounge* (Friday); *News Talk*, then *Stage, Screen and Studio* and *Groove Zone* (Saturday); and *Taiwan Economic Journal*, *Taipei Magazine*, *Sound Postcard* and *Hakka World* (Sunday). One hour to Europe, winter on 9355 kHz, and summer on 15600 kHz.

Radio Tirana, Albania. Monday through Saturday, winter only at this time. Thirty minutes of news, short features and Albanian music. To Europe on 7120 kHz. One hour earlier in summer.

Radio Budapest, Hungary. Winter only at this time. *News* and features, most of which are broadcast on a non-regular basis. Thirty minutes to Europe on 6025 kHz, and to southern Africa on 11965 (or 12010) kHz. One hour earlier in summer.

Voice of Turkey. Summer only at this time. *News*, then *Review of the Turkish Press* and features on Turkish history and culture. Selections of Turkish popular and classical music complete the program. Fifty minutes to Europe and eastern North America on 9830 kHz. One hour later during winter.

Radio Korea International, South Korea. Winter only at this hour. See 21:00 for specifics Thirty minutes to Europe on 3955 kHz, and one hour earlier in summer.

Radio Ukraine International. Winter only at this time. A potpourri of things Ukrainian, with the Sunday broadcast often featuring some excellent music. Sixty minutes to Europe and beyond on 5840 kHz. One hour earlier in summer.

All India Radio. The final half-hour of a transmission to Western Europe and Australasia, consisting mainly of news-related fare. To Western Europe on 7410, 9445, 9950 and 11620 kHz; and to Australasia on 9575, 9910, 11620 and 11715 kHz. Frequencies for Europe are audible in parts of eastern North America, while those for Australasia are also heard in Southeast Asia.

AFRTS Shortwave, USA. Network news, live sports, music and features in the upper-sideband mode from the Armed Forces Radio & Television Service. Transmitted from modestly powered U.S. Navy stations around the globe. Try 4319, 5446.5, 5765, 6350, 7590, 9980, 10320, 12133.5, 12579 and 13362 kHz.

22:30

Radio Sweden. Winter only at this time. Monday through Friday, it's *news* and features in *Sixty Degrees North*, concentrating heavily on Scandinavian topics. The Monday slot goes to *SportScan*, replaced Tuesday by *Close Up* or an alternative feature, and Wednesday by special features. Thursday's shows rotate from week to week—*Nordic Report*, *GreenScan*, *Heart Beat* or *S-Files*, while Friday offers a review of the week's news. Saturday's carousel is *Network Europe*, *Spectrum* (the arts), *Sweden Today* or *Studio 49*; and Sunday fare consists of *In Touch with Stockholm* (a

22:30–23:30

listener-response program) or the musical *Sounds Nordic*. Thirty minutes to Europe on 6065 kHz, and one hour earlier in summer.

Radio Prague, Czech Republic. *News*, then Monday through Friday there's *Current Affairs* followed by a feature or two. Monday's *Talking Point* is replaced Tuesday by *Czech Science* and *One on One* (interviews); Wednesday's slot is *Czechs in History*; *Czechs Today* or *Spotlight*; Thursday's feature is *Business Report*; and Friday, *The Arts*. Saturday fare is either the summer *Insight Central Europe* or the winter combo of *Magazine*, *Letter from Prague* and a repeat of Tuesday's *One on One*. Sunday's features are *Mailbox* and *ABC of Czech* followed by *Encore* (classical music), *Magic Carpet* (Czech world music) or *Czech Books*. A half hour to North America winter on 5915 and 7345 kHz, and summer on 7345 and 9415 kHz; also to West Africa winter on 9435 kHz.

Radio Canada International. *News* and a feature: *Media Zone* (Monday and Saturday), *The Maple Leaf Mailbag* (listener mail, Tuesday), *Spotlight* (Wednesday), *Business Sense* (Thursday), *Sci-Tech File* (Friday) and a comedy show on Sunday. Thirty minutes to East Asia winter on 7195 and 9730 kHz, and summer on 9525, 11810 and 12035 kHz.

22:45

All India Radio. The first 15 minutes of a much longer broadcast, consisting of Indian music, regional and international *news*, commentary, and a variety of talks and features of general interest. Continuous till 00:45. To East Asia on 9950, 11620 and 13605 kHz; and to Southeast Asia on 9705, 11620 and 13605 kHz.

23:00

■BBC World Service for the Americas. Monday through Thursday winter, a full hour of *The World Today*. On the remaining days, it's reduced to 30 minutes and followed by *Global Business* (Friday) or weekend features. Summer weekdays, opens with five minutes of *news*. Next comes the long-running *Outlook*,

and the hour is rounded off with ●*Off the Shelf* (readings from world literature. The best of the weekend programs are heard Sunday. Continuous to the Caribbean and eastern North America on 5975 kHz. Also audible in some areas on 12095 kHz, targeted at South America; a radio with synchronous selectable sideband helps reduce teletype interference.

Voice of Turkey. Winter only at this hour. See 22:00 for program details. Fifty minutes to western Europe and eastern North America on 7275 kHz. One hour earlier in summer.

■Deutsche Welle, Germany. *News*, then Monday through Friday (Tuesday through Saturday local date in the target area), it's ●*NewsLink*. The lineup for the second half-hour is ●*A World of Music* (Monday), *Arts on the Air* (Tuesday), ●*Living in Germany* and *Europe in Capitals* (Wednesday), *Cool* (a youth show, Thursday) and ●*Focus on Folk* (Friday). Weekends, Saturday's news is followed by *Hard to Beat* (sport), *German by Radio* and *Asia This Week*; and Sunday there's *Hard to Beat*, *Inspired Minds* and either *Hits in Germany* or *Melody Time*. Sixty minutes to Southeast Asia winter on 7250, 9815 and 12035 kHz; and summer on 7115, 9890 and 15135 kHz.

Radio Australia. *World News*, followed Sunday through Thursday by *Asia Pacific* (replaced Friday by *Country Breakfast*, and Saturday by *The Europeans*). On the half-hour, look for a feature: *Verbatim* (Sunday), *The Europeans* (Monday and Tuesday), *Rural Reporter* (Wednesday), *Arts on RA* (Thursday), *Hit Mix* (Friday) and *Innovations* on Saturday. Continuous to the Pacific on 9660, 12080, 13630, 15230, 17795 and 21740 kHz; to East Asia on 13630 and (till 23:30) 15240 kHz; and to Southeast Asia on 13620 and (from 23:30) 11695 and 17750 kHz. Listeners in North America should try 17795 and 21740 kHz, especially during summer.

China Radio International. Starts with *News*, followed Sunday through Thursday by special reports—current events, sports, business, culture, science and technology and press clippings. The rest of the broadcast is devoted to features. Regulars include ●*People in the Know* (Sunday), *Biz China* (Monday), *China*

Horizons (Tuesday), ●*Voices from Other Lands* (Wednesday), and *Life in China* on Thursday. On Friday and Saturday the news is followed by a shorter series of reports (current events and sport) and two features. Friday brings *Cutting Edge*, and *Listeners' Garden* (listener mail, Chinese folk music, a preview of the next week's programs, and a Chinese language lesson); replaced Saturday by *Reports on Developing Countries* and *In the Spotlight*, a series of mini-features: *Cultural Carousel*, *In Vogue*, *Writings from China*, *China Melody* and *Talking Point*. One hour to the United States and Caribbean on 5990, 6040 (winter), 6145 (summer) and 11970 (or 13680) kHz via CRI's Cuban and Canadian relays.

Radio Cairo, Egypt. The first hour of a 90-minute broadcast to eastern North America. A ten-minute *news* bulletin is aired at 23:15, with the remaining time taken up by short features on Egypt, the Middle East and Islam. For the intellectual listener there's *Literary Readings* at 23:45 Monday, and *Modern Arabic Poetry* at the same time Friday. More general fare is available in *Listener's Mail* at 23:25 Thursday and Saturday. On 11855 kHz (7260 kHz may be used in winter).

Radio Romania International. Starts with *Radio Newsreel*, a combination of news, commentary and press review. Features on Romania complete the broadcast. Monday, the lineup includes *Pro Memoria* (Romanian history), *Pages of Romanian Literature*, *Romanian Hits* and *Sports Roundup*. Regular features on other days include Tuesday's *Business Club* and *Visual Arts*, Wednesday's *Stage and Screen* and *Romanian Musicians*, Thursday's *Listeners Letterbox* and ●*Skylark* (Romanian folk music), and Friday's *Cultural Survey* and ●*The Folk Music Box*. Saturday fare includes *World of Culture*, *Roots*, *Radio Pictures* and *DX Mailbag*; and Sunday's broadcast has *Sunday Studio* and repeats of programs aired earlier in the week. Fifty-five minutes to western Europe winter on 6135 and 7105 kHz, and summer on 7280 and 9590 kHz; also to eastern North America winter on 6180 and 9610 kHz, and summer on 9645 and 11940 kHz.

Radio Bulgaria. Summer only at this time. Repeat of the 21:00 broadcast for Europe; see

there for specifics. Sixty minutes to eastern North America on 9700 and 11700 kHz. One hour later during winter.

Voice of America. Continues with programs aimed at East Asia and the Pacific on the same frequencies as at 22:00.

AFRTS Shortwave, USA. Network news, live sports, music and features in the upper-sideband mode from the Armed Forces Radio & Television Service. Transmitted from modestly powered U.S. Navy stations around the globe. Try 4319, 5446.5, 5765, 6350, 7590, 9980, 10320, 12133.5, 12579 and 13362 kHz.

23:30

Radio Prague, Czech Republic. Winter only at this time. See 2230 for specifics. Saturday programming at this hour is *Insight Central Europe*. A half hour to eastern North America on 5915 and 7345 kHz, and one hour earlier in summer.

Radio Vilnius, Lithuania. A half hour that's mostly *news* and background reports about events in Lithuania. Of broader appeal is *Mailbag*, aired every other Saturday. For some Lithuanian music, try the second half of Sunday's broadcast. To eastern North America on 9875 kHz.

All India Radio. Continuous programming to East and Southeast Asia. A potpourri of *news*, commentary, features and exotic Indian music. To East Asia on 9950, 11620 and 13605 kHz; and to Southeast Asia on 9705, 11620 and 13605 kHz.

Voice of Vietnam. *News*, then *Commentary* or *Weekly Review*. These are followed by short features and some pleasant Vietnamese music (especially at the weekend). A half hour to Southeast Asia on 9840 and 12020 kHz. Frequencies may vary slightly.

Prepared by Tony Jones and the staff of PASSPORT TO WORLD BAND RADIO.

Addresses PLUS—2005

Station Postal and Email Addresses . . . PLUS Webcasts, Websites, Who's Who, Phones, Faxes, Bureaus, Future Plans, Items for Sale, Giveaways . . . PLUS Summer and Winter Times in Each Country!

PASSPORT shows how stations reach out to you, but Addresses PLUS also shows how you can reach out to stations. This details, country by country, how broadcasters go beyond world band radio to keep in touch, inform and entertain.

"Applause" Replies

When radio broadcasting was in its infancy, listeners sent in "applause" cards to let stations how well they were being received. To say "thanks," stations would reply with a letter or illustrated card verifying ("QSLing" in Morse code) that the station the listener heard was, in fact, theirs. While they were at it, some would throw in a free souvenir—station calendar, pennant or sticker.

The tradition continues to this day, although obtaining QSLs is tougher than it used to be. You can learn how to provide feedback to stations by looking under "Verification" in Passport's "Worldly Words" glossary. Some stations also sell goods—radios, CDs, publications, clothing, tote bags, caps, watches, clocks, pens, knives, letter openers, lighters, refrigerator magnets and keyrings.

Paying Postfolk

Most stations reply to listener correspondence—even email—through the postal system. That way, they can send out printed schedules, verification cards and other "hands-on" souvenirs. Major stations usually do this for free, but smaller ones often seek reimbursement for postage.

> **Some stations give away or offer unusual items.**

Most effective, especially for Latin American and Indonesian stations, is to enclose some unused (mint) stamps from the station's country. These are available from Plum's Airmail Postage, 12 Glenn Road, Flemington NJ 08822 USA, plumdx@msn.com, phone +1 (908) 788-1020, fax +1 (908) 782 2612. One way to help ensure your return-postage stamps are properly used is to stick them onto a pre-addressed return airmail envelope—self-addressed stamped envelope, or SASE.

You can also prompt reluctant stations by donating one paper U.S. dollar, preferably hidden from prying eyes by a piece of foil-covered carbon paper or the like. Registration often helps, as cash tends to get stolen. In some countries, though, registered mail is a prime target for would-be thieves, especially in parts of Latin America. International Reply Coupons (IRCs), which recipients may exchange locally for air or surface stamps, are available at a number of post offices worldwide, particularly in large cities. Thing is, they're increasingly hard to find, relatively costly, not fully effective, and aren't accepted by postal authorities in some countries.

Gloria, Portugal may well have been the world's largest shortwave transmission facility before 1992. Like much else in the peaceful afterglow of European communism's defeat, this RFE facility was shut down by American officials in late 1995.

RFE-RL via D. Walcutt

Stamp Out Crime

Mail theft is still a problem in several countries. We identify these and offer proven countermeasures, but start by using common sense. For example, some postal employees are stamp collectors and steal mail with unusual stamps, so use everyday stamps. A postal meter, PC-generated postage or an aerogram are other options.

¿Que Hora Es?

World Time, explained in "Setting Your World Time Clock," is essential if you want to find out when your favorite station is on. But if you want to know what time it is in any given country, World Time and "Addresses PLUS" work together to provide a solution.

Here's how. So that you don't have to wrestle with seasonal changes in your own time, "Addresses PLUS" gives local times for each country in terms of hours' difference from World Time (which stays constant year-round). For example, if you look below under "Albania," you'll see that country is World Time +1; that is, one hour ahead of World Time. So, if World Time is 12:00, the local time in Albania is 13:00 (1:00 PM). On the other hand, México City is World Time –6; that is, six hours behind World Time. If World Time is 12:00, in México City it's 6:00 AM.

Local times shown in parentheses are for the middle of the year—roughly April-October; specific dates of seasonal-time changeovers for individual countries can be obtained at www.timeanddate.com/worldclock.

Spotted Something New?

Has something changed since we went to press? A missing detail? Please let us know! Your update information, especially photocopies of material received from stations, is highly valued. Contact the IBS Editorial Office, Box 300, Penn's Park, PA 18943 USA, fax +1 (215) 598 3794, email addresses@passband.com.

Muchas gracias to the kindly folks and helpful organizations mentioned at the end of this chapter for their tireless cooperation in the preparation of this section. Without you, none of this would have been possible.

Using PASSPORT's Addresses PLUS Section

Stations included: All stations are listed if known to reply, however erratically. Also, new stations which possibly may reply to correspondence from listeners.

Leased-time programs: Private organizations/NGOs that lease program time, but which possess no world band transmitters of their own, are usually not listed. However, they may be reached at the stations over which they are heard.

Postal addresses are given. These sometimes differ from transmitter locations in the Blue Pages.

Phone and fax numbers. To help avoid confusion, telephone numbers have hyphens, fax numbers don't. All are configured for international dialing once you add your country's International access code (011 in the United States and Canada, 010 in the United Kingdom, and so on). For domestic dialing within countries outside the United States, Canada and the Caribbean, replace the country code (1-3 digits preceded by a "+") by a zero.

Giveaways. If you want freebies, say so politely in your correspondence. These are usually available until supplies run out.

Webcasting. World band stations which simulcast and/or provide archived programming over the Internet are indicated by 📻.

Unless otherwise indicated, stations:

- Reply regularly within six months or so to most listeners' correspondence in English.

- Provide, upon request, free station schedules and verification ("QSL") postcards or letters (see "Verification" in the glossary). When other items are available for free or for purchase, it is specified.
- Do not require compensation for postage costs incurred in replying to you. Where compensation is required, details are provided.

Local times. These are given in difference from World Time. For example, "World Time –5" means that if you subtract five hours from World Time, you'll get the local time in that country. So, if it were 11:00 World Time, it would be 06:00 local time in that country. Times in (parentheses) are for the middle of the year—roughly April-October. For exact changeover dates, see above explanatory paragraph.

TIPS FOR EFFECTIVE CORRESPONDENCE

Golden Rule: Write unto others as you would have them write unto you. The milk of human kindness is mighty skim these days, so a considerate message stands out.

Be interesting and helpful from the recipient's point of view, yet friendly without being chummy. Comments on specific programs are almost always appreciated, even if you are sending in what is basically a technical report.

Incorporate language courtesies. Using the broadcaster's tongue is always a plus—Addresses PLUS indicates when it is a requirement—but English is usually the next-best bet. When writing in any language to Spanish-speaking countries, remember that what gringos think of as the "last name" is actually written as the penultimate name. Thus, Juan Antonio Vargas García, which can also be written as Juan Antonio Vargas G., refers to Sr. Vargas; so your salutation should read, *Estimado Sr. Vargas*.

What's that "García" doing there, then? That's *mamita's* father's family name. Latinos more or less solved the problem of gender fairness in names long before Anglos.

But, wait—what about Portuguese, used by all those stations in Brazil? Same concept, but in reverse. *Mamá's* father's family name is penultimate, and the "real" last name is where English-speakers are used to it, at the end.

In Chinese, the "last" name comes first. However, when writing in English, Chinese names are often reversed for the benefit of *weiguoren*—foreigners. For example, "Li" is a common Chinese last name, so if you see "Li Dan," it's "Mr. Li." But if it's "Dan Li"—and certainly if it's been Westernized into "Dan Lee"—he's already one step ahead of you, and it's still "Mr. Li" (or Lee). Less widely known is that the same can also occur in Hungarian. For example, "Bartók Béla" for Béla Bartók.

If in doubt, fall back on the ever-safe "Dear Sir" or "Dear Madam"—"Hi" is still not appropriate with most letters—or use email, where salutations are not expected. Avoid first names, too, especially for recipients outside the United States. However, if you know the recipient is an amateur radio operator ("ham"), it is safe to use the first name if you include ham call letters in the address; e.g., Norman Gorman, WA3CRN, Station Engineer.

Be patient, as replies by post take weeks, sometimes months. Slow responders, those that tend to take beaucoup months to reply, are cited in Addresses PLUS, as are erratic repliers.

ALBANIA   World Time +1 (+2 midyear)

⏻**Radio Tirana**, External Service, Rruga Ismail Qemali Nr. 11, Tirana, Albania. Phone: (general) +355 (42) 23-239; (Phone/ Fax, Technical Directorate) +355 (42) 26203. Fax: (External Service) +355 (42) 23650; (Technical Directorate) +355 (42) 27 745. Email: (general) radiotirana@radiotirana.net; radiotirana@interalb.net; (Technical Directorate) 113566.3011@compuserve.com; (Mandija) imandija@icc-al.org; or dcico@artv.tirana.al. Web: http://rtsh.sil.at; (RealAudio from Radio Tirana 1, domestic service) http:// rtsh.sil.at/online.htm. Contact: Astrit Ibro, Director of External Services; Adriana Bislea, English Department; Clara Ceska; Marjeta Thoma; Pandi Skaka, Producer; or Diana Koci; (Technical Directorate) Irfan Mandija, Technical Director ARTV; (Frequency Management) Mrs. Drita Cico, Head of RTV Monitoring Center. May send free stickers and postcards. Return postage helpful ($1 should be enough).
Trans World Radio—*see* Monaco.

ANGOLA   World Time +1

Rádio Ecclésia (if reactivated), Rua Comandante Bula 118, São Paulo, Luanda, Angola; or Caixa Postal 3579, Luanda, Angola. Phone: (general) +244 (2) 443-041; (studios) +244 (2) 445-484. Fax: +244 (2) 443 093. Email: ecclesia@snet.co.ao. Web: http://recclesia.org. Contact: Fr. Antônio Jaca, General Manager. A Catholic station founded in 1954 and which broadcast continuously from March 1955 until closed by presidential decree in 1978. Reestablished in March 1997, when it was granted a permit to operate on FM. Experimented with shortwave transmissions via Radio Nederland facilities during July 2000, but these were terminated for technical reasons. Restarted transmissions in April 2001 via facilities of Germany's T-Systems International (*see*) and switched to a South African relay in May 2002. Although these transmissions were also terminated, the station hopes to resume shortwave broadcasts via its own transmitter sometime in the future, if and when the current tight regulations in Angola are relaxed. According to press reports, the shortwave equipment has already been purchased by the Episcopal Conference of Portugal.

⏻**Rádio Nacional de Angola**, Caixa Postal 1329, Luanda, Angola. Fax: +244 (2) 391 234. Email: (general, including reception reports) diop@rna.ao; (Magalhães) josela30@hotmail.com; (technical) rochapinto@rna.ao; (reception reports only) departamento133@hotmail.com. Web: (includes RealAudio) www.rna.ao; if the audio link doesn't work, try www.netangola.com/p/default.htm. Contact: Júlio Mendonça, Diretor dos Serviços de Programas; [Ms.] Josefa Canzuela Magalhães, Departamento de Intercâmbio e Opinião Pública; or Manuel Rabelais, Diretor Geral; (technical) Cândido Rocha Pinto, Diretor dos Serviços Técnicos. Replies irregularly. Best is to correspond in Portuguese and include $1, return postage or 2 IRCs.

ANTARCTICA   World Time –3 Base Antárctica Esperanza

Radio Nacional Arcángel San Gabriel—LRA36, Base Esperanza, V9411XAD Antártida Argentina, Argentina. Phone/ Fax: +54 (2964) 421 519. Email: lra36@infovia.com.ar. Return postage required. Replies to correspondence in Spanish, and sometimes to correspondence in English and French, depending on who is at the station (the staff changes each year, usually around February). If no reply, try sending your correspondence (but don't write the station's name on the

envelope) and 2 IRCs via the helpful Gabriel Iván Barrera, Casilla 2868, C1000WBC Buenos Aires, Argentina.

ANGUILLA   World Time –4

Caribbean Beacon, Box 690, Anguilla, British West Indies. Phone: +1 (264) 497- 4340. Fax: +1 (264) 497 4311. Contact: Monsell Hazell, Chief Engineer. $2 or return postage helpful. Relays Dr. Gene Scott's University Network—*see* USA.

ANTIGUA   World Time –4

BBC World Service—Caribbean Relay Station, P.O. Box 1203, St. John's, Antigua. Phone: +1 (268) 462-0994. Fax: +1 (268) 462 0436. Contact: (technical) David George. Nontechnical correspondence should be sent to the BBC World Service in London (*see*).

Deutsche Welle—Relay Station Antigua—same address and contact as BBC World Service, above. Nontechnical correspondence should be sent to Deutsche Welle in Germany (*see*).

ARGENTINA   World Time –3

Radio Baluarte (when operating), Casilla de Correo 45, 3370 Puerto Iguazú, Provincia de Misiones, Argentina. Phone: +54 (3737) 422-557. Email: icnfuturo@hotmail.com. Contact: Hugo Eidinger, Director. Free tourist literature. Return postage helpful. The same programs are aired on 1610 kHz (Radio Maranatha) and 101.7 MHz (Radio Futuro), and all three outlets are believed to be unlicensed. However, given the current radio licensing situation in the country, this is not unusual.

Radiodifusión Argentina al Exterior—RAE, Casilla de Correos 555, C1000WBC Buenos Aires, Argentina. Phone/Fax: +54 (11) 4325-6368; (technical) +54 (11) 4325-5270. Email: (general) rae@radionacional.gov.ar; (technical) operativa@radionacional.gov.ar; (Marcela Campos) camposrae@fibertel.com.ar (this address is to be phased out). Web: www.radionacional.gov.ar/rae.asp. Contact: (general) John Anthony Middleton, Head of English Team; María Dolores López, Spanish Team; (administration) Marcela G. R. Campos, Directora; (technical) Gabriel Iván Barrera, DX Editor. Return postage (3 IRCs) appreciated. The station asks listeners not to send currency notes, as it's a breach of local postal regulations. Reports covering at least 20-30 minutes of reception are appreciated.

Radio Nacional Buenos Aires, Maipú 555, C1006ACE Buenos Aires, Argentina. Phone: +54 (11) 4325-9100. Fax: (management—Gerencia General) +54 (11) 4325 9433; (Director) +54 (11) 4325-4590, +54 (11) 4322-4313; (technical—Gerencia Operativa) +54 (11) 4325-5270. Email: (general) info@ radionacional.gov.ar; (Director) direccion@radionacional.gov.ar, or mariogiorgi@uol.com.ar; (technical) operativa@ radionacional.gov.ar. Web: www.radionacional.gov.ar. Contact: (general) Mario Giorgi, Director; (technical) Alberto Enríquez. Return postage (3 IRCs) helpful. Prefers correspondence in Spanish, and usually replies via RAE (*see* above). If no reply, try sending your correspondence (but don't write the station's name on your envelope) and 3 IRCs via the helpful Gabriel Iván Barrera, Casilla 2868, C1000WBC Buenos Aires, Argentina.

ARMENIA   World Time +4 (+5 midyear)

⏻**Public Radio of Armenia/Voice of Armenia**, Radio Agency, Alek Manoukyan Street 5, 375025 Yerevan, Armenia. Phone: +374 (1) 551-143. Fax: +374 (1) 554 600. Email: (General Di-

Bob Padula is founder and editor of EDXP, as well as a veteran activist in the Australian DX community. He appears to have set a new world's record for total station verifications: over 8,000 QSL cards and letters. R. Padula

rector) president@mediaconcern.am; (Foreign Broadcasts Department, reception reports and comments on programs) pr@armradio.am. Web: (includes Windows Media) www.armradio.am. Contact: V. Voskanian, Deputy Editor-in-Chief; R. Abalian, Editor-in-Chief; Armenag Sansaryan, International Relations Bureau; Laura Baghdassarian, Deputy Manager, Radioagency; or Armen Amiryan, Director. Free postcards and stamps. Requests 2 IRCs for postal reply. Replies slowly.

ASCENSION World Time exactly

BBC World Service—Atlantic Relay Station, English Bay, Ascension (South Atlantic Ocean). Fax: +247 6117. Contact: (technical) Jeff Cant, Staff Manager; M.R. Watkins, A/Assistant Resident Engineer; or Mrs. Nicola Nicholls, Transmitter Engineer. Nontechnical correspondence should be sent to the BBC World Service in London (see).

AUSTRALIA World Time +11 (+10 midyear) Victoria (VIC), New South Wales (NSW), Australian Capital Territory (ACT) and Tasmania (TAS); +10:30 (+9:30 midyear) South Australia (SA); +10 Queensland (QLD); +9:30 Northern Territory (NT); +8 Western Australia (WA)

Australian Broadcasting Corporation Northern Territory HF Service—ABC Radio 8DDD Darwin, Administrative Center for the Northern Territory Shortwave Service, ABC Box 9994, GPO Darwin NT 0820, Australia. Phone: +61 (8) 8943-3222; (engineering) +61 (8) 8943-3209. Fax: +61 (8) 8943 3235 or +61 (8) 8943 3208. Contact: (general) Tony Bowden, Branch Manager; (administration) Barbra Lilliebridge, Administration Officer; (technical) Peter Camilleri or Yvonne Corby. Free stick-

ers and postcards. "Traveller's Guide to ABC Radio" for $1. T-shirts US$20. Three IRCs or return postage helpful.
BBC World Service via Radio Australia—For verification direct from the Australian transmitters, contact John Westland, Director of English Programs at Radio Australia (see). Nontechnical correspondence should be sent to the BBC World Service in London (see).
CDRS—Community Development Radio Service, ARDS, Box 1671, Nhulunbuy NT 0881, Australia; or (street address) 19 Pera Circuit, Nhulunbuy NT 0880, Australia. Phone: +61 (8) 8987-3910. Fax: +61 (8) 8987 3912. Email: (general) nhulun@ards.com.au; (technical) dale@ards.com.au. Web: www.ards.com.au/cdrsframe.htm. Contact: Dale Chesson, Radio Service Manager.
EDXP News Report, 404 Mont Albert Road, Mont Albert, Victoria 3127, Australia. Phone/Fax: +61 (3) 9898-2906. Email: info@edxp.org. Web: http://edxp.org. Contact: Bob Padula. " EDXP News Report" is compiled by the "Electronic DX Press" and airs over several world band stations. Focuses on shortwave broadcasters beaming to, or located in Asia and the Pacific. Currently heard on Adventist World Radio, HCJB-Australia, HCJB-Ecuador, WINB, WWCR, World Harvest Radio, Radio Vlaanderen International and Radio Korea International. Verifies postal reports with full-detail "EDXP" QSL cards showing Australian fauna, flora, and scenery. Return postage required; four 50c stamps within Australia, and one IRC or US dollar elsewhere. Email reports welcome, and are confirmed with animated Web-delivered QSLs. Does not verify reports of Internet broadcasts.
HCJB Australia, P.O. Box 291, Kilsyth VIC 3137, Australia. Phone: +61 (3) 9761-4844. Fax: +61 (3) 9761 4061. Email: office@hcjb.org.au. Contact: Derek Kickbush, Director of Broad-

casting; Dennis Adams; or David Yetman, Frequency Manager. *VERIFICATION OF RECEPTION REPORTS:* Voice of the Great Southland, GPO Box 691, Melbourne VIC 3001, Australia. Email: english@hcjb.org.au; or (Yetman) dyetman@hcjb.org.au. One IRC required for postal reply.
NEW DELHI OFFICE: Radio GMTA, P.O. Box 4960, New Delhi 110 029 India.

Radio Australia

STUDIOS AND MAIN OFFICES: GPO Box 428G, Melbourne VIC 3001, Australia. Phone: ("Openline" voice mail for listeners' messages and requests) +61 (3) 9626-1825; (switchboard) +61 (3) 9626-1800; (English programs) +61 (3) 9626-1922; (marketing manager) +61 (3) 9626 1723; (engineering) +61 (3) 9626-1914. Fax and Faxpoll: (general) +61 (3) 9626 1899; (engineering) +61 (3) 9626 1917. Email: (general) english@ra.abc.net.au; (marketing manager) hutchins.andria@abc.net.au; (engineering) holmes.nigel@a2.abc.net.au; (Radio Australia transmissions and programs) raelp@radioaus.abc.net.au; (Pacific Services) rapac@radioaus.abc.net.au; (Internet and Web Coordinator) naughton.russell@a2.abc.net.au. Web: (includes RealAudio) www.abc.net.au/ra. Contact: (general) John Westland, Head, English Language Programming; Roger Broadbent, Producer "Feedback"; Tony Hastings, Director of Programs; Caroline Bilney, Information Officer; Kirsty Boyle, Transmission Performance Officer; Mark Hemetsberger, Marketing & Communications Manager; or Jean-Gabriel Manguy, General Manager; (technical) Nigel Holmes, Transmission Manager, Transmission Management Unit. Free stickers and sometimes pennants and souvenirs available. On-air language courses available in Chinese, Indonesian, Khmer and Vietnamese. Course notes available at cost price. Radio Australia will attempt to answer listener's letters even though this will largely depend on the availability of resources and a reply may no longer be possible in all cases. All reception reports received by Radio Australia will now be forwarded to the Australian Radio DX Club for assessment and checking. ARDXC will forward completed QSLs to Radio Australia for mailing. For further information, contact John Westland, Director of English Programs at Radio Australia (Email: westland.john@a2.abc.net.au); or John Wright, Secretary/Editor, ARDXC (Email: dxer@fl.net.au). Plans to add new aerials and re-locate 250 kW transmitters.
NEW YORK BUREAU, NONTECHNICAL: Room 2260, 630 Fifth Avenue, New York NY 10020 USA. Phone: (representative) +1 (212) 332-2540; or (correspondent) +1 (212) 332-2545. Fax: +1 (212) 332 2546. Contact: Maggie Jones, North American Representative.
LONDON BUREAU, NONTECHNICAL: 54 Portland Place, London W1N 4DY, United Kingdom. Phone: +44 (20) 7631-4456. Fax: (administration) +44 (20) 7323 0059, (news) +44 (20) 7323 1125. Contact: Robert Bolton, Manager.
BANGKOK BUREAU, NONTECHNICAL: 209 Soi Hutayana off Soi Suanplu, South Sathorn Road, Bangkok 10120, Thailand. Fax: +66 (2) 287 2040. Contact: Nicholas Stuart.
SAN FRANCISCO OFFICE, SCHEDULES: 2654 17th Avenue, San Francisco CA 94116 USA. Phone: +1 (415) 564-9968. Email: GPoppin@aol.com. Contact: George Poppin. This address, a volunteer office, only provides Radio Australia schedules to listeners. All other correspondence should be sent directly to the main office in Melbourne.

Voice International Limited (formerly Christian Voice International Australia)

MAIN OFFICE: Voice International TM, P.O. Box 1104, Buderim, QLD 4556, Australia; or (street address) Killick Street, Kunda Park, QLD 4556, Australia. Phone: +61 (7) 5477-1555. Fax: +61 (7) 5477 1727. Email: (general) voice@voice.com.au; (DXer contact) dxer@voice.com.au; (Hindi Service) mail@thevoiceasia.com. (Edmiston) mike.edmiston@voice.com.au; (Moti) raymoti@voice.com.au. Web: www.voice.com.au; (Hindi Service, includes MP3) www.the voiceasia. com. Contact: (general) Mike Edmiston, Director; Raymond Moti, Station Manager; or Richard Daniel, Corporate Relations Manager.
ADDRESSES IN INDIA: The Voice, P.O. Box 1, Kangra, Pin Code 176001, Himachal, India; or The Voice, P.O. Box 2, Ludhiana, Pin Code 141008, Punjab, India.
HONG KONG ADDRESS: Liu Sheng, Flat 1b, 67 Ha Heung Road, Kowloon, Hong Kong, China. Email: sheng@voice.com.au.
INDONESIAN ADDRESS: Suara International, P.O. Box 2634, Jakarta Pusat, 10026 Indonesia. Phone: +62 (21) 565-7819. Email: suara@voice.com.au.
INTERNATIONAL TOLL FREE NUMBERS: (Indonesia only) 001-803-61-555; (India, only) 000-800-610-1019.
TRANSMITTER SITE: Voice International, PMB 5777, Darwin NT 0801, Australia. Phone: (general) +61 (8) 8981-6591 or (operations manager) +61 (8) 8981-8822. Fax: +61 (8) 8981 2846. Contact: Mrs. Lorna Manning, Site Administrator; or Robert Egoroff, Operations Manager.

AUSTRIA   World Time +1 (+2 midyear)

Radio Afrika International (if reactivated), Radio Afrika Center, Margaretengürtel 100-110/3/3, A-1050 Vienna, Austria. Phone/Fax: +43 (1) 5052-924. Email: radio.afrikas@sil.at. Web: (includes RealAudio) www.radioafrika.net. Contact: Mathurin Butusolua; Alexis Neuberg. Suspended transmissions on shortwave in June 2003, but remains on mediumwave AM and the Internet. Is looking for new partners and donors to resume on shortwave.

Radio Austria International, Listener Service, Argentinierstrasse 30a, A-1040 Vienna, Austria. Phone: +43 (1) 50101-16060; (frequency management) +43 (1) 87878-12629. Fax: +43 (1) 50101 16066; (frequency management) +43 (1) 87878 12773. Email: (frequency schedules, comments, reception reports) roi.service@orf.at; (frequency management) hfbc@orf.at. Web: (includes RealAudio) http://oe1.orf.at/service/international_en. Contact: (general) Vera Bock, Listener Service; (English Department) David Ward; (technical) Ing. Ernst Vranka, Frequency Manager; Ing. Klaus Hollndonner, Chief Engineer; Martin Cargnelli, Monitoring Department.
WASHINGTON NEWS BUREAU: 1206 Eaton Ct. NW, Washington DC 20007 USA. Phone: +1 (202) 822-9570. Contact: Eugen Freund.

AZERBAIJAN   World Time +4 (+5 midyear)

Radio Dada Gorgud/Voice of Azerbaijan, Medhi Hüseyin küçäsi 1, 370011 Baku, Azerbaijan. Phone: +994 (12) 398-585. Fax: +994 (12) 395 452. Email: webmaster@aztv.az. Web: (State TV and Radio Broadcasting Company parent organization) www.aztv.az. Contact: Mrs. Tamam Bayatli-Öner, Director; Kamil Mamedov, Director of Division of International Relations; or Arzu Abdullayev. May run station contests at various times during the year. Free postcards and occasionally books. $1 or return postage helpful. Replies irregularly to correspondence in English.

BAHRAIN World Time +3
Radio Bahrain (when operating), Broadcasting and Television, Ministry of Information, P.O. Box 702, Al Manämah, Bahrain. Phone: (Arabic Service) +973 781-888; (English Ser-

Brussels' Grand Palace was initiated in 1402 and took half a century to construct. Although a French army officer ordered it destroyed in 1695, it was quickly rebuilt. Corbis

vice) +973 629-085. Fax: (Arabic Service) +973 681 544; (English Service) +973 780 911. Web: www.gna.gov.bn./brtc/radio.html. Contact: A. Suliman (for Director of Broadcasting). $1 or IRC required. Replies irregularly.

BANGLADESH World Time +6

Bangladesh Betar
NONTECHNICAL CORRESPONDENCE: External Services, Bangladesh Betar, Shahbagh Post Box No. 2204, Dhaka 1000, Bangladesh; (physical address) Betar Bhaban Sher-e-Bangla Nagar, Agargaon Road, Dhaka 1207, Bangladesh. Phone: (director general) +880 (2) 8615-294; (Rahman Khan) +880 (2) 8613-949; (external services) +880 (2) 8618-119. Fax:(director general) +880 (2) 8612 021. Email: (Office of Director General) dgbetar@bd.drik.net; (external services) ts-betar@bdonline.com. Contact: Mrs. Dilruba Begum, Director, External Services; Ashfaque-ur Rahman Khan, Director - Programmes; or (technical) Muhammed Nazrul Islam, Station Engineer. $1 helpful. For further technical contacts, *see* below.
RESEARCH AND RECEIVING CENTRE: Bangladesh Betar, 121 Kazi Nazrul Islam Avenue, Dhaka-1000, Bangladesh. Phone: +880 (2) 8625-538 or +880 (2) 8626-175. Fax: +880 (2) 8612 021. Email: rrc@dhaka.net or dgbetar@bd.drik.net. Contact: Md. Kamal Uddin.
TECHNICAL CORRESPONDENCE: National Broadcasting Authority, NBA Bhaban, 121 Kazi Nazrul Islam Avenue, Shahabagh, Dhaka 1000, Bangladesh. Phone: +880 (2) 500-143/7, +880 (2) 500-490, +880 (2) 500-810, +880 (2) 505-113 or +880 (2) 507-269; (Shakir) +880 (2) 818-734; (Das) +880 (2) 500-810. Fax: +880 (2) 817 850. Email: rrc@dhaka.net. Contact: Syed Abdus Shakir, Chief Engineer; (reception reports) Manoranjan Das, Station Engineer, Dhaka; or Muhammed Romizuddin Bhuiya, Senior Engineer (Research Wing). Verifications not common from this office.

BELARUS World Time +2 (+3 midyear)

Belarusian Radio—*see* Radio Station Belarus, below, for details.
Radio Grodno (Hrodna)—contact via Radio Station Belarus, below.

Radio Mogilev (Mahiliou)—contact via Radio Station Belarus, below.
▣Radio Station Belarus/Radio Minsk, 4, Krasnaya St., Minsk 220807, Belarus. Phone: (domestic Belarusian Radio) +375 (17) 239-5810; (external services, general) +375 (17) 239-5830; (English Service) +375 (17) 239-5831; (German Service) +375 (17) 239-5875. Fax: (all services) +375 (17) 284 8574. Email: (domestic Belarusian Radio) tvr@tvr.by; (external services) radio-minsk@tvr.by. Web: (includes Windows Media) www.tvr.by. Contact: Natalia Khlebus, Director; Grigori Mityushnikov, Editor, English Service; Ilia Dohel, English Program Director; Elena Khoroshevich, German Program Editor; or Jürgen Eberhardt, German Program Editor. Free Belarus stamps.

BELGIUM World Time +1 (+2 midyear)

▣RTBF-International, B-1044 Brussels, Belgium. Phone: +32 (2) 737-4024. Fax: +32 (2) 737 3032. Email: relint.r@rtbf.be, or rtbfi@rtbf.be. Web: (RTBF-International) www.rtbf.be/ri/; ("La Première") www.rtbf.be/premiere/; (RealAudio) www.rtbf.be/jp. Contact: Jean-Pol Hecq, Directeur des Relations Internationales (or "Head, International Service" if writing in English). Broadcasts are essentially a relay of news and information programs from the domestic channel "La Première" of RTBF (Radio-Télévision Belge de la Communauté Française) via facilities of T-Systems International (*see*) in Jülich, Germany. Return postage not required. Accepts email reports.
▣Radio Vlaanderen Internationaal (RVI)
NONTECHNICAL AND GENERAL TECHNICAL: B-1043 Brussels, Belgium; (English Section) RVI Brussels Calling, B-1043 Brussels, Belgium. Phone: +32 (2) 741-5611, +32 (2) 741-3806/7 or +32 (2) 741-3802. Fax: +32 (2) 741-4689. Email: info@rvi.be. Web: (includes RealAudio, Windows Media and online reception report form) www.rvi.be. Contact (general) Deanne Lehman, Producer, "Brussels 1043" letterbox program; Ximena Prieto, Head, Foreign Languages Desk; Maryse Jacob, Head, French Service; Martina Luxen, Head, German Service; or Wim Jansen, Station Manager; (general technical) Frans Vossen, Producer, "Radio World." Sells RVI T-shirts (large/extra large) for 400 Belgian francs. May send free music CD. Remarks and reception reports can also be sent c/o the following diplomatic addresses:

NIGERIA EMBASSY: Embassy of Belgium, 1A, Bak Road, Ikoyi-Island, Lagos, Nigeria.

ARGENTINA EMBASSY: Embajada de Bélgica, Defensa 113 - 8 Piso, 1065 Buenos Aires, Argentina.

FREQUENCY MANAGEMENT OFFICE: BRTN, August Reyerslaan 52, B-1043 Brussels, Belgium. Phone: +32 (2) 741-5020. Fax: +32 (2) 741 5567. Email: (De Cuyper) hector.decuyper@vrt.be. Contact: Hector De Cuyper, Frequency Manager.

TDP Radio, P.O. Box 1, 2310 Rijkevorsel, Belgium. Phone: +32 (3) 314-7800. Fax: +32 (3) 314 1212. Web: (includes Windows Media, MP3, RealAudio) www.tdpradio.com. Contact: Daniël Versmissen, Program Manager; or Ludo Maes, Technical Manager. Transmits via T-Systems International facilities in Jülich, Germany.

Transmitter Documentation Project (TDP), P.O. Box 1, 2310 Rijkevorsel, Belgium. Phone: +32 (3) 314-7800. Fax: +32 (3) 314 1212. Email: info@transmitter.org. Web: www.broadcast.be or www.airtime.be/schedule.html. Contact: Ludo Maes, Managing Director. A free online publication by Belgian Dxer Ludo Maes. TDP lists current and past shortwave transmitters used worldwide in country order with station name, transmitter site & geographical coordinates, transmitter type, power and year of installation etc. Also brokers leased airtime over world band transmitters, and verifies reception reports for client stations.

BENIN   World Time +1

Office de Radiodiffusion et Télévision du Benin, Boite Postale 366, Cotonou, Benin. Phone: +229 301-096, +229 301-347. Fax: +229 302 184, +229 300 448. Email: webmaster@ortb.org. Web: www.ortb.org. Contact: (Cotonou) Damien Zinsou Ala Hassa; Emile Desire Ologoudou, Directeur Generale; or Leonce Goohouede; (technical) Anastase Adjoko, Chef de Service Technique. Return postage, $1 or IRC required. Replies irregularly and slowly to correspondence in French.

PARAKOU REGIONAL STATION: ORTB-Parakou, Boite Postale 128, Parakou, Benin. Phone: +229 610-773, +229 611-096, +229 611080. Fax: +229 610 881. Contact: (general) J. de Matha, Le Chef de la Station; (technical) Léon Donou, Chef des Services Techniques. Return postage required. Replies tend to be extremely irregular, and a safer option is to send correspondence to the Cotonou address.

BHUTAN   World Time +6

Bhutan Broadcasting Service

STATION: Department of Information and Broadcasting, Ministry of Communications, P.O. Box 101, Thimphu, Bhutan. Phone: +975 (2) 323-071/72. Fax: +975 (2) 323 073. Email: (News and Current Affairs) news@bbs.com.bt; (Thinley Tobgay Dorji) thinley@bbs.com.bt; (Sonam Tobgay) toby@bbs.com.bt. Web: (includes news and songs in MP3) www.bbs.com.bt. Contact: (general) Thinley Tobgay Dorji, News Coordinator; or Kinga Singye, Executive Director; (technical) Dorji Wangchuk, Station Engineer. Two IRCs, return postage or $1 required. Replies irregularly; correspondence to the U.N. Mission (see following) may be more fruitful.

UNITED NATIONS MISSION: Permanent Mission of the Kingdom of Bhutan to the United Nations, Two United Nations Plaza, 27th Floor, New York NY 10017 USA. Fax: +1 (212) 826 2998. Contact: Mrs. Kunzang C. Namgyel, Third Secretary; Mrs. Sonam Yangchen, Attaché; Ms. Leki Wangmo, Second Secretary; or Hari K. Chhetri, Second Secretary. Free newspapers and booklet on the history of Bhutan.

BOLIVIA   World Time -4

NOTE ON STATION IDENTIFICATIONS: Many Bolivian stations listed as "Radio..." may also announce as "Radio Emisora..." or "Radiodifusora..."

Paititi Radiodifusión—see Radio Paititi, below.

Radio Abaroa (if reactivated), Calle Nicanor Gonzalo Salvatierra 249, Riberalta, Beni, Bolivia. Contact: René Arias Pacheco, Director. Return postage or $1 required. Replies occasionally to correspondence in Spanish.

Radio Animas (if reactivated), Chocaya, Animas, Potosí, Bolivia. Contact: Julio Acosta Campos, Director. Return postage or $1 required. Replies irregularly to correspondence in Spanish.

Radio Camargo—see Radio Emisoras Camargo, below.

Radio Centenario "La Nueva"

MAIN OFFICE: Casilla 818, Santa Cruz de la Sierra, Bolivia. Phone: +591 (33) 529-265. Fax: +591 (3) 524 747. Email: mision.eplabol@scbbs-bo.com. Contact: Napoleón Ardaya B., Director. May send a calendar. Free stickers. Return postage or $1 required. Audio cassettes of contemporary Christian music and Bolivian folk music $10, including postage; CDs of Christian folk music $15, including postage. Replies to correspondence in English and Spanish.

U.S. BRANCH OFFICE: LATCOM, 1218 Croton Avenue, New Castle PA 16101 USA. Phone: +1 (412) 652-0101. Fax: +1 (412) 652 4654. Contact: Hope Cummins.

Radio Eco (when operating)

MAIN ADDRESS: Correo Central, Reyes, Ballivián, Beni, Bolivia. Contact: Gonzalo Espinoza Cortés, Director. Free station literature. $1 or return postage required. Replies to correspondence in Spanish.

ALTERNATIVE ADDRESS: Rolmán Medina Méndez, Correo Central, Reyes, Ballivián, Bolivia.

Radio Eco San Borja (if reactivated), Correo Central, San Borja, Ballivián, Beni, Bolivia. Email: gonzaloeco@hotmail.com. Contact: Gonzalo Espinoza Cortés, Director. Free station poster promised to correspondents. Return postage appreciated. Replies slowly to correspondence in Spanish.

Radio Emisoras Ballivián (when operating), Correo Central, San Borja, Beni, Bolivia. Replies to correspondence in Spanish, and sometimes sends pennant.

Radio Emisora Padilla—see Radio Padilla, below.

Radio Emisoras Camargo, Casilla Postal 9, Camargo, Provincia Nor-Cinti, Chuquisaca, Bolivia. Email: jlgarpas@hotmail.com. Web: www.radiocamargo.cjb.net. Contact: Pablo García B., Gerente Propietario. Return postage or $1 required. Replies slowly to correspondence in Spanish.

Radio Emisoras Minería—see Radiodifusoras Minería.

◪Radio Fides, Casilla 9143, La Paz, Bolivia. Fax: +591 (2) 237 9030. Email: rafides@fidesbolivia.com (rafides@caoba.entelnet.bo may also work). Web: (includes RealAudio) http://fidesbolivia.com. Contact: R.P. Eduardo Pérez Iribarne, S.J., Director. Replies occasionally to correspondence in Spanish.

Radio Illimani, Casilla 1042, La Paz, Bolivia. Phone: +591 (2) 237-6364. Fax: +591 (2) 235 9275. Email: illimani@communica.gov.bo. Contact: Gabriel Astorga Guachala. $1 required, and your letter should be registered and include a tourist brochure or postcard from where you live. Replies irregularly to friendly correspondence in Spanish.

Radio Juan XXIII [Veintitrés], Avenida Santa Cruz al frente de la plaza principal, San Ignacio de Velasco, Santa Cruz, Bolivia. Phone: +591 (3962) 2087. Phone/Fax: +591 (3962) 2188. Contact: Pbro. Elías Cortezón, Director; or María Elffy Gutiérrez

Méndez, Encargada de la Discoteca. Return postage or $1 required. Replies occasionally to correspondence in Spanish.

📻Radio La Cruz del Sur, Casilla 1408, La Paz, Bolivia. Phone: +591 (2) 222-0541. Fax: +591 (2) 224 3337. Email: cruzdelsur@zuper.net. Web: (includes Real Audio) www.geocities.com/cruzdelsur2000. Contact: Carlos Montesinos, Director. Pennant $1 or return postage. Replies slowly to correspondence in Spanish.

Radio La Palabra (if reactivated), Parroquia de Santa Ana de Yacuma, Beni, Bolivia. Phone: +591 (3848) 2117. Contact: Padre Yosu Arketa, Director. Return postage necessary. Replies to correspondence in Spanish.

Radio Mallku (formerly Radio A.N.D.E.S.), Casilla No. 16, Uyuni, Provincia Antonio Quijarro, Departamento de Potosí, Bolivia. Phone: +591 (2693) 2145. Email: (FRUTCAS parent organization) frutcas@hotmail.es. Contact: Freddy Juárez Huarachi, Director; Erwin Freddy Mamani Machaca, Jefe de Prensa y Programación. Spanish preferred. Return postage in the form of two U.S. dollars appreciated, as the station depends on donations for its existence. Station owned by La Federación Unica de Trabajadores Campesinos del Altiplano Sud (FRUTCAS).

Radio Minería—*see* Radiodifusoras Minería.

Radio Mosoj Chaski, Casilla 4493, Cochabamba, Bolivia. Phone: +591 (442) 220-641 or +591 (442) 220-644. Fax: +591 (442) 251 041. Email: chaski@bo.net. Contact: Paul G. Pittman, Administrator. Replies to correspondence in Spanish and English.

NORTH AMERICAN OFFICE: Quechuan Radio, c/o SIM USA, P.O. Box 7900, Charlotte NC 28241 USA.

Radio Movima (if reactivated), Calle Baptista No. 24, Santa Ana de Yacuma, Beni, Bolivia. Contact: Rubén Serrano López, Director; Javier Roca Diaz, Director Gerente; or Mavis Serrano, Directora. Return postage or $1 required. Replies irregularly to correspondence in Spanish.

Radio Nacional de Huanuni, Casilla 681, Oruro, Bolivia. Contact: Rafael Linneo Morales, Director General; or Alfredo Murillo, Director. Return postage or $1 required. Replies irregularly to correspondence in Spanish.

Radio Norte (if reactivated), Calle Warnes 195, 2do piso del Cine Escorpio, Montero, Santa Cruz, Bolivia. Phone: +591 (3922) 20-970. Fax: +591 (3922) 21 062. Contact: Leonardo Arteaga Ríos, Director.

Radio Padilla (if reactivated), Padilla, Chuquisaca, Bolivia. Contact: Moisés Palma Salazar, Director. Return postage or $1 required. Replies to correspondence in Spanish.

Radio Paititi, Casilla 172, Guayaramerín, Beni, Bolivia. Contact: Armando Mollinedo Bacarreza, Director; Luis Carlos Santa Cruz Cuéllar, Director Gerente; or Ancir Vaca Cuéllar, Gerente-Propietario. Free pennants. Return postage or $3 required. Replies irregularly to correspondence in Spanish.

📻Radio Panamericana, Casilla 5263, La Paz, Bolivia; (physical address) Av. 16 de Julio, Edif. 16 de Julio, Of. 902, El Prado, La Paz, Bolivia. Phone: +591 (2) 231-2644, +591 (2) 231-1383 or +591 (2) 231-3980. Fax: +591 (2) 233-4271. Email: pana@panamericanabolivia.com. Web: (includes RealAudio) www.panamericanabolivia.com. Contact: Daniel Sánchez Rocha, Director. Replies irregularly, with correspondence in Spanish preferred. $1 or 2 IRCs helpful.

Radio Perla del Acre (when operating), Casilla 7, Cobija, Departamento de Pando, Bolivia. Return postage or $1 required. Replies irregularly to correspondence in Spanish.

Radio Pío XII [Doce], Siglo Veinte, Potosí, Bolivia. Phone: +591 (258) 20-250. Fax: +591 (258) 20 544. Email: radiopio@nogal.oru.entelnet.bo. Contact: Pbro. Roberto Durette, OMI, Director General; or José Blanco. Return postage necessary. As mail delivery to Siglo Veinte is erratic, latters may be sent instead to: Casilla 434, Oruro, Bolivia; to the attention of Abenor Alfaro Castillo, periodista de Radio Pío XX [Phone: +591 (252) 76-1630].

Radio San Gabriel, Casilla 4792, La Paz, Bolivia. Phone: +591 (22) 414-371. Phone/Fax: +591 (22) 411 174. Email: rsg@fundayni.rds.org.bo; (technical, including reception reports) remoc@entelnet.bo. Contact: (general) Hno. [Brother] José Canut Saurat, Director General; or Sra. Martha Portugal, Dpto. de Publicidad; (technical) Rómulo Copaja Alcón, Director Técnico. $1 or return postage helpful. Free book on station, Aymara calendars and *La Voz del Pueblo Aymara* magazine. Replies fairly regularly to correspondence in Spanish. Station of the Hermanos de la Salle Catholic religious order.

Radio San Miguel, Casilla 102, Riberalta, Beni, Bolivia. Phone: +591 (385) 8268 or +591 (385) 8363. Fax: +591 (385) 8268. Contact: Félix Alberto Rada Q., Director; or Gerin Pardo Molina, Director. Free stickers and pennants; has a different pennant each year. Return postage or $1 required. Replies irregularly to correspondence in Spanish. Feedback on program "Bolivia al Mundo" (aired 0200-0300 World Time) especially appreciated.

Radio Santa Ana, Calle Sucre No. 250, Santa Ana de Yacuma, Beni, Bolivia. Contact: Mario Roberto Suárez, Director; or Mariano Verdugo. Return postage or $1 required. Replies irregularly to correspondence in Spanish.

Radio Santa Cruz, Emisora del Instituto Radiofónico Fé y Alegría (IRFA), Casilla 672 (or 3213), Santa Cruz, Bolivia. Phone: +591 (33) 521-814. Fax: +591 (33) 532 257. Email: irfacruz@roble.scz.entelnet.bo. Contact: Padre Francisco Flores, S.J., Director General; Srta. María Yolanda Marcó Escobar, Secretaria de Dirección; Señora Mirian Suárez, Productor, "Protagonista Ud."; or Lic. Silvia Nava S. Free pamphlets, stickers and pennants. Welcomes correspondence in English, French and Spanish, but return postage required for a reply.

Radio Virgen de los Remedios, Casilla 198, Tupiza, Departamento de Potosí, Bolivia; or (physical address) Parroquia Nuestra Señora de la Candelaria, Tupiza, Departamento de Potosí, Bolivia. Phone: +591 (269) 44-662. Email: radiovirgenderemedios@hotmail.com. Contact: Padre Estanislao Odroniec.

Radio Yura (La Voz de los Ayllus), Casilla 326, Yura, Provincia Quijarro, Departamento de Potosí, Bolivia. Phone: +591 (281) 36-216. Email: canal18@cedro.pts.entelnet.bo. Contact: Rolando Cueto F., Director.

Radiodifusoras Minería, Casilla de Correo 247, Oruro, Bolivia. Phone: +591 (252) 77-736. Contact: Dr. José Carlos Gomez Espinoza, Gerente Propietario; or Srta. Costa Colque Flores, Responsable del programa "Minería Cultural." Free pennants. Replies to correspondence in Spanish.

Radiodifusoras Trópico, Casilla 60, Trinidad, Beni, Bolivia. Contact: Eduardo Avila Alberdi, Director. Replies slowly to correspondence in Spanish. Return postage required for reply.

BOTSWANA   World Time +2

Radio Botswana, (when operating) Private Bag 0060, Gaborone, Botswana. Phone: +267 352-541 or +267 352-861. Fax: +267 357 138. Contact: (general) Ted Makgekgenene, Director; or Monica Mphusu, Producer, "Maokaneng/Pleasure Mix"; (technical) Kingsley Reetsang, Principal Broadcasting

Engineer. Free stickers, pennants and pins. Return postage, $1 or 2 IRCs required. Replies slowly and irregularly.

Voice of America/IBB—Botswana Relay Station
TRANSMITTER SITE: Voice of America, Botswana Relay Station, Moepeng Hill, Selebi-Phikwe, Botswana; or VOA-Botswana Transmitting Station, Private Bag 38, Selebi-Phikwe, Botswana. Phone: +267 810-932. Contact: Station Manager. This address for specialized technical correspondence only, although some reception reports may be verified, depending on who is at the site. During 2001, a number of verifications were received from Gabriel Tjitjo, Supervisor, Transmission Plant. All other correspondence should be directed to the regular VOA or IBB addresses (*see* USA).

BRAZIL

World Time –1 (–2 midyear) Atlantic Islands; –2 (–3 midyear) Eastern, including Brasília and Rio de Janeiro; –3 (–4 midyear) Western; –4 Northwestern; –5 Acre. There are often slight variations from one year to the next. Information regarding Daylight Saving Time can be found at http://pcdsh01.on.br.

NOTE: Postal authorities recommend that, because of the level of theft in the Brazilian postal system, correspondence to Brazil be sent only via registered mail.

Emissora Rural A Voz do São Francisco, Caixa Postal 8, 56300-000 Petrolina PE, Brazil. Email: emissorarural@silcons.com.br. Contact: Maria Letecia de Andrade Nunes. Return postage necessary. Replies to correspondence in Portuguese.

Rádio Alvorada, Rua Dom Bosco 145, Bairro Iguaçu, 86060-340 Londrina PR, Brazil. Phone: +55 (43) 3347-0606. Fax: +55 (43) 3347 0303. Email: pascom@arquidiocesedelondrina.com.br. Web: www.dialogocomdeus.com.br/radio.html. Contact: Padre Silvio Andrei, Diretor; or Sonia López. $1 or return postage. Replies to correspondence in Portuguese.

Rádio Alvorada, Rua Governador Leopoldo Neves 516, 69151-460 Parintins AM, Brazil. Phone: +55 (92) 533-2002, +55 (92) 533-3097. Fax: +55 (92) 533 2004. Email: alvorada@jurupari.com.br. Contact: Raimunda Ribeira da Motta, Diretora; or M. Braga. Return postage required. Replies occasionally to correspondence in Portuguese.

Rádio Alvorada, Avenida Ceará 2150, Jardim Nazle, 69900-460 Rio Branco AC, Brazil. Phone: +55 (68) 226-2301. Email: severian_jose@brturbo.com. Contact: José Severiano, Diretor. Occasionally replies to correspondence in Portuguese.

Rádio Araguaia—FM sister-station to Rádio Anhanguera (*see* next entry) and sometimes relayed via the latter's shortwave outlet. Web: (general) www.opopular.com.br/araguaia/; (RealAudio) www2.opopular.com.br/radio.htm. Usually identifies as "Araguaia FM."

Rádio Anhanguera, BR-157 Km. 1103, Zona Rural, 77804-970 Araguaína TO, Brazil. Return postage required. Occasionally replies to correspondence in Portuguese. Sometimes airs programming from sister-station Rádio Araguaia, 97.1 FM (*see* previous item) or from the Rede Somzoomsat satellite network.

Rádio Anhanguera, Rua Thomaz Edson, Quadra 07, Setor Serrinha, 74835-130 Goiânia GO, Brazil; or Caixa Postal 13, 74823-000 Goiânia GO, Brazil. Web: (RealAudio only) www2.opopular.com.br/radio.htm. Contact: Fábio de Campos Roriz, Diretor; or Eng. Domingo Vicente Tinoco. Return postage required. Replies to correspondence in Portuguese. Although—like its namesake in Araguaína (*see*, above)—a member of the Sistema de Rádio da Organização Jaime Câmara, this station is also an affiliate of the CBN network and often identifies as "CBN Anhanguera," especially when airing news programming.

Rádio Aparecida, Avenida Getulio Vargas 185, 12570-000 Aparecida SP, Brazil; or Caixa Postal 2, 12570-970 Aparecida SP, Brazil. Phone/Fax: +55 (12) 564-4400. Email: (nontechnical) radioaparecida@redemptor.com.br; (Macedo) cassianomac@yahoo.com. Web: www.radioaparecida.com.br. Contact: Padre C. Cabral; Savio Trevisan, Departamento Técnico; Cassiano Alves Macedo, Producer, "Encontro DX" (aired 2200 Saturday; one hour earlier when Brazil on DST); Ana Cristina Carvalho, Secretária da Direção; Padre César Moreira; or João Climaco, Diretor Geral. Return postage or $1 required. Replies occasionally to correspondence in Portuguese.

Rádio Bandeirantes, Rua Radiantes 13, Bairro Morumbi, 01059-970 São Paulo SP, Brazil. Phone: +55 (11) 3745-7552. Fax: +55 (11) 3743 5391. Email: (general) rbnoar@band.com.br; (Huertas) ahuertas@band.com.br; (Dorin) ldorin@band.com.br. Web: (includes Windows Media) www.radiobandeirantes.com.br. Contact: Augusto Huertas, Coordenador Técnico; or Luciano Dorin, Apresentador. Free stickers, pennants and canceled Brazilian stamps. $1 or return postage required.

Rádio Baré Ondas Tropicais, Av. Carvalho Leal 250, Cachoeirinha, 69065-000 Manaus AM, Brazil; or Avenida Humaitá 336, Cachoeirinha, 69065-000 Manaus AM, Brazil. Phone: +55 (92) 231-1299; +55 (92) 231-1379. Fax: +55 (92) 234 0161. Email: proclip@argo.com.br. Contact: Rosivaldo Ferreira, Diretor da agência PROCLIP. A service for listeners in the interior of the state of Amazonas, produced and managed by PROCLIP, a local advertising agency. Replies to correspondence in Portuguese.

Rádio Boa Vontade, Av. São Paulo 722, 3º andar, 90230-160 Porto Alegre RS, Brazil. Phone: +55 (51) 3325-7019 or +55 (51) 3374-0203. Email: rbv1300am@hotmail.com. Web: www.redeboavontade.com.br. Contact: José Joaquim Martins Rodrigues, Gerente Administrativo.

Rádio Brasil, Caixa Postal 625, 13000-000 Campinas, São Paulo SP, Brazil. Contact: Wilson Roberto Correa Viana, Gerente. Return postage required. Replies to correspondence in Portuguese.

Rádio Brasil Central, Caixa Postal 330, 74001-970 Goiânia GO, Brazil. Web: www.agecom.go.gov.br/Web_AM. Contact: Ney Raymundo Fernández, Diretor Administrativo; Sergio Rubens da Silva; or Arizio Pedro Soárez, Diretor Gerente. Free stickers. $1 or return postage required. Replies to correspondence in Portuguese.

Rádio Brasil Tropical, Caixa Postal 405, 78005-970 Cuiabá MT, Brazil (street address: Rua Joaquim Murtinho 1456, 78020-830 Cuiabá MT, Brazil). Phone: +55 (65) 321-6882 or +55 (65) 321-6226. Fax: +55 (65) 624 3455. Email: rcultura@terra.com.br. Contact: Klécius Antonio dos Santos, Diretor Comercial; or Roberto Ferreira, Gerente Comercial. Free stickers. $1 required. Replies to correspondence in Portuguese. Shortwave sister-station to Rádio Cultura de Cuiabá (*see*).

Rádio Caiari, Rua das Crianças 4646, Bairro Areal da Floresta, 78912-210 Porto Velho RO, Brazil. Phone/Fax: +55 (69) 210-3621. Email: caiari@radiocaiari.com.br. Web: www.radiocaiari.com.br. Contact: Eudes Júnior. Free stickers. Return postage helpful. Replies irregularly to correspondence in Portuguese.

Rádio Canção Nova, Caixa Postal 57, 12630-000 Cachoeira Paulista SP, Brazil; (physical address) Rua João Paulo II s/n, Alto da Bela Vista, 12630-000 Cachoeira Paulista SP, Brazil. Phone: +55 (12) 560-2022. Fax: +55 (12) 561 2074. Email: (nontechnical) radio@cancaonova.org.br; (Director) adriana@

cancaonova.org.br; (reception reports) dx@cancaonova.com. Web: (includes RealAudio) www.cancaonova.org.br/cnova/radio. Contact: (general) Benedita Luiza Rodrigues; Ana Claudia de Santana; or Valera Guimarães Massafera, Secretária; (administration) Adriana Pereira, Diretora da Rádio; (reception reports) Eduardo Moura, Apresentador do programa "Além Fronteiras," aired 2200 UTC Saturday (one hour earlier when Brazil is on DST). Free stickers, pennants and station brochure sometimes given upon request. May send magazines. $1 helpful.

Rádio Capixaba, Caixa Postal 509, 29000-000 Vitória ES, Brazil; or (street address) Av. Santo Antônio 366, 29025-000 Vitória ES, Brazil. Email: radiocap@terra.com.br. Contact: Jairo Gouvea Maia, Diretor; or Sr. Sardinha, Técnico. Replies occasionally to correspondence in Portuguese.

Rádio Clube de Dourados, Rua Ciro Mello 2045, Dourados MS, Brazil. Web: (Windows Media) www.douranet.com.br/netshow/clube.asx. Replies irregularly to correspondence in Portuguese.

Rádio Clube de Rondonópolis (when operating), Caixa Postal 190, 78700-000 Rondonópolis MT, Brazil. Contact: Canário Silva, Departamento Comercial; or Saúl Feliz, Gerente-Geral. Return postage helpful. Replies to correspondence in Portuguese.

Rádio Clube de Varginha, Caixa Postal 102, 37000-000 Varginha MG, Brazil. Email: sistemaclube@varginha.com.br. Contact: Mariela Silva Gómez. Return postage necessary. Replies to correspondence in Spanish and Portuguese.

Rádio Clube do Pará, Av. Almirante Barroso 2190 - 3º andar, 66093-020 Belém PA, Brazil. Phone: +55 (91) 3084-0138. Fax: +55 (91) 276 2848. Email: timaocampeao@expert.com.br. Web: (includes Windows Media) www.radioclubedopara.com.br. Contact: Edyr Paiva Proença, Diretor Geral; or José Almeida Lima de Sousa. Return postage required. Replies irregularly to correspondence in Portuguese.

Radio Clube Paranaense, Rua Rockefeller 1311, Prado Velho, 80230-130 Curitiba PR, Brazil. Phone: +55 (41) 332-2772. Email: clubeb2@onda.com.br. Web: www.clubeb2.com.br. Contact: Vicente Mickosz, Superintendente.

Rádio Copacabana (when operating), Rua Visconde Inhauma 37 - 12º andar, Rio de Janeiro. Phone: +55 (21) 233-9269 or +55 (21) 263-8567. Replies slowly to correspondence in Portuguese.

Rádio Congonhas, Praça Basílica 130, 36404-000 Congonhas MG, Brazil. Replies to correspondence in Portuguese.

Rádio Cultura Araraquara, Avenida Feijó 583 (Centro), 14801-140 Araraquara SP, Brazil. Phone: +55 (16) 232-3790. Fax: +55 (16) 232 3475. Email: ouvintes@culturafmam.com.br (cultura@techs.com.br may also work). Web: (includes Windows Media) www.culturafmam.com.br. Contact: Antonio Carlos Rodrigues dos Santos, Diretor Artistico e Comercial. Return postage required. Replies slowly to correspondence in Portuguese.

Rádio Cultura de Campos (when operating), Caixa Postal 79, 28100-970 Campos RJ, Brazil. $1 or return postage necessary. Replies to correspondence in Portuguese.

Rádio Cultura de Cuiabá—AM sister-station of Rádio Brasil Tropical (*see*) and whose programming is partly relayed by RBT. Email: rcultura@terra.com.br. Web: www.grupocultura.com.br.

Rádio Cultura Filadelfia, Rua Antonio Barbosa 1353, Caixa Postal 89, 85851-090 Foz do Iguaçu PR, Brazil. Phone: +55 (45) 523-2930. A Finnish listener reported receiving a reply from Andre Antero (andreantero@hotmail.com); however, this person's connection with the station is unknown.

Rádio Cultura Ondas Tropicais, Rua Barcelos s/n - Praça 14, 69020-200 Manaus AM, Brazil. Phone: +55 (92) 621-0015. Fax: +55 (92) 633 3332, +55 (92) 633 2829. Web: (FUNTEC parent organization) www.tvculturaamazonas.br. Contact: Luíz Fernando de Souza Ferreira; or Maria Jerusalem dos Santos, Chefe da Divisão de Rádio. Replies to correspondence in Portuguese. Return postage appreciated. Station is part of the FUNTEC (Fundação Televisão e Rádio Cultura do Amazonas) network.

Rádio Cultura São Paulo, Rua Cenno Sbrighi 378, Agua Branca, 05036-900 São Paulo, Brazil; or Caixa Postal 11544, 05049-970 São Paulo, Brazil. Phone: (general) +55 (11) 3874-3122; (Cultura AM) +55 (11) 3874-3081; (Cultura FM) +55 (11) 3874-3082. Fax: +55 (11) 3611 2014. Email: (Cultura AM, relayed on 9615 and 17815 kHz) falecom@radiocultura.am.br; (Cultura FM, relayed on 6170 kHz) falecom@radioculturasp.fm.br. Web: (includes Windows Media) www.tvcultura.com.br. Contact: Thais de Almeida Dias, Chefe de Produção e Programação; Eduardo Weber; Sra. Maria Luíza Amaral Kfouri, Chefe de Produção; or Valvenio Martins de Almeida, Coordenador de Produção. $1 or return postage required. Replies slowly to postal correspondence in Portuguese.

Rádio Difusora 6 de Agosto, Rua Pio Nazário 31, 69930-000 Xapuri AC, Brazil. Contact: Francisco Evangelista de Abreu. Replies to correspondence in Portuguese.

Rádio Difusora Acreana, Rua Benjamin Constant 1232, 69900-161 Rio Branco AC, Brazil. Phone: +55 (68) 223-9696. Fax: +55 (68) 223 8610. Email: rda@osite.com.br. Contact: Washington Aquino, Diretor Geral. Replies irregularly to correspondence in Portuguese.

Rádio Difusora Cáceres, Caixa Postal 297, 78200-000 Cáceres MT, Brazil. Contact: Sra. Maridalva Amaral Vignardi. $1 or return postage required. Replies occasionally to correspondence in Portuguese.

Rádio Difusora de Aquidauana, Caixa Postal 18, 79200-000 Aquidauana MS, Brazil. Phone: +55 (67) 241-3956 or +55 (67) 241-3957. Contact: Joel Severino da Silva, Diretor Geral. Free tourist literature and used Brazilian stamps. $1 or return postage required. This station sometimes identifies during the program day as "Nova Difusora," but its sign-off announcement gives the official name as "Rádio Difusora, Aquidauana."

Rádio Difusora de Londrina, Caixa Postal 1870, 86000-000 Londrina PR, Brazil. Contact: Oscar Simões Costa, Gerente Administrativo. Free tourist brochure, which sometimes seconds as a verification. $1 or return postage helpful. Replies irregularly to correspondence in Portuguese.

Rádio Difusora de Macapá, Rua Cândido Mendes 525 - Centro, 68900-100 Macapá AP, Brazil. Phone: +55 (96) 212-1120 or +55 (96) 212-1118. Fax: +55 (96) 212 1116. Email: radio630@hotmail.com. Web: http://macapa-ap.com.br/ empresas/rdm.htm. Contact: Paulo Roberto Rodrigues, Gerente. $1 or return postage required. Replies irregularly to correspondence in Portuguese. Sometimes provides stickers, key rings and—on rare occasions—T-shirts.

Rádio Difusora de Poços de Caldas, Rua Rio Grande do Sul 631- 1º andar, Centro, 37701-001 Poços de Caldas MG, Brazil. Phone/Fax: +55 (35) 3722-1530. Email: difusora@ difusorapocos.com.br. Web: www.difusorapocos.com.br. Contact: (general) Orlando Cioffi, Diretor Geral; (technical) Ronaldo Cioffi, Diretor Técnico. $1 or return postage required. Replies to correspondence in Portuguese.

Rádio Difusora do Amazonas, Av. Eduardo Ribeiro 639 - 20º andar, Centro, 69010-001 Manaus AM, Brazil. Phone: +55 (92) 633-1001. Fax: +55 (92) 234 3750. Email: difusora@internext.com.br. Web: (includes Windows Media) www.difusoramanaus.com.br. Contact: J. Joaquim Marinho, Diretor. Joaquim Marinho is a keen collector and especially interested in Duck Hunting Permit Stamps, stamp booklets and stamp sheets. Will reply to correspondence in Portuguese or English. $1 or return postage helpful.

Rádio Difusora Roraima, Avenida Capitão Ene Garcez 830, São Francisco, 69301-160 Boa Vista RR, Brazil. Phone/Fax: +55 (95) 623-2259. Email: radiorr@technet.com.br. Web: www.radiororaima.com.br. Contact: Galvão Soares, Diretor Geral. Return postage required. Replies occasionally to correspondence in Portuguese.

Rádio Difusora Taubaté (when operating), Rua Dr. Sousa Alves 960, 12020-030 Taubaté SP, Brazil. Contact: Emilio Amadei Beringhs Neto, Diretor Superintendente. May send free stickers, pens, keychains and T-shirts. Return postage or $1 helpful.

Rádio Educação Rural, Avenida Mato Grosso 530, Centro, 79002-230 Campo Grande MS, Brazil. Phone: +55 (67) 384-3164, +55 (67) 382-2238 or +55 (67) 384-3345. Contact: Ailton Guerra, Gerente-Geral; Angelo Venturelli, Diretor. $1 or return postage required. Replies to correspondence in Portuguese.

Rádio Educação Rural, Praça São Sebastião 228, 69460-000 Coari AM, Brazil. Phone: +55 (97) 561-2474. Fax: +55 (97) 561 263. Email: radiocoari@portalcoari.com.br. Contact: Lino Rodrigues Pessoa, Diretor Comercial; or Elijane Martins Correa. $1 or return postage helpful. Replies irregularly to correspondence in Portuguese.

Rádio Educação Rural de Tefé, Caixa Postal 21, 69470-000 Tefé AM, Brazil; or (street address) 21Praça Santa Tereza 283,

Centro, 69470-000 Tefé AM, Brazil. Phone: +55 (97) 343-3017. Fax: +55 (97) 343 2663. Email: rert@osite.com.br; fjoaquim@mandic.com.br. Contact: Thomas Schwamborn, Diretor Administrativo.

Rádio Educadora de Bragança, Praça das Bandeiras s/n, 68600-000 Bragança PA, Brazil. Phone: +55 (91) 425-1295. Fax: +55 (91) 425 1702. Email: educadora@eletronet.com.br. Contact: José Rosendo de S. Neto; Zelina Cardoso Gonçalves; or Adelino Borges, Aux. Escritório. $1 or return postage required. Replies to correspondence in Portuguese.

Rádio Educadora de Guajará Mirim, Praça Mário Corrêa No.90, 78957-000 Guajará Mirim RO, Brazil. Phone: +55 (69) 541-2274. Fax: +55 (69) 541 6333. Email: educadora@ osite.com.br; comercial@radio-educadora.ht.st. Contact: Wilson Charles. Return postage helpful. Replies to correspondence in Portuguese.

Rádio Educadora de Limeira, Caixa Postal 105, 13480-970 Limeira SP, Brazil. Email: (Bortolan) bab@zaz.com.br. Contact: Bruno Arcaro Bortolan, Gerente.

Rádio Gaúcha, Avenida Ipiranga 1075 - 2º andar, Bairro Azenha, 90160-093 Porto Alegre RS, Brazil. Phone: +55 (51) 3218-6600. Fax: +55 (51) 3218 6680. Email: (general) gaucha@rdgaucha.com.br; (comments on program content) reportagem@rdgaucha.com.br; (technical) gilberto.kussler@ rdgaucha.com.br. Web: (includes RealAudio) http:// radiogaucha.clicrbs.com.br. Contact: Gilberto Kussler, Gerente Técnico. Replies to correspondence, preferably in Portuguese.

Rádio Gazeta, Avenida Paulista 900, 01310-940 São Paulo SP, Brazil. Phone: +55 (11) 3170-5757. Fax: +55 (11) 3170 5630. Email: (Fundação Cásper Líbero parent organization) fcl@fcl.com.br. Web: (Fundação Cásper Líbero parent organization) www.fcl.com.br. Contact: Shakespeare Ettinger, Supervisor Geral de Operação; Bernardo Leite da Costa; José Roberto Mignone Cheibub, Gerente Geral; or Ing. Aníbal Horta Figueiredo. Free stickers. $1 or return postage necessary. Replies to correspondence in Portuguese. Currently relays programming from the station's mediumwave AM station (Gazeta AM) after several years of leasing airtime to the "Deus é Amor" Pentecostal church.

Rádio Globo (when operating), Rua do Russel 434-Glória, 22210-210 Rio de Janeiro RJ, Brazil. Phone: +55 (21) 555-8375. Fax: +55 (21) 558 6385. Email: (administration) gerenciaamrio@radioglobo.com.br. Web: (includes RealAudio) www.radioglobo.com.br/globorio. Contact: Marcos Libretti, Diretor Geral. Replies irregularly to correspondence in Portuguese. Return postage helpful.

Rádio Globo, Rua das Palmeiras 315, Santa Cecilia, 01226-901 São Paulo SP, Brazil. Phone: +55 (11) 3824-3217. Fax: +55 (11) 3824 3210. Email: (Rapussi) margarete@ radioglobo.com.br. Web: (includes RealAudio) www.radioglobo.com.br. Contact: Ademar Dutra, Locutor, "Programa Ademar Dutra"; Margarete Rapussi; Guilherme Viterbo; or José Marques. Replies to correspondence, preferably in Portuguese.

Rádio Guaíba, Rua Caldas Júnior 219, 90019-900 Porto Alegre RS, Brazil. Phone: +55 (51) 3215-6222. Email: (administration) diretor@radioguaiba.com.br; (technical) centraltecnica@radioguaiba.com.br. Web: (includes RealAudio) www.radioguaiba.com.br. Return postage helpful.

Rádio Guarani (if reactivated), Avenida Assis Chateaubriand 499, Floresta, 30150-101 Belo Horizonte MG, Brazil. Phone: +55 (31) 3237-6000. Fax: +55 (31) 3237 6656. Email: guarani@guarani.com.br. Web: (includes RealAudio) www.guarani.com.br. Contact: Junara Belo, Setor de

Comunicações. Replies slowly to correspondence in Portuguese. Return postage helpful.

Rádio Guarujá, Caixa Postal 45, 88000-000 Florianópolis SC, Brazil. Email: guaruja@radioguaruja.com.br. Web: www.radioguaruja.com.br. Contact: Mario Silva, Diretor; Joana Sempre Bom Braz, Assessora de Marketing e Comunicação; or Rosa Michels de Souza. Return postage required. Replies irregularly to correspondence in Portuguese.

NEW YORK OFFICE: 45 West 46 Street, 5th Floor, Manhattan, NY 10036 USA.

Rádio Guarujá Paulista, Rua José Vaz Porto 175, Vila Santa Rosa, 11431-190 Guarujá SP, Brazil; or (technical, including reception reports) A/C Orivaldo Rampazzo, Rua Montenegro 196, 11410-040 Guarujá SP, Brazil. Phone: +55 (13) 3386-6092. Email: guarujaam@miranet.com.br. Contact: Orivaldo Rampazzo, Diretor. Replies to correspondence in Portuguese. Transmits via facilities of former world band stations in the state of São Paulo, which are fed via the Internet.

Rádio Iguatemi (when operating), Caixa Postal 66, 06001-970 Osasco SP, Brazil. Web: http:// radioiguatemi.cidadeinternet.com.br. Sometimes replaces Rádio Mundial (*see*) on 4975 kHz. Both stations belong to the same network, Rede CBS.

REDE CBS PARENT ORGANIZATION: Rede CBS, Av. Paulista, 2200 - 14° andar - Cerqueira César, 01310-300 São Paulo SP, Brazil. Phone: +55 (11) 3016 5999. Fax: +55 (11) 3016 5980. Web: www.redecbs.com.br.

Rádio Inconfidência, Avenida Raja Gabáglia 1666, Luxemburgo, 30350-540 Belo Horizonte MG, Brazil. Phone: +55 (31) 3297-7344. Fax: +55 (31) 3297 7348. Email: inconfidencia@inconfidencia.com.br. Web: www.inconfidencia.com.br. Contact: Isaias Lansky, Diretor; Manuel Emilio de Lima Torres, Dirctor Superintendente; Jairo Antolio Lima, Diretor Artístico; or Eugenio Silva. Free stickers and postcards. May send CD of Brazilian music. $1 or return postage helpful.

Rádio Integração (if reactivated), Rua Alagoas 270, Bairro Escola Técnica, 69980-000 Cruzeiro do Sul AC, Brazil. Phone: +55 (68) 322-4637. Fax: +55 (68) 322 6511. Email: rtvi@omegasul.com.br. Contact: Albelia Bezerra da Cunha. Return postage helpful.

Rádio Itatiaia, Rua Itatiaia 117, 31210-170 Belo Horizonte MG, Brazil. Fax: +55 (31) 446 2900. Email: itatiaia@itatiaia.com.br. Web: (includes RealAudio) www.itatiaia.com.br/am/index.html. Contact: Lúcia Araújo Bessa, Assistente da Diretória; or Claudio Carneiro.

Rádio Jornal "A Crítica" (when operating), Av. André Araujo 1024A, Aleixo, 69060-001 Manaus AM, Brazil. Phone: +55 (92) 642-4545. Fax: +55 (92) 642 2484. Contact: Rui Souto de Alencar, Diretor Executivo.

Rádio Liberal (if reactivated), C.P 498, 66017-970 Belém PA, Brazil; or (street address) Av. Nazaré 350, 66035-170 Belém PA, Brazil. Phone: +55 (91) 213-1500. Fax: +55 (91) 224 5240. Email: radio@radioliberal.com.br. Web: (includes RealAudio) www.radioliberal.com.br. Contact: Flavia Vasconcellos; Advaldo Castro, Diretor de Programação AM; João Carlos Silva Ribeiro, Coordenador de Programação AM. Currently off the air because of difficulty in obtaining parts for the transmitter.

Rádio Marumby, Caixa Postal 296, 88010-970 Florianópolis SC, Brazil; Rua Angelo Laporta 841, C. P. 62, 88020-600 Florianópolis SC, Brazil; or (missionary parent organization) Gideões Missionários da Última Hora—GMUH, Ministério Evangélico Mundial, Rua Joaquim Nunes 244, Caixa Postal 2004, 88340-000 Camboriú SC, Brazil. Email: (GMUH parent organization) gmuh@gmuh.com.br. Web: www.gmuh.com.br/ aradio.htm; www.gmuh.com.br/marumby.htm. Contact: Davi Campos, Diretor Artístico; Dr. Cesario Bernardino, Presidente, GMUH; or Jair Albano, Diretor. $1 or return postage required. Free diploma and stickers. Replies to correspondence in Portuguese.

Rádio Marumby, Curitiba—*see* Rádio Novas de Paz, Curitiba, below.

Rádio Meteorologia Paulista, Rua Capitão João Marques 89, Jardim Centenário, 14940-000 Ibitinga, São Paulo SP, Brazil. Phone: +55 (16) 242-3388. Fax: +55 (16) 242 5056. Email: radio.ibitinga@ibinet.com.br. Web: (includes RealAudio from Ternura FM, relayed several hours each day by Rádio Meteorologia Paulista) www.ibinet.com.br/radioibitinga. Contact: Roque de Rosa, Diretora. Replies to correspondence in Portuguese. $1 or return postage required.

Rádio Missões da Amazônia, Travessa Dr. Lauro Sodré 299, 68250-000 Óbidos PA, Brazil. Phone: +55 (93) 547-1698. Fax: +55 (93) 547-1699. Email: radiomissoes@eunet.com.br. Contact: Max Hamoy; Edérgio de Moras Pinto; or Maristela Hamoy. Return postage required. Replies occasionally to correspondence in Portuguese.

Rádio Mundial, Av. Paulista 2198-Térreo, Cerqueira César, 01310-300 São Paulo, Brazil. Phone: +55 (11) 3016 5999. Email: radiomundial@radiomundial.com. Web: www.radiomundial.com.br. Contact: (nontechnical) Luci Rothschild de Abreu, Diretora Presidente.

REDE CBS PARENT ORGANIZATION: Rede CBS, Av. Paulista, 2200 - 14° andar - Cerqueira César, 01310-300 São Paulo SP, Brazil. Phone: +55 (11) 3016 5999. Fax: +55 (11) 3016 5980. Web: www.redecbs.com.br.

Rádio Municipal, Avenida Alvaro Maia s/n, 69750-000 São Gabriel da Cachoeira AM, Brazil. Phone/Fax: +55 (97) 471-1768. Contact: Luíz dos Santos França, Gerente; or Valdir de Souza Marques. Return postage necessary. Replies to correspondence in Portuguese. Formerly Rádio Nacional de São Gabriel da Cachoeira, prior to the station's transfer from Radiobrás to the local municipality.

Rádio Nacional da Amazônia, SCRN 702/3 Bloco-B, Ed. Radiobrás, 70710-750 Brasília DF, Brazil; or (postal address) Caixa Postal 258, 70359-970 Brasília-DF, Brazil. Phone: +55 (61) 327-1981. Fax: +55 (61) 321 7602. Email: nacionaloc@radiobras.gov.br. Web: (includes Windows Media) www.radiobras.gov.br/nacional. Contact: (general) Luíz Otavio de Castro Souza, Diretor; Fernando Gómez da Câmara, Gerente de Escritório; or Januario Procopio Toledo, Diretor; (technical) Valmira Almeida, Chefe da Divisão de Ondas Curtas da Radiobrás. Free stickers, but no verifications.

Rádio Nacional do Brasil, Caixa Postal 257, 70160-000 Brasília-DF, Brazil. Email: radionacionaldobrasil@ radiobras.gov.br. Returned to the air in August 2003 after several years off the air.

Rádio Nacional São Gabriel da Cachoeira—*see* Rádio Municipal.

Rádio Novas de Paz, Avenida Paraná 1896, 82510-000 Curitiba PR, Brazil; or Caixa Postal 22, 80000-000 Curitiba PR, Brazil. Phone: +55 (41) 257-4109. Contact: João Falavinha Ienzen, Gerente. $1 or return postage required. Replies irregularly to correspondence in Portuguese.

Rádio Nova Visão

STUDIOS: Rua do Manifesto 1373, 04209-001 São Paulo SP, Brazil. Contact: José Eduardo Dias, Diretor Executivo. Return postage required. Replies to correspondence in Portuguese. Free stickers. Relays Rádio Trans Mundial fulltime.

TRANSMITTER: Caixa Postal 551, 97000-000 Santa Maria RS, Brazil; or Caixa Postal 6084, 90000-000 Porto Alegre RS, Brazil. Reportedly issues full-data verifications for reports in Portuguese or German, upon request, from this location. If no luck, try contacting, in English or Dutch, Tom van Ewijck, via email at egiaroll@mail.iss.lcca.usp.br. For further information, see the entry for Rádio Trans Mundial.

Rádio Novo Tempo, Caixa Postal 146, 79002-970 Campo Grande MS, Brazil; (street address) Rua Amando de Oliveira 135, Bairro Amambaí, 79005-370 Campo Grande MS, Brazil. Email: (Ramos) ellen.ramos@usb.org.br. Web: www.asm.org.br (click on the "Rádio Novo Tempo" link). Contact: Ellen Ramos, Locutora; or Pastor Paulo Melo. Return postage required. Replies to correspondence in Portuguese. A station of the Seventh Day Adventists.

Rádio Oito de Setembro (when operating), Caixa Postal 8, 13690-000 Descalvado SP, Brazil. Contact: Adonias Gomes. Replies to corrrespondence in Portuguese.

Rádio Pioneira de Teresina, Rua 24 de Janeiro 150 sul, 64001-230 Teresina PI, Brazil. Phone: +55 (86) 221-8121. Fax: +55 (86) 221 8122. Email: (general) online email form; (comments on programs) programacao@radiopioneira.am.br Web: www.radiopioneira.am.br. Contact: Luíz Eduardo Bastos; Padre Tony Batista, Diretor; or Joel Silva. $1 or return postage required. Replies slowly to correspondence in Portuguese.

Rádio Progresso (if reactivated), Estrada do Belmont s/n, B Nacional, 78903-400 Porto Velho RO, Brazil. Return postage required. Replies occasionally to correspondence in Portuguese.

Rádio Record
STATION: Caixa Postal 7920, 04084-002 São Paulo SP, Brazil. Email: radiorecord@rederecord.com.br. Contact: Mário Luíz Catto, Diretor Geral. Free stickers. Return postage or $1 required. Replies occasionally to correspondence in Portuguese.
NEW YORK OFFICE: 630 Fifth Avenue, Room 2607, New York NY 10111 USA.

Rádio Relógio, Rua Paramopama 131, Ribeira, Ilha do Governador, 21930-110 Rio de Janeiro RJ, Brazil. Phone: +55 (21) 467-0201. Fax: +55 (21) 467 4656. Email: radiorelogio@ig.com.br. Contact: Olindo Coutinho, Diretor Geral; or Renato Castro. Replies occasionally to correspondence in Portuguese.

Rádio Ribeirão Preto, Caixa Postal 1252, 14025-000 Ribeirão Preto SP, Brazil (physical address: Av. 9 de Julho 600, 14025-000 Ribeirão Preto SP, Brazil). Phone/Fax: +55 (16) 610-3511. Contact: Lucinda de Oliveira, Secretária; Luis Schiavone Junior; or Paulo Henríque Rocha da Silva. Replies to correspondence in Portuguese.

Rádio Rio Mar, Rua José Clemente 500, Centro, 69010-070 Manaus AM, Brazil. Phone: +55 (92) 633-2295; +55 (92) 633-5005. Fax: +55 (92) 232 7763. Email: riomar@bol.com.br; decom@auxiliadora.g12.br. Web: (includes Windows Media) www.geocities.com/radioriomar. Contact: Jairo de Sousa Coelho, Diretor de Programação e Jornalismo. Replies to correspondence in Portuguese. $1 or return postage helpful.

Rádio Rural Santarém, Rua São Sebastião 622 - Bloco A, 68005-090 Santarém PA, Brazil. Phone: +55 (93) 523-1006. Fax: +55 (93) 523 2685. Email: ruralsonia@hotmail.com. Contact: Edilberto Moura Sena, Diretor Executivo; João Elias B. Bentes, Gerente Geral; or Edsergio de Moraes Pinto. Replies slowly to correspondence in Portuguese. Free stickers. Return postage or $1 required.

Rádio Trans Mundial, Caixa Postal 18300, 04626-970 São Paulo SP, Brazil. Phone: +55 (11) 5031-3533. Fax: +55 (11) 5031 5271. Email: (general) rtm@transmundial.com.br; (technical) tecnica@transmundial.com.br; ("Amigos do Rádio" DX-program) amigosdoradio@transmundial.com.br. Web: (includes RealAudio) www.transmundial.com.br. Contact: José Eduardo Dias, Diretor; or Rudolf Grimm, programa "Amigos do Rádio." Sells religious books and casettes and CDs of religious music (from choral to bossa nova). Prices, in local currency, can be found at the Website (click on "catálogo"). Program provider for Rádio Nova Visão—*see,* above.

Rádio Cacique (when operating), Caixa Postal 486, 18090-970 Sorocaba SP, Brazil. Phone: +55 (15) 231-3712 or (15) 232-2922. Email: Online email form. Web: www.radiocacique.com.br.

Rádio Senado. Caixa Postal 070-747, 70359-970 Brasília DF, Brazil; or (physical address) Praça dos Três Poderes, Anexo II, Bloco B, Térreo, 70165-900 Brasília DF, Brazil. Phone: (shortwave department) +55 (61) 311-1238. Email: radio@senado.gov.br; (Fabiano) max@senado.gov.br. Web: (includes RealAudio) www.senado.gov.br/radio. Contact: Max Fabiano, Diretor; (technical) José Carlos Sigmaringa, Coordenador do Núcleo de Ondas Curtas.

Rádio Universo/Rádio Tupi, Rua Basilio Itiberê 1001, Rebouças, 80215-140 Curitiba PR, Brazil. Email: (Santana) billsantana2000@hotmail.com. Contact: Luíz Andreu Rúbio, Diretor; or Douglas Santana. Replies occasionally to correspondence in Portuguese. Rádio Universo's air time is leased to the "Deus é Amor" Pentecostal church, and programs originate from the Rádio Tupi network. Identifies on the air as "Rádio Tupi, Sistema Universo de Comunicação" or, more often, just as "Rádio Tupi."

Rádio Vale do Rio Madeiro (if activated), Rua Júlio de Oliveira 1323, São Pedro, 69800-000 Humaitá AM, Brazil. Phone/Fax: +55 (97) 373-2073. Email: radiovrm@dnknet.com.br. Although assigned a shortwave frequency years ago, the station never used it. Now, the station is again proposing to operate on shortwave, but only if it is granted a new frequency, for which it has already applied. In the meantime, broadcasts continue on 670 kHz AM.

Rádio Verdes Florestas, Rua Mário Lobão 81, 69980-000 Cruzeiro do Sul AC, Brazil; or Caixa Postal 53, 69981-970 Cruzeiro do Sul AC, Brazil. Phone: +55 (68) 322-3309, +55 (68) 322-2634. Email: florestas@nauanet.com.br. Contact: Marlene Valente de Andrade. Return postage required. Replies occasionally to correspondence in Portuguese.

Rádio Voz do Coração Imaculado, Caixa Postal 354, 75001-970 Anápolis GO, Brazil. Contact: P. Domingos M. Esposito A religious station which started shortwave operation in 1999 with the transmitter formerly used by Rádio Carajá. Operation tends to be irregular, as the station is funded entirely from donations.

Sistema LBV Mundial, Legião da Boa Vontade, Av. Sérgio Tomás 740, Bom Retiro, 01131-010 São Paulo SP, Brazil; or Rua Doraci 90, Bom Retiro, 01134-020 São Paulo SP, Brazil. Phone: 3225-4500. Fax: +55 (11) 3225 4639. Web: www.lbv.org. Contact: André Tiago, Diretor; Sandra Albuquerque, Secretária; or Gizelle Almeida, Gerente do Dept. de Rádio. Replies slowly to correspondence in all main languages. Program provider for Rádio Boa Vontade (*see*).
NEW YORK OFFICE: 383 5th Avenue, 2nd Floor, New York NY 10016 USA. Phone: +1 (212) 481-1004. Fax: +1 (212) 481 1005. Email: lgw2000@aol.com.

Voz de Libertação. Ubiquitous programming originating from the "Deus é Amor" Pentecostal church's Rádio Universo (1300 kHz) in São Bernardo do Campo, São Paulo, and heard over several shortwave stations, especially Rádio Universo, Curitiba (see). A RealAudio feed is available at the "Deus é Amor" Website, www.ipda.org.br.

Voz do Coração Imaculado—*see* Rádio Voz do Coração Imaculado.

BULGARIA   World Time +2 (+3 midyear)

⊠Radio Bulgaria
NONTECHNICAL AND TECHNICAL: P.O. Box 900, BG-1000, Sofia, Bulgaria; or (street address) 4 Dragan Tsankov Blvd., 1040 Sofia, Bulgaria. Phone: (general) +359 (2) 985-241; (Managing Director) +359 (2) 854-604. Fax: (general, usually weekdays only) +359 (2) 871 060, +359 (2) 871 061 or +359 (2) 650 560; (Managing Director) +359 (2) 946 1576; +359 (2) 988 5103; (Frequency Manager) +359 (2) 963 4464. Email: (English program and schedule information) english@bnr.bg (same format for other languages, e.g. french@...; spanish@...). Web: (includes RealAudio) www.bnr.bg. Contact: (general) Mrs. Iva Delcheva, English Section; Svilen Stoicheff, Head of English Section; (administration and technical) Anguel H. Nedyalkov, Managing Director; (technical) Atanas Tzenov, Director. Replies regularly, but sometimes slowly. Return postage helpful. Verifies email reports with QSL cards. For concerns about frequency usage, contact BTC, below, with copies to Messrs. Nedyalkov and Tzenov of Radio Bulgaria.
FREQUENCY MANAGEMENT AND TRANSMISSION OPERATIONS: Bulgarian Telecommunications Company (BTC), Ltd., 8 Totleben Blvd., 1606 Sofia, Bulgaria. Phone: +359 (2) 88-00-75. Fax: +359 (2) 87 58 85 or +359 (2) 80 25 80. Contact: Roumen Petkov, Frequency Manager; or Mrs. Margarita Krasteva, Radio Regulatory Department.

⊠Radio Varna, 22 Primorski blvd, 9000 Varna, Bulgaria. Phone: +359 (52) 602-802. Fax: +359 (52) 664 411. Email: bnr@radiovarna.com. Web: (includes live domestic programing in RealAudio) www.radiovarna.com. Contact: (technical) Kostadin Kovachev, Chief Engineer.

BURKINA FASO   World Time exactly

Radiodiffusion-Télévision Burkina, B.P. 7029, Ouagadougou, Burkina Faso. Phone: +226 310-441. Contact: (general) Raphael L. Onadia; Tahere Ouedraogo, Le Chef des Programs; or M. Pierre Tassembedo; (technical) Marcel Teho, Head of Transmitting Centre. Replies irregularly to correspondence in French. IRC or return postage helpful.

BURMA—*see* MYANMAR.

BURUNDI   World Time +2

La Voix de la Révolution, B.P. 1900, Bujumbura, Burundi. Phone: +257 22-37-42. Fax: +257 22 65 47 or +257 22 66 13. Email: rtnb@cbinf.com. Contact: (general) Grégoire Barampumba, Head of News Section; or Frederic Havugiyaremye, Journaliste; (administration) Gérard Mfuranzima, Le Directeur de la Radio; or Didace Baranderetse, Directeur Général de la Radio; (technical) Abraham Makuza, Le Directeur Technique. $1 required.

CAMBODIA   World Time +7

National Radio of Cambodia (when operating)
STATION ADDRESS: 106 Preah Kossamak Street, Monivong Boulevard, Phnom Penh, Cambodia. Phone: +855 (23) 423-

Dud American ordinance (UXO) in Cambodia has mostly been converted to peacetime use, including as life-giving planters.   M. Guha

369 or +855 (23) 422-869. Fax: + 855 (23) 427 319. Email: vocri@vocri.org. Web: www.vocri.org. Contact: (general) Miss Hem Bory, English Announcer; Kem Yan, Chief of External Relations; or Touch Chhatha, Producer, Art Department; (administration) In Chhay, Chief of Overseas Service; Som Sarun, Chief of Home Service; Van Sunheng, Deputy Director General, Cambodian National Radio and Television; or Ieng Muli, Minister of Information; (technical) Oum Phin, Chief of Technical Department. Free program schedule. Replies irregularly and slowly. Do not include stamps, currency, IRCs or dutiable items in envelope. Registered letters stand a much better chance of getting through. Has been increasingly off the air in recent years.

CAMEROON   World Time +1

NOTE: Any CRTV outlet is likely to be verified by contacting via registered mail, in English or French with $2 enclosed, James Achanyi-Fontem, Cameroon Link, Shortwave Monitors, P.O. Box 1460, Douala, Cameroon.

Cameroon Radio Television Corporation (CRTV)—Buea (when operating), P.M.B., Buea (Sud-Ouest), Cameroon. Contact: Ononino Oli Isidore, Chef Service Technique. Three IRCs, $1 or return postage required.

Cameroon Radio Television Corporation (CRTV)—Garoua (when operating), B.P. 103, Garoua (Nord/Adamawa),

Cameroon. Contact: Kadeche Manguele. Free cloth pennants. Three IRCs or return postage required. Replies irregularly and slowly to correspondence in French.

📻**Cameroon Radio Television Corporation (CRTV)—Yaoundé** (if reactivated), B.P. 1634, Yaoundé (Centre-Sud), Cameroon. Phone: +237 221-4035, +237 221-4077 or +237 221-4088. Fax: +237 220 4340. Email: crtv@crtv.cm. Web: (includes RealAudio and Windows Media) www.crtv.cm. Contact: (technical or nontechnical) Prof. Gervais Mendo Ze, Directeur-Général; (technical) Eyébé Tanga, Directeur Technique. $1 required. Replies slowly (sometimes extremely slowly) to correspondence in French.

CANADA
World Time –3:30 (–2:30 midyear) Newfoundland; –4 (–3 midyear) Atlantic; –5 (–4 midyear) Eastern, including Québec and Ontario; –6 (–5 midyear) Central; except Saskatchewan; –6 Saskatchewan; –7 (–6 midyear) Mountain; –8 (–7 midyear) Pacific, including Yukon.

📻**Canadian Broadcasting Corporation (CBC)—English Programs**, P.O. Box 500, Station A, Toronto, Ontario, M5W 1E6, Canada. Phone: (Audience Relations) +1 (416) 205-3700. Email: cbcinput@toronto.cbc.ca. Web: (includes RealAudio) www.radio.cbc.ca. CBC prepares some of the programs heard over Radio Canada International (see).
LONDON NEWS BUREAU: CBC, 43-51 Great Titchfield Street, London W1P 8DD, England. Phone: +44 (20) 7412-9200. Fax: +44 (20) 7631 3095.
PARIS NEWS BUREAU: CBC, 17 avenue Matignon, F-75008 Paris, France. Phone: +33 (1) 4421-1515. Fax: +33 (1) 4421 1514.
WASHINGTON NEWS BUREAU: CBC, National Press Building, Suite 500, 529 14th Street NW, Washington DC 20045 USA. Phone: +1 (202) 383-2900. Contact: Jean-Louis Arcand, David Hall or Susan Murray.

📻**Canadian Broadcasting Corporation (CBC)—French Programs**, Société Radio-Canada, C.P. 6000, succ. centre-ville, Montréal, Québec, H3C 3A8, Canada. Phone: (Audience Relations) +1 (514) 597-6000. Welcomes correspondence sent to this address but may not reply due to shortage of staff. CBC prepares some of the programs heard over Radio Canada International (see).
CBC Northern Québec Shortwave Service—*see* Radio Canada International, below.

📻**CFRX-CFRB**
MAIN ADDRESS: 2 St. Clair Avenue West, Toronto, Ontario, M4V 1L6, Canada. Phone:(main switchboard) +1 (416) 924-5711; (talk shows switchboard) +1 (416) 872-1010; (news centre) +1 (416) 924-6717; (CFRB information access line) +1 (416) 872-2372. Fax: (main fax line) +1 (416) 323 6830; (CFRB news fax line) +1 (416) 323 6816. Email: (comments on programs) cfrbcomments@cfrb.com; (News Director) news@cfrb.com; (general, nontechnical) info@cfrb.com; or opsmngr@cfrb.com; (technical) ian.sharp@cfrb.com. Web: (includes MP3) www.cfrb.com. Contact: (nontechnical) Carlo Massaro, Information Officer; or Steve Kowch, Operations Manager; (technical) Ian Sharp, Technical Supervisor. Reception reports should be sent to the verification address, below.
VERIFICATION ADDRESS: Ontario DX Association, 155 Main St. N., Apt. 313, Newmarket, Ontario, L3Y 8C2, Canada. Email: (including CFRB/CFRX reception reports) odxa@rogers.com. Web: www.odxa.on.ca. Contact: Steve Canney, VA3SC. ODXA is offering a three month free trial membership to the email version of *Listening In* which is the clubs monthly magazine. Contact them for the trial membership via their email address listed above.

CFVP-CKMX, AM 1060, Standard Broadcasting, P.O. Box 2750, Station 'M', Calgary, Alberta, T2P 4P8, Canada. Phone: (general) +1 (403) 240-5800; (news) +1 (403) 240-5844; (technical) +1 (403) 240-5867. Fax: (general and technical) +1 (403) 240 5801; (news) +1 (403) 246 7099. Contact: (general) Gary Russell, General Manager; or Beverley Van Tighem, Executive Assistant; (technical) Ken Pasolli, Technical Director.
CHU. Radio Station CHU, National Research Council of Canada, 1200 Montreal Road, Bldg M-36, Ottawa, Ontario, K1A 0R6, Canada. Phone: +1 (613) 993-5186. Fax: +1 (613) 952 1394. Email: radio.chu@nrc.ca. Web: http://inms-ienm.nrc-cnrc.gc.ca/time_services/shortwave_broadcasts_e.html. Contact: Dr. Rob Douglas; Dr. Jean-Simon Boulanger, Group Leader; or Ray Pelletier, Technical Officer. Official standard frequency and World Time station for Canada on 3330, 7335 and 14670 kHz. Brochure available upon request. Those with a personal computer, Bell 103 compatible modem and appropriate software can get the exact time, from CHU's cesium clock, via the telephone; details available upon request, or direct from the Website. Verifies reception reports with a QSL card.
📻**CKZN**, CBC Newfoundland and Labrador, P.O. Box 12010, Station 'A', St. John's, Newfoundland, A1B 3T8, Canada. Phone: +1 (709) 576-5155. Fax: +1 (709) 576 5099. Email: (administration) radiomgt@stjohns.cbc.ca; (engineer) keith_durnford@cbc.ca. Web: (includes RealAudio) www.stjohns.cbc.ca. Contact: (general) Heather Elliott, Communications Officer; (technical) Shawn R. Williams, Manager, Transmission and Distribution; Keith Durnford, Supervisor, Transmission Operations; Terry Brett, Transmitter Department; or Rosemary Sampson. Free CBC sticker and verification card with the history of Newfoundland included. Don't enclose money, stamps or IRCs with correspondence, as they will only have to be returned. Relays CBN (St. John's, 640 kHz) except at 1000-1330 World Time (one hour earlier in summer) when programming comes from CFGB Goose Bay.
CFGB ADDRESS: CBC Radio, Box 1029 Station 'C', Happy Valley, Goose Bay, Labrador, Newfoundland A0P 1C0, Canada.
📻**CKZU-CBU**, CBC, P.O. Box 4600, Vancouver, British Columbia, V6B 4A2, Canada—for verification of reception reports, mark the envelope, "Attention: Engineering." Phone: (general) +1 (604) 662-6000; (toll-free, U.S. and Canada only) 1-800-961-6161; (engineering) +1 (604) 662-6060. Fax: +1 (604) 662 6350. Email: (general) webmaster@vancouver.cbc.ca; (Newbury) newburyd@vancouver.cbc.ca. Web: (includes RealAudio) www.vancouver.cbc.ca. Contact: (general) Public Relations; (technical) Dave Newbury, Transmission Engineer.
High Adventure Gospel Communication Ministries—*see* Bible Voice Broadcasting, United Kingdom.

📻**Radio Canada International**
NOTE: (CBC Northern Québec Service) The following P. O Box 6000 postal address and street address are also valid for the Northern Québec Service, provided that you mention the name of the service and "17th Floor" on the envelope. RCI does not issue technical verifications for Northern Québec Service transmissions.
MAIN OFFICE: P.O. Box 6000, Montréal, Québec, H3C 3A8, Canada; or (street address) 1400 boulevard René Lévesque East, Level B Montréal, Québec, H2L 2M2, Canada. Phone: (general) +1 (514) 597-7500; (Audience Relations, Bill Westenhaver) +1 (514) 597-5899. Fax: (Audience Relations) +1 (514) 597 7760. Email: info@rcinet.ca. Web: (includes RealAudio, Window Media & MP3) www.rcinet.ca. Contact: (general and technical verifications) Bill Westenhaver, Audience Relations; Stéphane Parent, Producer/Host "Le courrier

mondial"; or Ian Jones, Producer/Host "The Maple Leaf Mailbag"; (administration) Jean Larin, Director. Free stickers & lapel pins on request.

TRANSMISSION OFFICE, INTERNATIONAL SERVICES, CBC TRANSMISSION: Room: B52-70, 1400 boulevard René Lévesque East, Montréal, Québec, H2L 2M2, Canada. Phone: +1 (514) 597-7618/19. Fax: +1 (514) 284 2052. Email: (Théorêt) gerald_theoret@radio-canada.ca; (Bouliane) jacques_bouliane@radio-canada.ca. Contact: (general) Gérald Théorêt, Frequency Manager, CBC Transmission Management; or Ms. Nicole Vincent, Frequency Management, (administration) Jacques Bouliane, Senior Manager, International Services. This office only for informing about transmitter-related problems (interference, modulation quality, etc.), especially by fax. Verifications not given out at this office; requests for verification should be sent to the main office, above.

TRANSMITTER SITE: CBC, P.O. Box 6131, Sackville New Brunswick, E4L 1G6, Canada. Phone: +1 (506) 536-2690/1. Fax: +1 (506) 536 2342. Contact: Raymond Bristol, Sackville Plant Manager, CBC Transmission. All correspondence not concerned with transmitting equipment should be directed to the appropriate address in Montréal, above. Free tours given during normal working hours.

MONITORING STATION: P.O. Box 460, Station Main Stittsville, Ontario, K2S 1A6, Canada. Phone: +1 (613) 831-4802. Fax: +1 (613) 831 0343. Email: derek.williams@cbc.ca. Contact: Derek Williams, Manager of Monitoring.

Radio Monte-Carlo Middle East (via Radio Canada International)—*see* France.

Shortwave Classroom, R. Tait McKenzie Public School, 175 Paterson Street, Almonte, Ontario, K0A 1A0, Canada. Phone: +1 (613) 256-8248. Fax: +1 (613) 256 4791. Email: neil.carletonn@ucdsb.on.ca. Contact: Neil Carleton, VE3NCE, Editor & Publisher. *The Shortwave Classroom* newsletter was published three times per year as a nonprofit volunteer project for teachers around the world that use shortwave listening in the classroom, or as a club activity, to teach about global perspectives, media studies, world geography, languages, social studies and other subjects. Although no longer published, a set of back issues with articles and classroom tips from teachers around the globe is available for $10.

CENTRAL AFRICAN REPUBLIC   World Time +1

Radio Centrafrique, Radiodiffusion-Télévision Centrafricaine, B.P. 940, Bangui, Central African Republic. Contact: (technical) Jacques Mbilo, Le Directeur des Services Techniques; or Michèl Bata, Services Techniques. Replies on rare occasions to correspondence in French. Return postage required.

Radio Ndeke Luka, PNUD, B.P. 872, Bangui, Central African Republic. Email: ndekeluka@hotmail.com. Contact: Cédrine Beney, Chargée de projet. Replies to correspondence in French, and may reply in French to correspondence in English. The station is managed by the Fondation Hirondelle, based in Switzerland, and operates under the aegis of the United Nations, in partnership with the UNDP (United Nations Development Programme). Its main transmitting studio is located in Bangui. Broadcasts domestically on FM, and produces a program aired via shortwave facilities in the United Kingdom or the United Arab Emirates, depending on the time of year.

FONDATION HIRONDELLE: 3 Rue Traversière, CH 1018-Lausanne, Switzerland. Phone: +41 (21) 647-2805. Fax: +41 (21) 647 4469. Email info@hirondelle.org. Web: www.hirondelle.org. Verifies reception reports.

CHAD   World Time +1

Radiodiffusion Nationale Tchadienne—N'djamena, B.P. 892, N'Djamena, Chad. Contact: Djimadoum Ngoka Kilamian; or Ousmane Mahamat. Two IRCs or return postage required. Replies slowly to correspondence in French.

CHILE   World Time –3 (–4 midyear)

Radio Esperanza

OFFICE: Casilla 830, Temuco, Chile. Phone: +56 (45) 213-790. Phone/Fax: +56 (45) 367-070. Email: esperanza@telsur.cl. Web: www.acym.cl/radio.htm. Contact: (general) Juanita Cárcamo, Departmento de Programación; Eleazar Jara, Dpto. de Programación; Ramón P. Woerner K., Publicidad; or Alberto Higueras Martínez, Locutor; (verifications) Rodolfo Campos, Director; Juanita Carmaco M., Dpto. de Programación; (technical) Juan Luis Puentes, Dpto. Técnico. Free pennants, stickers, bookmarks and tourist information. Two IRCs, $1 or 2 U.S. stamps appreciated. Replies, often slowly, to correspondence in Spanish or English.

STUDIO: Calle Luis Durand 03057, Temuco, Chile. Phone/Fax: +56 (45) 240-161.

Radio Parinacota, Casilla 82, Arica, Chile. Phone: +56 (58) 245-889. Phone/Fax: +56 (58) 245 986. Email: rparinacota@latinmail.com. Contact: Tomislav Simunovich Gran, Director.

Radio Voz Cristiana

ENGINEERING DEPARTMENT: Ryder Street, West Bromwich, West Midlands B70 0EJ, United Kingdom. Phone: +44 (121) 522-6087. Fax: +44 (121) 522 6083. Email: andrewflynn@ christianvision.com. Contact: Andrew Flynn, Head of Engineering.

TRANSMISSION FACILITIES: Casilla 395, Talagante, Santiago, Chile. Phone: (Engineering) +56 (2) 855-7046. Fax: +56 (2) 855 7053. Email: (Chief Engineer) antonio@vozcristiana.cl; (Frequency Manager) andrewflynn@christianvision.com; (Administration) admin@vozcristiana.cl. Contact: Antonio Reyes, Chief Engineer; Gisela Vergara, Transmissions Senior Engineer. Free program and frequency schedules. Sometimes sends small souvenirs. All QSL requests should be sent to the Miami address, below.

PROGRAM PRODUCTION: P.O. Box 2889, Miami FL 33144 USA; or (street address) 15485 Eagle Nest Lane, Suite 220, Miami Lakes FL 33014 USA. Phone: +1 (305) 231-7704; (Portuguese Service) +1 (305) 231-7742. Fax: +1 (305) 231 7447. Email: (listener feedback) comentarios@vozcristiana.com; (González) david@vozcristiana.com; (Portuguese Service) cv-usa@msn.com. Web: (includes RealAudio) www.vozcristiana.com. Contact: (administration) Juan Mark Gallardo, Director Regional; (technical and nontechnical) David González, Gerente de Programación. Verifies reception reports.

CHINA   World Time +8; still nominally +6 ("Urümqi Time") in the Xinjiang Uighur Autonomous Region, but in practice +8 is observed there, as well.

NOTE: China Radio International, the Central People's Broadcasting Station and certain regional outlets reply regularly to listeners' letters in a variety of languages. If a Chinese regional station does not respond to your correspondence within four months—and many will not, unless your letter is in Chinese or the regional dialect—try writing them c/o China Radio International.

Central People's Broadcasting Station (CPBS)—China National Radio (Zhongyang Renmin Guangbo Diantai), P.O.

Box 4501, Beijing 100866, China. Phone: +86 (10) 6851-2435 or +86 (10) 6851-5522. Fax: +86 (10) 6851 6630. Email: zhangzr@mail.cnradio.com.cn. Web: (includes RealAudio) www.cnradio.com; (services for Taiwan) www.nihaotw.com. Contact: Wang Changquan, Audience Department, China National Radio. Tape recordings of music and news $5 plus postage. CPBS T-shirts $10 plus postage; also sells ties and other items with CPBS logo. No credit cards. Free stickers, pennants and other small souvenirs. Return postage helpful. Responds regularly to correspondence in English and Standard Chinese (Mandarin). Although in recent years this station has officially been called "China National Radio" in English-language documents, all on-air identifications in Standard Chinese continue to be "Zhongyang Renmin Guangbo Dientai" (Central People's Broadcasting Station). To quote from the Website of China's State Administration of Radio, Film and TV: "The station moved to Beijing on March 25, 1949. It was renamed the Central People's Broadcasting Station (it [sic] English name was changed to China National Radio later on)..."

China Huayi Broadcasting Corporation, P.O. Box 251, Fuzhou, Fujian 350001, China. Email: (station) fm1071@chbcnews.com; (Yuan Jia) chrisyuanjia@sohu.com; (Qiao Xiaoli, reception reports) 2883752@163.com, dxswl@21cn.com. Web: (includes Windows Media) www.chbcnews.com (or www.chbc.cn). Contact: Lin Hai Chun, Announcer; Qiao Xiaoli QSL Manager; Yuan Jia, Program Manager; or Wu Gehong. Replies to correspondence in English and Chinese. Reception reports can be sent to Qiao Xiaoli, Feng Jing Xin Cun 3-4-304, Changshu, Jiangsu 215500, China (although verifications are sometimes received direct from the station). Return postage necessary and recordings accepted.

China National Radio—*see* Central People's Broadcasting Station (CPBS), above.

China Radio International

MAIN OFFICE, NON-CHINESE LANGUAGES SERVICE: 16A Shijingshan Street, Beijing 100040, China; or P.O. Box 4216, CRI-2 Beijing 100040 China. Phone: (Director's office) +86 (10) 6889-1625; (Audience Relations.) +86 (10) 6889-1617 or +86 (10) 6889-1652; (English newsroom/current affairs) +86 (10) 6889-1619; (Technical Director) +86 (10) 6609-2577. Fax: (Director's office) +86 (10) 6889 1582; (English Service) +86 (10) 6889 1378 or +86 (10) 6889 1379; (Audience Relations) +86 (10) 6889 3175; (administration) +86 (10) 6851 3174; (German Service) +86 (10) 6889 2053; (Spanish Service) +86 (10) 6889 1909. Email: (English) crieng@cri.com.cn; yinglian@cri.com.cn or msg@cri.com.cn; (Chinese) chn@cri.com.cn; (German) ger@box.cri.com.cn (*see* also the entry for the Berlin Bureau, below); (Japanese) jap@cri.com.cn; (Spanish) spa@cri.com.cn; ("Voices from Other Lands" program) voices@box.cri.com.cn. Web: (official, includes RealAudio) www.cri.com.cn; www.cirenglish.com; www.cri.cn; www.chinabroadcast.cn; (unofficial, but regularly updated) http://pw2.netcom.com/~jleq/cri1.htm. Contact: Ms. Wang Anjing, Director of Audience Relations, English Service; Ying Lian, English Service; Shang Chunyan, "Listener's Garden"; Yu Meng, Editor; or Li Ping, Director of English Service; (administration) Li Dan, President, China Radio International; Xia Jixuan, Chen Minyi, Chao Tieqi and Wang Dongmei, Deputy Directors, China Radio International; Xin Liancai, Director International Relations, China Radio International. Free bi-monthly *Messenger* newsletter for loyal listeners, pennants, stickers, desk calendars, pins and handmade papercuts. Every year, China Radio International holds contests and quizzes, with the overall winner getting a free trip to China. T-shirts for $8. Two-volume,

820-page set of *Day-to-Day Chinese* language-lesson books $15, including postage worldwide; a 155-page book, *Learn to Speak Chinese: Sentence by Sentence*, plus two cassettes for $15. Two Chinese music tapes for $15. Various other books (on arts, medicine, Chinese idioms etc.) in English available from Audience Relations Department, English Service, China Radio International, 100040 Beijing, China. Payment by postal money order to Mr. Li Yi. Every year, the Audience Relations Department will renew the mailing list of the *Messenger* newsletter. CRI is also relayed via shortwave transmitters in Canada, Cuba, France, French Guiana, Mali, Russia and Spain.

ARLINGTON NEWS BUREAU: 2000 South Eads Street APT#712, Arlington VA 22202 USA. Phone: +1 (703) 521-8689. Contact: Mr. Yongjing Li.

BERLIN BUREAU: Berliner Büro, Gürtelstr. 32 B, D-10247 Berlin, Germany. Phone: +49 (30) 2966-8998. Fax: +49 (30) 2966 8997. Email: deyubu@hotmail.com. Correspondence to CRI's German Service can be sent to this office.

CHINA (HONG KONG) NEWS BUREAU: 387 Queen's Road East, Room 1503, Hong Kong, China. Phone: +852 2834-0384. Contact: Ms. He Jincao.

JERUSALEM NEWS BUREAU: Flat 16, Hagdud Ha'ivri 12, Jerusalem 92345, Israel. Phone: +972 (2) 566-6084. Contact: Ms. Liu Suyun.

LONDON NEWS BUREAU: 13B Clifton Gardens, Golders Green, London NW11 7ER, United Kingdom. Phone: +44 (20) 8458-6943. Contact: Ms. Wu Manling.

NEW YORK NEWS BUREAU: 630 First Avenue #35K, New York NY 10016 USA. Fax: +1 (212) 889 2076. Contact: Mr Qian Jun.

SYDNEY NEWS BUREAU: Unit 53, Block A15 Herbert Street, St. Leonards NSW 2065, Australia. Phone: +61 (2) 9436-1493. Contact: Mr. Yang Binyuan.

SAN FRANCISCO OFFICE, SCHEDULES: 2654 17th Avenue, San Francisco CA 94116 USA. Phone: +1 (415) 564-9968. Email: GPoppin@aol.com. Contact: George Poppin. This address, a volunteer office, only provides CRI schedules to listeners. All other correspondence should be sent directly to the main office in Beijing.

FREQUENCY PLANNING DIVISION: Radio and Television of People's Republic of China, 2 Fuxingmenwai Street, Beijing 100866, China; or P.O. Box 2144, Beijing 100866, China. Phone: (Yang Minmin) +86 (10) 8606-2064; or (Zheng Shuguang & Pang Junhua) +86 (10) 8069-2120. Fax: +86 (10) 6609 2176. Email: (Yang Minmin) pdc@abrs.chinasartft. Contact: Ms. Yang Minmin, Manager, Frequency Coordination; Mr. Zheng Shuguang, Frequency Manager; Mrs. Ling Li Wen, Frequency Manager; or Ms. Pang Junhua, Frequency Manager.

MAIN OFFICE, CHINESE LANGUAGES SERVICE: China Radio International, Beijing 100040, China. Prefers correspondence in Chinese (Mandarin).

MONITORING CENTER: 2 Fuxingmenwai Street, Beijing 100866, China or P.O Box 4502 Beijing 100866, China. Phone: +86 (10) 8609-1745/6. Fax: +86 (10) 8609 2176 or +86 (10) 8609 3269. Email: mc@chinasarft.gov.cn or jczhxjch@public.fhnet.cn.net. Contact: Ms. Zhang Wei, Chief Engineer, Monitoring Department; Zhao Chengping, Monitoring Manager; or Ms. Xu Tao, Deputy Director of Monitoring Department.

Fujian People's Broadcasting Station, 2 Gutian Lu, Fuzhou, Fujian 350001, China. $1 or IRC helpful. Contact: Audience Relations. Replies occasionally and usually slowly. Prefers correspondence in Chinese.

Gannan People's Broadcasting Station, 49 Renmin Xije, Hezuo Zhen, Xiahe, Gian Su 747000, China. Verifies reception reports written in English. Return postage not required.

Gansu People's Broadcasting Station, 226 Donggang Xilu, Lanzhou 730000, China. Phone: +86 (931) 841-1054. Fax: +86 (931) 882 5834. Contact: Li Mei. IRC helpful.

Guangxi Foreign Broadcasting Station, 12 Min Zu Avenue, Nanning, Guangxi 530022, China. Phone: +86 (771) 585-4191, +86 (771) 585-4256 or +86 (771) 585-4403. Email: 101@gxfbs.com or 103@gxfbs.com; (Thanh Mai) thanhmai@gxfbs.com. Web: www.gxfbs.com. Contact: Thanh Mai, Vietnamese Section. Free stickers and handmade papercuts. IRC helpful. Replies irregularly. Broadcasts in Vietnamese and Cantonese to listeners in Vietnam.

Guangxi People's Broadcasting Station (if reactivated), 75 Min Zu Avenue, Nanning, Guangxi 530022, China. Email: gxbs@public.nn.gx.cn. Web: www.gxpbs.com. IRC helpful. Replies irregularly.

Guizhou People's Broadcasting Station (when operating), 259 Qingyun Lu, Guiyang, Guizhou 550002, China. Phone: +86 (851) 582-2495. Fax: +86 (851) 586 9983.

Heilongjiang People's Broadcasting Station, 181 Zhongshan Lu, Harbin, Heilongjiang 150001, China. Phone: +86 (451) 8289-3443. Fax: +86 (451) 8289 3539. Email: am621@sina.com. Web: (includes RealAudio) www.am621.com.cn. $1 or return postage helpful.

☞Hubei People's Broadcasting Station, 563 Jiefang Dadao, Wuhan, Hubei 430022, China. Web: (includes RealAudio) www.hbradio.com.cn.

Hunan People's Broadcasting Station, 27 Yuhua Lu, Changsha, Hunan 410007, China. Phone: +86 (731) 554-7202. Fax: +86 (731) 554 7220.

Jiangxi People's Broadcasting Station, 111 Hongdu Zhong Dadao, Nanchang, Jiangxi 330046, China. Email: gfzq@public.nc.jx.cn. Contact: Tang Ji Sheng, Editor, Chief Editor's Office. Free gold/red pins. Replies irregularly. Mr. Tang enjoys music, literature and stamps, so enclosing a small memento along these lines should help assure a speedy reply.

☞Nei Menggu (Inner Mongolia) People's Broadcasting Station, 19 Xinhua Darjie, Hohhot, Nei Menggu 010058, China. Web: (includes RealAudio) www.nmrb.cn. Contact: Zhang Xiang-Quen, Secretary; or Liang Yan. Replies irregularly.

Qinghai People's Broadcasting Station, 96 Kunlun Lu, Xining, Qinghai 810001, China. Contact: Liqing Fangfang; or Ghou Guo Liang, Director, Technical Department. $1 helpful.

Radio Television Hong Kong (when operating), C.P.O Box 70200, Kowloon, Hong Kong, China. Broadcasts weather reports for the South China Sea Yacht Race on 3940 kHz. Website for the race is: www.rhkyc.org.hk./chinacoastraceweek.htm.

CAPE D'AGUILAR HF STATION: P.O. Box 9896, GPO Hong Kong, China. Phone: +852 2888-1128. Fax: +852 2809 2434. Contact: Lam Chi Keung, Assistant Engineer or Ailsa Angus, Sailing Manager. This station provides the transmission facilities for the weather reports on the South China Sea Yacht Race. See previous entry.

Sichuan People's Broadcasting Station, 119-1 Hongxing Zhonglu, Chengdu, Sichuan 610017, China. Web: www.swww.com.cn/scsb. Replies occasionally.

Voice of Jinling (Jinling zhi Sheng), P.O. Box 268, Nanjing, Jiangsu 210002, China. Fax: +86 (25) 413 235. Contact: Strong Lee, Producer/Host, "Window of Taiwan." Free stickers and calendars, plus Chinese-language color station brochure and information on the Nanjing Technology Import and Export Corporation. Replies to correspondence in Chinese and to simple correspondence in English. $1, IRC or 1 yuan Chinese stamp required for return postage.

Jean-Gabriel Manguy, head of Radio Australia, greets local official Bruce Wilson at the 60th anniversary of RA's Shepparton facility. M. Hemetsberger

Voice of Pujiang (Pujiang zhi Sheng), P.O. Box 3064, Shanghai 200002, China. Phone: +86 (21) 6208-2797. Fax: +86 (21) 6208 2850. Contact: Jiang Bimiao, Editor and Reporter.

☞Voice of the Straits (Haixia zhi Sheng), P.O. Box 187, Fuzhou, Fujian 350012, China. Email: (English) vos@am666.net. Web: (includes RealAudio) www.vos.com.cn; (English) www.am666.net/enroot. Replies irregularly to correspondence in English.

Wenzhou People's Broadcasting Station, 19 Xianxue Qianlu, Wenzhou, Zhejiang 325000, China.

Xilingol People's Broadcasting Station, Xilin Dajie, Xilinhot, Nei Menggu 026000, China.

☞Xinjiang People's Broadcasting Station, 84 Tuanjie Lu, Urümqi, Xinjiang 830044, China. Phone: +86 (991) 256-1565. Email: mw738@21cn.com or habar@21cn.com. Web: (includes RealAudio) www.xjbs.com.cn. Contact: Zhao Ji-shu or Ms. Zhao Donglan, Editorial Office. Free tourist booklet, postcards and used Chinese stamps. Replies to correspondence in Chinese and to simple correspondence in English.

Xizang People's Broadcasting Station, 180 Beijing Zhonglu, Lhasa, Xizang 850000, China. Web: http://tibet.goldinfo.com.cn/diantai/diantai.htm. Contact: Lobsang Chonphel, Announcer; Tse Ring Yuzen, President; Tse Ring DeKy; or Miss Wenxin, host of "Tonight's Appointment" program. Free stickers and brochures. Enclosing an English-language magazine may help with a reply. Sometimes announces itself in English as "China Tibet Broadcasting Company" or "Tibet China Broadcasting Station."

"HOLY TIBET" ENGLISH PROGRAM: Foreign Affairs Office, China Tibet People's Broadcasting Company, 850000 Lhasa, China. Two IRCs requested. Contact: Mo Shuji; or Tse Shen

Yunnan People's Broadcasting Station, 73 Renmin Xilu, Central Building of Broadcasting and TV, Kunming, 650031 Yunnan, China. Phone: +86 (871) 531-0270. Fax: +86 (871) 531 0360. Contact: Sheng Hongpeng or F.K. Fan. Free Chi-

Carlson Wong interviews Erik Betterman, Director General of Deutsche Welle, for Radio Taiwan International's "Taipei Magazine." RTI

nese-language brochure on Yunnan Province, but no QSL cards. $1 or return postage helpful. Replies occasionally.
Zhejiang People's Broadcasting Station, 111 Moganshan Lu, Hangzhou, Zhejiang 310005, China. Phone: +86 (571) 807-7050. Email: radiozjy@163.com. Contact: Yin Weiling, Editor.

CHINA (TAIWAN)   World Time +8

Central Broadcasting System (CBS), 55 Pei'an Road, Tachih, Taipei 104, Taiwan, Republic of China. Phone: +886 (2) 2591-8161. Email: cbs@cbs.org.tw. Web: (includes RealAudio) www.cbs.org.tw. Contact: Lee Ming, Deputy Director. Free stickers.
China Radio, 53 Min Chuan West Road 9th Floor, Taipei 10418, Taiwan. Phone: +886 (2) 2598-1009. Fax: +886 (2) 2598 8348. Email: (Adams) readams@usa.net. Contact: Richard E. Adams, Station Director. Verifies reception reports. A religious broadcaster, sometimes referred to as "True Light Station," transmitting via leased facilities in Petropavlovsk-Kamchatskiy, Russia.
Radio Taiwan International (RTI), P.O. Box 24-38 (or P.O. Box 24-777), Taipei 106, Taiwan, Republic of China; (street address) 55 Pei-an Road, Taipei 104, Taiwan, Republic of China. Phone: +886 (2) 2885-6168, X-385 or X-387. Fax: +886 (2) 2886 2294 or +886 (2) 2886 7088. Email: cbs@cbs.org.tw or prog@cbs.org.tw. Web: (includes RealAudio and online reception report form) www.cbs.org.tw. Contact: (general)Wayne Wang Tao-Fang, Chief of International Affairs Section; (administration) Ling Feng-Jenq, Chairman; (technical) Peter Lee, Manager, Engineering Department. Free stickers. May send an annual diary, other publications and an occasional surprise gift. Broadcasts to the Americas are relayed via WYFR's Okeechobee site in the USA. Also uses relay facilities in France and the United Kingdom. RTI is the international arm of its parent organization, the Central Broadcasting System. Formerly known as Radio Taipei International.
BERLIN OFFICE: Postfach 30 92 43, D-10760 Berlin, Germany.
DAKAR OFFICE: B.P. 6867, Dakar, Senegal.
HANOI OFFICE: G.P.O Box 104 Hanoi, Vietnam.

NEW DELHI OFFICE: P. O. Box 4914, Safdarjung Enclave, New Delhi, 110 029 India.
SURABAYA OFFICE: P.O. Box 1024, Surabaya, 60008 Indonesia.
Voice of Han, 5F. No.3, Hsiu-Yi Road, Sec.1, Taipei, Taiwan, Republic of China. Phone: +886 (2) 2321-5053. Fax: +886 (2) 2393 0970. Email: voh_radio@sinamail.com. Web: (includes Windows Media) www.voh.com.tw.

CLANDESTINE

Clandestine broadcasts are often subject to abrupt change or termination. Being operated by anti-establishment political and/or military organizations, these groups tend to be suspicious of outsiders' motives. Thus, they are more likely to reply to contacts from those who communicate in the station's native tongue, and who are perceived to be at least somewhat favorably disposed to their cause. Most will provide, upon request, printed matter on their cause, though not necessarily in English.

For more detailed information on clandestine stations, refer to the annual publication, *Clandestine Stations List*, about $10 or 10 IRCs postpaid by air, published by the Danish Shortwave Clubs International, Tavleager 31, DK-2670 Greve, Denmark; phone (Denmark) +45 4290-2900; fax (via Germany) +49 6371 71790; email 100413.2375@compuserve.com. For CIA media contact information, *see* USA. Available on the Internet, *The Clandestine Radio Intel Webpage* specializes in background information on these stations and is organized by region and target country. The page can be accessed at: www.ClandestineRadio.com. Another informative Web page specializing in clandestine radio information and containing a twice monthly report on the latest news and developments affecting the study of clandestine radio is *Clandestine Radio Watch*, found at www.listen.to/qip.
"Arab Radio." Web: (includes RealAudio and Windows Media) www.arabicsyradio.org. Successor to the former "Voice of the Homeland" and opposes the Syrian government.
"Degar Radio," Montagnard Foundation, Inc., P.O. Box 171114, Spartanburg SC 29301 USA. Phone: +1 (864) 576-

0698. Fax: +1 (864) 595 1940. Email: degar@montagnard-foundation.org; (Kok Sor) kksor@montagnard-foundation.org. Web: (Montagnard Foundation parent organization) www.montagnard-foundation.org. Contact: Kok Sor, President, Montagnard Foundation.

☞"**Dejen Radio**" (when operating), Liberty Bell Communications, Inc., P.O. Box 792, Indianapolis IN 46206-0792 USA. Email: dejen@ethiopiancommentator.com. Web: (RealAudio) www.ethiopiancommentator.com/dejenradio.

☞"**Democratic Voice of Burma**" ("Democratic Myanmar a-Than"), P.O. Box 6720, St. Olavs Plass, N-0130 Oslo, Norway. Phone: (Director/Chief Editor) +47 (22) 868-486; (Aministration) +47 (22) 868-472. Email: (general) comment@dvb.no; (Director) director@dvb.no; (technical problems) comments@dvb.no. Web: (includes RealAudio and MP3) www.dvb.no. Contact: (general) Dr. Anng Kin, Listener Liaison; Aye Chan Naing, Daily Editor; or Thida, host for "Songs Request Program"; (administration) Harn Yawnghwe, Director; or Daw Khin Pyone, Manager; (technical) Saw Neslon Ku, Studio Technician; Petter Bernsten; or Technical Dept. Norwegian kroner requested for a reply, but presumably Norwegian mint stamps would also suffice. Programs produced by Burmese democratic movements, as well as professional and independent radio journalists, to provide informational and educational services for the democracy movement inside and outside Burma. Opposes the current Myanmar government. Transmitted originally via facilities in Norway, but more recently has broadcast from sites in Germany, Madagascar and Central Asia.

"**Minivan Radio.**" Promotes human rights in the Maldives and is opposed to the present government. Transmits via facilities of Germany's T-Systems International (see).

FRIENDS OF MALDIVES SPONSORING ORGANIZATION: 64 Milford Street, Salisbury SP1 2BP, United Kingdom. Phone: +44 (1722) 504-330. Email: admin@friendsofmaldives.co.uk. Web: www.friendsofmaldives.co.uk.

☞"**Hmong Lao Radio**," P.O. Box 6426, St. Paul MN 55106 USA. Phone: +1 (651) 292-0774. Fax: +1 (651) 292 0795. Email: (Lor) blor@hmonglaoradio.org; (Vang) cvang@hmonglaoradio.org. Web: (includes Windows Media) www.hmonglaoradio.org. Contact: Bee Lor; or Cha Vang. Verifies reception reports. Transmits via facilities in the United Kingdom and Taiwan.

"**Information Radio**" (when operating), 193rd Special Operations Wing, 81 Constellation Court, Middletown PA 17057 USA. Email: (Shank) edward.shank@paharr.ang.af.mil. Web: (193rd Special Operation Wing parent organization) www.paharr.ang.af.mil. Contact: Lt. Edward Shank, Public Affairs Officer. Psy-ops station operated by the 193rd Special Operations Wing of the Pennsylvania Air National Guard.

"**Information Radio**" (when operating). Email: (including reception reports) marlo@nsa.bahrain.navy.mil. Supposedly operates from ships in the Persian Gulf and Horn of Africa. Identifies as "Radio One" in English, but as "Information Radio" in other languages.

"**National Radio of the Democratic Saharan Arab Republic**"—see Radio Nacional de la República Arabe Saharaui Democrática, Western Sahara.

☞"**Radio Anternacional**," BM Box 1499, London WC1N 3XX, United Kingdom. Phone: +44 (20) 8962-2707. Fax: +44 (20) 8346 2203. Email: radio7520@yahoo.com; (Majedi) azarmajedi@yahoo.com. Web: (includes Windows Media) www.radio-international.org. Contact: Ms. Azar Majedi. Broadcast via a transmitter in Moldova. Has ties to the Worker-Communist Party of Iran.

"**Radio Free Afghanistan**"—see USA.

"**Radio Free Bougainville**" (when operating), 2 Griffith Avenue, Roseville NSW 2069, Australia. Phone/Fax: +61 (2) 9417-1066. Email: svoron@hotmail.com. Contact: Sam Voron, Australian Director. $5, AUS$5 or 5 IRCs required. Station is operated from Panguna, Central Bougainville by members of the Mekamui Defence Force led by Francis Ona. Opposed to the Papua New Guinea government.

"**Radio Free Syria**," Reform Party of Syria, P. O. Box 59730, Potomac, MD 20859 USA. Phone: +1 (301) 346-5000. Fax: +1 (301) 299 4955. Email: (English) webmaster@radiofreesyria.org; (Arabic) admin@radiofreesyria.net. Web: www.radiofreesyria.org; (Reform Party of Syria parent organization) www.reformsyria.org. Opposes the Ba'ath government of Syria. Transmits via facilities of Germany's T-Systems International (see).

"**Radio Freedom, Voice of the Ogadeni People**"—see "Radio Xoriyo"

"**Radio Independent Makumi**" (when operating)—see "Radio Free Bougainville" (which is sometimes operated under this name) for contact details.

"**Radio International**"—see "Radio Anternacional."

"**Radio Komala**" (when operating), c/o Representation of Komala Abroad, Postfach 800272, D-51002 Köln, Germany. Email: komala_radio@hotmail.com; radiokomala@komala.org. Web: www.komala.org. Replies to correspondence in English. Komala, one of the founder members of the Communist Party of Iran in 1982, left that organization in 2000. It now refers to itself in English as the "Revolutionary Organization of the People of Kurdistan."

"**Radio Nacional de la República Arabe Saharaui Democrática**"—see Western Sahara.

"**Radio New Sudan**," SNA/SAF, Culture and Information Office, Neguse Street Nr. 6/8 (or P.O. Box 9257), Asmara, Eritrea. Email: infosaf@eol.com.er. Web: (Sudan Alliance Forces) www.safsudan.com. Contact: Amir Babkir, Sudan Alliance Forces Secretary for Culture and Information. The Sudan Alliance Forces are an opposition guerrilla army of ex-government northern soldiers, affiliated to the Asmara, Eritrea-based National Democratic Alliance (NDA). Opposes the current Sudan government. Claims to operate in liberated areas on the Sudanese side of the Sudan-Eritrea border, but actual site seems to be in Asmara, Eritrea. Formerly known as "Voice of Freedom and Renewal."

"**Radio One**"—see "Information Radio" (second entry).

"**Radio Payam-e Dost**" (Bahá'í Radio International), P.O. Box 765, Great Falls VA 22066 USA. Phone: +1 (703) 671-8888. Fax: +1 (301) 292 6947. Email: payam@bahairadio.org. Web: www.bahairadio.org.

"**Radio Rainbow**" ("Kestedamena rediyo ye selamena yewendimamach dimtse"), c/o RAPEHGA, P.O. Box 140104, D-53056 Bonn, Germany. Contact: T. Assefa. Supposedly operated by an Ethiopian opposition group called Research and Action Group for Peace in Ethiopia and the Horn of Africa. Broadcasts via hired shortwave transmitters in Germany.

☞"**Radio Rhino International - Africa**," c/o Allerweltshaus e.V., Koernerstr. 77 - 79, D - 50823 Köln, Germany. Phone: +49 (162) 885-4486. Fax: +49 (221) 991 2907. Email: mail@radiorhino.org. Web: (includes MP3) www.radiorhino.org. Contact: Godfrey Ayoo, Director. Opposed to the Uganda government. Transmits via the Jülich facilities of Germany's T-Systems International (see).

"**Radio Sedaye Iran**"—see KRSI, USA.

"Radio Station Freedom, Voice of the Communist Party of Iraqi Kurdistan" ("Era ezgay azadiya, dengi hizbi shuyu'i kurdistani iraqa") (when operating).
KURDISTAN COMMUNIST PARTY-IRAQ (KCPI) PARENT ORGANIZATION: Web: http://user.tninet.se/~lto357q/framse4.
"Radio Voice of Hope"—*see* Netherlands.
"Radio Voice of the People." Email: voxpop@zol.co.zw (if this fails, try the online email form). Web: www.voxpop.co.zw. Contact: John Masuku. Airs via Radio Nederland facilities in Madagascar and is opposed to Zimbabwean president Mugabe.
MOVEMENT FOR DEMOCRATIC CHANGE PARENT ORGANIZATION: Harvest House, 6th Floor, N.Mandela Ave/Angwa St, Harare, Zimbabwe. Phone: +263 (91) 367-151/2/3 or +263 (4) 781-138/9. Email: support@mdc.co.zw. Web: www.mdczimbabwe.com.
"Radio VOP"—*see* "Radio Voice of the People," above.
🔊**"Radio Xoriyo,"** ("Halkani wa Radio Xoriyo, Codkii Ummadda Odageniya"). Email: radioxoriyo@ogaden.com; or ogaden@yahoo.com (some verifications received from these addresses). If these fail, try webmaster@ogaden.com. Web: (includes RealAudio) www.ogaden.com. Broadcasts are supportive of the Ogadenia National Liberation Front, and hostile to the Ethiopian government. Transmits via facilities of Germany's T-Systems International (*see*).
🔊**"SW Radio Africa"**
UNITED KINGDOM OFFICE: Phone: +44 (20) 8387-1441. Email: (general) views@swradioafrica.com; (technical) tech@swradioafrica.com. Web: (includes Windows Media) www.swradioafrica.com. Programs are produced in London and aired via a transmitter in South Africa. Run by exiled Zimbabweans and opposes the Mugabe government.
🔊**"Voice of Biafra International,"** 733 15th Street NW, Suite 700, Washington DC 20005 USA. Phone: +1 (202) 347-2983. Email: biafrafoundation@yahoo.com; (Nkwocha) oguchi@pacbell.net; oguchi@mbay.net. Web (includes Windows Media): www.biafraland.com/vobi.htm. Contact: Oguchi Nkwocha, M.D.; or Chima Osondu. A project of the Biafra Foundation, Ekwe Nche and the Biafra Actualization Forum.
"Voice of China" ("Zhongguo zhi Yin"), P.O. Box 273538, Concord CA 94527 USA; or (sponsoring organization) Foundation for China in the 21st Century, P.O. Box 11696, Berkeley CA 94701 USA. Web: www.china21century.org/default.asp?menu=xu (click on "VOC"). Contact: Lily Hu, Executive Director. Financial support from the Foundation for China in the 21st Century. Has "picked up the mission" of the earlier Voice of June 4th, but has no organizational relationship with it. Transmits via facilities of the Central Broadcasting System, Taiwan (*see*).
🔊**"Voice of Democratic Eritrea"** ("Sawt Eritrea al-Dimuqratiya-Sawtu Jabhat al-Tahrir al-Eritrea"), ELF-RC, Postfach 200434, D-53134 Bonn, Germany. Alternative address: Postfach 1946, D-65409 Ruesselheim, Germany. Phone: +49 (228) 356-181. Email: (Eritrean political opposition) meskerem@erols.com. Web: (includes RealAudio) www.meskerem.net. Contact: Seyoum O. Michael, Member of Executive Committee, ELF-RC; or Neguse Tseggon. Station of the Eritrean Liberation Front-Revolutionary Council, hostile to the government of Eritrea. Transmits via facilities of T-Systems International (*see*), in Germany.
🔊**"Voice of Ethiopian Medhin,"** P.O. Box 7968, Washington, DC 20044 USA Phone: +1 (301) 565-4011. Fax: +1 (301) 565 4031. Web: (includes RealAudio) www.medhin.com. Broadcast produced by overseas members of the Ethiopian Medhin Democratic Party based in the USA, a broad-based coalition of Ethiopians aiming to democratize their country and recognized by

the Ethiopian government in 2004 as an official opposition party.
MEDHIN GERMAN BRANCH: Postfach 111423, D-60049 Frankfurt/Main, Germany.
"Voice of Ethiopian Unity"—*see* "Voice of the Democratic Path of Ethiopian Unity.
"Voice of Iranian Kurdistan" ("Seda-ye Kordestan-e Iran")—Contact one of the PDKI (Democratic Party of Iranian Kurdistan parent organization) offices, below.
PDKI INTERNATIONAL BUREAU: AFK, Boite Postale 102, F-75623 Paris Cedex 13, France. Phone: +33 (1) 4585-6431. Fax: +33 (1) 4585 2093. Email: pdkiran@club-internet.fr. Web: www.pdk-iran.org.
PDKI AUSTRALIAN BUREAU: Web: www.pdkiran.org.
PDKI CANADA BUREAU: P.O. Box 29010, London, Ontario N6K 4L9, Canada. Phone/Fax: +1 (519) 680-7784. Email: pdkiontario@pdki.org. Web: www.pdki.org.
PDKI REPRESENTATIVE IN USA: Email: pdkiusa@pdki.org.
"Voice of Iraqi Kurdistan"—*see* Iraq.
"Voice of Jammu Kashmir Freedom" ("Sada-i Hurriyat-i Jammu Kashmir"), P.O. Box 102, Muzaffarabad, Azad Kashmir, via Pakistan. Contact: Islam-ud Din Butt. Pro-Moslem and favors Azad Kashmiri independence from India. Believed to transmit via facilities in Pakistan. Return postage not required.
HARKAT-UL-MUJAHIDEEN SPONSORING ORGANIZATION: Email: info@harkatulmujahideen.org. Web: www.ummah.net.pk/harkat.
🔊**"Voice of Khmer Krom,"** P.O. Box 121, Pensauken NJ 08110 USA. Email: vokk@khmerkrom.org. Web: (includes RealAudio) http://radio.khmerkrom.org. Targeted at the inhabitants of what used to be South Vietnam, and aired via facilities in the Russian Far East. Reception reports can be verified from: TDP, P.O. Box 1, 2310 Rijkevorsel, Belgium.
🔊**"Voice of Komalah"** ("Seda-ye Komalah") (when operating). Email: radiokom@radiokomaleh.com. Web: (includes RealAudio) www.radiokomaleh.com. Station of the Kurdish branch of the Communist Party of Iran.
KOMALAH PARENT ORGANIZATION (KURDISTAN): Email: komalah@hotmail.com.
SWEDISH OFFICE: P.O. Box 750 26, Uppsala, Sweden. Phone/Fax: +46 (18) 468-493. Email: komala@cpiran.org.
"Voice of Kurdistan Toilers" ("Aira dengi zahmatkishan-e kurdistana") (when operating).
KURDISTAN TOILERS PARTY PARENT ORGANIZATION: Email: info@ktp.nu. Web: www.ktp.nu.
🔊**"Voice of Liberty"** ("Dimtsi Harnet Ertra"). Email: volcomments@eritreaone.com.Reception reports can be verified from: TDP, P.O. Box 1, 2310 Rijkevorsel, Belgium. Supports the EPLF-DP faction of the Eritrean People's Liberation Front. Broadcasts via a transmitter in western Russia.
"Voice of Mesopotamia" ("Dengê Mezopotamya"), Phone: +32 (53) 648-827/29. Fax: +32 (53) 641 215. Email: info@denge-mezopotamya.com. Web: www.denge-mezopotamya.com. Contact: Ahmed Dicle, Director.
KURDISTAN WORKERS PARTY (PKK, also known as Kadek) SPONSORING ORGANIZATION: Email: serxwebun@serxwebun.com. Web: www.pkk.org.
ADDRESS FOR RECEPTION REPORTS: TDP, P.O. Box 1, 2310 Rijkevorsel, Belgium (*see*).
🔊**"Voice of Oromiyaa"** ("Sagalee Oromiyaa"). Email: sagaloromo@aol.com. Web: (includes RealAudio) www.voiceoforomiyaa.com.
🔊**"Voice of Oromo Liberation"** ("Sagalee Bilisummaa Oromoo"), Postfach 510610, D-13366 Berlin, Germany; or SBO,

Prinzenallee 81, D-13357 Berlin, Germany. Phone/Fax: +49 (30) 494 3372. Email: sbo13366@aol.com. Web: (includes RealAudio) www.oromoliberationfront.org/sbo.html. Contact: Taye Teferah, European Coordinator. Occasionally replies to correspondence in English or German. Return postage required. Station of the Oromo Liberation Front of Ethiopia, an Oromo nationalist organization. Via T-Systems International facilities in Germany.

OROMO LIBERATION FRONT USA OFFICE: P.O. Box 73247, Washington DC 20056 USA. Phone: +1 (202) 462-5477. Fax: +1 (202) 332 7011.

"Voice of the Communist Party of Iraqi Kurdistan"—*see* "Radio Station Freedom"

"Voice of the Communist Party of Iran" ("Seda-ye Hezb-e Komunist-e Iran")

COMMUNIST PARTY OF IRAN SPONSORING ORGANIZATION: C.D.C.R.I., Box 704 45, S-107 25 Stockholm, Sweden. Phone/Fax: +46 (8) 786-8054. Email: cpi@cpiran.org. Web: www.cpiran.org.

"Voice of the Democratic Path of Ethiopian Unity," Finote Democracy, P.O. Box 88675, Los Angeles CA 90009 USA. Email: efdpu@finote.org. Web: (includes RealAudio) www.finote.org. Transmits via German facilities of T-Systems International (*see*). *EUROPEAN ADDRESS:* Finote Democracy, Postbus 10573, 1001 EN, Amsterdam, Netherlands.

"Voice of the Iraqi People" (when operating), BM Al-Tariq, London WC1N 3XX, United Kingdom. Web: www.iraqcp.org/radicp; (RealAudio) http://icp42.tripod.com/icpradio; (Iraqi Communist Party sponsoring organization) www.iraqcp.org.

"Voice of the Kurdistan People"—*see* Iraq.

"Voice of the Worker" ("Seda-ye Kargar") (when operating). Web: (includes historical archives in TrueSpeech) www.kvwpiran.org.

WORKER-COMMUNIST PARTY OF IRAN (WPI) PARENT ORGANIZATION: Email: wpi@wpiran.org. Web: www.wpiran.org. *WPI INTERNATIONAL OFFICE:* WPI, Office of International Relations, Suite 730, 28 Old Brompton Road, South Kensington, London SW7 3SS, United Kingdom. Phone: +44 (77) 7989-8968. Fax: +44 (87) 0136 2182. Email: wpi.international.office@ukonline.co.uk.

"Voice of the Worker-Communist Party of Iraq" (Aira dangi kizb-e communist-e kargar-e iraqa") (when operating), WCPI Radio, Zargata, Sulaimania, Iraq. Email: radio@wpiraq.org; (WPCI parent organization) jamal@wpiraq.org. Web: (WCPI parent organization) www.wpiraq.org. Station of the Worker-Communist Party of Iraq.

WCPI CANADIAN OFFICE: P.O. Box 491, Don Mills Postal Station, North York, Ontario M3C 2T4, Canada.

WCPI GERMAN OFFICE: A.K.P.I., Postfach 160244, D-10336 Berlin, Germany.

WCPI SWEDISH OFFICE: W.P.C.I., Box 1211, SE-17224, Sundbyberg, Sweden.

"Voice of Tibet"

ADMINISTRATIVE OFFICE: Welhavensgate 1, N-0166 Oslo, Norway. Phone: (administration) +47 2211-2700; (studio) +47 2211-1209. Fax: +47 2211 5474. Email: voti@online.no; (Norbu) votibet@online.no. Web: (includes RealAudio) www.vot.org. Contact: Øystein Alme, Project Manager [sometimes referred to as "Director"]; or Chophel Norbu, Project Coordinator.

MAIN EDITORIAL OFFICE: Voice of Tibet, Editor-in-Chief, Narthang Building, Gangchen, Kyishong, Dharamsala-176 215 H.P., India. Phone: +91 (1892) 228-179 or +91 (1892) 222 384. Fax: +91 (1892) 24913. Email: vot@nde.vsnl.net.in. Contact: Sonam Dargyay. A joint venture of the Norwegian Human Rights House, Norwegian Tibet Committee and World-View International. Programs focus on Tibetan culture, education, human rights and news from Tibet. Opposed to Chinese control of Tibet. Those seeking a verification for this program should enclose a prepared card or letter. Return postage helpful. Verifications have been received from both addresses. Broadcasts via transmitters in the former Soviet Union.

"Voz de la Resistencia"

Email: (FARC-EP parent organization) farc-ep@comision.internal.org; or elbarcino@laneta.apc.org (updated transmission schedules and QSLs available from this address, but correspond in Spanish). Web: www.resistencianacional.org/radio.htm; www.radioresistencia.com; (FARC-EP parent organization) http://burn.ucsd.edu/~farc-ep. Contact: Olga Lucía Marín, Comisión Internacional de las FARC-EP. Station of the Fuerzas Armadas Revolucionarias de Colombia - Ejercito del Pueblo.

COLOMBIA World Time –5

NOTE: Colombia, the country, is always spelled with two o's. It should never be written as "Columbia."

Alcaravan Radio—*see* La Voz de Tu Conciencia.

Caracol Villavicencio—*see* La Voz de los Centauros.

Ecos del Atrato (when operating), Apartado Aéreo 196, Quibdó, Chocó, Colombia. Phone: +57 (49) 711-450. Contact: Absalón Palacios Agualimpia, Administrador. Free pennants. Replies to correspondence in Spanish.

La Voz de Tu Conciencia, Colombia para Cristo, Apartado Aéreo 95300, Santafé de Bogotá, D.C., Colombia. Phone: +57 (1) 338-4716. Email: info@fuerzadepaz.com. Web: www.fuerza de paz.com/emisoras.asp. Contact: Russel Martín Stendal, Administrador. Station is actually located in Puerto Lleras, in the guerrilla "combat zone." Sometimes carries programming from sister station Alcaravan Radio (1530 kHz).

La Voz de los Centauros (Caracol Villavicencio), Cra. 31 No. 37-71 Of. 1001, Villavicencio, Meta, Colombia. Phone: +57 (986) 214-995; (technical) +57 (986) 662-3666. Fax: +57 (986) 623 954. Contact: Carlos Torres Leyva, Gerencia; or Olga Arenas, Administradora. Replies to correspondence in Spanish.

La Voz del Guaviare, Carrera 22 con Calle 9, San José del Guaviare, Colombia. Phone: +57 (986) 840-153/4. Fax: +57 (986) 840 102. Contact: Luis Fernando Román Robayo, Director General. Replies slowly to correspondence in Spanish.

La Voz del Llano (when operating), Calle 41B No. 30-11, Barrio La Grama, Villavicencio, Meta, Colombia; or (postal address in Bogotá) Apartado Aéreo 67751, Santafé de Bogotá, Colombia. Phone: +57 (986) 624-102. Fax: +57 (986) 625 045. Contact: Manuel Buenaventura, Director; Rafael Rodríguez R., or Edgar Valenzuela Romero. Replies occasionally to correspondence in Spanish. $1 or return postage necessary.

Ondas del Orteguaza, Calle 16, No. 12-48, piso 2, Florencia, Caquetá, Colombia. Phone: +57 (88) 352-558. Contact: Sandra Liliana Vásquez, Secretaria; Señora Elisa Viuda de Santos; or Henry Valencia Vásquez. Free stickers. IRC, return postage or $1 required. Replies occasionally to correspondence in Spanish.

Radio Auténtica, Calle 38 No. 32-41, piso 7, Edif. Santander, Villavicencio, Meta, Colombia. Phone: +57 (986) 626-780. Phone/Fax: +57 (986) 624-507. Web: (Cadena Radial Auténtica de Colombia parent organization) www.cmb.org.co/cra. Contact: (general) Pedro Rojas Velásquez; or Carlos Alberto Pimienta, Gerente; (technical) Sra. Alba Nelly González de Rojas, Administradora. Sells religious audio cassettes for 3,000 pesos. Return postage required. Replies slowly to correspondence in Spanish.

CONGO (DEMOCRATIC REPUBLIC) (formerly Zaïre)
World Time +1 Western, including Kinshasa; +2 Eastern

Radio Bukavu (when active), B.P. 475, Bukavu, Democratic Republic of the Congo. $1 or return postage required. Replies slowly. Correspondence in French preferred.

Radio CANDIP, B.P. 373, Bunia, Democratic Republic of Congo. Letters should preferably be sent via registered mail. $1 or return postage required. Correspondence in French preferred.

Radio Kahuzi, c/o AIMServe, Box 63435 (BUKAVU), Nairobi, Kenya. Email: besi@alltell.net. Contact: Richard & Kathy McDonald.

Radio Lubumbashi, B.P. 7296, Lubumbashi, Democratic Republic of the Congo. Letters should be sent via registered mail. $1 or 3 IRCs helpful. Correspondence in French preferred.

Radio Okapi
Email: info@monuc.org. Web: (includes Windows Media) www.monuc.org/radio. A joint project involving the United Nations Mission in the Democratic Republic of the Congo (MONUC) and the Swiss-based Fondation Hirondelle.
MONUC PUBLIC INFORMATION OFFICES:
(USA) P.O. Box 4653, Grand Central Station, New York NY 10163-4653 USA. Phone: +1 (212) 963-0103. Fax: +1 (212) 963 0205.
(Congo) 12 Av. des Aviateurs, Kinshasa, Gombe, Democratic Republic of the Congo; or B.P. 8811, Kinshasa 1, Democratic Republic of the Congo. Phone: +39 0831 24 5000, X-56372 or X-56374. Contact: Georges Schleger, VE2EK, Communications Officer & Head of Technical Services.

Radio-Télévision Nationale Congolaise, B.P. 3171, Kinshasa-Gombe, Democratic Republic of the Congo. Letters should be sent via registered mail. $1 or 3 IRCs helpful. Correspondence in French preferred.

CONGO (REPUBLIC)   World Time +1

Radiodiffusion Nationale Congolaise (also announces as "Radio Nationale" or "Radio Congo"), Radiodiffusion-Télévision Congolaise, B.P. 2241, Brazzaville, Congo. Email: (technical) actu_rtnc@hotmail.com. Contact: Roger Olingou or Félix Lossombo, Le Directeur Administratif et Financier. Return postage required, but smallest denomination currency notes (e.g. $1US or 1 euro) reportedly cannot be changed into local currency. Replies irregularly to letters in French (and sometimes, English) sent via registered mail.

COSTA RICA   World Time –6

Faro del Caribe—TIFC, Apartado 2710, 1000 San José, Costa Rica. Phone: +506 226-4358, +506 227-5048, +506 286-1755. Fax: +506 227-1725. Email: tifc@farodelcaribe.org, tifccr@racsa.co.cr, radio@farodelcaribe.org; (technical) tecnico@farodelcaribe.org. Web: (includes Real Audio) www.farodelcaribe.org. Contact: Carlos A. Rozotto Piedrasanta, Director Administrativo; or Mauricio Ramires; (technical) Minor Enrique, Station Engineer. Free stickers, pennants, books and bibles. $1 or IRCs helpful.
U.S. OFFICE, NONTECHNICAL: Misión Latinoamericana, P.O. Box 620485, Orlando FL 32862 USA.

Radio Casino (when operating), Apartado 287, 7301 Puerto Limón, Costa Rica. Phone: +506 758-0029. Fax: +506 758 3029. Contact: Edwin Zamora, Departamento de Notícias; or Luis Grau Villalobos, Gerente; (technical) Ing. Jorge Pardo, Director Técnico; or Geraldo Moya, Técnico.

Radio Exterior de España—Cariari Relay Station, Cariari de Pococí, Costa Rica. Phone: +506 767-7308 or +506 767-7311. Fax: +506 225 2938.

Radio Universidad de Costa Rica, Apartado 1-06, 2060 Universidad de Costa Rica, San Pedro de Montes de Oca, San José, Costa Rica. Phone: (general) +506 207-4727; (studio) +506 225-3936. Fax: +506 207 5459. Email: radioucr@cariari.ucr.ac.cr. Web: http://cariari.ucr.ac.cr/~radioucr/radioucr. Contact: Marco González Muñoz; Henry Jones, Locutor de Planta; or Nora Garita B., Directora. Marco González is a radio amateur, call-sign TI3AGM. Free postcards, station brochure and stickers. Replies slowly to correspondence in Spanish or English. $1 or return postage required.

University Network—*see* USA.

CROATIA   World Time +1 (+2 midyear)

Croatian Radio-Television (Hrvatska Radio-Televizija, HRT)
MAIN OFFICE: Hrvatska Radio-Televizija (HRT), Prisavlje 3, HR-10000 Zagreb, Croatia. Phone: (operator) +385 (1) 634-3366; (Managing Director) +385 (1) 634-3308; (Technical Director) +385 (1) 634-3663. Fax: (Technical Director) +385 (1) 634 3636. Email: (Managing Director) i.lucev@hrt.hr; (Technical Director) nikola.percin@hrt.hr; (technical, including reception reports) z.klasan@hrt.hr. Web: (includes RealAudio) www.hrt.hr. Contact: (general) Ivanka Lucev, Managing Director; (Technical Director) Nikola Percin.
TRANSMITTING STATION DEANOVEC: P.O Box 3, 10313 Graberje Ivaanicko, Croatia. Phone: +385 (1) 283-0533. Fax: +385 (1) 283 0534. Email: dane.pavlic@oiv.hr. Contact: Dane Pavlic, Head of Station.
TRANSMISSION AUTHORITY: Odasiljaci i Veze D.O.O., Vlaska 106, HR-10000 Zagreb, Croatia. Phone: +385 (1) 464-6160. Fax: +385 (1) 464 6161. Email: Zelimir.Klasan@hrt.hr. Contact: Zelimir Klasan. This independent state-owned company replaces the former Transmitters and Communications Department of HRT.

Voice of Croatia (Glas Hrvatske)—same address as "Hrvatska Radio," above. Phone: (Editor-in-Chief) +385 (1) 634-2602; (Shortwave Technical Coordinator) +385 (1) 634-3428; (Shortwave Technical Coordinator, mobile) +385 9857-7565. Fax: (Editor-in-Chief) +385 (1) 634 3305; (Shortwave Technical Coordinator) +385 (1) 634 3347. Email: (Editor-in-Chief) ivana.jadresic@hrt.hr; (staff) kratki.val@hrt.hr; (Shortwave Technical Coordinator) z.klasan@hrt.hr. Contact: (Editor-in-Chief) Ivana Jadresic; (Shortwave Technical Coordinator, domestic & external) Zelimir Klasan.
Croatian Radio operates two services on world band: the domestic (first) national radio program, transmitted via HRT's Deanovec shortwave station for listeners in Europe and the Mediterranean; and a special service in Croatian, with news segments in English and Spanish for Croatian expatriates, which airs via facilities of T-Systems International (*see*) in Jülich, Germany and is sponsored by the Croatian Heritage Organization. The previous Croatian external broadcasting service known as "Radio Hrvatska" and produced by the Croatian Information Center (Hrvatski Informativni Centar, HIC) was discontinued on October 1st 2000. The external service resumed its transmissions on April 18th 2001 as Glas Hrvatske (Voice of Croatia) under the authority of HRT.
WASHINGTON NEWS BUREAU: Croatian-American Association, 2020 Pennsylvania Avenue NW, Suite 287, Washington DC 20006 USA. Phone: +1 (202) 429-5543. Fax: +1 (202) 429 5545. Email: 73150.3552@compuserve.com. Web: www.hrnet.org/CAA. Contact: Frank Brozovich, President.

CUBA   World Time –5 (–4 midyear)

Radio Habana Cuba, P.O. Box 6240, Habana, Cuba 10600. Phone: (general) +53 (7) 784-954 or +53 (7) 334-272; (English Department) +53 (7) 877-6628; (Coro) +53 (7) 814-243 or (home) +53 (7) 301-794. Fax: (general) +53 (7) 783 518; (English Department) +53 (7) 705 810. Email: (general) radiohc@ip.etecsa.cu; (English Service) radiohc@enet.cu; (Arnie Coro) arnie@rhc.cu or coro@enet.cu. Web: (includes Windows Media and online reception report form) www.radiohc.cu; (includes archived scripts of "DXers Unlimited") www.radiohc.org. Contact: (general) Lourdes López, Head of Correspondence Department; Juan Jacomino, Head of English Service; or Mike La Guardia, Senior Editor; (administration) Ms. Milagro Hernández Cuba, General Director; (technical) Arnaldo Coro Antich, ("Arnie Coro"), Producer, "DXers Unlimited"; or Arturo González, Head of Technical Department. Free wallet and wall calendars, pennants, stickers, keychains and pins. DX Listeners' Club. Free sample *Granma International* newspaper. Contests with various prizes, including trips to Cuba.

Radio Rebelde, Departamento de Relaciones Públicas, Apartado Postal 6277, 10600 Habana 6, Cuba; or (street address) Calle 23 No. 258 entre L y M, El Vedado, Habana, Cuba 10600. For technical correspondence (including reception reports), substitute "Servicio de Onda Corta" in place of "Departamento de Relaciones Públicas." Reception reports can also be emailed to Radio Habana Cuba's Arnie Coro (arnie@radiohc.org) for forwarding to Radio Rebelde. Phone: +53 (7) 831-3514. Fax: +53 (7) 334 270. Email: (nontechnical) webrebelde@rrebelde.icrt.cu. Web (includes RealAudio): www.radiorebelde.com.cu. Contact: Daimelis Monzón; Noemí Cairo Marín; Iberlise González Padua; or Marisel Ramos Soca (all from "Relaciones Públicas"); or Jorge Luis Más Zabala, Director, Relaciones Públicas. Replies slowly, with correspondence in Spanish preferred.

CYPRUS   World Time +2 (+3 midyear)

🎦**Bayrak Radio International** (when operating), BRTK Campus, Dr. Fazil Küçük Boulevard, P.O. Box 417, Lefkosa - T.R.N.C., via Mersin 10, Turkey. Phone: +90 (392) 225-5555. Fax: (general) +90 (392) 225 4581. Email: (general) brt@cc.emu.edu.tr; (technical, including reception reports) tosun@cc.emu.edu.tr. Web: (includes RealAudio) www.brt.gov.nc.tr. Contact: Mustafa Tosun, Head of Transmission Department; Halil Balbaz, Transmitter Manager; Ölfet Kortmaz, Head of Bayrak International.

BBC World Service—East Mediterranean Relay Station, P.O. Box 209, Limassol, Cyprus. Contact: Steve Welch. This address for technical matters only. Other correspondence should be sent to the BBC World Service in London (*see*).

🎦**Cyprus Broadcasting Corporation**, Broadcasting House, P.O. Box 4824, Nicosia 1397, Cyprus; or (physical address) RIK Street, Athalassa, Nicosia 2120, Cyprus. Phone: +357 (2) 862-000. Fax: +357 (2) 314 050. Email: rik@cybc.com.cy. Web: (includes RealAudio) www.cybc.com.cy. Contact: (general) Pavlos Soteriades, Director General; or Evangella Gregoriou, Head of Public and International Relations; (technical) Andreas Michaelides, Director of Technical Services. Free stickers. Replies occasionally, sometimes slowly. IRC or $1 helpful.

CZECH REPUBLIC   World Time +1 (+2 midyear)

🎦**Radio Prague**, Czech Radio, Vinohradská 12, 12099 Prague 2, Czech Republic. Phone: (Czech Department) +420 (2) 2155-2921; (English Department) +420 (2) 2155-2930; (German Department) +420 (2) 2155-2941; (French Department) +420 (2) 2155-2910; (Spanish Department) +420 (2) 2155-2950. Phone/Fax: (Oldrich Čip, technical) +420 (2) 2271-5005. Fax: (all languages) +420 (2) 2155 2903. Email: (general) cr@radio.cz; (Director) Miroslav.Krupicka@radio.cz; (English Department) english@radio.cz; (Program Director) David.Vaughan@radio.cz; (free news texts) robot@radio.cz, writing "Subscribe English" (or other desired language) within the subject line; (technical, chief engineer) cip@radio.cz. Web: (includes RealAudio and MP3) www.radio.cz; (text) ftp://ftp.radio.cz; gopher://gophcr.radio.cz. Contact: (general) Markéta Atanasová; David Vaughan, Editor-in-Chief; (administration) Miroslav Krupička, Director; (technical, all programs) Oldrich Čip, Chief Engineer. Free stickers; also key chains, pens, bookmarks and other souvenirs when available. Samples of *Welcome to the Czech Republic* and *Czech Life* available upon request from Orbis, Vinohradská 46, 120 41 Prague, Czech Republic.

RFE-RL—*see* USA.

DENMARK   World Time +1 (+2 midyear)

World Music Radio (when operating), P. O. Box 112, DK-8900 Randers, Denmark. Phone: (Monday through Friday, 0800-1400 World Time) +45 70 222 222. Fax: +45 70 222 888. E-mail: wmr@wmr.dk. URL: www.wmr.dk. Contact: Stig Hartvig Nielsen. Return postage required. An independent station, WMR first went on the air in 1967 from the Netherlands, from where broadcasting continued until August 1973. Later programs were aired via the facilities of Radio Andorra (in 1976 and 1980), Radio Milano International (1982-1983) and Radio Dublin (1983-1989). In 1997, WMR returned to the air between May 31 and August 24 from a new HQ in Denmark, leasing airtime over powerful transmitters in South Africa. These broadcasts ceased due to lack of commercial advertising. The station tested during 2003 and 2004 from its own transmitter. Plans to commence regular transmissions.

DOMINICAN REPUBLIC   World Time –4

Radio Amanecer Internacional, Apartado Postal 4680, Santo Domingo, Dominican Republic. Phone: +1 (809) 688-5600, +1 (809) 688-5609, +1 (809) 688-8067. Fax: +1 (809) 227 1869. Web: www.tricom.net/amanecer. Contact: (general) Señora Ramona C. de Subervi, Directora; (technical) Ing. Sócrates Domínguez. $1 or return postage required. Replies slowly to correspondence in Spanish.

Radio Barahona (when operating), Apartado 201, Barahona, Dominican Republic; or Gustavo Mejía Ricart No. 293, Apto. 2-B, Ensanche Quisqueya, Santo Domingo, Dominican Republic. Phone: +1 (809) 524-4040. Fax: +1 (809) 524 5461. Contact: (general) Rodolfo Z. Lama Jaar, Administrador; (technical) Ing. Roberto Lama Sajour, Administrador General. Free stickers. Letters should be sent via registered mail. $1 or return postage helpful. Replies to correspondence in Spanish.

EMPRESAS RADIOFÓNICAS PARENT ORGANIZATION: Empresas Radiofónicas S.A., Apartado Postal 20339, Santo Domingo, Dominican Republic. Phone: +1 (809) 567-9698. Fax: +1 (809) 472-3313. Web: www.suprafm.com.

Radio Cima Cien (when operating), Apartado 804, Santo Domingo, Dominican Republic. Fax: +1 (809) 541 1088. Contact: Roberto Vargas, Director. Free pennants, postcards, coins and taped music. Roberto likes collecting stamps and coins.

Radio Cristal Internacional, Apartado Postal 894, Santo Domingo, Dominican Republic; or (street address) Calle Pepillo

Salcedo No. 18, Altos, Santo Domingo, Dominican Republic. Phone: +1 (809) 565-1460 or +1 (809) 566-5411. Fax: +1 (809) 567 9107. Contact: (general) Fernando Hermón Gross, Director de Programas; or Margarita Reyes, Secretaria; or (administration) Darío Badía, Director General; or Héctor Badía, Director de Administración. Seeks reception reports. Return postage of $2 appreciated.

ECUADOR   World Time –5 (–4 sometimes, in times of drought); –6 Galapagos

NOTE: According to HCJB's "DX Party Line," during periods of drought, such as caused by "El Niño," electricity rationing causes periods in which transmitters cannot operate because of inadequate hydroelectric power, as well as spikes which occasionally damage transmitters. Accordingly, many Ecuadorian stations tend to be irregular, or even entirely off the air, during drought conditions.

NOTE: According to veteran Dxer Harald Kuhl in Hard-Core-DX of Kotanet Communications Ltd., IRCs are exchangeable only in the cities of Quito and Guayaquil. Too, overseas airmail postage is very expensive now in Ecuador; so when in doubt, enclosing $2 for return postage is appropriate.

Emisoras Luz y Vida, Casilla 11-01-222, Loja, Ecuador. Phone: +593 (7) 570-426. Contact: Hermana [Sister] Ana Maza Reyes, Directora; or Lic. Guida Carrión H., Directora de Programas. Return postage required. Replies irregularly to correspondence in Spanish.

Escuelas Radiofónicas Populares del Ecuador, Juan de Velasco 4755 y Guayaquil, Casilla Postal 06-01-341, Riobamba, Ecuador. Phone: +593 (3) 961-608 or +593 (3) 960-247. Fax: +593 (3) 961 625. Email: admin@esrapoec.ecuanex.net.ec. Web: www.ded.org.ec/essapa01.htm. Contact: Juan Pérez Sarmiento, Director Ejecutivo; or María Ercilia López, Secretaria. Free pennants and key rings. "Chimborazo" cassette of Ecuadorian music for 10,000 sucres plus postage; T-shirts for 12,000 sucres plus postage; and caps with station logo for 8,000 sucres plus postage. Return postage helpful. Replies to correspondence in Spanish.

HCJB World Radio, The Voice of the Andes

STATION: Casilla 17-17-691, Quito, Ecuador. Phone: (general) +593 (2) 226-6808 (X-4441, 1300-2200 World Time Monday through Friday, for the English Dept.); (Frequency Management) +593 (2) 226-6808 (X-4627); (*DX Partyline* English program, toll-free, U.S. only, for reception reports, loggings and other correspondence) +1 866 343-0791. Fax: (general) +593 (2) 226 7263; (Frequency Manager) +593 (2) 226 3267. Email: (Graham) agraham@hcjb.org.ec; (Frequency Management) irops@hcjb.org.ec or dweber@hcjb.org.ec; (language sections) format is language@hcjb.org.ec; so to reach, say, the Spanish Department, it would be spanish@hcjb.org.ec. Web: (English, includes RealAudio and online reception report form) www.hcjb.org; (Spanish) www.hcjb.org.ec. Contact: (general) English [or other language] Department; (administration) Jim Estes, Director of Broadcasting; Alex Saks, Station Manager; Curt Cole, Programme Director, or Allen Graham, Ecuador National Director; (technical) Douglas Weber, Frequency Manager. Free religious brochures, calendars, stickers and pennants; free email *The Andean Herald* newsletter. *Catch the Vision* book $8, postpaid. IRC or unused U.S. or Canadian stamps appreciated for airmail reply.

INTERNATIONAL HEADQUARTERS: HCJB World Radio, Inc., P.O. Box 39800, Colorado Springs CO 80949-9800 USA. Phone: +1 (719) 590-9800. Fax: +1 (719) 590 9801. Email: info@hcjb.org. Contact: Andrew Braio, Public Information; (administration)

Richard D. Jacquin, Director, International Operations. Various items sold via U.S. address—catalog available. This address is not a mail drop, so listeners' correspondence, except those concerned with purchasing HCJB items, should be directed to the usual Quito address.

ENGINEERING CENTER: 2830 South 17th Street, Elkhart IN 46517 USA. Phone: +1 (219) 294-8201. Fax: +1 (219) 294 8391. Email: info@hcjbeng.org. Web: www.hcjbeng.org. Contact: Dave Pasechnik, Project Manager; or Bob Moore, Engineering. This address only for those professionally concerned with the design and manufacture of transmitter and antenna equipment. Listeners' correspondence should be directed to the usual Quito address.

REGIONAL OFFICES: Although HCJB has over 20 regional offices throughout the world, the station wishes that all listener correspondence be directed to the station in Quito, as the regional offices do not serve as mail drops for the station.

La Voz de Saquisilí—Radio Libertador (when operating), Calle 24 de Mayo, Saquisilí, Cotopaxi, Ecuador. Phone: +593 (3) 721-035. Contact: Arturo Mena Herrera, Gerente-Propietario. Reception reports actively solicited. Return postage, in the form of $2 or mint Ecuadorian stamps, appreciated; IRCs difficult to exchange. Spanish strongly preferred.

La Voz del Napo, Misión Josefina, Tena, Napo, Ecuador. Phone: +593 (6) 886-356. Email: coljav20@yahoo.es. Contact: Padre Humberto Dorigatti, Director. Free pennants and stickers. $2 or return postage required. Replies occasionally to correspondence in Spanish.

La Voz del Río Tarqui (when operating), Manuel Vega 653 y Presidente Córdova, Cuenca, Ecuador. Phone: +593 (7) 822-132. Contact: Sra. Alicia Pulla Célleri, Gerente. Replies irregularly to correspondence in Spanish. Has ties with station WKDM in New York.

La Voz del Upano

STATION: Vicariato Apostólico de Méndez, Misión Salesiana, 10 de Agosto s/n, Macas, Provincia de Morona Santiago, Ecuador. Phone: +593 (7) 505-247. Email: radioupano@easynet.net.ec. Contact: Sra. Leonor Guzmán, Directora. Free pennants and calendars. On one occasion, not necessarily to be repeated, sent tape of Ecuadorian folk music for $2. Otherwise, $2 required. Replies to correspondence in Spanish.

QUITO OFFICE: Procura Salesiana, Equinoccio 623 y Queseras del Medio, Quito, Ecuador. Phone: +593 (2) 551-012.

Radio Buen Pastor—*see* Radio El Buen Pastor.

Radio Centinela del Sur (C.D.S. Internacional), Casilla 11-01-106, Loja, Ecuador; or (studios) Olmedo 11-56 y Mercadillo, Loja, Ecuador. Phone: +593 (7) 561-166 or +593 (7) 570-211. Fax: +593 (7) 562 270. Contact: (general) Marcos G. Coronel V., Director de Programas; or José A. Coronel V., Director del programa "Ovación"; (technical) José A. Coronel Illescas, Gerente General. Return postage required. Replies occasionally to correspondence in Spanish.

Radio Centro, Casilla 18-01-574, Ambato, Ecuador. Phone: +593 (3) 822-240 or +593 (3) 841-126. Fax: +593 (3) 829 824. Contact: Luis Alberto Gamboa Tello, Director Gerente; or Lic. María Elena de López. Free stickers. Return postage appreciated. Replies to correspondence in Spanish.

Radiodifusora Cultural Católica La Voz del Upano—*see* La Voz del Upano, above.

Radiodifusora Cultural, La Voz del Napo—*see* La Voz del Napo, above.

Radio El Buen Pastor, Asociación Cristiana de Indígenas Saraguros (ACIS), Reino de Quito y Azuay, Correo Central, Saraguro, Loja, Ecuador. Phone: +593 (2) 00-146. Contact:

(general) Dean Pablo Davis, Sub-director; Segundo Poma, Director; Mark Vogan, OMS Missionary; Mike Schrode, OMS Ecuador Field Director; Juana Guamán, Secretaria; or Zoila Vacacela, Secretaria; (technical) Miguel Kelly. $2 or return postage in the form of mint Ecuadorian stamps required, as IRCs are difficult to exchange in Ecuador. Station is keen to receive reception reports; may respond to English, but correspondence in Spanish preferred. $10 required for QSL card and pennant.

Radio Federación Shuar (Shuara Tuntuiri), Casilla 17-01-1422, Quito, Ecuador. Phone/Fax: +593 (2) 504-264. Contact: Manuel Jesús Vinza Chacucuy, Director; Yurank Tsapak Rubén Gerardo, Director; or Prof. Albino M. Utitiaj P., Director de Medios. Return postage or $2 required. Replies irregularly to correspondence in Spanish.

Radio La Voz del Río Tarqui—*see* La Voz del Rio Tarqui.

Radio Luz y Vida—*see* Emisoras Luz y Vida, above.

Radio María

GUAYAQUIL OFFICE: P. Icaza 437 y G. Córdova, Guayaquil, Ecuador. Phone: +593 (4) 568-172. Fax: +593 (4) 568 176. Email: radiomaria@radiomariaecuador.org. Web: (includes RealAudio) www.radiomariaecuador.org; (Windows Media and MP3 audio) www.radiomaria.org/media/index.asp?LNG=SPA.

QUITO OFFICE: Baquerizo Moreno 281 y Leonidas Plaza, Quito, Ecuador. Phone: +593 (2) 564-714, +593 (2) 564-719 or +593 (2) 558-702. Fax: +593 (2) 237 630. Email: radmaria@andinanet.net

A Catholic radio network currently leasing airtime over La Voz del Napo (*see*), but which is looking into the possiblity of setting up its own shortwave station.

Radio Oriental, Casilla 260, Tena, Napo, Ecuador. Phone: +593 (6) 886-033 or +593 (6) 886-388. Contact: Luis Enrique Espín Espinosa, Gerente General. $2 or return postage helpful. Reception reports welcome.

Radio Quito, Casilla 17-21-1971, Quito, Ecuador. Phone/Fax: +593 (2) 508-301. Email: radioquito@elcomercio.com. Contact: Xavier Almeida, Gerente General; or José Almeida, Subgerente. Free stickers. Return postage normally required, but occasionally verifies email reports. Replies slowly, but regularly.

EGYPT   World Time +2 (+3 midyear)

WARNING: MAIL THEFT. Feedback from PASSPORT readership indicates that money is sometimes stolen from envelopes sent to Radio Cairo.

Egyptian Radio, P.O. Box 1186, 11511 Cairo, Egypt. Email: ertu@ertu.gov.eg. Web: www.ertu.gov.eg. For additional details, *see* Radio Cairo, below.

Radio Cairo

NONTECHNICAL: P.O. Box 566, Cairo 11511, Egypt. Phone: +20 (2) 677-8945. Fax: +20 (2) 575 9553. Email: (Spanish Service) radioelcairoespa@yahoo.com; (African services) radiocairo@hotmail.com. Contact: Mrs. Amal Badr, Head of English Programme; Mrs. Sahar Kalil, Director of English Service to North America and Producer, "Questions and Answers"; or Mrs. Magda Hamman, Secretary. Free stickers, postcards, stamps, maps, papyrus souvenirs, calendars and *External Services of Radio Cairo* book. Free booklet and individually tutored Arabic-language lessons with loaned textbooks from Kamila Abdullah, Director General, Arabic by Radio, Radio Cairo, P.O. Box 325, Cairo, Egypt. Arabic-language religious, cultural and language-learning audio and video tapes from the Egyptian Radio and Television Union sold via Sono Cairo Audio-Video, P.O. Box 2017, Cairo, Egypt; when ordering video tapes, inquire to ensure they function on the television standard (NTSC,

PAL or SECAM) in your country. Once replied regularly, if slowly, but recently replies have been increasingly scarce. Comments welcomed about audio quality—*see TECHNICAL*, below. Avoid enclosing money (*see WARNING*, above).

TECHNICAL: Broadcast Engineering Department, 24th Floor—TV Building (Maspiro), Egyptian Radio and Television Union, P.O. Box 1186, 11511 Cairo, Egypt. Phone/Fax: +20 (2) 574-6840. Email: (general) freqmeg@yahoo.com; (Lawrence) niveenl@hotmail.com. Contact: Hamdy Emara, Chairman of Engineering Sector; Mrs. Rokaya M. Kamel, Head of Engineering & Training, Mrs.Laila Hamdalla, Director of Monitoring & Frequency Management; or Mrs. Niveen W. Lawrence, Director of Shortwave Department. Comments and suggestions on audio quality and level especially welcomed. One PASSPORT reader reported that his letter to this address was returned by the Egyptian postal authorities, but we have not received any other reports of returned mail.

EL SALVADOR   World Time –6

Radio Imperial (when operating), Apartado 56, Sonsonante, El Salvador. Fax: +503 450-0189. Contact: (general) Nubia Ericka García, Directora; Pastor Pedro Mendoza; (technical) Moisés B. Cruz G., Ingeniero. Replies to correspondence in English and Spanish, and verifies reception reports by fax, if number provided. $1 helpful.

ENGLAND—*see* UNITED KINGDOM.

EQUATORIAL GUINEA   World Time +1

Radio Africa (when operating)

TRANSMISSION OFFICE: Apartado 851, Malabo, Isla Bioko, Equatorial Guinea.

U.S. OFFICE FOR CORRESPONDENCE AND VERIFICATIONS: Pan American Broadcasting, 20410 Town Center Lane #200, Cupertino CA 95014 USA. Phone: +1 (408) 996-2033; (toll-free, U.S. only) 1-800-726-2620. Fax: +1 (408) 252 6855. Email: pabcomain@aol.com. Web: www.radiopanam.com. Contact: (listener correspondence) Terry Kraemer; (general) Carmen Jung, Office and Sales Administrator; or James Manero. $1 in cash or unused U.S. stamps, or 2 IRCs, required for reply.

Radio East Africa—same details as "Radio Africa," above.

Radio Nacional de Guinea Ecuatorial—Bata ("Radio Bata"), Apartado 749, Bata, Río Muni, Equatorial Guinea. Phone: +240 (8) 2592. Fax: +240 (8) 2093. Contact: José Mba Obama, Director. If no response try sending your letter c/o Spanish Embassy, Bata, enclosing $1 for return postage. Spanish preferred.

Radio Nacional de Guinea Ecuatorial—Malabo ("Radio Malabo"), Apartado 195, Malabo, Isla Bioko, Equatorial Guinea. Phone: +240 (9) 2260. Fax: (general) +240 (9) 2097; (technical) +240 (9) 3122. Contact: (general) Román Manuel Mané-Abaga, Jefe de Programación; Ciprano Somon Suakin; or Manuel Sobede, Inspector de Servicios de Radio y TV; (technical) Hermenegildo Moliko Chele, Jefe Servicios Técnicos de Radio y Televisión. $1 or return postage required. Replies irregularly to correspondence in Spanish.

ERITREA   World Time +3

Radio UNMEE—*see* United Nations.

Voice of the Broad Masses of Eritrea (Dimtsi Hafash), Ministry of Information, Radio Division, P.O. Box 872, Asmara, Eritrea; or Ministry of Information, Technical Branch, P.O. Box 243, Asmara, Eritrea. Phone: +291 (1) 116-084 or +291 (1)

120-497. Fax: +291 (1) 126 747. Email: nesredin1@dehai.org. Web: (including RealAudio) www.dehai.org/dhe/dhe.htm. Contact: Ghebreab Ghebremedhin; or Berhane Gerzgiher, Director, Engineering Division. Return postage or $1 helpful. Free information on history of the station and about Eritrea.

ETHIOPIA World Time +3

Radio Ethiopia: (external service) P.O. Box 654; (domestic service) P.O. Box 1020—both in Addis Ababa, Ethiopia (address your correspondence to "Audience Relations"). Phone: (main office) +251 (1) 116-427 or +251 (1) 551-011; (engineering) +251 (1) 200-948. Fax: +251 (1) 552 263. Web: www.angelfire.com/biz/radioethiopia. Contact: (external service, general) Kahsai Tewoldemedhin, Program Director; Ms. Woinshet Woldeyes, Secretary, Audience Relations; Ms. Ellene Mocria, Head of Audience Relations; or Yohaness Ruphael, Producer, "Contact"; (administration) Kasa Miliko, Head of Station; (technical) Terefe Ghebre Medhin or Zegeye Solomon. Free stickers and tourist brochures. Poor replier.

Radio Fana (Radio Torch), P.O. Box 30702, Addis Ababa, Ethiopia. Phone: +251 (1) 516-777. Email: radio-fana@telecom.net.et. Contact: Woldu Yemessel, General Manager; Mesfin Alemayehu, Head, External Relations; or Girma Lema, Head, Planning and Research Department. Station is autonomous and receives its income from non-governmental educational sponsorship. Seeks help with obtaining vehicles, recording equipment and training materials.

Voice of the Tigray Revolution, P.O. Box 450, Mek'ele, Tigray, Ethiopia. Contact: Fre Tesfamichael, Director. $1 helpful.

FINLAND World Time +2 (+3 midyear)

☞YLE Radio Finland

MAIN OFFICE: Box 78, FIN-00024 Yleisradio, Finland. Phone: (general, 24-hour English speaking switchboard for both Radio Finland and Yleisradio Oy) +358 (9) 14801; (international information) +358 (9) 1480-3729; (administration) +358 (9) 1480-4320 or +358 (9) 1480-4316; (Technical Customer Service) +358 (9) 1480-3213; (comments on programs) +358 (9) 1480-5490. Fax: (general) +358 (9) 148 1169; (international information) +358 (9) 1480 3391; (Technical Affairs) +358 (9) 1480 3588. Email: (general) rfinland@yle.fi, or rfinland@aol.com; (comments on programs) christina.rockstroh@yle.fi; (Yleisradio Oy parent organization) fbc@yle.fi; (reception reports) raimoe.makela@yle.fi. To contact individuals, the format is firstname.lastname@yle.fi; so to reach, say, Pertti Seppä, it would be pertti.seppa@yle.fi. Web: (includes RealAudio) www.yle.fi/rfinland; (online reception report form) www.yle.fi/sataradio/receptionreport.html. Contact—Radio Finland: (administration) Juhani Niinistö, Head of International Radio; (comments on programs) Mrs. Christina Rockstroh, Managing Editor, foreign language radio. Contact—Yleisradio Oy parent organization: (general) Marja Salusjärvi, Head of International PR; (administration) Arne Wessberg, Managing Director; or Tapio Siikala, Director for Domestic and International Radio. Sometimes provides free stickers and small souvenirs, as well as tourist and other magazines. For a free color catalog of souvenirs, clothes, toys, timepieces, binoculars, CDs, tapes and other merchandise, contact the YLE Shop, Yleisradio, Pl 77, FIN-00003 Helsinki, Finland. Phone: +358 (9) 1480-3555. Fax: +358 (9) 1480 3466 or go to www.yle.fi/yleshop. Replies to correspondence. For verification of reception reports, *see* Transmission Facility, below. YLE Radio Finland external broadcasting is a part of YLE and not a separate administrative unit. Radio Finland itself is not a legal entity.

NUNTII LATINI (Program in Latin): P.O. Box 99, FIN- 00024 Yleisradio, Finland. Fax: +358 (9) 1480 3391. Email: nuntii.latini@yle.fi. Web: www.yle.fi/fbc/nuntii.html. Six years of Nuntii Latini now available in books I to III at US$30 each from: Bookstore Tiedekirja, Kirkkokatu 14, FIN-00170 Helsinki, Finland; Fax: +358 (9) 635 017. VISA/MC/EURO.

NETWORK PLANNING: Digita, Wireless Networks, P.O. Box 135, FIN-00521 Helsinki, Finland. Phone: (Huuhka) +358 (20) 411-7287; (Hautala) +358 (20) 411-7282. Fax: +358 (9) 148 5260. Email: esko.huuhka@digita.fi or kari.hautala@digita.fi. Contact: Esko Huuhka, Head of Network Planning; or Kari Hautala, Frequency Manager.

TRANSMISSION FACILITY: Digita Shortwave Centre, Makholmantie 79, FIN-28660 Pori; or (verifications) Pori SW Base, Preiviikki, FIN-28660 Pori, Finland—Attention: Raimo Mäkelä. (Email: raimoe.makela@yle.fi). Web: (Digita Oy) www.digita.fi; www.yle.fi/sataradio/preiviiki.html. Contact: Kalevi Vahtera, Station Manager; or Raimo Mäkelä (QSL-verifications). Issues full-data verification cards for good reception reports, and provides free illustrated booklets about the transmitting station.

NORTH AMERICAN OFFICE—LISTENER and MEDIA LIAISON: P.O. Box 462, Windsor CT 06095 USA. Phone: +1 (860) 688-5540 or +1 (860) 688-5098. Phone/Fax: (24-hour toll-free within U.S. and Canada for recorded schedule and voice mail) 1-800-221-9539. Fax: +1 (860) 688 0113. Email: yleus@aol.com. Contact: John Berky, YLE Finland Transcriptions. Free *YLE North America* newsletter. This office does not verify reception reports.

Scandinavian Weekend Radio, P.O. Box 35, FIN-40321, Jyväskylä, Finland. Phone: (when on air) +358 (400) 995-559. Fax: (when on air) +358 (3) 475 5776. Email: (general) info@swradio.net; (technical) esa.saunamaki@swradio.net; (reception reports) online report form at the station's Website: www.swradio.net. Two IRCs, $2 or 2 euros required for verification card.

FRANCE World Time +1 (+2 midyear)

☞Radio France Internationale (RFI)

MAIN OFFICE: B.P. 9516, F-75016 Paris Cedex 16, France; (street address) 116, avenue du président Kennedy, F-75016 Paris, France. Phone: (general) +33 (1) 56-40-12-12; (International Affairs and Program Placement) +33 (1) 44-30-89-32 or +33 (1) 44-30-89-49; (Service de la communication) +33 (1) 42-30-29-51; (Audience Relations) +33 (1) 44-30-89-69/70/71; (Media Relations) +33 (1) 42-30-29-85; (Développement et de la communication) +33 (1) 44-30-89-21; *(Fréquence Monde)* +33 (1) 42-30-10-86; (English Service) +33 (1) 56-40-30-62; (Spanish Department) +33 (1) 42-30-30-48. Fax: (general) +33 (1) 56 40 47 59; (International Affairs and Program Placement) +33 (1) 44 30 89 20; (Audience Relations) +33 (1) 44 30 89 99; (other nontechnical) +33 (1) 42 30 44 81; (English Service) +33 (1) 56 40 26 74; (Spanish Department) +33 (1) 42 30 46 69. Email: (Audience Relations) courrier.auditeurs@rfi.fr; (English Service) english.service@rfi.fr, english.features@rfi.fr; (Spanish Service) service.amerique.latine@rfi.fr. Web: (includes RealAudio) www.rfi.fr. Contact: John Maguire, Editor, English Language Service; J.P. Charbonnier, Producer, "Lettres des Auditeurs"; Joël Amar, International Affairs/Program Placement Department; Arnaud Littardi, Directeur du développement et de la communication; Nicolas Levkov, Rédactions en Langues Etrangères; Daniel Franco, Rédaction en français; Mme. Anne Toulouse, Rédacteur en chef du Service Mondiale en français;

Christine Berbudeau, Rédacteur en chef, *Fréquence* **Monde**; or Marc Verney, Attaché de Presse; (administration) Jean-Paul Cluzel, Président-Directeur Général; (technical) M. Raymond Pincon, Producer, "Le Courrier Technique." Free *Fréquence* **Monde** bi-monthly magazine in French upon request. Free souvenir keychains, pins, lighters, pencils, T-shirts and stickers have been received by some—especially when visiting the headquarters at 116 avenue du Président Kennedy, in the 16th Arrondissement. Can provide supplementary materials for "Dites-moi tout" French-language course; write to the attention of Mme. Chantal de Grandpre, "Dites-moi tout." "Le Club des Auditeurs" French-language listener's club ("Club 9516" for English-language listeners); applicants must provide name, address and two passport-type photos, whereupon they will receive a membership card and the club bulletin. RFI exists primarily to defend and promote Francophone culture, but also provides meaningful information and cultural perspectives in non-French languages.

TRANSMISSION OFFICE, TECHNICAL: TéléDiffusion de France, Direction de la Production et des Méthodes, Service ondes courtes, 10 rue d'Oradour sur Glane, 75732 Paris Cedex 15, France. Phone: (Gruson) +33 (1) 5595-1553; (Meunier) +33 (1) 5595-1161. Fax: +33 (1) 5595 2137. Email: (Gruson) jacques.gruson@tdf.fr; (Meunier) a_meunier@compuserve.com or (Penneroux) michel.penneroux@tdf.fr. Contact: Jacques Gruson; Alain Meunier; Michel Penneroux, Business Development Manager AM-HF; Mme Annick Daronian or Mme Sylvie Greuillet (short wave service). This office is for informing about transmitter-related problems (interference, modulation quality), and also for reception reports and verifications.

UNITED STATES PROMOTIONAL, SCHOOL LIAISON, PROGRAM PLACEMENT AND CULTURAL EXCHANGE OFFICES:

NEW ORLEANS: Services Culturels, Suite 2105, Ambassade de France, 300 Poydras Street, New Orleans LA 70130 USA. Phone: +1 (504) 523-5394. Phone/Fax: +1 (504) 529-7502. Contact: Adam-Anthony Steg, Attaché Audiovisuel. This office promotes RFI, especially to language teachers and others in the educational community within the southern United States, and arranges for bi-national cultural exchanges. It also sets up RFI feeds to local radio stations within the southern United States.

NEW YORK: Audiovisual Bureau, Radio France Internationale, 972 Fifth Avenue, New York NY 10021 USA. Phone: +1 (212) 439-1452. Fax: +1 (212) 439 1455. Contact: Gérard Blondel or Julien Vin. This office promotes RFI, especially to language teachers and others within the educational community outside the southern United States, and arranges for bi-national cultural exchanges. It also sets up RFI feeds to local radio stations within much of the United States.

NEW YORK NEWS BUREAU: 1290 Avenue of the Americas, New York NY 10019 USA. Phone: +1 (212) 581-1771. Fax: +1 (212) 541 4309. Contact: Ms. Auberi Edler, Reporter; or Bruno Albin, Reporter.

WASHINGTON NEWS BUREAU: 529 14th Street NW, Suite 1126, Washington DC 20045 USA. Phone: +1 (202) 879-6706. Contact: Pierre J. Cayrol.

SAN FRANCISCO OFFICE, SCHEDULES: 2654 17th Avenue, San Francisco CA 94116 USA. Phone: +1 (415) 564-9968. Email: GPoppin@aol.com. Contact: George Poppin. This address, a volunteer office, only provides RFI schedules to listeners. All other correspondence should be sent directly to the main office in Paris.

Radio Monte Carlo-Middle East
MAIN OFFICE: Radio Monte Carlo-Moyen Orient, 116 avenue du président Kennedy, F-75116 Paris, France; or B.P. 371, Paris

16, France. Email: contact@rmc-mo.com. Web: (includes RealAudio) www.rmc-mo.com. A station of the RFI group whose programs are produced in Paris and aired via a mediumwave AM transmitter in Cyprus; also via FM in France and parts of the Middle East. Provides programs for RFI's Arabic service. A daily Arabic program is also broadcast on shortwave to North America via Radio Canada International's Sackville facilitities.

CYPRUS ADDRESS: P.O. Box 2026, Nicosia, Cyprus. Contact: M. Pavlides, Chef de Station. Reception reports have sometimes been verified via this address.

Trans World Radio

Voice of Orthodoxy—*see* Voix de l'Orthodoxie, below.

Voix de l'Orthodoxie, B.P. 416-08, F-75366 Paris Cedex 08, France. Email: irinavo@wanadoo.fr. Contact: Michel Solovieff, General Secretary. An organization that has long broadcast religious programming to Russia via shortwave transmitters in various countries, most recently via Kazakstan. Verifies reception reports, including those written in English.

RUSSIAN OFFICE: Nab. Leitenanta Shmidta 39, St. Petersburg 199034, Russia.

FRENCH GUIANA World Time –3

Radio France Internationale Guyane Relay Station, TDF, Montsinéry, French Guiana. Contact: (technical) Chef des Services Techniques, RFI Guyane. All correspondence concerning non-technical matters should be sent directly to the main addresses (*see*) for Radio France Internationale in France. Can consider replies only to technical correspondence in French.

RFO Guyane, 43 bis, rue du Docteur-Gabriel-Devèze, B.P. 7013 - Cayenne Cedex, French Guiana. Phone: +595 299-900 or +594 299-907. Fax: +594 299 958. Web: (text plus news summaries in Quick-Time audio) www.rfo.fr/guyane/guyane.htm; (streaming in RealAudio, Windows Media and Quick-Time) www.rfo.fr/emissions/emis_s_radio.htm. Contact: (administration) George Chow-Toun, Directeur Régional; (editorial) Claude Joly, Rédacteur en Chef; (technical) Charles Diony, Directeur Technique. Free stickers. Replies occasionally and sometimes slowly; correspondence in French preferred, but English often okay.

GABON World Time +1

Afrique Numéro Un, B.P. 1, Libreville, Gabon. Fax: +241 742 133. Email: africagc@cql-internet.fr. Web: www.africa1.com. Contact: (general) Gaston Didace Singangoye; or Jean Félix Ngawin Ndong; (technical) Mme. Marguerite Bayimbi, Le Directeur [sic] Technique. Free calendars and bumper stickers. $1, 2 IRCs or return postage helpful. Replies very slowly.

RTV Gabonaise (when operating), B.P. 10150, Libreville, Gabon. Contact: André Ranaud-Renombo, Le Directeur Technique, Adjoint Radio. Free stickers. $1 required. Replies occasionally, but slowly, to correspondence in French.

GEORGIA World Time +3 (+4 midyear)

Georgian Radio, TV-Radio Tbilisi, ul. M. Kostava 68, Tbilisi 380071, Republic of Georgia. Phone: (domestic service) +995 (32) 368-362; (external service) +995 (32) 360-063. Fax: +995 (32) 955 137. Email: office@geotvr.ge. Web: (includes MP3) www.geotvr.ge. Contact: (external service) Helena Apkhadze, Foreign Editor; Tamar Shengelia; Mrs. Natia Datuaschwili, Secretary; or Maya Chihradze; (domestic service) Lia Uumlaelsa, Manager; or V. Khundadze, Acting Director of Television and

Monika Lindenberg, program secretary and editorial assistant, works behind the scenes at Deutsche Welle's feature and magazine production section.

DW

Radio Department. External Service may be closed down in the near future. Replies erratically and slowly, in part due to financial restrictions. Return postage or $1 helpful.

Radio Hara, Rustaveli Ave. 52, II Floor, Apt. 211-212, Tbilisi, Georgia. Email: league@geoconst.org.ge. Contact: Nino Berdznishvili, Program Manager; or Zourab Shengelia. Programs are produced by the Georgian-Abkhazian Relations Institute.

Republic of Abkhazia Radio, Abkhaz State Radio and TV Co., Aidgylara Street 34, Sukhum 384900, Republic of Abkhazia; or Zvanba Street 8, Sukhum 384900, Republic of Abkhazia. However, given the problems in getting mail to Abkhazia, the station requests that reception reports be sent to the following address: National Library of Abkhazia, Krasnodar District, P.O. Box 964, 354000 Sochi, Russia. Phone: +995 (881) 24-867 or +995 (881) 25-321. Fax: +995 (881) 21 144. Contact: Zurab Argun, Director. A 1992 uprising in northwestern Georgia drove the majority of ethnic Georgians from the region. This area remains virtually autonomous from Georgia.

GERMANY   World Time +1 (+2 midyear)

📻Adventist World Radio

AWR GERMAN LANGUAGE OFFICE: Stimme der Hoffnung, Am Elfengrund 66, D-64297 Darmstadt, Germany. Phone: (listener services) +49 (6151) 9544-0; (technical) +49 (6151) 954-465. Fax: (listener services) +61 (6151) 954 470; (technical) +61 (6151) 539 3365. Email: (listener services) service@stimme-der-hoffnung.de; (technical) dxer@stimme-der-hoffnung.de. Web: (includes RealAudio) www.stimme-der-hoffnung.de/rs. Contact: (technical) Lothar Klepp. Note that only German should be used to contact this office; all listener mail in English should be sent to: Adventist World Radio, 39 Brendon Street, London W1H 5HD, United Kingdom. *See* other AWR listings under Guam, Kenya, Madagascar, United Kingdom and USA.

AWR EUROPE FREQUENCY MANAGEMENT OFFICE: Postfach 100252, D-64202 Darmstadt, Germany. Phone: (Dedio) +49 (6151) 953-151; (Crillo) +49 (6151) 953-153. Fax: +61 (6151) 953 152. Email: (Dedio) 102555.257@compuserve.com; or dedio@awr.org; (Cirillo) pino@awr.org. Contact: Claudius Dedio, Frequency Coordinator; or Giuseppe Cirillo, Monitoring Engineer.

📻Bayerischer Rundfunk, Rundfunkplatz 1, D-80300 München, Germany. Phone: +49 (89) 5900-01. Fax: +49 (89) 5900 2375. Email: (general) info@br-online.de; (technical) techinfo@br-mail.de; or techinfo@brnet.de. Web: (includes RealAudio) www.br-online.de. Contact: Dr. Gualtiero Guidi; or Jutta Paue, Engineering Adviser. Free stickers and 250-page program schedule book. Replies to correspondence in English and German. Verifies email reports with QSL cards, if requested.

Christliche Wissenschaft (Christian Science), Radiosendungen, E. Bethmann, P.O. Box 7330, D-22832 Norderstedt, Germany; or CS-Radiosendungen, Alexanderplatz 2, D-20099 Hamburg, Germany. Contact: Erich Bethmann. A program aired intermittently via the Jülich facilities of T-Systems International (*see*).

T-Systems International. *See* "Shortwave Radio Station Jülich—T-Systems International AG."

📻Deutsche Welle

MAIN OFFICE: Kurt-Schumacher-Str. 3, D-53113 Bonn, Germany; or (postal address) DW, D-53110, Bonn, Germany. Phone: +49 (228) 429-0; (English Service) +49 (228) 429-4144. Fax: +1 (228) 429 3000; (English Service) +49 (228) 429 4155. Email: online@dw-world.de; (English Service) feedback.english@dw-world.de. To reach specific individuals by email at Deutsche Welle the format is: firstname.lastname@dw-world.de. For language courses: feedback.radio@dw-world.de. Web: www.dw-world.de. Contact: Erik Bettermann, Director General; or Uta Thofern, Head of English Service.

Broadcasts via transmitters in Germany, Antigua, Canada, Madagascar, Portugal, Russia, Rwanda, Singapore and Sri Lanka.

TECHNICAL ADVISORY SERVICE: Phone: +49 (228) 429-3208. Fax: +49 (228) 429 3220. Email: tb@dw-world.de. All technical mail and QSL-reports should be sent to the Technical Advisory Service.

U.S./CANADIAN LISTENER CONTACT OFFICE: 2000 M Street, NW, Suite 335, Washington DC 20036 USA. Phone: +1 (202) 785-5730. Fax: +1 (202) 785 5735.

Deutschlandfunk, Raderberggürtel 40, D-50968 Köln, Germany. Phone: +49 (221) 345-0. Fax: +49 (221) 345 4802. Email: (program information) deutschlandfunk@dradio.de. Web: www.dradio.de/dlf/themen.

DeutschlandRadio-Berlin, Hans-Rosenthal-Platz, D-10825 Berlin Schönberg, Germany. Phone: +49 (30) 8503-0. Fax: +49 (30) 8503 6168. Email: dlrb@dlf.de; online@dlf.de; (program information) deutschlandradioberlin@dradio.de. Web: www.dradio.de/dlrb/index.html. Contact: Dr. Karl-Heinz Stamm; or Ulrich Reuter. Correspondence in English accepted. Sometimes sends stickers, pens, magazines and other souvenirs. Verifies email reports with a QSL card.

Evangeliums-Rundfunk—*see* Monaco (Trans World Radio).

Evangeliums-Radio-Hamburg, Postfach 920741, D-21137 Hamburg, Germany. Phone: +49 (40) 702-7025. Fax: +49 (40) 8540 8861. Email: evangeliums-radio-hamburg@t-online.de. Web: www.evr-hamburg.de. Verifies reports in German, and possibly, English. Airs via T-Systems International's Jülich facilities, and locally on FM and cable.

Missionswerk Friedensstimme, Postfach 100 638, D-51606 Gummersbach, Germany; or (physical address) Gimborner Str. 20, D-51709 Marienheide, Germany. Phone: +49 (2261) 24717. Fax: +49 (2261) 60170. Broadcasts to Russia via T-Systems International's Jülich facilities.

Shortwave Radio Station Jülich—T-Systems International
JÜLICH ADDRESS: Rundfunksendestelle Jülich, Merscher Höehe D-52428 Jülich, Germany. Phone: (head of station) +49 (2461)

697-310; (Technical Engineer) +49 (2461) 697-330; (manager sales and marketing all sw stations) +49 (2461) 697-350; (Ralf Weyl, back office) +49 (2461) 697-340. Fax: (all offices) +49 (2461) 697 371. Email: (Hirte) guenter.hirte@t-systems.com; (Goslawski) roman.goslawski@t-systems.com; (Brodowsky) walter.brodowsky@t-systems.com; (Weyl) ralf.weyl@t-systems.com. Contact: Günter Hirte, Head of Shortwave Radio Station Jülich; Roman Goslawski, Deputy Head of Shortwave Radio Station Jülich; Horst Tobias, Frequency Manager; (technical) Walter Brodowsky, Manager Sales and Marketing all SW Stations; or (nontechnical) Ralf Weyl, Customer Services. Reception reports accepted by mail or fax, and should be clearly marked to the attention of Walter Brodowsky.
KÖLN ADDRESS: Niederlassung 2 Köln, Service Centre Rundfunk, D-50482 Köln Germany. Phone: (Kraus) +49 (221) 575-4000; (Hufschlag) +49 (221) 575-4011. Fax: +49 (221) 575 4090. Email: info@dtag.de. Web: www.dtag.de; www.telekom.de. Contact: Egon Kraus, Head of Broadcasting Service Centre; or Josef Hufschlag, Customer Advisor for High Frequency Broadcasting. This organization operates transmitters on German soil used by Deutsche Welle, as well as those leased to various international world band stations.
📻**Radio Santec**, Marienstrasse 1, D-97070 Würzburg, Germany. Phone: (0800-1600 Central European Time, Monday through Friday) +49 (931) 3903-264. Fax: +49 (931) 3903 195. Email: info@radio-santec.com. Web: (includes RealAudio) www.radio-santec.com. Reception reports verified with QSL cards only if requested. Radio Santec, constituted as a separate legal entity in 1999, is the radio branch of Universelles Leben (Universal Life).
Stimme des Evangeliums, Evangelische Missions-Gemeinden, Jahnstrasse 9, D-89182 Bernstadt, Germany. Phone: +49 (7348) 948-026. Fax: +49 (7348) 948-027. Contact: Pastor Albert Giessler. Replies to correspondence in German, and verifies reception reports. A broadcast of the Evangelical Missions Congregations in Germany, and aired via facilities of T-Systems International (*see*) in Jülich.
📻**Südwestrundfunk**, Neckarstrasse 230, D-70190 Stuttgart, Germany. Phone +49 (711) 929-0. Fax: +49 (711) 929 2600. Email: (general) info@swr-online.de; (technical) technik@swr-online.de. Web: (includes RealAudio) www.swr-online.de. Sometimes sends stickers and postcards. Return postage not required.
SWR BADEN-BADEN: Hans-Bredow-Strasse, D-76530 Baden-Baden, Germany. Phone: +49 (7221) 929-0.
This station is the result of a merger between the former Süddeutscher Rundfunk and Südwestfunk. Based in Stuttgart, transmissions under the new banner commenced in September 1998.

GHANA   World Time exactly

WARNING—CONFIDENCE ARTISTS: Attempted correspondence with Radio Ghana may result in requests, perhaps resulting from mail theft, from skilled confidence artists for money, free electronic or other products, publications or immigration sponsorship. To help avoid this, correspondence to Radio Ghana should be sent via registered mail.
📻**Ghana Broadcasting Corporation**, Broadcasting House, P.O. Box 1633, Accra, Ghana. Phone: +233 (21) 221-161. Fax: +233 (21) 221 153 or +233 (21) 773 227. Web: (not updated) www.gbc.com.gh. Contact: (general) Mrs. Maud Blankson-Mills, Director of Corporate Affairs; (administration) Cris Tackie, Acting Director of Radio; (technical) K.D. Frimpong, Director of Engineering; or E. Heneath, Propagation Department. Re-

plies tend to be erratic, and reception reports are best sent to the attention of the Propagation Engineer, GBC Monitoring Station. Enclosing an IRC, return postage or $1 and registering your letter should improve the chances of a reply.

GREECE   World Time +2 (+3 midyear)

📻**Foni tis Helladas** (Voice of Greece)
NONTECHNICAL: Hellenic Radio-Television, ERA-5, The Voice of Greece, 432 Mesogion Av., 15342 Athens, Greece; or P.O. Box 60019, 15310 Aghia Paraskevi, Athens, Greece. Phone: +30 (210) 606-6310. Fax: +30 (210) 606 6309. Email: era5@ert.gr; (Foreign Language News Department) interprogram@ert.gr. Web: (includes Windows Media) www.ert.gr/radio/era5. Contact: Angeliki Barka, Head of Programmes. Ioannis Koutzouradis, Managing Director; or Gina Vogiatzoglou, Programme Director. Free tourist literature.
TECHNICAL: Elliniki Radiophonia—ERA-5, General Technical Directorate, ERT/ERA Hellenic Radio Television SA, Mesogion 402, 15342 Athens, Greece. Phone: (Charalambopoulos) +30 (210) 606-6257; (Vorgias) +30 (210) 606-6256 or +30 (210) 606-6263. Fax: +30 (210) 606 6243. Email: (reception reports) era5@ert.gr; (Vorgias) svorgias@ert.gr; (Charalambopoulos) bcharalabopoulos@ert.gr. Contact: Charalambos Charalambopoulos or Sotiris Vorgias, Planning Engineer; (administration) Th. Kokossis, General Director; or Nicolas Yannakakis, Director. Technical reception reports may be sent via mail, fax or email. Taped reports not accepted.
Radiophonikos Stathmos Makedonias—ERT-3, Angelaki 2, 546 21 Thessaloniki, Greece. Phone: +30 (310) 244-979. Fax: +30 (310) 236 370. Email: charter3@compulink.gr. Web: (includes Windows Media) www.ert3.gr. Contact: (general) Mrs. Tatiana Tsioli, Program Director; or Lefty Kongalides, Head of International Relations; (technical) Dimitrios Keramidas, Engineer. Free booklets, stickers and other small souvenirs.

GUAM   World Time +10

Adventist World Radio—KSDA
AWR-Asia, P.O. Box 8990, Agat, GU 96928 USA. Phone: +1 (671) 565-2000. Fax: +1 (671) 565 2983. Email: english@awr.org. Web: www.awr.org. Contact: Elvin Vence, Chief Engineer. All listener mail should be sent to: Adventist World Radio, 39 Brendon Street, London W1H 5HD, United Kingdom. Also, *see* AWR listings under Germany, Kenya, Madagascar, United Kingdom and USA.
Trans World Radio—KTWR
MAIN OFFICE, ENGINEERING INQUIRIES & FREQUENCY COORDINATION ONLY: P.O. Box 8780, Agana, GU 96928 USA. Phone: +1 (671) 828-8638. Fax: +1 (671) 828 8636. Email: cwhite@guam.twr.org or ktwrfreq@guam.twr.org. Web: (schedule) www.gospelcom.net/twr/broadcasts/guam.htm. Contact: (technical) Chuck White, Chief Engineer/Station Manager; or George Ross, Frequency Coordinator Manager. This office will also verify email reports with a QSL card. Requests reports covering 15-30 minutes of programming. All English listener mail of a nontechnical nature should now be sent to the Australian office (*see* next entry). Addresses for listener mail in other languages will be found in the broadcasts. Also, *see* USA.
ENGLISH LISTENER MAIL, NONTECHNICAL: Trans World Radio ANZ, 2-6 Albert Street, Blackburn, Victoria 3130, Australia; or P.O. Box 390, Box Hill, Victoria 3128, Australia. Phone: +61 (3) 9878-5922. Fax: +61 (3) 9878 5944. Email: info@twradio.org. Web: www.twradio.org. Contact: John Reeder, National Director.

PROGRAMMING INQUIRES & REGIONAL HEADQUARTERS: Trans World Radio, 75 High Street #04-00 Wisma Sugnomal, Singapore 179435, Singapore.
CHINA (HONG KONG) OFFICE: TWR-CMI, P.O. Box 98697, Tsimshatsui Post Office, Kowloon, Hong Kong. Phone: +852 2780-8336. Fax: +852 2385 5045. Email: (general) info@twr.org.hk; (Ko) simon_ko@compuserve.com; (Lok) joycelok@compuserve.com. Web: www.twr.org.hk. Contact: Simon Ko, Acting Area Director; or Joyce Lok, Programming/ Follow -up Director.
NEW DELHI OFFICE: P.O. Box 4310, New Delhi-110 019, India. Contact: N. Emil Jebasingh, Vishwa Vani; or S. Stanley.
TOKYO OFFICE: Pacific Broadcasting Association, C.P.O. Box 1000, Tokyo 100-91, Japan. Phone +81 (3) 3295-4921. Fax: +81 (3) 3233 2650. Email: pba@path.ne.jp. Contact: (administration) Nobuyoshi Nakagawa.

GUATEMALA   World Time –6

La Voz de Nahualá, Nahualá, Sololá, Guatemala. Phone: +502 763-0115 or +502 763-0163. Contact: (technical) Juan Fidel Lepe Juárez, Técnico Auxiliar; or F. Manuel Esquipulas Carrillo Tzep. Return postage required. Correspondence in Spanish preferred.
Radio Amistad
ADDRESS FOR RECEPTION REPORTS: David Daniell, Asesor de Comunicaciones, Apartado Postal 25, Bulevares MX, 53140 Mexico. Phone/Fax: +52 (5) 572-9633. Email: dpdaniell@aol.com. Replies to correspondence in English or Spanish.
Radio Buenas Nuevas, 13020 San Sebastián, Huehuetenango, Guatemala. Contact: Israel G. Rodas Mérida, Gerente. $1 or return postage helpful. Free religious and station information in Spanish. Sometimes includes a small pennant. Replies to correspondence in Spanish.
Radio Chortís (when operating), Centro Social, 20004 Jocotán, Chiquimula, Guatemala. Contact: Padre Juan María Boxus, Director. $1 or return postage required. Replies irregularly to correspondence in Spanish.
Radio Cultural—TGNA, Apartado 601, 01901 Guatemala City, Guatemala. Phone: +502 472-1745; (English) +502 471-0807. Fax: +502 440-0260. Email: tgn@radiocultural.net; tgna@guate.net. Web: www.radiocultural.net. Contact: Wayne Berger, Chief Engineer. Free religious printed matter. Return postage or $1 appreciated.
Radio K'ekchi—TGVC, 3ra Calle 7-15, Zona 1, 16015 Fray Bartolomé de las Casas, Alta Verapaz, Guatemala; (Media Consultant) David Daniell, Asesor de Comunicaciones, Apartado Postal 25, Bulevares MX, 53140 Mexico. Phone: (station) +502 950-0299; (Daniell, Phone/Fax) +52 (5) 572-9633. Fax: (station) +502 950 0398. Email: dpdaniell@aol.com. Contact: (general) Gilberto Sun Xicol, Gerente; Ancelmo Cuc Chub, Director; or Mateo Botzoc, Director de Programas; (technical) Larry Baysinger, Ingeniero Jefe. Free paper pennant. $1 or return postage required. Replies to correspondence in Spanish.
Radio Maya de Barillas—TGBA, 13026 Villa de Barillas, Huehuetenango, Guatemala. Contact: José Castañeda, Pastor Evangélico y Gerente. Free pennants and pins. Station is very interested in receiving reception reports. $1 or return postage required. Replies occasionally to correspondence in Spanish.
Radio Verdad, Apartado Postal 5, Chiquimula, Guatemala. Email: radioverdad@chiquimula.zzn.com. Contact: Dr. Édgar Amílcar Madrid Morales, Gerente. May send free pennants & calendars. Replies to correspondence in Spanish and English;

return postage appreciated. An evangelical and educational station.

GUINEA   World Time exactly

Radiodiffusion-Télévision Guinéenne, B.P. 391, Conakry, Guinea. If no reply is forthcoming from this address, try sending your letter to: D.G.R./P.T.T., B.P. 3322, Conakry, Guinea. Phone/Fax: +224 451-408. Email: (Issa Conde, Directeur) issaconde@yahoo.fr. Contact: (general) Yaoussou Diaby, Journaliste Sportif; Boubacar Yacine Diallo, Directeur Général/ ORTG; Issa Conde, Directeur; or Seny Camara; (administration) Momo Toure, Chef Services Administratifs; (technical, studio) Mbaye Gagne, Chef de Studio; (technical, overall) Direction des Services Techniques. Return postage or $1 required. Replies very irregularly to correspondence in French.

GUYANA   World Time –3

Voice of Guyana, Guyana Broadcasting Corporation, Broadcasting House, P.O. Box 10760, Georgetown, Guyana. Phone: +592 (2) 258-734, +592 (2) 258-083 or +592 (2) 262-691. Fax: +592 (2) 258 756, but persist as the fax machine appears to be switched off much of the time. Contact: (general) Indira Anandjit, Personnel Assistant; or M. Phillips; (technical) Roy Marshall, Senior Technician; or Shiroxley Goodman, Chief Engineer. $1 or IRC helpful. Sending a spare sticker from another station helps assure a reply. Note that when the station's mediumwave AM transmitter is down because of a component fault, parts of the shortwave unit are sometimes 'borrowed' until spares become available. As a result, the station is sometimes off shortwave for several weeks at a time.

HOLLAND—*see* NETHERLANDS

HONDURAS   World Time –6

La Voz de la Mosquitia (if reactivated)
STATION: Puerto Lempira, Dpto. Gracias a Dios, Honduras. Contact: Sammy Simpson, Director; or Larry Sexton. Free pennants.
U.S. OFFICE: Global Outreach, Box 1, Tupelo MS 38802 USA. Phone: +1 (601) 842-4615. Another U.S. contact is Larry Hooker, who occasionally visits the station, and who can be reached at +1 (334) 694-7976.
La Voz Evangélica—HRVC
MAIN OFFICE: Apartado Postal 3252, Tegucigalpa, M.D.C., Honduras. Phone: +504 234-3468/69/70. Fax: +504 233 3933. Email: hrvc@infanet.hn. Web (includes RealAudio): www.hrvc.org. Contact: (general) Srta. Orfa Esther Durón Mendoza, Secretaria; Tereso Ramos, Director de Programación; Alan Maradiaga; or Modesto Palma, Jefe, Depto. Tráfico; (technical) Carlos Paguada, Director del Dpto. Técnico; (administration) Venancio Mejía, Gerente; or Nelson Perdomo, Director. Free calendars. Three IRCs or $1 required. Replies to correspondence in English, Spanish, Portuguese and German.
REGIONAL OFFICE, SAN PEDRO SULA: Apartado 2336, San Pedro Sula, Honduras. Phone: +504 557-5030. Contact: Hernán Miranda, Director.
REGIONAL OFFICE, LA CEIBA: Apartado 164, La Ceiba, Honduras. Phone: +504 443-2390. Contact: José Banegas, Director.
Radio Costeña—relays Radio Ebenezer (1220 kHz mediumwave AM), and all correspondence should be sent to the latter's address: Radio Ebenezer 1220 AM, Apartado 3466, San Pedro Sula, Honduras. Email: ebenezer@globalnet.hn; or

pastor@ebenezer.hn. Web: www.ebenezer.hn. Contact: Germán Ponce, Gerente. According to a Swedish DXer, a reply was received from Iván Franco at casasps@yahoo.com, but it's not known what relation this person has with the station.

Radio HRMI, Radio Misiones Internacionales
STATION: Apartado Postal 20583, Comayaguela, M.D.C., Honduras. Phone: +504 233-9029. Contact: Wayne Downs, Director. $1 or return postage helpful.
U.S. OFFICE: IMF World Missions, P.O. Box 6321, San Bernardino CA 92412, USA. Phone +1 (909) 370-4515. Fax: +1 (909) 370 4862. Email: jkpimf@msn.com. Contact: Dr. James K. Planck, President; or Gustavo Roa, Coordinator.

Radio Litoral—HRLW, Apartado Postal 888, La Ceiba, Provincia Atlántida, Honduras. Phone: +504 443-0039. Email: radiolitoral@psinet.hn. Contact: Vicente Pintor, Gerente. Free postcards. 1$ or return postage required. Replies to correspondence in Spanish.

Radio Luz y Vida—HRPC, Apartado 369, San Pedro Sula, Honduras. Phone: +504 654-1221. Fax: +504 557 0394. Email: efmhonduras@globalnet.hn. Contact: Don Moore, Station Director; Cristóbal "Chris" Fleck; Ubaldo Zaldívar; or, to have your letter read over the air, "English Friendship Program." Return postage or $1 appreciated.

HUNGARY   World Time +1 (+2 midyear)

🔊Radio Budapest
STATION OFFICES: Bródy Sándor utca 5-7, H-1800 Budapest, Hungary. Phone: (general) +36 (1) 328-7224, +36 (1) 328-8328, +36 (1) 328-7357 +36 (1) 328-8588, +36 (1) 328-7710 or +36 (1) 328-7723; (voice mail, English) +36 (1) 328-8320; (voice mail, German) +36 (1) 328-7325; (administration) +36 (1) 328-7503 or +36 (1) 328-8415; (technical) +36 (1) 328-7226 or +36 (1) 328-8923. Fax: (general) +36 (1) 328 8517; (administration) +36 (1) 328 8838; (technical) +36 (1) 328 7105. Email: (English) english@kaf.radio.hu; (German) nemet1@kaf.radio.hu; (Spanish) espanol@kaf.radio.hu; (Hungarian Information Resources) avadasz@bluemoon.sma.com; (technical) (Füszfás) Fuszfasla@muszak.radio.hu. Web: (includes RealAudio) www.english.radio.hu/index.php?rovat_id=1059. Contact: (English Language Service) Ágnes Kevi, Correspondence; Louis Horváth, DX Editor; or Sándor Laczkó, Editor; (administration) László Krassó, Director, Foreign Broadcasting; Dr. Zsuzsa Mészáros, Vice-Director, Foreign Broadcasting; János Szirányi, President, Magyar Rádió; or János Simkó, Vice President, Magyar Rádió; (technical) László Füszfás, Deputy Technical Director, Magyar Rádió; Külföldi Adások Főszerkesztősége; or Lajos Horváth, Műszaki Igazgatósá; (Hungarian Information Resources) Andrew Vadasz.
COMMUNICATION AUTHORITY: P.O. Box 75, H-1525 Budapest, Hungary. Phone: +36 (1) 457-7178. Fax: +36 (1) 457 7120 or 36 (1) 356 5520. Email: czuprak@hif.hu. Contact: Ernö Czuprák.
TRANSMISSION AUTHORITY: Ministry of Transport, Communications and Water Management, P.O. Box 87, H-1400 Budapest, Hungary. Phone: +36 (1) 461-3390. Fax: +36 (1) 461 3392. Email: horvathf@cms.khvm.hu. Contact: Ferenc Horváth, Frequency Manager, Radio Communications Engineering Services.

ICELAND   World Time exactly

🔊Ríkisútvarpid, International Relations Department, Efstaleiti 1, IS-150 Reykjavik, Iceland. Phone: +354 515-3000. Fax: +354 515 3010. Email: isradio@ruv.is. Web: (includes RealAudio) www.ruv.is/utvarpid. Contact: Dóra Ingvadóttir, Head of International Relations; or Markús Öern Antonsson, Director.

INDIA   World Time +5:30

WARNING—MAIL THEFT: PASSPORT readers report that letters to India containing IRCs and other valuables have disappeared en route when not registered. Best is either to register your letter or to send correspondence in an unsealed envelope, and without enclosures.
EMAIL ADDRESSES: Several email addresses for regional stations listed below have been reported as not being in use, at least temporarily. Rejection messages include: "Mailbox temporarily disabled," "Over quota," and "Account has been disabled."
VERIFICATION OF REGIONAL STATIONS: All Indian regional stations can be verified via New Delhi (*see* All India Radio—External Services Division for contact details), but some listeners prefer contacting each station individually, in the hope of receiving a direct QSL. Well-known Indian DXer Jose Jacob makes the following suggestions: address your report to the station engineer of the respective station; specify the time of reception in both World Time (UTC) and Indian Standard Time (IST); instead of using the SINPO code, write a brief summary of reception quality; and if possible, report on local programs rather than relays of national programming from New Delhi. Jose adds that reports should be written in English, and return postage is not required (although an IRC or mint Indian stamps may sometimes help).

🔊Akashvani—All India Radio
ADMINISTRATION/ENGINEERING: Directorate General of All India Radio, Akashvani Bhawan, 1 Sansad Marg, New Delhi-110 001, India. Phone: +91 (11) 2342-1006 or +91 (11) 2371-5413; (Director General) +91 (11) 2371-0300 Ext. 102; (Engineer-in-Chief) +91 (11) 2342-1058 or (Phone/Fax) +91 (11) 2342-1459; (Director, Spectrum Management) +91 (11) 2342-1062 or +91 (11) 2342-1145. Fax: +91 (11) 2371 11956; (Director General) +91 (11) 2342 1956. Email: airlive@air.org.in; (Director General) dgair@air.org.in; (Engineer-in-Chief) einc@air.org.in; (Director, Spectrum Management) faair@nda.vsnl.net.in. Web: (includes live audio) www.allindiaradio.org. Contact: (technical) K.M. Paul, Engineer-in-Chief; A.K. Bhatnagar, Director, Spectrum Management; or Devendra Singh, Deputy Director, Spectrum Management.
AUDIENCE RESEARCH: Audience Research Unit, All India Radio, Press Trust of India Building, 2nd floor, Sansad Marg, New Delhi-110 001, India. Phone: (general) +91 (11) 2371-0033 or +91 (11) 2371-9215; (Director) +91 (11) 2338-6506. Contact: Ramesh Chandra, Director.
CENTRAL MONITORING STATION: All India Radio, Ayanagar, New Delhi-110 047, India. Phone: +91 (11) 2650-2955 or +91 (11) 2650 1763. Contact: P.S. Bhatnagar, Director.
COMMERCIAL SERVICE: Vividh Bharati Service, AIR, P.O. Box 11497, 101 M.K. Road, Mumbai-400 020, India. Phone: +91 (22) 2203-7193.
INTERNATIONAL MONITORING STATION—MAIN OFFICE: International Monitoring Station, All India Radio, Dr. K.S. Krishnan Road, Todapur, New Delhi-110 097, India. Phone: +91 (11) 2584-2939. Contact: B.L. Kasturiya, Deputy Director; D.P. Chhabra or R.K. Malviya, Assistant Research Engineers—Frequency Planning.
NATIONAL CHANNEL: AIR, Gate 22, Jawaharlal Nehru Stadium, Lodhi Road, New Delhi-110 003. Phone: +91 (11) 2584-3825; (station engineer) +91 (11) 2584-3207. Contact: J.K. Das, Director; or V.D. Sharma, Station Engineer.
NEWS SERVICES DIVISION: News Services Division, Broadcasting House, 1 Sansad Marg, New Delhi-110 001, India. Phone:

(newsroom) +91 (11) 2342-1006 or +91 (11) 2371-5413; (Special Director General—News) +91 (11) 2371-0084 or +91 (11) 2373-1510; (News on phone in English) +91 (11) 2332-4343; (News on phone in Hindi) +91 (11) 2332-4242. Fax: +91 (11) 2371 1196. Email: nsdair@giasdl01.vsnl.net.in. Contact: B.I. Saini, Special Director General—News.

PROGRAMMING: Broadcasting House, 1 Sansad Marg, New Delhi-110 001 India. Phone: (general) +91 (11) 2371-5411.

RESEARCH AND DEVELOPMENT: Office of the Chief Engineer R&D, All India Radio, 14-B Ring Road, Indraprastha Estate, New Delhi-110 002, India. Phone: (general) +91 (11) 2337-8211/12; (Chief Engineer) +91 (11) 2337 9255 or +91 (11) 2337-9329. Fax: +91 (11) 2331 8329 or +91 (11) 2331 6674. Email: rdair@nda.vsnl.net.in. Web: www.air.kode.net. Contact: B.L. Mathur, Chief Engineer.

TRANSCRIPTION AND PROGRAM EXCHANGE SERVICES: Akashvani Bhavan, 1 Sansad Marg, New Delhi-110 001, India. Phone: (Director, Transcription & Program Exchange Services: V.A. Magazine) +91 (11) 2342-1927. Contact: D.P. Jadav, Director.

All India Radio—Aizawl, Radio Tila, Tuikhuahtlang, Aizawl-796 001, Mizoram, India. Phone: +91 (389) 2322-415. Fax: +91 (389) 2322 114. Email: airzawl@sancharnet.in. Contact: (technical) S. Nellai Nayagam, Station Engineer.

All India Radio—Aligarh, Anoopshahar Road, Aligarh-202 001, Uttar Pradesh, India. Phone: +91 (571) 2401-993. Phone/Fax: +91 (571) 2400-972.

All India Radio—Bangalore Shortwave Transmitting Centre

HEADQUARTERS: see All India Radio—External Services Division.

AIR OFFICE NEAR TRANSMITTER: Superintending Engineer, Super Power Transmitters, All India Radio, Yelahanka New Town, Bangalore-560 064, Karnataka, India. Phone/Fax: +91 (80) 2846-0379. Email: sptairynk@vsnl.com. Contact: (technical) R. Narasimha Swamy, Superintending Engineer.

All India Radio—Bhopal, Akashvani Bhavan, Shamla Hills, Bhopal-462 002, Madhya Pradesh, India. Phone: +91 (755) 2540-041. Email: airbhopal@vsnl.com. Contact: (technical) S.K. Gaur, Station Engineer.

All India Radio—Chennai

EXTERNAL SERVICES: see All India Radio—External Services Division.

DOMESTIC SERVICE: Avadi, Chennai-100 062, Tamil Nadu, India. Phone/Fax: +91 (44) 2638-3204. Email: airavadi@vsnl.com. Contact: (technical) S.R.M Sastry, Superintending Engineer; or K. Palanisamy, Assistant Station Engineer.

All India Radio—External Services Division

MAIN ADDRESS: Broadcasting House, 1 Sansad Marg, P.O. Box 500, New Delhi-110 001, India. Phone: (general) +91 (11) 2371-5411; (Director) +91 (11) 2371-0057. Contact: (general) P.P. Setia, Director of External Services; or S.C. Panda, Audience Relations Officer; (technical) Rakesh Tyagi, Assistant Director Engineering (F.A.). Email (Research Dept.): rdair@giasdl01.vsnl.net.in; (comments on programs) air@kode.net. Web: (includes RealAudio in English and other languages) www.allindiaradio.com; http://air.kode.net; (unofficial, but contains updated schedule information) www.angelfire.com/in/alokdg/air.html. Free monthly *India Calling* magazine and stickers. Replies erratic. Except for stations listed below, correspondence to domestic stations is more likely to be responded to if it is sent via the External Services Division; request that your letter be forwarded to the appropriate domestic station.

VERIFICATION ADDRESS: Prasar Bharati Corporation of India, Akashvani Bhavan, Room 204, Sansad Marg, New Delhi-110 001, India; or P.O. Box 500, New Delhi-110 001, India. Fax: +91 (11) 2342 1062 or +91 (11) 2342 1145. Email: faair@nda.vsnl.net.in; spectrum-manager@air.org.in; or faair@giasdl01.vsnl.net.in; (Bhatnagar) akb@air.org.in. Contact: A. K. Bhatnagar, Director, Spectrum Management & Synergy.

All India Radio—Gangtok, Old MLA Hostel, Gangtok-737 101, Sikkim, India. Phone: +91 (359) 222-636. Email: airgtk@dte.vsnl.net.in. Contact: (general) Y.P. Yolmo, Station Director; (technical) A. Bhatnagar, Station Engineer.

All India Radio—Gorakhpur

NEPALESE EXTERNAL SERVICE: see All India Radio—External Services Division.

DOMESTIC SERVICE: Town Hall, Post Bag 26, Gorakhpur-273 001, Uttar Pradesh, India. Phone/Fax: +91 (551) 2337-401. Fax: +91 (551) 2333 618. Contact: (technical) Dr. S.M. Pradhan, Superintending Engineer; or P.P. Shukle, Station Engineer.

All India Radio—Guwahati, P.O. Box 28, Chandmari, Guwahati-781 003, Assam, India. Phone/Fax: +91 (361) 2540-135. Fax: +91 (361) 2540 378 or +91 (361) 2540 426. Email: airgau@sancharnet.in. Contact: (technical) P.C. Sanghi, Superintending Engineer; or H.S. Dhillon, Station Engineer.

All India Radio—Hyderabad, Rocklands, Saifabad, Hyderabad-500 004, Andhra Pradesh, India. Phone: +91 (40) 2323-4904. Fax: +91 (40) 2323 2239 or +91 (40) 2323 4282. Email: airhyd@hd2.vsnl.net.in. Contact: (technical) P. Vishwanathan, Superintending Engineer.

All India Radio—Imphal, Palau Road, Imphal-795 001, Manipur, India. Phone: +91 (385) 220-534. Email: airimfal@dte.vsnl.net.in. Contact: (technical) M. Jayaraman, Superintending Engineer.

All India Radio—Itanagar, Naharlagun, Itanagar-791 110, Arunachal Pradesh, India. Phone: +91 (360) 2213-007. Fax: +91 (360) 2213 008 or +91 (360) 2212 933. Contact: J.T. Jirdoh, Station Director; or P. Sanghi, Superintending Engineer. Verifications direct from station are difficult, as engineering is done by staff visiting from the Regional Engineering Headquarters at AIR—Guwahati (*see*); that address might be worth contacting if all else fails.

All India Radio—Jaipur, 5 Park House, Mirza Ismail Road, Jaipur-302 001, Rajasthan, India. Phone: +91 (141) 2366-623. Fax: +91 (141) 2363 196. Email: airjpr@jp1.dot.net.in. Contact: (technical) S.C. Sharma, Station Engineer; or C.L. Goel, Assistant Station Engineer.

All India Radio—Jammu—*see* Radio Kashmir—Jammu.

All India Radio—Jeypore, Jeypore-764 005, Orissa, India. Phone: +91 (685) 2432-524. Fax: +91 (685) 2432 358. Email: airjeyp@dte.vsn1.net.in; airjeyp@sancharnet.in. Contact: M.P. Singh, Superintending Engineer; P. Subramanium, Assistant Station Engineer; A. Chanti Babu, Assistant Station Engineer; or K. Naryan Das, Assistant Station Engineer.

All India Radio—Kohima, P.O. Box 42, Kohima-797 001, Nagaland, India. Phone/Fax: +91 (370) 222-121. Fax: +91 (370) 222 109. Contact: (technical) M. Tyagi, Superintending Engineer; K.K Jose, Assistant Engineer; or K. Morang, Assistant Station Engineer. Return postage, $1 or IRC helpful.

All India Radio—Kolkata, G.P.O. Box 696, Kolkata—700 001, West Bengal, India. Phone: +91 (33) 2248-9131. Email: aircal@cal.vsnl.net.in. Contact: (technical) S.K. Pal, Superintending Engineer.

All India Radio—Kurseong, Mehta Club Building, Kurseong-734 203, Darjeeling District, West Bengal, India. Phone: +91 (3554) 24350. Contact: (general) George Kuruvilla, Assistant

Director; (technical) R.K. Sinha, Chief Engineer; or B.K. Behara, Station Engineer.

All India Radio—Leh—*see* Radio Kashmir—Leh.

All India Radio—Lucknow, 18 Vidhan Sabha Marg, Lucknow-226 001, Uttar Pradesh, India. Phone: +91 (522) 2244-130 or +91 (522) 2237-476. Fax: +91 (522) 2237 470. Email: airlko@sancharnet.in. Contact: Dr. S.M. Pradhan, Superintending Engineer. This station now appears to be replying via the External Services Division, New Delhi.

All India Radio—Mumbai

EXTERNAL SERVICES: see All India Radio External Services Division.

COMMERCIAL SERVICE (VIVIDH BHARATI): All India Radio, P.O. Box 11497, 101 M K Road, Mumbai-400 0020, Maharashtra, India. Phone: (general) +91 (22) 2203-1341 or +91 (22) 2203-594; (Phone/Fax, Director) +91 (22) 2203-7702; (Phone/Fax, Superintending Engineer) +91 (22) 2882-1867. Fax: +91 (22) 2287 6040. Email: (general) vbs@vsnl.com; (Manuswamy) mindiran@yahoo.co.uk. Contact: Vijayalakshmi Sinha, Director; or Indiran Munuswamy, Superintending Engineer.

DOMESTIC SERVICE: P.O. Box 13034, Mumbai-400 020, Maharashtra, India. Phone: +91 (22) 2202-9853. Email: (general) sdairmumbai@vsnl.net; (Manuswamy) mindiran@yahoo.co.uk. Contact:Indiran Munuswamy, Superintending Engineer; or Lak Bhatnagar, Supervisor, Frequency Assignments.

All India Radio—New Delhi, P.O. Box 70, New Delhi-110 011, India. Phone: (general) +91 (11) 2371-6249. Fax: +91 (11) 2371 0113. Email: (reception reports) faair@nda.vsnl.net.in. Contact: (technical) V. Chaudhry, Superintending Engineer.

All India Radio—Panaji Shortwave Transmitting Centre

HEADQUARTERS: see All India Radio—External Services Division, above.

AIR OFFICE NEAR TRANSMITTER: P.O. Box 220, Altinho, Panaji-403 001, Goa, India. Phone: +91 (832) 2225-623 or +91 (832) 2230-696. Fax: +91 (832) 2225 662 or +91 (832) 2225 351. Email: airtrgoa@goatelecom.com. Contact: (technical) V.K. Singhla, Station Engineer; V. Punnose, Superintending Engineer; or G.N. Shetti, Assistant Engineer.

All India Radio—Port Blair, Haddo Post, Dilanipur, Port Blair-744 102, South Andaman, Andaman and Nicobar Islands, Union Territory, India. Phone: +91 (3192) 30-682. Fax: +91 (3192) 230 260. Email: pblairpb@sancharnet.in. Contact: (technical) Station Engineer (K.S. Venkateraslu retires by early 2005; replacement unknown). Registering letters appears to be useful.

All India Radio—Ranchi, 6 Ratu Road, Ranchi-834 001, Jharkhand, India. Phone: +91 (651) 2283-310 or +91 (651) 2208-558. Fax: +91 (651) 2301 666 or +91 (651) 2301 957. Contact: (technical) H.K. Sinha, Superintending Engineer.

All India Radio—Shillong, P.O. Box 14, Shillong-793 001, Meghalaya, India. Phone: +91 (364) 2224-443 or +91 (364) 2222-781. Fax: +91 (364) 2222 781. Email: air_neschillong@yahoo.com. Contact: (general) C. Lalsaronga, Director NEIS; (technical) R. Venugopal, Superintending Engineer; or H. Diengdoh, Station Engineer. Free booklet on station's history. Replies tend to be rare, due to a shortage of staff.

All India Radio—Shimla, Choura Maidan, Simla-171 004, Himachal Pradesh, India. Phone: +91 (177) 24809 or +91 (177) 2211-355. Fax: +91 (177) 2204 400. Contact: (technical) V.K. Upadhayay, Superintending Engineer; or Krishna Murari, Assistant Engineer. Return postage helpful.

All India Radio—Srinagar—*see* Radio Kashmir—Srinagar.

All India Radio—Thiruvananthapuram, P.O. Box 403, Bhakti Vilas, Vazuthacaud, Thiruvananthapuram-695 014, Kerala, India. Phone: +91 (471) 2325-009. Fax: +91 (471) 2324 406 or +91 (471) 2324 982. Email: airtvpm@md4.vsnl.net.in; (Station Engineer) tvm_airtvpm@sancharnet.in. Contact: (general) K. Srinivasa Raghavan, Station Director; (technical) T.S. Sreekumar, Assistant Station Engineer.

Radio Kashmir—Leh, Leh-194 101, Ladakh District, Jammu and Kashmir, India. Phone: +91 (198) 2252-063. Fax: +91 (198) 2252 234. Contact: (technical) L.K. Gandotar, Station Engineer; T.S. Sreekumar, Assistant Station Engineer.

Radio Kashmir—Srinagar, Sherwani Road, Srinagar-190 001, Jammu and Kashmir, India. Phone: +91 (194) 271-460. Phone/Fax: +91 (194) 2452-100. Fax: +91 (194) 2452 168. Email: akashvani@nde.com. Contact: L. Rehman, Station Director; or P.M. Bansal, Station Engineer.

INDONESIA
World Time +7 Western: Waktu Indonesia Bagian Barat (Jawa, Sumatera); +8 Central: Waktu Indonesia Bagian Tengal (Bali, Kalimantan, Sulawesi, Nusa Tenggara); +9 Eastern: Waktu Indonesia Bagian Timur (Papua, Maluku)

NOTE: Except where otherwise indicated, Indonesian stations, especially those of the Radio Republik Indonesia (RRI) network, will reply to at least some correspondence in English. However, correspondence in Indonesian is more likely to ensure a reply.

Kang Guru II Radio English, KANGURU, JALF, Kotak Pos 3095, Denpasar 80030, Bali, Indonesia. Phone: +62 (361) 225-243. Fax: +62 (361) 263 509. Email: kangguru@ialfbali.co.id. Web: www.kanguru.org. Contact: Walter Slamer, Kang Guru Project Manager; or Ogi Yutarini, Administration Officer. Free "KANGURU" magazine. This program is aired over various RRI outlets, including Jakarta and Sorong. Continuation of this project, currently sponsored by Australia's AusAID, will depend upon whether adequate supplementary funding can be made available.

Radio Pemerintah Daerah Kabupaten TK II—RPDK Manggarai, Ruteng, Flores, Nusa Tenggara Timur, Indonesia. Contact: Simon Saleh, B.A. Return postage required.

Radio Pemerintah Daerah Kabupaten TK II—RSPK Ngada, Jalan Soekarno-Hatta, Bjawa, Flores, Nusa Tenggara Tengah, Indonesia. Phone: +62 (384) 21-142. Contact: Drs. Petrus Tena, Kepala Studio.

Radio Republik Indonesia—RRI Ambon (when operating), Jalan Jendral Akhmad Yani 1, Ambon 97124, Maluku, Indonesia. Phone: +62 (911) 52-740, +62 (911) 53-261 or +62 (911) 53-263. Fax: +62 (911) 53 262. Contact: Drs. H. Ali Amran or Pirla C. Noija, Kepala Seksi Siaran. A very poor replier to correspondence in recent years. Correspondence in Indonesian and return postage essential.

Radio Republik Indonesia—RRI Banda Aceh (when operating), Kotak Pos 112, Banda Aceh 23243, Aceh, Indonesia. Phone: +62 (651) 22-116/156. Contact: Parmono Prawira, Technical Director; or S.H. Rosa Kim. Return postage helpful.

Radio Republik Indonesia—Bandar Lampung, *see* RRI Tanjung Karang listing below.

Radio Republik Indonesia—RRI Bandung (when operating), Stasiun Regional 1, Kotak Pos 1055, Bandung 40122, Jawa Barat, Indonesia. Email: rribandung@yahoo.com. Web: www.kanguru.org/rristationprofiles.htm. Contact: Drs. Idrus Alkaf, Kepala Stasiun; Mrs. Ati Kusmiati; or Eem Suhaemi, Kepala Seksi Siaran. Return postage or IRC helpful.

Radio Republik Indonesia—RRI Banjarmasin (when operating), Stasiun Nusantara 111, Kotak Pos 117, Banjarmasin 70234, Kalimantan Selatan, Indonesia. Phone: +62 (511) 268-601 or +62 (511) 261-562. Fax: +62 (511) 252 238. Contact:

Deutsche Welle's international team includes editors of the German and Chinese services. DW

Jul Chaidir, Stasiun Kepala; or Harmyn Husein. Free stickers. Return postage or IRCs helpful.

Radio Republik Indonesia—RRI Bengkulu, Stasiun Regional 1, Kotak Pos 13 Kawat, Kotamadya Bengkulu 38227, Indonesia. Phone: +62 (736) 350-811. Fax: +62 (736) 350 927. Contact: Drs. Drs. Jasran Abubakar, Kepala Stasiun. Free picture postcards, decals and tourist literature. Return postage or 2 IRCs helpful.

Radio Republik Indonesia—RRI Biak (when operating), Kotak Pos 505, Biak 98117, Papua, Indonesia. Phone: +62 (981) 21-211 or +62 (981) 21-197. Fax: +62 (981) 21 905. Contact: Butje Latuperissa, Kepala Seksi Siaran; or Drs. D.A. Siahainenia, Kepala Stasiun. Correspondence in Indonesian preferred.

Radio Republik Indonesia—RRI Bukittinggi (when operating), Stasiun Regional 1 Bukittinggi, Jalan Prof. Muhammad Yamin 199, Aurkuning, Bukittinggi 26131, Propinsi Sumatera Barat, Indonesia. Phone: +62 (752) 21-319 or +62 (752) 21-320. Fax: +62 (752) 367 132. Contact: Mr. Effendi, Sekretaris; Zul Arifin Mukhtar, SH; or Samirwan Sarjana Hukum, Producer, "Phone in Program." Replies to correspondence in Indonesian or English. Return postage helpful.

Radio Republik Indonesia—RRI Denpasar (when operating), Kotak Pos 3031, Denpasar 80233, Bali, Indonesia. Phone: +62 (361) 222-161 or +62 (361) 223-087. Fax: +62 (361) 227 312. Contact: I Gusti Ngurah Oka, Kepala Stasiun. Replies slowly to correspondence in Indonesian. Return postage or IRCs helpful.

Radio Republik Indonesia—RRI Dili (when operating), Stasiun Regional 1 Dili, Jalan Kaikoli, Kotak Pos 103, Dili 88000, Timor-Timur, Indonesia. Contact: Harry A. Silalahi, Kepala Stasiun; Arnoldus Klau; or Paul J. Amalo, BA. Return postage or $1 helpful. Replies occasionally to correspondence in Indonesian.

Radio Republik Indonesia—RRI Fak Fak, Jalan Kapten P. Tendean, Kotak Pos 54, Fak-Fak 98612, Papua, Indonesia. Phone: +62 (956) 22-519 or +62 (956) 22-521. Contact: Bahrun Siregar, Kepala Stasiun; Aloys Ngotra, Kepala Seksi Siaran; Drs. Tukiran Erlantoko; or Richart Tan, Kepala Sub Seksi Siaran Kata. Station plans to upgrade its transmitting facilities with

the help of the Japanese government. Return postage required. Replies occasionally.

Radio Republik Indonesia—RRI Gorontalo, Jalan Jendral Sudirman 30, Gorontalo 96115, Sulawesi Utara, Indonesia. Fax: +62 (435) 821 590/91. Contact: Drs. Bagus Edi Asmoro; Drs. Muhammad. Assad, Kepala Stasiun; or Saleh S. Thalib, Technical Manager. Return postage helpful. Replies occasionally, preferably to correspondence in Indonesian.

Radio Republik Indonesia—RRI Jakarta

STATION: Stasiun Nasional Jakarta, Kotak Pos 356, Jakarta 10110, Daerah Khusus Jakarta Raya, Indonesia; or (street address) Jalan Medan Merdeka Barat 4-5, Jakarta 10110, Indonesia. Phone: +62 (21) 345-9091 or +62 (21) 384-6817. Fax: +62 (21) 345 7132 or +62 (21) 345 7134. Email: rri@rrionline.com; rri@rri-online.com. Web: (includes Windows Media) www.rri.online.com; (includes MP3) www.rri-online.com (Note: www.rrionline.com and www.rri-online.com are two very different sites). Contact: Drs. Beni Koesbani, Kepala Stasiun; or Drs. Nuryudi, MM. Return postage helpful. Replies irregularly.

"DATELINE" ENGLISH PROGRAM: see Kang Guru II Radio English.
TRANSMITTERS DIVISION: Jalan Merdeka Barat 4-5, Jakarta 10110 Indonesia. Phone/Fax: +62 (21) 385-7831. Email: sruslan@yahoo.com or sruslan@msn.com. Contact: Sunarya Ruslan, Head of Transmitters Division.
"U.N. CALLING ASIA" ENGLISH PROGRAM: Program via RRI Jakarta Programa Ibukota Satu, every Sunday. Contact address same as United Nations Radio (see).

Radio Republik Indonesia—RRI Jambi (when operating), Jalan Jendral A. Yani 5, Telanaipura, Jambi 36122, Propinsi Jambi, Indonesia. Contact: M. Yazid, Kepala Siaran; H. Asmuni Lubis, BA; or Byamsuri, Acting Station Manager. Return postage helpful.

Radio Republik Indonesia—RRI Jayapura, Kotak Pos 1077, Jayapura 99200, Papua, Indonesia. Phone: +62 (967) 33-339. Fax: +62 (967) 33 439. Contact: Harry Liborang, Direktorat Radio; Hartono, Bidang Teknik; or Dr. David Alex Siahainenia, Kepala. Return postage of $1 helpful. Replies to correspondence in Indonesian or English.

Radio Republik Indonesia—RRI Kendari, Kotak Pos 7, Kendari 93111, Sulawesi Tenggara, Indonesia. Phone: +62 (401) 21-464. Fax: +62 (401) 21 730. Contact: H. Sjahbuddin, BA; Muniruddin Amin, Programmer; or Drs. Supandi. Return postage required. Replies slowly to correspondence in Indonesian.

Radio Republik Indonesia—RRI Kupang (Regional I) (when operating), Jalan Tompello 8, Kupang 85225, Timor, Indonesia. Phone: +62 (380) 821-437 or +62 (380) 825-444. Fax: +62 (380) 833 149. Contact: Drs. P.M. Tisera, Kepala Stasiun; Qustigap Bagang, Kepala Seksi Siaran; or Said Rasyid, Kepala Studio. Return postage helpful. Correspondence in Indonesian preferred. Replies occasionally.

Radio Republik Indonesia—RRI Madiun (when operating), Jalan Mayjend Panjaitan 10, Madiun 63133, Jawa Timur, Indonesia. Phone: +62 (351) 464-419, +62 (351) 459-198, +62 (351) 462-726 or +62 (351) 459-495. Fax: +62 (351) 464 964. Web: www.kanguru.org/rristationprofiles.htm. Contact: Sri Lestari, SS or Imam Soeprapto, Kepala Seksi Siaran. Replies to correspondence in English or Indonesian. Return postage helpful.

Radio Republik Indonesia—RRI Makassar, Jalan Riburane 3, Makassar, 90111, Sulawesi Selatan, Indonesia. Phone: +62 (411) 321-853. Contact: H. Kamaruddin Alkaf Yasin, Head of Broadcasting Department; L.A. Rachim Ganie; Ashan Muhammad, Kepala Bidang Teknik; Salam Hormat, Head of Station; or Drs. Bambang Pudjono. Return postage, $1 or IRCs helpful. Replies irregularly and sometimes slowly.

Radio Republik Indonesia—RRI Malang (when operating), Kotak Pos 78, Malang 65140, Jawa Timur, Indonesia; or Jalan Candi Panggung No. 58, Mojolangu, Malang 65142, Indonesia. Email: makobu@mlg.globalxtrem.net. Contact: Drs.Tjutju Tjuar Na Adikorya, Kepala Stasiun; Ml. Mawahib, Kepala Seksi Siaran; or Dra Hartati Soekemi, Mengetahui. Return postage required. Free history and other booklets. Replies irregularly to correspondence in Indonesian.

Radio Republik Indonesia—RRI Manado (when operating), Kotak Pos 1110, Manado 95124 Propinsi Sulawesi Utara, Indonesia. Phone: +62 (431) 863-392. Fax: +62 (431) 863 492. Contact: Costher H. Gulton, Kepala Stasiun; or Untung Santoso, Kepala Seksi Teknik. Free stickers and postcards. Return postage or $1 required. Replies occasionally to correspondence in Indonesian.

Radio Republik Indonesia—RRI Manokwari (when operating), Regional II, Jalan Merdeka 68, Manokwari 98311, Papua, Indonesia. Phone: +62 (962) 21-343. Contact: Eddy Kusbandi, Manager; or Nurdin Mokogintu. Return postage helpful.

Radio Republik Indonesia—RRI Mataram (when operating), Stasiun Regional I Mataram, Jalan Langko 83 Ampenan, Mataram 83114, Nusa Tenggara Barat, Indonesia. Phone: +62 (370) 23-713 or +62 (370) 21-355. Contact: Drs. Hamid Djasman, Kepala; or Bochri Rachman, Ketua Dewan Pimpinan Harian. Free stickers. Return postage required. With sufficient return postage or small token gift, sometimes sends tourist information and Batik print. Replies to correspondence in Indonesian.

Radio Republik Indonesia—RRI Medan (when operating), Jalan Letkol Martinus Lubis 5, Medan 20232, Sumatera, Indonesia. Phone: +62 (61) 324-222/441. Fax: +62 (61) 512 161. Contact: Kepala Stasiun, Ujamalul Abidin Ass; Drs. S. Parlin Tobing, SH, Produsennya, "Kontak Pendengar"; Drs. H. Suryanta Saleh; or Suprato. Free stickers. Return postage required. Replies to correspondence in Indonesian.

Radio Republik Indonesia—RRI Merauke, Stasiun Regional 1, Kotak Pos 11, Merauke 99611, Papua, Indonesia. Phone: +62 (971) 21-396 or +62 (971) 21-376. Contact: (general) Drs.

Buang Akhir, Direktor; Achmad Ruskaya B.A., Kepala Stasiun, Drs.Tuanakotta Semuel, Kepala Seksi Siaran; or John Manuputty, Kepala Subseksi Pemancar; (technical) Daf'an Kubangun, Kepala Seksi Tehnik. Return postage helpful.

Radio Republik Indonesia—RRI Nabire (when operating), Kotak Pos 110, Jalan Merdeka 74 Nabire 98811, Papua, Indonesia. Phone: +62 (984) 21-013. Contact: Muchtar Yushaputra, Kepala Stasiun. Free stickers and occasional free picture postcards. Return postage or IRCs helpful.

Radio Republik Indonesia—RRI Padang, Kotak Pos 77, Padang 25111, Sumatera Barat, Indonesia. Phone: +61 (751) 28-363, +62 (751) 21-030 or +62 (751) 27-482. Contact: H. Hutabarat, Kepala Stasiun; or Amir Hasan, Kepala Seksi Siaran. Return postage helpful.

Radio Republik Indonesia—RRI Palangkaraya (when operating), Jalan M. Husni Thamrin 1, Palangkaraya 73111, Kalimantan Tengah, Indonesia. Phone: +62 (536) 21-779. Fax: +62 (536) 21 778. Contact: Andy Sunandar; Drs.Amiruddin; S. Polin; A.F. Herry Purwanto; Meyiwati SH; Supardal Djojosubrojo, Sarjana Hukum; Dr. S. Parlin Tobing, Station Manager; Murniaty Oesin, Transmission Department Engineer; Gumer Kamis; or Ricky D. Wader, Kepala Stasiun. Return postage helpful. Will respond to correspondence in Indonesian or English.

Radio Republik Indonesia—RRI Palembang (when operating), Jalan Radio 2, Km. 4, Palembang 30128, Sumatera Selatan, Indonesia. Phone: +62 (711) 350-811, +62 (711) 309-977 or +62 (711) 350-927. Contact: Drs. H. Mursjid Noor, Kepala Stasiun; H.Ahmad Syukri Ahkab, Kepala Seksi Siaran; or H.Iskandar Suradilaga. Return postage helpful. Replies slowly and occasionally.

Radio Republik Indonesia—RRI Palu, Jalan R.A. Kartini 39, Palu 94112, Sulawesi Tengah, Indonesia. Phone: +62 (451) 21-621 or +62 (451) 94-112. Contact: Akson Boole; Nyonyah Netty Ch. Soriton, Kepala Seksi Siaran; Gugun Santoso; Untung Santoso, Kepala Seksi Teknik; or M. Hasjim, Head of Programming. Return postage required. Replies slowly to correspondence in Indonesian.

Radio Republik Indonesia—RRI Pekanbaru (when operating), Kotak Pos 51, Pekanbaru 28113, Kepulauan Riau, Indonesia. Phone: +62 (761) 22-081, +62 (761) 23-606 or +62 (761) 25-111. Fax: +62 (761) 23 605. Contact: (general) Hendri Yunis, ST, Kepala Stasiun, Ketua DPH; Arisun Agus, Kepala Seksi Siaran; Drs. H. Syamsidi, Kepala Supag Tata Usaha; or Zainal Abbas. Return postage helpful.

Radio Republik Indonesia—RRI Pontianak, Kotak Pos 1005, Pontianak 78117, Kalimantan Barat, Indonesia. Phone: +62 (561) 734-987. Fax: +62 (561) 734 659. Contact: Ruddy Banding, Kepala Seksi Siaran; Achmad Ruskaya, BA; Drs. Effendi Afati, Producer, "Dalam Acara Kantong Surat"; Subagio, Kepala Sub Bagian Tata Usaha; Augustwus Campek; Rahayu Widati; Suryadharma, Kepala Sub Seksi Programa; or Muchlis Marzuki B.A. Return postage or $1 helpful. Replies some of the time to correspondence in Indonesian (preferred) or English.

Radio Republik Indonesia—RRI Samarinda, Kotak Pos 45, Samarinda, Kalimantan Timur 75110, Indonesia. Phone: +62 (541) 743-495. Fax: +62 (541) 741 693. Contact: Siti Thomah, Kepala Seksi Siaran; Tyranus Lenjau, English Announcer; S. Yati; Marthin Tapparan; or Sunendra, Kepala Stasiun. May send tourist brochures and maps. Return postage helpful. Replies to correspondence in Indonesian.

Radio Republik Indonesia—RRI Semarang (when operating), Kotak Pos 1073, Semarang 50241, Jawa Tengah, Indonesia. Phone: +62 (24) 831-6686, +62 (24) 831-6661 or +62 (24)

831-6330. (Phone/Fax, marketing) +62 (24) 831-6330. Web: www.kanguru.org/rristationprofiles.htm. Contact: Djarwanto, SH; Drs. Sabeni, Doktorandus; Drs. Purwadi, Program Director; Dra. Endang Widiastuti, Kepala Sub Seksi Periklanan Jasa dan Hak Cipta; H. Sutakno, Kepala Stasiun; or Mardanon, Kepala Teknik. Return postage helpful.

Radio Republik Indonesia—RRI Serui, Jalan Pattimura Kotak Pos 19, Serui 98213, Papua, Indonesia. Phone: +62 (983) 31-150 or +62 (983) 31-121. Contact: Agus Raunsai, Kepala Stasiun; J. Lolouan, BA, Kepala Studio; Ketua Tim Pimpinan Harian, Kepala Seksi Siaran; Yance Yebi-Yebi; Natalis Edowai; Albertus Corputty; or Drs. Jasran Abubakar. Replies occasionally to correspondence in Indonesian. IRC or return postage helpful.

Radio Republik Indonesia—RRI Sibolga (when operating), Jalan Ade Irma Suryani, Nasution No. 11, Sibolga 22513, Sumatera Utara, Indonesia. Phone: +61 (631) 21-183, +62 (631) 22-506 or +62 (631) 22-947. Contact: Mrs. Laiya, Mrs. S. Sitoupul or B.A. Tanjung. Return postage required. Replies occasionally to correspondence in Indonesian.

Radio Republik Indonesia—RRI Sorong

STATION: Kotak Pos 146, Sorong 98414, Papua, Indonesia. Phone: +62 (951) 21-003, +62 (951) 22-111, or +62 (951) 22-611. Contact: Drs. Sallomo Hamid; Tetty Rumbay S., Kasubsi Siaran Kata; Mrs. Tien Widarsanto, Resa Kasi Siaran; Ressa Molle; Mughpar Yushaputra, Kepala Stasiun; Umar Solle, Station Manager; or Linda Rumbay. Return postage helpful. Replies to correspondence in English.

"DATELINE" ENGLISH PROGRAM: See Kang Guru II Radio English.

Radio Republik Indonesia—RRI Sumenep (when operating), Jalan Urip Sumoharjo 26, Sumenep 69411, Madura, Jawa Timur, Indonesia. Phone: +62 (328) 62-317, +62 (328) 21-811, +62 (328) 21-317 or +62 (328) 66-768. Contact: Dian Irianto, Kepala Stasiun. Return postage helpful.

Radio Republik Indonesia—RRI Surabaya, (when operating) Stasiun Regional 1, Kotak Pos 239, Surabaya 60271, Jawa Timur, Indonesia. Phone: +62 (31) 534-1327, +62 (31) 534-2327, +62 (31) 534-1327, +62 (31) 534-5474, +62 (31) 534-0478 or +62 (31) 547-3610. Fax: +62 (31) 534 2351. Contact: Zainal Abbas, Kepala Stasiun; Usmany Johozua, Kepala Seksi Siaran; Drs. E. Agus Widjaja, MM, Kasi Siaran; Pardjingat, Kepala Seksi Teknik; or Ny Koen Tarjadi. Return postage or IRCs helpful.

Radio Republik Indonesia—RRI Surakarta (when operating), Kotak Pos 40, Surakarta 57133, Jawa Tengah, Indonesia. Phone: +62 (271) 634-004/05, +62 (271) 638-145, +62 (271) 654-399 or +62 (271) 641-178. Fax: +62 (271) 642 208. Contact: H. Tomo, B.A., Head of Broadcasting; or Titiek Sudartik, S.H., Kepala. Return postage helpful.

Radio Republik Indonesia—RRI Tanjungkarang, Kotak Pos 24, Bandar Lampung 35213, Indonesia. Phone: +62 (721) 555-2280 or +62 (721) 569-720. Fax: +62 (721) 562 767. Contact: M. Nasir Agun, Kepala Stasiun; Hi Hanafie Umar; Djarot Nursinggih, Tech. Transmission; Drs. Doewadji, Kepala Seksi Siaran; Drs. Zulhaqqi Hafiz, Kepala Sub Seksi Periklanan; or Asmara Haidar Manaf. Return postage helpful. Also identifies as RRI Bandar Lampung. Replies in Indonesian to correspondence in English or Indonesian.

Radio Republik Indonesia—RRI Tanjungpinang, Stasiun RRI Regional II Tanjungpinang, Kotak Pos 8, Tanjungpinang 29123, Kepulauan Riau, Indonesia. Phone: +62 (771) 21-278, +62 (771) 21-540, +62 (771) 21-916 or +62 (771) 29-123. Contact: M. Yazid, Kepala Stasiun; Wan Suhardi, Produsennya, "Siaran

Bahasa Melayu"; or Rosakim, Sarjana Hukum. Return postage helpful. Replies occasionally to correspondence in Indonesian or English.

Radio Republik Indonesia—RRI Ternate (when operating), Jalan Sultan Khairun, Kedaton, Ternate 97720 (Ternate), Maluku Utara, Indonesia. Phone: +62 (921) 21-582, +62 (921) 21-762 or +62 (921) 25-525. Contact: (general) Abd. Latief Kamarudin, Kepala Stasiun; (technical) Rusdy Bachmid, Head of Engineering; or Abubakar Alhadar. Return postage helpful.

Radio Republik Indonesia—RRI Tual (when operating), Watden, Pulau Kai, Tual 97661 Maluku, Indonesia.

Radio Republik Indonesia—RRI Wamena (when operating), RRI Regional II, Kotak Pos 10, Wamena, Papua 99511, Indonesia. Phone: +62 (969) 31-380. Fax: +62 (969) 31 299. Contact: Yoswa Kumurawak, Penjab Subseksi Pemancar. Return postage helpful.

Radio Republik Indonesia—RRI Yogyakarta (when operating), Jalan Amat Jazuli 4, Kotak Pos 18, Yogyakarta 55224, Jawa Tengah, Indonesia. Fax: +62 (274) 2784. Phone: +62 (274) 512-783/85 or +62 (274) 580-333. Email: rri-yk@yogya.wasantara.net.id. Contact: Phoenix Sudomo Sudaryo; Tris Mulyanti, Seksi Programa Siaran; Martono, ub. Kabid Penyelenggaraan Siaran; Mr. Kadis, Technical Department; or Drs. H. Hamdan Sjahbeni, Kepala Stasiun. IRC, return postage or $1 helpful. Replies occasionally to correspondence in Indonesian or English.

Radio Siaran Pemerintah Daerah TK II—RSPD Halmahera Tengah, Soasio, Jalan A. Malawat, Soasio, Maluku Tengah 97812, Indonesia. Contact: Drs. S. Chalid A. Latif, Kepala Badan Pengelola.

📻**Voice of Indonesia**, Kotak Pos 1157, Jakarta 10001, Daerah Khusus Jakarta Raya, Indonesia; (street address) Jalan Medan Merdeka Barat No. 4-5, Jakarta 10110 Indonesia. Phone: +62 (21) 345-6811. Fax: +62 (21) 350 0990. Email: voi@rri-online.com. Web: (includes Windows Media) www.rrionline.com (Note: www.rrionline.com and www.rri-online.com are two different sites). Contact: Anastasia Yasmine, Head of Foreign Affairs Section; or Amy Aisha, Presenter, "Listeners Mailbag." Free stickers and calendars. Be careful when addressing your letters to the station as mail sent to the Voice of Indonesia, Japanese Section, has sometimes been incorrectly delivered to NHK's Jakarta Bureau. Very slow in replying but enclosing 4 IRCs may help speed things up.

IRAN   World Time +3:30 (+4:30 midyear)

📻**Voice of the Islamic Republic of Iran**

MAIN OFFICE: IRIB External Services, P.O. Box 19395-6767, Tehran, Iran; or P.O. Box 19395-3333, Tehran, Iran. Phone: (IRIB Public Relations) +98 (21) 204-001/2/3 and +98 (21) 204-6894/5. Fax: (external services) +98 (21) 205 1635, +98 (21) 204 1097 or + 98 (21) 291 095; (IRIB Public Relations) +98 (21) 205 3305/7; (IRIB Central Administration) +98 (21) 204 1051; (technical) +98 (21) 654 841. Email: (general) irib@dci.iran.com; (all technical matters) sw@irib.ir; (Research Centre) iribrec@dci.iran.com; (English Service) englishradio@irib.ir (same format for German and Spanish, e.g. germanradio@irib.ir); (French Service) radio_fr@irib.ir. Web: (includes RealAudio) www.irib.ir/worldservice. Contact: (general) Hamid Yasamin, Public Affairs; Ali Larijani, Head; or Hameed Barimani, Producer, "Listeners Special"; (administration) J. Ghanbari, Director General; or J. Sarafraz, Deputy Managing Director; (technical) M. Ebrahim Vassigh, Frequency Manager. Free seven-volume set of books on Islam, magazines, calen-

dars, book markers, tourist literature and postcards. Verifications require a minimum of two days' reception data on two or more separate broadcasts, plus return postage. Station is currently asking their listeners to send in their telephone numbers so that they can call and talk to them directly. Upon request they will even broadcast your conversation on air. You can send your phone number to the postal address above or you can fax it to: + 98 (21) 205 1635. If the English Service doesn't reply, then try writing to the French Service in French.
ENGINEERING ACTIVITIES, TEHRAN: IRIB, P.O. Box 15875-4344, Tehran, Iran. Phone: +98 (21) 2196-6127. Fax: +98 (21) 204 1051, +98 (21) 2196 6268 or +98 (21) 172 924. Contact: Mrs. Niloufar Parviz.
ENGINEERING ACTIVITIES, HESSARAK/KARAJ: IRIB, P.O. Box 155, Hessarak/Karaj, Iran. Phone: (Frequency Control & Design Bureau) +98 (21) 216-3762; (Majid Farahmandnia) +98 (21) 216-3772; or (Yousef Ghadaksaz) +98 (21) 216-3742. Fax: (Frequency Design Bureau) +98 (21) 201 3649. Email: rezairib@dci.iran.com; (Ali Akbar Sabouri) sabouri@takta.net; (Yousef Ghadaksaz) ghadaksaz@irib.ir; or (Majid Farahmandnia) farahmand@irib.ir. Contact: Yousef Ghadaksaz, Manager of Shortwave Radio Department; Saeed Alavivafa, Head of Shortwave Frequency Management; Ali Akbar Sabouri, Head of Karaj Station; Navid Homayouni, Planning Engineer; M. Ebrahim Vasigh; or Majid Farahmandnia, Manager, Frequency Control and Design Bureau.
SIRJAN TRANSMITTING STATION: P.O. Box 369, Sirjan, Iran. Phone: +98 (21) 216-3744. Contact: Ebrahim Safabahar, Head of Sirjan Station; or Saeed Safizadeh, Technical Engineer.
Mashhad Regional Radio, P.O. Box 555, Mashhad Center, Jomhoriye Eslame, Iran. Contact: J. Ghanbari, General Director.

IRAQ   World Time +3 (+4 midyear)

INDIA ADDRESS: P.O. Box 3044, New Delhi 110003, India.
Radio Kurdistan ("Aira dangi kurdistana, dangi hizbi socialisti democrati kurdistan") (when active). Web: (KSDP parent organization) www.ksdp.net. Station is run by the Kurdistan Socialist Democratic Party.
Voice of Iraqi Kurdistan ("Aira dangi Kurdestana Iraqiyah") (when active). Sponsored by the Kurdistan Democratic Party-Iraq (KDP), led by Masoud Barzani, and the National Democratic Iraqi Front. Broadcasts from its own transmitting facilities, reportedly located in the Kurdish section of Iraq. To contact the station or to obtain verification of reception reports, try going via one of the following KDP offices (the Swedish office is known to verify email reception reports):
KURDISTAN-SALAHEDDIN CENTRAL MEDIA AND CULTURE OFFICE: Phone: +873 (761) 610-320. Fax: +873 (761) 610 321. Email: kdppress@aol.com.
KDP LONDON OFFICE: KDP International Relations Committee-London, P.O. Box 7725, London SW1V 3ZD, United Kingdom. Phone: +44 (20) 7498-2664. Fax: +44 (20) 7498 2531. Email: kdpeurope@aol.com.
KDP MADRID OFFICE: PDK Comité de Relaciones Internacionales-España, Avenida Papa Negro, 20-1°-105ª, E-28043 Madrid, Spain. Phone: +34 (91) 759-9475. Fax: +34 (91) 300 1638. Email: pdk@futurnet.es. Web: http://usuarios.futurnet.es/p/pdk.
KDP WASHINGTON OFFICE: KDP International Relations Committee-Washington, 1015 18th Street, NW, Suite 704, Washington DC 20036 USA. Phone: +1 (202) 331-9505. Fax: +1 (202) 331 9506. Email: kdpusa@aol.com. Contact: Namat Sharif, Kurdistan Democratic Party.

KDP-CANADA OFFICE: Phone: +1 (905) 387-3759. Fax: +1 (905) 387 3756. Email: kdpcanada@hotmail.com. Web: www.geocities.com/Paris/Gallery/3209.
KDP-DENMARK OFFICE: Postbox 437, DK-3000 Helsingor, Denmark; or Postbox 551, DK-2620 Albertslund, Denmark. Phone/Fax: +45 5577-9761. Email: kdpdenmark@hotmail.com. Web: http://members.tripod.com/kdpDenmark.
KDP-SWEDEN OFFICE: Box 2017, SE-145 02 Norsborg, Sweden. Phone: +46 (8) 361-446. Fax: +46 (8) 367 844. Email: party@kdp.pp.se; (Atroushi) atrushi@iname.com. Web: (includes Windows Media) www.kdp.pp.se. Contact: Alex Atroushi, who will verify email reports sent to the "party" address.
Voice of the Kurdistan People—*see* Voice of the People of Kurdistan, below.
Voice of the People of Kurdistan ("Aira dangi gelli kurdistana"). Email: said@aha.ru; or puk@puk.org. Web: www.aha.ru/~said/dang.htm; (PUK parent organization) www.puk.org. Official radio station of the Patriotic Union of Kurdistan (PUK) led by Jalal Talabani. Originally called "Voice of the Iraqi Revolution."
PUK GERMAN OFFICE: Patriotische Union Kurdistans (PUK), Postfach 21 0231, D-10502 Berlin, Germany. Phone: +49 (30) 3409-7850. Fax: +49 (30) 3409 7849. Email: pukoffice@pukg.de. Contact: Dara Gafori. Replies to correspondence in English and German, and verifies reception reports.

ISRAEL   World Time +2 (+3 midyear)

Bezeq—Israel Telecommunication Corp. Ltd., Engineering and Planning Division, Radio and T.V. Broadcasting Section, P.O. Box 62081, Tel-Aviv 61620, Israel. Phone: +972 (3) 626-4562 or +972 (3) 626-4500. Fax: +972 (3) 626 4559. Email: (Oren) mosheor@bezeq.com; or rms2@bezeqint.net. Web: www.bezeq.co.il. Contact: Moshe Oren, Frequency Manager. Bezeq is responsible for transmitting the programs of the Israel Broadcasting Authority (IBA), which *inter alia* parents Kol Israel. This address only for pointing out transmitter-related problems (interference, modulation quality, network mixups, etc.), especially by fax, of transmitters based in Israel. Does not verify reception reports.
Galei Zahal (Israel Defence Forces Radio), Zahal, Military Mail No. 01005, Israel. Phone: +972 (3) 512-6666. Fax: +972 (3) 512 6760. Email: glz@galatz.co.il. Web: (includes Windows Media) www.glz.msn.co.il.
Kol Israel (Israel Radio International)
STUDIOS: Kol Israel, P.O. Box 1082, Jerusalem 91010, Israel. Phone: (general) +972 (2) 530-2222; (Engineering Dept.) +972 (2) 501-3453; (Hebrew voice mail for Reshet Bet program "The Israel Connection") +972 (3) 765-1929. Fax: (English Service) +972 (2) 530 2424. Email: (general) ask@israel-info.gov.il; (English Service) englishradio@iba.org.il; (correspondence relating to reception problems, only) engineering@israelradio.org; (Reshet Bet program for Israelis abroad) kesherisraeli@yahoo.com. Web: (Hebrew) www.kolisrael.org.il; (English, includes RealAudio) www.israelradio.org.il; (RealAudio and Windows Media) www.iba.org.il. Contact: Edmond Sehayeq, Head of Programming, Arabic, Persian and Yemenite broadcasts; Yishai Eldar, Reporter, English News Department; Steve Linde, Head of English News Department; or Sara Gabbai, Head of Western Broadcasting Department; (administration) Yonni Ben-Menachem, Director of External Broadcasting; (technical, frequency management) Raphael Kochanowski, Director of Liaison and Coordination, Engineering Dept. No verifications or freebies, due to limited budget.

Yukuko Tsuji, narrator, and Toshimichi Ohtake, editor, of the Far Eastern DX Report for AWR's "WaveScan." They man the Japan Shortwave Club's booth at the 2004 Tokyo Ham Fair. T. Ohtake

SAN FRANCISCO OFFICE, SCHEDULES: 2654 17th Avenue, San Francisco CA 94116 USA. Phone: +1 (415) 564-9968. Email: GPoppin@aol.com. Contact: George Poppin. This address, a volunteer office, only provides KOL Israel schedules to listeners. All other correspondence should be sent directly to the main office in Jerusalem.

ITALY   World Time +1 (+2 midyear)

⌨**Italian Radio Relay Service**, IRRS-Shortwave, Nexus-IBA, C.P. 10980, I-20110 Milano, Italy. Phone: +39 (02) 266-6971. Fax: +39 (02) 7063 8151. Email: (general) info@nexus.org; (reception reports) reports@nexus.org; (Cotroneo) aec@nexus.org; (Norton) ron@nexus.org. Web:www.nexus.org/radio.htm; (MP3) http://mp3.nexus.org; (European Gospel Radio) www.egradio.org. Contact: (general) Vanessa Dickinson; Ron Norton, Verification Manager; Anna S. Boschetti, President; Alfredo E. Cotroneo, CEO; (technical) Ron Norton. For budget reasons, this station cannot assure a reply to all listeners' mail. Email correspondence and reception reports by email are answered promptly and at no charge. For verification also send letters to program producers mentioned on air. Small program producer initiative (International Public Access Radio) at www.nexus.org/IPAR. Check website for details. Two IRCs or $1 helpful.

⌨**Radio Roma-RAI International** (external services)
MAIN OFFICE: External/Foreign Service, Centro RAI, Saxa Rubra, 00188 Rome, Italy; or P.O. Box 320, Correspondence Sector, 00100 Rome, Italy. Phone: +39 (06) 33-17-2360. Fax: +39 (06) 33 17 18 95 or +39 (06) 322 6070. Email: raiinternational@rai.it. Web: (shortwave) www.raiinternational.rai.it/radio/indexoc.htm. Contact: (general) Rosaria Vassallo, Correspondence Sector; or Augusto Milana, Editor-in-Chief, Shortwave Programs in Foreign Languages; Esther Casas, Servicio Español; (administration) Angela Buttiglione, Managing Director; or Gabriella Tambroni, Assistant Director. Free stickers, banners, calendars and *RAI Calling from Rome* magazine. Can provide supplementary materials, including on VHS and CD-ROM, for Italian-language video course, "Viva l' italiano," with an audio equivalent soon to be offered, as well. Is constructing "a new,

more powerful and sophisticated shortwave transmitting center" in Tuscany; when this is activated, RAI International plans to expand news, cultural items and music in Italian and various other language services—including Spanish & Portuguese, plus new services in Chinese and Japanese. Responses can be very slow. Pictures of RAI's Shortwave Center at Prato Smeraldo can be found at www.mediasuk.org/rai.

SHORTWAVE FREQUENCY MONITORING OFFICE: RaiWay Monitoring Centre, Centro di Controllo, Via Mirabellino 1, 20052 Monza (MI), Italy. Phone: +39 (039) 388-389. Phone/Fax (ask for fax): +39 (039) 386-222. Email: raiway.hfmonitoring@rai.it or cqmonza@rai.it. Contact: Mrs. Lucia Luisa La Franceschina; or Mario Ballabio.

ENGINEERING OFFICE, ROME: Via Teulada 66, 00195 Rome, Italy. Phone: +39 (06) 331-70721. Fax: +39 (06) 331 75142 or +39 (06) 372 3376. Email: isola@rai.it. Contact: Clara Isola.

ENGINEERING OFFICE, TURIN: Via Cernaia 33, 10121 Turin, Italy. Phone: +39 (011) 810-2293. Fax: +39 (011) 575 9610. Email: allamano@rai.it. Contact: Giuseppe Allamano, HF Frequency Planning.

NEW YORK OFFICE, NONTECHNICAL: 1350 Avenue of the Americas—21st floor, New York NY 10019 USA. Phone: +1 (212) 468-2500. Fax: +1 (212) 765 1956. Contact: Umberto Bonetti, Deputy Director of Radio Division. RAI caps, aprons and tote bags for sale at Boutique RAI, c/o the aforementioned New York address.

SAN FRANCISCO OFFICE, SCHEDULES: 2654 17th Avenue, San Francisco CA 94116 USA. Phone: +1 (415) 564-9968. Email: GPoppin@aol.com. Contact: George Poppin. This address, a volunteer office, only provides RAI schedules to listeners. All other correspondence should be sent directly to the main office in Rome.

RTV Italiana-RAI (domestic service)
ROME: Centro RAI, Saxa Rubra, 00188 Rome, Italy. Fax: +39 (06) 322 6070. Email: grr@rai.it. Web: www.rai.it.

JAPAN   World Time +9

NHK Fukuoka, 1-1-10 Ropponmatsu, Chuo-ku, Fukuoka-shi, Fukuoka 810-8577, Japan. Phone: +81 (92) 724-2800. Web: www.nhk.or.jp/fukuoka.

NHK Nagoya, 13-3 Higashisakura 1-chome, Higashi-ku, Nagoya 461-8725, Japan. Phone: +81 (52) 952-7111. Fax: +81 (52) 952 7268. Web: www.nhk.or.jp/nagoya.

NHK Osaka, 3-43 Bamba-cho, Chuo-ku, Osaka 540-8501, Japan. Fax: +81 (6) 6941 0612. Web: www.nhk.or.jp/osaka. Contact: (technical) Technical Bureau. IRC or $1 helpful.

NHK Sapporo, 1-1-1 Ohdori Nishi, Chuo-ku, Sapporo 060-8703, Japan. Fax: +81 (11) 232 5951. Web: www.nhk.or.jp/sapporo. Sometimes sends postcards, stickers or other small souvenirs.

NHK Tokyo/Shobu-Kuki, 3047-1 Oaza-Sanga, Shobu-cho, Minamisaitama-gun, Saitama 346-0104, Japan. Fax: +81 (3) 3481 4985 or +81 (480) 85 1508. Web: www.nhk.or.jp. IRC or $1 helpful. Replies occasionally. Letters should be sent via registered mail.

⌨**Radio Japan/NHK World** (external service)
MAIN OFFICE: NHK World, Nippon Hoso Kyokai, Tokyo 150-8001, Japan. Phone: +81 (3) 3465-1111. Fax: (general) +81 (3) 3481 1350; ("Hello from Tokyo" and Production Center) +81 (3) 3465 0966. Email: (general) info@intl.nhk.or.jp; ("Hello from Tokyo" program) hello@intl.nhk.or.jp; (Spanish Section) latin@intl.nhk.or.jp. Web: (includes RealAudio and Windows Media) www.nhk.or.jp/nhkworld. Contact: (administration) Isao Kitamoto, Deputy Director General; Hisashi Okawa, Se-

nior Director International Planning; (general) Yoshiki Fushimi; H. Kawamoto, English Service; Ms. Kyoko Hirotani, Programming Division; or K. Terasaka, Programming Division.
ENGINEERING ADMINISTRATION DEPARTMENT: Nippon Hoso Kyokai, Tokyo 150-8001, Japan. Phone: +81 (3) 5455-5395, +81 (3) 5455-5384, +81 (3) 5455-5376 or +81 (3) 5455-2288. Fax: +81 (3) 3485 0952 or +81 (3) 3481 4985. Email: (general) rj-freq@eng.nhk.or.jp; yoshimi@eng.nhk.or.jp or kurasima@eng.nhk.or.jp. Contact: Fujimoto Hiroki, Frequency Manager; Akira Mizuguchi, Transmissions Manager; Tetsuya Itsuk or Toshiki Kurashima.
MONITORING DIVISION: NHK World/Radio Japan. Fax: +81 (3) 3481 1877.
HONG KONG OFFICE: Phone: +852 2577-5999.
LONDON OFFICE: Phone: +44 (20) 7334-0909.
LOS ANGELES OFFICE: Phone: +1 (310) 816-0300.
NEW YORK OFFICE: Phone: +1 (212) 755-3907.
SINGAPORE OFFICE: Phone: +65 225-0667.
◻**Radio Nikkei**, Nikkei Radio Broadcasting Company, 9-15 Akasaka 1-chome, Minato-ku, Tokyo 107-8373, Japan. Fax: +81 (3) 3583 9062. Web: (includes Windows Media) www.radionikkei.jp. Contact: H. Nagao, Public Relations; M. Teshima; Ms. Terumi Onoda; or H. Ono. Sending a reception report may help with a reply. Free stickers and Japanese stamps. $1 or 2 IRCs helpful.
NEW YORK NEWS BUREAU: 1325 Avenue of the Americas #2403, New York NY 10019 USA. Fax: +1 (212) 261 6449. Contact: Noboru Fukui, reporter.

JORDAN World Time +2 (+3 midyear)

Radio Jordan, P.O. Box 909, Amman, Jordan; or P.O. Box 1041, Amman, Jordan. Phone: (general) +962 (6) 477-4111; (International Relations) +962 (6) 477-8578; (English Service) +962 (6) 475-7410 or +962 (6) 477-3111; (Arabic Service) +962 (6) 463-6454; (Saleh) +962 (6) 474-8048; or (Al-Arini) +962 (6) 474 9161. Fax: (general) +962 (6) 478 8115; (English Service) +962 (6) 420 7862; (Al-Arini) +962 (6) 474 9190. Email: (general) general@jrtv.gov.jo; (programs) rj@jrtv.gov.jo; (schedule) feedback@jrtv.gov.jo; (technical) eng@jrtv.gov.jo; (Director of Radio TV Engineering) arini@jrtv.gov.jo. Web: www.jrtv.com/radio.htm. Contact: (general) Jawad Zada, Director of Foreign Service; Mrs. Hryal Zamakhshari, Director of Arabic Programs; or Qasral Mushatta; (administrative) Hashem Khresat, Director of Radio; Mrs. Fatima Massri, Director of International Relations; or Muwaffaq al-Rahayifah, Director of Shortwave Services; (technical) Youssef Al-Arini, Director of Radio TV Engineering. Free stickers. Replies irregularly and slowly. Enclosing $1 helps.

KENYA World Time +3

Adventist World Radio, AWR Africa, P.O. Box 42276, Nairobi, Kenya. Phone: +254 (2) 573-277. Fax: +254 (2) 568 433. Web: www.awr.org. Contact: (general) Samuel Misiani, Regional Director. Free home Bible study guides, program schedule and other small items. Return postage (IRCs or 1$) appreciated. This office will sometimes verify reception reports direct, but replies are slow. Also, *see* AWR listings under Germany, Guam, Madagascar, United Kingdom and USA.
◻**Kenya Broadcasting Corporation**, P.O. Box 30456, Harry Thuku Road, Nairobi, Kenya. Phone: +254 (2) 334-567. Fax: +254 (2) 220 675. Email: (general) kbc@swiftkenya.com; (management) mdkbc@swiftkenya.com; (technical services) kbctechnical@swiftkenya.com. Web: (general) www.kbc.co.ke;

(RealAudio) www.africaonline.co.ke/AfricaOnline/netradio.html. Contact: (general) Henry Makokha, Liaison Office; (administration) Joe Matano Khamisi, Managing Director; (technical) Nathan Lamu, Senior Principal Technical Officer; Augustine Kenyanjier Gochui; Lawrence Holnati, Engineering Division; or Daniel Githua, Assistant Manager Technical Services (Radio). IRC required. Replies irregularly. If all you want is verfication of your reception report(s), you may have better luck sending your letter to: Engineer in Charge, Maralal Radio Station, P.O. Box 38, Maralal, Kenya.

KIRIBATI World Time +12

Radio Kiribati (if reactivated), Broadcasting & Publications Authority, P.O. Box 78, Bairiki, Tarawa, Republic of Kiribati. Phone: +686 21187. Fax: +686 21096. Email: bpa@tskl.net.ki. Contact: (general) Atiota Bauro, Programme Organiser; Mrs. Otiri Laboia; Batiri Bataua, News Editor; or Moia Tetoa, Radio Manager; (technical) Tooto Kabwebwenibeia, Broadcast Engineer; Martin Ouma Ojwach, Senior Superintendent of Electronics; Kautabuki Rubeiarki, Senior Technician; or T. Fakaofo, Technical Staff. Cassettes of local songs available for purchase. $1 or return postage required for a reply (IRCs not accepted). Currently off the air due to transmitter problems.

KOREA (DPR) World Time +9

Voice of Korea, External Service, Korean Central Broadcasting Station, Pyongyang, Democratic People's Republic of Korea (*not* "North Korea"). Phone: +850 (2) 381-6035. Fax: +850 (2) 381 4416. Phone and fax numbers valid only in those countries with direct telephone service to North Korea. Web: (unofficial) www.hikoryo.com/ser/vok.htm. Free publications, pennants, calendars, newspapers, artistic prints and pins. Do not include dutiable items in your envelope. Replies are irregular, as mail from countries not having diplomatic relations with North Korea is sent via circuitous routes and apparently does not always arrive. Indeed, some PASSPORT readers continue to report that mail to the station results in their receiving anti-communist literature from *South* Korea, which indicates that mail interdiction has not ceased. One way around the problem is to add "VIA BEIJING, CHINA" to the address, but replies via this route tend to be slow in coming. According to some listeners sending your letters via the English Section of China Radio International in a separate envelope addressed to the Voice of Korea asking them to forward your letter on to

Pyongyang. Explain the mail situation to the good folks in Beijing and you may have success. Another gambit is to send your correspondence to an associate in a country—such as China, Ukraine or India—having reasonable relations with North Korea, and ask that it be forwarded. If you don't know anyone in these countries, try using the good offices of the following person: Willi Passman, Oberhausener Str. 100, D-45476, Mülheim, Germany. Send correspondence in a sealed envelope without any address on the back. That should be sent inside another envelope. Include 2 IRCs to cover the cost of forwarding.

Regional Korean Central Broadcasting Stations—Not known to reply, but a long-shot possibility is to try corresponding in Korean to: Korean Central Broadcasting Station, Ministry of Posts and Telecommunications, Chongsung-dong, Moranbong District, Pyongyang, Democratic People's Republic of Korea.

KOREA (REPUBLIC) World Time +9

Korean Broadcasting System (KBS), 18 Yoido-dong, Youngdeungpo-Gu, Seoul, Republic of Korea 150-790. Phone: +82 (2) 781-1000; (duty officer) +82 (2) 781-1711/1792; (news desk) +82 (2) 781-4444; (overseas assistance) +82 (2) 781-1473/1497. Fax: +82 (2) 781 1698 or +82 (2) 781 2399. Email: pr@kbs.co.kr. Web: (includes Windows Media) http://kbs.co.kr.

Radio Korea International
MAIN OFFICE, INTERNATIONAL BROADCASTING DEPARTMENT: Radio Korea International, Global Center, Korean Broadcasting System, Yoido-dong 18, Youngdeungpo-Gu, Seoul, Republic of Korea 150-790. Phone: (general) +82 (2) 781-3650/60/70; (English Section) +82 (2) 781-3674/5/6; (Korean Section) +82 (2) 781-3669/71/73; (German Section) +82 (2) 781-3682/3/9; (Japanese Section) +82 (2) 781-3654/5/6 (Spanish Section) +82 (2) 781-3679/81/97. Fax: (general) +82 (2) 781 3694/5/6. Email: (general) rki@kbs.co.kr; (English) english@kbs.co.kr; (German) german@kbs.co.kr; (Japanese) rkijp@kbs.co.kr; (Spanish) spanish@kbs.co.kr; (Executive Director) hheejoo@kbs.co.kr. Web: (includes Windows Media) http://rki.kbs.co.kr. Contact: Ms. Hee Joo Han, Executive Director, KBS World-External Radio & TV; (administration) Mr. Ahn Jung-won, Director Division 1; or Mr. Sang Myung Kim; (English Section) Mr. Chae Hong-Pyo, Manager; Ms. Seung Joo (Sophia) Hong, Producer; Mr. Chun Hye-Jin, DX Editor, *Seoul Calling*; (Korean Section) Mr. Hae Ok Lee, Producer; (Japanese Section) Ms. Hye Young Kim, Producer; (Spanish Section) Ms. Sujin Cho, Producer; (German Section) Mr. Chung Soon Wan, Manager; Mr. Lee Bum Suk, Producer; Mr. Sabastian Ratzer, Journalist.
ENGINEERING DEPARTMENT: IBC, Center, Korean Broadcasting System, Yoido-dong 18, Youngdeungpo-Gu, Seoul, Republic of Korea 150-790. Phone: (general) +82 (2) 781-5141/5137; (Radio Transmission Division) +82 (2) 781-5663. Fax: +82 (2) 781 5159. Email: (Radio Transmission Division) poeto@hanmail.net; (Frequency Manager) kdhy@kbs.co.kr; (Planning Engineer) pulo5@kbs.co.kr. Contact: Mr. Oh Daesik, Radio Transmission Division; Mr. Dae-hyun Kim, Frequency Manager; or Mr. Chun-soo Lee, Planning Engineer.
QSLs, time/frequency schedule, station stickers, calendars, *Let's Learn Korean* book and a wide variety of other small souvenirs. *History of Korea* is available on CD-ROM (upon request) and via the station's Website.

KUWAIT World Time +3

Ministry of Information, P.O. Box 193, 13002 Safat, Kuwait. Phone: +965 241-5301. Fax: +965 243 4511. Web:

www.moinfo.gov.kw. Contact: Sheik Nasir Al-Sabah, Minister of Information.
TRANSMISSION AND FREQUENCY MANAGEMENT SECTION: Ministry of Information, P.O. Box 967 13010 Safat, Kuwait. Phone: +965 241-3590 or +965 241-7830. Fax: +965 241 5498. Email: kwtfreq@yahoo.com. Contact: Ahmed J. Alawdhi, Head of Frequency Section; Abdel Amir Mohamed Ali, Head of Frequency Planning; Nasser Al-Saffar, Frequency Manager; or Muhamad Abdullah, Director of Transmitting Stations.
Radio Kuwait, P.O. Box 397, 13004 Safat, Kuwait; (technical) Department of Frequency Management, P.O. Box 967, 13010 Safat, Kuwait. Phone: (general) +965 242-3774; (technical) +965 241-0301. Fax: (general) +965 245 6660; (technical) +965 241 5946. Email: (technical, including reception reports) kwtfreq@hotmail.com; (general) radiokuwait@radiokuwait.org or info@moinfo.gov.kw. Web: (news in RealAudio) www.radiokuwait.org; (live in Windows Media) www.media.gov.kw. Contact: (general) Manager, External Service; (technical) Wessam Najaf. Sometimes gives away stickers, calendars, pens or key chains.

KYRGYZSTAN World Time +5 (+6 midyear)

Kyrgyz Radio, Kyrgyz TV and Radio Center, 59 Jash Gvardiya Boulevard, 720010 Bishkek, Kyrgyzstan. Phone: (general) +996 (312) 253-404 or +996 (312) 255-741; (Director) +996 (312) 255-700 or +996 (312) 255-709; (Assemov) +996 (312) 650-7341 or +996 (312) 255-703; (Atakanova) +996 (312) 251-927; (technical) +996 (312) 257-771. Fax: +996 (312) 257 952. Note that from a few countries, the dialing code is still the old +7 (3312). Email: trk@kyrnet.kg. Web: www.ktr.kg. Contact: (administration) Moldoseyit Mambetakunov, Vice-Chairman - Kyrgyz Radio; or Eraly Ayilchiyev, Director; (general) Talant Assemov, Editor - Kyrgyz/Russian/German news; Gulnara Abdulaeva, Announcer - Kyrgyz/Russian/German news; (technical) Mirbek Uursabekov, Technical Director. Kyrgyz and Russian preferred, but correspondence in English and German can also be processed. For quick processing of reception reports, use email in German to Talant Assemov.
TRANSMISSION FACILITIES: Ministry of Transport and Communications, 42 Issanova Street, 720000 Bishkek, Kyrgyzstan. Phone: +996 (312) 216-672. Fax: +996 (312) 213 667. Contact: Jantoro Satybaldiyev, Minister. The shortwave transmitting station is located at Krasnaya-Rechka (Red River), a military encampment in the Issk-Ata region, about 40 km south of Bishkek.

LAO PEOPLE'S DEMOCRATIC REPUBLIC
World Time +7

NOTE: Although universally known as Laos, the official name of the country is "Lao People's Democratic Republic." English has now replaced French as the preferred foreign language.
Houa Phanh Provincial Radio Station, Sam Neua, Houa Phanh Province, Lao P.D.R. Phone: +856 (64) 312-008. Fax: +856 (21) 312 017. Contact: Mr. Veeyang, Hmong Announcer, and the only person who speaks English at the station; Ms. Nouan Thong, Lao Announcer; Mr. Vilaphone Bounsouvanh, Director; or Mr. Khong Kam, Engineer.
Lao National Radio
PROGRAM OFFICE AND NATIONAL STUDIOS: Lao National Radio, Phangkham Road, Ban Sisaket, Chanthabouri District, Vientiane, Lao P.D.R; or P.O. Box 310, Vientiane, Lao P.D.R. Phone: +856 (21) 212-097/428/429/431/432; (Head of English service & External Relations) +856 (21) 252-863. Fax:

+856 (21) 212 430. Email: natradio@laonet.net or (Head of English Service) inpanhs@hotmail.com. Contact: Mr. Bounthan Inthaxay, Director General; Mr. Inpanh Satchaphansy, Head of English Service & External relations; Mr. Vorasak Pravongviengkham, Head of French Service; Ms. Mativarn Simanithone, Deputy Head, English Section; Ms Chanthery Vichitsavanh, Announcer, English Section. Sometimes includes a program schedule and Laotian stamps when replying.
HF TRANSMITTER SITE: Transmitting Station KM6, Phone Tong Road, Ban Chommany Neuk, Vientiane Province, Lao P.D.R. Phone: +856 (21) 710-181. Contact: Mr. Sysamone Phommaxay, Station Engineer.
TECHNICAL OFFICE: Mass Media Department, Ministry of Information & Culture, 01000 Thanon Setthathirath, Vientiane, Lao P.D.R.; or P.O. Box 122, Vientiane, Lao P.D.R. Phone/Fax: +856 (21) 212-424. Email: dy_sisombath@yahoo.com. Contact: Mr. Dy Sisombath, Deputy Director General & Manager, Technical Network Expansion Planning.
LATVIA World Time +2 (+3 midyear)
KREBS TV, P.O. Box 371, LV-1010 Riga, Latvia. This company holds the license, and brokers airtime, for the shortwave transmitter formerly used by Latvian Radio. Reception reports should be sent to the individual program producers or stations which hire airtime over the transmitter.

LEBANON   World Time +2 (+3 midyear)

Radio Voice of Charity, Rue Fouad Chéhab, B.P. 850, Jounieh, Lebanon. Phone: +961 (9) 914-901 or +961 (9) 918-090. Email: email@radiocharity.org.lb. Web: (includes Windows Media) www.radiocharity.org. Contact: Frère Elie Nakhoul, Managing Director. Operates domestically on FM, and airs a 30-minute daily Arabic broadcast via the shortwave facilities of Vatican Radio. Replies to correspondence in English, French and Arabic, and verifies reception reports.

LESOTHO   World Time +2

Radio Lesotho (when operating), P.O. Box 552, Maseru 100, Lesotho. Phone: +266 323-371 or +266 323-561. Fax: +266 323 003. Web: www.radioles.co.ls. Contact: (general) Mamonyane Matsaba, Acting Programming Director; or Sekhonyana Motlohi, Producer, "What Do Listeners Say?"; (administration) Ms. Mpine Tente, Principal Secretary, Ministry of Information and Broadcasting; (technical) Lebohang Monnapula, Chief Engineer; Emmanuel Rametse, Transmitter Engineer; or Motlatsi Monyane, Studio Engineer. Return postage necessary, but do not include currency notes—local currency exchange laws are very strict.

LIBERIA   World Time exactly

NOTE: Mail sent to Liberia may be returned as undeliverable.
Radio ELWA, c/o SIM Liberia, 08 B.P. 886, Abidjan 08, Côte d'Ivoire. Contact: Moses T. Nyantee, Station Manager; or Chief Technician.
Radio Veritas (when operating), P.O. Box 3569, Monrovia, Liberia. Phone: +231 226-979. Contact: Steve Kenneh, Manager.

LIBYA   World Time +2

Libyan Jamahiriyah Broadcasting Corporation, P.O. Box 9333, Soug al Jama, Tripoli, Libya. Phone: +218 (21) 361-4508. Fax: +218 (21) 489 4240. Email: info@ljbc.net. Web: www.ljbc.net. Contact: Youssef Aimoujrab.

The Lao National Culture Hall is neither Lao nor cultural. Built by China, this empty edifice is used for gatherings.   M. Guha

Voice of Africa, P.O. Box 4677/4386 or 2009, Soug al Jama, Tripoli, Libya. Phone: +218 (21) 444-0112, +218 (21) 444-9106 or +218 (21) 444-9872. Fax: +218 (21) 444 9875. Email: africavoice@hotmail.com. The external service of Libyan Jamahiriyah Broadcasting identifies as "Voice of Africa" in its English and French programs, while in Arabic it may use the same identification as the domestic service or refer to itself as the "Voice of Libya." Replies slowly and irregularly.
MALTA OFFICE: P.O. Box 17, Hamrun, Malta. Replies tend to be more forthcoming from this address than direct from Libya.

LITHUANIA   World Time +2 (+3 midyear)

Radio Vilnius, Lietuvos Radijas, Konarskio 49, LT-2600 Vilnius, Lithuania. Phone: +370 (5) 236-3079. Email: ravil@lrt.lt. Contact: Ms. Ilona Rukiene, Head of English Department. Free stickers, pennants, Lithuanian stamps and other souvenirs.

MADAGASCAR   World Time +3

Adventist World Radio
ADMINISTRATION: B.P. 700, Antananarivo, Madagascar. Phone: +261 (2022) 404-65.
STUDIO: B.P. 460, Antananarivo, Madagascar.
TECHNICAL AND NON-TECHNICAL (e.g. comments on programs)—see United Kingdom and USA. AWR broadcasts in

Malagasy and French on leased airtime from Radio Nederland's Madagascar Relay. Reception reports concerning these broadcasts are best sent to the AWR U.K. office. Also, *see* AWR listings under Germany, Guam, Kenya, United Kingdom and USA.
Radio Madagasikara, B.P. 442 - Anosy, 101 Antananarivo, Madagascar. Phone: +261 2022-21745. Fax: +261 2022 32715. Email: (Director's Office) mmdir@dts.mg; (Editorial Dept.) mminfo@dts.mg; (Program Dept.) mmprog@dts.mg; (Webmaster) radmad@dts.mg. Web: http://takelaka.dts.mg/radmad. Contact: Mlle. Rakotonirina Soa Herimanitia, Secrétaire de Direction, a young lady who collects stamps; Mamy Rafenomanantsoa, Directeur; or J.J. Rakotonirina, who has been known to request hi-fi catalogs. $1 required, and enclosing used stamps from various countries may help. Tape recordings accepted. Replies slowly and somewhat irregularly, usually to correspondence in French.
Radio Nederland Wereldomroep—Madagascar Relay, B.P. 404, Antananarivo, Madagascar. Contact: (technical) Rahamefy Eddy, Technische Dienst; or J.A. Ratobimiarana, Chief Engineer. Nontechnical correspondence should be sent to Radio Nederland Wereldomreop in the Netherlands (*see*).

MALAWI   World Time +2

Malawi Broadcasting Corporation (when operating), P.O. Box 30133, Chichiri, Blantyre 3, Malawi. Phone: (general) +265 671-222; (transmitting station) +265 694-208. Fax: +265 671 257 or +265 671 353. Email: dgmbc@malawi.net. Web: www.mbcradios.com. Contact: (general) Wilson Bankuku, Director General; J.O. Mndeke; or T.J. Sineta; (technical) Abraham E. Nsapato, Controller of Transmitters; Phillip Chinseu, Engineering Consultant; or Joseph Chikagwa, Director of Engineering. Tends to be irregular due to lack of transmitter spares. Return postage or $1 helpful, as the station is underfunded.

MALAYSIA   World Time +8

Asia-Pacific Broadcasting Union (ABU), P.O. Box 1164, 59700 Kuala Lumpur, Malaysia; or (street address) 2nd Floor, Bangunan IPTAR, Angkasapuri, 50614 Kuala Lumpur, Malaysia. Phone: (general) +60 (3) 2282-3592; (Programme Department)+60 (3) 2282-2480; (Technical Department) +60 (3) 2282-3108. Fax: +60 (3) 2282 5292. Email: (Office of Secretary-General) sg@abu.org.my; (Programme Department) prog@abu.org.my; (Technical Department) tech@abu.org.my. Web: www.abu.org.my. Contact: (administration) David Astley, Secretary-General; (technical) Sharad Sadhu and Rukmin Wijemanne, Senior Engineers, Technical Department.
Radio Malaysia Kota Kinabalu, RTM Sabah, 2.4 km Jalan Tuaran, 88614 Kota Kinabalu, Sabah, Malaysia. Phone: +60 (88) 213-444. Fax: +60 (88) 223 493. Email: rtmkk@rtm.net.my. Web: www.p.sabah.gov.my/rtm. Contact: Benedict Janil, Director of Broadcasting; Hasbullah Latiff; or Mrs. Angrick Saguman. Registering your letter may help. $1 or return postage required.
☎Radio Malaysia, Kuala Lumpur
MAIN OFFICE: RTM, Angkasapuri, Bukit Putra, 50614 Kuala Lumpur, Malaysia. Phone: +60 (3) 2282-5333 or +60 (3) 2282-4976. Fax: +60 (3) 2282 4735, +60 (3) 2282 5103 or +60 (3) 2282 5859. Email: sabariah@rtm.net.my or helpdesk@rtm.net.my. Web: www.rtm.net.my. Contact: (general) Madzhi Johari, Director of Radio; (technical) Ms. Aminah Din, Deputy Director Engineering (Radio); Abdullah Bin Shahadan, Engineer, Transmission and Monitoring; or Ong Poh,

Chief Engineer. May sell T-shirts and key chains. Return postage required.
ENGINEERING DIVISION: 3rd Floor, Angkasapum, 50616 Kuala Lumpur, Malaysia. Phone: +60 (3) 2285-7544. Fax: +60 (3) 2283 2446. Email: zulrahim@rtm.net.my. Contact: Zulkifli Ab Rahim.
RADIO 1 (MALAY): Wisma Radio Angkasapuri, P.O. Box 11272, 50740 Kuala Lumpur, Malaysia. Phone: +60 (3) 2288-7841 or +60 (3) 2288-7261. Fax: +60 (3) 2284 7593. Email: komit@radio1.com.my. Web: www.rtm.net.my/radio1; (includes Windows Media) www.radio1.com.my.
RADIO 4 (ENGLISH): Same address as Radio 1, above. Phone: +60 (3) 2288-7282/3/4/5 or +60 (3) 2288-7663. Fax: +60 (3) 2284 5750. Email: radio4@rtm.net.my. Web: www.rtm.net.my/radio4.
RADIO 6 (TAMIL): Same address as Radios 1 and 4, above. Phone: +60 (3) 2288-7279. Fax: +60 (3) 2284 9137. Web: www.rtm.net.my/radio6.
TRANSMISSION OFFICE: Controller of Engineering, Department of Broadcasting (RTM), 43000 Kajang, Selangor Darul Ehsan, Malaysia. Phone: +60 (3) 8736-1530 or +60 (3) 8736-1530/1863. Fax: +60 (3) 8736 1226/7. Email: rtmkjg@rtm.net.my. Contact: Jeffrey Looi; or Ab Wahid Bin Hamid, Supervisor, Transmission Engineering.
Radio Malaysia Sarawak (Kuching), RTM Sarawak, Jalan Satok, 93614 Kuching, Sarawak, Malaysia. Phone: +60 (82) 248-422. Fax: +60 (82) 241 914. Email: rtmkuc@rtm.net.my. Contact: (general) Yusof Ally, Director of Broadcasting; Mohd. Hulman Abdollah; or Human Resources Development; (technical, but also nontechnical) Colin A. Minoi, Technical Correspondence; (technical) Kho Kwang Khoon, Deputy Director of Engineering. Return postage helpful.
Radio Malaysia Sarawak (Miri), RTM Miri, Bangunan Penyiaran, 98000 Miri, Sarawak, Malaysia. Phone: +60 (85) 422-524 or +60 (85) 423-645. Fax: +60 (85) 411 430. Contact: Clement Stia. $1 or return postage helpful.
Radio Malaysia Sarawak (Sibu), RTM Sibu, Bangunan Penyiaran, 96009 Sibu, Sarawak, Malaysia. Phone: +60 (84) 323-566. Fax: +60 (84) 321 717. Contact: Clement Stia, Divisional Controller, Broadcasting Department. $1 or return postage required. Replies irregularly and slowly.
Voice of Islam—Program of the Voice of Malaysia (*see*, below).
Voice of Malaysia, Suara Malaysia, Wisma Radio Angkasapuri, P.O. Box 11272, 50740 Kuala Lumpur, Malaysia. Phone: (general) +60 (3) 2288-7824; (English Service) +60 (3) 2282-7826. Fax: +60 (3) 2284 7594. Email: vom@rtm.net.my; (technical, Kajang transmitter site) rtmkjg@po.jaring.my. Web:www.rtm.net.my/vom/utama.htm. Contact: (general) Mrs. Mahani bte Ujang, Supervisor, English Service; Hajjah Wan Chuk Othman, English Service; (administration) Santokh Singh Gill, Director; or Mrs. Adilan bte Omar, Assistant Director; (technical) Lin Chew, Director of Engineering; (Kajang transmitter site) Kok Yoon Yeen, Technical Assistant. Free calendars and stickers. Two IRCs or return postage helpful. Replies slowly and irregularly.

MALI   World Time exactly

Radiodiffusion Télévision Malienne, B.P. 171, Bamako, Mali. Phone: +223 212-019 or +223 212-474. Fax: +223 214 205. Email: (general) ortm@cafib.com; (Traore) cotraore@sotelma.ml. Contact: Karamoko Issiaka Daman, Directeur des Programmes; (administration) Abdoulaye Sidibe, Directeur General; (Technical) Nouhoum Traore. $1 or IRC helpful. Replies slowly and irregularly to correspondence in French. English is accepted.

MAURITANIA   World Time exactly

Radio Mauritanie, B.P. 200, Nouakchott, Mauritania. Phone: +222 (2) 52287. Fax: +222 (2) 51264. Email: rm@mauritania.mr. Contact: Madame Amir Feu; Lemrabott Boukhary; Madame Fatimetou Fall Dite Ami, Secretaire de Direction; Mr. El Hadj Diagne; or Mr. Hane Abou. Return postage or $1 required. Rarely replies.

MEXICO   World Time –6 (–5 midyear) Central, South and Eastern, including D.F.; –7 (–6 midyear) Mountain; –7 Sonora; –8 (–7 midyear) Pacific

Candela FM—*see* RASA Onda Corta.
La Hora Exacta—XEQK (if reactivated), Real de Mayorazgo 83, Barrio de Xoco, 03330-México D.F., Mexico. Phone: +52 (55) 628-1731, +52 (55) 628-1700 Ext. 1648 or 1659. Fax: +52 (55) 604 8292. Web: www.imer.gob.mx (click on "Radiodifusoras"). Contact: Lic. Santiago Ibarra Ferrer, Gerente.
La Jarocha—XEFT (if reactivated), Apartado Postal 21, 91701-Veracruz, VER, Mexico. Phone: +52 (229) 322-250. Contact: C.P. Miguel Rodríguez Sáez, Sub-Director; or Lic. Juan de Dios Rodríguez Díaz, Director. Free tourist guide to Veracruz. Return postage, IRC or $1 probably helpful. Likely to reply to correspondence in Spanish.
Radio Educación Onda Corta—XEPPM, Apartado Postal 21-940, 04021-México D.F., Mexico. Phone: (general) +52 (55) 559-6169. Phone/Fax: (Director's Office) +52 (55) 575-6566. Email: (general) radioe@conaculta.gob.mx; (Lidia Camacho) lidiac@conaculta.gob.mx. Web: www.cnca.gob.mx/cnca/buena/radio; (includes Windows Media) www.radioeducacion.edu.mx. Contact: (general) Lic. María Del Carmen Limón Celorio, Directora de Producción y Planeación; (administration) Lic. Lidia Camacho Camacho, Directora General; (technical) Ing. Jesús Aguilera Jiménez, Subdirector de Desarrollo Técnico. Free stickers, calendars and station photo. Return postage or $1 required. Replies, sometimes slowly, to correspondence in English, Spanish, Italian or French.
Radio Huayacocotla—XEJN
STATION ADDRESS: "Radio Huaya," Dom. Gutiérrez Najera s/n, Apartado Postal 13, 92600-Huayacocotla, VER, Mexico. Phone: +52 (775) 80067. Fax: +52 (775) 80178. Email: radiohua@sjsocial.org, or framos@ubiero.uia.mx. Web: www.sjsocial.org/Radio/huarad.html. Contact: Pedro Ruperto Albino, Coordinador. Return postage or $1 helpful. Replies irregularly to correspondence in Spanish.
Radio Mil Onda Corta—XEOI, NRM, Avda. Insurgentes Sur 1870, Col. Florida, 01030- México D.F., Mexico; or Apartado Postal 21-1000, 04021-México, D.F., Mexico (this address for reception reports and listeners' correspondence on the station's shortwave broadcasts, and mark the envelope to the attention of Dr. Julián Santiago Díez de Bonilla). Phone: (station) +52 (55) 662-1000 or +52 (55) 662-1100; (Núcleo Radio Mil network) +52 (55) 662-6060, +52 (55) 663-0739 or +52 (55) 663 0590. Fax: (station) +52 (55) 662 0974; (Núcleo Radio Mil network) +52 (55) 662 0979. Email: info@nrm.com.mx. Web: www.nrm.com.mx/estaciones/radiomil. Contact: (administration) Edilberto Huesca P., Vicepresidente Ejecutivo del Núcleo Radio Mil; or Lic. Gustavo Alvite Martínez, Director; (shortwave service) Dr. Julián Santiago Díez de Bonilla. Free stickers. $1 or return postage required.
Radio Transcontinental—XERTA (when operating), Plaza de San Juan 5, Primer piso, Despacho 2, Esquina con Ayuntamiento, Centro, 06070-México D.F., Mexico. Phone: +52 (55) 5518-4938. Email: xerta@radiodifusion.com. Web: (includes

RealAudio) www.misionradio.com. Contact: Verónica Coria Miranda, Representante Ejecutiva.
Radio UNAM [Universidad Autónoma de México]—XEYU (when operating), Adolfo Prieto 133, Colonia del Valle, 03100-México D.F., Mexico. Phone: +52 (55) 523-2633. Email: (general) radiounam@www.unam.mx; (Director) fes@servidor.unam.mx. Web: (includes RealAudio and MP3) www.unam.mx/radiounam. Contact: (general) Lic. Fernando Escalante Sobrino, Director General de Radio UNAM; (technical) Ing. Gustavo Carreño, Departamento Técnico. Free tourist literature and stickers. $1 or return postage required. Replies irregularly to correspondence in Spanish.
Radio Universidad—XEXQ Onda Corta, Arista 245, Centro Histórico, Apartado Postal 456, 78000-San Luis Potosí, SLP, Mexico. Phone: +52 (444) 826-1345. Fax: +52 (444) 826 1388. Web: www.uaslp.mxmx/rtu. Contact: Lic. Leticia Zavala Pérez, Coordinadora; Lizbeth Deyanira Tapia Hernández, Radio Operadora.
RASA Onda Corta—XEQM (when operating), Apartado Postal 217, 97001-Mérida, YUC, Mexico. Phone: +52 (999) 236-155. Fax: +52 (999) 280 680. Contact: Lic. Bernardo Laris Rodríguez, Director General del Grupo RASA Mérida. Replies irregularly to correspondence in Spanish. Currently relays programs from FM sister station "Candela Tropicaliente," but hopes eventually to produce its own programming based on the best programs of each station in the network.

MOLDOVA   World Time +2 (+3 midyear)

Radio DMR, Rose Luxembourg Street 10, Tiraspol 3300, Republic of Moldova. Email: radiopmr@inbox.ru. Web: www.president-pmr.org. Contact: Arkady D Shablienko, Director; Ms. Antonina N. Voronkova, Editor-in-Chief; Ernest A. Vardanean, Editor and Translator; Vadim A. Rudomiotov, Announcer; Vlad Butuk, Technician Engineer. Replies to correspondence in English and Russian. Return postage helpful. Broadcasts from the separatist, pro-Russian, "Dniester Moldavian Republic" (also known as "Trans-Dniester Moldavian Republic").

MONACO   World Time +1 (+2 midyear)

Trans World Radio
MAIN OFFICE: B.P. 349, MC-98007 Monte-Carlo, Monaco-Cedex. Phone: +377 (92) 16-56-00. Fax: +377 (92) 16 56 01. Web: (transmission schedule) www.gospelcom.net/twr/broadcasts/europe.htm. Contact: (general) Mrs. Jeanne Olson; (administration) Richard Olson, Station Manager; (Technical) *see* Vienna address, below. Free paper pennant. IRC or $1 helpful. Also, *see* USA. Uses the transmitting facilities of Radio Monte Carlo, across the border in Fontbonne, France.
GERMAN OFFICE: Evangeliums-Rundfunk, Postfach 1444, D-35573 Wetzlar, Germany. Phone: +49 (6441) 957-0. Fax: +49 (6441) 957 120. Email: erf@erf.de; or siemens@arf.de. Web: (includes RealAudio) www.erf.de. Contact: Jürgen Werth, Direktor.
NETHERLANDS OFFICE, NONTECHNICAL: Postbus 176, NL-3780 BD Voorthuizen, Netherlands. Phone: +31 (0) 3429-2727. Fax: +31 (0) 3429 6727. Contact: Beate Kiebel, Manager Broadcast Department; or Felix Widmer.
VIENNA OFFICE, TECHNICAL: Postfach 141, A-1235 Vienna, Austria. Phone: (Schraut) +43 (1) 863-1216: (Dobos) +43 (1) 863-1221; +43 (1) 863-1233; +43 (1) 863-1247 or (Baertschi) +43 (1) 863-1258. Fax: +43 (1) 863 1220. Email: (Menzel) 100615.1511@compuserve.com; (Schraut) twr_euro_bschraut@

compuserve.com; bschraut@twr-europe.at; (Baertschi) rbaertsc@twr-europe.net; (Dobos) kdobos@twr-europe.at. Contact: Helmut Menzel, Director of Engineering; Bernhard Schraut, Deputy Technical Director; Rudolf Baertschi, Technical Director; or Kalman Dobos, Frequency Coordinator. *SWISS OFFICE:* Evangelium in Radio und Fernsehen, Witzbergstrasse 23, CH-8330 Pfäffikon ZH, Switzerland. Phone: +41 (951) 0500. Fax: +41 (951) 0540. Email: erf@erf.ch. Web: www.erf.ch.

MONGOLIA   World Time +8 (+9 midyear)

Mongolian Radio (Postal and email addresses same as Voice of Mongolia, *see* below). Phone: (administration) +976 (11) 323-520 or +976 (11) 328-978; (editorial) +976 (11) 329-766; (MRTV parent organization) +976 (11) 326-663. Fax: +976 (11) 327 234. Email: mr@mongol.net. Contact: A. Buidakhmet, Director.
Voice of Mongolia, C.P.O. Box 365, Ulaanbaatar 13, Mongolia. Phone: +976 (1) 321-624 or (English Section) +976 (11) 327-900. Fax: +976 (11) 323 096 or (English Section) +976 (11) 327 234. Email: mr@mongol.net. Contact: (general) Mrs. Narantuya, Chief of Foreign Service; Z. Densmaa, Mail Editor; Mrs. Oyunchimeg Alagsai, Head of English Department; or Ms. Tsegmid Burmaa, Japanese Department; (administration) Ch. Surenjav, Director; (technical) Ing. Ganhuu, Chief of Technical Department. Correpondence should be directed to the relevant language section and 2 IRCs or 1$ appreciated. Sometimes very slow in replying. Accepts taped reception reports, preferably containing five-minute excerpts of the broadcast(s) reported, but cassettes cannot be returned. Free pennants, postcards, newspapers and Mongolian stamps.
TECHNICAL DEPARTMENT: C.P.O Box 1126, Ulaanbaatar Mongolia. Phone: +976 (11) 363-584. Fax: +976 (11) 327 900. Email: aem@mongol.net. Contact: Mr. Tumurbaatar Gantumur, Director of Technical Department; or Ms. Buyanbaatar Unur, Engineer, Technical Center of Transmission System.

MOROCCO   World Time exactly

☐Radio Medi Un
MAIN OFFICE: B.P. 2055, Tanger, Morocco (physical location: 3, rue Emsallah, 90000 Tanger, Morocco). Phone/Fax: +212 (9) 936-363 or +212 (9) 935-755. Email: (general) medi1@medi1.com; (technical) technique@medi1.com. Web: (includes RealAudio) www.medi1.com; www.medi1.co.ma. Contact: J. Dryk, Responsable Haute Fréquence. Two IRCs helpful. Free stickers. Correspondence in French preferred.
PARIS BUREAU, NONTECHNICAL: 78 Avenue Raymond Poincaré, F-75016 Paris, France. Phone: +33 (1) 45-01-53-30. Correspondence in French preferred.
Radio Méditerranée Internationale—*see* Radio Medi Un.
Radiodiffusion-Télévision Marocaine, 1 rue El Brihi, Rabat, Morocco. Phone: +212 (7) 766-881/83/85, +212 (7) 701-740 or +212 (7) 201-404. Fax: +212 (7) 722 047, or +212 (7) 703 208. Email: rtm@rtm.gov.ma; (technical) hammouda@rtm.gov.ma.Contact: (nontechnical and technical) Ms. Naaman Khadija, Ingénieur d'Etat en Télécommunication; Abed Bendalh; or Rahal Sabir; (technical) Tanone Mohammed Jamaledine, Technical Director; Hammouda Mohammed, Engineer; or N. Read. Correspondence welcomed in English, French, Arabic or Berber.
Voice of America/IBB—Morocco Relay Station, Briech. Phone: (office) +212 (9) 93-24-81. Fax: +212 (9) 93 55 71. Contact: Station Manager. These numbers for urgent technical matters only. Otherwise, does not welcome direct correspon-dence; *see* USA for acceptable VOA and IBB Washington addresses and related information.

MYANMAR (BURMA)   World Time +6:30

Radio Myanmar
STATION: GPO Box 1432, Yangon-11181, Myanmar; or 426, Pyay Road, Yangon-11041, Myanmar. Phone: +95 (1) 531-850. Fax: +95 (1) 525 428. Web: www.myanmar.com/RADIO_TV.HTM. Contact: Ko Ko Htway, Director (Broadcasting).

NAGORNO-KARABAGH   World Time +4 (+5 midyear)

Voice of Justice, Tigranmetz Street 23a, Stepanakert, Nagorno-Karabagh. Contact: Michael Hajiyan, Station Manager. Replies to correspondence in Armenian, Azeri, Russian and German.

NAMIBIA   World Time +2 (+1 midyear)

Radio Namibia/Namibian Broadcasting Corporation (when operating), P.O. Box 321, Windhoek 9000, Namibia. Phone: (general) +264 (61) 291-3111; (National Radio—English Service) +264 (61) 291-2440; (German Service) +264 (61) 291-2330; (Schachtschneider) +264 (61) 291-2188. Fax: (general) +264 (61) 217 760; (German Service) +264 (61) 291 2291; (Duwe, technical) +264 (61) 231 881. Email: (general) webmaster@nbc.com.na. To contact individuals, the format is initiallastname@nbc.com.na; so to reach, say, Peter Schachtschneider, it would be pschachtschneider@nbc.com.na. Web: www.nbc.com.na/index.html. Contact: (general) Corry Tjaveondja, Manager, National Radio; (technical) Peter Schachtschneider, Manager, Transmitter Maintenance; Joe Duwe, Chief Technician. Free stickers.

NEPAL   World Time +5:45

☐Radio Nepal, P.O. Box 634, Singha Durbar, Kathmandu, Nepal. Phone: (general) +977 (1) 223-910, +977 (1) 243-569; (engineering) +977 (1) 225-467. Fax: +977 (1) 221 952. Email: radio@rne.wlink.com.np; (engineering) radio@engg.wlink.com.np. Web: (includes RealAudio in English and Nepali) www.radionepal.org. Contact: (general) S.R. Sharma, Executive Director; M.P. Adhikari, Deputy Executive Director; Jayanti Rajbhandari, Director - Programming; or S.K. Pant, Producer, "Listener's Mail"; (technical) Ram Sharan Kharki, Director - Engineering. 3 IRCs necessary, but station urges that neither mint stamps nor cash be enclosed, as this invites theft by Nepalese postal employees.

NETHERLANDS   World Time +1 (+2 midyear)

☐Radio Nederland Wereldomroep (Radio Netherlands)
MAIN OFFICE: P.O. Box 222, 1200 JG Hilversum, The Netherlands. Phone: (general) +31 (35) 672-4211; (English Language Service) +31 (35) 672-4242; (24-hour listener Answerline) +31 (35) 672-4222. Fax: (general) +31 (35) 672 4207, but indicate destination department on fax cover sheet; (English Language Service) +31 (35) 672 4239. Email: (English Service) letters@rnw.nl; ("Media Network") media@rnw.nl. Web: (includes RealAudio, Windows Media and MP3) www.rnw.nl. Contact: (management) Jan Hoek, Acting Director-General; Mike Shaw, Head of English Language Service; Ginger da Silva, Network Manager English. Full-data verification cards for reception reports, following guidelines in the RNW folder, "Writing Useful Reception Reports," available on the Media Network

Website. Semi-annual *On Target* newsletter also free upon request, as are stickers and booklets. Other language departments have their own newsletters. The Radio Netherlands Music Department produces concerts heard on many NPR stations in North America, as well as a line of CDs, mainly of classical, jazz, world music and the Euro Hit 40. Most of the productions are only for rebroadcasting on other stations, but recordings on the NM Classics label are for sale. More details are available at the RNW Website (www.rnmusic.nl). Visitors welcome, but must call in advance.

PROGRAMME DISTRIBUTION, NETWORK AND FREQUENCY PLANNING: P.O. Box 222, 1200 JG Hilversum, The Netherlands. Phone: +31 (35) 672-4422. Fax: +31 (35) 672 4429. Email: nfp@rnw.nl. Contact: Leo van der Woude, Frequency Manager; or Jan Willem Drexhage, Head of Programme Distribution.

NEW DELHI OFFICE: (local correspondence only) P.O. Box 5257, Chanakya Puri Post Office, New Delhi, 110 021, India. Forwards mail from Indian listeners to the Netherlands every three weeks.

📻**Radio Voice of Hope**, Plot No. 15, Komi Crescent, Lusira, 338829 Kampala, Uganda. Phone: +256 (41) 220-334. Email: webmaster@radiovoiceofhope.net; hope@africaonline.co.ug; or (Namadi) jnamadi@excite.com. Web: (includes RealAudio) www.radiovoiceofhope.net. Contact: Jane Namadi, Editor. Return postage requested. Programs are produced by the New Sudan Council of Churches (NSCC) at studios in the Netherlands and Uganda. Identifies as "Radio Voice of Hope for the voiceless in southern Sudan." Transmits via the Radio Nederland relay station in Madagascar, and is a project sponsored by the Dutch public broadcaster NCRV and supported by Pax Christi and the Interchurch Organization for Development Corporation.

KENYA ADDRESS: P.O.Box 66168, Nairobi, Kenya. Phone: +254 (2) 446-966 or +254 (2) 448-141/2. Fax: +254 (2) 447 015. Email: nscc-nbo@maf.org.

NETHERLANDS ANTILLES   World Time –4

Radio Nederland Wereldomroep—Bonaire Relay, P.O. Box 45, Kralendijk, Netherlands Antilles. Contact: Leo Kool, Manager. Nontechnical correspondence should be sent to Radio Nederland Wereldomreop in the Netherlands (*see*).

NEW ZEALAND   World Time +13 (+12 midyear)

📻**Radio New Zealand International (Te Reo Irirangi O Aotearoa, O Te Moana-nui-a-kiwa)**, P.O. Box 123, Wellington, New Zealand. Phone: +64 (4) 474-1437. Fax: +64 (4) 474 1433 or +64 (4) 474 1886. Email: info@rnzi.com. Web: (includes RealAudio and online reception report form) www.rnzi.com. Contact: Florence de Ruiter, Listener Mail; Myra Oh, Producer, "Mailbox"; or Walter Zweifel, News Editor; (administration) Ms. Linden Clark, Manager; (technical) Adrian Sainsbury, Technical Manager. Free stickers, schedule/flyer about station, map of New Zealand and tourist literature available. English/Maori T-shirts for US$20; sweatshirts $40; interesting variety of CDs, as well as music cassettes and spoken programs, in Domestic "Replay Radio" catalog (VISA/MC). Two IRCs or $2 for QSL card, one IRC for schedule/catalog. Email reports verified by email only.

Radio Reading Service—ZLXA, P.O. Box 360, Levin 5500, New Zealand. Phone: (general) +64 (6) 368-2229; (engineering) +64 (25) 985-360. Fax: +64 (6) 368 7290. Email: (general, including reception reports) info@radioreading.org; (Bell) abell@radioreading.org; (Stokoe) bstokoe@radioreading.org.

Web: www.radioreading.org. Contact: (general) Ash Bell, Manager/Station Director; (technical, including reception reports) Brian Stokoe. Operated by volunteers 24 hours a day, seven days a week. Station is owned by the "New Zealand Radio for the Print Disabled Inc." Free brochure, postcards and stickers. $1, return postage or 3 IRCs appreciated.

NICARAGUA   World Time –6

Radio Miskut (when operating), Barrio Pancasan, Puerto Cabezas, R.A.A.N., Nicaragua. Phone: +505 (282) 2443. Fax: +505 (267) 3032. Contact: Evaristo Mercado Pérez, Director de Operación y de Programas; or Abigail Zúñiga Fagoth. T-shirts $10, and *Resumen Mensual del Gobierno y Consejo Regional* and *Revista Informativa Detallada de las Gestiones y Logros* $10 per copy. Station has upgraded to a new shortwave transmitter and is currently improving its shortwave antenna. Replies slowly and irregularly to correspondence in English and Spanish. $2 helpful, as is registering your letter.

NIGER   World Time +1

La Voix du Sahel, O.R.T.N., B.P. 361, Niamey, Niger. Fax: +227 72 35 48. Contact: (general) Adamou Oumarou; Issaka Mamadou; Zakari Saley; Souley Boubacou; or Mounkaïla Inazadan, Producer, "Inter-Jeunes Variétés"; (administration) Oumar Tiello, Directeur; (technical) Afo Sourou Victor. $1 helpful. Correspondence in French preferred. Correspondence by males with this station may result in requests for certain unusual types of magazines and photographs.

NIGERIA   World Time +1

WARNING—MAIL THEFT: For the time being, correspondence from abroad to Nigerian addresses has a relatively high probability of being stolen.

WARNING—CONFIDENCE ARTISTS: For years, now, correspondence with Nigerian stations has sometimes resulted in letters from highly skilled "pen pal" confidence artists. These typically offer to send you large sums of money, if you will provide details of your bank account or similar information (after which they clean out your account). Other scams are disguised as tempting business proposals; or requests for money, free electronic or other products, publications or immigration sponsorship. Persons thus approached should contact their country's diplomatic offices. For example, Americans should contact the Diplomatic Security Section of the Department of State [phone +1 (202) 647-4000], or an American embassy or consulate.

Radio Nigeria—Enugu (when operating), P.M.B. 1051, Enugu (Anambra), Phone: +234 (42) 254-137. Fax: +234 (42) 255 354. Nigeria. Contact: Engr. Louis Nnamuchi, Deputy Director Engineering Services. Two IRCs, return postage or $1 required. Replies slowly.

Radio Nigeria—Ibadan, Broadcasting House, P.M.B. 5003, Ibadan, Oyo State, Nigeria. Phone: +234 (22) 241-4093 or +234 (22) 241-4106. Fax: +234 (22) 241 3930. Contact: V.A. Kalejaiye, Technical Services Department; Rev. Olukunle Ajani, Executive Director; Nike Adegoke, Executive Director; or Dare Folarin, Principal Public Affairs Officer. $1 or return postage required. Replies slowly.

Radio Nigeria—Kaduna, P.O. Box 250, Kaduna (Kaduna), Nigeria. Contact: R.B. Jimoh, Assistant Director Technical Service; or Shehu Muhammad, Chief Technical Officer, Studio Link and Outside Broadcasts. May send sticker celebrating 30 years

Mt. Fuji is Japan's most familiar icon and geographic feature. It has been featured on numerous Radio Japan verification cards over the years.

T. Ohtake

of broadcasting. $1 or return postage required. Replies slowly.
Radio Nigeria—Lagos, P.M.B. 12504, Ikoyi, Lagos, Nigeria. Phone: +234 (1) 269-0301. Fax: +234 (1) 269 0073. Contact: Willie Egbe, Assistant Director for Programmes; Babatunde Olalekan Raji, Monitoring Unit. Two IRCs or return postage helpful. Replies slowly and irregularly.

Voice of Nigeria
ABUJA OFFICE: 6th Floor, Radio House Herbert Macaulay, Garki-Abuja, Nigeria. Phone: +234 (9) 234-6973, +234 (9) 234-4017. Fax: +234 (9) 234 6970. Email: (general) dgovon@nigol.net.ng, vonabuja@rosecom.net; (Idowu) tidowu@yahoo.com. Web: www.voiceofnigeria.org. Contact: Ayodele Suleiman, Director of Programming; Tope Idowu, Editor *"Voice Of Nigeria Airwaves"* program magazine & Special Assistant to the Director General; Frank Iloye, Station Manager; (technical) Timothy Gyang, Deputy Director, Engineering.
LAGOS OFFICE: P.M.B. 40003, Falomo, Lagos, Nigeria. Phone: +234 (1) 269-3075 or +234 (1) 269-3078. Fax: +234 (1) 269 3078, +234 (9) 269 1944. Email: vonlagos@fiberia.com.
Replies from the station tend to be erratic, but continue to generate unsolicited correspondence from supposed "pen pals" (*see WARNING—CONFIDENCE ARTISTS, above*); faxes, which are much less likely to be intercepted, may be more fruitful. Two IRCs or return postage helpful.

NORTHERN MARIANA ISLANDS World Time +10

Far East Broadcasting Company—Radio Station KFBS, P.O. Box 500209, Saipan, Mariana Islands MP 96950 USA. Phone:

+1 (670) 322-3841. Fax: +1 (670) 322 3060. Email: saipan@febc.org. Web: www.febc.org. Contact: Robert Springer, Director; or Irene Gabbie, QSL Secretary. Replies sometimes take months. Also, *see* FEBC Radio International, USA.

NORWAY World Time +1 (+2 midyear).

UKEsenderen, Elgesetergate 1, N-7030 Trondheim, Norway. Email: uka@uka.no. Web: www.uka.ntnu.no. A student station which operates on 7215 kHz for approximately three weeks (mid-October to early November) in odd-numbered years.

OMAN World Time +4

☞**Radio Sultanate of Oman**, Ministry of Information, P.O. Box 600, Muscat, Post Code 113, Sultanate of Oman. Phone: +968 602-494 or +968 603-222. Fax: (general) +968 602 055, +968 693 770 or +968 602 831; (technical) +968 604 629 or +968 607 239. Email: (general) tvradio@omantel.net.om; (Frequency Management) sjnomani@omantel.net.om; or abulukman@hotmail.com. Web: (includes RealAudio) www.oman-radio.gov.om. Contact: (Directorate General of Technical Affairs) Abdallah Bin Saif Al-Nabhani, Acting Chief Engineer; Salim Al-Nomani, Director of Frequency Management; or Ahmed Mohamed Al-Balushi, Head of Studio's Engineering. Replies regularly, and responses are from one to two weeks. $1, mint stamps or 3 IRCs helpful.

PAKISTAN World Time +5 (+6 midyear)

Azad Kashmir Radio, Muzaffarabad, Azad Kashmir, Pakistan. Contact: (technical) M. Sajjad Ali Siddiqui, Director of Engineering; or Liaquatullah Khan, Engineering Manager. Registered mail helpful. Rarely replies to correspondence.
☞**Pakistan Broadcasting Corporation**—same address, fax and contact details as "Radio Pakistan," below. Web: (includes RealAudio) www.radio.gov.pk.
Radio Pakistan, P.O. Box 1393, Islamabad 44000, Pakistan. Phone: +92 (51) 921-6942 or +92 (51) 921-7321. Fax: +92 (51) 920 1861, +92 (51) 920 1118 or +92 (51) 922 3877. Email: (general) cnoradio@isb.comsats.net.pk; (technical) cfmpbchq@isb.comsats.net.pk (reception reports to this address have been verified with QSL cards). Web: www.radio.gov.pk/exter.html. Contact: (technical) Ahmed Nawaz, Senior Broadcast Engineer, Room No. 324, Frequency Management Cell; Iftikhar Malik, Senior Broadcast Engineer & Frequency Manager, Frequency Management Cell; Ajmal Kokhar, Controller of Frequency Management; Syed Asmat Ali Shah, Senior Broadcasting Engineer; Zulfiqar Ahmad, Director of Engineering; or Nasirahmad Bajwa, Frequency Management. Free stickers, pennants and *Pakistan Calling* magazine. May also send pocket calendar. Replies irregularly to postal correspondence; better is to use email if you can. Plans to replace two 50 kW transmitters with 500 kW units if and when funding is forthcoming.

PALAU World Time +9

Radio Station T8BZ (formerly KHBN and name still used), P.O. Box 66, Koror, Palau PW 96940. Phone: +680 488-2162 or +680 544-1050. Fax: (main office) +680 488 2163; (engineering) +680 544 1008. Email:(general) hamadmin@ palaunet.com or highadventure@fastmail.fm; (technical) cacciatore@lineone.net. Contact: (technical) Ben Chen, Engineering Manager. IRC requested.

PAPUA NEW GUINEA   World Time +10

NOTE: Stations are sometimes off the air due to financial or technical problems which can take weeks or months to resolve.

Catholic Radio Network
STATION: Web: www.catholicpng.org.pg.
RECEPTION REPORTS: Email: wwilson@tepng.com. Contact: Wayne Wilson, Construction Manager, TE(PNG).
KBBN ("Krai Bilong Baibel Bradkesting Netwok") (if activated on shortwave), P.O. Box 617, Mt. Hagen W.H.P., Papua New Guinea. Email: bwells@daltron.com.pg. Contact: Brad Wells. A bible radio ministry initially broadcasting on FM, but which eventually hopes to add a shortwave transmitter.

National Broadcasting Corporation of Papua New Guinea, P.O. Box 1359, Boroko 111 NCD, Papua New Guinea. Phone: +675 325-5233, + 675 325-5949 or +675 325-6779. Fax: +675 323 0404, +675 325 0796 or +675 325 6296. Email: pom@nbc.com.pg. Web: www.nbc.com.pg. Contact: (general) Renagi R. Lohia, CBE, Managing Director and C.E.O.; or Ephraim Tammy, Director, Radio Services; (technical) Bob Kabewa, Sr. Technical Officer; or F. Maredey, Chief Engineer. Two IRCs or return postage helpful. Replies irregularly.

Radio Bougainville, P.O. Box 35, Buka, North Solomons Province (NSP), Papua New Guinea. Contact: Aloysius Rumina, Provincial Programme Manager; Ms. Christine Talei, Assistant Provincial Manager; Mark Nikis, Acting Director, provincial Radio; or Aloysius Laukai, Senior Programme Officer. Replies irregularly.

Radio Central (when operating), P.O. Box 1359, Boroko, NCD, Papua New Guinea. Contact: Steven Gamini, Station Manager; Lahui Lovai, Provincial Programme Manager; or Amos Langit, Technician. $1, 2 IRCs or return postage helpful. Replies irregularly.

Radio Eastern Highlands (when operating), P.O. Box 311, Goroka, EHP, Papua New Guinea. Phone: +675 732-1533, +675 732-1733. Contact: Tony Mill, Station Manager; Tonko Nonao, Program Manager; Ignas Yanam, Technical Officer; or Kiri Nige, Engineering Division. $1 or return postage required. Replies irregularly.

Radio East New Britain (when operating), P.O. Box 393, Rabaul, ENBP, Papua New Guinea. Contact: Esekia Mael, Station Manager; or Oemas Kumaina, Provincial Program Manager. Return postage required. Replies slowly.

Radio East Sepik, P.O. Box 65, Wewak, E.S.P., Papua New Guinea. Contact: Elias Albert, Assistant Provincial Program Manager; or Luke Umbo, Station Manager.

Radio Enga, P.O. Box 300, Wabag, Enga Province, Papua New Guinea. Phone: +675 547-1213. Contact: (general) John Lyein Kur, Station Manager; or Robert Papuvo, (technical) Gabriel Paiao, Station Technician.

Radio Gulf (when operating), P.O. Box 36, Kerema, Gulf, Papua New Guinea. Contact: Tmothy Akia, Station Manager; or Timothy Akia, Provincial Program Manager.

Radio Madang, P.O. Box 2138, Madang, Papua New Guinea. Phone: +675 852-2415. Fax: +675 852 2360. Contact: (general) Damien Boaging, Senior Programme Officer; Geo Gedabing, Provincial Programme Manager; Peter Charlie Yannum, Assistant Provincial Programme Manager; or James Steve Valakvi, Senior Programme Officer; (technical) Lloyd Guvil, Technician.

Radio Manus, P.O. Box 505, Lorengau, Manus, Papua New Guinea. Phone: +675 470-9029. Fax: +675 470 9079. Contact: (technical and nontechnical) John P. Mandrakamu, Provincial Program Manager. Station is seeking the help of DXers and broadcasting professionals in obtaining a second hand, but still usable broadcasting quality CD player that could be donated to Radio Manus. Replies regularly. Return postage appreciated.

Radio Milne Bay (when operating), P.O. Box 111, Alotau, Milne Bay, Papua New Guinea. Contact: (general) Trevor Webumo, Assistant Manager; Simon Muraga, Station Manager; or Raka Petuely, Program Officer; (technical) Philip Maik, Technician. Return postage in the form of mint stamps helpful.

Radio Morobe, P.O. Box 1262, Lae, Morobe, Papua New Guinea. Fax: +675 472 6423. Contact: Ken L. Tropu, Assistant Program Manager; Peter W. Manua, Program Manager; Kekalem M. Meruk, Assistant Provincial Program Manager; or Aloysius R. Nasc, Station Manager.

Radio New Ireland (when operating), P.O. Box 140, Kavieng, New Ireland, Papua New Guinea. Contact: Otto A. Malatana, Station Manager; or Ruben Bale, Provincial Program Manager. Currently off air due to a shortage of transmitter spares. Return postage or $1 helpful.

Radio Northern (when operating), Voice of Oro, P.O. Box 137, Popondetta, Oro, Papua New Guinea. Contact: Roma Tererembo, Assistant Provincial Programme Manager; or Misael Pendaia, Station Manager. Return postage required.

Radio Sandaun, P.O. Box 37, Vanimo, Sandaun Province, Papua New Guinea. Contact: (nontechnical) Gabriel Deckwalen, Station Manager; Zacharias Nauot, Acting Assistant Manager; Celina Korei, Station Journalist; Elias Rathley, Provincial Programme Manager; Mrs. Maria Nauot, Secretary; (technical) Paia Ottawa, Technician. $1 helpful.

Radio Simbu, P.O. Box 228, Kundiawa, Chimbu, Papua New Guinea. Phone: +675 735-1038 or +675 735-1082. Fax: +675 735 1012. Contact: (general) John Bare, Manager; Tony Mill Waine, Provincial Programme Manager; Felix Tsiki; or Thomas Ghiyandiule, Producer, "Pasikam Long ol Pipel." Cassette recordings $5. Free two-Kina banknotes.

Radio Southern Highlands (when operating), P.O. Box 104, Mendi, SHP, Papua New Guinea. Contact: (general) Andrew Meles, Provincial Programme Manager; Miriam Piapo, Programme Officer; Benard Kagaro, Programme Officer; Lucy Aluy, Programme Officer; Jacob Mambi, Shift Officer; or Nicholas Sambu, Producer, "Questions and Answers"; (technical) Ronald Helori, Station Technician. $1 or return postage helpful; or donate a wall poster of a rock band, singer or American landscape.

Radio Western, P.O. Box 23, Daru, Western Province, Papua New Guinea. Contact: Robin Wainetti, Manager; (technical) Samson Tobel, Technician. $1 or return postage required. Replies irregularly.

Radio Western Highlands (when operating), P.O. Box 311, Mount Hagen, WHP, Papua New Guinea. Contact: (general) Anna Pundia, Station Manager; (technical) Esau Okole, Technician. $1 or return postage helpful. Replies occasionally. Often off the air because of theft, armed robbery or inadequate security for the station's staff.

Radio West New Britain, P.O. Box 412, Kimbe, WNBP, Papua New Guinea. Fax: +675 983 5600. Contact: Valuka Lowa, Provincial Station Manager; Darius Gilime, Provincial Program Manager; Lemeck Kuam, Producer, "Questions and Answers"; or Esekial Mael. Return postage required.

Wantok Radio Light—PNG Christian Broadcasting Network (if activated on shortwave)
U.S. SPONSORING ORGANIZATION: Life Radio Ministries, Inc., Joe Emert, P.O. Box 2020, Griffin GA 30223 USA. Phone: +1 (770) 229-9267. Email: jemert@wmvv.com. Web: www.wmvv.com/intmin.htm. Contact: Joe Emert. Currently

operates on FM, but has been granted permission to operate a 100 kW shortwave transmitter. A joint project involving Life Radio Ministries, HCJB World Radio and others.

PARAGUAY   World Time –3 (–4 midyear)

Radio América (when operating), Casilla de Correo 2220, Asunción, Paraguay. Fax: +595 (21) 963-149. Email: radioamerica@lycos.com, ramerica@rieder.net.py. Contact: Adán Mur, Asesor Técnico. Replies to correspondence in Spanish and English. Operates on legally assigned 1480 kHz on mediumwave AM, but is believed to be unlicensed on shortwave.

Radio Nacional del Paraguay (when operating), Blas Garay 241 entre Yegros e Iturbe, Asunción, Paraguay. Phone: +595 (21) 449-213. Fax: +595 (21) 332 750. Free tourist brochure. $1 or return postage required. Replies, sometimes slowly, to correspondence in Spanish.

PERU   World Time –5

NOTE: Obtaining replies from Peruvian stations calls for creativity, tact, patience—and the proper use of Spanish, not form letters and the like.

CPN Radio (if reactivated), Cadena Peruana de Noticias, Gral. Salaverry 156, Miraflores, Lima, Peru. Phone: +51 (1) 446-1554 or +51 (1) 445-7770. Email: webmastercpn@gestion.com.pe. Web: www.cpnradio.com.pe. Contact: Oscar Romero Caro, Gerente General; or Zenaida Solís, Directora de Programas.

Estación C (if reactivated), Casilla de Correo 210, Moyobamba, San Martín, Peru. Contact: Porfirio Centurión, Propietario.

Estación Wari (when operating), Calle Nazareno 108, Ayacucho, Peru. Phone: +51 (64) 813-039. Contact: Walter Muñoz Ynga I., Gerente.

Estación X (Equis) (when operating), Calle Argentina 198, Bagua, Departamento de Amazonas, Peru.

Frecuencia Líder (Radio Bambamarca), Jirón Jorge Chávez 416, Bambamarca, Hualgayoc, Cajamarca, Peru. Phone: (office) +51 (74) 713-260; (studio) +51 (74) 713-249. Contact: (general) Valentín Peralta Díaz, Gerente; Irma Peralta Rojas; or Carlos Antonio Peralta Rojas; (technical) Oscar Lino Peralta Rojas. Free station photos. *La Historia de Bambamarca* book for 5 Soles; cassettes of Peruvian and Latin American folk music for 4 Soles each; T-shirts for 10 Soles each (sending US$1 per Sol should suffice and cover foreign postage costs, as well). Replies occasionally to correspondence in Spanish. Considering replacing their transmitter to improve reception.

Frecuencia San Ignacio (when operating), Jirón Villanueva Pinillos 330, San Ignacio, Cajamarca, Peru. Contact: Franklin R. Hoyos Cóndor, Director Gerente; or Ignacio Gómez Torres, Técnico de Sonido. Replies to correspondence in Spanish. $1 or return postage necessary.

Frecuencia VH—*see* Radio Frecuencia VH.

La Super Radio San Ignacio (when operating), Avenida Víctor Larco 104, a un costado del campo deportivo, San Ignacio, Distrito de Sinsicap, Provincia de Otuzco, La Libertad, Peru.

La Voz de Anta, Distrito de Anta, Provincia de Acobamba, Departamento de Huancavelica. Phone: +51 (64) 750-201.

La Voz de la Selva—*see* Radio La Voz de la Selva.

La Voz de San Juan—*see* Radio La Voz de San Juan.

La Voz del Campesino—*see* Radio La Voz del Campesino.

La Voz del Marañon—*see* Radio La Voz del Marañon.

Ondas del Suroriente—*see* Radio Ondas del Suroriente, below.

Radio Adventista Mundial—La Voz de la Esperanza (when operating), Jirón Dos de Mayo No. 218, Celendín, Cajamarca,

Peru. Contact: Francisco Goicochea Ortiz, Director; or Lucas Solano Oyarce, Director de Ventas.

Radio Altura, Casilla de Correo 140, Cerro de Pasco, Pasco, Peru. Phone: +51 (64) 721-875, +51 (64) 722-398. Contact: Oswaldo de la Cruz Vásquez, Gerente General. Replies to correspondence in Spanish.

Radio Altura, Antonio Raymondi 3ra Cuadra, Distrito de Huarmaca, Provincia de Huancabamba, Piura, Peru.

Radio Amauta del Perú, (when operating), Jirón Manuel Iglesias s/n, a pocos pasos de la Plazuela San Juan, San Pablo, Cajamarca, Nor Oriental del Marañón, Peru.

Radio Amistad, Manzana I-11, Lote 6, Calle 22, Urbanización Mariscal Cáceres, San Juan de Lurigancho, Lima, Peru. Phone: +51 (1) 392-3640. Email: radioamistad@peru.com. Contact: Manuel Mejía Barboza. Accepts email reception reports.

Radio Ancash, Casilla de Correo 221, Huaraz, Peru. Phone: +51 (44) 721-381,+51 (44) 721-359, +51 (44) 721-487, +51 (44) 722-512. Fax: +51 (44) 722 992. Contact: Armando Moreno Romero, Gerente General. Replies to correspondence in Spanish.

Radio Andahuaylas, Jr. Ayacucho No. 248, Andahuaylas, Apurímac, Peru. Contact: Sr. Daniel Andréu C., Gerente. $1 required. Replies irregularly to correspondence in Spanish.

Radio Andina, Huáscar 201, Huancabamba, Piura, Peru. According to an on-air announcement, the station is expected to move to Avenida Ramón Castilla 254. Phone: +51 (74) 473-104. Contact: Manuel Campos Ojeda, Director.

Radio Andina, Real 175, Huancayo, Junín, Peru. Phone: +51 (64) 231-123. Replies infrequently to correspondence in Spanish.

Radio Apurímac (when operating), Jirón Cusco 206 (or Ovalo El Olivo No. 23), Abancay, Apurímac, Peru. Contact: Antero Quispe Allca, Director General.

Radio Atlántida

STATION: Jirón Arica 441, Iquitos, Loreto, Peru. Phone: +51 (94) 234-452, +51 (94) 234-962. Contact: Pablo Rojas Bardales.

LISTENER CORRESPONDENCE: Sra. Carmela López Paredes, Directora del prgrama "Trocha Turística," Jirón Arica 1083, Iquitos, Loreto, Peru. Free pennants and tourist information. $1 or return postage required. Replies to most correspondence in Spanish, the preferred language, and some correspondence in English.

Radio Bambamarca—*see* Frecuencia Líder, above.

Radio Bethel—*see* Radio Bethel Arequipa, below.

Radio Bethel Arequipa, Avenida Unión 215, 3er piso, Distrito Miraflores, Arequipa, Peru. Contact: Josué Ascarruz Pacheco. Usually announces as "Radio Bethel" and belongs to the "Movimiento Misionero Mundial" evangelistic organization.

Radio Bolívar, Correo Central, Bolívar, Provincia de Bolívar, Departamento de La Libertad, Peru. Contact: Julio Dávila Echevarría, Gerente. May send free pennant. Return postage helpful.

Radio Cajamarca, Jirón La Mar 675, Cajamarca, Peru. Phone: +51 (44) 921-014. Contact: Porfirio Cruz Potosí.

Radio Chanchamayo (when operating), Jirón Tarma 551, La Merced, Junín, Peru.

Radio Chaski, Baptist Mid-Missions, Apartado Postal 368, Cusco, Peru; or Alameda Pachacútec s/n B-5, Cusco, Peru. Phone: +51 (84) 225-052. Contact: Andrés Tuttle H., Gerente; or Felipe S. Velarde Hinojosa M., Representante Legal.

Radio Chincheros, Jirón Apurímac s/n, Chincheros, Departamento de Apurímac, Peru.

Radio Chota, Jirón Anaximandro Vega 690, Apartado Postal 3, Chota, Cajamarca, Peru. Phone: +51 (44) 771-240. Contact:

Aladino Gavidia Huamán, Administrador. $1 or return postage required. Replies slowly to correspondence in Spanish.

Radio Comas (if reactivated on shortwave), Avenida Estados Unidos 327, Urbanización Huaquillay, km 10 de la Avenida Túpac Amaru, Distrito de Comas, Lima, Peru. Phone: +51 (1) 525-0859. Fax: +51 (1) 525 0094. Email: rtcomas@terra.com.pe. Web: (includes MP3) www.radiocomas.com. Contact: Edgar Saldaña R.; Juan Rafael Saldaña Reátegui (Relaciones Públicas) or Gamaniel Francisco Chahua, Productor-Programador General.

Radio Comercial Naranjos (when operating), Avenida Cajamarca 464, Distrito de Pardo Miguel Naranjos, Provincia de Rioja, San Martín, Peru. Contact: Mario Cusma Vasquez, Propietario; Esperanza Galo Gomez, Gerente Admnitrativo; or Pepe Vasquez, Jefe de Producciones.

Radio CORA (when operating), Compañía Radiofónica Lima, S.A., Paseo de la República 144, Centro Cívico, Oficina 5, Lima 1, Peru. Phone: +51 (1) 433-5005, +51 (1) 433-1188 or +51 (1) 433-0848. Fax: +51 (1) 433 6134. Email: cora@peru.itete.com.pe; cora@lima.business.com.pe. Contact: (general) Dra. Lylian Ramírez M., Directora de Prensa y Programación; Juan Ramírez Lazo, Director Gerente; or Srta. Angelina María Abie; (technical) Srta. Sylvia Ramírez M., Directora Técnica. Free station sticky-label pads, bumper stickers and may send large certificate suitable for framing. Audio cassettes with extracts from their programs $20 plus $2 postage; women's hair bands $2 plus $1 postage. Two IRCs or $1 required. Replies slowly to correspondence in English, Spanish, French, Italian and Portuguese.

Radio Coremarca (if reactivated), Jirón Jaime de Martínez, Bambamarca, Peru. Contact: Virgilio Carranza Tello, Director. A small educational station, so include return postage with your correspondence.

Radio Cultural Amauta, Jr. Cahuide 278, Apartado Postal 24, Huanta, Ayacucho, Peru. Phone/Fax: +51 (64) 832-153. Email: arca@terra.com.pe or (Montes Sinforoso) montessd@terra.com.pe. Web: (includes RealAudio) www.rca.es.vg. Contact: Demetria Montes Sinforoso (Administradora); Vicente Saico Tinco.

Radio Cusco, Apartado Postal 251, Cusco, Peru. Phone: (general)+51 (84) 225-851; (management) +51 (84) 232-457. Fax: +51 (84) 223 308. Contact: Sra. Juana Huamán Yépez, Administradora; or Raúl Siú Almonte, Gerente General; (technical) Benjamín Yábar Alvarez. Free pennants, postcards and key rings. Audio cassettes of Peruvian music $10 plus postage. $1 or return postage required. Replies irregularly to correspondence in English or Spanish. Station is looking for folk music recordings from around the world to use in their programs.

Radio del Pacífico, Apartado Postal 4236, Lima 1, Peru. Phone: +51 (1) 433-3275. Fax: +51 (1) 433 3276. Contact: J. Petronio Allauca, Secretario, Departamento de Relaciones Públicas; or Julio Villarreal. $1 or return postage required. Replies occasionally to correspondence in Spanish.

Radio El Sol de los Andes, Jirón 2 de Mayo 257, Juliaca, Peru. Phone: +51 (54) 321-115. Fax: +51 (54) 322 981. Contact: Armando Alarcón Velarde.

Radio Estación Uno, Barrio Altos, Distrito de Pucará, Provincia Jaén, Nor Oriental del Marañón, Peru.

Radio Estudio 2000, Distrito Miguel Pardo Naranjos, Provincia de Rioja, Departamento de San Martín, Peru.

Radio Frecuencia VH ("La Voz de Celendín"; "RVC"), Jirón José Gálvez 1030, Celendín, Cajamarca, Peru. Contact: Fernando Vásquez Castro, Propietario.

Radio Frecuencia San Ignacio—see Frecuencia San Ignacio.

Radio Horizonte, Apartado Postal 69 (or Jirón Amazonas 1177), Chachapoyas, Amazonas, Peru. Phone: +51 (74) 757-793. Fax: +51 (74) 757 004. Contact: Sra. Rocío García Rubio, Ing. Electrónico, Directora; Percy Chuquizuta Alvarado, Locutor; María Montaldo Echaiz, Locutora; Marcelo Mozambite Chavarry, Locutor; Ing. María Dolores Gutiérrez Atienza, Administradora; Juan Nancy Ruíz de Valdez, Secretaria; Yoel Toro Morales, Técnico de Transmisión; or María Soledad Sánchez Castro, Administradora. Replies to correspondence in English, French, German and Spanish. $1 required.

Radio Horizonte, Jirón Incanato 387 Altos, Distrito José Leonardo Ortiz, Chiclayo, Lambayeque, Peru. Phone: +51 (74) 252-917. Contact: Enrique Becerra Rojas, Owner and General Manager. Return postage required.

Radio Hualgayoc (if reactivated), Jirón San Martín s/n, Hualgayoc, Cajamarca, Peru. Contact: Máximo Zamora Medina, Director Propietario.

Radio Huamachuco (if reactivated), Jirón Bolívar 937, Huamachuco, La Libertad, Peru. Contact: Manuel D. Gil Gil, Director Propietario.

Radio Huanta 2000, Jirón Gervacio Santillana 455, Huanta, Peru. Phone: +51 (64) 932-105. Fax: +51 (64) 832 105. Contact: Ronaldo Sapaico Maravi, Departmento Técnico; or Sra. Lucila Orellana de Paz, Administradora. Free photo of staff. Return postage or $1 appreciated. Replies to correspondence in Spanish.

Radio Huarmaca, Av. Grau 454 (detrás de Inversiones La Loretana), Distrito de Huarmaca, Provincia de Huancabamba, Región Grau, Peru. Contact: Simón Zavaleta Pérez. Return postage helpful.

Radio Ilucán, Jirón Lima 290, Cutervo, Región Nororiental del Marañón, Peru. Phone: +51 (44) 737-010 or +51 (44) 737-231. Email: radioilucan@hotmail.com. Contact: José Gálvez Salazar, Gerente Administrativo. $1 required. Replies occasionally to correspondence in Spanish.

Radio Imagen (when operating), Casilla de Correo 42, Tarapoto, San Martín, Peru; Jirón San Martín 328, Tarapoto, San Martín, Peru; or Apartado Postal 254, Tarapoto, San Martín, Peru. Phone: +51 (94) 522-696. Contact: Adith Chumbe Vásquez, Secretaria; or Jaime Ríos Tapullima, Gerente General. Replies irregularly to correspondence in Spanish. $1 or return postage helpful.

Radio Integración, Av. Seoane 200, Apartado Postal 57, Abancay, Departamento de Apurímac, Peru. Contact: Zenón Hernán Farfán Cruzado, Propietario.

Radio Internacional (if activated), Apartado Postal 105, Serpost, Cercado, Arequipa, Peru. Email: radiovozdesalvacion@iglesia-dios.org; (Vera) joseveravera@iglesia-dios.org; (Quiroz) pilarquiroz@iglesia-dios.org. Web: www.radiovozdesalvacion.100megas.com/index.html. Contact: José Manuel Vera Vera, Director General; or Hna. [Sister] Pilar Quiroz, Asistente de Programas Internacionales. Plans to operate on 6035 kHz.

Radio Internacional Cristiana—see Radio Internacional, above.

Radio Internacional del Perú (if reactivated), Jirón Bolognesi 532, San Pablo, Cajamarca, Peru.

Radio Jaén (La Voz de la Frontera), Calle Mariscal Castilla 439, Jaén, Cajamarca, Peru. Contact: Luis A. Vilchez Ochoa, Administrador.

Radio Juliaca (La Decana), Jirón Ramón Castilla 949, Apartado Postal 67, Juliaca, San Román, Puno, Peru. Phone: +51 (54) 321-372. Fax: +51 (54) 332 386. Contact: Robert Theran Escobedo, Director.

Vientiane's ornate Patousai arch was built in 1958. It is an Oriental variation on France's Arc de Triomphe in Paris.

M. Guha

Radio JVL (when operating), Jirón Túpac Amaru 105, Consuelo, Distrito de San Pablo, Provincia de Bellavista, Departamento de San Martín, Peru. Contact: John Wiley Villanueva Lara—a student of electronic engineering—who currently runs the station, and whose initials make up the station name. Replies to correspondence in Spanish. Return Postage required.

Radio La Hora, Av. Garcilaso 180, Cusco, Peru. Phone: +51 (84) 225-615 or +51 (84) 231-371. Contact: (general) Edmundo Montesinos G., Gerente; (reception reports) Carlos Gamarra Moscoso, who is also a DXer. Free stickers, pins, pennants and postcards of Cusco. Return postage required. Replies to correspondence in Spanish. Reception reports are best sent direct to Carlos Gamarra's home address: Av. Garcilaso 411, Wanchaq, Cusco, Peru. The station hopes to increase transmitter power to 2 kw if and when the economic situation improves.

Radio La Inmaculada (if reactivated), Parroquia La Inmaculada Concepción, Frente de la Plaza de Armas, Santa Cruz, Provincia de Santa Cruz, Departamento de Cajamarca, Peru. Phone: +51 (74) 714-051. Contact: Reverendo Padre Angel Jorge Carrasco, Gerente; or Gabino González Vera, Locutor.

Radio Lajas, Jirón Rosendo Mendívil 589, Lajas, Chota, Cajamarca, Nor Oriental del Marañón, Peru. Contact: Alfonso Medina Burga, Gerente Propietario.

Radio La Merced, Junín 163, La Merced, Junín, Peru. Phone: +51 (64) 531-199. Occasionally replies to correspondence in Spanish.

Radio La Oroya, Calle Lima 190, Tercer Piso Of. 3, Apartado Postal 88, La Oroya, Provincia de Yauli, Departamento de Junín, Peru. Phone: +51 (64) 391-401. Fax: +51 (64) 391 440. Email: rlofigu@net.cosapidata.com.pe. Contact: Jacinto Manuel Figueroa Yauri, Gerente-Propietario. Free pennants. $1 or return postage necessary. Replies to correspondence in Spanish.

Radio La Voz, Andahuaylas, Apurímac, Peru. Contact: Lucio Fuentes, Director Gerente.

Radio La Voz de Abancay, Avenida Noviembre Lote 6, Urbanización Micaela Bastidas, Abancay, Departamento de Apurímac, Peru. Contact: Lucio Fuentes, Propietario.

Radio La Voz de Chiriaco (when operating), Jirón Ricardo Palma s/n, Chiriaco, Distrito de Imaza, Provincia de Bagua, Departamento de Amazonas, Peru. Contact: Hildebrando López

Pintado, Director; Santos Castañeda Cubas, Director Gerente; or Fidel Huamuro Curinambe, Técnico de Mantenimiento. $1 or return postage helpful.

Radio La Voz de Cutervo (if reactivated), Jirón María Elena Medina 644-650, Cutervo, Cajamarca, Peru.

Radio La Voz de la Selva, Jirón Abtao 255, Casilla de Correo 207, Iquitos, Loreto, Peru. Phone: +51 (94) 265-245. Fax: +51 (94) 264 531. Email: lvsradio@terra.com.pe. Contact: Julia Jáuregui Rengifo, Directora; Marcelino Esteban Benito, Director; Pedro Sandoval Guzmán, Announcer; or Mery Blas Rojas. Replies to correspondence in Spanish.

Radio La Voz de las Huarinjas, Barrio El Altillo s/n, Huancabamba, Piura, Peru. Phone: +51 (74) 473-126 or +51 (74) 473-259. Contact: Alfonso García Silva, Gerente Director (also the owner of the station); or Bill Yeltsin, Administrador. Replies to correspondence in Spanish.

Radio La Voz de Oxapampa (if reactivated), Av. Mullenbruck 469, Oxapampa, Pasco, Peru. Contact: Pascual Villafranca Guzmán, Director Propietario.

Radio La Voz de San Juan (if reactivated), 28 de Julio 420, Lonya Grande, Provincia de Utcubamba, Región Nororiental del Marañón, Peru. Contact: Prof. Víctor Hugo Hidrovo; or Edilberto Ortiz Chávez, Locutor. Formerly known as Radio San Juan.

Radio La Voz de Santa Cruz (if reactivated), Av. Zarumilla 190, Santa Cruz, Cajamarca, Peru.

Radio La Voz del Campesino, Av. Ramón Castilla s/n en la salida a Chiclayo, Huarmaca, Provincia de Huancabamba, Piura, Peru. Contact: Hernando Huancas Huancas.

Radio La Voz del Marañón (if reactivated), Jirón Bolognesi 130, Barrio La Alameda, Cajamarca, Nor Oriental del Marañón, Peru. Contact: Eduardo Díaz Coronado.

Radio Libertad de Junín, Cerro de Pasco 528, Apartado Postal 2, Junín, Peru. Phone: +51 (64) 344-026. Contact: Mauro Chaccha G., Director Gerente. Replies slowly to correspondence in Spanish. Return postage necessary.

Radio Líder, Portal Belén 115, 2do piso, Cusco, Peru. Contact: Mauro Calvo Acurio, Propietario.

Radio Lircay (when operating), Barrio Maravillas, Lircay, Provincia de Angaraes, Huancavelica, Peru.

Radio Los Andes (Huamachuco), Pasaje Damián Nicolau 108-110, 2do piso, Huamachuco, La Libertad, Peru. Phone: +51

(44) 441-240 or +51 (44) 441-502. Fax: +51 (44) 441 214. Email: radiolosandes@starmedia.com. Contact: Monseñor Sebastián Ramis Torerns.

Radio Los Andes (Huarmaca), Huarmaca, Provincia de Huancabamba, Región Grau, Peru. Contact: William Cerro Calderón.

Radio Luz y Sonido, Apartado Postal 280, Huánuco, Peru; or (street address) Jirón Dos de Mayo 1286, Oficina 205, Huánuco, Peru. Phone: +51 (64) 512-394 or +51 (64) 518-500. Fax: +51 (64) 511 985. Contact: (technical) Jorge Benavides Moreno; (nontechnical) Pedro Martínez Tineo, Director Ejecutivo; Lic. Orlando Bravo Jesús; or Seydel Saavedra Cabrera, Operador/ Locutor. Return postage or $2 required. Replies to correspondence in Spanish, Italian and Portuguese. Sells video cassettes of local folk dances and religious and tourist themes.

Radio Macedonia (when operating), Seminario Bautista Macedonia, Casilla 1677, Arequipa, Peru. Phone/Fax: +51 (54) 444-376. Email: (W.A. Gardner) gardner@world-evangelism.com. Contact: W. Austin Gardner; or Chris Gardner. Replies to correspondence in Spanish or English.

U.S. PARENT ORGANIZATION: Macedonia World Baptist Missions Inc., P.O. Box 519, Braselton GA 30517 USA. Phone: +1 (706) 654-2818. Fax: +1 (706) 654 2816. Email: mwbm@mwbm.org. Web: http://mwbm.org.

Radio Madre de Dios, Daniel Alcides Carrión 385, Apartado Postal 37, Puerto Maldonado, Madre de Dios, Peru. Phone: +51 (84) 571-050. Fax: +51 (84) 571 018 or +51 (84) 573 542. Contact: (administration) Padre Rufino Lobo Alonso, Director; (general) Alcides Arguedas Márquez, Director del programa "Un Festival de Música Internacional," heard Mondays 0100 to 0200 World Time. Sr. Arguedas is interested in feedback for this letterbox program. Replies to correspondence in Spanish. $1 or return postage appreciated.

Radio Majestad (if reactivated), Calle Real 1033, Oficina 302, Huancayo, Junín, Peru.

Radio Marañón, Apartado Postal 50, Jaén, Cajamarca, Peru; or (street address) Francisco de Orellana 343, Jaén, Cajamarca, Peru. Phone: +51 (44) 731-147 or +51 (44) 732-168. Fax: +51 (44) 732 580. Email: (general) correo@radiomaranon.org.pe; (Director) pmaguiro@radiomaranon.org.pe. Web: www.radiomaranon.org.pe. Contact: Francisco Muguiro Ibarra S.J., Director. Return postage necessary. May send free pennant. Replies slowly to correspondence in Spanish and (sometimes) English.

Radio Marginal, San Martín 257, Tocache, San Martín, Peru. Phone: +51 (94) 551-031. Rarely replies.

Radio Máster (when operating), Jirón 20 de Abril 308, Moyobamba, Departamento de San Martín, Peru. Contact: Américo Vásquez Hurtado, Director.

Radio Melodía, San Camilo 501, Arequipa, Peru. Phone: +51 (54) 232-071, +51 (54) 232-327 or +51 (54) 285-152. Fax: +51 (54) 237 312. Contact: Hermógenes Delgado Torres, Director; or Señora Elba Alvarez de Delgado. Replies to correspondence in Spanish.

Radio Moderna, Jirón Arequipa 323, 2do piso, Celendín, Cajamarca, Peru.

Radio Mundial Adventista (if activated), Colegio Adventista de Titicaca, Casilla 4, Juliaca, Peru. Currently on mediumwave (AM) only, but hopes to add shortwave sometime in the future.

Radio Naylamp (when operating), Avenida Andrés Avelino Cáceres 800, Lambayeque, Peru. Phone: +51 (74) 283-353. Contact: Dr. Juan José Grández Vargas, Director Gerente; or Delicia Coronel Muñoz, who is interested in receiving postcards and the like. Free stickers, pennants and calendars. Return postage necessary.

Radio Nor Andina, Jirón José Gálvez 602, Celendín, Cajamarca, Peru. Contact: Misael Alcántara Guevara, Gerente; or Víctor B. Vargas C., Departamento de Prensa. Free calendar. $1 required. Donations (registered mail best) sought for the Committee for Good Health for Children, headed by Sr. Alcántara, which is active in saving the lives of hungry youngsters in poverty-stricken Cajamarca Province. Replies irregularly to casual or technical correspondence in Spanish, but regularly to Children's Committee donors and helpful correspondence in Spanish.

Radio Nor Peruana, Emisora Municipal, Jirón Ortiz Arrieta 588, 1er. piso del Concejo Provincial de Chachapoyas, Chachapoyas, Amazonas, Peru. Contact: Carlos Poema, Administrador; or Edgar Villegas, program host for "La Voz de Chachapoyas," (Sundays, 1100-1300).

Radio Nuevo Horizonte, Consorcio Minero Horizonte, Minera Aurífera Retamas, Distrito de Parcoy, Provincia de Pataz, Departamento de La Libertad, Peru.

Radio Ondas del Huallaga, Jirón Leoncio Prado 723, Apartado Postal 343, Huánuco, Peru. Phone: +51 (64) 511-525 or +51 (64) 512-428. Contact: Flaviano Llanos Malpartida, Representante Legal. $1 or return postage required. Replies to correspondence in Spanish.

Radio Ondas del [Río] Marañón (if reactivated), Jirón Amazonas 315, Distrito de Aramango, Provincia de Bagua, Departamento de Amazonas, Región Nororiental del Marañón, Peru. Contact: Agustín Tongod, Director Propietario. "Río"—river—is sometimes, but not always, used in on-air identification.

Radio Ondas del Río Mayo, Jirón Huallaga 348, Nueva Cajamarca, San Martín, Peru. Phone: +51 (94) 556-006. Contact: Edilberto Lucío Peralta Lozada, Gerente; or Víctor Huaras Rojas, Locutor. Free pennants. Return postage helpful. Replies slowly to correspondence in Spanish.

Radio Ondas del Suroriente (when operating), Jirón Ricardo Palma 510, Quillabamba, La Convención, Cusco, Peru.

Radio Oriente, Vicariato Apostólico, Avenida Progreso 114, Yurimaguas, Loreto, Peru. Phone: +51 (94) 352-156. Fax: +51 (94) 352 128. Email: rovay@qnet.co.pe. Web: www.dxing.info/ radio/oriente. Contact: (general) Sra. Elisa Cancino Hidalgo; or Juan Antonio López-Manzanares M., Director, (technical) Pedro Capo Moragues, Gerente Técnico. $1 or return postage required. Replies occasionally to correspondence in English, French, Spanish and Catalan.

Radio Origen (if reactivated), Acobamba, Departamento de Huancavelica, Peru.

Radio Perú ("Perú, la Radio")
STUDIO ADDRESS: Jirón Atahualpa 191, San Ignacio, Región Nororiental del Marañón, Peru.
ADMINISTRATION: Avenida San Ignacio 493, San Ignacio, Región Nororiental del Marañón, Peru. Contact: Oscar Vásquez Chacón, Director General; or Idelso Vásquez Chacón, Director Propietario. Sometimes relays the FM outlet, "Estudio 97."

Radio Quillabamba, Jirón Ricardo Palma 432, Apartado Postal 76, Quillabamba, La Convención, Cusco, Peru. Phone: +51 (84) 281-002. Fax: +51 (84) 281 771. Contact: Padre Francisco Javier Panera, Director. Replies very irregularly to correspondence in Spanish.

Radio Reina de la Selva, Jirón Ayacucho 944, Plaza de Armas, Chachapoyas, Región Nor Oriental del Marañón, Peru. Phone: +51 (74) 757-203. Contact: José David Reina Noriega, Gerente General; or Jorge Oscar Reina Noriega, Director General. Replies irregularly to correspondence in Spanish. Return postage necessary.

Radio San Antonio (Callalli), Parroquia San Antonio de Padua, Plaza Principal s/n, Callalli, Departamento de Arequipa, Peru. Contact: Hermano [Brother] Rolando.

Radio San Antonio (Villa Atalaya), Jirón Iquitos s/n, Villa Atalaya, Departamento de Ucayali, Peru. Email: (Zerdin) zerdin@terra.com.pe. Contact: Gerardo Zerdin.

Radio San Francisco Solano (when operating), Parroquia de Sóndor, Calle San Miguel No. 207, Distrito de Sóndor, Huancabamba, Piura, Peru. Contact: Reverendo Padre Manuel José Rosas Castillo, Vicario Parroquial. Station operated by the Franciscan Fathers. Replies to correspondence in Spanish. $1 helpful.

Radio San Ignacio, Jirón Victoria 277, San Ignacio, Región Nororiental del Marañón, Peru. Contact: César Colunche Bustamante, Director Propietario; or his son, Fredy Colunche, Director de Programación.

Radio San Miguel, Av. Huayna Cápac 146, Huánchac, Cusco, Peru. Contact: Sra. Catalina Pérez de Alencastre, Gerente General; or Margarita Mercado. Replies to correspondence in Spanish.

Radio San Miguel (when operating), Jirón Alfonso Ugarte 668, San Miguel, Cajamarca, Peru.

Radio San Miguel de El Faique (if reactivated), Distrito de El Faique, Provincia de Huancabamba, Departamento de Piura, Peru.

Radio San Nicolás, Jirón Amazonas 114, Rodríguez de Mendoza, Peru. Contact: Juan José Grández Santillán, Gerente; or Violeta Grández Vargas, Administradora. Return postage necessary.

Radio Santa Mónica, Urbanización Marcavalle P-20, Cusco, Peru. Phone:+ 51 (84) 225-357.

Radio Santa Rosa, Jirón Camaná 170, Casilla 4451, Lima 01, Peru. Phone: +51 (1) 427-7488. Fax: +51 (1) 426 9219. Email: radiosantarosa@terra.com.pe. Web: http:// barrioperu.terra.com.pe/radiosantarosa. Contact: Padre Juan Sokolich Alvarado, Director; or Lucy Palma Barreda. Free stickers and pennants. $1 or return postage necessary. 180-page book commemorating station's 35th anniversary $10. Replies to correspondence in Spanish.

Radio Satélite (when operating), Jirón Cuervo No. 543, Provincia de Santa Cruz, Cajamarca, Peru. Phone: +51 (74) 714-074, +51 (74) 714-169. Contact: Sabino Llamo Chávez, Gerente. Free tourist brochure. $1 or return postage required. Replies to correspondence in Spanish.

Radio Sicuani, Jirón 2 de Mayo 212, Sicuani, Canchis, Cusco, Peru; or Apartado Postal 45, Sicuani, Peru. Phone: +51 (84) 351-136 or +51 (84) 351-698. Fax: +51 (84) 351 697. Email: cecosda@mail.cosapidata.com.pe. Contact: Mario Ochoa Vargas, Director.

Radio Soledad (if reactivated), Centro Minero de Retama, Distrito de Parcoy, Provincia de Pataz, La Libertad, Peru. Contact: Vicente Valdivieso, Locutor. Return postage necessary.

Radio Sudamérica, Jirón Ramón Castilla 491, tercer nivel, Plaza de Armas, Cutervo, Cajamarca, Peru. Phone: +51 (74) 736-090 or +51 (74) 737-443. Contact: Jorge Luis Paredes Guerra, Administrador; or Amadeo Mario Muñoz Guivar, Propietario.

Radio Superior, Jirón San Martín 229, Provincia de Bolívar, Departamento de La Libertad, Peru.

Radio Tacna, Aniceto Ibarra 436, Casilla de Correo 370, Tacna, Peru. Phone: +51 (54) 714-871. Fax: +51 (54) 723 745. Email: scaceres@viabcp.com. Contact: (nontechnical and technical) Ing. Alfonso Cáceres Contreras, Gerente de Operaciones; (administration) Yolanda Vda. de Cáceres C., Directora Gerente.

Free stickers and samples of *Correo* local newspaper. $1 or return postage helpful. Audio cassettes of Peruvian and other music $2 plus postage. Replies irregularly to correspondence in English and Spanish.

Radio Tawantinsuyo, Av. Sol 806, Cusco, Peru. Phone: +51 (84) 226-955 or +51 (84) 228-411. Contact: Ing. Raul Montesinos Espejo, Director Gerente. Has a very attractive QSL card, but only replies occasionally to correspondence, which should be in Spanish.

Radio Tarma, Jirón Molino del Amo 167, Apartado Postal 167, Tarma, Peru. Phone/Fax: +51 (64) 321-167 or +51 (64) 321-510. Contact: Mario Monteverde Pomareda, Gerente General. Sometimes sends 100 Inti banknote in return when $1 enclosed. Free stickers. $1 or return postage required. Replies irregularly to correspondence in Spanish.

Radio Tayacaja (when operating), Correo Central, Distrito de Pampas, Tayacaja, Huancavelica, Peru. Phone: +51 (64) 220-217, Anexo 238. Contact: (general) J. Jorge Flores Cárdenas; (technical) Ing. Larry Guido Flores Lezama. Free stickers and pennants. Replies to correspondence in Spanish. Hopes to replace transmitter.

Radio Tingo María (when operating), Jirón Callao 115 (or Av. Raimondi No. 592), Casilla de Correo 25, Tingo María, Leoncio Prado, Departamento de Huánuco, Peru. Contact: Gina A. de la Cruz Ricalde, Administradora; or Ricardo Abad Vásquez, Gerente. Free brochures. $1 required. Replies slowly to correspondence in Spanish.

Radio Tropical (if reactivated), Casilla de Correo 31, Tarapoto, Peru. Phone: +51 (94) 522-083 or +51 (94) 524-689. Fax: +51 (94) 522 155. Contact: Mery A. Rengifo Tenazoa, Secretaria; or Luis F. Mori Reátegui, Gerente. Free stickers, occasionally free pennants, and station history booklet. $1 or return postage required. Replies occasionally to correspondence in Spanish.

Radio Unión, Apartado Postal 833, Lima 27, Peru; or (street address) Avenida Central 717 - Piso 12, San Isidro, Lima 27, Peru. Phone: +51 (1) 221-3158/9, +51 (1) 440-1785. Fax: +51 (1) 221 0888. Contact: Raúl Rubbeck Jiménez, Director Gerente; Juan Zubiaga Santiváñez, Gerente; Natividad Albizuri Salinas, Secretaria; or Juan Carlos Sologuren, Dpto. de Administración, who collects stamps. Free satin pennants and stickers. IRC required, and enclosing used or new stamps from various countries is especially appreciated. Replies irregularly to correspondence and tape recordings, with Spanish preferred.

Radio Uno, Av. Balta 1480, 3er piso, frente al Mercado Modelo, Chiclayo, Peru. Phone: +51 (74) 224-967. Contact: Luz Angela Romero, Directora del noticiero "Encuentros"; Plutarco Chamba Febres, Director Propietario; Juan Vargas, Administrador; or Filomena Saldívar Alarcón, Pauta Comercial. Return postage required.

Radio Victoria, Jr.Reynel 320, Mirones Bajo, Lima 1, Peru. Phone: +51 (1) 336-5448. Fax: +51 (1) 427 1195. Email: soermi@mixmail.com. Contact: Marta Flores Ushinahua. This station is owned by the Brazilian-run Pentecostal Church "Dios Es Amor," with local headquarters at Av. Arica 248, Lima; Phone: +51 (1) 330-8023. Their program "La Voz de la Liberación" is produced locally and aired over numerous Peruvian shortwave stations.

Radio Virgen del Carmen ("RVC"), Jirón Virrey Toledo 466, Huancavelica, Peru. Phone: +51 (64) 752-740. Contact: Rvdo. Samuel Morán Cárdenas, Gerente.

Radiodifusoras Huancabamba (if reactivated), Calle Unión 409, Huancabamba, Piura, Peru. Phone: +51 (74) 473-233. Contact: Federico Ibáñez Maticorena, Director.

Radiodifusoras Paratón, Jirón Alfonso Ugarte 1090, contiguo al Parque Leoncio Prado, Huarmaca, Provincia de Huancabamba, Piura, Peru. Contact: Prof. Hernando Huancas Huancas, Gerente General; or Prof. Rómulo Chincay Huamán, Gerente Administrativo.

PHILIPPINES World Time +8

NOTE: Philippine stations sometimes send publications with lists of Philippine young ladies seeking "pen pal" courtships.
DUR2—Philippine Broadcasting Service (when operating), Bureau of Broadcasting Services, Media Center, Bohol Avenue, Quezon City, Philippines. Relays DZRB Radio ng Bayan and DZRM Radio Manila.
Far East Broadcasting Company—FEBC Radio International (External Service)
MAIN OFFICE: P.O. Box 1, Valenzuela, Metro Manila, Philippines 0560. Phone: (general) +63 (2) 292-5603, +63 (2) 292-9403 or +63 (2) 292-5790; (International Broadcast Manager) +63 (2) 292-5603 ext. 158. Fax: +63 (2) 292 9430; +63 (2) 291 4982 (International Broadcast Manager) +63 (2) 292 9724, but lacks funds to provide faxed replies. Email: febcomphil@febc.org.ph; (Peter McIntyre) pm@febc.jfm.org.ph; (Larry Podmore) lpodmore@febc.jmf.org.ph; (Chris Cooper) ccooper@febc.org.ph. Web: www.febc.org; www.febc.ph. Contact: (general) Peter McIntyre, Manager, International Operations Division; (administration) Carlos Peña, Managing Director; Chris Cooper, International Broadcast Manager; (engineering) Ing. Renato Valentin, Frequency Manager; Larry Podmore, IBG Chief Engineer. Free stickers and calendar cards. Three IRCs appreciated for airmail reply. Plans to add a new 100 kW shortwave transmitter.
INTERNATIONAL SCHEDULLING OFFICE: FEBC, 20 Ayer Rajah Crescent, Technopreneur Center, #09-22, Singapore 139964, Singapore. Phone: +65 6773-9017. Fax: +65 6773 9018. Email: phsu@febc.org. Contact: Peter C. Hsu, International Schedule Manager.
NEW DELHI BUREAU, NONTECHNICAL: c/o FEBC, Box 6, New Delhi-110 001, India.
Radyo Pilipinas, the Voice of Democracy, Philippine Broadcasting Service, 4th Floor, PIA Building, Visayas Avenue, Quezon City 1100, Metro Manila, Philippines. Phone: (general) +63 (2) 924-2620; +63 (2) 920-3963; or +63 (2) 924-2548; (engineering) +63 (2) 924-2268. Fax: +63 (2) 924 2745. Email: pbs.pao@pbs.gov.ph. Contact: (nontechnical) Joy Montero; Evelyn Salvador Agato, Officer-in-Charge; Mercy Lumba; Leo Romano, Producer, "Listeners and Friends"; Tanny V. Rodriguez, Station Manager; or Richard G. Lorenzo, Production Coordinator; (technical) Danilo Alberto, Supervisor; or Mike Pangilinan, Engineer. Free postcards and stickers.
Radio Veritas Asia
STUDIOS AND ADMINISTRATIVE HEADQUARTERS: P.O. Box 2642, Quezon City, 1166 Philippines. Phone: +63 (2) 939-0011 to 14, +63 (2) 939-4692. Fax: (general) +63 (2) 938 1940; (Frequency Planning and Monitoring) +63 (2) 939 7556. Email: (general) rveritas-asia@veritas-asia.org; (Program Dept.) rvaprogram@rveritas-asia.org; (Audience Research) rva-ars@rveritas-asia.org; (technical) technical@rveritas-asia.org. Web: www.rveritas-asia.org. Contact: (administration) Ms. Erlinda G. So, Manager; (general) Ms. Cleofe R. Labindao, Audience Relations Officer; Mrs. Regie de Juan Galindez; or Msgr. Pietro Nguyen Van Tai, Program Director; (technical) Honorio L. Llavore, Technical Director; Alex M. Movilla, Assistant Technical Director; or Alfonso L. Macaranas, Station Operating Engineer. Free caps, T-shirts, stickers, pennants, rulers, pens,

postcards and calendars. Free bi-monthly newsletter *UPLINK.* Return postage appreciated.
TRANSMITTER SITE: Radio Veritas Asia, Palauig, Zambales, Philippines. Contact: Fr. Hugo Delbaere, CICM, Technical Consultant.
BRUSSELS BUREAUS AND MAIL DROPS: Catholic Radio and Television Network, 32-34 Rue de l' Association, B-1000 Brussels, Belgium; or UNDA, 12 Rue de l'Orme, B-1040 Brussels, Belgium.
Voice of Friendship—*see* FEBC Radio International.

PIRATE

Pirate radio stations are usually one-person operations airing home-brew entertainment and/or iconoclastic viewpoints. In order to avoid detection by the authorities, they tend to appear irregularly, with little concern for the niceties of conventional program scheduling. Most are found in Europe chiefly on weekends, and mainly during evenings in North America, often just above 6200 kHz, just below 7000 kHz and just above 7375 kHz. These *sub rosa* stations and their addresses are subject to unusually abrupt change or termination, sometimes as a result of forays by radio authorities.
A worthy source of current addresses and other information on American pirate radio activity is: A*C*E, P.O. Box 12112, Norfolk VA 23541 USA (email: pradio@erols.com; Web: www.frn.net/ace/), a club which publishes a periodical ($20/year U.S., US$21 Canada, $27 elsewhere) for serious pirate radio enthusiasts.
For Europirate DX news, try:
SRSNEWS, Swedish Report Service, Ostra Porten 29, SE-442 54 Ytterby, Sweden. Email: srs@ice.warp.slink.se. Web: www-pp.kdt.net/jonny/index.html.
Pirate Connection, P.O. Box 4580, SE-203 20 Malmoe, Sweden; or P.O. Box 7085, Kansas City, Missouri 64113 USA. Phone: (home, Sweden) +46 (40) 611-1775; (mobile, Sweden) +46 (70) 581-5047. Email: etoxspz@eto.ericsson.se, xtdspz@lmd.ericsson.se or spz@exallon.se. Web: www-pp.hogia.net/jonny/pc. Six issues annually for about $23. Related to SRSNEWS, above.
FRS Goes DX, P.O. Box 2727, NL-6049 ZG Herten, Netherlands. Email: FRSH@pi.net; or peter.verbruggen@tip.nl. Web: http://home.pi.net/~freak55/home.htm.
Free-DX, 3 Greenway, Harold Park, Romford, Essex, RM3 OHH, United Kingdom.
FRC-Finland, P.O. Box 82, FIN-40101 Jyvaskyla, Finland.
Pirate Express, Postfach 220342, Wuppertal, Germany.
For up-to-date listener discussions and other pirate-radio information on the Internet, the usenet URLs are: alt.radio.pirate and rec.radio.pirate.

POLAND World Time +1 (+2 midyear)

Radio Polonia
STATION: External Service, P.O. Box 46, PL-00-977 Warsaw, Poland. Phone: (general) +48 (22) 645-9305 or +48 (22) 444-123; (English Section) +48 (22) 645-9262; (German Section) +48 (22) 645-9333; (placement liaison) +48 (22) 645-9002. Fax: (general and administration) +48 (22) 645 5917 or +48 (22) 645 5919; (placement liaison) +48 (2) 645 5906. Email (general): piatka@radio.com.pl; (Polish Section) polonia@radio.com.pl; (English Section) english.section@radio.com.pl; (German Section) deutsche.redaktion@radio.com.pl; (Esperanto Section) esperanto.redakcio@radio.com.pl. Web: (includes RealAudio and Windows Media) www.radio.com.pl/polonia. Contact:

"Jolly Joe" Adamov's career began as Hitler's forces approached Moscow, making him today's elder statesman of world band radio. He later survived an alley encounter with dreaded NKVD henchman Lavrenti P. Beria. *Voice of Russia*

(general) Rafał Kiepuszewski, Head, English Section and Producer, "Postbag"; Peter Gentle, Presenter, "Postbag"; or Ann Flapan, Corresponding Secretary; (administration) Jerzy M. Nowakowski, Managing Director; Wanda Samborska, Managing Director; Bogumiła Berdychowska, Deputy Managing Director; or Maciej Lętowski, Executive Manager. On-air Polish language course with free printed material. Free stickers, pens, key rings and possibly T-shirts depending on financial cutbacks. DX Listeners' Club.

TRANSMISSION AUTHORITY: PAR (National Radiocommunication Agency), ul. Kasprzaka 18/20, PL-01-211 Warsaw, Poland. Phone: +48 (22) 608-8139/40, +48 (22) 608-8174 or +48 (22) 608-8191. Fax: +48 (22) 608 8195. Email: the format is initial.last name@par.gov.pl, so to reach, say, Filomena Grodzicka, it would be f.grodzicka@par.gov.pl. Contact: Mrs. Filomena Grodzicka, Head of BC Section; Lukasz Trzos; Mrs. Katalin Jaros; Ms. Urszula Rzepa or Jan Kondej. Responsible for coordinating Radio Polonia's frequencies.

PORTUGAL   World Time exactly (+1 midyear); Azores World Time –1 (World Time midyear)

📻RDP Internacional—Rádio Portugal, Av. Marechal Gomes da Costa nº 37, 1849-030 Lisbon, Portugal. Phone: (general) +351 (21) 382-0000. Fax: (general) +351 (21) 382 0165. Email: (general) rdpinternacional@rdp.pt; (reception reports and listener correspondence) isabelsaraiva@rdp.pt, or christianehaupt@rdp.pt. Web: (includes Windows Media and bilingual English-Portuguese online reception report form) http://programas.rtp.pt/EPG/radio. Contact: (administration) Jaime Marques de Almeida, Director; (general) Isabel Saraiva

or Christiane Haupt, Listener's Service Department; (technical) Eng. Francisco Mascarenhas, Technical Director. Free stickers. May also send literature from the Portuguese National Tourist Office.

DIRECÇÀO TÉCNICA-GRUPO REDES DE EMISSORES: Av. Marechal Gomes da Costa, 37, Bloco B-2º 1849-030 Lisbon Portugal. Phone: +351 (21) 382-0228. Fax: +351 (21) 382 0098. Email: teresaabreu@rdp.pt or paulacarvalho@rdp.pt. Contact: Mrs. Teresa Beatriz Abreu, Frequency Manager; or Ms. Paula Carvalho.

Radio Trans Europe (transmission facilities), 6º esq., Rua Braamcamp 84, 1200 Lisbon, Portugal. Transmitters located at Sines, and used by RDP Internacional and Germany's Deutsche Welle (*see*).

ROMANIA   World Time +2 (+3 midyear)

📻Radio Romãnia International

STATION: 60-62 Berthelot St., RO-70747 Bucharest, Romania; P.O. Box 111, RO-70756 Bucharest, Romania; or Romanian embassies worldwide. Phone: (general) +40 (21) 222-2556, +40 (21) 303-1172, +40 (21) 303-1488 or +40 (21) 312-3645; (English Department) +40 (21) 303-1357; (engineering) +40 (21) 303-1193. Fax: (general) +40 (21) 223 2613 [if no connection, try via the office of the Director General of Radio Romãnia, but mark fax "Pentru RRI"; that fax is +40 (21) 222 5641]; (Engineering Services) +40 (21) 312 1056/7 or +40 (21) 615 6992. Email: (general) rri@rri.ro; (English Service) engl@rri.ro; (Nisipeanu) mnisipeanu@radio.rornet.ro; (Ianculescu) rianculescu@rri.ro. Web: (includes RealAudio) www.rri.ro. Contact: (communications in English or Romanian) Dan Balamat, "Listeners' Letterbox"; or Ioana Masariu, Head of the English Service; (radio enthusiasts' issues, English only) "DX Mailbox," English Department; (communications in French or Romanian) Doru Vasile Ionescu, Deputy General Director; (listeners' letters) or Dan Dumitrescu; (technical) Sorin Floricu, Head of Broadcasting Department; Radu Ianculescu, HF Planning & Monitoring; or Marius Nisipeanu, Director, Production & Broadcasting. Listeners' Club. Annual contests. Rarely replies. Concerns about frequency management should be directed to the PTT (*see* below), with copies to the Romanian Autonomous Company (*see* farther below) and to a suitable official at RRI.

TRANSMISSION AND FREQUENCY MANAGEMENT, PTT: General Directorate of Regulations, Ministry of Communications, 14a Al. Libertatii, R-70060 Bucharest, Romania. Phone: +40 (21) 400-1312 or +40 (21) 400-177. Fax: +40 (21) 400 1230. Email: marian@snr.ro. Contact: Mrs. Elena Danila, Head of Frequency Management Department.

TRANSMISSION AND FREQUENCY MANAGEMENT, AUTONOMOUS COMPANY: Romanian Autonomous Company for Radio Communications, 14a Al. Libertatii, R-70060 Bucharest, Romania. Phone: +40 (21) 400-1072. Fax: +40 (21) 400 1228 or +40 (1) 335 5965. Email: marian@snr.ro. Contact: Mr. Marian Ionitá, Executive Director of Operations.

RUSSIA   (Times given for republics, oblasts and krays):

• World Time +2 (+3 midyear) Kaliningradskaya;
• World Time +3 (+4 midyear) Adygeya, Arkhangelskaya, Astrakhanskaya, Belgorodskaya, Bryanskaya, Chechnya, Chuvashiya, Dagestan, Ingushetiya, Kabardino-Balkariya, Kalmykiya, Kaluzhskaya, Karachayevo-Cherkesiya, Ivanovskaya, Karelia, Kirovskaya, Komi, Kostromskaya, Krasnodarskiy, Kurskaya, Leningradskaya (including St. Petersburg), Lipetskaya, Mariy-El, Mordoviya, Moskovskaya (in-

cluding the capital, Moscow), Murmanskaya, Nenetskiy, Nizhegorodskaya, Novgorodskaya, Severnaya Osetiya, Orlovskaya, Penzenskaya, Pskovskaya, Rostovskaya, Ryazanskaya, Saratovskaya, Smolenskaya, Stavropolskiy, Tambovskaya, Tatarstan, Tulskaya, Tverskaya, Ulyanovskaya, Vladimirskaya, Volgogradskaya, Vologodskaya, Voronezhskaya, Yaroslavskaya;

- World Time +4 (+5 midyear) Samarskaya, Udmurtiya;
- World Time +5 (+6 midyear) Bashkortostan, Chelyabinskaya, Khanty-Mansiyskiy, Komi-Permyatskiy, Kurganskaya, Orenburgskaya, Permskaya, Sverdlovskaya, Tyumenskaya, Yamalo-Nenetskiy;
- World Time +6 (+7 midyear) Altayskiy, Novosibirskaya, Omskaya, Tomskaya;
- World Time +7 (+8 midyear) Evenkiyskiy, Kemerovskaya, Khakasiya, Krasnoyarskiy, Taymyrskiy, Tyva;
- World Time +8 (+9 midyear) Buryatiya, Irkutskaya, Ust-Ordynskiy;
- World Time +9 (+10 midyear) Aginskiy-Buryatskiy, Amurskaya, Chitinskaya, Sakha;
- World Time +10 (+11 midyear) Khabarovskiy, Primorskiy, Yevreyskaya;
- World Time +11 (+12 midyear) Magadanskaya, Sakhalinskaya;
- World Time +12 (+13 midyear) Chukotskiy, Kamchatskaya, Koryakskiy.

C.I.S. FREQUENCY MANAGEMENT ENGINEERING OFFICE: General Radio Frequency Center, 25 Pyatnitskaya Str., 113326 Moscow, Russia. Phone: +7 (095) 950-6022; Phone/Fax: +7 (095) 789-3587. Email: (Titov) a_titov@vor.ru. Web: (General Radio Frequency Center parent organization) www.grfc.ru. Contact: (general) Mrs. Nina Bykova, Monitoring Coordinator; (administration) Anatoliy T. Titov, Chief of Division for SW and MW Frequency Broadcasting Schedules. This office is responsible for the operation of radio broadcasting in the Russian Federation, as well as for frequency usage of transmitters throughout much of the C.I.S. Correspondence should be concerned only with significant technical observations or engineering suggestions concerning frequency management improvement—not regular requests for verifications. Correspondence in Russian preferred, but English accepted.

Adygey Radio—*see* Maykop Radio.

Amur Radio—*see* Blagoveschensk Radio.

Arkhangel'sk Radio, GTRK "Pomorye," ul. Popova 2, 163061 Arkhangel'sk, Arkhangel'skaya Oblast, Russia; or U1PR, Valentin G. Kalasnikov, ul. Suvorov 2, kv. 16, Arkhangel'sk, Arkhangel'skaya Oblast, Russia. Replies irregularly to correspondence in Russian.

Blagoveschensk Radio, GTRK "Amur," per Svyatitelya Innokentiya 15, 675000 Blagoveschensk, Russia. Contact: V.I. Kal'chenko, Chief Engineer.

Buryat Radio—*see* Ulan-Ude Radio.

Kabardino-Balkar Radio—*see* Nalchik Radio.

Kamchatka Rybatskaya—a special service for fishermen off the coasts of China, Japan and western North America; *see* Petropavlovsk-Kamchatskiy Radio for contact details.

Khabarovsk Radio (if reactivated on shortwave), GTRK "Dalnevostochnaya," ul. Lenina 4, 682632 Khabarovsk, Khabarovskiy Kray, Russia; or Dom Radio, pl. Slavy, 682632 Khabarovsk, Khabarovskiy Kray, Russia. Web: (program schedule only) www.khb.ru/Afisha/Radio/kabar.htm. Contact: (technical) V.N. Kononov, Glavnyy Inzhener.

Khanty-Mansiysk Radio, GTRK "Yugoriya," ul. Mira 7, 626200 Khanty-Mansiysk, Russia. Contact: (technical) Vladimir Sokolov, Engineer.

Krasnoyarsk Radio, Krasnoyarskaya GTRK, "Tsentr Rossii," ul. Mechnikova 44A, 666001, Krasnoyarsk 28, Krasnoyarsky Kray, Russia. Email: postmaster@telegid.krasnoyarsk.su. Contact: Valeriy Korotchenko; or Anatoliy A. Potehin, RAØAKE. Free local information booklets in English/Russian. Replies in Russian to correspondence in English or Russian. Return postage helpful.

Kyzyl Radio, GTRK "Tyva," ul. Gornaya 31, 667003 Kyzyl, Respublika Tyva, Russia. Email: tv@tuva.ru. Replies to correspondence in Russian.

Magadan Radio, GTRK "Magadan," ul. Kommuny 8/12, 685024 Magadan, Magadanskaya Oblast, Russia. Contact: Viktor Loktionov or V.G. Kuznetsov. Return postage helpful. Occasionally replies to correspondence in Russian.

Mariy Radio—*see* Yoshkar-Ola Radio.

Mayak—*see* Radiostantsiya Mayak.

Maykop Radio, GTRK "Adygeya," ul. Zhukovskogo 24, 385000 Maykop, Republic of Adygeya, Russia. Contact: A.T. Kerashev, Chairman. English accepted but Russian preferred. Return postage helpful.

Murmansk Radio, GTRK "Murman," per. Rusanova 7, 183032 Murmansk, Murmanskaya Oblast, Russia. Phone: +7 (8152) 561-527. Phone/Fax: +7 (8152) 459-770. Fax: +7 (8152) 231 913. Email: tvmurman@sampo.ru; tvmurman@sampo.karelia.ru; murmantv@com.mels.ru. Web: www.sampo.ru/~tvmurman/radio/rmain.html. Contact: D. Pemaredi (chairman).

Nalchik Radio, GTRK "Kabbalk Teleradio," pr. Lenina 3, 360000 Nalchik, Republic of Kabardino-Balkariya, Russia. Contact: Kamal Makitov, Vice-Chairman. Replies to correspondence in Russian.

Palana Radio (if reactivated), Koryakskaya GTRK "Palana," ul. Obukhova 4, 684620 Palana, Koryakskiy avt. Okrug, Russia.

Perm Radio, Permskaya GTRK "T-7," ul. Tekhnicheskaya 7, 614070 Perm, Permskaya Oblast, Russia. Contact: M. Levin, Senior Editor; or A. Losev, Acting Chief Editor.

Petropavlovsk-Kamchatskiy Radio, GTRK "Kamchatka," ul. Sovetskaya 62, 683000 Petropavlovsk-Kamchatskiy, Kamchatskaya Oblast, Russia. Contact: A.F. Borodin, Head of GTRK "Kamchatka." Email: gtrkbuh@mail.iks.ru. $1 required for postal reply. Replies in Russian to correspondence in Russian or English. Currently inactive on shortwave, apart from a special program for fishermen—*see* Kamchatka Rybatskaya.

Radio Gardarika (when operating), Radio Studio Dom Radio, Ligovsky Prospekt 174, 197002 St. Petersburg, Russia. Email: studiosw@metroclub.ru. Contact: Suvorov Alexey, Shortwave Project Manager. Replies to correspondence in Russian and English. Return postage helpful.

☞**Radio Miks-Master** (when operating), ul. Oktyabr'skaya 20/1, 677027 Yakutsk, Respublika Sakha, Russia. Phone: +7 (4112) 420-302. Email: mix_radio@rambler.ru. Web: (includes MP3) http://mixmaster.ykt.ru.

Radio Nalchik—*see* Radio Kabardino-Balkar, above.

☞**Radio Rossii** (Russia's Radio), GRK "Radio Rossii," Yamskogo Polya 5-YA ul. 19/21, 125040 Moscow, Russia. Phone: +7 (095) 213-1054, +7 (095) 250-0511 or +7 (095) 251-4050. Fax: +7 (095) 250 0105, +7 (095) 233 6449 or +7 (095) 214 4767. Email: mail@radiorus.ru. Web: (includes Windows Media) www.radiorus.ru. Contact: Sergei Yerofeyev, Director of International Operations [sic]; or Sergei Davidov, Director. Free English-language information sheet. For verification of reception from transmitters located in St. Petersburg and Kaliningrad, *see NOTE*, above, shortly after the country heading, "RUSSIA."

Radio Studio—*see* Radio Gardarika.

Voice of Russia announcers (from left) Michael Chernikh, Anastasia Mironova, Ivan Sedov and Irene Larina. VoR

Radiostantsiya Tikhiy Okean ("Radio Station Pacific Ocean") (when operating), RTV Center, ul. Uborevieha 20A, 690000 Vladivostok, Primorskiy Kray, Russia. Once a regular broadcaster, but now restricted to special transmissions.

Sakhalin Radio, GTRK "Sakhalin," ul. Komsomolskaya 209, 693000 Yuzhno-Sakhalinsk, Sakhalinskaya Oblast, Russia. Web: www.nbcsakha.ru/radio.htm. Phone: (Director of Radio) +7 (42422) 729-349. Phone/Fax: (GTRK parent company) +7 (42422) 35286. Email: gtrk@sakhalin.ru; (Romanov) romanov@gtrk.sakhalin.su. Web: www.gtrk.ru/RV/radio.htm. Contact: S. Romanov, Director of Radio.

Tatarstan Wave ("Tatarstan Dulkynda"), GTRK "Tatarstan," ul. Gor'kogo 15, 420015 Kazan, Tatarstan, Russia. Phone: (general) +7 (8432) 384-846; (editorial) +7 (8432) 367-493. Fax: +7 (8432) 361 283. Email: root@gtrkrt.kazan.su; postmaster@stvcrt.kazan.su. Contact: Hania Hazipovna Galinova. Formerly known as Voice of Tatarstan.
ADDRESS FOR RECEPTION REPORTS: QSL Manager, P.O. Box 134, 420136 Kazan, Tatarstan, Russia. Contact: Ildus Ibatullin, QSL Manager. Offers an honorary diploma in return for 12 correct reports in a given year. The diploma costs 2 IRCs for Russia and 4 IRCs elsewhere. All reports to the QSL Manager address listed above. Accepts reports in English and Russian. Return postage helpful.

Tura Radio (if reactivated), Evenkiyskaya GTRK "Kheglen," ul. 50 Let Oktyabrya 28, 663370 Tura, Russia.

Ufa Radio (if reactivated), GTRK "Bashkortostan," ul. Gafuri 9/1, 450076 Ufa, Respublika Bashkortostan, Russia. Email: gtrk@bashinform.ru. Replies to correspondence in Russian.

Ulan-Ude Radio, Buryatskaya GTRK, ul. Erbanova 7, 670000 Ulan-Ude, Republic of Buryatia, Russia. Contact: Z.A. Telin; Mrs. M.V. Urbaeva, 1st Vice-Chairman; or L.S. Shikhanova.

Voice of Russia, GRK "Golos Rossii," ul. Pyatnitskaya 25, Moscow 115326, Russia. Phone: (Chairman) +7 (095) 950-6331; (International Relations Department) +7 (095) 950-6440; (Technical Department) +7 (095) 950-6115. Fax: (Chairman & World Service in English) +7 (095) 230 2828; Email: letters@vor.ru. Web: (includes RealAudio) www.vor.ru. Contact: (Letters Department, World Service in English) Olga Troshina, Elena Osipova or Elena Frolovskaya; (Chairman) Armen Oganesyan; (International Relations Department) Vic-

tor Kopytin, Director; (Technical Department) Ms. Rachel Staviskaya, Director; (World Service in English) Vladimir Zhamkin, Director. For language services other than English contact the International Relations Department.
SAN FRANCISCO OFFICE, SCHEDULES: 2654 17th Avenue, San Francisco CA 94116 USA. Phone: +1 (415) 564-9968. Email: GPoppin@aol.com. Contact: George Poppin. This address, a volunteer office, only provides Voice of Russia schedules to listeners. All other correspondence should be sent directly to the Voice of Russia in Moscow.

Yakutsk Radio, NVK "Sakha," ul. Ordzhonikidze 48, 677007 Yakutsk, Respublika Sakha, Russia. Contact: (general) Alexandra Borisova; Lia Sharoborina, Advertising Editor; or Albina Danilova, Producer, "Your Letters"; (technical) Sergei Bobnev, Technical Director. Russian books $15; audio cassettes $10. Free station stickers and original Yakutian souvenirs. Replies to correspondence in English.

RWANDA   World Time +2

Deutsche Welle—Relay Station Kigali—Correspondence should be directed to the main offices in Cologne, Germany *(see)*.

Radio Rwanda, B.P. 83, Kigali, Rwanda. Phone: +250 76540. Fax: +250 76185. Email: (Rwandan Information Office) imvaho2002@yahoo.fr. Web: (includes RealAudio) www.orinfor.gov.rw/radiorwanda.htm. Contact: Marcel Singirankabo. $1 required. Rarely replies, with correspondence in French preferred.

SAO TOME E PRINCIPE   World Time exactly

Voice of America/IBB—São Tomé Relay Station, P.O. Box 522, São Tomé, São Tomé e Príncipe. Contact: Manuel Neves, Transmitter Plant Technician. Replies direct if $1 included with correspondence, otherwise all communications should be directed to the usual VOA or IBB addresses in Washington *(see USA)*.

SAUDI ARABIA   World Time +3

Broadcasting Service of the Kingdom of Saudi Arabia, P.O. Box 61718, Riyadh-11575, Saudi Arabia. Phone: (general) +966 (1) 404-2795; (administration) +966 (1) 442-5493. Fax: (general) +966 (1) 402 8177. Web: (MP3 only) www.saudiradio.net. Contact: (general) Mutlaq A. Albegami. Free travel information and book on Saudi history. For technical contacts including Engineering and Frequency Management, see the next entry.

Saudi Arabian Radio & Television, P.O. Box 8525, Riyadh-11492, Saudi Arabia. Phone: (technical & frequency managementl) +966 (1) 442-5170. Fax: (technical & frequency management) +966 (1) 404 1692. Email: alsamnan@yahoo.com or inform.eng@suhuf.net.sa. Contact: Suleiman Al-Samnan, Director of Engineering and Frequency Management; Suleiman Al-Kalifa, General Manager; Suleiman Al Haidari, Engineer; or Youssef Dhim.

SERBIA AND MONTENEGRO   World Time +1 (+2 midyear)

International Radio of Serbia and Montenegro, Hilendarska 2/IV, P.O. Box 200, 11000 Beograd, Serbia and Montenegro. Phone: +381 (11) 324-4455. Fax: +381 (11) 323 2014. Email: radioyu@bitsyu.net. Web: (includes RealAudio) www.radioyu.org. Contact: (general) Milena Jokich, Director

& Editor-in-Chief; Aleksandar Georgiev; Aleksandar Popovic, Head of Public Relations; Pance Zafirovski, Head of Programs; or Slobodan Topović, Producer, "Post Office Box 200/Radio Hams' Corner"; (technical) B. Miletic, Operations Manager of HF Broadcasting; Technical Department; or Rodoljub Medan, Chief Engineer. Free pennants, stickers, pins and tourist information. $1 helpful. Formerly known as Radio Yugoslavia.

SEYCHELLES   World Time +4

BBC World Service—Indian Ocean Relay Station, P.O. Box 448, Victoria, Mahé, Seychelles; or Grand Anse, Mahé, Seychelles. Phone: +248 78-269. Fax: +248 78 500. Contact: (administration) Peter J. Loveday, Station Manager; (technical) Peter Lee, Resident Engineer; Nigel Bird, Resident Engineer; or Steve Welch, Assistant Resident Engineer. Nontechnical correspondence should be sent to the BBC World Service in London (*see*).

SIERRA LEONE   World Time exactly

Radio UNAMSIL (when operating), Mammy Yoko Hotel, P.O. Box 5, Freetown, Sierra Leone. Email: info@unamsil.org; or patrickcoker@unamsil.org. Web: (UNAMSIL parent organization) www.unamsil.org. Contact: Patrick Coker or Sheila Dallas, Station Manager & Executive Producer. Station of the United Nations Mission in Sierra Leone.
Sierra Leone Broadcasting Service (when operating), New England, Freetown, Sierra Leone. Phone: +232 (22) 240-123; +232 (22) 240-173; +232 (22) 240-497 or 232 (22) 241-919. Fax: +232 (22) 240 922. Contact: Cyril Juxon-Smith, Officer in Charge; or Henry Goodaig Hjax, Assistant Engineer.

SINGAPORE   World Time +8

BBC World Service—Far Eastern Relay Station, VT Merlin Communications, 51 Turut Track, Singapore 718930, Singapore. Phone: + 65 6793-7511/3. Fax: +65 6793 7834. Email: wuipin@singnet.com.sg. Contact: (technical) Mr. Wui Pin Yong, Operations Manager; or Far East Resident Engineer. Nontechnical correspondence should be sent to the BBC World Service in London (*see*).
MediaCorp Radio, Farrer Road, P.O. Box 968, Singapore 912899, Singapore; or (street address) Caldecott Broadcast Centre, Caldecott Hill, Andrew Road, Singapore 299939, Singapore. Phone: (general) +65 6251-8622; (Fern) +65 6359-7577; (transmitting station) +65 6793-7651. Fax: +65 6256 9533. Email: (Fern) cherfern@mediacorpradio.com. Web: (includes Windows Media) www.mediacorpradio.com. Contact: (administration) Peh Cher Fern, Corporate Communications Senior Executive. Free regular and Post-It stickers, pens, umbrellas, mugs, towels, wallets and lapel pins. Do not include currency in envelope. Successor to the former Radio Corporation of Singapore.
Radio Singapore International, Farrer Road, P.O. Box 5300, Singapore 912899, Singapore; or (street address) Caldecott Broadcast Centre, Annex Building Level 1, Andrew Road, Singapore 299939, Singapore. Phone: (general) + 65 6359-7662; (English Service) + 65 6359-7675. Fax: +65 6259 1357 or +65 6259 1380. Email: info@rsi.com.sg; or (English Service) english@rsi.com.sg. Web: (includes Windows Media) www.rsi.com.sg. Contact: (general) Augustine Anthuvan, Assistant Programme Director, English Service; (technical) Lim Wing Kee, RSI Engineering. Free souvenir T-shirts and key chains to selected listeners. Do not include currency in envelope.

SLOVAKIA   World Time +1 (+2 midyear)

Radio Slovakia International, Mýtna 1, P.O. Box 55, 817 55 Bratislava 15, Slovakia. Phone: (Editor-in-Chief) +421 (2) 5727-3730; (English Service) +421 (2) 5727-3736 or +421 (2) 5727-2737; (technical) +421 (2) 5727-3251. Fax: +421 (2) 5249 6282 or +421 (2) 5249 8247; (technical) +421 (2) 5249 7659. Email: (English Section) englishsection@slovakradio.sk; for other language sections, the format is rsi_language@ slovakradio.sk, where the language is written in English (e.g. rsi_spanish@slovakradio.sk); (Frequency Manager) chocholata@slovakradio.sk. Web: (includes RealAudio and online reception-report form) www.rsi.sk. Contact: Oxana Ferjenčíková, Director of English Broadcasting; (administration) PhDr. Karol Palkovič, Head of External Broadcasting; or Dr. Slavomira Kubickova, Head of International Relations; (technical) Ms. Edita Chocholatá, Frequency Manager.

SOLOMON ISLANDS   World Time +11

Solomon Islands Broadcasting Corporation (Radio Happy Isles), P.O. Box 654, Honiara, Solomon Islands. Phone: +677 20051. Fax: +677 23159 or +677 25652. Email: sibcnews@solomon.com.sb. Web: (SIBC news in text format) www.sibconline.com.sb. Contact: (general) David Palapu, Manager Broadcast Operations; Julian Maka'a, Producer, "Listeners From Far Away"; Walter Nalangu, News & Current Affairs; Rachel Rahi'i, Commercial/Advertising; or Bart Basi, Programmes; (administration) Grace Ngatulu; Johnson Honimae, General Manager; (technical) Cornelius Rathamana, Technical Division. IRC or $1 helpful. Problems with the domestic mail system may cause delays. Plans to reactivate shortwave frequency 9545kHz.

SOMALIA   World Time +3

Radio Banaadir—*see* Radio Banadir, below.
Radio Banadir (when operating), Kaaraan (Beexaani), Mogadishu, Somalia. Phone: +2525 944-156 or +2525 960-368. Email: radiobanadir@somalinternet.com. Web: (includes RealAudio) www.radiobanadir.com.
Radio Galkayo (when operating), 2 Griffith Avenue, Roseville NSW 2069, Australia. Phone/Fax: +61 (2) 9417-1066. Email: svoron@hotmail.com. Web: (includes RealAudio and online email form) www. radiogalkayo.com. Contact: Sam Voron, VK2BVS, 6O0A, Australian Director. $5, AUS$5 or 5 IRCs required for return postage or replies free via the Internet. A community radio station in the Mudug region, Puntland State, northern Somalia and supported by local and overseas volunteers. Seeks volunteers and donations of radio equipment, airline tickets and is setting up a Radio Galkayo Amateur Radio club Station.
Radio Shabele, Global Building, 3rd Floor, Mogadishu, Somalia. Phone: +2521 659-699, +22521 227-733 or +2521 933-111. Email: radio@shabele.com. Web: (includes RealAudio) www.shabele.com. Contact:Abdi Malik Yusuf Mahmuud, Chairman.

SOMALILAND   World Time +3

NOTE: "Somaliland," claimed as an independent nation, is diplomatically recognized only as part of Somalia.
Radio Hargeysa, P.O. Box 14, Hargeysa, Somaliland, Somalia. Email: no known direct mail address, but try admin@radiohargeysa.com or radio@somaliland.com. Web: (includes RealAudio) www.radiohargeysa.com; (RealAudio ar-

America's exceptionally effective international broadcasting facility, at Playa de Pals in Spain, was eliminated just before 9/11.

Nick Olguin via Jack Quinn

chives only) www.radiosomaliland.com. Contact: Sulayman Abdel-Rahman, announcer. More likely to respond to correspondence in Somali or Arabic.

SOUTH AFRICA World Time +2

BBC World Service via South Africa—For verification direct from the South African transmitters, contact Sentech (*see* below). Nontechnical correspondence should be sent to the BBC World Service in London (*see*).

⊞Channel Africa, P.O. Box 91313, Auckland Park 2006, South Africa. Phone: (executive editor) +27 (11) 714-2255; (technical) +27 (11) 714-2614. Fax: (executive editor) +27 (11) 714 2072. Email: (general) africancan@channelafrica.org; (news desk) news.africa@channelafrica.org; (technical) meyerhelen@channelafrica.org. Web: (includes Windows Media) www.channelafrica.org. Contact: (general) Promise Zamesa, Executive Editor; (technical) Mrs. Helen Meyer, Supervisor Operations. Reception reports are best directed to Sentech (*see*), which operates the transmission facilities.

Radio Veritas, P.O. Box 53687, Troyeville 2139, South Africa; or (street address) 36 Beelaerts Street, Troyeville 2094, South Africa. Phone: +27 (11) 624-2516; (studio) +27 (11) 614-6225. Fax: +27 (11) 614 7711. Email: info@radioveritas.co.za; (Fr. Blaser) eblaser@iafrica.com. Web: www.radioveritas.co.za. Contact: Fr. Emil Blaser OP, Director. Return postage helpful. Reception reports can also be directed to Sentech (*see*), which operates the transmission facilities.

⊞Radiosondergrense (Radio Without Boundaries), Posbus 91312, Auckland Park 2006, South Africa. Phone: (general) +27 (89) 110-2525; (live studio on-air line) +27 (89) 110-4553; (station manager) +27 (11) 714-2702. Fax: (general) +27 (11) 714 6445; (station manager) +27 (11) 714 3472. Email: (general) info@rsg.co.za; (Myburgh) sarel@rsg.co.za. Web: (includes Windows Media) www.rsg.co.za. Contact: Sarel Myburgh, Station Manager. Reception reports are best directed to Sentech (*see*, below), which operates the shortwave transmission facilities. A domestic service of the South African Broadcasting Corporation, and formerly known as Afrikaans Stereo. The shortwave operation is scheduled to be eventually replaced by a satellite and FM network.

Sentech Ltd, Transmission Planning, Private Bag X06, Honeydew 2040, South Africa. Phone: (general) +27 (11) 471-4400 or +27 (11) 691-7000; (shortwave) +27 (11) 471-4658. Fax: (shortwave) +27 (11) 471 4754. Email: (Kathy Otto) ottok@sentech.co.za; (Smuts) smutsn@sentech.co.za. Web: (schedules & frequencies) www.sentech.co.za. Contact: Mr. Neël Smuts, Managing Director; Rodgers Gamuti, Client Manager; or Kathy Otto, HF Coverage Planner. Sentech issues veri-

fication letters for reception reports on transmissions from the Meyerton shortwave facilities.

South African Radio League—Amateur Radio Mirror International, P.O. Box 90438, Garsfontein 0042, South Africa. Email: armi@intekom.co.za; armi@sarl.org.za. Web: www.sarl.org.za/public/ARMI/ARMI.asp. Amateur Radio Mirror International is a weekly broadcast aired via Sentech's Meyerton facilities.

Trans World Radio Africa

NONTECHNICAL CORRESPONDENCE: Trans World Radio—South Africa, Private Bag 987, Pretoria 0001, South Africa. Phone: +27 (12) 807-0053. Fax: +27 (12) 807 1266. Web: (includes online email form) www.twrafrica.org.

TECHNICAL CORRESPONDENCE: Reception reports and other technical correspondence are best directed to Sentech (*see*, above) or to TWR's Swaziland office (*see*). Also, *see* USA.

SPAIN World Time +1 (+2 midyear)

⊞Radio Exterior de España (Spanish National Radio, World Service)

MAIN OFFICE: Apartado de Correos 156.202, E-28080 Madrid, Spain. Phone: (general) +34 (91) 346-1081/1083; (Audience Relations) +34 (91) 346-1149. Fax: +34 (91) 346 1815. Email: (Director) dir_ree.rne@rtve.es; (Spanish programming, listener feedback) ree.rne@rtve.es. Web: (includes RealAudio, MP3 and Windows Media) www.ree.rne.es. Contact: (Audience Relations) Pilar Salvador M.; (Assistant Director) Pedro Fernández Céspedes; (Director) Francisco Fernández Oria. Free stickers and tourist information. Verification of reception reports is temporarily suspended due to "staffing and budget constraints." Listeners are requested not to send cash or IRCs, since the limited services which still exist are free. An alternative, for those who speak and write Spanish, is to send a reception report on the program "Españoles en la Mar" which is produced in the Canary Islands. Times and frequencies can be found at the REE Website. Reports should be sent to: Programa "Españoles en la Mar," Apartado Postal 1233, Santa Cruz de Tenerife, Spain. Magazines and small souvenirs are sometimes included with verifications from this address.

TRANSCRIPTION SERVICE: Radio Nacional de España, Servicio de Transcripciones, Apartado 156.200, Casa de la Radio (Prado del Rey), E-28223 Madrid, Spain.

HF FREQUENCY PLANNING OFFICE: Prado del Rey. Pozuelo de Alarcom, E-28223 Madrid, Spain. Phone: (Huerta) +34 (91) 346-1276; (Arlanzón) +34 (91) 346-1639; or (Almarza) +34 (91) 346-1978. Fax: (Huerta & Almarza) +34 (91) 346 1402 or (Alanzón) +34 (91) 346 1275. Email: (Almarza) planif_red2.rne@rtve.es; or (Huerta & Arlanzón) plan_red.rne@rtve.es. Contact: Fernando Almarza, Frequency Planning; Salvador Arlanzón, HF Frequency Manager; or José Maria Huerta, Technical Director.

NOBLEJAS TRANSMITTER SITE: Centro Emisor de RNE en Onda Corta, Ctra. Dos Barrios s/n, E-45350 Noblejas-Toledo, Spain.
COSTA RICA RELAY FACILITY—see Costa Rica.
MOSCOW OFFICE: P.O Box 88, 109044 Moscow, Russia.
WASHINGTON NEWS BUREAU: National Press Building, 529 14th Street NW, Suite 1288, Washington DC 20045 USA. Phone: +1 (202) 783-0768. Contact: Luz María Rodríguez.

SRI LANKA   World Time +6:00

Deutsche Welle—Relay Station Sri Lanka, 92/2 D.S. Senanayake Mawatha, Colombo 08, Sri Lanka. Phone: +94 (1) 699-449. Fax: +94 (1) 699 450. Contact: R. Groschkus, Resident Engineer. Nontechnical correspondence should be sent to Deutsche Welle in Germany (*see*).

Radio Japan/NHK, c/o SLBC, P.O. Box 574, Torrington Square, Colombo 7, Sri Lanka. This address for technical correspondence only. General nontechnical listener correspondence should be sent to the usual Radio Japan address in Japan. News-oriented correspondence may also be sent to the NHK Bangkok Bureau (*see* Radio Japan, Japan).

Sri Lanka Broadcasting Corporation (also announces as "Radio Sri Lanka" in the external service), P.O. Box 574, Independence (Torrington) Square, Colombo 7, Sri Lanka. Phone: (general) +94 (1) 697-491 or +94 (1) 697-493; (Director General) +94 (1) 696-140. Fax: (general) +94 (1) 697 150 or +94 (1) 698 576; (Director General) +94 (1) 695 488; (Sooryia, Phone/Fax) +94 (1) 696-1311. Email: slbc@sri.lanka.net; slbcweb@sri.lanka.net. Web: www.infolanka.com/people/sisira/slbc.html. Contact: Icumar Ratnayake, Controller, "Mailbag Program"; (SLBC administration) Eric Fernando, Director General; Newton Gunaratne, Deputy Director-General; (technical) H.M.N.R. Jayawardena, Engineer - Training and Frequency Management; Wimala Sooriya, Deputy Director - Engineering; or A.M.W. Gunaratne, Station Engineer, Ekala.

Voice of America/IBB—Iranawila Relay Station.
ADDRESS: Station Manager, IBB Sri Lanka Transmitting Station, c/o U.S. Embassy, 210 Galle Road, Colombo 3, Sri Lanka. Contact: Walter Patterson, Station Manager. Verifies reception reports. Nontechnical correspondence should be sent to the VOA address in Washington.

SUDAN   World Time +3

Sudan National Radio Corporation, P.O. Box 572, Omdurman, Sudan. Phone: (general) +249 (11) 553-151 or +249 (11) 552-100. (Phone/Fax, technical) +249 (11) 550- 492. Email: (general) snrc@sudanmail.net; has2000@hotmail.com; (technical) salihb@maktoob.com. Web: www.srtc.info/radio. Contact: (general) Mohammed Elfatih El Sumoal; (technical) Abbas Sidig, Director General, Engineering and Technical Affairs; Mohammed Elmahdi Khalil, Administrator, Engineering and Technical Affairs; Saleh Al-Hay; Bachir Saleh, Deputy Director of Engineering; or Adil Didahammed, Engineering Department. Replies irregularly. Return postage necessary.

SURINAME   World Time –3

Radio Apintie, Postbus 595, Paramaribo, Suriname. Phone: +597 400-500, +597 400-450 or +597 401-400. Fax: +597 400 684. Email: apintie@sr.net. Web: (includes Windows Media) www.apintie.sr. Contact: Charles E. Vervuurt, Director. Free

pennant. Return postage or $1 required. Email reception reports preferred, since local mail service is unreliable.

SWAZILAND   World Time +2

Trans World Radio—Swaziland
MAIN OFFICE: P.O. Box 64, Manzini, Swaziland. Phone: +268 505-2781/2/3. Fax: +268 505 5333. Email: (Chief Engineer) sstavrop@twr.org; (Mrs. L. Stavropoulos, DX Secretary) lstavrop@twr.org; (Greg Shaw, Follow-up Department) gshaw@twr.org. Web: (transmission schedule) www.gospelcom.net/twr/broadcasts/africa.htm. Contact: (general) Greg Shaw, Follow-up Department; G.J. Alary, Station Director; or Joseph Ndzinisa, Program Manager; (technical) Mrs. L. Stavropoulos, DX Secretary; Chief Engineer. Free stickers, postcards and calendars. A free Bible Study course is available. May swap canceled stamps. $1, return postage or 3 IRCs required. Also, *see* USA.
AFRICA REGIONAL OFFICE: P.O. Box 4232,Kempton Park 1610, South Africa. Phone: +27 (11) 974-2885. Fax: +27 (11) 974 9960. Email: jburnett@twraro.org.za. Contact: James Burnett, Regional Engineer & Frequency Manager; Stephen Boakye-Yiadom, African Regional Director.
CÔTE D'IVOIRE OFFICE: B.P. 2131, Abidjan 06, Côte d'Ivoire.
KENYA OFFICE: P.O. Box 21514 Nairobi, Kenya.
MALAWI OFFICE: P. O. Box 52 Lilongwe, Malawi.
SOUTH AFRICA OFFICE: P.O. Box 36000, Menlo Park 0102, South Africa.
ZIMBABWE OFFICE: P.O. Box H-74, Hatfield, Harare, Zimbabwe.

SWEDEN   World Time +1 (+2 midyear)

IBRA Radio, SE-141 99 Stockholm, Sweden. Phone: +46 (8) 608-9600. Fax: +46 (8) 608 9650. Email: ibra@ibra.se. Web: www.ibra.se; www.ibra.org. Contact: Mikael Stjernberg, Public Relations Manager; or Helene Hasslof. Free pennants and stickers. IBRA Radio's programs are aired over various world band stations, including Trans World Radio and FEBA Radio; and also broadcast independently via transmitters in Germany and Russia. Accepts email reception reports.

Radio Sweden, SE-105 10 Stockholm, Sweden. Phone: (general) +46 (8) 784-7200, +46 (8) 784-7207, +46 (8) 784-7288 or +46 (8) 784-5000; (listener voice mail) +46 (8) 784-7287; (technical department) +46 (8) 784-7286. Fax: (general) +46 (8) 667 6283; (polling to receive schedule) +46 8 660 2990. Email: (general) radiosweden@sr.se; (In Touch) intouch@p6.sr.se; (schedule on demand) english@rs.sr.se; (Roxström) sarah.roxstrom@rs.sr.se; (Hagström) nidia.hagstrom@rs.sr.se; (Wood) george.wood@p6.sr.se; (Sounds Nordic) sono@p6.sr.se); (Beckman, technical manager) rolf-b@stab.sr.se. Web: (includes RealAudio) www.sr.se/rs.Contact: (general) Nidia Hagström, Host, "In Touch with Stockholm" [include your telephone number]; Sarah Roxström, Head, English Service; Greta Grandin, Program Assistant, English Service; Gabby Katz, Presenter of Heartbeat; Bill Schiller, Spectrum presenter; George Wood; Olimpia Seldon, Assistant to the Director; or Frida Sjolander, Public Relations and Information; (administration) Finn Norgren, Director General; (technical) Rolf Erik Beckman, Head, Technical Department; or Anders Baecklin, Editor, Technical Administration. T-shirts (three sizes) $10 or £8. Payment for T-shirts may be made by international money order, Swedish postal giro account No. 43 36 56-6 or internationally negotiable bank check.
NEW YORK NEWS BUREAU: Swedish Broadcasting, 747 Third Avenue, 8th floor, New York NY 10022 USA. Phone: +1 (212)

Bangkok is a Wild East of unbounded entrepreneurial activity. M. Guha

644-1224. Fax: +1 (212) 644 1227. Contact: Elizabeth Johansson.

WASHINGTON NEWS BUREAU: Swedish Broadcasting, 2030 M Street NW, Suite 700, Washington DC 20036 USA. Phone: +1 (202) 785-1727. Contact: Folke Rydén, Lisa Carlsson or Steffan Ekendahl.

TRANSMISSION AUTHORITY: TERACOM, Svensk Rundradio AB, P.O. Box 17666, SE-118 92 Stockholm, Sweden. Phone: (general) +46 (8) 555-420-00; (Wiberg) +46 (8) 555-420-66. Fax: (general) +46 (8) 555 420 01; (Wiberg) +46 (8) 555 20 60. Email: (general) info@teracom.se; (Wiberg) magnus.wiberg@teracom.se. Web: www.teracom.se. Contact: (Frequency Planning Dept.—Head Office): Magnus Wiberg; (Engineering) Hakan Widenstedt, Chief Engineer. Free stickers; sometimes free T-shirts to those monitoring during special test transmissions. Seeks monitoring feedback for new frequency usages.

SWITZERLAND   World Time +1 (+2 midyear)

European Broadcasting Union, 17A Ancienne Route, CH-1218 Grand-Saconnex, Geneva, Switzerland; or Case Postal 67, CH-1218 Grand-Saconnex, Geneva, Switzerland. Phone: +41 (22) 717-2111. Fax: +41 (22) 747 4000. Email: ebu@ebu.ch. Web: www.ebu.ch. Contact: Mr. Jean Stock, Secretary-General; or Robin Levey, Strategic Information Service Database

Manager. Umbrella organization for broadcasters in 49 European and Mediterranean countries.

International Telecommunication Union, Place des Nations, CH-1211 Geneva 20, Switzerland. Phone: (switchboard) +41 (22) 730-5111; (Broadcasting Services Division) +41 (22) 730-5933 or +41 (22) 730-6136; (Terrestrial Services Department) +41 (22) 730-5514. Fax: (general) +41 (22) 733 7256; (Broadcasting Services Division) +41 (22) 730 5785. Email: (schedules and reference tables) brmail@itu.int; (Broadcasting Services Division) jacques.fonteyne@itu.int or pham.hai@itu.int; (Terrestrial Services Department) nedialko.miltchev@itu.int. Web: www.itu.int. Contact: Jacques Fonteyne, Head of Broadcasting Services Division; Hai Pham, Broadcasting Services Division; or Nedialko Miltchev, Engineer, Terrestrial Services Department. The ITU is the world's official regulatory body for all telecommunication activities, including world band radio. Offers a wide range of official multilingual telecommunication publications in print and/or digital formats.

Radio Réveil, Paroles, Les Chapons 4, CH-2022 Bevaix, Switzerland. Phone: +41 (32) 846-1655. Fax: +41 (32) 846 2547. Email: contact@paroles.ch. Web (includes RealAudio): www.paroles.ch. An evangelical radio ministry, part of the larger Radio Réveil Paroles de Vie organization, which apart from broadcasting to much of Europe on longwave, mediumwave AM and FM, also targets an African audience via the shortwave facilities of Germany's T-Systems International (*see*).

SYRIA   World Time +2 (+3 midyear)

Radio Damascus, Syrian Radio and Television, P.O. Box 4702, Damascus, Syria. Phone: +963 (11) 221-7653. Fax: +963 (11) 222 2692. Email: tv-radio@net.sy; mostafab@scs-net.org. Web: www.rtv.gov.sy. Contact: Mr. Afaf, Director General; Mr. Mazen Al-Achhab, Head of Frequency Department; Adnan Salhab; Mr. Farid Shalash; or Mr. Mohamed Hamida. Free stickers, paper pennants and *The Syria Times* newspaper. Replies can be highly erratic, but as of late have been more regular, if sometimes slow.

TAIWAN—*see* CHINA (TAIWAN)

TAJIKISTAN   World Time +5

Radio Tajikistan, Chapaev Street 31, 734025 Dushanbe, Tajikistan; or English Service, International Service, Radio Tajikistan, P.O. Box 108, 734025 Dushanbe, Tajikistan. Phone: (Director) +992 (372) 210-877 or +992 (372) 277-417; (English Department) +992 (372) 277-417; (Ramazonov) +992 (372) 277-667 or +992 (372) 277-347. Fax: +992 (372) 211 198. Email: treng@td.silk.org. Web: http://radio.tojikiston.com. Contact: (administration) Mansur Sultanov, Director - Tajik Radio; Nasrullo Ramazonov, Foreign Relations Department. Correspondence in Russian or Tajik preferred. There is no official policy for verification of listeners' reports, so try sending reception reports and correspondence in English to the attention of Mr. Ramazonov, who is currently the sole English speaker at the station. Caution should be exercised when contacting him via email, as it is his personal account and he is charged for both incoming and outgoing mail. In addition, all email is routinely monitored and censored. Return postage (IRCs) helpful.

Tajik Radio, ul. Chapaeva 31, 734025 Dushanbe, Tajikistan. Contact information as for Radio Tajikistan, above.

TANZANIA   World Time +3

Radio Tanzania, Nyerere Road, P.O. Box 9191, Dar es Salaam, Tanzania. Phone: +255 (51) 860-760. Fax: +255 (51) 865 577. Email: radiotanzania@raha.com. Contact: (general) Abdul Ngarawa, Director of Broadcasting; Mrs. Edda Sanga, Controller of Programs; N. Nyamwocha; Ms. Penzi Nyamungumi, Head of English Service and International Relations Unit; or Ahmed Jongo, Producer, "Your Answer"; (technical) Taha Usi, Chief Engineer; or Emmanuel Mangula, Deputy Chief Engineer. Replies to correspondence in English.

Voice of Tanzania Zanzibar, Department of Broadcasting, Radio Tanzania Zanzibar, P.O. Box 2503, Zanzibar, Tanzania—if this address brings no reply, try P.O. Box 1178; (Ali Bakari Muombwa, personal address) P.O. Box 2068, Zanzibar, Tanzania. Phone: +255 (54) 231-088. Fax: + 255 (54) 257 207. Contact: (general) Seti Suleiman, Director; Ndaro Nyamwolha; Ali Bakari Muombwa; Abdulrah'man M. Said; or Kassim S. Kassim; (technical) Khalid Hassan Rajab, Shortwave Transmitter Engineer; Nassor M. Suleiman, Maintenance Engineer. $1 return postage helpful.

THAILAND   World Time +7

BBC World Service—Asia Relay Station, P.O. Box 20, Muang, Nakhon Sawan 60000, Thailand; (physical address) Mu 1, Tambon Ban Kaeng, Muang District, Nakhon Sawan 6000, Thailand. Phone: +66 5622-7275/6. Contact: Jaruwan Meesaurtong, Personal Assistant. Verifies reception reports.

Radio Thailand World Service, 236 Vibhavadi Rangsit Road, Din Daeng, Bangkok 10400, Thailand. Phone: +66 (2) 277-0943, +66 (2) 277-4022 X-2223. Phone/Fax: +66 (2) 277-6139, +66 (2) 274-9099. Email: (general) (Samosorn) amporns@mozart.inet.co.th. Web: www.hsk9.com. Contact: Mrs. Amporn Samosorn, Chief of External Services; Mr. Santi Charoenjai, Head of Shortwave Transmitter Station; or Patra Lamjiack. Free pennants. Replies irregularly, especially to those who persist.

TOGO   World Time exactly

Radio Lomé, B.P. 434, Lomé, Togo. Phone: +228 212-492. Return postage, $1 or 2 IRCs helpful. French preferred, but English accepted.

TUNISIA   World Time +1

Arab States Broadcasting Union, 6, rue des Enterpreneurs, Z.I. Ariana Cedex, TN-1080 Tunis, Tunisia. Phone: +216 (71) 703-855. Fax: +216 (71) 704 203. Email: a.suleiman@asbu.intl.tn. Contact: Abdelrahim Suleiman, Director, Technical Department; or Bassil Ahmad Zoubi, Head of Transmission Department.

⬛Radiodiffusion Télévision Tunisienne, 71 Avenue de la Liberté, TN-1070 Tunis, Tunisia. Phone: +216 (1) 801-177. Fax: +216 (1) 781 927. Email: info@radiotunis.com. Web: (includes RealAudio) www.radiotunis.com/news.html. Contact: Mongai Caffai, Director General; Mohamed Abdelkafi, Director; Kamel Cherif, Directeur; Masmoudi Mahmoud; Mr. Bechir Betteib, Director of Operations; or Smaoui Sadok, Le Sous-Directeur Technique. Replies irregularly and slowly to correspondence in French or Arabic. $1 helpful. For reception reports try: Le Chef de Service du Controle de la Récepcion de l'Office National de la Télédiffusion, O.N.T, Cité Ennassim I, Bourjel, B.P. 399, TN-1080 Tunis, Tunisia. Phone: +216 (1) 801-177. Fax: +216 (1) 781 927. Email: ont.@ati.tn. Contact: Abdesselem Slim.

TURKEY   World Time +2 (+3 midyear)

Meteorolojı Sesi Radyosu (Voice of Meteorology), T.C. Tarim Bakanliği, Devlet Meteorolojı İşleri, Genel Müdürlüğü, P.K. 401, Ankara, Turkey. Phone: +90 (312) 359-7545, X-281. Fax: +90 (312) 314 1196. Email: info@meteor.gov.tr; e-mail@meteor.gov.tr. Contact: Prof. Atila Dorum. Free tourist literature. Return postage helpful.

⬛Voice of Turkey (Turkish Radio-Television Corporation External Service)
MAIN OFFICE, NONTECHNICAL: TRT External Services Department, TRT Sitesi, Turan Güneş Blv., Or-An Çankaya, 06450 Ankara, Turkey; or P.K. 333, Yenişehir, 06443 Ankara, Turkey. Phone: (general) +90 (312) 490-9800/9801; (English desk) +90 (312) 490-9842. Fax: (English desk) +90 (312) 490 9846. Email: (English desk) englishdesk@trt.net.tr; (Spanish Service) espanol@trt.net.tr. Web: (includes Windows Media) www.trt.net.tr. *WARNING: This site can only be viewed using Microsoft's Internet Explorer, and is not easy to navigate.* Contact: (English and non-technical) Mr. Osman Erkan, Chief, English desk; or Michael Daventry, English Announcer. Technical correspondence, such as on reception quality should be directed to: Ms. Sedef Somaltin *(see next entry below).* On-air language courses offered in Arabic and German, but no printed course material. Free stickers, pennants, and tourist literature.
MAIN OFFICE, TECHNICAL (FOR EMIRLER AND ÇAKIRLAR TRANSMITTER SITES AND FOR FREQUENCY MANAGEMENT): TRT Teknik Yardimcilik, TRT Sitesi, Kat: 5/C, 06109 ORAN, Ankara, Turkey. Phone: +90 (312) 490-1732. Fax: +90 (312) 490 1733. Email: sedef.somaltin@trt.net.tr or kiymet.erdal@trt.net.tr. Contact: Mr. Haluk Buran, TRT Deputy Director General (Head of Engineering); Ms. Sedef Somaltin, Engineer & Frequency Manager; or Ms. Kiymet Erdal, Engineer & Frequency Manager. The HFBC seasonal schedules can be reached directly from: www.trt.net.tr/duyurufiles/vot.htm.
SAN FRANCISCO OFFICE, SCHEDULES: 2654 17th Avenue, San Francisco CA 94116 USA. Phone: +1 (415) 564-9968. Email: GPoppin@aol.com. Contact: George Poppin. This address, a volunteer office, only provides TRT schedules to listeners. All other correspondence should be sent directly to Ankara.

TURKMENISTAN   World Time +5

Radio Turkmenistan, National TV and Radio Broadcasting Company, Mollanepes St. 3, 744000 Ashgabat, Turkmenistan. Phone: +993 (12) 251-515. Fax: +993 (12) 251 421. Contact: (administration) Yu M. Pashaev, Deputy Chairman of State Television and Radio Company; (technical) G. Khanmamedov; Kakali Karayev, Chief of Technical Department; or A.A Armanklichev, Deputy Chief, Technical Department. This country is currently under strict censorship and media people are closely watched. A lot of foreign mail addressed to a particular person may attract the attention of the security services. Best is not to address your mail to particular individuals but to the station itself.

UGANDA   World Time +3

Radio Uganda
GENERAL OFFICE: P.O. Box 7142, Kampala, Uganda. Phone: +256 (41) 257-256. Fax: +256 (41) 256 888. Email: ugabro@infocom.co.ug. Contact: (general) Charles Byekwaso, Controller of Programmes; Machel Rachel Makibuuka; or Mrs. Florence Sewanyana, Head of Public Relations. $1 or return postage required. Replies infrequently and slowly. Correspon-

dence to this address has sometimes been returned with the annotation "storage period overdue"—presumably because the mail is not collected on a regular basis.

ENGINEERING DIVISION: P.O. Box 2038, Kampala, Uganda. Phone: +256 (41) 256-647. Contact: Leopold B. Lubega, Principal Broadcasting Engineer; or Rachel Nakibuuka, Secretary. Four IRCs or $2 required. Enclosing a self addressed envelope may also help to get a reply.

UKRAINE   World Time +2 (+3 midyear)

WARNING-MAIL THEFT: For the time being, letters to Ukrainian stations, especially containing funds or IRCs, are more likely to arrive safely if sent by registered mail.

Government Transmission Authority: RRT/Concern of Broadcasting, Radiocommunication and Television, 10 Dorogajtshaya St., 254112 Kyiv, Ukraine. Phone: +380 (44) 226-2260 or +380 (44) 444-6900. Fax: +380 (44) 440 8722; or +380 (44) 452 6784. Email: (Kurilov) ak@cbrt.freenet.kiev.ua. Contact: Mr. Mykola Kyryliuk, Deputy Director, Technical Operations & Management Centre; Alexej M. Kurilov; Alexey Karpenko; Alexander Serdiuk, Director, Technical Operations & Management Centre; Nikolai P. Kiriliuk, Head of Operative Management Service; or Mrs. Liudmila Deretskaya, Interpreter. This agency is responsible for choosing the frequencies used by Radio Ukraine International.

Radio Ukraine International, Kreshchatyk str., 26, 01001 Kyiv, Ukraine. Phone: (Ukrainian section) +380 (44) 229-1757; (English section) + 380 (44) 228-5484; (German section) +380 (44) 229-3134. Fax: (Ukrainian section) +380 (44) 228 7894; (English section) +380 (44) 228 7356. Email: (Ukrainian section) marinenko@nrcu.gov.ua; (English section, including QSL cards & complete schedules) vsru@nrcu.gov.ua; (reception reports) egorov@nrcu.gov.ua; mo@ukrradio.ru.kiev.ua; (German section) rui@nrcu.gov.ua; (Director) dykyi@nrcu.gov.ua. Web: (includes RealAudio) www.nrcu.gov.ua. Contact: (administration) Olexander Dykyi, Director; Inna Chichinadze, Deputy-Director; Mykola Marynenko, Editor-in-Chief, Ukrainian Section; Georgiy Mykhailov, Editor-in-Chief, German Section; or Zhanna Mescherska, Editor-in-Chief, English Section. Free stickers, calendars and Ukrainian stamps.

UNITED ARAB EMIRATES   World Time +4

Emirates Radio, P.O. Box 1695, Dubai, United Arab Emirates. Phone: +971 (4) 370-255. Fax: +971 (4) 374 111, +971 (4) 370 283 or +971 (4) 371 079. Email: radio@dubaitv.gov.ae; radio@dubaidd.org.ae. Web: www.dubaitv.gov.ae. Contact: Ms. Khulud Halaby; or Sameer Aga, Producer, "Cassette Club Cinarabic"; (technical) K.F. Fenner, Chief Engineer—Radio; or Ahmed Al Muhaideb, Assistant Controller, Engineering. Free pennants. Replies irregularly.

UNITED KINGDOM   World Time exactly (+1 midyear)

Adventist World Radio, 39 Brendon Street, London W1H 5HD, United Kingdom. Phone: +44 (1344) 401-401. Fax: +44 (1344) 401 419. Email: english@awr.org. Web: www.awr.org. Contact: Victor Hulbert, Director of English Language Service. All mail addressed to AWR and written in English is processed at this address. Also, *see* AWR listings under Germany, Guam, Kenya, Madagascar and USA.

BBC Monitoring, Caversham Park, Reading, Berkshire RG4 8TZ, United Kingdom. Phone: (switchboard) +44 (118) 948-6000; (Media Services—monitoring) +44 (118) 948-6261; Mar-

keting Department) +44 (118) 948-6289. Fax: (Media Services) +44 (118) 946 1993; (Marketing Department) +44 (118) 946 3823. Email: (Marketing Department) marketing@mon.bbc.co.uk; (Media Services/World Media) mediaservices@mon.bbc.co.uk; (publications and real time services) marketing@ mon.bbc.co.uk; or (director) chris.wescott@bbc.co.uk. Web: www.monitor.bbc.co.uk. Contact: (administration) Chris Wescott, Director of Monitoring; (Media Services) Chris McWhinnie, Editor "World Media," or Peter Feuilherade; (Publication Sales) Stephen Innes, Marketing. BBC Monitoring produces the weekly publication *World Media* which reports political, economic, legal, organisational, programming and technical developments in the world's electronic media. Its reports are based on material broadcast or published by radio and TV stations, news agencies, Websites and publications; other information issued but not necessarily broadcast by such sources and by other relevant bodies; and information obtained by BBC Monitoring's own observations of foreign media. Available on yearly subscription, costing £410.00. Price excludes postage overseas. *World Media* is also available online through the Internet or via a direct dial-in bulletin board at an annual cost of £425.00. VISA/MC/AX.

▣BBC World Service

MAIN OFFICE, NONTECHNICAL: Bush House, Strand, London WC2B 4PH, United Kingdom. Phone: (general) +44 (20) 7240-3456; (Press Office) +44 (20) 7557-2947/1; (International Marketing) +44 (20) 7557-1143. Fax: (Audience Relations) +44 (20) 7557 1258; ("Write On" listeners' letters program) +44 (20) 7436 2800; (Audience and Market Research) +44 (20) 7557 1254; (International Marketing) +44 (20) 7557 1254. Email: (general listener correspondence) worldservice.letters@ bbc.co.uk; ("Write On") writeon@bbc.co.uk. Web: (general, including RealAudio and Windows Media) www.bbc.co.uk/ worldservice/; (RealAudio) www.broadcast.com/bbc; (entertainment and information) www.beeb.com. Contact: Patrick Condren, Presenter, of "Write On"; Alan Booth, Controller, Marketing & Communications; Richard Sambrook, Director; Miles Palmer, Head of Business Development. Offers *BBC On Air* magazine (*see* below). Also, *see* Antigua, Ascension, Oman, Seychelles, Singapore and Thailand. Does not verify reception reports due to budget limitations.

SAN FRANCISCO OFFICE, SCHEDULES: 2654 17th Avenue, San Francisco CA 94116 USA. Phone: +1 (415) 564-9968. Email: GPoppin@aol.com. Contact: George Poppin. This address, a volunteer office, only provides BBC World Service schedules to listeners. All other correspondence should be sent directly to the main office in London.

TECHNICAL: See VT Merlin Communications.

BBC WORLD SERVICE—PUBLICATION AND PRODUCT SALES

BBC World Service Shop, Bush House Arcade, Strand, London WC2B 4PH, United Kingdom. Phone: +44 (20) 7557-2576. Fax: +44 (20) 7240 4811. Sells numerous audio/video cassettes (video, PAL/VHS only), publications, portable world band radios, T-shirts, sweatshirts and other BBC souvenirs available by mail order to UK addresses only.

"BBC On Air" (monthly program magazine), P.O. Box 76, Bush House, Strand, London WC2B 4PH, United Kingdom. Phone: +44 (20) 7557-2211 or +44 (20) 7557-2803. Fax: +44 (20) 7240 4899. Email: bbconair@bbc.co.uk. Web: www.bbconair.co.uk. Contact: Millie Patrick, Marketing Manager, BBC On Air magazine. Subscription $35 or £22 per year, and can be processed online. VISA/MC/AX/Barclay/EURO/Access, Postal Order, International Money Draft or cheque in pounds sterling or U.S. dollars.

BFBS—British Forces Broadcasting Service (when operating), Services Sound and Vision, Chalfont Grove, Narcot Lane, Chalfont St. Peter, Gerrards Cross, Buckinghamshire SL9 8TN, United Kingdom; or BFBS Worldwide, P.O. Box 903, Gerrards Cross, Buckinghamshire SL9 8TN, United Kingdom. Email: (general) marina.haward@bfbs.com. Web: (includes Windows Media) www.ssvc.com/bfbs. Normally only on satellite and FM, but hires additional shortwave facilities when British troops are fighting overseas.

Bible Voice Broadcasting
EUROPEAN OFFICE: P. O. Box 220, Leeds LS26 0WW, United Kingdom. Phone: +44 (1900) 827-355. Email: mail@biblevoice.org.
Web: www.biblevoice.org. Contact: Martin and Liz Thompson.
NORTH AMERICAN OFFICE: High Adventure Gospel Communication Ministries, P.O. Box 425, Station E, Toronto, ON M6H 4E3, Canada.
Phone: +1 (905) 898-5447; (toll-free, U.S. and Canada only) 1-800-550-4670. Email: highadventure@sympatico.ca. Contact: Don and Marty McLaughlin.
Bible Voice Broadcasting is a partnership between Bible Voice (U.K.) and High Adventure Gospel Communication Ministries (Canada).

Commonwealth Broadcasting Association, CBA Secretariat, 17 Fleet Street, London EC4Y 1AA, United Kingdom. Phone: +44 (20) 7583-5550. Fax: +44 (20) 7583 5549. Email: cba@cba.org.uk. Web: www.cba.org.uk. Publishes the annual *Commonwealth Broadcaster Directory* and the quarterly *Commonwealth Broadcaster* (online subscription form available).

Far East Broadcasting Association (FEBA), Ivy Arch Road, Worthing, West Sussex BN14 8BX, United Kingdom. Phone: +44 (1903) 237-281. Fax: +44 (1903) 205 294. Email: reception@feba.org.uk or (Richard Whittington) rwhittington@feba.org.uk. Web: www.feba.org.uk. Contact: Tony Ford, Director of Programming; or Richard Whittington, Schedule Engineer. Does not verify reception reports. Try sending reports to individual program producers (addresses are usually given over the air).

IBC-Tamil, 3 College Fields, Prince George's Road, Colliers Wood, London SW19 2PT, United Kingdom. Phone: +44 (20) 8100-0012. Fax: +44 (20) 8100 0003. Email: radio@ibctamil.co.uk. Web: (includes RealAudio) www.ibctamil.co.uk. Contact: A.C. Tarcisius, Managing Director; S. Shivaranjith, Manager; K. Pillai; or Public Relations Officer.

Radio Ezra (when operating). Fax: +44 (1642) 887 546. Email: info@radioezra.com. Web: www.radioezra.com. Contact: John D. Hill. Broadcasts irregularly via transmitters in the former Sovet Union. Welcomes reception reports via fax or email, and verifies with a QSL certificate. Describes itself as a "counter-missionary station."

VT Merlin Communications Limited, 20 Lincoln's Inn Fields, London WC2A 3ED, United Kingdom. Phone: +44 (20) 7969-0000. Fax: +44 (20) 7396 6223. Email: marketing@merlincommunications.com. Web: www.vtplc.com/merlin. Contact: Fiona Lowry, Chief Executive; Rory Maclachlan, Director of International Communications & Digital Services; Ciaran Fitzgerald, Head of Engineering & Operations; Richard Hurd, Head of Transmission Sales; Laura Jelf, Marketing Manager; or Anna Foakes, Marketing Department. Formerly known as Merlin Communications International. Does not verify reception reports.

Wales Radio International, Preseli Radio Productions, Pros Kairon, Crymych, Pembrokeshire, SA41 3QE, Wales, United Kingdom. Phone: +44 (1437) 563-361. Fax: +44 (1239) 831 390. Email: jenny@wri.cymru.net. Web: (includes MP3) http://wri.cymru.net. Contact: Jenny O'Brien. A weekly broadcast via the facilities of VT Merlin Communications (*see*, above).

World Radio Network, P.O. Box 1212, London SW8 2ZF, United Kingdom. Phone: +44 (20) 7896-9000. Fax: + 44 (20) 7896 9007. Email: (general) email@wrn.org; (Ayris) tim.ayris@wrn.org. Web: (includes RealAudio and Windows Media) www.wrn.org. Contact: Tim Ayris, Broadcast Sales Manager for WRN's networks. Provides Webcasts and program placements for international broadcasters.

UNITED NATIONS World Time –5 (–4 midyear)

Radio UNMEE
Web: (MP3) www.un.org/Depts/dpko/unmee/radio.htm; (UNMEE general information) www.un.org/Depts/dpko/unmee/unmeeN.htm.
NEW YORK OFFICE: Same contact details as United Nations Radio, below.
ERITREA OFFICE: P.O. Box 5805, Asmara, Eritrea. Phone: +291 (1) 151-908. Email: kellyb@un.org.
ETHIOPIA OFFICE: ECA Building, P.O. Box 3001, Addis Ababa, Ethiopia. Phone: +251 (1) 443-396. Email: walkera@un.org.
Radio service of the United Nations Mission in Eritrea and Ethiopia (UNMEE). Aired via facilities in the United Arab Emirates, and also relayed over Eritrea's national radio, Voice of the Broad Masses of Eritrea.

United Nations Radio, Secretariat Building, Room S-850-M, United Nations, New York NY 10017 USA; or write to the station over which UN Radio was heard. Phone: +1 (212) 963-5201. Fax: +1 (212) 963 1307. Email: (general) unradio@un.org; (comments on programs) audio-visual@un.org; (reception reports) smithd@un.org; or (Villanueva) villanueva1@un.org. Web: (general) www.un.org/av/radio; (RealAudio) www.wrn.org/ondemand/unitednations.html; www.internetbroadcast.com/un. Contact: (general) Sylvester E. Rowe, Chief, Radio and Video Service; or Ayman El-Amir, Chief, Radio Section, Department of Public Information; (reception reports) David Smith; or Trixie Villanueva; (technical and nontechnical) Sandra Guy, Secretary. Free stamps and *UN Frequency* publication. Reception reports (including those sent by email) are verified with a QSL card.
GENEVA OFFICE: Room G209, Palais des Nations, CH-1211 Geneva 10, Switzerland. Phone: +41 (22) 917-4222. Fax: +41 (22) 917 0123.
PARIS OFFICE: UNESCO Radio, 7 Place de Fontenoy, F-75007 Paris, France. Fax: +33 (1) 45 67 30 72. Contact: Erin Faherty, Executive Radio Producer.

URUGUAY World Time –3

Banda Oriental—*see* Radio Sarandí del Yí.
Emisora Ciudad de Montevideo, Canelones 2061, 11200 Montevideo, Uruguay. Phone: +598 (2) 402-0142 or +598 (2) 402-4242. Fax: +598 (2) 402 0700. Email: online form. Web: (includes MP3) www.emisoraciudaddemontevideo.com.uy. Contact: Aramazd Yizmeyian, Director General. Free stickers. Return postage helpful.
La Voz de Artigas (if reactivated), Av. Lecueder 483, 55000 Artigas, Uruguay. Phone: +598 (772) 2447 or +598 (772) 3445. Fax: +598 (772) 4744. Email: lavozart@adinet.com.uy. Contact: (general) Sra. Solange Murillo Ricciardi, Co-Propietario; or Luis Murillo; (technical) Roberto Murillo Ricciardi, Director. Free stickers and pennants. Replies to correspondence written in English, Spanish, French, Italian and Portuguese.

Radiodifusion Nacional—*see* S.O.D.R.E.

☞Radio Monte Carlo, Av. 18 de Julio 1224 piso 1, 11100 Montevideo, Uruguay. Phone: +598 (2) 901-4433 or +598 (2) 908-3987. Fax: +598 (2) 901 7762. Email: cx20@netgate.com.uy. Contact: Ana Ferreira de Errázquin, Secretaria, Departamento de Prensa de la Cooperativa de Radioemisoras; Gustavo Cirino, Jefe Técnico; Déborah Ibarra, Secretaria; Emilia Sánchez Vega, Secretaria; or Ulises Graceras. Correspondence in Spanish preferred.

☞Radio Oriental (when operating), Calle Cerrito 475, 11000 Montevideo, Uruguay. Phone/Fax: +598 (2) 916-1130. Email: (Management) director@oriental.com.uy; (general) info@oriental.com.uy, or secretaria@oriental.com.uy. Web: www.oriental.com.uy. Contact: Presbítero Jorge Techera, Director; (technical) José A. Porro, Technician. Correspondence in Spanish preferred. Formerly a commercial station, Radio Oriental was purchased by the Uruguayan Catholic Church in 2003.

Radio Sarandí del Yí (when operating), Sarandí 328, 97100 Sarandí del Yí, Uruguay. Phone/Fax: +598 (367) 9155. Email: (owner) norasan@adinet.com.uy. Contact: Nora San Martín de Porro, Propietaria.

Radio Universo (when activated), Ferrer 1265, 27000 Castillos, Dpto. de Rocha, Uruguay. Email: am1480@ adinet.com.uy. Contact: Juan Héber Brañas, Propietario. Currently only on 1480 kHz mediumwave AM, but has been granted a license to operate on shortwave.

S.O.D.R.E., Radiodifusión Nacional, Casilla 1412, 11000 Montevideo, Uruguay. Phone: +598 (2) 916-1933; (technical) +598 (2) 915-7865. Email: info@sodre.gub.uy. Web: www.sodre.gub.uy. Contact: (management) Julio César Ocampos, Director de Radiodifusión Nacional; (technical) José Cuello, División Técnica Radio. Reception reports may also be sent to the "Radioactividades" program (*see*, below).

MEDIA PROGRAM: "Radioactividades," Casilla 7011, 11000 Montevideo, Uruguay. Fax: +598 (2) 575 4640. Email: radioact@chasque.apc.org. Web: www.chasque.org/radioact.

USA World Time −4 Atlantic, including Puerto Rico and Virgin Islands; −5 (−4 midyear) Eastern, excluding Indiana; −5 Indiana, except northwest and southwest portions; −6 (−5 midyear) Central, including northwest and southwest Indiana; −7 (−6 midyear) Mountain, except Arizona; −7 Arizona; −8 (−7 midyear) Pacific; −9 (−8 midyear) Alaska, except Aleutian Islands; −10 (−9 midyear) Aleutian Islands; −10 Hawaii; −11 Samoa

☞Adventist World Radio

HEADQUARTERS: 12501 Old Columbia Pike, Silver Spring MD 20904 USA. Email: english@awr.org. Web: (includes RealAudio and Windows Media) www.awr.org; (Chinese service, English/Chinese text) www.vohc.com—worth a visit just for the graphics. Send all letters and reception reports to: AWR, 39 Brendon Street, London W1H 5HD, United Kingdom.

INTERNATIONAL RELATIONS: Box 29235, Indianapolis IN 46229 USA. Phone/Fax: +1 (317) 891-8540. Email: adrian@awr.org. Contact: Dr. Adrian M. Peterson, International Relations Coordinator. Provides publications with regular news releases and technical information. Sometimes issues special verification cards. QSL stamps and certificates also available from this address in return for reception reports.

OPERATIONS AND ENGINEERING: 3060 Noble Court, Boulder CO 80301 USA. Phone: +1 (303) 448-1875. Fax: +1 (303) 998 0259. Email: hodgson@awr.org. Contact: Greg Hodgson

DX PROGRAM: "Wavescan," prepared by Adrian Peterson; aired on all AWR facilities and other stations. Also available in RealAudio at the AWR Website, www.awr.org. Also, *see* AWR listings under Germany, Guam, Kenya, Madagascar and United Kingdom.

☞AFRTS-American Forces Radio and Television Service (Shortwave), Naval Media Center, NDW Anacostia Annex, 2713 Mitscher Road SW, Washington DC 20373-5819 USA. For verification of reception, be sure to mark the envelope, "Attn: Short Wave Reception Reports." Email: (verifications) qsl@mediacen.navy.mil. Web: http://myafn.dodmedia.osd.mil/radio/shortwave; (AFRTS parent organization) www.afrts.osd.mil; (2-minute news clips in RealAudio): www.defenselink.mil/news/radio/; (Naval Media Center) www.mediacen.navy.mil. The Naval Media Center is responsible for all AFRTS broadcasts aired on shortwave.

FLORIDA ADDRESS: NCTS-Jacksonville-Detachment Key West, Building A 1004, Naval Air Station Boca Chica, Key West, FL 33040 USA.

Aurora Communications, Mile 129, Sterling Highway, Ninilchik, Alaska, USA. Plans to commence broadcasts to Russia when circumstances allow.

Broadcasting Board of Governors (BBG), 330 Independence Avenue SW, Room 3360, Washington DC 20237 USA. Phone: +1 (202) 619-2538. Fax: +1 (202) 619 1241. Email: pubaff@ibb.gov. Web: www.bbg.gov. Contact: Kathleen Harrington, Public Relations. The BBG, created in 1994 and headed by nine members nominated by the President, is the overseeing agency for all official non-military United States international broadcasting operations, including the VOA, RFE-RL, Radio Martí and Radio Free Asia.

☞Family Radio Worldwide:

NONTECHNICAL: Family Stations, Inc., 290 Hegenberger Road, Oakland CA 94621-1436 USA; or P.O. Box 2140 Oakland CA 94621-9985 USA. Phone: (general) +1 (510) 568-6200; (toll-free, U.S. only) 1-800-543-1495; (engineering) +1 (510) 568-6200 ext. 240. Fax: (main office) +1 (510) 568 6200; (engineering) +1 (510) 562 1023. Email: (general) famradio@familyradio.com; (international department) international@familyradio.com; (shortwave program schedules) shortwave@familyradio.com. Web: (includes RealAudio and MP3) www.familyradio.com. Contact: (general) Harold Camping, General Manager; or David Hoff, Manager of International Department. Free gospel tracts (33 languages), books, booklets, quarterly *Family Radio News* magazine and frequency schedule. 2 IRCs helpful.

TECHNICAL: WYFR—Family Radio, 10400 NW 240th Street, Okeechobee FL 34972 USA. Phone: +1 (863) 763-0281. Fax: +1 (863) 763 8867. Email: (technical) fsiyfr@okeechobee.com; (frequency schedule) wyfr@okeechobee.com. Contact: Dan Elyea, Engineering Manager; or Edward F. Dearborn, Chief Operator; (frequency schedule) Evelyn Marcy.

FEBC Radio International

INTERNATIONAL HEADQUARTERS: Far East Broadcasting Company, Inc., P.O. Box 1, La Mirada CA 90637 USA. Phone: +1 (310) 947-4651. Fax: +1 (310) 943 0160. Email: febc@febc.org. Web: www.febc.org. Operates world band stations in the Northern Mariana Islands, the Philippines and the Seychelles. Does not verify reception reports from this address.

RUSSIAN OFFICE: P.O. Box 2128, Khabarovsk 680020, Russia. Email: khabarovsk@febc.org.

Federal Communications Commission, 445 12th Street SW, Washington DC 20554 USA. Phone: +1 (202) 418-0190; (toll-free, U.S. only) 1-888-225-5322. Fax: +1 (202) 418 0232. Email:

(general information and inquiries) fccinfo@fcc.gov; (Freedom of Information Act requests) FOIA@fcc.gov; (Polzin) tpolzin@fcc.gov. Web: (general) www.fcc.gov; (high frequency operating schedules) www.fcc.gov/ib/pnd/neg/hf_web/seasons.html; (FTP) ftp://ftp.fcc.gov/pub. Contact: (International Bureau, technical) Thomas E. Polzin.

📻Fundamental Broadcasting Network, Grace Missionary Baptist Church, 520 Roberts Road, Newport NC 28570 USA. Phone: +1 (252) 223-6088; (toll-free, U.S. only) 1-800-245-9685; (Robinson) +1 (252) 223-4600. Email: (general) fbn@clis.com; (technical, David Robinson) davidwr@clis.com. Web: (includes MP3) www.fbnradio.com. Contact: Pastor Clyde Eborn; (technical) David Robinson, Chief Engineer. Verifies reception reports if an IRC or (within the USA) an SASE is included. Accepts email reports. A religious and educational non-commercial broadcasting network which operates sister stations WBOH and WTJC.

Gospel for Asia, 1800 Golden Trail Court, Carrollton TX 75010 USA. Phone: +1 (972) 300-7777; (toll-free, U.S. only) 1-800-946-2742. Email: info@gfa.org. Web: www.gfa.org. Transmits via facilities in Jülich, Germany, and Dhabayya, U.A.E.
CALIFORNIA OFFICE: P.O. Box 1210 Somis, California 93066 USA. Email: gfaradio@mygfa.org. Contact: Rhonda Penland, Coordinator.
CANADIAN OFFICE: 245 King Street E., Stoney Creek, ON L8G 1L9, Canada. Phone: +1 (905) 662-2101. Email: infocanada@gfa.org.
UNITED KINGDOM OFFICE: P.O. Box 166, York YO10 5WA, United Kingdom. Phone: +44 (1904) 643-233. Email: infouk@gfa.org.

High Adventure Ministries
MAIN OFFICE: P.O. Box 197569, Louisville KY 40259 USA. Phone: +1 (502) 968-7550; (toll-free, U.S. only) 1-800-517-4673. Fax: +1 (502) 968 7580. Email: mail@highadventure.net. Web: www.highadventure.net. Contact: Jackie Yockey.
MIDDLE EAST OFFICE: P.O. Box 53379, Limassol, Cyprus. Phone: +972 (9) 767-0835. Fax: +972 (9) 765 1407. Email: gronberg@zahav.net.il. Contact: Isaac Gronberg.
SINGAPORE OFFICE, NONTECHNICAL: 265B/C South Bridge Road - Eu Yan Sang Annexe, Singapore 058814, Singapore. Phone: + 65 221-2054. Fax: +65 221 2059. Email: csarch@singnet.com.sg. Contact: Cyril Seah.

International Broadcasting Bureau (IBB)—Reports to the Broadcasting Board of Governors (see), and includes, among others, the Voice of America, RFE-RL, Radio Martí and Radio Free Asia. IBB Engineering (Office of Engineering and Technical Operations) provides broadcast services for these stations. Contact: (administration) Brian Conniff, Director; or Joseph O'Connell, Director of External Affairs. Web: www.ibb.gov/ibbpage.html.
FREQUENCY AND MONITORING OFFICE, TECHNICAL:
IBB/EOF: Spectrum Management Division, International Broadcasting Bureau (IBB), Room 4611 Cohen Bldg., 330 Independence Avenue SW, Washington DC 20237 USA. Phone: +1 (202) 619-1669. Fax: +1 (202) 619 1680. Email: (scheduling) dferguson@ibb.gov; (monitoring) bw@his.com. Web: (general) http://monitor.ibb.gov; (email reception report form) http://monitor.ibb.gov/now_you_try_it.html. Contact: Dan Ferguson (dferguson@ibb.gov); or Bill Whitacre (bw@his.com).

KAIJ
ADMINISTRATION OFFICE: Two-if-by-Sea Broadcasting Co., 22720 SE 410th St., Enumclaw WA 89022 USA. Phone/Fax: (Mike Parker, California) +1 (818) 606-1254; (Washington State office, if and when operating) +1 (206) 825 4517. Contact: Mike Parker (mark envelope, "please forward"). Relays programs of Dr. Gene Scott's University Network (see). Replies occasionally.
STUDIO: Faith Center, 1615 S. Glendale Avenue, Glendale CA 91025 USA. Phone: +1 (818) 246-8121. Contact: Dr. Gene Scott, President.
TRANSMITTER SITE: RR#3 Box 120, Frisco TX 75034 USA; or Highway 380 West, Prosper TX 75078 USA (physical location: Highway 380, 3.6 miles west of State Rt. 289, near Denton TX; transmitters and antennas located on Belt Line Road along the lake in Coppell TX). Phone: +1 (972) 346-2758. Contact: Walt Green or Fred Bithell. Station encourages mail to be sent to the administration office, which seldom replies, or the studio (see above).

KIMF (under construction): International Fellowship of Churches, Radio Station KIMF, 9746 6th Street, Rancho Cucamonga CA 91730 USA.
ALTERNATIVE ADDRESS: IMF World Missions, P.O. Box 6321, San Bernardino CA 92412, USA. Phone +1 (909) 370-4515. Fax: +1 (909) 370 4862. Email: jkpimf@msn.com. Contact: Dr. James K. Planck, President.
TRANSMITTER SITE: Intersection Spring Mesa Road & State Road 506, Pinon NM, USA.

KJES—King Jesus Eternal Savior

STATION: The Lord's Ranch, 230 High Valley Road, Vado NM 88072 USA. Phone: +1 (505) 233-2090. Fax: +1 (505) 233 3019. Email: KJES@aol.com. Contact: Michael Reuter, Manager. $1 or return postage appreciated.

SPONSORING ORGANIZATION: Our Lady's Youth Center, P.O. Box 1422, El Paso TX 79948 USA. Phone: +1 (915) 533-9122.

KNLS—New Life Station

OPERATIONS CENTER: World Christian Broadcasting, 605 Bradley Ct., Franklin TN 37067 USA (letters sent to the Alaska transmitter site are usually forwarded to Franklin). Phone: +1 (615) 371-8707 ext.140. Fax: +1 (615) 371 8791. Email: knls@aol.com. Web: (includes sample programs in RealAudio) www.knls.org. Contact: (general) Dale R. Ward, Executive Producer; L. Wesley Jones, Director of Follow-Up Teaching; or Rob Scobey, Senior Producer, English Language Service; (technical) F.M. Perry, Frequency Coordinator. Free *Alaska Calling!* newsletter and station pennants. Free spiritual literature and bibles in Russian, Mandarin and English. Free Alaska books, tapes, postcards and cloth patches. Two free DX books for beginners. Special, individually numbered, limited edition, verification cards issued for each new transmission period to the first 200 listeners providing confirmed reception reports. Stamp and postcard exchange. Return postage appreciated.

TRANSMITTER SITE: P.O. Box 473, Anchor Point AK 99556 USA. Phone: +1 (907) 235-8262. Fax: +1 (907) 235 2326. Contact: (technical) Kevin Chambers, Chief Engineer.

⬛KRSI—Radio Sedaye Iran (when operating), Suite 207, 9744 Wilshire Boulevard, Beverly Hills CA 90212-1812 USA. Phone: +1 (310) 888-2818. Fax: +1 (310) 859 8444. Web: (includes Windows Media and online email form) www.krsi.net. Normally operates via a closed broadcasting system and the Internet, but started shortwave broadcasts during 2000. Hires airtime via facilities in Moldova or France (occasionally both).

⬛KTBN—Trinity Broadcasting Network:

GENERAL CORRESPONDENCE: P.O. Box A, Santa Ana CA 92711 USA. Phone: +1 (714) 832-2950. Fax: +1 (714) 730 0661. Email: comments@tbn.org. Web: (Trinity Broadcasting Network, including RealAudio) www.tbn.org; (KTBN) www.tbn.org/watch/how2watch/sw_radio/index.htm. Contact: Dr. Paul F. Crouch, Managing Director. Monthly TBN newsletter. Free booklets, stickers and small souvenirs sometimes available.

TECHNICAL CORRESPONDENCE: Engineering/QSL Department, 2442 Michelle Drive, Tustin CA 92780-7015 USA. Phone: +1 (714) 665-2145. Fax: +1 (714) 730 0661. Email: lreyes@tbn.org. Contact: Laura Reyes, QSL Manager; or Ben Miller, Vice President, Engineering. Responds to reception reports. Write to: Trinity Broadcasting Network, Attention: Superpower KTBN Radio QSL Manager, Laura Reyes, 2442 Michelle Drive, Tustin CA 92780 USA. Return postage (IRC or SASE) helpful. Although a California operation, KTBN's shortwave transmitter is located at Salt Lake City, Utah.

KVOH—La Voz de Restauración, 4409 W. Adams Blvd., Los Angeles CA 90016 USA. Phone: +1 (323) 766-2454. Email: informacion@restauracion.com. Web: (includes Windows Media) www.restauracion.com.

⬛KWHR-World Harvest Radio:

ADMINISTRATION OFFICE: See World Harvest Radio.

TRANSMITTER: Although located 6 1/2 miles southwest of Naalehu, 8 miles north of South Cape, and 2000 feet west of South Point (Ka La) Road (the antennas are easily visible from this road) on Big Island, Hawaii, the operators of this rural transmitter site maintain no post office box in or near Naalehu, and their telephone number is unlisted, Best bet is to contact

them via their administration office (*see* WHRI), or to drive in unannounced (it's just off South Point Road) the next time you vacation on Big Island.

Leading The Way, P.O. Box 20100, Atlanta GA 30325 USA. Phone: +1 (404) 841-0100. Email: mholler@leadingtheway.org. Web: www.leadingtheway.org; www.oneplace.com/ministries/leading_the_way. Broadcasts via transmitters in the United Kingdom.

Leinwoll (Stanley)—Telecommunication Consultant, 305 E. 86th Street, Suite 21S-W, New York NY 10028 USA. Phone: +1 (212) 987-0456. Fax: +1 (212) 987 3532. Email: stanL00011@aol.com. Contact: Stanley Leinwoll, President. This firm provides frequency management and other engineering services for some private U.S. world band stations, but does not correspond with the general public.

National Association of Shortwave Broadcasters, 10400 NW 20th Street, Okeechobee, FL 34972 USA; P.O. Box 8700, Cary NC 27512 USA. Phone: +1 (863) 763-0281. Fax: +1 (863) 763 8867. Email: nasbmem@rocketmail.com. Web: www.shortwave.org. Contact: Dan Elyea, Secretary-Treasurer. Association of most private U.S. world band stations, as well as a group of other international broadcasters, equipment manufacturers and organizations related to shortwave broadcasting. Includes committees on various subjects, such as digital shortwave radio. Interfaces with the Federal Communications Commission's International Bureau and other broadcasting-related organizations to advance the interests of its members. Publishes *NASB Newsletter* for members and associates and is available for free via their website. Annual one-day convention held in Washington DC early each spring; non-members wishing to attend should contact the Secretary-Treasurer in advance; convention fee typically $50 per person.

⬛Overcomer Ministry ("Voice of the Last Day Prophet of God"), P.O. Box 691, Walterboro SC 29488 USA. Phone: (0900-1700 local time, Sunday through Friday) +1 (803) 538-3892. Email: (general) brotherstair@overcomerministry.com; (reception reports) overcomer@overcomerministry.com. Web: (includes RealAudio) www.overcomerministry.com. Contact: Brother R.G. Stair. Sample "Overcomer" newsletter and various pamphlets free upon request. Sells a Sangean shortwave radio for $50, plus other items of equipment and various publications at appropriate prices. Via T-Systems International, Germany, and WWCR, USA.

Pan American Broadcasting, 20410 Town Center Lane #200, Cupertino CA 95014 USA. Phone: +1 (408) 996-2033; (toll-free, U.S. only) 1-800-726-2620. Fax: +1 (408) 252 6855. Email: info@panambc.com; pabcomain@aol.com; (Bernald) gbernald@panambc.com. Web: www.panambc.com. Contact: (listener correspondence) Terry Kraemer; (general) Carmen Jung, Office and Sales Administrator; or Gene Bernald. $1 in cash or unused U.S. stamps, or 2 IRCs, required for reply. Operates transmitters in Equatorial Guinea (*see*) and hires airtime over a number of world band stations, plus T-Systems International facilities in Germany.

Radio Africa International (if reactivated), General Board of Global Ministries, United Methodist Church, 475 Riverside Drive, New York NY 10115 USA. Phone: (toll-free, U.S. only) 1-800-862-4246; (Media Contact) +1 (212) 870 3803. Fax: +1 (212) 870 3748. Email: radio@gbgm-umc.org. Web: (GBGM-UMC parent organization) www.gbgm-umc.org. Contact: Donna Niemann, Executive Producer; Raphael Mbadinga, Senior Producer. Sells calendars, magazines, books, videos and CDs of Christian music. Transmits via Jülich, Germany, when active.

Radio Amani, 41-36 College Point Blvd., Suite #2A, Flushing NY 11355 USA. Phone: +1 (718) 461-6799. Fax: +1 (718) 886 8616. Email: info@radioamani.com. Web: (includes MP3) www.radioamani.com.

AFGHANISTAN PEACE ASSOCIATION (APA) PARENT ORGANIZA-TION: Same postal address and phone/fax numbers as Radio Amani. Email: info@afghanistanpeace.com. Web: www.afghanistanpeace.com.

Radio Farda—a joint venture between Radio Free Europe-Radio Liberty (*see*) and the Voice of America (*see*). Email: comment@radiofarda.com. Web: (includes RealAudio and online email form) www.radiofarda.com. Broadcasts a mix of news, information and popular Iranian and western music to younger audiences in Iran.

Radio Free Afghanistan—a service of Radio Free Europe-Radio Liberty (*see*). Web: (includes RealAudio) www.azadiradio.org.

Radio Free Asia, Suite 300, 2025 M Street NW, Washington DC 20036 USA. Phone: (general) +1 (202) 530-4900; (president) +1 (202) 457-4901;(vice president of editorial) +1 (202) 530-4907; (vice-president of administration) +1 (202) 530-4902); (chief technology officer) +1 (202) 530-4958; (manager of production support) +1 (202) 530-4943. Fax: +1 (202) 530 7794 or +1 (202) 721 7468. Email: (individuals) the format is lastnameinitial@rfa.org; so to reach, say the CTO, David Baden, it would be badend@rfa.org; (language sections) the format is language@rfa.org; so to contact, say, the Vietnamese section, address your message to vietnamese@rfa.org; (general) communications@rfa.org; (reception reports) qsl@rfa.org. Web: (includes AudioActive and RealAudio) www.rfa.org; (automated reception report system) www.techweb.rfa.org. Contact: (administration) Richard Richter, President; or Daniel Southerland, Vice President of Editorial; Libby Liu, Vice-President of Administration; (technical) David M. Baden, Chief Technology Officer; A. J. Janitschek, Manager of Production Support. RFA, originally created in 1996 as the Asia Pacific Network, is funded as a private nonprofit U.S. corporation by a grant from the Broadcasting Board of Governors (*see*).

HONG KONG OFFICE: Room 904, Mass Mutal Tower, 38 Gloucester Road, Wanchai, Hong Kong, China.

THAILAND OFFICE: Maxim House, 112 Witthayu Road, Pathomwan, Bangkok 10330, Thailand.

Radio Free Europe-Radio Liberty/RFE-RL

PRAGUE HEADQUARTERS: Vinohradská 1, 110 00 Prague 1, Czech Republic. Phone: +420 (2) 2112-1111; (president) +420 (2) 2112-3000; (news desk) +420 (2) 2112-3629; (public relations) +420 (2) 2112-3012; (technical operations) +420 (2) 2112-3700; (broadcast operations) +420 (2) 2112-3550; (affiliate relations). +420 (2) 2112-2539. Fax: +420 (2) 2112 3013; (president) +420 (2) 2112 3002; (news desk) +420 (2) 2112 3613; (public relations) +420 (2) 2112 2995; (technical operations) +420 (2) 2112 3702; (broadcast operations) +420 (2) 2112 3540; (affiliate operations) +420 (2) 2112 4563. Email: the format is lastnameinitial@rferl.org; so to reach, say, Luke Springer, it would be springerl@rferl.org. Web: (general, including RealAudio) www.rferl.org; (broadcast services) www.rferl.org/bd. Contact: Thomas A. Dine, President; Kestutis Girnius, Managing Editor, News and Current Affairs; Luke Springer, Deputy Director, Technology; Jana Horakova, Public Relations Coordinator; Uldis Grava, Marketing Director; or Christopher Carzoli, Broadcast Operations Director.

WASHINGTON OFFICE: 1201 Connecticut Avenue NW, Washington DC 20036 USA. Phone: +1 (202) 457-6900; (newsdesk) +1 (202) 457-6950; (technical) +1 (202) 457-6963. Fax: +1 (202)

Mother Angelica, the foundress of EWTN Global Catholic Network. EWTN

457 6992; (news desk) +1 (202) 457 6997; (technical) +1 (202) 457 6913. Email and Web: *see* above. Contact: Jane Lester, Secretary of the Corporation; Ken Morehouse, Director of Technology Systems; or Paul Goble, Director of Communications; (news) Oleh Zwadiuk, Washington Bureau Chief. A private nonprofit corporation funded by a grant from the Broadcasting Board of Governors, RFE/RL broadcasts in 21 languages (but not English) from transmission facilities now part of the International Broadcasting Bureau (IBB), *see*.

Radio Martí, Office of Cuba Broadcasting, 4201 N.W. 77th Avenue, Miami FL 33166 USA. Phone: +1 (305) 437-7000; (Director) +1 (305) 437-7117; (Technical Operations) +1 (305) 437-7051. Fax: +1 (305) 437 7016. Email: martinoticias@ocb.ibb.gov. Web: (includes RealAudio and Windows Media) www.martinoticias.com/radio.asp. Contact: (technical) Michael Pallone, Director, Engineering and Technical Operations; or Tom Warden, Chief of Radio Operations.

Sudan Radio Service, Education Development Center, 1000 Potomac Street NW, Suite 350, Washington DC 20007 USA. Phone: +1 (202) 572-3700. Fax: +1 (202) 223 4059. Email: srs@edc.org; (Groce) jgroce@edc.org or jgroce@sudanradio.org. (Laflin) mlaflin@edc.org. Web: (includes Windows Media) www.sudanradio.org. Contact: Jeremy Groce, Radio Programming Advisor, EDC; or Mike Laflin, Director, EDC. Web: (EDC parent organization) www.edc.org.

PRODUCTION STUDIOS, KENYA: c/o EDC, P.O. Box 4392, 00100 Nairobi Kenya. Phone: +254 (20) 570-906 or +254 (20) 572-2269. Fax: +254 (20) 576 520. Contact: Mike Kuenzli.

Trans World Radio, International Headquarters, P.O. Box 8700, Cary NC 27512-8700 USA. Phone: +1 (919) 460-3700; (toll-free, U.S. only) 1-800-456-7897. Fax: +1 (919) 460 3702. Email: info2@twr.org. Web: (includes sample programs in

RealAudio) www.gospelcom.net/twr. Contact: (general) Jon Vaught, Public Relations; Richard Greene, Director, Public Relations; Joe Fort, Director, Broadcaster Relations; or Bill Danick; (technical) Glenn W. Sink, Assistant Vice President, International Operations. Free "Towers to Eternity" publication for those living in the U.S. Technical correspondence should be sent to the office nearest the country where the transmitter is located—Guam, Monaco or Swaziland. For information on offices in Asia and Australasia, refer to the entry under "Guam." *CANADIAN OFFICE:* P.O. Box 444, Niagara Falls ON, L2E 6T8 Canada. Web: http://twrcan.ca.

University Network, P.O. Box 1, Los Angeles CA 90053 USA. Phone: (toll-free, U.S. only) 1-800-338-3030. Web: (includes RealAudio and Windows Media) www.drgenescott.com. Transmits over KAIJ and WWCR (USA); Caribbean Beacon (Anguilla, West Indies); the former AWR facilities in Cahuita, Costa Rica; and a transmitter in Samara, Russia. Does not verify reception reports.

USA Radio Network, 2290 Springlake Road, Suite 107, Dallas TX 75234 USA. Toll-free phone (.U.S. only) 1-800-829-8111. Email: (complaints/suggestions) tim@usaradio.com; (technical) david@usaradio.com. Web: (includes RealAudio and MP3) www.usaradio.com. Contact: (general) Tim Maddoux. Does not broadcast direct on shortwave, but some of its news and other programs are heard via U.S. stations KWHR, WHRA, WHRI and WWCR.

Voice of America—All Transmitter Locations
MAIN OFFICE: 330 Independence Avenue SW, Washington DC 20237 USA. If contacting the VOA directly is impractical, write c/o the American Embassy in your country. Phone: (Office of Public Affairs) +1 (202) 401-7000; (Audience Mail Division) +1 (202) 619-2770; (Africa Division) +1 (202) 619-1666 or +1 (202) 619-2879; (Office of Research) +1 (202) 619-4965; (administration) +1 (202) 619-1088. Fax: (Office of Public Affairs) +1 (202) 619 1241; (Africa Division) +1 (202) 619 1664; (Audience Mail Division and Office of Research) +1 (202) 619 0211. Email: (general business) pubaff@voa.gov; (reception reports and schedule requests) letters@voa.gov; (automatic reply back email schedules for "VOA News Now") schedule@voanews.com or cwschedule@voa.gov; ("VOA News Now") newsnow@voanews.com; (VOA Special English) special@voa.gov; (VOA English to Africa) africanews@voa.gov. Web: (includes RealAudio) www.voa.gov. Contact: Mrs. Betty Lacy Thompson, Chief, Audience Mail Division, B/K. G759A Cohen; Larry James, Director, English Programs Division; Leo Sarkisian; Rita Rochelle, Africa Division; George Mackenzie, Audience Research Officer; (reception reports) Mrs. Irene Greene, QSL Desk, Audience Mail Division, Room G-759-C. Free stickers and calendars. If you're an American and miffed because you can't receive these goodies from the VOA, don't blame the station—they're only following the law. The VOA occasionally hosts international broadcasting conventions, and as of 1996 has been accepting limited supplemental funding from the U.S. Agency for International Development (AID). Also, *see* Botswana, Greece, Morocco, Philippines, São Tomé e Príncipe, Sri Lanka and Thailand.

Voice of America/IBB—Delano Relay Station, Rt. 1, Box 1350, Delano CA 93215 USA; (physical address) 11015 Melcher Road, Delano CA 93215 USA. Phone: +1 (805) 725-0150. Fax: +1 (805) 725 6511. Email: (Vodenik) jvodenik@del.ibb.gov, k9hsp@juno.com. Contact: (technical) John Vodenik, Engineer. Photos of this facility can be seen at the following Website: www.hawkins.pair.com/voadelano.shtml. Nontechnical correspondence should be sent to the VOA address in Washington.

Voice of America/IBB—Greenville Relay Station, P.O. Box 1826, Greenville NC 27834 USA. Phone: (site A) +1 (252) 752-7115 or (site B) +1 (252) 752-7181. Fax: (site A) +1 (252) 758 8742 or (site B) +1 (252) 752 5959. Contact: (technical) Bruce Hunter, Manager; or Glenn Ruckleson. Nontechnical correspondence should be sent to the VOA address in Washington.

WBCQ—"The Planet," 97 High Street, Kennebunk ME 04043 USA. Phone: +1 (207) 985-7547; (transmitter site, urgent technical matters only) +1 (207) 538-9180. Email: wbcq@gwi.net. Web: http://theplanet.wbcq.net. Contact: Allan H. Weiner, Owner; or Elayne Star, Assistant Manager. Verifies reception reports if 1 IRC or (within USA) an SASE is included.

WBOH—*see* Fundamental Broadcasting Network.

WEWN—EWTN Global Catholic Radio, 5817 Old Leeds Rd., Birmingham AL 35210 USA.

Phone: (general) +1 (205) 271-2900; (Station Manager) +1 (205) 271-2943; (Chief Engineer) +1 (205) 271-2959; (Marketing Manager) +1 (205) 271-2982; (Program Director, English) +1 (205) 271-2944; (Program Director, Spanish) +1 (205) 271-2900 ext. 2073; (Frequency Manager) +1 (205) 795-5779. Fax: (general) +1 (205) 271 2926; (Marketing) +1 (205) 271 2925; (Engineering and Frequency Management) +1 (205) 271 2953. Email: (general) wewn@ewtn.com; (technical) radio@ewtn.com; (Spanish) rcm@ewtn.com. To contact individuals, the format is initiallastname@ewtn.com; so to reach, say, Thom Price, it would be tprice@ewtn.com. Web: (includes RealAudio and online reception-report form) www.ewtn.com/wewn. Contact: (general) Thom Price, Director of English Programming; or Doug Archer, Director of Spanish Programming; (marketing) Bernard Lockhart, Radio Marketing Manager; (administration) William Steltemeier, President; or Frank Leurck, Station Manager; (technical) Terry Borders, Vice President Engineering; Glen Tapley, Frequency Manager; or Dennis Dempsey, Chief Engineer. Listener correspondence welcomed; responds to correspondence on-air and by mail. Free bumper stickers, program schedules and (sometimes) other booklets or publications. Sells numerous religious books, CDs, audio and video cassettes, T-shirts, sweatshirts and various other religious articles; list available upon request (VISA/MC). IRC or return postage appreciated for correspondence. Although a Catholic entity, WEWN is not an official station of the Vatican, which operates its own Vatican Radio (*see*). Rather, WEWN reflects the activities of Mother M. Angelica and the Eternal Word Foundation, Inc. Donations and bequests accepted by the Eternal Word Foundation.
CANADA ADDRESS: P.O. Box 157, Station A, Etobicoke, Ontario, MC9C 4V2, Canada. Phone: +1 (205) 271-2900.

WHRA-World Harvest Radio:
ADMINISTRATION OFFICE: See World Harvest Radio.
TRANSMITTERS: Located in Greenbush, Maine. Technical and other correspondence should be sent to the main office of World Harvest Radio (*see*).

WINB—World International Broadcasters, 2900 Windsor Road, P.O. Box 88, Red Lion PA 17356 USA. Phone: (all departments) +1 (717) 244-5360. Fax: +1 (717) 246 0363. Email: (reception reports) winb40th@yahoo.com. Web: www.winb.com. Contact: (general) Mrs. Sally Spyker, Manager; (sales & Frequency Manager) Hans Johnson; (technical) Fred W. Wise, Technical Director; or John H. Norris, Owner. Return postage helpful outside United States. No giveaways or items for sale.

WJIE Shortwave, P.O. Box 197309, Louisville KY 40259 USA. Phone: +1 (502) 965-1220. Fax: +1 (502) 964 4228. Email: wjiesw@hotmail.com. (Freeman, technical) morgan@wjie.org. Web: www.wjiesw.com. Contact: Morgan Freeman. Transmitting equipment purchased from former world band station WJCR.

☞WMLK—Assemblies of Yahweh, 190 Frantz Road, P.O. Box C, Bethel PA 19507 USA. Phone: +1 (717) 933-4518, +1 (717) 933-4880; (toll-free, U.S. only) 1-800-523-3827. Email: (general) aoy@wmlkradio.net; (technical) technician@wmlkradio.net; (Elder Meyer) jacobmeyer@assembliesofyahweh.com; or jacobmeyer@wmlkradio.net; (McAvin) garymcavin@wmlkradio.net. Web: (includes MP3) http://wmlkradio.net; (Assemblies of Yahweh parent organization) www.assembliesofyahweh.com. Contact: (general) Elder Jacob O. Meyer, Manager and Producer of "The Open Door to the Living World"; (technical) Gary McAvin, Station Manager. Free *The Sacred Name Broadcaster* magazine published monthly, stickers and religious material. Bibles, audio and video (VHS) tapes and religious paperback books offered. Enclosing return postage ($1 or IRCs) helps speed things up.

☞World Harvest Radio, LeSEA Broadcasting, 61300 Ironwood Road, South Bend IN 46614 USA. Phone: +1 (219) 291-8200. Fax: +1 (219) 291 9043. Email: whr@lesea.com. Web: (includes RealAudio): www.whr.org; (Parent Organization, LeSEA Broadcasting) www.lesea.com. Contact: (general manager) Pete Sumrall; (technical) Douglas Garlinger, Chief Engineer. World Harvest Radio T-shirts available. Return postage appreciated. *ENGINEERING DEPARTMENT:* P.O. Box 50450, Indianapolis, IN 46250 USA.

WRMI—Radio Miami International, 175 Fontainebleau Blvd., Suite 1N4, Miami FL 33172 USA; or P.O. Box 526852, Miami FL 33152 USA. Phone: (general) +1 (305) 559-9764; (Engineering) +1 (305) 827-2234. Fax: (general) +1 (305) 559 8186; (Engineering) +1 (305) 819 8756. Email: info@wrmi.net. Web: www.wrmi.net. Contact: (technical and nontechnical) Jeff White, General Manager/Sales Manager; (technical) Indalecio "Kiko" Espinosa, Chief Engineer. Free station stickers and tourist brochures. Sells "public access" airtime to nearly anyone to say virtually anything for $1 per minute.

WRNO WORLDWIDE (when operating)
TRANSMITTER SITE: 4539 I-10 Service Road North, Metairie LA 70006 USA.
GOOD NEWS WORLDWIDE, PARENT ORGANIZATION: P.O. Box 895, Fort Worth TX 76101 USA. Phone: +1 (817) 801-8322. Fax: +1 (817) 492 7015. Email: hope@goodnewsworld.org. Web: www.goodnewsworld.org.

☞WSHB-World Harvest Radio:
ADMINISTRATION OFFICE: See World Harvest Radio.
TRANSMITTERS: Located in Cypress Creek, South Carolina. Technical and other correspondence should be sent to the main office of World Harvest Radio (*see*)

WTJC—*see* Fundamental Broadcasting Network.

WWBS (if reactivated), P.O. Box 18174. Macon GA 31209 USA. Phone: +1 (912) 477-3433. Email: wwbsradio@aol.com. Contact: Joanne Josey. Include return postage if you want your reception reports verified.

WWCR—World Wide Christian Radio, F.W. Robbert Broadcasting Co., 1300 WWCR Avenue, Nashville TN 37218 USA. Phone: (general) +1 (615) 255-1300. Fax: +1 (615) 255 1311. Email: (general) wwcr@wwcr.com; ("Ask WWCR" program) askwwcr@wwcr.com. Web: www.wwcr.com. Contact: (administration) George McClintock, K4BTY, General Manager; Adam W. Lock, Sr., WA2JAL, Head of Operations; or Dawn Keen, Program Director; (technical) William Hair, Chief Engineer. Free program guides, updated monthly. Return postage helpful. For items sold on the air and tapes of programs, contact the producers of the programs, and *not* WWCR. Replies as time permits. Carries programs from various political organizations, which may be contacted directly.

WWRB—World Wide Religious Broadcasters, c/o Airline Transport Communications, Box 7, Manchester TN 37349 USA. Phone/Fax: +1 (931) 841-0492. Email: dfrantz@tennessee.com. Web: www.wwrb.org. Contact: Dave Frantz, Chief Engineer; or Angela Frantz. Verifies reception reports with a large certificate and automatic membership of the WWRB Shortwave Listener's Club. Does not accept email reports.

WWV/WWVB (official time and frequency stations): NIST Radio Station WWV, 2000 East County Road #58, Ft. Collins CO 80524 USA. Phone: +1 (303) 497-3914. Fax: +1 (303) 497 4063. Email: nist.radio@boulder.nist.gov; (Deutch) deutch@boulder.nist.gov. Web: http://tf.nist.gov/timefreq/stations/wwv.html. Contact: Matt Deutch, Engineer-in-Charge; or John S. Milton. Along with branch sister station WWVH in Hawaii (*see* below), WWV and WWVB are the official time and frequency stations of the United States, operating over longwave (WWVB) on 60 kHz, and over shortwave (WWV) on 2500, 5000, 10000, 15000 and 20000 kHz. *PARENT ORGANIZATION:* National Institute of Standards and Technology, Time and Frequency Division, 325 Broadway, Boulder CO 80305-3328 USA. Phone: +1 (303) 497-5453. Email: (Lowe) lowe@boulder.nist.gov. Contact: John Lowe, Group Leader.

WWVH (official time and frequency station): NIST Radio Station WWVH, P.O. Box 417, Kekaha, Kauai HI 96752 USA. Phone: +1 (808) 335-4361; (live audio) +1 (808) 335-4363. Fax: +1 (808) 335 4747. Email: nistwwvh@gte.net; (Okayama) okayama@boulder.nist.gov. Web: http://tf.nist.gov/stations/wwvh.htm. Contact: (technical) Dean T. Okayama, Engineer-in-Charge. Along with headquarters sister stations WWV and WWVB (*see* preceding), WWVH is the official time and frequency station of the United States, operating on 2500, 5000, 10000 and 15000 kHz.

WYFR—Family Radio—*see* Family Radio Worldwide.

UZBEKISTAN   World Time +5

Radio Tashkent, Khorazm Street 49, Tashkent 700047, Uzbekistan. Phone: +998 (71) 139-9657; (Chief Editor, English Service) +998 (71) 133-9221; (Chief, English Department) +998 (71) 139-9643. Fax: +998 (71) 133 6068. Email: ino@uzpak.uz. Web: http://ino.uzpak.uz. Contact: Sherzat Gulyamov, Director International Service; Mirtuichi Agzamov, Chief of English Department; Ms. Nargiza Kamilova, Chief Editor, English and German Services. Correspondence is welcomed in English, German, Russian, Uzbek and nine other languages broadcast by Radio Tashkent. Reception reports are verified with colorful QSL cards. Free pennants, badges, wallet calendars and postcards. Has quizzes from time to time with prizes and souvenirs. Books in English by Uzbek writers are apparently available for purchase. Station offers free membership to the "Salum Aleikum Listeners' Club" for regular listeners. Now refers to itself as "Radio Tashkent International" in official publications, but still announces as "Radio Tashkent" on the air.

VANUATU   World Time +12 (+11 midyear)

Radio Vanuatu, Information and Public Relations, Private Mail Bag 049, Port Vila, Vanuatu. Phone: +678 22999 or +678 23026. Fax: +678 22026. Contact: Maxwell E. Maltok, General Manager; Ambong Thompson, Head of Programmes; or Allan Kalfabun, Sales and Marketing Consultant, who is interested in exchanging letters and souvenirs from other countries; (technical) K.J. Page, Principal Engineer; Marianne Berukilkilu, Technical Manager; or Willie Daniel, Technician.

VATICAN CITY STATE   World Time +1 (+2 midyear)

▣Radio Vaticana (Vatican Radio)
MAIN AND PROMOTION OFFICES: 00120 Città del Vaticano, Vatican City State. Phone: (general) +39 (06) 6988-3551; (Director General) +39 (06) 6988-3945; (Programme Director) +39 (06) 6988-3996; (Publicity and Promotion Department) +39 (06) 6988-3045; (technical, general) +39 (06) 6988-4897; (frequency management) +39 (06) 6988-5258. Fax: (general) +39 (06) 6988 4565; (frequency management) +39 (06) 6988 5062. Email: sedoc@vatiradio.va; sedoc@vaticanradio-us.org; (Director General) dirigen@vatiradio.va; (frequency management) mc6790@mclink.it; or gestfreq@vatiradio.va; (technical direction, general) sectec@vatiradio.va; (Programme Director) dirpro@vatiradio.va; (Publicity and Promotion Department) promo@vatiradio.va; (English Section) englishpr@vatiradio.va; (French Section) magfra@vatiradio.va; (German Section) deutsch@vatiradio.va; (Japanese Section) japan@vatiradio.va. Web: (general, including multilingual news and live broadcasts in RealAudio) www.vatican.va/news_services/radio/; www.vaticanradio.org; (RealAudio in English and other European languages, plus text) www.wrn.org/vatican-radio. Contact: (general) Elisabetta Vitalini Sacconi, Promotion Office and schedules; Eileen O'Neill, Head of Program Development, English Service; Fr. Lech Rynkiewicz S.J., Head of Promotion Office; Fr. Federico Lombardi, S.J., Program Director; Solange de Maillardoz, Head of International Relations; Sean Patrick Lovett, Head of English Service; or Veronica Scarisbrick, Producer, "On the Air;" (administration) Fr. Pasquale Borgomeo, S.J., Director General; (technical) Sergio Salvatori, Assistant Frequency Manager, Direzione Tecnica; Fr. Eugenio Matis S.J., Technical Director; or Giovanni Serra, Frequency Management Department. Correspondence sought on religious and programming matters, rather than the technical minutiae of radio. Free station stickers and paper pennants. Music CDs $13; *Pope John Paul II: The Pope of the Rosary* double CD/cassette $19.98 plus shipping; "Sixty Years . . . a Single Day" PAL video on Vatican Radio for 15,000 lire, including postage, from the Promotion Office.
INDIA OFFICE: Loyola College, P.B. No 3301, Chennai-600 03, India. Fax: +91 (44) 2825 7340. Email: (Tamil) tamil@vatiradio.va; (Hindi) hindi@vatiradio.va; (English) india@vatiradio.va.
REGIONAL OFFICE, INDIA: Pastoral Orientation Centre, P.B. No 2251, Palarivattom, India. Fax: +91 (484) 2336 227. Email: (Malayalam) malayalam@vatiradio.va.
JAPAN OFFICE: 2-10-10 Shiomi, Koto-ku, Tokyo 135, Japan. Fax: +81 (3) 5632 4457.
POLAND OFFICE: Warszawskie Biuro Sekcji Polskiej Radia Watykanskiego, ul. Skwer Ks. Kard. S, Warsaw, Poland. Phone: +48 (22) 838-8796.

VENEZUELA   World Time –4

Ecos del Torbes (when operating), Apartado 152, San Cristóbal 5001-A, Táchira, Venezuela. Phone: (general) +58 (276) 438-244; (studio): +58 (276) 421-949. Contact: (general) Licenciada Dinorah González Zerpa, Gerente; Simón Zaidman Krenter; (technical) Ing. Iván Escobar S., Jefe Técnico.
Observatorio Cagigal—YVTO, Apartado 6745, Armada 84-DHN, Caracas 103, Venezuela. Phone: +58 (212) 481-2761. Email: armdhn@ven.net. Contact: Jesús Alberto Escalona, Director Técnico; or Gregorio Pérez Moreno, Director. $1 or return postage helpful.
Radio Amazonas, Av. Simón Bolívar 4, Puerto Ayacucho 7101, Amazonas, Venezuela. Contact: Angel María Pérez, Propietario.

ADDRESS FOR RECEPTION REPORTS: Sr. Jorge García Rangel, Radio Amazonas QSL Manager, Calle Roma, Qta: Costa Rica No. A-16, Urbanización Alto Barinas, Barinas 5201, Venezuela. Two IRC's or $2 required.
Radio Nacional de Venezuela (when operating), Final Calle Las Marías, El Pedregal de Chapellín, 1050 Caracas, Venezuela. If this fails, try: Director de la Onda Corta, Apartado Postal 3979, Caracas 1010-A, Venezuela. Phone: +58 (212) 730-6022, +58 (212) 730-6666. Email: ondacortavenezuela@hotmail.com. Contact: Ali Méndez Martínez, Representativo de onda corta. Currently broadcasts via the transmission facilities of Radio Habana Cuba.
Radio Táchira (when operating), Apartado 152, San Cristóbal 5001-A, Táchira, Venezuela. Phone: +58 (276) 430-009. Contact: Desirée González Zerpa, Directora; Sra. Albertina, Secretaria; or Eleázar Silva Malavé, Gerente.
Radio Valera (when operating), Av. 10 No. 9-31, Valera 3102, Trujillo, Venezuela. Phone: +58 (271) 53-744. Contact: Gladys Barroeta; or Mariela Leal. Replies to correspondence in Spanish. Return postage required. This station has been on the same world band frequency for almost 50 years, which is a record for Latin America.

VIETNAM   World Time +7

Bac Thai Broadcasting Service—contact via Voice of Vietnam—Overseas Service, below.
Lai Chau Broadcasting Service—contact via Voice of Vietnam—Overseas Service, below.
Lam Dong Broadcasting Service, Da Lat, Vietnam. Contact: Hoang Van Trung. Replies slowly to correspondence in Vietnamese, but French may also suffice.
Son La Broadcasting Service, Son La, Vietnam. Contact: Nguyen Hang, Director. Replies slowly to correspondence in Vietnamese, but French may also suffice.
Voice of Vietnam—Domestic Service (Dài Tiêng Nói Viêt Nam, TNVN)—Addresses and contact numbers as for all sections of Voice of Vietnam—Overseas Service, below. Contact: Phan Quang, Director General.
▣Voice of Vietnam—Overseas Service
TRANSMISSION FACILITY (MAIN ADDRESS FOR NONTECHNICAL CORRESPONDENCE AND GENERAL VERIFICATIONS): 58 Quán Sú, Hànôi, Vietnam. Phone: +84 (4) 824-0044. Fax: +84 (4) 826 1122. Email: qhqt.vov@hn.vnn.vn; rtc.vov@hn.vnn.vn or ktpt@hn.vnn.vn. Web: (English text) www.vov.org.vn/docs1/english/; (Vietnamese text and RealAudio in English and Vietnamese) www.vov.org.vn. Contact: Ms. Hoang Minh Nguyet, Director of International Relations.
STUDIOS (NONTECHNICAL CORRESPONDENCE AND GENERAL VERIFICATIONS): 45 Ba Trieu Street, Hànôi, Vietnam. Phone: (director) +84 (4) 825-7870; (English service) +84 (4) 934-2456 or +84 (4) 825-4482; (newsroom) +84 (4) 825-5761 or +84 (4) 825-5862. Fax: (English service) +84 (4) 826 6707. Email: btdn.vov@hn.vnn.vn. Contact: Ms. Nguyen Thi Hue, Director, Overseas Service. Voice of Vietnam Overseas Service broadcasts in 11 foreign languages namely English, French, Japanese, Russian, Spanish, Mandarin, Cantonese, Indonesian, Lao, Thai, Khmer and Vietnamese for overseas Vietnamese.
TECHNICAL CORRESPONDENCE: Office of Radio Reception Quality, Central Department of Radio and Television Broadcast Engineering, Vietnam General Corporation of Posts and Telecommunications, Hànôi, Vietnam.
Yen Bai Broadcasting Station—contact via Voice of Vietnam, Overseas Service, above.

WESTERN SAHARA   World Time exactly

Radio Nacional de la República Arabe Saharaui Democrática, Directeur d'Information, Frente Polisario, B.P. 10, El-Mouradia, 16000 Algiers, Algeria; or c/o Ambassade de la République Arabe Saharaui Démocratique, 1 Av. Franklin Roosevelt, 16000 Algiers, Algeria. Phone (Algeria): +213 (2) 747-907. Fax, when operating (Algeria): +213 (2) 747 984. Email: rasdradio@yahoo.es. Web: (includes a RealAudio recording made in the station's studios) http://web.jet.es/rasd/amateur4.htm. Contact: Mohammed Baali. Two IRCs helpful. Pro-Polisario Front, and supported by the Algerian government. Operates from Rabuni, near Tindouf, on the Algerian side of the border with Western Sahara.

YEMEN   World Time +3

Republic of Yemen Radio, Ministry of Information, P.O. Box 2182 (or P.O. Box 2371), Sana'a-al Hasbah, Yemen. Phone: (general) +967 (1) 282-005; (engineering) +967 (1) 230-751. Fax: (general) +967 (1) 230 761; (engineering) +967 (1) 251 628. Email: yradio@y.net.ye or hussein3itu@y.net.ye. Web: (includes RealAudio) www.yradio.gov.ye. Contact: (general) English Service; (administration) Mohammed Dahwan, General Director of Sana'a Radio; Adel Affara; or Abdulrahman Al-Haimi; (technical) Mohammed H. Bather, Engineer; Esmail Hussein Al Nomo, Head of Transmitting Station; Mohamed Al Aryani, Chief Engineer; or Mohamed Al Sammann, Chairman of Engineering Sector.

ZAMBIA   World Time +2

The Voice - Africa
STATION: Private Bag E606, Lusaka, Zambia. Phone: +260 (1) 274-251. Fax: +260 (1) 274 526. Email: cvoice@zamnet.zm. Web: (includes MP3) www.voiceglobal.net. Contact: Philip Haggar, Station Manager; Beatrice Phiri; or Lenganji Nanyangwe, Assistant to Station Manager. Free calendars and stickers; pens, as available. Free religious books and items under selected circumstances. Sells T-shirts and sundry other items. $1 or 2 IRCs appreciated for reply. Broadcasts Christian teachings and music, as well as news and programs on farming, sport, education, health, business and children's affairs. Formerly known as Radio Christian Voice, and sometimes still identifies as such on the air.
U. K. OFFICE: The Voice, P.O. Box 3040, West Bromwich, West Midlands, B70 0EJ, United Kingdom. Phone:+44 (121) 224-1614. Fax: +44 (121) 224 1613. Email: feedback@voiceafrica.net; (Joynes) sandra@voiceafrica.net. Contact: Sandra Joynes, Office Administrator.
Radio Zambia, Mass Media Complex, Alick Nkhata Road, P.O. Box 50015, Lusaka 10101, Zambia. Phone: (general) +260 (1) 254-989, +260 (1) 253-301 or +260 (1) 252-005; (Public Relations) +260 (1) 254-989, X-216; (engineering) +260 (1) 250-380. Fax: +260 (1) 254 317 or +260 (1) 254 013. Email: (general) znbc@microlink.zm (zambroad@zamnet.zm may also work); (Nkula, technical) pnkula@yahoo.com. Web: www. znbc.co.zm. Contact: (general) Keith M. Nalumango, Director of Programmes; or Lawson Chishimba, Public Relations Manager; (administration) Duncan H. Mbazima, Director-General; (technical) Patrick Nkula, Director of Engineering; or Malolela Lusambo. Free *Zamwaves* newsletter. Sometimes gives away stickers, postcards and small publications. $1 required, and postal correspondence should be sent via registered mail. Tours given of the station Tuesdays to Fridays between 9:00 AM and noon local time; inquire in advance. Used to reply slowly and irregularly, but seems to be better now.

ZIMBABWE   World Time +2

Zimbabwe Broadcasting Corporation, P.O. Box HG444, Highlands, Harare, Zimbabwe; or P.O. Box 2271, Harare, Zimbabwe. Phone: +263 (4) 498-610 or +263 (4) 498-630. Fax: +263 (4) 498 613. Email: zbc@zbc.co.zw; (general enquiries) pr@zbc.co.zw; (news) hnn@zbc.co.zw; (Engineering) hbt@zbc.co.zw. Web: (includes Windows Media) www.zbc.co.zw. Contact: (general) Rugare Sangomoyo; or Lydia Muzenda; (administration) Alum Mpofu, Chief Executive Officer; (news details) Munyaradzi Hwengwere; (Broadcasting Technology, Engineering) Craig Matambo. $1 helpful.

CREDITS: Craig Tyson (Australia), Editor, with Tony Jones (Paraguay). Special thanks to Gabriel Iván Barrera (Argentina), Swopan Chakroborty David Crystal (Israel), Graeme Dixon (New Zealand), Jose Jacob (India), Marie Lamb (USA), Gary Neal (USA), Fotios Padazopulos (USA), George Poppin (USA), Paulo Roberto e Souza (Brazil) and Célio Romais (Brazil); also the following organizations for their support and cooperation: Jembatan DX/Juichi Yamada (Japan) and RUS-DX/Anatoly Klepov (Russia).

Worldwide Broadcasts in English— 2005

Country-by-Country Guide to Best-Heard Stations

Dozens of countries reach out in English, and here are the times and frequencies to hear them. If you want to know which shows are on hour-by-hour, check out "What's On Tonight."

• **When and where:** "Best Times and Frequencies," earlier in this edition, pinpoints where each world band segment is found and gives tuning tips. Best is late afternoon and evening, when most programs are beamed your way. Tune world band segments within the 5730–10000 kHz range in winter, 5730–15800 kHz during summer. Around breakfast, you can also explore segments within the 5730–17900 kHz range for fewer but intriguing catches.

• **Strongest (and weakest) frequencies:** Frequencies shown in italics—say, *5965* kHz—tend to be best, as they are from relay transmitters that may be located near you. However, other frequencies beamed your way might do almost as well. Some signals not beamed to you can also be heard, especially when they are targeted to nearby parts of the world. Frequencies with no target zones are typically for domestic coverage, so they are unlikely to be heard unless you're in or near that country.

Program Times

Times and days of the week are in World Time, explained in "Setting Your World Time Clock" and PASSPORT's glossary; for local times in each country, see "Addresses PLUS." Midyear, some stations are an hour earlier (⬜) or later (⬜) because of daylight saving/summer time. Those used only seasonally are labeled **S** for summer (midyear, typically the last Sunday in March until the last Sunday in October) and **W** for winter. Stations may also extend their hours of transmission, or air special programs, for national holidays, emergencies or sports events.

> **Best are late afternoon and evening. Daytime succeeds, too.**

Indigenous Music

Broadcasts in other than English? Turn to the next section, "Voices from Home," or the Blue Pages. Keep in mind that stations for kinsfolk abroad sometimes carry delightful chunks of native music. They make for enjoyable listening, regardless of language.

Schedules for Entire Year

To be as useful as possible over the months to come, PASSPORT's schedules consist not just of observed activity, but also that which we have creatively opined will take place during the forthcoming year. This predictive material is based on decades of experience and is original from us. Although inherently not as exact as real-time data, over the years it's been of tangible value to PASSPORT readers.

T. Ohtake

ALBANIA

RADIO TIRANA

0245-0300 &		
0330-0400	▣	Tu-Su 6115 & Tu-Su 7160 (E North Am)
1845-1900	🅂	M-Sa 9520 (W Europe)
1945-2000	▣	M-Sa 7210 (W Europe)
1945-2000	🅆	M-Sa 6115 (W Europe)
2130-2200	🅂	M-Sa 7130 (W Europe)
2230-2300	🅆	M-Sa 7120 (W Europe)

ARGENTINA

RADIO ARGENTINA AL EXTERIOR-RAE

0200-0300	Tu-Sa 11710 (Americas)
1800-1900	M-F 9690 (Europe & N Africa), M-F 15345 (Europe)

ARMENIA

VOICE OF ARMENIA

0910-0930	▣	Su 4810 (E Europe, Mideast & W Asia), Su 15270 (Europe)
2040-2100	▣	M-Sa 4810 (E Europe, Mideast & W Asia), M-Sa 9960 (Europe)

AUSTRALIA

HCJB AUSTRALIA

0000-0100	15525 (E Asia)
0100-0230	15560 (S Asia)
0700-1100	11750 (Australasia)
1100-1230	15425 (SE Asia)
1430-1800	15390 (S Asia)
2230-2400	15525 (E Asia)

RADIO AUSTRALIA

0000-0130	17775 (SE Asia)
0000-0200	17715 (E Asia & Pacific), 17795 (Pacific & W North Am)
0000-0300	21725 (Pacific & E Asia)
0000-0800	9660 & 15240 (Pacific)
0000-0900	12080 (S Pacific), 17750 (SE Asia)
0000-1100	13630 (Pacific & E Asia)
0030-0400	15415 (SE Asia)
0200-0700	15515 (Pacific & N America)
0300-0500	21725 (SE Asia)
0430-0500	15415 (SE Asia)
0500-0800	15160 (Pacific & N America)
0530-0800	15415 (SE Asia)
0600-0800	11880 (Pacific & E Asia)
0800-0830	Sa/Su 15415 (SE Asia)
0800-0900	5995 & 9710 (Pacific)
0800-1130	*15240* (E Asia)
0800-1400	9580 (Pacific & N America)
0800-1600	9590 (Pacific & W North Am)
0830-0900	15415 (SE Asia)
0900-0930	Sa/Su 15415 (SE Asia)
0900-1300	11880 (SE Asia)
0930-1100	15415 (SE Asia)
1100-1200	12080 (S Pacific)
1100-1300	9475 (SE Asia)
1100-1400	5995 (Pacific), 6020 (Pacific & W North Am), 6035 (Pacific), 9560 (E Asia & Pacific)
1400-1600	11750 (SE Asia)
1400-1800	5995 (Pacific & W North Am), 6080 (SE Asia), 7240 (Pacific & W North Am)
1430-1700	11660 (SE Asia)
1430-1900	9475 (SE Asia)
1600-2000	9710 (Pacific)
1700-2100	11880 (Pacific & W North Am)
1800-2000	6080 (Pacific & E Asia), 7240 (Pacific)
1800-2100	9580 (Pacific)
1900-2130	9500 (SE Asia)
2000-2100	F/Sa 6080 & F/Sa 7240 (Pacific)
2000-2200	11650 (Pacific), 12080 (S Pacific)
2100-2200	9660 (Pacific)
2100-2300	11880 & 13630 (Pacific)
2200-2330	*15240* (E Asia)
2200-2400	13620 (SE Asia), 15230 (Pacific), 21740 (Pacific & N America)
2300-2400	9660 (Pacific), 12080 (S Pacific), 13630 (Pacific & E Asia), 17795 (Pacific & W North Am)
2330-2400	11695 & 17750 (SE Asia)

VOICE INTERNATIONAL

0900-1100	11955 (SE Asia)
0900-1400	13685 (E Asia)
1100-1800	13635 (S Asia & SE Asia)
1800-2100	6115/11865 (S Asia & SE Asia)

AUSTRIA

RADIO AUSTRIA INTERNATIONAL

0005-0015	🅂	Su/M 9870 (C America), 🅆 Su/M 13730 (S America)
0015-0030	🅂	9870 (C America), 🅆 13730 (S America)

0035-0045	**S** Su/M 9870 (C America), **W** Su/M 13730 (S America)
0045-0100	**W** 13730 (S America)
0105-0115	**W** Su/M 7325 & **S** Su/M 9870 (E North Am), **W** Su/M 9870 (C America)
0115-0130	**W** 7325 & **S** 9870 (E North Am), **W** 9870 (C America)
0135-0145	**W** Su/M 7325 & **S** Su/M 9870 (E North Am), **W** Su/M 9870 (C America)
0145-0200	**W** 7325 & **S** 9870 (E North Am), **W** 9870 (C America)
0605-0630 &	
0635-0700 ▭	Su 17870 (Mideast)
1205-1215	**S** Sa/Su 17715 (S Asia, SE Asia & Australasia)
1215-1230	**S** 17715 (S Asia, SE Asia & Australasia)
1235-1245	**S** Sa/Su 17715 (S Asia, SE Asia & Australasia)
1245-1300	**S** 17715 (S Asia, SE Asia & Australasia)
1305-1315	**W** Sa/Su 17855 (S Asia, SE Asia & Australasia)
1305-1330 ▭	Sa/Su 6155 & Sa/Su 13730 (Europe)
1315-1330	**W** 17855 (S Asia, SE Asia & Australasia)
1335-1345 ▭	Sa/Su 6155 & Sa/Su 13730 (Europe)
1335-1345	**W** Sa/Su 17855 (S Asia, SE Asia & Australasia)
1345-1400 ▭	6155 & 13730 (Europe)
1345-1400	**W** 17855 (S Asia, SE Asia & Australasia)
1505-1530	**S** Sa/Su *13755* (W North Am)
1510-1525	**S** M-F *13755* (W North Am)
1535-1600	**S** Sa/Su *13755* (W North Am)
1540-1555	**S** M-F *13755* (W North Am)
1605-1630	**W** Sa/Su *13675* (W North Am)
1610-1625	**W** M-F *13675* (W North Am)
1635-1700	**W** Sa/Su *13675* (W North Am)
1640-1655	**W** M-F *13675* (W North Am)
2305-2315	**S** Sa/Su 9870 (S America)
2315-2330	**S** 9870 (S America)
2335-2345	**S** Sa/Su 9870 (S America)
2345-2400	**S** 9870 (S America)

BANGLADESH

BANGLADESH BETAR

1230-1300	7185 & 9550 (SE Asia)
1745-1815 &	
1815-1900	7185 & 9550 (Europe)

BELARUS

RADIO BELARUS

0430-0500 ▭	M-W/F/Sa 5970 (W Europe & Atlantic), M-W/F/Sa 7210 (N Europe)
2000-2030 ▭	Su-Tu/Th/F 7105 (Europe), Su-Tu/Th/F 7210 (N Europe)

BELGIUM

RADIO VLAANDEREN INTERNATIONAAL

0400-0430	**S** *11635* (W North Am)
0500-0530	**W** *9590* (W North Am)
0700-0730	**S** *5985* (Europe)
0800-0830	**W** *5965* (Europe)
1130-1200	*9940/9945* (E Asia, SE Asia & Australasia)
1730-1800	**S** *9925* (Europe), **S** *11640* (S Europe & Mideast)
1830-1900	**W** *5910* (S Europe & Mideast), **W** *7330/7490* (Europe)
1930-2000	**S** *9925* (Europe)
2030-2100	**W** *7330/7490* (Europe)
2200-2230	**W** *9590/11730* & **S** *11635* (N America)

BULGARIA

RADIO BULGARIA

0000-0100	**W** 7400 & **W** 9400 (E North Am)
0200-0300	**S** 9700 & **S** 11700 (E North Am)
0300-0400	**W** 7400 & **W** 9400 (E North Am)
0730-0800 ▭	11600 & 13600 (W Europe)
1230-1300 ▭	11700 & 15700 (W Europe)
1730-1800	**S** 9500 & **S** 11500 (W Europe)
1830-1900	**W** 5800 & **W** 7500 (W Europe)
2200-2300 ▭	5800 & 7500 (W Europe)
2300-2400	**S** 9700 & **S** 11700 (E North Am)

CANADA

CANADIAN BROADCASTING CORP—(E North Am)

0000-0300 ▭	Su 9625
0200-0300 ▭	Tu-Sa 9625
0300-0310 &	
0330-0609 ▭	M 9625

Maria Chen hosts Indonesian shows from Radio Taiwan International. RTI is easily heard in North America, Europe, Asia and the Pacific.   RTI

0400-0609 🔲	Su 9625	
0500-0609 🔲	Tu-Sa 9625	
1200-1255 🔲	M-F 9625	
1200-1505 🔲	Sa 9625	
1200-1700 🔲	Su 9625	
1600-1615 &		
1700-1805 🔲	Sa 9625	
1800-2400 🔲	Su 9625	
1945-2015,		
2200-2225 &		
2240-2330 🔲	M-F 9625	

CFRX-CFRB—(E North Am)
24 Hr   6070

CFVP-CKMX—(W North Am)
0600-0400 🔲 6030

CKZN—(E North Am)
24 Hr   6160

CKZU-CBU—(W North Am)
24 Hr   6160

RADIO CANADA INTERNATIONAL
0000-0100   🅂 9640 (E Asia & SE Asia), 🆆 9755, 🆆 9880 & 🅂 15205 (SE Asia)
0000-0200   🅂 13710 (W North Am)
0030-0200   🅂 11990 (C America & S America)
0100-0300 🔲 9755 (N America & C America)
0100-0300   🆆 6190 (E North Am & C America), 🆆 9810 (W North Am)

0130-0300   🆆 11840 (S America)
1200-1300   9660/9670 (E Asia), 🆆 11730 (SE Asia), 🅂 15190 (E Asia & SE Asia), 🅂 M-F 17800 (C America)
1300-1400 🔲 M-F 9515 (E North Am), M-F 13655 (E North Am & C America)
1300-1400   🆆 M-F 17820 (C America)
1300-1500   🅂 17800 (C America)
1400-1600 🔲 9515 & 13655 (E North Am & C America)
1400-1600   🆆 17820 (C America)
1500-1600   🆆 9635, 🆆 11730, 🅂 15455 & 🅂 17720 (S Asia), 🅂 Sa/Su 17800 (C America)
1600-1700 🔲 Sa/Su 9515 & Sa/Su 13655 (E North Am & C America)
1600-1700   🆆 Sa/Su 17820 (C America)
1800-1900   🆆 7370, 🅂 9530 & 🆆 9770 (E Africa), 🅂 11770 (E Africa & C Africa), 🆆 11875 (C Africa & E Africa), 🅂 13730 (C Africa & S Africa), 🆆 15140 (W Africa & C Africa), 🅂 15255 (W Africa)
1900-2200   🅂 17765 (C America)
2000-2100   🅂 5995 (N Africa), 🅂 7235 & 🅂 11690 (Europe & Mideast), 🅂 13700 (W Europe)
2000-2300   🆆 15180 (C America)

2100-2200 ⬅ *5850* (W Europe)
2100-2200 W *7425* (Mideast & E Africa), W *9770* (W Europe)
2200-2230 S 15170 (C America & S America)
2200-2400 S 5960 (E North Am), S 13785 (E North Am & C America)
2230-2300 W *7195*, S *9525* & W *9730* (E Asia & SE Asia), S *11810* (E Asia), S *12035* (E Asia & SE Asia)

CHINA

CHINA RADIO INTERNATIONAL

0000-0100 9515 (S Asia), S 13600 (Europe)
0000-0200 W 7345 (Europe)
0100-0200 *9580* (E North Am), *9790* (W North Am), S 13600 (Europe)
0100-0400 11770 (S Asia)
0300-0400 *9690* (N America & C America), *9790* (W North Am), 15110 (S Asia)
0400-0500 *9755* (W North Am)
0400-0600 *6190* (W North Am)
0400-0800 S 17490 (W Europe)
0500-0600 *9560* (W North Am)
0500-0700 13720 (S Asia)
0500-0900 15350 & 17540 (S Asia)
0600-0700 S 11740, 13620 & W 15190 (E Africa)
0600-0900 15465 (S Asia)
0800-1300 17490 (W Europe)
0900-1100 15210 & 17690 (Australasia)
1000-1200 S *6040* (E North Am)
1100-1200 W *5960* (E North Am)
1200-1300 9730 (SE Asia), 15415 (Australasia)
1200-1400 11760 (Australasia), 11980 (SE Asia)
1200-1500 9795 (Europe)
1300-1400 9570 & S *9650* (E North Am), W *11885* (W North Am), 11900 (Australasia), 15180 (SE Asia), S *15260* (E North Am & C America)
1300-1500 W *9755* (E North Am & C America)
1300-1700 S 17490 (W Europe)
1400-1500 9560, 11675 & 11765 (S Asia), W *13675* (W North Am)

1400-1600 ⬅ 7405 (W North Am)
1400-1600 W 7285 & 11775 (S Asia), *13685* (E Africa), *13740/17730* (W North Am), S 13775 (S Asia), *15125* (C Africa & E Africa)
1500-1600 W 7160 & 9785 (S Asia)
1500-1700 W 9430, W 9525 & S 13640 (Europe)
1600-1800 9570 (E Africa & S Africa), S 11900 (S Africa), S 11940 (Europe)
1800-1900 S 13830 (Europe)
1900-2000 9585 (Mideast)
1900-2100 7140/7295 & 9440 (N Africa)
2000-2130 *11640 & 13630* (E Africa & S Africa)
2000-2200 W 5965, 7190 & 9600 (Europe), W 9855 (W Europe), S 11790 (Europe)
2200-2300 W *7170* & S *9880/7175* (N Europe)
2300-2400 *5990* (C America), W *6040* & S *6145* (E North Am), *13680* (W North Am)

CHINA (TAIWAN)

RADIO TAIWAN INTERNATIONAL

0200-0300 *5950* (E North Am), *9680* (N America), 11875 (SE Asia), 15465 (E Asia)
0300-0400 *5950* (W North Am), *15215* (S America), 15320 (SE Asia)
0700-0800 *5950* (W North Am)
0800-0900 9610 (Australasia)
1100-1200 7105 (SE Asia)
1200-1300 7130 (E Asia)
1400-1500 15265 (SE Asia)
1600-1700 11815 (E Asia & S Asia)
1800-1900 *3965* (W Europe)
2200-2300 W *9355* & S *15600* (Europe)

CROATIA

VOICE OF CROATIA

0215-0230 S *9925* (N America & S America)
0315-0330 W *7285* (N America & S America)
2215-2230 S *7285* (S America)
2315-2330 W *7285* (S America)

Radio France Internationale's rotatable curtain antenna at Issodun, France. It allows RFI's signals to be beamed in any direction—important in an unpredictable world.

George Woodard

CUBA

RADIO HABANA CUBA

0100-0500	6000 (E North Am), 9820 (N America)
0500-0700	9550 (C America), 9820 (W North Am)
2030-2130	11760 (Europe & E North Am)

CZECH REPUBLIC

RADIO PRAGUE

0000-0030	[S] 7345 (N America & C America), [S] 9440 (Americas)
0100-0130	6200 (N America & C America), 7345 (N America)
0200-0230	[W] 6200 (N America & C America), [W] 7345 (N America)
0300-0330	[S] 7345 (N America), [S] 9870 (W North Am & C America)
0330-0400	[S] 11600 (Mideast), [S] 15600 (Mideast & S Asia)
0400-0430	[W] 6200 (W North Am & C America), [W] 7345 (N America)
0430-0500	[W] 9865 (Mideast), [W] 11600 (Mideast & S Asia)
0700-0730	[S] 11600 (W Europe)
0800-0830 ⬅	9880 (W Europe)
0800-0830	[W] 7345 (W Europe)
0900-0930	[S] 21745 (S Asia & W Africa)
1000-1030	[W] 21745 (S Asia & W Africa)
1030-1100	[S] 9880 & [S] 11615 (N Europe)
1130-1200	[W] 11640 (N Europe), [W] 21745 (E Africa & Mideast)
1300-1330	[S] 13580 (N Europe), [S] 21745 (S Asia)
1400-1430	[W] 21745 (N America & E Africa)
1600-1630	[S] 17485 (E Africa)
1700-1730 ⬅	5930 (W Europe)
1700-1730	[W] 15710 (W Africa & C Africa), [S] 17485 (C Africa)
1800-1830 ⬅	5930 (W Europe)
1800-1830	[W] 9415 (Asia & Australasia)
2000-2030	[S] 11600 (SE Asia & Australasia)
2100-2130 ⬅	5930 (W Europe)
2100-2130	[W] 9430 (SE Asia & Australasia)
2230-2300	[W] 5930 (N America), 7345 (E North Am & C America), [S] 9415 (N America)
2330-2400	[W] 5930 (N America), [W] 7345 (E North Am & C America)

ECUADOR

HCJB-VOICE OF THE ANDES

1100-1330	[W] 12005 & [S] 15115 (Americas), 21455 USB (Europe & Australasia)

EGYPT

RADIO CAIRO

0000-0030	[W] 7115 & [S] 11725 (N America)
0200-0330	11855/7260 (N America)
1215-1330	17670 (S Asia & SE Asia)
1630-1830	9855 (S Africa)
2030-2200	15375 (W Africa)
2115-2245	9990 (Europe)
2300-2400	[W] 7115 & [S] 11725 (N America)

ETHIOPIA

RADIO ETHIOPIA

1030-1100	M-F 5990, M-F 7110, M-F 9704
1600-1700	7165 & 9560 (E Africa)

FRANCE

RADIO FRANCE INTERNATIONALE

0400-0430	[S] M-F *7280*, [W] M-F 9555/ 11995 & [S] M-F 11700 (Irr) (E Africa)

0500-0530	**S** M-F *11685/15605* & **W** M-F *11850* (E Africa & S Africa), **W** M-F 11995/15155 & **S** M-F 15155 (E Africa)
0600-0630	**S** M-F *11665* & **W** M-F *11725* (W Africa), **W** M-F 15155, M-F 17800 & **S** M-F 21620 (E Africa)
0700-0800	**W** *11725* & *15605* (W Africa)
1200-1230	*17815* (W Africa), **S** 21620/25820 & **W** 21620 (E Africa)
1400-1500	**W** *7180/9580* & **S** *9580/11610* (S Asia), **S** 15615/17515 & **W** 17620 (Mideast)
1600-1700	**W** 9590 (N Africa), *9730* (S Africa), 11615 (N Africa), *15160* (W Africa & C Africa), **W** 15365/21580 & 17850 (C Africa & S Africa)
1600-1730	**W** 11615 & **S** 15605 (Mideast), **W** 15605 & **S** 17605 (E Africa)

GERMANY
DEUTSCHE WELLE

0000-0100	**W** *6030*, **S** *7130*, **W** 7290, **S** *9505* & **S** 9825 (S Asia)
0400-0500	**W** *6180* (E Africa), **S** *7225* (C Africa & E Africa), **W** *9545* & **S** *9630* (E Africa & Mideast), **W** 9710 (C Africa & S Africa), **S** 11945 (E Africa)
0500-0600	**W** 7285 (C Africa & S Africa), **W** *9565* (C Africa & E Africa), **S** *9630* (C Africa & S Africa), **S** *9700* (C Africa & E Africa), **W** *12035* & **S** *12045* (S Africa), **S** *15410* (E Africa), **W** *15410* (C Africa & E Africa), **S** *17860* (C Africa & S Africa)
0600-0700	**S** *7170* & **W** 7225 (W Africa), **W** 11785 (W Africa & C Africa), **S** 15275 (W Africa), **W** *15410* & **S** *17860* (W Africa & C Africa)
0600-1000	6140 (Europe)
1000-1030	**W** *6205* (E Asia), **S** *15350* (E Asia & SE Asia), *17820* (E Asia)
1100-1200	**S** *15105*, **W** *15410*, **S** *17820* & **S** *21820* (SE Asia)
1300-1600	6140 (Europe)

1600-1700	*6170/6180* & *7225* (S Asia), **W** 11695 (S Asia, SE Asia & Australasia), **S** *17595* (S Asia)
1900-2000	**W** *6180*, **S** *7225* & **W** *11865* (C Africa & E Africa), **S** 13590 (Mideast & E Africa), **W** 13780 (E Africa), **S** *15545* & **S** *17770* (C Africa & E Africa), **W** *17800* (C Africa & S Africa)
2000-2100	**S** *7130* & **W** *12025* (S Africa), **W** 13780 (C Africa & S Africa), **S** 13820 & **S** 15205 (C Africa & E Africa), **W** 15205 (C Africa & S Africa), **W** *15410* (C Africa)
2100-2200	**S** 9440, **W** 9615 & **S** *11865* (W Africa), **W** *13780* (W Africa & C Africa), **S** *15205* & **W** *15410* (W Africa)
2200-2300	**W** *6180* (E Asia & SE Asia), **S** *7115* (E Asia), **S** 9720 (E Asia & SE Asia)
2300-2400	**S** *7115*, **W** *7250*, **W** *9815*, **S** *9890*, **W** *12035* & **S** *15135* (SE Asia)

GHANA
GHANA BROADCASTING CORPORATION

0530-0900	4915, 6130/3366
0900-1200	Sa/Su/Holidays 4915
1200-1700	6130
1700-2400	3366, 4915

GUYANA
VOICE OF GUYANA

24 Hr	3291

HUNGARY
RADIO BUDAPEST

0100-0130	**S** 9590 (N America)
0200-0230	**W** 9775 (N America)
0230-0300	**S** 9570 (N America)
0330-0400	**W** 9775 (N America)
1500-1530	**S** Su 9715 (N Europe)
1600-1630	▪ Su 6025 (Europe)
1600-1630	**W** Su 9580 (N Europe)
1900-1930	**S** 11720 (W Europe)
2000-2030	▪ 3975 & 6025 (Europe)
2100-2130	**S** 11830 (S Africa)
2200-2230	▪ 6025 (Europe)
2200-2230	**W** 11965/12010 (S Africa)

INDIA

ALL INDIA RADIO

0000-0045 9705 (E Asia & SE Asia), 9950 (E Asia), 11620 (E Asia & SE Asia), 11645 (E Asia), 13605 (E Asia & SE Asia)
1000-1100 13695 (Australasia), 13710 (E Asia & Australasia), 15020 (E Asia), 15260 (S Asia), 15410 (E Asia), 17510 (Australasia), 17800 (E Asia), 17895 (Australasia)
1330-1500 9690, 11620 & 13710 (SE Asia)
1745-1945 7410 (Europe), 9445 (W Africa), 9950 & 11620 (Europe), 11935 (E Africa), 13605 (W Africa), 15075 (E Africa), 15155 (W Africa), 17670 (E Africa)
2045-2230 7410 & 9445 (Europe), 9910 (Australasia), 9950 (Europe), 11620 & 11715 (Australasia)
2245-2400 9705 (E Asia & SE Asia), 9950 (E Asia), 11620 (E Asia & SE Asia), 11645 (E Asia), 13605 (E Asia & SE Asia)

INDONESIA

VOICE OF INDONESIA

0100-0200 9525 & 11785 (E Asia, SE Asia & Pacific)
0800-0900 9525 & 11785 (Australasia)
2000-2100 9525, 11785 & 15150 (Europe)

IRAN

VOICE OF THE ISLAMIC REPUBLIC

1030-1130 [W] 15460, [W] 15480, [S] 15600 & [S] 17660 (S Asia)
1530-1630 [W] 9610, [S] 9635, [W] 9940 & [S] 11650 (S Asia & SE Asia)
1930-2030 9800, [W] 11695 & [S] 11750 (S Africa)

ISRAEL

KOL ISRAEL

0330-0345 [S] 11585 (W Europe & E North Am)
0430-0445 ⬅ 15640/17600 (Australasia)
0430-0445 [W] 6280 (W Europe & E North Am)
1900-1925 [S] 11605 (W Europe & E North Am), [S] 15615 (S Africa), [S] 17535 (W Europe & E North Am)
2000-2025 [W] 6280 & [W] 9435 (W Europe & E North Am), [W] 15640 (S Africa)

ITALY

RAI INTERNATIONAL

0055-0115 11800 (N America)
0445-0500 [W] 5965 (S Europe & N Africa), [W] 6100 & [S] 6110 (N Africa), [W] 7230, [S] 7235 & [S] 9875 (S Europe & N Africa)
1935-1955 [S] 5970, [W] 6035, [S] 9605 & [W] 9760 (W Europe)
2025-2045 [W] 6040, [S] 6185 & 11880 (Mideast)
2205-2230 11895 (E Asia)

JAPAN

RADIO JAPAN

0000-0015 13650 & 17810 (SE Asia)
0000-0100 *6145* (E North Am)
0100-0200 [S] *6025* & [W] *6030* (Mideast), *11860* (SE Asia), 15325 (S Asia), 17560 (Mideast), 17685 (Australasia), 17810 (SE Asia), 17825 (W North Am & C America), 17835 (S America), 17845 (E Asia)
0300-0400 21610 (Australasia)
0500-0600 *5975* (W Europe), *6110* (W North Am), 17810 (SE Asia)
0500-0700 *7230* (Europe), 15195 (E Asia), 21755 (Australasia)
0600-0700 [W] 11690 (W North Am & C America), 11715 (E Asia), *11740* (SE Asia), 11760 (E Asia), [S] 13630 (W North Am & C America), 17870 (Pacific)
1000-1100 *17585* (Europe), *17720* (Mideast), 21755 (Australasia)
1000-1200 *6120* (E North Am), 9695 (SE Asia), 11730 (E Asia)
1400-1500 *11840* (Australasia)
1400-1600 7200 (SE Asia), [W] 9845 & [S] 11730 (S Asia)
1500-1600 6190 (E Asia), 9505 (W North Am & C America)

Sumo matches are as distinctly Japanese as football is American. Fans are just as rabid, too.

T. Ohtake

1700-1800	9535 (W North Am & C America), 11970 (Europe), *15355* (S Africa)
2100-2200	[S] *6035* (Australasia), [S] *6055* & [W] *6090* (W Europe), *6180* (Europe), *11855* (C Africa), [W] *11920* (Australasia), 17825 (W North Am), 21670 (Pacific)

JORDAN

RADIO JORDAN—(W Europe & E North Am)

1400-1730 ⬅	11690

KOREA (DPR)

VOICE OF KOREA

0100-0200	3560 & 6195/9720 (E Asia), 6520/13760 (C America & S America), 7140 (E Asia), 7580/15180 (C America), 9345 (E Asia), 11735 (C America & S America)
0200-0300	4405 (E Asia), 9325/11845 & 11335/15230 (SE Asia)
0300-0400	3560, 6195/9720, 7140 & 9345 (E Asia)
1000-1100	3560 (E Asia), 9335/15180 (C America), 9850/13650 (SE Asia), 11710 (C America), 11735 (SE Asia)
1300-1400 & 1500-1600	4405 (E Asia), 9325/13760 (Europe), 9335 (N America), 11335/15245 (Europe), 11710 (N America)
1600-1700	3560 (E Asia), 9975 & 11735 (Mideast & Africa)
1900-2000	4405 (E Asia), 9325/13760 & 11335/15245 (Europe), 11710/9660 (Africa)
2100-2200	4405 (E Asia), 9325/13760 & 11335/15245 (Europe)

KOREA (REPUBLIC)

RADIO KOREA INTERNATIONAL

0200-0300	*9560* (W North Am), 11810 (E Asia & S America), 15575 (N America)
0800-0900	9570 (SE Asia), 13670 (Europe)
1200-1300	*9650* (E North Am)
1300-1400	9570 & 13670/9700 (SE Asia)
1600-1700	5975 (E Asia), [W] 7255 (E Africa & S Africa), 9870 (Mideast)
1900-2000	5975 (E Asia), 7275 (Europe)
2100-2130	[S] *3955* (W Europe)
2200-2230	[W] *3955* (W Europe)

LITHUANIA

RADIO VILNIUS

0030-0100	[W] 7325 & [S] 11690 (E North Am)
0930-1000 ⬅	9710 (W Europe)
2330-2400	9875 (E North Am)

MALAYSIA

VOICE OF MALAYSIA

0300-0600 & 0600-0825	6175 & 9750 (SE Asia), 15295 (Australasia)

MONGOLIA

VOICE OF MONGOLIA
1000-1030	12085/12015 (E Asia, SE Asia & Australasia)
1500-1530	9720 (C Asia)
2000-2030	9720 (E Europe & W Asia)

NETHERLANDS

RADIO NEDERLAND
0000-0100	*9845* (E North Am)
0100-0200	▥ *6165* & ▨ *9845* (N America)
0400-0500	*6165 & 9590* (W North Am)
1000-1100	▥ *7315* (E Asia), *9785/9790* (Australasia), ▨ *12065* (E Asia), ▥ *12065* & ▨ *13710* (E Asia & SE Asia), *13820* (E Asia)
1200-1300 ▤	*11675* (E North Am)
1400-1600	▨ *9890*, ▨ *11835*, ▥ *12070*, ▨ *12075*, ▥ *12080* & ▥ *15595* (S Asia)
1800-1900	*6020* (S Africa)
1800-2000	▥ 9895 & 11655 (E Africa)
1800-2100	▨ *9895* (W Africa & C Africa)
1900-2100	*7120* (C Africa & S Africa), Sa/Su *15315* (N America), ▨ Sa/Su *17660* (W North Am), ▥ Sa/Su *17725* & ▨ Sa/Su *17735* (E North Am), *17810* (W Africa), ▥ Sa/Su *17875* (W North Am)
2000-2100	▥ 9895 & ▨ 11655 (W Africa), ▥ *11655* (W Africa & C Africa)

Tatyana Shvetsova, Lyubov Tsarevskaya, Olga Troshina, Larisa Avrutina, Elena Biryukova; back row Olga Shapovalova, Branislav Siljkovic, Elena Osipova, Anatoly Morozov and Elena Frolovskaya. Voice of Russia

NEW ZEALAND

RADIO NEW ZEALAND INTERNATIONAL—
(Pacific)
0000-0400	▥ 17675
0000-0500	▨ 15720
0400-0800	▥ 15340
0500-0705	▨ 9615/11820
0706-0800	▨ 9885
0800-1100	9885/9815
1100-1300	▨ 9885 & ▥ 15530
1300-1750	▥ 9870/9815
1300-1850	▨ 6095
1750-1950	▥ 11980
1851-1950	▨ 9845/9885
1921-2050	▨ 11725
1950-2238	▥ 15265
2051-2400	▨ 15720
2236-2400	▥ 17675

NIGERIA

VOICE OF NIGERIA—(N Africa & Europe)
0500-1000	15120/17800
1500-2000	15120
2000-2300	15120/17800

PHILIPPINES

RADYO PILIPINAS—(S Asia & Mideast)
0200-0330	▨ 11885, ▥ 12015, 15120 & 15270

POLAND

RADIO POLONIA
1300-1330 ▤	11820 (W Europe)
1300-1400 ▤	9525 (W Europe)
1700-1800	▨ 7285 (N Europe)
1800-1900 ▤	5995 (W Europe)
1800-1900	▥ 7170 (N Europe)

ROMANIA

RADIO ROMANIA INTERNATIONAL
0100-0200	▥ 6140 (E North Am), ▥ 9510 (Australasia), 9690 (E North Am), ▥ 11740 (Australasia), ▨ 11940 (E North Am), ▨ 15430 & ▨ 17760 (Australasia)
0400-0500	▥ 6125, ▥ 9515 & ▨ 11820 (W North Am), ▥ 11870 & ▨ 15140 (S Asia), ▨ 15235 (W North Am), ▥ 15250 & ▨ 17860 (S Asia)

0630-0700	**W** 9565 & **W** 11710 (W Europe)
0700-0730	**S** 11830 & **S** 15150 (W Europe)
1300-1400	**S** 11830, 15105 & **W** 17745 (W Europe)
1800-1900	**W** 5965, **W** 7130, **S** 11940 & **S** 15380 (W Europe)
2130-2200	**W** 6015 (E North Am), **W** 6055, **S** 7130/7230, **W** 7145 & **S** 7285 (W Europe), **W** 9540 (E North Am), **S** 9725 (W Europe), **S** 11750 & **S** 15285 (E North Am)
2300-2400	**W** 6135 (W Europe), **W** 6180 (E North Am), **W** 7105, **S** 7280 & **S** 9590 (W Europe), **W** 9610, **S** 9645 & **S** 11940 (E North Am)

RUSSIA

VOICE OF RUSSIA

0100-0300	**S** *5945* (Mideast)
0100-0500	**S** *9665/7180* (E North Am), **S** 17660 (W North Am)
0200-0400	**W** *5995* (Mideast), **S** *9860* (E North Am)
0200-0600 ◄▬	15595 (W North Am)
0200-0600	**W** *7180* (E North Am), **W** 15445 (W North Am)
0300-0500	**W** *7350* & **S** 9880/7300 (E North Am), **S** 15455 (W North Am)
0400-0600	**W** 7240 (E North Am), **W** 12010 (W North Am)
0500-0600 &	
0600-0900	21790 (Australasia)
0600-1000	**W** 11820 (W Europe)
0700-0900	**S** 17635 (Australasia)
0800-1000 ◄▬	*17495 & 17525* (SE Asia & Australasia)
0800-1000	**W** 17665 (Australasia), **W** 17850 (SE Asia)
1400-1500	**S** 9745 (S Asia), **S** 12055 (SE Asia), **S** 15605 (S Asia), **S** 17645 (S Asia & SE Asia)
1400-1600	**S** 7390 (E Asia & SE Asia)
1500-1600	**W** 6205 (SE Asia), **W** 7315 (W Asia & S Asia), **S** 7325 (Mideast), **W** 7350 (S Asia), *11500* (SE Asia)
1500-1800	**S** 11985 (Mideast & E Africa)
1600-1700 ◄▬	*4940, 4965 & 4975* (W Asia & S Asia)
1600-1700	**W** 6005 (Mideast), **S** 12055 (W Asia & S Asia), **S** 15540 (Mideast)
1600-1800	**S** 9405 (S Asia)
1600-1900	**W** 9830 (Mideast, E Africa & S Africa)
1700-1800 ◄▬	5945 (S Asia)
1700-1800	**S** Sa/Su 9480/9820 & **S** Sa/Su 11675/7350 (N Europe)
1700-1900	**W** 5910 (S Asia)
1700-2000	**S** 9890 (Europe)
1800-1900	**W** Sa/Su 5950, **W** Sa/Su 6175 & **S** 9480/9820 (N Europe), **S** 9745 (E Africa), **S** 11630/9480 (Europe)
1800-2000 ◄▬	*11510* (E Africa & S Africa)
1800-2200	**W** 7290 (N Europe)
1900-2000	**W** 7335 (E Africa & S Africa), **W** 7360 & **S** 7440 (Europe)
1900-2100	**S** 12070/7310 (Europe)
1900-2200	**W** 6175 (N Europe), **W** 6235 (W Europe)
2000-2100	**W** 6145 & **S** 15455/11980 (Europe)
2000-2200	**W** 7340 (Europe)
2100-2200	**W** 7300 (Europe)

SERBIA AND MONTENEGRO

INTERNATIONAL RADIO OF SERBIA & MONTENEGRO

0000-0030	**S** M-Sa *9580* (E North Am)
0100-0130	**W** M-Sa *7115* (E North Am)
0200-0230	**W** M-Sa *7130* (W North Am)
0430-0500	**S** *9580* (W North Am)
1330-1400	**W** *11835* (Australasia)
1930-2000 &	
2200-2230 ◄▬	*6100* (Europe)
2200-2230	**S** Su-F *7230* (Australasia)

SINGAPORE

MEDIACORP RADIO

1400-1600 &	
2300-1100	6150

RADIO SINGAPORE INTERNATIONAL—(SE Asia)

1100-1400	6080 & 6150

SLOVAKIA

RADIO SLOVAKIA INTERNATIONAL

0100-0130	5930 (N America), 9440 (S America)

0700-0730	[S] 9440, [W] 13715 & 15460 (Australasia)
1630-1700	[S] 5920 (W Europe)
1730-1800 ←	7345 (W Europe)
1730-1800	[W] 5915 (W Europe)
1830-1900	[S] 5920 & [S] 6055 (W Europe)
1930-2000	[W] 5915 & [W] 7345 (W Europe)

SOLOMON ISLANDS

SOLOMON ISLANDS BROADCASTING

0000-0030	5020
0030-0038	Sa/Su 5020
0038-0130	5020
0130-0145	Sa/Su 5020
0145-0230	5020
0230-0245	Sa/Su 5020
0240-0330	5020
0330-0338	Sa/Su 5020
0338-0430	5020
0430-0438	Sa/Su 5020
0438-0545	5020
0545-0600	Sa/Su 5020
0600-0648	5020
0648-0700	Sa/Su 5020
0700-0800	5020
0800-0830	Sa/Su 5020
0830-0945	5020
0945-1000	Su-F 5020
1000-1010	5020
1010-1030	Sa/Su 5020
1030-1100, 1100-1900, 1900-1930 & 1945-2030	5020
2030-2045	F/Sa 5020
2045-2130	5020
2130-2138	F/Sa 5020
2138-2230	5020
2230-2238	F/Sa 5020
2238-2330	5020
2330-2345	F/Sa 5020
2345-2400	5020

SOUTH AFRICA

CHANNEL AFRICA

0300-0355	[S] 6160 & [W] 7390 (E Africa)
0300-0500	3345 (S Africa)
0500-0555	[S] 9770 & [W] 11875 (W Africa)
0500-0700	[S] 7210 & [W] 7240 (S Africa)
0600-0655	[S] 15215 & [W] 15220 (W Africa)
0700-0800, 1000-1200 & 1400-1600	11825 (S Africa)
1500-1555	17770 (C Africa & E Africa)
1700-1755	[S] 15265 & [W] 15285 (W Africa)
1900-2200	3345 (S Africa)

SOUTH AFRICAN RADIO LEAGUE

0800-0900	Su 9750 (S Africa), [W] Su 17780 & [S] Su 17815 (E Africa)
1900-2000	M 3215 (S Africa)

SPAIN

RADIO EXTERIOR DE ESPAÑA

0000-0100	[W] 6055 (N America), [S] 15385 (N America & C America)
2000-2100	[S] M-F 9570 & [W] M-F 9595 (N Africa & W Africa), [W] M-F 9680 & [S] M-F 15290 (Europe)
2100-2200	[S] Sa/Su 9570 (N Africa & W Africa), [S] Sa/Su 9840 (Europe)
2200-2300	[W] Sa/Su 9595 (N Africa & W Africa), [W] Sa/Su 9680 (Europe)

SRI LANKA

SRI LANKA BROADCASTING CORPORATION

0030-0430 & 1230-1530	6005, 9770 & 15745 (S Asia)
1900-2000	Sa *6010* (W Europe)

SWEDEN

RADIO SWEDEN

0130-0200	[S] *6010* (E North Am), [S] 9435 & [W] 9435 (S Asia)
0230-0300	[S] *6010* & [W] *9495* (N America)
0330-0400	[W] *9495* (W North Am)
1230-1300	[S] 13580 (E Asia & Australasia), [S] 15240 (N America), [S] 15735 (Asia & Australasia)
1330-1400	[W] 9430 (E Asia & Australasia), [S] *15240* (N America), [S] 15735 (Mideast, SE Asia & Australasia), [W] 17505 (SE Asia & Australasia), [W] 18960 (N America)
1430-1500	[W] 17505 (Asia & Australasia), [W] 18960 (N America)

1830-1900 ▭ M-Sa 6065 (Europe)
2030-2100 ▭ 6065 (Europe)
2030-2100 Ⓦ 9415/9400 (SE Asia & Australasia)
2130-2200 Ⓢ 9880 (E Asia & Australasia)
2230-2300 ▭ 6065 (Europe)

SYRIA

RADIO DAMASCUS
2005-2105 12085 (Irr) & 13610 (Europe)
2110-2210 12085 (Irr) & 13610 (N America & Australasia)

THAILAND

RADIO THAILAND
0000-0030 Ⓢ 9570 & Ⓦ 9680 (E Africa & S Africa)
0030-0100 *5890* (E North Am)
0300-0330 *5890* (W North Am)
0530-0600 Ⓦ 13780 & Ⓢ 21795 (Europe)
1230-1300 Ⓦ 9810 & Ⓢ 9855 (SE Asia & Australasia)
1400-1430 Ⓦ 9560 & Ⓢ 9830 (SE Asia & Australasia)
1900-2000 Ⓢ 7155 & Ⓦ 9840 (N Europe)
2030-2045 Ⓦ 9535 & Ⓢ 9680 (Europe)

TURKEY

VOICE OF TURKEY
0300-0350 Ⓢ 6140 (W Europe & E North Am), Ⓢ 7270 (Mideast)
0400-0450 Ⓦ 6020 (Europe & N America), Ⓦ 7240 (Mideast)
1230-1325 Ⓢ 15225 (Europe), Ⓢ 15535 (S Asia, SE Asia & Australasia)
1330-1425 Ⓦ 15155 (W Europe), Ⓦ 15195 (S Asia, SE Asia & Australasia)
1830-1920 Ⓢ 9785 (W Europe)
1930-2020 Ⓦ 6055 (W Europe)
2030-2120 Ⓢ 7170 (S Asia, SE Asia & Australasia)
2130-2220 Ⓦ 9525 (S Asia, SE Asia & Australasia)
2200-2250 Ⓢ 9830 (W Europe & E North Am)
2300-2350 Ⓦ 7275 (W Europe & E North Am)

UKRAINE

RADIO UKRAINE
0000-0100 Ⓢ 7545 (E North Am)

Pathumthani antenna, Thailand.

M. Guha

0100-0200 Ⓦ 5910 (E North Am)
0300-0400 Ⓢ 7545 (E North Am)
0400-0500 Ⓦ 5910 (E North Am)
1100-1200 Ⓢ 15415 (W Europe)
1200-1300 Ⓦ 13585 (W Europe)
2100-2200 Ⓢ 7420 (W Europe)
2200-2300 Ⓦ 5840 (W Europe)

UNITED KINGDOM

BBC WORLD SERVICE
0000-0030 *3915* (SE Asia), *11945* (E Asia)
0000-0100 *5970* (S Asia), *9740* (SE Asia), *11955* (S Asia), *17615* (E Asia)

0000-0200	*6195* (SE Asia), *9410* (W Asia)
0000-0300	9825 (S America), ◨ *11835* (W North Am & C America), 12095 (S America), *15310* (S Asia), *15360* (SE Asia), *17790* (S Asia)
0000-0400	*5975* (C America & N America)
0000-0530	*15280* (E Asia)
0100-0300	*11955* (S Asia)
0100-0400	◫ *9525* (C America & W North Am)
0200-0300	◨ *6195* (E Europe), ◫ 6195 & ◨ *9410* (Europe), ◫ *9410* (Mideast & W Asia), *9750* (E Africa), ◨ *11760* (Mideast)
0300-0400	*6005* (S Africa), 9750, ◨ *12035* & ◫ *12035* (E Africa), ◨ *12095* (E Europe)
0300-0500	3255 (S Africa), ◨ *7120* (W Africa), ◨ *11760* (W Asia), ◫ *11760* (Mideast), ◫ *11765* (W Africa), ◨ *11835* (W North Am & C America), *15360* (SE Asia), ◨ *15575* (Mideast), *17760* & *21660* (E Asia), *21830* (W Asia & S Asia)
0300-0600	6195 (Europe), *15310* (S Asia)
0300-0700	*7160* (W Africa & C Africa), *9410* (Europe), *17790* (S Asia)
0300-2200	*6190* (S Africa)
0330-0600	*15420* (E Africa)
0400-0500	*5975* (W North Am, C America & S America), ◫ *12035* & ◨ *17640* (E Africa)
0400-0600	◫ *6135* (W North Am & C America), ◨ *12095* (Europe)
0400-0720	*6005* (W Africa)
0500-0700	*11765* (W Africa), ◨ 15565 (E Europe), ◫ *15565* (N Europe & E Europe), *17640* (E Africa)
0500-0730	*15575* (W Asia)
0500-0800	*21660* (E Asia)
0500-0900	*11955* (SE Asia), *15360* (E Asia, SE Asia & Australasia)
0500-1000	*17760* (E Asia & SE Asia)
0500-1400	*11760* (Mideast)
0500-1700	*11940* (S Africa)
0530-0600	M-F *17885* (E Africa)
0600-0700	◨ 15485 (W Europe & N Africa)
0600-0800	◫ *6195* (W Europe)
0600-1700	12095 (Europe)
0600-1800	*15310* (S Asia)
0630-0700	*15400* (W Africa & C Africa)
0700-0800	*11765* (W Africa)
0700-0900	◫ 9410 (Europe)
0700-1000	*15400* (W Africa)
0700-1500	17640 (E Europe & W Asia)
0700-1600	*17790* (S Asia)
0700-1700	15485 (W Europe & N Africa)
0700-1800	15565 (E Europe)
0730-0900	Sa/Su *15575* (W Asia)
0800-0900	◨ 21830 (W Asia & S Asia)
0800-1000	*17830* (W Africa & C Africa)
0800-1100	*17885* (E Africa), *21660* (E Asia)
0800-1300	*21470* (S Africa)
0900-1000	*15190* (S America)
0900-1030	*15360* (E Asia)
0900-1100	6195 (SE Asia), *9605* (E Asia)
0900-1200	*15575* (W Asia)
0900-1600	*9740* (SE Asia & Australasia)
1000-1100	Sa/Su *15190* (S America), Sa/Su *15400* (W Africa), Sa/Su *17830* (W Africa & C Africa)
1000-1400	6195 (C America & N America), *17760* (E Asia)
1030-1100	*11945* & *15285* (E Asia)
1100-1130	*15400* (W Africa), *17790* (S America)
1100-1200	17885 (E Africa)
1100-1700	6195 (SE Asia), *15190* (C America & S America)
1100-2100	*17830* (W Africa & C Africa)
1130-1145	*7135* (E Asia), ◫ *11750* & ◨ *11920* (SE Asia)
1200-1400	*17885* (E Africa)
1200-1500	*15575* (Mideast)
1300-1400	*15420* (E Africa)
1300-1900	*21470* (S Africa)
1330-1345	*15105* (W Africa & C Africa), *21640* (W Africa)
1400-1600	◨ *6135* & ◨ *7160* (E Asia), *21660* (E Africa)
1445-1500	◫ M-Sa *6140*, M-Sa *7205* & M-Sa *15245* (S Asia)
1500-1530	*11860*, *15420* & *21490* (E Africa)
1500-1600	*5975* (S Asia), ◫ *9410* (Europe)
1500-2300	*15400* (W Africa)
1600-1700	◨ *9410* (W Europe), 17790 (W Asia & S Asia), ◫ *21660* (E Africa)
1600-1800	*3915* & *7160* (SE Asia), *9510* (S Asia)
1600-1830	*5975* (S Asia)

The London Eye holds 25 people in each capsule, with one trip around the Ferris-like wheel taking half an hour. It offers spectacular views of the city by day—even more so by night. T. Ohtake

1615-1700	Sa/Su *11860* & Sa/Su *21490* (E Africa)
1700-1745	*6005* & *9630* (E Africa)
1700-1800	🅂 15485 (W Europe & N Africa)
1700-1900	12095 (E Europe), *15420* (C Africa & E Africa)
1700-2200	*3255* (S Africa), 6195 & *9410* (Europe)
1800-2000	*15310* (Mideast)
1830-2100	*6005* & *9630* (E Africa)
1900-2100	*12095* (S Africa)
2100-2200	*3915* (S Asia & SE Asia), *6005* (S Africa), 🅆 *6110* (E Asia), *6195* (SE Asia), 🅂 *11945* (E Asia)
2100-2300	🅆 *9605* (W Africa)
2100-2400	*5965* (E Asia), *5975* (C America & N America), *12095* (S America), 🅂 *17830* (W Africa)
2115-2130	M-F *11675* & M-F *15390* (C America)
2130-2145	🅆 Tu/F 11680 & 🅂 Tu/F 11720 (Atlantic & S America)
2200-2300	🅂 *6195* (W Europe), *7105*, *9660* & *11955* (SE Asia), *12080* (S Pacific)
2200-2400	🅆 6195 (N Europe & W Europe), *6195* & *9740* (SE Asia)

2300-2400	*3915* (SE Asia), *11945* (E Asia), *11955* (SE Asia), *15280* (E Asia)
2330-2400	🅆 *6035* & 🅂 *9580* (E Asia)

WALES RADIO INTERNATIONAL

0200-0230	🅂 Sa 9795 (N America)
0300-0330	🅆 Sa 9735 (N America)
1130-1200	🅆 Sa 17625 (Australasia)
1230-1300	🅂 Sa 17745 (Australasia)
2030-2100	🅂 F *7150* (W Europe), 🅂 F *7325* (Europe)
2130-2200	🅆 F 5970 & 🅆 F 7110/5995 (Europe)

UNITED NATIONS
UNITED NATIONS RADIO

1730-1745	🅂 M-F *7150* & 🅆 M-F *7170* (S Africa), M-F *15495* (Mideast), M-F *17810* (W Africa & C Africa)

USA
ADVENTIST WORLD RADIO

0200-0230	🅆 *6175* & 🅂 *9820* (W Asia & S Asia)
1000-1030	🅂 *11560* (E Asia), 🅆 *11870* (SE Asia), 🅆 *11900* (E Asia), 🅂 *11930* (SE Asia)
1130-1200	🅆 *15260* & 🅂 *15435* (SE Asia)

Mark Fine demonstrates DRM reception at the 2004 Kulpsville Fest, an annual spring gathering of radio enthusiasts and professionals. Information on future Fests is at swlfest.com.   L. Magne

1200-1230	*15135* (S Asia)
1330-1400	*11980* (E Asia), 🅂 M/Tu/Th-Sa *15275* & 🅆 M/Tu/Th-Sa *15660* (S Asia)
1530-1600	*15225* (S Asia)
1600-1630	🅆 *15495/15480* (S Asia)
1600-1700	🅂 *15235* (S Asia)
1630-1700	🅂 *11975* & 🅆 *11980* (S Asia)
1730-1800	🅂 *9385* & 🅆 *11560* (Mideast)
1800-1830	*3215* & *3345* (S Africa), 🅆 W/F *9530* & 🅂 W/F *15470* (C Africa)
1800-1900	🅆 *11925* & 🅂 *12130* (E Africa)
2000-2100	🅂 *7170* & 🅆 *15295* (C Africa)
2100-2200	🅆 *9830* & 🅂 *15130* (W Africa)
2130-2200	🅂 *11850*, *11980* & 🅆 *12010* (E Asia)
2230-2300	*11850* & *15320* (SE Asia)

AFRTS-AMERICAN FORCES RADIO & TV SERVICE

0000-0500	🅂 *13855* (Irr) USB (Atlantic)
24 Hr	*4319/12579* USB (S Asia), 5447 USB (C America), *5765/13362* USB & 6350/10320 USB (Pacific), 7507 USB (C America), *7590* USB & *9980* USB (Atlantic), 12134 USB (Americas)
2100-2400	🅂 *13855* (Irr) USB (Atlantic)

FAMILY RADIO

0000-0100	🅂 6065 & 🅆 6085 (E North Am), 🅆 11720 & 🅂 15130 (S America)
0000-0445	9505 (N America)
0100-0200	*15195* (S Asia)
0100-0445	6065 (E North Am)
0200-0300	5985 & 11855 (C America), 🅂 15255 (S America)
0300-0400	🅆 9985 (S America), 11740 (C America)
0400-0500	7355 (Europe), 9715 (W North Am)
0400-0600	6855 (E North Am)
0500-0600	🅆 7520 & 🅂 9355 (Europe)
0600-0700	🅆 5850 (C America), 9680 (N America), 🅂 11530 (C Africa & S Africa), 🅆 11530 & 🅂 11580 (Europe), 🅆 11580 (C Africa & S Africa)
0600-0745	7355 (Europe)
0700-0745	5985 (N America)
0700-0800	🅆 9495 (C America), 9715 (W North Am)
0700-0845	🅂 9930 & 🅆 9985 (W Africa)
0700-1100	🅆 6855 (E North Am)
0800-1045	🅆 7455 (N America)
0800-1145	🅆 5950 (W North Am & C America)
1000-1145	🅂 9755 (W North Am)
1000-1245	🅂 5950 & 🅆 6890 (E North Am)
1100-1200	🅂 7355 (C America), 🅆 9555 (S America), 🅆 11725 (C America), 🅆 11830 & 🅂 11855 (S America)
1100-1245	🅂 5850 & 🅂 6015 (N America)
1100-1345	🅆 7355 (N America)
1200-1300	🅆 11530 (S America)
1200-1345	🅆 11970 (W North Am)
1200-1645	🅂 17750 (W North Am)

1300-1400	11830 & 🅂 11865 (N America)
1300-1500	*11560* (S Asia), 🅂 11970 (E North Am)
1300-1600	🅆 11855 (E North Am)
1400-1500	13695 (E North Am)
1400-1645	🅆 11615 (N America), 🅆 17760 (W North Am)
1500-1545	🅆 15210 (S America)
1500-1600	*6280* (S Asia)
1500-1700	*15520* (S Asia)
1600-1645	11830 & 🅂 11865 (N America)
1600-1700	6085 (C America), 🅂 15130 (W North Am), 🅆 17690 (C Africa), 🅂 21525 (C Africa & S Africa)
1600-1800	21455 (Europe)
1600-1945	13695 (E North Am), 18980 (Europe)
1700-1800	*21680* (C Africa & E Africa)
1700-2145	🅆 17510 & 🅂 17795 (W North Am)
1800-2100	🅆 15115 (W Africa)
1800-2145	🅆 17535 (N America)
1900-1945	6085 (C America), 🅂 15130 (W North Am), 🅆 15565 (Europe)
1900-2045	🅂 17750 (Europe)
1900-2100	*3230 & 6020* (S Africa)
1900-2200	🅂 17845 (W Africa)
1945-2145	🅂 18980 (Europe)
2000-2100	*15195* (C Africa)
2000-2200	🅆 5820 (Europe), 🅂 *7350* & 🅆 *7360* (W Europe), 🅆 7580 (Europe), 🅆 17575 & 🅂 17725 (S America)
2100-2200	🅆 15565 (W Africa), 🅂 18930 (Europe)
2200-2245	🅂 15695 (Europe), 🅂 15770 & 🅆 21525 (C Africa & S Africa)
2200-2300	🅆 9690 (S America)
2200-2345	11740 (N America)
2300-2400	5985 & 11855 (C America), 🅆 15170, 🅂 15255, 🅆 15400 & 🅂 17750 (S America)

KAIJ—(N America)

0000-0200	5755/13815
0200-1200	5755
1200-1400	5755/13815
1400-2400	13815

KJES

0100-0230	7555 (W North Am)
1300-1400	11715 (N America)
1400-1500	11715 (W North Am)
1800-1900	15385 (Australasia)

KTBN—(E North Am)

0000-0100	🅆 7505 & 🅂 15590
0100-1500	7505
1500-1600	🅆 7505 & 🅂 15590
1600-2400	15590

TRANS WORLD RADIO

0430-0500	🅂 M-F *3200*, M-F *4775* & 🅆 M-F *6120* (S Africa)
0500-0630	🅂 *4775 & 6120* (S Africa)
0500-0900	🅆 *7205* (S Africa), *9500* (S Africa & E Africa)
0600-0635	M-Sa *11640* (W Africa)
0630-0900	🅂 *6120* (S Africa)
0730-0740	Sa/Su *15205* (SE Asia)
0740-0900	*15205* (SE Asia)
0745-0755 ▭	Sa/Su *9870* (W Europe)
0745-0755	Sa/Su *11865* (W Europe)
0745-0815	M-F *11840* (Australasia & S Pacific)
0755-0850 ▭	*9870* (W Europe)
0755-0850	*11865* (W Europe)
0815-0930	*11840* (Australasia & S Pacific)
0850-0920 ▭	Su-F *9870* (W Europe)
0850-0920	Su-F *11865* (W Europe)
1215-1230	🅆 Sa/Su *7560* (S Asia)
1500-1600	*12105* (S Asia)
1630-1715	*6130* (S Africa)
1710-1725 ▭	*5855* (W Asia & C Asia)
1715-2045	*3200* (S Africa)
1730-1900	*9500* (E Africa)

UNIVERSITY NETWORK

0000-0200	*13750* (C America)
0000-1200	*5029* (C America), *6150* (C America & S America), *7375* (S America)
24 Hr	*9725* (N America)
0300-1600	🅂 *17765* (S Asia)
1200-2400	*11869* (S Asia)
2000-2400	*13750* (C America)

VOA-VOICE OF AMERICA

0000-0030	*11995* (W Asia & S Asia)
0000-0100	*7215* & 🅆 *9890* (SE Asia), *15185* (SE Asia & S Pacific), *15290 & 17820* (E Asia)
0030-0100	🅂 *9780* (S Asia & SE Asia), *11760* (SE Asia), *17740* (E Asia & S Pacific)
0100-0200	🅂 *7115*, 🅆 *7200*, 🅆 *7255*, 🅆 *9850*, 🅂 *9885*, 11705, 🅂 *11725*, 🅆 *11820*, 🅆 *15250*, 🅆 *15290*, 🅆 *17740* & 🅆 *17820* (S Asia)

Radio cognoscente Hans Johnson visits WRNO's transmitter building. The Louisiana station aired football, Cajun music and more, but after the owner died it was donated to the Catholic Church and fell into disrepair.

H. Johnson

0130-0200	Tu-Sa 7405, Tu-Sa 9775 & Tu-Sa 13740 (C America & S America)
0200-0300	**S** M-F *7115*, **W** M-F *7200*, **W** M-F *7255*, **W** M-F *9850*, **S** M-F *9885*, M-F 11705, **S** M-F *11725*, **W** M-F *11820*, **W** M-F 15250, **W** M-F 15290, **W** M-F *17740* & **W** M-F *17820* (S Asia)
0300-0330	M-F *7340* (C Africa & E Africa)
0300-0400	**W** *4960* (W Africa & C Africa), **W** M-F *6035* (E Africa & S Africa), **S** M-F *7105* (C Africa & S Africa)
0300-0430	M-F *9885* (C Africa)
0300-0500	M-F *6080* (C Africa & S Africa), **W** M-F *7290* (C Africa & E Africa), **W** M-F *7415* (C Africa & S Africa), **S** *11695* (Mideast), **S** M-F *17895* (C Africa & E Africa)
0300-0600	**S** M-F *7290* (C Africa & S Africa)
0300-0630	**S** M-F *12080* (E Africa & S Africa)
0400-0500	*4960* & 9575 (W Africa & C Africa), **W** M-F *9775* (C Africa & E Africa), **S** M-F *11835* (Africa)
0400-0600	**W** *15205* (E Europe & W Asia)
0400-0700	**W** *7170* (N Africa)

0500-0600	**S** M-F *6080* (C Africa & S Africa), **W** *9700* (N Africa & W Africa)
0500-0630	M-F 6035 & **W** M-F *6105* (W Africa & C Africa), **S** M-F *6180* (W Africa), **W** M-F *7295* (W Africa & C Africa), **W** M-F *13710* (C Africa & E Africa)
0600-0630	**W** M-F *11995* (C Africa & E Africa)
0600-0700	**W** *5995* (N Africa), Sa/Su *6080* (W Africa), **S** *7290* (W Africa & C Africa), **W** Sa/Su *11835* (C Africa & S Africa)
1200-1300	**W** *6110* & **S** *6160* (SE Asia), **W** *11715* (E Asia & Australasia), **S** *15240* & **W** *15665* (E Asia)
1200-1400	*9645* (SE Asia & Australasia)
1200-1500	*9760* (E Asia, S Asia & SE Asia), **W** *11705* (E Asia)
1300-1600	**W** *6110* (S Asia & SE Asia)
1400-1500	**W** *9645* (S Asia), *15425* (SE Asia & Pacific)
1400-1800	**S** *6160* (S Asia & SE Asia), *7125* (S Asia)
1500-1600	**S** *9590* & **S** *9760* (S Asia & SE Asia), **W** *9760* (E Asia, S Asia & SE Asia), **W** *9795*, **W** *9825*, **S** *9845* & **S** *12040* (E Asia), **W** *15460* & **S** *15550* (SE Asia & Australasia)

1500-1700	[W] 9645 (S Asia), [W] 9685 (Mideast & S Asia)
1600-1700	[W] 6035 (W Africa), [S] 9670 & [S] 9700 (Mideast & S Asia), 9760 (S Asia & SE Asia), [W] 9855 (Mideast), [S] 12080 (C Africa & S Africa), [S] 13600 (SE Asia), [W] 13600 (S Africa), [S] 15225 (C Africa & S Africa), [W] 15255 (Mideast), [S] 15410 (C Africa & E Africa), [W] 17640 (E Africa), [W] 17715 (C Africa), [S] 17895 (C Africa & S Africa), [W] 17895 (C Africa & E Africa)
1600-1800	[S] 15255 (E Europe & W Asia), [W] 15445 (E Africa)
1600-2000	[W] 13710 (E Africa & S Africa), [S] 15580 (Africa)
1600-2100	[S] 9850 (S Africa)
1600-2200	[W] 15240 (Africa)
1700-1800	M-F 5990 (SE Asia & Australasia), [W] 6040 (N Africa & Mideast), [W] M-F 6045 (E Asia & Australasia), 9645 (S Asia), [S] 9700 (Mideast & S Asia), [W] M-F 9760 (S Asia & SE Asia), [W] M-F 11955 (E Asia & SE Asia), [W] M-F 12005 (SE Asia), [W] M-F 15230 (E Asia & Australasia), [W] 15255 (Mideast)
1700-2100	[S] 6040 (Mideast), [S] 9760 (N Africa & Mideast), [W] 9760 (Mideast & S Asia)
1700-2200	[S] 15410 (Africa)
1740-1800	11975 & 17895 (S Africa)
1800-1900	[W] 9530 (W Asia), [S] 9770 (Mideast), [W] 11665 (N Africa & Mideast)
1800-2000	[S] 17895 (W Africa), [W] 17895 (C Africa & E Africa)
1800-2200	[W] 6035 (W Africa), 11975 (C Africa & E Africa), [W] 15580 (W Africa & C Africa)
1900-2000	[S] 7260, [S] 9670, [W] 9785, [W] 12015, [S] 13635 & [W] 13640 (Mideast)
1900-2030	4940 (W Africa & C Africa)
1900-2100	[W] 9690 (Mideast & S Asia), [S] 9770 (N Africa & E Africa)
1900-2200	[W] 7415 (E Africa & S Africa), [S] 13670 (E Africa), [S] 15445 (W Africa)
2000-2030	[S] 11855 (W Africa)
2000-2100	6095 (Mideast), [S] 17745 (W Africa & C Africa)
2000-2200	[W] 13710 & [W] 17895 (W Africa & C Africa)
2030-2100	Sa/Su 4940 (W Africa & C Africa)
2030-2230	11835 (W Asia & S Asia)
2100-2200	[W] 6040, [W] 6095 & [W] 9595 (Mideast), [W] 15385 (C Africa & E Africa)
2200-2300	[W] 6045 (E Asia)
2200-2400	7215 (SE Asia), [W] 9670 (SE Asia & Australasia), [W] 9890 & [W] 11760 (SE Asia), 15185 (SE Asia & S Pacific), 15290 (E Asia), 15305 (E Asia & SE Asia), [W] 17735 (SE Asia), 17740 (E Asia & S Pacific), 17820 (E Asia)
2230-2300	[S] 13755 (E Asia)
2230-2330	[S] 9560 & [W] 9780 (E Asia), 11935 (W Asia & S Asia), [S] 15145 & [W] 15150 (E Asia)
2300-2330	[S] 13755 (E Asia)
2300-2400	[W] 6180, [W] 7205 & [W] 11655 (E Asia)
2330-2400	[W] 7130, [S] 7225, [S] 7260, [W] 9620 & 11805 (SE Asia), 11995 (W Asia & S Asia), [W] 13640, [S] 13725 & 15205 (SE Asia)

WBCQ-"THE PLANET"—(N America)

0000-0100	[◄] 5105
0000-0230	[◄] 9330 LSB
0000-0530	[◄] 7415
0100-0500	[◄] M/Sa 5105
0230-0500	[◄] Tu-Su 9330 LSB
0530-0600	[◄] Su/M 7415
0600-0800	[◄] Su 7415
1700-2030	[◄] M-F 17495
1945-2100	[◄] M-F 7415 & M-F 9330 LSB
2030-2200	[◄] M-Sa 17495
2100-2200	[◄] M-Sa 7415
2100-2400	[◄] M-F 5105 & 9330 LSB
2200-2400	[◄] 7415 & M-F 17495

WBOH—(C America)

0200-1105 &	
1200-0100	[◄] 5920

WEWN

0000-1000	5825 (N America)
0500-0800	[W] 7570 (Europe)
0600-0900	[S] 7580 (Europe)
1000-1300	[W] 5825 (N America)

1000-1400	⬛ 7520 (N America)
1300-1400	⬛ 9955 (N America)
1400-1600	9955 (N America)
1600-2000	⬛ 15695 (Europe)
1600-2200	13615 (N America)
1700-2000	⬛ 15685 (Europe)
2000-2200	17595 (W Africa)
2200-2400	9975 (N America), ⬛ 15695 (Europe), ⬛ 15745 (W Africa)

WINB-WORLD INTERNATIONAL BROADCASTERS—(C America & W North Am)

1200-1300 ⬛	Sa/Su 9320
1300-2300 ⬛	13570
2300-0500 ⬛	9320

WJIE SHORTWAVE

24 Hr	7490 (E North Am), 13595 (W North Am)

WMLK—(Europe, Mideast & N America)

1600-2100	Su-F 9465

WORLD HARVEST RADIO

0000-0030	Su-F 17510 (E Asia)
0000-0200	Tu-Su 7315 (C America & S America)
0000-0500	7580 (Europe & Mideast)
0000-1000	7535 (E North Am)
0030-0230	17510 (E Asia)
0200-0800	7315 (C America & S America)
0230-0300	Su/M 17510 (E Asia)
0300-0400	17510 (E Asia)
0400-0530	17780 (E Asia)
0500-1000	⬛ 7580 & ⬛ 11730 (Africa)
0530-0600	Su-F 17780 (E Asia)
0600-0800	17780 (E Asia)
0700-1045	11565 (Australasia)
0800-0900	⬛ 9930 & ⬛ 17780 (E Asia)
0800-1000	M-Sa 7315 (C America & S America)
0900-1000	⬛ Su-F 9930 & ⬛ Su-F 17780 (E Asia)
1000-1030	Su-F 9930 (E Asia)
1000-1300	9495/7315 (C America), ⬛ 9850/7535 (E North Am)
1000-1600	⬛ 9840 (E North Am)
1045-1300	Sa/Su 11565 (Australasia)
1130-1230	9930 (E Asia)
1230-1300	Su 9930 (E Asia & SE Asia)
1300-1330	Sa/Su 9930 (E Asia & SE Asia)
1300-1500	⬛ 11670/9850 (E North Am), 17560 (Europe & Mideast)
1300-1700	15105 (C America & S America)
1330-1400	Su 9930 (E Asia & SE Asia)
1500-1600	⬛ 13760 (E North Am & W Europe), ⬛ 17560 (Europe & Mideast)
1500-1900	⬛ 17650 (Africa)
1600-1700	Sa/Su 9930 (E Asia)
1600-1900	⬛ 17650 (Europe & Mideast)
1600-2000	13760 (E North Am & W Europe)
1700-1800	⬛ 15105 & ⬛ 15565 (C America & S America)
1800-2200	15565 (C America & S America)
1900-2300	17650 (Africa)
2000-2100	⬛ 13760 (E North Am & W Europe)
2100-2200	⬛ 13770 (E North Am & Europe)
2200-2300	Su-F 9495 (C America & S America), 17510 (E Asia & SE Asia)
2200-2400	⬛ M-F 9430 (E North Am), ⬛ Sa/Su 13770 (E North Am & Europe)
2300-2345	Sa/Su 9495 (C America & S America)
2300-2400	7580 (Europe & Mideast), Su-F 17510 (E Asia & SE Asia)
2345-2400	9495 (C America & S America)

WRMI-RADIO MIAMI INTERNATIONAL

0000-0300 ⬛	Tu-Sa 6870 (N America)
0300-0330 ⬛	M-Sa 6870 (N America)
0330-1000 ⬛	6870 (N America)
1300-2300 ⬛	15725 (N America)
2300-2400 ⬛	M-F 15725 (N America)

WTJC—(E North Am)

0400-0300 ⬛	9370

WWCR

0000-0100	⬛ 3210/9475 & ⬛ 3210 (E North Am)
0000-0200	5935/13845 & ⬛ 7465 (E North Am)
0000-1200	5070 (E North Am)
0100-0900	3210 (E North Am)
0200-0400	5765/7465 (E North Am)
0200-1200	5935 (E North Am)
0400-1000	5765 (E North Am)
0900-1000	⬛ 3210 & ⬛ 9475 (E North Am)
1000-1100	⬛ 9985 & ⬛ Su-F 15825 (E North Am)
1000-1300	5765/7465 (E North Am)

1100-1130 [S] Sa/Su 15825 (E North Am)
1100-1200 [W] Su-F 15825 (E North Am)
1130-1200 [S] 15825 (E North Am)
1200-1230 [S] 15825 & [W] Sa/Su 15825 (E North Am)
1200-1300 [W] 5070 (E North Am)
1200-1400 5935/13845 (E North Am)
1230-2100 15825 (E North Am)
1300-1500 7465 (E North Am)
1300-1600 ⇦ 9985 (E North Am)
1400-2400 13845 (E North Am)
1500-1600 [W] 7465 (E North Am), [S] 12160 (E North Am & Europe)
1500-2400 [S] 9475 (E North Am)
1600-2200 [W] 9985 (E North Am), 12160 (E North Am & Europe)
2100-2145 [S] Sa/Su 15825 (E North Am)
2100-2200 [W] 15825 (Irr) (E North Am)
2145-2200 [S] 15825 (E North Am)
2200-2245 [W] Sa/Su 9985 (E North Am)
2200-2400 5070/12160 (E North Am & Europe), [W] 7465 (E North Am)
2300-2400 [W] 3210/9985 (E North Am)

WWRB

0000-0500 5050 & 5745 (N America)
0000-0600 5085 & 6890 (E North Am & N Europe)
1600-2230 Su-F 9320 (E North Am & N Europe)
1600-2300 Su-F 12172 (E North Am, Europe & N Africa)
2300-2400 [W] 5085 & 6890 (E North Am & N Europe), [S] 12172 (E North Am, Europe & N Africa)

UZBEKISTAN

RADIO TASHKENT

0100-0130 [W] 5975 (S Asia), [W] 6165 (W Asia & S Asia), [W] 7135 & [W] 7160 (S Asia), [S] 7190 & [S] 9715 (W Asia & S Asia)
1200-1230 &
1330-1400 [W] 5060, [W] 5975, [W] 6025, [S] 7285, 9715 & [S] 15295 (S Asia), [S] 17775 (S Asia & SE Asia)
2030-2100 5025, [W] 7105, [W] 7185 & 11905 (Europe)
2130-2200 5025, [W] 7185 & [S] 11905 (Europe)

VATICAN STATE

VATICAN RADIO

0250-0310 7305 (E North Am), 9605 (E North Am & C America)
0500-0530 [W] 7360 (E Africa), 9660 (Africa), 11625 & 15570 (E Africa)
0600-0620 ⇦ 4005 (Europe), 5890 (W Europe)
0630-0645 [S] M-Sa 9645 (S Europe & N Africa)
0730-0745 ⇦ M-Sa 4005 (Europe), M-Sa 5890 (W Europe), M-Sa 7250 (Europe), M-Sa 11740 (W Europe & N Africa), M-Sa 15595 (Mideast)
0730-0745 [W] M-Sa 9645 (W Europe)
1120-1130 ⇦ M-Sa 7250 (Europe), M-Sa 11740 (W Europe)
1615-1630 [S] 7250 (N Europe)
1715-1730 ⇦ 4005 (Europe), 5890 & 9645 (W Europe)
1715-1730 [W] 7250 (Mideast)
2050-2110 ⇦ 4005 & 5890 (Europe)

VIETNAM

VOICE OF VIETNAM

0100-0130,
0230-0300 &
0330-0400 *6175* (E North Am & C America)
1100-1130 7285 (SE Asia)
1230 1300 9840 & 12020 (SE Asia)
1500-1530 7285, 9840 & 12020 (SE Asia)
1600-1630 7220 (W Africa & C Africa), [W] 7280 (Europe), 9550 (W Africa & C Africa), 9730 & [S] 13740 (Europe)
1700-1730 [S] *9725* (W Europe)
1800-1830 [W] *5955* (W Europe), [W] 7280, 9730 & [S] 13740 (Europe)
1900-1930 &
2000-2030 [W] 7280, 9730 & [S] 13740 (Europe)
2030-2100 7220 & 9550 (W Africa & C Africa)
2330-2400 9840 & 12020 (SE Asia)

YEMEN

REPUBLIC OF YEMEN RADIO—(Mideast & E Africa)

1800-1900 9780

Voices from Home—2005

Country-by-Country Guide to Native Broadcasts

For some, English offerings are merely icing on the cake. Their real interest is in eavesdropping on broadcasts for *nativos*—the home folks. These can be enjoyable regardless of language, especially when they offer traditional music.

Some you'll hear, many you won't, depending on your location and equipment. Keep in mind that native-language broadcasts are sometimes weaker than those in English, so you may need more patience and better hardware. PASSPORT REPORTS shows which radios and antennas work best.

When to Tune

Some broadcasts come in better during the day within world band segments from 9300 to 21850 kHz. However, signals from Latin America and Africa peak near or during darkness, especially from 4700 to 5100 kHz. See "Best Times and Frequencies" for specifics.

Times and days of the week are in World Time, explained in "Setting Your World Time Clock" and PASSPORT's glossary; for local times in each country, see "Addresses PLUS." Midyear, some stations are an hour earlier (◧) or later (◨) because of daylight saving/summer time. Those used only seasonally are labeled ▪ for summer (midyear, typically the last Sunday in March until the last Sunday in October) and ▪ for winter. Stations may also extend their hours for holidays, emergencies or sports events.

Frequencies in *italics* may be best, as they come from relay transmitters that could be near you, although other frequencies beamed your way might do almost as well. Some signals not beamed to you can also be heard, especially when they are for audiences in nearby parts of the world. Frequencies with no target zones are usually for domestic coverage, so they are the least likely to be heard unless you're in or near that country.

Nativo **broadcasts are enjoyed worldwide.**

Schedules for Entire Year

To be as useful as possible over the months to come, PASSPORT's schedules consist not just of observed activity, but also that which we have creatively opined will take place during the forthcoming year. This predictive material is based on decades of experience and is original from us. Although inherently not as exact as real-time data, over the years it's been of tangible value to PASSPORT readers.

Despite years of destruction by hostile armies, looters, vandals and nature, much Buddhist sculpture remains throughout Southeast Asia.

M. Guha

ALBANIA—Albanian

RADIO TIRANA

0000-0130 ⬅	6115 & 7270 (E North Am)
0630-0900	[S] 7110 (Europe)
0730-1000	[W] 7105 (Europe)
2130-2300 ⬅	6100 & 7295/6205 (Europe)

ARGENTINA—Spanish

RADIO ARGENTINA AL EXTERIOR-RAE

1200-1400	M-F 11710 (S America)
2200-2400	M-F 6060 (C America & S America), M-F 11710 (Europe & N Africa), M-F 15345 (Europe)

RADIO NACIONAL

0000-0100	M 11710 (S America)
0000-0230	Su/M 6060 (C America & S America), Su/M 15345 (Americas)
0230-0300	M 6060 (C America & S America), M 15345 (Americas)
0900-1200	6060 (S America)
1800-2000	Su 6060 & Su 11710 (S America), Su 15345 (Europe)
2000-2200	Sa/Su 11710 (S America)
2000-2400	Sa/Su 6060 (S America), Sa/Su 15345 (Europe)
2200-2400	Su 11710 (S America)

ARMENIA—Armenian

VOICE OF ARMENIA

0300-0330 ⬅	4810 (Irr) (E Europe, Mideast & W Asia), 9965 (S America)
0400-0430 ⬅	9965 (Irr) (S America)
0800-0830 ⬅	Su 4810 (E Europe, Mideast & W Asia), Su 15270 (Europe)
1930-2000 ⬅	M-Sa 4810 (E Europe, Mideast & W Asia), M-Sa 9960 (Europe)

AUSTRIA—German

RADIO AUSTRIA INTERNATIONAL

0000-0015	[S] Tu-Sa 9870 (C America)
0005-0015 & 0035-0045	[W] Tu-Sa 13730 (S America)
0100-0115	[S] Tu-Sa 9870 (E North Am), [W] Tu-Sa 9870 (C America)
0105-0115	[W] Tu-Sa 7325 (E North Am)
0135-0145	[W] Tu-Sa 7325 & [S] Tu-Sa 9870 (E North Am), [W] Tu-Sa 9870 (C America)
0500-1305 ⬅	6155 & 13730 (Europe)
0600-0700 ⬅	M-Sa 17870 (Mideast)
1200-1215 & 1230-1245	[S] M-F 17715 (S Asia, SE Asia & Australasia)
1300-1315	[W] M-F 17855 (S Asia, SE Asia & Australasia)
1305-1330 & 1330-1345 ⬅	M-F 6155 & M-F 13730 (Europe)
1330-1345	[W] M-F 17855 (S Asia, SE Asia & Australasia)
1400-1830 ⬅	13730 (Europe)
1400-2308 ⬅	6155 (Europe)
1500-1510 & 1525-1540	[S] M-F *13755* (W North Am)
1600-1610 & 1625-1640	[W] M-F *13675* (W North Am)
1830-2308 ⬅	5945 (Europe, N Africa & Mideast)
2305-2315 & 2335-2345	[S] M-F 9870 (S America)

BANGLADESH—Bangla

BANGLADESH BETAR

1630-1730	7185 & 9550 (Mideast)
1915-2000	7185 & 9550 (Europe)

BELGIUM

RADIO VLAANDEREN INTERNATIONAAL

Dutch

0430-0500	[S] *11635* (W North Am)
0500-0530	[S] *9925* (C Africa)
0500-0700	[S] *9590* (Europe)
0500-0800	[S] *15195* (Europe)
0530-0600	[W] *9590* (W North Am)
0600-0630	[W] *17730/15530* (C Africa)
0600-0800	[W] *5965* (S Europe & Mideast)
0600-0900	[W] *9925* (Europe)
0700-0800	[S] *9590* (W Europe & N Africa)
0800-0900	[W] *9590* (S Europe & W Africa)
1100-1130	[S] *15195* (W Europe & N Africa), [S] *15450* (Europe)
1100-1200 ⬅	Su *21630/17745* (C Africa)
1200-1230 ⬅	*21630/17745* (C Africa)
1200-1230	*9940/9945* (E Asia, SE Asia & Australasia), [W] *13690* (S Europe & W Africa), [W] *15160* (Europe), [W] *17690* (SE Asia), [S] *17695* (SE Asia & Australasia)
1300-1600	[S] Su *15160* (W Europe & N Africa), [S] Su *15195* (Europe)

1400-1700   [W] Su *9590* (W Europe & N Africa), [W] Su *13800* (Europe)

1700-1800   [S] *13690* (W Europe & N Africa)

1800-1900   [S] *9925* (Europe), [S] *11640* (S Europe & Mideast), [S] *13690* (W Europe & N Africa), [S] *15325* (C Africa)

1800-2000   [S] Sa *5910* (W Europe), [W] *13790/13690* (W Europe & W Africa)

1900-2000   [W] *5910* (S Europe & Mideast), [W] *7330/7490* (Europe), [W] *13690/13790* (C Africa)

1900-2100   [W] Sa *5985* (Europe)

2000-2100   [S] *9840* (W Europe & N Africa), [S] *9925* (Europe)

2100-2200   [W] *5960* (S Europe & W Africa), [W] *7330/7490* (Europe)

2230-2300   [W] *9590/11730* & [S] *11635* (N America)

RTBF INTERNATIONAL
French

0550-0700 [↔] Su-F 9970 (S Europe)
0600-0812 [↔] *17580* (C Africa)
0700-1800 [↔] 9970 (S Europe)
0812-1100 [↔] Sa/Su *17580* (C Africa)
1100-1230 [↔] *21565* (C Africa)
1530-1600 [↔] M-F *17570* (C Africa)
1600-1805 [↔] *17570* (C Africa)
1800-2100 [↔] M-Sa 9970 (S Europe)
1805-1902 [↔] M-F *17570* (C Africa)
2100-2200 [↔] Sa 9970 (S Europe)

BRAZIL—Portuguese

RADIO BANDEIRANTES
24 Hr   6090, 9645, 11925

RADIO BRASIL CENTRAL
0000-0200 [→] 4985
0000-0330 [→] 11815
0200-0600 [→] 4985 (Irr)
0330-0600 [→] 11815 (Irr)
0600-2400 [→] 4985, 11815

RADIO CULTURA
0000-0200 [→] 6170, 9615, 17815
0700-2400 [→] 9615, 17815
0800-2400 [→] 6170

RADIO GUAIBA
0700-0300 [→] 6000, 11785

RADIO NACIONAL DA AMAZONIA
0000-0050   6180/6190
0000-0230 [→] 11780

0230-0700 [→] Su 11780
0700-0800 [W] 6180/6190
0700-2400 [→] 11780
0800-1850 &
2110-2400   6180/6190

BULGARIA—Bulgarian

RADIO BULGARIA
0000-0100   [S] 9700 & [S] 11700 (E North Am)

0100-0200 [↔] 9500 & 11600/11500 (S America)

0100-0200   [W] 7400 & [W] 9400 (E North Am)

0400-0430   [S] Sa/Su 7200 (S Europe), [S] Sa/Su 11500 (W Europe)

0430-0500   [S] 7200 (S Europe), [S] 11500 (W Europe)

0500-0530 [↔] Sa/Su 7500 & Sa/Su 9400 (E Europe), Sa/Su 9500 (W Europe)

0500-0530   [W] Sa/Su 5800 (W Europe), [W] Sa/Su 5900 (S Europe)

0530-0600 [↔] 7500 & 9400 (E Europe), 9500 (W Europe)

0530-0600   [W] 5800 (W Europe), [W] 5900 (S Europe)

1100-1130 [↔] 7200 (S Europe), 11600 (E Europe), 11700 (W Europe), 13600 (E Europe), 15700 (W Europe)

1300-1500 [↔] 11700 & 15700 (W Europe)

1500-1600   [S] 7200 (S Europe), [S] 9400 (E Europe), [S] 15700 (Mideast)

1600-1700 [↔] 7500 (E Europe), 17500 (S Africa)

1600-1700   [W] 5800 (E Europe), [W] 5900 (S Europe), [W] 9400 (Mideast)

1900-2000 [↔] 5900 (S Europe)

1900-2100 [↔] 7200 (W Europe), 7400 (Mideast)

CANADA—French

CANADIAN BROADCASTING CORP—(E North Am)
0100-0300 [↔] M 9625
0300-0400 [↔] Su 9625 & Tu-Sa 9625
1300-1310 &
1500-1555 [↔] M-F 9625
1700-1715 [↔] Su 9625
1900-1945 [↔] M-F 9625
1900-2310 [↔] Sa 9625

RADIO CANADA INTERNATIONAL

1000-1200	🅂 11945 (E North Am & C America)
1100-1300	🅆 9515 (C America)
1200-1300	🅂 Sa/Su 11945 (E North Am & C America)
1300-1400	🅆 Sa/Su 9515 (E North Am & C America)
1500-1600	🅂 M-F 17765 (C America)
1600-1700	🅆 M-F 17835 (C America)
1600-1900	🅂 17765 (C America)
1700-2000	🅆 17835 (C America)
1900-2000	🅂 5995 (Europe), 🅂 7235 (W Europe & N Africa), 🅆 11845 (C Africa), 🅆 13650 (W Africa), 🅂 13700 (W Europe), 🅆 15140 (W Africa & C Africa), 🅆 17735 (W Africa)
1900-2100	🅂 15325 (W Europe & N Africa)
2000-2100 ⬅	5850 (W Europe)
2000-2100	🅆 7235, 🅆 9710 & 🅆 11725 (W Europe), 🅂 11890/11965 (N Africa & W Africa)
2100-2200	🅆 7235, 🅆 9565 & 🅆 11845 (N Africa)
2200-2300	🅂 9390 & 🅆 9665 (W Africa), 🅂 11755 & 🅆 11835 (W Africa & C Africa), 🅂 15300 (C America)
2300-2400	🅆 15180 (C America)

CHINA

CHINA RADIO INTERNATIONAL
Chinese

0000-0100	🅂 5960 & 🅆 6040 (E North Am), 🅆 11730 & 🅂 11930 (W North Am)
0100-0200	🅆 7180 & 🅂 13640 (S Asia)
0200-0300	9580 (E North Am), 9690 (N America & C America), 17680/11695 (S America)
0300-0400	🅆 9590 (Europe), 9720 (W North Am), 🅂 13600 (Europe)
0600-0800	17650 (W Europe)
0900-1000	9665 & 15110 (E Asia), 15125 & 15440 (Australasia)
0900-1100	11980, 15340 & 17785 (SE Asia)
1000-1200	17650 (W Europe)
1200-1400	11875 (Australasia), 15340 & 17785 (SE Asia)

1400-1600	🅆 6075 & 🅂 9610 (S Asia), 🅂 17650 (W Europe)
1500-1600	7265 & 9560 (S Asia), 🅆 13675 (W North Am)
1600-1700	🅆 17735 (W North Am)
1730-1830	🅆 6150 & 🅆 7120 (Europe), 🅆 7160 (Mideast), 🅆 7315 (N Africa), 9645 (W Africa & C Africa), 🅂 9685 (Europe), 9745 (Mideast & N Africa), 🅂 11660 (Europe), 🅂 11760 & 🅂 11835 (Mideast & N Africa)
1800-2000	🅂 11940 (Europe)
2000-2100	7245 (Mideast & N Africa), 🅆 7335 (Europe), 9685 & 9865 (Mideast), 🅂 13775 (Europe)
2200-2300	5955 (E Asia), 🅆 5975 (E Africa), 6140 & 🅂 7180 (SE Asia), 🅆 7180 (E Asia), 7190 (E Africa & S Africa), 🅆 7220 (SE Asia), 7265 (Mideast & W Asia), 9460 & 9550 (SE Asia), 🅂 9695 (E Asia), 11945, 15260 & 15400 (SE Asia)
2230-2300	15505 (W Africa, C Africa & E Africa)
2230-2400	11975 (N Africa)
2300-2400	7170 (W Africa)

CHINA (TAIWAN)

CENTRAL BROADCASTING SYSTEM-CBS
Chinese

0000-0200	11640 & 11885/11985 (E Asia)
0000-0300	9660/9680 & 11710 (E Asia)
0100-0200	🅆 11825, 15215 & 🅂 17845 (S America)
0100-0500	11940 (E Asia)
0200-0500	15290 (E Asia)
0300-0500	15215 (E Asia)
0400-0500	5950 (W North Am), 9680 (N America), 15270 & 15320 (SE Asia)
0400-0600	11640, M-F 11985/11970 & 15430/15335 (E Asia)
0400-0900	Sa/Su 11730 (E Asia)
0500-0600	🅆 9495 & 🅂 11740 (C America), 15270 (SE Asia)
0500-0800	Sa/Su 15215 (E Asia)
0600-0900	Sa/Su 15430/15335 (E Asia)
0600-1000	Sa/Su 11640 & 11795/11775 (E Asia)

0900-1000	Sa/Su 6085, Sa/Su 7185 & 11605 (E Asia), 11635 (SE Asia), Sa/Su 11665 (E Asia), 11715 (Australasia), 11940 & 15525 (SE Asia)
0900-1100	9415 (E Asia)
0900-1300	15395/15215 (E Asia)
0900-1400	7270 (E Asia)
0900-1700	9780 (E Asia)
1000-1400	11640 (E Asia)
1000-1500	6085 (E Asia)
1000-1700	7185 & 11665 (E Asia)
1100-1200	11715 (Australasia)
1100-1400	11875/11855 (E Asia)
1100-1700	11780/11770 (E Asia)
1200-1300	11605 (E Asia), 15465 (SE Asia)
1300-1400	15265 (SE Asia)
1300-1500	7105 (SE Asia)
1400-1700	9680 (E Asia)
1400-1800	6145 & 7130 (E Asia)
1900-2000	9565, ◼ *15600* & ◻ *17760* (Europe)
2200-2300	*3965* (W Europe)
2200-2400	*5950* (E North Am), 11635 (SE Asia), 11710 (E Asia), *15440* (W North Am)
2230-2400	6150 & 11885/11985 (E Asia)
2300-2400	9660/9680 (E Asia), 9790 (SE Asia), 15345/15245 (E Asia)

VOICE OF HAN—(E Asia)
Chinese

0655-0105	9745
0655-1500 &	
2100-0105	6105

CROATIA—Croatian

CROATIAN RADIO

0400-1000	◼ 13830 (Europe)
0500-1000	◻ 7365 (Europe & Mideast)
0500-1800 ▭	9830 (Europe & Mideast)
0500-2400 ▭	6165 (Europe)
1000-2200	13830 (Europe & Mideast)
2200-2300	◼ 13830 (Europe)

VOICE OF CROATIA

0000-0100	◼ *9925* (E North Am & S America)
0000-0200	◻ *7285* (E North Am & S America)
0100-0215 &	
0250-0300	◼ *9925* (N America & S America)
0300-0500	◼ *9925* (W North Am)

0350-0400	◻ *7285* (N America & S America)
0400-0600	◻ *7285* (W North Am)
0500-0800 ▭	*9470* (Australasia)
0600-1000	*13820/12110* (Australasia)
2200-2215 &	
2250-2300	◼ *9925* (S America)
2300-2315	◻ *7285* (S America)
2300-2400	◼ *9925* (E North Am & S America)
2350-2400	◻ *7285* (S America)

CUBA—Spanish

RADIO HABANA CUBA

0000-0100 ▭	Tu-Sa 6000 & Tu-Sa 11875 (E North Am)
0000-0100	9820 (N America)
0000-0500	5965 (C America & W North Am), 9505 (C America), 9600 (S America), 11760 (E North Am), 15230 (S America)
0200-0500	9550 (C America)
0300-0500	11875 (S America)
1100-1400	6000 & 9820/9550 (C America)
1100-1500	11705 (S America), 11760 (Americas), 15230 (S America)
1400-1830	Su 11670 (C America), Su 11875 (S America), Su 13680 (C America), Su 13750 & ◼ Su 17750 (N America)
2100-2300	9550 (C America), 15120 (Europe), 15230 (S America)
2300-2400 ▭	M-F 6000 & M-F 11875 (E North Am)

RADIO REBELDE

24 Hr	5025
0300-0400	6120 (C America)
1100-1300	6140/11655 & 9600 (C America)
1700-1800	11655 & 15570 (C America)

CZECH REPUBLIC—Czech

RADIO PRAGUE

0030-0100	◻ 5930 (S America), ◻ 7345 (N America)
0130-0200	◼ 6200 (N America & C America), ◼ 7345 (S America)
0230-0300	◻ 6200 (N America & C America), ◼ 7345 (N America), ◻ 7345 (S America), ◼ 9870 (W North Am & C America)

0330-0400   [W] 6200 (W North Am & C America), [W] 7345 (N America)
0830-0900   [S] 21745 (E Africa & Mideast)
0930-1000 [←] 11600 (W Europe)
0930-1000   [S] 21745 (S Asia & W Africa), [W] 21745 (E Africa & Mideast)
1030-1100   [W] 21745 (S Asia & W Africa)
1100-1130   [S] 11615 (N Europe), [S] 21745 (S Asia)
1200-1230   [W] 11640 (N Europe), [W] 21745 (S Asia, SE Asia & Australasia)
1330-1400 [←] 6055 (Europe), 7345 (W Europe)
1330-1400   [S] 13580 (N Europe), [S] 21745 (S Asia)
1430-1500   [W] 21745 (N America & E Africa)
1530-1600   [S] 17485 (E Africa)
1630-1700 [←] 5930 (W Europe)
1630-1700   [W] 15710 (W Africa & C Africa)
1730-1800   [S] 5930 (E Europe, Asia & Australasia), [S] 17485 (C Africa)
1830-1900   [W] 5930 (W Europe), [W] 9415 (Asia & Australasia)
1930-2000   [S] 11600 (SE Asia & Australasia)
2030-2100 [←] 5930 (W Europe)
2030-2100   [W] 9430 (SE Asia & Australasia)
2100-2130   [S] 9800 (W Africa), [S] 11600 (SE Asia & Australasia)
2200-2230   [W] 5930 (W Europe), [W] 9435 (W Europe & S America)
2330-2400   [S] 7345 & [S] 9440 (S America)

EGYPT—Arabic

EGYPTIAN RADIO
0000-0030 [←] 11665 (E Africa)
0000-0400 [←] 12050 (Europe & E North Am)
0700-1100 [←] 15115 (W Africa)
1200-2400 [←] 12050 (Europe & E North Am)
1900-2400 [←] 11665 (E Africa)

RADIO CAIRO
0000-0045   9735 & 11755 (S America)
0030-0430   7115 (N America)
1015-1215   17775 (Mideast)
1300-1600   15365 (C Africa)
2000-2200   7270/9750 (Australasia)
2330-2400   9735 & 11755 (S America)

FINLAND—Finnish & Swedish

YLE RADIO FINLAND
0200-0300   [S] 5955 (E Europe)
0300-0500   [S] 11995 (Mideast), [S] 13685 (E Africa)

0345-0400   [S] 5955 (E Europe)
0400-0600   [S] 9655/6120 (E Europe & Mideast), [W] 9815 (E Africa & S Africa), [W] 11865 (E Africa)
0400-0700   [W] 6120 (E Europe & Mideast)
0400-2100   6120 (Europe)
0500-0600   [S] 11755 (Europe)
0600-0800   [S] 15135/9560 (W Europe & Australasia)
0600-1900   11755 (Europe)
0630-0700   [S] Sa 17715 (SE Asia & Australasia)
0700-0800   [S] Sa/Su 17715 (SE Asia & Australasia)
0700-0900   [W] 9560 (W Europe & Australasia)
0730-0900   [W] Sa/Su 21800 (SE Asia & Australasia)
0800-0900 [←] Su 6180 (E Europe)
0830-1000   [S] 17655 (E Asia)
0930-1100   [W] 17730 (E Asia)
0945-1000   [W] 17810 (C Asia & E Asia)
1000-1100   [S] Su 15530 (Europe), [S] 17710 (SE Asia & Australasia)
1100-1200 [←] 21800 (E Africa & S Africa)
1100-1200   [S] Su 15490 & [W] 17820 (E Asia, SE Asia & Australasia)
1200-1300 [←] 21800 (S America)
1200-1300   [S] 13665 (N America), [W] Su 15330 (E Asia, SE Asia & Australasia), [S] 15400 (E North Am)
1300-1400   [S] 9630 (W Europe), [W] 15400 (N America), [S] 17625 (W Asia & S Asia)
1300-1500   [S] 9705 (E Europe), [W] 17840 (E North Am)
1345-1400   [W] 9595 (E Europe)
1400-1600   [W] 7195 (E Europe)
1400-1800   9630 (W Europe)
1500-1600 [←] 11755 (E Africa)
1500-1600   [S] 15400 (N America)
1600-1700   [W] 13665 (W North Am), [S] Sa/Su 15400 (N America), [W] 17730 (S America)
1700-1800   [W] 9610 (E Africa & S Africa), [S] 17710 (E Africa)
1800-1850   [S] 15335 (E Africa & S Africa)
1800-1900   [W] 7270 (W Asia & S Asia), [S] 9630 (W Europe)
1900-1950   [W] 9805 (Mideast & E Africa)
1900-2000   [S] 11755 (Europe)
2100-2300   [S] 6120 (Europe)

2130-2200	[W] 7160 (E Asia)
2200-2230	[W] 5970 (Europe)
2230-2300	[S] 9895 (SE Asia & Australasia), [S] 11895 (E Asia)
2330-2400	[W] 9730 & [S] 11895 (E Asia, SE Asia & Australasia)

FRANCE—French

RADIO FRANCE INTERNATIONALE

0000-0030	*17710* (SE Asia)
0000-0100	[W] *12025* & [S] *15535* (SE Asia)
0100-0200	[W] *15605* & [S] *17710* (S Asia)
0130-0200	[W] *5920* & [S] *11665* (C America)
0300-0400	[S] *5925* (C Africa & E Africa), [W] 5945 (Mideast), [W] *7135* (C Africa & E Africa), [W] 7315 (Mideast), [S] 9790/11700 & [W] 9790 (E Africa), [S] 9845/ 7315 (Mideast)
0300-0500	7135 (C Africa)
0300-0600	9790 (C Africa)
0330-0400	[S] 6045, [S] 7280 & [S] 9745 (E Europe)
0400-0430	[W] Sa/Su 9555/11995, M-F *9805* & [S] Sa/Su 11700 (Irr) (E Africa)
0400-0445	[S] 6045 (E Europe)
0400-0500	[S] 3965/5925 & [W] 3965 (N Africa), [S] *7150* & [W] *7270* (C Africa & S Africa), [W] 7315/ 9555 & [S] 9825/11685 (Mideast)
0400-0600	*4890* (C Africa), *15210* (E Africa)
0430-0500	[W] 5990 & [W] 6045 (E Europe), [W] 9555/11995 & [S] 11700 (Irr) (E Africa)
0500-0530	[W] Sa/Su 11995/15155 & [S] Sa/Su 15155 (E Africa)
0500-0545	[W] 5990 (E Europe)
0500-0600	[W] *6175* (C Africa), [W] 7135 (N Africa), [W] 9555/11685 (Mideast), 11700 & [S] 15300 (C Africa & S Africa), [S] 15605/11685 (Mideast)
0530-0600	[W] 11995/15155 & [S] 15155 (E Africa)
0600-0630	[S] Sa/Su *11665* & [W] Sa/Su *11725* (W Africa), [S] Sa/Su 21620 (E Africa)
0600-0700	[W] 5925 (N Africa), 9790 & [S] 11700 (N Africa & W Africa), [W] 11700 & 15300 (C Africa &

	S Africa), [S] 15315 (W Africa), *17770* (C Africa), [S] 17850 (C Africa & S Africa)
0600-0800	[W] 7135 (N Africa)
0630-0700	[S] *11665* & [W] *11725* (W Africa), [S] 21620 (E Africa)
0700-0800	[W] 9790 (N Africa), 11700 (N Africa & W Africa), *15170* (W Africa & C Africa), [S] 15300 (N Africa & W Africa), [S] 17620 (W Africa), 17850 (C Africa & S Africa)
0700-0900	15315 (W Africa)
0700-1600	21580 (C Africa & S Africa)
0800-1000	17620 (W Africa)
0800-1200	15300 (N Africa & W Africa)
0800-1600	11845 (N Africa)
0900-1200	[W] 21685 (W Africa)
1000-1100	[S] 17620 (W Africa), 17850 (C Africa & S Africa)
1030-1200	[W] *7140/9830* & [S] *9830* (E Asia), [S] *15215/11890* (SE Asia)
1100-1200	6175 (W Europe & Atlantic), *11600* (SE Asia), [W] *11670* & *13640* (C America), [W] 15515 (E North Am & C America), [S] *15515* (C America), [S] 17570 (E North Am & C America), *17850* (C Africa)
1100-1400	17620 (W Africa)
1130-1200	[W] 17610 (E North Am & C America), [S] *21645* (C America)
1200-1400	[S] 15300 (N Africa & W Africa), [W] 15300 (W Africa), *17850* (W Africa & C Africa)
1200-1500	21685 (W Africa)
1230-1300	*15515* (C America), [S] 21620/ 25820 & [W] 21620 (E Africa), *21760* (W Africa & C Africa)
1230-1330	*17860* (C America)
1300-1400	[S] *15515/21645* & [W] *15515* (C America)
1330-1400	M-Sa *17860* (C America)
1400-1600	15300 & [S] 17620 (W Africa)
1500-1600	17850 (C Africa & S Africa), [W] 21685 (W Africa)
1600-1700	*6090* (SE Asia), [S] 15300 (W Africa), [W] 15300 (Africa), 17620 (W Africa), [S] 21580 (C Africa & S Africa)
1700-1800	[S] 11700 (N Africa), 15300 (Africa), [S] 17620 (W Africa & E Africa)

The IBB's Biblis Transmitting Station, near Mannheim in Germany. It uses 100 kW transmitters to reach throughout Europe. RFE-RL via D. Walcutt

1700-2000	🔳 11965 (W Africa)
1730-1800	🔳 15605 & 🅂 17605 (E Africa)
1800-1900	🔳 9790 (N Africa & W Africa), 🅂 *9790* (W Africa), 🅂 11615 (N Africa & W Africa), 🔳 *11955* (W Africa), 🔳 11995 (E Africa), 🅂 15300 (Africa), 🔳 15300 (C Africa & S Africa), 🅂 15605 (W Africa)
1800-2000	🔳 7315 (N Africa)
1800-2200	11705 (C Africa & S Africa)
1900-2000	🅂 9790 (N Africa), 🔳 9790 (Africa), 🅂 11615 (W Africa)
1900-2100	🔳 6175 (N Africa), *11955* (W Africa), 11995 (E Africa), 🅂 15300 (C Africa & S Africa)
1900-2200	*7160* (C Africa)
2000-2100	🅂 6175/9805 (E Europe), 7315 (N Africa)
2000-2200	9790 (Africa)
2100-2200	🔳 3965 & 6175 (N Africa), 7315 (N Africa & W Africa), 🅂 *11955* (W Africa)
2300-2400	🔳 *12025*, 🔳 *12075*, 🅂 *15535*, 🅂 *15595* & *17710* (SE Asia)

GABON—French

AFRIQUE NUMERO UN
0500-2300	9580 (C Africa)
0700-1600	17630 (W Africa)
1600-1700	15475 (W Africa & E North Am)
1700-1900	15475 (Irr) (W Africa & E North Am)

GERMANY—German

BAYERISCHER RUNDFUNK
| 0500-2300 🔲 | 6085 |

DEUTSCHE WELLE
0000-0200	🔳 *6100* (N America), 9545 (E North Am & S America), 🅂 *9640* (E North Am), 🔳 *9655* (C America), 🔳 *11690* & 🅂 *11865* (S America), 🅂 *11960* (N America), 🅂 *15275* (C America & S America)
24 Hr	6075 (Europe)
0200-0400	🔳 6075 (Mideast & W Asia), *6100* (N America), 🔳 6145 (E North Am), 🔳 *9870* (C America)
0200-0600	🔳 *9640* & 🅂 *9735* (N America)
0400-0500	🔳 *6100* (W North Am)
0400-0600	🅂 6100 (E North Am), 🔳 6145 (N America)
0500-0600	🔳 *6100* (W North Am)
0600-0800	9735 & *11985* (Australasia)
0600-1000	*9690* (Australasia), *21640* (SE Asia & Australasia)
0600-1800	13780 (Mideast)
0600-2000	9545 (S Europe & Atlantic)
0700-0800	🔳 3995 (Europe)
0800-1000	🔳 9735 (Australasia)
1000-1200	🔳 *15605* (E Asia & SE Asia), 🔳 21840 (SE Asia & Australasia), 🅂 21840 (Irr) (E Asia)
1000-1400	🔳 *5910* (E Asia), 🔳 *7400* (E Asia & SE Asia), 🅂 *7430* (E Asia), 🅂 *9900*, 🅂 *17485/17635*, 🔳 *17845* & 🅂 *21640* (E Asia & SE Asia)
1200-1400	🔳 *9395* (E Asia & SE Asia), 🔳 17630 (S Asia, SE Asia & Australasia), 🅂 17845 (E Europe, W Asia & C Asia)
1400-1600	🔳 13780 (S Asia, SE Asia & Australasia), 🅂 15275 (Mideast & E Africa), 🔳 *15275* (Mideast & W Asia), 🔳 15680 (S Asia, SE Asia & Australasia)
1400-1800	*9655* (S Asia & C Asia), 🅂 15275 (S Asia & SE Asia), 🅂 *17845* (Mideast, W Asia & C Asia)
1600-1800	🔳 9545 (S Asia & SE Asia), 🔳 *11795* (Mideast & W Asia)
1800-2000	🅂 6075 (Mideast), 🔳 *15275* (E Africa)

1800-2200	[S] *7185* (S Africa), [S] 9735 (C Africa & S Africa), [W] 9735 (W Africa & E Africa), [S] 11795 (Africa), [W] 11795 (C Africa & S Africa), [W] *11945* (S Africa), [S] 13780 (Africa), [S] 13810 (W Africa & S America), *17860* (W Africa, C America & S America)
2000-2200	9545 (Atlantic & S America)
2200-2400	[W] *6225* (E Asia), 9545 (S America), [W] *9780* (E North Am), [S] *11690* (E North Am & C America), [W] *11690* & [S] *11865* (S America), [W] *11955* & [W] *11990* (C America), [S] *15275* (C America & S America), [S] *15410* (E North Am), [S] *17860* (W Africa & C America)

DEUTSCHLANDRADIO—(Europe)

24 Hr	6005

GREECE—Greek

FONI TIS HELLADAS

0000-0350	7475 (N America)
0000-0400	[W] 9375 (W Africa & S America), 15630 (Mideast, S Asia & Australasia)
0000-0550	[W] 5865 (W Europe & Atlantic)
0350-0550	[W] 7475 (N America)
0400-0550	[S] 9420 (Europe)
0400-0600	[S] 15630 (W Europe & Atlantic)
0400-0700	17520 (Mideast, S Asia & Australasia)
0400-0800	21530 (Mideast, S Asia & Australasia)
0550-0650	[S] 9420 (Europe)
0600-0650	15630 (W Europe & Atlantic)
0600-0800	[W] 9420 (Europe), [W] *11750* & [S] *17705* (E Asia & Australasia)
0650-0700	[W] 15630 (W Europe & Atlantic)
0700-0800	[S] W-M 15630 & [W] 15630 (W Europe & Atlantic), [W] 17520 (Mideast, S Asia & Australasia)
0800-0830	W-M 15630 (W Europe & Atlantic)
0800-0930	[W] W-M 9420 (Europe)
0830-0900	[W] W-M 15630 (W Europe & Atlantic)
0900-0930	W-M 15630 (W Europe & Atlantic)
0930-1000	[S] W-M 15630 (W Europe & Atlantic)
1100-1200	[W] W-M 15630 (W Europe & Atlantic)
1100-1250	[S] 12105 (Europe)
1200-1300	[W] 9420 (Europe), [W] 15630 (W Europe & Atlantic)
1200-1500	*9690* (N America)
1300-1400 ←	15650 (Mideast & C Asia)
1300-1600	9420 (Europe), 15630 (W Europe & Atlantic)
1600-1700	9420 (Europe), 15630 (W Europe & Atlantic)
1600-2200	[W] *17705* (N America)
1700-1800	9420 (Europe), 15630 (W Europe & Atlantic)
1800-1850	[W] 15630 (W Europe & Atlantic)
1800-1900	9420 (Europe), 15630 (W Europe & Atlantic)
1900-2000	[W] 5865 (W Europe & Atlantic), 9420 (Europe)
1900-2050	[S] 12105 (Europe), [S] 15630 (W Europe & Atlantic)
2000-2100	[W] 5865 (W Europe & Atlantic), [W] 7475 & 9420 (Europe)
2000-2200	*17565* (S America)
2100-2300	9420 & [S] 12110 (Australasia)
2100-2400	[W] 5865 & [S] 9375 (W Europe & Atlantic), [W] 15650 (Australasia)
2300-2400	7475 (W Europe & Atlantic), [W] 9375, [S] 12105 & [S] 12110 (W Africa & S America)

HUNGARY—Hungarian

RADIO BUDAPEST

0000-0100	[W] M 9580 (S America), [S] 9800 (N America), [W] M 12010 (S America)
0100-0200	[W] 9835/9870 (N America)
0130-0230	[S] 9570 (N America)
0230-0330	[W] 9775 (N America)
0500-1300 ←	Su 6025 (Europe)
1200-1300 ←	21560 (Australasia)
1400-1500 ←	Su 6025 (Europe)
1700-1800	[S] 15335 (S Africa)
1800-1900	[S] 7235 (N Europe)
1900-2000 ←	3975 & 6025 (Europe)
1900-2000	[W] 11755/11835 (Australasia)
2000-2100	[W] 11785 (S Africa), [S] 12020 (N America)
2100-2200	[S] 9780 (Australasia)
2200-2300	[W] 9825 (N America), [S] 9850 & [S] 11990 (S America)

2300-2400 ⇦ 6025 (Europe)
2300-2400 [W] 9580, [S] Su 9850, [S] Su 11990 & [W] 12010 (S America)

ISRAEL

GALEI ZAHAL—(Europe)
Hebrew
24 Hr 6973/15785

KOL ISRAEL
Arabic
0345-2210 ⇦ 5915 (Mideast)
Hebrew
0000-0330 11585 (W Europe & E North Am)
0000-0500 [W] 9345 (W Europe & E North Am)
0000-0600 [W] 7545 (W Europe & E North Am)
0330-0500 [S] 11590 (W Europe & E North Am)
0330-0600 [W] 11585 (W Europe & E North Am)
0500-1900 ⇦ 15760 (W Europe & E North Am)
0600-1030 & 1115-1500 ⇦ 17535 (W Europe & N America)
1500-1900 [W] 17535 (W Europe & N America)
1700-2355 [W] 9390 (W Europe & N America)
1800-1830 [S] 11585 (W Europe & E North Am)
1800-2400 [W] 9345 (W Europe & E North Am)
1830-2400 11585 (W Europe & E North Am)
2000-2400 [S] 13635 (W Europe & N America)
2025-2400 [W] 6280 (W Europe & E North Am)
Yiddish
1600-1625 [S] 11605 (E Europe), [S] 17535 (Europe & E North Am)
1700-1725 [W] 9435 (E Europe), [W] 15640 (Europe & E North Am)

ITALY—Italian

RAI INTERNATIONAL
0000-0055 9840 (S America), 11800 (N America)
0130-0230 *6110* (S America), *11765* (C America)
0130-0315 9840 (S America), 11800 (N America)
0435-0445 [W] 5965 (S Europe & N Africa), [W] 6100 & [S] 6110 (N Africa), [W] 7230, [S] 7235 & [S] 9875 (S Europe & N Africa)
0455-0530 [S] 11900 & [W] 11985 (E Africa)
0630-1300 9670 (E Europe)
1000-1100 *11920* (Australasia)
1250-1630 [S] Su 11775 (E Africa), [S] Su 17780 (N America)
1350-1730 ⇦ Su 9670 (W Europe), Su 21535 (S America), Su 21710 (C Africa & S Africa)
1350-1730 [W] Su 21520 (N America)
1400-1425 M-Sa 17780 (N America)
1400-1430 M-Sa 21520 (N America)
1500-1525 M-Sa 9670 (S Europe & N Africa), [S] M-Sa 11795 (N Africa & Mideast), [W] M-Sa 11800 & [S] M-Sa 11855 (S Europe & N Africa), [W] M-Sa 11900 (N Africa & Mideast)
1555-1625 [W] M-Sa 5985, M-Sa 9670 & M-Sa 11855 (W Europe)
1700-1800 [W] M-Sa 6140 (Mideast), [S] 9670 & [W] M-Sa 9755 (S Europe & N Africa), [S] 11670 (E Africa), [S] 11725 (S Europe & N Africa), [W] 11875 (E Africa), [W] 11895 (S Europe & N Africa), [W] 15250 (C Africa), *15320* & [S] 17800 (C Africa & S Africa)
1830-1905 [W] 11800, [W] 15250, [S] 17780 & [S] 21520 (N America)
2240-2400 9840 (S America), 11800 (N America)

RAI-RADIOTELEVISIONE ITALIANA—(Europe, Mideast & N Africa)
0000-0003, 0012-0103, 0112-0203, 0212-0303, 0312-0403, 0412-0500 & 2300-2400 ⇦ 6060

JAPAN—Japanese

RADIO JAPAN
0200-0300 *11860* (SE Asia), 17835 (S America), 17845 (E Asia)

0200-0500	*5960* (E North Am), 15195 (E Asia), 15325 (S Asia), 17810 (SE Asia)
0300-0400	*9660* (S America)
0300-0500	17560 (Mideast), 17685 (Australasia), 17825 (W North Am & C America)
0700-0800	6145, 6165 & 15195 (E Asia), 17870 (Pacific)
0700-0900	17860 (SE Asia)
0700-1000	*11740* (SE Asia), *11920* & 21755 (Australasia)
0800-1000	*9530* (S America), 9540 (W North Am & C America), 9825 (Pacific & S America), *11710* (Europe), 15590 (S Asia), *17650* (W Africa), *17720* (Mideast)
0800-1700	9750 (E Asia)
0900-1600	11815 (SE Asia)
1300-1500	*11705* (E North Am)
1500-1700	9535 (W North Am & C America), *12045* (S Asia), *21630* (C Africa)
1600-1700	🗖 9845 (S Asia)
1600-1900	6035 (E Asia), 7200 (SE Asia)
1700-1800	*9750* (Europe), *11865* (S Asia), *21600* (S America)
1700-1900	*6175* (W Europe), 7140 (Australasia), 9835 (Pacific & S America), 🗖 *11880* (Mideast), 🖪 *13670* (Mideast & N Africa)
1800-1900	*15355* (S Africa)
1900-2000	🗖 *11675* (Australasia)
1900-2100	🖪 *6035* (Australasia)
2000-2100	6165 (E Asia), 11830 (Europe), 🗖 *11920* (Australasia)
2000-2200	🗖 7225 & 11665 (SE Asia)
2000-2400	11910 (E Asia), 🖪 13680 (SE Asia)
2100-2200	9560 (E Asia)
2200-2300	*6115* (W Europe), 🖪 *9650* (Mideast), 🗖 *11770* (Australasia), *11895* (C America), 🗖 *11920* (Australasia), *15220* (S America), 17825 (W North Am)
2200-2400	🗖 11665 (SE Asia)
2300-2400	*17605* (S America)

RADIO NIKKEI

0000-0800	3925, Sa/Su 9760
0000-0900	Sa/Su 3945, Sa/Su 6115
0000-1400	6055, 9595
0800-1400 &	
2030-2300	3925
2030-2400	6055, 9595
2300-2400	3925, F/Sa 3945, F/Sa 6115, F/Sa 9760

JORDAN—Arabic

RADIO JORDAN

0500-0810 ▭	11810 (Mideast, S Asia & Australasia)
0600-0815 ▭	11960 (E Europe)
1130-1300 ▭	15290 (N Africa & C America)
1200-1600 ▭	11810 (Mideast, S Asia & Australasia)
1845-2100 ▭	9830 (W Europe)
1845-2300 ▭	11810 (Mideast, S Asia & Australasia)
2100-2300 ▭	15435 (S America)

KOREA (DPR)—Korean

KOREAN CENTRAL BROADCASTING STATION

0000-0630	6100
0000-0930	9665
0000-1800	2850, 11680
0900-0950	4405, 7140 & 9345 (E Asia)
1200-1250	3560 (E Asia), 9335/15180 (C America), 9850/13650 (SE Asia), 11710 (C America), 11735 (SE Asia)
1400-1450	3560 (E Asia), 9850/13650 & 11735 (SE Asia)
1500-1800	6100
1700-1750	4405 (E Asia), 9325/13760 (Europe), 9335 (N America), 11335/15245 (Europe), 11710 (N America)
2000-2050	3560 (E Asia), 6520/9640 (C Africa), 6575/9325 & 7505/11845 (E Europe), 9975 (Mideast & Africa), 11710 (Africa), 11735 (Mideast & Africa)
2000-2400	2850, 6100, 9665, 11680
2300-2350	3560, 4405 & 7140 (E Asia), 9325/13760 (Europe), 9345 & 9975 (E Asia), 11335/15245 (Europe), 11735 (E Asia)

PYONGYANG BROADCASTING STATION

0000-0050	3560, 7140 & 9345 (E Asia)
0000-0100	6195/9720 (E Asia)
0000-0925	6248 (E Asia)
0000-1800	6398 (E Asia)

0000-1900	3320 (E Asia)
0200-0630	3250 (E Asia)
0700-0750	4405, 7140 & 9345 (E Asia)
0900-0950	3560 (E Asia), 9325/13760 (E Europe & Asia), 9975 (E Asia), 11335/15245 (E Europe), 11735/6575 (E Asia)
1000-1050 &	
1200-1250	4405, 7140 & 9345 (E Asia)
1300-1350	6575/9325 & 7505/11845 (E Europe)
1500-1900	6248 (E Asia)
1500-2030	3250 (E Asia)
2100-2400	3320, 6248 & 6398 (E Asia)

KOREA (REPUBLIC)—Korean

RADIO KOREA INTERNATIONAL

0100-0200	15575 (N America)
0300-0400	*9650* (E North Am), 11810 (E Asia & S America)
0700-0800	*9535* (Europe)
0900-1000	15210 (Europe)
0900-1100	5975 & 7275 (E Asia), 9570 (SE Asia), 13670 (Europe)
1200-1300	7275 (E Asia)
1600-1800	7275 (Europe), **S** 15575 (Mideast & Africa)
1700-1900	5975 (E Asia), 7150 (Mideast), 9515 (Europe)
1800-2000	9870 (Mideast)
2100-2300	5975 (E Asia)

KUWAIT—Arabic

RADIO KUWAIT

0200-0500	6055 (Mideast & W Asia)
0200-0530	11675 (W North Am)
0200-1305	15495 (N Africa)
0400-0740	15505 (E Europe & W Asia)
0800-0925	15110 (S Asia & SE Asia)
0900-1305	6055 (Mideast & W Asia)
1015-1740	15505 (W Africa & C Africa)
1200-1505	17885 (E Asia & Australasia)
1300-1605	13620/11990 (Europe & E North Am)
1315-1600	15110 (S Asia)
1615-1800	11990 (Europe & E North Am)
1730-2130	9880 (N Africa)
1745-2130	15505 (Europe & E North Am)
1800-2400	15495 (W Africa & C Africa)
1815-2400	9855 (Europe & E North Am)

LIBYA—Arabic

RADIO JAMAHIRIYA

1000-1400	*21695* (E Africa)
1100-1230	**S** *15610*, *17695* & **W** *21485* (W Africa)
1100-1500	*21675* (C Africa)
1200-1300	11660/17660 USB & 11890 USB (Mideast)
1600-1700	**W** *15220* (W Africa)
1600-1900	**S** *15660* & **S** *17695* (W Africa)
1700-1800	**W** *15220* (C Africa), **W** *15615* (W Africa), **W** *15660* (E Africa), **S** *17880* (C Africa)
1700-1900	**W** *11860* (W Africa), **S** *17635* (E Africa)
1800-1900	11180 USB, 11660 & 11890/9605 USB (Mideast)
1800-2000	**W** *11635* & **S** *15205* (C Africa)
1800-2030	**W** *11715* (E Africa)
1900-2030	**S** *15315* (E Africa)
2000-2130	*11635* (C Africa)

LITHUANIA—Lithuanian

RADIO VILNIUS

0000-0030	**W** *7325* & **S** 11690 (E North Am)
0900-0930	▢ 9710 (W Europe)
2300-2330	9875 (E North Am)

MEXICO—Spanish

RADIO EDUCACION

0000-0830	▢ 6185
0830-0900	▢ Th-Tu 6185
0900-1200	▢ 6185

MOROCCO

RADIO MEDI UN—(Europe & N Africa)
Arabic & French

0500-0400	9575

RTV MAROCAINE
Arabic

0000-0500	**W** *5980* & **S** 11920 (N Africa & Mideast)
0900-2200	15345 (N Africa & Mideast)
1100-1500	15335 (Europe)
2200-2400	7135 (Europe)

NETHERLANDS—Dutch

RADIO NEDERLAND

0300-0400	*6165* (N America), *9590* (C America)

0500-0600	⬛ 6015 (S Europe), ⬛ *6165* (W North Am)
0600-0700 ◧	*5955 & 7125 (Europe)*
0600-0700	⬜ *6165* (W North Am), ⬛ *11655* (N Europe)
0600-0800	⬜ 6015 & ⬛ 11935 (S Europe)
0600-0900 ◧	9895 (S Europe)
0700-0800	*9625 & 11655* (Australasia)
0700-1800 ◧	5955 (W Europe)
0800-0900	⬜ 11935 (S Europe)
0900-1600 ◧	Sa/Su 9895 & Sa/Su 13700 (S Europe)
0930-1015	M-Sa *6020* (C America)
1100-1200	⬛ *9895* (E North Am)
1200-1300	⬜ *9890* (E North Am)
1300-1400	*7380* & ⬜ *9865/9940* (E Asia & SE Asia), ⬛ *12065* (SE Asia), ⬜ *12070* (S Asia), ⬛ *13695* (E Asia & S Asia), ⬛ *17580* & ⬜ *17815* (SE Asia), *21480* (S Asia)
1600-1700	⬜ 11655 (S Europe), *13840* (Mideast), ⬛ *15335* (Europe, Mideast & E Africa)
1600-1800 ◧	9895 (S Europe), 13700 (S Europe & Mideast)
1700-1800	*6020* (S Africa), 11655 (E Africa)
2100-2200	*7120 & 9895* (C Africa), *15315* (S America), *17810* (W Africa)
2200-2300	*15315* (S America)
2300-2400	*9525* (C America & S America), *15315* (S America)

OMAN—Arabic

RADIO SULTANATE OF OMAN

0000-0200	9760 (Europe & Mideast)
0200-0300	15355 (E Africa)
0200-0400	6085 (Mideast)
0400-0600	9515 (Mideast), 17590 (E Africa)
0600-1000	17630 (Europe & Mideast)
0600-1400	13640 (Mideast)
1400-1800	15375 (E Africa)
1500-1800	15140 (Europe & Mideast)
1800-2000	6190 & 15355 (E Africa)
2000-2200	6085 (E Africa), 13640 (Europe & Mideast)
2200-2400	⬜ 13755 & ⬛ 15355 (Europe & Mideast)
2300-2400	9760 (Europe & Mideast)

PARAGUAY—Spanish

RADIO NACIONAL—(S America)
24 Hr	9737 (Irr)

POLAND—Polish

RADIO POLONIA

1130-1200 ◧	7285 (E Europe)
1130-1200	⬜ 5965 (Europe)
1530-1630	⬛ 5965 (W Europe)
1630-1730	⬜ 6035 (W Europe)
2100-2200	⬛ 7265 (W Europe)
2200-2300 ◧	6050 (E Europe)
2200-2300	⬜ 7285 (W Europe)

PORTUGAL—Portuguese

RDP INTERNATIONAL

0000-0200	⬛ Tu-Sa 13660 & ⬛ Tu-Sa 15295 (S America), ⬛ Tu-Sa 15480 (W North Am)
0000-0300 ◧	Tu-Sa 9715 (E North Am), Tu-Sa 13700 (C America)
0000-0300	⬜ Tu-Sa 11655/9410 (W North Am), ⬜ Tu-Sa 11980 & ⬜ Tu-Sa 13770 (S America)
0500-0700	⬛ M-F 7240 (W Europe)
0500-0755	⬛ M-F 9815 & ⬛ M-F 9840 (Europe)
0600-0855	⬜ M-F 9755 (Europe)
0600-1300	⬜ M-F 9815 (Europe)
0645-0800	⬛ M-F 11850 (Europe)
0700-0800	⬛ Sa/Su 12020 (Europe)
0700-1345	⬛ Sa/Su 13640 (Europe)
0745-0900	⬜ M-F 11660 (Europe)
0800-0900	⬜ Sa/Su 11875 (Europe)
0800-1100 ◧	Sa/Su 17710 (W Africa & S America), Sa/Su 21830 (E Africa & S Africa)
0800-1200	⬛ 12020 (Europe)
0800-1455	⬜ Sa/Su 15575 (Europe)
0830-1000	⬛ Sa/Su 11995 (Europe)
0900-1255	⬜ 11875 (Europe)
0930-1100	⬜ Sa/Su 9815 (Europe)
1100-1300 ◧	21655 & M-F 21725 (W Africa & S America), 21830 (E Africa & S Africa)
1100-1300	⬜ M-F 15140 (Europe)
1200-1355	⬛ Sa/Su 12020 (Europe)
1200-2000	⬛ Sa/Su/Holidays 17575 (N America), ⬛ Sa/Su/Holidays 17615 (C America)
1255-1455	⬜ Sa/Su 11875 (Europe)
1300-1700 ◧	Sa/Su 21655 (W Africa & S America)
1300-1700	⬜ Sa/Su/Holidays 15575 (E North Am), ⬜ Sa/Su 21800 (W Africa & S America)

1300-1755 ◧	Sa/Su 21830 (E Africa & S Africa)
1300-1800	W Sa/Su/Holidays 17745 (C America)
1400-1600 ◧	M-F 21810/17810 (Mideast & S Asia)
1400-2000	S Sa/Su 13770 & S Sa/Su 15555 (Europe)
1500-1700	W Sa/Su 11960 (Europe)
1500-1800	W Sa/Su 11775 (Europe)
1600-1900	S M-F 13770 & S M-F 15525 (Europe)
1700-1800 ◧	M-F 17680 (E Africa & S Africa)
1700-1800	W M-F 11740 & W 11960 (Europe)
1700-1900	W Sa/Su/Holidays 17825 (E North Am), S M-F 21540 (Irr) (C America)
1700-2000 ◧	21655 & 21800 (W Africa & S America)
1800-2000 ◧	17680 (E Africa & S Africa)
1800-2000	W 11740 & W M-F 11960 (Europe), W Sa/Su/Holidays 15450 (C America)
1800-2100	W Sa/Su 11630 (Europe)
1900-2300	S 11945 (Irr) (S Africa), S 13720 (Irr) & S M-F 15445 (Irr) (Europe), S 21540 (Irr) (C America)
1900-2400	W 15540 (Irr) (E North Am)
2000-2100 ◧	Sa/Su 17680 & M-F 17680 (Irr) (E Africa & S Africa), Sa/Su 21655 (W Africa & S America)
2000-2100	W Sa/Su 11740 (Europe)
2000-2300	S Sa/Su 15555 (Irr) (Europe), S 17575 (Irr) (E North Am)
2000-2400 ◧	21800 (Irr) (W Africa & S America)
2000-2400	W 11630/9835 (Irr) & W 12040/9795 (Europe), W M-F 13820 (E Europe), W 15450 (Irr) (C America), W 15555 (Irr) (W Africa & S America)
2100-2400 ◧	17680 (Irr) (E Africa & S Africa)
2300-2400	S M-F 13660 & S M-F 15295 (S America), S M-F 15480 (W North Am)

ROMANIA—Romanian

RADIO ROMANIA

0800-0900	S Su 11830 (Mideast), S Su 15270 (W Asia & S Asia), Su 15370 (Mideast), W Su 15430, W Su 17735 & S Su 17805 (W Asia & S Asia), W Su 17810 (Mideast)
0900-1000	W Su 15380 (N Africa & Mideast), Su 15430 (Mideast), S Su 15450 & W Su 17745 (N Africa & Mideast), W Su 17775 (Mideast), S Su 17855 (N Africa & Mideast)
1000-1100	S Su 11830, S Su 15250 & W Su 15260 (W Europe), Su 15380, W Su 17735 & S Su 17740 (S Europe & Atlantic), W Su 17825 (W Europe)

RADIO ROMANIA INTERNATIONAL

0200-0300	S 9620 & S 11895 (W Asia & C Asia)
1200-1300	S 9760 & S 11830 (W Europe)
1300-1400	W 15170 & W 17825 (W Europe)
1400-1500	S 9760 & S 11830 (W Europe)
1500-1600	W 11740 & W 15150 (W Europe)
1600-1700	S 9690 & S 11960 (Mideast)
1700-1800	W 6055 (Mideast), W 6110 (W Europe), W 7220 (Mideast), S 9530 (W Europe)
1700-1900	S 11765 (W Europe)
1800-1900	W 6040, W 7140 & S 9755 (W Europe)
1900-2000	W 6140 & W 7125 (W Europe)

RUSSIA—Russian

RADIO ROSSII

0000-1300	S 5920 (E Asia)
0000-1400	W 6075 (E Asia)
0100-0600	S 9480 (Europe & W Africa)
0200-0500	W 5925 (Europe & W Africa)
0520-0800	W 12075 (Europe & W Africa)
0620-1500	S 13665 (Europe & W Africa)
0820-1500	W 17600 (Europe & W Africa)
1520-1800	W 7310 (Europe & W Africa)
1520-2100	S 9450 (Europe & W Africa)
1700-2400	S 5920 (E Asia)
1800-2400	W 6075 (E Asia)
1820-2200	W 5895 (Europe & W Africa)

RUSSIAN INTERNATIONAL RADIO

0000-0600 ◧	*7125* (E North Am)
1400-1500	S *15430* (Mideast)
1500-1600	W *9555* (Mideast)
1900-2100	S *5985* & S *9825* (Mideast)
2000-2100	S *7260* (Mideast)
2000-2200	W *5965* & W *5975* (Mideast)
2100-2200	W *5990* (Mideast)

VOICE OF RUSSIA

0100-0200	**S** *11825* (E North Am)
0100-0300	**S** 9470 (S America), **S** 9725 & **S** 9880/7300 (E North Am), **S** 12070/7260 (C America & S America), **S** 15425 & **S** 15455 (W North Am)
0200-0300	**W** 6195 & 7330 (S America), **W** *9765* (E North Am)
0200-0400	**W** 6115 & **W** 7240 (E North Am), **W** 7260 (C America & S America), **W** 12010 & **W** 13665 (W North Am)
0300-0400	**W** 7330 (S America)
1000-1200	**W** 11770 (E Europe)
1200-1400	**S** 7390 (E Asia & SE Asia), **S** 9480 (E Asia & Australasia), **S** 9745 (S Asia), **S** 11640 (SE Asia & Australasia), **S** 15470 (E Asia)
1200-1500	**S** 9875 (C Asia), **S** 9920 (C Asia & S Asia)
1300-1400	**W** 6145 (E Asia), **S** 17645 (S Asia & SE Asia)
1300-1500	**W** 7155 (Australasia), **W** 7260 (E Asia & SE Asia), **W** 9450 (E Asia), **W** 15460/17570 (S Asia & SE Asia)
1300-1600	**W** 7365 (C Asia)
1300-1800	**W** 6185 (C Asia)
1300-1900	**S** 7370 (Europe)
1400-1500	**W** 6205 (SE Asia), **W** 7315 (W Asia & S Asia)
1400-1700	**S** 11830 (Mideast)
1400-1900	**S** 9820/9450 (Europe)
1400-2000	**W** 6045 (N Europe & E Europe)
1500-1600	**S** 12055 (W Asia & S Asia), **S** 15440/7130 (Mideast & W Asia), **S** 15540 (Mideast)
1500-1700	**S** 9865 (C Asia)
1500-1900	**W** 5995 (C Asia)
1500-2000	**W** 7170 (N Europe & E Europe)
1500-2200	**W** 7445 (Mideast & W Asia)
1600-1700	**◄█** 5945 (S Asia)
1600-1700	**W** 7315 (W Asia & S Asia)
1700-1800	**S** 11630/9480 (Europe), **S** 15540 (Mideast)
1700-2100	**S** 12055 (Mideast & E Africa)
1800-1900	**W** 7360 (Europe)
1900-2000	**S** *5950* (S Europe, N Africa & Mideast), **S** 11630/9480 & **S** 11745/12020 (Europe)
2000-2100	**W** *6170* (S Europe, N Africa & Mideast), **W** 7310 & **W** 7360 (Europe)

SAUDI ARABIA—Arabic

BROADCASTING SERVICE OF THE KINGDOM

0300-0600	9580 (Mideast & E Africa), 15170 (E Europe & W Asia)
0300-0800	17895 (C Asia & E Asia)
0300-0900	9675 (Mideast)
0600-0900	15380 (Mideast), 17730 (N Africa), 17740 (W Europe)
0600-1700	11855 (Mideast & E Africa)
0900-1200	11935 (Mideast), 17615 (S Asia & SE Asia), 17805 (N Africa), 21495 (E Asia & SE Asia), 21705 (W Europe)
0900-1600	9675 (Mideast)
1200-1400	15380 (Mideast), 21600 (SE Asia)
1200-1500	17895 & 21505 (N Africa), 21705 (W Europe)
1300-1600	21460 (E Africa)
1500-1800	13710 & 15315 (N Africa), 15435 (W Europe)
1600-1800	15205 (W Europe), 17560 (C Africa & W Africa)
1700-2200	9580 (Mideast & E Africa)
1800-2300	9555 (N Africa), 9870 (W Europe), 11740 (C Africa & W Africa), 11820 (W Europe), 11915 (N Africa)

SERBIA AND MONTENEGRO—Serbian

INTERNATIONAL RADIO OF SERBIA & MONTENEGRO

0000-0030	**S** Su *9580* (E North Am)
0030-0100	**W** *7115* & **S** *9580* (E North Am)
0100-0130	**W** Su *7115* (E North Am)
0130-0200	**W** *7115* (E North Am)
1400-1430	**W** *11835* (Australasia)
2030-2100	**◄█▶** *6100* (Europe)
2100-2130	**◄█▶** Sa *6100* (Europe)
2130-2200	**S** *7230* (Australasia)
2200-2230	**S** Sa *7230* (Australasia)
2330-2400	**S** *9580* (E North Am)

SINGAPORE—Chinese

MEDIACORP RADIO

1400-1600 & 2300-1100	6000

RADIO SINGAPORE INTERNATIONAL—(SE Asia)
1100-1400   6000 & 6185

SLOVAKIA—Slovak
RADIO SLOVAKIA INTERNATIONAL
0130-0200	5930 (N America), 9440 (S America)
0730-0800	**S** 9440, **W** 13715 & 15460 (Australasia)
1530-1600	**S** 5920 (W Europe)
1630-1700	**◄** 7345 (W Europe)
1630-1700	**W** 5915 (W Europe)
1900-1930	**S** 5920 & **S** 6055 (W Europe)
2000-2030	**W** 5915 & **W** 7345 (W Europe)

SPAIN
RADIO EXTERIOR DE ESPAÑA
Galician, Catalan & Basque

1240-1255	**S** M-F *9765* (C America), **S** M-F *11815* (C America & S America), **S** M-F 13720 (W Europe), **S** M-F *15170* (W North Am), **S** M-F 15585 (Europe), **S** M-F 21540 (C Africa & S Africa), **S** M-F 21570 (S America), **S** M-F 21610 (Mideast), **S** M-F 21700 (N America & C America)
1340-1355	**W** M-F *5970* (C America), **W** M-F *15170* (W North Am), **W** M-F 15585 (Europe), **W** M-F 17595 (N America), **W** M-F 21540 (C Africa & S Africa), **W** M-F 21570 (S America), **W** M-F 21610 (Mideast)

Spanish

0000-0200	**S** 11680 & **W** 11945 (S America)
0000-0400	**S** *6020* & **W** *11815* (C America & S America)
0000-0500	**S** 9535 & **W** 9540 (N America & C America), 9620 (S America), 15160 (C America & S America)
0100-0600	6055 (N America)
0200-0600	**S** *3350* & **W** *6040* (C America), **S** *6125* & **W** *11880* (N America)
0500-0600	**S** 12035 (Europe)
0500-0700	11890 (Mideast)
0600-0700	**W** 13720 (W Europe)
0600-0800	**W** Sa/Su 5985 (W Europe), **W** Sa/Su 9710 (Europe)
0600-0900	12035 (Europe)
0700-0900	17770 & Sa/Su 21610 (Australasia)
0700-1240	13720 (W Europe)
0800-1000	M-F 21570 (S America)
0900-1240	15585 (Europe), 21540 (C Africa & S Africa), 21610 (Mideast)
1000-1200	*9660* (E Asia), M-F *11815* (C America & S America)
1000-1240	21570 (S America), **S** M-F 21700 (N America & C America)
1000-1300	**W** M-F 17595 (N America & C America)
1100-1200	**W** M-F *5970* (C America)
1100-1240	**S** M-F *9765* (C America), M-F *15170* (W North Am)
1200-1240	**S** M-F *11815* (C America & S America)
1200-1300	**W** M-Sa *5970* (C America)
1200-1400	**S** Su *9765* (C America), *11910* (SE Asia)
1200-1500	Su *15170* (W North Am & C America), Sa/Su 21700 (C America & S America)
1200-1600	**S** Su *11815* & **W** Su *15125* (C America & S America)
1240-1255	**W** 13720 (W Europe), **W** M-F *15170* (W North Am), **S** Sa/Su 15585 & **W** 15585 (Europe), **S** Sa/Su 21540 & **W** 21540 (C Africa & S Africa), **S** Sa/Su 21570 & **W** 21570 (S America), **S** Sa/Su 21610 & **W** 21610 (Mideast)
1240-1300	**S** Sa/Su 13720 (W Europe)
1255-1340	M-F *15170* (W North Am), 15585 (Europe), 21540 (C Africa & S Africa), 21570 (S America), 21610 (Mideast)
1255-1400	**S** M-F *9765* (C America)
1300-1340	**W** M-F *5970* (C America), **W** M-F 17595 (N America)
1300-1400	Sa/Su 13720 (W Europe)
1300-1500	**W** Su *5970* (C America), **S** 17595 (N America)
1340-1355	**S** M-F *15170* (W North Am), **S** 15585 & **W** Sa/Su 15585 (Europe), **S** 21540 & **W** Sa/Su 21540 (C Africa & S Africa), **S** 21570 & **W** Sa/Su 21570 (S America), **S** 21610 & **W** Sa/Su 21610 (Mideast)

1355-1500	M-F 17595 (N America), 21610 (Mideast)
1355-1700	15585 (Europe), 21570 (S America)
1400-1500	[S] Sa 15385 (W Africa & C Africa), [S] 17755 & [W] 21540 (C Africa & S Africa)
1500-1600	Su *9765* (C America), Su *17850* (W North Am)
1500-1700	M-Sa 15385 (W Africa & C Africa), 21610 (Mideast)
1500-1800	21700 (C America & S America)
1500-1900	17755 (C Africa & S Africa)
1600-1800	Sa/Su *9765* (C America), [S] Sa/Su *11815* & [W] Sa/Su *15125* (C America & S America), Sa/Su *17850* (W North Am)
1700-1900	17715 (S America)
1700-2000	Sa/Su 9665 (Europe)
1700-2300	7275 (Europe)
1800-2000	*9765* (C America), [S] *11815* & [W] *15125* (C America & S America), *17850* (W North Am)
1800-2100	Sa/Su 21700 (C America & S America)
1800-2230	M-F 21700 (Irr) (C America & S America)
1900-2100	Su 17755 (C Africa & S Africa)
1900-2300	15110 (N America & C America)
2000-2100	[S] Sa 9665 & [W] Sa/Su 9665 (Europe)
2000-2230	M-F *9765* (Irr) (C America), [S] M-F *11815* (Irr) & [W] M-F *15125* (Irr) (C America & S America), M-F *17850* (Irr) (W North Am)
2000-2300	Sa/Su *9765* (C America), [S] Sa/Su *11815* & [W] Sa/Su *15125* (C America & S America), Sa/Su *17850* (W North Am)
2100-2200	[W] Sa 9665 (Europe), [W] M-F 11625 (C Africa)
2100-2300	[W] Sa/Su 21700 (C America & S America)
2200-2300	7270 (N Africa & W Africa), [W] Sa 11625 (C Africa)
2300-2400	[S] 9535 & [W] 9540 (N America & C America), 9620, [S] 11680 & [W] 11945 (S America), [W] Su *15125* (Irr) & 15160 (C America & S America), Su *17850* (Irr) (W North Am)

SWEDEN—Swedish

RADIO SWEDEN

0000-0030	[S] *9490* & [W] *9495* (S America)
0100-0130	[S] *6010* (E North Am), [S] *9435* (S Asia), [W] *9495* (S America), *12060* (S Asia)
0130-0200	[W] *12060* (S Asia)
0200-0230	[S] *6010* & [W] *9495* (N America)
0300-0330	[S] *9490* (S America), [W] *9495* (W North Am)
0330-0500	[S] M-F 9435 (Mideast & E Africa)
0430-0600	[W] M-F 11775 (Mideast & E Africa)
0500-0600	[W] M-F 5840 (Europe)
0500-0700 [▪]	M-F 6065 (Europe)
0600-0700 [▪]	M-F 9490 (W Europe & W Africa)
0600-0700	[S] M-Sa 9490 (Europe & N Africa)
0600-0800	[S] Sa 17505 (Mideast & Africa)
0700-0800	[S] Sa/Su 9490 (Europe & N Africa)
0700-0900	[W] Sa 6065 (Europe), [W] Sa 9490/13790 (Europe & N Africa), [S] Su 17505 (Mideast & Africa)
0800-0900	[S] Su 9490 (Europe & N Africa)
0800-1000	[W] Su 6065 (Europe), [W] Su 9490/13790 (Europe & N Africa)
1000-1010	[S] 15735 (Asia & Australasia)
1010-1030	[S] Sa/Su 15735 (Asia & Australasia)
1030-1040	[S] 15735 (E Asia & Australasia), [S] 18960 (C America & S America)
1040-1100	[S] Sa/Su 15735 (E Asia & Australasia), [S] Sa/Su 18960 (C America & S America)
1100-1110 [▪]	9490 (Europe), 21810 (Africa)
1100-1110	[W] 9920 (E Asia & Australasia), [S] 15240 (E North Am)
1110-1130 [▪]	Sa/Su 9490 (Europe), Sa/Su 21810 (Africa)
1110-1130	[W] Sa/Su 9920 (E Asia & Australasia), [S] Sa/Su 15240 (E North Am)
1130-1140	[W] 17505 (SE Asia & Australasia), [W] 21810 (C America & S America)
1140-1200	[W] Sa/Su 17505 (SE Asia & Australasia), [W] Sa/Su 21810 (C America & S America)

HFCC conference at DW Bockhaken: from left, Steffen Hilbig (DW-MES), Milan Prezelj (Hrvatski Informativni Centar), Zelimir Klasan (OiV, Croatia, Frequency Manager) and Dane Pavlic (Head of OiV Deanovec Station). M. Prezelj

1200-1215	**S** 15240 (E North Am), **S** 15735 (Asia & Australasia)
1200-1230	**W** 18960 (E North Am & C America)
1215-1230	**S** M-F 15240 (N America), **S** Sa/Su 15240 (E North Am), **S** M-F 15735 (E Asia & Australasia), **S** Sa/Su 15735 (Asia & Australasia)
1300-1315	**W** 9920 & **S** 15735 (E Asia & Australasia)
1300-1330	**S** *15240* & **W** 18960 (N America)
1315-1330	**W** Sa/Su 9920 (E Asia & Australasia), **S** M-F 15735 (SE Asia & Australasia), **S** Sa/Su 15735 (E Asia & Australasia), **W** M-F 17505 (SE Asia & Australasia)
1400-1415	**W** 17505 (SE Asia & Australasia)
1400-1430	**S** 15735 (Mideast, SE Asia & Australasia), 18960 (N America)
1415-1430	**W** M-F 9920 (E Asia & Australasia), **W** Sa/Su 17505 (SE Asia & Australasia)
1445-1500	**S** 15240 (N America)
1500-1530 ◻	17505 (Mideast, Asia & Australasia)
1500-1530	**S** 9410 (E Europe), **W** 17505 (Mideast, Asia & Australasia), **W** 18960 (N America)
1545-1600	**S** 13580 (Mideast), **S** 15735 (W Europe & W Africa), **W** 18960 (N America)
1545-1700 ◻	6065 (Europe)
1600-1615	**S** M-F 13580 (Mideast), **S** M-F 15735 (W Europe & W Africa)
1600-1630	**W** 5850 (E Europe & Mideast), **S** Su 13580 (Mideast)
1615-1630	**S** M 13580 (Mideast)
1645-1700	**W** 7420 (Mideast), **W** 13580 (W Europe & W Africa)
1700-1715 ◻	M-Sa 6065 (Europe)
1700-1715	**W** M-F 7420 (Mideast), **W** M-F 13580 (W Europe & W Africa)
1730-1800 ◻	6065 (Europe)
1800-1830	**S** 11600 (Mideast), **S** 13800 (Europe & Africa)
1800-1900 ◻	Su 6065 (Europe)
1900-1930 ◻	6065 (Europe)
1900-1930	**W** 7375 (N Africa & Mideast), **W** 9375 (W Europe & W Africa)
1900-2000	**S** 11595 (Africa)
2000-2030	**W** 9415/9445 (SE Asia & Australasia)
2000-2100	**S** 9390 (W Africa & S America), **S** 13580 (W Europe & W Africa)
2100-2130	**S** 9930 (E Asia & Australasia)
2100-2200	**W** 9490/9510 (W Africa & S America)
2100-2230 ◻	6065 (Europe)

THAILAND—Thai

RADIO THAILAND

0100-0200	*5890* (E North Am)
0330-0430	*5890* (W North Am)
1000-1100	**W** 7285 & **S** 11870 (SE Asia & Australasia)
1330-1400	**W** 7160 & **S** 11685 (E Asia)
1800-1900	**S** 9695 & **W** 11855 (Mideast)
2045-2115	**W** 9535 & **S** 9680 (Europe)

TUNISIA—Arabic

RTV TUNISIENNE

0200-0500	9720 & 12005 (N Africa & Mideast)
0400-0700	7190 (N Africa)
0400-0800	7275 (W Europe)
1200-1600	15450 & 17735 (N Africa & Mideast)
1400-1700	11730 (W Europe)
1400-1900	11950 (N Africa)
1600-2100	9720 & 12005 (N Africa & Mideast)
1700-2300	7225 (W Europe)
1900-2300	7190 (N Africa)

TURKEY—Turkish

VOICE OF TURKEY

0000-0700	[S] 9460 (Europe & E North Am)
0000-0800	[W] 7300 (W Europe & N America)
0400-0700	[S] 15425 (W Asia & C Asia)
0400-0900	[S] 11750 (Mideast)
0500-0800	[W] 17690 (W Asia & C Asia)
0500-1000	[W] 11925 (Mideast)
0800-1700 ⇦	11955 (N Africa & Mideast), 15350 (Europe)
0900-1200	[S] 21715 (Australasia)
1000-1300	[W] 17720 (Australasia)
1000-1500	[S] F 17705 (N Africa)
1100-1600	[W] F 17860 (N Africa)
1200-1600	[S] 13655 (Australasia)
1300-1700	[W] 9625 (Australasia)
1600-2100	[S] 9460 (Europe)
1600-2200	[S] 5960 (Mideast)
1700-2200	[W] 5980 (Europe), [S] 7215 (N Africa & W Africa)
1700-2300 ⇦	9560 (S Asia, SE Asia & Australasia)
1700-2300	[W] 6120 (Mideast)
1800-2300	[W] 9840 (N Africa & W Africa)
2100-2400	[S] 9460 (Europe & E North Am)
2200-2400	[W] 7300 (W Europe & N America)

UKRAINE—Ukrainian

RADIO UKRAINE

0000-0100	[W] 5910 (E North Am)
0000-0400	[S] 9385 (W Asia)
0100-0300	[S] 7545 (E North Am)
0100-0500	[W] 7420 (W Asia)
0200-0400	[W] 5910 (E North Am)
0400-0700	[S] 9945 (W Europe)
0500-0800	[W] 7420 (W Europe)
0700-1100	[S] 15415 (W Europe)
0800-1200	[W] 13585 (W Europe)
1200-1300	[S] 15415 (W Europe)
1300-1400	[W] 13585 (W Europe)
1400-1800 ⇦	7425 (W Asia)
1800-2000	[S] 11550 (W Europe)
1900-2100	[W] 7510 (W Europe)
2200-2300	[S] 7420 (W Europe)
2300-2400	[W] 5840 (W Europe), [S] 7545 (E North Am)

UNITED ARAB EMIRATES—Arabic

EMIRATES RADIO

0000-0200	13675/13650 (Irr) (E North Am & C America)
0200-0340	12005, 13675/13650 & 15400/15395 (E North Am & C America)
0400-0530	21700 (Australasia)
0400-0540	15435 (Australasia), 17830 (E Asia)
0600-1700	21605 (Europe)
0600-2050	13675/13650 & 15395/15435 (Europe)
1030-1200	15370 (N Africa)
1200-2050	13630 (N Africa)
1700-2050	11950 (Europe)
2050-2400	13675/13650 (Irr) (E North Am & C America)

VIETNAM—Vietnamese

VOICE OF VIETNAM

0000-0100	7285 (SE Asia)
0130-0230	*6175* (E North Am & C America)
0430-0530	*6175* (N America & C America)
1330-1430	7285 (SE Asia)
1500-1600	7220 & 9550 (W Africa & C Africa)
1700-1800	[W] 7280, 9730 & [S] 13740 (Europe)
1730-1830	[S] *9725* (W Europe)
1830-1930	[W] *5955* (W Europe)
1930-2030	[S] *9725* (S Europe)
2030-2130	[W] *5970* (S Europe)

YEMEN—Arabic

REPUBLIC OF YEMEN RADIO

0300-0600, 1100-1800 & 1900-2208	9780 (Mideast & E Africa)

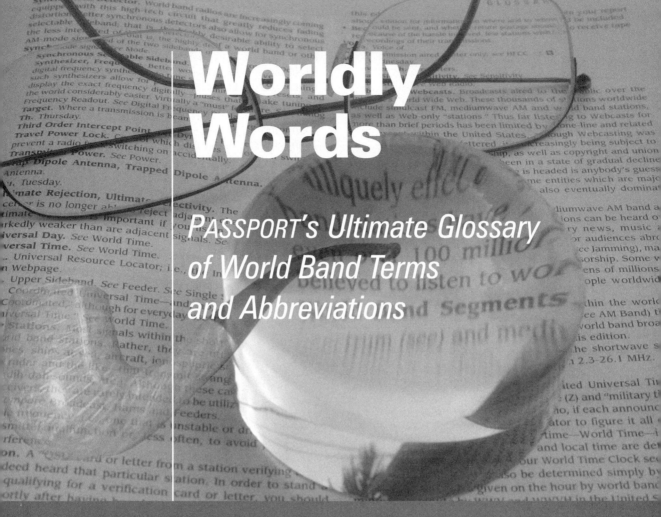

Worldly Words

PASSPORT's Ultimate Glossary of World Band Terms and Abbreviations

Lots of helpful terms and abbreviations are used in world band radio. Some are specialized and benefit from explanation; several are foreign words that need translation; and yet others are simply adaptations of everyday usage.

Here, then, is PASSPORT's A-Z guide to what's what in world band buzzwords. For a thorough analysis of technical terms and norms used in evaluating world band radios, see the Radio Database International White Paper, *How to Interpret Receiver Lab Tests and Measurements.*

A. Summer schedule season for world band stations. *See* 🄢. *See* HFCC. *Cf.* B.

Absorption. Reduction in signal strength during bounces (refraction) off the earth's ionosphere (*see* Propagation) or the earth itself.

AC. Alternating ("household" or "mains") current, 120V throughout North America, 100V in Japan and 220-240V in much of the rest of the world.

Active Antenna. An antenna that electronically amplifies signals. Active, or amplified, antennas are typically mounted indoors, but some models can also be erected outdoors. Active antennas take up relatively little space, but their amplification circuits may introduce certain problems that can result in unwanted sounds being heard. *Cf.* Passive Antenna. *See* Feedline.

Adjacent-Channel Interference. *See* Interference.

Adjacent-Channel Rejection. *See* Selectivity.

AGC. *See* Automatic Gain Control.

AGC Threshold. The threshold at which the automatic gain control (AGC), *see*, chooses to act relates to both listening pleasure and audible sensitivity. If the threshold is too low, the AGC will tend to act on internal receiver noise and minor static, desensitizing the receiver. However, if the threshold is too high, variations in loudness will be uncomfortable to the ear, forcing the listener to manually twiddle with the volume control to do, in effect, what the AGC should be doing automatically. Measured in µV (microvolts).

Alt. Freq. Alternative frequency or channel. Frequency or channel that may be used in place of the regularly scheduled one.

Amateur Radio. *See* Hams.

AM Band. The popular radio band that runs from 520–1705 kHz within the mediumwave spectrum, or Medium Frequency (MF) range of the radio spectrum, from 0.3-3.0 MHz (300-3,000 kHz). Outside North America, it is usually called the mediumwave (MW) band. However, in parts of Latin America it is sometimes called, by the general public and a few stations, *onda larga*—longwave—strictly speaking, a misnomer. In the United States, federal travelers' information services have primary status on 1610 kHz.

AM Equivalent (AME). *See* Single Sideband (second paragraph).

AM Mode. *See* Mode.

Amplified Antenna. *See* Active Antenna.

Analog Frequency Readout. This type of received-frequency indication is used on radios having needle-and-dial or "slide-rule" tuning. It is much less handy than digital frequency readout. *See* Synthesizer. *Cf.* Digital Frequency Display.

Antenna. *See* Active Antenna, Feedline, Passive Antenna.

Antennae. The accepted spelling for feelers protruding from insects. In electronics, the preferred plural for "antenna" is "antennas."

Antenna Polarization. *See* Polarization.

Arrestor. *See* MOV.

Attenuator. A circuit, typically switched with one or more levels, to desensitize a receiver by reducing the strength of all incoming signals. *See* RF Gain.

Audio Quality. At PASSPORT, audio quality refers to what in computer testing is called "benchmark" quality. This means, primarily, the freedom from distortion of a signal fed through a receiver's entire circuitry—*not* just the audio stage—from the antenna input through to the speaker terminals. A lesser characteristic of audio quality is the audio bandwidth needed for pleasant world band reception of music. Also, *see* Enhanced Fidelity.

Automatic Gain Control (AGC). Smooths out fluctuations in signal strength brought about by fading (*see*), a regular occurrence with world band signals, so a receiver's audio level

tends to stay relatively constant. This is accomplished by AGC attack, then AGC hang, and finally AGC decay. Each of these three actions involved in smoothing a fade has a micro-time preset at the factory for optimum performance, but top-end receivers often provide for user control of at least the decay time—with a few rarified models, all three times. *See* AGC Threshold.

AV. A Voz—Portuguese for "The Voice." In PASSPORT, this term is also used to represent "The Voice of."

B. Winter schedule season for world band stations, typically valid from the last Sunday in October until the last Sunday in March. *See* 🄦. *See* HFCC. *Cf.* A.

Balun. BALanced-to-UNbalanced device to match the two. Typically, a balun is placed between an unbalanced antenna feedline and a balanced antenna input, or *vice versa*.

Bands, Shortwave Broadcasting. *See* World Band Segments.

Bandwidth. A key variable that determines selectivity (*see*), bandwidth is the amount of radio signal, at –6 dB (-3 dB with professional gear), a radio's circuitry will let pass, and thus be heard. With world band channel spacing at 5 kHz, the best single bandwidths are usually in the vicinity of 3 to 6 kHz. Better radios offer two or more selectable bandwidths: at least one of 5 to 9 kHz or so for when a station is in the clear, and one or more others between 2 to 6 kHz for when a station is hemmed in by other signals next to it; with synchronous selectable sideband (*see* Synchronous Detector), these bandwidths can safely be at the upper ends of these ranges to provide enhanced fidelity. Proper selectivity is a key determinant of the aural quality of what you hear, and some newer models of tabletop receivers have dozens of bandwidths.

Bandscanning. Fishing for stations by continuously tuning up and/or down a given world band segment (*see*), such as in concert with PASSPORT's Blue Pages.

Baud. Measurement of the speed by which radioteletype (*see*), radiofax (*see*) and other digital data are transmitted. Baud is properly written entirely in lower case, and thus is abbreviated as b (baud), kb (kilobaud) or Mb (Megabaud). Baud rate standards are usually set by the international CCITT regulatory body.

BC. Broadcaster, Broadcasters, Broadcasting, Broadcasting Company, Broadcasting Corporation.

BCB (Broadcast Band). *See* AM Band.

BFO (beat-frequency oscillator). Carrier generated within a receiver. *Inter alia*, this replaces a received signal's full or vestigial transmitted carrier when a receiver is in the single-sideband mode (*see*) or synchronous selectable mode (*see*).

Birdie. A silent spurious signal, similar to a station's open carrier, created by circuit interaction within a receiver. The fewer and weaker the birdies within a receiver's tuning range, the better, although in reality birdies rarely degrade reception.

Blocking. The ability of a receiver to avoid being desensitized by powerful adjacent signals or signals from other nearby frequencies. Measured in dB (decibels) at 100 kHz signal spacing.

Boat Anchor. Radio slang for a classic or vintage tube-type communications receiver. These huge, heavy monsters were manufactured mainly from before World War II through the mid-1970s, although a few continued to be available up to a decade later. The definitive reference for collectors of elder receivers is *Shortwave Receivers Past & Present* by Universal Radio.

Broadcast. A radio or television transmission meant for the general public. *Cf.* Utility Stations, Hams.

BS. Broadcasting Station, Broadcasting Service.

Buzz. Noise typically generated by digital electronic circuitry. *See* Noise.

Carrier. *See* Mode.

Cd. Ciudad—Spanish for "City."

Buddhism in Laos diminished under Marxist pressure, but young monks are once again becoming numerous. M. Guha

Cellular Telephone Bands. In the United States, the cellular telephone bands are 824-849 and 869-894 MHz. Years ago, when analog cell transmissions were the norm, a powerful senator was overheard engaged in an awkward conversation. Shortly thereafter, receivers which could tune cellular frequencies were made illegal in the United States. As a practical matter, eavesdropping on these bands yields nothing intelligible because of the encrypted nature of the digital cellular transmissions that by now have become all but standard. Receivers tuning these "forbidden" ranges are readily acquired in Canada and nearly every other part of the world except North Korea.

Channel. An everyday term to indicate where a station is supposed to be located on the dial. World band channels are spaced exactly 5 kHz apart. Stations operating outside this norm are "off-channel" (for these, PASSPORT provides resolution to better than 1 kHz to aid in station identification).

Chuffing, Chugging. The sound made by some synthesized tuning systems when the tuning knob is turned. Called "chugging" or "chuffing," as it is suggestive of the rhythmic "chuf, chuf" sound of steam locomotives or "chugalug" gulping of beverages.

Cl. Club, Clube.

Co-Channel Interference. See Interference.

Coordinated Universal Time. See UTC, World Time.

Cult. Cultura, Cultural.

CW. Continuous wave, or telegraph-type ("Morse code," etc.) communication by telegraph key that opens and closes an unmodulated signal to create variations of long and short bursts that on a radio with a BFO (see) sound like dih-dah "beeps." Used mainly by hams (see), occasionally by utility stations (see).

DAB. Digital audio broadcasting. See Digital Radio Mondiale.

DC. Direct current, such as emanates from batteries. Cf. AC.

DC-to-Daylight. Hyperbolic slang for an exceptionally wide frequency tuning range. For example, some wideband receivers will tune from under 10 kHz to over 3 GHz (see). However, in the United States it is illegal to sell new radios to the public that tune the cellular telephone bands (see).

Default. The setting at which a control of a digitally operated electronic device, including many world band radios, normally operates, and to which it will eventually return (e.g., when the radio is next switched on).

Digital Frequency Display, Digital Frequency Readout. Indicates that a receiver displays the tuned frequency digitally, usually in kilohertz (see). Because this is so much handier than an analog frequency readout, all models included in PASSPORT REPORTS have digital frequency readout. See Synthesizer.

Digital Radio Mondiale (DRM). International organization (www.drm.org) seeking to convert world band transmissions from traditional analog mode to DRM digital mode, which is moving from its test phase to limited regular use. As DRM transmissions—unlike the conventional analog variety—are easily jammed, DRM appears to be finding support among nations hoping to limit what can be heard from unapproved sources. See Mode.

Digital Signal Processing (DSP). Where digital circuitry and software are used to perform radio circuit functions traditionally done using analog circuits. Used on certain world band receivers; also, available as an add-on accessory for audio processing only.

Dipole Antenna. See Passive Antenna.

Distortion. See Overall Distortion.

Domestic Service. See DS.

Double Conversion a/k/a **Dual Conversion.** See IF.

DRM. See Digital Radio Mondiale.

DS. Domestic Service—Broadcasting intended primarily for audiences in the broadcaster's home country. However, some domestic programs are beamed on world band to expatriates and other kinfolk abroad, as well as interested foreigners. Cf. ES.

DSP. See Digital Signal Processing.

Dual Conversion a/k/a/ **Double Conversion.** See IF.

DX, DXers, DXing. From an old telegraph abbreviation for distance (D) unknown (X); thus, to DX is to communicate over a great distance. DXers are those who specialize in finding distant or exotic stations that are considered to be rare catches. Few world band listeners are considered to be regular DXers, but many others seek out DX stations every now and then—usually by bandscanning, which is facilitated by PASSPORT's Blue Pages.

DXpedition. Typically, a gathering of DXers that camp out in a remote location favorable to catching the toughest of stations; these DX bases are usually far away from electrically noisy power and cable TV lines. Although Finns, Scandinavians and North Americans are known for doing this in groups, Jack Perolo, a legendary Brazilian DXer, decades ago used to vanish for weeks by himself in the Amazonian wilderness, toting a cache of lightweight homemade DX supersets that could operate seemingly forever off a set of batteries.

Dynamic Range. The ability of a receiver to handle weak signals in the presence of strong competing signals within or near the same world band segment (see World Band Spectrum). Sets with inferior dynamic range sometimes "overload," especially with external antennas, causing a mishmash of false signals up and down—and even beyond—the segment being received. Dynamic range is closely related to the third-order intercept point, or IP3. Where possible, PASSPORT measures dynamic range and IP3 at the traditional 20 kHz and more challenging 5 kHz signal-separation points.

Earliest Heard (or Latest Heard). See key at the bottom of each Blue Page. If the PASSPORT monitoring team cannot establish the definite sign-on (or sign-off) time of a station, the earliest (or latest) time that the station could be traced is indicated by a left-facing or right-facing "arrowhead flag." This means that the station almost certainly operates beyond the time shown by that "flag." It also means that, unless you live relatively close to the station, you're unlikely to be able to hear it beyond that "flagged" time.

EBS. Economic Broadcasting Station, a type of station found in China.

ECSS (Exalted-Carrier Selectable Sideband). Manual tuning of a conventional AM-mode signal, using a receiver's single-sideband circuitry to zero-beat *(see)* the receiver's BFO with the transmitted signal's carrier. The better-sounding of the signal's sidebands is then selected by the listener. *See* Synchronous Detector.

Ed, Educ. Educational, Educação, Educadora.

Electrical Noise. *See* Noise.

Elevation Panel, Elevation Rod. Plastic panel or metal rod which flips out from a receiver's panel to angle the radio to a comfortable operating angle.

Em. Emissora, Emisora, Emissor, Emetteur—in effect, "station" in various languages.

Enhanced Fidelity. Radios with good audio performance and certain types of high-tech circuitry can improve the fidelity of world band signals. Among the newer fidelity-enhancing techniques is synchronous detection *(see* Synchronous Detector), especially when coupled with selectable sideband. Another potential technological advance to improve fidelity is digital world band transmission, which is actively being researched and tested *(see* Digital Radio Mondiale*).*

EP. Emissor Provincial—Portuguese for "Provincial Station."

ER. Emissor Regional—Portuguese for "Regional Station."

Ergonomics. How handy and comfortable—intuitive—a set is to operate, especially hour after hour.

ES. External Service—Broadcasting intended primarily for audiences abroad. *Cf.* DS.

Exalted-Carrier Selectable Sideband. *See* ECSS.

External Service. *See* ES.

F. Friday.

Fading. Signals which scatter off the ionosphere *(see* Propagation) are subject to some degree of phase mismatch as the scattered bits of signal arrive at a receiver at minutely varying times. This causes fading, where signal strength varies anywhere from a few times per minute to many times per second, the latter being known as "flutter fading" and often caused by disruption by the earth's geomagnetic field *(see* Great Circle Path). "Selective fading" is a special type that is audible on shortwave and mediumwave AM when a fade momentarily sweeps across a signal's three components (lower sideband, carrier, upper sideband), attenuating the carrier more than the sidebands; with the carrier thus attenuated, the result is "selective-fading distortion." *See* Automatic Gain Control, Propagation.

Fax. *See* Radiofax.

Feeder, Shortwave. A utility *(see)* shortwave transmission from the broadcaster's home country to a shortwave or other relay site or local placement facility *(see)* some distance away. Although these specialized transmissions carry world band programs, they are not intended to be received by the general public. Many world band radios can process these quasi-broadcasts anyway. Shortwave feeders operate in lower sideband (LSB), upper sideband (USB) or independent sideband (termed ISL if heard on the lower side, ISU if heard on the upper side) modes. Feeders are now via satellites and Internet audio, but a few stations keep shortwave feeders in reserve should their satellite/Internet feeders fail. *See* Single Sideband, Utility Stations, NBFM.

Feedline. The wire or cable that runs between an antenna's receiving element(s) and a receiver. For sophisticated antennas, twin-lead ribbon feedlines are unusually efficient, and can reject much nearby electrical noise via phasing. However, coaxial cable feedlines are generally superior in high-local-electrical-noise environments.

First IF Rejection. A relatively uncommon source of false signals occurs when powerful transmitters operate on the same frequency as a receiver's first intermediate frequency (IF). The ability of receiving circuitry to avoid such transmitters' causing reception problems is called "IF rejection."

Flutter Fading. *See* Fading.

FM. The FM broadcast band is now standardized at 87.5-108 MHz worldwide except in Japan (76-90 MHz) and parts of the former Warsaw Pact (66-74 MHz). Also, for communications FM mode *see* NBFM.

Frequency. The standard term to indicate where a station is located within the radio spectrum—regardless of whether it is "on-channel" or "off-channel" *(see* Channel). Below 30 MHz this is customarily expressed in kilohertz (kHz, *see*), but some receivers display in Megahertz (MHz, *see*). These differ only in the placement of a decimal; e.g., 5970 kHz is the same as 5.97 MHz. Either measurement is equally valid, but to minimize confusion PASSPORT and most stations designate frequencies only in kHz.

Frequency Synthesizer. *See* Synthesizer, Frequency.

Front-End Selectivity. The ability of the initial stage of receiving circuitry to admit only limited frequency ranges into succeeding stages of circuitry. Good front-end selectivity keeps signals from other, powerful bands or segments from being superimposed upon the frequency range you're tuning. For example, a receiver with good front-end selectivity will receive only shortwave signals within the range 3200-3400 kHz. However, a receiver with mediocre front-end selectivity might allow powerful local mediumwave AM stations from 520-1700 kHz to be heard "ghosting in" between 3200 and 3400 kHz, along with the desired shortwave signals. Obviously, mediumwave AM signals don't belong on shortwave. Receivers with inadequate front-end selectivity can benefit from the addition of a preselector *(see)* or a high-pass filter.

GHz. Gigahertz, equivalent to 1,000 MHz *(see).*

GMT. Greenwich Mean Time. *See* World Time.

Great Circle Path. The shortest route a signal takes to arrive at a receiving location, following the circumference of the earth. Normal printed maps are too distorted for this purpose, but an ideal solution is to take a globe and run a string from a station's transmitter site *(see* PASSPORT's Blue Pages) to your location. Among other things, the closer a signal's path is to the geomagnetic North Pole, the greater the chance of its being disrupted by flutter fading *(see* Fading) during geomagnetic propagational disturbances *(see* Propagation). A Web search can turn up several software programs to generate great circle maps centered at your location, but for most a globe and string are more visually intuitive.

Hams. Government-licensed amateur radio hobbyists who *transmit* to each other by radio, often by single sideband *(see)*, within special amateur bands. Many of these bands are within the shortwave spectrum *(see)*. This spectrum is also used by world band radio, but world band radio and ham radio, which laymen sometimes confuse with each other, are two very separate entities. The easiest way is to think of hams as making something like phone calls, whereas world band stations are like long-distance versions of ordinary mediumwave AM stations.

Harmonic, Harmonic Radiation, Harmonic Signal. Usually, an unwanted weak spurious repeat of a signal in multiple(s) of the fundamental, or "real," frequency. Thus, the third harmonic of a mediumwave AM station on 1120 kHz might be heard on 4480 kHz within the world band spectrum. Stations almost always try to minimize harmonic radiation, as it wastes energy and spectrum space. However, in rare cases stations have been known to amplify a harmonic signal so they can operate inexpensively on a second frequency. Also, *see* Subharmonic.

Hash. Electrical buzzing noise. *See* Noise.

Hertz. *See* Hz.

Heterodyne. A whistle equal in pitch to the separation between two carriers. Thus, two world band stations 5 kHz apart will generate a 5000 Hz whistle unless receiver circuitry (e.g., *see* Notch Filter) keeps this from being audible.

High Fidelity. *See* Enhanced Fidelity.

High-Pass Filter. A filter which lets frequencies pass unattenuated only if they are above a designated frequency. For world band receivers and antennas, 2 MHz or thereabouts is the norm for high-pass filters, as this keeps out mediumwave AM and longwave signals.

HF (High Frequency). Shortwave. *See* Shortwave Spectrum.

HFCC (High Frequency Co-ordination Conference). Founded in 1990 and headquartered in Prague, the HFCC (www.hfcc.org) helps coordinate frequency usage by dozens of broadcasting organizations from numerous countries. These represent a solid majority of the global output for international shortwave broadcasting. Coordination meetings take place twice yearly: once for the "A" (summer) schedule season from the last Sunday in March until the last Sunday in October, another for "B" (winter), and these gatherings have been a great help in preventing frequency conflicts.

Hz. Hertz, a unit of frequency measurement formerly known as cycles per second (c/s). A thousand Hertz is equivalent to 1 kHz *(see)*.

IBS. International Broadcasting Services, Ltd., publishers of PASSPORT TO WORLD BAND RADIO.

IF (Intermediate Frequency). Virtually all world band receivers use the "superheterodyne" principle, where tuned radio frequencies are converted to a single intermediate frequency to facilitate reception, then amplified and detected to produce audio. In virtually all world band portables and most tabletop models, this frequency is either 455 kHz or 450 kHz. If this is not complemented by a second and higher intermediate frequency (double conversion), "images" readily occur at twice the IF; i.e., 910 kHz or 900 kHz. *See* Image.

IF Shift. *See* Passband Offset.

Image. A common type of spurious signal found on low-cost "single conversion" (single IF) radios where a strong signal appears at reduced strength, usually on a frequency 910 kHz or 900 kHz lower down. For example, the BBC on 5875 kHz might repeat on 4965 kHz, its "image frequency." Double-conversion (two IF) receivers have little problem with images, but the additional IF circuitry adds to manufacturing cost. *See* IF, Spurious-Signal Rejection.

Impedance. Opposition, expressed in ohms, to the flow of alternating current. Components work best when impedance is comparable from one to another; so, for example, a receiver with a 75-ohm antenna socket will work best with antennas having a similar feedline impedance. Antenna tuning units can resolve this, albeit at the cost of added operational complexity.

Independent Sideband. *See* Single Sideband.

Interference. Sounds from other signals, notably on the same frequency ("co-channel interference"), or on an adjacent or other nearby channel(s) ("adjacent-channel interference"), that disturb the station you are trying to hear. Worthy radios reduce interference by having good selectivity (*see*) and synchronous selectable sideband (*see* Synchronous Detector). Nearby television sets and cable television wiring may also generate a special type of radio interference called TVI, a "growl," typically from a television horizontal oscillator, heard every 15 kHz or so. Sometimes referred to as QRM, a term based on Morse-code shorthand.

Intermediate Frequency. *See* IF.

International Reply Coupon (IRC). Sold by selected post offices in most parts of the world, IRCs amount to official international "scrip" that may be exchanged for postage in most countries of the world. Because they amount to an international form of postage repayment, they are handy for listeners trying to encourage foreign stations to write them back. However, IRCs are very costly for the amount in stamps that is provided in return. Too, an increasing number of countries are not forthcoming about "cashing in" IRCs. Specifics on this and related matters are provided in the Addresses PLUS section of this book.

International Telecommunication Union (ITU). The regulatory body, headquartered in Geneva, for all international telecommunications, including world band radio. Sometimes incorrectly referred to as the "International Telecommunications Union." In recent years, the ITU has become increasingly ineffective as a regulatory body for world band radio, with much of its former role having been taken up by the HFCC *(see)*.

Internet Radio. *See* Web radio.

Inverted-L Antenna. *See* Passive Antenna.

Ionosphere. *See* Propagation.

IP3. Third-order intercept point. *See* Dynamic Range.

IRC. *See* International Reply Coupon.

Irr. Irregular operation or hours of operation; i.e., schedule tends to be unpredictable.

ISB. Independent sideband. *See* Single Sideband.

ISL. Independent sideband, lower. *See* Feeder.

ISU. Independent sideband, upper. *See* Feeder.

ITU. *See* International Telecommunication Union.

Jamming. Deliberate interference to a transmission with the intent of discouraging listening. However, shortwave broadcasts are uniquely resistant to jamming. This ability to avoid "gatekeeping" is a major reason why shortwave continues to be the workhorse for international broadcasting. For now, jamming is practiced much less than it was during the Cold War.

Keypad. On a world band radio, like a cell phone, a keypad can be used to control many variables. Radio keypads are used primarily so you can enter a station's frequency for reception, and the best keypads have real keys (not a membrane) in the standard telephone format of 3x4 with "zero" under the "8" key. Many keypads are also used for presets, but this means you have to remember code numbers for stations (e.g., BBC 5975 kHz is "07"); handier radios have separate keys for presets, while some others use LCD-displayed "pages" to access presets.

kHz. Kilohertz, the most common unit for measuring where a station is located on the world band dial if it is below 30,000 kHz. Formerly known as "kilocycles per second," or kc/s. 1,000 kilohertz equals one Megahertz. *See* Frequency. *Cf.* MHz.

kilohertz. *See* kHz. The "k" in "kilo" is not properly capitalized, although the computer modem industry got it wrong years back and most modem firms have as yet to correct the error.

kW. A kilowatt(s), the most common unit of measurement for transmitter power *(see)*.

LCD. Liquid-crystal display. LCDs, if properly designed, are fairly easily seen in bright light, but require illumination under darker conditions. LCDs—typically monochrome and gray on gray—also tend to have mediocre contrast, and sometimes can be read from only a certain angle or angles, but they consume nearly no battery power.

LED. Light-emitting diode. LEDs have a long life and are very easily read in the dark or in normal room light, but consume more battery power than LCDs and are hard to read in bright ambient light.

Lightning Arrestor. *See* MOV.

Line Output. Fixed-level audio output typically used to feed a recorder or outboard audio amplifier-speaker system.

Location. The physical location of a station's transmitter, which may be different from the studio location. Transmitter location is useful as a guide to reception quality. For example, if you're in eastern North America and wish to listen to the Voice of Russia, a transmitter located in St. Petersburg will almost certainly provide better reception than, say, one located in Siberia.

Longwave (LW) Band. The 148.5–283.5 kHz portion of the low-frequency (LF) radio spectrum used for domestic broadcasting in Europe, the Near East, North Africa, Russia and Mongolia. As a practical matter, these longwave signals, which have nothing to do with world band or other shortwave signals, are not usually audible in other parts of the world.

Longwire Antenna. *See* Passive Antenna.

Loop Antenna. Round (like a hula hoop) or square antenna often used for reception of longwave, mediumwave AM and even shortwave signals. These can be highly directive below around 2 MHz, and even up to roughly 6 MHz. For this reason, most such antennas can be rotated and even tilted manually or with an antenna rotor. Loops tend to have low gain, and thus need electrical amplification in order to reach their potential. When properly designed and mounted, they can produce superior signal-to-noise ratios that help with weak-signal (DX) reception. Strictly speaking, ferrite-rod antennas, found inside nearly every mediumwave AM radio as well as some specialty outboard antennas, are not "loops." However, in everyday parlance these tiny antennas are referred to as "loops" or "loopsticks."

Low-Pass Filter. A filter which lets frequencies pass unattenuated only if they are below a designated frequency. For world band receivers and antennas, 30 MHz or thereabouts is the norm for low-pass filters, as this keeps out VHF/UHF signals.

LSB. Lower Sideband. *See* Mode, Single Sideband, Feeder.

LV. La Voix, La Voz—French and Spanish for "The Voice." In PASSPORT, this term is also used to represent "The Voice of."

LW. *See* Longwave (LW) Band.

M. Monday.

Mains. *See* AC.

Manual Selectable Sideband. *See* ECSS.

Mediumwave Band, Mediumwave AM Band, Mediumwave Spectrum. *See* AM Band.

Megahertz. *See* MHz.

Memory, Memories. *See* Preset.

Meters. An outdated unit of measurement used for individual world band segments of the shortwave spectrum. The frequency range covered by a given meters designation—also known as "wavelength"—can be gleaned from the following formula: *frequency (kHz) = 299,792 ÷ meters.* Thus, 49 meters comes out to a frequency of 6118 kHz—well within the range of frequencies included in that segment (*see* World Band Spectrum). Inversely, meters can be derived from the following: *meters = 299,792 ÷ frequency (kHz).* The figure 299,792 is based on the speed of light as agreed upon internationally in 1983. However, in practice this awkward figure is usually rounded to 300,000 for computational purposes.

MHz. Megahertz, a common unit to measure where a station is located on the dial, especially above 30 MHz, although in the purest sense all measurements above 3 MHz are supposed to be in MHz. Formerly known as "Megacycles per second," or Mc/s. One Megahertz equals 1,000 kilohertz. *See* Frequency. *Cf.* kHz.

Mode. Method of transmission of radio signals. World band radio broadcasts are almost always in the analog AM (amplitude modulation) mode, the same mode used in the mediumwave AM band (*see*). The AM mode consists of three components: two "sidebands," plus one "carrier" that resides between the two sidebands. Each sideband contains the same programming as the other, and the carrier carries no programming, so a few stations have experimented with the single-sideband (SSB) mode. SSB contains only one sideband, either the lower sideband (LSB) or upper sideband (USB), and a reduced carrier. It requires special radio circuitry to be demodulated, or made intelligible, which is the main reason SSB is unlikely to be widely adopted as a world band mode. However, major efforts are currently underway to implement digital-mode world band transmissions (*see* Digital Radio Mondiale). There are yet other

modes used on shortwave, but not for world band. These include CW (Morse-type code), radiofax, RTTY (radioteletype) and narrow-band FM used by utility and ham stations. Narrow-band FM is not used for music, and is different from usual FM. *See* Single Sideband, NBFM, ISB, ISL, ISU, LSB and USB.

Modulation. The sounds contained in a radio signal.

MOV. Often used in power-line and antenna surge arrestors (a/k/a lightning arrestors) to shunt static and line-power surges to ground. MOVs perform well and are inexpensive, but tend to lose their effectiveness with use; costlier alternatives are thus sometimes worth considering. On rare occasion they also appear to have been implicated in starting fires, so a UL or other recognized certification is helpful. For both these reasons MOV-based arrestors should be replaced at least once every decade that they are in service.

MW. Mediumwave AM band; *see* AM Band. Also, Megawatt, which equals 1,000 kW; *see* kilowatt.

N. New, Nueva, Nuevo, Nouvelle, Nacional, National, Nationale.

Nac. Nacional. Spanish and Portuguese for "National."

Narrow-band FM. *See* NBFM.

Nat, Natl, Nat'l. National, Nationale.

NB. *See* Noise Blanker.

NBFM. Narrow-band FM, used within the shortwave spectrum by some "utility" stations, including (between 25-30 MHz) point-to-point broadcast station remote links. These links are documented by Guido Schotmans at http://dxing.hypermart.net.

Noise. Static, buzzes, pops and the like caused by the earth's atmosphere (typically lightning), and to a lesser extent by galactic noise. Also, electrical noise emanates from such man-made sources as electric blankets, fish-tank heaters, heating pads, electrical and gasoline motors, light dimmers, flickering light bulbs, non-incandescent lights, computers and computer peripherals, office machines, electric fences, and faulty electric utility wiring and related components. Sometimes referred to as QRN, a term based on Morse-code shorthand.

Noise Blanker. Receiver circuit, often found on costly tabletop and profession models, that reduces the impact of pulse-type electrical noises (nearby light dimmers, etc.) or certain unusual types of pulse transmissions. In practice, these circuits use long-established designs which act only on pulses which are greater in strength than the received signal, although designs without this limitation exist on paper.

Noise Floor. *See* Sensitivity.

Notch Filter, Tunable. A feature found on some tabletop and professional receivers for reducing or rejecting annoying heterodyne (*see*) interference—the whistles, howls and squeals for which shortwave has traditionally been notorious. Some noise filters operate within the IF (*see*) stage, whereas others operate as audio filters. IF notch filters tend to respond exceptionally well where there is fading, whereas audio filters usually have more capacity to attack higher-pitched heterodynes.

Other. Programs are in a language other than one of the world's primary languages.

Overall Distortion. Nothing makes listening quite so tiring as distortion. PASSPORT has devised techniques to measure overall cumulative distortion from signal input through audio output—not just distortion within the audio stage. This level of distortion is thus equal to what is heard by the ear.

Overloading. *See* Dynamic Range.

Passband Offset. Continuously variable control that can be user-adjusted such that only the best-sounding portion of a given sideband is heard when the receiver is in either the single-sideband mode (*see*) or the synchronous selectable sideband mode (*see*). This allows for a finer degree of control over adjacent-channel interference and tonal response than does a simple LSB or USB switch associated with a fixed BFO (*see*).

Also known as Passband Tuning, Passband Shift and IF Shift. The same nomenclature is sometimes used to describe variable-bandwidth circuitry.

Passband Tuning. *See* Passband Offset.

Passive Antenna. An antenna that is not electronically amplified. Typically, these are mounted outdoors, although the "tape-measure" type that comes as an accessory with some portables is usually strung indoors. For world band reception, virtually all outboard models for consumers are made from wire, rather than rods or tubular elements. The two most common designs are the inverted-L (so-called "longwire") and trapped dipole (mounted either horizontally or as a "sloper"). These antennas are preferable to active antennas (*cf.*), and are reviewed in detail in the Radio Database International White Paper, PASSPORT *Evaluation of Popular Outdoor Antennas (Unamplified)*. *See* Feedline.

PBS. In China, People's Broadcasting Station.

Phase Cancellation. In synchronous selectable sideband, two identical wave patterns (lower and upper sidebands) are brought together 180 degrees out of phase so as to cancel out the unwanted sideband. This is a less costly way of sideband attenuation than through the use of discrete IF filtering.

Phase Noise. Synthesizers and other circuits can create a "rushing" noise that is usually noticed only when the receiver is tuned alongside the edge of a powerful broadcast or other carrier. In effect, the signal becomes "modulated" by the noise. Phase noise is a useful measurement if you tune weak signals alongside powerful signals. Measured in dBc (decibels below carrier).

Pirate. Illegal radio station operated by enthusiasts with little if any political purpose other than to defy radio laws. Programs typically consist of music, satire or comments relevant to pirate colleagues.

Placement Facility. Typically a local FM or mediumwave AM station which leases airtime for one or more programs or program segments from an international broadcaster. These programs are usually fed by feeders (*see*), although some placement facilities pick up the programs via world band radio.

PLL (Phase-Locked Loop). With world band receivers, a PLL circuit means that the radio can be tuned digitally, often using a number of handy tuning techniques, such as a keypad (*see*) and presets (*see*).

Polarization. Radio and other over-the-air signals tend to be either horizontally or vertically polarized. Unsurprisingly, stations which transmit using vertical antennas produce vertically polarized signals, and so on. World band transmissions are almost always transmitted as horizontally polarized, so most outdoor receiving antennas are also horizontal. However, the scattering effects of the ionosphere turn the single horizontal transmitted signal, like a bread slicer, into numerous bits (*see* Fading). Some continue on as horizontal while others morph into vertical, but most fall somewhere in between. As a result, the angle of receiving antenna elements tends to be noncritical for reception of long-distance shortwave signals.

Power. Transmitter power *before* antenna gain, expressed in kilowatts (kW). The present range of world band powers is 0.01 to 1,000 kW.

Power Lock. *See* Travel Power Lock.

PR. People's Republic.

Preamplifier. An inboard or outboard broadband amplifier to increase the strength of signals fed into a receiver's circuitry. Active antennas (*see*) incorporate a preamplifier or an amplified preselector (*see*).

Preselector. A circuit—outboard as an accessory, or inboard as part of the receiver—that effectively limits the range of frequencies which can enter a receiver's circuitry or the circuitry of an active antenna (*see*); that is, which improves

front-end selectivity (*see*). For example, a preselector may let in the range 15000-16000 kHz, thus helping ensure that your receiver or active antenna will not encounter problems within that range caused by signals from, say, 5730-6250 kHz or local mediumwave AM signals (520-1705 kHz). This range usually can be varied, manually or automatically, according to the frequency to which the receiver is being tuned. A preselector may be passive (unamplified) or active (amplified).

Preset. Allows you to select a station pre-stored in a radio's memory. The handiest presets require only one push of a button, as on a car radio.

Propagation. World band signals travel, like a basketball, up and down from the station to your radio. The "floor" below is the earth's surface, whereas the "player's hand" on high is the *ionosphere*, a gaseous layer that envelops the planet. While the earth's surface remains pretty much the same from day to day, the ionosphere—nature's own passive "satellite"—varies in how it propagates radio signals, depending on how much sunlight hits the "bounce points."

Thus, some world band segments do well mainly by day, whereas others are best by night. During winter there's less sunlight, so the "night bands" become unusually active, whereas the "day bands" become correspondingly less useful (*see* World Band Spectrum). Day-to-day changes in the sun's weather also cause short-term changes in world band radio reception; this explains why some days you can hear rare signals.

Additionally, the 11-year sunspot cycle has a long term effect on propagation, with sunspot maximum greatly enhancing reception on higher world band segments. The last maximum was in late 2000, while the next minimum is expected in mid-2006.

These bounce, or refraction, points are not absolutely efficient. Some loss comes about from absorption (*see*), and signal scattering brings about fading (*see*).

Propagation, like the weather, varies considerably, which adds to the intrigue of world band radio. The accepted standard for propagation prediction is WWV (and sometimes WWVH) on 2500, 5000, 10000, 15000 and 20000 kHz. An explanation of prediction measurements is at www.boulder.nist.gov/timefreq/stations/iform.html#geo. But before going to that site, view the excellent primer on propagation at www.ac4rv.com/tn/propflash.htm, then go on to www.sunspotcycle.com.

PS. Provincial Station, Pangsong.

Pto. Puerto, Porto.

QRM. *See* Interference.

QRN. *See* Noise.

QSL. *See* Verification.

R. Radio, Radiodiffusion, Radiodifusora, Radiodifusão, Radiophonikos, Radiostantsiya, Radyo, Radyosu, and so forth.

Radiofax, Radio Facsimile. Like ordinary telefax (facsimile by telephone lines), but by radio.

Radioteletype (RTTY). Characters, but not illustrations, transmitted by radio. *See* Baud.

RDI. Radio Database International®, a registered trademark of International Broadcasting Services, Ltd.

Receiver. Synonym for a radio, but sometimes—especially when called a "communications receiver"—implying a radio with superior tough-signal and utility-signal performance.

Reception Report. *See* Verification.

Reduced Carrier. *See* Single Sideband.

Reg. Regional.

Relay. A retransmission facility, often highlighted in "Worldwide Broadcasts in English" and "Voices from Home" in PASSPORT's WorldScan® section. Relay facilities are generally considered to be located outside the broadcaster's country. Being closer to the target audience, they usually provide superior reception. *See* Feeder.

Rep. Republic, République, República.
RF Gain. A variable control to reduce the gain of a receiver's earliest amplification, in the RF stage. However, modern receivers often function better without an RF stage, in which case an RF gain control usually acts as a variable attenuator *(see)*.
RN. *See* R and N.
RS. Radio Station, Radiostantsiya, Radiostudiya, Radiophonikos Stathmos.
RT, RTV. Radiodiffusion Télévision, Radio Télévision, and so forth.
RTTY. *See* Radioteletype.
🅂 Transmission aired summer (midyear) only, typically from the last Sunday in March until the last Sunday in October; *see* "HFCC." *Cf.* 🅆
S. San, Santa, Santo, São, Saint, Sainte. Also, South.
Sa. Saturday.
SASE. Self-addressed, stamped envelope. *See* introduction to Addresses PLUS in this Passport.
Scan, Scanning. Circuitry within a radio that allows it to bandscan or memory scan automatically.
Season, Schedule Season. *See* HFCC.
Segments. *See* Shortwave Spectrum.
Selectivity. The ability of a radio to reject interference *(see)* from signals on adjacent channels. Thus, also known as adjacent-channel rejection, a key variable in radio quality. *See* Bandwidth. *See* Shape Factor. *See* Ultimate Rejection. *See* Synchronous Detector.
Sensitivity. The ability of a radio to receive weak signals; thus, also known as weak-signal sensitivity. Of special importance if you are listening during the day or tuning domestic tropical band broadcasts—or if you are located in such parts of the world as Western North America, Hawaii or Australasia, where signals tend to be relatively weak. The best measurement of sensitivity is the noise floor.
Shape Factor. Skirt selectivity helps reduce interference and increase audio fidelity. It is important if you will be tuning stations that are weaker than adjacent-channel signals. Skirt selectivity is measured by the shape factor, the ratio between the bandwidth at –6 dB (adjacent signal at about the same strength as the received station) and –60 dB (adjacent signal relatively much stronger), although with professional receivers and in parts of Europe –3 dB is used in lieu of –6 dB. A good shape factor provides the best defense against adjacent powerful signals' muscling their way in to disturb reception of the desired signal.
SHF. Super high frequency, 3-30 GHz.
Shortwave Spectrum. The shortwave spectrum—also known as the High Frequency (HF) spectrum—is that portion of the radio spectrum from 3 MHz through 30 MHz (3,000-30,000 kHz). The shortwave spectrum is occupied not only by world band radio (*see* World Band Segments), but also hams (*see*) and utility stations (*see*).
Sideband. *See* Mode.
Signal Polarization. *See* Polarization.
Signal-to-Noise Ratio. A common form of noise comes from a radio's (and/or active antenna's) electronic circuitry and usually sounds like "hiss." Depending upon its antenna's location, a receiver may also pick up and reproduce noise from nearby electrical and electronic sources, such as power and cable TV lines, light dimmers and digital electronic products. A third type of noise, galactic, is rarely a problem, and even then can be heard only above 20 MHz. Thus, a key part of enjoyable radio reception is to have a worthy signal-to-noise ratio; that is, where the received radio signal is strong enough relative to the various noises that it drowns out the noises.
Single Sideband, Independent Sideband. Spectrum- and power-conserving modes of transmission commonly used by

Dubai is prosperous and modern, but values its traditions. Here, dancers perform in time-honored fashion.   M. Prezelj

utility stations *(see)* and hams *(see)*. Single-sideband transmitted signals usually consist of one full sideband (lower sideband, LSB; or, more typically, upper sideband, USB) and a reduced or suppressed carrier, but no second sideband. Very few broadcasters (e.g., the American AFRTS) use, or are expected ever to use, the single-sideband mode. Many world band radios are already capable of demodulating single-sideband transmissions, and some can even process independent-sideband signals.

Independent-sideband (ISB) signals are like single-sideband signals, but with both sidebands. Content is usually different in the two sidebands—for stereo, as in the Kahn AM-stereo system where the left channel can be LSB, right channel USB. More typically, entirely different programming may be carried by each sideband, such as in a shortwave feed to a relay facility that retransmits two entirely different programs. *See* Feeder, Mode.

Certain world band broadcasters and time-standard stations emit single-sideband transmissions which have virtually no carrier reduction, or a minimum of reduction; say, 3 or 6 dB. These "AM equivalent" (AME) signals can be listened to, with slightly added distortion, on ordinary radios not equipped to demodulate pure single sideband signals. Properly designed synchronous detectors (*see*) help reduce distortion with AME transmissions. A variety of AME signals, called "compatible AM," include a minor FM component to help improve reception fidelity. These were experimented with by Leonard Kahn and the VOA decades ago, but were not found to offer any meaningful improvement over ordinary AME transmissions.
Site. *See* Location.
Skirt Selectivity. *See* Shape Factor.
Slew Controls. Elevator-button-type up and down controls to tune a radio. On many radios with synthesized tuning, slewing is used in lieu of tuning by knob. Better is when slew controls are complemented by a tuning knob, which is more versatile.
Sloper Antenna. *See* Passive Antenna.
Solar Cycle. Synonym for "sunspot cycle." *See* Propagation.
SPR. Spurious (false) extra signal from a transmitter actually operating on another frequency. One such type is harmonic (*see*).
Spur. *See* SPR.

Spurious Signal. *See* SPR.

Spurious-Signal Rejection. The ability of a radio receiver to avoid producing false signals, such as images *(see)* and birdies *(see)*, that might otherwise interfere with the clarity of the station you're trying to hear.

Squelch. A circuit which mutes a receiver until the received signal's strength exceeds a specified threshold, which is usually user-adjustable.

SSB. *See* Single Sideband.

St, Sta, Sto. Abbreviations for words that mean "Saint."

Stability. The ability of a receiver to rest exactly the tuned frequency without drifting.

Static. *See* Noise.

Static Arrestor. *See* MOV.

Su. Sunday.

Subharmonic. A harmonic heard at 1.5 or 0.5 times the operating frequency. This anomaly is caused by the way signals are generated within vintage-model transmitters, and thus cannot take place with modern transmitters. For example, the subharmonic of a station on 3360 kHz might be heard faintly on 5040 or 1680 kHz. Also, *see* Harmonic.

Sunspot Cycle. *See* Propagation.

Superheterodyne. *See* IF.

Surge Arrestor. *See* MOV.

SW. *See* Shortwave Spectrum.

SWL. Shortwave listener. The preponderance of shortwave listening is to world band stations, but some radio enthusiasts also eavesdrop on utility stations *(see)* and hams *(see)*.

Synchronous Detector. World band radios are increasingly coming equipped with this high-tech circuit that greatly reduces fading distortion. Better synchronous detectors also allow for synchronous selectable sideband; that is, the ability to select the less-interfered of the two sidebands of a world band or other AM-mode signal. *See* Mode, Phase Cancellation.

Synchronous Selectable Sideband. The best feature, derived from synchronous detection circuitry, greatly reduces the impact of adjacent-channel interference *(see)* on listening. *See* Synchronous Detector.

Synthesizer, Frequency. Better world band receivers utilize a digital frequency synthesizer to tune signals. Among other things, such synthesizers allow for pushbutton tuning and presets, and display the exact frequency digitally—pluses that make tuning to the world considerably easier. Virtually a "must" feature. *See* Analog Frequency Readout. *See* Digital Frequency Display.

Target. Where a transmission is beamed, a/k/a target zone.

Th. Thursday.

Third Order Intercept Point. *See* Dynamic Range.

Travel Power Lock. Control which disables the on/off switch to prevent a radio from switching on accidentally.

Transmitter Power. *See* Power.

Trap Dipole Antenna, Trapped Dipole Antenna. Dipole antenna with several coil "traps" that allow for optimum reception on several world band or other segments or bands. *See* Passive Antenna.

Tropical Band Segments. *See* World Band Segments.

Tu. Tuesday.

UHF. Ultra High Frequency, 300 MHz through 3 GHz.

Ultimate Rejection, Ultimate Selectivity. The point at which a receiver is no longer able to reject adjacent-channel interference. Ultimate rejection is important if you listen to signals that are markedly weaker than are adjacent signals. *See* Selectivity.

Universal Day. *See* World Time.

Universal Time. *See* World Time.

URL. Universal Resource Locator; i.e., the Internet address for a given Webpage.

USB. Upper Sideband. *See* Mode, Single Sideband, Feeder.

UTC. Coordinated Universal Time—and, no, it's *never* "Universal Time Coordinated," although for everyday use it's okay to refer simply to "Universal Time." *See* World Time.

Utility Stations. Most signals within the shortwave spectrum are not world band stations. Rather, they are utility stations—radio telephones, ships at sea, aircraft, ionospheric sounders, over-the-horizon radar and the like—that transmit strange sounds (growls, gurgles, dih-dah sounds, etc.). Although these can be picked up on many receivers, they are rarely intended to be utilized by the general public. *Cf.* Broadcast, Hams and Feeders.

v. Variable frequency; i.e., one that is unstable or drifting because of a transmitter malfunction or, less often, to avoid jamming or other interference.

Verification. A "QSL" card or letter from a station verifying that a listener indeed heard that particular station. In order to stand a chance of qualifying for a verification card or letter, you should respond with a reception report shortly after having heard the transmission. You need to provide the station heard with, at a minimum, the following information in a three-number "SIO" code, in which "SIO 555" is best and "SIO 111" is worst:

- **S**ignal strength, with 5 being of excellent quality, comparable to that of a local mediumwave AM station, and 1 being inaudible or at least so weak as to be virtually unintelligible, 2 (faint, but somewhat intelligible), 3 (moderate strength) and 4 (good strength) represent the signal-strength levels usually encountered with world band stations.
- **I**nterference from other stations, with 5 indicating no interference whatsoever, and 1 indicating such extreme interference that the desired signal is virtually drowned out. Ratings of 2 (heavy interference), 3 (moderate interference) and 4 (slight interference) represent the differing degrees of interference more typically encountered with world band signals. If possible, indicate the names of the interfering station(s) and the channel(s) they are on. Otherwise, at least describe what the interference sounds like.
- **O**verall quality of the signal, with 5 being best, 1 worst.
- In addition to providing SIO findings, you should indicate which programs you've heard, as well as comments on how you liked or disliked those programs. Refer to the Addresses PLUS section of this edition for information on where and to whom your report should be sent, and whether return postage should be included.
- Expanded versions of the SIO reporting code are the SINPO and SINFO codes, where "N" refers to atmospheric noise, "F" to fading and "P" to propagation conditions. As atmospheric noise is rarely audible below 20 MHz and propagation conditions are highly subjective, SIO tends to provide more accurate feedback. Fading, however, is not hard for an experienced monitor to rate, but a SIFO code has never caught on.
- Few stations wish to receive unsolicited tape (cassette) recordings of their transmissions. However, some actively seek MP3, RealAudio or other Internet-sent files or mailed CD recordings of certain transmissions.

VHF. Very high frequency spectrum, 30-300 MHz, which starts just above the shortwave spectrum *(see)* and ends at the UHF spectrum. *See* FM, which operates within the VHF spectrum. Somewhat confusingly, in German VHF is known as UKW (Ultra Short Wave), which is different from UHF (Ultra High Frequency).

Vo. Voice of.

◪ Transmission aired winter only, typically from the last Sunday in October until the last Sunday in March; *see* HFCC. *Cf.* ◪

W. Wednesday.

Wavelength. *See* Meters.

Weak-Signal Sensitivity. *See* Sensitivity.

Webcasting. *See* Web Radio.

Web Radio, Webcasts. Broadcasts aired to the public over the Internet's World Wide Web. These thousands of stations worldwide include simulcast FM, mediumwave AM and world band stations, as well as Web-only "stations." Although Webcasting was originally unfettered, it is increasingly being subject to official gatekeeping, or censorship, as well as unique and steep copyright and union royalties that have all but killed off Web simulcasting by AM/FM stations in the United States. PASSPORT lists URL information for world band stations which Webcast live or on-demand.

World Band Radio. Broadcasts (news, music, sports and so forth) transmitted within and just below the shortwave spectrum *(see)*. Virtually all are found within 14 world band segments *(see)*. These broadcasting stations are similar to regular mediumwave AM band and FM band broadcasters, except that world band stations can be heard over enormous distances. As a result, they often carry programs created especially for audiences abroad. World band is also difficult to "jam" *(see* Jamming), making it uniquely effective in outflanking official censorship. Some world band stations have regular audiences in the tens of millions, and even over 100 million. Although world band lacks the glamour of new broadcasting technologies, around 600 million people worldwide continue to listen.

World Band Segments. Fourteen slices within the shortwave spectrum *(see)* and upper reaches of the mediumwave spectrum *(see* AM Band) that are used almost exclusively for world band broadcasts. Those below 5.1 MHz are called "Tropical Band Segments." *See* "Best Times and Frequencies" sidebar elsewhere within this PASSPORT.

World Band Spectrum. *See* World Band Segments.

World Day. *See* World Time.

World Time. Also known as Coordinated Universal Time (UTC), Greenwich Mean Time (GMT), Zulu time (Z) and "military time." With over 150 countries on world band radio, if each announced its own local time you would need a calculator to figure it all out. To get around this, a single international time—World Time—is used. The differences between World Time and local time are detailed in the Addresses PLUS and Setting Your World Time Clock sections of this edition. World Time can also be determined simply by listening to time announcements given on the hour by world band stations—or minute by minute by WWV in the United States on 2500, 5000, 10000, 15000 and 20000 kHz; WWVH in Hawaii on 2500, 5000, 10000 and 15000 kHz; and CHU in Canada on 3330, 7335 and 14670 kHz. A 24-hour clock format is used, so "1800 World Time" means 6:00 PM World Time. If you're in, say, North America, Eastern Time is five hours behind World Time winters and four hours behind World Time summers, so 1800 World Time would be 1:00 PM EST or 2:00 PM EDT. The easiest solution is to use a 24-hour digital clock set to World Time. Many radios already have these built in, and World Time clocks are also available as accessories. World Time also applies to the days of the week. So if it's 9:00 PM (21:00) Wednesday in New York during the winter, it's 0200 *Thursday* World Time.

WS. World Service.

X-Band. The recently implemented extended mediumwave AM band segment from 1605-1705 kHz in the Western Hemisphere, Australia and ultimately beyond. In the United States, federal travelers' information services have primary status on 1610 kHz.

Zero beat. When tuning a world band or other AM-mode signal in the single-sideband mode, there is a whistle, or "beat," whose pitch is the result of the difference in frequency between the receiver's internally generated carrier (BFO, or beat-frequency oscillator) and the station's transmitted carrier. By tuning carefully, the listener can reduce the difference between these two carriers to the point where the whistle is deeper and deeper, to the point where it no longer audible. This silent sweet spot is known as "zero beat." *See* ECSS.

Zulu Time. *See* World Time.

Printed in Canada

PASSPORT's Blue Pages

Frequency Guide to World Band Schedules

Bandscanning can be frustrating if you don't have a "map"—PASSPORT's Blue Pages. Let's say you've stumbled across something Asian-sounding on 7410 kHz at 2035 World Time. The Blue Pages show All India Radio beamed to Western Europe, with 250 kW of power from Delhi. These suggest this is probably what you're hearing, even if you're not in Europe. You can also see that English from India will begin on that same channel in about ten minutes.

DRM Transmissions

Digital (DRM) transmissions change often, as the technology is being sorted out. By next year DRM receivers may be available, but in the meantime those who wish to experiment with the technology (*see* PASSPORT REPORTS) can get frequency information from www.drm.org/livebroadcast/globlivebroadcast.htm and www.rnw.nl/realradio/html/drm_schedule.html.

Schedules for Entire Year

Times and days of the week are in World Time, explained in "Setting Your World Time Clock" and PASSPORT's glossary; for local times in each country, see "Addresses PLUS." Midyear, some stations are an hour earlier (◧) or later (◨) because of daylight saving/summer time. Those used only seasonally are labeled **S** for summer (midyear, typically the last Sunday in March until the last Sunday in October) and **W** for winter. Stations may also extend their hours of transmission, or air special programs, for national holidays, emergencies or sports events.

To be as useful as possible over the months to come, PASSPORT's schedules consist not just of observed activity, but also that which we have creatively opined will take place during the forthcoming year. This predictive material is based on decades of experience and is original from us. Although inherently not as exact as real-time data, over the years it's been of tangible value to PASSPORT readers.

Guide to Blue Pages Format

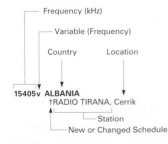

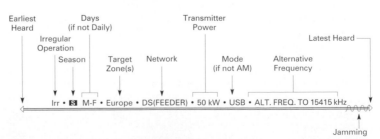

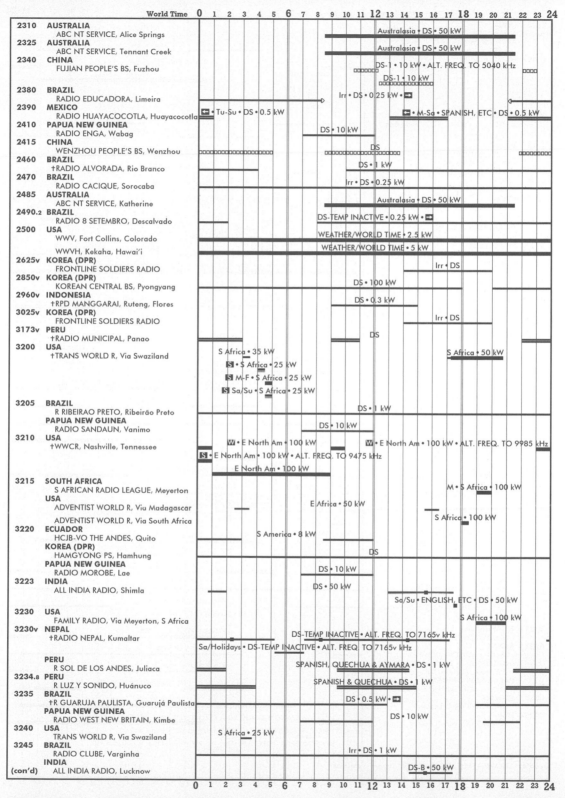

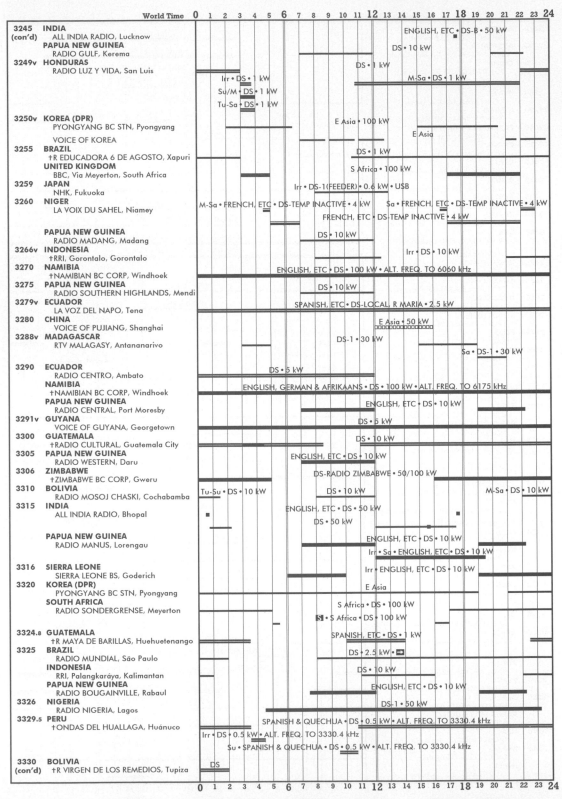

World Time	0 1 2 3 4 5 6 7 8 9 10 11 12 13 14 15 16 17 18 19 20 21 22 23 24
3245 **INDIA** (con'd) ALL INDIA RADIO, Lucknow	ENGLISH, ETC • DS-B • 50 kW
PAPUA NEW GUINEA RADIO GULF, Kerema	DS • 10 kW
3249v HONDURAS RADIO LUZ Y VIDA, San Luis	DS • 1 kW / Irr • DS • 1 kW / M-Sa • DS • 1 kW / Su/M • DS • 1 kW / Tu-Sa • DS • 1 kW
3250v KOREA (DPR) PYONGYANG BC STN, Pyongyang	E Asia • 100 kW / E Asia
VOICE OF KOREA	
3255 BRAZIL †R EDUCADORA 6 DE AGOSTO, Xapuri	DS • 1 kW
UNITED KINGDOM BBC, Via Meyerton, South Africa	S Africa • 100 kW
3259 JAPAN NHK, Fukuoka	Irr • DS-1(FEEDER) • 0.6 kW • USB
3260 NIGER LA VOIX DU SAHEL, Niamey	M-Sa • FRENCH, ETC • DS-TEMP INACTIVE • 4 kW / Sa • FRENCH, ETC • DS-TEMP INACTIVE • 4 kW / FRENCH, ETC • DS-TEMP INACTIVE • 4 kW
PAPUA NEW GUINEA RADIO MADANG, Madang	DS • 10 kW
3266v INDONESIA †RRI, Gorontalo, Gorontalo	Irr • DS • 10 kW
3270 NAMIBIA †NAMIBIAN BC CORP, Windhoek	ENGLISH, ETC • DS • 100 kW • ALT. FREQ. TO 6060 kHz
3275 PAPUA NEW GUINEA RADIO SOUTHERN HIGHLANDS, Mendi	DS • 10 kW
3279v ECUADOR LA VOZ DEL NAPO, Tena	SPANISH, ETC • DS-LOCAL R MARIA • 2.5 kW
3280 CHINA VOICE OF PUJIANG, Shanghai	E Asia • 50 kW
3288v MADAGASCAR RTV MALAGASY, Antananarivo	DS-1 • 30 kW / Sa • DS-1 • 30 kW
3290 ECUADOR RADIO CENTRO, Ambato	DS • 5 kW
NAMIBIA †NAMIBIAN BC CORP, Windhoek	ENGLISH, GERMAN & AFRIKAANS • DS • 100 kW • ALT. FREQ. TO 6175 kHz
PAPUA NEW GUINEA RADIO CENTRAL, Port Moresby	ENGLISH, ETC • DS • 10 kW
3291v GUYANA VOICE OF GUYANA, Georgetown	DS • 5 kW
3300 GUATEMALA †RADIO CULTURAL, Guatemala City	DS • 10 kW
3305 PAPUA NEW GUINEA RADIO WESTERN, Daru	ENGLISH, ETC • DS • 10 kW
3306 ZIMBABWE †ZIMBABWE BC CORP, Gweru	DS-RADIO ZIMBABWE • 50/100 kW
3310 BOLIVIA RADIO MOSOJ CHASKI, Cochabamba	Tu-Su • DS • 10 kW / DS • 10 kW / M-Sa • DS • 10 kW
3315 INDIA ALL INDIA RADIO, Bhopal	ENGLISH, ETC • DS • 50 kW / DS • 50 kW
PAPUA NEW GUINEA RADIO MANUS, Lorengau	ENGLISH, ETC • DS • 10 kW / Irr • Sa • ENGLISH, ETC • DS • 10 kW
3316 SIERRA LEONE SIERRA LEONE BS, Goderich	Irr • ENGLISH, ETC • DS • 10 kW
3320 KOREA (DPR) PYONGYANG BC STN, Pyongyang	E Asia
SOUTH AFRICA RADIO SONDERGRENSE, Meyerton	S Africa • DS • 100 kW / S Africa • DS • 100 kW
3324.8 GUATEMALA †R MAYA DE BARILLAS, Huehuetenango	SPANISH, ETC • DS • 1 kW
3325 BRAZIL RADIO MUNDIAL, São Paulo	DS • 2.5 kW • ➡
INDONESIA RRI, Palangkaráya, Kalimantan	DS • 10 kW
PAPUA NEW GUINEA RADIO BOUGAINVILLE, Rabaul	ENGLISH, ETC • DS • 10 kW
3326 NIGERIA RADIO NIGERIA, Lagos	DS-1 • 50 kW
3329.5 PERU †ONDAS DEL HUALLAGA, Huánuco	SPANISH & QUECHUA • DS • 0.5 kW • ALT. FREQ. TO 3330.4 kHz / Irr • DS • 0.5 kW • ALT. FREQ. TO 3330.4 kHz / Su • SPANISH & QUECHUA • DS • 0.5 kW • ALT. FREQ. TO 3330.4 kHz
3330 BOLIVIA (con'd) †R VIRGEN DE LOS REMEDIOS, Tupiza	DS
	0 1 2 3 4 5 6 7 8 9 10 11 12 13 14 15 16 17 18 19 20 21 22 23 24

ENGLISH ▬ ARABIC ⁵⁵⁵ CHINESE □□□ FRENCH ▭ GERMAN ▭ RUSSIAN ═ SPANISH ▭ OTHER ▬

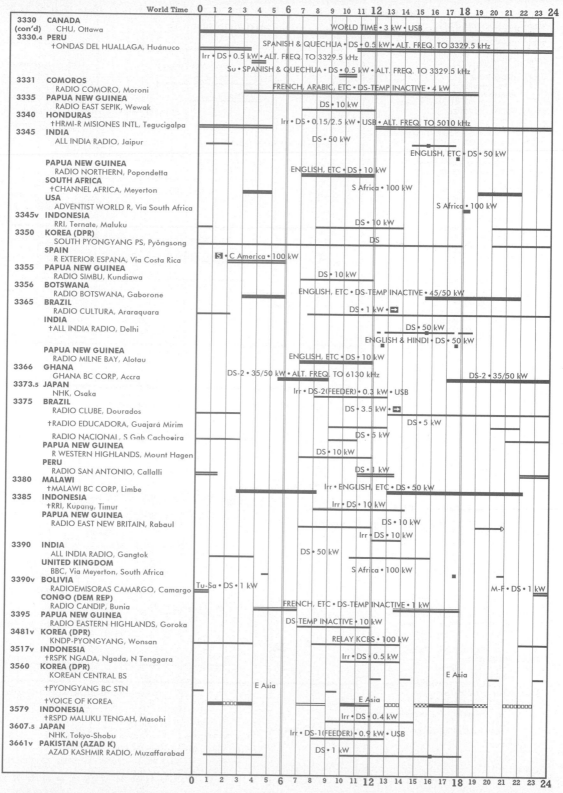

World Time 0 1 2 3 4 5 6 7 8 9 10 11 12 13 14 15 16 17 18 19 20 21 22 23 24

Freq	Country / Station	Notes
3330 (con'd)	**CANADA** — CHU, Ottawa	WORLD TIME • 3 kW • USB
3330.4	**PERU** — †ONDAS DEL HUALLAGA, Huánuco	SPANISH & QUECHUA • DS • 0.5 kW • ALT. FREQ. TO 3329.5 kHz — Irr • DS • 0.5 kW • ALT. FREQ. TO 3329.5 kHz — Su • SPANISH & QUECHUA • DS • 0.5 kW • ALT. FREQ. TO 3329.5 kHz
3331	**COMOROS** — RADIO COMORO, Moroni	FRENCH, ARABIC, ETC • DS-TEMP INACTIVE • 4 kW
3335	**PAPUA NEW GUINEA** — RADIO EAST SEPIK, Wewak	DS • 10 kW
3340	**HONDURAS** — †HRMI-R MISIONES INTL, Tegucigalpa	Irr • DS • 0.15/2.5 kW • USB • ALT. FREQ. TO 5010 kHz
3345	**INDIA** — ALL INDIA RADIO, Jaipur	DS • 50 kW — ENGLISH, ETC • DS • 50 kW
	PAPUA NEW GUINEA — RADIO NORTHERN, Popondetta	ENGLISH, ETC • DS • 10 kW
	SOUTH AFRICA — †CHANNEL AFRICA, Meyerton	S Africa • 100 kW
	USA — ADVENTIST WORLD R, Via South Africa	S Africa • 100 kW
3345v	**INDONESIA** — RRI, Ternate, Maluku	DS • 10 kW
3350	**KOREA (DPR)** — SOUTH PYONGYANG PS, Pyŏngsong	DS
	SPAIN — R EXTERIOR ESPANA, Via Costa Rica	S • C America • 100 kW
3355	**PAPUA NEW GUINEA** — RADIO SIMBU, Kundiawa	DS • 10 kW
3356	**BOTSWANA** — RADIO BOTSWANA, Gaborone	ENGLISH, ETC • DS-TEMP INACTIVE • 45/50 kW
3365	**BRAZIL** — RADIO CULTURA, Araraquara	DS • 1 kW • ⇨
	INDIA — †ALL INDIA RADIO, Delhi	DS • 50 kW — ENGLISH & HINDI • DS • 50 kW
	PAPUA NEW GUINEA — RADIO MILNE BAY, Alotau	ENGLISH, ETC • DS • 10 kW
3366	**GHANA** — GHANA BC CORP, Accra	DS-2 • 35/50 kW • ALT. FREQ. TO 6130 kHz — DS-2 • 35/50 kW
3373.5	**JAPAN** — NHK, Osaka	Irr • DS-2(FEEDER) • 0.3 kW • USB
3375	**BRAZIL** — RADIO CLUBE, Dourados	DS • 3.5 kW • ⇨
	†RADIO EDUCADORA, Guajará Mirim	DS • 5 kW
	RADIO NACIONAL, S Gab Cachoeira	DS • 5 kW
	PAPUA NEW GUINEA — R WESTERN HIGHLANDS, Mount Hagen	DS • 10 kW
	PERU — RADIO SAN ANTONIO, Callalli	DS • 1 kW
3380	**MALAWI** — †MALAWI BC CORP, Limbe	Irr • ENGLISH, ETC • DS • 50 kW
3385	**INDONESIA** — †RRI, Kupang, Timur	Irr • DS • 10 kW
	PAPUA NEW GUINEA — RADIO EAST NEW BRITAIN, Rabaul	DS • 10 kW — Irr • DS • 10 kW
3390	**INDIA** — ALL INDIA RADIO, Gangtok	DS • 50 kW
	UNITED KINGDOM — BBC, Via Meyerton, South Africa	S Africa • 100 kW
3390v	**BOLIVIA** — RADIOEMISORAS CAMARGO, Camargo	Tu-Sa • DS • 1 kW — M-F • DS • 1 kW
	CONGO (DEM REP) — RADIO CANDIP, Bunia	FRENCH, ETC • DS-TEMP INACTIVE • 1 kW
3395	**PAPUA NEW GUINEA** — RADIO EASTERN HIGHLANDS, Goroka	DS-TEMP INACTIVE • 10 kW
3481v	**KOREA (DPR)** — KNDP-PYONGYANG, Wonsan	RELAY KCBS • 100 kW
3517v	**INDONESIA** — †RSPK NGADA, Ngada, N Tenggara	Irr • DS • 0.5 kW
3560	**KOREA (DPR)** — KOREAN CENTRAL BS	E Asia
	†PYONGYANG BC STN	E Asia
	†VOICE OF KOREA	E Asia — E Asia
3579	**INDONESIA** — †RSPD MALUKU TENGAH, Masohi	Irr • DS • 0.4 kW
3607.5	**JAPAN** — NHK, Tokyo-Shobu	Irr • DS-1(FEEDER) • 0.9 kW • USB
3661v	**PAKISTAN (AZAD K)** — AZAD KASHMIR RADIO, Muzaffarabad	DS • 1 kW

0 1 2 3 4 5 6 7 8 9 10 11 12 13 14 15 16 17 18 19 20 21 22 23 24

SEASONAL S OR W   1-HR TIMESHIFT MIDYEAR ⇦ OR ⇨   JAMMING / OR ∧   EARLIEST HEARD ◁   LATEST HEARD ▷   NEW FOR 2005 †

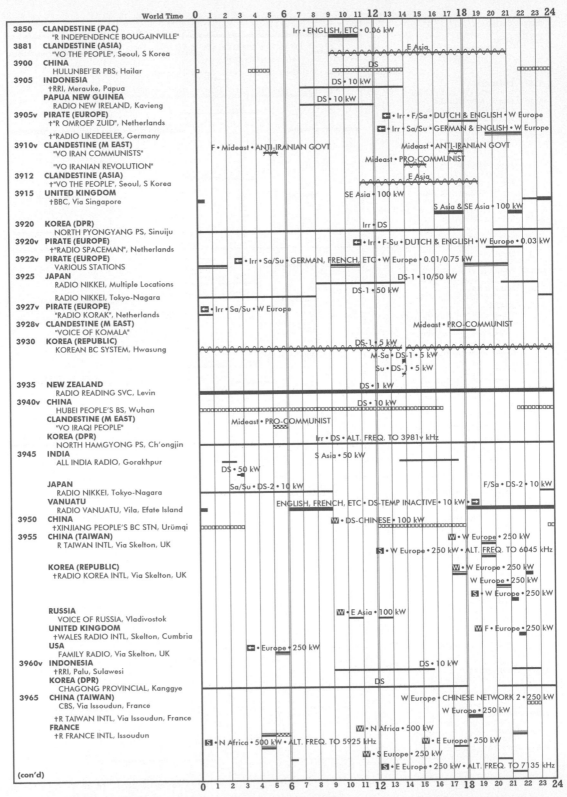

ENGLISH ▬ ARABIC ▨ CHINESE □□□ FRENCH ▬ GERMAN ▬ RUSSIAN ═ SPANISH ▬ OTHER ▬

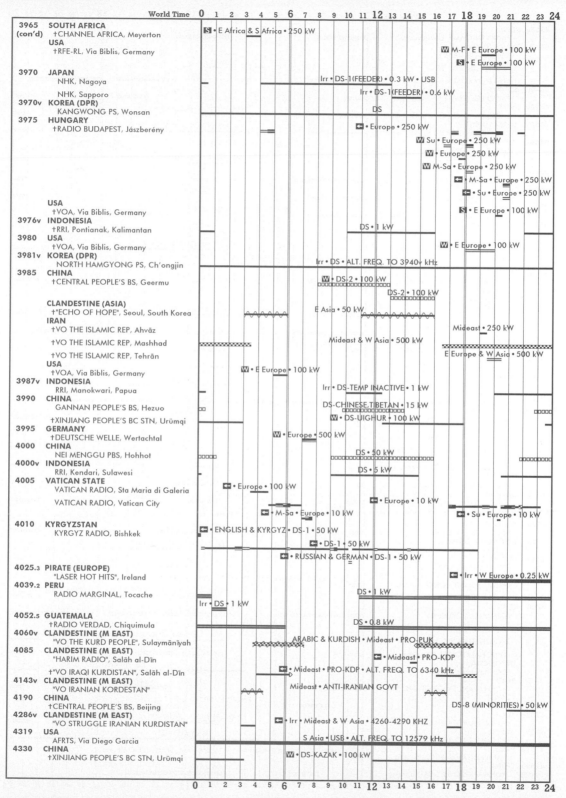

World Time | 0 1 2 3 4 5 6 7 8 9 10 11 12 13 14 15 16 17 18 19 20 21 22 23 24

3965	SOUTH AFRICA
(con'd)	†CHANNEL AFRICA, Meyerton
	USA
	†RFE-RL, Via Biblis, Germany
3970	JAPAN
	NHK, Nagoya
	NHK, Sapporo
3970v	KOREA (DPR)
	KANGWONG PS, Wonsan
3975	HUNGARY
	†RADIO BUDAPEST, Jászberény
	USA
	†VOA, Via Biblis, Germany
3976v	INDONESIA
	†RRI, Pontianak, Kalimantan
3980	USA
	†VOA, Via Biblis, Germany
3981v	KOREA (DPR)
	NORTH HAMGYONG PS, Ch'ongjin
3985	CHINA
	†CENTRAL PEOPLE'S BS, Geermu
	CLANDESTINE (ASIA)
	†"ECHO OF HOPE", Seoul, South Korea
	IRAN
	†VO THE ISLAMIC REP, Ahvāz
	†VO THE ISLAMIC REP, Mashhad
	†VO THE ISLAMIC REP, Tehrān
	USA
	†VOA, Via Biblis, Germany
3987v	INDONESIA
	RRI, Manokwari, Papua
3990	CHINA
	GANNAN PEOPLE'S BS, Hezuo
	†XINJIANG PEOPLE'S BC STN, Urümqi
3995	GERMANY
	†DEUTSCHE WELLE, Wertachtal
4000	CHINA
	NEI MENGGU PBS, Hohhot
4000v	INDONESIA
	RRI, Kendari, Sulawesi
4005	VATICAN STATE
	VATICAN RADIO, Sta Maria di Galeria
	VATICAN RADIO, Vatican City
4010	KYRGYZSTAN
	KYRGYZ RADIO, Bishkek
4025.3	PIRATE (EUROPE)
	"LASER HOT HITS", Ireland
4039.2	PERU
	RADIO MARGINAL, Tocache
4052.5	GUATEMALA
	†RADIO VERDAD, Chiquimula
4060v	CLANDESTINE (M EAST)
	"VO THE KURD PEOPLE", Sulaymānīyah
4085	CLANDESTINE (M EAST)
	"HARIM RADIO", Salāh al-Dīn
	†"VO IRAQI KURDISTAN", Salāh al-Dīn
4143v	CLANDESTINE (M EAST)
	"VO IRANIAN KORDESTAN"
4190	CHINA
	†CENTRAL PEOPLE'S BS, Beijing
4286v	CLANDESTINE (M EAST)
	"VO STRUGGLE IRANIAN KURDISTAN"
4319	USA
	AFRTS, Via Diego Garcia
4330	CHINA
	†XINJIANG PEOPLE'S BC STN, Urümqi

Chart annotations:

- S • E Africa & S Africa • 250 kW
- W M-F • E Europe • 100 kW
- S • E Europe • 100 kW
- Irr • DS-1(FEEDER) • 0.3 kW • USB
- Irr • DS-1(FEEDER) • 0.6 kW
- DS
- ⮕ • Europe • 250 kW
- W Su • Europe • 250 kW
- W • Europe • 250 kW
- W M-Sa • Europe • 250 kW
- ⮕ • M-Sa • Europe • 250 kW
- ⮕ • Su • Europe • 250 kW
- S • E Europe • 100 kW
- DS • 1 kW
- W • E Europe • 100 kW
- Irr • DS • ALT. FREQ. TO 3940v kHz
- W • DS-2 • 100 kW
- DS-2 • 100 kW
- E Asia • 50 kW
- Mideast • 250 kW
- Mideast & W Asia • 500 kW
- E Europe & W Asia • 500 kW
- W • E Europe • 100 kW
- Irr • DS-TEMP INACTIVE • 1 kW
- DS-CHINESE,TIBETAN • 15 kW
- W • DS-UIGHUR • 100 kW
- W • Europe • 500 kW
- DS • 50 kW
- DS • 5 kW
- ⮕ • Europe • 100 kW
- ⮕ • Europe • 10 kW
- ⮕ • M-Sa • Europe • 10 kW
- ⮕ • Su • Europe • 10 kW
- ⮕ • ENGLISH & KYRGYZ • DS-1 • 50 kW
- ⮕ • DS-1 • 50 kW
- ⮕ • RUSSIAN & GERMAN • DS-1 • 50 kW
- ⮕ • Irr • W Europe • 0.25 kW
- DS • 1 kW
- Irr • DS • 1 kW
- DS • 0.8 kW
- ARABIC & KURDISH • Mideast • PRO-PUK
- ⮕ • Mideast • PRO-KDP
- ⮕ • Mideast • PRO-KDP • ALT. FREQ. TO 6340 kHz
- Mideast • ANTI-IRANIAN GOVT
- DS-8 (MINORITIES) • 50 kW
- ⮕ • Irr • Mideast & W Asia • 4260-4290 KHZ
- S Asia • USB • ALT. FREQ. TO 12579 kHz
- W • DS-KAZAK • 100 kW

World Time | 0 1 2 3 4 5 6 7 8 9 10 11 12 13 14 15 16 17 18 19 20 21 22 23 24

SEASONAL S OR W   1-HR TIMESHIFT ⮕ OR ⮕   JAMMING / OR ∧   EARLIEST HEARD ◁   LATEST HEARD ▷   NEW FOR 2005 †

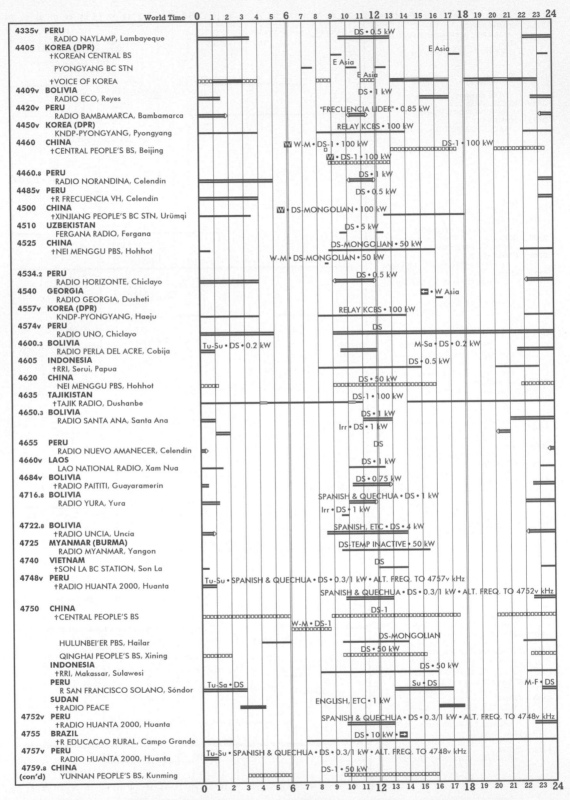

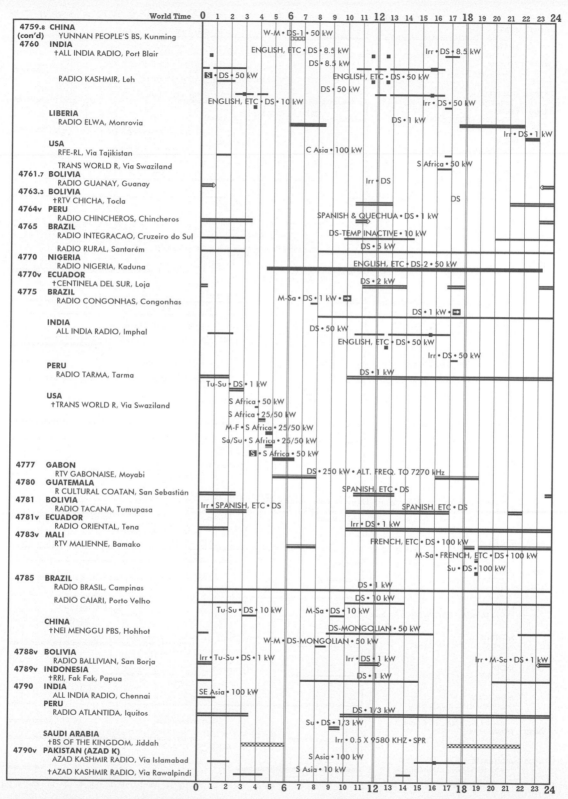

World Time 0 1 2 3 4 5 6 7 8 9 10 11 12 13 14 15 16 17 18 19 20 21 22 23 24

4759.8 CHINA
(con'd)   YUNNAN PEOPLE'S BS, Kunming — W-M • DS-1 • 50 kW
4760 INDIA
        †ALL INDIA RADIO, Port Blair — ENGLISH, ETC • DS • 8.5 kW — Irr • DS • 8.5 kW
        DS • 8.5 kW

        RADIO KASHMIR, Leh — S • DS • 50 kW — ENGLISH, ETC • DS • 50 kW — DS • 50 kW
        ENGLISH, ETC • DS • 10 kW — Irr • DS • 50 kW

        LIBERIA
        RADIO ELWA, Monrovia — DS • 1 kW — Irr • DS • 1 kW

        USA
        RFE-RL, Via Tajikistan — C Asia • 100 kW
        TRANS WORLD R, Via Swaziland — S Africa • 50 kW
4761.7 BOLIVIA
        RADIO GUANAY, Guanay — Irr • DS
4763.3 BOLIVIA
        †RTV CHICHA, Tocla — DS
4764v PERU
        RADIO CHINCHEROS, Chincheros — SPANISH & QUECHUA • DS • 1 kW
4765 BRAZIL
        RADIO INTEGRACAO, Cruzeiro do Sul — DS-TEMP INACTIVE • 10 kW

        RADIO RURAL, Santarém — DS • 5 kW
4770 NIGERIA
        RADIO NIGERIA, Kaduna — ENGLISH, ETC • DS-2 • 50 kW
4770v ECUADOR
        †CENTINELA DEL SUR, Loja — DS • 2 kW
4775 BRAZIL
        RADIO CONGONHAS, Congonhas — M-Sa • DS • 1 kW • ➡
        DS • 1 kW • ➡

        INDIA
        ALL INDIA RADIO, Imphal — DS • 50 kW — ENGLISH, ETC • DS • 50 kW — Irr • DS • 50 kW

        PERU
        RADIO TARMA, Tarma — DS • 1 kW

        USA
        †TRANS WORLD R, Via Swaziland — Tu-Su • DS • 1 kW
        S Africa • 50 kW
        S Africa • 25/50 kW
        M-F • S Africa • 25/50 kW
        Sa/Su • S Africa • 25/50 kW
        S • S Africa • 50 kW
4777 GABON
        RTV GABONAISE, Moyabi — DS • 250 kW • ALT. FREQ. TO 7270 kHz
4780 GUATEMALA
        R CULTURAL COATAN, San Sebastián — SPANISH, ETC • DS
4781 BOLIVIA
        RADIO TACANA, Tumupasa — Irr • SPANISH, ETC • DS — SPANISH, ETC • DS
4781v ECUADOR
        RADIO ORIENTAL, Tena — Irr • DS • 1 kW
4783v MALI
        RTV MALIENNE, Bamako — FRENCH, ETC • DS • 100 kW
        M-Sa • FRENCH, ETC • DS • 100 kW
        Su • DS • 100 kW
4785 BRAZIL
        RADIO BRASIL, Campinas — DS • 1 kW

        RADIO CAIARI, Porto Velho — DS • 10 kW
        Tu-Su • DS • 10 kW — M-Sa • DS • 10 kW

        CHINA
        †NEI MENGGU PBS, Hohhot — DS-MONGOLIAN • 50 kW
        W-M • DS-MONGOLIAN • 50 kW
4788v BOLIVIA
        RADIO BALLIVIAN, San Borja — Irr • Tu-Su • DS • 1 kW — Irr • DS • 1 kW — Irr • M-Sa • DS • 1 kW
4789v INDONESIA
        †RRI, Fak Fak, Papua — DS • 1 kW
4790 INDIA
        ALL INDIA RADIO, Chennai — SE Asia • 100 kW
        PERU
        RADIO ATLANTIDA, Iquitos — DS • 1/3 kW
        Su • DS • 1/3 kW

        SAUDI ARABIA
        †BS OF THE KINGDOM, Jiddah — Irr • 0.5 X 9580 KHZ • SPR
4790v PAKISTAN (AZAD K)
        AZAD KASHMIR RADIO, Via Islamabad — S Asia • 100 kW
        †AZAD KASHMIR RADIO, Via Rawalpindi — S Asia • 10 kW

0 1 2 3 4 5 6 7 8 9 10 11 12 13 14 15 16 17 18 19 20 21 22 23 24

SEASONAL S OR W   1-HR TIMESHIFT MIDYEAR ➡ OR ➡   JAMMING / OR ∧   EARLIEST HEARD ◁   LATEST HEARD ▷   NEW FOR 2005 †

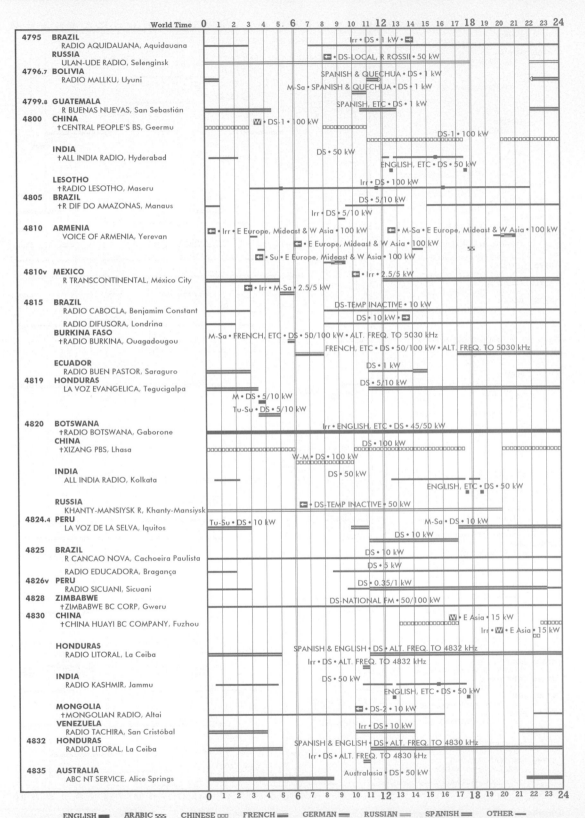

World Time 0 1 2 3 4 5 6 7 8 9 10 11 12 13 14 15 16 17 18 19 20 21 22 23 24

4795 BRAZIL
RADIO AQUIDAUANA, Aquidauana — Irr • DS • 1 kW • ⮌
RUSSIA
ULAN-UDE RADIO, Selenginsk — ⮌ • DS-LOCAL, R ROSSII • 50 kW
4796.7 BOLIVIA
RADIO MALLKU, Uyuni — SPANISH & QUECHUA • DS • 1 kW
M-Sa • SPANISH & QUECHUA • DS • 1 kW
4799.8 GUATEMALA
R BUENAS NUEVAS, San Sebastián — SPANISH, ETC • DS • 1 kW
4800 CHINA
†CENTRAL PEOPLE'S BS, Geermu — ☐ • DS-1 • 100 kW   DS-1 • 100 kW
INDIA
†ALL INDIA RADIO, Hyderabad — DS • 50 kW
ENGLISH, ETC • DS • 50 kW
LESOTHO
†RADIO LESOTHO, Maseru — Irr • DS • 100 kW
4805 BRAZIL
†R DIF DO AMAZONAS, Manaus — DS • 5/10 kW
Irr • DS • 5/10 kW
4810 ARMENIA
VOICE OF ARMENIA, Yerevan — ⮌ • Irr • E Europe, Mideast & W Asia • 100 kW   ⮌ • M-Sa • E Europe, Mideast & W Asia • 100 kW
⮌ • E Europe, Mideast & W Asia • 100 kW
⮌ • Su • E Europe, Mideast & W Asia • 100 kW
4810v MEXICO
R TRANSCONTINENTAL, México City — ⮌ • Irr • 2.5/5 kW
⮌ • Irr • M-Sa • 2.5/5 kW
4815 BRAZIL
RADIO CABOCLA, Benjamim Constant — DS-TEMP INACTIVE • 10 kW
RADIO DIFUSORA, Londrina — DS • 10 kW • ⮌
BURKINA FASO
†RADIO BURKINA, Ouagadougou — M-Sa • FRENCH, ETC • DS • 50/100 kW • ALT. FREQ. TO 5030 kHz
FRENCH, ETC • DS • 50/100 kW • ALT. FREQ. TO 5030 kHz
ECUADOR
RADIO BUEN PASTOR, Saraguro — DS • 1 kW
4819 HONDURAS
LA VOZ EVANGELICA, Tegucigalpa — DS • 5/10 kW
M • DS • 5/10 kW
Tu-Su • DS • 5/10 kW
4820 BOTSWANA
†RADIO BOTSWANA, Gaborone — Irr • ENGLISH, ETC • DS • 45/50 kW
CHINA
†XIZANG PBS, Lhasa — DS • 100 kW
W-M • DS • 100 kW
INDIA
ALL INDIA RADIO, Kolkata — DS • 50 kW
ENGLISH, ETC • DS • 50 kW
RUSSIA
KHANTY-MANSIYSK R, Khanty-Mansiysk — ⮌ • DS-TEMP INACTIVE • 50 kW
4824.4 PERU
LA VOZ DE LA SELVA, Iquitos — Tu-Su • DS • 10 kW   M-Sa • DS • 10 kW
DS • 10 kW
4825 BRAZIL
R CANCAO NOVA, Cachoeira Paulista — DS • 10 kW
RADIO EDUCADORA, Bragança — DS • 5 kW
4826v PERU
RADIO SICUANI, Sicuani — DS • 0.35/1 kW
4828 ZIMBABWE
†ZIMBABWE BC CORP, Gweru — DS-NATIONAL FM • 50/100 kW
4830 CHINA
†CHINA HUAYI BC COMPANY, Fuzhou — ☐ • E Asia • 15 kW
Irr • ☐ • E Asia • 15 kW
HONDURAS
RADIO LITORAL, La Ceiba — SPANISH & ENGLISH • DS • ALT. FREQ. TO 4832 kHz
Irr • DS • ALT. FREQ. TO 4832 kHz
INDIA
RADIO KASHMIR, Jammu — DS • 50 kW
ENGLISH, ETC • DS • 50 kW
MONGOLIA
†MONGOLIAN RADIO, Altai — ⮌ • DS-2 • 10 kW
VENEZUELA
RADIO TACHIRA, San Cristóbal — Irr • DS • 10 kW
4832 HONDURAS
RADIO LITORAL, La Ceiba — SPANISH & ENGLISH • DS • ALT. FREQ. TO 4830 kHz
Irr • DS • ALT. FREQ. TO 4830 kHz
4835 AUSTRALIA
ABC NT SERVICE, Alice Springs — Australasia • DS • 50 kW

0 1 2 3 4 5 6 7 8 9 10 11 12 13 14 15 16 17 18 19 20 21 22 23 24

ENGLISH ▬▬ ARABIC ≋≋ CHINESE ▫▫▫ FRENCH ══ GERMAN ▭▭ RUSSIAN ══ SPANISH ▬▬ OTHER ──

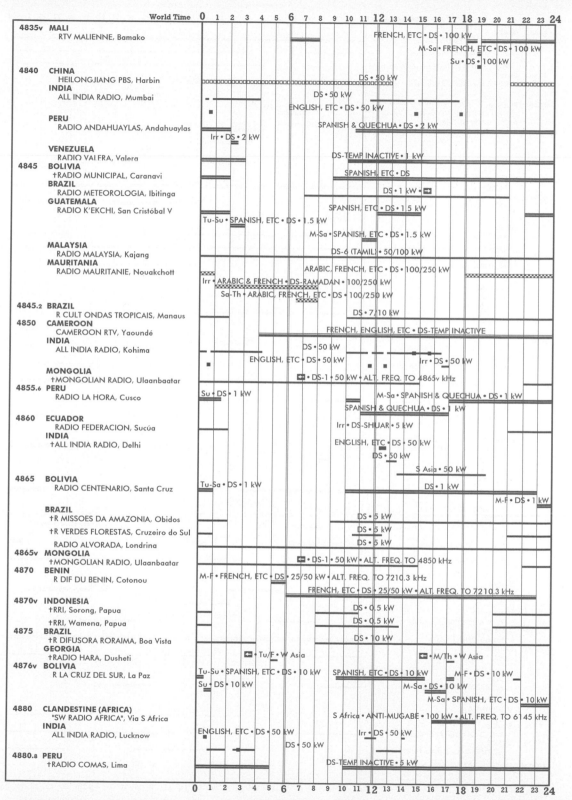

World Time 0 1 2 3 4 5 6 7 8 9 10 11 12 13 14 15 16 17 18 19 20 21 22 23 24

4835v MALI
RTV MALIENNE, Bamako — FRENCH, ETC • DS • 100 kW / M-Sa • FRENCH, ETC • DS • 100 kW / Su • DS • 100 kW

4840 CHINA
HEILONGJIANG PBS, Harbin — DS • 50 kW
INDIA
ALL INDIA RADIO, Mumbai — DS • 50 kW / ENGLISH, ETC • DS • 50 kW
PERU
RADIO ANDAHUAYLAS, Andahuaylas — SPANISH & QUECHUA • DS • 2 kW / Irr • DS • 2 kW

VENEZUELA
RADIO VALERA, Valera — DS-TEMP INACTIVE • 1 kW
4845 BOLIVIA
†RADIO MUNICIPAL, Caranavi — SPANISH, ETC • DS
BRAZIL
RADIO METEOROLOGIA, Ibitinga — DS • 1 kW • ⇨
GUATEMALA
RADIO K'EKCHI, San Cristóbal V — SPANISH, ETC • DS • 1.5 kW / Tu-Su • SPANISH, ETC • DS • 1.5 kW / M-Sa • SPANISH, ETC • DS • 1.5 kW

MALAYSIA
RADIO MALAYSIA, Kajang — DS-6 (TAMIL) • 50/100 kW
MAURITANIA
RADIO MAURITANIE, Nouakchott — ARABIC, FRENCH, ETC • DS • 100/250 kW / Irr • ARABIC & FRENCH • DS-RAMADAN • 100/250 kW / Sa-Th • ARABIC, FRENCH, ETC • DS • 100/250 kW

4845.2 BRAZIL
R CULT ONDAS TROPICAIS, Manaus — DS • 7/10 kW
4850 CAMEROON
CAMEROON RTV, Yaoundé — FRENCH, ENGLISH, ETC • DS-TEMP INACTIVE
INDIA
ALL INDIA RADIO, Kohima — DS • 50 kW / ENGLISH, ETC • DS • 50 kW / Irr • DS • 50 kW

MONGOLIA
†MONGOLIAN RADIO, Ulaanbaatar — ⬅ • DS-1 • 50 kW • ALT. FREQ. TO 4865v kHz
4855.6 PERU
RADIO LA HORA, Cusco — Su • DS • 1 kW / M-Sa • SPANISH & QUECHUA • DS • 1 kW / SPANISH & QUECHUA • DS • 1 kW

4860 ECUADOR
RADIO FEDERACION, Sucúa — Irr • DS-SHUAR • 5 kW
INDIA
†ALL INDIA RADIO, Delhi — ENGLISH, ETC • DS • 50 kW / DS • 50 kW / S Asia • 50 kW

4865 BOLIVIA
RADIO CENTENARIO, Santa Cruz — Tu-Sa • DS • 1 kW / DS • 1 kW / M-F • DS • 1 kW

BRAZIL
†R MISSOES DA AMAZONIA, Obidos — DS • 5 kW
†R VERDES FLORESTAS, Cruzeiro do Sul — DS • 5 kW
RADIO ALVORADA, Londrina — DS • 5 kW
4865v MONGOLIA
†MONGOLIAN RADIO, Ulaanbaatar — ⬅ • DS-1 • 50 kW • ALT. FREQ. TO 4850 kHz
4870 BENIN
R DIF DU BENIN, Cotonou — M-F • FRENCH, ETC • DS • 25/50 kW • ALT. FREQ. TO 7210.3 kHz / FRENCH, ETC • DS • 25/50 kW • ALT. FREQ. TO 7210.3 kHz

4870v INDONESIA
†RRI, Sorong, Papua — DS • 0.5 kW
†RRI, Wamena, Papua — DS • 0.5 kW
4875 BRAZIL
†R DIFUSORA RORAIMA, Boa Vista — DS • 10 kW
GEORGIA
†RADIO HARA, Dusheti — ⬅ • Tu/F • W Asia / ⬅ • M/Th • W Asia
4876v BOLIVIA
R LA CRUZ DEL SUR, La Paz — Tu-Su • SPANISH, ETC • DS • 10 kW / SPANISH, ETC • DS • 10 kW / M-F • DS • 10 kW / Su • DS • 10 kW / M-Sa • DS • 10 kW / M-Sa • SPANISH, ETC • DS • 10 kW

4880 CLANDESTINE (AFRICA)
"SW RADIO AFRICA", Via S Africa — S Africa • ANTI-MUGABE • 100 kW • ALT. FREQ. TO 6145 kHz
INDIA
ALL INDIA RADIO, Lucknow — ENGLISH, ETC • DS • 50 kW / Irr • DS • 50 kW / DS • 50 kW

4880.8 PERU
†RADIO COMAS, Lima — DS-TEMP INACTIVE • 5 kW

0 1 2 3 4 5 6 7 8 9 10 11 12 13 14 15 16 17 18 19 20 21 22 23 24

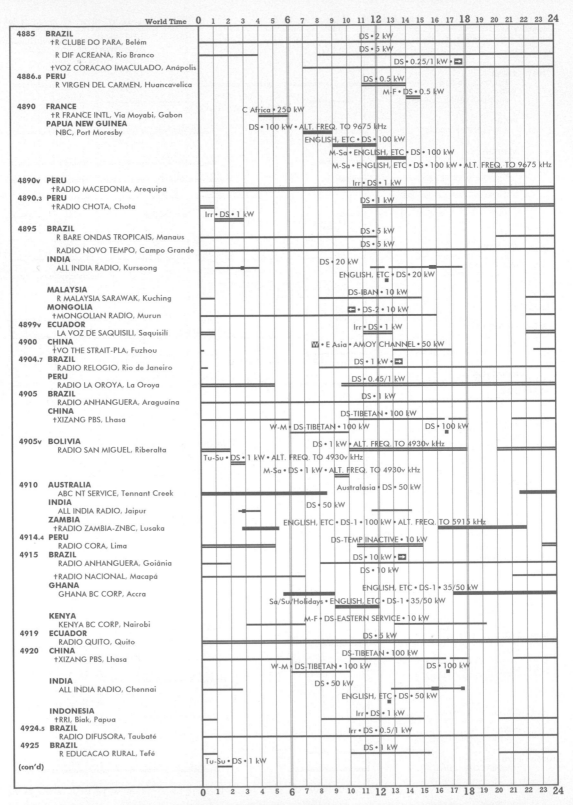

World Time 0 1 2 3 4 5 6 7 8 9 10 11 12 13 14 15 16 17 18 19 20 21 22 23 24

4885 BRAZIL
†R CLUBE DO PARA, Belém — DS • 2 kW
R DIF ACREANA, Rio Branco — DS • 5 kW
†VOZ CORACAO IMACULADO, Anápolis — DS • 0.25/1 kW ▶
4886.8 PERU
R VIRGEN DEL CARMEN, Huancavelica — DS • 0.5 kW
M-F • DS • 0.5 kW
4890 FRANCE
†R FRANCE INTL, Via Moyabi, Gabon — C Africa • 250 kW
PAPUA NEW GUINEA
NBC, Port Moresby — DS • 100 kW • ALT. FREQ. TO 9675 kHz
ENGLISH, ETC • DS • 100 kW
M-Sa • ENGLISH, ETC • DS • 100 kW
M-Sa • ENGLISH, ETC • DS • 100 kW • ALT. FREQ. TO 9675 kHz
4890v PERU
†RADIO MACEDONIA, Arequipa — Irr • DS • 1 kW
4890.3 PERU
†RADIO CHOTA, Chota — DS • 1 kW
Irr • DS • 1 kW
4895 BRAZIL
R BARE ONDAS TROPICAIS, Manaus — DS • 5 kW
RADIO NOVO TEMPO, Campo Grande — DS • 5 kW
INDIA
ALL INDIA RADIO, Kurseong — DS • 20 kW
ENGLISH, ETC • DS • 20 kW
MALAYSIA
R MALAYSIA SARAWAK, Kuching — DS-IBAN • 10 kW
MONGOLIA
†MONGOLIAN RADIO, Murun — ◀ • DS-2 • 10 kW
4899v ECUADOR
LA VOZ DE SAQUISILI, Saquisili — Irr • DS • 1 kW
4900 CHINA
†VO THE STRAIT-PLA, Fuzhou — W • E Asia • AMOY CHANNEL • 50 kW
4904.7 BRAZIL
RADIO RELOGIO, Rio de Janeiro — DS • 1 kW • ▶
PERU
RADIO LA OROYA, La Oroya — DS • 0.45/1 kW
4905 BRAZIL
RADIO ANHANGUERA, Araguaina — DS • 1 kW
CHINA
†XIZANG PBS, Lhasa — DS-TIBETAN • 100 kW
W-M • DS-TIBETAN • 100 kW — DS • 100 kW
4905v BOLIVIA
RADIO SAN MIGUEL, Riberalta — DS • 1 kW • ALT. FREQ. TO 4930v kHz
Tu-Su • DS • 1 kW • ALT. FREQ. TO 4930v kHz
M-Sa • DS • 1 kW • ALT. FREQ. TO 4930v kHz
4910 AUSTRALIA
ABC NT SERVICE, Tennant Creek — Australasia • DS • 50 kW
INDIA
ALL INDIA RADIO, Jaipur — DS • 50 kW
ZAMBIA
†RADIO ZAMBIA-ZNBC, Lusaka — ENGLISH, ETC • DS-1 • 100 kW • ALT. FREQ. TO 5915 kHz
4914.4 PERU
RADIO CORA, Lima — DS-TEMP INACTIVE • 10 kW
4915 BRAZIL
RADIO ANHANGUERA, Goiânia — DS • 10 kW • ▶
†RADIO NACIONAL, Macapá — DS • 10 kW
GHANA
GHANA BC CORP, Accra — ENGLISH, ETC • DS-1 • 35/50 kW
Sa/Su/Holidays • ENGLISH, ETC • DS-1 • 35/50 kW
KENYA
KENYA BC CORP, Nairobi — M-F • DS-EASTERN SERVICE • 10 kW
4919 ECUADOR
RADIO QUITO, Quito — DS • 5 kW
4920 CHINA
†XIZANG PBS, Lhasa — DS-TIBETAN • 100 kW
W-M • DS-TIBETAN • 100 kW — DS • 100 kW
INDIA
ALL INDIA RADIO, Chennai — DS • 50 kW
ENGLISH, ETC • DS • 50 kW
INDONESIA
†RRI, Biak, Papua — Irr • DS • 1 kW
4924.5 BRAZIL
RADIO DIFUSORA, Taubaté — Irr • DS • 0.5/1 kW
4925 BRAZIL
R EDUCACAO RURAL, Tefé — DS • 1 kW
Tu-Su • DS • 1 kW

(con'd)

0 1 2 3 4 5 6 7 8 9 10 11 12 13 14 15 16 17 18 19 20 21 22 23 24

ENGLISH ▬▬ ARABIC ⌇⌇⌇ CHINESE □□□ FRENCH ▬▬ GERMAN ▬▬ RUSSIAN ══ SPANISH ══ OTHER ──

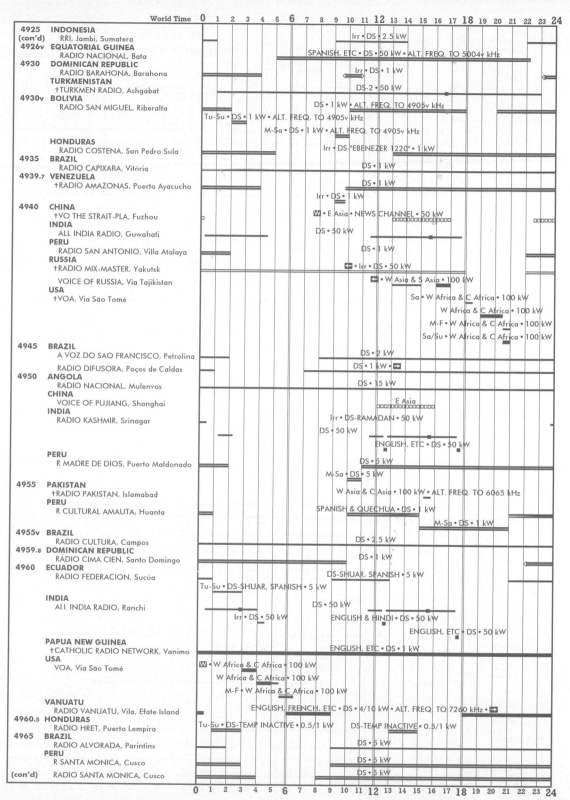

4925 **INDONESIA**	
(con'd) RRI, Jambi, Sumatera	Irr • DS • 2.5 kW
4926v **EQUATORIAL GUINEA**	
RADIO NACIONAL, Bata	SPANISH, ETC • DS • 50 kW • ALT. FREQ. TO 5004v kHz
4930 **DOMINICAN REPUBLIC**	
RADIO BARAHONA, Barahona	Irr • DS • 1 kW
TURKMENISTAN	
†TURKMEN RADIO, Ashgabat	DS-2 • 50 kW
4930v **BOLIVIA**	
RADIO SAN MIGUEL, Riberalta	DS • 1 kW • ALT. FREQ. TO 4905v kHz
	Tu-Su • DS • 1 kW • ALT. FREQ. TO 4905v kHz
	M-Sa • DS • 1 kW • ALT. FREQ. TO 4905v kHz
HONDURAS	
RADIO COSTENA, San Pedro Sula	Irr • DS-"EBENEZER 1220" • 1 kW
4935 **BRAZIL**	
RADIO CAPIXABA, Vitória	DS • 1 kW
4939.7 **VENEZUELA**	
†RADIO AMAZONAS, Puerto Ayacucho	DS • 1 kW
	Irr • DS • 1 kW
4940 **CHINA**	
†VO THE STRAIT-PLA, Fuzhou	W • E Asia • NEWS CHANNEL • 50 kW
INDIA	
ALL INDIA RADIO, Guwahati	DS • 50 kW
PERU	
RADIO SAN ANTONIO, Villa Atalaya	DS • 1 kW
RUSSIA	
†RADIO MIX-MASTER, Yakutsk	Irr • DS • 50 kW
VOICE OF RUSSIA, Via Tajikistan	W Asia & S Asia • 100 kW
USA	
†VOA, Via São Tomé	Sa • W Africa & C Africa • 100 kW
	W Africa & C Africa • 100 kW
	M-F • W Africa & C Africa • 100 kW
	Sa/Su • W Africa & C Africa • 100 kW
4945 **BRAZIL**	
A VOZ DO SAO FRANCISCO, Petrolina	DS • 2 kW
RADIO DIFUSORA, Poços de Caldas	DS • 1 kW
4950 **ANGOLA**	
RADIO NACIONAL, Mulenvos	DS • 15 kW
CHINA	
VOICE OF PUJIANG, Shanghai	E Asia
INDIA	
RADIO KASHMIR, Srinagar	Irr • DS-RAMADAN • 50 kW
	DS • 50 kW
	ENGLISH, ETC • DS • 50 kW
PERU	
R MADRE DE DIOS, Puerto Maldonado	DS • 5 kW
	M-Sa • DS • 5 kW
4955 **PAKISTAN**	
†RADIO PAKISTAN, Islamabad	W Asia & C Asia • 100 kW • ALT. FREQ. TO 6065 kHz
PERU	
R CULTURAL AMAUTA, Huanta	SPANISH & QUECHUA • DS • 1 kW
	M-Sa • DS • 1 kW
4955v **BRAZIL**	
RADIO CULTURA, Campos	DS • 2.5 kW
4959.8 **DOMINICAN REPUBLIC**	
RADIO CIMA CIEN, Santo Domingo	DS • 1 kW
4960 **ECUADOR**	
RADIO FEDERACION, Sucúa	DS-SHUAR, SPANISH • 5 kW
	Tu-Su • DS-SHUAR, SPANISH • 5 kW
INDIA	
ALL INDIA RADIO, Ranchi	DS • 50 kW
	Irr • DS • 50 kW
	ENGLISH & HINDI • DS • 50 kW
	ENGLISH, ETC • DS • 50 kW
PAPUA NEW GUINEA	
†CATHOLIC RADIO NETWORK, Vanimo	ENGLISH, ETC • DS • 1 kW
USA	
VOA, Via São Tomé	W • W Africa & C Africa • 100 kW
	W Africa & C Africa • 100 kW
	M-F • W Africa & C Africa • 100 kW
VANUATU	
RADIO VANUATU, Vila, Efate Island	ENGLISH, FRENCH, ETC • DS • 4/10 kW • ALT. FREQ. TO 7260 kHz
4960.5 **HONDURAS**	
RADIO HRET, Puerto Lempira	Tu-Su • DS-TEMP INACTIVE • 0.5/1 kW DS-TEMP INACTIVE • 0.5/1 kW
4965 **BRAZIL**	
RADIO ALVORADA, Parintins	DS • 5 kW
PERU	
R SANTA MONICA, Cusco	DS • 5 kW
(con'd) RADIO SANTA MONICA, Cusco	DS • 5 kW

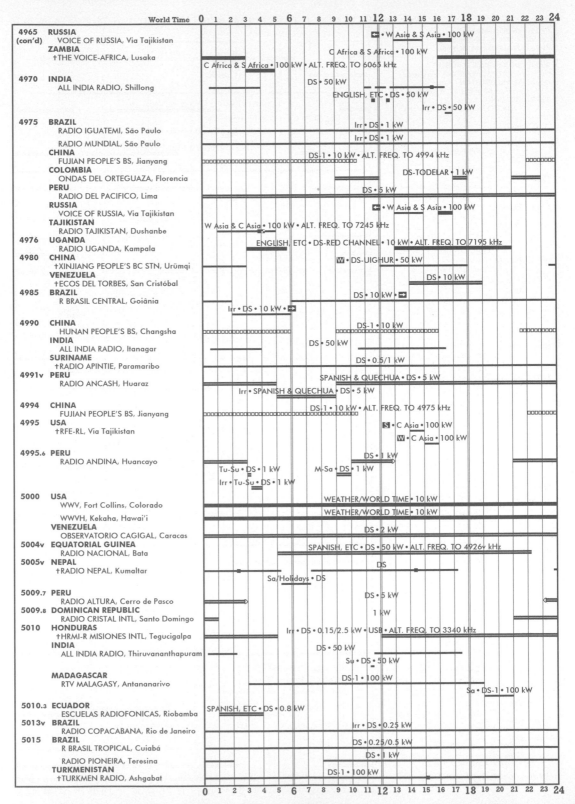

World Time 0 1 2 3 4 5 6 7 8 9 10 11 12 13 14 15 16 17 18 19 20 21 22 23 24

4965 (con'd) RUSSIA
VOICE OF RUSSIA, Via Tajikistan — W Asia & S Asia • 100 kW

ZAMBIA
†THE VOICE-AFRICA, Lusaka — C Africa & S Africa • 100 kW
C Africa & S Africa • 100 kW • ALT. FREQ. TO 6065 kHz

4970 INDIA
ALL INDIA RADIO, Shillong — DS • 50 kW
ENGLISH, ETC • DS • 50 kW
Irr • DS • 50 kW

4975 BRAZIL
RADIO IGUATEMI, São Paulo — Irr • DS • 1 kW
RADIO MUNDIAL, São Paulo — Irr • DS • 1 kW

CHINA
FUJIAN PEOPLE'S BS, Jianyang — DS-1 • 10 kW • ALT. FREQ. TO 4994 kHz

COLOMBIA
ONDAS DEL ORTEGUAZA, Florencia — DS-TODELAR • 1 kW

PERU
RADIO DEL PACIFICO, Lima — DS • 5 kW

RUSSIA
VOICE OF RUSSIA, Via Tajikistan — W Asia & S Asia • 100 kW

TAJIKISTAN
RADIO TAJIKISTAN, Dushanbe — W Asia & C Asia • 100 kW • ALT. FREQ. TO 7245 kHz

4976 UGANDA
RADIO UGANDA, Kampala — ENGLISH, ETC • DS-RED CHANNEL • 10 kW • ALT. FREQ. TO 7195 kHz

4980 CHINA
†XINJIANG PEOPLE'S BC STN, Urümqi — W • DS-UIGHUR • 50 kW

VENEZUELA
†ECOS DEL TORBES, San Cristóbal — DS • 10 kW

4985 BRAZIL
R BRASIL CENTRAL, Goiânia — DS • 10 kW
Irr • DS • 10 kW

4990 CHINA
HUNAN PEOPLE'S BS, Changsha — DS-1 • 10 kW

INDIA
ALL INDIA RADIO, Itanagar — DS • 50 kW

SURINAME
†RADIO APINTIE, Paramaribo — DS • 0.5/1 kW

4991v PERU
RADIO ANCASH, Huaraz — SPANISH & QUECHUA • DS • 5 kW
Irr • SPANISH & QUECHUA • DS • 5 kW

4994 CHINA
FUJIAN PEOPLE'S BS, Jianyang — DS-1 • 10 kW • ALT. FREQ. TO 4975 kHz

4995 USA
†RFE-RL, Via Tajikistan — S • C Asia • 100 kW
W • C Asia • 100 kW

4995.6 PERU
RADIO ANDINA, Huancayo — DS • 1 kW
Tu-Su • DS • 1 kW
M-Sa • DS • 1 kW
Irr • Tu-Su • DS • 1 kW

5000 USA
WWV, Fort Collins, Colorado — WEATHER/WORLD TIME • 10 kW
WWVH, Kekaha, Hawai'i — WEATHER/WORLD TIME • 10 kW

VENEZUELA
OBSERVATORIO CAGIGAL, Caracas — DS • 2 kW

5004v EQUATORIAL GUINEA
RADIO NACIONAL, Bata — SPANISH, ETC • DS • 50 kW • ALT. FREQ. TO 4926v kHz

5005v NEPAL
†RADIO NEPAL, Kumaltar — DS
Sa/Holidays • DS

5009.7 PERU
RADIO ALTURA, Cerro de Pasco — DS • 5 kW

5009.8 DOMINICAN REPUBLIC
RADIO CRISTAL INTL, Santo Domingo — 1 kW

5010 HONDURAS
†HRMI-R MISIONES INTL, Tegucigalpa — Irr • DS • 0.15/2.5 kW • USB • ALT. FREQ. TO 3340 kHz

INDIA
ALL INDIA RADIO, Thiruvananthapuram — DS • 50 kW
Su • DS • 50 kW

MADAGASCAR
RTV MALAGASY, Antananarivo — DS-1 • 100 kW
Sa • DS-1 • 100 kW

5010.3 ECUADOR
ESCUELAS RADIOFONICAS, Riobamba — SPANISH, ETC • DS • 0.8 kW

5013v BRAZIL
RADIO COPACABANA, Rio de Janeiro — Irr • DS • 0.25 kW

5015 BRAZIL
R BRASIL TROPICAL, Cuiabá — DS • 0.25/0.5 kW
RADIO PIONEIRA, Teresina — DS • 1 kW

TURKMENISTAN
†TURKMEN RADIO, Ashgabat — DS-1 • 100 kW

0 1 2 3 4 5 6 7 8 9 10 11 12 13 14 15 16 17 18 19 20 21 22 23 24

ENGLISH ▬   ARABIC ∿∿   CHINESE □□□   FRENCH ▬   GERMAN ▬   RUSSIAN ═   SPANISH ▬   OTHER ─

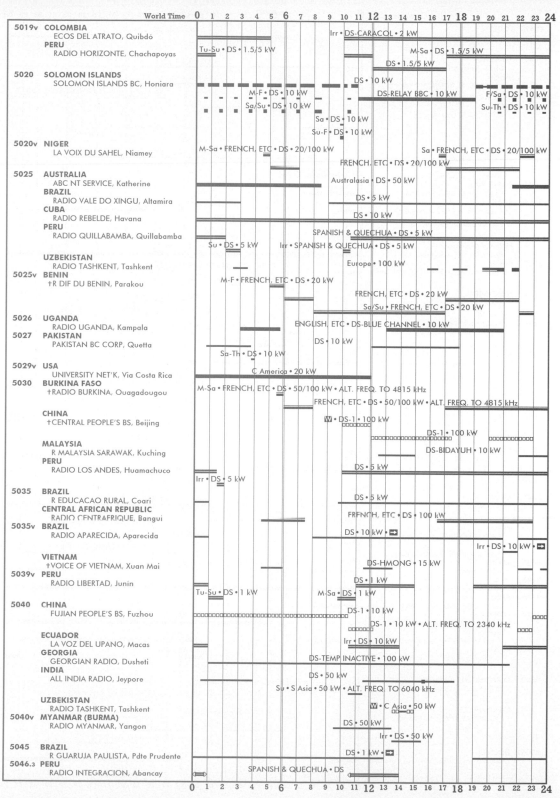

World Time 0 1 2 3 4 5 6 7 8 9 10 11 12 13 14 15 16 17 18 19 20 21 22 23 24

5019v COLOMBIA
ECOS DEL ATRATO, Quibdó — Irr • DS-CARACOL • 2 kW
PERU
RADIO HORIZONTE, Chachapoyas — Tu-Su • DS • 1.5/5 kW / M-Sa • DS • 1.5/5 kW / DS • 1.5/5 kW

5020 SOLOMON ISLANDS
SOLOMON ISLANDS BC, Honiara — DS • 10 kW / M-F • DS • 10 kW / DS-RELAY BBC • 10 kW / F/Sa • DS • 10 kW / Sa/Su • DS • 10 kW / Su-Th • DS • 10 kW / Sa • DS • 10 kW / Su-F • DS • 10 kW

5020v NIGER
LA VOIX DU SAHEL, Niamey — M-Sa • FRENCH, ETC • DS • 20/100 kW / Sa • FRENCH, ETC • DS • 20/100 kW / FRENCH, ETC • DS • 20/100 kW

5025 AUSTRALIA
ABC NT SERVICE, Katherine — Australasia • DS • 50 kW
BRAZIL
RADIO VALE DO XINGU, Altamira — DS • 5 kW
CUBA
RADIO REBELDE, Havana — DS • 10 kW
PERU
RADIO QUILLABAMBA, Quillabamba — SPANISH & QUECHUA • DS • 5 kW / Su • DS • 5 kW / Irr • SPANISH & QUECHUA • DS • 5 kW

UZBEKISTAN
RADIO TASHKENT, Tashkent — Europe • 100 kW
5025v BENIN
†R DIF DU BENIN, Parakou — M-F • FRENCH, ETC • DS • 20 kW / FRENCH, ETC • DS • 20 kW / Sa/Su • FRENCH, ETC • DS • 20 kW

5026 UGANDA
RADIO UGANDA, Kampala — ENGLISH, ETC • DS-BLUE CHANNEL • 10 kW
5027 PAKISTAN
PAKISTAN BC CORP, Quetta — DS • 10 kW / Sa-Th • DS • 10 kW

5029v USA
UNIVERSITY NET'K, Via Costa Rica — C America • 20 kW
5030 BURKINA FASO
†RADIO BURKINA, Ouagadougou — M-Sa • FRENCH, ETC • DS • 50/100 kW • ALT. FREQ. TO 4815 kHz / FRENCH, ETC • DS • 50/100 kW • ALT. FREQ. TO 4815 kHz

CHINA
†CENTRAL PEOPLE'S BS, Beijing — W • DS-1 • 100 kW / DS-1 • 100 kW

MALAYSIA
R MALAYSIA SARAWAK, Kuching — DS-BIDAYUH • 10 kW
PERU
RADIO LOS ANDES, Huamachuco — DS • 5 kW / Irr • DS • 5 kW

5035 BRAZIL
R EDUCACAO RURAL, Coari — DS • 5 kW
CENTRAL AFRICAN REPUBLIC
RADIO CENTRAFRIQUE, Bangui — FRENCH, ETC • DS • 100 kW
5035v BRAZIL
RADIO APARECIDA, Aparecida — DS • 10 kW • ➡ / Irr • DS • 10 kW • ➡

VIETNAM
†VOICE OF VIETNAM, Xuan Mai — DS-HMONG • 15 kW
5039v PERU
RADIO LIBERTAD, Junin — DS • 1 kW / Tu-Su • DS • 1 kW / M-Sa • DS • 1 kW

5040 CHINA
FUJIAN PEOPLE'S BS, Fuzhou — DS-1 • 10 kW / DS-1 • 10 kW • ALT. FREQ. TO 2340 kHz

ECUADOR
LA VOZ DEL UPANO, Macas — Irr • DS • 10 kW
GEORGIA
GEORGIAN RADIO, Dusheti — DS-TEMP INACTIVE • 100 kW
INDIA
ALL INDIA RADIO, Jeypore — DS • 50 kW / Su • S Asia • 50 kW • ALT. FREQ. TO 6040 kHz

UZBEKISTAN
RADIO TASHKENT, Tashkent — W • C Asia • 50 kW
5040v MYANMAR (BURMA)
RADIO MYANMAR, Yangon — DS • 50 kW / Irr • DS • 50 kW

5045 BRAZIL
R GUARUJA PAULISTA, Pdte Prudente — DS • 1 kW • ➡
5046.3 PERU
RADIO INTEGRACION, Abancay — ⬅➡ • SPANISH & QUECHUA • DS • ◁▷

0 1 2 3 4 5 6 7 8 9 10 11 12 13 14 15 16 17 18 19 20 21 22 23 24

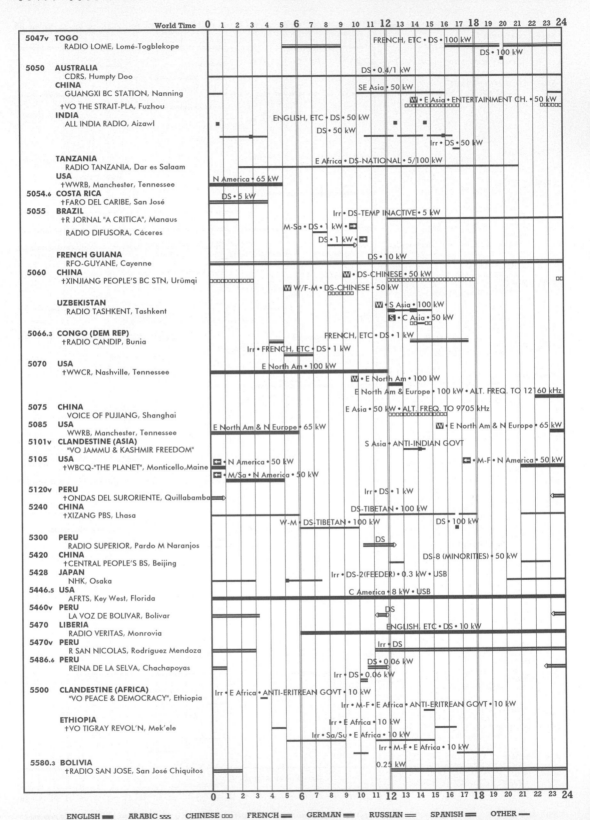

ENGLISH ▬   ARABIC ﹏   CHINESE ▫▫▫   FRENCH ═   GERMAN ▭   RUSSIAN ⹀   SPANISH ▬   OTHER —

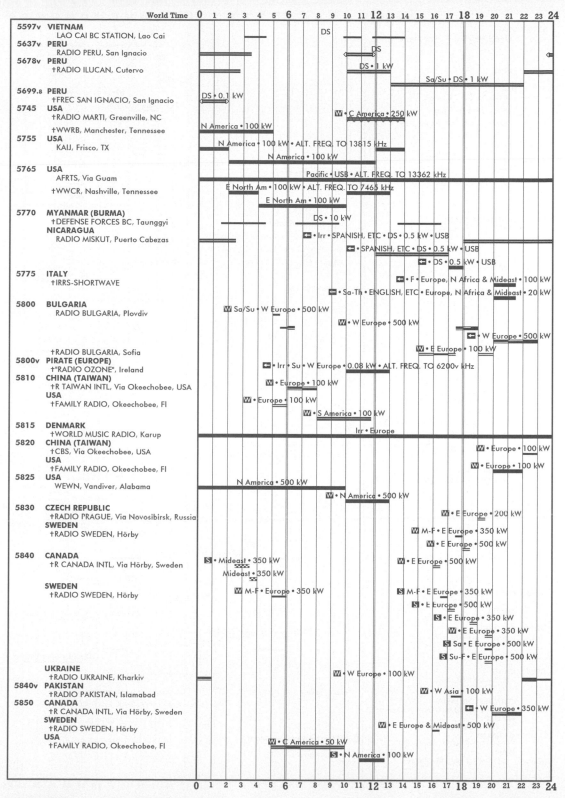

World Time: 0 1 2 3 4 5 6 7 8 9 10 11 12 13 14 15 16 17 18 19 20 21 22 23 24

5597v VIETNAM
  LAO CAI BC STATION, Lao Cai — DS

5637v PERU
  RADIO PERU, San Ignacio — DS

5678v PERU
  †RADIO ILUCAN, Cutervo — DS • 1 kW / Sa/Su • DS • 1 kW

5699.8 PERU
  †FREC SAN IGNACIO, San Ignacio — DS • 0.1 kW

5745 USA
  †RADIO MARTI, Greenville, NC — W • C America • 250 kW
  †WWRB, Manchester, Tennessee — N America • 100 kW

5755 USA
  KAIJ, Frisco, TX — N America • 100 kW • ALT. FREQ. TO 13815 kHz / N America • 100 kW

5765 USA
  AFRTS, Via Guam — Pacific • USB • ALT. FREQ. TO 13362 kHz
  †WWCR, Nashville, Tennessee — E North Am • 100 kW • ALT. FREQ. TO 7465 kHz / E North Am • 100 kW

5770 MYANMAR (BURMA)
  †DEFENSE FORCES BC, Taunggyi — DS • 10 kW
NICARAGUA
  RADIO MISKUT, Puerto Cabezas — Irr • SPANISH, ETC • DS • 0.5 kW • USB / SPANISH, ETC • DS • 0.5 kW • USB / DS • 0.5 kW • USB

5775 ITALY
  †IRRS-SHORTWAVE — F • Europe, N Africa & Mideast • 100 kW / Sa-Th • ENGLISH, ETC • Europe, N Africa & Mideast • 20 kW

5800 BULGARIA
  RADIO BULGARIA, Plovdiv — W Sa/Su • W Europe • 500 kW / W • W Europe • 500 kW / W • W Europe • 500 kW
  †RADIO BULGARIA, Sofia — W • E Europe • 100 kW

5800v PIRATE (EUROPE)
  †"RADIO OZONE", Ireland — Irr • Su • W Europe • 0.08 kW • ALT. FREQ. TO 6200v kHz

5810 CHINA (TAIWAN)
  †R TAIWAN INTL, Via Okeechobee, USA — W • Europe • 100 kW
USA
  †FAMILY RADIO, Okeechobee, Fl — W • Europe • 100 kW / W • S America • 100 kW

5815 DENMARK
  †WORLD MUSIC RADIO, Karup — Irr • Europe

5820 CHINA (TAIWAN)
  †CBS, Via Okeechobee, USA — W • Europe • 100 kW
USA
  †FAMILY RADIO, Okeechobee, Fl — W • Europe • 100 kW

5825 USA
  WEWN, Vandiver, Alabama — N America • 500 kW / W • N America • 500 kW

5830 CZECH REPUBLIC
  †RADIO PRAGUE, Via Novosibirsk, Russia — W • E Europe • 200 kW
SWEDEN
  †RADIO SWEDEN, Hörby — W M-F • E Europe • 350 kW / W • E Europe • 500 kW

5840 CANADA
  †R CANADA INTL, Via Hörby, Sweden — S • Mideast • 350 kW / Mideast • 350 kW / W • E Europe • 500 kW
SWEDEN
  †RADIO SWEDEN, Hörby — W M-F • Europe • 350 kW / S M-F • E Europe • 350 kW / S • E Europe • 500 kW / S • E Europe • 350 kW / W • E Europe • 350 kW / S Sa • E Europe • 500 kW / S Su-F • E Europe • 500 kW
UKRAINE
  †RADIO UKRAINE, Kharkiv — W • W Europe • 100 kW

5840v PAKISTAN
  †RADIO PAKISTAN, Islamabad — W • W Asia • 100 kW

5850 CANADA
  †R CANADA INTL, Via Hörby, Sweden — W Europe • 350 kW
SWEDEN
  †RADIO SWEDEN, Hörby — W • E Europe & Mideast • 500 kW
USA
  †FAMILY RADIO, Okeechobee, Fl — W • C America • 50 kW / S • N America • 100 kW

0 1 2 3 4 5 6 7 8 9 10 11 12 13 14 15 16 17 18 19 20 21 22 23 24

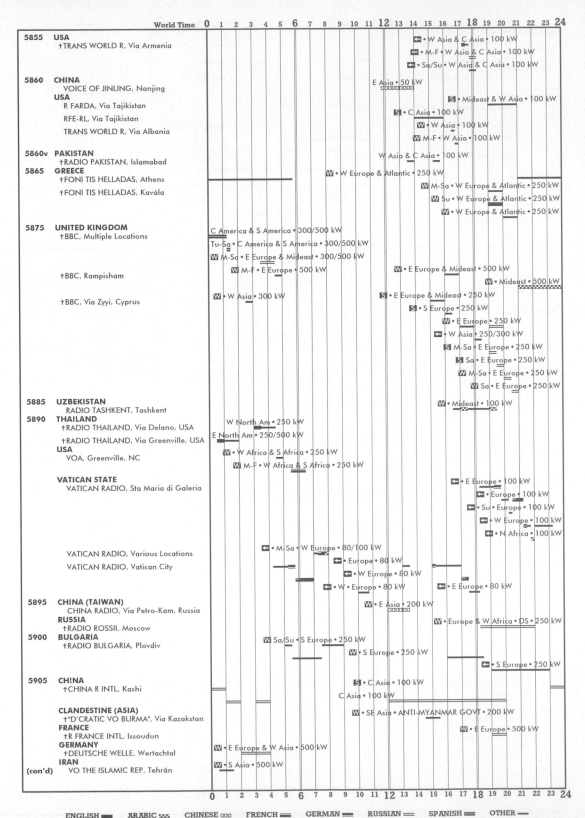

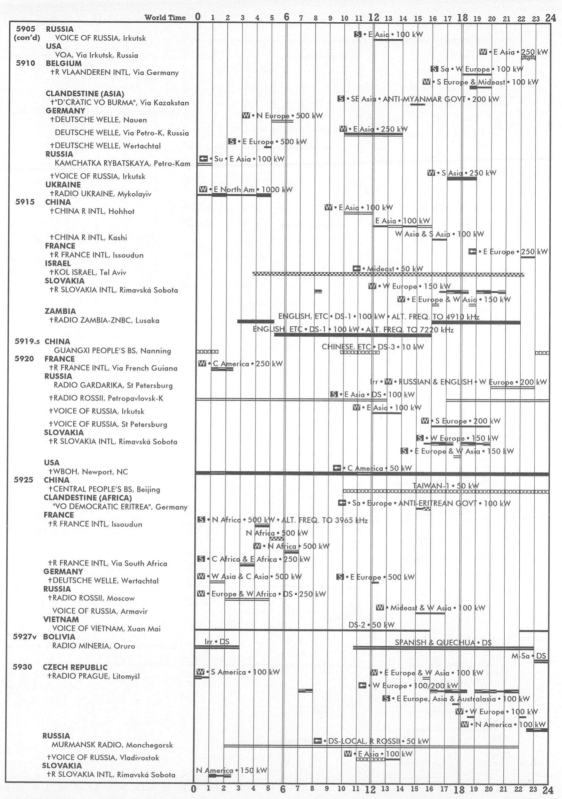

World Time   0 1 2 3 4 5 6 7 8 9 10 11 12 13 14 15 16 17 18 19 20 21 22 23 24

5905 RUSSIA
(con'd) VOICE OF RUSSIA, Irkutsk — S • E Asia • 100 kW
USA
   VOA, Via Irkutsk, Russia — W • E Asia • 250 kW
5910 BELGIUM
   †R VLAANDEREN INTL, Via Germany — S • Sa • W Europe • 100 kW
   W • S Europe & Mideast • 100 kW

   CLANDESTINE (ASIA)
   †"D'CRATIC VO BURMA", Via Kazakstan — S • SE Asia • ANTI-MYANMAR GOVT • 200 kW
GERMANY
   †DEUTSCHE WELLE, Nauen — W • N Europe • 500 kW
   DEUTSCHE WELLE, Via Petro-K, Russia — W • E Asia • 250 kW
   †DEUTSCHE WELLE, Wertachtal — S • E Europe • 500 kW
RUSSIA
   KAMCHATKA RYBATSKAYA, Petro-Kam — Su • E Asia • 100 kW

   †VOICE OF RUSSIA, Irkutsk — W • S Asia • 250 kW
UKRAINE
   †RADIO UKRAINE, Mykolayiv — W • E North Am • 1000 kW
5915 CHINA
   †CHINA R INTL, Hohhot — W • E Asia • 100 kW
   E Asia • 100 kW

   †CHINA R INTL, Kashi — W Asia & S Asia • 100 kW
FRANCE
   †R FRANCE INTL, Issoudun — E Europe • 250 kW
ISRAEL
   †KOL ISRAEL, Tel Aviv — Mideast • 50 kW
SLOVAKIA
   †R SLOVAKIA INTL, Rimavská Sobota — W • W Europe • 150 kW
   W • E Europe & W Asia • 150 kW

   ZAMBIA
   †RADIO ZAMBIA-ZNBC, Lusaka — ENGLISH, ETC • DS-1 • 100 kW • ALT. FREQ. TO 4910 kHz
   ENGLISH, ETC • DS-1 • 100 kW • ALT. FREQ. TO 7220 kHz

5919.5 CHINA
   GUANGXI PEOPLE'S BS, Nanning — CHINESE, ETC • DS-3 • 10 kW
5920 FRANCE
   †R FRANCE INTL, Via French Guiana — W • C America • 250 kW
RUSSIA
   RADIO GARDARIKA, St Petersburg — Irr • W • RUSSIAN & ENGLISH • W Europe • 200 kW
   †RADIO ROSSII, Petropavlovsk-K — S • E Asia • DS • 100 kW

   †VOICE OF RUSSIA, Irkutsk — W • E Asia • 100 kW

   †VOICE OF RUSSIA, St Petersburg — W • S Europe • 200 kW
SLOVAKIA
   †R SLOVAKIA INTL, Rimavská Sobota — S • W Europe • 150 kW
   S • E Europe & W Asia • 150 kW

   USA
   †WBOH, Newport, NC — C America • 50 kW
5925 CHINA
   †CENTRAL PEOPLE'S BS, Beijing — TAIWAN-1 • 50 kW
   CLANDESTINE (AFRICA)
   "VO DEMOCRATIC ERITREA", Germany — S • Sa • Europe • ANTI-ERITREAN GOVT • 100 kW
FRANCE
   †R FRANCE INTL, Issoudun — S • N Africa • 500 kW • ALT. FREQ. TO 3965 kHz
   N Africa • 500 kW
   W • N Africa • 500 kW

   †R FRANCE INTL, Via South Africa — S • C Africa & E Africa • 250 kW
GERMANY
   †DEUTSCHE WELLE, Wertachtal — W • W Asia & C Asia • 500 kW
   S • E Europe • 500 kW
RUSSIA
   †RADIO ROSSII, Moscow — W • Europe & W Africa • DS • 250 kW

   VOICE OF RUSSIA, Armavir — W • Mideast & W Asia • 100 kW
VIETNAM
   VOICE OF VIETNAM, Xuan Mai — DS-2 • 50 kW
5927v BOLIVIA
   RADIO MINERIA, Oruro — Irr • DS   SPANISH & QUECHUA • DS
   M-Sa • DS

5930 CZECH REPUBLIC
   †RADIO PRAGUE, Litomyšl — W • S America • 100 kW
   W • E Europe & W Asia • 100 kW
   W Europe • 100/200 kW
   S • E Europe, Asia & Australasia • 100 kW
   W • W Europe • 100 kW
   W • N America • 100 kW

   RUSSIA
   MURMANSK RADIO, Monchegorsk — DS-LOCAL, R ROSSII • 50 kW
   †VOICE OF RUSSIA, Vladivostok — W • E Asia • 100 kW
SLOVAKIA
   †R SLOVAKIA INTL, Rimavská Sobota — N America • 150 kW

   0 1 2 3 4 5 6 7 8 9 10 11 12 13 14 15 16 17 18 19 20 21 22 23 24

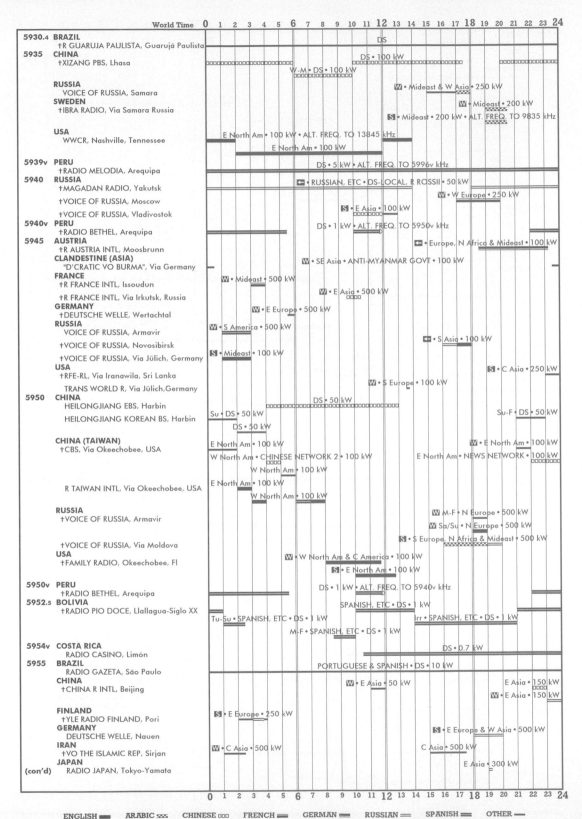

World Time 0 1 2 3 4 5 6 7 8 9 10 11 12 13 14 15 16 17 18 19 20 21 22 23 24

5930.4 BRAZIL
  †R GUARUJÁ PAULISTA, Guarujá Paulista — DS
5935 CHINA
  †XIZANG PBS, Lhasa — DS • 100 kW / W-M • DS • 100 kW
  RUSSIA
  VOICE OF RUSSIA, Samara — W • Mideast & W Asia • 250 kW
  SWEDEN
  †IBRA RADIO, Via Samara Russia — W • Mideast • 200 kW / S • Mideast • 200 kW • ALT. FREQ. TO 9835 kHz
  USA
  WWCR, Nashville, Tennessee — E North Am • 100 kW • ALT. FREQ. TO 13845 kHz / E North Am • 100 kW
5939v PERU
  †RADIO MELODIA, Arequipa — DS • 5 kW • ALT. FREQ. TO 5996v kHz
5940 RUSSIA
  †MAGADAN RADIO, Yakutsk — RUSSIAN, ETC • DS-LOCAL, R ROSSII • 50 kW
  †VOICE OF RUSSIA, Moscow — W • W Europe • 250 kW
  †VOICE OF RUSSIA, Vladivostok — S • E Asia • 100 kW
5940v PERU
  †RADIO BETHEL, Arequipa — DS • 1 kW • ALT. FREQ. TO 5950v kHz
5945 AUSTRIA
  †R AUSTRIA INTL, Moosbrunn — Europe, N Africa & Mideast • 100 kW
  CLANDESTINE (ASIA)
  "D'CRATIC VO BURMA", Via Germany — W • SE Asia • ANTI-MYANMAR GOVT • 100 kW
  FRANCE
  †R FRANCE INTL, Issoudun — W • Mideast • 500 kW
  †R FRANCE INTL, Via Irkutsk, Russia — W • E Asia • 500 kW
  GERMANY
  †DEUTSCHE WELLE, Wertachtal — W • E Europe • 500 kW
  RUSSIA
  VOICE OF RUSSIA, Armavir — W • S America • 500 kW
  †VOICE OF RUSSIA, Novosibirsk — S Asia • 100 kW
  †VOICE OF RUSSIA, Via Jülich, Germany — S • Mideast • 100 kW
  USA
  †RFE-RL, Via Iranawila, Sri Lanka — S • C Asia • 250 kW
  TRANS WORLD R, Via Jülich, Germany — W • S Europe • 100 kW
5950 CHINA
  HEILONGJIANG EBS, Harbin — DS • 50 kW / Su • DS • 50 kW / Su-F • DS • 50 kW
  HEILONGJIANG KOREAN BS, Harbin — DS • 50 kW
  CHINA (TAIWAN)
  †CBS, Via Okeechobee, USA — E North Am • 100 kW / W • E North Am • 100 kW
  W North Am • CHINESE NETWORK 2 • 100 kW / E North Am • NEWS NETWORK • 100 kW
  W North Am • 100 kW
  R TAIWAN INTL, Via Okeechobee, USA — E North Am • 100 kW / W North Am • 100 kW
  RUSSIA
  †VOICE OF RUSSIA, Armavir — W M-F • N Europe • 500 kW / W Sa/Su • N Europe • 500 kW
  †VOICE OF RUSSIA, Via Moldova — S • S Europe, N Africa & Mideast • 500 kW
  USA
  †FAMILY RADIO, Okeechobee, Fl — W • W North Am & C America • 100 kW / S • E North Am • 100 kW
5950v PERU
  †RADIO BETHEL, Arequipa — DS • 1 kW • ALT. FREQ. TO 5940v kHz
5952.5 BOLIVIA
  †RADIO PIO DOCE, Llallagua-Siglo XX — SPANISH, ETC • DS • 1 kW / Tu-Su • SPANISH, ETC • DS • 1 kW / Irr • SPANISH, ETC • DS • 1 kW / M-F • SPANISH, ETC • DS • 1 kW
5954v COSTA RICA
  RADIO CASINO, Limón — DS • 0.7 kW
5955 BRAZIL
  RADIO GAZETA, São Paulo — PORTUGUESE & SPANISH • DS • 10 kW
  CHINA
  †CHINA R INTL, Beijing — W • E Asia • 50 kW / E Asia • 150 kW / W • E Asia • 150 kW
  FINLAND
  †YLE RADIO FINLAND, Pori — S • E Europe • 250 kW
  GERMANY
  DEUTSCHE WELLE, Nauen — S • E Europe & W Asia • 500 kW
  IRAN
  †VO THE ISLAMIC REP, Sirjan — W • C Asia • 500 kW / C Asia • 500 kW
  JAPAN
(con'd) RADIO JAPAN, Tokyo-Yamata — E Asia • 300 kW

0 1 2 3 4 5 6 7 8 9 10 11 12 13 14 15 16 17 18 19 20 21 22 23 24

ENGLISH ▬ ARABIC ▧ CHINESE ▫▫▫ FRENCH ▬ GERMAN ▬ RUSSIAN ═ SPANISH ▬ OTHER ▬

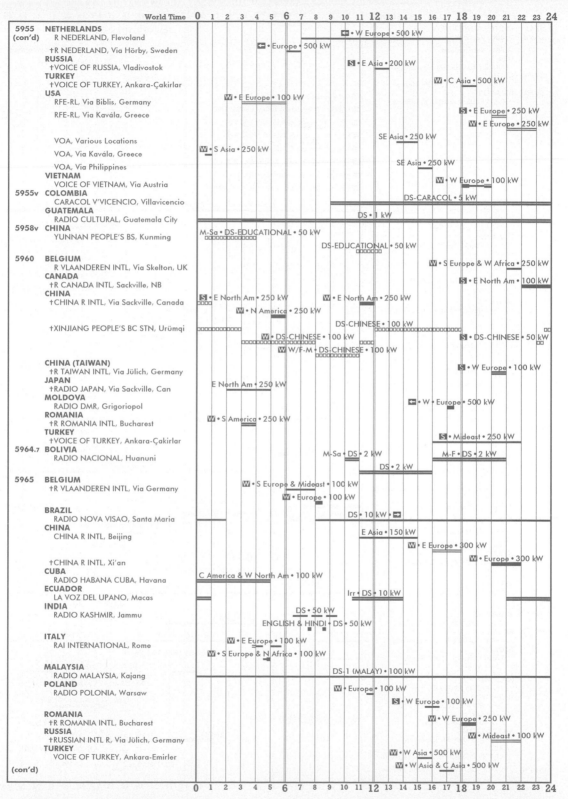

World Time 0 1 2 3 4 5 6 7 8 9 10 11 12 13 14 15 16 17 18 19 20 21 22 23 24

5955	**NETHERLANDS**	
(con'd)	R NEDERLAND, Flevoland	⬅ • W Europe • 500 kW
	†R NEDERLAND, Via Hörby, Sweden	⬅ • Europe • 500 kW
	RUSSIA	
	†VOICE OF RUSSIA, Vladivostok	Ⓢ • E Asia • 200 kW
	TURKEY	
	†VOICE OF TURKEY, Ankara-Çakirlar	Ⓦ • C Asia • 500 kW
	USA	
	RFE-RL, Via Biblis, Germany	Ⓦ • E Europe • 100 kW
	RFE-RL, Via Kavála, Greece	Ⓢ • E Europe • 250 kW
		Ⓦ • E Europe • 250 kW
	VOA, Various Locations	SE Asia • 250 kW
	VOA, Via Kavála, Greece	Ⓦ • S Asia • 250 kW
	VOA, Via Philippines	SE Asia • 250 kW
	VIETNAM	
	VOICE OF VIETNAM, Via Austria	Ⓦ • W Europe • 100 kW
5955v	**COLOMBIA**	
	CARACOL V'VICENCIO, Villavicencio	DS-CARACOL • 5 kW
	GUATEMALA	
	RADIO CULTURAL, Guatemala City	DS • 1 kW
5958v	**CHINA**	
	YUNNAN PEOPLE'S BS, Kunming	M-Sa • DS-EDUCATIONAL • 50 kW
		DS-EDUCATIONAL • 50 kW
5960	**BELGIUM**	
	R VLAANDEREN INTL, Via Skelton, UK	Ⓦ • S Europe & W Africa • 250 kW
	CANADA	
	†R CANADA INTL, Sackville, NB	Ⓢ • E North Am • 100 kW
	CHINA	
	†CHINA R INTL, Via Sackville, Canada	Ⓢ • E North Am • 250 kW Ⓦ • E North Am • 250 kW
		Ⓦ • N America • 250 kW
	†XINJIANG PEOPLE'S BC STN, Urümqi	DS-CHINESE • 100 kW
		Ⓦ • DS-CHINESE • 100 kW Ⓢ • DS-CHINESE • 50 kW
		Ⓦ W/F-M • DS-CHINESE • 100 kW
	CHINA (TAIWAN)	
	†R TAIWAN INTL, Via Jülich, Germany	Ⓢ • W Europe • 100 kW
	JAPAN	
	†RADIO JAPAN, Via Sackville, Can	E North Am • 250 kW
	MOLDOVA	
	RADIO DMR, Grigoriopol	⬅ • W • Europe • 500 kW
	ROMANIA	
	†R ROMANIA INTL, Bucharest	Ⓦ • S America • 250 kW
	TURKEY	
	†VOICE OF TURKEY, Ankara-Çakirlar	Ⓢ • Mideast • 250 kW
5964.7	**BOLIVIA**	
	RADIO NACIONAL, Huanuni	M-Sa • DS • 2 kW M-F • DS • 2 kW
		DS • 2 kW
5965	**BELGIUM**	
	†R VLAANDEREN INTL, Via Germany	Ⓦ • S Europe & Mideast • 100 kW
		Ⓦ • Europe • 100 kW
	BRAZIL	
	RADIO NOVA VISAO, Santa Maria	DS • 10 kW • ➡
	CHINA	
	CHINA R INTL, Beijing	E Asia • 150 kW
		Ⓦ • E Europe • 300 kW
	†CHINA R INTL, Xi'an	Ⓦ • Europe • 300 kW
	CUBA	
	RADIO HABANA CUBA, Havana	C America & W North Am • 100 kW
	ECUADOR	
	LA VOZ DEL UPANO, Macas	Irr • DS • 10 kW
	INDIA	
	RADIO KASHMIR, Jammu	DS • 50 kW
		ENGLISH & HINDI • DS • 50 kW
	ITALY	
	RAI INTERNATIONAL, Rome	Ⓦ • E Europe • 100 kW
		Ⓦ • S Europe & N Africa • 100 kW
	MALAYSIA	
	RADIO MALAYSIA, Kajang	DS-1 (MALAY) • 100 kW
	POLAND	
	RADIO POLONIA, Warsaw	Ⓦ • Europe • 100 kW
		Ⓢ • W Europe • 100 kW
	ROMANIA	
	†R ROMANIA INTL, Bucharest	Ⓦ • W Europe • 250 kW
	RUSSIA	
	†RUSSIAN INTL R, Via Jülich, Germany	Ⓦ • Mideast • 100 kW
	TURKEY	
	VOICE OF TURKEY, Ankara-Emirler	Ⓦ • W Asia • 500 kW
		Ⓦ • W Asia & C Asia • 500 kW
(con'd)		

0 1 2 3 4 5 6 7 8 9 10 11 12 13 14 15 16 17 18 19 20 21 22 23 24

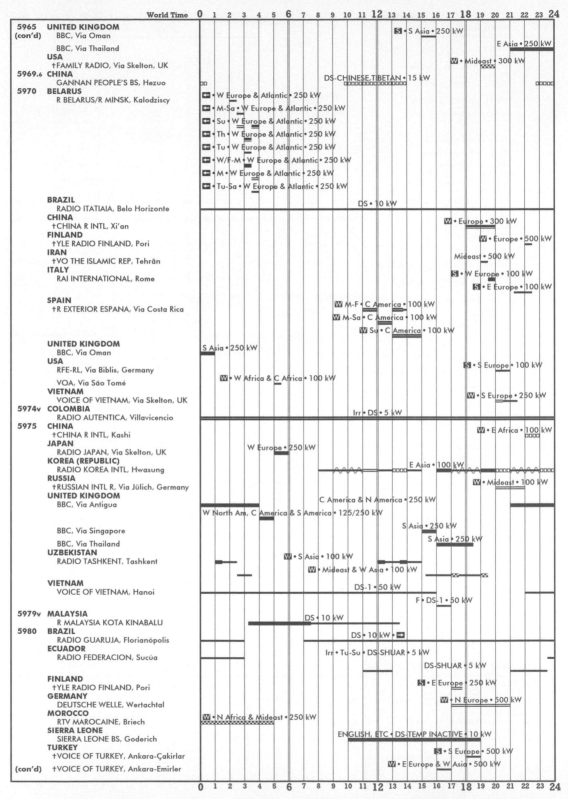

| | World Time | 0 | 1 | 2 | 3 | 4 | 5 | 6 | 7 | 8 | 9 | 10 | 11 | 12 | 13 | 14 | 15 | 16 | 17 | 18 | 19 | 20 | 21 | 22 | 23 | 24 |

5965 **UNITED KINGDOM**
(con'd)　　BBC, Via Oman — S Asia • 250 kW

　　　　BBC, Via Thailand — E Asia • 250 kW

USA
　　†FAMILY RADIO, Via Skelton, UK — W • Mideast • 300 kW

5969.6 CHINA
　　GANNAN PEOPLE'S BS, Hezuo — DS-CHINESE, TIBETAN • 15 kW

5970 BELARUS
　　R BELARUS/R MINSK, Kalodziscy — W Europe & Atlantic • 250 kW
　　　　M-Sa • W Europe & Atlantic • 250 kW
　　　　Su • W Europe & Atlantic • 250 kW
　　　　Th • W Europe & Atlantic • 250 kW
　　　　Tu • W Europe & Atlantic • 250 kW
　　　　W/F-M • W Europe & Atlantic • 250 kW
　　　　M • W Europe & Atlantic • 250 kW
　　　　Tu-Sa • W Europe & Atlantic • 250 kW

BRAZIL
　　RADIO ITATIAIA, Belo Horizonte — DS • 10 kW

CHINA
　　†CHINA R INTL, Xi'an — W • Europe • 300 kW

FINLAND
　　†YLE RADIO FINLAND, Pori — W • Europe • 500 kW

IRAN
　　†VO THE ISLAMIC REP, Tehrän — Mideast • 500 kW

ITALY
　　RAI INTERNATIONAL, Rome — S • W Europe • 100 kW
　　　　S • E Europe • 100 kW

SPAIN
　　†R EXTERIOR ESPANA, Via Costa Rica — W M-F • C America • 100 kW
　　　　W M-Sa • C America • 100 kW
　　　　W Su • C America • 100 kW

UNITED KINGDOM
　　BBC, Via Oman — S Asia • 250 kW

USA
　　RFE-RL, Via Biblis, Germany — S • S Europe • 100 kW

　　VOA, Via São Tomé — W • W Africa & C Africa • 100 kW

VIETNAM
　　VOICE OF VIETNAM, Via Skelton, UK — W • S Europe • 250 kW

5974v COLOMBIA
　　RADIO AUTENTICA, Villavicencio — Irr • DS • 5 kW

5975 CHINA
　　†CHINA R INTL, Kashi — W • E Africa • 100 kW

JAPAN
　　RADIO JAPAN, Via Skelton, UK — W Europe • 250 kW

KOREA (REPUBLIC)
　　RADIO KOREA INTL, Hwasung — E Asia • 100 kW

RUSSIA
　　†RUSSIAN INTL R, Via Jülich, Germany — W • Mideast • 100 kW

UNITED KINGDOM
　　BBC, Via Antigua — C America & N America • 250 kW
　　　　W North Am, C America & S America • 125/250 kW

　　BBC, Via Singapore — S Asia • 250 kW

　　BBC, Via Thailand — S Asia • 250 kW

UZBEKISTAN
　　RADIO TASHKENT, Tashkent — W • S Asia • 100 kW
　　　　W • Mideast & W Asia • 100 kW

VIETNAM
　　VOICE OF VIETNAM, Hanoi — DS-1 • 50 kW
　　　　F • DS-1 • 50 kW

5979v MALAYSIA
　　R MALAYSIA KOTA KINABALU — DS • 10 kW

5980 BRAZIL
　　RADIO GUARUJA, Florianópolis — DS • 10 kW

ECUADOR
　　RADIO FEDERACION, Sucúa — Irr • Tu-Su • DS-SHUAR • 5 kW
　　　　DS-SHUAR • 5 kW

FINLAND
　　†YLE RADIO FINLAND, Pori — S • E Europe • 250 kW

GERMANY
　　DEUTSCHE WELLE, Wertachtal — W • N Europe • 500 kW

MOROCCO
　　RTV MAROCAINE, Briech — W • N Africa & Mideast • 250 kW

SIERRA LEONE
　　SIERRA LEONE BS, Goderich — ENGLISH, ETC • DS-TEMP INACTIVE • 10 kW

TURKEY
　　†VOICE OF TURKEY, Ankara-Çakirlar — S • S Europe • 500 kW

(con'd)　†VOICE OF TURKEY, Ankara-Emirler — W • E Europe & W Asia • 500 kW

| | 0 | 1 | 2 | 3 | 4 | 5 | 6 | 7 | 8 | 9 | 10 | 11 | 12 | 13 | 14 | 15 | 16 | 17 | 18 | 19 | 20 | 21 | 22 | 23 | 24 |

ENGLISH ▬　ARABIC ≋　CHINESE ▫▫▫　FRENCH ▬　GERMAN ═　RUSSIAN ═　SPANISH ═　OTHER ▬

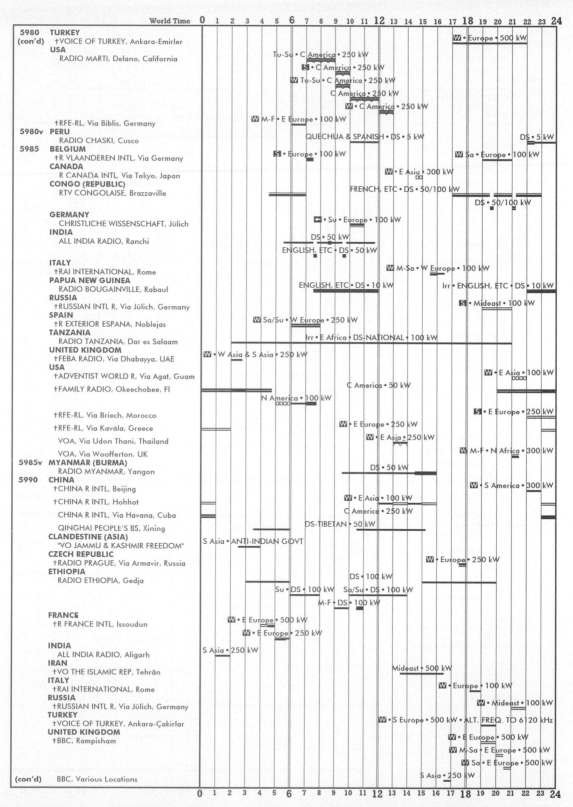

| | | World Time | 0 | 1 | 2 | 3 | 4 | 5 | 6 | 7 | 8 | 9 | 10 | 11 | 12 | 13 | 14 | 15 | 16 | 17 | 18 | 19 | 20 | 21 | 22 | 23 | 24 |

5980 TURKEY
(con'd) †VOICE OF TURKEY, Ankara-Emirler
 W • Europe • 500 kW
USA
 RADIO MARTI, Delano, California
 Tu-Su • C America • 250 kW
 S • C America • 250 kW
 W Tu-Su • C America • 250 kW
 C America • 250 kW
 W • C America • 250 kW

 †RFE-RL, Via Biblis, Germany
 W M-F • E Europe • 100 kW
5980v PERU
 RADIO CHASKI, Cusco
 QUECHUA & SPANISH • DS • 5 kW   DS • 5 kW
5985 BELGIUM
 †R VLAANDEREN INTL, Via Germany
 S • Europe • 100 kW   W Sa • Europe • 100 kW
CANADA
 R CANADA INTL, Via Tokyo, Japan
 W • E Asia • 300 kW
CONGO (REPUBLIC)
 RTV CONGOLAISE, Brazzaville
 FRENCH, ETC • DS • 50/100 kW
 DS • 50/100 kW

GERMANY
 CHRISTLICHE WISSENSCHAFT, Jülich
 ◄ • Su • Europe • 100 kW
INDIA
 ALL INDIA RADIO, Ranchi
 DS • 50 kW
 ENGLISH, ETC • DS • 50 kW

ITALY
 †RAI INTERNATIONAL, Rome
 W M-Sa • W Europe • 100 kW
PAPUA NEW GUINEA
 RADIO BOUGAINVILLE, Rabaul
 ENGLISH, ETC • DS • 10 kW   Irr • ENGLISH, ETC • DS • 10 kW
RUSSIA
 †RUSSIAN INTL R, Via Jülich, Germany
 S • Mideast • 100 kW
SPAIN
 †R EXTERIOR ESPANA, Noblejas
 W Sa/Su • W Europe • 250 kW
TANZANIA
 RADIO TANZANIA, Dar es Salaam
 Irr • E Africa • DS-NATIONAL • 100 kW
UNITED KINGDOM
 †FEBA RADIO, Via Dhabayya, UAE
 W • W Asia & S Asia • 250 kW
USA
 †ADVENTIST WORLD R, Via Agat, Guam
 W • E Asia • 100 kW
 †FAMILY RADIO, Okeechobee, Fl
 C America • 50 kW
 N America • 100 kW

 †RFE-RL, Via Briech, Morocco
 S • E Europe • 250 kW
 †RFE-RL, Via Kavála, Greece
 W • E Europe • 250 kW
 VOA, Via Udon Thani, Thailand
 W • E Asia • 250 kW
 VOA, Via Woofferton, UK
 W M-F • N Africa • 300 kW
5985v MYANMAR (BURMA)
 RADIO MYANMAR, Yangon
 DS • 50 kW
5990 CHINA
 †CHINA R INTL, Beijing
 W • S America • 300 kW
 †CHINA R INTL, Hohhot
 W • E Asia • 100 kW
 CHINA R INTL, Via Havana, Cuba
 C America • 250 kW
 QINGHAI PEOPLE'S BS, Xining
 DS-TIBETAN • 50 kW
CLANDESTINE (ASIA)
 "VO JAMMU & KASHMIR FREEDOM"
 S Asia • ANTI-INDIAN GOVT
CZECH REPUBLIC
 †RADIO PRAGUE, Via Armavir, Russia
 W • Europe • 250 kW
ETHIOPIA
 RADIO ETHIOPIA, Gedja
 DS • 100 kW
 Su • DS • 100 kW   Sa/Su • DS • 100 kW
 M-F • DS • 100 kW
FRANCE
 †R FRANCE INTL, Issoudun
 W • E Europe • 500 kW
 W • E Europe • 250 kW

INDIA
 ALL INDIA RADIO, Aligarh
 S Asia • 250 kW
IRAN
 †VO THE ISLAMIC REP, Tehrān
 Mideast • 500 kW
ITALY
 †RAI INTERNATIONAL, Rome
 W • Europe • 100 kW
RUSSIA
 †RUSSIAN INTL R, Via Jülich, Germany
 W • Mideast • 100 kW
TURKEY
 †VOICE OF TURKEY, Ankara-Çakirlar
 W • S Europe • 500 kW • ALT. FREQ. TO 6120 kHz
UNITED KINGDOM
 †BBC, Rampisham
 W • E Europe • 500 kW
 W M-Sa • E Europe • 500 kW
 W Sa • E Europe • 500 kW

(con'd) BBC, Various Locations
 S Asia • 250 kW

| | World Time | 0 | 1 | 2 | 3 | 4 | 5 | 6 | 7 | 8 | 9 | 10 | 11 | 12 | 13 | 14 | 15 | 16 | 17 | 18 | 19 | 20 | 21 | 22 | 23 | 24 |

SEASONAL S OR W   1-HR TIMESHIFT MIDYEAR ◄ OR ►   JAMMING / OR ∧   EARLIEST HEARD ◄   LATEST HEARD ►   NEW FOR 2005 †

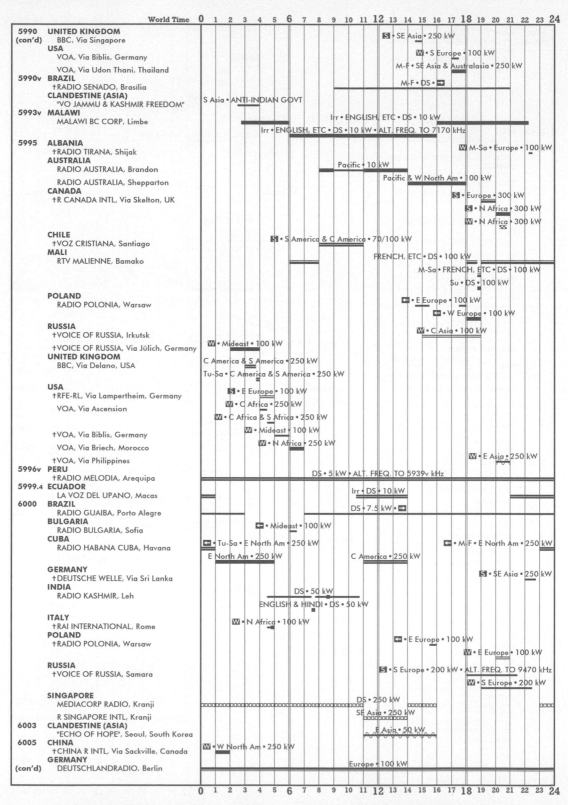

World Time 0 1 2 3 4 5 6 7 8 9 10 11 12 13 14 15 16 17 18 19 20 21 22 23 24

5990 UNITED KINGDOM
(con'd)   BBC, Via Singapore   S • SE Asia • 250 kW
      USA
           VOA, Via Biblis, Germany   W • S Europe • 100 kW
           VOA, Via Udon Thani, Thailand   M-F • SE Asia & Australasia • 250 kW
5990v BRAZIL
           †RADIO SENADO, Brasilia   M-F • DS • ⟹
      CLANDESTINE (ASIA)
           "VO JAMMU & KASHMIR FREEDOM"   S Asia • ANTI-INDIAN GOVT
5993v MALAWI
           MALAWI BC CORP, Limbe   Irr • ENGLISH, ETC • DS • 10 kW
                                          Irr • ENGLISH, ETC • DS • 10 kW • ALT. FREQ. TO 7170 kHz
5995 ALBANIA
           †RADIO TIRANA, Shijak   W • M-Sa • Europe • 100 kW
      AUSTRALIA
           RADIO AUSTRALIA, Brandon   Pacific • 10 kW
           RADIO AUSTRALIA, Shepparton   Pacific & W North Am • 100 kW
      CANADA
           †R CANADA INTL, Via Skelton, UK   S • Europe • 300 kW
                                                  S • N Africa • 300 kW
                                                  W • N Africa • 300 kW
      CHILE
           †VOZ CRISTIANA, Santiago   S • S America & C America • 70/100 kW
      MALI
           RTV MALIENNE, Bamako   FRENCH, ETC • DS • 100 kW
                                                  M-Sa • FRENCH, ETC • DS • 100 kW
                                                  Su • DS • 100 kW
      POLAND
           RADIO POLONIA, Warsaw   ⟸ • E Europe • 100 kW
                                                  ⟸ • W Europe • 100 kW
      RUSSIA
           †VOICE OF RUSSIA, Irkutsk   W • C Asia • 100 kW
           †VOICE OF RUSSIA, Via Jülich, Germany W • Mideast • 100 kW
      UNITED KINGDOM
           BBC, Via Delano, USA   C America & S America • 250 kW
                                         Tu-Sa • C America & S America • 250 kW
      USA
           †RFE-RL, Via Lampertheim, Germany   S • E Europe • 100 kW
           VOA, Via Ascension   W • C Africa • 250 kW
                                            W • C Africa & S Africa • 250 kW
           †VOA, Via Biblis, Germany   W • Mideast • 100 kW
           VOA, Via Briech, Morocco   W • N Africa • 250 kW
           †VOA, Via Philippines   W • E Asia • 250 kW
5996v PERU
           †RADIO MELODIA, Arequipa   DS • 5 kW • ALT. FREQ. TO 5939v kHz
5999.4 ECUADOR
           LA VOZ DEL UPANO, Macas   Irr • DS • 10 kW
6000 BRAZIL
           RADIO GUAIBA, Porto Alegre   DS • 7.5 kW • ⟹
      BULGARIA
           RADIO BULGARIA, Sofia   ⟸ • Mideast • 100 kW
      CUBA
           RADIO HABANA CUBA, Havana   ⟸ • Tu-Sa • E North Am • 250 kW   ⟸ • M-F • E North Am • 250 kW
                                           E North Am • 250 kW   C America • 250 kW
      GERMANY
           †DEUTSCHE WELLE, Via Sri Lanka   S • SE Asia • 250 kW
      INDIA
           RADIO KASHMIR, Leh   DS • 50 kW
                                           ENGLISH & HINDI • DS • 50 kW
      ITALY
           †RAI INTERNATIONAL, Rome   W • N Africa • 100 kW
      POLAND
           †RADIO POLONIA, Warsaw   ⟸ • E Europe • 100 kW
                                                  W • E Europe • 100 kW
      RUSSIA
           †VOICE OF RUSSIA, Samara   S • S Europe • 200 kW • ALT. FREQ. TO 9470 kHz
                                                  W • S Europe • 200 kW
      SINGAPORE
           MEDIACORP RADIO, Kranji   DS • 250 kW
           R SINGAPORE INTL, Kranji   SE Asia • 250 kW
6003 CLANDESTINE (ASIA)
           "ECHO OF HOPE", Seoul, South Korea   E Asia • 50 kW
6005 CHINA
           †CHINA R INTL, Via Sackville, Canada   W • W North Am • 250 kW
      GERMANY
(con'd)   DEUTSCHLANDRADIO, Berlin   Europe • 100 kW

0 1 2 3 4 5 6 7 8 9 10 11 12 13 14 15 16 17 18 19 20 21 22 23 24

ENGLISH ▬▬   ARABIC ≋≋   CHINESE □□□   FRENCH ▬▬   GERMAN ══   RUSSIAN ══   SPANISH ══   OTHER ──

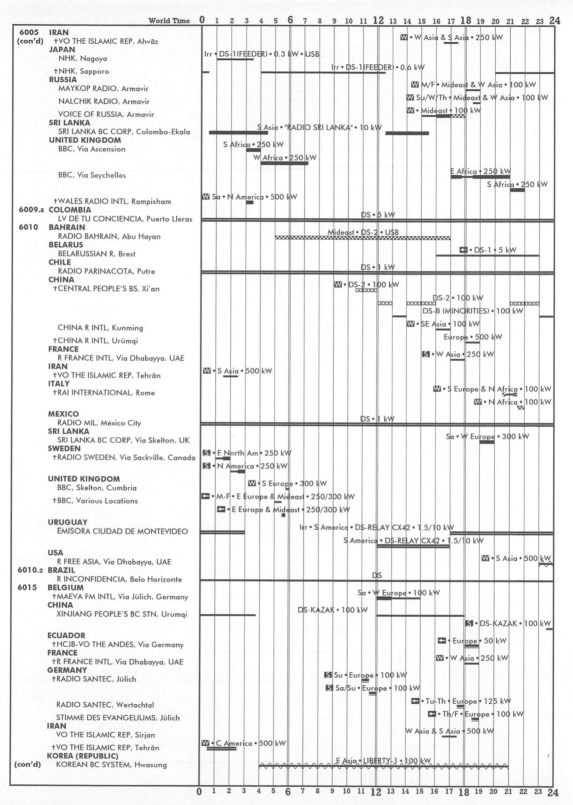

World Time 0 1 2 3 4 5 6 7 8 9 10 11 12 13 14 15 16 17 18 19 20 21 22 23 24

6005 **IRAN**
(con'd)   †VO THE ISLAMIC REP, Ahvāz   W • W Asia & S Asia • 250 kW
    JAPAN
      NHK, Nagoya   Irr • DS-1(FEEDER) • 0.3 kW • USB
      †NHK, Sapporo   Irr • DS-1(FEEDER) • 0.6 kW
    RUSSIA
      MAYKOP RADIO, Armavir   W M/F • Mideast & W Asia • 100 kW
      NALCHIK RADIO, Armavir   W Su/W/Th • Mideast & W Asia • 100 kW
      VOICE OF RUSSIA, Armavir   W • Mideast • 100 kW
    SRI LANKA
      SRI LANKA BC CORP, Colombo-Ekala   S Asia • "RADIO SRI LANKA" • 10 kW
    UNITED KINGDOM
      BBC, Via Ascension   S Africa • 250 kW
           W Africa • 250 kW
      BBC, Via Seychelles   E Africa • 250 kW
           S Africa • 250 kW
      †WALES RADIO INTL, Rampisham   W Sa • N America • 500 kW
6009.8 **COLOMBIA**
      LV DE TU CONCIENCIA, Puerto Lleras   DS • 5 kW
6010 **BAHRAIN**
      RADIO BAHRAIN, Abu Hayan   Mideast • DS-2 • USB
    BELARUS
      BELARUSSIAN R, Brest   ← • DS-1 • 5 kW
    CHILE
      RADIO PARINACOTA, Putre   DS • 1 kW
    CHINA
      †CENTRAL PEOPLE'S BS, Xi'an   W • DS-2 • 100 kW
           DS-2 • 100 kW
           DS-8 (MINORITIES) • 100 kW
      CHINA R INTL, Kunming   W • SE Asia • 100 kW
      †CHINA R INTL, Urümqi   Europe • 500 kW
    FRANCE
      R FRANCE INTL, Via Dhabayya, UAE   S • W Asia • 250 kW
    IRAN
      †VO THE ISLAMIC REP, Tehrān   W • S Asia • 500 kW
    ITALY
      †RAI INTERNATIONAL, Rome   W • S Europe & N Africa • 100 kW
           W • N Africa • 100 kW
    MEXICO
      RADIO MIL, México City   DS • 1 kW
    SRI LANKA
      SRI LANKA BC CORP, Via Skelton, UK   Sa • W Europe • 300 kW
    SWEDEN
      †RADIO SWEDEN, Via Sackville, Canada   S • E North Am • 250 kW
           S • N America • 250 kW
    UNITED KINGDOM
      BBC, Skelton, Cumbria   W • S Europe • 300 kW
      †BBC, Various Locations   ← • M-F • E Europe & Mideast • 250/300 kW
           ← • E Europe & Mideast • 250/300 kW
    URUGUAY
      EMISORA CIUDAD DE MONTEVIDEO   Irr • S America • DS-RELAY CX42 • 1.5/10 kW
           S America • DS-RELAY CX42 • 1.5/10 kW
    USA
      R FREE ASIA, Via Dhabayya, UAE   W • S Asia • 500 kW
6010.2 **BRAZIL**
      R INCONFIDENCIA, Belo Horizonte   DS
6015 **BELGIUM**
      †MAEVA FM INTL, Via Jülich, Germany   Sa • W Europe • 100 kW
    CHINA
      XINJIANG PEOPLE'S BC STN, Urumqi   DS-KAZAK • 100 kW
           S • DS-KAZAK • 100 kW
    ECUADOR
      †HCJB-VO THE ANDES, Via Germany   ← • Europe • 50 kW
    FRANCE
      †R FRANCE INTL, Via Dhabayya, UAE   W • W Asia • 250 kW
    GERMANY
      †RADIO SANTEC, Jülich   S Su • Europe • 100 kW
           S Sa/Su • Europe • 100 kW
      RADIO SANTEC, Wertachtal   ← • Tu-Th • Europe • 125 kW
      STIMME DES EVANGELIUMS, Jülich   ← • Th/F • Europe • 100 kW
    IRAN
      VO THE ISLAMIC REP, Sirjan   W Asia & S Asia • 500 kW
      †VO THE ISLAMIC REP, Tehrān   W • C America • 500 kW
    KOREA (REPUBLIC)
(con'd)   KOREAN BC SYSTEM, Hwasung   E Asia • LIBERTY-1 • 100 kW

0 1 2 3 4 5 6 7 8 9 10 11 12 13 14 15 16 17 18 19 20 21 22 23 24

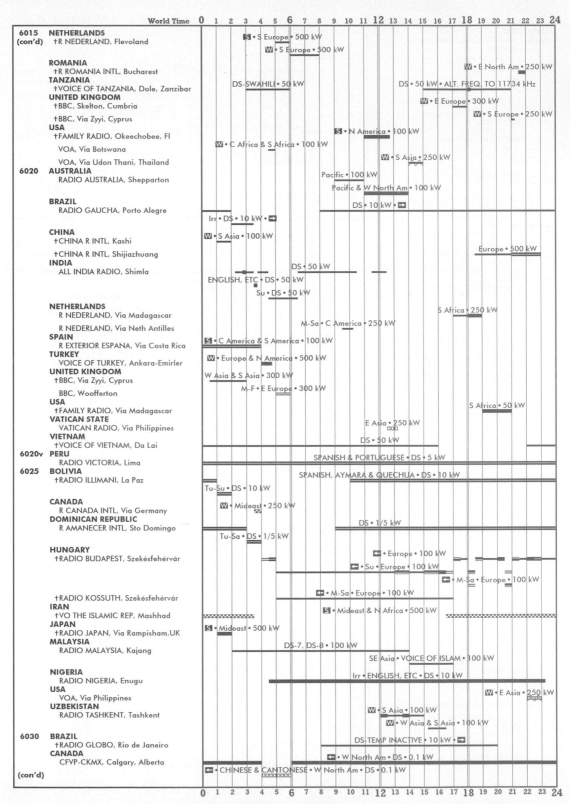

World Time 0 1 2 3 4 5 6 7 8 9 10 11 12 13 14 15 16 17 18 19 20 21 22 23 24

6015
(con'd) **NETHERLANDS**
 †R NEDERLAND, Flevoland — S • S Europe • 500 kW / W • S Europe • 500 kW

ROMANIA
 †R ROMANIA INTL, Bucharest — W • E North Am • 250 kW
TANZANIA
 †VOICE OF TANZANIA, Dole, Zanzibar — DS-SWAHILI • 50 kW / DS • 50 kW • ALT. FREQ. TO 11734 kHz
UNITED KINGDOM
 †BBC, Skelton, Cumbria — W • E Europe • 300 kW
 †BBC, Via Zyyi, Cyprus — W • S Europe • 250 kW
USA
 †FAMILY RADIO, Okeechobee, Fl — S • N America • 100 kW
 VOA, Via Botswana — W • C Africa & S Africa • 100 kW
 VOA, Via Udon Thani, Thailand — W • S Asia • 250 kW
6020 **AUSTRALIA**
 RADIO AUSTRALIA, Shepparton — Pacific • 100 kW / Pacific & W North Am • 100 kW

BRAZIL
 RADIO GAUCHA, Porto Alegre — DS • 10 kW • ⮕

 Irr • DS • 10 kW • ⮕
CHINA
 †CHINA R INTL, Kashi — W • S Asia • 100 kW
 †CHINA R INTL, Shijiazhuang — Europe • 500 kW
INDIA
 ALL INDIA RADIO, Shimla — DS • 50 kW / ENGLISH, ETC • DS • 50 kW / Su • DS • 50 kW

NETHERLANDS
 R NEDERLAND, Via Madagascar — S Africa • 250 kW
 R NEDERLAND, Via Neth Antilles — M-Sa • C America • 250 kW
SPAIN
 R EXTERIOR ESPANA, Via Costa Rica — S • C America & S America • 100 kW
TURKEY
 VOICE OF TURKEY, Ankara-Emirler — W • Europe & N America • 500 kW
UNITED KINGDOM
 †BBC, Via Zyyi, Cyprus — W Asia & S Asia • 300 kW
 BBC, Woofferton — M-F • E Europe • 300 kW
USA
 †FAMILY RADIO, Via Madagascar — S Africa • 50 kW
VATICAN STATE
 VATICAN RADIO, Via Philippines — E Asia • 250 kW
VIETNAM
 †VOICE OF VIETNAM, Da Lai — DS • 50 kW
6020v **PERU**
 RADIO VICTORIA, Lima — SPANISH & PORTUGUESE • DS • 5 kW
6025 **BOLIVIA**
 †RADIO ILLIMANI, La Paz — SPANISH, AYMARA & QUECHUA • DS • 10 kW

 Tu-Su • DS • 10 kW
CANADA
 R CANADA INTL, Via Germany — W • Mideast • 250 kW
DOMINICAN REPUBLIC
 R AMANECER INTL, Sto Domingo — DS • 1/5 kW

 Tu-Sa • DS • 1/5 kW
HUNGARY
 †RADIO BUDAPEST, Székésfehérvár — ⮕ • Europe • 100 kW / ⮕ • Su • Europe • 100 kW / ⮕ • M-Sa • Europe • 100 kW

 †RADIO KOSSUTH, Székésfehérvár — ⮕ • M-Sa • Europe • 100 kW
IRAN
 †VO THE ISLAMIC REP, Mashhad — S • Mideast & N Africa • 500 kW
JAPAN
 †RADIO JAPAN, Via Rampisham, UK — S • Mideast • 500 kW
MALAYSIA
 RADIO MALAYSIA, Kajang — DS-7, DS-8 • 100 kW / SE Asia • VOICE OF ISLAM • 100 kW

NIGERIA
 RADIO NIGERIA, Enugu — Irr • ENGLISH, ETC • DS • 10 kW
USA
 VOA, Via Philippines — W • E Asia • 250 kW
UZBEKISTAN
 RADIO TASHKENT, Tashkent — W • S Asia • 100 kW / W • W Asia & S Asia • 100 kW

6030 **BRAZIL**
 †RADIO GLOBO, Rio de Janeiro — DS-TEMP INACTIVE • 10 kW • ⮕
CANADA
 CFVP-CKMX, Calgary, Alberta — ⮕ • W North Am • DS • 0.1 kW

(con'd) — ⮕ • CHINESE & CANTONESE • W North Am • DS • 0.1 kW

0 1 2 3 4 5 6 7 8 9 10 11 12 13 14 15 16 17 18 19 20 21 22 23 24

ENGLISH ▬ ARABIC ▨ CHINESE ▫▫▫ FRENCH ▬ GERMAN ▬ RUSSIAN ═ SPANISH ▬ OTHER ▬

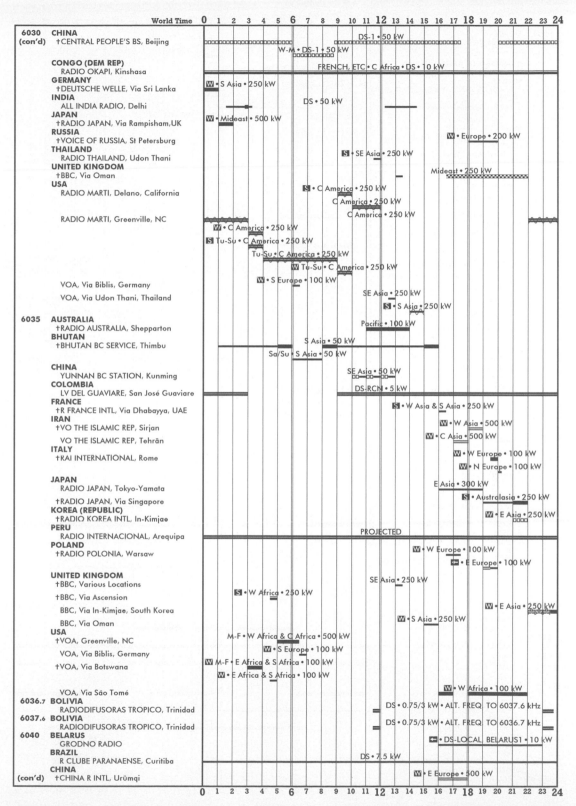

| | | World Time | 0 | 1 | 2 | 3 | 4 | 5 | 6 | 7 | 8 | 9 | 10 | 11 | 12 | 13 | 14 | 15 | 16 | 17 | 18 | 19 | 20 | 21 | 22 | 23 | 24 |

6030
(con'd)

| **CHINA** |
| †CENTRAL PEOPLE'S BS, Beijing | DS-1 • 50 kW / W-M • DS-1 • 50 kW |
| **CONGO (DEM REP)** |
| RADIO OKAPI, Kinshasa | FRENCH, ETC • C Africa • DS • 10 kW |
| **GERMANY** |
| †DEUTSCHE WELLE, Via Sri Lanka | W • S Asia • 250 kW |
| **INDIA** |
| ALL INDIA RADIO, Delhi | DS • 50 kW |
| **JAPAN** |
| †RADIO JAPAN, Via Rampisham,UK | W • Mideast • 500 kW |
| **RUSSIA** |
| †VOICE OF RUSSIA, St Petersburg | W • Europe • 200 kW |
| **THAILAND** |
| RADIO THAILAND, Udon Thani | S • SE Asia • 250 kW |
| **UNITED KINGDOM** |
| †BBC, Via Oman | Mideast • 250 kW |
| **USA** |
RADIO MARTI, Delano, California	S • C America • 250 kW / C America • 250 kW / C America • 250 kW
RADIO MARTI, Greenville, NC	W • C America • 250 kW / S Tu-Su • C America • 250 kW / Tu-Su • C America • 250 kW / W Tu-Su • C America • 250 kW
VOA, Via Biblis, Germany	W • S Europe • 100 kW
VOA, Via Udon Thani, Thailand	SE Asia • 250 kW / S • S Asia • 250 kW

6035

| **AUSTRALIA** |
| †RADIO AUSTRALIA, Shepparton | Pacific • 100 kW |
| **BHUTAN** |
| †BHUTAN BC SERVICE, Thimbu | S Asia • 50 kW / Sa/Su • S Asia • 50 kW |
| **CHINA** |
| YUNNAN BC STATION, Kunming | SE Asia • 50 kW |
| **COLOMBIA** |
| LV DEL GUAVIARE, San José Guaviare | DS-RCN • 5 kW |
| **FRANCE** |
| †R FRANCE INTL, Via Dhabayya, UAE | S • W Asia & S Asia • 250 kW |
| **IRAN** |
| †VO THE ISLAMIC REP, Sirjan | W • W Asia • 500 kW |
| VO THE ISLAMIC REP, Tehrān | W • C Asia • 500 kW |
| **ITALY** |
| †RAI INTERNATIONAL, Rome | W • W Europe • 100 kW / W • N Europe • 100 kW |
| **JAPAN** |
| RADIO JAPAN, Tokyo-Yamata | E Asia • 300 kW |
| †RADIO JAPAN, Via Singapore | S • Australasia • 250 kW |
| **KOREA (REPUBLIC)** |
| †RADIO KOREA INTL, In-Kimjae | W • E Asia • 250 kW |
| **PERU** |
| RADIO INTERNACIONAL, Arequipa | PROJECTED |
| **POLAND** |
| †RADIO POLONIA, Warsaw | W • W Europe • 100 kW / • E Europe • 100 kW |
| **UNITED KINGDOM** |
†BBC, Various Locations	SE Asia • 250 kW
†BBC, Via Ascension	S • W Africa • 250 kW
BBC, Via In-Kimjae, South Korea	W • E Asia • 250 kW
BBC, Via Oman	W • S Asia • 250 kW
USA
†VOA, Greenville, NC	M-F • W Africa & C Africa • 500 kW
VOA, Via Biblis, Germany	W • S Europe • 100 kW
†VOA, Via Botswana	W M-F • E Africa & S Africa • 100 kW / W • E Africa & S Africa • 100 kW
VOA, Via São Tomé	W • W Africa • 100 kW

6036.7
| **BOLIVIA** |
| RADIODIFUSORAS TROPICO, Trinidad | DS • 0.75/3 kW • ALT. FREQ. TO 6037.6 kHz |

6037.6
| **BOLIVIA** |
| RADIODIFUSORAS TROPICO, Trinidad | DS • 0.75/3 kW • ALT. FREQ. TO 6036.7 kHz |

6040
| **BELARUS** |
| GRODNO RADIO | • DS-LOCAL, BELARUS1 • 10 kW |
| **BRAZIL** |
| R CLUBE PARANAENSE, Curitiba | DS • 7.5 kW |

(con'd)
| **CHINA** |
| †CHINA R INTL, Urümqi | W • E Europe • 500 kW |

| | | 0 | 1 | 2 | 3 | 4 | 5 | 6 | 7 | 8 | 9 | 10 | 11 | 12 | 13 | 14 | 15 | 16 | 17 | 18 | 19 | 20 | 21 | 22 | 23 | 24 |

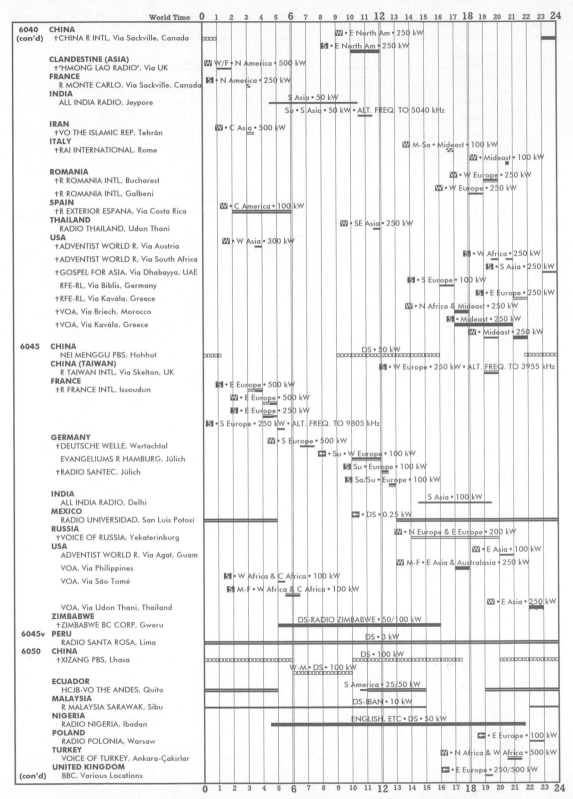

	World Time	0 1 2 3 4 5 6 7 8 9 10 11 12 13 14 15 16 17 18 19 20 21 22 23 24
6040 (con'd)	CHINA †CHINA R INTL, Via Sackville, Canada	W • E North Am • 250 kW / S • E North Am • 250 kW
	CLANDESTINE (ASIA) †"HMONG LAO RADIO", Via UK	W W/F • N America • 500 kW
	FRANCE R MONTE CARLO, Via Sackville, Canada	S • N America • 250 kW
	INDIA ALL INDIA RADIO, Jeypore	S Asia • 50 kW / Su • S Asia • 50 kW • ALT. FREQ. TO 5040 kHz
	IRAN †VO THE ISLAMIC REP, Tehrān	W • C Asia • 500 kW
	ITALY †RAI INTERNATIONAL, Rome	W M-Sa • Mideast • 100 kW / W • Mideast • 100 kW
	ROMANIA †R ROMANIA INTL, Bucharest	W • W Europe • 250 kW
	†R ROMANIA INTL, Galbeni	W • W Europe • 250 kW
	SPAIN †R EXTERIOR ESPANA, Via Costa Rica	W • C America • 100 kW
	THAILAND RADIO THAILAND, Udon Thani	W • SE Asia • 250 kW
	USA †ADVENTIST WORLD R, Via Austria	W • W Asia • 300 kW
	†ADVENTIST WORLD R, Via South Africa	S • W Africa • 250 kW
	†GOSPEL FOR ASIA, Via Dhabayya, UAE	S • S Asia • 250 kW
	RFE-RL, Via Biblis, Germany	S • S Europe • 100 kW
	†RFE-RL, Via Kavála, Greece	S • E Europe • 250 kW
	†VOA, Via Briech, Morocco	W • N Africa & Mideast • 250 kW
	†VOA, Via Kavála, Greece	S • Mideast • 250 kW
		W • Mideast • 250 kW
6045	CHINA NEI MENGGU PBS, Hohhot	DS • 50 kW
	CHINA (TAIWAN) R TAIWAN INTL, Via Skelton, UK	S • W Europe • 250 kW • ALT. FREQ. TO 3955 kHz
	FRANCE †R FRANCE INTL, Issoudun	S • E Europe • 500 kW / W • E Europe • 500 kW / W • E Europe • 250 kW / S • S Europe • 250 kW • ALT. FREQ. TO 9805 kHz
	GERMANY †DEUTSCHE WELLE, Wertachtal	W • S Europe • 500 kW
	EVANGELIUMS R HAMBURG, Jülich	• Su • W Europe • 100 kW
	†RADIO SANTEC, Jülich	S Su • Europe • 100 kW / S Sa/Su • Europe • 100 kW
	INDIA ALL INDIA RADIO, Delhi	S Asia • 100 kW
	MEXICO RADIO UNIVERSIDAD, San Luis Potosí	• DS • 0.25 kW
	RUSSIA †VOICE OF RUSSIA, Yekaterinburg	W • N Europe & E Europe • 200 kW
	USA ADVENTIST WORLD R, Via Agat, Guam	W • E Asia • 100 kW / W M-F • E Asia & Australasia • 250 kW
	VOA, Via Philippines	S • W Africa & C Africa • 100 kW
	VOA, Via São Tomé	S M-F • W Africa & C Africa • 100 kW
	VOA, Via Udon Thani, Thailand	W • E Asia • 250 kW
	ZIMBABWE †ZIMBABWE BC CORP, Gweru	DS-RADIO ZIMBABWE • 50/100 kW
6045v	PERU RADIO SANTA ROSA, Lima	DS • 3 kW
6050	CHINA †XIZANG PBS, Lhasa	DS • 100 kW / W-M • DS • 100 kW
	ECUADOR HCJB-VO THE ANDES, Quito	S America • 25/50 kW
	MALAYSIA R MALAYSIA SARAWAK, Sibu	DS-IBAN • 10 kW
	NIGERIA RADIO NIGERIA, Ibadan	ENGLISH, ETC • DS • 50 kW
	POLAND RADIO POLONIA, Warsaw	• E Europe • 100 kW
	TURKEY VOICE OF TURKEY, Ankara-Çakirlar	W • N Africa & W Africa • 500 kW
	UNITED KINGDOM	• E Europe • 250/500 kW
(con'd)	BBC, Various Locations	

0 1 2 3 4 5 6 7 8 9 10 11 12 13 14 15 16 17 18 19 20 21 22 23 24

ENGLISH ▄▄   ARABIC ▨▨   CHINESE ▭▭▭   FRENCH ▬▬   GERMAN ▭▭   RUSSIAN ══   SPANISH ▭▭   OTHER ──

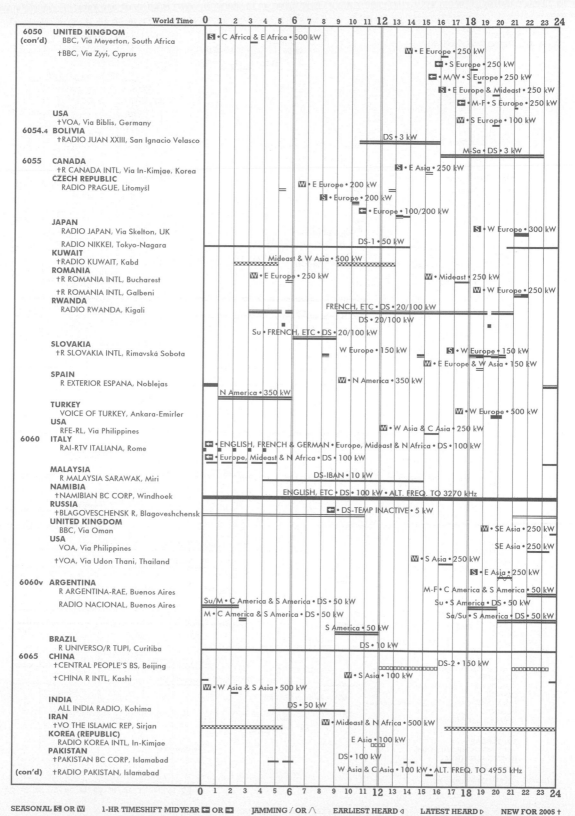

World Time

6050 (con'd)	UNITED KINGDOM
	BBC, Via Meyerton, South Africa
	†BBC, Via Zyyi, Cyprus
	USA
	†VOA, Via Biblis, Germany
6054.4	BOLIVIA
	†RADIO JUAN XXIII, San Ignacio Velasco
6055	CANADA
	†R CANADA INTL, Via In-Kimjae, Korea
	CZECH REPUBLIC
	RADIO PRAGUE, Litomyšl
	JAPAN
	RADIO JAPAN, Via Skelton, UK
	RADIO NIKKEI, Tokyo-Nagara
	KUWAIT
	†RADIO KUWAIT, Kabd
	ROMANIA
	†R ROMANIA INTL, Bucharest
	†R ROMANIA INTL, Galbeni
	RWANDA
	RADIO RWANDA, Kigali
	SLOVAKIA
	†R SLOVAKIA INTL, Rimavská Sobota
	SPAIN
	R EXTERIOR ESPANA, Noblejas
	TURKEY
	VOICE OF TURKEY, Ankara-Emirler
	USA
	RFE-RL, Via Philippines
6060	ITALY
	RAI-RTV ITALIANA, Rome
	MALAYSIA
	R MALAYSIA SARAWAK, Miri
	NAMIBIA
	†NAMIBIAN BC CORP, Windhoek
	RUSSIA
	†BLAGOVESCHENSK R, Blagoveshchensk
	UNITED KINGDOM
	BBC, Via Oman
	USA
	VOA, Via Philippines
	†VOA, Via Udon Thani, Thailand
6060v	ARGENTINA
	R ARGENTINA-RAE, Buenos Aires
	RADIO NACIONAL, Buenos Aires
	BRAZIL
	R UNIVERSO/R TUPI, Curitiba
6065	CHINA
	†CENTRAL PEOPLE'S BS, Beijing
	†CHINA R INTL, Kashi
	INDIA
	ALL INDIA RADIO, Kohima
	IRAN
	†VO THE ISLAMIC REP, Sirjan
	KOREA (REPUBLIC)
	RADIO KOREA INTL, In-Kimjae
	PAKISTAN
	†PAKISTAN BC CORP, Islamabad
(con'd)	†RADIO PAKISTAN, Islamabad

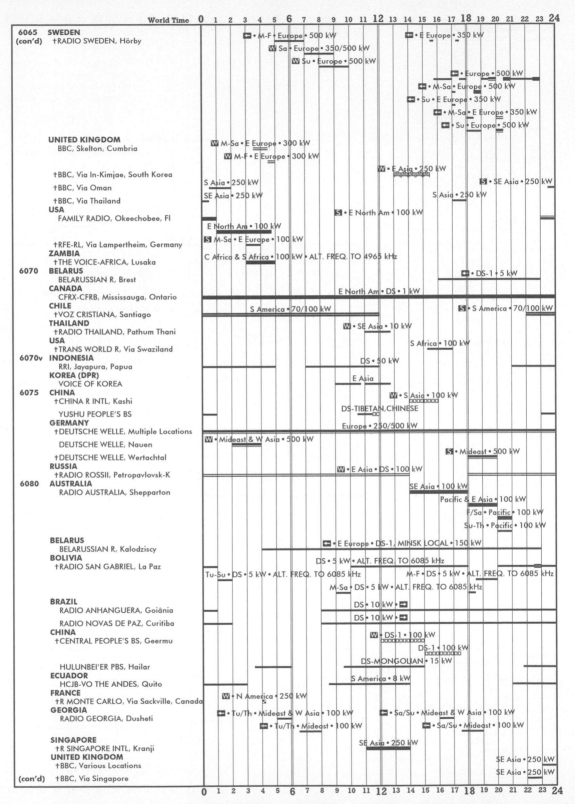

World Time 0 1 2 3 4 5 6 7 8 9 10 11 12 13 14 15 16 17 18 19 20 21 22 23 24

6065
(con'd) **SWEDEN**
          †RADIO SWEDEN, Hörby
          ◧ • M-F • Europe • 500 kW
          W • Sa • Europe • 350/500 kW
          W • Su • Europe • 500 kW
          ◧ • E Europe • 350 kW
          ◧ • Europe • 500 kW
          ◧ • M-Sa • Europe • 500 kW
          ◧ • Su • E Europe • 350 kW
          ◧ • M-Sa • E Europe • 350 kW
          ◧ • Su • Europe • 500 kW

UNITED KINGDOM
          BBC, Skelton, Cumbria
          W • M-Sa • E Europe • 300 kW
          W • M-F • E Europe • 300 kW

          †BBC, Via In-Kimjae, South Korea
          W • E Asia • 250 kW

          †BBC, Via Oman
          S Asia • 250 kW   S • SE Asia • 250 kW

          †BBC, Via Thailand
          SE Asia • 250 kW   S Asia • 250 kW

USA
          FAMILY RADIO, Okeechobee, Fl
          S • E North Am • 100 kW
          E North Am • 100 kW

          †RFE-RL, Via Lampertheim, Germany
          S • M-Sa • E Eurpe • 100 kW

ZAMBIA
          †THE VOICE-AFRICA, Lusaka
          C Africa & S Africa • 100 kW • ALT. FREQ. TO 4965 kHz

6070 **BELARUS**
          BELARUSSIAN R, Brest
          ◧ • DS-1 • 5 kW

CANADA
          CFRX-CFRB, Mississauga, Ontario
          E North Am • DS • 1 kW

CHILE
          †VOZ CRISTIANA, Santiago
          S America • 70/100 kW   S • S America • 70/100 kW

THAILAND
          †RADIO THAILAND, Pathum Thani
          W • SE Asia • 10 kW

USA
          †TRANS WORLD R, Via Swaziland
          S Africa • 100 kW

6070v **INDONESIA**
          RRI, Jayapura, Papua
          DS • 50 kW

KOREA (DPR)
          VOICE OF KOREA
          E Asia

6075 **CHINA**
          †CHINA R INTL, Kashi
          W • S Asia • 100 kW

          YUSHU PEOPLE'S BS
          DS-TIBETAN,CHINESE

GERMANY
          †DEUTSCHE WELLE, Multiple Locations
          Europe • 250/500 kW

          DEUTSCHE WELLE, Nauen
          W • Mideast & W Asia • 500 kW

          †DEUTSCHE WELLE, Wertachtal
          S • Mideast • 500 kW

RUSSIA
          †RADIO ROSSII, Petropavlovsk-K
          W • E Asia • DS • 100 kW

6080 **AUSTRALIA**
          RADIO AUSTRALIA, Shepparton
          SE Asia • 100 kW
          Pacific & E Asia • 100 kW
          F/Sa • Pacific • 100 kW
          Su-Th • Pacific • 100 kW

BELARUS
          BELARUSSIAN R, Kalodziscy
          ◧ • E Europe • DS-1, MINSK LOCAL • 150 kW

BOLIVIA
          †RADIO SAN GABRIEL, La Paz
          DS • 5 kW • ALT. FREQ. TO 6085 kHz
          Tu-Su • DS • 5 kW • ALT. FREQ. TO 6085 kHz   M-F • DS • 5 kW • ALT. FREQ. TO 6085 kHz
          M-Sa • DS • 5 kW • ALT. FREQ. TO 6085 kHz

BRAZIL
          RADIO ANHANGUERA, Goiânia
          DS • 10 kW • ➡

          RADIO NOVAS DE PAZ, Curitiba
          DS • 10 kW • ➡

CHINA
          †CENTRAL PEOPLE'S BS, Geermu
          W • DS-1 • 100 kW
          DS-1 • 100 kW

          HULUNBEI'ER PBS, Hailar
          DS-MONGOLIAN • 15 kW

ECUADOR
          HCJB-VO THE ANDES, Quito
          S America • 8 kW

FRANCE
          †R MONTE CARLO, Via Sackville, Canada
          W • N America • 250 kW

GEORGIA
          RADIO GEORGIA, Dusheti
          ◧ • Tu/Th • Mideast & W Asia • 100 kW   ◧ • Sa/Su • Mideast & W Asia • 100 kW
          ◧ • Tu/Th • Mideast • 100 kW   ◧ • Sa/Su • Mideast • 100 kW

SINGAPORE
          †R SINGAPORE INTL, Kranji
          SE Asia • 250 kW

UNITED KINGDOM
          †BBC, Various Locations
          SE Asia • 250 kW

(con'd) †BBC, Via Singapore
          SE Asia • 250 kW

0 1 2 3 4 5 6 7 8 9 10 11 12 13 14 15 16 17 18 19 20 21 22 23 24

ENGLISH ▬▬   ARABIC ⧆⧆⧆   CHINESE □□□   FRENCH ═══   GERMAN ▭▭   RUSSIAN ══   SPANISH ▭▭   OTHER ──

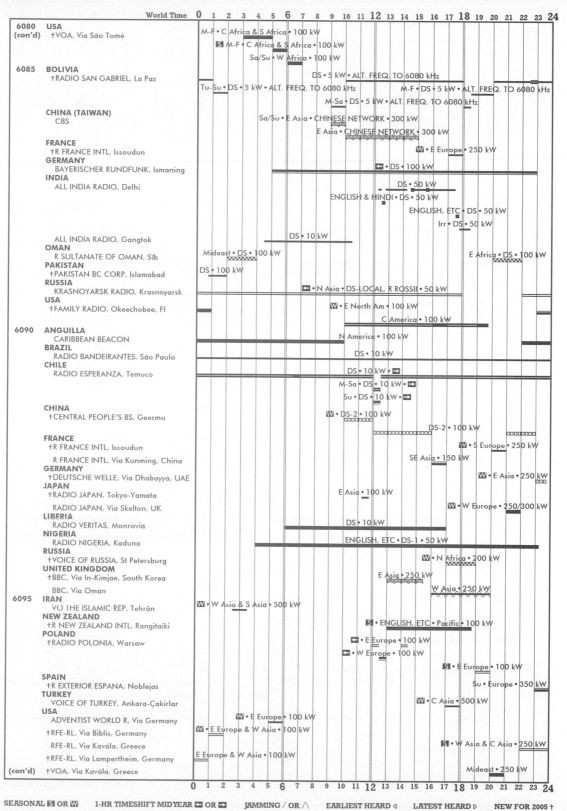

World Time 0 1 2 3 4 5 6 7 8 9 10 11 12 13 14 15 16 17 18 19 20 21 22 23 24

6080 USA
(con'd) †VOA, Via São Tomé
- M-F • C Africa & S Africa • 100 kW
- S M-F • C Africa & S Africa • 100 kW
- Sa/Su • W Africa • 100 kW

6085 BOLIVIA
†RADIO SAN GABRIEL, La Paz
- DS • 5 kW • ALT. FREQ. TO 6080 kHz
- Tu-Su • DS • 5 kW • ALT. FREQ. TO 6080 kHz
- M-F • DS • 5 kW • ALT. FREQ. TO 6080 kHz
- M-Sa • DS • 5 kW • ALT. FREQ. TO 6080 kHz

CHINA (TAIWAN)
CBS
- Sa/Su • E Asia • CHINESE NETWORK • 300 kW
- E Asia • CHINESE NETWORK • 300 kW

FRANCE
†R FRANCE INTL, Issoudun
- W • E Europe • 250 kW

GERMANY
BAYERISCHER RUNDFUNK, Ismaning
- DS • 100 kW

INDIA
ALL INDIA RADIO, Delhi
- DS • 50 kW
- ENGLISH & HINDI • DS • 50 kW
- ENGLISH, ETC • DS • 50 kW
- Irr • DS • 50 kW

ALL INDIA RADIO, Gangtok
- DS • 10 kW

OMAN
R SULTANATE OF OMAN, Sīb
- Mideast • DS • 100 kW
- E Africa • DS • 100 kW

PAKISTAN
†PAKISTAN BC CORP, Islamabad
- DS • 100 kW

RUSSIA
KRASNOYARSK RADIO, Krasnoyarsk
- N Asia • DS-LOCAL, R ROSSII • 50 kW

USA
†FAMILY RADIO, Okeechobee, Fl
- W • E North Am • 100 kW
- C America • 100 kW

6090 ANGUILLA
CARIBBEAN BEACON
- N America • 100 kW

BRAZIL
RADIO BANDEIRANTES, São Paulo
- DS • 10 kW

CHILE
RADIO ESPERANZA, Temuco
- DS • 10 kW •
- M-Sa • DS • 10 kW •
- Su • DS • 10 kW •

CHINA
†CENTRAL PEOPLE'S BS, Geermu
- W • DS-2 • 100 kW
- DS-2 • 100 kW

FRANCE
†R FRANCE INTL, Issoudun
- W • S Europe • 250 kW

R FRANCE INTL, Via Kunming, China
- SE Asia • 150 kW

GERMANY
†DEUTSCHE WELLE, Via Dhabayya, UAE
- W • E Asia • 250 kW

JAPAN
†RADIO JAPAN, Tokyo-Yamata
- E Asia • 100 kW

RADIO JAPAN, Via Skelton, UK
- W • W Europe • 250/300 kW

LIBERIA
RADIO VERITAS, Monrovia
- DS • 10 kW

NIGERIA
RADIO NIGERIA, Kaduna
- ENGLISH, ETC • DS-1 • 50 kW

RUSSIA
†VOICE OF RUSSIA, St Petersburg
- W • N Africa • 200 kW

UNITED KINGDOM
†BBC, Via In-Kimjae, South Korea
- E Asia • 250 kW

BBC, Via Oman
- W Asia • 250 kW

6095 IRAN
VO THE ISLAMIC REP, Tehrān
- W • W Asia & S Asia • 500 kW

NEW ZEALAND
†R NEW ZEALAND INTL, Rangitaiki
- S • ENGLISH, ETC • Pacific • 100 kW

POLAND
†RADIO POLONIA, Warsaw
- E Europe • 100 kW
- W Europe • 100 kW
- S • E Europe • 100 kW

SPAIN
†R EXTERIOR ESPANA, Noblejas
- Su • Europe • 350 kW

TURKEY
VOICE OF TURKEY, Ankara-Çakirlar
- W • C Asia • 500 kW

USA
ADVENTIST WORLD R, Via Germany
- W • E Europe • 100 kW

†RFE-RL, Via Biblis, Germany
- W • E Europe & W Asia • 100 kW

RFE-RL, Via Kavála, Greece
- S • W Asia & C Asia • 250 kW

†RFE-RL, Via Lampertheim, Germany
- E Europe & W Asia • 100 kW

(con'd) †VOA, Via Kavála, Greece
- Mideast • 250 kW

0 1 2 3 4 5 6 7 8 9 10 11 12 13 14 15 16 17 18 19 20 21 22 23 24

SEASONAL S OR W   1-HR TIMESHIFT MIDYEAR ⬅ OR ➡   JAMMING / OR ∧   EARLIEST HEARD ◁   LATEST HEARD ▷   NEW FOR 2005 †

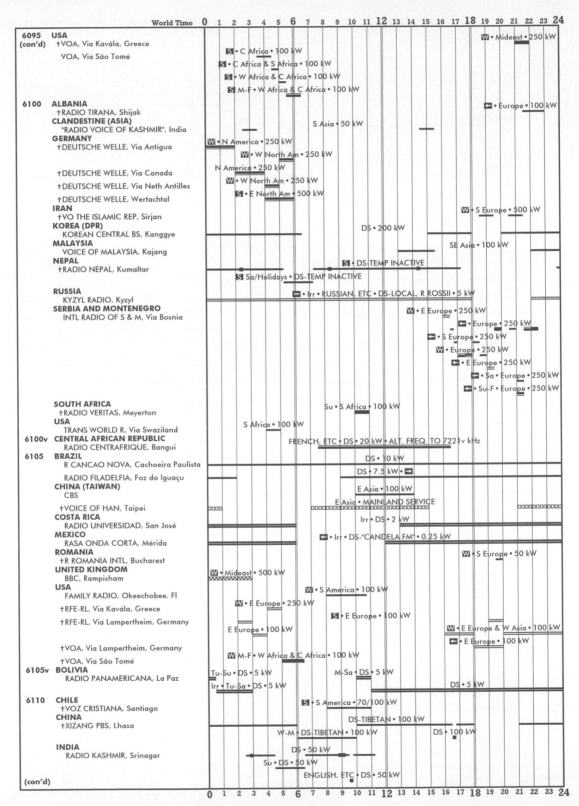

	World Time	0 1 2 3 4 5 6 7 8 9 10 11 12 13 14 15 16 17 18 19 20 21 22 23 24

6095 USA
(con'd) †VOA, Via Kavála, Greece — W • Mideast • 250 kW
          VOA, Via São Tomé — S • C Africa • 100 kW
                              S • C Africa & S Africa • 100 kW
                              S • W Africa & C Africa • 100 kW
                              S M-F • W Africa & C Africa • 100 kW

6100 ALBANIA
      †RADIO TIRANA, Shijak — ← • Europe • 100 kW
      CLANDESTINE (ASIA) — S Asia • 50 kW
      "RADIO VOICE OF KASHMIR", India
      GERMANY
      †DEUTSCHE WELLE, Via Antigua — W • N America • 250 kW
                                     W • W North Am • 250 kW
      †DEUTSCHE WELLE, Via Canada — N America • 250 kW
      †DEUTSCHE WELLE, Via Neth Antilles — W • W North Am • 250 kW
      †DEUTSCHE WELLE, Wertachtal — S • E North Am • 500 kW
      IRAN
      †VO THE ISLAMIC REP, Sirjan — W • S Europe • 500 kW
      KOREA (DPR)
      KOREAN CENTRAL BS, Kanggye — DS • 200 kW
      MALAYSIA
      VOICE OF MALAYSIA, Kajang — SE Asia • 100 kW
      NEPAL
      †RADIO NEPAL, Kumaltar — S • DS-TEMP INACTIVE
                               S • Sa/Holidays • DS-TEMP INACTIVE
      RUSSIA
      KYZYL RADIO, Kyzyl — ← • Irr • RUSSIAN, ETC • DS-LOCAL, R ROSSII • 5 kW
      SERBIA AND MONTENEGRO
      INTL RADIO OF S & M, Via Bosnia — W • E Europe • 250 kW
                                        ← • Europe • 250 kW
                                        ← • S Europe • 250 kW
                                        W • Europe • 250 kW
                                        ← • E Europe • 250 kW
                                        ← • Sa • Europe • 250 kW
                                        ← • Su-F • Europe • 250 kW

      SOUTH AFRICA
      †RADIO VERITAS, Meyerton — Su • S Africa • 100 kW
      USA
      TRANS WORLD R, Via Swaziland — S Africa • 100 kW
6100v CENTRAL AFRICAN REPUBLIC — FRENCH, ETC • DS • 20 kW • ALT. FREQ. TO 7221v kHz
      RADIO CENTRAFRIQUE, Bangui
6105 BRAZIL
      R CANCAO NOVA, Cachoeira Paulista — DS • 10 kW
      RADIO FILADELFIA, Foz do Iguaçu — DS • 7.5 kW • →
      CHINA (TAIWAN)
      CBS — E Asia • 100 kW
      †VOICE OF HAN, Taipei — E Asia • MAINLAND SERVICE
      COSTA RICA
      RADIO UNIVERSIDAD, San José — Irr • DS • 2 kW
      MEXICO
      RASA ONDA CORTA, Mérida — ← • Irr • DS-"CANDELA FM" • 0.25 kW
      ROMANIA
      †R ROMANIA INTL, Bucharest — W • S Europe • 50 kW
      UNITED KINGDOM
      BBC, Rampisham — W • Mideast • 500 kW
      USA
      FAMILY RADIO, Okeechobee, Fl — W • S America • 100 kW
      †RFE-RL, Via Kavála, Greece — W • E Europe • 250 kW
      †RFE-RL, Via Lampertheim, Germany — S • E Europe • 100 kW
                                          E Europe • 100 kW
                                          W • E Europe & W Asia • 100 kW
                                          ← • E Europe • 100 kW
      †VOA, Via Lampertheim, Germany
      †VOA, Via São Tomé — W M-F • W Africa & C Africa • 100 kW
6105v BOLIVIA
      RADIO PANAMERICANA, La Paz — Tu-Su • DS • 5 kW
                                   M-Sa • DS • 5 kW
                                   Irr • Tu-Sa • DS • 5 kW
                                   DS • 5 kW
6110 CHILE
      †VOZ CRISTIANA, Santiago — S • S America • 70/100 kW
      CHINA
      †XIZANG PBS, Lhasa — DS-TIBETAN • 100 kW
                           W-M • DS-TIBETAN • 100 kW
                           DS • 100 kW
      INDIA
      RADIO KASHMIR, Srinagar — DS • 50 kW
                                Su • DS • 50 kW
                                ENGLISH, ETC • DS • 50 kW

(con'd)

	0 1 2 3 4 5 6 7 8 9 10 11 12 13 14 15 16 17 18 19 20 21 22 23 24

ENGLISH ▬ ARABIC ⟋⟍ CHINESE □□□ FRENCH ▭▭ GERMAN ▬ RUSSIAN ▭ SPANISH ▭ OTHER ▬

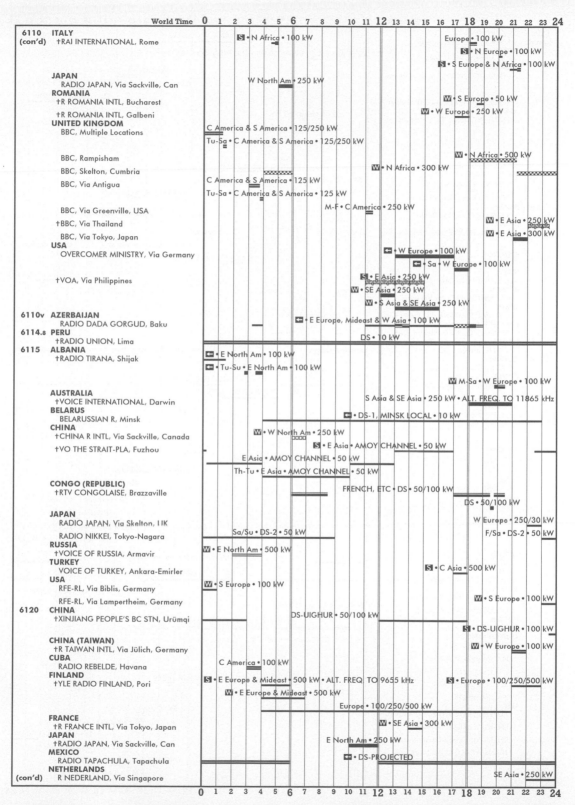

6110	**ITALY**
(con'd)	†RAI INTERNATIONAL, Rome
	JAPAN
	RADIO JAPAN, Via Sackville, Can
	ROMANIA
	†R ROMANIA INTL, Bucharest
	†R ROMANIA INTL, Galbeni
	UNITED KINGDOM
	BBC, Multiple Locations
	BBC, Rampisham
	BBC, Skelton, Cumbria
	BBC, Via Antigua
	BBC, Via Greenville, USA
	†BBC, Via Thailand
	BBC, Via Tokyo, Japan
	USA
	OVERCOMER MINISTRY, Via Germany
	†VOA, Via Philippines
6110v	**AZERBAIJAN**
	RADIO DADA GORGUD, Baku
6114.8	**PERU**
	†RADIO UNION, Lima
6115	**ALBANIA**
	†RADIO TIRANA, Shijak
	AUSTRALIA
	†VOICE INTERNATIONAL, Darwin
	BELARUS
	BELARUSSIAN R, Minsk
	CHINA
	†CHINA R INTL, Via Sackville, Canada
	†VO THE STRAIT-PLA, Fuzhou
	CONGO (REPUBLIC)
	†RTV CONGOLAISE, Brazzaville
	JAPAN
	RADIO JAPAN, Via Skelton, UK
	RADIO NIKKEI, Tokyo-Nagara
	RUSSIA
	†VOICE OF RUSSIA, Armavir
	TURKEY
	VOICE OF TURKEY, Ankara-Emirler
	USA
	RFE-RL, Via Biblis, Germany
	RFE-RL, Via Lampertheim, Germany
6120	**CHINA**
	†XINJIANG PEOPLE'S BC STN, Urümqi
	CHINA (TAIWAN)
	†R TAIWAN INTL, Via Jülich, Germany
	CUBA
	RADIO REBELDE, Havana
	FINLAND
	†YLE RADIO FINLAND, Pori
	FRANCE
	†R FRANCE INTL, Via Tokyo, Japan
	JAPAN
	†RADIO JAPAN, Via Sackville, Can
	MEXICO
	RADIO TAPACHULA, Tapachula
	NETHERLANDS
(con'd)	R NEDERLAND, Via Singapore

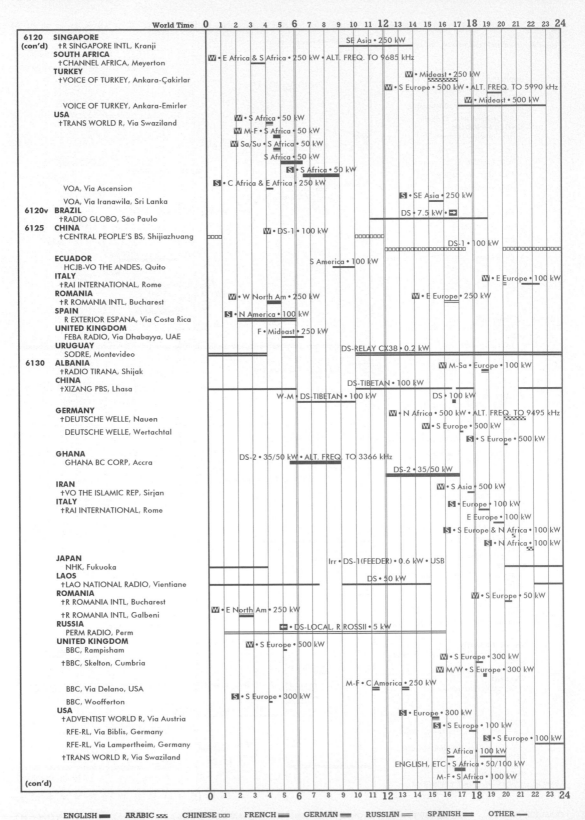

World Time

6120 **SINGAPORE**
(con'd) †R SINGAPORE INTL, Kranji — SE Asia • 250 kW
SOUTH AFRICA
†CHANNEL AFRICA, Meyerton — W • E Africa & S Africa • 250 kW • ALT. FREQ. TO 9685 kHz
TURKEY
†VOICE OF TURKEY, Ankara-Çakirlar — W • Mideast • 250 kW
— W • S Europe • 500 kW • ALT. FREQ. TO 5990 kHz
VOICE OF TURKEY, Ankara-Emirler — W • Mideast • 500 kW
USA
†TRANS WORLD R, Via Swaziland — W • S Africa • 50 kW
— W • M-F • S Africa • 50 kW
— W • Sa/Su • S Africa • 50 kW
— S Africa • 50 kW
— S • S Africa • 50 kW
— S • C Africa & E Africa • 250 kW
VOA, Via Ascension
VOA, Via Iranawila, Sri Lanka — S • SE Asia • 250 kW
6120v **BRAZIL**
†RADIO GLOBO, São Paulo — DS • 7.5 kW • ⇒
6125 **CHINA**
†CENTRAL PEOPLE'S BS, Shijiazhuang — W • DS-1 • 100 kW
— DS-1 • 100 kW
ECUADOR
HCJB-VO THE ANDES, Quito — S America • 100 kW
ITALY
†RAI INTERNATIONAL, Rome — W • E Europe • 100 kW
ROMANIA
†R ROMANIA INTL, Bucharest — W • W North Am • 250 kW — W • E Europe • 250 kW
SPAIN
R EXTERIOR ESPANA, Via Costa Rica — S • N America • 100 kW
UNITED KINGDOM
FEBA RADIO, Via Dhabayya, UAE — F • Mideast • 250 kW
URUGUAY
SODRE, Montevideo — DS-RELAY CX38 • 0.2 kW
6130 **ALBANIA**
†RADIO TIRANA, Shijak — W • M-Sa • Europe • 100 kW
CHINA
†XIZANG PBS, Lhasa — DS-TIBETAN • 100 kW
— W-M • DS-TIBETAN • 100 kW — DS • 100 kW
GERMANY
†DEUTSCHE WELLE, Nauen — W • N Africa • 500 kW • ALT. FREQ. TO 9495 kHz
DEUTSCHE WELLE, Wertachtal — W • S Europe • 500 kW
— S • S Europe • 500 kW
GHANA
GHANA BC CORP, Accra — DS-2 • 35/50 kW • ALT. FREQ. TO 3366 kHz
— DS-2 • 35/50 kW
IRAN
†VO THE ISLAMIC REP, Sirjan — W • S Asia • 500 kW
ITALY
†RAI INTERNATIONAL, Rome — S • Europe • 100 kW
— E Europe • 100 kW
— S • S Europe & N Africa • 100 kW
— S • N Africa • 100 kW
JAPAN
NHK, Fukuoka — Irr • DS-1 (FEEDER) • 0.6 kW • USB
LAOS
†LAO NATIONAL RADIO, Vientiane — DS • 50 kW
ROMANIA
†R ROMANIA INTL, Bucharest — W • S Europe • 50 kW
†R ROMANIA INTL, Galbeni — W • E North Am • 250 kW
RUSSIA
PERM RADIO, Perm — DS-LOCAL, R ROSSII • 5 kW
UNITED KINGDOM
BBC, Rampisham — W • S Europe • 500 kW
†BBC, Skelton, Cumbria — W • S Europe • 300 kW
— W • M/W • S Europe • 300 kW
BBC, Via Delano, USA — M-F • C America • 250 kW
BBC, Woofferton — S • S Europe • 300 kW
USA
†ADVENTIST WORLD R, Via Austria — S • Europe • 300 kW
RFE-RL, Via Biblis, Germany — S • S Europe • 100 kW
RFE-RL, Via Lampertheim, Germany — S • S Europe • 100 kW
†TRANS WORLD R, Via Swaziland — S Africa • 100 kW
— ENGLISH, ETC • S Africa • 50/100 kW
— M-F • S Africa • 100 kW

(con'd)

ENGLISH ▬ ARABIC � CHINESE □□□ FRENCH ▬ GERMAN ▬ RUSSIAN ═ SPANISH ▬ OTHER ▬

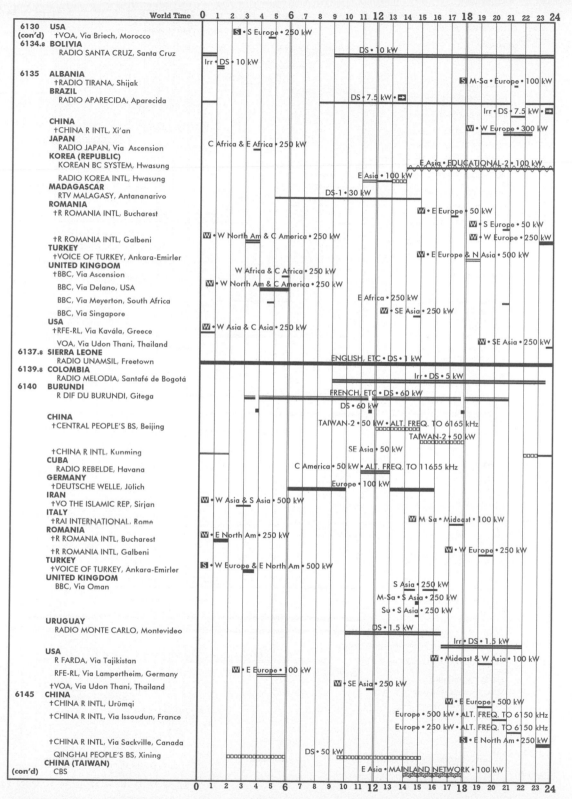

World Time 0 1 2 3 4 5 6 7 8 9 10 11 12 13 14 15 16 17 18 19 20 21 22 23 24

6130 **USA**
(con'd) †VOA, Via Briech, Morocco — S·S Europe·250 kW
6134.8 **BOLIVIA**
RADIO SANTA CRUZ, Santa Cruz — DS·10 kW — Irr·DS·10 kW

6135 **ALBANIA**
†RADIO TIRANA, Shijak — S·M-Sa·Europe·100 kW
BRAZIL
RADIO APARECIDA, Aparecida — DS·7.5 kW· — Irr·DS·7.5 kW·

CHINA
†CHINA R INTL, Xi'an — W·W Europe·300 kW
JAPAN
RADIO JAPAN, Via Ascension — C Africa & E Africa·250 kW
KOREA (REPUBLIC)
KOREAN BC SYSTEM, Hwasung — E Asia·EDUCATIONAL-2·100 kW

RADIO KOREA INTL, Hwasung — E Asia·100 kW
MADAGASCAR
RTV MALAGASY, Antananarivo — DS-1·30 kW
ROMANIA
†R ROMANIA INTL, Bucharest — W·E Europe·50 kW
— W·S Europe·50 kW

†R ROMANIA INTL, Galbeni — W·W North Am & C America·250 kW — W·W Europe·250 kW
TURKEY
†VOICE OF TURKEY, Ankara-Emirler — W·E Europe & N Asia·500 kW
UNITED KINGDOM
†BBC, Via Ascension — W Africa & C Africa·250 kW

BBC, Via Delano, USA — W·W North Am & C America·250 kW

BBC, Via Meyerton, South Africa — E Africa·250 kW

BBC, Via Singapore — W·SE Asia·250 kW
USA
†RFE-RL, Via Kavála, Greece — W·W Asia & C Asia·250 kW

VOA, Via Udon Thani, Thailand — W·SE Asia·250 kW
6137.8 **SIERRA LEONE**
RADIO UNAMSIL, Freetown — ENGLISH, ETC·DS·1 kW
6139.8 **COLOMBIA**
RADIO MELODIA, Santafé de Bogotá — Irr·DS·5 kW
6140 **BURUNDI**
R DIF DU BURUNDI, Gitega — FRENCH, ETC·DS·60 kW
— DS·60 kW

CHINA
†CENTRAL PEOPLE'S BS, Beijing — TAIWAN-2·50 kW·ALT. FREQ. TO 6165 kHz
— TAIWAN-2·50 kW

†CHINA R INTL, Kunming — SE Asia·50 kW
CUBA
RADIO REBELDE, Havana — C America·50 kW·ALT. FREQ. TO 11655 kHz
GERMANY
†DEUTSCHE WELLE, Jülich — Europe·100 kW
IRAN
†VO THE ISLAMIC REP, Sirjan — W·W Asia & S Asia·500 kW
ITALY
†RAI INTERNATIONAL, Rome — W·M Sa·Mideast·100 kW
ROMANIA
†R ROMANIA INTL, Bucharest — W·E North Am·250 kW

†R ROMANIA INTL, Galbeni — W·W Europe·250 kW
TURKEY
†VOICE OF TURKEY, Ankara-Emirler — S·W Europe & E North Am·500 kW
UNITED KINGDOM
BBC, Via Oman — S Asia·250 kW
— M-Sa·S Asia·250 kW
— Su·S Asia·250 kW

URUGUAY
RADIO MONTE CARLO, Montevideo — DS·1.5 kW
— Irr·DS·1.5 kW

USA
R FARDA, Via Tajikistan — W·Mideast & W Asia·100 kW

RFE-RL, Via Lampertheim, Germany — W·E Europe·100 kW

†VOA, Via Udon Thani, Thailand — W·SE Asia·250 kW
6145 **CHINA**
†CHINA R INTL, Urümqi — W·E Europe·500 kW

†CHINA R INTL, Via Issoudun, France — Europe·500 kW·ALT. FREQ. TO 6150 kHz
— Europe·250 kW·ALT. FREQ. TO 6150 kHz

†CHINA R INTL, Via Sackville, Canada — S·E North Am·250 kW

QINGHAI PEOPLE'S BS, Xining — DS·50 kW
CHINA (TAIWAN)
(con'd) CBS — E Asia·MAINLAND NETWORK·100 kW

0 1 2 3 4 5 6 7 8 9 10 11 12 13 14 15 16 17 18 19 20 21 22 23 24

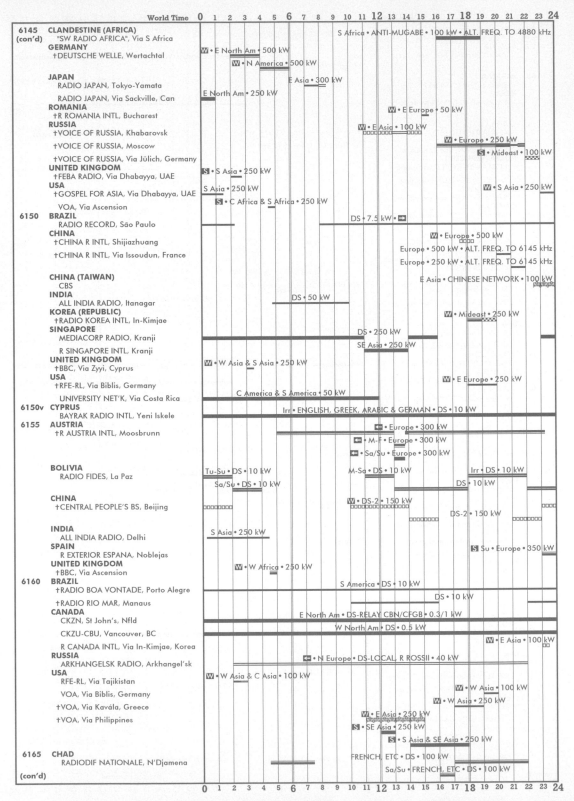

World Time   0 1 2 3 4 5 6 7 8 9 10 11 12 13 14 15 16 17 18 19 20 21 22 23 24

6145
(con'd) **CLANDESTINE (AFRICA)**
  "SW RADIO AFRICA", Via S Africa — S Africa • ANTI-MUGABE • 100 kW • ALT. FREQ. TO 4880 kHz
GERMANY
  †DEUTSCHE WELLE, Wertachtal — W • E North Am • 500 kW
                              W • N America • 500 kW
JAPAN
  RADIO JAPAN, Tokyo-Yamata — E Asia • 300 kW
  RADIO JAPAN, Via Sackville, Can — E North Am • 250 kW
ROMANIA
  †R ROMANIA INTL, Bucharest — W • E Europe • 50 kW
RUSSIA
  †VOICE OF RUSSIA, Khabarovsk — W • E Asia • 100 kW
  †VOICE OF RUSSIA, Moscow — W • Europe • 250 kW
  †VOICE OF RUSSIA, Via Jülich, Germany — S • Mideast • 100 kW
UNITED KINGDOM
  †FEBA RADIO, Via Dhabayya, UAE — S • S Asia • 250 kW
USA
  †GOSPEL FOR ASIA, Via Dhabayya, UAE — S Asia • 250 kW
                              W • S Asia • 250 kW
  VOA, Via Ascension — S • C Africa & S Africa • 250 kW
6150 **BRAZIL**
  RADIO RECORD, São Paulo — DS • 7.5 kW •
CHINA
  †CHINA R INTL, Shijiazhuang — W • Europe • 500 kW
  †CHINA R INTL, Via Issoudun, France — Europe • 500 kW • ALT. FREQ. TO 6145 kHz
                              Europe • 250 kW • ALT. FREQ. TO 6145 kHz
CHINA (TAIWAN)
  CBS — E Asia • CHINESE NETWORK • 100 kW
INDIA
  ALL INDIA RADIO, Itanagar — DS • 50 kW
KOREA (REPUBLIC)
  †RADIO KOREA INTL, In-Kimjae — W • Mideast • 250 kW
SINGAPORE
  MEDIACORP RADIO, Kranji — DS • 250 kW
  R SINGAPORE INTL, Kranji — SE Asia • 250 kW
UNITED KINGDOM
  †BBC, Via Zyyi, Cyprus — W • W Asia & S Asia • 250 kW
USA
  †RFE-RL, Via Biblis, Germany — W • E Europe • 250 kW
  UNIVERSITY NET'K, Via Costa Rica — C America & S America • 50 kW
6150v **CYPRUS**
  BAYRAK RADIO INTL, Yeni Iskele — Irr • ENGLISH, GREEK, ARABIC & GERMAN • DS • 10 kW
6155 **AUSTRIA**
  †R AUSTRIA INTL, Moosbrunn — • Europe • 300 kW
                              • M-F • Europe • 300 kW
                              • Sa/Su • Europe • 300 kW
BOLIVIA
  RADIO FIDES, La Paz — Tu-Su • DS • 10 kW   M-Sa • DS • 10 kW   Irr • DS • 10 kW
                       Sa/Su • DS • 10 kW   DS • 10 kW
CHINA
  †CENTRAL PEOPLE'S BS, Beijing — W • DS-2 • 150 kW
                              DS-2 • 150 kW
INDIA
  ALL INDIA RADIO, Delhi — S Asia • 250 kW
SPAIN
  R EXTERIOR ESPANA, Noblejas — S • Su • Europe • 350 kW
UNITED KINGDOM
  †BBC, Via Ascension — W • W Africa • 250 kW
6160 **BRAZIL**
  †RADIO BOA VONTADE, Porto Alegre — S America • DS • 10 kW
  †RADIO RIO MAR, Manaus — DS • 10 kW
CANADA
  CKZN, St John's, Nfld — E North Am • DS-RELAY CBN/CFGB • 0.3/1 kW
  CKZU-CBU, Vancouver, BC — W North Am • DS • 0.5 kW
  R CANADA INTL, Via In-Kimjae, Korea — W • E Asia • 100 kW
RUSSIA
  ARKHANGELSK RADIO, Arkhangel'sk — • N Europe • DS-LOCAL, R ROSSII • 40 kW
USA
  RFE-RL, Via Tajikistan — W • W Asia & C Asia • 100 kW
  VOA, Via Biblis, Germany — W • W Asia • 100 kW
  †VOA, Via Kavála, Greece — W • W Asia • 250 kW
  †VOA, Via Philippines — W • E Asia • 250 kW
                          S • SE Asia • 250 kW
                          S • S Asia & SE Asia • 250 kW
6165 **CHAD**
  RADIODIF NATIONALE, N'Djamena — FRENCH, ETC • DS • 100 kW
                                Sa/Su • FRENCH, ETC • DS • 100 kW
(con'd)

0 1 2 3 4 5 6 7 8 9 10 11 12 13 14 15 16 17 18 19 20 21 22 23 24

ENGLISH ▬   ARABIC ⋙   CHINESE □□□   FRENCH ══   GERMAN ▬▬   RUSSIAN ══   SPANISH ▬   OTHER ──

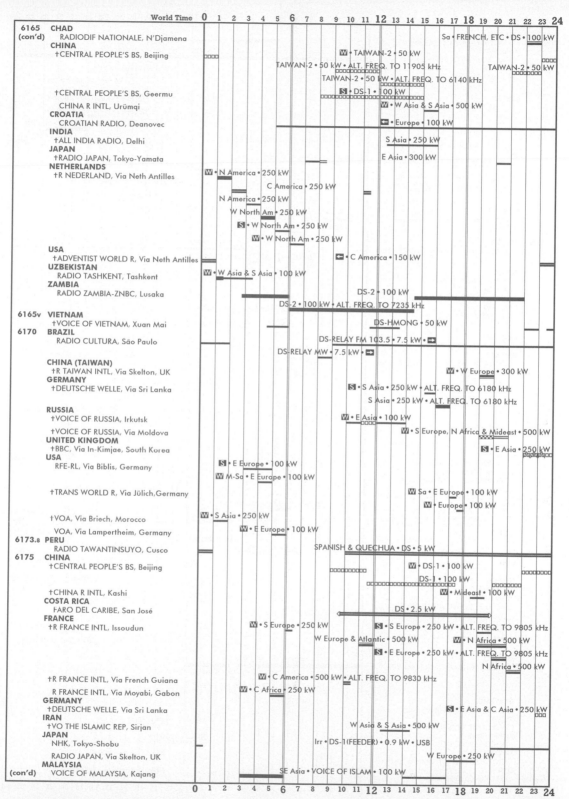

World Time 0 1 2 3 4 5 6 7 8 9 10 11 12 13 14 15 16 17 18 19 20 21 22 23 24

6165 CHAD
(con'd) RADIODIF NATIONALE, N'Djamena — Sa • FRENCH, ETC • DS • 100 kW
CHINA
†CENTRAL PEOPLE'S BS, Beijing — W • TAIWAN-2 • 50 kW
TAIWAN-2 • 50 kW • ALT. FREQ. TO 11905 kHz — TAIWAN-2 • 50 kW
TAIWAN-2 • 50 kW • ALT. FREQ. TO 6140 kHz
†CENTRAL PEOPLE'S BS, Geermu — S • DS-1 • 100 kW
CHINA R INTL, Urümqi — W • W Asia & S Asia • 500 kW
CROATIA
CROATIAN RADIO, Deanovec — ⇦ • Europe • 100 kW
INDIA
†ALL INDIA RADIO, Delhi — S Asia • 250 kW
JAPAN
†RADIO JAPAN, Tokyo-Yamata — E Asia • 300 kW
NETHERLANDS
†R NEDERLAND, Via Neth Antilles — W • N America • 250 kW
C America • 250 kW
N America • 250 kW
W North Am • 250 kW
S • W North Am • 250 kW
W • W North Am • 250 kW
USA
†ADVENTIST WORLD R, Via Neth Antilles — ⇦ • C America • 150 kW
UZBEKISTAN
RADIO TASHKENT, Tashkent — W • W Asia & S Asia • 100 kW
ZAMBIA
RADIO ZAMBIA-ZNBC, Lusaka — DS-2 • 100 kW
DS-2 • 100 kW • ALT. FREQ. TO 7235 kHz

6165v VIETNAM
†VOICE OF VIETNAM, Xuan Mai — DS-HMONG • 50 kW
6170 BRAZIL
RADIO CULTURA, São Paulo — DS-RELAY FM 103.5 • 7.5 kW • ⇨
DS-RELAY MW • 7.5 kW • ⇨
CHINA (TAIWAN)
†R TAIWAN INTL, Via Skelton, UK — W • W Europe • 300 kW
GERMANY
†DEUTSCHE WELLE, Via Sri Lanka — S • S Asia • 250 kW • ALT. FREQ. TO 6180 kHz
S Asia • 250 kW • ALT. FREQ. TO 6180 kHz
RUSSIA
†VOICE OF RUSSIA, Irkutsk — W • E Asia • 100 kW
†VOICE OF RUSSIA, Via Moldova — W • S Europe, N Africa & Mideast • 500 kW
UNITED KINGDOM
†BBC, Via In-Kimjae, South Korea — S • E Asia • 250 kW
USA
RFE-RL, Via Biblis, Germany — S • E Europe • 100 kW
W • M-Sa • E Europe • 100 kW
†TRANS WORLD R, Via Jülich, Germany — W Sa • E Europe • 100 kW
W • Europe • 100 kW
†VOA, Via Briech, Morocco — W • S Asia • 250 kW
VOA, Via Lampertheim, Germany — W • E Europe • 100 kW
6173.8 PERU
RADIO TAWANTINSUYO, Cusco — SPANISH & QUECHUA • DS • 5 kW
6175 CHINA
†CENTRAL PEOPLE'S BS, Beijing — W • DS-1 • 100 kW
DS-1 • 100 kW
†CHINA R INTL, Kashi — W • Mideast • 100 kW
COSTA RICA
†FARO DEL CARIBE, San José — DS • 2.5 kW
FRANCE
†R FRANCE INTL, Issoudun — W • S Europe • 250 kW
S • S Europe • 250 kW • ALT. FREQ. TO 9805 kHz
W Europe & Atlantic • 500 kW
W • N Africa • 500 kW
S • E Europe • 250 kW • ALT. FREQ. TO 9805 kHz
N Africa • 500 kW
†R FRANCE INTL, Via French Guiana — W • C America • 500 kW • ALT. FREQ. TO 9830 kHz
R FRANCE INTL, Via Moyabi, Gabon — W • C Africa • 250 kW
GERMANY
†DEUTSCHE WELLE, Via Sri Lanka — S • E Asia & C Asia • 250 kW
IRAN
†VO THE ISLAMIC REP, Sirjan — W Asia & S Asia • 500 kW
JAPAN
NHK, Tokyo-Shobu — Irr • DS-1 (FEEDER) • 0.9 kW • USB
RADIO JAPAN, Via Skelton, UK — W Europe • 250 kW
MALAYSIA
(con'd) VOICE OF MALAYSIA, Kajang — SE Asia • VOICE OF ISLAM • 100 kW

0 1 2 3 4 5 6 7 8 9 10 11 12 13 14 15 16 17 18 19 20 21 22 23 24

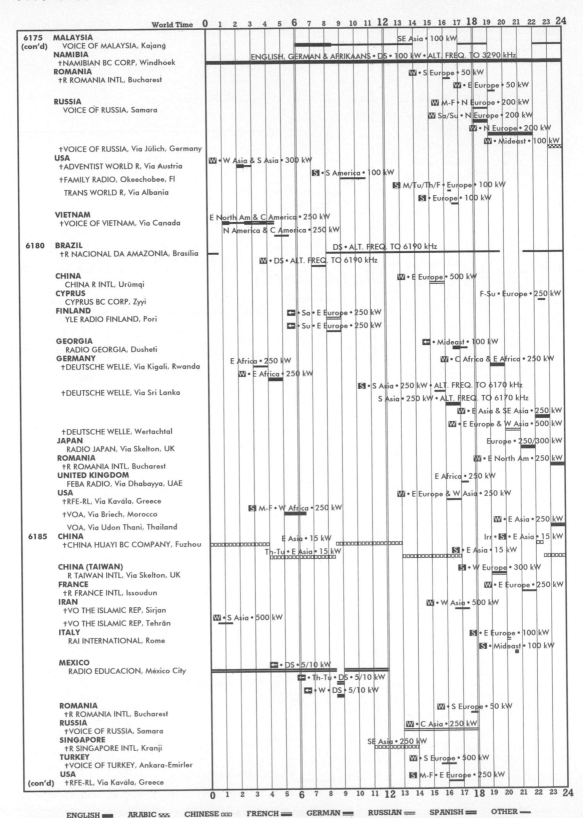

World Time 0 1 2 3 4 5 6 7 8 9 10 11 12 13 14 15 16 17 18 19 20 21 22 23 24

6175
(con'd) **MALAYSIA**
   VOICE OF MALAYSIA, Kajang — SE Asia • 100 kW
NAMIBIA
   †NAMIBIAN BC CORP, Windhoek — ENGLISH, GERMAN & AFRIKAANS • DS • 100 kW • ALT. FREQ. TO 3290 kHz
ROMANIA
   †R ROMANIA INTL, Bucharest — W • S Europe • 50 kW / W • E Europe • 50 kW
RUSSIA
   VOICE OF RUSSIA, Samara — W • M-F • N Europe • 200 kW / W • Sa/Su • N Europe • 200 kW / W • N Europe • 200 kW / W • Mideast • 100 kW
   †VOICE OF RUSSIA, Via Jülich, Germany
USA
   †ADVENTIST WORLD R, Via Austria — W • W Asia & S Asia • 300 kW
   †FAMILY RADIO, Okeechobee, Fl — S • S America • 100 kW
   TRANS WORLD R, Via Albania — S • M/Tu/Th/F • Europe • 100 kW / S • Europe • 100 kW
VIETNAM
   †VOICE OF VIETNAM, Via Canada — E North Am & C America • 250 kW / N America & C America • 250 kW

6180 **BRAZIL**
   †R NACIONAL DA AMAZONIA, Brasília — DS • ALT. FREQ. TO 6190 kHz / W • DS • ALT. FREQ. TO 6190 kHz
CHINA
   CHINA R INTL, Urümqi — W • E Europe • 500 kW
CYPRUS
   CYPRUS BC CORP, Zyyi — F-Su • Europe • 250 kW
FINLAND
   YLE RADIO FINLAND, Pori — Sa • E Europe • 250 kW / Su • E Europe • 250 kW
GEORGIA
   RADIO GEORGIA, Dusheti — Mideast • 100 kW
GERMANY
   †DEUTSCHE WELLE, Via Kigali, Rwanda — E Africa • 250 kW / W • E Africa • 250 kW / W • C Africa & E Africa • 250 kW
   †DEUTSCHE WELLE, Via Sri Lanka — S • S Asia • 250 kW • ALT. FREQ. TO 6170 kHz / S Asia • 250 kW • ALT. FREQ. TO 6170 kHz / W • E Asia & SE Asia • 250 kW / W • E Europe & W Asia • 500 kW
   †DEUTSCHE WELLE, Wertachtal
JAPAN
   RADIO JAPAN, Via Skelton, UK — Europe • 250/300 kW
ROMANIA
   †R ROMANIA INTL, Bucharest — W • E North Am • 250 kW
UNITED KINGDOM
   FEBA RADIO, Via Dhabayya, UAE — E Africa • 250 kW
USA
   †RFE-RL, Via Kavála, Greece — W • E Europe & W Asia • 250 kW
   †VOA, Via Briech, Morocco — S • M-F • W Africa • 250 kW
   VOA, Via Udon Thani, Thailand — W • E Asia • 250 kW

6185 **CHINA**
   †CHINA HUAYI BC COMPANY, Fuzhou — E Asia • 15 kW / Th-Tu • E Asia • 15 kW / Irr • S • E Asia • 15 kW / S • E Asia • 15 kW
CHINA (TAIWAN)
   R TAIWAN INTL, Via Skelton, UK — S • W Europe • 300 kW
FRANCE
   †R FRANCE INTL, Issoudun — W • E Europe • 250 kW
IRAN
   †VO THE ISLAMIC REP, Sirjan — W • W Asia • 500 kW
   †VO THE ISLAMIC REP, Tehrān — W • S Asia • 500 kW
ITALY
   RAI INTERNATIONAL, Rome — S • E Europe • 100 kW / S • Mideast • 100 kW
MEXICO
   RADIO EDUCACION, México City — DS • 5/10 kW / Th-Tu • DS • 5/10 kW / W • DS • 5/10 kW
ROMANIA
   †R ROMANIA INTL, Bucharest — W • S Europe • 50 kW
RUSSIA
   †VOICE OF RUSSIA, Samara — W • C Asia • 250 kW
SINGAPORE
   †R SINGAPORE INTL, Kranji — SE Asia • 250 kW
TURKEY
   †VOICE OF TURKEY, Ankara-Emirler — W • S Europe • 500 kW
USA
(con'd) †RFE-RL, Via Kavála, Greece — S • M-F • E Europe • 250 kW

0 1 2 3 4 5 6 7 8 9 10 11 12 13 14 15 16 17 18 19 20 21 22 23 24

ENGLISH ▪▪▪ ARABIC ░░░ CHINESE □□□ FRENCH ▬▬ GERMAN ▬▬ RUSSIAN ══ SPANISH ▬▬ OTHER —

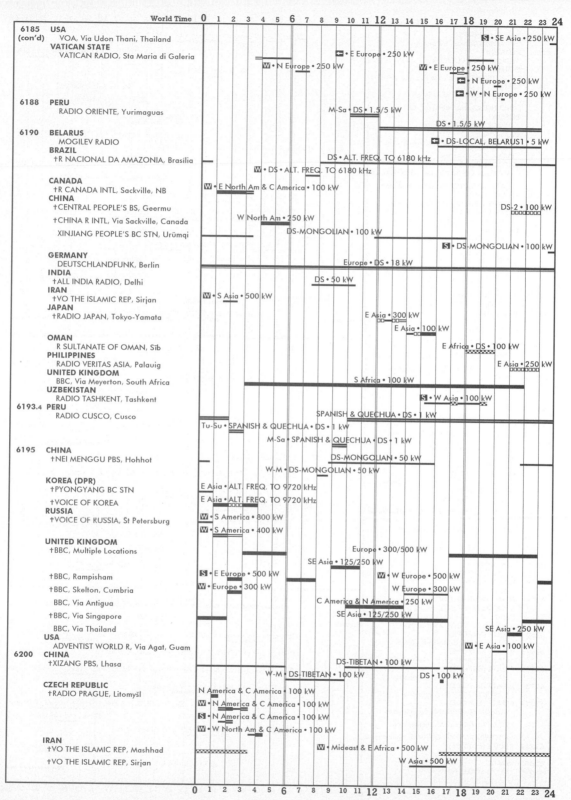

World Time 0 1 2 3 4 5 6 7 8 9 10 11 12 13 14 15 16 17 18 19 20 21 22 23 24

6185 **USA**
(con'd) VOA, Via Udon Thani, Thailand — **S** • SE Asia • 250 kW
VATICAN STATE
VATICAN RADIO, Sta Maria di Galeria — • E Europe • 250 kW
W • N Europe • 250 kW — **W** • E Europe • 250 kW
• N Europe • 250 kW
• W • N Europe • 250 kW

6188 **PERU**
RADIO ORIENTE, Yurimaguas M-Sa • DS • 1.5/5 kW
DS • 1.5/5 kW

6190 **BELARUS**
MOGILEV RADIO • DS-LOCAL, BELARUS1 • 5 kW
BRAZIL
†R NACIONAL DA AMAZONIA, Brasilia DS • ALT. FREQ. TO 6180 kHz
W • DS • ALT. FREQ. TO 6180 kHz
CANADA
†R CANADA INTL, Sackville, NB **W** • E North Am & C America • 100 kW
CHINA
†CENTRAL PEOPLE'S BS, Geermu DS-2 • 100 kW
†CHINA R INTL, Via Sackville, Canada W North Am • 250 kW
XINJIANG PEOPLE'S BC STN, Urümqi DS-MONGOLIAN • 100 kW
S • DS-MONGOLIAN • 100 kW
GERMANY
DEUTSCHLANDFUNK, Berlin Europe • DS • 18 kW
INDIA
†ALL INDIA RADIO, Delhi DS • 50 kW
IRAN
†VO THE ISLAMIC REP, Sirjan **W** • S Asia • 500 kW
JAPAN
†RADIO JAPAN, Tokyo-Yamata E Asia • 300 kW
E Asia • 100 kW
OMAN
R SULTANATE OF OMAN, Sib E Africa • DS • 100 kW
PHILIPPINES
RADIO VERITAS ASIA, Palauig E Asia • 250 kW
UNITED KINGDOM
BBC, Via Meyerton, South Africa S Africa • 100 kW
UZBEKISTAN
RADIO TASHKENT, Tashkent **S** • W Asia • 100 kW
6193.4 PERU
RADIO CUSCO, Cusco SPANISH & QUECHUA • DS • 1 kW
Tu-Su • SPANISH & QUECHUA • DS • 1 kW
M-Sa • SPANISH & QUECHUA • DS • 1 kW

6195 **CHINA**
†NEI MENGGU PBS, Hohhot DS-MONGOLIAN • 50 kW
W-M • DS-MONGOLIAN • 50 kW
KOREA (DPR)
†PYONGYANG BC STN E Asia • ALT. FREQ. TO 9720 kHz
†VOICE OF KOREA E Asia • ALT. FREQ. TO 9720 kHz
RUSSIA
†VOICE OF RUSSIA, St Petersburg **W** • S America • 800 kW
W • S America • 400 kW
UNITED KINGDOM
†BBC, Multiple Locations Europe • 300/500 kW
SE Asia • 125/250 kW
†BBC, Rampisham **S** • E Europe • 500 kW **W** • W Europe • 500 kW
†BBC, Skelton, Cumbria **W** • Europe • 300 kW W Europe • 300 kW
BBC, Via Antigua C America & N America • 250 kW
†BBC, Via Singapore SE Asia • 125/250 kW
BBC, Via Thailand SE Asia • 250 kW
USA
ADVENTIST WORLD R, Via Agat, Guam **W** • E Asia • 100 kW
6200 **CHINA**
†XIZANG PBS, Lhasa DS-TIBETAN • 100 kW
W-M • DS-TIBETAN • 100 kW DS • 100 kW
CZECH REPUBLIC
†RADIO PRAGUE, Litomyšl N America & C America • 100 kW
W • N America & C America • 100 kW
S • N America & C America • 100 kW
W • W North Am & C America • 100 kW
IRAN
†VO THE ISLAMIC REP, Mashhad **W** • Mideast & E Africa • 500 kW
†VO THE ISLAMIC REP, Sirjan W Asia • 500 kW

0 1 2 3 4 5 6 7 8 9 10 11 12 13 14 15 16 17 18 19 20 21 22 23 24

SEASONAL **S** OR **W** 1-HR TIMESHIFT MIDYEAR ⇐ OR ⇒ JAMMING / OR /\ EARLIEST HEARD ◁ LATEST HEARD ▷ NEW FOR 2005 †

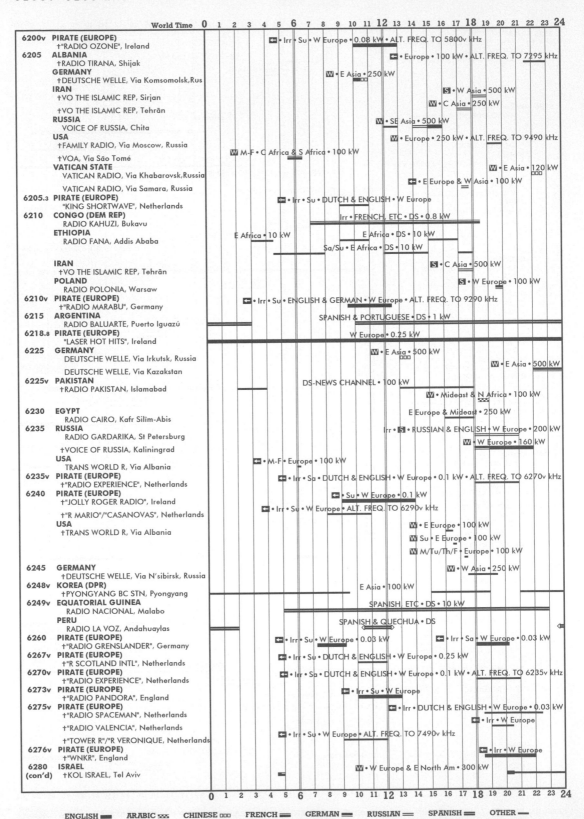

World Time 0 1 2 3 4 5 6 7 8 9 10 11 12 13 14 15 16 17 18 19 20 21 22 23 24

6200v **PIRATE (EUROPE)**
       †"RADIO OZONE", Ireland
6205   **ALBANIA**
       †RADIO TIRANA, Shijak
       GERMANY
       †DEUTSCHE WELLE, Via Komsomolsk,Rus
       IRAN
       †VO THE ISLAMIC REP, Sirjan
       †VO THE ISLAMIC REP, Tehrãn
       RUSSIA
       VOICE OF RUSSIA, Chita
       USA
       †FAMILY RADIO, Via Moscow, Russia
       †VOA, Via São Tomé
       VATICAN STATE
       VATICAN RADIO, Via Khabarovsk,Russia
       VATICAN RADIO, Via Samara, Russia
6205.3 **PIRATE (EUROPE)**
       "KING SHORTWAVE", Netherlands
6210   **CONGO (DEM REP)**
       RADIO KAHUZI, Bukavu
       ETHIOPIA
       RADIO FANA, Addis Ababa
       IRAN
       †VO THE ISLAMIC REP, Tehrãn
       POLAND
       RADIO POLONIA, Warsaw
6210v **PIRATE (EUROPE)**
       †"RADIO MARABU", Germany
6215   **ARGENTINA**
       RADIO BALUARTE, Puerto Iguazú
6218.8 **PIRATE (EUROPE)**
       "LASER HOT HITS", Ireland
6225   **GERMANY**
       DEUTSCHE WELLE, Via Irkutsk, Russia
       DEUTSCHE WELLE, Via Kazakstan
6225v **PAKISTAN**
       †RADIO PAKISTAN, Islamabad
6230   **EGYPT**
       RADIO CAIRO, Kafr Silim-Abis
6235   **RUSSIA**
       RADIO GARDARIKA, St Petersburg
       †VOICE OF RUSSIA, Kaliningrad
       USA
       TRANS WORLD R, Via Albania
6235v **PIRATE (EUROPE)**
       †"RADIO EXPERIENCE", Netherlands
6240   **PIRATE (EUROPE)**
       †"JOLLY ROGER RADIO", Ireland
       †"R MARIO"/"CASANOVAS", Netherlands
       USA
       †TRANS WORLD R, Via Albania
6245   **GERMANY**
       †DEUTSCHE WELLE, Via N'sibirsk, Russia
6248v **KOREA (DPR)**
       †PYONGYANG BC STN, Pyongyang
6249v **EQUATORIAL GUINEA**
       RADIO NACIONAL, Malabo
       PERU
       RADIO LA VOZ, Andahuaylas
6260   **PIRATE (EUROPE)**
       †"RADIO GRENSLANDER", Germany
6267v **PIRATE (EUROPE)**
       †"R SCOTLAND INTL", Netherlands
6270v **PIRATE (EUROPE)**
       †"RADIO EXPERIENCE", Netherlands
6273v **PIRATE (EUROPE)**
       †"RADIO PANDORA", England
6275v **PIRATE (EUROPE)**
       †"RADIO SPACEMAN", Netherlands
       †"RADIO VALENCIA", Netherlands
       †"TOWER R"/"R VERONIQUE", Netherlands
6276v †"WNKR", England
6280   **ISRAEL**
(con'd) †KOL ISRAEL, Tel Aviv

0 1 2 3 4 5 6 7 8 9 10 11 12 13 14 15 16 17 18 19 20 21 22 23 24

ENGLISH ━━ ARABIC ⋙ CHINESE ▫▫▫ FRENCH ═══ GERMAN ▬▬ RUSSIAN ══ SPANISH ━━ OTHER ──

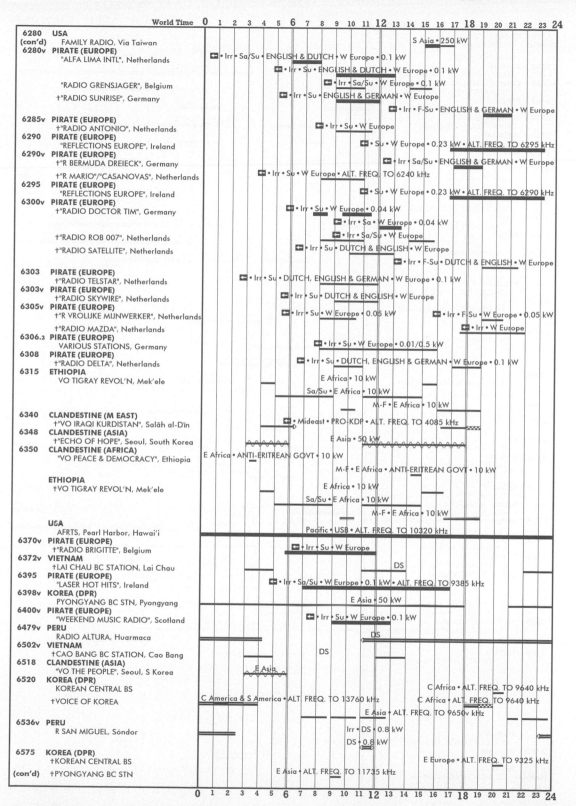

World Time	0 1 2 3 4 5 6 7 8 9 10 11 12 13 14 15 16 17 18 19 20 21 22 23 24
6280 USA	
(con'd) FAMILY RADIO, Via Taiwan	S Asia • 250 kW
6280v PIRATE (EUROPE)	⇐ • Irr • Sa/Su • ENGLISH & DUTCH • W Europe • 0.1 kW
"ALFA LIMA INTL", Netherlands	⇐ • Irr • Su • ENGLISH & DUTCH • W Europe • 0.1 kW
"RADIO GRENSJAGER", Belgium	⇐ • Irr • Sa/Su • W Europe • 0.1 kW
†"RADIO SUNRISE", Germany	⇐ • Irr • Su • ENGLISH & GERMAN • W Europe
	⇐ • Irr • F-Su • ENGLISH & GERMAN • W Europe
6285v PIRATE (EUROPE)	
†"RADIO ANTONIO", Netherlands	⇐ • Irr • Su • W Europe
6290 PIRATE (EUROPE)	
"REFLECTIONS EUROPE", Ireland	⇐ • Su • W Europe • 0.23 kW • ALT. FREQ. TO 6295 kHz
6290v PIRATE (EUROPE)	⇐ • Irr • Sa/Su • ENGLISH & GERMAN • W Europe
†"R BERMUDA DREIECK", Germany	
†"R MARIO"/"CASANOVAS", Netherlands	⇐ • Irr • Su • W Europe • ALT. FREQ. TO 6240 kHz
6295 PIRATE (EUROPE)	
"REFLECTIONS EUROPE", Ireland	⇐ • Su • W Europe • 0.23 kW • ALT. FREQ. TO 6290 kHz
6300v PIRATE (EUROPE)	⇐ • Irr • Su • W Europe • 0.04 kW
†"RADIO DOCTOR TIM", Germany	⇐ • Irr • Sa • W Europe • 0.04 kW
†"RADIO ROB 007", Netherlands	⇐ • Irr • Sa/Su • W Europe
†"RADIO SATELLITE", Netherlands	⇐ • Irr • Su • DUTCH & ENGLISH • W Europe
	⇐ • Irr • F-Su • DUTCH & ENGLISH • W Europe
6303 PIRATE (EUROPE)	
†"RADIO TELSTAR", Netherlands	⇐ • Irr • Su • DUTCH, ENGLISH & GERMAN • W Europe • 0.1 kW
6303v PIRATE (EUROPE)	
†"RADIO SKYWIRE", Netherlands	⇐ • Irr • Su • DUTCH & ENGLISH • W Europe
6305v PIRATE (EUROPE)	⇐ • Irr • Su • W Europe • 0.05 kW ⇐ • Irr • F-Su • W Europe • 0.05 kW
†"R VROLIJKE MIJNWERKER", Netherlands	
†"RADIO MAZDA", Netherlands	⇐ • Irr • W Europe
6306.3 PIRATE (EUROPE)	
VARIOUS STATIONS, Germany	⇐ • Irr • Su • W Europe • 0.01/0.5 kW
6308 PIRATE (EUROPE)	
†"RADIO DELTA", Netherlands	⇐ • Irr • Su • DUTCH, ENGLISH & GERMAN • W Europe • 0.1 kW
6315 ETHIOPIA	
VO TIGRAY REVOL'N, Mek'ele	E Africa • 10 kW
	Sa/Su • E Africa • 10 kW
	M-F • E Africa • 10 kW
6340 CLANDESTINE (M EAST)	
†"VO IRAQI KURDISTAN", Salāh al-Dīn	⇐ • Mideast • PRO-KDP • ALT. FREQ. TO 4085 kHz
6348 CLANDESTINE (ASIA)	
†"ECHO OF HOPE", Seoul, South Korea	E Asia • 50 kW
6350 CLANDESTINE (AFRICA)	
"VO PEACE & DEMOCRACY", Ethiopia	E Africa • ANTI-ERITREAN GOVT • 10 kW
	M-F • E Africa • ANTI-ERITREAN GOVT • 10 kW
ETHIOPIA	
†VO TIGRAY REVOL'N, Mek'ele	E Africa • 10 kW
	Sa/Su • E Africa • 10 kW
	M-F • E Africa • 10 kW
USA	
AFRTS, Pearl Harbor, Hawai'i	Pacific • USB • ALT. FREQ. TO 10320 kHz
6370v PIRATE (EUROPE)	
†"RADIO BRIGITTE", Belgium	⇐ • Irr • Su • W Europe
6372v VIETNAM	
†LAI CHAU BC STATION, Lai Chau	DS
6395 PIRATE (EUROPE)	
"LASER HOT HITS", Ireland	⇐ • Irr • Sa/Su • W Europe • 0.1 kW • ALT. FREQ. TO 9385 kHz
6398v KOREA (DPR)	
PYONGYANG BC STN, Pyongyang	E Asia • 50 kW
6400v PIRATE (EUROPE)	
"WEEKEND MUSIC RADIO", Scotland	⇐ • Irr • Su • W Europe • 0.1 kW
6479v PERU	
RADIO ALTURA, Huarmaca	DS
6502v VIETNAM	
†CAO BANG BC STATION, Cao Bang	DS
6518 CLANDESTINE (ASIA)	
"VO THE PEOPLE", Seoul, S Korea	E Asia
6520 KOREA (DPR)	
KOREAN CENTRAL BS	C Africa • ALT. FREQ. TO 9640 kHz
†VOICE OF KOREA	C America & S America • ALT. FREQ. TO 13760 kHz C Africa • ALT. FREQ. TO 9640 kHz
	E Asia • ALT. FREQ. TO 9650v kHz
6536v PERU	
R SAN MIGUEL, Sóndor	Irr • DS • 0.8 kW
	DS • 0.8 kW
6575 KOREA (DPR)	
†KOREAN CENTRAL BS	E Europe • ALT. FREQ. TO 9325 kHz
(con'd) †PYONGYANG BC STN	E Asia • ALT. FREQ. TO 11735 kHz

0 1 2 3 4 5 6 7 8 9 10 11 12 13 14 15 16 17 18 19 20 21 22 23 24

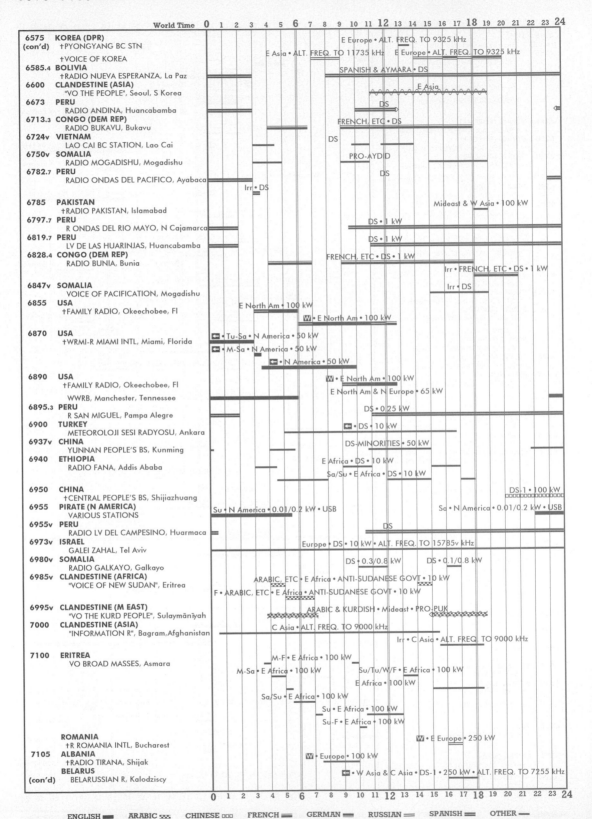

6575	**KOREA (DPR)**	
(con'd)	†PYONGYANG BC STN	E Europe • ALT. FREQ. TO 9325 kHz
		E Asia • ALT. FREQ. TO 11735 kHz E Europe • ALT. FREQ. TO 9325 kHz
	†VOICE OF KOREA	
6585.4	**BOLIVIA**	SPANISH & AYMARA • DS
	†RADIO NUEVA ESPERANZA, La Paz	
6600	**CLANDESTINE (ASIA)**	E Asia
	"VO THE PEOPLE", Seoul, S Korea	
6673	**PERU**	DS
	RADIO ANDINA, Huancabamba	
6713.3	**CONGO (DEM REP)**	FRENCH, ETC • DS
	RADIO BUKAVU, Bukavu	
6724v	**VIETNAM**	DS
	LAO CAI BC STATION, Lao Cai	
6750v	**SOMALIA**	PRO-AYDID
	RADIO MOGADISHU, Mogadishu	
6782.7	**PERU**	DS
	RADIO ONDAS DEL PACIFICO, Ayabaca	
		Irr • DS
6785	**PAKISTAN**	Mideast & W Asia • 100 kW
	†RADIO PAKISTAN, Islamabad	
6797.7	**PERU**	DS • 1 kW
	R ONDAS DEL RIO MAYO, N Cajamarca	
6819.7	**PERU**	DS • 1 kW
	LV DE LAS HUARINJAS, Huancabamba	
6828.4	**CONGO (DEM REP)**	FRENCH, ETC • DS • 1 kW
	RADIO BUNIA, Bunia	Irr • FRENCH, ETC • DS • 1 kW
6847v	**SOMALIA**	Irr • DS
	VOICE OF PACIFICATION, Mogadishu	
6855	**USA**	E North Am • 100 kW
	†FAMILY RADIO, Okeechobee, Fl	W • E North Am • 100 kW
6870	**USA**	Tu-Sa • N America • 50 kW
	†WRMI-R MIAMI INTL, Miami, Florida	M-Sa • N America • 50 kW
		• N America • 50 kW
6890	**USA**	W • E North Am • 100 kW
	†FAMILY RADIO, Okeechobee, Fl	E North Am & N Europe • 65 kW
	WWRB, Manchester, Tennessee	
6895.3	**PERU**	DS • 0.25 kW
	R SAN MIGUEL, Pampa Alegre	
6900	**TURKEY**	DS • 10 kW
	METEOROLOJI SESI RADYOSU, Ankara	
6937v	**CHINA**	DS-MINORITIES • 50 kW
	YUNNAN PEOPLE'S BS, Kunming	
6940	**ETHIOPIA**	E Africa • DS • 10 kW
	RADIO FANA, Addis Ababa	Sa/Su • E Africa • DS • 10 kW
6950	**CHINA**	DS-1 • 100 kW
	†CENTRAL PEOPLE'S BS, Shijiazhuang	
6955	**PIRATE (N AMERICA)**	Su • N America • 0.01/0.2 kW • USB Sa • N America • 0.01/0.2 kW • USB
	VARIOUS STATIONS	
6955v	**PERU**	DS
	RADIO LV DEL CAMPESINO, Huarmaca	
6973v	**ISRAEL**	Europe • DS • 10 kW • ALT. FREQ. TO 15785v kHz
	GALEI ZAHAL, Tel Aviv	
6980v	**SOMALIA**	DS • 0.3/0.8 kW DS • 0.1/0.8 kW
	RADIO GALKAYO, Galkayo	
6985v	**CLANDESTINE (AFRICA)**	ARABIC, ETC • E Africa • ANTI-SUDANESE GOVT • 10 kW
	"VOICE OF NEW SUDAN", Eritrea	F • ARABIC, ETC • E Africa • ANTI-SUDANESE GOVT • 10 kW
6995v	**CLANDESTINE (M EAST)**	ARABIC & KURDISH • Mideast • PRO-PUK
	"VO THE KURD PEOPLE", Sulaymānīyah	
7000	**CLANDESTINE (ASIA)**	C Asia • ALT. FREQ. TO 9000 kHz
	"INFORMATION R", Bagram, Afghanistan	Irr • C Asia • ALT. FREQ. TO 9000 kHz
7100	**ERITREA**	M-F • E Africa • 100 kW
	VO BROAD MASSES, Asmara	M-Sa • E Africa • 100 kW Su/Tu/W/F • E Africa • 100 kW
		E Africa • 100 kW
		Sa/Su • E Africa • 100 kW
		Su • E Africa • 100 kW
		Su-F • E Africa • 100 kW
	ROMANIA	W • E Europe • 250 kW
	†R ROMANIA INTL, Bucharest	
7105	**ALBANIA**	W • Europe • 100 kW
	†RADIO TIRANA, Shijak	
	BELARUS	• W Asia & C Asia • DS-1 • 250 kW • ALT. FREQ. TO 7255 kHz
(con'd)	BELARUSSIAN R, Kalodziscy	

ENGLISH ▬ ARABIC ░░ CHINESE ▫▫▫ FRENCH ══ GERMAN ▬ RUSSIAN ═ SPANISH ▬ OTHER ─

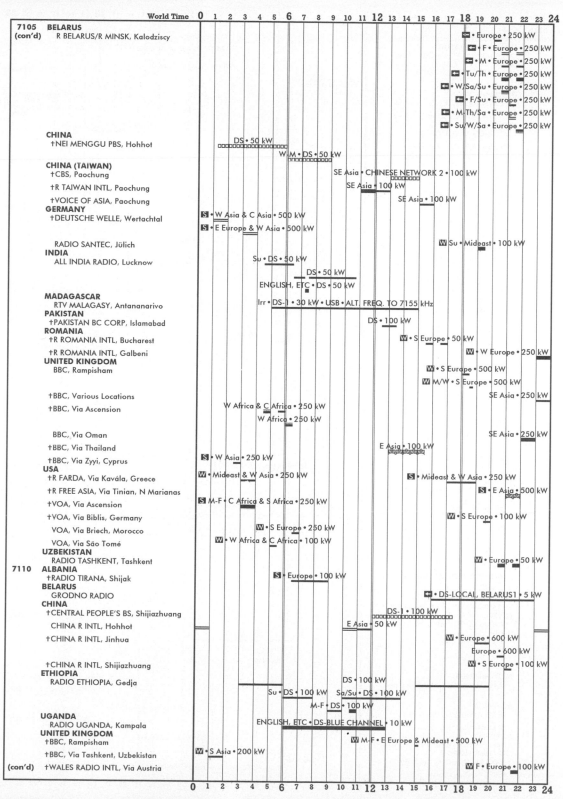

World Time 0 1 2 3 4 5 6 7 8 9 10 11 12 13 14 15 16 17 18 19 20 21 22 23 24

7105
(con'd)   BELARUS
           R BELARUS/R MINSK, Kalodziscy

           CHINA
             †NEI MENGGU PBS, Hohhot

           CHINA (TAIWAN)
             †CBS, Paochung
             †R TAIWAN INTL, Paochung
             †VOICE OF ASIA, Paochung
           GERMANY
             †DEUTSCHE WELLE, Wertachtal

             RADIO SANTEC, Jülich
           INDIA
             ALL INDIA RADIO, Lucknow

           MADAGASCAR
             RTV MALAGASY, Antananarivo
           PAKISTAN
             †PAKISTAN BC CORP, Islamabad
           ROMANIA
             †R ROMANIA INTL, Bucharest
             †R ROMANIA INTL, Galbeni
           UNITED KINGDOM
             BBC, Rampisham

             †BBC, Various Locations
             †BBC, Via Ascension

             BBC, Via Oman
             †BBC, Via Thailand
             †BBC, Via Zyyi, Cyprus
           USA
             †R FARDA, Via Kavála, Greece
             †R FREE ASIA, Via Tinian, N Marianas
             †VOA, Via Ascension
             †VOA, Via Biblis, Germany
             VOA, Via Briech, Morocco
             VOA, Via São Tomé
           UZBEKISTAN
             RADIO TASHKENT, Tashkent
7110   ALBANIA
             †RADIO TIRANA, Shijak
           BELARUS
             GRODNO RADIO
           CHINA
             †CENTRAL PEOPLE'S BS, Shijiazhuang
             CHINA R INTL, Hohhot
             †CHINA R INTL, Jinhua

             †CHINA R INTL, Shijiazhuang
           ETHIOPIA
             RADIO ETHIOPIA, Gedja

           UGANDA
             RADIO UGANDA, Kampala
           UNITED KINGDOM
             †BBC, Rampisham
             †BBC, Via Tashkent, Uzbekistan
(con'd)   †WALES RADIO INTL, Via Austria

0 1 2 3 4 5 6 7 8 9 10 11 12 13 14 15 16 17 18 19 20 21 22 23 24

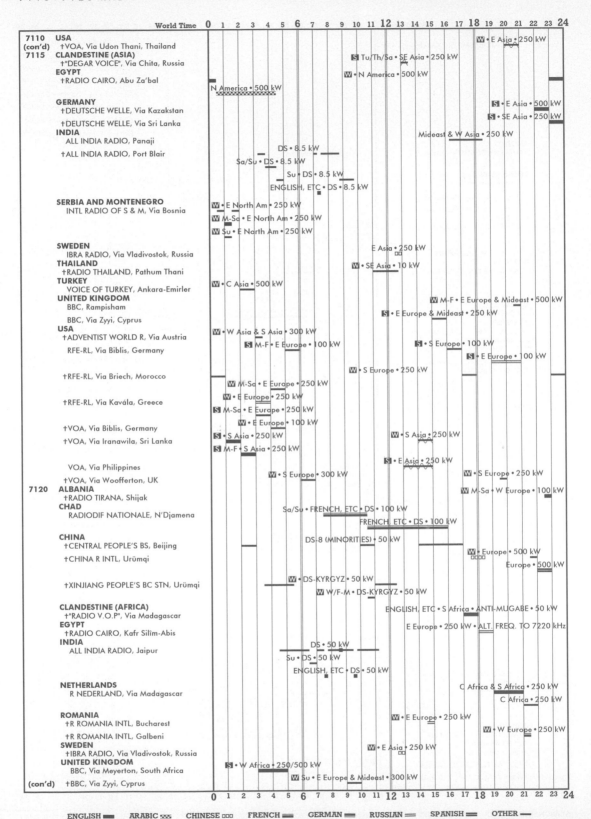

World Time	0 1 2 3 4 5 6 7 8 9 10 11 12 13 14 15 16 17 18 19 20 21 22 23 24

7110
(con'd)
USA
†VOA, Via Udon Thani, Thailand — **W** • E Asia • 250 kW

7115
CLANDESTINE (ASIA)
†"DEGAR VOICE", Via Chita, Russia — **S** Tu/Th/Sa • SE Asia • 250 kW

EGYPT
†RADIO CAIRO, Abu Za'bal — **W** • N America • 500 kW

N America • 500 kW

GERMANY
†DEUTSCHE WELLE, Via Kazakstan — **S** • E Asia • 500 kW

†DEUTSCHE WELLE, Via Sri Lanka — **S** • SE Asia • 250 kW

INDIA
ALL INDIA RADIO, Panaji — Mideast & W Asia • 250 kW

†ALL INDIA RADIO, Port Blair — DS • 8.5 kW
Sa/Su • DS • 8.5 kW
Su • DS • 8.5 kW
ENGLISH, ETC • DS • 8.5 kW

SERBIA AND MONTENEGRO
INTL RADIO OF S & M, Via Bosnia — **W** • E North Am • 250 kW
W M-Sa • E North Am • 250 kW
W Su • E North Am • 250 kW

SWEDEN
IBRA RADIO, Via Vladivostok, Russia — E Asia • 250 kW

THAILAND
†RADIO THAILAND, Pathum Thani — **W** • SE Asia • 10 kW

TURKEY
VOICE OF TURKEY, Ankara-Emirler — **W** • C Asia • 500 kW

UNITED KINGDOM
BBC, Rampisham — **W** M-F • E Europe & Mideast • 500 kW

BBC, Via Zyyi, Cyprus — **S** • E Europe & Mideast • 250 kW

USA
†ADVENTIST WORLD R, Via Austria — **W** • W Asia & S Asia • 300 kW

RFE-RL, Via Biblis, Germany — **S** M-F • E Europe • 100 kW
S • S Europe • 100 kW
S • E Europe • 100 kW

†RFE-RL, Via Briech, Morocco — **W** • S Europe • 250 kW
W M-Sa • E Europe • 250 kW

†RFE-RL, Via Kavála, Greece — **W** • E Europe • 250 kW
S M-Sa • E Europe • 250 kW
W • E Europe • 100 kW

†VOA, Via Biblis, Germany — **S** • S Asia • 250 kW

†VOA, Via Iranawila, Sri Lanka — **S** M-F • S Asia • 250 kW
W • S Asia • 250 kW

VOA, Via Philippines — **S** • E Asia • 250 kW

†VOA, Via Woofferton, UK — **W** • S Europe • 300 kW
W • S Europe • 250 kW

7120
ALBANIA
†RADIO TIRANA, Shijak — **W** M-Sa • W Europe • 100 kW

CHAD
RADIODIF NATIONALE, N'Djamena — Sa/Su • FRENCH, ETC • DS • 100 kW
FRENCH, ETC • DS • 100 kW

CHINA
†CENTRAL PEOPLE'S BS, Beijing — DS-8 (MINORITIES) • 50 kW

†CHINA R INTL, Urümqi — **W** • Europe • 500 kW
Europe • 500 kW

†XINJIANG PEOPLE'S BC STN, Urümqi — **W** • DS-KYRGYZ • 50 kW
W W/F-M • DS-KYRGYZ • 50 kW

CLANDESTINE (AFRICA)
†"RADIO V.O.P", Via Madagascar — ENGLISH, ETC • S Africa • ANTI-MUGABE • 50 kW

EGYPT
†RADIO CAIRO, Kafr Silim-Abis — E Europe • 250 kW • ALT. FREQ. TO 7220 kHz

INDIA
ALL INDIA RADIO, Jaipur — DS • 50 kW
Su • DS • 50 kW
ENGLISH, ETC • DS • 50 kW

NETHERLANDS
R NEDERLAND, Via Madagascar — C Africa & S Africa • 250 kW
C Africa • 250 kW

ROMANIA
†R ROMANIA INTL, Bucharest — **W** • E Europe • 250 kW

†R ROMANIA INTL, Galbeni — **W** • W Europe • 250 kW

SWEDEN
†IBRA RADIO, Via Vladivostok, Russia — **W** • E Asia • 250 kW

UNITED KINGDOM
BBC, Via Meyerton, South Africa — **S** • W Africa • 250/500 kW

(con'd)   †BBC, Via Zyyi, Cyprus — **W** Su • E Europe & Mideast • 300 kW

	0 1 2 3 4 5 6 7 8 9 10 11 12 13 14 15 16 17 18 19 20 21 22 23 24

ENGLISH ■■   ARABIC ▧▧   CHINESE ▭▭▭   FRENCH ══   GERMAN ▬▬   RUSSIAN ══   SPANISH ══   OTHER ──

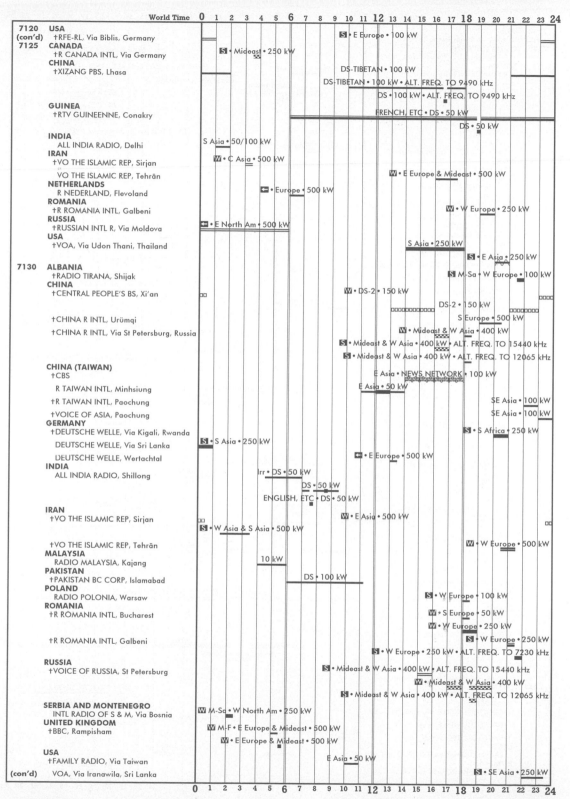

World Time | 0 1 2 3 4 5 6 7 8 9 10 11 12 13 14 15 16 17 18 19 20 21 22 23 24

7120 **USA**
(con'd) †RFE-RL, Via Biblis, Germany — S • E Europe • 100 kW
7125 **CANADA**
 †R CANADA INTL, Via Germany — S • Mideast • 250 kW
 CHINA
 †XIZANG PBS, Lhasa — DS-TIBETAN • 100 kW
 DS-TIBETAN • 100 kW • ALT. FREQ. TO 9490 kHz
 DS • 100 kW • ALT. FREQ. TO 9490 kHz

 GUINEA
 †RTV GUINEENNE, Conakry — FRENCH, ETC • DS • 50 kW
 DS • 50 kW

 INDIA
 ALL INDIA RADIO, Delhi — S Asia • 50/100 kW
 IRAN
 †VO THE ISLAMIC REP, Sirjan — W • C Asia • 500 kW
 VO THE ISLAMIC REP, Tehrān — W • E Europe & Mideast • 500 kW
 NETHERLANDS
 R NEDERLAND, Flevoland — • Europe • 500 kW
 ROMANIA
 †R ROMANIA INTL, Galbeni — W • W Europe • 250 kW
 RUSSIA
 †RUSSIAN INTL R, Via Moldova — • E North Am • 500 kW
 USA
 †VOA, Via Udon Thani, Thailand — S Asia • 250 kW
 S • E Asia • 250 kW

7130 **ALBANIA**
 †RADIO TIRANA, Shijak — S • M-Sa • W Europe • 100 kW
 CHINA
 †CENTRAL PEOPLE'S BS, Xi'an — W • DS-2 • 150 kW
 DS-2 • 150 kW
 †CHINA R INTL, Urümqi — S Europe • 500 kW
 †CHINA R INTL, Via St Petersburg, Russia — W • Mideast & W Asia • 400 kW
 S • Mideast & W Asia • 400 kW • ALT. FREQ. TO 15440 kHz
 S • Mideast & W Asia • 400 kW • ALT. FREQ. TO 12065 kHz
 CHINA (TAIWAN)
 †CBS — E Asia • NEWS NETWORK • 100 kW
 R TAIWAN INTL, Minhsiung — E Asia • 50 kW
 †R TAIWAN INTL, Paochung — SE Asia • 100 kW
 †VOICE OF ASIA, Paochung — SE Asia • 100 kW
 GERMANY
 †DEUTSCHE WELLE, Via Kigali, Rwanda — S • S Africa • 250 kW
 DEUTSCHE WELLE, Via Sri Lanka — S • S Asia • 250 kW
 DEUTSCHE WELLE, Wertachtal — • E Europe • 500 kW
 INDIA
 ALL INDIA RADIO, Shillong — Irr • DS • 50 kW
 DS • 50 kW
 ENGLISH, ETC • DS • 50 kW
 IRAN
 †VO THE ISLAMIC REP, Sirjan — W • E Asia • 500 kW
 S • W Asia & S Asia • 500 kW
 †VO THE ISLAMIC REP, Tehrān — W • W Europe • 500 kW
 MALAYSIA
 RADIO MALAYSIA, Kajang — 10 kW
 PAKISTAN
 †PAKISTAN BC CORP, Islamabad — DS • 100 kW
 POLAND
 RADIO POLONIA, Warsaw — S • W Europe • 100 kW
 ROMANIA
 †R ROMANIA INTL, Bucharest — W • S Europe • 50 kW
 W • W Europe • 250 kW
 S • W Europe • 250 kW
 †R ROMANIA INTL, Galbeni — S • W Europe • 250 kW • ALT. FREQ. TO 7230 kHz
 RUSSIA
 †VOICE OF RUSSIA, St Petersburg — S • Mideast & W Asia • 400 kW • ALT. FREQ. TO 15440 kHz
 W • Mideast & W Asia • 400 kW
 S • Mideast & W Asia • 400 kW • ALT. FREQ. TO 12065 kHz
 SERBIA AND MONTENEGRO
 INTL RADIO OF S & M, Via Bosnia — W • M-Sa • W North Am • 250 kW
 UNITED KINGDOM
 †BBC, Rampisham — W • M-F • E Europe & Mideast • 500 kW
 W • E Europe & Mideast • 500 kW
 USA
 †FAMILY RADIO, Via Taiwan — E Asia • 50 kW
(con'd) VOA, Via Iranawila, Sri Lanka — S • SE Asia • 250 kW

0 1 2 3 4 5 6 7 8 9 10 11 12 13 14 15 16 17 18 19 20 21 22 23 24

SEASONAL S OR W   1-HR TIMESHIFT MIDYEAR ◨ OR ▣   JAMMING / OR ∧   EARLIEST HEARD ◁   LATEST HEARD ▷   NEW FOR 2005 †

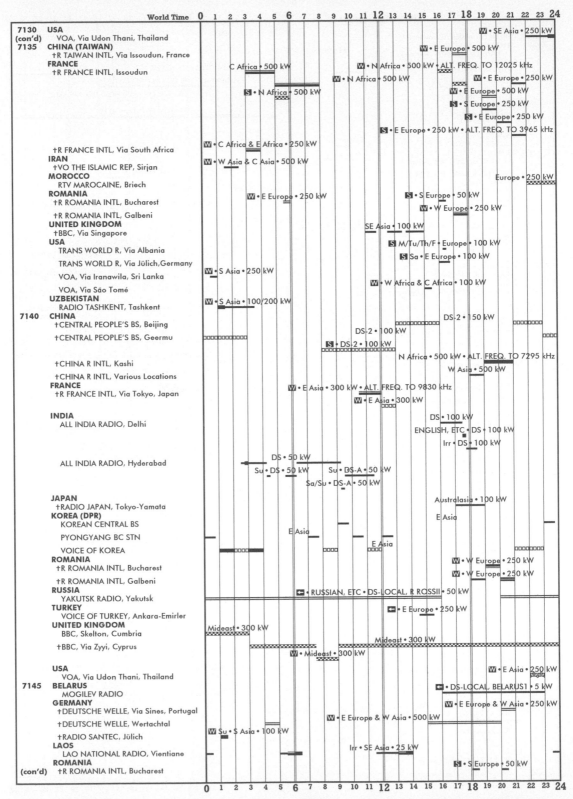

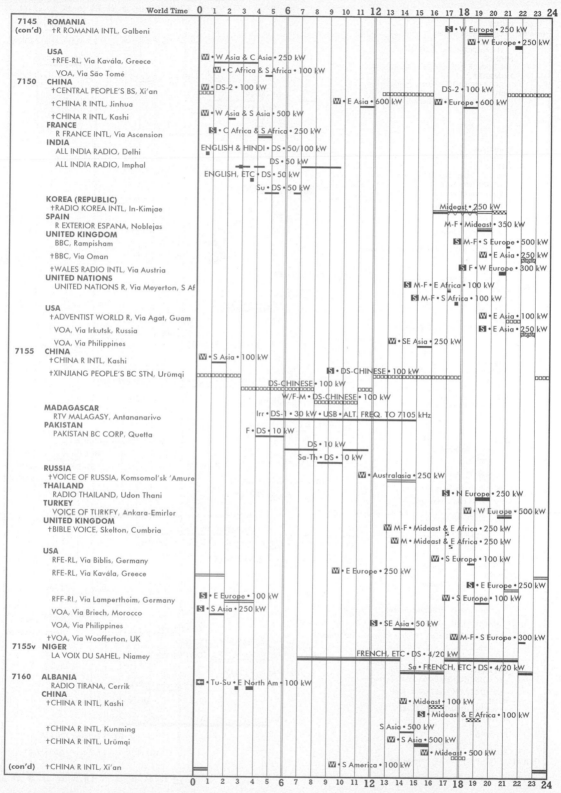

World Time | 0 1 2 3 4 5 6 7 8 9 10 11 12 13 14 15 16 17 18 19 20 21 22 23 24

7145 **ROMANIA**
(con'd) †R ROMANIA INTL, Galbeni — Ⓢ • W Europe • 250 kW; Ⓦ • W Europe • 250 kW

USA
†RFE-RL, Via Kavála, Greece — Ⓦ • W Asia & C Asia • 250 kW
VOA, Via São Tomé — Ⓦ • C Africa & S Africa • 100 kW

7150 **CHINA**
†CENTRAL PEOPLE'S BS, Xi'an — Ⓦ • DS-2 • 100 kW; DS-2 • 100 kW
†CHINA R INTL, Jinhua — Ⓦ • E Asia • 600 kW; Ⓦ • Europe • 600 kW
†CHINA R INTL, Kashi — Ⓦ • W Asia & S Asia • 500 kW

FRANCE
R FRANCE INTL, Via Ascension — Ⓢ • C Africa & S Africa • 250 kW

INDIA
ALL INDIA RADIO, Delhi — ENGLISH & HINDI • DS • 50/100 kW
ALL INDIA RADIO, Imphal — DS • 50 kW; ENGLISH, ETC • DS • 50 kW; Su • DS • 50 kW

KOREA (REPUBLIC)
†RADIO KOREA INTL, In-Kimjae — Mideast • 250 kW

SPAIN
R EXTERIOR ESPANA, Noblejas — M-F • Mideast • 350 kW

UNITED KINGDOM
BBC, Rampisham — Ⓢ M-F • S Europe • 500 kW
†BBC, Via Oman — Ⓦ • E Asia • 250 kW
†WALES RADIO INTL, Via Austria — Ⓢ F • W Europe • 300 kW

UNITED NATIONS
UNITED NATIONS R, Via Meyerton, S Af — Ⓢ M-F • E Africa • 100 kW; Ⓢ M-F • S Africa • 100 kW

USA
†ADVENTIST WORLD R, Via Agat, Guam — Ⓦ • E Asia • 100 kW
VOA, Via Irkutsk, Russia — Ⓢ • E Asia • 250 kW
VOA, Via Philippines — Ⓦ • SE Asia • 250 kW

7155 **CHINA**
†CHINA R INTL, Kashi — Ⓦ • S Asia • 100 kW
†XINJIANG PEOPLE'S BC STN, Urümqi — Ⓢ • DS-CHINESE • 100 kW; DS-CHINESE • 100 kW; W/F-M • DS-CHINESE • 100 kW

MADAGASCAR
RTV MALAGASY, Antananarivo — Irr • DS • 30 kW • USB • ALT. FREQ. TO 7105 kHz

PAKISTAN
PAKISTAN BC CORP, Quetta — F • DS • 10 kW; DS • 10 kW; Sa-Th • DS • 10 kW

RUSSIA
†VOICE OF RUSSIA, Komsomol'sk 'Amure — Ⓦ • Australasia • 250 kW

THAILAND
RADIO THAILAND, Udon Thani — Ⓢ • N Europe • 250 kW

TURKEY
VOICE OF TURKEY, Ankara-Emirler — Ⓦ • W Europe • 500 kW

UNITED KINGDOM
†BIBLE VOICE, Skelton, Cumbria — Ⓦ M-F • Mideast & E Africa • 250 kW; Ⓦ M • Mideast & E Africa • 250 kW

USA
RFE-RL, Via Biblis, Germany — Ⓦ • S Europe • 100 kW
RFE-RL, Via Kavála, Greece — Ⓦ • E Europe • 250 kW; Ⓢ • E Europe • 250 kW
RFF-RL, Via Lampertheim, Germany — Ⓢ • E Europe • 100 kW; Ⓦ • S Europe • 100 kW
VOA, Via Briech, Morocco — Ⓢ • S Asia • 250 kW
VOA, Via Philippines — Ⓢ • SE Asia • 50 kW
†VOA, Via Woofferton, UK — Ⓦ M-F • S Europe • 300 kW

7155v **NIGER**
LA VOIX DU SAHEL, Niamey — FRENCH, ETC • DS • 4/20 kW; Sa • FRENCH, ETC • DS • 4/20 kW

7160 **ALBANIA**
RADIO TIRANA, Cerrik — ⇆ • Tu-Su • E North Am • 100 kW

CHINA
†CHINA R INTL, Kashi — Ⓦ • Mideast • 100 kW; Ⓢ • Mideast & E Africa • 100 kW
†CHINA R INTL, Kunming — S Asia • 500 kW
†CHINA R INTL, Urümqi — Ⓦ • S Asia • 500 kW; Ⓦ • Mideast • 500 kW
(con'd) †CHINA R INTL, Xi'an — Ⓦ • S America • 100 kW

World Time | 0 1 2 3 4 5 6 7 8 9 10 11 12 13 14 15 16 17 18 19 20 21 22 23 24

SEASONAL Ⓢ OR Ⓦ   1-HR TIMESHIFT MIDYEAR ⇆ OR ⇨   JAMMING / OR ∧   EARLIEST HEARD ◁   LATEST HEARD ▷   NEW FOR 2005 †

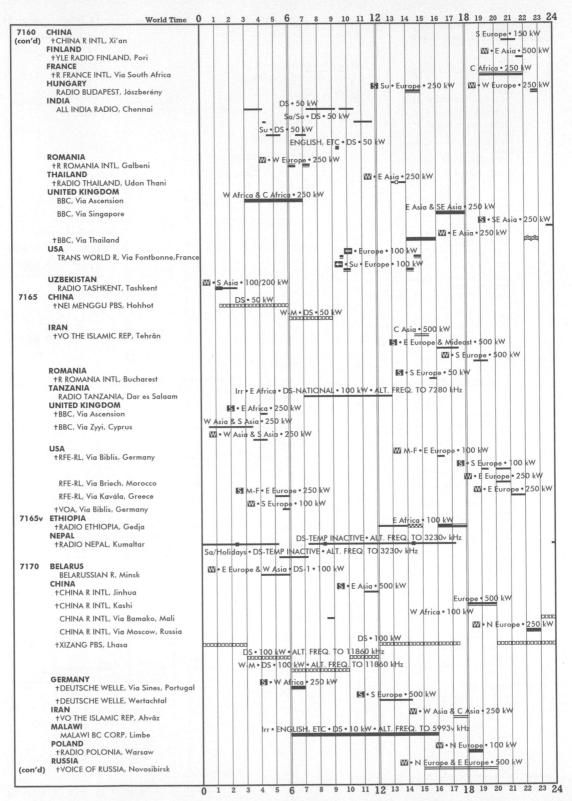

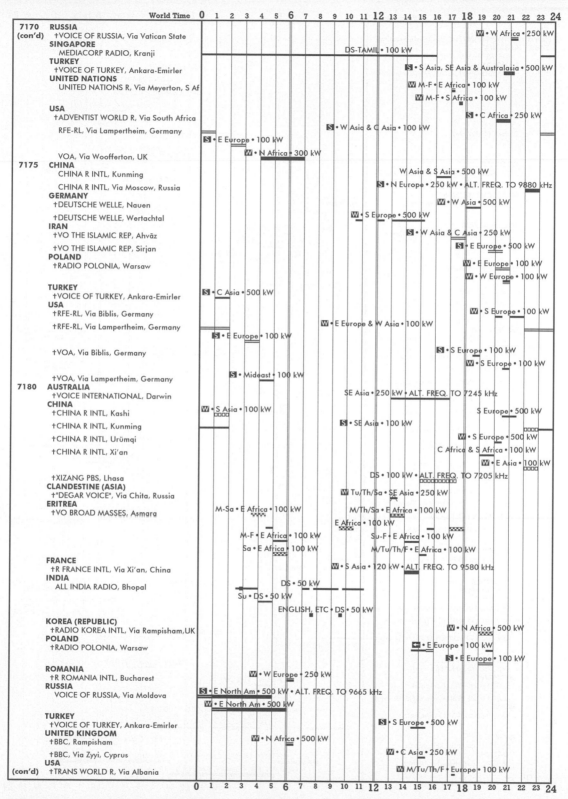

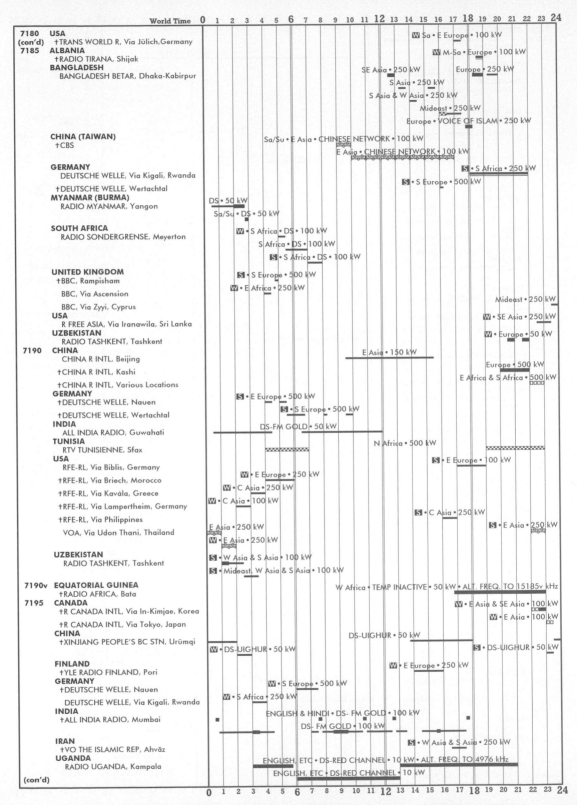

| | | World Time | 0 | 1 | 2 | 3 | 4 | 5 | 6 | 7 | 8 | 9 | 10 | 11 | 12 | 13 | 14 | 15 | 16 | 17 | 18 | 19 | 20 | 21 | 22 | 23 | 24 |

7180 **USA**
(con'd) †TRANS WORLD R, Via Jülich, Germany — W Sa • E Europe • 100 kW
7185 **ALBANIA**
  †RADIO TIRANA, Shijak — W M-Sa • Europe • 100 kW
  BANGLADESH
  BANGLADESH BETAR, Dhaka-Kabirpur — SE Asia • 250 kW · Europe • 250 kW · S Asia • 250 kW · S Asia & W Asia • 250 kW · Mideast • 250 kW · Europe • VOICE OF ISLAM • 250 kW

  CHINA (TAIWAN)
  †CBS — Sa/Su • E Asia • CHINESE NETWORK • 100 kW · E Asia • CHINESE NETWORK • 100 kW

  GERMANY
  DEUTSCHE WELLE, Via Kigali, Rwanda — S • S Africa • 250 kW
  †DEUTSCHE WELLE, Wertachtal — S • S Europe • 500 kW
  MYANMAR (BURMA)
  RADIO MYANMAR, Yangon — DS • 50 kW · Sa/Su • DS • 50 kW

  SOUTH AFRICA
  RADIO SONDERGRENSE, Meyerton — W • S Africa • DS • 100 kW · S Africa • DS • 100 kW · S • S Africa • DS • 100 kW

  UNITED KINGDOM
  †BBC, Rampisham — S • S Europe • 500 kW
  BBC, Via Ascension — W • E Africa • 250 kW
  BBC, Via Zyyi, Cyprus — Mideast • 250 kW
  USA
  R FREE ASIA, Via Iranawila, Sri Lanka — W • SE Asia • 250 kW
  UZBEKISTAN
  RADIO TASHKENT, Tashkent — W • Europe • 50 kW
7190 **CHINA**
  CHINA R INTL, Beijing — E Asia • 150 kW
  †CHINA R INTL, Kashi — Europe • 500 kW
  †CHINA R INTL, Various Locations — E Africa & S Africa • 500 kW
  GERMANY
  †DEUTSCHE WELLE, Nauen — S • E Europe • 500 kW
  †DEUTSCHE WELLE, Wertachtal — S • S Europe • 500 kW
  INDIA
  ALL INDIA RADIO, Guwahati — DS-FM GOLD • 50 kW
  TUNISIA
  RTV TUNISIENNE, Sfax — N Africa • 500 kW
  USA
  RFE-RL, Via Biblis, Germany — S • E Europe • 100 kW
  †RFE-RL, Via Briech, Morocco — W • E Europe • 250 kW
  †RFE-RL, Via Kavála, Greece — W • C Asia • 250 kW
  †RFE-RL, Via Lampertheim, Germany — W • C Asia • 100 kW · S • C Asia • 250 kW
  †RFE-RL, Via Philippines — S • E Asia • 250 kW
  VOA, Via Udon Thani, Thailand — E Asia • 250 kW · W • E Asia • 250 kW
  UZBEKISTAN
  RADIO TASHKENT, Tashkent — S • W Asia & S Asia • 100 kW · S • Mideast, W Asia & S Asia • 100 kW
7190v **EQUATORIAL GUINEA**
  †RADIO AFRICA, Bata — W Africa • TEMP INACTIVE • 50 kW • ALT. FREQ. TO 15185v kHz
7195 **CANADA**
  †R CANADA INTL, Via In-Kimjae, Korea — W • E Asia & SE Asia • 100 kW
  †R CANADA INTL, Via Tokyo, Japan — W • E Asia • 100 kW
  CHINA
  †XINJIANG PEOPLE'S BC STN, Urümqi — DS-UIGHUR • 50 kW · W • DS-UIGHUR • 50 kW · S • DS-UIGHUR • 50 kW
  FINLAND
  †YLE RADIO FINLAND, Pori — W • E Europe • 250 kW
  GERMANY
  †DEUTSCHE WELLE, Nauen — W • S Europe • 500 kW
  DEUTSCHE WELLE, Via Kigali, Rwanda — W • S Africa • 250 kW
  INDIA
  †ALL INDIA RADIO, Mumbai — ENGLISH & HINDI • DS- FM GOLD • 100 kW · DS- FM GOLD • 100 kW
  IRAN
  †VO THE ISLAMIC REP, Ahvāz — S • W Asia & S Asia • 250 kW
  UGANDA
  RADIO UGANDA, Kampala — ENGLISH, ETC • DS-RED CHANNEL • 10 kW • ALT. FREQ. TO 4976 kHz · ENGLISH, ETC • DS-RED CHANNEL • 10 kW

(con'd)

| | World Time | 0 | 1 | 2 | 3 | 4 | 5 | 6 | 7 | 8 | 9 | 10 | 11 | 12 | 13 | 14 | 15 | 16 | 17 | 18 | 19 | 20 | 21 | 22 | 23 | 24 |

ENGLISH ▬   ARABIC ⬚⬚⬚   CHINESE □□□   FRENCH ▬▬   GERMAN ▬▬   RUSSIAN ═   SPANISH ═   OTHER ▬

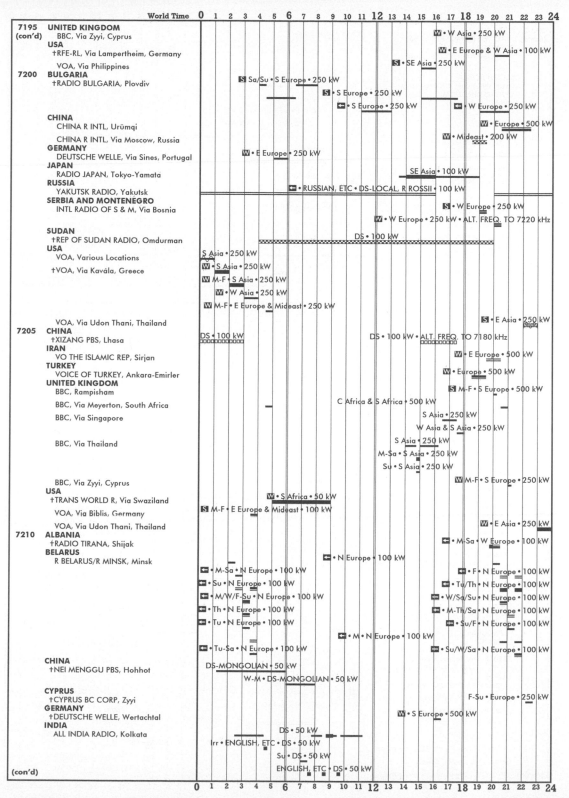

World Time	0 1 2 3 4 5 6 7 8 9 10 11 12 13 14 15 16 17 18 19 20 21 22 23 24
7195 **UNITED KINGDOM**	
(con'd) BBC, Via Zyyi, Cyprus	W • W Asia • 250 kW
USA	
†RFE-RL, Via Lampertheim, Germany	W • E Europe & W Asia • 100 kW
VOA, Via Philippines	S • SE Asia • 250 kW
7200 BULGARIA	
†RADIO BULGARIA, Plovdiv	S Sa/Su • S Europe • 250 kW
	S • S Europe • 250 kW
	⇦ • S Europe • 250 kW ⇦ • W Europe • 250 kW
CHINA	
CHINA R INTL, Urümqi	W • Europe • 500 kW
CHINA R INTL, Via Moscow, Russia	W • Mideast • 200 kW
GERMANY	
DEUTSCHE WELLE, Via Sines, Portugal	W • E Europe • 250 kW
JAPAN	
RADIO JAPAN, Tokyo-Yamata	SE Asia • 100 kW
RUSSIA	
YAKUTSK RADIO, Yakutsk	⇦ • RUSSIAN, ETC • DS-LOCAL, R ROSSII • 100 kW
SERBIA AND MONTENEGRO	
INTL RADIO OF S & M, Via Bosnia	S • W Europe • 250 kW
	W • W Europe • 250 kW • ALT. FREQ. TO 7220 kHz
SUDAN	
†REP OF SUDAN RADIO, Omdurman	DS • 100 kW
USA	
VOA, Various Locations	S Asia • 250 kW
	W • S Asia • 250 kW
†VOA, Via Kavála, Greece	W M-F • S Asia • 250 kW
	W • W Asia • 250 kW
	W M-F • E Europe & Mideast • 250 kW
VOA, Via Udon Thani, Thailand	S • E Asia • 250 kW
7205 CHINA	
†XIZANG PBS, Lhasa	DS • 100 kW DS • 100 kW • ALT. FREQ. TO 7180 kHz
IRAN	
VO THE ISLAMIC REP, Sirjan	W • E Europe • 500 kW
TURKEY	
VOICE OF TURKEY, Ankara-Emirler	W • Europe • 500 kW
UNITED KINGDOM	
BBC, Rampisham	W M-F • S Europe • 500 kW
BBC, Via Meyerton, South Africa	C Africa & S Africa • 500 kW
BBC, Via Singapore	S Asia • 250 kW
	W Asia & S Asia • 250 kW
BBC, Via Thailand	S Asia • 250 kW
	M-Sa • S Asia • 250 kW
	Su • S Asia • 250 kW
BBC, Via Zyyi, Cyprus	W M-F • S Europe • 250 kW
USA	
†TRANS WORLD R, Via Swaziland	W • S Africa • 50 kW
VOA, Via Biblis, Germany	S M-F • E Europe & Mideast • 100 kW
VOA, Via Udon Thani, Thailand	W • E Asia • 250 kW
7210 ALBANIA	
†RADIO TIRANA, Shijak	⇦ • M-Sa • W Europe • 100 kW
BELARUS	
R BELARUS/R MINSK, Minsk	⇦ • N Europe • 100 kW
	⇦ • M-Sa • N Europe • 100 kW ⇦ • F • N Europe • 100 kW
	⇦ • Su • N Europe • 100 kW ⇦ • Tu/Th • N Europe • 100 kW
	⇦ • M/W/F-Su • N Europe • 100 kW ⇦ • W/Sa/Su • N Europe • 100 kW
	⇦ • Th • N Europe • 100 kW ⇦ • M-Th/Sa • N Europe • 100 kW
	⇦ • Tu • N Europe • 100 kW ⇦ • Su/F • N Europe • 100 kW
	⇦ • M • N Europe • 100 kW
	⇦ • Tu-Sa • N Europe • 100 kW ⇦ • Su/W/Sa • N Europe • 100 kW
CHINA	
†NEI MENGGU PBS, Hohhot	DS-MONGOLIAN • 50 kW
	W-M • DS-MONGOLIAN • 50 kW
CYPRUS	
†CYPRUS BC CORP, Zyyi	F-Su • Europe • 250 kW
GERMANY	
†DEUTSCHE WELLE, Wertachtal	W • S Europe • 500 kW
INDIA	
ALL INDIA RADIO, Kolkata	DS • 50 kW
	Irr • ENGLISH, ETC • DS • 50 kW
	Su • DS • 50 kW
	ENGLISH, ETC • DS • 50 kW
(con'd)	0 1 2 3 4 5 6 7 8 9 10 11 12 13 14 15 16 17 18 19 20 21 22 23 24

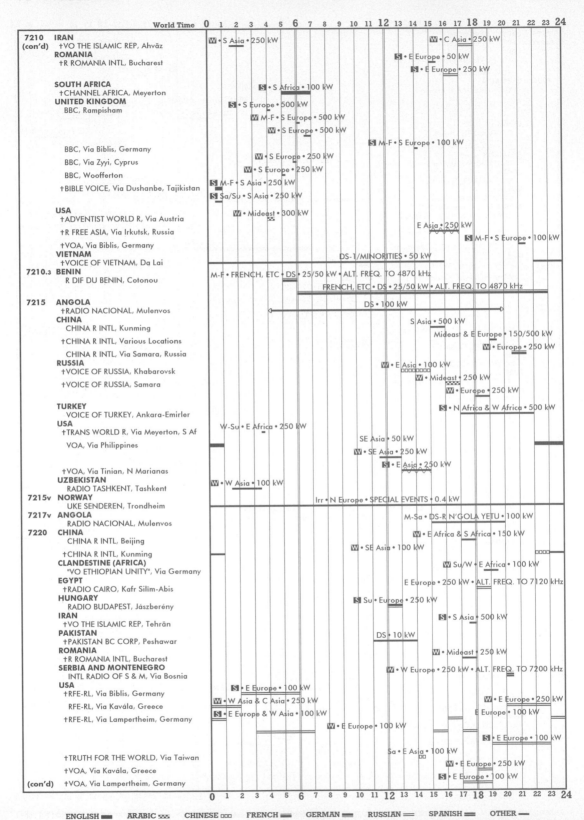

World Time 0 1 2 3 4 5 6 7 8 9 10 11 12 13 14 15 16 17 18 19 20 21 22 23 24

7210 **IRAN**
(con'd) †VO THE ISLAMIC REP, Ahvāz — W • S Asia • 250 kW ... W • C Asia • 250 kW
ROMANIA
 †R ROMANIA INTL, Bucharest — S • E Europe • 50 kW ; S • E Europe • 250 kW

SOUTH AFRICA
 †CHANNEL AFRICA, Meyerton — S • S Africa • 100 kW
UNITED KINGDOM
 BBC, Rampisham — S • S Europe • 500 kW ; W • M-F • S Europe • 500 kW ; W • S Europe • 500 kW ; S M-F • S Europe • 100 kW

 BBC, Via Biblis, Germany — W • S Europe • 250 kW
 BBC, Via Zyyi, Cyprus — W • S Europe • 250 kW
 BBC, Woofferton
 †BIBLE VOICE, Via Dushanbe, Tajikistan — S M-F • S Asia • 250 kW ; S Sa/Su • S Asia • 250 kW

USA
 †ADVENTIST WORLD R, Via Austria — W • Mideast • 300 kW
 †R FREE ASIA, Via Irkutsk, Russia — E Asia • 250 kW
 †VOA, Via Biblis, Germany — S M-F • S Europe • 100 kW
VIETNAM
 †VOICE OF VIETNAM, Da Lai — DS-1/MINORITIES • 50 kW
7210.3 BENIN
 R DIF DU BENIN, Cotonou — M-F • FRENCH, ETC • DS • 25/50 kW • ALT. FREQ. TO 4870 kHz ; FRENCH, ETC • DS • 25/50 kW • ALT. FREQ. TO 4870 kHz

7215 ANGOLA
 †RADIO NACIONAL, Mulenvos — DS • 100 kW
CHINA
 CHINA R INTL, Kunming — S Asia • 500 kW
 †CHINA R INTL, Various Locations — Mideast & E Europe • 150/500 kW ; W • Europe • 250 kW
 CHINA R INTL, Via Samara, Russia
RUSSIA
 †VOICE OF RUSSIA, Khabarovsk — W • E Asia • 100 kW ; W • Mideast • 250 kW
 †VOICE OF RUSSIA, Samara — W • Europe • 250 kW

TURKEY
 VOICE OF TURKEY, Ankara-Emirler — S • N Africa & W Africa • 500 kW
USA
 †TRANS WORLD R, Via Meyerton, S Af — W-Su • E Africa • 250 kW
 VOA, Via Philippines — SE Asia • 50 kW ; W • SE Asia • 250 kW ; S • E Asia • 250 kW

 †VOA, Via Tinian, N Marianas
UZBEKISTAN
 RADIO TASHKENT, Tashkent — W • W Asia • 100 kW
7215v NORWAY
 UKE SENDEREN, Trondheim — Irr • N Europe • SPECIAL EVENTS • 0.4 kW
7217v ANGOLA
 RADIO NACIONAL, Mulenvos — M-Sa • DS-R N'GOLA YETU • 100 kW
7220 CHINA
 CHINA R INTL, Beijing — W • E Africa & S Africa • 150 kW
 †CHINA R INTL, Kunming — W • SE Asia • 100 kW
CLANDESTINE (AFRICA)
 "VO ETHIOPIAN UNITY", Via Germany — W Su/W • E Africa • 100 kW
EGYPT
 †RADIO CAIRO, Kafr Silim-Abis — E Europe • 250 kW • ALT. FREQ. TO 7120 kHz
HUNGARY
 RADIO BUDAPEST, Jászberény — S Su • Europe • 250 kW
IRAN
 †VO THE ISLAMIC REP, Tehrān — S • S Asia • 500 kW
PAKISTAN
 †PAKISTAN BC CORP, Peshawar — DS • 10 kW
ROMANIA
 †R ROMANIA INTL, Bucharest — W • Mideast • 250 kW
SERBIA AND MONTENEGRO
 INTL RADIO OF S & M, Via Bosnia — W • W Europe • 250 kW • ALT. FREQ. TO 7200 kHz
USA
 †RFE-RL, Via Biblis, Germany — S • E Europe • 100 kW ; W • E Europe • 250 kW
 RFE-RL, Via Kavála, Greece — W • W Asia & C Asia • 250 kW ; E Europe • 100 kW
 †RFE-RL, Via Lampertheim, Germany — S • E Europe & W Asia • 100 kW ; W • E Europe • 100 kW ; S • E Europe • 100 kW

 †TRUTH FOR THE WORLD, Via Taiwan — Sa • E Asia • 100 kW
 †VOA, Via Kavála, Greece — W • E Europe • 250 kW
(con'd) †VOA, Via Lampertheim, Germany — S • E Europe • 100 kW

0 1 2 3 4 5 6 7 8 9 10 11 12 13 14 15 16 17 18 19 20 21 22 23 24

ENGLISH ▬ ARABIC ▨ CHINESE ▫▫▫ FRENCH ▬ GERMAN ▬ RUSSIAN ═ SPANISH ▬ OTHER ▬

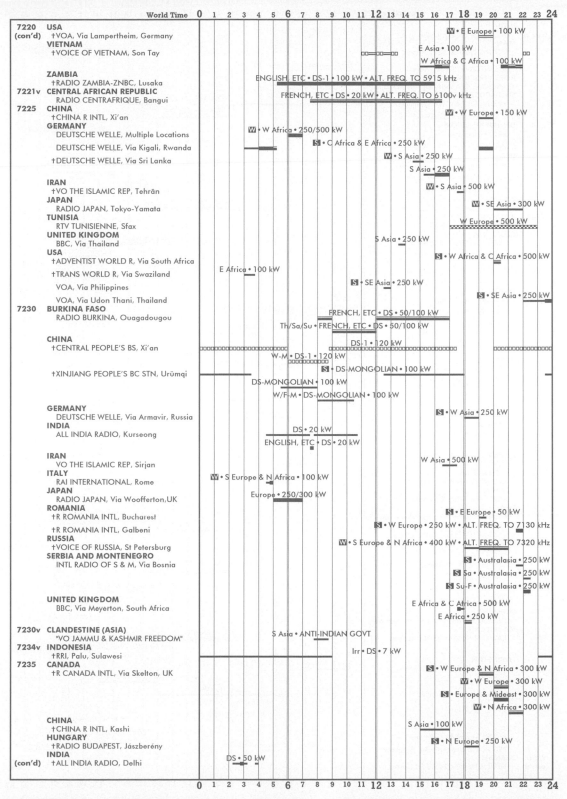

World Time 0 1 2 3 4 5 6 7 8 9 10 11 12 13 14 15 16 17 18 19 20 21 22 23 24

Freq	Country / Station	Details
7220 (con'd)	USA †VOA, Via Lampertheim, Germany	W • E Europe • 100 kW
	VIETNAM †VOICE OF VIETNAM, Son Tay	E Asia • 100 kW / W Africa & C Africa • 100 kW
	ZAMBIA †RADIO ZAMBIA-ZNBC, Lusaka	ENGLISH, ETC • DS-1 • 100 kW • ALT. FREQ. TO 5915 kHz
7221v	CENTRAL AFRICAN REPUBLIC RADIO CENTRAFRIQUE, Bangui	FRENCH, ETC • DS • 20 kW • ALT. FREQ. TO 6100v kHz
7225	CHINA †CHINA R INTL, Xi'an	W • W Europe • 150 kW
	GERMANY DEUTSCHE WELLE, Multiple Locations	W • W Africa • 250/500 kW
	DEUTSCHE WELLE, Via Kigali, Rwanda	S • C Africa & E Africa • 250 kW
	†DEUTSCHE WELLE, Via Sri Lanka	W • S Asia • 250 kW / S Asia • 250 kW
	IRAN †VO THE ISLAMIC REP, Tehrān	W • S Asia • 500 kW
	JAPAN RADIO JAPAN, Tokyo-Yamata	W • SE Asia • 300 kW
	TUNISIA RTV TUNISIENNE, Sfax	W Europe • 500 kW
	UNITED KINGDOM BBC, Via Thailand	S Asia • 250 kW
	USA †ADVENTIST WORLD R, Via South Africa	S • W Africa & C Africa • 500 kW
	†TRANS WORLD R, Via Swaziland	E Africa • 100 kW
	VOA, Via Philippines	S • SE Asia • 250 kW
	VOA, Via Udon Thani, Thailand	S • SE Asia • 250 kW
7230	BURKINA FASO RADIO BURKINA, Ouagadougou	FRENCH, ETC • DS • 50/100 kW / Th/Sa/Su • FRENCH, ETC • DS • 50/100 kW
	CHINA †CENTRAL PEOPLE'S BS, Xi'an	DS-1 • 120 kW / W-M • DS-1 • 120 kW
	†XINJIANG PEOPLE'S BC STN, Urümqi	S • DS-MONGOLIAN • 100 kW / DS-MONGOLIAN • 100 kW / W/F-M • DS-MONGOLIAN • 100 kW
	GERMANY DEUTSCHE WELLE, Via Armavir, Russia	S • W Asia • 250 kW
	INDIA ALL INDIA RADIO, Kurseong	DS • 20 kW / ENGLISH, ETC • DS • 20 kW
	IRAN VO THE ISLAMIC REP, Sirjan	W Asia • 500 kW
	ITALY RAI INTERNATIONAL, Rome	W • S Europe & N Africa • 100 kW
	JAPAN RADIO JAPAN, Via Woofferton, UK	Europe • 250/300 kW
	ROMANIA †R ROMANIA INTL, Bucharest	S • E Europe • 50 kW
	†R ROMANIA INTL, Galbeni	S • W Europe • 250 kW • ALT. FREQ. TO 7130 kHz
	RUSSIA †VOICE OF RUSSIA, St Petersburg	W • S Europe & N Africa • 400 kW • ALT. FREQ. TO 7320 kHz
	SERBIA AND MONTENEGRO INTL RADIO OF S & M, Via Bosnia	S • Australasia • 250 kW / S Sa • Australasia • 250 kW / S Su-F • Australasia • 250 kW
	UNITED KINGDOM BBC, Via Meyerton, South Africa	E Africa & C Africa • 500 kW / E Africa • 250 kW
7230v	CLANDESTINE (ASIA) "VO JAMMU & KASHMIR FREEDOM"	S Asia • ANTI-INDIAN GOVT
7234v	INDONESIA †RRI, Palu, Sulawesi	Irr • DS • 7 kW
7235	CANADA †R CANADA INTL, Via Skelton, UK	S • W Europe & N Africa • 300 kW / W • W Europe • 300 kW / S • Europe & Mideast • 300 kW / W • N Africa • 300 kW
	CHINA †CHINA R INTL, Kashi	S Asia • 100 kW
	HUNGARY †RADIO BUDAPEST, Jászberény	S • N Europe • 250 kW
(con'd)	INDIA †ALL INDIA RADIO, Delhi	DS • 50 kW

0 1 2 3 4 5 6 7 8 9 10 11 12 13 14 15 16 17 18 19 20 21 22 23 24

SEASONAL S OR W   1-HR TIMESHIFT MIDYEAR ⇦ OR ⇨   JAMMING / OR /\   EARLIEST HEARD ◁   LATEST HEARD ▷   NEW FOR 2005 †

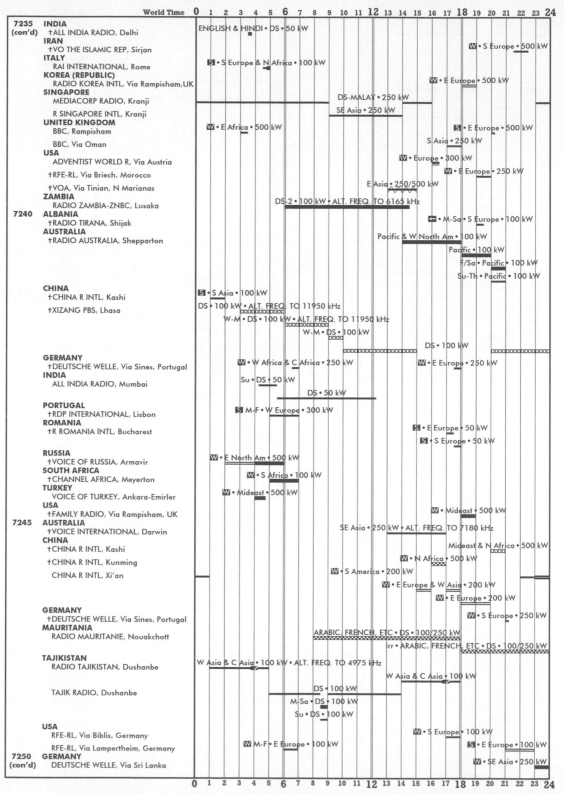

World Time	0 1 2 3 4 5 6 7 8 9 10 11 12 13 14 15 16 17 18 19 20 21 22 23 24

7235 **INDIA**
(con'd) †ALL INDIA RADIO, Delhi — ENGLISH & HINDI • DS • 50 kW
IRAN
†VO THE ISLAMIC REP, Sirjan — W • S Europe • 500 kW
ITALY
RAI INTERNATIONAL, Rome — S • S Europe & N Africa • 100 kW
KOREA (REPUBLIC)
RADIO KOREA INTL, Via Rampisham, UK — W • E Europe • 500 kW
SINGAPORE
MEDIACORP RADIO, Kranji — DS-MALAY • 250 kW
R SINGAPORE INTL, Kranji — SE Asia • 250 kW
UNITED KINGDOM
BBC, Rampisham — W • E Africa • 500 kW / S • E Europe • 500 kW
BBC, Via Oman — S Asia • 250 kW
USA
ADVENTIST WORLD R, Via Austria — W • Europe • 300 kW
†RFE-RL, Via Briech, Morocco — W • E Europe • 250 kW
†VOA, Via Tinian, N Marianas — E Asia • 250/500 kW
ZAMBIA
RADIO ZAMBIA-ZNBC, Lusaka — DS-2 • 100 kW • ALT. FREQ. TO 6165 kHz
7240 **ALBANIA**
†RADIO TIRANA, Shijak — M-Sa • S Europe • 100 kW
AUSTRALIA
†RADIO AUSTRALIA, Shepparton — Pacific & W North Am • 100 kW
— Pacific • 100 kW
— F/Sa • Pacific • 100 kW
— Su-Th • Pacific • 100 kW
CHINA
†CHINA R INTL, Kashi — S • S Asia • 100 kW
†XIZANG PBS, Lhasa — DS • 100 kW • ALT. FREQ. TO 11950 kHz
— W-M • DS • 100 kW • ALT. FREQ. TO 11950 kHz
— W-M • DS • 100 kW
— DS • 100 kW
GERMANY
†DEUTSCHE WELLE, Via Sines, Portugal — W • W Africa & C Africa • 250 kW / W • E Europe • 250 kW
INDIA
ALL INDIA RADIO, Mumbai — Su • DS • 50 kW
— DS • 50 kW
PORTUGAL
†RDP INTERNATIONAL, Lisbon — S • M-F • W Europe • 300 kW
ROMANIA
†R ROMANIA INTL, Bucharest — S • E Europe • 50 kW
— S • S Europe • 50 kW
RUSSIA
†VOICE OF RUSSIA, Armavir — W • E North Am • 500 kW
SOUTH AFRICA
†CHANNEL AFRICA, Meyerton — W • S Africa • 100 kW
TURKEY
VOICE OF TURKEY, Ankara-Emirler — W • Mideast • 500 kW
USA
†FAMILY RADIO, Via Rampisham, UK — W • Mideast • 500 kW
7245 **AUSTRALIA**
†VOICE INTERNATIONAL, Darwin — SE Asia • 250 kW • ALT. FREQ. TO 7180 kHz
CHINA
†CHINA R INTL, Kashi — Mideast & N Africa • 500 kW
†CHINA R INTL, Kunming — W • N Africa • 500 kW
CHINA R INTL, Xi'an — W • S America • 200 kW
— W • E Europe & W Asia • 200 kW
— W • E Europe • 200 kW
GERMANY
†DEUTSCHE WELLE, Via Sines, Portugal — W • S Europe • 250 kW
MAURITANIA
RADIO MAURITANIE, Nouakchott — ARABIC, FRENCH, ETC • DS • 100/250 kW
— Irr • ARABIC, FRENCH, ETC • DS • 100/250 kW
TAJIKISTAN
RADIO TAJIKISTAN, Dushanbe — W Asia & C Asia • 100 kW • ALT. FREQ. TO 4975 kHz
— W Asia & C Asia • 100 kW
TAJIK RADIO, Dushanbe — DS • 100 kW
— M-Sa • DS • 100 kW
— Su • DS • 100 kW
USA
RFE-RL, Via Biblis, Germany — W • S Europe • 100 kW
RFE-RL, Via Lampertheim, Germany — W • M-F • E Europe • 100 kW
— S • E Europe • 100 kW
7250 **GERMANY**
(con'd) DEUTSCHE WELLE, Via Sri Lanka — W • SE Asia • 250 kW

World Time	0 1 2 3 4 5 6 7 8 9 10 11 12 13 14 15 16 17 18 19 20 21 22 23 24

ENGLISH ▬   ARABIC ﹏   CHINESE ▯▯▯   FRENCH ▬▬   GERMAN ▬   RUSSIAN ▭▭   SPANISH ▬   OTHER ▬

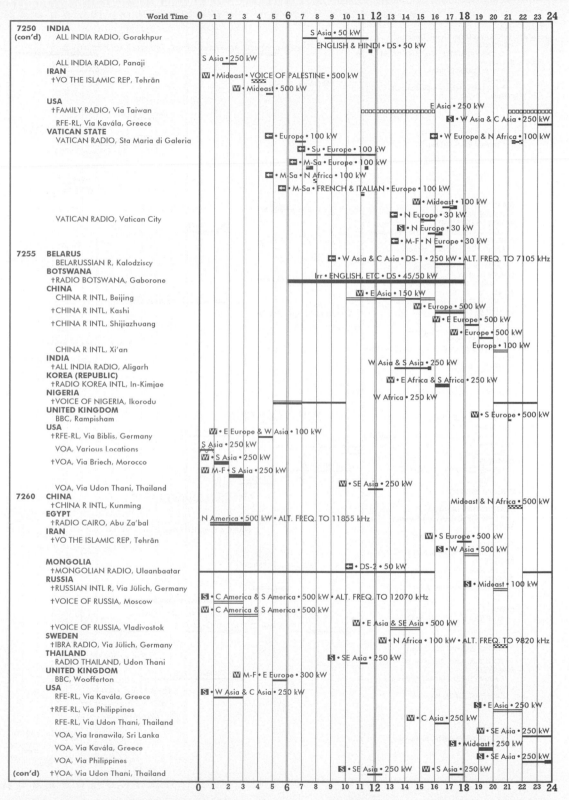

World Time   0 1 2 3 4 5 6 7 8 9 10 11 12 13 14 15 16 17 18 19 20 21 22 23 24

7250   **INDIA**
(con'd)   ALL INDIA RADIO, Gorakhpur   S Asia • 50 kW
                                  ENGLISH & HINDI • DS • 50 kW
       ALL INDIA RADIO, Panaji   S Asia • 250 kW
      IRAN
       †VO THE ISLAMIC REP, Tehrān   W • Mideast • VOICE OF PALESTINE • 500 kW
                           W • Mideast • 500 kW
      USA
       †FAMILY RADIO, Via Taiwan   E Asia • 250 kW
       RFE-RL, Via Kavála, Greece   S • W Asia & C Asia • 250 kW
      VATICAN STATE
       VATICAN RADIO, Sta Maria di Galeria   • Europe • 100 kW   • W Europe & N Africa • 100 kW
                        • Su • Europe • 100 kW
                       • M-Sa • Europe • 100 kW
                 • M-Sa • N Africa • 100 kW
                   • M-Sa • FRENCH & ITALIAN • Europe • 100 kW
                              W • Mideast • 100 kW
       VATICAN RADIO, Vatican City   • N Europe • 30 kW
                            S • N Europe • 30 kW
                          • M-F • N Europe • 30 kW

7255   **BELARUS**
       BELARUSSIAN R, Kalodziscy   • W Asia & C Asia • DS-1 • 250 kW • ALT. FREQ. TO 7105 kHz
      BOTSWANA
       †RADIO BOTSWANA, Gaborone   Irr • ENGLISH, ETC • DS • 45/50 kW
      CHINA
       †CHINA R INTL, Beijing   W • E Asia • 150 kW
       †CHINA R INTL, Kashi   W • Europe • 500 kW
       †CHINA R INTL, Shijiazhuang   W • E Europe • 500 kW
                               W • Europe • 500 kW
       CHINA R INTL, Xi'an   Europe • 100 kW
      INDIA
       †ALL INDIA RADIO, Aligarh   W Asia & S Asia • 250 kW
      KOREA (REPUBLIC)
       †RADIO KOREA INTL, In-Kimjae   W • E Africa & S Africa • 250 kW
      NIGERIA
       †VOICE OF NIGERIA, Ikorodu   W Africa • 250 kW
      UNITED KINGDOM
       BBC, Rampisham   W • S Europe • 500 kW
      USA
       †RFE-RL, Via Biblis, Germany   W • E Europe & W Asia • 100 kW
       VOA, Various Locations   S Asia • 250 kW
       †VOA, Via Briech, Morocco   W • S Asia • 250 kW
                      W M-F • S Asia • 250 kW
       VOA, Via Udon Thani, Thailand   W • SE Asia • 250 kW

7260   **CHINA**
       †CHINA R INTL, Kunming   Mideast & N Africa • 500 kW
      EGYPT
       †RADIO CAIRO, Abu Za'bal   N America • 500 kW • ALT. FREQ. TO 11855 kHz
      IRAN
       †VO THE ISLAMIC REP, Tehrān   W • S Europe • 500 kW
                              S • W Asia • 500 kW
      MONGOLIA
       †MONGOLIAN RADIO, Ulaanbaatar   • DS-2 • 50 kW
      RUSSIA
       †RUSSIAN INTL R, Via Jülich, Germany   S • Mideast • 100 kW
       †VOICE OF RUSSIA, Moscow   S • C America & S America • 500 kW • ALT. FREQ. TO 12070 kHz
                      W • C America & S America • 500 kW
       †VOICE OF RUSSIA, Vladivostok   W • E Asia & SE Asia • 500 kW
      SWEDEN
       †IBRA RADIO, Via Jülich, Germany   W • N Africa • 100 kW • ALT. FREQ. TO 9820 kHz
      THAILAND
       RADIO THAILAND, Udon Thani   S • SE Asia • 250 kW
      UNITED KINGDOM
       BBC, Woofferton   W M-F • E Europe • 300 kW
      USA
       RFE-RL, Via Kavála, Greece   S • W Asia & C Asia • 250 kW
       †RFE-RL, Via Philippines   S • E Asia • 250 kW
       RFE-RL, Via Udon Thani, Thailand   W • C Asia • 250 kW
       VOA, Via Iranawila, Sri Lanka   W • SE Asia • 250 kW
       VOA, Via Kavála, Greece   S • Mideast • 250 kW
       VOA, Via Philippines   S • SE Asia • 250 kW
      (con'd)   †VOA, Via Udon Thani, Thailand   S • SE Asia • 250 kW   W • S Asia • 250 kW

      0 1 2 3 4 5 6 7 8 9 10 11 12 13 14 15 16 17 18 19 20 21 22 23 24

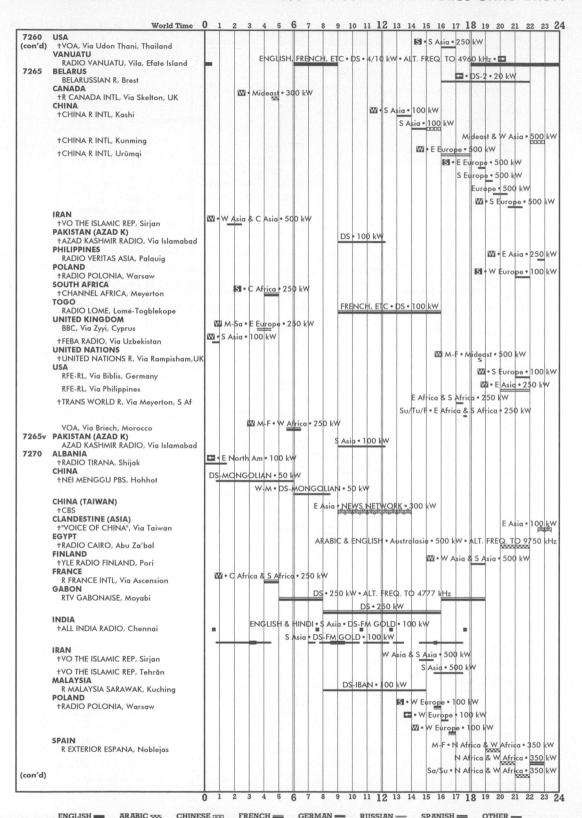

World Time 0 1 2 3 4 5 6 7 8 9 10 11 12 13 14 15 16 17 18 19 20 21 22 23 24

7260   **USA**
(con'd)   †VOA, Via Udon Thani, Thailand   S • S Asia • 250 kW
           VANUATU
           RADIO VANUATU, Vila, Efate Island   ENGLISH, FRENCH, ETC • DS • 4/10 kW • ALT. FREQ. TO 4960 kHz •
7265   **BELARUS**
           BELARUSSIAN R, Brest   DS-2 • 20 kW
           CANADA
           †R CANADA INTL, Via Skelton, UK   W • Mideast • 300 kW
           CHINA
           †CHINA R INTL, Kashi   W • S Asia • 100 kW
                                                  S Asia • 100 kW

           †CHINA R INTL, Kunming   Mideast & W Asia • 500 kW
           †CHINA R INTL, Urümqi   W • E Europe • 500 kW
                                                       S • E Europe • 500 kW
                                                       S Europe • 500 kW
                                                       Europe • 500 kW
                                                       W • S Europe • 500 kW

           IRAN
           †VO THE ISLAMIC REP, Sirjan   W • W Asia & C Asia • 500 kW
           PAKISTAN (AZAD K)
           †AZAD KASHMIR RADIO, Via Islamabad   DS • 100 kW
           PHILIPPINES
           RADIO VERITAS ASIA, Palauig   W • E Asia • 250 kW
           POLAND
           †RADIO POLONIA, Warsaw   S • W Europe • 100 kW
           SOUTH AFRICA
           †CHANNEL AFRICA, Meyerton   S • C Africa • 250 kW
           TOGO
           RADIO LOME, Lomé-Togblekope   FRENCH, ETC • DS • 100 kW
           UNITED KINGDOM
           BBC, Via Zyyi, Cyprus   W • M-Sa • E Europe • 250 kW
           †FEBA RADIO, Via Uzbekistan   W • S Asia • 100 kW
           UNITED NATIONS
           †UNITED NATIONS R, Via Rampisham,UK   W • M-F • Mideast • 500 kW
           USA
           RFE-RL, Via Biblis, Germany   W • S Europe • 100 kW
           RFE-RL, Via Philippines   W • E Asia • 250 kW
           †TRANS WORLD R, Via Meyerton, S Af   E Africa & S Africa • 250 kW
                                                    Su/Tu/F • E Africa & S Africa • 250 kW
           VOA, Via Briech, Morocco   W • M-F • W Africa • 250 kW
7265v **PAKISTAN (AZAD K)**
           AZAD KASHMIR RADIO, Via Islamabad   S Asia • 100 kW
7270   **ALBANIA**
           †RADIO TIRANA, Shijak   • E North Am • 100 kW
           CHINA
           †NEI MENGGU PBS, Hohhot   DS-MONGOLIAN • 50 kW
                                              W-M • DS-MONGOLIAN • 50 kW

           CHINA (TAIWAN)
           †CBS   E Asia • NEWS NETWORK • 300 kW
           CLANDESTINE (ASIA)
           †"VOICE OF CHINA", Via Taiwan   E Asia • 100 kW
           EGYPT
           †RADIO CAIRO, Abu Za'bal   ARABIC & ENGLISH • Australasia • 500 kW • ALT. FREQ. TO 9750 kHz
           FINLAND
           †YLE RADIO FINLAND, Pori   W • W Asia & S Asia • 500 kW
           FRANCE
           R FRANCE INTL, Via Ascension   W • C Africa & S Africa • 250 kW
           GABON
           RTV GABONAISE, Moyabi   DS • 250 kW • ALT. FREQ. TO 4777 kHz
                                                DS • 250 kW
           INDIA
           †ALL INDIA RADIO, Chennai   ENGLISH & HINDI • S Asia • DS-FM GOLD • 100 kW
                                          S Asia • DS-FM GOLD • 100 kW
           IRAN
           †VO THE ISLAMIC REP, Sirjan   W Asia & S Asia • 500 kW
           †VO THE ISLAMIC REP, Tehrān   S Asia • 500 kW
           MALAYSIA
           R MALAYSIA SARAWAK, Kuching   DS-IBAN • 100 kW
           POLAND
           †RADIO POLONIA, Warsaw   S • W Europe • 100 kW
                                                   • W Europe • 100 kW
                                                   W • W Europe • 100 kW

           SPAIN
           R EXTERIOR ESPANA, Noblejas   M-F • N Africa & W Africa • 350 kW
                                                   N Africa & W Africa • 350 kW
                                                   Sa/Su • N Africa & W Africa • 350 kW
(con'd)

0 1 2 3 4 5 6 7 8 9 10 11 12 13 14 15 16 17 18 19 20 21 22 23 24

ENGLISH ▬▬   ARABIC ▧▧▧   CHINESE □□□   FRENCH ▬▬   GERMAN ▬▬   RUSSIAN ══   SPANISH ▬▬   OTHER ▬▬

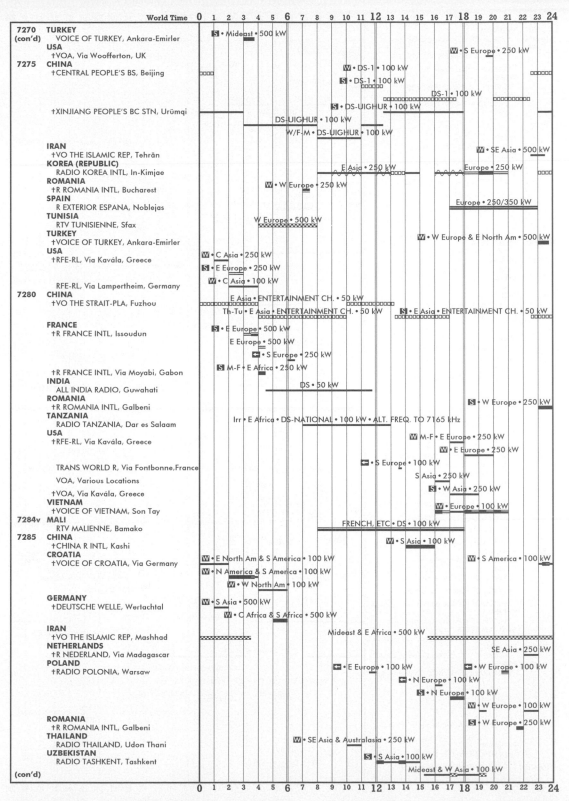

World Time 0 1 2 3 4 5 6 7 8 9 10 11 12 13 14 15 16 17 18 19 20 21 22 23 24

kHz	Country / Station	Schedule
7270 (con'd)	**TURKEY**	
	VOICE OF TURKEY, Ankara-Emirler	[S] • Mideast • 500 kW
	USA	
	†VOA, Via Woofferton, UK	[W] • S Europe • 250 kW
7275	**CHINA**	
	†CENTRAL PEOPLE'S BS, Beijing	[W] • DS-1 • 100 kW
		[S] • DS-1 • 100 kW
		DS-1 • 100 kW
	†XINJIANG PEOPLE'S BC STN, Urümqi	[S] • DS-UIGHUR • 100 kW
		DS-UIGHUR • 100 kW
		W/F-M • DS-UIGHUR • 100 kW
	IRAN	
	†VO THE ISLAMIC REP, Tehrān	[W] • SE Asia • 500 kW
	KOREA (REPUBLIC)	
	RADIO KOREA INTL, In-Kimjae	E Asia • 250 kW
		Europe • 250 kW
	ROMANIA	
	†R ROMANIA INTL, Bucharest	[W] • W Europe • 250 kW
	SPAIN	
	R EXTERIOR ESPANA, Noblejas	Europe • 250/350 kW
	TUNISIA	
	RTV TUNISIENNE, Sfax	W Europe • 500 kW
	TURKEY	
	†VOICE OF TURKEY, Ankara-Emirler	[W] • W Europe & E North Am • 500 kW
	USA	
	†RFE-RL, Via Kavála, Greece	[W] • C Asia • 250 kW
		[S] • E Europe • 250 kW
	RFE-RL, Via Lampertheim, Germany	[W] • C Asia • 100 kW
7280	**CHINA**	
	†VO THE STRAIT-PLA, Fuzhou	E Asia • ENTERTAINMENT CH. • 50 kW
		Th-Tu • E Asia • ENTERTAINMENT CH. • 50 kW
		[S] • E Asia • ENTERTAINMENT CH. • 50 kW
	FRANCE	
	†R FRANCE INTL, Issoudun	[S] • E Europe • 500 kW
		E Europe • 500 kW
		[←] • S Europe • 250 kW
	†R FRANCE INTL, Via Moyabi, Gabon	[S] M-F • E Africa • 250 kW
	INDIA	
	ALL INDIA RADIO, Guwahati	DS • 50 kW
	ROMANIA	
	†R ROMANIA INTL, Galbeni	[S] • W Europe • 250 kW
	TANZANIA	
	RADIO TANZANIA, Dar es Salaam	Irr • E Africa • DS-NATIONAL • 100 kW • ALT. FREQ. TO 7165 kHz
	USA	
	†RFE-RL, Via Kavála, Greece	[W] M-F • E Europe • 250 kW
		[W] • E Europe • 250 kW
	TRANS WORLD R, Via Fontbonne, France	[←] • S Europe • 100 kW
	VOA, Various Locations	S Asia • 250 kW
	†VOA, Via Kavála, Greece	[S] • W Asia • 250 kW
	VIETNAM	
	†VOICE OF VIETNAM, Son Tay	[W] • Europe • 100 kW
7284v	**MALI**	
	RTV MALIENNE, Bamako	FRENCH, ETC • DS • 100 kW
7285	**CHINA**	
	†CHINA R INTL, Kashi	[W] • S Asia • 100 kW
	CROATIA	
	†VOICE OF CROATIA, Via Germany	[W] • E North Am & S America • 100 kW
		[W] • S America • 100 kW
		[W] • N America & S America • 100 kW
		[W] • W North Am • 100 kW
	GERMANY	
	†DEUTSCHE WELLE, Wertachtal	[W] • S Asia • 500 kW
		[W] • C Africa & S Africa • 500 kW
	IRAN	
	†VO THE ISLAMIC REP, Mashhad	Mideast & E Africa • 500 kW
	NETHERLANDS	
	†R NEDERLAND, Via Madagascar	SE Asia • 250 kW
	POLAND	
	†RADIO POLONIA, Warsaw	[←] • E Europe • 100 kW
		[←] • W Europe • 100 kW
		[←] • N Europe • 100 kW
		[S] • N Europe • 100 kW
		[W] • W Europe • 100 kW
	ROMANIA	
	†R ROMANIA INTL, Galbeni	[S] • W Europe • 250 kW
	THAILAND	
	RADIO THAILAND, Udon Thani	[W] • SE Asia & Australasia • 250 kW
	UZBEKISTAN	
	RADIO TASHKENT, Tashkent	[S] • S Asia • 100 kW
(con'd)		Mideast & W Asia • 100 kW

0 1 2 3 4 5 6 7 8 9 10 11 12 13 14 15 16 17 18 19 20 21 22 23 24

SEASONAL [S] OR [W] 1-HR TIMESHIFT MIDYEAR [←] OR [→] JAMMING / OR /\ EARLIEST HEARD ◁ LATEST HEARD ▷ NEW FOR 2005 †

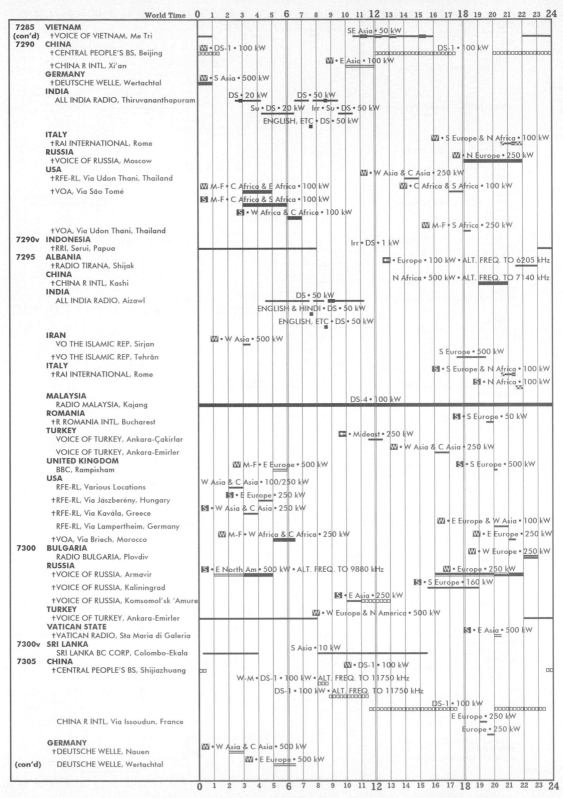

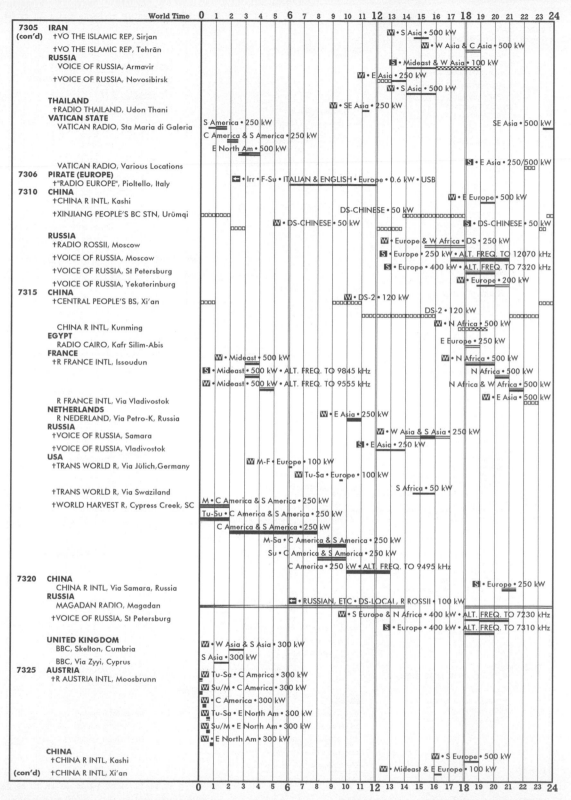

World Time 0 1 2 3 4 5 6 7 8 9 10 11 12 13 14 15 16 17 18 19 20 21 22 23 24

7305 **IRAN**
(con'd)   †VO THE ISLAMIC REP, Sirjan — Ⓦ • S Asia • 500 kW
          †VO THE ISLAMIC REP, Tehrān — Ⓦ • W Asia & C Asia • 500 kW
          RUSSIA
          VOICE OF RUSSIA, Armavir — Ⓢ • Mideast & W Asia • 100 kW
          †VOICE OF RUSSIA, Novosibirsk — Ⓦ • E Asia • 250 kW
                                         — Ⓦ • S Asia • 500 kW
          THAILAND
          †RADIO THAILAND, Udon Thani — Ⓦ • SE Asia • 250 kW
          VATICAN STATE
          VATICAN RADIO, Sta Maria di Galeria — S America • 250 kW
                                                SE Asia • 500 kW
                                                C America & S America • 250 kW
                                                E North Am • 500 kW
          VATICAN RADIO, Various Locations — Ⓢ • E Asia • 250/500 kW
7306 **PIRATE (EUROPE)**
          †"RADIO EUROPE", Pioltello, Italy — ⇆ • Irr • F-Su • ITALIAN & ENGLISH • Europe • 0.6 kW • USB
7310 **CHINA**
          †CHINA R INTL, Kashi — Ⓦ • E Europe • 500 kW
          †XINJIANG PEOPLE'S BC STN, Urümqi — DS-CHINESE • 50 kW
                                               Ⓦ • DS-CHINESE • 50 kW
                                               Ⓢ • DS-CHINESE • 50 kW
          RUSSIA
          †RADIO ROSSII, Moscow — Ⓦ • Europe & W Africa • DS • 250 kW
          †VOICE OF RUSSIA, Moscow — Ⓢ • Europe • 250 kW • ALT. FREQ. TO 12070 kHz
          †VOICE OF RUSSIA, St Petersburg — Ⓢ • Europe • 400 kW • ALT. FREQ. TO 7320 kHz
          †VOICE OF RUSSIA, Yekaterinburg — Ⓦ • Europe • 200 kW
7315 **CHINA**
          †CENTRAL PEOPLE'S BS, Xi'an — Ⓦ • DS-2 • 120 kW
                                         DS-2 • 120 kW
          CHINA R INTL, Kunming — Ⓦ • N Africa • 500 kW
          EGYPT
          RADIO CAIRO, Kafr Silīm-Abis — E Europe • 250 kW
          FRANCE
          †R FRANCE INTL, Issoudun — Ⓦ • Mideast • 500 kW
                                      Ⓦ • N Africa • 500 kW
                                      Ⓢ • Mideast • 500 kW • ALT. FREQ. TO 9845 kHz
                                      N Africa • 500 kW
                                      Ⓦ • Mideast • 500 kW • ALT. FREQ. TO 9555 kHz
                                      N Africa & W Africa • 500 kW
                                      Ⓦ • E Asia • 500 kW
          R FRANCE INTL, Via Vladivostok
          NETHERLANDS
          R NEDERLAND, Via Petro-K, Russia — Ⓦ • E Asia • 250 kW
          RUSSIA
          †VOICE OF RUSSIA, Samara — Ⓦ • W Asia & S Asia • 250 kW
          †VOICE OF RUSSIA, Vladivostok — Ⓢ • E Asia • 250 kW
          USA
          †TRANS WORLD R, Via Jülich, Germany — Ⓦ • M-F • Europe • 100 kW
                                                 Ⓦ • Tu-Sa • Europe • 100 kW
          †TRANS WORLD R, Via Swaziland — S Africa • 50 kW
          †WORLD HARVEST R, Cypress Creek, SC — M • C America & S America • 250 kW
                                                 Tu-Su • C America & S America • 250 kW
                                                 C America & S America • 250 kW
                                                 M-Sa • C America & S America • 250 kW
                                                 Su • C America & S America • 250 kW
                                                 C America • 250 kW • ALT. FREQ. TO 9495 kHz
7320 **CHINA**
          CHINA R INTL, Via Samara, Russia — Ⓢ • Europe • 250 kW
          RUSSIA
          MAGADAN RADIO, Magadan — ⇆ • RUSSIAN, ETC • DS-LOCAL, R ROSSII • 100 kW
          †VOICE OF RUSSIA, St Petersburg — Ⓦ • S Europe & N Africa • 400 kW • ALT. FREQ. TO 7230 kHz
                                             Ⓢ • Europe • 400 kW • ALT. FREQ. TO 7310 kHz
          UNITED KINGDOM
          BBC, Skelton, Cumbria — Ⓦ • W Asia & S Asia • 300 kW
          BBC, Via Zyyi, Cyprus — S Asia • 300 kW
7325 **AUSTRIA**
          †R AUSTRIA INTL, Moosbrunn — Ⓦ • Tu-Sa • C America • 300 kW
                                        Ⓦ • Su/M • C America • 300 kW
                                        Ⓦ • C America • 300 kW
                                        Ⓦ • Tu-Sa • E North Am • 300 kW
                                        Ⓦ • Su/M • E North Am • 300 kW
                                        Ⓦ • E North Am • 300 kW
          CHINA
          †CHINA R INTL, Kashi — Ⓦ • S Europe • 500 kW
(con'd)   †CHINA R INTL, Xi'an — Ⓦ • Mideast & E Europe • 100 kW

0 1 2 3 4 5 6 7 8 9 10 11 12 13 14 15 16 17 18 19 20 21 22 23 24

SEASONAL Ⓢ OR Ⓦ   1-HR TIMESHIFT MIDYEAR ⇆ OR ⇄   JAMMING / OR ∧   EARLIEST HEARD ◁   LATEST HEARD ▷   NEW FOR 2005 †

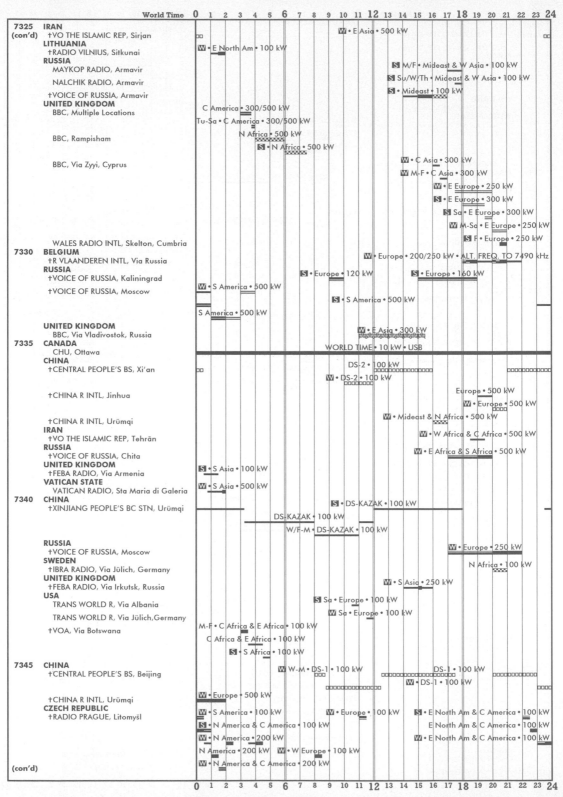

World Time	0 1 2 3 4 5 6 7 8 9 10 11 12 13 14 15 16 17 18 19 20 21 22 23 24
7325 IRAN	
(con'd) †VO THE ISLAMIC REP, Sirjan	W • E Asia • 500 kW
LITHUANIA	
†RADIO VILNIUS, Sitkunai	W • E North Am • 100 kW
RUSSIA	
MAYKOP RADIO, Armavir	S M/F • Mideast & W Asia • 100 kW
NALCHIK RADIO, Armavir	S Su/W/Th • Mideast & W Asia • 100 kW
†VOICE OF RUSSIA, Armavir	S • Mideast • 100 kW
UNITED KINGDOM	
BBC, Multiple Locations	C America • 300/500 kW
	Tu-Sa • C America • 300/500 kW
BBC, Rampisham	N Africa • 500 kW
	S • N Africa • 500 kW
BBC, Via Zyyi, Cyprus	W • C Asia • 300 kW
	W M-F • C Asia • 300 kW
	W • E Europe • 250 kW
	S • E Europe • 300 kW
	S Sa • E Europe • 300 kW
	W M-Sa • E Europe • 250 kW
	S F • E Europe • 250 kW
WALES RADIO INTL, Skelton, Cumbria	
7330 BELGIUM	
†R VLAANDEREN INTL, Via Russia	W • Europe • 200/250 kW • ALT. FREQ. TO 7490 kHz
RUSSIA	
†VOICE OF RUSSIA, Kaliningrad	S • Europe • 120 kW S • Europe • 160 kW
†VOICE OF RUSSIA, Moscow	W • S America • 500 kW
	S • S America • 500 kW
	S America • 500 kW
UNITED KINGDOM	
BBC, Via Vladivostok, Russia	W • E Asia • 300 kW
7335 CANADA	
CHU, Ottawa	WORLD TIME • 10 kW • USB
CHINA	
†CENTRAL PEOPLE'S BS, Xi'an	DS-2 • 100 kW
	W • DS-2 • 100 kW
†CHINA R INTL, Jinhua	Europe • 500 kW
	W • Europe • 500 kW
†CHINA R INTL, Ürümqi	W • Mideast & N Africa • 500 kW
IRAN	
†VO THE ISLAMIC REP, Tehrän	W • W Africa & C Africa • 500 kW
RUSSIA	
†VOICE OF RUSSIA, Chita	W • E Africa & S Africa • 500 kW
UNITED KINGDOM	
†FEBA RADIO, Via Armenia	S • S Asia • 100 kW
VATICAN STATE	
VATICAN RADIO, Sta Maria di Galeria	S • S Asia • 500 kW
7340 CHINA	
†XINJIANG PEOPLE'S BC STN, Ürümqi	S • DS-KAZAK • 100 kW
	DS-KAZAK • 100 kW
	W/F-M • DS-KAZAK • 100 kW
RUSSIA	
†VOICE OF RUSSIA, Moscow	W • Europe • 250 kW
SWEDEN	
†IBRA RADIO, Via Jülich, Germany	N Africa • 100 kW
UNITED KINGDOM	
†FEBA RADIO, Via Irkutsk, Russia	W • S Asia • 250 kW
USA	
TRANS WORLD R, Via Albania	S Sa • Europe • 100 kW
TRANS WORLD R, Via Jülich, Germany	W Sa • Europe • 100 kW
†VOA, Via Botswana	M-F • C Africa & E Africa • 100 kW
	C Africa & E Africa • 100 kW
	S • S Africa • 100 kW
7345 CHINA	
†CENTRAL PEOPLE'S BS, Beijing	W W-M • DS-1 • 100 kW DS-1 • 100 kW
	W • DS-1 • 100 kW
†CHINA R INTL, Ürümqi	W • Europe • 500 kW
CZECH REPUBLIC	
†RADIO PRAGUE, Litomyšl	W • S America • 100 kW W • Europe • 100 kW S • E North Am & C America • 100 kW
	S • N America & C America • 100 kW E North Am & C America • 100 kW
	W • N America • 200 kW W • E North Am & C America • 100 kW
	N America • 200 kW W • W Europe • 100 kW
(con'd)	W • N America & C America • 200 kW

	0 1 2 3 4 5 6 7 8 9 10 11 12 13 14 15 16 17 18 19 20 21 22 23 24

ENGLISH ▬▬   ARABIC ﹏﹏   CHINESE ▭▭▭   FRENCH ▬▬   GERMAN ▬▬   RUSSIAN ═══   SPANISH ▬▬   OTHER ▬▬

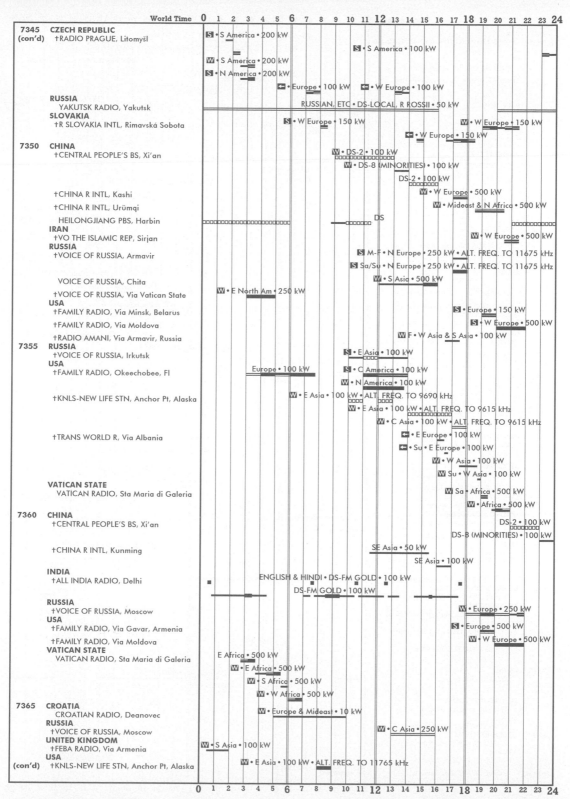

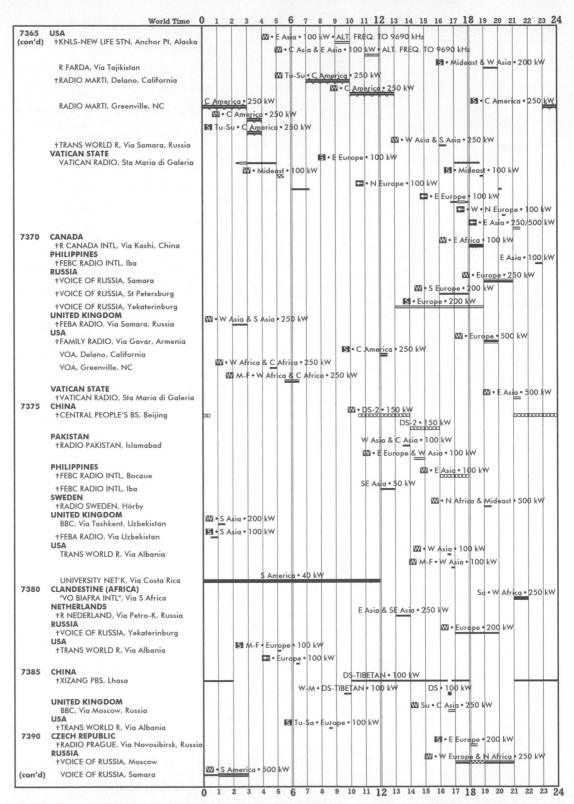

World Time 0 1 2 3 4 5 6 7 8 9 10 11 12 13 14 15 16 17 18 19 20 21 22 23 24

7365	USA
(con'd)	†KNLS-NEW LIFE STN, Anchor Pt, Alaska
	R FARDA, Via Tajikistan
	†RADIO MARTI, Delano, California
	RADIO MARTI, Greenville, NC
	†TRANS WORLD R, Via Samara, Russia
	VATICAN STATE
	VATICAN RADIO, Sta Maria di Galeria
7370	CANADA
	†R CANADA INTL, Via Kashi, China
	PHILIPPINES
	†FEBC RADIO INTL, Iba
	RUSSIA
	†VOICE OF RUSSIA, Samara
	†VOICE OF RUSSIA, St Petersburg
	†VOICE OF RUSSIA, Yekaterinburg
	UNITED KINGDOM
	†FEBA RADIO, Via Samara, Russia
	USA
	†FAMILY RADIO, Via Gavar, Armenia
	VOA, Delano, California
	VOA, Greenville, NC
	VATICAN STATE
	†VATICAN RADIO, Sta Maria di Galeria
7375	CHINA
	†CENTRAL PEOPLE'S BS, Beijing
	PAKISTAN
	†RADIO PAKISTAN, Islamabad
	PHILIPPINES
	†FEBC RADIO INTL, Bocaue
	†FEBC RADIO INTL, Iba
	SWEDEN
	†RADIO SWEDEN, Hörby
	UNITED KINGDOM
	BBC, Via Tashkent, Uzbekistan
	†FEBA RADIO, Via Uzbekistan
	USA
	TRANS WORLD R, Via Albania
	UNIVERSITY NET'K, Via Costa Rica
7380	CLANDESTINE (AFRICA)
	"VO BIAFRA INTL", Via S Africa
	NETHERLANDS
	†R NEDERLAND, Via Petro-K, Russia
	RUSSIA
	†VOICE OF RUSSIA, Yekaterinburg
	USA
	†TRANS WORLD R, Via Albania
7385	CHINA
	†XIZANG PBS, Lhasa
	UNITED KINGDOM
	BBC, Via Moscow, Russia
	USA
	†TRANS WORLD R, Via Albania
7390	CZECH REPUBLIC
	†RADIO PRAGUE, Via Novosibirsk, Russia
	RUSSIA
	†VOICE OF RUSSIA, Moscow
(con'd)	VOICE OF RUSSIA, Samara

W • E Asia • 100 kW • ALT. FREQ. TO 9690 kHz
W • C Asia & E Asia • 100 kW • ALT. FREQ. TO 9690 kHz
S • Mideast & W Asia • 200 kW
W Tu-Su • C America • 250 kW
W • C America • 250 kW
C America • 250 kW
W • C America • 250 kW
S Tu-Su • C America • 250 kW
S • C America • 250 kW
W • W Asia & S Asia • 250 kW
S • E Europe • 100 kW
W • Mideast • 100 kW
S • Mideast • 100 kW
• N Europe • 100 kW
• E Europe • 100 kW
• W • N Europe • 100 kW
• E Asia • 250/500 kW
W • E Africa • 100 kW
E Asia • 100 kW
W • Europe • 250 kW
W • S Europe • 200 kW
S • Europe • 200 kW
W • W Asia & S Asia • 250 kW
W • Europe • 500 kW
S • C America • 250 kW
W • W Africa & C Africa • 250 kW
W M-F • W Africa & C Africa • 250 kW
W • E Asia • 500 kW
W • DS-2 • 150 kW
DS-2 • 150 kW
W Asia & C Asia • 100 kW
W • E Europe & W Asia • 100 kW
W • E Asia • 100 kW
SE Asia • 50 kW
W • N Africa & Mideast • 500 kW
W • S Asia • 200 kW
S • S Asia • 100 kW
W • W Asia • 100 kW
W M-F • W Asia • 100 kW
S America • 40 kW
Sa • W Africa • 250 kW
E Asia & SE Asia • 250 kW
W • Europe • 200 kW
S M-F • Europe • 100 kW
• Europe • 100 kW
DS-TIBETAN • 100 kW
W-M • DS-TIBETAN • 100 kW
DS • 100 kW
W Su • C Asia • 250 kW
S Tu-Sa • Europe • 100 kW
S • E Europe • 200 kW
W • W Europe & N Africa • 250 kW
W • S America • 500 kW

0 1 2 3 4 5 6 7 8 9 10 11 12 13 14 15 16 17 18 19 20 21 22 23 24

ENGLISH ▬   ARABIC ⧓⧓⧓   CHINESE □□□   FRENCH ▬   GERMAN ▬   RUSSIAN ═   SPANISH ▬   OTHER ▬

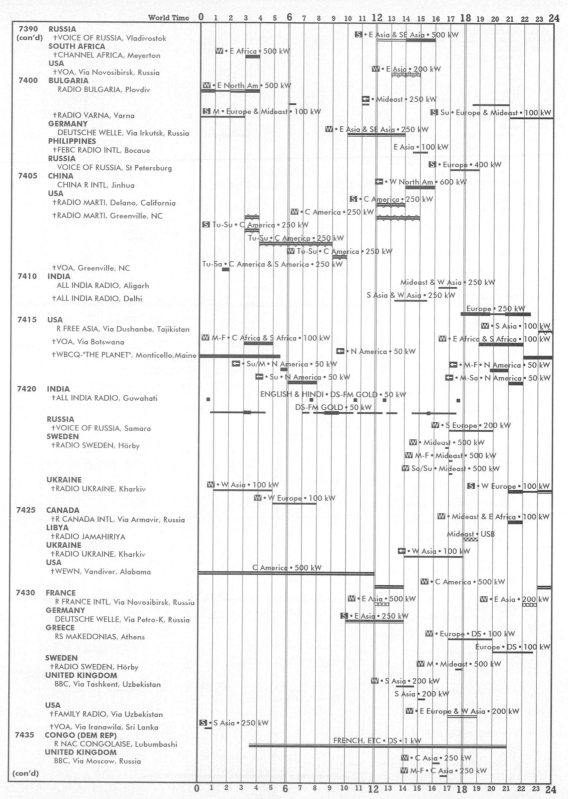

World Time 0 1 2 3 4 5 6 7 8 9 10 11 12 13 14 15 16 17 18 19 20 21 22 23 24

7390 (con'd)	RUSSIA
	†VOICE OF RUSSIA, Vladivostok	S • E Asia & SE Asia • 500 kW
	SOUTH AFRICA
	†CHANNEL AFRICA, Meyerton	W • E Africa • 500 kW
	USA
	†VOA, Via Novosibirsk, Russia	W • E Asia • 200 kW
7400	BULGARIA
	RADIO BULGARIA, Plovdiv	W • E North Am • 500 kW
		⮂ • Mideast • 250 kW
	†RADIO VARNA, Varna	S • M • Europe & Mideast • 100 kW S • Su • Europe & Mideast • 100 kW
	GERMANY
	DEUTSCHE WELLE, Via Irkutsk, Russia	W • E Asia & SE Asia • 250 kW
	PHILIPPINES
	†FEBC RADIO INTL, Bocaue	E Asia • 100 kW
	RUSSIA
	VOICE OF RUSSIA, St Petersburg	S • Europe • 400 kW
7405	CHINA
	CHINA R INTL, Jinhua	⮂ • W North Am • 600 kW
	USA
	†RADIO MARTI, Delano, California	S • C America • 250 kW
	†RADIO MARTI, Greenville, NC	W • C America • 250 kW
		S Tu-Su • C America • 250 kW
		Tu-Su • C America • 250 kW
		W Tu-Su • C America • 250 kW
	†VOA, Greenville, NC	Tu-Sa • C America & S America • 250 kW
7410	INDIA
	ALL INDIA RADIO, Aligarh	Mideast & W Asia • 250 kW
	†ALL INDIA RADIO, Delhi	S Asia & W Asia • 250 kW
7415	USA	Europe • 250 kW
	R FREE ASIA, Via Dushanbe, Tajikistan	W • S Asia • 100 kW
	†VOA, Via Botswana	W M-F • C Africa & S Africa • 100 kW W • E Africa & S Africa • 100 kW
	†WBCQ-"THE PLANET", Monticello, Maine	⮂ • N America • 50 kW
		⮂ • Su/M • N America • 50 kW ⮂ • M-F • N America • 50 kW
		⮂ • Su • N America • 50 kW ⮂ • M-Sa • N America • 50 kW
7420	INDIA
	†ALL INDIA RADIO, Guwahati	ENGLISH & HINDI • DS-FM GOLD • 50 kW
		DS-FM GOLD • 50 kW
	RUSSIA
	†VOICE OF RUSSIA, Samara	W • S Europe • 200 kW
	SWEDEN
	†RADIO SWEDEN, Hörby	W • Mideast • 500 kW
		W M-F • Mideast • 500 kW
		W Sa/Su • Mideast • 500 kW
	UKRAINE
	†RADIO UKRAINE, Kharkiv	W • W Asia • 100 kW S • W Europe • 100 kW
		W • W Europe • 100 kW
7425	CANADA
	†R CANADA INTL, Via Armavir, Russia	W • Mideast & E Africa • 100 kW
	LIBYA
	†RADIO JAMAHIRIYA	Mideast • USB
	UKRAINE
	†RADIO UKRAINE, Kharkiv	⮂ • W Asia • 100 kW
	USA
	†WEWN, Vandiver, Alabama	C America • 500 kW
7430	FRANCE	W • C America • 500 kW
	R FRANCE INTL, Via Novosibirsk, Russia	W • E Asia • 500 kW W • E Asia • 200 kW
	GERMANY
	DEUTSCHE WELLE, Via Petro-K, Russia	S • E Asia • 250 kW
	GREECE
	RS MAKEDONIAS, Athens	W • Europe • DS • 100 kW
		Europe • DS • 100 kW
	SWEDEN
	†RADIO SWEDEN, Hörby	W M • Mideast • 500 kW
	UNITED KINGDOM
	BBC, Via Tashkent, Uzbekistan	W • S Asia • 200 kW
		S Asia • 200 kW
	USA
	†FAMILY RADIO, Via Uzbekistan	W • E Europe & W Asia • 200 kW
	†VOA, Via Iranawila, Sri Lanka	S • S Asia • 250 kW
7435	CONGO (DEM REP)
	R NAC CONGOLAISE, Lubumbashi	FRENCH, ETC • DS • 1 kW
	UNITED KINGDOM
	BBC, Via Moscow, Russia	W • C Asia • 250 kW
		W M-F • C Asia • 250 kW
(con'd)

0 1 2 3 4 5 6 7 8 9 10 11 12 13 14 15 16 17 18 19 20 21 22 23 24

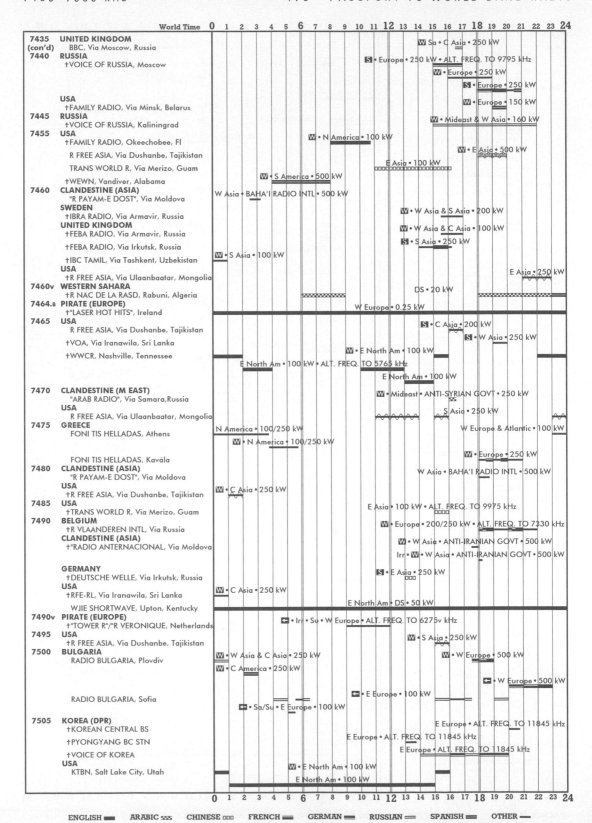

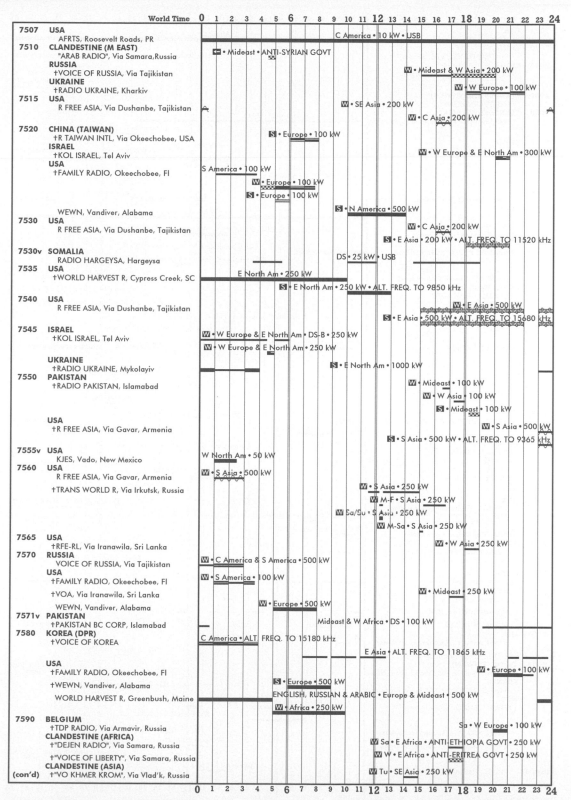

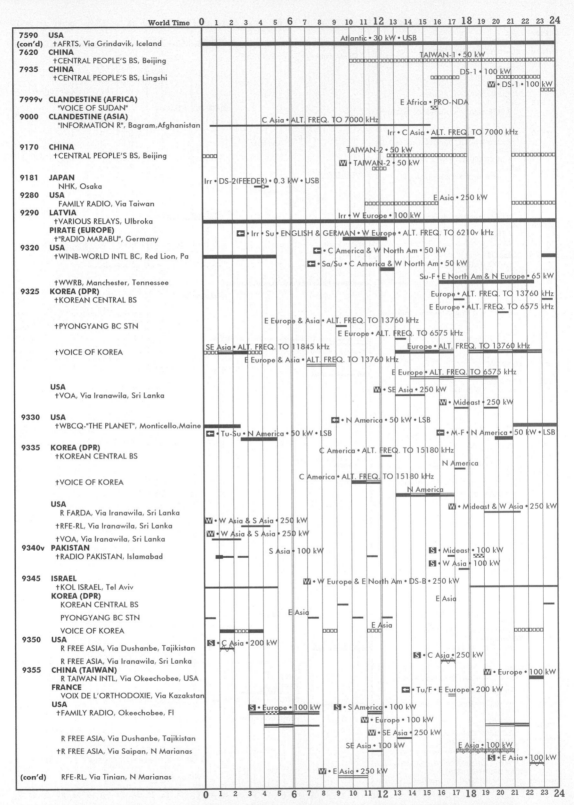

	World Time	0 1 2 3 4 5 6 7 8 9 10 11 12 13 14 15 16 17 18 19 20 21 22 23 24
7590 (con'd)	USA †AFRTS, Via Grindavik, Iceland	Atlantic • 30 kW • USB
7620	CHINA †CENTRAL PEOPLE'S BS, Beijing	TAIWAN-1 • 50 kW
7935	CHINA †CENTRAL PEOPLE'S BS, Lingshi	DS-1 • 100 kW
		W • DS-1 • 100 kW
7999v	CLANDESTINE (AFRICA) "VOICE OF SUDAN"	E Africa • PRO-NDA
9000	CLANDESTINE (ASIA) "INFORMATION R", Bagram, Afghanistan	C Asia • ALT. FREQ. TO 7000 kHz
		Irr • C Asia • ALT. FREQ. TO 7000 kHz
9170	CHINA †CENTRAL PEOPLE'S BS, Beijing	TAIWAN-2 • 50 kW
		W • TAIWAN-2 • 50 kW
9181	JAPAN NHK, Osaka	Irr • DS-2(FEEDER) • 0.3 kW • USB
9280	USA FAMILY RADIO, Via Taiwan	E Asia • 250 kW
9290	LATVIA †VARIOUS RELAYS, Ulbroka	Irr • W Europe • 100 kW
	PIRATE (EUROPE) †"RADIO MARABU", Germany	Irr • Su • ENGLISH & GERMAN • W Europe • ALT. FREQ. TO 6210v kHz
9320	USA †WINB-WORLD INTL BC, Red Lion, Pa	C America & W North Am • 50 kW
		Sa/Su • C America & W North Am • 50 kW
	†WWRB, Manchester, Tennessee	Su-F • E North Am & N Europe • 65 kW
9325	KOREA (DPR) †KOREAN CENTRAL BS	Europe • ALT. FREQ. TO 13760 kHz
		E Europe • ALT. FREQ. TO 6575 kHz
	†PYONGYANG BC STN	E Europe & Asia • ALT. FREQ. TO 13760 kHz
		E Europe • ALT. FREQ. TO 6575 kHz
	†VOICE OF KOREA	SE Asia • ALT. FREQ. TO 11845 kHz
		Europe • ALT. FREQ. TO 13760 kHz
		E Europe & Asia • ALT. FREQ. TO 13760 kHz
		E Europe • ALT. FREQ. TO 6575 kHz
	USA †VOA, Via Iranawila, Sri Lanka	W • SE Asia • 250 kW
		W • Mideast • 250 kW
9330	USA †WBCQ-"THE PLANET", Monticello, Maine	N America • 50 kW • LSB
		Tu-Su • N America • 50 kW • LSB
		M-F • N America • 50 kW • LSB
9335	KOREA (DPR) †KOREAN CENTRAL BS	C America • ALT. FREQ. TO 15180 kHz
		N America
	†VOICE OF KOREA	C America • ALT. FREQ. TO 15180 kHz
		N America
	USA R FARDA, Via Iranwila, Sri Lanka	W • Mideast & W Asia • 250 kW
	†RFE-RL, Via Iranawila, Sri Lanka	W • W Asia & S Asia • 250 kW
	†VOA, Via Iranawila, Sri Lanka	W • W Asia & S Asia • 250 kW
9340v	PAKISTAN †RADIO PAKISTAN, Islamabad	S Asia • 100 kW
		S • Mideast • 100 kW
		S • W Asia • 100 kW
9345	ISRAEL †KOL ISRAEL, Tel Aviv	W • W Europe & E North Am • DS-B • 250 kW
	KOREA (DPR) KOREAN CENTRAL BS	E Asia
	PYONGYANG BC STN	E Asia
	VOICE OF KOREA	E Asia
9350	USA R FREE ASIA, Via Dushanbe, Tajikistan	S • C Asia • 200 kW
	R FREE ASIA, Via Iranawila, Sri Lanka	S • C Asia • 250 kW
9355	CHINA (TAIWAN) R TAIWAN INTL, Via Okeechobee, USA	W • Europe • 100 kW
	FRANCE VOIX DE L'ORTHODOXIE, Via Kazakstan	Tu/F • E Europe • 200 kW
	USA †FAMILY RADIO, Okeechobee, Fl	S • Europe • 100 kW
		S • S America • 100 kW
		W • Europe • 100 kW
		W • SE Asia • 250 kW
	R FREE ASIA, Via Dushanbe, Tajikistan	SE Asia • 100 kW
	†R FREE ASIA, Via Saipan, N Marianas	E Asia • 100 kW
		S • E Asia • 100 kW
(con'd)	RFE-RL, Via Tinian, N Marianas	W • E Asia • 250 kW

0 1 2 3 4 5 6 7 8 9 10 11 12 13 14 15 16 17 18 19 20 21 22 23 24

ENGLISH ▬▬   ARABIC ⌇⌇⌇   CHINESE ▫▫▫   FRENCH ══   GERMAN ▬▬   RUSSIAN ══   SPANISH ══   OTHER ──

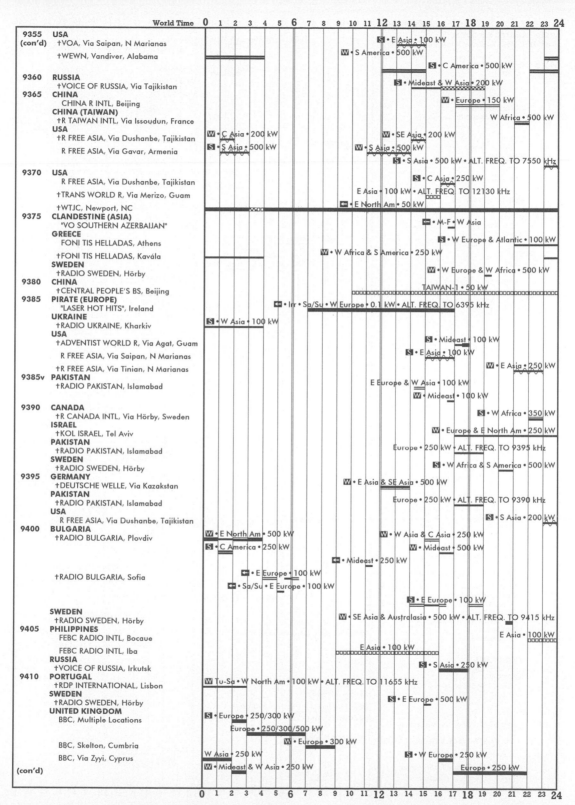

World Time 0 1 2 3 4 5 6 7 8 9 10 11 12 13 14 15 16 17 18 19 20 21 22 23 24

9355 USA
(con'd)
  †VOA, Via Saipan, N Marianas — S • E Asia • 100 kW
  †WEWN, Vandiver, Alabama — W • S America • 500 kW / S • C America • 500 kW

9360 RUSSIA
  †VOICE OF RUSSIA, Via Tajikistan — S • Mideast & W Asia • 200 kW
9365 CHINA
  CHINA R INTL, Beijing — W • Europe • 150 kW
  CHINA (TAIWAN)
  †R TAIWAN INTL, Via Issoudun, France — W Africa • 500 kW
  USA
  †R FREE ASIA, Via Dushanbe, Tajikistan — W • C Asia • 200 kW / W • SE Asia • 200 kW
  R FREE ASIA, Via Gavar, Armenia — S • S Asia • 500 kW / W • S Asia • 500 kW / S • S Asia • 500 kW • ALT. FREQ. TO 7550 kHz

9370 USA
  R FREE ASIA, Via Dushanbe, Tajikistan — S • C Asia • 250 kW
  †TRANS WORLD R, Via Merizo, Guam — E Asia • 100 kW • ALT. FREQ. TO 12130 kHz
  †WTJC, Newport, NC — ⬅ • E North Am • 50 kW
9375 CLANDESTINE (ASIA)
  "VO SOUTHERN AZERBAIJAN" — ⬅ • M-F • W Asia
  GREECE
  FONI TIS HELLADAS, Athens — S • W Europe & Atlantic • 100 kW
  †FONI TIS HELLADAS, Kavála — W • W Africa & S America • 250 kW
  SWEDEN
  †RADIO SWEDEN, Hörby — W • W Europe & W Africa • 500 kW
9380 CHINA
  †CENTRAL PEOPLE'S BS, Beijing — TAIWAN-1 • 50 kW
9385 PIRATE (EUROPE)
  "LASER HOT HITS", Ireland — ⬅ • Irr • Sa/Su • W Europe • 0.1 kW • ALT. FREQ. TO 6395 kHz
  UKRAINE
  †RADIO UKRAINE, Kharkiv — S • W Asia • 100 kW
  USA
  †ADVENTIST WORLD R, Via Agat, Guam — S • Mideast • 100 kW
  R FREE ASIA, Via Saipan, N Marianas — S • E Asia • 100 kW
  †R FREE ASIA, Via Tinian, N Marianas — W • E Asia • 250 kW
9385v PAKISTAN
  †RADIO PAKISTAN, Islamabad — E Europe & W Asia • 100 kW / W • Mideast • 100 kW

9390 CANADA
  †R CANADA INTL, Via Hörby, Sweden — S • W Africa • 350 kW
  ISRAEL
  †KOL ISRAEL, Tel Aviv — W • Europe & E North Am • 250 kW
  PAKISTAN
  †RADIO PAKISTAN, Islamabad — Europe • 250 kW • ALT. FREQ. TO 9395 kHz
  SWEDEN
  †RADIO SWEDEN, Hörby — S • W Africa & S America • 500 kW
9395 GERMANY
  †DEUTSCHE WELLE, Via Kazakstan — W • E Asia & SE Asia • 500 kW
  PAKISTAN
  †RADIO PAKISTAN, Islamabad — Europe • 250 kW • ALT. FREQ. TO 9390 kHz
  USA
  R FREE ASIA, Via Dushanbe, Tajikistan — S • S Asia • 200 kW
9400 BULGARIA
  †RADIO BULGARIA, Plovdiv — W • E North Am • 500 kW / W • W Asia & C Asia • 250 kW
  — S • C America • 250 kW / W • Mideast • 500 kW
  — ⬅ • Mideast • 250 kW
  †RADIO BULGARIA, Sofia — ⬅ • E Europe • 100 kW
  — ⬅ • Sa/Su • E Europe • 100 kW
  — S • E Europe • 100 kW
  SWEDEN
  †RADIO SWEDEN, Hörby — W • SE Asia & Australasia • 500 kW • ALT. FREQ. TO 9415 kHz
9405 PHILIPPINES
  FEBC RADIO INTL, Bocaue — E Asia • 100 kW
  FEBC RADIO INTL, Iba — E Asia • 100 kW
  RUSSIA
  †VOICE OF RUSSIA, Irkutsk — S • S Asia • 250 kW
9410 PORTUGAL
  †RDP INTERNATIONAL, Lisbon — W • Tu-Sa • W North Am • 100 kW • ALT. FREQ. TO 11655 kHz
  SWEDEN
  †RADIO SWEDEN, Hörby — S • E Europe • 500 kW
  UNITED KINGDOM
  BBC, Multiple Locations — S • Europe • 250/300 kW
  — Europe • 250/300/500 kW
  BBC, Skelton, Cumbria — W • Europe • 300 kW
  BBC, Via Zyyi, Cyprus — W Asia • 250 kW / S • W Europe • 250 kW
  — W • Mideast & W Asia • 250 kW / Europe • 250 kW
(con'd)

0 1 2 3 4 5 6 7 8 9 10 11 12 13 14 15 16 17 18 19 20 21 22 23 24

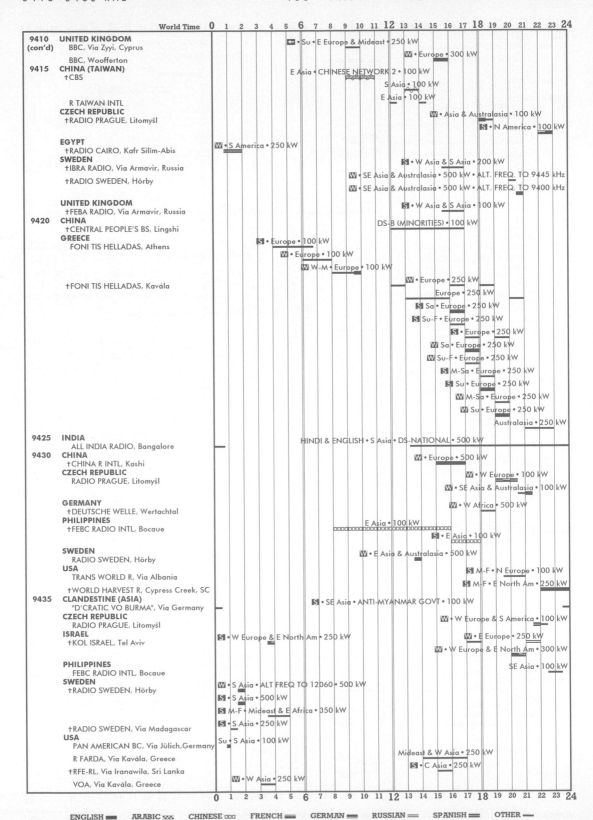

World Time 0 1 2 3 4 5 6 7 8 9 10 11 12 13 14 15 16 17 18 19 20 21 22 23 24

Freq	Country / Station	Details
9410 (con'd)	**UNITED KINGDOM** BBC, Via Zyyi, Cyprus	☐ • Su • E Europe & Mideast • 250 kW
	BBC, Woofferton	W • Europe • 300 kW
9415	**CHINA (TAIWAN)** †CBS	E Asia • CHINESE NETWORK 2 • 100 kW
		S Asia • 100 kW
		E Asia • 100 kW
	R TAIWAN INTL	
	CZECH REPUBLIC †RADIO PRAGUE, Litomyšl	W • Asia & Australasia • 100 kW
		S • N America • 100 kW
	EGYPT †RADIO CAIRO, Kafr Silim-Abis	W • S America • 250 kW
	SWEDEN †IBRA RADIO, Via Armavir, Russia	S • W Asia & S Asia • 200 kW
	†RADIO SWEDEN, Hörby	W • SE Asia & Australasia • 500 kW • ALT. FREQ. TO 9445 kHz
		W • SE Asia & Australasia • 500 kW • ALT. FREQ. TO 9400 kHz
	UNITED KINGDOM †FEBA RADIO, Via Armavir, Russia	S • W Asia & S Asia • 100 kW
9420	**CHINA** †CENTRAL PEOPLE'S BS, Lingshi	DS-B (MINORITIES) • 100 kW
	GREECE FONI TIS HELLADAS, Athens	S • Europe • 100 kW
		W • Europe • 100 kW
		W W-M • Europe • 100 kW
	†FONI TIS HELLADAS, Kavála	W • Europe • 250 kW
		Europe • 250 kW
		S Sa • Europe • 250 kW
		S Su-F • Europe • 250 kW
		S • Europe • 250 kW
		W Sa • Europe • 250 kW
		W Su-F • Europe • 250 kW
		S M-Sa • Europe • 250 kW
		S Su • Europe • 250 kW
		W M-Sa • Europe • 250 kW
		W Su • Europe • 250 kW
		Australasia • 250 kW
9425	**INDIA** ALL INDIA RADIO, Bangalore	HINDI & ENGLISH • S Asia • DS-NATIONAL • 500 kW
9430	**CHINA** †CHINA R INTL, Kashi	W • Europe • 500 kW
	CZECH REPUBLIC RADIO PRAGUE, Litomyšl	W • W Europe • 100 kW
		W • SE Asia & Australasia • 100 kW
	GERMANY †DEUTSCHE WELLE, Wertachtal	W • W Africa • 500 kW
	PHILIPPINES †FEBC RADIO INTL, Bocaue	E Asia • 100 kW
		S • E Asia • 100 kW
	SWEDEN RADIO SWEDEN, Hörby	W • E Asia & Australasia • 500 kW
	USA TRANS WORLD R, Via Albania	S M-F • N Europe • 100 kW
	†WORLD HARVEST R, Cypress Creek, SC	S M-F • E North Am • 250 kW
9435	**CLANDESTINE (ASIA)** "D'CRATIC VO BURMA", Via Germany	S • SE Asia • ANTI-MYANMAR GOVT • 100 kW
	CZECH REPUBLIC RADIO PRAGUE, Litomyšl	W • W Europe & S America • 100 kW
	ISRAEL †KOL ISRAEL, Tel Aviv	S • W Europe & E North Am • 250 kW
		W • E Europe • 250 kW
		W • W Europe & E North Am • 300 kW
	PHILIPPINES FEBC RADIO INTL, Bocaue	SE Asia • 100 kW
	SWEDEN †RADIO SWEDEN, Hörby	W • S Asia • ALT FREQ TO 12060 • 500 kW
		S • S Asia • 500 kW
		S M-F • Mideast & E Africa • 350 kW
	†RADIO SWEDEN, Via Madagascar	S • S Asia • 250 kW
	USA PAN AMERICAN BC, Via Jülich, Germany	Su • S Asia • 100 kW
	R FARDA, Via Kavála, Greece	Mideast & W Asia • 250 kW
	†RFE-RL, Via Iranawila, Sri Lanka	S • C Asia • 250 kW
	VOA, Via Kavála, Greece	W • W Asia • 250 kW

0 1 2 3 4 5 6 7 8 9 10 11 12 13 14 15 16 17 18 19 20 21 22 23 24

ENGLISH ▬   ARABIC ⌇⌇⌇   CHINESE ▢▢▢   FRENCH ══   GERMAN ▬▬   RUSSIAN ══   SPANISH ══   OTHER ─

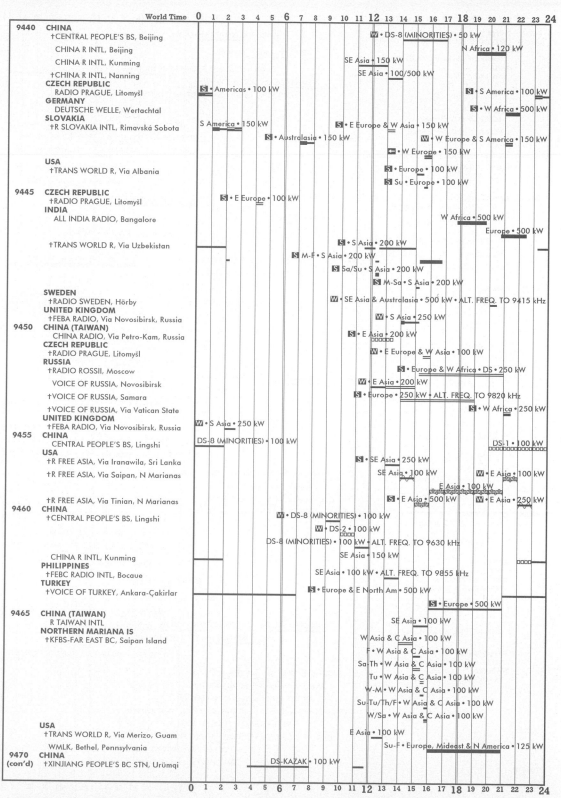

World Time 0 1 2 3 4 5 6 7 8 9 10 11 12 13 14 15 16 17 18 19 20 21 22 23 24

9440 **CHINA**
†CENTRAL PEOPLE'S BS, Beijing — W • DS-8 (MINORITIES) • 50 kW
CHINA R INTL, Beijing — N Africa • 120 kW
CHINA R INTL, Kunming — SE Asia • 150 kW
†CHINA R INTL, Nanning — SE Asia • 100/500 kW
CZECH REPUBLIC
RADIO PRAGUE, Litomyšl — S • Americas • 100 kW   S • S America • 100 kW
GERMANY
DEUTSCHE WELLE, Wertachtal — S • W Africa • 500 kW
SLOVAKIA
†R SLOVAKIA INTL, Rimavská Sobota — S America • 150 kW   S • E Europe & W Asia • 150 kW
S • Australasia • 150 kW   W • W Europe & S America • 150 kW
⇦ • W Europe • 150 kW
USA
†TRANS WORLD R, Via Albania — S • Europe • 100 kW
S • Su • Europe • 100 kW

9445 **CZECH REPUBLIC**
†RADIO PRAGUE, Litomyšl — S • E Europe • 100 kW
INDIA
ALL INDIA RADIO, Bangalore — W Africa • 500 kW
Europe • 500 kW
†TRANS WORLD R, Via Uzbekistan — S • S Asia • 200 kW
S • M-F • S Asia • 200 kW
S • Sa/Su • S Asia • 200 kW
S • M-Sa • S Asia • 200 kW
SWEDEN
†RADIO SWEDEN, Hörby — W • SE Asia & Australasia • 500 kW • ALT. FREQ. TO 9415 kHz
UNITED KINGDOM
†FEBA RADIO, Via Novosibirsk, Russia — W • S Asia • 250 kW
9450 **CHINA (TAIWAN)**
CHINA RADIO, Via Petro-Kam, Russia — S • E Asia • 200 kW
CZECH REPUBLIC
†RADIO PRAGUE, Litomyšl — W • E Europe & W Asia • 100 kW
RUSSIA
†RADIO ROSSII, Moscow — S • Europe & W Africa • DS • 250 kW
VOICE OF RUSSIA, Novosibirsk — W • E Asia • 200 kW
†VOICE OF RUSSIA, Samara — S • Europe • 250 kW • ALT. FREQ. TO 9820 kHz
†VOICE OF RUSSIA, Via Vatican State — S • W Africa • 250 kW
UNITED KINGDOM
†FEBA RADIO, Via Novosibirsk, Russia — W • S Asia • 250 kW
9455 **CHINA**
CENTRAL PEOPLE'S BS, Lingshi — DS-8 (MINORITIES) • 100 kW   DS-1 • 100 kW
USA
†R FREE ASIA, Via Iranawila, Sri Lanka — S • SE Asia • 250 kW
†R FREE ASIA, Via Saipan, N Marianas — SE Asia • 100 kW   W • E Asia • 100 kW
E Asia • 100 kW
†R FREE ASIA, Via Tinian, N Marianas — S • E Asia • 500 kW   W • E Asia • 250 kW
9460 **CHINA**
†CENTRAL PEOPLE'S BS, Lingshi — W • DS-8 (MINORITIES) • 100 kW
W • DS-2 • 100 kW
DS-8 (MINORITIES) • 100 kW • ALT. FREQ. TO 9630 kHz
CHINA R INTL, Kunming — SE Asia • 150 kW
PHILIPPINES
†FEBC RADIO INTL, Bocaue — SE Asia • 100 kW • ALT. FREQ. TO 9855 kHz
TURKEY
†VOICE OF TURKEY, Ankara-Çakirlar — S • Europe & E North Am • 500 kW
S • Europe • 500 kW
9465 **CHINA (TAIWAN)**
R TAIWAN INTL — SE Asia • 100 kW
NORTHERN MARIANA IS
†KFBS-FAR EAST BC, Saipan Island — W Asia & C Asia • 100 kW
F • W Asia & C Asia • 100 kW
Sa-Th • W Asia & C Asia • 100 kW
Tu • W Asia & C Asia • 100 kW
W-M • W Asia & C Asia • 100 kW
Su-Tu/Th/F • W Asia & C Asia • 100 kW
W/Sa • W Asia & C Asia • 100 kW
USA
†TRANS WORLD R, Via Merizo, Guam — E Asia • 100 kW
WMLK, Bethel, Pennsylvania — Su-F • Europe, Mideast & N America • 125 kW
9470 **CHINA**
(con'd) †XINJIANG PEOPLE'S BC STN, Urümqi — DS-KAZAK • 100 kW

0 1 2 3 4 5 6 7 8 9 10 11 12 13 14 15 16 17 18 19 20 21 22 23 24

SEASONAL S OR W   1-HR TIMESHIFT MIDYEAR ⇦ OR ⇨   JAMMING / OR /\   EARLIEST HEARD ◁   LATEST HEARD ▷   NEW FOR 2005 †

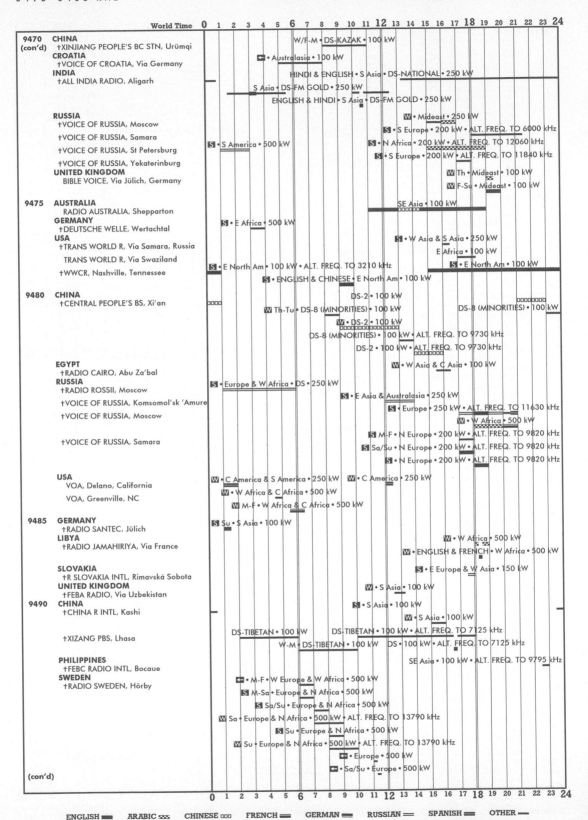

	World Time	0 1 2 3 4 5 6 7 8 9 10 11 12 13 14 15 16 17 18 19 20 21 22 23 24

9470 **CHINA**
(con'd) †XINJIANG PEOPLE'S BC STN, Urümqi — W/F-M • DS-KAZAK • 100 kW
CROATIA
†VOICE OF CROATIA, Via Germany — ☜ • Australasia • 100 kW
INDIA
†ALL INDIA RADIO, Aligarh — HINDI & ENGLISH • S Asia • DS-NATIONAL • 250 kW
— S Asia • DS-FM GOLD • 250 kW
— ENGLISH & HINDI • S Asia • DS-FM GOLD • 250 kW

RUSSIA
†VOICE OF RUSSIA, Moscow — W • Mideast • 250 kW
— S • S Europe • 200 kW • ALT. FREQ. TO 6000 kHz
†VOICE OF RUSSIA, Samara — S • S America • 500 kW   S • N Africa • 200 kW • ALT. FREQ. TO 12060 kHz
†VOICE OF RUSSIA, St Petersburg
†VOICE OF RUSSIA, Yekaterinburg — S • S Europe • 200 kW • ALT. FREQ. TO 11840 kHz
UNITED KINGDOM
BIBLE VOICE, Via Jülich, Germany — W • Th • Mideast • 100 kW
— W • F-Su • Mideast • 100 kW

9475 **AUSTRALIA**
RADIO AUSTRALIA, Shepparton — SE Asia • 100 kW
GERMANY
†DEUTSCHE WELLE, Wertachtal — S • E Africa • 500 kW
USA
†TRANS WORLD R, Via Samara, Russia — S • W Asia & S Asia • 250 kW
TRANS WORLD R, Via Swaziland — E Africa • 100 kW
— S • E North Am • 100 kW • ALT. FREQ. TO 3210 kHz   S • E North Am • 100 kW
†WWCR, Nashville, Tennessee — S • ENGLISH & CHINESE • E North Am • 100 kW

9480 **CHINA**
†CENTRAL PEOPLE'S BS, Xi'an — DS-2 • 100 kW
— W • Th-Tu • DS-8 (MINORITIES) • 100 kW   DS-8 (MINORITIES) • 100 kW
— W • DS-2 • 100 kW
— DS-8 (MINORITIES) • 100 kW • ALT. FREQ. TO 9730 kHz
— DS-2 • 100 kW • ALT. FREQ. TO 9730 kHz

EGYPT
†RADIO CAIRO, Abu Za'bal — W • W Asia & C Asia • 100 kW
RUSSIA
†RADIO ROSSII, Moscow — S • Europe & W Africa • DS • 250 kW
†VOICE OF RUSSIA, Komsomol'sk 'Amure — S • E Asia & Australasia • 250 kW
†VOICE OF RUSSIA, Moscow — S • Europe • 250 kW • ALT. FREQ. TO 11630 kHz
— W • W Africa • 500 kW
†VOICE OF RUSSIA, Samara — S • M-F • N Europe • 200 kW • ALT. FREQ. TO 9820 kHz
— S • Sa/Su • N Europe • 200 kW • ALT. FREQ. TO 9820 kHz
— S • N Europe • 200 kW • ALT. FREQ. TO 9820 kHz

USA
VOA, Delano, California — W • C America & S America • 250 kW   W • C America • 250 kW
VOA, Greenville, NC — W • W Africa & C Africa • 500 kW
— W • M-F • W Africa & C Africa • 500 kW

9485 **GERMANY**
†RADIO SANTEC, Jülich — S • Su • S Asia • 100 kW
LIBYA
†RADIO JAMAHIRIYA, Via France — W • W Africa • 500 kW
— W • ENGLISH & FRENCH • W Africa • 500 kW
SLOVAKIA
†R SLOVAKIA INTL, Rimavská Sobota — S • E Europe & W Asia • 150 kW
UNITED KINGDOM
†FEBA RADIO, Via Uzbekistan — W • S Asia • 100 kW
9490 **CHINA**
†CHINA R INTL, Kashi — S • S Asia • 100 kW
— W • S Asia • 100 kW
†XIZANG PBS, Lhasa — DS-TIBETAN • 100 kW   DS-TIBETAN • 100 kW • ALT. FREQ. TO 7125 kHz
— W-M • DS-TIBETAN • 100 kW   DS • 100 kW • ALT. FREQ. TO 7125 kHz
— SE Asia • 100 kW • ALT. FREQ. TO 9795 kHz

PHILIPPINES
†FEBC RADIO INTL, Bocaue
SWEDEN
†RADIO SWEDEN, Hörby — ☜ • M-F • W Europe & W Africa • 500 kW
— S • M-Sa • Europe & N Africa • 500 kW
— S • Sa/Su • Europe & N Africa • 500 kW
— W • Sa • Europe & N Africa • 500 kW • ALT. FREQ. TO 13790 kHz
— S • Su • Europe & N Africa • 500 kW
— W • Su • Europe & N Africa • 500 kW • ALT. FREQ. TO 13790 kHz
— ☜ • Europe • 500 kW
— ☜ • Sa/Su • Europe • 500 kW

(con'd)

	0 1 2 3 4 5 6 7 8 9 10 11 12 13 14 15 16 17 18 19 20 21 22 23 24

ENGLISH ▬   ARABIC ▨   CHINESE □□□   FRENCH ═   GERMAN ▬   RUSSIAN ══   SPANISH ▬   OTHER ─

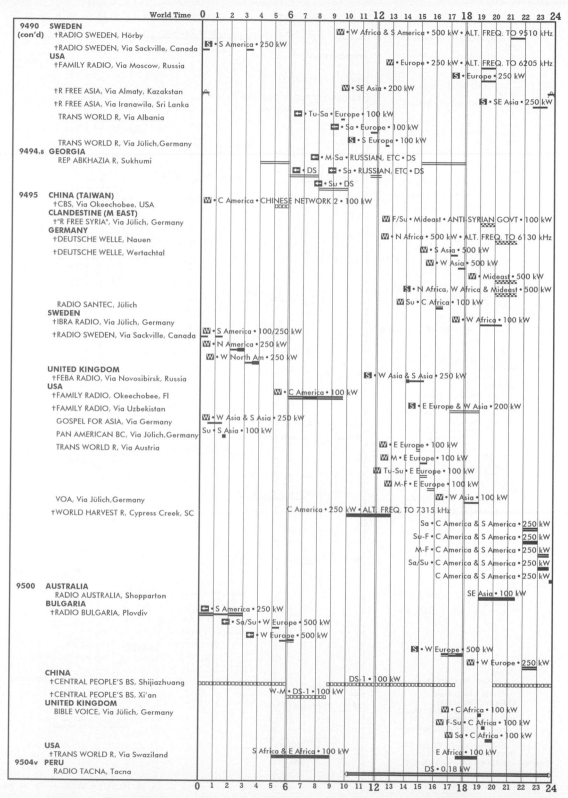

		World Time
9490 (con'd)	SWEDEN	
	†RADIO SWEDEN, Hörby	W • W Africa & S America • 500 kW • ALT. FREQ. TO 9510 kHz
	†RADIO SWEDEN, Via Sackville, Canada	S • S America • 250 kW
USA		
	†FAMILY RADIO, Via Moscow, Russia	W • Europe • 250 kW • ALT. FREQ. TO 6205 kHz
		S • Europe • 250 kW
	†R FREE ASIA, Via Almaty, Kazakhstan	W • SE Asia • 200 kW
	†R FREE ASIA, Via Iranawila, Sri Lanka	S • SE Asia • 250 kW
	TRANS WORLD R, Via Albania	⬅ Tu-Sa • Europe • 100 kW
		Sa • Europe • 100 kW
	TRANS WORLD R, Via Jülich, Germany	S • S Europe • 100 kW
9494.8	GEORGIA	
	REP ABKHAZIA R, Sukhumi	⬅ • M-Sa • RUSSIAN, ETC • DS
		⬅ • DS ⬅ • Sa • RUSSIAN, ETC • DS
		⬅ • Su • DS
9495	CHINA (TAIWAN)	
	†CBS, Via Okeechobee, USA	W • C America • CHINESE NETWORK 2 • 100 kW
	CLANDESTINE (M EAST)	
	†"R FREE SYRIA", Via Jülich, Germany	W F/Su • Mideast • ANTI-SYRIAN GOVT • 100 kW
	GERMANY	
	†DEUTSCHE WELLE, Nauen	W • N Africa • 500 kW • ALT. FREQ. TO 6130 kHz
	†DEUTSCHE WELLE, Wertachtal	W • S Asia • 500 kW
		W • W Asia • 500 kW
		W • Mideast • 500 kW
		S • N Africa, W Africa & Mideast • 500 kW
		W Su • C Africa • 100 kW
	RADIO SANTEC, Jülich	
	SWEDEN	
	†IBRA RADIO, Via Jülich, Germany	W • W Africa • 100 kW
	†RADIO SWEDEN, Via Sackville, Canada	W • S America • 100/250 kW
		W • N America • 250 kW
		W • W North Am • 250 kW
	UNITED KINGDOM	
	†FEBA RADIO, Via Novosibirsk, Russia	S • W Asia & S Asia • 250 kW
	USA	
	†FAMILY RADIO, Okeechobee, Fl	W • C America • 100 kW
	†FAMILY RADIO, Via Uzbekistan	S • E Europe & W Asia • 200 kW
	GOSPEL FOR ASIA, Via Germany	W • W Asia & S Asia • 250 kW
	PAN AMERICAN BC, Via Jülich, Germany	Su • S Asia • 100 kW
	TRANS WORLD R, Via Austria	W • E Europe • 100 kW
		W M • E Europe • 100 kW
		W Tu-Su • E Europe • 100 kW
		W M-F • E Europe • 100 kW
	VOA, Via Jülich, Germany	W • W Asia • 100 kW
	†WORLD HARVEST R, Cypress Creek, SC	C America • 250 kW • ALT. FREQ. TO 7315 kHz
		Sa • C America & S America • 250 kW
		Su-F • C America & S America • 250 kW
		M-F • C America & S America • 250 kW
		Sa/Su • C America & S America • 250 kW
		C America & S America • 250 kW
9500	AUSTRALIA	
	RADIO AUSTRALIA, Shepparton	SE Asia • 100 kW
	BULGARIA	
	†RADIO BULGARIA, Plovdiv	⬅ • S America • 250 kW
		⬅ • Sa/Su • W Europe • 500 kW
		⬅ • W Europe • 500 kW
		S • W Europe • 500 kW
		W • W Europe • 250 kW
	CHINA	
	†CENTRAL PEOPLE'S BS, Shijiazhuang	DS-1 • 100 kW
	†CENTRAL PEOPLE'S BS, Xi'an	W-M • DS-1 • 100 kW
	UNITED KINGDOM	
	BIBLE VOICE, Via Jülich, Germany	W • C Africa • 100 kW
		W F-Su • C Africa • 100 kW
		W Sa • C Africa • 100 kW
	USA	
	†TRANS WORLD R, Via Swaziland	S Africa & E Africa • 100 kW E Africa • 100 kW
9504v	PERU	
	RADIO TACNA, Tacna	DS • 0.18 kW

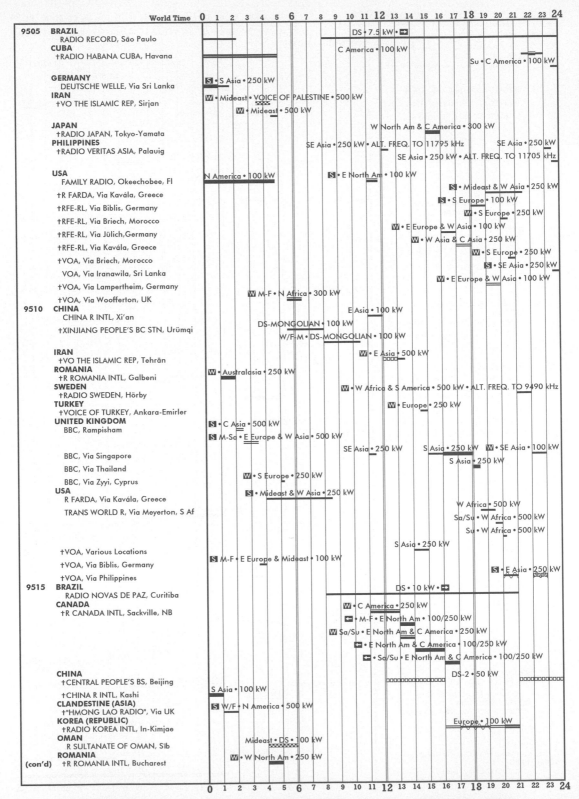

| World Time | 0 1 2 3 4 5 6 7 8 9 10 11 12 13 14 15 16 17 18 19 20 21 22 23 24 |

9505 BRAZIL
RADIO RECORD, São Paulo — DS • 7.5 kW •

CUBA
†RADIO HABANA CUBA, Havana — C America • 100 kW; Su • C America • 100 kW

GERMANY
DEUTSCHE WELLE, Via Sri Lanka — S • S Asia • 250 kW

IRAN
†VO THE ISLAMIC REP, Sirjan — W • Mideast • VOICE OF PALESTINE • 500 kW; W • Mideast • 500 kW

JAPAN
†RADIO JAPAN, Tokyo-Yamata — W North Am & C America • 300 kW

PHILIPPINES
†RADIO VERITAS ASIA, Palauig — SE Asia • 250 kW • ALT. FREQ. TO 11795 kHz; SE Asia • 250 kW; SE Asia • 250 kW • ALT. FREQ. TO 11705 kHz

USA
FAMILY RADIO, Okeechobee, Fl — N America • 100 kW; S • E North Am • 100 kW
†R FARDA, Via Kavála, Greece — S • Mideast & W Asia • 250 kW
†RFE-RL, Via Biblis, Germany — S • S Europe • 100 kW
†RFE-RL, Via Briech, Morocco — S • S Europe • 250 kW
†RFE-RL, Via Jülich, Germany — W • E Europe & W Asia • 100 kW
†RFE-RL, Via Kavála, Greece — W • W Asia & C Asia • 250 kW; W • S Europe • 250 kW
†VOA, Via Briech, Morocco — S • SE Asia • 250 kW
VOA, Via Iranawila, Sri Lanka — W • E Europe & W Asia • 100 kW
†VOA, Via Lampertheim, Germany
†VOA, Via Woofferton, UK — W M-F • N Africa • 300 kW

9510 CHINA
CHINA R INTL, Xi'an — E Asia • 100 kW
†XINJIANG PEOPLE'S BC STN, Urümqi — DS-MONGOLIAN • 100 kW; W/F-M • DS-MONGOLIAN • 100 kW

IRAN
†VO THE ISLAMIC REP, Tehrān — W • E Asia • 500 kW

ROMANIA
†R ROMANIA INTL, Galbeni — W • Australasia • 250 kW

SWEDEN
†RADIO SWEDEN, Hörby — W • W Africa & S America • 500 kW • ALT. FREQ. TO 9490 kHz

TURKEY
†VOICE OF TURKEY, Ankara-Emirler — W • Europe • 250 kW

UNITED KINGDOM
BBC, Rampisham — S • C Asia • 500 kW; S M-Sa • E Europe & W Asia • 500 kW
BBC, Via Singapore — SE Asia • 250 kW; S Asia • 250 kW; W • SE Asia • 100 kW
BBC, Via Thailand — S Asia • 250 kW
BBC, Via Zyyi, Cyprus — W • S Europe • 250 kW

USA
R FARDA, Via Kavála, Greece — S • Mideast & W Asia • 250 kW
TRANS WORLD R, Via Meyerton, S Af — W Africa • 500 kW; Sa/Su • W Africa • 500 kW; Su • W Africa • 500 kW
†VOA, Various Locations — S Asia • 250 kW
†VOA, Via Biblis, Germany — S M-F • E Europe & Mideast • 100 kW
†VOA, Via Philippines — S • E Asia • 250 kW

9515 BRAZIL
RADIO NOVAS DE PAZ, Curitiba — DS • 10 kW •

CANADA
†R CANADA INTL, Sackville, NB — W • C America • 250 kW; M-F • E North Am • 100/250 kW; W Sa/Su • E North Am & C America • 250 kW; E North Am & C America • 100/250 kW; Sa/Su • E North Am & C America • 100/250 kW

CHINA
†CENTRAL PEOPLE'S BS, Beijing — DS-2 • 50 kW
†CHINA R INTL, Kashi — S Asia • 100 kW

CLANDESTINE (ASIA)
†"HMONG LAO RADIO", Via UK — S W/F • N America • 500 kW

KOREA (REPUBLIC)
†RADIO KOREA INTL, In-Kimjae — Europe • 100 kW

OMAN
R SULTANATE OF OMAN, Sīb — Mideast • DS • 100 kW

ROMANIA
(con'd) †R ROMANIA INTL, Bucharest — W • W North Am • 250 kW

| 0 1 2 3 4 5 6 7 8 9 10 11 12 13 14 15 16 17 18 19 20 21 22 23 24 |

ENGLISH ▬   ARABIC ⌇⌇⌇   CHINESE ▯▯▯   FRENCH ▬▬   GERMAN ▬▬   RUSSIAN ═══   SPANISH ▬▬   OTHER ▬

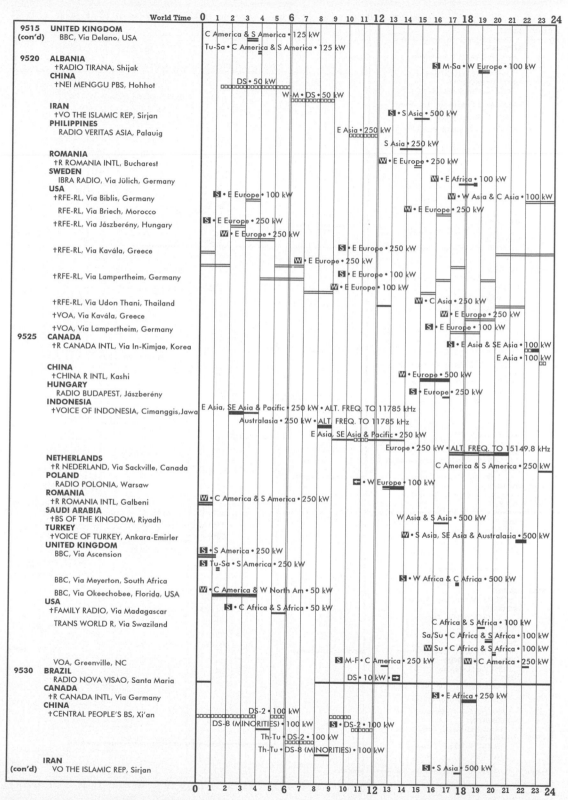

World Time	9515 UNITED KINGDOM (con'd) BBC, Via Delano, USA	Schedule

9515 **UNITED KINGDOM**
(con'd) BBC, Via Delano, USA — C America & S America • 125 kW / Tu-Sa • C America & S America • 125 kW

9520 **ALBANIA**
†RADIO TIRANA, Shijak — S M-Sa • W Europe • 100 kW
CHINA
†NEI MENGGU PBS, Hohhot — DS • 50 kW / W-M • DS • 50 kW

IRAN
†VO THE ISLAMIC REP, Sirjan — S • S Asia • 500 kW
PHILIPPINES
RADIO VERITAS ASIA, Palauig — E Asia • 250 kW / S Asia • 250 kW

ROMANIA
†R ROMANIA INTL, Bucharest — W • E Europe • 250 kW
SWEDEN
IBRA RADIO, Via Jülich, Germany — W • E Africa • 100 kW
USA
†RFE-RL, Via Biblis, Germany — S • E Europe • 100 kW / W • W Asia & C Asia • 100 kW
RFE-RL, Via Briech, Morocco — W • E Europe • 250 kW
†RFE-RL, Via Jászberény, Hungary — S • E Europe • 250 kW / W • E Europe • 250 kW

†RFE-RL, Via Kavála, Greece — S • E Europe • 250 kW / W • E Europe • 250 kW
†RFE-RL, Via Lampertheim, Germany — S • E Europe • 100 kW / W • E Europe • 100 kW

†RFE-RL, Via Udon Thani, Thailand — W • C Asia • 250 kW
†VOA, Via Kavála, Greece — W • E Europe • 250 kW
†VOA, Via Lampertheim, Germany — S • E Europe • 100 kW

9525 **CANADA**
†R CANADA INTL, Via In-Kimjae, Korea — S • E Asia & SE Asia • 100 kW / E Asia • 100 kW

CHINA
†CHINA R INTL, Kashi — W • Europe • 500 kW
HUNGARY
RADIO BUDAPEST, Jászberény — S • Europe • 250 kW
INDONESIA
†VOICE OF INDONESIA, Cimanggis, Jawa — E Asia, SE Asia & Pacific • 250 kW • ALT. FREQ. TO 11785 kHz / Australasia • 250 kW • ALT. FREQ. TO 11785 kHz / E Asia, SE Asia & Pacific • 250 kW / Europe • 250 kW • ALT. FREQ. TO 15149.8 kHz

NETHERLANDS
†R NEDERLAND, Via Sackville, Canada — C America & S America • 250 kW
POLAND
RADIO POLONIA, Warsaw — • W Europe • 100 kW
ROMANIA
†R ROMANIA INTL, Galbeni — W • C America & S America • 250 kW
SAUDI ARABIA
†BS OF THE KINGDOM, Riyadh — W Asia & S Asia • 500 kW
TURKEY
†VOICE OF TURKEY, Ankara-Emirler — W • S Asia, SE Asia & Australasia • 500 kW
UNITED KINGDOM
BBC, Via Ascension — S • S America • 250 kW / S Tu-Sa • S America • 250 kW

BBC, Via Meyerton, South Africa — S • W Africa & C Africa • 500 kW
BBC, Via Okeechobee, Florida, USA — W • C America & W North Am • 50 kW
USA
†FAMILY RADIO, Via Madagascar — S • C Africa & S Africa • 50 kW
TRANS WORLD R, Via Swaziland — C Africa & S Africa • 100 kW / Sa/Su • C Africa & S Africa • 100 kW / W Su • C Africa & S Africa • 100 kW

VOA, Greenville, NC — S M-F • C America • 250 kW / W • C America • 250 kW

9530 **BRAZIL**
RADIO NOVA VISAO, Santa Maria — DS • 10 kW •
CANADA
†R CANADA INTL, Via Germany — S • E Africa • 250 kW
CHINA
†CENTRAL PEOPLE'S BS, Xi'an — DS-2 • 100 kW / DS-8 (MINORITIES) • 100 kW / S • DS-2 • 100 kW / Th-Tu • DS-2 • 100 kW / Th-Tu • DS-8 (MINORITIES) • 100 kW

IRAN
(con'd) VO THE ISLAMIC REP, Sirjan — S • S Asia • 500 kW

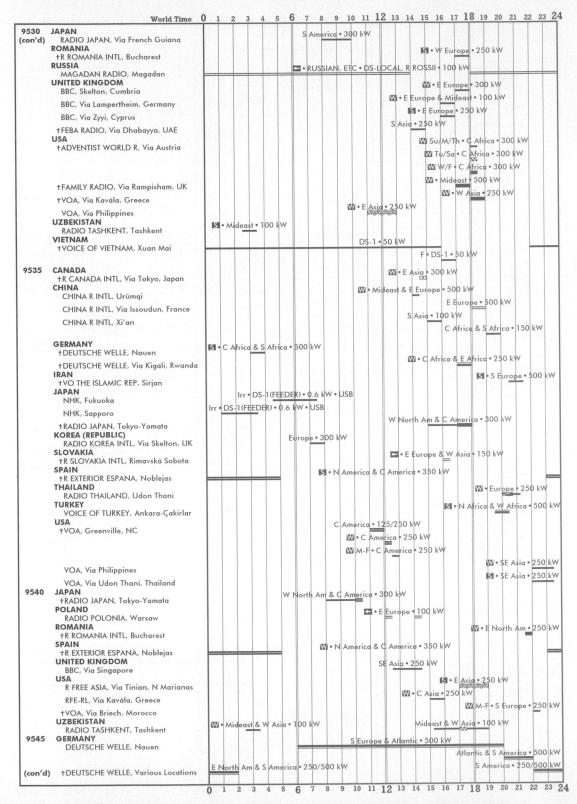

	World Time	0 1 2 3 4 5 6 7 8 9 10 11 12 13 14 15 16 17 18 19 20 21 22 23 24
9530	**JAPAN**	
(con'd)	RADIO JAPAN, Via French Guiana	S America • 300 kW
	ROMANIA	
	†R ROMANIA INTL, Bucharest	S • W Europe • 250 kW
	RUSSIA	
	MAGADAN RADIO, Magadan	• RUSSIAN, ETC • DS-LOCAL, R ROSSII • 100 kW
	UNITED KINGDOM	
	BBC, Skelton, Cumbria	W • E Europe • 300 kW
	BBC, Via Lampertheim, Germany	W • E Europe & Mideast • 100 kW
	BBC, Via Zyyi, Cyprus	S • E Europe • 250 kW
	†FEBA RADIO, Via Dhabayya, UAE	S Asia • 250 kW
	USA	
	†ADVENTIST WORLD R, Via Austria	W • Su/M/Th • C Africa • 300 kW
		W • Tu/Sa • C Africa • 300 kW
		W • W/F • C Africa • 300 kW
	†FAMILY RADIO, Via Rampisham, UK	W • Mideast • 500 kW
	†VOA, Via Kavála, Greece	W • W Asia • 250 kW
	VOA, Via Philippines	W • E Asia • 250 kW
	UZBEKISTAN	
	RADIO TASHKENT, Tashkent	S • Mideast • 100 kW
	VIETNAM	
	†VOICE OF VIETNAM, Xuan Mai	DS-1 • 50 kW
		F • DS-1 • 50 kW
9535	**CANADA**	
	†R CANADA INTL, Via Tokyo, Japan	W • E Asia • 300 kW
	CHINA	
	CHINA R INTL, Urümqi	W • Mideast & E Europe • 500 kW
	CHINA R INTL, Via Issoudun, France	E Europe • 500 kW
	CHINA R INTL, Xi'an	S Asia • 100 kW
		C Africa & S Africa • 150 kW
	GERMANY	
	†DEUTSCHE WELLE, Nauen	S • C Africa & S Africa • 500 kW
	†DEUTSCHE WELLE, Via Kigali, Rwanda	W • C Africa & E Africa • 250 kW
	IRAN	
	†VO THE ISLAMIC REP, Sirjan	S • S Europe • 500 kW
	JAPAN	
	NHK, Fukuoka	Irr • DS-1(FEEDER) • 0.6 kW • USB
	NHK, Sapporo	Irr • DS-1(FEEDER) • 0.6 kW • USB
	†RADIO JAPAN, Tokyo-Yamata	W North Am & C America • 300 kW
	KOREA (REPUBLIC)	
	RADIO KOREA INTL, Via Skelton, UK	Europe • 300 kW
	SLOVAKIA	
	†R SLOVAKIA INTL, Rimavská Sobota	• E Europe & W Asia • 150 kW
	SPAIN	
	†R EXTERIOR ESPANA, Noblejas	S • N America & C America • 350 kW
	THAILAND	
	RADIO THAILAND, Udon Thani	W • Europe • 250 kW
	TURKEY	
	VOICE OF TURKEY, Ankara-Çakirlar	S • N Africa & W Africa • 500 kW
	USA	
	†VOA, Greenville, NC	C America • 125/250 kW
		W • C America • 250 kW
		W • M-F • C America • 250 kW
	VOA, Via Philippines	W • SE Asia • 250 kW
	VOA, Via Udon Thani, Thailand	S • SE Asia • 250 kW
9540	**JAPAN**	
	†RADIO JAPAN, Tokyo-Yamata	W North Am & C America • 300 kW
	POLAND	
	RADIO POLONIA, Warsaw	• E Europe • 100 kW
	ROMANIA	
	†R ROMANIA INTL, Bucharest	W • E North Am • 250 kW
	SPAIN	
	†R EXTERIOR ESPANA, Noblejas	W • N America & C America • 350 kW
	UNITED KINGDOM	
	BBC, Via Singapore	SE Asia • 250 kW
	USA	
	R FREE ASIA, Via Tinian, N Marianas	S • E Asia • 250 kW
	RFE-RL, Via Kavála, Greece	W • C Asia • 250 kW
	†VOA, Via Briech, Morocco	W • M-F • S Europe • 250 kW
	UZBEKISTAN	
	RADIO TASHKENT, Tashkent	W • Mideast & W Asia • 100 kW
		Mideast & W Asia • 100 kW
9545	**GERMANY**	
	DEUTSCHE WELLE, Nauen	S Europe & Atlantic • 500 kW
		Atlantic & S America • 500 kW
(con'd)	†DEUTSCHE WELLE, Various Locations	E North Am & S America • 250/500 kW
		S America • 250/500 kW
		0 1 2 3 4 5 6 7 8 9 10 11 12 13 14 15 16 17 18 19 20 21 22 23 24

ENGLISH ▬   ARABIC ⁑⁑   CHINESE □□□   FRENCH ═══   GERMAN ▬▬   RUSSIAN ═══   SPANISH ═══   OTHER ▬

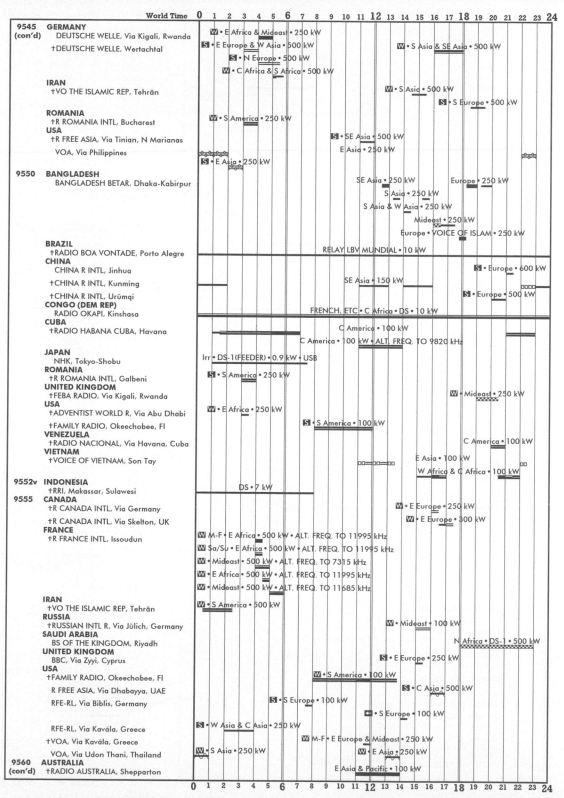

World Time 0 1 2 3 4 5 6 7 8 9 10 11 12 13 14 15 16 17 18 19 20 21 22 23 24

9545
(con'd) GERMANY
   DEUTSCHE WELLE, Via Kigali, Rwanda — W • E Africa & Mideast • 250 kW
   †DEUTSCHE WELLE, Wertachtal — S • E Europe & W Asia • 500 kW / W • S Asia & SE Asia • 500 kW
   S • N Europe • 500 kW
   W • C Africa & S Africa • 500 kW

IRAN
   †VO THE ISLAMIC REP, Tehrān — W • S Asia • 500 kW / S • S Europe • 500 kW

ROMANIA
   †R ROMANIA INTL, Bucharest — W • S America • 250 kW
USA
   †R FREE ASIA, Via Tinian, N Marianas — S • SE Asia • 500 kW
   VOA, Via Philippines — E Asia • 250 kW
   S • E Asia • 250 kW

9550 BANGLADESH
   BANGLADESH BETAR, Dhaka-Kabirpur — SE Asia • 250 kW / Europe • 250 kW
   S Asia • 250 kW
   S Asia & W Asia • 250 kW
   Mideast • 250 kW
   Europe • VOICE OF ISLAM • 250 kW

BRAZIL
   †RADIO BOA VONTADE, Porto Alegre — RELAY LBV MUNDIAL • 10 kW
CHINA
   CHINA R INTL, Jinhua — S • Europe • 600 kW
   †CHINA R INTL, Kunming — SE Asia • 150 kW
   †CHINA R INTL, Urümqi — S • Europe • 500 kW
CONGO (DEM REP)
   RADIO OKAPI, Kinshasa — FRENCH, ETC • C Africa • DS • 10 kW
CUBA
   †RADIO HABANA CUBA, Havana — C America • 100 kW
   C America • 100 kW • ALT. FREQ. TO 9820 kHz

JAPAN
   NHK, Tokyo-Shobu — Irr • DS-1 (FEEDER) • 0.9 kW • USB
ROMANIA
   †R ROMANIA INTL, Galbeni — S • S America • 250 kW
UNITED KINGDOM
   †FEBA RADIO, Via Kigali, Rwanda — W • Mideast • 250 kW
USA
   †ADVENTIST WORLD R, Via Abu Dhabi — W • E Africa • 250 kW
   †FAMILY RADIO, Okeechobee, Fl — S • S America • 100 kW
VENEZUELA
   †RADIO NACIONAL, Via Havana, Cuba — C America • 100 kW
VIETNAM
   †VOICE OF VIETNAM, Son Tay — E Asia • 100 kW
   W Africa & C Africa • 100 kW

9552v INDONESIA
   †RRI, Makassar, Sulawesi — DS • 7 kW
9555 CANADA
   †R CANADA INTL, Via Germany — W • E Europe • 250 kW
   †R CANADA INTL, Via Skelton, UK — W • E Europe • 300 kW
FRANCE
   †R FRANCE INTL, Issoudun — W M-F • E Africa • 500 kW • ALT. FREQ. TO 11995 kHz
   W Sa/Su • E Africa • 500 kW • ALT. FREQ. TO 11995 kHz
   W • Mideast • 500 kW • ALT. FREQ. TO 7315 kHz
   W • E Africa • 500 kW • ALT. FREQ. TO 11995 kHz
   W • Mideast • 500 kW • ALT. FREQ. TO 11685 kHz

IRAN
   †VO THE ISLAMIC REP, Tehrān — W • S America • 500 kW
RUSSIA
   †RUSSIAN INTL R, Via Jülich, Germany — W • Mideast • 100 kW
SAUDI ARABIA
   BS OF THE KINGDOM, Riyadh — N Africa • DS-1 • 500 kW
UNITED KINGDOM
   BBC, Via Zyyi, Cyprus — S • E Europe • 250 kW
USA
   †FAMILY RADIO, Okeechobee, Fl — W • S America • 100 kW
   R FREE ASIA, Via Dhabayya, UAE — S • C Asia • 500 kW
   RFE-RL, Via Biblis, Germany — S • S Europe • 100 kW
    • S Europe • 100 kW
   RFE-RL, Via Kavála, Greece — S • W Asia & C Asia • 250 kW
   †VOA, Via Kavála, Greece — W M-F • E Europe & Mideast • 250 kW
   VOA, Via Udon Thani, Thailand — W • S Asia • 250 kW / W • E Asia • 250 kW
9560 AUSTRALIA
(con'd) †RADIO AUSTRALIA, Shepparton — E Asia & Pacific • 100 kW

0 1 2 3 4 5 6 7 8 9 10 11 12 13 14 15 16 17 18 19 20 21 22 23 24

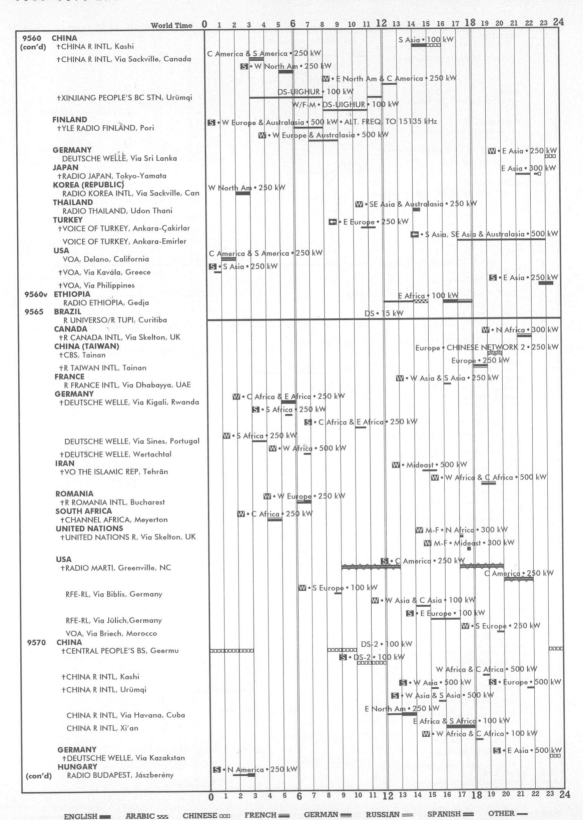

World Time 0 1 2 3 4 5 6 7 8 9 10 11 12 13 14 15 16 17 18 19 20 21 22 23 24

9560
(con'd) **CHINA**
†CHINA R INTL, Kashi — S Asia • 100 kW
†CHINA R INTL, Via Sackville, Canada — C America & S America • 250 kW
S • W North Am • 250 kW
W • E North Am & C America • 250 kW

†XINJIANG PEOPLE'S BC STN, Urümqi — DS-UIGHUR • 100 kW
W/F-M • DS-UIGHUR • 100 kW

FINLAND
†YLE RADIO FINLAND, Pori — S • W Europe & Australasia • 500 kW • ALT. FREQ. TO 15135 kHz
W • W Europe & Australasia • 500 kW

GERMANY
DEUTSCHE WELLE, Via Sri Lanka — W • E Asia • 250 kW
JAPAN
†RADIO JAPAN, Tokyo-Yamata — E Asia • 300 kW
KOREA (REPUBLIC)
RADIO KOREA INTL, Via Sackville, Can — W North Am • 250 kW
THAILAND
RADIO THAILAND, Udon Thani — W • SE Asia & Australasia • 250 kW
TURKEY
†VOICE OF TURKEY, Ankara-Çakirlar — E Europe • 250 kW
VOICE OF TURKEY, Ankara-Emirler — S Asia, SE Asia & Australasia • 500 kW
USA
VOA, Delano, California — C America & S America • 250 kW
†VOA, Via Kavála, Greece — S • S Asia • 250 kW
†VOA, Via Philippines — S • E Asia • 250 kW
9560v ETHIOPIA
RADIO ETHIOPIA, Gedja — E Africa • 100 kW
9565 BRAZIL
R UNIVERSO/R TUPI, Curitiba — DS • 15 kW
CANADA
†R CANADA INTL, Via Skelton, UK — W • N Africa • 300 kW
CHINA (TAIWAN)
†CBS, Tainan — Europe • CHINESE NETWORK 2 • 250 kW
†R TAIWAN INTL, Tainan — Europe • 250 kW
FRANCE
R FRANCE INTL, Via Dhabayya, UAE — W • W Asia & S Asia • 250 kW
GERMANY
†DEUTSCHE WELLE, Via Kigali, Rwanda — W • C Africa & E Africa • 250 kW
S • S Africa • 250 kW
S • C Africa & E Africa • 250 kW
DEUTSCHE WELLE, Via Sines, Portugal — W • S Africa • 250 kW
W • W Africa • 500 kW
†DEUTSCHE WELLE, Wertachtal
IRAN
†VO THE ISLAMIC REP, Tehrān — W • Mideast • 500 kW
W • W Africa & C Africa • 500 kW
ROMANIA
†R ROMANIA INTL, Bucharest — W • W Europe • 250 kW
SOUTH AFRICA
†CHANNEL AFRICA, Meyerton — W • C Africa • 250 kW
UNITED NATIONS
†UNITED NATIONS R, Via Skelton, UK — W M-F • N Africa • 300 kW
W M-F • Mideast • 300 kW
USA
†RADIO MARTI, Greenville, NC — S • C America • 250 kW
C America • 250 kW
RFE-RL, Via Biblis, Germany — W • S Europe • 100 kW
W • W Asia & C Asia • 100 kW
S • E Europe • 100 kW
RFE-RL, Via Jülich, Germany — W • S Europe • 250 kW
VOA, Via Briech, Morocco
9570 CHINA
†CENTRAL PEOPLE'S BS, Geermu — DS-2 • 100 kW
S • DS-2 • 100 kW
†CHINA R INTL, Kashi — W Africa & C Africa • 500 kW
S • W Asia • 500 kW
S • Europe • 500 kW
†CHINA R INTL, Urümqi — S • W Asia & S Asia • 500 kW
CHINA R INTL, Via Havana, Cuba — E North Am • 250 kW
CHINA R INTL, Xi'an — E Africa & S Africa • 100 kW
W • W Africa & C Africa • 100 kW
GERMANY
†DEUTSCHE WELLE, Via Kazakstan — S • E Asia • 500 kW
HUNGARY
(con'd) RADIO BUDAPEST, Jászberény — S • N America • 250 kW

0 1 2 3 4 5 6 7 8 9 10 11 12 13 14 15 16 17 18 19 20 21 22 23 24

ENGLISH ▬ ARABIC ░ CHINESE ▫▫▫ FRENCH ═ GERMAN ▬ RUSSIAN ═ SPANISH ▬ OTHER ─

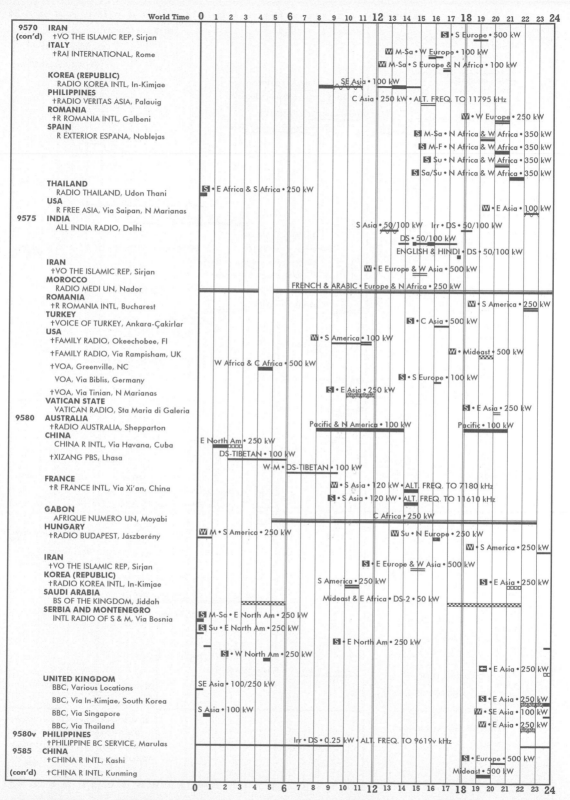

	9570	IRAN
	(con'd)	†VO THE ISLAMIC REP, Sirjan — S • S Europe • 500 kW
		ITALY
		†RAI INTERNATIONAL, Rome — W M-Sa • W Europe • 100 kW
		W M-Sa • S Europe & N Africa • 100 kW
		KOREA (REPUBLIC)
		RADIO KOREA INTL, In-Kimjae — SE Asia • 100 kW
		PHILIPPINES
		†RADIO VERITAS ASIA, Palauig — C Asia • 250 kW • ALT. FREQ. TO 11795 kHz
		ROMANIA
		†R ROMANIA INTL, Galbeni — W • W Europe • 250 kW
		SPAIN
		R EXTERIOR ESPANA, Noblejas — S M-Sa • N Africa & W Africa • 350 kW
		S M-F • N Africa & W Africa • 350 kW
		S Su • N Africa & W Africa • 350 kW
		S Sa/Su • N Africa & W Africa • 350 kW
		THAILAND
		RADIO THAILAND, Udon Thani — S • E Africa & S Africa • 250 kW
		USA
		R FREE ASIA, Via Saipan, N Marianas — W • E Asia • 100 kW
	9575	INDIA
		ALL INDIA RADIO, Delhi — S Asia • 50/100 kW Irr • DS • 50/100 kW
		DS • 50/100 kW
		ENGLISH & HINDI • DS • 50/100 kW
		IRAN
		†VO THE ISLAMIC REP, Sirjan — W • E Europe & W Asia • 500 kW
		MOROCCO
		RADIO MEDI UN, Nador — FRENCH & ARABIC • Europe & N Africa • 250 kW
		ROMANIA
		†R ROMANIA INTL, Bucharest — W • S America • 250 kW
		TURKEY
		†VOICE OF TURKEY, Ankara-Çakirlar — S • C Asia • 500 kW
		USA
		†FAMILY RADIO, Okeechobee, Fl — W • S America • 100 kW
		†FAMILY RADIO, Via Rampisham, UK — W • Mideast • 500 kW
		†VOA, Greenville, NC — W Africa & C Africa • 500 kW
		VOA, Via Biblis, Germany — S • S Europe • 100 kW
		VOA, Via Tinian, N Marianas — S • E Asia • 250 kW
		VATICAN STATE
		VATICAN RADIO, Sta Maria di Galeria — S • E Asia • 250 kW
	9580	AUSTRALIA
		†RADIO AUSTRALIA, Shepparton — Pacific & N America • 100 kW Pacific • 100 kW
		CHINA
		CHINA R INTL, Via Havana, Cuba — E North Am • 250 kW
		†XIZANG PBS, Lhasa — DS-TIBETAN • 100 kW
		W-M • DS-TIBETAN • 100 kW
		FRANCE
		†R FRANCE INTL, Via Xi'an, China — W • S Asia • 120 kW • ALT. FREQ. TO 7180 kHz
		S • S Asia • 120 kW • ALT. FREQ. TO 11610 kHz
		GABON
		AFRIQUE NUMERO UN, Moyabi — C Africa • 250 kW
		HUNGARY
		†RADIO BUDAPEST, Jászberény — W M • S America • 250 kW W Su • N Europe • 250 kW
		W • S America • 250 kW
		IRAN
		†VO THE ISLAMIC REP, Sirjan — S • E Europe & W Asia • 500 kW
		KOREA (REPUBLIC)
		†RADIO KOREA INTL, In-Kimjae — S America • 250 kW S • E Asia • 250 kW
		SAUDI ARABIA
		BS OF THE KINGDOM, Jiddah — Mideast & E Africa • DS-2 • 50 kW
		SERBIA AND MONTENEGRO
		INTL RADIO OF S & M, Via Bosnia — S M-Sa • E North Am • 250 kW
		S Su • E North Am • 250 kW
		S • E North Am • 250 kW
		S • W North Am • 250 kW
		E Asia • 250 kW
		UNITED KINGDOM
		BBC, Various Locations — SE Asia • 100/250 kW
		BBC, Via In-Kimjae, South Korea — S • E Asia • 250 kW
		BBC, Via Singapore — S Asia • 100 kW W • SE Asia • 100 kW
		BBC, Via Thailand — W • E Asia • 250 kW
	9580v	PHILIPPINES
		†PHILIPPINE BC SERVICE, Marulas — Irr • DS • 0.25 kW • ALT. FREQ. TO 9619v kHz
	9585	CHINA
		†CHINA R INTL, Kashi — S • Europe • 500 kW
	(con'd)	†CHINA R INTL, Kunming — Mideast • 500 kW

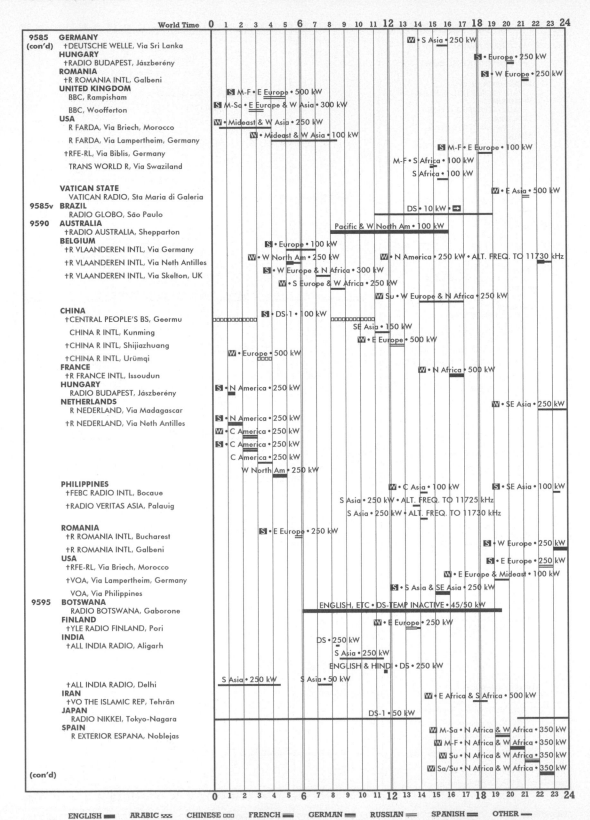

	World Time	0 1 2 3 4 5 6 7 8 9 10 11 12 13 14 15 16 17 18 19 20 21 22 23 24

9585 (con'd) **GERMANY**
†DEUTSCHE WELLE, Via Sri Lanka — W • S Asia • 250 kW

HUNGARY
†RADIO BUDAPEST, Jászberény — S • Europe • 250 kW

ROMANIA
†R ROMANIA INTL, Galbeni — S • W Europe • 250 kW

UNITED KINGDOM
BBC, Rampisham — S M-F • E Europe • 500 kW
BBC, Woofferton — S M-Sa • E Europe & W Asia • 300 kW

USA
R FARDA, Via Briech, Morocco — W • Mideast & W Asia • 250 kW
R FARDA, Via Lampertheim, Germany — W • Mideast & W Asia • 100 kW
†RFE-RL, Via Biblis, Germany — S M-F • E Europe • 100 kW
TRANS WORLD R, Via Swaziland — M-F • S Africa • 100 kW / S Africa • 100 kW

VATICAN STATE
VATICAN RADIO, Sta Maria di Galeria — W • E Asia • 500 kW

9585v BRAZIL
RADIO GLOBO, São Paulo — DS • 10 kW ➡

9590 AUSTRALIA
†RADIO AUSTRALIA, Shepparton — Pacific & W North Am • 100 kW

BELGIUM
†R VLAANDEREN INTL, Via Germany — S • Europe • 100 kW
†R VLAANDEREN INTL, Via Neth Antilles — W • W North Am • 250 kW / W • N America • 250 kW • ALT. FREQ. TO 11730 kHz
†R VLAANDEREN INTL, Via Skelton, UK — S • W Europe & N Africa • 300 kW / W • S Europe & W Africa • 250 kW / W Su • W Europe & N Africa • 250 kW

CHINA
†CENTRAL PEOPLE'S BS, Geermu — S • DS-1 • 100 kW
CHINA R INTL, Kunming — SE Asia • 150 kW
†CHINA R INTL, Shijiazhuang — W • E Europe • 500 kW
†CHINA R INTL, Urümqi — W • Europe • 500 kW

FRANCE
†R FRANCE INTL, Issoudun — W • N Africa • 500 kW

HUNGARY
RADIO BUDAPEST, Jászberény — S • N America • 250 kW

NETHERLANDS
R NEDERLAND, Via Madagascar — W • SE Asia • 250 kW
†R NEDERLAND, Via Neth Antilles — S • N America • 250 kW / W • C America • 250 kW / S • C America • 250 kW / C America • 250 kW / W North Am • 250 kW

PHILIPPINES
†FEBC RADIO INTL, Bocaue — W • C Asia • 100 kW / S • SE Asia • 100 kW
†RADIO VERITAS ASIA, Palauig — S Asia • 250 kW • ALT. FREQ. TO 11725 kHz / S Asia • 250 kW • ALT. FREQ. TO 11730 kHz

ROMANIA
†R ROMANIA INTL, Bucharest — S • E Europe • 250 kW
†R ROMANIA INTL, Galbeni — S • W Europe • 250 kW / S • E Europe • 250 kW

USA
†RFE-RL, Via Briech, Morocco — W • E Europe & Mideast • 100 kW
†VOA, Via Lampertheim, Germany — S • S Asia & SE Asia • 250 kW
VOA, Via Philippines

9595 BOTSWANA
RADIO BOTSWANA, Gaborone — ENGLISH, ETC • DS-TEMP INACTIVE • 45/50 kW

FINLAND
†YLE RADIO FINLAND, Pori — W • E Europe • 250 kW

INDIA
†ALL INDIA RADIO, Aligarh — DS • 250 kW / S Asia • 250 kW / ENGLISH & HINDI • DS • 250 kW
†ALL INDIA RADIO, Delhi — S Asia • 250 kW / S Asia • 50 kW

IRAN
†VO THE ISLAMIC REP, Tehrān — W • E Africa & S Africa • 500 kW

JAPAN
RADIO NIKKEI, Tokyo-Nagara — DS-1 • 50 kW

SPAIN
R EXTERIOR ESPANA, Noblejas — W M-Sa • N Africa & W Africa • 350 kW / W M-F • N Africa & W Africa • 350 kW / W Su • N Africa & W Africa • 350 kW / W Sa/Su • N Africa & W Africa • 350 kW

(con'd)

	0 1 2 3 4 5 6 7 8 9 10 11 12 13 14 15 16 17 18 19 20 21 22 23 24

ENGLISH ▬   ARABIC ▨▨▨   CHINESE □□□   FRENCH ▬▬   GERMAN ▬▬   RUSSIAN ═══   SPANISH ▬▬   OTHER ▬

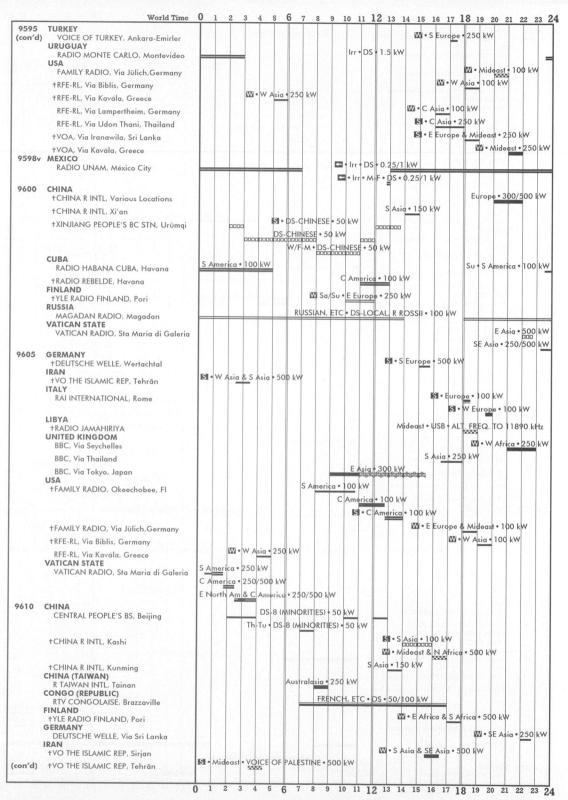

| | World Time | 0 | 1 | 2 | 3 | 4 | 5 | 6 | 7 | 8 | 9 | 10 | 11 | 12 | 13 | 14 | 15 | 16 | 17 | 18 | 19 | 20 | 21 | 22 | 23 | 24 |

9595 TURKEY
(con'd)   VOICE OF TURKEY, Ankara-Emirler — W • S Europe • 250 kW

URUGUAY
   RADIO MONTE CARLO, Montevideo — Irr • DS • 1.5 kW

USA
   FAMILY RADIO, Via Jülich, Germany — W • Mideast • 100 kW
   †RFE-RL, Via Biblis, Germany — W • W Asia • 100 kW
   †RFE-RL, Via Kavála, Greece — W • W Asia • 250 kW
   RFE-RL, Via Lampertheim, Germany — W • C Asia • 100 kW
   RFE-RL, Via Udon Thani, Thailand — S • C Asia • 250 kW
   †VOA, Via Iranawila, Sri Lanka — S • E Europe & Mideast • 250 kW
   †VOA, Via Kavála, Greece — W • Mideast • 250 kW

9598v MEXICO
   RADIO UNAM, México City — Irr • DS • 0.25/1 kW — Irr • M-F • DS • 0.25/1 kW

9600 CHINA
   †CHINA R INTL, Various Locations — Europe • 300/500 kW
   †CHINA R INTL, Xi'an — S Asia • 150 kW
   †XINJIANG PEOPLE'S BC STN, Urümqi — S • DS-CHINESE • 50 kW / DS-CHINESE • 50 kW / W/F-M • DS-CHINESE • 50 kW

CUBA
   RADIO HABANA CUBA, Havana — S America • 100 kW — Su • S America • 100 kW
   †RADIO REBELDE, Havana — C America • 100 kW

FINLAND
   †YLE RADIO FINLAND, Pori — W • Sa/Su • E Europe • 250 kW

RUSSIA
   MAGADAN RADIO, Magadan — RUSSIAN, ETC • DS-LOCAL, R ROSSII • 100 kW

VATICAN STATE
   VATICAN RADIO, Sta Maria di Galeria — E Asia • 500 kW / SE Asia • 250/500 kW

9605 GERMANY
   †DEUTSCHE WELLE, Wertachtal — S • S Europe • 500 kW

IRAN
   †VO THE ISLAMIC REP, Tehrān — S • W Asia & S Asia • 500 kW

ITALY
   RAI INTERNATIONAL, Rome — S • Europe • 100 kW / S • W Europe • 100 kW

LIBYA
   †RADIO JAMAHIRIYA — Mideast • USB • ALT. FREQ. TO 11890 kHz

UNITED KINGDOM
   BBC, Via Seychelles — W • W Africa • 250 kW
   BBC, Via Thailand — S Asia • 250 kW
   BBC, Via Tokyo, Japan — E Asia • 300 kW

USA
   †FAMILY RADIO, Okeechobee, Fl — S America • 100 kW / C America • 100 kW / S • C America • 100 kW
   †FAMILY RADIO, Via Jülich, Germany — W • E Europe & Mideast • 100 kW
   †RFE-RL, Via Biblis, Germany — W • W Asia • 100 kW
   RFE-RL, Via Kavála, Greece — W • W Asia • 250 kW

VATICAN STATE
   VATICAN RADIO, Sta Maria di Galeria — S America • 250 kW / C America • 250/500 kW / E North Am & C America • 250/500 kW

9610 CHINA
   CENTRAL PEOPLE'S BS, Beijing — DS-8 (MINORITIES) • 50 kW / Th-Tu • DS-8 (MINORITIES) • 50 kW
   †CHINA R INTL, Kashi — S • S Asia • 100 kW / W • Mideast & N Africa • 500 kW
   †CHINA R INTL, Kunming — S Asia • 150 kW

CHINA (TAIWAN)
   R TAIWAN INTL, Tainan — Australasia • 250 kW

CONGO (REPUBLIC)
   RTV Congolaise, Brazzaville — FRENCH, ETC • DS • 50/100 kW

FINLAND
   †YLE RADIO FINLAND, Pori — W • E Africa & S Africa • 500 kW

GERMANY
   DEUTSCHE WELLE, Via Sri Lanka — W • SE Asia • 250 kW

IRAN
   †VO THE ISLAMIC REP, Sirjan — W • S Asia & SE Asia • 500 kW
(con'd)   †VO THE ISLAMIC REP, Tehrān — S • Mideast • VOICE OF PALESTINE • 500 kW

| | World Time | 0 | 1 | 2 | 3 | 4 | 5 | 6 | 7 | 8 | 9 | 10 | 11 | 12 | 13 | 14 | 15 | 16 | 17 | 18 | 19 | 20 | 21 | 22 | 23 | 24 |

SEASONAL **S** OR **W**   1-HR TIMESHIFT MIDYEAR ⬅ OR ➡   JAMMING / OR /\   EARLIEST HEARD ◁   LATEST HEARD ▷   NEW FOR 2005 †

World Time 0 1 2 3 4 5 6 7 8 9 10 11 12 13 14 15 16 17 18 19 20 21 22 23 24

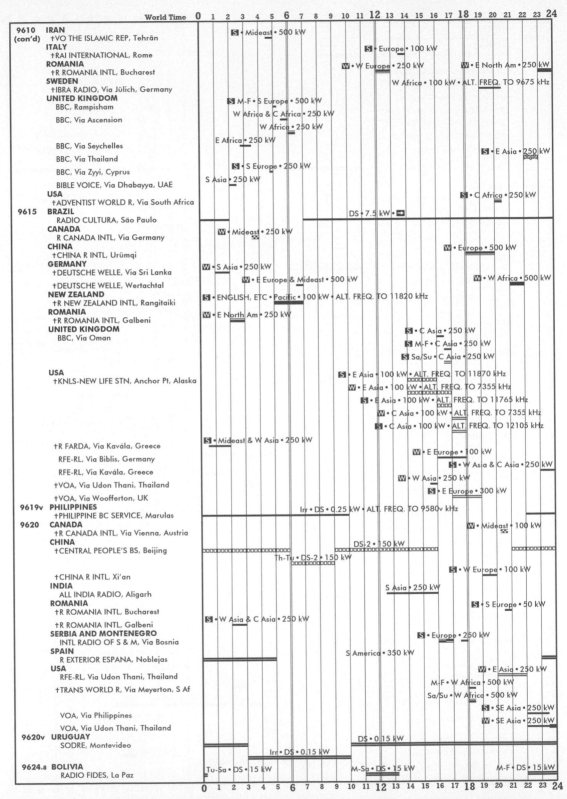

9610
(con'd) **IRAN**
    †VO THE ISLAMIC REP, Tehrān — S • Mideast • 500 kW
    ITALY
    †RAI INTERNATIONAL, Rome — S • Europe • 100 kW
    ROMANIA
    †R ROMANIA INTL, Bucharest — W • W Europe • 250 kW   W • E North Am • 250 kW
    SWEDEN
    †IBRA RADIO, Via Jülich, Germany — W Africa • 100 kW • ALT. FREQ. TO 9675 kHz
    UNITED KINGDOM
    BBC, Rampisham — S • M-F • S Europe • 500 kW
    BBC, Via Ascension — W Africa & C Africa • 250 kW
        W Africa • 250 kW
    BBC, Via Seychelles — E Africa • 250 kW
    BBC, Via Thailand — S • E Asia • 250 kW
    BBC, Via Zyyi, Cyprus — S • S Europe • 250 kW
    BIBLE VOICE, Via Dhabayya, UAE — S Asia • 250 kW
    USA
    †ADVENTIST WORLD R, Via South Africa — S • C Africa • 250 kW

9615 **BRAZIL**
    RADIO CULTURA, São Paulo — DS • 7.5 kW • ⇒
    CANADA
    R CANADA INTL, Via Germany — W • Mideast • 250 kW
    CHINA
    †CHINA R INTL, Urümqi — W • Europe • 500 kW
    GERMANY
    †DEUTSCHE WELLE, Via Sri Lanka — W • S Asia • 250 kW
    †DEUTSCHE WELLE, Wertachtal — W • E Europe & Mideast • 500 kW   W • W Africa • 500 kW
    NEW ZEALAND
    †R NEW ZEALAND INTL, Rangitaiki — S • ENGLISH, ETC • Pacific • 100 kW • ALT. FREQ. TO 11820 kHz
    ROMANIA
    †R ROMANIA INTL, Galbeni — W • E North Am • 250 kW
    UNITED KINGDOM
    BBC, Via Oman — S • C Asia • 250 kW
        S • M-F • C Asia • 250 kW
        S • Sa/Su • C Asia • 250 kW
    USA
    †KNLS-NEW LIFE STN, Anchor Pt, Alaska — S • E Asia • 100 kW • ALT. FREQ. TO 11870 kHz
        W • E Asia • 100 kW • ALT. FREQ. TO 7355 kHz
        S • E Asia • 100 kW • ALT. FREQ. TO 11765 kHz
        W • C Asia • 100 kW • ALT. FREQ. TO 7355 kHz
        S • C Asia • 100 kW • ALT. FREQ. TO 12105 kHz
    †R FARDA, Via Kavála, Greece — S • Mideast & W Asia • 250 kW
    RFE-RL, Via Biblis, Germany — W • E Europe • 100 kW
    RFE-RL, Via Kavála, Greece — S • W Asia & C Asia • 250 kW
    †VOA, Via Udon Thani, Thailand — W • W Asia • 250 kW
    †VOA, Via Woofferton, UK — S • E Europe • 300 kW

9619v **PHILIPPINES**
    †PHILIPPINE BC SERVICE, Marulas — Irr • DS • 0.25 kW • ALT. FREQ. TO 9580v kHz
9620 **CANADA**
    †R CANADA INTL, Via Vienna, Austria — W • Mideast • 100 kW
    CHINA
    †CENTRAL PEOPLE'S BS, Beijing — DS-2 • 150 kW
        Th-Tu • DS-2 • 150 kW
    †CHINA R INTL, Xi'an — S • W Europe • 100 kW
    INDIA
    ALL INDIA RADIO, Aligarh — S Asia • 250 kW
    ROMANIA
    †R ROMANIA INTL, Bucharest — S • S Europe • 50 kW
    †R ROMANIA INTL, Galbeni — S • W Asia & C Asia • 250 kW
    SERBIA AND MONTENEGRO
    INTL RADIO OF S & M, Via Bosnia — S • Europe • 250 kW
    SPAIN
    R EXTERIOR ESPANA, Noblejas — S America • 350 kW
    USA
    RFE-RL, Via Udon Thani, Thailand — W • E Asia • 250 kW
    †TRANS WORLD R, Via Meyerton, S Af — M-F • W Africa • 500 kW
        Sa/Su • W Africa • 500 kW
    VOA, Via Philippines — S • SE Asia • 250 kW
    VOA, Via Udon Thani, Thailand — W • SE Asia • 250 kW

9620v **URUGUAY**
    SODRE, Montevideo — DS • 0.15 kW
        Irr • DS • 0.15 kW

9624.8 **BOLIVIA**
    RADIO FIDES, La Paz — Tu-Sa • DS • 15 kW   M-Sa • DS • 15 kW   M-F • DS • 15 kW

0 1 2 3 4 5 6 7 8 9 10 11 12 13 14 15 16 17 18 19 20 21 22 23 24

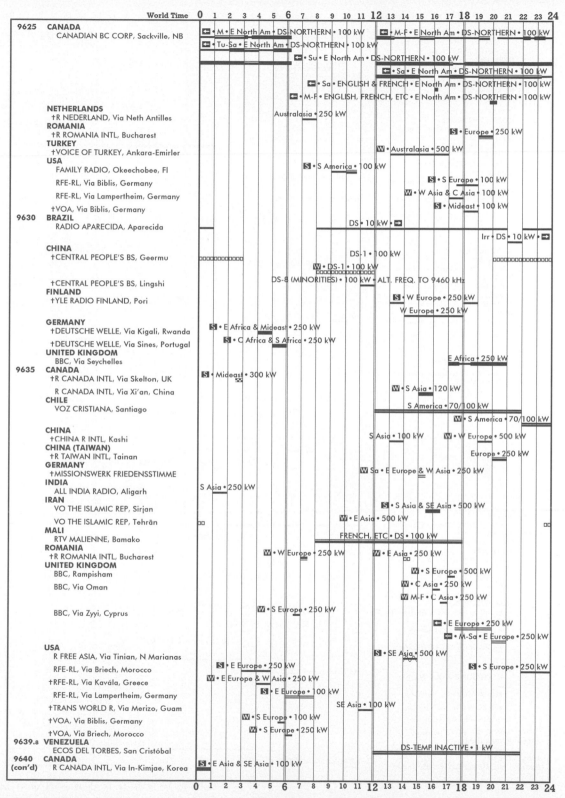

World Time 0 1 2 3 4 5 6 7 8 9 10 11 12 13 14 15 16 17 18 19 20 21 22 23 24

9625 CANADA
CANADIAN BC CORP, Sackville, NB
◁ • M • E North Am • DS-NORTHERN • 100 kW ... ◁ • M-F • E North Am • DS-NORTHERN • 100 kW
◁ • Tu-Sa • E North Am • DS-NORTHERN • 100 kW
◁ • Su • E North Am • DS-NORTHERN • 100 kW
◁ • Sa • E North Am • DS-NORTHERN • 100 kW
◁ • Sa • ENGLISH & FRENCH • E North Am • DS-NORTHERN • 100 kW
◁ • M-F • ENGLISH, FRENCH, ETC • E North Am • DS-NORTHERN • 100 kW

NETHERLANDS
†R NEDERLAND, Via Neth Antilles
Australasia • 250 kW
ROMANIA
†R ROMANIA INTL, Bucharest
S • Europe • 250 kW
TURKEY
†VOICE OF TURKEY, Ankara-Emirler
W • Australasia • 500 kW
USA
FAMILY RADIO, Okeechobee, Fl
S • S America • 100 kW
RFE-RL, Via Biblis, Germany
S • S Europe • 100 kW
RFE-RL, Via Lampertheim, Germany
W • W Asia & C Asia • 100 kW
†VOA, Via Biblis, Germany
S • Mideast • 100 kW

9630 BRAZIL
RADIO APARECIDA, Aparecida
DS • 10 kW • ▷
Irr • DS • 10 kW • ▷

CHINA
†CENTRAL PEOPLE'S BS, Geermu
DS-1 • 100 kW
W • DS-1 • 100 kW
†CENTRAL PEOPLE'S BS, Lingshi
DS-8 (MINORITIES) • 100 kW • ALT. FREQ. TO 9460 kHz
FINLAND
†YLE RADIO FINLAND, Pori
S • W Europe • 250 kW
W Europe • 250 kW
GERMANY
†DEUTSCHE WELLE, Via Kigali, Rwanda
S • E Africa & Mideast • 250 kW
†DEUTSCHE WELLE, Via Sines, Portugal
S • C Africa & S Africa • 250 kW
UNITED KINGDOM
BBC, Via Seychelles
E Africa • 250 kW

9635 CANADA
†R CANADA INTL, Via Skelton, UK
S • Mideast • 300 kW
R CANADA INTL, Via Xi'an, China
W • S Asia • 120 kW
CHILE
VOZ CRISTIANA, Santiago
S America • 70/100 kW
W • S America • 70/100 kW

CHINA
†CHINA R INTL, Kashi
S Asia • 100 kW
W • W Europe • 500 kW
CHINA (TAIWAN)
†R TAIWAN INTL, Tainan
Europe • 250 kW
GERMANY
†MISSIONSWERK FRIEDENSSTIMME
W • Sa • E Europe & W Asia • 250 kW
INDIA
ALL INDIA RADIO, Aligarh
S Asia • 250 kW
IRAN
VO THE ISLAMIC REP, Sirjan
S • S Asia & SE Asia • 500 kW
VO THE ISLAMIC REP, Tehrän
W • E Asia • 500 kW
MALI
RTV MALIENNE, Bamako
FRENCH, ETC • DS • 100 kW
ROMANIA
†R ROMANIA INTL, Bucharest
W • W Europe • 250 kW
W • E Asia • 250 kW
UNITED KINGDOM
BBC, Rampisham
W • S Europe • 500 kW
BBC, Via Oman
W • C Asia • 250 kW
W • M-F • C Asia • 250 kW
BBC, Via Zyyi, Cyprus
W • S Europe • 250 kW
◁ • E Europe • 250 kW
◁ • M-Sa • E Europe • 250 kW

USA
R FREE ASIA, Via Tinian, N Marianas
S • SE Asia • 500 kW
RFE-RL, Via Briech, Morocco
S • E Europe • 250 kW
S • S Europe • 250 kW
†RFE-RL, Via Kavála, Greece
W • E Europe & W Asia • 250 kW
RFE-RL, Via Lampertheim, Germany
S • E Europe • 100 kW
†TRANS WORLD R, Via Merizo, Guam
SE Asia • 100 kW
†VOA, Via Biblis, Germany
W • S Europe • 100 kW
†VOA, Via Briech, Morocco
W • S Europe • 250 kW

9639.8 VENEZUELA
ECOS DEL TORBES, San Cristóbal
DS-TEMP INACTIVE • 1 kW

9640 CANADA
(con'd) R CANADA INTL, Via In-Kimjae, Korea
S • E Asia & SE Asia • 100 kW

0 1 2 3 4 5 6 7 8 9 10 11 12 13 14 15 16 17 18 19 20 21 22 23 24

SEASONAL S OR W   1-HR TIMESHIFT MIDYEAR ◁ OR ▷   JAMMING / OR /\   EARLIEST HEARD ◁   LATEST HEARD ▷   NEW FOR 2005 †

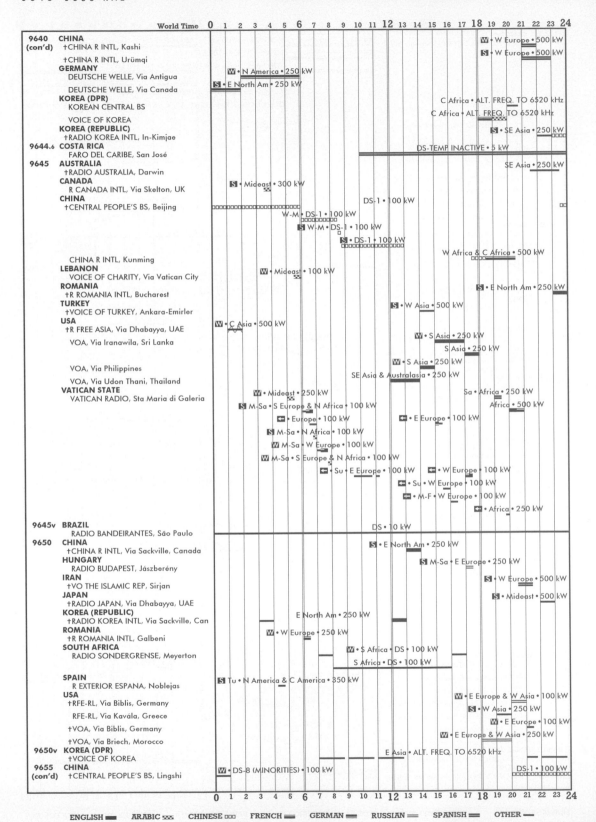

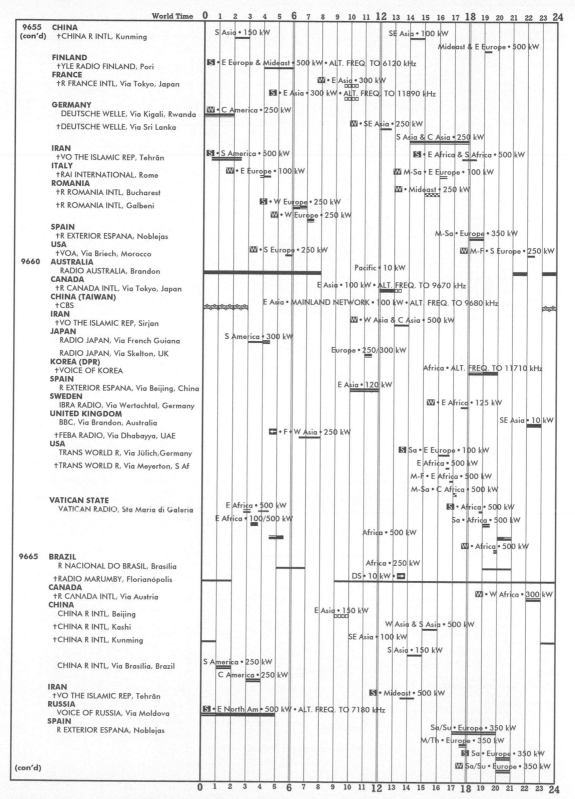

| World Time | 0 | 1 | 2 | 3 | 4 | 5 | 6 | 7 | 8 | 9 | 10 | 11 | 12 | 13 | 14 | 15 | 16 | 17 | 18 | 19 | 20 | 21 | 22 | 23 | 24 |

9655 CHINA
(con'd) †CHINA R INTL, Kunming — S Asia • 150 kW — SE Asia • 100 kW — Mideast & E Europe • 500 kW

FINLAND
   †YLE RADIO FINLAND, Pori — S • E Europe & Mideast • 500 kW • ALT. FREQ. TO 6120 kHz

FRANCE
   †R FRANCE INTL, Via Tokyo, Japan — W • E Asia • 300 kW; S • E Asia • 300 kW • ALT. FREQ. TO 11890 kHz

GERMANY
   DEUTSCHE WELLE, Via Kigali, Rwanda — W • C America • 250 kW

   †DEUTSCHE WELLE, Via Sri Lanka — W • SE Asia • 250 kW; S Asia & C Asia • 250 kW

IRAN
   †VO THE ISLAMIC REP, Tehrãn — S • S America • 500 kW — S • E Africa & S Africa • 500 kW

ITALY
   †RAI INTERNATIONAL, Rome — W • E Europe • 100 kW — W M-Sa • E Europe • 100 kW

ROMANIA
   †R ROMANIA INTL, Bucharest — W • Mideast • 250 kW

   †R ROMANIA INTL, Galbeni — S • W Europe • 250 kW; W • W Europe • 250 kW

SPAIN
   †R EXTERIOR ESPANA, Noblejas — M-Sa • Europe • 350 kW

USA
   †VOA, Via Briech, Morocco — W • S Europe • 250 kW — W M-F • S Europe • 250 kW

9660 AUSTRALIA
   RADIO AUSTRALIA, Brandon — Pacific • 10 kW

CANADA
   †R CANADA INTL, Via Tokyo, Japan — E Asia • 100 kW • ALT. FREQ. TO 9670 kHz

CHINA (TAIWAN)
   †CBS — E Asia • MAINLAND NETWORK • 100 kW • ALT. FREQ. TO 9680 kHz

IRAN
   †VO THE ISLAMIC REP, Sirjan — W • W Asia & C Asia • 500 kW

JAPAN
   RADIO JAPAN, Via French Guiana — S America • 300 kW

   RADIO JAPAN, Via Skelton, UK — Europe • 250/300 kW

KOREA (DPR)
   †VOICE OF KOREA — Africa • ALT. FREQ. TO 11710 kHz

SPAIN
   R EXTERIOR ESPANA, Via Beijing, China — E Asia • 120 kW

SWEDEN
   IBRA RADIO, Via Wertachtal, Germany — W • E Africa • 125 kW

UNITED KINGDOM
   BBC, Via Brandon, Australia — SE Asia • 10 kW

   †FEBA RADIO, Via Dhabayya, UAE — ◄ • F • W Asia • 250 kW

USA
   TRANS WORLD R, Via Jülich, Germany — S Sa • E Europe • 100 kW; E Africa • 500 kW; M-F • E Africa • 500 kW; M-Sa • C Africa • 500 kW

   †TRANS WORLD R, Via Meyerton, S Af —

VATICAN STATE
   VATICAN RADIO, Sta Maria di Galeria — E Africa • 500 kW; E Africa • 100/500 kW; S • Africa • 500 kW; Sa • Africa • 500 kW; Africa • 500 kW; W • Africa • 500 kW

9665 BRAZIL
   R NACIONAL DO BRASIL, Brasília — Africa • 250 kW

   †RADIO MARUMBY, Florianópolis — DS • 10 kW • ►

CANADA
   †R CANADA INTL, Via Austria — W • W Africa • 300 kW

CHINA
   CHINA R INTL, Beijing — E Asia • 150 kW

   †CHINA R INTL, Kashi — W Asia & S Asia • 500 kW

   †CHINA R INTL, Kunming — SE Asia • 100 kW; S Asia • 150 kW

   CHINA R INTL, Via Brasília, Brazil — S America • 250 kW; C America • 250 kW

IRAN
   †VO THE ISLAMIC REP, Tehrãn — S • Mideast • 500 kW

RUSSIA
   VOICE OF RUSSIA, Via Moldova — S • E North Am • 500 kW • ALT. FREQ. TO 7180 kHz

SPAIN
   R EXTERIOR ESPANA, Noblejas — Sa/Su • Europe • 350 kW; M/Th • Europe • 350 kW; S Sa • Europe • 350 kW; W Sa/Su • Europe • 350 kW

(con'd)

| | 0 | 1 | 2 | 3 | 4 | 5 | 6 | 7 | 8 | 9 | 10 | 11 | 12 | 13 | 14 | 15 | 16 | 17 | 18 | 19 | 20 | 21 | 22 | 23 | 24 |

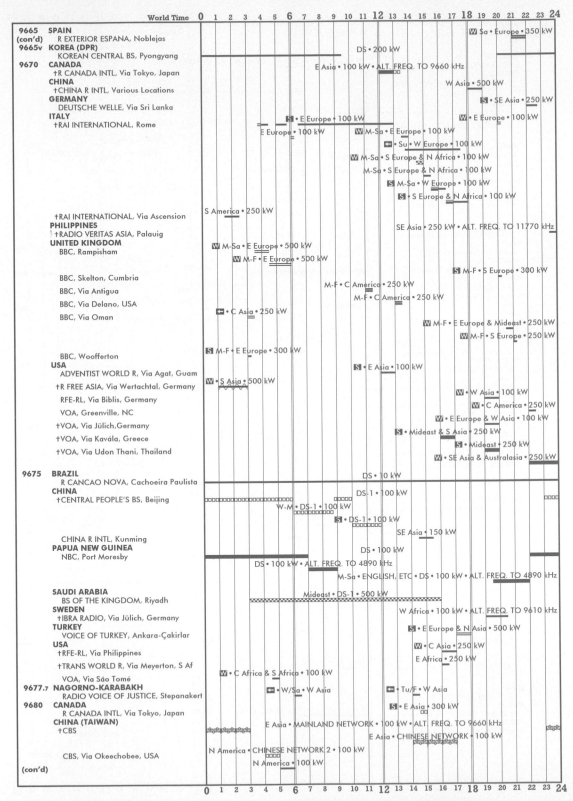

| | | World Time | 0 | 1 | 2 | 3 | 4 | 5 | 6 | 7 | 8 | 9 | 10 | 11 | 12 | 13 | 14 | 15 | 16 | 17 | 18 | 19 | 20 | 21 | 22 | 23 | 24 |

9665 **SPAIN**
(con'd) R EXTERIOR ESPANA, Noblejas — W Sa • Europe • 350 kW
9665v **KOREA (DPR)**
KOREAN CENTRAL BS, Pyongyang — DS • 200 kW
9670 **CANADA**
†R CANADA INTL, Via Tokyo, Japan — E Asia • 100 kW • ALT. FREQ. TO 9660 kHz
CHINA
†CHINA R INTL, Various Locations — W Asia • 500 kW
GERMANY
DEUTSCHE WELLE, Via Sri Lanka — S • SE Asia • 250 kW
ITALY
†RAI INTERNATIONAL, Rome — S • E Europe • 100 kW ; W • E Europe • 100 kW
E Europe • 100 kW
W M-Sa • E Europe • 100 kW
S • Su • W Europe • 100 kW
W M-Sa • S Europe & N Africa • 100 kW
M-Sa • S Europe & N Africa • 100 kW
S • M-Sa • W Europe • 100 kW
S • S Europe & N Africa • 100 kW

†RAI INTERNATIONAL, Via Ascension — S America • 250 kW
PHILIPPINES
†RADIO VERITAS ASIA, Palauig — SE Asia • 250 kW • ALT. FREQ. TO 11770 kHz
UNITED KINGDOM
BBC, Rampisham — W M-Sa • E Europe • 500 kW
W M-F • E Europe • 500 kW

BBC, Skelton, Cumbria — S M-F • S Europe • 300 kW
BBC, Via Antigua — M-F • C America • 250 kW
BBC, Via Delano, USA — M-F • C America • 250 kW
BBC, Via Oman — S • C Asia • 250 kW
W M-F • E Europe & Mideast • 250 kW
W M-F • S Europe • 250 kW

BBC, Woofferton — S M-F • E Europe • 300 kW
USA
ADVENTIST WORLD R, Via Agat, Guam — S • E Asia • 100 kW
†R FREE ASIA, Via Wertachtal, Germany — W • S Asia • 500 kW
RFE-RL, Via Biblis, Germany — W • W Asia • 100 kW
VOA, Greenville, NC — W • C America • 250 kW
†VOA, Via Jülich, Germany — W • E Europe & W Asia • 100 kW
†VOA, Via Kavála, Greece — S • Mideast & S Asia • 250 kW
†VOA, Via Udon Thani, Thailand — S • Mideast • 250 kW
W • SE Asia & Australasia • 250 kW

9675 **BRAZIL**
R CANCAO NOVA, Cachoeira Paulista — DS • 10 kW
CHINA
†CENTRAL PEOPLE'S BS, Beijing — DS-1 • 100 kW
W-M • DS-1 • 100 kW
S • DS-1 • 100 kW

CHINA R INTL, Kunming — SE Asia • 150 kW
PAPUA NEW GUINEA
NBC, Port Moresby — DS • 100 kW
DS • 100 kW • ALT. FREQ. TO 4890 kHz
M-Sa • ENGLISH, ETC • DS • 100 kW • ALT. FREQ. TO 4890 kHz

SAUDI ARABIA
BS OF THE KINGDOM, Riyadh — Mideast • DS-1 • 500 kW
SWEDEN
†IBRA RADIO, Via Jülich, Germany — W Africa • 100 kW • ALT. FREQ. TO 9610 kHz
TURKEY
VOICE OF TURKEY, Ankara-Çakirlar — S • E Europe & N Asia • 500 kW
USA
†RFE-RL, Via Philippines — W • C Asia • 250 kW
E Africa • 250 kW
†TRANS WORLD R, Via Meyerton, S Af — W • C Africa & S Africa • 100 kW
VOA, Via São Tomé
9677.7 **NAGORNO-KARABAKH** — S • W/Sa • W Asia ; S • Tu/F • W Asia
RADIO VOICE OF JUSTICE, Stepanakert
9680 **CANADA** — S • E Asia • 300 kW
R CANADA INTL, Via Tokyo, Japan
CHINA (TAIWAN)
†CBS — E Asia • MAINLAND NETWORK • 100 kW • ALT. FREQ. TO 9660 kHz
E Asia • CHINESE NETWORK • 100 kW

CBS, Via Okeechobee, USA — N America • CHINESE NETWORK 2 • 100 kW
N America • 100 kW

(con'd)

ENGLISH ▬   ARABIC ⬚⬚⬚   CHINESE □□□   FRENCH ═══   GERMAN ▬▬   RUSSIAN ══   SPANISH ▬▬   OTHER ──

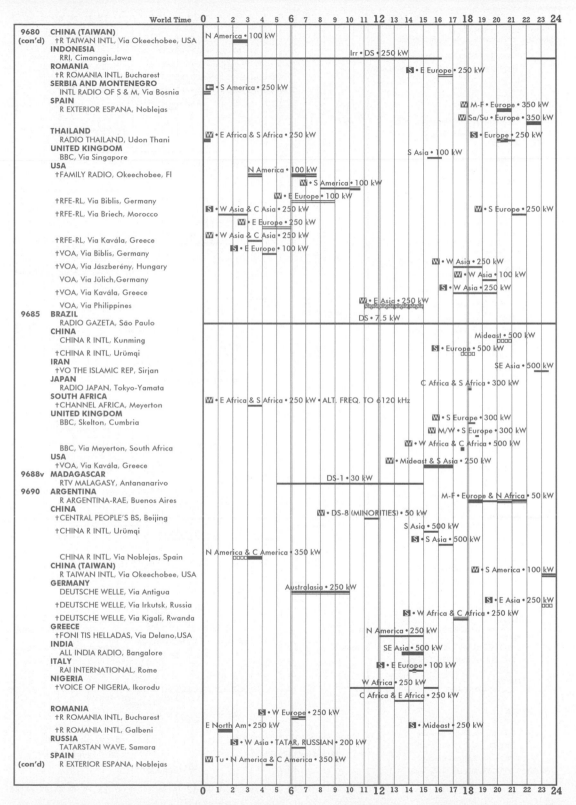

World Time 0 1 2 3 4 5 6 7 8 9 10 11 12 13 14 15 16 17 18 19 20 21 22 23 24

9680 **CHINA (TAIWAN)**
(con'd) †R TAIWAN INTL, Via Okeechobee, USA — N America • 100 kW
  INDONESIA
  RRI, Cimanggis, Jawa — Irr • DS • 250 kW
  ROMANIA
  †R ROMANIA INTL, Bucharest — S • E Europe • 250 kW
  SERBIA AND MONTENEGRO
  INTL RADIO OF S & M, Via Bosnia — • S America • 250 kW
  SPAIN
  R EXTERIOR ESPANA, Noblejas — W M-F • Europe • 350 kW
  W Sa/Su • Europe • 350 kW
  THAILAND
  RADIO THAILAND, Udon Thani — W • E Africa & S Africa • 250 kW — S • Europe • 250 kW
  UNITED KINGDOM
  BBC, Via Singapore — S Asia • 100 kW
  USA
  †FAMILY RADIO, Okeechobee, Fl — N America • 100 kW
  W • S America • 100 kW
  W • E Europe • 100 kW
  †RFE-RL, Via Biblis, Germany — S • W Asia & C Asia • 250 kW   W • S Europe • 250 kW
  W • E Europe • 250 kW
  †RFE-RL, Via Briech, Morocco
  †RFE-RL, Via Kavála, Greece — W • W Asia & C Asia • 250 kW
  †VOA, Via Biblis, Germany — S • E Europe • 100 kW
  †VOA, Via Jászberény, Hungary — W • W Asia • 250 kW
  VOA, Via Jülich, Germany — W • W Asia • 100 kW
  †VOA, Via Kavála, Greece — S • W Asia • 250 kW
  VOA, Via Philippines — W • E Asia • 250 kW
9685 **BRAZIL**
  RADIO GAZETA, São Paulo — DS • 7.5 kW
  CHINA
  CHINA R INTL, Kunming — Mideast • 500 kW
  †CHINA R INTL, Urümqi — S • Europe • 500 kW
  IRAN
  †VO THE ISLAMIC REP, Sirjan — SE Asia • 500 kW
  JAPAN
  RADIO JAPAN, Tokyo-Yamata — C Africa & S Africa • 300 kW
  SOUTH AFRICA
  †CHANNEL AFRICA, Meyerton — W • E Africa & S Africa • 250 kW • ALT. FREQ. TO 6120 kHz
  UNITED KINGDOM
  BBC, Skelton, Cumbria — W • S Europe • 300 kW
  W M/W • S Europe • 300 kW
  BBC, Via Meyerton, South Africa — W • W Africa & C Africa • 500 kW
  USA
  †VOA, Via Kavála, Greece — W • Mideast & S Asia • 250 kW
9688v MADAGASCAR
  RTV MALAGASY, Antananarivo — DS-1 • 30 kW
9690 ARGENTINA
  R ARGENTINA-RAE, Buenos Aires — M-F • Europe & N Africa • 50 kW
  CHINA
  †CENTRAL PEOPLE'S BS, Beijing — W • DS-8 (MINORITIES) • 50 kW
  †CHINA R INTL, Urümqi — S Asia • 500 kW
  S • S Asia • 500 kW
  CHINA R INTL, Via Noblejas, Spain — N America & C America • 350 kW
  CHINA (TAIWAN)
  R TAIWAN INTL, Via Okeechobee, USA — W • S America • 100 kW
  GERMANY
  DEUTSCHE WELLE, Via Antigua — Australasia • 250 kW
  †DEUTSCHE WELLE, Via Irkutsk, Russia — S • E Asia • 250 kW
  †DEUTSCHE WELLE, Via Kigali, Rwanda — S • W Africa & C Africa • 250 kW
  GREECE
  †FONI TIS HELLADAS, Via Delano, USA — N America • 250 kW
  INDIA
  ALL INDIA RADIO, Bangalore — SE Asia • 500 kW
  ITALY
  RAI INTERNATIONAL, Rome — S • E Europe • 100 kW
  NIGERIA
  †VOICE OF NIGERIA, Ikorodu — W Africa • 250 kW
  C Africa & E Africa • 250 kW
  ROMANIA
  †R ROMANIA INTL, Bucharest — S • W Europe • 250 kW
  †R ROMANIA INTL, Galbeni — E North Am • 250 kW   S • Mideast • 250 kW
  RUSSIA
  TATARSTAN WAVE, Samara — S • W Asia • TATAR, RUSSIAN • 200 kW
  SPAIN
(con'd) R EXTERIOR ESPANA, Noblejas — W Tu • N America & C America • 350 kW

0 1 2 3 4 5 6 7 8 9 10 11 12 13 14 15 16 17 18 19 20 21 22 23 24

SEASONAL S OR W   1-HR TIMESHIFT MIDYEAR ⇐ OR ⇒   JAMMING / OR ∧   EARLIEST HEARD ◁   LATEST HEARD ▷   NEW FOR 2005 †

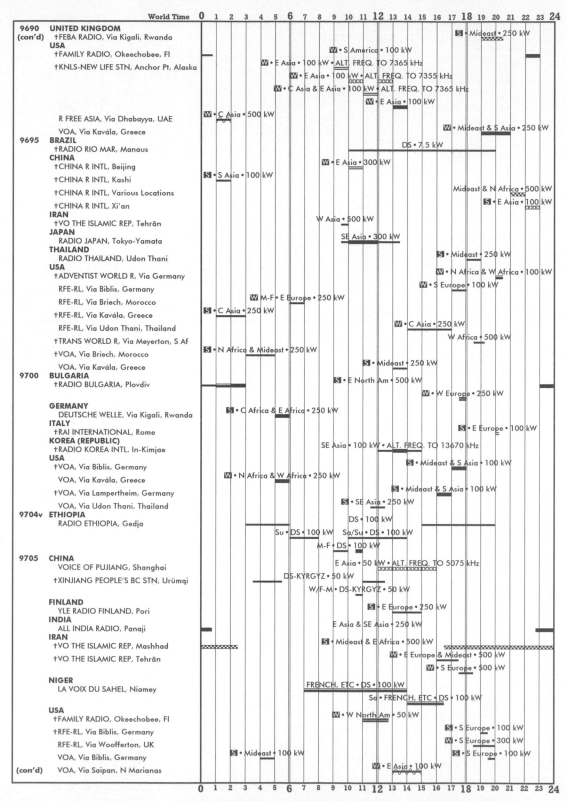

| World Time | 0 | 1 | 2 | 3 | 4 | 5 | 6 | 7 | 8 | 9 | 10 | 11 | 12 | 13 | 14 | 15 | 16 | 17 | 18 | 19 | 20 | 21 | 22 | 23 | 24 |

9690 UNITED KINGDOM
(con'd)   †FEBA RADIO, Via Kigali, Rwanda   S • Mideast • 250 kW
        USA
         †FAMILY RADIO, Okeechobee, Fl   W • S America • 100 kW
         †KNLS-NEW LIFE STN, Anchor Pt, Alaska   W • E Asia • 100 kW • ALT. FREQ. TO 7365 kHz
                                                   W • E Asia • 100 kW • ALT. FREQ. TO 7355 kHz
                                                   W • C Asia & E Asia • 100 kW • ALT. FREQ. TO 7365 kHz
                                                   W • E Asia • 100 kW
         R FREE ASIA, Via Dhabayya, UAE   W • C Asia • 500 kW
         VOA, Via Kavála, Greece   W • Mideast & S Asia • 250 kW

9695 BRAZIL
         †RADIO RIO MAR, Manaus   DS • 7.5 kW
        CHINA
         †CHINA R INTL, Beijing   W • E Asia • 300 kW
         †CHINA R INTL, Kashi   S • S Asia • 100 kW
         †CHINA R INTL, Various Locations   Mideast & N Africa • 500 kW
         †CHINA R INTL, Xi'an   S • E Asia • 100 kW
        IRAN
         †VO THE ISLAMIC REP, Tehrān   W Asia • 500 kW
        JAPAN
         RADIO JAPAN, Tokyo-Yamata   SE Asia • 300 kW
        THAILAND
         RADIO THAILAND, Udon Thani   S • Mideast • 250 kW
        USA
         †ADVENTIST WORLD R, Via Germany   W • N Africa & W Africa • 100 kW
         RFE-RL, Via Biblis, Germany   W • S Europe • 100 kW
         RFE-RL, Via Briech, Morocco   W M-F • E Europe • 250 kW
         †RFE-RL, Via Kavála, Greece   S • C Asia • 250 kW
         RFE-RL, Via Udon Thani, Thailand   W • C Asia • 250 kW
         †TRANS WORLD R, Via Meyerton, S Af   W Africa • 500 kW
         †VOA, Via Briech, Morocco   S • N Africa & Mideast • 250 kW
         VOA, Via Kavála, Greece   S • Mideast • 250 kW

9700 BULGARIA
         †RADIO BULGARIA, Plovdiv   S • E North Am • 500 kW
                                                   W • W Europe • 250 kW
        GERMANY
         DEUTSCHE WELLE, Via Kigali, Rwanda   S • C Africa & E Africa • 250 kW
        ITALY
         †RAI INTERNATIONAL, Rome   S • E Europe • 100 kW
        KOREA (REPUBLIC)
         †RADIO KOREA INTL, In-Kimjae   SE Asia • 100 kW • ALT. FREQ. TO 13670 kHz
        USA
         †VOA, Via Biblis, Germany   S • Mideast & S Asia • 100 kW
         VOA, Via Kavála, Greece   W • N Africa & W Africa • 250 kW
         †VOA, Via Lampertheim, Germany   S • Mideast & S Asia • 100 kW
         VOA, Via Udon Thani, Thailand   S • SE Asia • 250 kW

9704v ETHIOPIA
         RADIO ETHIOPIA, Gedja   DS • 100 kW
                                                   Su • DS • 100 kW   Sa/Su • DS • 100 kW
                                                   M-F • DS • 100 kW

9705 CHINA
         VOICE OF PUJIANG, Shanghai   E Asia • 50 kW • ALT. FREQ. TO 5075 kHz
         †XINJIANG PEOPLE'S BC STN, Urümqi   DS-KYRGYZ • 50 kW
                                                   W/F-M • DS-KYRGYZ • 50 kW
        FINLAND
         YLE RADIO FINLAND, Pori   S • E Europe • 250 kW
        INDIA
         ALL INDIA RADIO, Panaji   E Asia & SE Asia • 250 kW
        IRAN
         †VO THE ISLAMIC REP, Mashhad   S • Mideast & E Africa • 500 kW
         †VO THE ISLAMIC REP, Tehrān   W • E Europe & Mideast • 500 kW
                                                   W • S Europe • 500 kW
        NIGER
         LA VOIX DU SAHEL, Niamey   FRENCH, ETC • DS • 100 kW
                                                   Sa • FRENCH, ETC • DS • 100 kW
        USA
         †FAMILY RADIO, Okeechobee, Fl   W • W North Am • 50 kW
         †RFE-RL, Via Biblis, Germany   S • S Europe • 100 kW
         RFE-RL, Via Woofferton, UK   W • S Europe • 300 kW
         VOA, Via Biblis, Germany   S • Mideast • 100 kW
(con'd) VOA, Via Saipan, N Marianas   W • E Asia • 100 kW

| 0 | 1 | 2 | 3 | 4 | 5 | 6 | 7 | 8 | 9 | 10 | 11 | 12 | 13 | 14 | 15 | 16 | 17 | 18 | 19 | 20 | 21 | 22 | 23 | 24 |

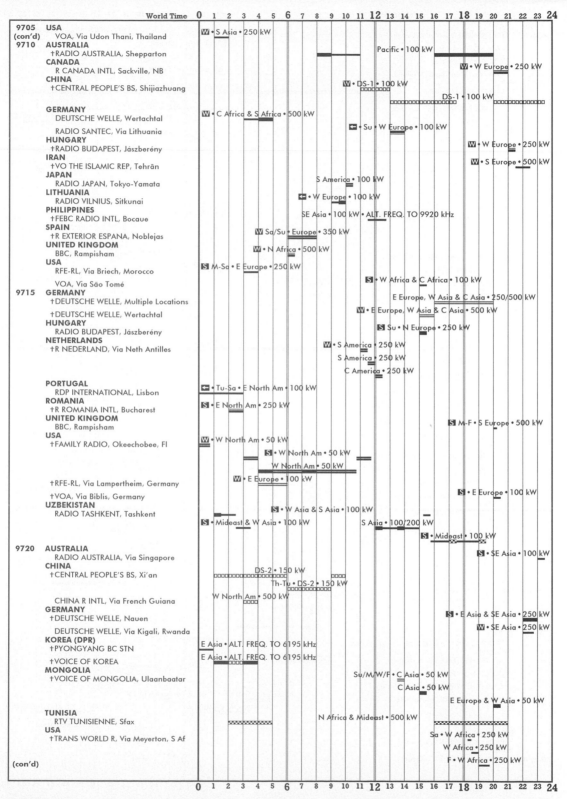

| World Time | 0 | 1 | 2 | 3 | 4 | 5 | 6 | 7 | 8 | 9 | 10 | 11 | 12 | 13 | 14 | 15 | 16 | 17 | 18 | 19 | 20 | 21 | 22 | 23 | 24 |

9705 USA
(con'd) VOA, Via Udon Thani, Thailand — W • S Asia • 250 kW

9710 AUSTRALIA
†RADIO AUSTRALIA, Shepparton — Pacific • 100 kW

CANADA
R CANADA INTL, Sackville, NB — W • W Europe • 250 kW

CHINA
†CENTRAL PEOPLE'S BS, Shijiazhuang — W • DS-1 • 100 kW / DS-1 • 100 kW

GERMANY
DEUTSCHE WELLE, Wertachtal — W • C Africa & S Africa • 500 kW

RADIO SANTEC, Via Lithuania — • Su • W Europe • 100 kW

HUNGARY
†RADIO BUDAPEST, Jászberény — W • W Europe • 250 kW

IRAN
†VO THE ISLAMIC REP, Tehrān — W • S Europe • 500 kW

JAPAN
RADIO JAPAN, Tokyo-Yamata — S America • 100 kW

LITHUANIA
RADIO VILNIUS, Sitkunai — • W Europe • 100 kW

PHILIPPINES
†FEBC RADIO INTL, Bocaue — SE Asia • 100 kW • ALT. FREQ. TO 9920 kHz

SPAIN
†R EXTERIOR ESPANA, Noblejas — W Sa/Su • Europe • 350 kW

UNITED KINGDOM
BBC, Rampisham — W • N Africa • 500 kW

USA
RFE-RL, Via Briech, Morocco — S M-Sa • E Europe • 250 kW

VOA, Via São Tomé — S • W Africa & C Africa • 100 kW

9715 GERMANY
†DEUTSCHE WELLE, Multiple Locations — E Europe, W Asia & C Asia • 250/500 kW

†DEUTSCHE WELLE, Wertachtal — W • E Europe, W Asia & C Asia • 500 kW

HUNGARY
RADIO BUDAPEST, Jászberény — S Su • N Europe • 250 kW

NETHERLANDS
†R NEDERLAND, Via Neth Antilles — W • S America • 250 kW / S America • 250 kW / C America • 250 kW

PORTUGAL
RDP INTERNATIONAL, Lisbon — • Tu-Sa • E North Am • 100 kW

ROMANIA
†R ROMANIA INTL, Bucharest — S • E North Am • 250 kW

UNITED KINGDOM
BBC, Rampisham — S M-F • S Europe • 500 kW

USA
†FAMILY RADIO, Okeechobee, Fl — W • W North Am • 50 kW / S • W North Am • 50 kW / W North Am • 50 kW

†RFE-RL, Via Lampertheim, Germany — W • E Europe • 100 kW

†VOA, Via Biblis, Germany — S • E Europe • 100 kW

UZBEKISTAN
RADIO TASHKENT, Tashkent — S • W Asia & S Asia • 100 kW

9720 AUSTRALIA
RADIO AUSTRALIA, Via Singapore — S • Mideast & W Asia • 100 kW / S Asia • 100/200 kW / S • Mideast • 100 kW / S • SE Asia • 100 kW

CHINA
†CENTRAL PEOPLE'S BS, Xi'an — DS-2 • 150 kW / Th-Tu • DS-2 • 150 kW

CHINA R INTL, Via French Guiana — W North Am • 500 kW

GERMANY
†DEUTSCHE WELLE, Nauen — S • E Asia & SE Asia • 250 kW

DEUTSCHE WELLE, Via Kigali, Rwanda — W • SE Asia • 250 kW

KOREA (DPR)
†PYONGYANG BC STN — E Asia • ALT. FREQ. TO 6195 kHz

†VOICE OF KOREA — E Asia • ALT. FREQ. TO 6195 kHz

MONGOLIA
†VOICE OF MONGOLIA, Ulaanbaatar — Su/M/W/F • C Asia • 50 kW / C Asia • 50 kW / E Europe & W Asia • 50 kW

TUNISIA
RTV TUNISIENNE, Sfax — N Africa & Mideast • 500 kW

USA
†TRANS WORLD R, Via Meyerton, S Af — Sa • W Africa • 250 kW / W Africa • 250 kW / F • W Africa • 250 kW

(con'd)

| World Time | 0 | 1 | 2 | 3 | 4 | 5 | 6 | 7 | 8 | 9 | 10 | 11 | 12 | 13 | 14 | 15 | 16 | 17 | 18 | 19 | 20 | 21 | 22 | 23 | 24 |

SEASONAL S OR W   1-HR TIMESHIFT MIDYEAR ⇐ OR ⇒   JAMMING / OR /\   EARLIEST HEARD ◁   LATEST HEARD ▷   NEW FOR 2005 †

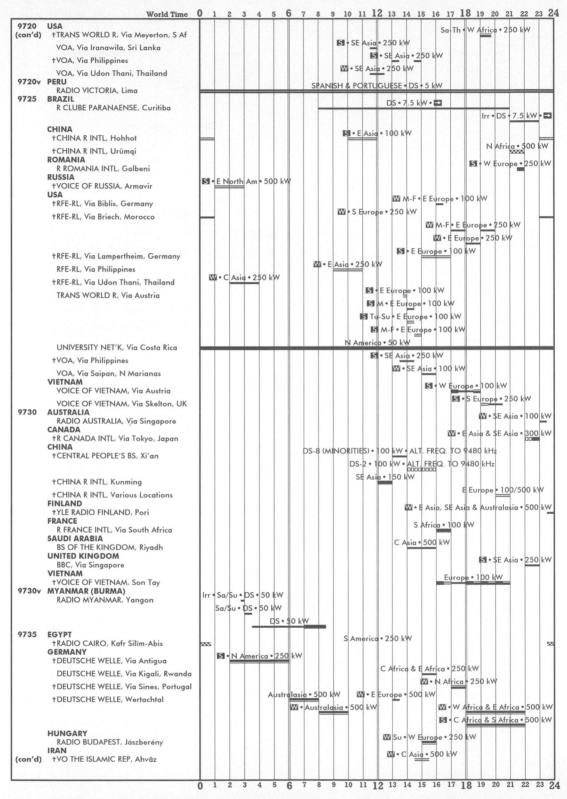

World Time 0 1 2 3 4 5 6 7 8 9 10 11 12 13 14 15 16 17 18 19 20 21 22 23 24

9720
(con'd) USA
  †TRANS WORLD R, Via Meyerton, S Af — Sa-Th • W Africa • 250 kW
  VOA, Via Iranawila, Sri Lanka — S • SE Asia • 250 kW
  †VOA, Via Philippines — S • SE Asia • 250 kW
  VOA, Via Udon Thani, Thailand — W • SE Asia • 250 kW
9720v PERU
  RADIO VICTORIA, Lima — SPANISH & PORTUGUESE • DS • 5 kW
9725 BRAZIL
  R CLUBE PARANAENSE, Curitiba — DS • 7.5 kW • ⇨ / Irr • DS • 7.5 kW • ⇨

  CHINA
  †CHINA R INTL, Hohhot — S • E Asia • 100 kW
  †CHINA R INTL, Urümqi — N Africa • 500 kW
  ROMANIA
  R ROMANIA INTL, Galbeni — S • W Europe • 250 kW
  RUSSIA
  †VOICE OF RUSSIA, Armavir — S • E North Am • 500 kW
  USA
  †RFE-RL, Via Biblis, Germany — W M-F • E Europe • 100 kW
  †RFE-RL, Via Briech, Morocco — W • S Europe • 250 kW
    W M-F • E Europe • 250 kW
    W • E Europe • 250 kW
  †RFE-RL, Via Lampertheim, Germany — S • E Europe • 100 kW
  RFE-RL, Via Philippines — W • E Asia • 250 kW
  †RFE-RL, Via Udon Thani, Thailand — W • C Asia • 250 kW
  TRANS WORLD R, Via Austria — S • E Europe • 100 kW
    S M • E Europe • 100 kW
    S Tu-Su • E Europe • 100 kW
    S M-F • E Europe • 100 kW
  UNIVERSITY NET'K, Via Costa Rica — N America • 50 kW
  †VOA, Via Philippines — S • SE Asia • 250 kW
  VOA, Via Saipan, N Marianas — W • SE Asia • 100 kW
  VIETNAM
  VOICE OF VIETNAM, Via Austria — S • W Europe • 100 kW
  VOICE OF VIETNAM, Via Skelton, UK — S • S Europe • 250 kW
9730 AUSTRALIA
  RADIO AUSTRALIA, Via Singapore — W • SE Asia • 100 kW
  CANADA
  †R CANADA INTL, Via Tokyo, Japan — W • E Asia & SE Asia • 300 kW
  CHINA
  †CENTRAL PEOPLE'S BS, Xi'an — DS-8 (MINORITIES) • 100 kW • ALT. FREQ. TO 9480 kHz
    DS-2 • 100 kW • ALT. FREQ. TO 9480 kHz
  †CHINA R INTL, Kunming — SE Asia • 150 kW
  †CHINA R INTL, Various Locations — E Europe • 100/500 kW
  FINLAND
  †YLE RADIO FINLAND, Pori — W • E Asia, SE Asia & Australasia • 500 kW
  FRANCE
  R FRANCE INTL, Via South Africa — S Africa • 100 kW
  SAUDI ARABIA
  BS OF THE KINGDOM, Riyadh — C Asia • 500 kW
  UNITED KINGDOM
  BBC, Via Singapore — S • SE Asia • 250 kW
  VIETNAM
  †VOICE OF VIETNAM, Son Tay — Europe • 100 kW
9730v MYANMAR (BURMA)
  RADIO MYANMAR, Yangon — Irr • Sa/Su • DS • 50 kW
    Sa/Su • DS • 50 kW
    DS • 50 kW
9735 EGYPT
  †RADIO CAIRO, Kafr Silim-Abis — S America • 250 kW
  GERMANY
  †DEUTSCHE WELLE, Via Antigua — S • N America • 250 kW
  DEUTSCHE WELLE, Via Kigali, Rwanda — C Africa & E Africa • 250 kW
  †DEUTSCHE WELLE, Via Sines, Portugal — W • N Africa • 250 kW
  †DEUTSCHE WELLE, Wertachtal — Australasia • 500 kW / W • E Europe • 500 kW
    W • Australasia • 500 kW
    W • W Africa & E Africa • 500 kW
    S • C Africa & S Africa • 500 kW
  HUNGARY
  RADIO BUDAPEST, Jászberény — W Su • W Europe • 250 kW
  IRAN
  **(con'd) †VO THE ISLAMIC REP, Ahvāz — W • C Asia • 500 kW

0 1 2 3 4 5 6 7 8 9 10 11 12 13 14 15 16 17 18 19 20 21 22 23 24

ENGLISH ▬ ARABIC ⌇⌇ CHINESE ▫▫▫ FRENCH ▬ GERMAN ▬ RUSSIAN ═ SPANISH ▬ OTHER ▬

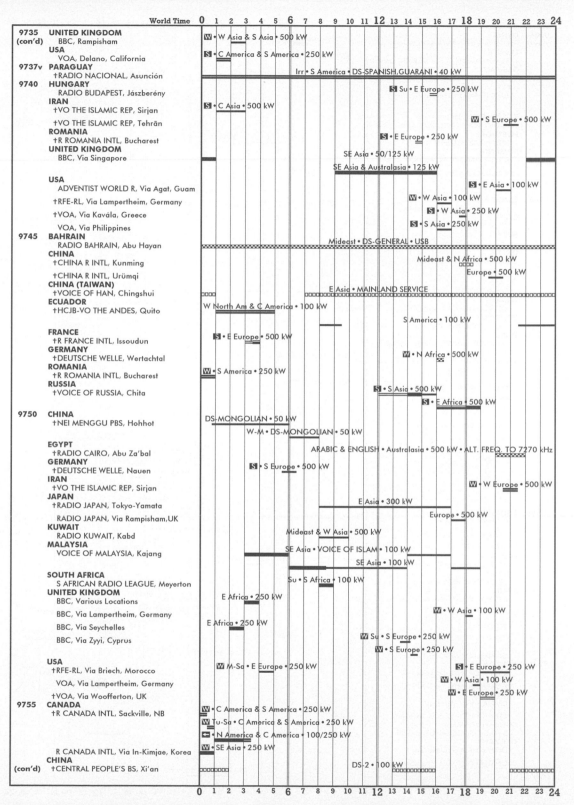

World Time	0 1 2 3 4 5 6 7 8 9 10 11 12 13 14 15 16 17 18 19 20 21 22 23 24
9735 UNITED KINGDOM	
(con'd) BBC, Rampisham	W • W Asia & S Asia • 500 kW
USA	
VOA, Delano, California	S • C America & S America • 250 kW
9737v PARAGUAY	
†RADIO NACIONAL, Asunción	Irr • S America • DS-SPANISH, GUARANI • 40 kW
9740 HUNGARY	
RADIO BUDAPEST, Jászberény	S • Su • E Europe • 250 kW
IRAN	
†VO THE ISLAMIC REP, Sirjan	S • C Asia • 500 kW
†VO THE ISLAMIC REP, Tehrān	W • S Europe • 500 kW
ROMANIA	
†R ROMANIA INTL, Bucharest	S • E Europe • 250 kW
UNITED KINGDOM	
BBC, Via Singapore	SE Asia • 50/125 kW
	SE Asia & Australasia • 125 kW
USA	
ADVENTIST WORLD R, Via Agat, Guam	S • E Asia • 100 kW
†RFE-RL, Via Lampertheim, Germany	W • W Asia • 100 kW
†VOA, Via Kavála, Greece	S • W Asia • 250 kW
VOA, Via Philippines	S • S Asia • 250 kW
9745 BAHRAIN	
RADIO BAHRAIN, Abu Hayan	Mideast • DS-GENERAL • USB
CHINA	
†CHINA R INTL, Kunming	Mideast & N Africa • 500 kW
†CHINA R INTL, Urümqi	Europe • 500 kW
CHINA (TAIWAN)	
†VOICE OF HAN, Chingshui	E Asia • MAINLAND SERVICE
ECUADOR	
†HCJB-VO THE ANDES, Quito	W North Am & C America • 100 kW
	S America • 100 kW
FRANCE	
†R FRANCE INTL, Issoudun	S • E Europe • 500 kW
GERMANY	
†DEUTSCHE WELLE, Wertachtal	W • N Africa • 500 kW
ROMANIA	
†R ROMANIA INTL, Bucharest	W • S America • 250 kW
RUSSIA	
†VOICE OF RUSSIA, Chita	S • S Asia • 500 kW
	S • E Africa • 500 kW
9750 CHINA	
†NEI MENGGU PBS, Hohhot	DS-MONGOLIAN • 50 kW
	W-M • DS-MONGOLIAN • 50 kW
EGYPT	
†RADIO CAIRO, Abu Za'bal	ARABIC & ENGLISH • Australasia • 500 kW • ALT. FREQ. TO 7270 kHz
GERMANY	
†DEUTSCHE WELLE, Nauen	S • S Europe • 500 kW
IRAN	
†VO THE ISLAMIC REP, Sirjan	W • W Europe • 500 kW
JAPAN	
†RADIO JAPAN, Tokyo-Yamata	E Asia • 300 kW
RADIO JAPAN, Via Rampisham, UK	Europe • 500 kW
KUWAIT	
RADIO KUWAIT, Kabd	Mideast & W Asia • 500 kW
MALAYSIA	
VOICE OF MALAYSIA, Kajang	SE Asia • VOICE OF ISLAM • 100 kW
	SE Asia • 100 kW
SOUTH AFRICA	
S AFRICAN RADIO LEAGUE, Meyerton	Su • S Africa • 100 kW
UNITED KINGDOM	
BBC, Various Locations	E Africa • 250 kW
BBC, Via Lampertheim, Germany	W • W Asia • 100 kW
BBC, Via Seychelles	E Africa • 250 kW
BBC, Via Zyyi, Cyprus	W Su • S Europe • 250 kW
	W • S Europe • 250 kW
USA	
†RFE-RL, Via Briech, Morocco	W M-Sa • E Europe • 250 kW
VOA, Via Lampertheim, Germany	S • E Europe • 250 kW
†VOA, Via Woofferton, UK	W • W Asia • 100 kW
	W • E Europe • 250 kW
9755 CANADA	
†R CANADA INTL, Sackville, NB	W • C America & S America • 250 kW
	W Tu-Sa • C America & S America • 250 kW
	← N America & C America • 100/250 kW
R CANADA INTL, Via In-Kimjae, Korea	W • SE Asia • 250 kW
CHINA	
(con'd) †CENTRAL PEOPLE'S BS, Xi'an	DS-2 • 100 kW
	0 1 2 3 4 5 6 7 8 9 10 11 12 13 14 15 16 17 18 19 20 21 22 23 24

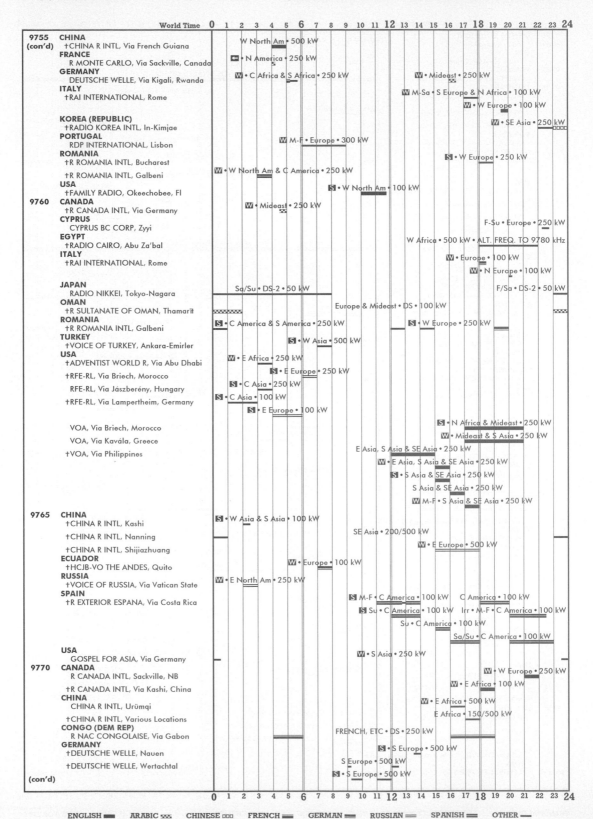

| | World Time | 0 | 1 | 2 | 3 | 4 | 5 | 6 | 7 | 8 | 9 | 10 | 11 | 12 | 13 | 14 | 15 | 16 | 17 | 18 | 19 | 20 | 21 | 22 | 23 | 24 |

9755
(con'd) CHINA
  †CHINA R INTL, Via French Guiana — W North Am • 500 kW
FRANCE
  R MONTE CARLO, Via Sackville, Canada — N America • 250 kW
GERMANY
  DEUTSCHE WELLE, Via Kigali, Rwanda — W • C Africa & S Africa • 250 kW — W • Mideast • 250 kW
ITALY
  †RAI INTERNATIONAL, Rome — W M-Sa • S Europe & N Africa • 100 kW
  — W • W Europe • 100 kW
KOREA (REPUBLIC)
  †RADIO KOREA INTL, In-Kimjae — W • SE Asia • 250 kW
PORTUGAL
  RDP INTERNATIONAL, Lisbon — W M-F • Europe • 300 kW
ROMANIA
  †R ROMANIA INTL, Bucharest — S • W Europe • 250 kW
  †R ROMANIA INTL, Galbeni — W • W North Am & C America • 250 kW
USA
  †FAMILY RADIO, Okeechobee, Fl — S • W North Am • 100 kW

9760 CANADA
  †R CANADA INTL, Via Germany — W • Mideast • 250 kW
CYPRUS
  CYPRUS BC CORP, Zyyi — F-Su • Europe • 250 kW
EGYPT
  †RADIO CAIRO, Abu Za'bal — W Africa • 500 kW • ALT. FREQ. TO 9780 kHz
ITALY
  †RAI INTERNATIONAL, Rome — W • Europe • 100 kW
  — W • N Europe • 100 kW
JAPAN
  RADIO NIKKEI, Tokyo-Nagara — Sa/Su • DS-2 • 50 kW — F/Sa • DS-2 • 50 kW
OMAN
  †R SULTANATE OF OMAN, Thamarit — Europe & Mideast • DS • 100 kW
ROMANIA
  †R ROMANIA INTL, Galbeni — S • C America & S America • 250 kW — S • W Europe • 250 kW
TURKEY
  †VOICE OF TURKEY, Ankara-Emirler — S • W Asia • 500 kW
USA
  †ADVENTIST WORLD R, Via Abu Dhabi — W • E Africa • 250 kW
  †RFE-RL, Via Briech, Morocco — S • E Europe • 250 kW
  RFE-RL, Via Jászberény, Hungary — S • C Asia • 250 kW
  †RFE-RL, Via Lampertheim, Germany — S • C Asia • 100 kW
  — S • E Europe • 100 kW
  VOA, Via Briech, Morocco — S • N Africa & Mideast • 250 kW
  VOA, Via Kavála, Greece — W • Mideast & S Asia • 250 kW
  †VOA, Via Philippines — E Asia, S Asia & SE Asia • 250 kW
  — W • E Asia, S Asia & SE Asia • 250 kW
  — S • S Asia & SE Asia • 250 kW
  — S Asia & SE Asia • 250 kW
  — W M-F • S Asia & SE Asia • 250 kW

9765 CHINA
  †CHINA R INTL, Kashi — S • W Asia & S Asia • 100 kW
  †CHINA R INTL, Nanning — SE Asia • 200/500 kW
  †CHINA R INTL, Shijiazhuang — W • E Europe • 500 kW
ECUADOR
  †HCJB-VO THE ANDES, Quito — W • Europe • 100 kW
RUSSIA
  †VOICE OF RUSSIA, Via Vatican State — W • E North Am • 250 kW
SPAIN
  †R EXTERIOR ESPANA, Via Costa Rica — S M-F • C America • 100 kW — C America • 100 kW
  — S Su • C America • 100 kW — Irr • M-F • C America • 100 kW
  — Su • C America • 100 kW
  — Sa/Su • C America • 100 kW
USA
  GOSPEL FOR ASIA, Via Germany — W • S Asia • 250 kW

9770 CANADA
  R CANADA INTL, Sackville, NB — W • W Europe • 250 kW
  †R CANADA INTL, Via Kashi, China — W • E Africa • 100 kW
CHINA
  CHINA R INTL, Urümqi — W • E Africa • 500 kW
  †CHINA R INTL, Various Locations — E Africa • 150/500 kW
CONGO (DEM REP)
  R NAC CONGOLAISE, Via Gabon — FRENCH, ETC • DS • 250 kW
GERMANY
  †DEUTSCHE WELLE, Nauen — S • S Europe • 500 kW
  †DEUTSCHE WELLE, Wertachtal — S Europe • 500 kW
  — S • S Europe • 500 kW

(con'd)

| | 0 | 1 | 2 | 3 | 4 | 5 | 6 | 7 | 8 | 9 | 10 | 11 | 12 | 13 | 14 | 15 | 16 | 17 | 18 | 19 | 20 | 21 | 22 | 23 | 24 |

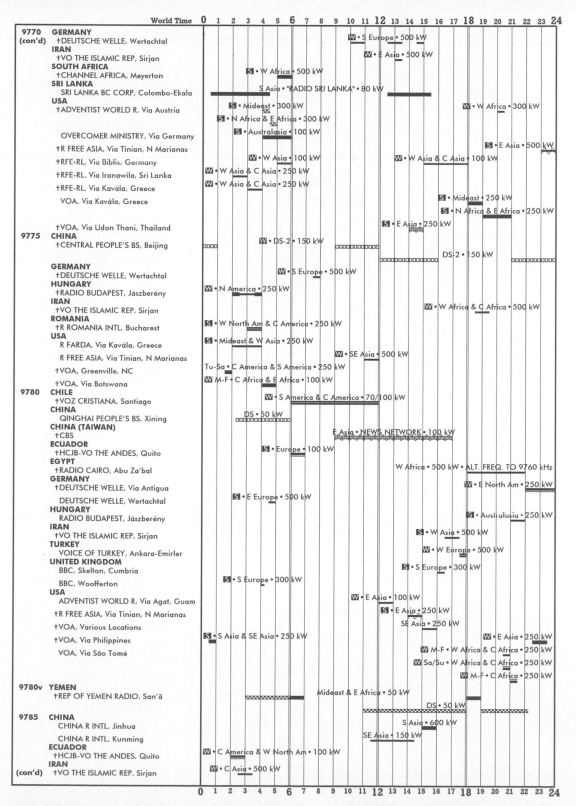

World Time   0 1 2 3 4 5 6 7 8 9 10 11 12 13 14 15 16 17 18 19 20 21 22 23 24

9770 GERMANY
(con'd) †DEUTSCHE WELLE, Wertachtal — W • S Europe • 500 kW
IRAN
   †VO THE ISLAMIC REP, Sirjan — W • E Asia • 500 kW
SOUTH AFRICA
   †CHANNEL AFRICA, Meyerton — S • W Africa • 500 kW
SRI LANKA
   SRI LANKA BC CORP, Colombo-Ekala — S Asia • "RADIO SRI LANKA" • 80 kW
USA
   †ADVENTIST WORLD R, Via Austria — S • Mideast • 300 kW   W • W Africa • 300 kW
         S • N Africa & E Africa • 300 kW
   OVERCOMER MINISTRY, Via Germany — S • Australasia • 100 kW
   †R FREE ASIA, Via Tinian, N Marianas — S • E Asia • 500 kW
   †RFE-RL, Via Biblis, Germany — W • W Asia • 100 kW   W • W Asia & C Asia • 100 kW
   †RFE-RL, Via Iranawila, Sri Lanka — W • W Asia & C Asia • 250 kW
   †RFE-RL, Via Kavála, Greece — W • W Asia & C Asia • 250 kW
   VOA, Via Kavála, Greece — S • Mideast • 250 kW
         S • N Africa & E Africa • 250 kW
   †VOA, Via Udon Thani, Thailand — S • E Asia • 250 kW
9775 CHINA
   †CENTRAL PEOPLE'S BS, Beijing — W • DS-2 • 150 kW   DS-2 • 150 kW
GERMANY
   †DEUTSCHE WELLE, Wertachtal — W • S Europe • 500 kW
HUNGARY
   †RADIO BUDAPEST, Jászberény — W • N America • 250 kW
IRAN
   †VO THE ISLAMIC REP, Sirjan — W • W Africa & C Africa • 500 kW
ROMANIA
   †R ROMANIA INTL, Bucharest — S • W North Am & C America • 250 kW
USA
   R FARDA, Via Kavála, Greece — S • Mideast & W Asia • 250 kW
   R FREE ASIA, Via Tinian, N Marianas — W • SE Asia • 500 kW
   †VOA, Greenville, NC — Tu-Sa • C America & S America • 250 kW
   †VOA, Via Botswana — W M-F • C Africa & E Africa • 100 kW
9780 CHILE
   †VOZ CRISTIANA, Santiago — W • S America & C America • 70/100 kW
CHINA
   QINGHAI PEOPLE'S BS, Xining — DS • 50 kW
CHINA (TAIWAN)
   †CBS — E Asia • NEWS NETWORK • 100 kW
ECUADOR
   †HCJB-VO THE ANDES, Quito — S • Europe • 100 kW
EGYPT
   †RADIO CAIRO, Abu Za'bal — W Africa • 500 kW • ALT. FREQ. TO 9760 kHz
GERMANY
   †DEUTSCHE WELLE, Via Antigua — W • E North Am • 250 kW
   DEUTSCHE WELLE, Wertachtal — S • E Europe • 500 kW
HUNGARY
   RADIO BUDAPEST, Jászberény — S • Australasia • 250 kW
IRAN
   †VO THE ISLAMIC REP, Sirjan — S • W Asia • 500 kW
TURKEY
   VOICE OF TURKEY, Ankara-Emirler — W • W Europe • 500 kW
UNITED KINGDOM
   BBC, Skelton, Cumbria — S • S Europe • 300 kW
   BBC, Woofferton — S • S Europe • 300 kW
USA
   ADVENTIST WORLD R, Via Agat, Guam — W • E Asia • 100 kW
   †R FREE ASIA, Via Tinian, N Marianas — S • E Asia • 250 kW
         SE Asia • 250 kW
   †VOA, Various Locations — S • S Asia & SE Asia • 250 kW
   †VOA, Via Philippines — W • E Asia • 250 kW
   VOA, Via São Tomé — W M-F • W Africa & C Africa • 250 kW
         W Sa/Su • W Africa & C Africa • 250 kW
         W M-F • C Africa • 250 kW
9780v YEMEN
   †REP OF YEMEN RADIO, San'ā — Mideast & E Africa • 50 kW   DS • 50 kW
9785 CHINA
   CHINA R INTL, Jinhua — S Asia • 600 kW
   CHINA R INTL, Kunming — SE Asia • 150 kW
ECUADOR
   †HCJB-VO THE ANDES, Quito — W • C America & W North Am • 100 kW
IRAN
(con'd) †VO THE ISLAMIC REP, Sirjan — W • C Asia • 500 kW

0 1 2 3 4 5 6 7 8 9 10 11 12 13 14 15 16 17 18 19 20 21 22 23 24

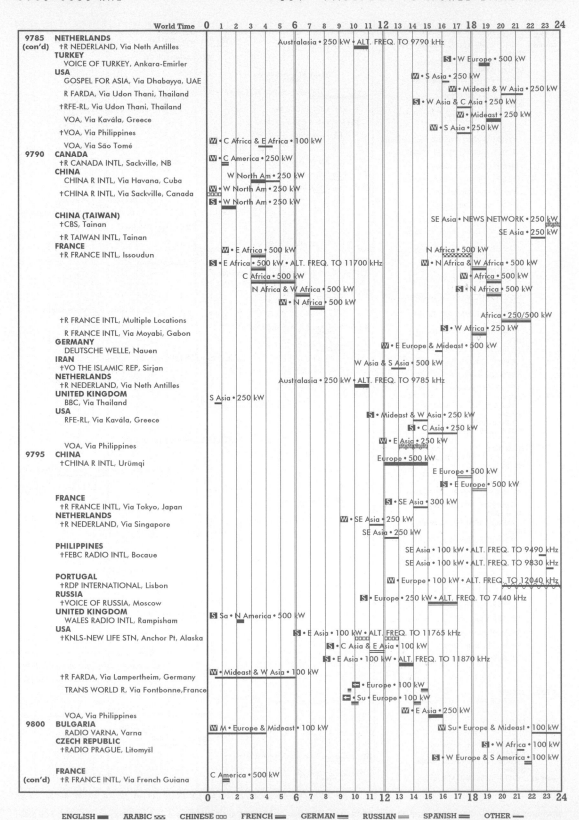

World Time 0 1 2 3 4 5 6 7 8 9 10 11 12 13 14 15 16 17 18 19 20 21 22 23 24

9785
(con'd) NETHERLANDS
  †R NEDERLAND, Via Neth Antilles — Australasia • 250 kW • ALT. FREQ. TO 9790 kHz
TURKEY
  VOICE OF TURKEY, Ankara-Emirler — **S** • W Europe • 500 kW
USA
  GOSPEL FOR ASIA, Via Dhabayya, UAE — **W** • S Asia • 250 kW
  R FARDA, Via Udon Thani, Thailand — **W** • Mideast & W Asia • 250 kW
  †RFE-RL, Via Udon Thani, Thailand — **S** • W Asia & C Asia • 250 kW
  VOA, Via Kavála, Greece — **W** • Mideast • 250 kW
  †VOA, Via Philippines — **W** • S Asia • 250 kW
  VOA, Via São Tomé — **W** • C Africa & E Africa • 100 kW

9790 CANADA
  †R CANADA INTL, Sackville, NB — **W** • C America • 250 kW
CHINA
  CHINA R INTL, Via Havana, Cuba — W North Am • 250 kW
  †CHINA R INTL, Via Sackville, Canada — **W** • W North Am • 250 kW / **S** • W North Am • 250 kW

CHINA (TAIWAN)
  †CBS, Tainan — SE Asia • NEWS NETWORK • 250 kW
  †R TAIWAN INTL, Tainan — SE Asia • 250 kW
FRANCE
  †R FRANCE INTL, Issoudun — **W** • E Africa • 500 kW / N Africa • 500 kW
    S • E Africa • 500 kW • ALT. FREQ. TO 11700 kHz / **W** • N Africa & W Africa • 500 kW
    C Africa • 500 kW / **W** • Africa • 500 kW
    N Africa & W Africa • 500 kW / **S** • N Africa • 500 kW
    W • N Africa • 500 kW
  †R FRANCE INTL, Multiple Locations — Africa • 250/500 kW
  R FRANCE INTL, Via Moyabi, Gabon — **S** • W Africa • 250 kW
GERMANY
  DEUTSCHE WELLE, Nauen — **W** • E Europe & Mideast • 500 kW
IRAN
  †VO THE ISLAMIC REP, Sirjan — W Asia & S Asia • 500 kW
NETHERLANDS
  †R NEDERLAND, Via Neth Antilles — Australasia • 250 kW • ALT. FREQ. TO 9785 kHz
UNITED KINGDOM
  BBC, Via Thailand — S Asia • 250 kW
USA
  RFE-RL, Via Kavála, Greece — **S** • Mideast & W Asia • 250 kW
    S • C Asia • 250 kW
  VOA, Via Philippines — **W** • E Asia • 250 kW

9795 CHINA
  †CHINA R INTL, Urümqi — Europe • 500 kW
    E Europe • 500 kW
    S • E Europe • 500 kW
FRANCE
  †R FRANCE INTL, Via Tokyo, Japan — **S** • SE Asia • 300 kW
NETHERLANDS
  †R NEDERLAND, Via Singapore — **W** • SE Asia • 250 kW
    SE Asia • 250 kW
PHILIPPINES
  †FEBC RADIO INTL, Bocaue — SE Asia • 100 kW • ALT. FREQ. TO 9490 kHz
    SE Asia • 100 kW • ALT. FREQ. TO 9830 kHz
PORTUGAL
  †RDP INTERNATIONAL, Lisbon — **W** • Europe • 100 kW • ALT. FREQ. TO 12040 kHz
RUSSIA
  †VOICE OF RUSSIA, Moscow — **S** • Europe • 250 kW • ALT. FREQ. TO 7440 kHz
UNITED KINGDOM
  WALES RADIO INTL, Rampisham — **S** Sa • N America • 500 kW
USA
  †KNLS-NEW LIFE STN, Anchor Pt, Alaska — **S** • E Asia • 100 kW • ALT. FREQ. TO 11765 kHz
    S • C Asia & E Asia • 100 kW
    S • E Asia • 100 kW • ALT. FREQ. TO 11870 kHz
  †R FARDA, Via Lampertheim, Germany — **W** • Mideast & W Asia • 100 kW
  TRANS WORLD R, Via Fontbonne, France — ▭ • Europe • 100 kW
    ▭ • Su • Europe • 100 kW
  VOA, Via Philippines — **W** • E Asia • 250 kW

9800 BULGARIA
  RADIO VARNA, Varna — **W** M • Europe & Mideast • 100 kW / **W** Su • Europe & Mideast • 100 kW
CZECH REPUBLIC
  †RADIO PRAGUE, Litomyšl — **S** • W Africa • 100 kW
    S • W Europe & S America • 100 kW
FRANCE
(con'd) †R FRANCE INTL, Via French Guiana — C America • 500 kW

0 1 2 3 4 5 6 7 8 9 10 11 12 13 14 15 16 17 18 19 20 21 22 23 24

ENGLISH ▬ ARABIC ⋙ CHINESE ▭▭▭ FRENCH ▬▬ GERMAN ▬▬ RUSSIAN ═══ SPANISH ═══ OTHER ▬

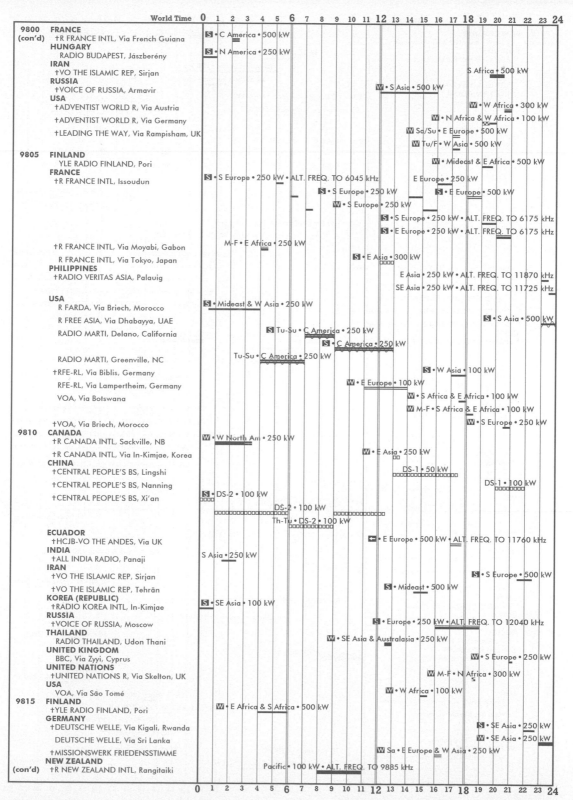

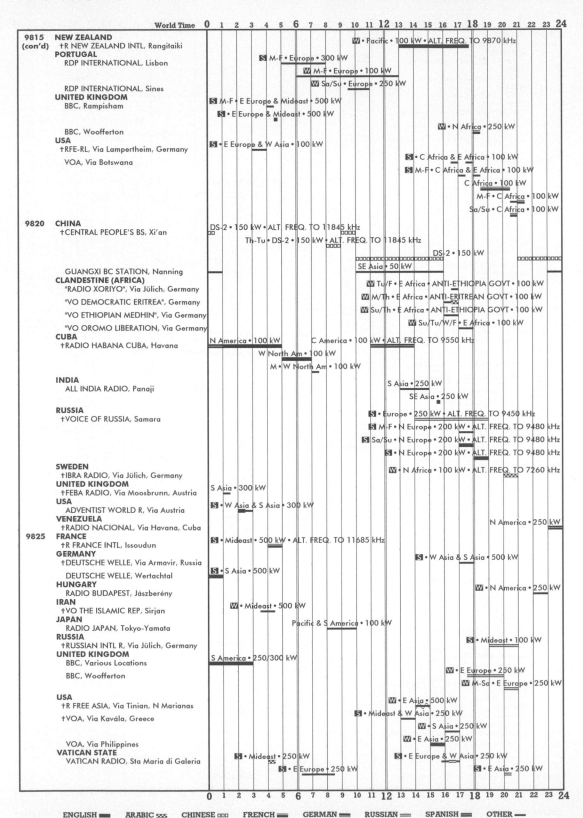

World Time　0　1　2　3　4　5　6　7　8　9　10　11　12　13　14　15　16　17　18　19　20　21　22　23　24

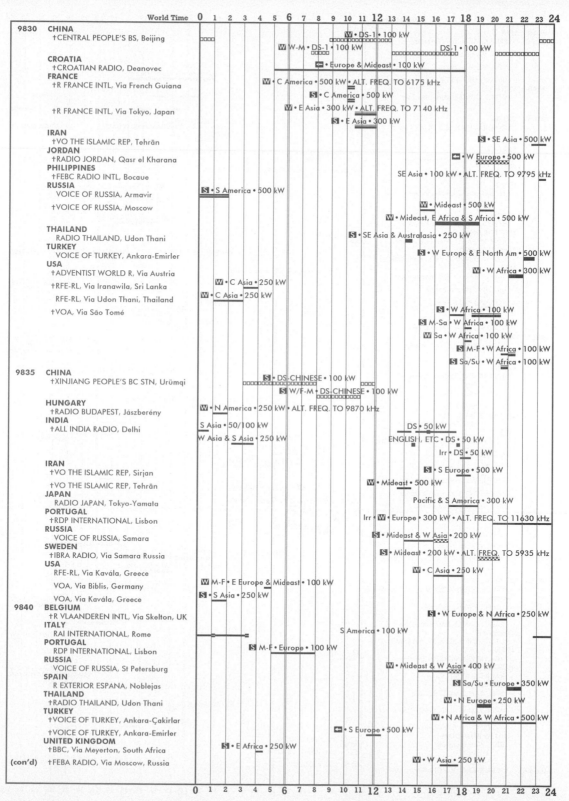

9830　CHINA
　†CENTRAL PEOPLE'S BS, Beijing
　　W • DS-1 • 100 kW
　　W-M • DS-1 • 100 kW
　　DS-1 • 100 kW

　CROATIA
　†CROATIAN RADIO, Deanovec
　　• Europe & Mideast • 100 kW
　FRANCE
　†R FRANCE INTL, Via French Guiana
　　W • C America • 500 kW • ALT. FREQ. TO 6175 kHz
　　S • C America • 500 kW

　†R FRANCE INTL, Via Tokyo, Japan
　　W • E Asia • 300 kW • ALT. FREQ. TO 7140 kHz
　　S • E Asia • 300 kW

　IRAN
　†VO THE ISLAMIC REP, Tehrān
　　S • SE Asia • 500 kW
　JORDAN
　†RADIO JORDAN, Qasr el Kharana
　　• W Europe • 500 kW
　PHILIPPINES
　†FEBC RADIO INTL, Bocaue
　　SE Asia • 100 kW • ALT. FREQ. TO 9795 kHz
　RUSSIA
　VOICE OF RUSSIA, Armavir
　　S • S America • 500 kW

　†VOICE OF RUSSIA, Moscow
　　W • Mideast • 500 kW
　　W • Mideast, E Africa & S Africa • 500 kW

　THAILAND
　RADIO THAILAND, Udon Thani
　　S • SE Asia & Australasia • 250 kW
　TURKEY
　VOICE OF TURKEY, Ankara-Emirler
　　S • W Europe & E North Am • 500 kW
　USA
　†ADVENTIST WORLD R, Via Austria
　　W • W Africa • 300 kW

　†RFE-RL, Via Iranawila, Sri Lanka
　　W • C Asia • 250 kW
　RFE-RL, Via Udon Thani, Thailand
　　W • C Asia • 250 kW

　†VOA, Via São Tomé
　　S • W Africa • 100 kW
　　S M-Sa • W Africa • 100 kW
　　W Sa • W Africa • 100 kW
　　S M-F • W Africa • 100 kW
　　S Sa/Su • W Africa • 100 kW

9835　CHINA
　†XINJIANG PEOPLE'S BC STN, Urümqi
　　S • DS-CHINESE • 100 kW
　　S W/F-M • DS-CHINESE • 100 kW

　HUNGARY
　†RADIO BUDAPEST, Jászberény
　　W • N America • 250 kW • ALT. FREQ. TO 9870 kHz
　INDIA
　†ALL INDIA RADIO, Delhi
　　S Asia • 50/100 kW
　　W Asia & S Asia • 250 kW
　　DS • 50 kW
　　ENGLISH, ETC • DS • 50 kW
　　Irr • DS • 50 kW

　IRAN
　†VO THE ISLAMIC REP, Sirjan
　　S • S Europe • 500 kW

　†VO THE ISLAMIC REP, Tehrān
　　W • Mideast • 500 kW
　JAPAN
　RADIO JAPAN, Tokyo-Yamata
　　Pacific & S America • 300 kW
　PORTUGAL
　†RDP INTERNATIONAL, Lisbon
　　Irr • W • Europe • 300 kW • ALT. FREQ. TO 11630 kHz
　RUSSIA
　VOICE OF RUSSIA, Samara
　　S • Mideast & W Asia • 200 kW
　SWEDEN
　†IBRA RADIO, Via Samara Russia
　　S • Mideast • 200 kW • ALT. FREQ. TO 5935 kHz
　USA
　RFE-RL, Via Kavála, Greece
　　W • C Asia • 250 kW

　VOA, Via Biblis, Germany
　　W M-F • E Europe & Mideast • 100 kW

　VOA, Via Kavála, Greece
　　S • S Asia • 250 kW

9840　BELGIUM
　†R VLAANDEREN INTL, Via Skelton, UK
　　S • W Europe & N Africa • 250 kW
　ITALY
　RAI INTERNATIONAL, Rome
　　S America • 100 kW
　PORTUGAL
　RDP INTERNATIONAL, Lisbon
　　S M-F • Europe • 100 kW
　RUSSIA
　VOICE OF RUSSIA, St Petersburg
　　W • Mideast & W Asia • 400 kW
　SPAIN
　R EXTERIOR ESPANA, Noblejas
　　S Sa/Su • Europe • 350 kW
　THAILAND
　†RADIO THAILAND, Udon Thani
　　W • N Europe • 250 kW
　TURKEY
　†VOICE OF TURKEY, Ankara-Çakirlar
　　W • N Africa & W Africa • 500 kW

　†VOICE OF TURKEY, Ankara-Emirler
　　• S Europe • 500 kW
　UNITED KINGDOM
　†BBC, Via Meyerton, South Africa
　　S • E Africa • 250 kW

(con'd)　†FEBA RADIO, Via Moscow, Russia
　　W • W Asia • 250 kW

0　1　2　3　4　5　6　7　8　9　10　11　12　13　14　15　16　17　18　19　20　21　22　23　24

SEASONAL S OR W　　1-HR TIMESHIFT MIDYEAR ⊏ OR ⊐　　JAMMING / OR ∧　　EARLIEST HEARD ◁　　LATEST HEARD ▷　　NEW FOR 2005 †

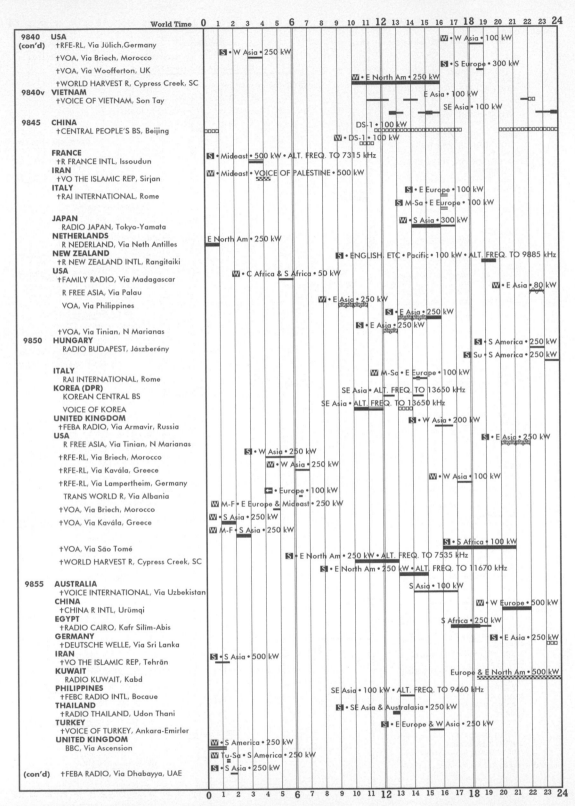

World Time 0 1 2 3 4 5 6 7 8 9 10 11 12 13 14 15 16 17 18 19 20 21 22 23 24

9840
(con'd) **USA**
  †RFE-RL, Via Jülich, Germany — W • W Asia • 100 kW
  †VOA, Via Briech, Morocco — S • W Asia • 250 kW
  †VOA, Via Woofferton, UK — S • S Europe • 300 kW
  †WORLD HARVEST R, Cypress Creek, SC — W • E North Am • 250 kW
9840v **VIETNAM**
  †VOICE OF VIETNAM, Son Tay — E Asia • 100 kW / SE Asia • 100 kW

9845 **CHINA**
  †CENTRAL PEOPLE'S BS, Beijing — DS-1 • 100 kW / W • DS-1 • 100 kW
  FRANCE
  †R FRANCE INTL, Issoudun — S • Mideast • 500 kW • ALT. FREQ. TO 7315 kHz
  IRAN
  †VO THE ISLAMIC REP, Sirjan — W • Mideast • VOICE OF PALESTINE • 500 kW
  ITALY
  †RAI INTERNATIONAL, Rome — S • E Europe • 100 kW / S M-Sa • E Europe • 100 kW
  JAPAN
  RADIO JAPAN, Tokyo-Yamata — W • S Asia • 300 kW
  NETHERLANDS
  R NEDERLAND, Via Neth Antilles — E North Am • 250 kW
  NEW ZEALAND
  †R NEW ZEALAND INTL, Rangitaiki — S • ENGLISH, ETC • Pacific • 100 kW • ALT. FREQ. TO 9885 kHz
  USA
  †FAMILY RADIO, Via Madagascar — W • C Africa & S Africa • 50 kW / W • E Asia • 80 kW
  R FREE ASIA, Via Palau — W • E Asia • 250 kW
  VOA, Via Philippines — S • E Asia • 250 kW / S • E Asia • 250 kW
  †VOA, Via Tinian, N Marianas
9850 **HUNGARY**
  RADIO BUDAPEST, Jászberény — S • S America • 250 kW / S Su • S America • 250 kW
  ITALY
  RAI INTERNATIONAL, Rome — W M-Sa • E Europe • 100 kW
  KOREA (DPR)
  KOREAN CENTRAL BS — SE Asia • ALT. FREQ. TO 13650 kHz
  VOICE OF KOREA — SE Asia • ALT. FREQ. TO 13650 kHz
  UNITED KINGDOM
  †FEBA RADIO, Via Armavir, Russia — S • W Asia • 200 kW
  USA
  R FREE ASIA, Via Tinian, N Marianas — S • E Asia • 250 kW
  †RFE-RL, Via Briech, Morocco — S • W Asia • 250 kW
  †RFE-RL, Via Kavála, Greece — W • W Asia • 250 kW
  †RFE-RL, Via Lampertheim, Germany — W • W Asia • 100 kW
  TRANS WORLD R, Via Albania — • Europe • 100 kW
  †VOA, Via Briech, Morocco — W M-F • E Europe & Mideast • 250 kW
  †VOA, Via Kavála, Greece — W • S Asia • 250 kW / W M-F • S Asia • 250 kW
  †VOA, Via São Tomé — S • S Africa • 100 kW
  †WORLD HARVEST R, Cypress Creek, SC — S • E North Am • 250 kW • ALT. FREQ. TO 7535 kHz / S • E North Am • 250 kW • ALT. FREQ. TO 11670 kHz

9855 **AUSTRALIA**
  †VOICE INTERNATIONAL, Via Uzbekistan — S Asia • 100 kW
  CHINA
  †CHINA R INTL, Urümqi — W • W Europe • 500 kW
  EGYPT
  †RADIO CAIRO, Kafr Silim-Abis — S Africa • 250 kW
  GERMANY
  †DEUTSCHE WELLE, Via Sri Lanka — S • E Asia • 250 kW
  IRAN
  †VO THE ISLAMIC REP, Tehrān — S • S Asia • 500 kW
  KUWAIT
  RADIO KUWAIT, Kabd — Europe & E North Am • 500 kW
  PHILIPPINES
  †FEBC RADIO INTL, Bocaue — SE Asia • 100 kW • ALT. FREQ. TO 9460 kHz
  THAILAND
  †RADIO THAILAND, Udon Thani — S • SE Asia & Australasia • 250 kW
  TURKEY
  †VOICE OF TURKEY, Ankara-Emirler — S • E Europe & W Asia • 250 kW
  UNITED KINGDOM
  BBC, Via Ascension — W • S America • 250 kW / W Tu-Sa • S America • 250 kW / S • S Asia • 250 kW
(con'd) †FEBA RADIO, Via Dhabayya, UAE

0 1 2 3 4 5 6 7 8 9 10 11 12 13 14 15 16 17 18 19 20 21 22 23 24

ENGLISH ▬   ARABIC ⋙   CHINESE □□□   FRENCH ▬▬   GERMAN ▬▬   RUSSIAN ═   SPANISH ▬▬   OTHER ▬

World Time 0 1 2 3 4 5 6 7 8 9 10 11 12 13 14 15 16 17 18 19 20 21 22 23 24

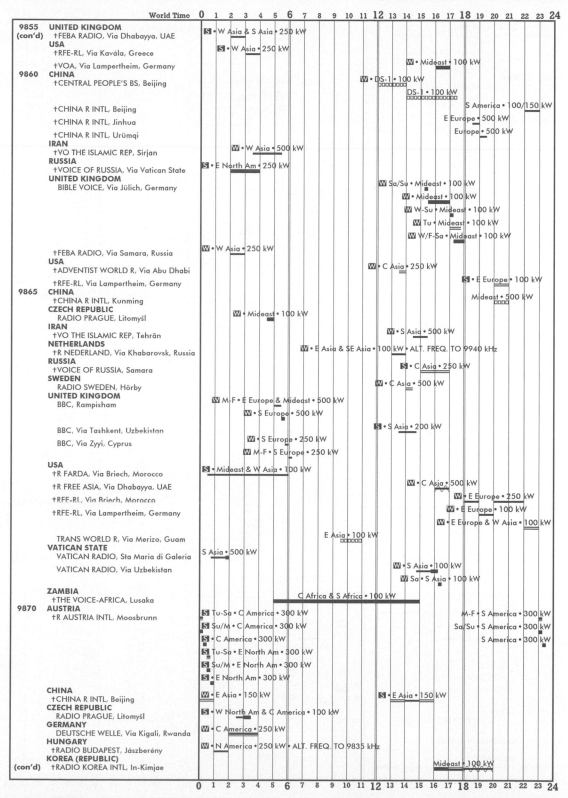

9855 UNITED KINGDOM
(con'd) †FEBA RADIO, Via Dhabayya, UAE — S • W Asia & S Asia • 250 kW
USA
†RFE-RL, Via Kavála, Greece — S • W Asia • 250 kW
†VOA, Via Lampertheim, Germany — W • Mideast • 100 kW
9860 CHINA
†CENTRAL PEOPLE'S BS, Beijing — W • DS-1 • 100 kW
DS-1 • 100 kW
†CHINA R INTL, Beijing — S America • 100/150 kW
†CHINA R INTL, Jinhua — E Europe • 500 kW
†CHINA R INTL, Urümqi — Europe • 500 kW
IRAN
†VO THE ISLAMIC REP, Sirjan — W • W Asia • 500 kW
RUSSIA
†VOICE OF RUSSIA, Via Vatican State — S • E North Am • 250 kW
UNITED KINGDOM
BIBLE VOICE, Via Jülich, Germany — W Sa/Su • Mideast • 100 kW
W • Mideast • 100 kW
W-Su • Mideast • 100 kW
W Tu • Mideast • 100 kW
W/F-Sa • Mideast • 100 kW
†FEBA RADIO, Via Samara, Russia — W • W Asia • 250 kW
USA
†ADVENTIST WORLD R, Via Abu Dhabi — W • C Asia • 250 kW
†RFE-RL, Via Lampertheim, Germany — S • E Europe • 100 kW
9865 CHINA
†CHINA R INTL, Kunming — Mideast • 500 kW
CZECH REPUBLIC
RADIO PRAGUE, Litomyšl — W • Mideast • 100 kW
IRAN
†VO THE ISLAMIC REP, Tehrān — W • S Asia • 500 kW
NETHERLANDS
†R NEDERLAND, Via Khabarovsk, Russia — W • E Asia & SE Asia • 100 kW • ALT. FREQ. TO 9940 kHz
RUSSIA
†VOICE OF RUSSIA, Samara — S • C Asia • 250 kW
SWEDEN
RADIO SWEDEN, Hörby — W • C Asia • 500 kW
UNITED KINGDOM
BBC, Rampisham — W M-F • E Europe & Mideast • 500 kW
W • S Europe • 500 kW
BBC, Via Tashkent, Uzbekistan — S • S Asia • 200 kW
BBC, Via Zyyi, Cyprus — W • S Europe • 250 kW
W M-F • S Europe • 250 kW
USA
†R FARDA, Via Briech, Morocco — S • Mideast & W Asia • 100 kW
†R FREE ASIA, Via Dhabayya, UAE — W • C Asia • 500 kW
†RFE-RL, Via Briech, Morocco — W • E Europe • 250 kW
†RFE-RL, Via Lampertheim, Germany — W • E Europe • 100 kW
W • E Europe & W Asia • 100 kW
TRANS WORLD R, Via Merizo, Guam — E Asia • 100 kW
VATICAN STATE
VATICAN RADIO, Sta Maria di Galeria — S Asia • 500 kW
VATICAN RADIO, Via Uzbekistan — W • S Asia • 100 kW
W Sa • S Asia • 100 kW
ZAMBIA
†THE VOICE-AFRICA, Lusaka — C Africa & S Africa • 100 kW
9870 AUSTRIA
†R AUSTRIA INTL, Moosbrunn — S Tu-Sa • C America • 300 kW
M-F • S America • 300 kW
S Su/M • C America • 300 kW
Sa/Su • S America • 300 kW
S • C America • 300 kW
S America • 300 kW
S Tu-Sa • E North Am • 300 kW
S Su/M • E North Am • 300 kW
S • E North Am • 300 kW
CHINA
†CHINA R INTL, Beijing — W • E Asia • 150 kW
S • E Asia • 150 kW
CZECH REPUBLIC
RADIO PRAGUE, Litomyšl — S • W North Am & C America • 100 kW
GERMANY
DEUTSCHE WELLE, Via Kigali, Rwanda — W • C America • 250 kW
HUNGARY
†RADIO BUDAPEST, Jászberény — W • N America • 250 kW • ALT. FREQ. TO 9835 kHz
KOREA (REPUBLIC)
(con'd) †RADIO KOREA INTL, In-Kimjae — Mideast • 100 kW

0 1 2 3 4 5 6 7 8 9 10 11 12 13 14 15 16 17 18 19 20 21 22 23 24

SEASONAL S OR W   1-HR TIMESHIFT MIDYEAR ⇦ OR ⇨   JAMMING / OR ∧   EARLIEST HEARD ◁   LATEST HEARD ▷   NEW FOR 2005 †

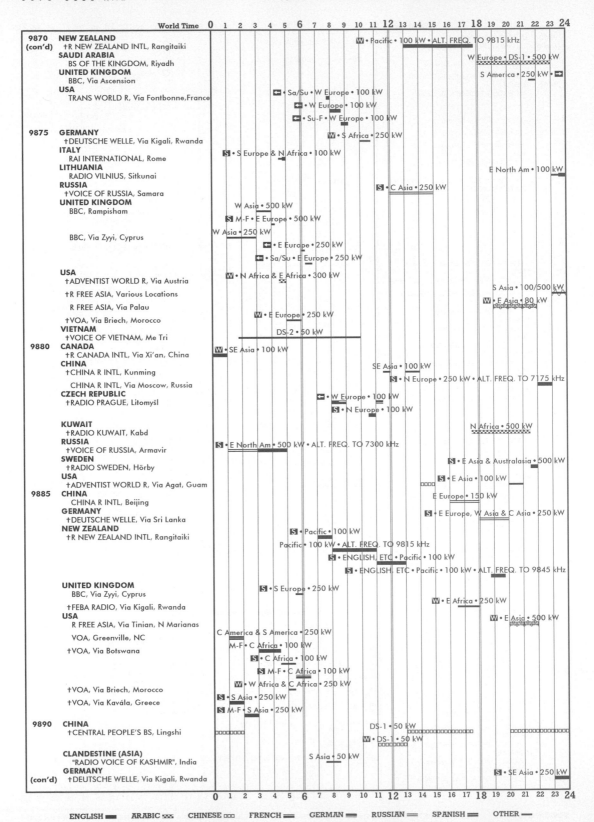

World Time   0 1 2 3 4 5 6 7 8 9 10 11 12 13 14 15 16 17 18 19 20 21 22 23 24

9870   **NEW ZEALAND**
(con'd)   †R NEW ZEALAND INTL, Rangitaiki   W • Pacific • 100 kW • ALT. FREQ. TO 9815 kHz
     SAUDI ARABIA   W Europe • DS-1 • 500 kW
     BS OF THE KINGDOM, Riyadh
     UNITED KINGDOM   S America • 250 kW
     BBC, Via Ascension
     USA
     TRANS WORLD R, Via Fontbonne, France   • Sa/Su • W Europe • 100 kW
     • W Europe • 100 kW
     • Su-F • W Europe • 100 kW

9875   **GERMANY**
     †DEUTSCHE WELLE, Via Kigali, Rwanda   W • S Africa • 250 kW
     ITALY
     RAI INTERNATIONAL, Rome   S • S Europe & N Africa • 100 kW
     LITHUANIA
     RADIO VILNIUS, Sitkunai   E North Am • 100 kW
     RUSSIA
     †VOICE OF RUSSIA, Samara   S • C Asia • 250 kW
     UNITED KINGDOM
     BBC, Rampisham   W Asia • 500 kW
     S • M-F • E Europe • 500 kW

     BBC, Via Zyyi, Cyprus   W Asia • 250 kW
     • E Europe • 250 kW
     • Sa/Su • E Europe • 250 kW

     USA
     †ADVENTIST WORLD R, Via Austria   W • N Africa & E Africa • 300 kW
     †R FREE ASIA, Various Locations   S Asia • 100/500 kW
     R FREE ASIA, Via Palau   W • E Asia • 80 kW
     †VOA, Via Briech, Morocco   W • E Europe • 250 kW
     VIETNAM
     †VOICE OF VIETNAM, Me Tri   DS-2 • 50 kW
9880   **CANADA**
     †R CANADA INTL, Via Xi'an, China   W • SE Asia • 100 kW
     CHINA
     †CHINA R INTL, Kunming   SE Asia • 100 kW
     CHINA R INTL, Via Moscow, Russia   S • N Europe • 250 kW • ALT. FREQ. TO 7175 kHz
     CZECH REPUBLIC
     †RADIO PRAGUE, Litomyšl   • W Europe • 100 kW
     S • N Europe • 100 kW

     KUWAIT
     †RADIO KUWAIT, Kabd   N Africa • 500 kW
     RUSSIA
     †VOICE OF RUSSIA, Armavir   S • E North Am • 500 kW • ALT. FREQ. TO 7300 kHz
     SWEDEN
     †RADIO SWEDEN, Hörby   S • E Asia & Australasia • 500 kW
     USA
     †ADVENTIST WORLD R, Via Agat, Guam   S • E Asia • 100 kW
9885   **CHINA**
     CHINA R INTL, Beijing   E Europe • 150 kW
     GERMANY
     †DEUTSCHE WELLE, Via Sri Lanka   S • E Europe, W Asia & C Asia • 250 kW
     NEW ZEALAND
     †R NEW ZEALAND INTL, Rangitaiki   S • Pacific • 100 kW
     Pacific • 100 kW • ALT. FREQ. TO 9815 kHz
     S • ENGLISH, ETC • Pacific • 100 kW
     S • ENGLISH, ETC • Pacific • 100 kW • ALT. FREQ. TO 9845 kHz

     UNITED KINGDOM
     BBC, Via Zyyi, Cyprus   S • S Europe • 250 kW
     †FEBA RADIO, Via Kigali, Rwanda   W • E Africa • 250 kW
     USA
     R FREE ASIA, Via Tinian, N Marianas   W • E Asia • 500 kW
     VOA, Greenville, NC   C America & S America • 250 kW
     †VOA, Via Botswana   M-F • C Africa • 100 kW
     S • C Africa • 100 kW
     S • M-F • C Africa • 100 kW
     W • W Africa & C Africa • 250 kW
     †VOA, Via Briech, Morocco   S • S Asia • 250 kW
     †VOA, Via Kavála, Greece   S • M-F • S Asia • 250 kW

9890   **CHINA**
     †CENTRAL PEOPLE'S BS, Lingshi   DS-1 • 50 kW
     W • DS-1 • 50 kW

     CLANDESTINE (ASIA)
     "RADIO VOICE OF KASHMIR", India   S Asia • 50 kW
     GERMANY
(con'd)   †DEUTSCHE WELLE, Via Kigali, Rwanda   S • SE Asia • 250 kW

0 1 2 3 4 5 6 7 8 9 10 11 12 13 14 15 16 17 18 19 20 21 22 23 24

ENGLISH ▬▬   ARABIC ░░░   CHINESE ▫▫▫   FRENCH ▬▬   GERMAN ▬▬   RUSSIAN ══   SPANISH ══   OTHER ──

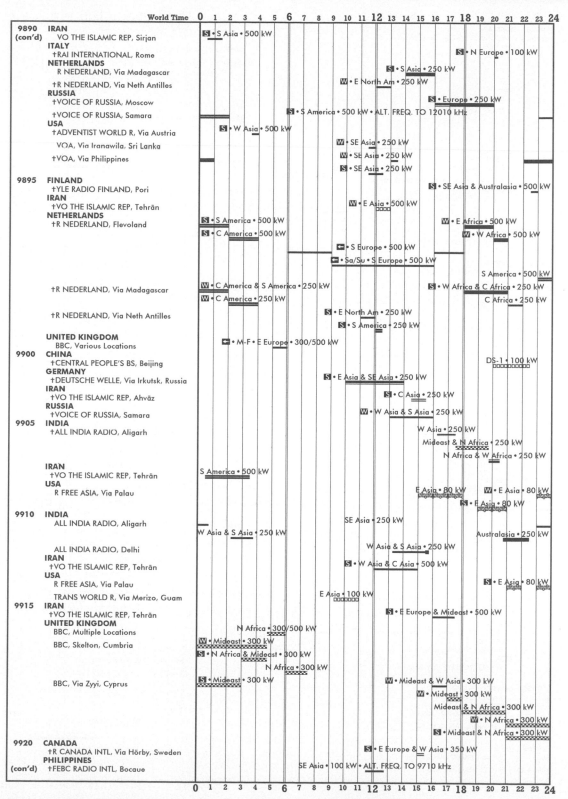

World Time

9890
IRAN
(con'd)   VO THE ISLAMIC REP, Sirjan — S • S Asia • 500 kW
ITALY
   †RAI INTERNATIONAL, Rome — S • N Europe • 100 kW
NETHERLANDS
   R NEDERLAND, Via Madagascar — S • S Asia • 250 kW
   †R NEDERLAND, Via Neth Antilles — W • E North Am • 250 kW
RUSSIA
   †VOICE OF RUSSIA, Moscow — S • Europe • 250 kW
   †VOICE OF RUSSIA, Samara — S • S America • 500 kW • ALT. FREQ. TO 12010 kHz
USA
   †ADVENTIST WORLD R, Via Austria — S • W Asia • 500 kW
   VOA, Via Iranawila, Sri Lanka — W • SE Asia • 250 kW
   †VOA, Via Philippines — W • SE Asia • 250 kW
     S • SE Asia • 250 kW

9895
FINLAND
   †YLE RADIO FINLAND, Pori — S • SE Asia & Australasia • 500 kW
IRAN
   †VO THE ISLAMIC REP, Tehrān — W • E Asia • 500 kW
NETHERLANDS
   †R NEDERLAND, Flevoland — S • S America • 500 kW
     S • C America • 500 kW
     W • E Africa • 500 kW
     W • W Africa • 500 kW
     ⇦ • S Europe • 500 kW
     ⇦ • Sa/Su • S Europe • 500 kW
     S America • 500 kW
   †R NEDERLAND, Via Madagascar — W • C America & S America • 250 kW
     S • W Africa & C Africa • 250 kW
     W • C America • 250 kW
     C Africa • 250 kW
   †R NEDERLAND, Via Neth Antilles — S • E North Am • 250 kW
     S • S America • 250 kW
UNITED KINGDOM
   BBC, Various Locations — ⇦ • M-F • E Europe • 300/500 kW

9900
CHINA
   †CENTRAL PEOPLE'S BS, Beijing — DS-1 • 100 kW
GERMANY
   †DEUTSCHE WELLE, Via Irkutsk, Russia — S • E Asia & SE Asia • 250 kW
IRAN
   †VO THE ISLAMIC REP, Ahvāz — S • C Asia • 250 kW
RUSSIA
   †VOICE OF RUSSIA, Samara — W • W Asia & S Asia • 250 kW
9905
INDIA
   †ALL INDIA RADIO, Aligarh — W Asia • 250 kW
     Mideast & N Africa • 250 kW
     N Africa & W Africa • 250 kW
IRAN
   †VO THE ISLAMIC REP, Tehrān — S America • 500 kW
USA
   R FREE ASIA, Via Palau — E Asia • 80 kW
     W • E Asia • 80 kW
     S • E Asia • 80 kW

9910
INDIA
   ALL INDIA RADIO, Aligarh — SE Asia • 250 kW
     W Asia & S Asia • 250 kW
     Australasia • 250 kW
   ALL INDIA RADIO, Delhi — W Asia & S Asia • 250 kW
IRAN
   †VO THE ISLAMIC REP, Tehrān — S • W Asia & C Asia • 500 kW
USA
   R FREE ASIA, Via Palau — S • E Asia • 80 kW
   TRANS WORLD R, Via Merizo, Guam — E Asia • 100 kW

9915
IRAN
   †VO THE ISLAMIC REP, Tehrān — S • E Europe & Mideast • 500 kW
UNITED KINGDOM
   BBC, Multiple Locations — N Africa • 300/500 kW
   BBC, Skelton, Cumbria — W • Mideast • 300 kW
     S • N Africa & Mideast • 300 kW
     N Africa • 300 kW
   BBC, Via Zyyi, Cyprus — S • Mideast • 300 kW
     W • Mideast & W Asia • 300 kW
     W • Mideast • 300 kW
     Mideast & N Africa • 300 kW
     W • N Africa • 300 kW
     S • Mideast & N Africa • 300 kW

9920
CANADA
   †R CANADA INTL, Via Hörby, Sweden — S • E Europe & W Asia • 350 kW
PHILIPPINES
(con'd)   †FEBC RADIO INTL, Bocaue — SE Asia • 100 kW • ALT. FREQ. TO 9710 kHz

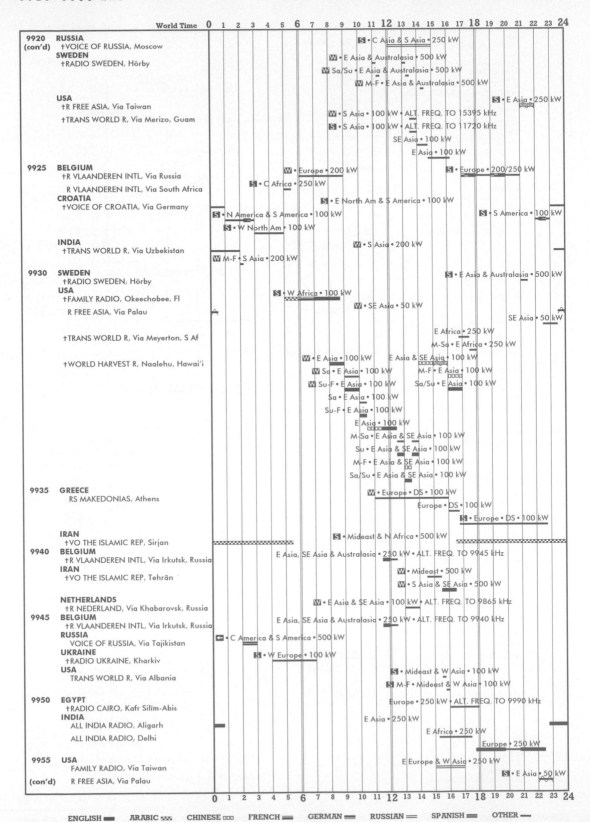

| World Time | 0 | 1 | 2 | 3 | 4 | 5 | 6 | 7 | 8 | 9 | 10 | 11 | 12 | 13 | 14 | 15 | 16 | 17 | 18 | 19 | 20 | 21 | 22 | 23 | 24 |

9920
(con'd) RUSSIA
†VOICE OF RUSSIA, Moscow — S • C Asia & S Asia • 250 kW

SWEDEN
†RADIO SWEDEN, Hörby — W • E Asia & Australasia • 500 kW
W Sa/Su • E Asia & Australasia • 500 kW
W M-F • E Asia & Australasia • 500 kW

USA
†R FREE ASIA, Via Taiwan — S • E Asia • 250 kW
†TRANS WORLD R, Via Merizo, Guam — W • S Asia • 100 kW • ALT. FREQ. TO 15395 kHz
S • S Asia • 100 kW • ALT. FREQ. TO 11720 kHz
SE Asia • 100 kW
E Asia • 100 kW

9925 BELGIUM
†R VLAANDEREN INTL, Via Russia — W • Europe • 200 kW
S • Europe • 200/250 kW
R VLAANDEREN INTL, Via South Africa — S • C Africa • 250 kW
CROATIA
†VOICE OF CROATIA, Via Germany — S • E North Am & S America • 100 kW
S • N America & S America • 100 kW
S • S America • 100 kW
S • W North Am • 100 kW

INDIA
†TRANS WORLD R, Via Uzbekistan — W • S Asia • 200 kW
W M-F • S Asia • 200 kW

9930 SWEDEN
†RADIO SWEDEN, Hörby — S • E Asia & Australasia • 500 kW
USA
†FAMILY RADIO, Okeechobee, Fl — S • W Africa • 100 kW
R FREE ASIA, Via Palau — W • SE Asia • 50 kW
SE Asia • 50 kW

†TRANS WORLD R, Via Meyerton, S Af — E Africa • 250 kW
M-Sa • E Africa • 250 kW

†WORLD HARVEST R, Naalehu, Hawai'i — W • E Asia • 100 kW   E Asia & SE Asia • 100 kW
W Sa • E Asia • 100 kW   M-F • E Asia • 100 kW
W Su-F • E Asia • 100 kW   Sa/Su • E Asia • 100 kW
Sa • E Asia • 100 kW
Su-F • E Asia • 100 kW
E Asia • 100 kW
M-Sa • E Asia & SE Asia • 100 kW
Su • E Asia & SE Asia • 100 kW
M-F • E Asia & SE Asia • 100 kW
Sa/Su • E Asia & SE Asia • 100 kW

9935 GREECE
RS MAKEDONIAS, Athens — W • Europe • DS • 100 kW
Europe • DS • 100 kW
S • Europe • DS • 100 kW

IRAN
†VO THE ISLAMIC REP, Sirjan — S • Mideast & N Africa • 500 kW
9940 BELGIUM
†R VLAANDEREN INTL, Via Irkutsk, Russia — E Asia, SE Asia & Australasia • 250 kW • ALT. FREQ. TO 9945 kHz
IRAN
†VO THE ISLAMIC REP, Tehrān — W • Mideast • 500 kW
W • S Asia & SE Asia • 500 kW

NETHERLANDS
†R NEDERLAND, Via Khabarovsk, Russia — W • E Asia & SE Asia • 100 kW • ALT. FREQ. TO 9865 kHz
9945 BELGIUM
†R VLAANDEREN INTL, Via Irkutsk, Russia — E Asia, SE Asia & Australasia • 250 kW • ALT. FREQ. TO 9940 kHz
RUSSIA
VOICE OF RUSSIA, Via Tajikistan — C America & S America • 500 kW
UKRAINE
†RADIO UKRAINE, Kharkiv — S • W Europe • 100 kW
USA
TRANS WORLD R, Via Albania — S • Mideast & W Asia • 100 kW
S M-F • Mideast & W Asia • 100 kW

9950 EGYPT
†RADIO CAIRO, Kafr Silīm-Abis — Europe • 250 kW • ALT. FREQ. TO 9990 kHz
INDIA
ALL INDIA RADIO, Aligarh — E Asia • 250 kW
ALL INDIA RADIO, Delhi — E Africa • 250 kW
Europe • 250 kW

9955 USA
FAMILY RADIO, Via Taiwan — E Europe & W Asia • 250 kW
(con'd) R FREE ASIA, Via Palau — S • E Asia • 50 kW

| | 0 | 1 | 2 | 3 | 4 | 5 | 6 | 7 | 8 | 9 | 10 | 11 | 12 | 13 | 14 | 15 | 16 | 17 | 18 | 19 | 20 | 21 | 22 | 23 | 24 |

ENGLISH ▬ ARABIC ▨ CHINESE □□□ FRENCH ▬ GERMAN ▬ RUSSIAN ▬ SPANISH ▬ OTHER ▬

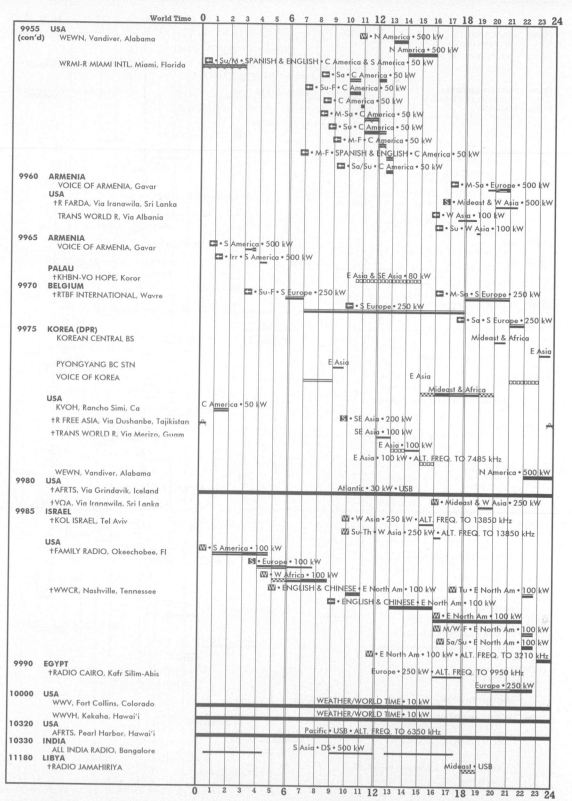

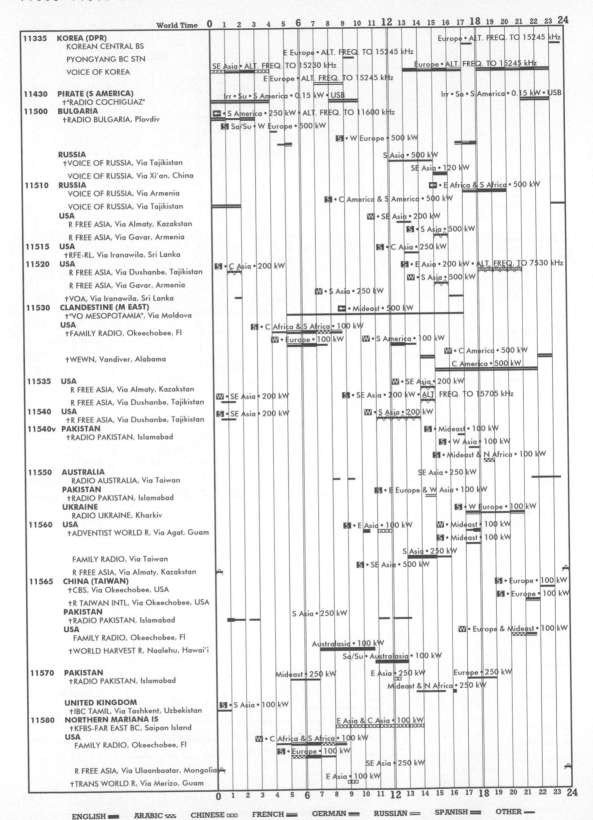

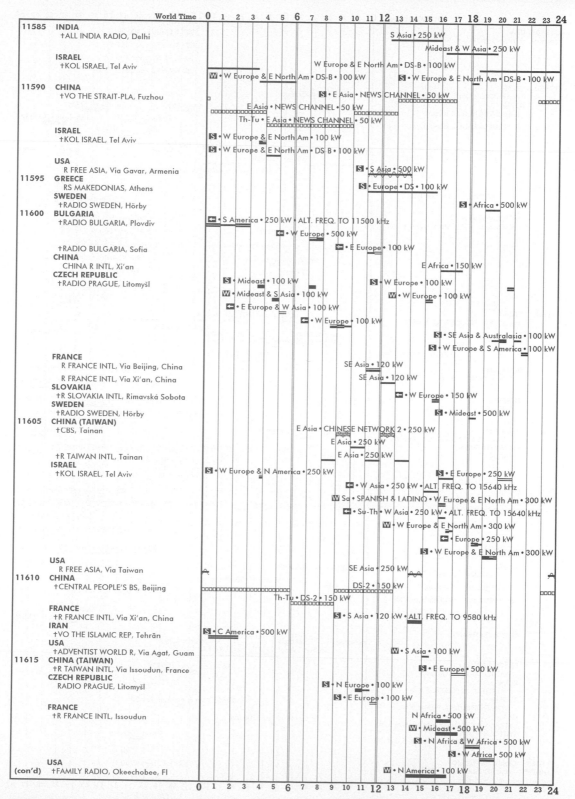

11585	**INDIA** †ALL INDIA RADIO, Delhi	S Asia • 250 kW Mideast & W Asia • 250 kW
	ISRAEL †KOL ISRAEL, Tel Aviv	W Europe & E North Am • DS-B • 100 kW
11590	**CHINA** †VO THE STRAIT-PLA, Fuzhou	W • W Europe & E North Am • DS-B • 100 kW S • W Europe & E North Am • DS-B • 100 kW S • E Asia • NEWS CHANNEL • 50 kW E Asia • NEWS CHANNEL • 50 kW Th-Tu • E Asia • NEWS CHANNEL • 50 kW
	ISRAEL †KOL ISRAEL, Tel Aviv	W • W Europe & E North Am • 100 kW W • W Europe & E North Am • DS-B • 100 kW
	USA R FREE ASIA, Via Gavar, Armenia	S • S Asia • 500 kW
11595	**GREECE** RS MAKEDONIAS, Athens	S • Europe • DS • 100 kW
	SWEDEN †RADIO SWEDEN, Hörby	S • Africa • 500 kW
11600	**BULGARIA** †RADIO BULGARIA, Plovdiv	S America • 250 kW • ALT. FREQ. TO 11500 kHz
		• W Europe • 500 kW
	†RADIO BULGARIA, Sofia	• E Europe • 100 kW
	CHINA CHINA R INTL, Xi'an	E Africa • 150 kW
	CZECH REPUBLIC †RADIO PRAGUE, Litomyšl	S • Mideast • 100 kW S • W Europe • 100 kW W • Mideast & S Asia • 100 kW W • W Europe • 100 kW • E Europe & W Asia • 100 kW • W Europe • 100 kW S • SE Asia & Australasia • 100 kW S • W Europe & S America • 100 kW
	FRANCE R FRANCE INTL, Via Beijing, China	SE Asia • 120 kW
	R FRANCE INTL, Via Xi'an, China	SE Asia • 120 kW
	SLOVAKIA †R SLOVAKIA INTL, Rimavská Sobota	• W Europe • 150 kW
	SWEDEN †RADIO SWEDEN, Hörby	S • Mideast • 500 kW
11605	**CHINA (TAIWAN)** †CBS, Tainan	E Asia • CHINESE NETWORK 2 • 250 kW E Asia • 250 kW
	†R TAIWAN INTL, Tainan	E Asia • 250 kW
	ISRAEL †KOL ISRAEL, Tel Aviv	S • W Europe & N America • 250 kW S • E Europe • 250 kW • W Asia • 250 kW • ALT. FREQ. TO 15640 kHz W Sa • SPANISH & LADINO • W Europe & E North Am • 300 kW • Su-Th • W Asia • 250 kW • ALT. FREQ. TO 15640 kHz W • W Europe & E North Am • 300 kW • Europe • 250 kW S • W Europe & E North Am • 300 kW
	USA R FREE ASIA, Via Taiwan	SE Asia • 250 kW
11610	**CHINA** †CENTRAL PEOPLE'S BS, Beijing	DS-2 • 150 kW Th-Tu • DS-2 • 150 kW
	FRANCE †R FRANCE INTL, Via Xi'an, China	S • S Asia • 120 kW • ALT. FREQ. TO 9580 kHz
	IRAN †VO THE ISLAMIC REP, Tehrān	S • C America • 500 kW
	USA †ADVENTIST WORLD R, Via Agat, Guam	W • S Asia • 100 kW
11615	**CHINA (TAIWAN)** †R TAIWAN INTL, Via Issoudun, France	S • E Europe • 500 kW
	CZECH REPUBLIC RADIO PRAGUE, Litomyšl	S • N Europe • 100 kW S • E Europe • 100 kW
	FRANCE †R FRANCE INTL, Issoudun	N Africa • 500 kW W • Mideast • 500 kW S • N Africa & W Africa • 500 kW S • W Africa • 500 kW
(con'd)	**USA** †FAMILY RADIO, Okeechobee, Fl	W • N America • 100 kW

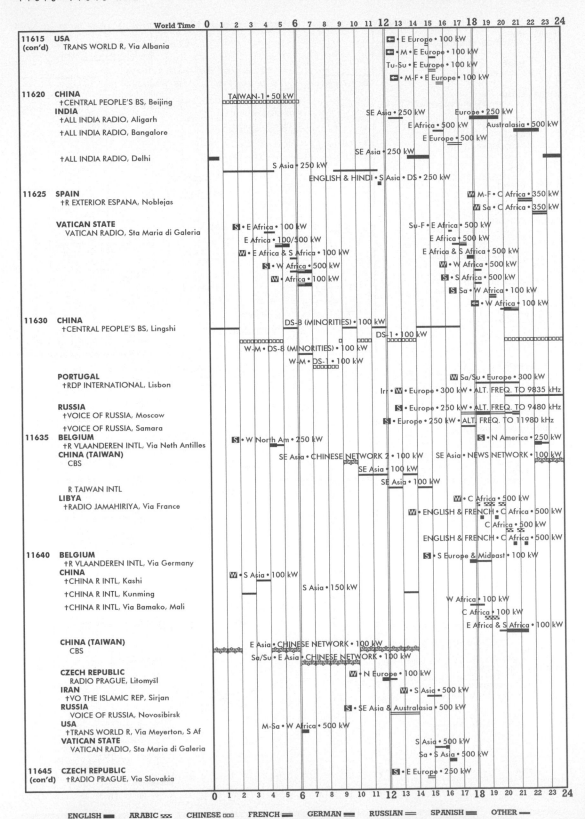

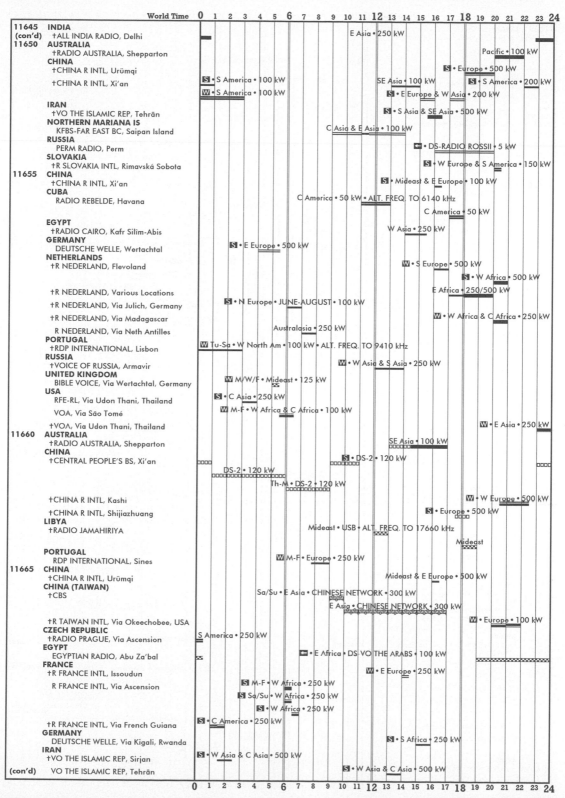

World Time: 0 1 2 3 4 5 6 7 8 9 10 11 12 13 14 15 16 17 18 19 20 21 22 23 24

11645 INDIA
(con'd) †ALL INDIA RADIO, Delhi — E Asia • 250 kW
11650 AUSTRALIA
  †RADIO AUSTRALIA, Shepparton — Pacific • 100 kW
CHINA
  †CHINA R INTL, Urümqi — S • Europe • 500 kW
  †CHINA R INTL, Xi'an — S • S America • 100 kW / SE Asia • 100 kW / S • S America • 200 kW
                                    W • S America • 100 kW / S • E Europe & W Asia • 200 kW
IRAN
  †VO THE ISLAMIC REP, Tehrān — S • S Asia & SE Asia • 500 kW
NORTHERN MARIANA IS
  KFBS-FAR EAST BC, Saipan Island — C Asia & E Asia • 100 kW
RUSSIA
  PERM RADIO, Perm — DS-RADIO ROSSII • 5 kW
SLOVAKIA
  †R SLOVAKIA INTL, Rimavská Sobota — S • W Europe & S America • 150 kW
11655 CHINA
  †CHINA R INTL, Xi'an — S • Mideast & E Europe • 100 kW
CUBA
  RADIO REBELDE, Havana — C America • 50 kW • ALT. FREQ. TO 6140 kHz
                                    C America • 50 kW
EGYPT
  †RADIO CAIRO, Kafr Silim-Abis — W Asia • 250 kW
GERMANY
  DEUTSCHE WELLE, Wertachtal — S • E Europe • 500 kW
NETHERLANDS
  †R NEDERLAND, Flevoland — W • S Europe • 500 kW
                                    S • W Africa • 500 kW
                                    E Africa • 250/500 kW
  †R NEDERLAND, Various Locations
  †R NEDERLAND, Via Julich, Germany — S • N Europe • JUNE-AUGUST • 100 kW
  †R NEDERLAND, Via Madagascar — W • W Africa & C Africa • 250 kW
  R NEDERLAND, Via Neth Antilles — Australasia • 250 kW
PORTUGAL
  †RDP INTERNATIONAL, Lisbon — W • Tu-Sa • W North Am • 100 kW • ALT. FREQ. TO 9410 kHz
RUSSIA
  †VOICE OF RUSSIA, Armavir — W • W Asia & S Asia • 250 kW
UNITED KINGDOM
  BIBLE VOICE, Via Wertachtal, Germany — W • M/W/F • Mideast • 125 kW
USA
  RFE-RL, Via Udon Thani, Thailand — S • C Asia • 250 kW
  VOA, Via São Tomé — W • M-F • W Africa & C Africa • 100 kW
  †VOA, Via Udon Thani, Thailand — W • E Asia • 250 kW
11660 AUSTRALIA
  †RADIO AUSTRALIA, Shepparton — SE Asia • 100 kW
CHINA
  †CENTRAL PEOPLE'S BS, Xi'an — S • DS-2 • 120 kW
                                    DS-2 • 120 kW
                                    Th-M • DS-2 • 120 kW
  †CHINA R INTL, Kashi — W • W Europe • 500 kW
  †CHINA R INTL, Shijiazhuang — S • Europe • 500 kW
LIBYA
  †RADIO JAMAHIRIYA — Mideast • USB • ALT. FREQ. TO 17660 kHz
                                    Mideast
PORTUGAL
  RDP INTERNATIONAL, Sines — W • M-F • Europe • 250 kW
11665 CHINA
  †CHINA R INTL, Urümqi — Mideast & E Europe • 500 kW
CHINA (TAIWAN)
  †CBS — Sa/Su • E Asia • CHINESE NETWORK • 300 kW
                                    E Asia • CHINESE NETWORK • 300 kW
  †R TAIWAN INTL, Via Okeechobee, USA — W • Europe • 100 kW
CZECH REPUBLIC
  †RADIO PRAGUE, Via Ascension — S America • 250 kW
EGYPT
  EGYPTIAN RADIO, Abu Za'bal — E Africa • DS-VO THE ARABS • 100 kW
FRANCE
  †R FRANCE INTL, Issoudun — W • E Europe • 250 kW
  R FRANCE INTL, Via Ascension — S • M-F • W Africa • 250 kW
                                    S • Sa/Su • W Africa • 250 kW
                                    S • W Africa • 250 kW
  †R FRANCE INTL, Via French Guiana — S • C America • 250 kW
GERMANY
  DEUTSCHE WELLE, Via Kigali, Rwanda — S • S Africa • 250 kW
IRAN
  †VO THE ISLAMIC REP, Sirjan — S • W Asia & C Asia • 500 kW
(con'd) VO THE ISLAMIC REP, Tehrān — S • W Asia & C Asia • 500 kW

0 1 2 3 4 5 6 7 8 9 10 11 12 13 14 15 16 17 18 19 20 21 22 23 24

SEASONAL ⑤ OR Ⓦ   1-HR TIMESHIFT MIDYEAR ⬅ OR ➡   JAMMING / OR ∧   EARLIEST HEARD ◁   LATEST HEARD ▷   NEW FOR 2005 †

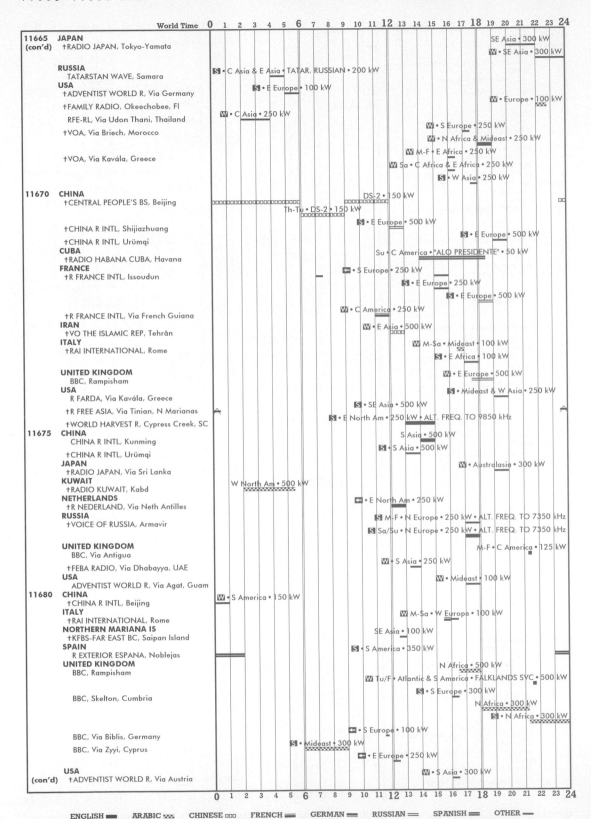

World Time 0 1 2 3 4 5 6 7 8 9 10 11 12 13 14 15 16 17 18 19 20 21 22 23 24

11665 **JAPAN**
(con'd)   †RADIO JAPAN, Tokyo-Yamata — SE Asia • 300 kW / W • SE Asia • 300 kW

RUSSIA
   TATARSTAN WAVE, Samara — S • C Asia & E Asia • TATAR, RUSSIAN • 200 kW
USA
   †ADVENTIST WORLD R, Via Germany — S • E Europe • 100 kW
   †FAMILY RADIO, Okeechobee, Fl — W • Europe • 100 kW
   RFE-RL, Via Udon Thani, Thailand — W • C Asia • 250 kW
   †VOA, Via Briech, Morocco — W • S Europe • 250 kW / W • N Africa & Mideast • 250 kW
   †VOA, Via Kavála, Greece — W M-F • E Africa • 250 kW / W Sa • C Africa & E Africa • 250 kW / S • W Asia • 250 kW

11670 **CHINA**
   †CENTRAL PEOPLE'S BS, Beijing — DS-2 • 150 kW / Th-Tu • DS-2 • 150 kW
   †CHINA R INTL, Shijiazhuang — S • E Europe • 500 kW
   †CHINA R INTL, Urümqi — S • E Europe • 500 kW
CUBA
   †RADIO HABANA CUBA, Havana — Su • C America • "ALO PRESIDENTE" • 50 kW
FRANCE
   †R FRANCE INTL, Issoudun — S • S Europe • 250 kW / S • E Europe • 250 kW / S • E Europe • 500 kW
   †R FRANCE INTL, Via French Guiana — W • C America • 250 kW
IRAN
   †VO THE ISLAMIC REP, Tehrān — W • E Asia • 500 kW
ITALY
   †RAI INTERNATIONAL, Rome — W M-Sa • Mideast • 100 kW / S • E Africa • 100 kW
UNITED KINGDOM
   BBC, Rampisham — W • E Europe • 500 kW
USA
   R FARDA, Via Kavála, Greece — S • Mideast & W Asia • 250 kW
   †R FREE ASIA, Via Tinian, N Marianas — S • SE Asia • 500 kW
   †WORLD HARVEST R, Cypress Creek, SC — S • E North Am • 250 kW • ALT. FREQ. TO 9850 kHz

11675 **CHINA**
   CHINA R INTL, Kunming — S Asia • 500 kW
   †CHINA R INTL, Urümqi — S • S Asia • 500 kW
JAPAN
   †RADIO JAPAN, Via Sri Lanka — W • Australasia • 300 kW
KUWAIT
   †RADIO KUWAIT, Kabd — W North Am • 500 kW
NETHERLANDS
   †R NEDERLAND, Via Neth Antilles — • E North Am • 250 kW
RUSSIA
   †VOICE OF RUSSIA, Armavir — S M-F • N Europe • 250 kW • ALT. FREQ. TO 7350 kHz / S Sa/Su • N Europe • 250 kW • ALT. FREQ. TO 7350 kHz
UNITED KINGDOM
   BBC, Via Antigua — M-F • C America • 125 kW
   †FEBA RADIO, Via Dhabayya, UAE — W • S Asia • 250 kW
USA
   ADVENTIST WORLD R, Via Agat, Guam — W • Mideast • 100 kW

11680 **CHINA**
   †CHINA R INTL, Beijing — W • S America • 150 kW
ITALY
   †RAI INTERNATIONAL, Rome — W M-Sa • W Europe • 100 kW
NORTHERN MARIANA IS
   †KFBS-FAR EAST BC, Saipan Island — SE Asia • 100 kW
SPAIN
   R EXTERIOR ESPANA, Noblejas — S • S America • 350 kW
UNITED KINGDOM
   BBC, Rampisham — N Africa • 500 kW / W Tu/F • Atlantic & S America • FALKLANDS SVC • 500 kW
   BBC, Skelton, Cumbria — S • S Europe • 300 kW / N Africa • 300 kW / S • N Africa • 300 kW
   BBC, Via Biblis, Germany — • S Europe • 100 kW
   BBC, Via Zyyi, Cyprus — S • Mideast • 300 kW / • E Europe • 250 kW
USA
(con'd)   †ADVENTIST WORLD R, Via Austria — W • S Asia • 300 kW

0 1 2 3 4 5 6 7 8 9 10 11 12 13 14 15 16 17 18 19 20 21 22 23 24

ENGLISH ▬   ARABIC ▨   CHINESE ☐☐☐   FRENCH ═   GERMAN ▬   RUSSIAN ═   SPANISH ═   OTHER ─

World Time 0 1 2 3 4 5 6 7 8 9 10 11 12 13 14 15 16 17 18 19 20 21 22 23 24

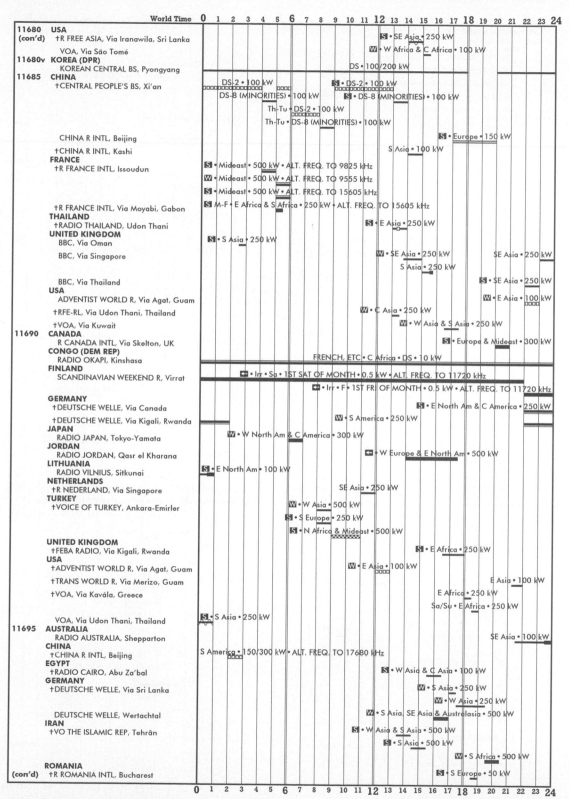

11680	USA	
(con'd)	†R FREE ASIA, Via Iranawila, Sri Lanka	§•SE Asia•250 kW
	VOA, Via São Tomé	W•W Africa & C Africa•100 kW
11680v	KOREA (DPR)	
	KOREAN CENTRAL BS, Pyongyang	DS•100/200 kW
11685	CHINA	
	†CENTRAL PEOPLE'S BS, Xi'an	DS-2•100 kW / §•DS-2•100 kW
		DS-8 (MINORITIES)•100 kW / §•DS-8 (MINORITIES)•100 kW
		Th-Tu•DS-2•100 kW
		Th-Tu•DS-8 (MINORITIES)•100 kW
	CHINA R INTL, Beijing	§•Europe•150 kW
	†CHINA R INTL, Kashi	S Asia•100 kW
	FRANCE	
	†R FRANCE INTL, Issoudun	§•Mideast•500 kW•ALT. FREQ. TO 9825 kHz
		W•Mideast•500 kW•ALT. FREQ. TO 9555 kHz
		§•Mideast•500 kW•ALT. FREQ. TO 15605 kHz
		§•M-F•E Africa & S Africa•250 kW•ALT. FREQ. TO 15605 kHz
	THAILAND	
	†RADIO THAILAND, Udon Thani	§•E Asia•250 kW
	UNITED KINGDOM	
	BBC, Via Oman	§•S Asia•250 kW
	BBC, Via Singapore	W•SE Asia•250 kW / SE Asia•250 kW
		S Asia•250 kW
	BBC, Via Thailand	§•SE Asia•250 kW
	USA	
	ADVENTIST WORLD R, Via Agat, Guam	W•E Asia•100 kW
	†RFE-RL, Via Udon Thani, Thailand	W•C Asia•250 kW
	†VOA, Via Kuwait	W•W Asia & S Asia•250 kW
11690	CANADA	
	R CANADA INTL, Via Skelton, UK	§•Europe & Mideast•300 kW
	CONGO (DEM REP)	
	RADIO OKAPI, Kinshasa	FRENCH, ETC•C Africa•DS•10 kW
	FINLAND	
	SCANDINAVIAN WEEKEND R, Virrat	⇆•Irr•Sa•1ST SAT OF MONTH•0.5 kW•ALT. FREQ. TO 11720 kHz
		⇆•Irr•F•1ST FRI OF MONTH•0.5 kW•ALT. FREQ. TO 11720 kHz
	GERMANY	
	†DEUTSCHE WELLE, Via Canada	§•E North Am & C America•250 kW
	†DEUTSCHE WELLE, Via Kigali, Rwanda	W•S America•250 kW
	JAPAN	
	RADIO JAPAN, Tokyo-Yamata	W•W North Am & C America•300 kW
	JORDAN	
	RADIO JORDAN, Qasr el Kharana	⇆•W Europe & E North Am•500 kW
	LITHUANIA	
	RADIO VILNIUS, Sitkunai	§•E North Am•100 kW
	NETHERLANDS	
	†R NEDERLAND, Via Singapore	SE Asia•250 kW
	TURKEY	
	†VOICE OF TURKEY, Ankara-Emirler	W•W Asia•500 kW
		§•S Europe•250 kW
		§•N Africa & Mideast•500 kW
	UNITED KINGDOM	
	†FEBA RADIO, Via Kigali, Rwanda	§•E Africa•250 kW
	USA	
	†ADVENTIST WORLD R, Via Agat, Guam	W•E Asia•100 kW
	†TRANS WORLD R, Via Merizo, Guam	E Asia•100 kW
	†VOA, Via Kavála, Greece	E Africa•250 kW
		Sa/Su•E Africa•250 kW
	VOA, Via Udon Thani, Thailand	§•S Asia•250 kW
11695	AUSTRALIA	
	RADIO AUSTRALIA, Shepparton	SE Asia•100 kW
	CHINA	
	†CHINA R INTL, Beijing	S America•150/300 kW•ALT. FREQ. TO 17680 kHz
	EGYPT	
	†RADIO CAIRO, Abu Za'bal	§•W Asia & C Asia•100 kW
	GERMANY	
	†DEUTSCHE WELLE, Via Sri Lanka	W•S Asia•250 kW
		W•W Asia•250 kW
	DEUTSCHE WELLE, Wertachtal	W•S Asia, SE Asia & Australasia•500 kW
	IRAN	
	†VO THE ISLAMIC REP, Tehrān	§•W Asia & S Asia•500 kW
		§•S Asia•500 kW
		W•S Africa•500 kW
	ROMANIA	
(con'd)	†R ROMANIA INTL, Bucharest	§•S Europe•50 kW

0 1 2 3 4 5 6 7 8 9 10 11 12 13 14 15 16 17 18 19 20 21 22 23 24

SEASONAL § OR W   1-HR TIMESHIFT MIDYEAR ⇆ OR ⇒   JAMMING / OR ∧   EARLIEST HEARD ◁   LATEST HEARD ▷   NEW FOR 2005 †

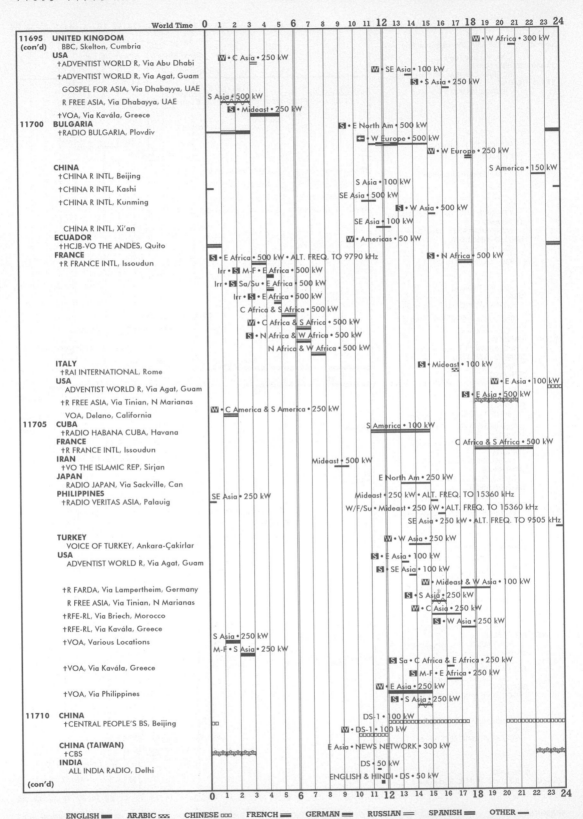

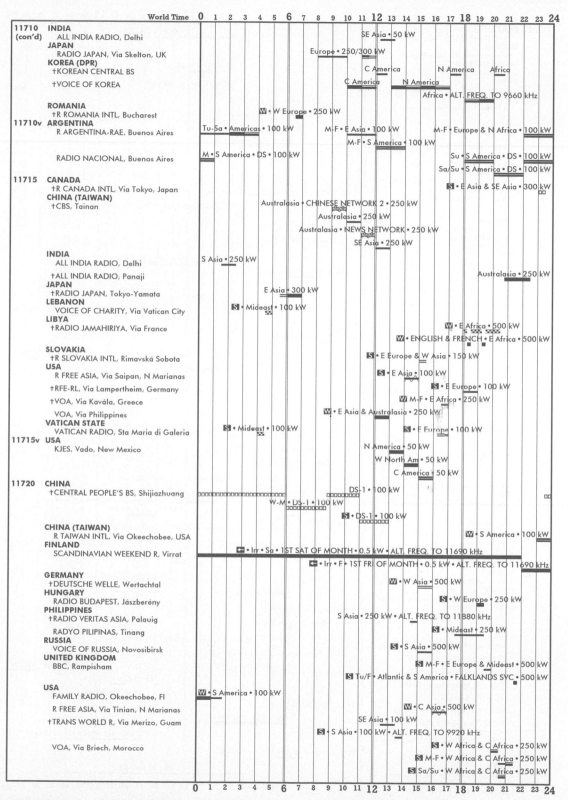

World Time 0 1 2 3 4 5 6 7 8 9 10 11 12 13 14 15 16 17 18 19 20 21 22 23 24

11710 INDIA	
(con'd) ALL INDIA RADIO, Delhi	SE Asia • 50 kW
JAPAN	
RADIO JAPAN, Via Skelton, UK	Europe • 250/300 kW
KOREA (DPR)	
†KOREAN CENTRAL BS	C America / N America / Africa
†VOICE OF KOREA	C America / N America
	Africa • ALT. FREQ. TO 9660 kHz
ROMANIA	
†R ROMANIA INTL, Bucharest	W • W Europe • 250 kW
11710v ARGENTINA	
R ARGENTINA-RAE, Buenos Aires	Tu-Sa • Americas • 100 kW / M-F • E Asia • 100 kW / M-F • Europe & N Africa • 100 kW
	M-F • S America • 100 kW
RADIO NACIONAL, Buenos Aires	M • S America • DS • 100 kW / Su • S America • DS • 100 kW
	Sa/Su • S America • DS • 100 kW
11715 CANADA	
†R CANADA INTL, Via Tokyo, Japan	S • E Asia & SE Asia • 300 kW
CHINA (TAIWAN)	
†CBS, Tainan	Australasia • CHINESE NETWORK 2 • 250 kW
	Australasia • 250 kW
	Australasia • NEWS NETWORK • 250 kW
	SE Asia • 250 kW
INDIA	
ALL INDIA RADIO, Delhi	S Asia • 250 kW
†ALL INDIA RADIO, Panaji	Australasia • 250 kW
JAPAN	
†RADIO JAPAN, Tokyo-Yamata	E Asia • 300 kW
LEBANON	
VOICE OF CHARITY, Via Vatican City	S • Mideast • 100 kW
LIBYA	
†RADIO JAMAHIRIYA, Via France	W • E Africa • 500 kW
	W • ENGLISH & FRENCH • E Africa • 500 kW
SLOVAKIA	
†R SLOVAKIA INTL, Rimavská Sobota	S • E Europe & W Asia • 150 kW
USA	
R FREE ASIA, Via Saipan, N Marianas	S • E Asia • 100 kW
†RFE-RL, Via Lampertheim, Germany	S • E Europe • 100 kW
†VOA, Via Kavála, Greece	W M-F • E Africa • 250 kW
VOA, Via Philippines	W • E Asia & Australasia • 250 kW
VATICAN STATE	
VATICAN RADIO, Sta Maria di Galeria	S • Mideast • 100 kW / S • E Europe • 100 kW
11715v USA	
KJES, Vado, New Mexico	N America • 50 kW
	W North Am • 50 kW
	C America • 50 kW
11720 CHINA	
†CENTRAL PEOPLE'S BS, Shijiazhuang	DS-1 • 100 kW
	W-M • DS-1 • 100 kW
	S • DS-1 • 100 kW
CHINA (TAIWAN)	
R TAIWAN INTL, Via Okeechobee, USA	W • S America • 100 kW
FINLAND	
SCANDINAVIAN WEEKEND R, Virrat	⇨ • Irr • Sa • 1ST SAT OF MONTH • 0.5 kW • ALT. FREQ. TO 11690 kHz
	⇨ • Irr • F • 1ST FRI OF MONTH • 0.5 kW • ALT. FREQ. TO 11690 kHz
GERMANY	
†DEUTSCHE WELLE, Wertachtal	W • W Asia • 500 kW
HUNGARY	
RADIO BUDAPEST, Jászberény	S • W Europe • 250 kW
PHILIPPINES	
†RADIO VERITAS ASIA, Palauig	S Asia • 250 kW • ALT. FREQ. TO 11880 kHz
RADYO PILIPINAS, Tinang	S • Mideast • 250 kW
RUSSIA	
VOICE OF RUSSIA, Novosibirsk	S • S Asia • 500 kW
UNITED KINGDOM	
BBC, Rampisham	S M-F • E Europe & Mideast • 500 kW
	S Tu/F • Atlantic & S America • FALKLANDS SVC • 500 kW
USA	
FAMILY RADIO, Okeechobee, Fl	W • S America • 100 kW
R FREE ASIA, Via Tinian, N Marianas	W • C Asia • 500 kW
†TRANS WORLD R, Via Merizo, Guam	SE Asia • 100 kW
	S • S Asia • 100 kW • ALT. FREQ. TO 9920 kHz
VOA, Via Briech, Morocco	S • W Africa & C Africa • 250 kW
	S M-F • W Africa & C Africa • 250 kW
	S Sa/Su • W Africa & C Africa • 250 kW

0 1 2 3 4 5 6 7 8 9 10 11 12 13 14 15 16 17 18 19 20 21 22 23 24

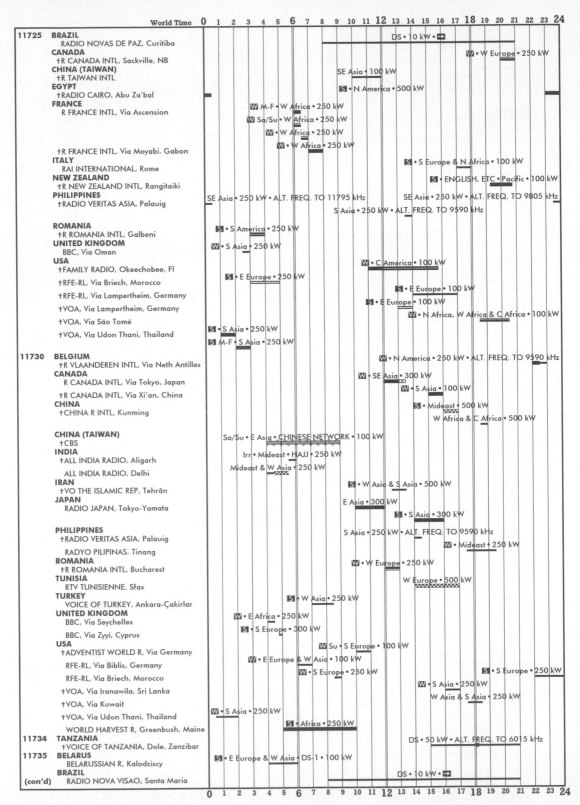

World Time   0 1 2 3 4 5 6 7 8 9 10 11 12 13 14 15 16 17 18 19 20 21 22 23 24

11725 BRAZIL
  RADIO NOVAS DE PAZ, Curitiba — DS • 10 kW •
CANADA
  †R CANADA INTL, Sackville, NB — W • W Europe • 250 kW
CHINA (TAIWAN)
  †R TAIWAN INTL — SE Asia • 100 kW
EGYPT
  †RADIO CAIRO, Abu Za'bal — S • N America • 500 kW
FRANCE
  R FRANCE INTL, Via Ascension — W M-F • W Africa • 250 kW
                                 W Sa/Su • W Africa • 250 kW
                                 W • W Africa • 250 kW
  †R FRANCE INTL, Via Moyabi, Gabon — W • W Africa • 250 kW
ITALY
  RAI INTERNATIONAL, Rome — S • S Europe & N Africa • 100 kW
NEW ZEALAND
  †R NEW ZEALAND INTL, Rangitaiki — S • ENGLISH, ETC • Pacific • 100 kW
PHILIPPINES
  †RADIO VERITAS ASIA, Palauig — SE Asia • 250 kW • ALT. FREQ. TO 11795 kHz   SE Asia • 250 kW • ALT. FREQ. TO 9805 kHz
                                 S Asia • 250 kW • ALT. FREQ. TO 9590 kHz
ROMANIA
  †R ROMANIA INTL, Galbeni — S • S America • 250 kW
UNITED KINGDOM
  BBC, Via Oman — W • S Asia • 250 kW
USA
  †FAMILY RADIO, Okeechobee, Fl — W • C America • 100 kW
  †RFE-RL, Via Briech, Morocco — S • E Europe • 250 kW
  †RFE-RL, Via Lampertheim, Germany — S • E Europe • 100 kW
  †VOA, Via Lampertheim, Germany — S • E Europe • 100 kW
  †VOA, Via São Tomé — W • N Africa, W Africa & C Africa • 100 kW
  †VOA, Via Udon Thani, Thailand — S • S Asia • 250 kW
                                   S M-F • S Asia • 250 kW

11730 BELGIUM
  †R VLAANDEREN INTL, Via Neth Antilles — W • N America • 250 kW • ALT. FREQ. TO 9590 kHz
CANADA
  R CANADA INTL, Via Tokyo, Japan — W • SE Asia • 300 kW
  †R CANADA INTL, Via Xi'an, China — W • S Asia • 100 kW
CHINA
  †CHINA R INTL, Kunming — S • Mideast • 500 kW
                           W Africa & C Africa • 500 kW
CHINA (TAIWAN)
  †CBS — Sa/Su • E Asia • CHINESE NETWORK • 100 kW
INDIA
  †ALL INDIA RADIO, Aligarh — Irr • Mideast • HAJJ • 250 kW
  ALL INDIA RADIO, Delhi — Mideast & W Asia • 250 kW
IRAN
  †VO THE ISLAMIC REP, Tehrān — S • W Asia & S Asia • 500 kW
JAPAN
  RADIO JAPAN, Tokyo-Yamata — E Asia • 300 kW
                              S • S Asia • 300 kW
PHILIPPINES
  †RADIO VERITAS ASIA, Palauig — S Asia • 250 kW • ALT. FREQ. TO 9590 kHz
  RADYO PILIPINAS, Tinang — W • Mideast • 250 kW
ROMANIA
  †R ROMANIA INTL, Bucharest — W • W Europe • 250 kW
TUNISIA
  RTV TUNISIENNE, Sfax — W Europe • 500 kW
TURKEY
  VOICE OF TURKEY, Ankara-Çakirlar — S • W Asia • 250 kW
UNITED KINGDOM
  BBC, Via Seychelles — W • E Africa • 250 kW
  BBC, Via Zyyi, Cyprus — S • S Europe • 300 kW
USA
  †ADVENTIST WORLD R, Via Germany — W Su • S Europe • 100 kW
  RFE-RL, Via Biblis, Germany — W • E Europe & W Asia • 100 kW
  RFE-RL, Via Briech, Morocco — W • S Europe • 250 kW   S • S Europe • 250 kW
  †VOA, Via Iranawila, Sri Lanka — W • S Asia • 250 kW
                                   W Asia & S Asia • 250 kW
  †VOA, Via Kuwait
  †VOA, Via Udon Thani, Thailand — W • S Asia • 250 kW
  WORLD HARVEST R, Greenbush, Maine — S • Africa • 250 kW
11734 TANZANIA
  †VOICE OF TANZANIA, Dole, Zanzibar — DS • 50 kW • ALT. FREQ. TO 6015 kHz
11735 BELARUS
  BELARUSSIAN R, Kalodziscy — S • E Europe & W Asia • DS-1 • 100 kW
BRAZIL
(con'd) RADIO NOVA VISAO, Santa Maria — DS • 10 kW •

World Time   0 1 2 3 4 5 6 7 8 9 10 11 12 13 14 15 16 17 18 19 20 21 22 23 24

ENGLISH ▬▬   ARABIC ▨▨   CHINESE ▫▫▫   FRENCH ══   GERMAN ▬▬   RUSSIAN ══   SPANISH ══   OTHER ──

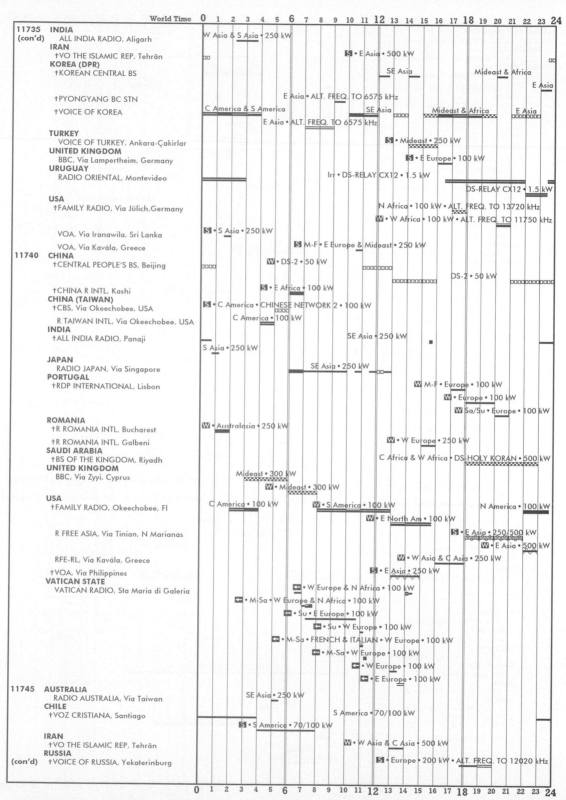

World Time 0 1 2 3 4 5 6 7 8 9 10 11 12 13 14 15 16 17 18 19 20 21 22 23 24

11735 INDIA
(con'd)   ALL INDIA RADIO, Aligarh — W Asia & S Asia • 250 kW
IRAN
   †VO THE ISLAMIC REP, Tehrān — S • E Asia • 500 kW
KOREA (DPR)
   †KOREAN CENTRAL BS — SE Asia / Mideast & Africa / E Asia

   †PYONGYANG BC STN — E Asia • ALT. FREQ. TO 6575 kHz

   †VOICE OF KOREA — C America & S America / SE Asia / Mideast & Africa / E Asia
     E Asia • ALT. FREQ. TO 6575 kHz

TURKEY
   VOICE OF TURKEY, Ankara-Çakirlar — S • Mideast • 250 kW
UNITED KINGDOM
   BBC, Via Lampertheim, Germany — S • E Europe • 100 kW
URUGUAY
   RADIO ORIENTAL, Montevideo — Irr • DS-RELAY CX12 • 1.5 kW / DS-RELAY CX12 • 1.5 kW

USA
   †FAMILY RADIO, Via Jülich, Germany — N Africa • 100 kW • ALT. FREQ. TO 13720 kHz
     W • W Africa • 100 kW • ALT. FREQ. TO 11750 kHz

   VOA, Via Iranawila, Sri Lanka — S • S Asia • 250 kW
   VOA, Via Kavála, Greece — S • M-F • E Europe & Mideast • 250 kW
11740 CHINA
   †CENTRAL PEOPLE'S BS, Beijing — W • DS-2 • 50 kW / DS-2 • 50 kW

   †CHINA R INTL, Kashi — S • E Africa • 100 kW
CHINA (TAIWAN)
   †CBS, Via Okeechobee, USA — S • C America • CHINESE NETWORK 2 • 100 kW

   R TAIWAN INTL, Via Okeechobee, USA — C America • 100 kW
INDIA
   †ALL INDIA RADIO, Panaji — SE Asia • 250 kW

JAPAN
   RADIO JAPAN, Via Singapore — S Asia • 250 kW / SE Asia • 250 kW
PORTUGAL
   †RDP INTERNATIONAL, Lisbon — W • M-F • Europe • 100 kW
     W • Europe • 100 kW
     W • Sa/Su • Europe • 100 kW

ROMANIA
   †R ROMANIA INTL, Bucharest — W • Australasia • 250 kW

   †R ROMANIA INTL, Galbeni — W • W Europe • 250 kW
SAUDI ARABIA
   †BS OF THE KINGDOM, Riyadh — C Africa & W Africa • DS-HOLY KORAN • 500 kW
UNITED KINGDOM
   BBC, Via Zyyi, Cyprus — Mideast • 300 kW
     W • Mideast • 300 kW

USA
   †FAMILY RADIO, Okeechobee, Fl — C America • 100 kW / W • S America • 100 kW / N America • 100 kW
     W • E North Am • 100 kW

   R FREE ASIA, Via Tinian, N Marianas — S • E Asia • 250/500 kW
     W • E Asia • 500 kW

   RFE-RL, Via Kavála, Greece — W • W Asia & C Asia • 250 kW
   †VOA, Via Philippines — S • E Asia • 250 kW
VATICAN STATE
   VATICAN RADIO, Sta Maria di Galeria — • W Europe & N Africa • 100 kW
     • M-Sa • W Europe & N Africa • 100 kW
     • Su • E Europe • 100 kW
     • Su • W Europe • 100 kW
     • M-Sa • FRENCH & ITALIAN • W Europe • 100 kW
     • M-Sa • W Europe • 100 kW
     • W Europe • 100 kW
     • E Europe • 100 kW

11745 AUSTRALIA
   RADIO AUSTRALIA, Via Taiwan — SE Asia • 250 kW
CHILE
   †VOZ CRISTIANA, Santiago — S America • 70/100 kW
     S • S America • 70/100 kW

IRAN
   †VO THE ISLAMIC REP, Tehrān — W • W Asia & C Asia • 500 kW
RUSSIA
(con'd)   †VOICE OF RUSSIA, Yekaterinburg — S • Europe • 200 kW • ALT. FREQ. TO 12020 kHz

0 1 2 3 4 5 6 7 8 9 10 11 12 13 14 15 16 17 18 19 20 21 22 23 24

SEASONAL S OR W   1-HR TIMESHIFT MIDYEAR ⬅ OR ➡   JAMMING / OR /\   EARLIEST HEARD ◁   LATEST HEARD ▷   NEW FOR 2005 †

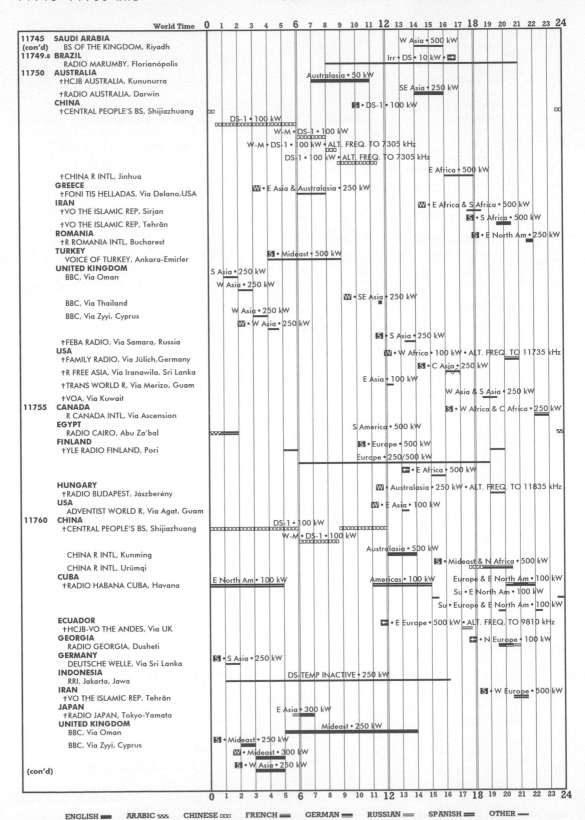

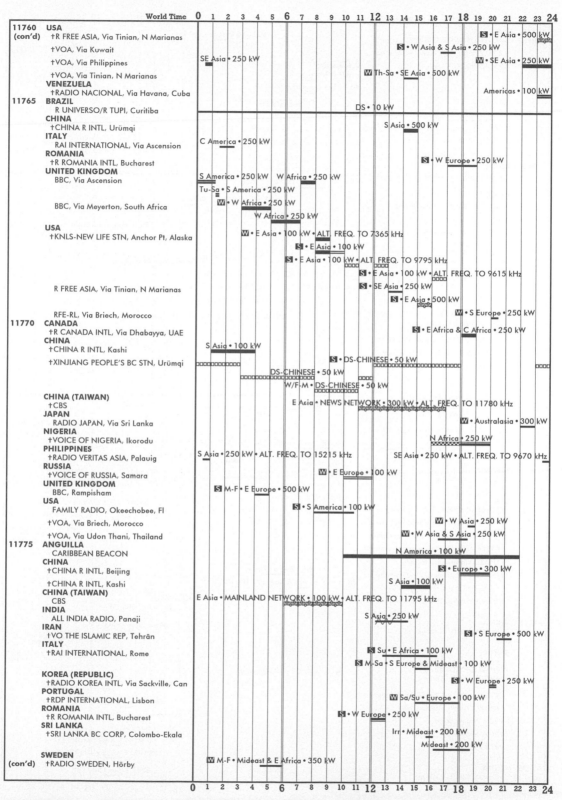

World Time

11760 USA
(con'd)   †R FREE ASIA, Via Tinian, N Marianas — 🅂 • E Asia • 500 kW

          †VOA, Via Kuwait — 🅂 • W Asia & S Asia • 250 kW

          †VOA, Via Philippines — SE Asia • 250 kW / 🅆 • SE Asia • 250 kW

          †VOA, Via Tinian, N Marianas — 🅆 Th-Sa • SE Asia • 500 kW
VENEZUELA
          †RADIO NACIONAL, Via Havana, Cuba — Americas • 100 kW
11765 BRAZIL
          R UNIVERSO/R TUPI, Curitiba — DS • 10 kW
CHINA
          †CHINA R INTL, Urümqi — S Asia • 500 kW
ITALY
          RAI INTERNATIONAL, Via Ascension — C America • 250 kW
ROMANIA
          †R ROMANIA INTL, Bucharest — 🅂 • W Europe • 250 kW
UNITED KINGDOM
          BBC, Via Ascension — S America • 250 kW / W Africa • 250 kW
                                Tu-Sa • S America • 250 kW
          BBC, Via Meyerton, South Africa — 🅆 • W Africa • 250 kW
                                W Africa • 250 kW
USA
          †KNLS-NEW LIFE STN, Anchor Pt, Alaska — 🅆 • E Asia • 100 kW • ALT. FREQ. TO 7365 kHz
                                🅂 • E Asia • 100 kW
                                🅂 • E Asia • 100 kW • ALT. FREQ. TO 9795 kHz
                                🅂 • E Asia • 100 kW • ALT. FREQ. TO 9615 kHz
          R FREE ASIA, Via Tinian, N Marianas — 🅂 • SE Asia • 250 kW
                                🅂 • E Asia • 500 kW
          RFE-RL, Via Briech, Morocco — 🅆 • S Europe • 250 kW
11770 CANADA
          †R CANADA INTL, Via Dhabayya, UAE — 🅂 • E Africa & C Africa • 250 kW
CHINA
          †CHINA R INTL, Kashi — S Asia • 100 kW
          †XINJIANG PEOPLE'S BC STN, Urümqi — 🅂 • DS-CHINESE • 50 kW
                                DS-CHINESE • 50 kW
                                W/F-M • DS-CHINESE • 50 kW
CHINA (TAIWAN)
          †CBS — E Asia • NEWS NETWORK • 300 kW • ALT. FREQ. TO 11780 kHz
JAPAN
          RADIO JAPAN, Via Sri Lanka — 🅆 • Australasia • 300 kW
NIGERIA
          †VOICE OF NIGERIA, Ikorodu — N Africa • 250 kW
PHILIPPINES
          †RADIO VERITAS ASIA, Palauig — S Asia • 250 kW • ALT. FREQ. TO 15215 kHz / SE Asia • 250 kW • ALT. FREQ. TO 9670 kHz
RUSSIA
          †VOICE OF RUSSIA, Samara — 🅆 • E Europe • 100 kW
UNITED KINGDOM
          BBC, Rampisham — 🅂 M-F • E Europe • 500 kW
USA
          FAMILY RADIO, Okeechobee, Fl — 🅂 • S America • 100 kW
          †VOA, Via Briech, Morocco — 🅆 • W Asia • 250 kW
          †VOA, Via Udon Thani, Thailand — 🅆 • W Asia & S Asia • 250 kW
11775 ANGUILLA
          CARIBBEAN BEACON — N America • 100 kW
CHINA
          †CHINA R INTL, Beijing — 🅂 • Europe • 300 kW
          †CHINA R INTL, Kashi — S Asia • 100 kW
CHINA (TAIWAN)
          CBS — E Asia • MAINLAND NETWORK • 100 kW • ALT. FREQ. TO 11795 kHz
INDIA
          ALL INDIA RADIO, Panaji — S Asia • 250 kW
IRAN
          †VO THE ISLAMIC REP, Tehrān — 🅂 • S Europe • 500 kW
ITALY
          †RAI INTERNATIONAL, Rome — 🅂 Su • E Africa • 100 kW
                                🅂 M-Sa • S Europe & Mideast • 100 kW
KOREA (REPUBLIC)
          †RADIO KOREA INTL, Via Sackville, Can — 🅂 • W Europe • 250 kW
PORTUGAL
          †RDP INTERNATIONAL, Lisbon — 🅆 Sa/Su • Europe • 100 kW
ROMANIA
          †R ROMANIA INTL, Bucharest — 🅂 • W Europe • 250 kW
SRI LANKA
          †SRI LANKA BC CORP, Colombo-Ekala — Irr • Mideast • 200 kW
                                Mideast • 200 kW
SWEDEN
(con'd)   †RADIO SWEDEN, Hörby — 🅆 M-F • Mideast & E Africa • 350 kW

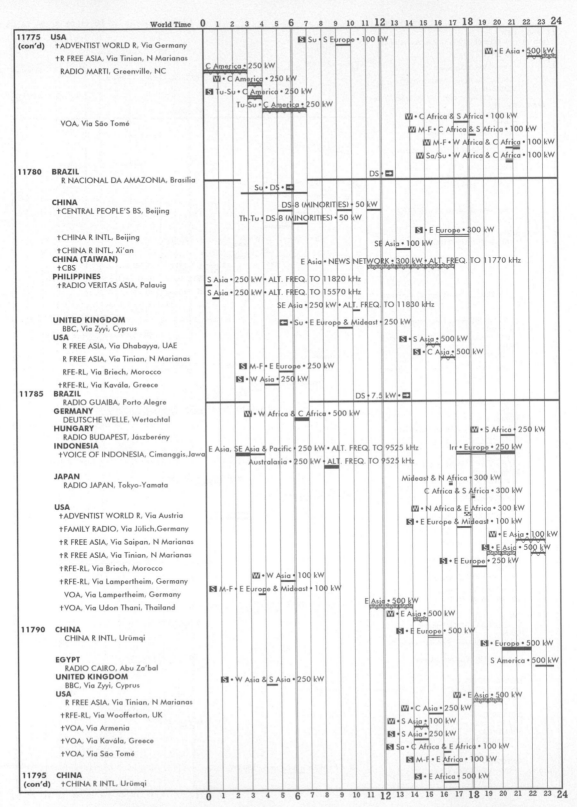

World Time 0 1 2 3 4 5 6 7 8 9 10 11 12 13 14 15 16 17 18 19 20 21 22 23 24

11775 USA
(con'd) †ADVENTIST WORLD R, Via Germany
         †R FREE ASIA, Via Tinian, N Marianas
         RADIO MARTI, Greenville, NC

         VOA, Via São Tomé

11780 BRAZIL
         R NACIONAL DA AMAZONIA, Brasilia

         CHINA
         †CENTRAL PEOPLE'S BS, Beijing

         †CHINA R INTL, Beijing
         †CHINA R INTL, Xi'an
         CHINA (TAIWAN)
         †CBS
         PHILIPPINES
         †RADIO VERITAS ASIA, Palauig

         UNITED KINGDOM
         BBC, Via Zyyi, Cyprus
         USA
         R FREE ASIA, Via Dhabayya, UAE
         R FREE ASIA, Via Tinian, N Marianas
         RFE-RL, Via Briech, Morocco
         †RFE-RL, Via Kavála, Greece

11785 BRAZIL
         RADIO GUAIBA, Porto Alegre
         GERMANY
         DEUTSCHE WELLE, Wertachtal
         HUNGARY
         RADIO BUDAPEST, Jászberény
         INDONESIA
         †VOICE OF INDONESIA, Cimanggis,Jawa

         JAPAN
         RADIO JAPAN, Tokyo-Yamata

         USA
         †ADVENTIST WORLD R, Via Austria
         †FAMILY RADIO, Via Jülich,Germany
         †R FREE ASIA, Via Saipan, N Marianas
         †R FREE ASIA, Via Tinian, N Marianas
         †RFE-RL, Via Briech, Morocco
         †RFE-RL, Via Lampertheim, Germany
         VOA, Via Lampertheim, Germany
         †VOA, Via Udon Thani, Thailand

11790 CHINA
         CHINA R INTL, Urümqi

         EGYPT
         RADIO CAIRO, Abu Za'bal
         UNITED KINGDOM
         BBC, Via Zyyi, Cyprus
         USA
         R FREE ASIA, Via Tinian, N Marianas
         †RFE-RL, Via Woofferton, UK
         †VOA, Via Armenia
         †VOA, Via Kavála, Greece
         †VOA, Via São Tomé

11795 CHINA
(con'd) †CHINA R INTL, Urümqi

0 1 2 3 4 5 6 7 8 9 10 11 12 13 14 15 16 17 18 19 20 21 22 23 24

ENGLISH ▬   ARABIC ░░░   CHINESE □□□   FRENCH ▬   GERMAN ▬   RUSSIAN ═══   SPANISH ▬   OTHER ▬

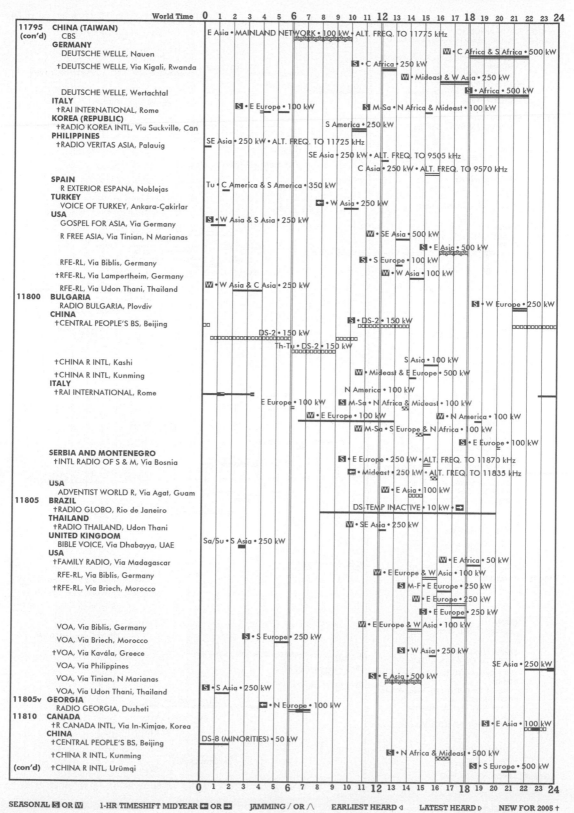

World Time 0 1 2 3 4 5 6 7 8 9 10 11 12 13 14 15 16 17 18 19 20 21 22 23 24

11795 CHINA (TAIWAN)
(con'd) CBS — E Asia • MAINLAND NETWORK • 100 kW • ALT. FREQ. TO 11775 kHz
GERMANY
DEUTSCHE WELLE, Nauen — W • C Africa & S Africa • 500 kW
†DEUTSCHE WELLE, Via Kigali, Rwanda — S • C Africa • 250 kW
— W • Mideast & W Asia • 250 kW
DEUTSCHE WELLE, Wertachtal — S • Africa • 500 kW
ITALY
†RAI INTERNATIONAL, Rome — S • E Europe • 100 kW — S M-Sa • N Africa & Mideast • 100 kW
KOREA (REPUBLIC)
†RADIO KOREA INTL, Via Sackville, Can — S America • 250 kW
PHILIPPINES
†RADIO VERITAS ASIA, Palauig — SE Asia • 250 kW • ALT. FREQ. TO 11725 kHz
— SE Asia • 250 kW • ALT. FREQ. TO 9505 kHz
— C Asia • 250 kW • ALT. FREQ. TO 9570 kHz
SPAIN
R EXTERIOR ESPANA, Noblejas — Tu • C America & S America • 350 kW
TURKEY
VOICE OF TURKEY, Ankara-Çakirlar — • W Asia • 250 kW
USA
GOSPEL FOR ASIA, Via Germany — S • W Asia & S Asia • 250 kW
R FREE ASIA, Via Tinian, N Marianas — W • SE Asia • 500 kW
— S • E Asia • 500 kW
RFE-RL, Via Biblis, Germany — S • S Europe • 100 kW
†RFE-RL, Via Lampertheim, Germany — W • W Asia • 100 kW
RFE-RL, Via Udon Thani, Thailand — W • W Asia & C Asia • 250 kW
11800 BULGARIA
RADIO BULGARIA, Plovdiv — S • W Europe • 250 kW
CHINA
†CENTRAL PEOPLE'S BS, Beijing — S • DS-2 • 150 kW
— DS-2 • 150 kW
— Th-Tu • DS-2 • 150 kW
†CHINA R INTL, Kashi — S Asia • 100 kW
†CHINA R INTL, Kunming — W • Mideast & E Europe • 500 kW
ITALY
†RAI INTERNATIONAL, Rome — N America • 100 kW
— E Europe • 100 kW — S M-Sa • N Africa & Mideast • 100 kW
— W • E Europe • 100 kW — W • N America • 100 kW
— W M-Sa • S Europe & N Africa • 100 kW
— S • E Europe • 100 kW
SERBIA AND MONTENEGRO
†INTL RADIO OF S & M, Via Bosnia — S • E Europe • 250 kW • ALT. FREQ. TO 11870 kHz
— • Mideast • 250 kW • ALT. FREQ. TO 11835 kHz
USA
ADVENTIST WORLD R, Via Agat, Guam — W • E Asia • 100 kW
11805 BRAZIL
†RADIO GLOBO, Rio de Janeiro — DS-TEMP INACTIVE • 10 kW •
THAILAND
†RADIO THAILAND, Udon Thani — W • SE Asia • 250 kW
UNITED KINGDOM
BIBLE VOICE, Via Dhabayya, UAE — Sa/Su • S Asia • 250 kW
USA
†FAMILY RADIO, Via Madagascar — W • E Africa • 50 kW
RFE-RL, Via Biblis, Germany — W • E Europe & W Asia • 100 kW
†RFE-RL, Via Briech, Morocco — S M-F • E Europe • 250 kW
— W • E Europe • 250 kW
— S • E Europe • 250 kW
VOA, Via Biblis, Germany — W • E Europe & W Asia • 100 kW
VOA, Via Briech, Morocco — S • S Europe • 250 kW
†VOA, Via Kavála, Greece — S • W Asia • 250 kW
VOA, Via Philippines — SE Asia • 250 kW
VOA, Via Tinian, N Marianas — S • E Asia • 500 kW
VOA, Via Udon Thani, Thailand — S • S Asia • 250 kW
11805v GEORGIA
RADIO GEORGIA, Dusheti — • N Europe • 100 kW
11810 CANADA
†R CANADA INTL, Via In-Kimjae, Korea — S • E Asia • 100 kW
CHINA
†CENTRAL PEOPLE'S BS, Beijing — DS-8 (MINORITIES) • 50 kW
†CHINA R INTL, Kunming — S • N Africa & Mideast • 500 kW
(con'd) †CHINA R INTL, Urümqi — S • S Europe • 500 kW

0 1 2 3 4 5 6 7 8 9 10 11 12 13 14 15 16 17 18 19 20 21 22 23 24

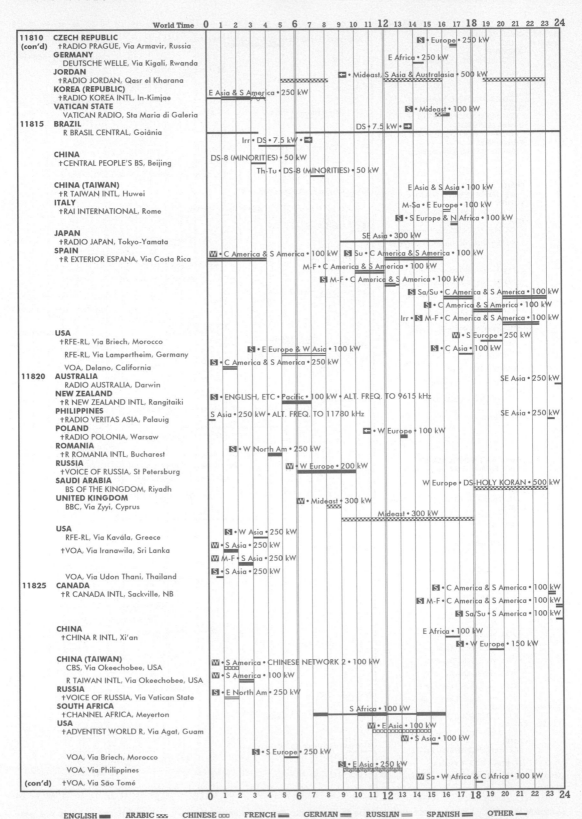

	World Time	0 1 2 3 4 5 6 7 8 9 10 11 12 13 14 15 16 17 18 19 20 21 22 23 24
11810 (con'd)	**CZECH REPUBLIC** †RADIO PRAGUE, Via Armavir, Russia	S • Europe • 250 kW
	GERMANY DEUTSCHE WELLE, Via Kigali, Rwanda	E Africa • 250 kW
	JORDAN †RADIO JORDAN, Qasr el Kharana	• Mideast, S Asia & Australasia • 500 kW
	KOREA (REPUBLIC) †RADIO KOREA INTL, In-Kimjae	E Asia & S America • 250 kW
	VATICAN STATE VATICAN RADIO, Sta Maria di Galeria	S • Mideast • 100 kW
11815	**BRAZIL** R BRASIL CENTRAL, Goiânia	DS • 7.5 kW •
		Irr • DS • 7.5 kW •
	CHINA †CENTRAL PEOPLE'S BS, Beijing	DS-8 (MINORITIES) • 50 kW
		Th-Tu • DS-8 (MINORITIES) • 50 kW
	CHINA (TAIWAN) †R TAIWAN INTL, Huwei	E Asia & S Asia • 100 kW
	ITALY †RAI INTERNATIONAL, Rome	M-Sa • E Europe • 100 kW
		S • S Europe & N Africa • 100 kW
	JAPAN †RADIO JAPAN, Tokyo-Yamata	SE Asia • 300 kW
	SPAIN †R EXTERIOR ESPANA, Via Costa Rica	W • C America & S America • 100 kW S • Su • C America & S America • 100 kW
		M-F • C America & S America • 100 kW
		S • M-F • C America & S America • 100 kW
		Sa/Su • C America & S America • 100 kW
		S • C America & S America • 100 kW
		Irr • S • M-F • C America & S America • 100 kW
	USA †RFE-RL, Via Briech, Morocco	W • S Europe • 250 kW
	RFE-RL, Via Lampertheim, Germany	S • E Europe & W Asia • 100 kW S • C Asia • 100 kW
	VOA, Delano, California	S • C America & S America • 250 kW
11820	**AUSTRALIA** RADIO AUSTRALIA, Darwin	SE Asia • 250 kW
	NEW ZEALAND †R NEW ZEALAND INTL, Rangitaiki	S • ENGLISH, ETC • Pacific • 100 kW • ALT. FREQ. TO 9615 kHz
	PHILIPPINES †RADIO VERITAS ASIA, Palauig	S Asia • 250 kW • ALT. FREQ. TO 11780 kHz SE Asia • 250 kW
	POLAND †RADIO POLONIA, Warsaw	• W Europe • 100 kW
	ROMANIA †R ROMANIA INTL, Bucharest	S • W North Am • 250 kW
	RUSSIA †VOICE OF RUSSIA, St Petersburg	W • W Europe • 200 kW
	SAUDI ARABIA BS OF THE KINGDOM, Riyadh	W Europe • DS-HOLY KORAN • 500 kW
	UNITED KINGDOM BBC, Via Zyyi, Cyprus	W • Mideast • 300 kW Mideast • 300 kW
	USA RFE-RL, Via Kavála, Greece	S • W Asia • 250 kW
	†VOA, Via Iranawila, Sri Lanka	W • S Asia • 250 kW
		W • M-F • S Asia • 250 kW
	VOA, Via Udon Thani, Thailand	S • S Asia • 250 kW
11825	**CANADA** †R CANADA INTL, Sackville, NB	S • C America & S America • 100 kW
		S • M-F • C America & S America • 100 kW
		S • Sa/Su • S America • 100 kW
	CHINA †CHINA R INTL, Xi'an	E Africa • 100 kW
		S • W Europe • 150 kW
	CHINA (TAIWAN) CBS, Via Okeechobee, USA	W • S America • CHINESE NETWORK 2 • 100 kW
	R TAIWAN INTL, Via Okeechobee, USA	W • S America • 100 kW
	RUSSIA †VOICE OF RUSSIA, Via Vatican State	S • E North Am • 250 kW
	SOUTH AFRICA †CHANNEL AFRICA, Meyerton	S Africa • 100 kW
	USA †ADVENTIST WORLD R, Via Agat, Guam	W • E Asia • 100 kW
		W • S Asia • 100 kW
	VOA, Via Briech, Morocco	S • S Europe • 250 kW
	VOA, Via Philippines	S • E Asia • 250 kW
(con'd)	†VOA, Via São Tomé	W • Sa • W Africa & C Africa • 100 kW

0 1 2 3 4 5 6 7 8 9 10 11 12 13 14 15 16 17 18 19 20 21 22 23 24

ENGLISH ▬   ARABIC ▨▨   CHINESE ▢▢▢   FRENCH ═   GERMAN ▬   RUSSIAN ▬   SPANISH ═   OTHER ▬

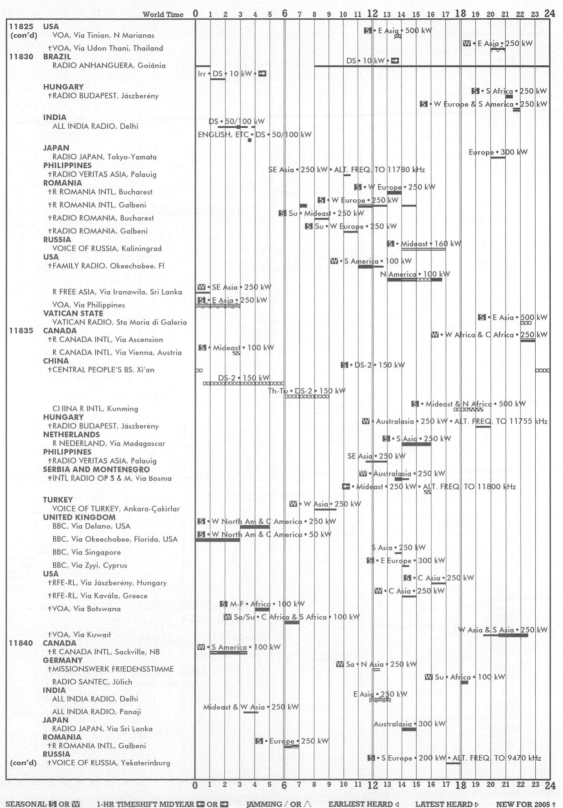

World Time 0 1 2 3 4 5 6 7 8 9 10 11 12 13 14 15 16 17 18 19 20 21 22 23 24

11825	**USA**
(con'd)	VOA, Via Tinian, N Marianas — S • E Asia • 500 kW
	†VOA, Via Udon Thani, Thailand — W • E Asia • 250 kW
11830	**BRAZIL**
	RADIO ANHANGUERA, Goiânia — DS • 10 kW
	Irr • DS • 10 kW
	HUNGARY
	†RADIO BUDAPEST, Jászberény — S • S Africa • 250 kW / S • W Europe & S America • 250 kW
	INDIA
	ALL INDIA RADIO, Delhi — DS • 50/100 kW / ENGLISH, ETC • DS • 50/100 kW
	JAPAN
	RADIO JAPAN, Tokyo-Yamata — Europe • 300 kW
	PHILIPPINES
	†RADIO VERITAS ASIA, Palauig — SE Asia • 250 kW • ALT. FREQ. TO 11780 kHz
	ROMANIA
	†R ROMANIA INTL, Bucharest — S • W Europe • 250 kW
	†R ROMANIA INTL, Galbeni — S • W Europe • 250 kW
	†RADIO ROMANIA, Bucharest — S Su • Mideast • 250 kW
	†RADIO ROMANIA, Galbeni — S Su • W Europe • 250 kW
	RUSSIA
	VOICE OF RUSSIA, Kaliningrad — S • Mideast • 160 kW
	USA
	†FAMILY RADIO, Okeechobee, Fl — W • S America • 100 kW / N America • 100 kW
	R FREE ASIA, Via Iranawila, Sri Lanka — W • SE Asia • 250 kW
	VOA, Via Philippines — S • E Asia • 250 kW
	VATICAN STATE
	VATICAN RADIO, Sta Maria di Galeria — S • E Asia • 500 kW
11835	**CANADA**
	†R CANADA INTL, Via Ascension — W • W Africa & C Africa • 250 kW
	R CANADA INTL, Via Vienna, Austria — S • Mideast • 100 kW
	CHINA
	†CENTRAL PEOPLE'S BS, Xi'an — S • DS-2 • 150 kW / DS-2 • 150 kW / Th-Tu • DS-2 • 150 kW
	CHINA R INTL, Kunming — S • Mideast & N Africa • 500 kW
	HUNGARY
	†RADIO BUDAPEST, Jászberény — W • Australasia • 250 kW • ALT. FREQ. TO 11755 kHz
	NETHERLANDS
	R NEDERLAND, Via Madagascar — S • S Asia • 250 kW
	PHILIPPINES
	†RADIO VERITAS ASIA, Palauig — SE Asia • 250 kW
	SERBIA AND MONTENEGRO
	†INTL RADIO OF S & M, Via Bosnia — W • Australasia • 250 kW / ⟵ • Mideast • 250 kW • ALT. FREQ. TO 11800 kHz
	TURKEY
	VOICE OF TURKEY, Ankara-Çakirlar — W • W Asia • 250 kW
	UNITED KINGDOM
	BBC, Via Delano, USA — S • W North Am & C America • 250 kW
	BBC, Via Okeechobee, Florida, USA — S • W North Am & C America • 50 kW
	BBC, Via Singapore — S Asia • 250 kW
	BBC, Via Zyyi, Cyprus — S • E Europe • 300 kW
	USA
	†RFE-RL, Via Jászberény, Hungary — S • C Asia • 250 kW
	†RFE-RL, Via Kavála, Greece — W • C Asia • 250 kW
	†VOA, Via Botswana — S M-F • Africa • 100 kW / W Sa/Su • C Africa & S Africa • 100 kW
	†VOA, Via Kuwait — W Asia & S Asia • 250 kW
11840	**CANADA**
	†R CANADA INTL, Sackville, NB — W • S America • 100 kW
	GERMANY
	†MISSIONSWERK FRIEDENSSTIMME — W Sa • N Asia • 250 kW
	RADIO SANTEC, Jülich — W Su • Africa • 100 kW
	INDIA
	ALL INDIA RADIO, Delhi — E Asia • 250 kW
	ALL INDIA RADIO, Panaji — Mideast & W Asia • 250 kW
	JAPAN
	RADIO JAPAN, Via Sri Lanka — Australasia • 300 kW
	ROMANIA
	†R ROMANIA INTL, Galbeni — S • Europe • 250 kW
	RUSSIA
(con'd)	†VOICE OF RUSSIA, Yekaterinburg — S • S Europe • 200 kW • ALT. FREQ. TO 9470 kHz

0 1 2 3 4 5 6 7 8 9 10 11 12 13 14 15 16 17 18 19 20 21 22 23 24

SEASONAL S OR W   1-HR TIMESHIFT MIDYEAR ⟵ OR ⟶   JAMMING / OR ∧   EARLIEST HEARD ◁   LATEST HEARD ▷   NEW FOR 2005 †

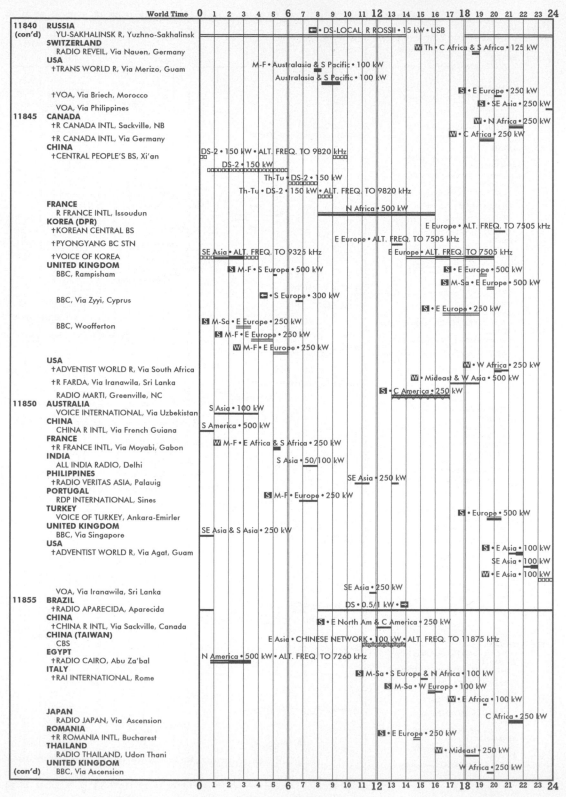

World Time   0   1   2   3   4   5   6   7   8   9   10   11   12   13   14   15   16   17   18   19   20   21   22   23   24

11840 (con'd)   **RUSSIA**
YU-SAKHALINSK R, Yuzhno-Sakhalinsk — · DS-LOCAL R ROSSII · 15 kW · USB
SWITZERLAND
RADIO REVEIL, Via Nauen, Germany — W Th · C Africa & S Africa · 125 kW
USA
†TRANS WORLD R, Via Merizo, Guam — M-F · Australasia & S Pacific · 100 kW
Australasia & S Pacific · 100 kW

†VOA, Via Briech, Morocco — S · E Europe · 250 kW
VOA, Via Philippines — S · SE Asia · 250 kW
11845   **CANADA**
†R CANADA INTL, Sackville, NB — W · N Africa · 250 kW
†R CANADA INTL, Via Germany — W · C Africa · 250 kW
CHINA
†CENTRAL PEOPLE'S BS, Xi'an — DS-2 · 150 kW · ALT. FREQ. TO 9820 kHz
DS-2 · 150 kW
DS-2 · 150 kW
Th-Tu · DS-2 · 150 kW
Th-Tu · DS-2 · 150 kW · ALT. FREQ. TO 9820 kHz
FRANCE
R FRANCE INTL, Issoudun — N Africa · 500 kW
KOREA (DPR)
†KOREAN CENTRAL BS — E Europe · ALT. FREQ. TO 7505 kHz
†PYONGYANG BC STN — E Europe · ALT. FREQ. TO 7505 kHz
†VOICE OF KOREA — SE Asia · ALT. FREQ. TO 9325 kHz   E Europe · ALT. FREQ. TO 7505 kHz
UNITED KINGDOM
BBC, Rampisham — S M-F · S Europe · 500 kW   S · E Europe · 500 kW
S M-Sa · E Europe · 500 kW
BBC, Via Zyyi, Cyprus — · S Europe · 300 kW   S · E Europe · 250 kW
BBC, Woofferton — S M-Sa · E Europe · 250 kW
S M-F · E Europe · 250 kW
W M-F · E Europe · 250 kW
USA
†ADVENTIST WORLD R, Via South Africa — W · W Africa · 250 kW
†R FARDA, Via Iranawila, Sri Lanka — W · Mideast & W Asia · 500 kW
RADIO MARTI, Greenville, NC — S · C America · 250 kW
11850   **AUSTRALIA**
VOICE INTERNATIONAL, Via Uzbekistan — S Asia · 100 kW
CHINA
CHINA R INTL, Via French Guiana — S America · 500 kW
FRANCE
†R FRANCE INTL, Via Moyabi, Gabon — W M-F · E Africa & S Africa · 250 kW
INDIA
ALL INDIA RADIO, Delhi — S Asia · 50/100 kW
PHILIPPINES
†RADIO VERITAS ASIA, Palauig — SE Asia · 250 kW
PORTUGAL
RDP INTERNATIONAL, Sines — S M-F · Europe · 250 kW
TURKEY
VOICE OF TURKEY, Ankara-Emirler — S · Europe · 500 kW
UNITED KINGDOM
BBC, Via Singapore — SE Asia & S Asia · 250 kW
USA
†ADVENTIST WORLD R, Via Agat, Guam — S · E Asia · 100 kW
SE Asia · 100 kW
W · E Asia · 100 kW
VOA, Via Iranawila, Sri Lanka — SE Asia · 250 kW
11855   **BRAZIL**
†RADIO APARECIDA, Aparecida — DS · 0.5/1 kW · —
CHINA
†CHINA R INTL, Via Sackville, Canada — S · E North Am & C America · 250 kW
CHINA (TAIWAN)
CBS — E Asia · CHINESE NETWORK · 100 kW · ALT. FREQ. TO 11875 kHz
EGYPT
†RADIO CAIRO, Abu Za'bal — N America · 500 kW · ALT. FREQ. TO 7260 kHz
ITALY
†RAI INTERNATIONAL, Rome — S M-Sa · S Europe & N Africa · 100 kW
S M-Sa · W Europe · 100 kW
W · E Africa · 100 kW
JAPAN
RADIO JAPAN, Via Ascension — C Africa · 250 kW
ROMANIA
†R ROMANIA INTL, Bucharest — S · E Europe · 250 kW
THAILAND
RADIO THAILAND, Udon Thani — W · Mideast · 250 kW
UNITED KINGDOM
(con'd)   BBC, Via Ascension — W Africa · 250 kW

0   1   2   3   4   5   6   7   8   9   10   11   12   13   14   15   16   17   18   19   20   21   22   23   24

ENGLISH ▬   ARABIC ▨   CHINESE ▯▯▯   FRENCH ▬   GERMAN ▬   RUSSIAN ═   SPANISH ▬   OTHER ▬

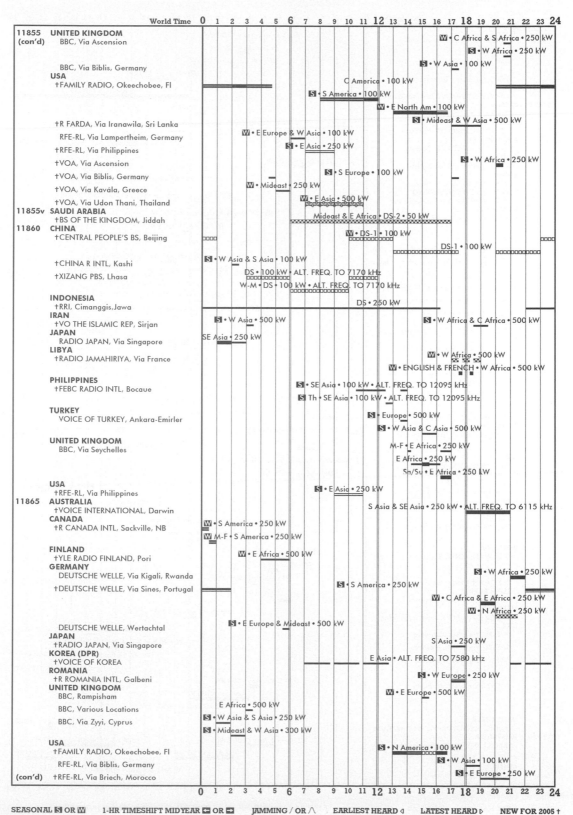

World Time 0 1 2 3 4 5 6 7 8 9 10 11 12 13 14 15 16 17 18 19 20 21 22 23 24

11855 UNITED KINGDOM
(con'd)   BBC, Via Ascension
    W•C Africa & S Africa • 250 kW
    S•W Africa • 250 kW

    BBC, Via Biblis, Germany
    S•W Asia • 100 kW
USA
    †FAMILY RADIO, Okeechobee, Fl
    C America • 100 kW
    S • S America • 100 kW
    W • E North Am • 100 kW
    †R FARDA, Via Iranawila, Sri Lanka
    S • Mideast & W Asia • 500 kW
    RFE-RL, Via Lampertheim, Germany
    W • E Europe & W Asia • 100 kW
    †RFE-RL, Via Philippines
    S • E Asia • 250 kW
    †VOA, Via Ascension
    S • W Africa • 250 kW
    †VOA, Via Biblis, Germany
    S • S Europe • 100 kW
    †VOA, Via Kavála, Greece
    W • Mideast • 250 kW
    †VOA, Via Udon Thani, Thailand
    W • E Asia • 500 kW
11855v SAUDI ARABIA
    †BS OF THE KINGDOM, Jiddah
    Mideast & E Africa • DS-2 • 50 kW
11860 CHINA
    †CENTRAL PEOPLE'S BS, Beijing
    W • DS-1 • 100 kW
    DS-1 • 100 kW
    †CHINA R INTL, Kashi
    S • W Asia & S Asia • 100 kW
    †XIZANG PBS, Lhasa
    DS • 100 kW • ALT. FREQ. TO 7170 kHz
    W-M • DS • 100 kW • ALT. FREQ. TO 7170 kHz
INDONESIA
    †RRI, Cimanggis, Jawa
    DS • 250 kW
IRAN
    †VO THE ISLAMIC REP, Sirjan
    S • W Asia • 500 kW
    S • W Africa & C Africa • 500 kW
JAPAN
    RADIO JAPAN, Via Singapore
    SE Asia • 250 kW
LIBYA
    †RADIO JAMAHIRIYA, Via France
    W • W Africa • 500 kW
    W • ENGLISH & FRENCH • W Africa • 500 kW
PHILIPPINES
    †FEBC RADIO INTL, Bocaue
    S • SE Asia • 100 kW • ALT. FREQ. TO 12095 kHz
    S Th • SE Asia • 100 kW • ALT. FREQ. TO 12095 kHz
TURKEY
    VOICE OF TURKEY, Ankara-Emirler
    S • Europe • 500 kW
    S • W Asia & C Asia • 500 kW
UNITED KINGDOM
    BBC, Via Seychelles
    M-F • E Africa • 250 kW
    E Africa • 250 kW
    Sa/Su • E Africa • 250 LW
USA
    †RFE-RL, Via Philippines
    S • E Asia • 250 kW
11865 AUSTRALIA
    †VOICE INTERNATIONAL, Darwin
    S Asia & SE Asia • 250 kW • ALT. FREQ. TO 6115 kHz
CANADA
    †R CANADA INTL, Sackville, NB
    W • S America • 250 kW
    W M-F • S America • 250 kW
FINLAND
    †YLE RADIO FINLAND, Pori
    W • E Africa • 500 kW
GERMANY
    DEUTSCHE WELLE, Via Kigali, Rwanda
    S • W Africa • 250 kW
    †DEUTSCHE WELLE, Via Sines, Portugal
    S • S America • 250 kW
    W • C Africa & E Africa • 250 kW
    W • N Africa • 250 kW
    DEUTSCHE WELLE, Wertachtal
    S • E Europe & Mideast • 500 kW
JAPAN
    †RADIO JAPAN, Via Singapore
    S Asia • 250 kW
KOREA (DPR)
    †VOICE OF KOREA
    E Asia • ALT. FREQ. TO 7580 kHz
ROMANIA
    †R ROMANIA INTL, Galbeni
    S • W Europe • 250 kW
UNITED KINGDOM
    BBC, Rampisham
    W • E Europe • 500 kW
    BBC, Various Locations
    E Africa • 500 kW
    BBC, Via Zyyi, Cyprus
    S • W Asia & S Asia • 250 kW
    S • Mideast & W Asia • 300 kW
USA
    †FAMILY RADIO, Okeechobee, Fl
    S • N America • 100 kW
    RFE-RL, Via Biblis, Germany
    S • W Asia • 100 kW
(con'd) †RFE-RL, Via Briech, Morocco
    S • E Europe • 250 kW

0 1 2 3 4 5 6 7 8 9 10 11 12 13 14 15 16 17 18 19 20 21 22 23 24

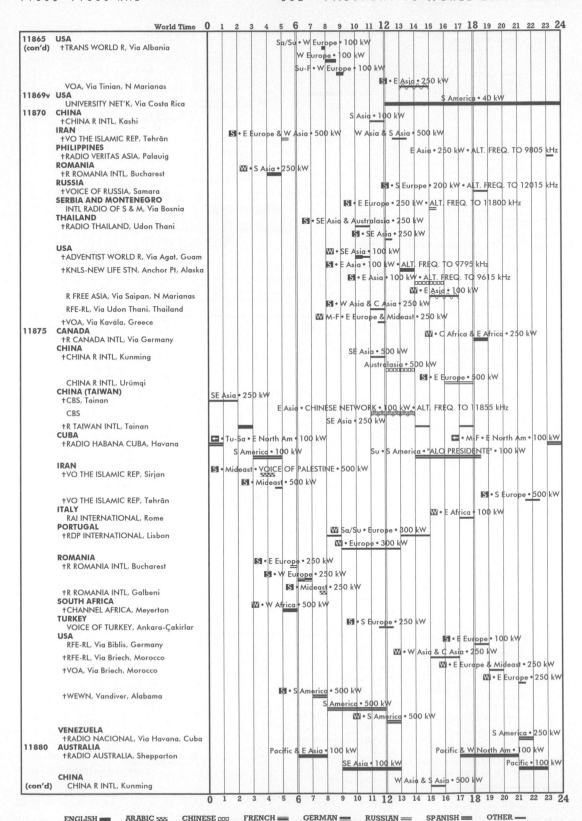

11865 (con'd)	USA	†TRANS WORLD R, Via Albania
		VOA, Via Tinian, N Marianas
11869v	USA	UNIVERSITY NET'K, Via Costa Rica
11870	CHINA	†CHINA R INTL, Kashi
	IRAN	†VO THE ISLAMIC REP, Tehrān
	PHILIPPINES	†RADIO VERITAS ASIA, Palauig
	ROMANIA	†R ROMANIA INTL, Bucharest
	RUSSIA	†VOICE OF RUSSIA, Samara
	SERBIA AND MONTENEGRO	INTL RADIO OF S & M, Via Bosnia
	THAILAND	†RADIO THAILAND, Udon Thani
	USA	†ADVENTIST WORLD R, Via Agat, Guam
		†KNLS-NEW LIFE STN, Anchor Pt, Alaska
		R FREE ASIA, Via Saipan, N Marianas
		RFE-RL, Via Udon Thani, Thailand
		†VOA, Via Kavála, Greece
11875	CANADA	†R CANADA INTL, Via Germany
	CHINA	†CHINA R INTL, Kunming
		CHINA R INTL, Urümqi
	CHINA (TAIWAN)	†CBS, Tainan
		CBS
		†R TAIWAN INTL, Tainan
	CUBA	†RADIO HABANA CUBA, Havana
	IRAN	†VO THE ISLAMIC REP, Sirjan
		†VO THE ISLAMIC REP, Tehrān
	ITALY	RAI INTERNATIONAL, Rome
	PORTUGAL	†RDP INTERNATIONAL, Lisbon
	ROMANIA	†R ROMANIA INTL, Bucharest
		†R ROMANIA INTL, Galbeni
	SOUTH AFRICA	†CHANNEL AFRICA, Meyerton
	TURKEY	VOICE OF TURKEY, Ankara-Çakirlar
	USA	RFE-RL, Via Biblis, Germany
		†RFE-RL, Via Briech, Morocco
		†VOA, Via Briech, Morocco
		†WEWN, Vandiver, Alabama
	VENEZUELA	†RADIO NACIONAL, Via Havana, Cuba
11880	AUSTRALIA	†RADIO AUSTRALIA, Shepparton
(con'd)	CHINA	CHINA R INTL, Kunming

World Time 0 1 2 3 4 5 6 7 8 9 10 11 12 13 14 15 16 17 18 19 20 21 22 23 24

Sa/Su • W Europe • 100 kW
W Europe • 100 kW
Su-F • W Europe • 100 kW
Ⓢ • E Asia • 250 kW
S America • 40 kW
S Asia • 100 kW
Ⓢ • E Europe & W Asia • 500 kW   W Asia & S Asia • 500 kW
E Asia • 250 kW • ALT. FREQ. TO 9805 kHz
Ⓦ • S Asia • 250 kW
Ⓢ • S Europe • 200 kW • ALT. FREQ. TO 12015 kHz
Ⓢ • E Europe • 250 kW • ALT. FREQ. TO 11800 kHz
Ⓢ • SE Asia & Australasia • 250 kW
Ⓢ • SE Asia • 250 kW
Ⓦ • SE Asia • 100 kW
Ⓢ • E Asia • 100 kW • ALT. FREQ. TO 9795 kHz
Ⓢ • E Asia • 100 kW • ALT. FREQ. TO 9615 kHz
Ⓦ • E Asia • 100 kW
Ⓢ • W Asia & C Asia • 250 kW
Ⓦ M-F • E Europe & Mideast • 250 kW
Ⓦ • C Africa & E Africa • 250 kW
SE Asia • 500 kW
Australasia • 500 kW
Ⓢ • E Europe • 500 kW
SE Asia • 250 kW
E Asia • CHINESE NETWORK • 100 kW • ALT. FREQ. TO 11855 kHz
SE Asia • 250 kW
Ⓔ • Tu-Sa • E North Am • 100 kW   Ⓔ • M-F • E North Am • 100 kW
S America • 100 kW   Su • S America • "ALO PRESIDENTE" • 100 kW
Ⓢ • Mideast • VOICE OF PALESTINE • 500 kW
Ⓢ • Mideast • 500 kW
Ⓢ • S Europe • 500 kW
Ⓦ • E Africa • 100 kW
Ⓦ Sa/Su • Europe • 300 kW
Ⓦ • Europe • 300 kW
Ⓢ • E Europe • 250 kW
Ⓢ • W Europe • 250 kW
Ⓢ • Mideast • 250 kW
Ⓦ • W Africa • 500 kW
Ⓢ • S Europe • 250 kW
Ⓢ • E Europe • 100 kW
Ⓦ • W Asia & C Asia • 250 kW
Ⓦ • E Europe & Mideast • 250 kW
Ⓦ • E Europe • 250 kW
Ⓢ • S America • 500 kW
S America • 500 kW
Ⓦ • S America • 500 kW
S America • 250 kW
Pacific & E Asia • 100 kW   Pacific & W North Am • 100 kW
SE Asia • 100 kW   Pacific • 100 kW
W Asia & S Asia • 500 kW

0 1 2 3 4 5 6 7 8 9 10 11 12 13 14 15 16 17 18 19 20 21 22 23 24

ENGLISH ▬ ARABIC ▨ CHINESE ⬚⬚⬚ FRENCH ▬ GERMAN ▭ RUSSIAN ═ SPANISH ▬ OTHER ▬

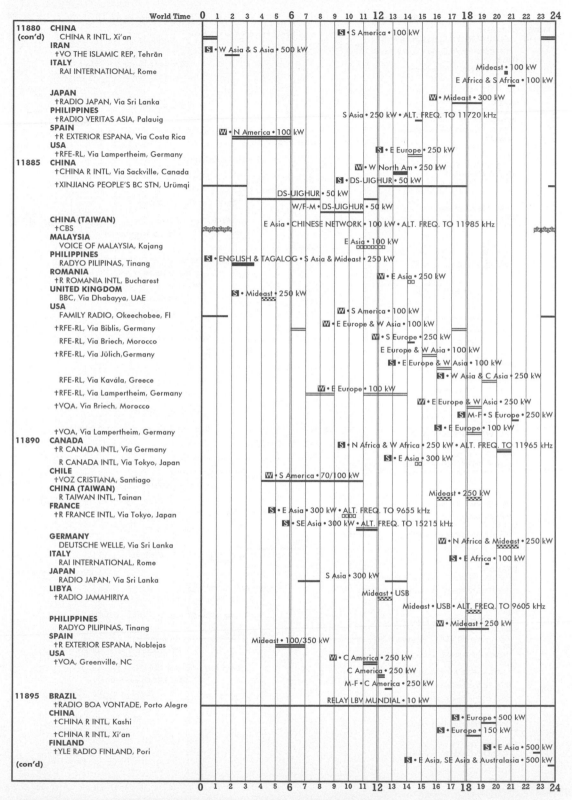

World Time 0 1 2 3 4 5 6 7 8 9 10 11 12 13 14 15 16 17 18 19 20 21 22 23 24

11880 **CHINA**
(con'd)   CHINA R INTL, Xi'an — S America • 100 kW
         IRAN
         †VO THE ISLAMIC REP, Tehrān — [S] • W Asia & S Asia • 500 kW
         ITALY
         RAI INTERNATIONAL, Rome — Mideast • 100 kW
                                  E Africa & S Africa • 100 kW
         JAPAN
         †RADIO JAPAN, Via Sri Lanka — [W] • Mideast • 300 kW
         PHILIPPINES
         †RADIO VERITAS ASIA, Palauig — S Asia • 250 kW • ALT. FREQ. TO 11720 kHz
         SPAIN
         †R EXTERIOR ESPANA, Via Costa Rica — [W] • N America • 100 kW
         USA
         †RFE-RL, Via Lampertheim, Germany — [S] • E Europe • 250 kW

11885 **CHINA**
         †CHINA R INTL, Via Sackville, Canada — [W] • W North Am • 250 kW
         †XINJIANG PEOPLE'S BC STN, Urümqi — [S] • DS-UIGHUR • 50 kW
                                            DS-UIGHUR • 50 kW
                                            W/F-M • DS-UIGHUR • 50 kW
         CHINA (TAIWAN)
         †CBS — E Asia • CHINESE NETWORK • 100 kW • ALT. FREQ. TO 11985 kHz
         MALAYSIA
         VOICE OF MALAYSIA, Kajang — E Asia • 100 kW
         PHILIPPINES
         RADYO PILIPINAS, Tinang — [S] • ENGLISH & TAGALOG • S Asia & Mideast • 250 kW
         ROMANIA
         †R ROMANIA INTL, Bucharest — [W] • E Asia • 250 kW
         UNITED KINGDOM
         BBC, Via Dhabayya, UAE — [S] • Mideast • 250 kW
         USA
         FAMILY RADIO, Okeechobee, Fl — [W] • S America • 100 kW
         †RFE-RL, Via Biblis, Germany — [W] • E Europe & W Asia • 100 kW
         RFE-RL, Via Briech, Morocco — [W] • S Europe • 250 kW
         †RFE-RL, Via Jülich, Germany — E Europe & W Asia • 100 kW
                                        [S] • E Europe & W Asia • 100 kW
         RFE-RL, Via Kavála, Greece — [S] • W Asia & C Asia • 250 kW
         †RFE-RL, Via Lampertheim, Germany — [W] • E Europe • 100 kW
         †VOA, Via Briech, Morocco — [W] • E Europe & W Asia • 250 kW
                                     [S] M-F • S Europe • 250 kW
         †VOA, Via Lampertheim, Germany — [S] • E Europe • 100 kW

11890 **CANADA**
         †R CANADA INTL, Via Germany — [S] • N Africa & W Africa • 250 kW • ALT. FREQ. TO 11965 kHz
         R CANADA INTL, Via Tokyo, Japan — [S] • E Asia • 300 kW
         CHILE
         †VOZ CRISTIANA, Santiago — [W] • S America • 70/100 kW
         CHINA (TAIWAN)
         R TAIWAN INTL, Tainan — Mideast • 250 kW
         FRANCE
         †R FRANCE INTL, Via Tokyo, Japan — [S] • E Asia • 300 kW • ALT. FREQ. TO 9655 kHz
                                            [S] • SE Asia • 300 kW • ALT. FREQ. TO 15215 kHz
         GERMANY
         DEUTSCHE WELLE, Via Sri Lanka — [W] • N Africa & Mideast • 250 kW
         ITALY
         RAI INTERNATIONAL, Rome — [S] • E Africa • 100 kW
         JAPAN
         RADIO JAPAN, Via Sri Lanka — S Asia • 300 kW
         LIBYA
         †RADIO JAMAHIRIYA — Mideast • USB
                             Mideast • USB • ALT. FREQ. TO 9605 kHz
         PHILIPPINES
         RADYO PILIPINAS, Tinang — [W] • Mideast • 250 kW
         SPAIN
         †R EXTERIOR ESPANA, Noblejas — Mideast • 100/350 kW
         USA
         †VOA, Greenville, NC — [W] • C America • 250 kW
                               C America • 250 kW
                               M-F • C America • 250 kW

11895 **BRAZIL**
         †RADIO BOA VONTADE, Porto Alegre — RELAY LBV MUNDIAL • 10 kW
         CHINA
         †CHINA R INTL, Kashi — [S] • Europe • 500 kW
         †CHINA R INTL, Xi'an — [S] • Europe • 150 kW
         FINLAND
         †YLE RADIO FINLAND, Pori — [S] • E Asia • 500 kW
                                    [S] • E Asia, SE Asia & Australasia • 500 kW
(con'd)

0 1 2 3 4 5 6 7 8 9 10 11 12 13 14 15 16 17 18 19 20 21 22 23 24

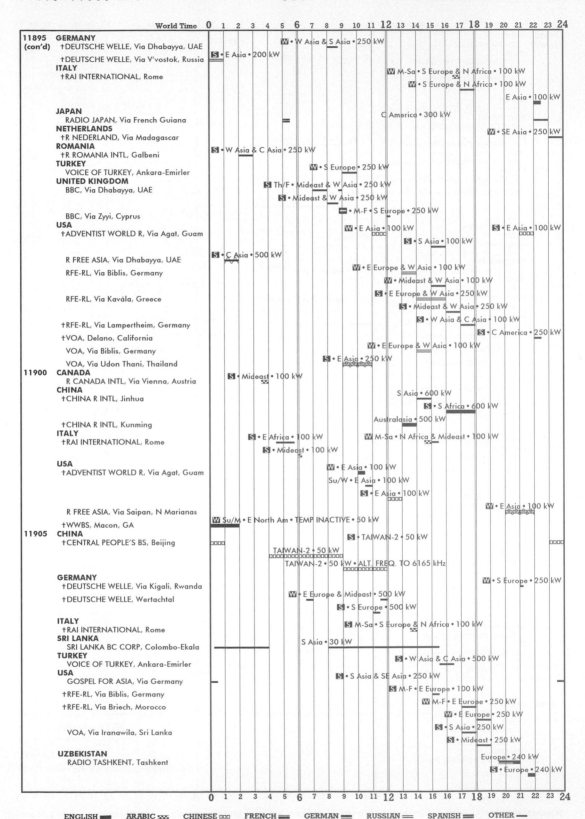

| | World Time | 0 | 1 | 2 | 3 | 4 | 5 | 6 | 7 | 8 | 9 | 10 | 11 | 12 | 13 | 14 | 15 | 16 | 17 | 18 | 19 | 20 | 21 | 22 | 23 | 24 |

11895 GERMANY
(con'd) †DEUTSCHE WELLE, Via Dhabayya, UAE — W • W Asia & S Asia • 250 kW
†DEUTSCHE WELLE, Via V'vostok, Russia — S • E Asia • 200 kW
ITALY
†RAI INTERNATIONAL, Rome — W M-Sa • S Europe & N Africa • 100 kW
W • S Europe & N Africa • 100 kW
E Asia • 100 kW
JAPAN
RADIO JAPAN, Via French Guiana — C America • 300 kW
NETHERLANDS
†R NEDERLAND, Via Madagascar — W • SE Asia • 250 kW
ROMANIA
†R ROMANIA INTL, Galbeni — S • W Asia & C Asia • 250 kW
TURKEY
VOICE OF TURKEY, Ankara-Emirler — W • S Europe • 250 kW
UNITED KINGDOM
BBC, Via Dhabayya, UAE — S • Th/F • Mideast & W Asia • 250 kW
S • Mideast & W Asia • 250 kW
BBC, Via Zyyi, Cyprus — • M-F • S Europe • 250 kW
USA
†ADVENTIST WORLD R, Via Agat, Guam — W • E Asia • 100 kW
S • E Asia • 100 kW
S • S Asia • 100 kW
R FREE ASIA, Via Dhabayya, UAE — S • C Asia • 500 kW
RFE-RL, Via Biblis, Germany — W • E Europe & W Asia • 100 kW
W • Mideast & W Asia • 100 kW
RFE-RL, Via Kavála, Greece — S • E Europe & W Asia • 250 kW
S • Mideast & W Asia • 250 kW
†RFE-RL, Via Lampertheim, Germany — S • W Asia & C Asia • 100 kW
†VOA, Delano, California — S • C America • 250 kW
VOA, Via Biblis, Germany — W • E Europe & W Asia • 100 kW
VOA, Via Udon Thani, Thailand — S • E Asia • 250 kW
11900 CANADA
R CANADA INTL, Via Vienna, Austria — S • Mideast • 100 kW
CHINA
†CHINA R INTL, Jinhua — S Asia • 600 kW
S • S Africa • 600 kW
†CHINA R INTL, Kunming — Australasia • 500 kW
ITALY
†RAI INTERNATIONAL, Rome — S • E Africa • 100 kW
W M-Sa • N Africa & Mideast • 100 kW
S • Mideast • 100 kW
USA
†ADVENTIST WORLD R, Via Agat, Guam — W • E Asia • 100 kW
Su/W • E Asia • 100 kW
S • E Asia • 100 kW
R FREE ASIA, Via Saipan, N Marianas — W • E Asia • 100 kW
†WWBS, Macon, GA — W Su/M • E North Am • TEMP INACTIVE • 50 kW
11905 CHINA
†CENTRAL PEOPLE'S BS, Beijing — S • TAIWAN-2 • 50 kW
TAIWAN-2 • 50 kW
TAIWAN-2 • 50 kW • ALT. FREQ. TO 6165 kHz
GERMANY
†DEUTSCHE WELLE, Via Kigali, Rwanda — W • S Europe • 250 kW
†DEUTSCHE WELLE, Wertachtal — W • E Europe & Mideast • 500 kW
S • S Europe • 500 kW
ITALY
†RAI INTERNATIONAL, Rome — S M-Sa • S Europe & N Africa • 100 kW
SRI LANKA
SRI LANKA BC CORP, Colombo-Ekala — S Asia • 30 kW
TURKEY
VOICE OF TURKEY, Ankara-Emirler — S • W Asia & C Asia • 500 kW
USA
GOSPEL FOR ASIA, Via Germany — S • S Asia & SE Asia • 250 kW
†RFE-RL, Via Biblis, Germany — S M-F • E Europe • 100 kW
†RFE-RL, Via Briech, Morocco — W M-F • E Europe • 250 kW
W • E Europe • 250 kW
VOA, Via Iranawila, Sri Lanka — S • S Asia • 250 kW
S • Mideast • 250 kW
UZBEKISTAN
RADIO TASHKENT, Tashkent — Europe • 240 kW
S • Europe • 240 kW

| | World Time | 0 | 1 | 2 | 3 | 4 | 5 | 6 | 7 | 8 | 9 | 10 | 11 | 12 | 13 | 14 | 15 | 16 | 17 | 18 | 19 | 20 | 21 | 22 | 23 | 24 |

ENGLISH ▬ ARABIC ⁓ CHINESE ▫▫▫ FRENCH ▬ GERMAN ▬ RUSSIAN ▬ SPANISH ▬ OTHER ▬

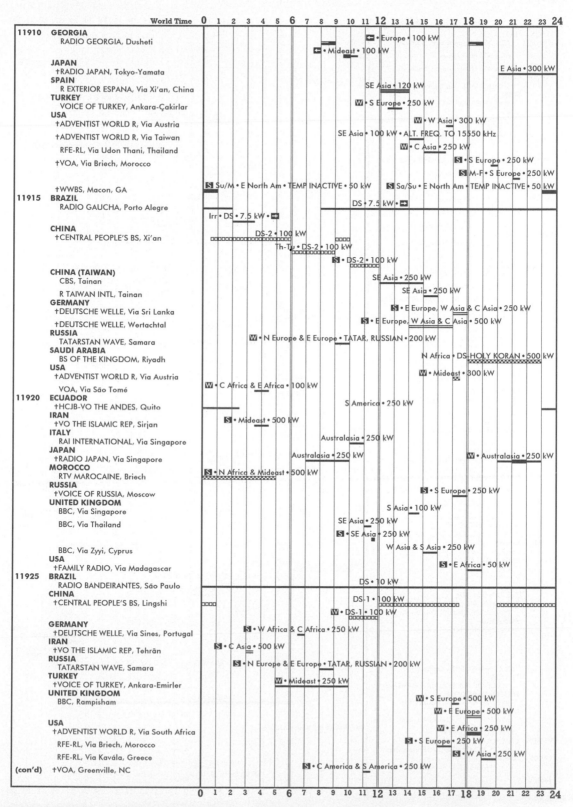

World Time 0 1 2 3 4 5 6 7 8 9 10 11 12 13 14 15 16 17 18 19 20 21 22 23 24

11910 GEORGIA
RADIO GEORGIA, Dusheti — Europe • 100 kW
— Mideast • 100 kW

JAPAN
†RADIO JAPAN, Tokyo-Yamata — E Asia • 300 kW
SPAIN
R EXTERIOR ESPANA, Via Xi'an, China — SE Asia • 120 kW
TURKEY
VOICE OF TURKEY, Ankara-Çakirlar — W • S Europe • 250 kW
USA
†ADVENTIST WORLD R, Via Austria — W • W Asia • 300 kW
†ADVENTIST WORLD R, Via Taiwan — SE Asia • 100 kW • ALT. FREQ. TO 15550 kHz
RFE-RL, Via Udon Thani, Thailand — W • C Asia • 250 kW
†VOA, Via Briech, Morocco — S • S Europe • 250 kW
— M-F • S Europe • 250 kW
†WWBS, Macon, GA — S • Su/M • E North Am • TEMP INACTIVE • 50 kW — S • Sa/Su • E North Am • TEMP INACTIVE • 50 kW

11915 BRAZIL
RADIO GAUCHA, Porto Alegre — DS • 7.5 kW •
Irr • DS • 7.5 kW •

CHINA
†CENTRAL PEOPLE'S BS, Xi'an — DS-2 • 100 kW
Th-Tu • DS-2 • 100 kW
S • DS-2 • 100 kW

CHINA (TAIWAN)
CBS, Tainan — SE Asia • 250 kW
R TAIWAN INTL, Tainan — SE Asia • 250 kW
GERMANY
†DEUTSCHE WELLE, Via Sri Lanka — S • E Europe, W Asia & C Asia • 250 kW
†DEUTSCHE WELLE, Wertachtal — S • E Europe, W Asia & C Asia • 500 kW
RUSSIA
TATARSTAN WAVE, Samara — W • N Europe & E Europe • TATAR, RUSSIAN • 200 kW
SAUDI ARABIA
BS OF THE KINGDOM, Riyadh — N Africa • DS-HOLY KORAN • 500 kW
USA
†ADVENTIST WORLD R, Via Austria — W • Mideast • 300 kW
VOA, Via São Tomé — W • C Africa & E Africa • 100 kW

11920 ECUADOR
†HCJB-VO THE ANDES, Quito — S America • 250 kW
IRAN
†VO THE ISLAMIC REP, Sirjan — S • Mideast • 500 kW
ITALY
RAI INTERNATIONAL, Via Singapore — Australasia • 250 kW
JAPAN
†RADIO JAPAN, Via Singapore — Australasia • 250 kW — W • Australasia • 250 kW
MOROCCO
RTV MAROCAINE, Briech — S • N Africa & Mideast • 500 kW
RUSSIA
†VOICE OF RUSSIA, Moscow — S • S Europe • 250 kW
UNITED KINGDOM
BBC, Via Singapore — S Asia • 100 kW
BBC, Via Thailand — SE Asia • 250 kW
S • SE Asia • 250 kW
BBC, Via Zyyi, Cyprus — W Asia & S Asia • 250 kW
USA
†FAMILY RADIO, Via Madagascar — S • E Africa • 50 kW

11925 BRAZIL
RADIO BANDEIRANTES, São Paulo — DS • 10 kW
CHINA
†CENTRAL PEOPLE'S BS, Lingshi — DS-1 • 100 kW
W • DS-1 • 100 kW
GERMANY
†DEUTSCHE WELLE, Via Sines, Portugal — S • W Africa & C Africa • 250 kW
IRAN
†VO THE ISLAMIC REP, Tehrān — S • C Asia • 500 kW
RUSSIA
TATARSTAN WAVE, Samara — S • N Europe & E Europe • TATAR, RUSSIAN • 200 kW
TURKEY
†VOICE OF TURKEY, Ankara-Emirler — W • Mideast • 250 kW
UNITED KINGDOM
BBC, Rampisham — W • S Europe • 500 kW
W • E Europe • 500 kW
USA
†ADVENTIST WORLD R, Via South Africa — W • E Africa • 250 kW
RFE-RL, Via Briech, Morocco — S • S Europe • 250 kW
RFE-RL, Via Kavála, Greece — S • W Asia • 250 kW
(con'd) †VOA, Greenville, NC — S • C America & S America • 250 kW

0 1 2 3 4 5 6 7 8 9 10 11 12 13 14 15 16 17 18 19 20 21 22 23 24

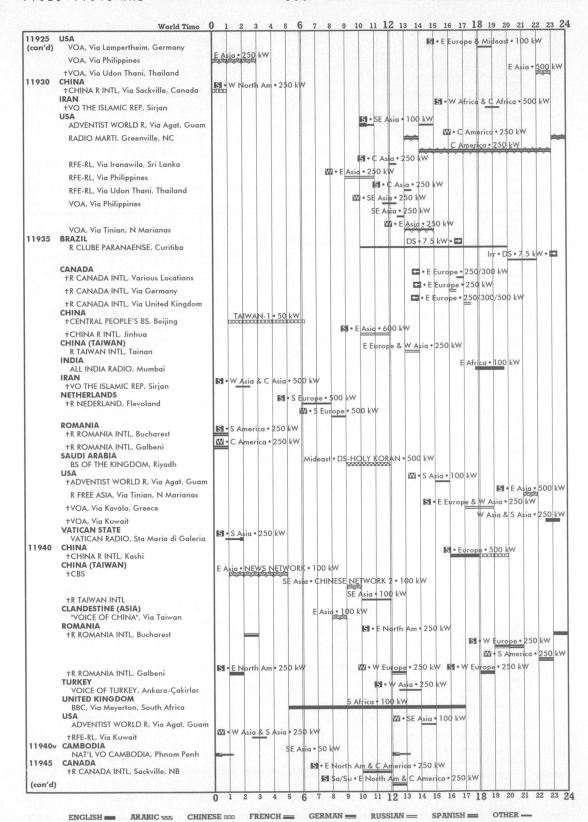

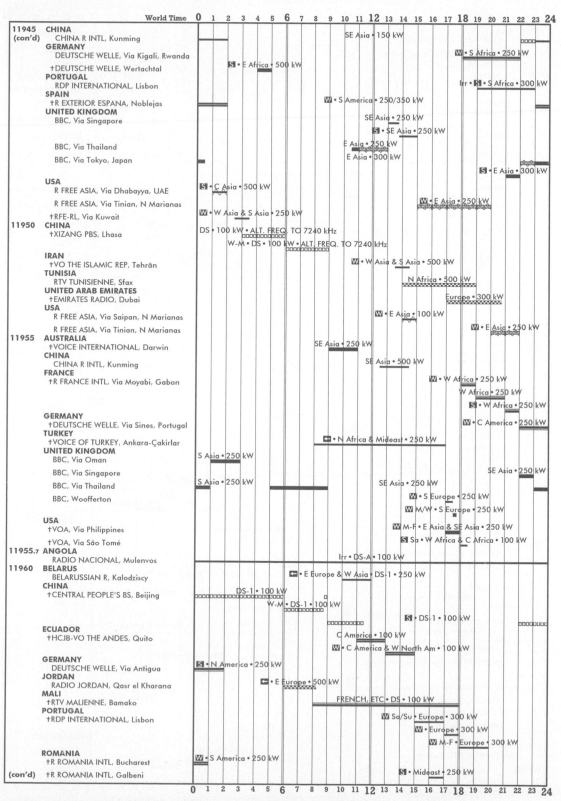

World Time

11945	**CHINA**	
(con'd)	CHINA R INTL, Kunming	SE Asia • 150 kW
	GERMANY	
	DEUTSCHE WELLE, Via Kigali, Rwanda	W • S Africa • 250 kW
	†DEUTSCHE WELLE, Wertachtal	S • E Africa • 500 kW
	PORTUGAL	
	RDP INTERNATIONAL, Lisbon	Irr • S • S Africa • 300 kW
	SPAIN	
	†R EXTERIOR ESPANA, Noblejas	W • S America • 250/350 kW
	UNITED KINGDOM	
	BBC, Via Singapore	SE Asia • 250 kW / S • SE Asia • 250 kW
	BBC, Via Thailand	E Asia • 250 kW
	BBC, Via Tokyo, Japan	E Asia • 300 kW / S • E Asia • 300 kW
	USA	
	R FREE ASIA, Via Dhabayya, UAE	S • C Asia • 500 kW
	R FREE ASIA, Via Tinian, N Marianas	W • E Asia • 250 kW
	†RFE-RL, Via Kuwait	W • W Asia & S Asia • 250 kW
11950	**CHINA**	
	†XIZANG PBS, Lhasa	DS • 100 kW • ALT. FREQ. TO 7240 kHz / W-M • DS • 100 kW • ALT. FREQ. TO 7240 kHz
	IRAN	
	†VO THE ISLAMIC REP, Tehrān	W • W Asia & S Asia • 500 kW
	TUNISIA	
	RTV TUNISIENNE, Sfax	N Africa • 500 kW
	UNITED ARAB EMIRATES	
	†EMIRATES RADIO, Dubai	Europe • 300 kW
	USA	
	R FREE ASIA, Via Saipan, N Marianas	W • E Asia • 100 kW
	R FREE ASIA, Via Tinian, N Marianas	W • E Asia • 250 kW
11955	**AUSTRALIA**	
	†VOICE INTERNATIONAL, Darwin	SE Asia • 250 kW
	CHINA	
	CHINA R INTL, Kunming	SE Asia • 500 kW
	FRANCE	
	†R FRANCE INTL, Via Moyabi, Gabon	W • W Africa • 250 kW / W Africa • 250 kW / S • W Africa • 250 kW
	GERMANY	
	†DEUTSCHE WELLE, Via Sines, Portugal	W • C America • 250 kW
	TURKEY	
	†VOICE OF TURKEY, Ankara-Çakirlar	⬅ • N Africa & Mideast • 250 kW
	UNITED KINGDOM	
	BBC, Via Oman	S Asia • 250 kW
	BBC, Via Singapore	SE Asia • 250 kW
	BBC, Via Thailand	S Asia • 250 kW / SE Asia • 250 kW
	BBC, Woofferton	W • S Europe • 250 kW / W M/W • S Europe • 250 kW
	USA	
	†VOA, Via Philippines	W M-F • E Asia & SE Asia • 250 kW
	†VOA, Via São Tomé	S Sa • W Africa & C Africa • 100 kW
11955.7	**ANGOLA**	
	RADIO NACIONAL, Mulenvos	Irr • DS-A • 100 kW
11960	**BELARUS**	
	BELARUSSIAN R, Kalodziscy	⬅ • E Europe & W Asia • DS-1 • 250 kW
	CHINA	
	†CENTRAL PEOPLE'S BS, Beijing	DS-1 • 100 kW / W-M • DS-1 • 100 kW / S • DS-1 • 100 kW
	ECUADOR	
	†HCJB-VO THE ANDES, Quito	C America • 100 kW / W • C America & W North Am • 100 kW
	GERMANY	
	DEUTSCHE WELLE, Via Antigua	S • N America • 250 kW
	JORDAN	
	RADIO JORDAN, Qasr el Kharana	⬅ • E Europe • 500 kW
	MALI	
	†RTV MALIENNE, Bamako	FRENCH, ETC • DS • 100 kW
	PORTUGAL	
	†RDP INTERNATIONAL, Lisbon	W Sa/Su • Europe • 300 kW / W • Europe • 300 kW / W M-F • Europe • 300 kW
	ROMANIA	
	†R ROMANIA INTL, Bucharest	W • S America • 250 kW
(con'd)	†R ROMANIA INTL, Galbeni	S • Mideast • 250 kW

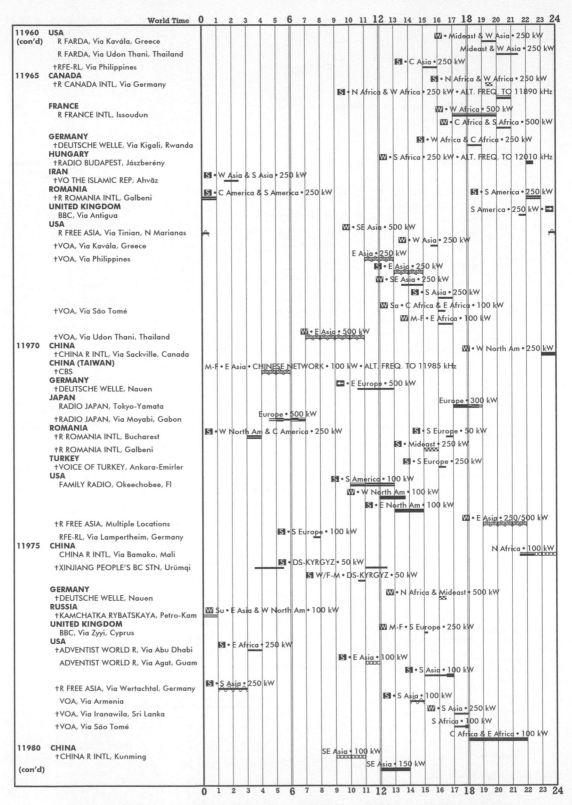

World Time 0 1 2 3 4 5 6 7 8 9 10 11 12 13 14 15 16 17 18 19 20 21 22 23 24

11960 USA
(con'd)
  R FARDA, Via Kavála, Greece — W • Mideast & W Asia • 250 kW
  R FARDA, Via Udon Thani, Thailand — Mideast & W Asia • 250 kW
  †RFE-RL, Via Philippines — S • C Asia • 250 kW
11965 CANADA
  †R CANADA INTL, Via Germany — S • N Africa & W Africa • 250 kW
  — S • N Africa & W Africa • 250 kW • ALT. FREQ. TO 11890 kHz

FRANCE
  R FRANCE INTL, Issoudun — W • W Africa • 500 kW
  — W • C Africa & S Africa • 500 kW

GERMANY
  †DEUTSCHE WELLE, Via Kigali, Rwanda — S • W Africa & C Africa • 250 kW
HUNGARY
  †RADIO BUDAPEST, Jászberény — W • S Africa • 250 kW • ALT. FREQ. TO 12010 kHz
IRAN
  †VO THE ISLAMIC REP, Ahvāz — S • W Asia & S Asia • 250 kW
ROMANIA
  †R ROMANIA INTL, Galbeni — S • C America & S America • 250 kW — S • S America • 250 kW
UNITED KINGDOM
  BBC, Via Antigua — S America • 250 kW •
USA
  R FREE ASIA, Via Tinian, N Marianas — W • SE Asia • 500 kW
  — W • W Asia • 250 kW
  †VOA, Via Kavála, Greece — E Asia • 250 kW
  †VOA, Via Philippines — S • E Asia • 250 kW
  — W • SE Asia • 250 kW
  — S • S Asia • 250 kW
  †VOA, Via São Tomé — W • Sa • C Africa & E Africa • 100 kW
  — W • M-F • E Africa • 100 kW
  †VOA, Via Udon Thani, Thailand — W • E Asia • 500 kW
11970 CHINA
  †CHINA R INTL, Via Sackville, Canada — W • W North Am • 250 kW
CHINA (TAIWAN)
  †CBS — M-F • E Asia • CHINESE NETWORK • 100 kW • ALT. FREQ. TO 11985 kHz
GERMANY
  †DEUTSCHE WELLE, Nauen — E Europe • 500 kW
JAPAN
  RADIO JAPAN, Tokyo-Yamata — Europe • 500 kW
  — Europe • 300 kW
  †RADIO JAPAN, Via Moyabi, Gabon
ROMANIA
  †R ROMANIA INTL, Bucharest — S • W North Am & C America • 250 kW
  †R ROMANIA INTL, Galbeni — S • S Europe • 50 kW
  — S • Mideast • 250 kW
TURKEY
  †VOICE OF TURKEY, Ankara-Emirler — S • S Europe • 250 kW
USA
  FAMILY RADIO, Okeechobee, Fl — S • S America • 100 kW
  — W • W North Am • 100 kW
  — S • E North Am • 100 kW
  — W • E Asia • 250/500 kW
  †R FREE ASIA, Multiple Locations — S • S Europe • 100 kW
  RFE-RL, Via Lampertheim, Germany
11975 CHINA
  CHINA R INTL, Via Bamako, Mali — N Africa • 100 kW
  †XINJIANG PEOPLE'S BC STN, Urümqi — S • DS-KYRGYZ • 50 kW
  — S • W/F-M • DS-KYRGYZ • 50 kW
GERMANY
  †DEUTSCHE WELLE, Nauen — W • N Africa & Mideast • 500 kW
RUSSIA
  †KAMCHATKA RYBATSKAYA, Petro-Kam — W • Su • E Asia & W North Am • 100 kW
UNITED KINGDOM
  BBC, Via Zyyi, Cyprus — W • M-F • S Europe • 250 kW
USA
  †ADVENTIST WORLD R, Via Abu Dhabi — S • E Africa • 250 kW
  ADVENTIST WORLD R, Via Agat, Guam — S • E Asia • 100 kW
  — S • S Asia • 100 kW
  †R FREE ASIA, Via Wertachtal, Germany — S • S Asia • 250 kW
  VOA, Via Armenia — S • S Asia • 100 kW
  †VOA, Via Iranawila, Sri Lanka — W • S Asia • 250 kW
  †VOA, Via São Tomé — S Africa • 100 kW
  — C Africa & E Africa • 100 kW
11980 CHINA
  †CHINA R INTL, Kunming — SE Asia • 100 kW
  — SE Asia • 150 kW
(con'd)

World Time 0 1 2 3 4 5 6 7 8 9 10 11 12 13 14 15 16 17 18 19 20 21 22 23 24

ENGLISH ▬▬ ARABIC ⋙ CHINESE ▫▫▫ FRENCH ═══ GERMAN ▬▬ RUSSIAN ═══ SPANISH ▬▬ OTHER ▬▬

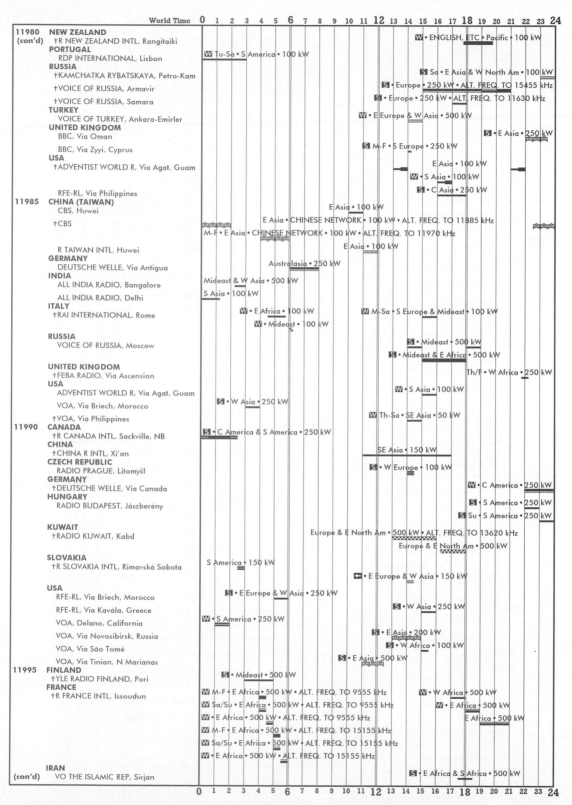

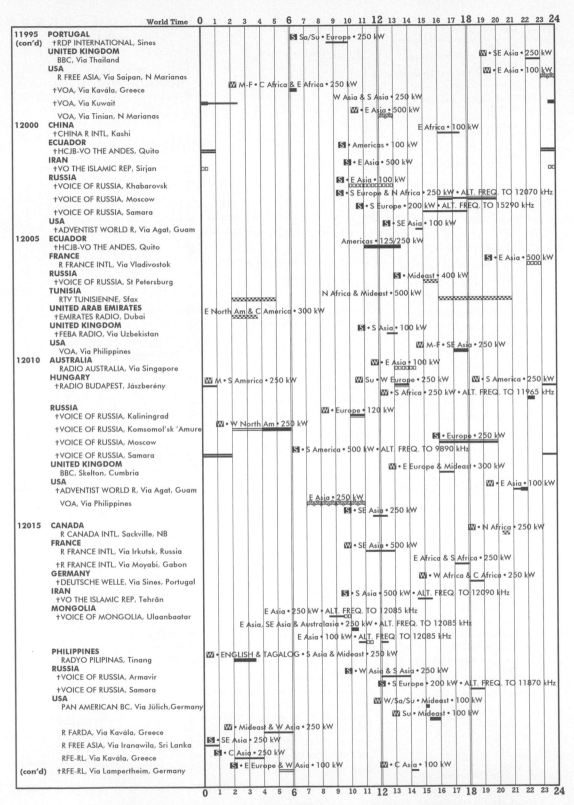

		World Time	0 1 2 3 4 5 6 7 8 9 10 11 12 13 14 15 16 17 18 19 20 21 22 23 24

11995
(con'd) PORTUGAL
    †RDP INTERNATIONAL, Sines — S Sa/Su • Europe • 250 kW
  UNITED KINGDOM
    BBC, Via Thailand — W • SE Asia • 250 kW
  USA
    R FREE ASIA, Via Saipan, N Marianas — W • E Asia • 100 kW
    †VOA, Via Kavála, Greece — W M-F • C Africa & E Africa • 250 kW
    †VOA, Via Kuwait — W Asia & S Asia • 250 kW
    VOA, Via Tinian, N Marianas — W • E Asia • 500 kW

12000 CHINA
    †CHINA R INTL, Kashi — E Africa • 100 kW
  ECUADOR
    †HCJB-VO THE ANDES, Quito — S • Americas • 100 kW
  IRAN
    †VO THE ISLAMIC REP, Sirjan — S • E Asia • 500 kW
  RUSSIA
    †VOICE OF RUSSIA, Khabarovsk — S • E Asia • 100 kW
    †VOICE OF RUSSIA, Moscow — S • S Europe & N Africa • 250 kW • ALT. FREQ. TO 12070 kHz
    †VOICE OF RUSSIA, Samara — S • S Europe • 200 kW • ALT. FREQ. TO 15290 kHz
  USA
    †ADVENTIST WORLD R, Via Agat, Guam — S • SE Asia • 100 kW

12005 ECUADOR
    †HCJB-VO THE ANDES, Quito — Americas • 125/250 kW
  FRANCE
    R FRANCE INTL, Via Vladivostok — S • E Asia • 500 kW
  RUSSIA
    †VOICE OF RUSSIA, St Petersburg — S • Mideast • 400 kW
  TUNISIA
    RTV TUNISIENNE, Sfax — N Africa & Mideast • 500 kW
  UNITED ARAB EMIRATES
    †EMIRATES RADIO, Dubai — E North Am & C America • 300 kW
  UNITED KINGDOM
    †FEBA RADIO, Via Uzbekistan — S • S Asia • 100 kW
  USA
    VOA, Via Philippines — W M-F • SE Asia • 250 kW

12010 AUSTRALIA
    RADIO AUSTRALIA, Via Singapore — W • E Asia • 100 kW
  HUNGARY
    †RADIO BUDAPEST, Jászberény — W M • S America • 250 kW   W Su • W Europe • 250 kW   W • S America • 250 kW
                                   W • S Africa • 250 kW • ALT. FREQ. TO 11965 kHz
  RUSSIA
    †VOICE OF RUSSIA, Kaliningrad — W • Europe • 120 kW
    †VOICE OF RUSSIA, Komsomol'sk 'Amure — W • W North Am • 250 kW
    †VOICE OF RUSSIA, Moscow — S • Europe • 250 kW
    †VOICE OF RUSSIA, Samara — S • S America • 500 kW • ALT. FREQ. TO 9890 kHz
  UNITED KINGDOM
    BBC, Skelton, Cumbria — W • E Europe & Mideast • 300 kW
  USA
    †ADVENTIST WORLD R, Via Agat, Guam — W • E Asia • 100 kW
    VOA, Via Philippines — E Asia • 250 kW   S • SE Asia • 250 kW

12015 CANADA
    R CANADA INTL, Sackville, NB — W • N Africa • 250 kW
  FRANCE
    R FRANCE INTL, Via Irkutsk, Russia — W • SE Asia • 500 kW
    †R FRANCE INTL, Via Moyabi, Gabon — E Africa & S Africa • 250 kW
  GERMANY
    †DEUTSCHE WELLE, Via Sines, Portugal — W • W Africa & C Africa • 250 kW
  IRAN
    †VO THE ISLAMIC REP, Tehrān — S • S Asia • 500 kW • ALT. FREQ. TO 12090 kHz
  MONGOLIA
    †VOICE OF MONGOLIA, Ulaanbaatar — E Asia • 250 kW • ALT. FREQ. TO 12085 kHz
                             E Asia, SE Asia & Australasia • 250 kW • ALT. FREQ. TO 12085 kHz
                             E Asia • 100 kW • ALT. FREQ. TO 12085 kHz
  PHILIPPINES
    RADYO PILIPINAS, Tinang — W • ENGLISH & TAGALOG • S Asia & Mideast • 250 kW
  RUSSIA
    †VOICE OF RUSSIA, Armavir — S • W Asia & S Asia • 250 kW
    †VOICE OF RUSSIA, Samara — S • S Europe • 200 kW • ALT. FREQ. TO 11870 kHz
  USA
    PAN AMERICAN BC, Via Jülich, Germany — W/Sa/Su • Mideast • 100 kW
                                  W Su • Mideast • 100 kW
    R FARDA, Via Kavála, Greece — W • Mideast & W Asia • 250 kW
    R FREE ASIA, Via Iranawila, Sri Lanka — S • SE Asia • 250 kW
    RFE-RL, Via Kavála, Greece — S • C Asia • 250 kW
  (con'd) †RFE-RL, Via Lampertheim, Germany — S • E Europe & W Asia • 100 kW   W • C Asia • 100 kW

ENGLISH ■■■   ARABIC ▨▨▨   CHINESE □□□   FRENCH ▬▬▬   GERMAN ▭▭▭   RUSSIAN ═══   SPANISH ▬▬▬   OTHER ─

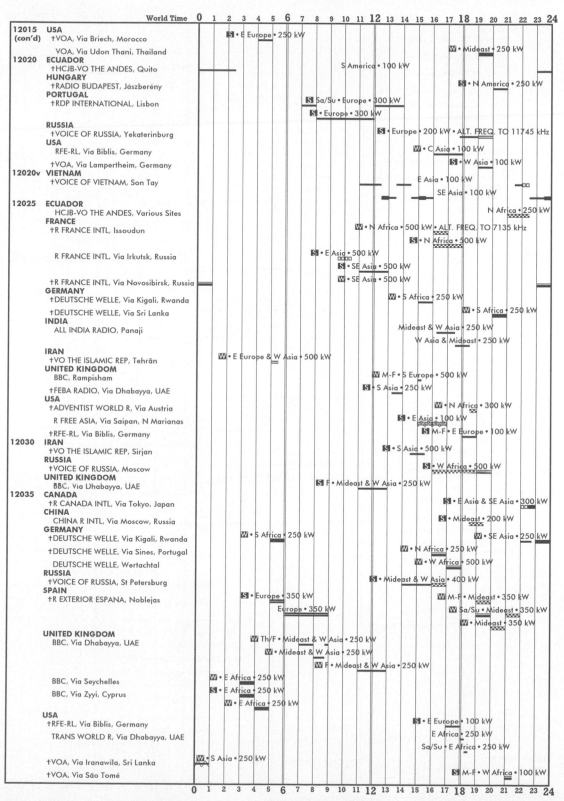

12015	USA			
(con'd)	†VOA, Via Briech, Morocco		S • E Europe • 250 kW	
	VOA, Via Udon Thani, Thailand			W • Mideast • 250 kW
12020	ECUADOR			
	†HCJB-VO THE ANDES, Quito		S America • 100 kW	
	HUNGARY			
	†RADIO BUDAPEST, Jászberény			S • N America • 250 kW
	PORTUGAL			
	†RDP INTERNATIONAL, Lisbon		S Sa/Su • Europe • 300 kW	
			S • Europe • 300 kW	
	RUSSIA			
	†VOICE OF RUSSIA, Yekaterinburg			S • Europe • 200 kW • ALT. FREQ. TO 11745 kHz
	USA			
	RFE-RL, Via Biblis, Germany			W • C Asia • 100 kW
	†VOA, Via Lampertheim, Germany			S • W Asia • 100 kW
12020v	VIETNAM			
	†VOICE OF VIETNAM, Son Tay		E Asia • 100 kW	
			SE Asia • 100 kW	
12025	ECUADOR			
	HCJB-VO THE ANDES, Various Sites			N Africa • 250 kW
	FRANCE			
	†R FRANCE INTL, Issoudun		W • N Africa • 500 kW • ALT. FREQ. TO 7135 kHz	
			S • N Africa • 500 kW	
	R FRANCE INTL, Via Irkutsk, Russia		S • E Asia • 500 kW	
			S • SE Asia • 500 kW	
	†R FRANCE INTL, Via Novosibirsk, Russia		W • SE Asia • 500 kW	
	GERMANY			
	†DEUTSCHE WELLE, Via Kigali, Rwanda		W • S Africa • 250 kW	
	†DEUTSCHE WELLE, Via Sri Lanka			W • S Africa • 250 kW
	INDIA			
	ALL INDIA RADIO, Panaji		Mideast & W Asia • 250 kW	
			W Asia & Mideast • 250 kW	
	IRAN			
	†VO THE ISLAMIC REP, Tehrān		W • E Europe & W Asia • 500 kW	
	UNITED KINGDOM			
	BBC, Rampisham		W M-F • S Europe • 500 kW	
	†FEBA RADIO, Via Dhabayya, UAE		S • S Asia • 250 kW	
	USA			
	†ADVENTIST WORLD R, Via Austria		W • N Africa • 300 kW	
	R FREE ASIA, Via Saipan, N Marianas		S • E Asia • 100 kW	
	†RFE-RL, Via Biblis, Germany		S M-F • E Europe • 100 kW	
12030	IRAN			
	†VO THE ISLAMIC REP, Sirjan		S • S Asia • 500 kW	
	RUSSIA			
	†VOICE OF RUSSIA, Moscow		S • W Africa • 500 kW	
	UNITED KINGDOM			
	BBC, Via Dhabayya, UAE		S F • Mideast & W Asia • 250 kW	
12035	CANADA			
	†R CANADA INTL, Via Tokyo, Japan		S • E Asia & SE Asia • 300 kW	
	CHINA			
	CHINA R INTL, Via Moscow, Russia		S • Mideast • 200 kW	
	GERMANY			
	†DEUTSCHE WELLE, Via Kigali, Rwanda		W • S Africa • 250 kW	
	†DEUTSCHE WELLE, Via Sines, Portugal		W • N Africa • 250 kW	
	DEUTSCHE WELLE, Wertachtal		W • W Africa • 500 kW	
	RUSSIA			
	†VOICE OF RUSSIA, St Petersburg		S • Mideast & W Asia • 400 kW	
	SPAIN			
	†R EXTERIOR ESPANA, Noblejas		S • Europe • 350 kW	W M-F • Mideast • 350 kW
			Europe • 350 kW	W Sa/Su • Mideast • 350 kW
				W • Mideast • 350 kW
	UNITED KINGDOM			
	BBC, Via Dhabayya, UAE		W Th/F • Mideast & W Asia • 250 kW	
			W • Mideast & W Asia • 250 kW	
			W F • Mideast & W Asia • 250 kW	
	BBC, Via Seychelles		W • E Africa • 250 kW	
	BBC, Via Zyyi, Cyprus		S • E Africa • 250 kW	
			W • E Africa • 250 kW	
	USA			
	†RFE-RL, Via Biblis, Germany		S • E Europe • 100 kW	
	TRANS WORLD R, Via Dhabayya, UAE		E Africa • 250 kW	
			Sa/Su • E Africa • 250 kW	
	†VOA, Via Iranawila, Sri Lanka		W • S Asia • 250 kW	
	†VOA, Via São Tomé		S M-F • W Africa • 100 kW	

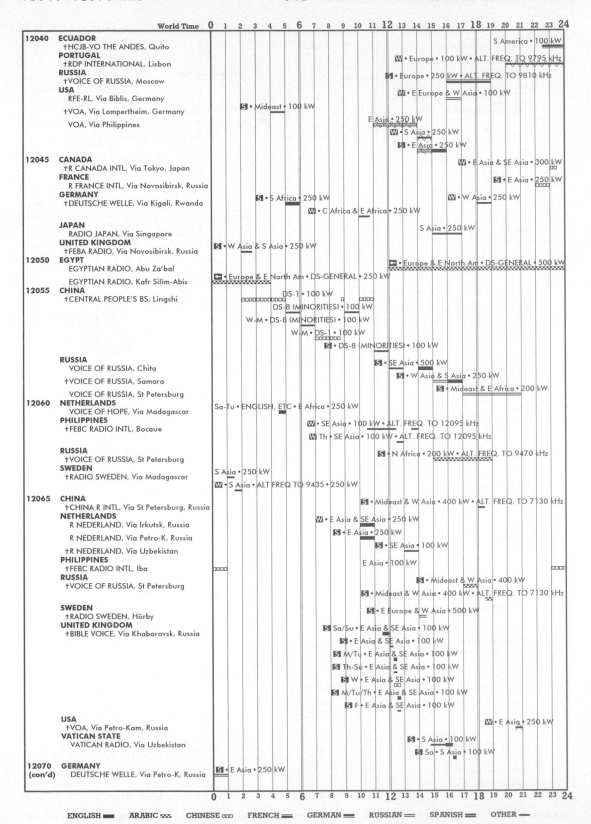

	World Time	0 1 2 3 4 5 6 7 8 9 10 11 12 13 14 15 16 17 18 19 20 21 22 23 24
12040	ECUADOR	
	†HCJB-VO THE ANDES, Quito	S America • 100 kW
	PORTUGAL	
	†RDP INTERNATIONAL, Lisbon	W • Europe • 100 kW • ALT. FREQ. TO 9795 kHz
	RUSSIA	
	†VOICE OF RUSSIA, Moscow	S • Europe • 250 kW • ALT. FREQ. TO 9810 kHz
	USA	
	RFE-RL, Via Biblis, Germany	W • E Europe & W Asia • 100 kW
	†VOA, Via Lampertheim, Germany	S • Mideast • 100 kW
	VOA, Via Philippines	E Asia • 250 kW
		W • S Asia • 250 kW
		S • E Asia • 250 kW
12045	CANADA	
	†R CANADA INTL, Via Tokyo, Japan	W • E Asia & SE Asia • 300 kW
	FRANCE	
	R FRANCE INTL, Via Novosibirsk, Russia	S • E Asia • 250 kW
	GERMANY	
	†DEUTSCHE WELLE, Via Kigali, Rwanda	S • S Africa • 250 kW
		W • W Asia • 250 kW
		W • C Africa & E Africa • 250 kW
	JAPAN	
	RADIO JAPAN, Via Singapore	S Asia • 250 kW
	UNITED KINGDOM	
	†FEBA RADIO, Via Novosibirsk, Russia	S • W Asia & S Asia • 250 kW
12050	EGYPT	
	EGYPTIAN RADIO, Abu Za'bal	□ • Europe & E North Am • DS-GENERAL • 500 kW
	EGYPTIAN RADIO, Kafr Silim-Abis	□ • Europe & E North Am • DS-GENERAL • 250 kW
12055	CHINA	
	†CENTRAL PEOPLE'S BS, Lingshi	DS-1 • 100 kW
		DS-8 (MINORITIES) • 100 kW
		W-M • DS-8 (MINORITIES) • 100 kW
		W-M • DS-1 • 100 kW
		S • DS-8 (MINORITIES) • 100 kW
	RUSSIA	
	VOICE OF RUSSIA, Chita	S • SE Asia • 500 kW
	†VOICE OF RUSSIA, Samara	S • W Asia & S Asia • 250 kW
	VOICE OF RUSSIA, St Petersburg	S • Mideast & E Africa • 200 kW
12060	NETHERLANDS	
	VOICE OF HOPE, Via Madagascar	Sa-Tu • ENGLISH, ETC • E Africa • 250 kW
	PHILIPPINES	
	†FEBC RADIO INTL, Bocaue	W • SE Asia • 100 kW • ALT. FREQ. TO 12095 kHz
		W Th • SE Asia • 100 kW • ALT. FREQ. TO 12095 kHz
	RUSSIA	
	†VOICE OF RUSSIA, St Petersburg	S • N Africa • 200 kW • ALT. FREQ. TO 9470 kHz
	SWEDEN	
	†RADIO SWEDEN, Via Madagascar	S Asia • 250 kW
		W • S Asia • ALT FREQ TO 9435 • 250 kW
12065	CHINA	
	†CHINA R INTL, Via St Petersburg, Russia	S • Mideast & W Asia • 400 kW • ALT. FREQ. TO 7130 kHz
	NETHERLANDS	
	R NEDERLAND, Via Irkutsk, Russia	W • E Asia & SE Asia • 250 kW
	R NEDERLAND, Via Petro-K, Russia	S • E Asia • 250 kW
	†R NEDERLAND, Via Uzbekistan	S • SE Asia • 100 kW
	PHILIPPINES	
	†FEBC RADIO INTL, Iba	E Asia • 100 kW
	RUSSIA	
	†VOICE OF RUSSIA, St Petersburg	S • Mideast & W Asia • 400 kW
		S • Mideast & W Asia • 400 kW • ALT. FREQ. TO 7130 kHz
	SWEDEN	
	†RADIO SWEDEN, Hörby	S • E Europe & W Asia • 500 kW
	UNITED KINGDOM	
	†BIBLE VOICE, Via Khabarovsk, Russia	S Sa/Su • E Asia & SE Asia • 100 kW
		S • E Asia & SE Asia • 100 kW
		S M/Tu • E Asia & SE Asia • 100 kW
		S Th-Su • E Asia & SE Asia • 100 kW
		S W • E Asia & SE Asia • 100 kW
		S M/Tu/Th • E Asia & SE Asia • 100 kW
		S F • E Asia & SE Asia • 100 kW
	USA	
	†VOA, Via Petro-Kam, Russia	W • E Asia • 250 kW
	VATICAN STATE	
	VATICAN RADIO, Via Uzbekistan	S • S Asia • 100 kW
		S Sa • S Asia • 100 kW
12070 (con'd)	GERMANY	
	DEUTSCHE WELLE, Via Petro-K, Russia	S • E Asia • 250 kW

| | World Time | 0 1 2 3 4 5 6 7 8 9 10 11 12 13 14 15 16 17 18 19 20 21 22 23 24 |

ENGLISH ■■   ARABIC ▧▧   CHINESE □□□   FRENCH ═══   GERMAN ━━   RUSSIAN ═══   SPANISH ══   OTHER ───

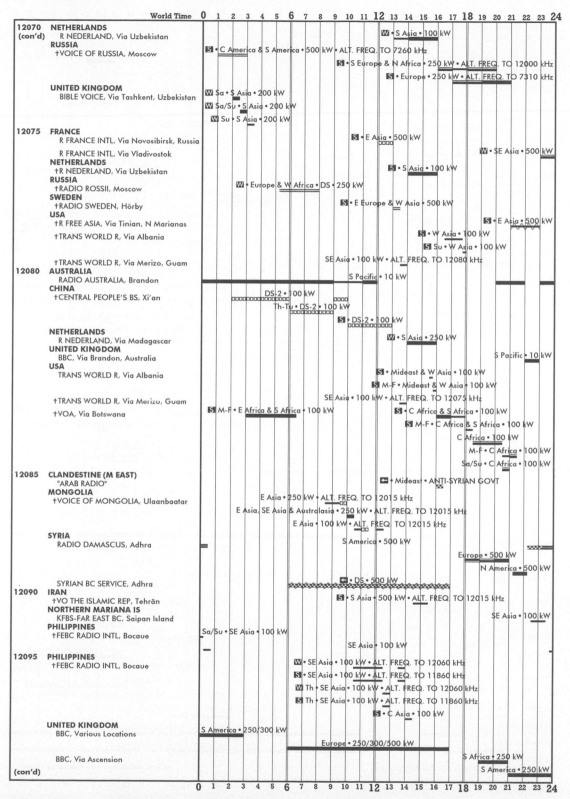

World Time   0 1 2 3 4 5 6 7 8 9 10 11 12 13 14 15 16 17 18 19 20 21 22 23 24

12070 **NETHERLANDS**
(con'd)   R NEDERLAND, Via Uzbekistan
   RUSSIA
   †VOICE OF RUSSIA, Moscow

   UNITED KINGDOM
   BIBLE VOICE, Via Tashkent, Uzbekistan

12075 **FRANCE**
   R FRANCE INTL, Via Novosibirsk, Russia

   R FRANCE INTL, Via Vladivostok
   NETHERLANDS
   †R NEDERLAND, Via Uzbekistan
   RUSSIA
   †RADIO ROSSII, Moscow
   SWEDEN
   †RADIO SWEDEN, Hörby
   USA
   †R FREE ASIA, Via Tinian, N Marianas

   †TRANS WORLD R, Via Albania

   †TRANS WORLD R, Via Merizo, Guam
12080 **AUSTRALIA**
   RADIO AUSTRALIA, Brandon
   CHINA
   †CENTRAL PEOPLE'S BS, Xi'an

   NETHERLANDS
   R NEDERLAND, Via Madagascar
   UNITED KINGDOM
   BBC, Via Brandon, Australia
   USA
   TRANS WORLD R, Via Albania

   †TRANS WORLD R, Via Merizo, Guam

   †VOA, Via Botswana

12085 **CLANDESTINE (M EAST)**
   "ARAB RADIO"
   MONGOLIA
   †VOICE OF MONGOLIA, Ulaanbaatar

   SYRIA
   RADIO DAMASCUS, Adhra

   SYRIAN BC SERVICE, Adhra
12090 **IRAN**
   †VO THE ISLAMIC REP, Tehrān
   NORTHERN MARIANA IS
   KFBS-FAR EAST BC, Saipan Island
   PHILIPPINES
   †FEBC RADIO INTL, Bocaue

12095 **PHILIPPINES**
   †FEBC RADIO INTL, Bocaue

   UNITED KINGDOM
   BBC, Various Locations

   BBC, Via Ascension

(con'd)

   0 1 2 3 4 5 6 7 8 9 10 11 12 13 14 15 16 17 18 19 20 21 22 23 24

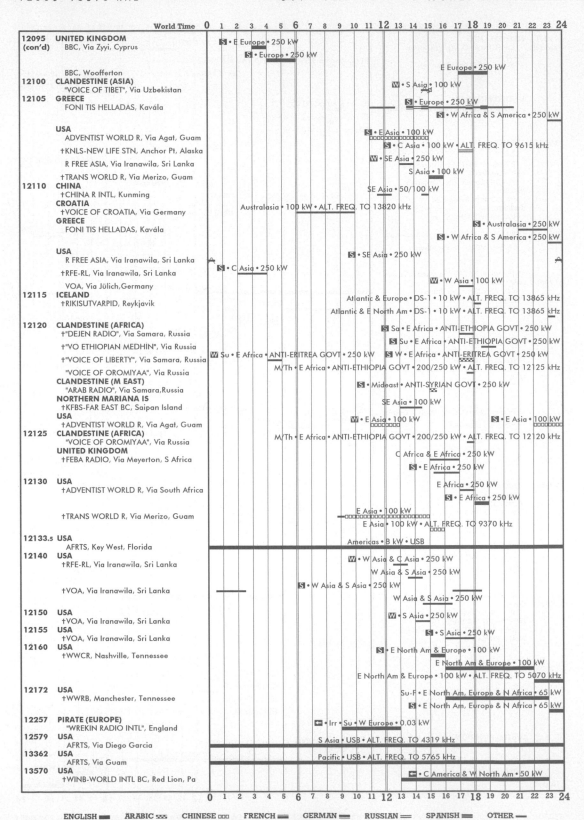

	World Time	0 1 2 3 4 5 6 7 8 9 10 11 12 13 14 15 16 17 18 19 20 21 22 23 24
12095	UNITED KINGDOM	
(con'd)	BBC, Via Zyyi, Cyprus	S • E Europe • 250 kW
		S • Europe • 250 kW
	BBC, Woofferton	E Europe • 250 kW
12100	CLANDESTINE (ASIA)	
	"VOICE OF TIBET", Via Uzbekistan	W • S Asia • 100 kW
12105	GREECE	
	FONI TIS HELLADAS, Kavála	S • Europe • 250 kW
		S • W Africa & S America • 250 kW
	USA	
	ADVENTIST WORLD R, Via Agat, Guam	S • E Asia • 100 kW
	†KNLS-NEW LIFE STN, Anchor Pt, Alaska	S • C Asia • 100 kW • ALT. FREQ. TO 9615 kHz
	R FREE ASIA, Via Iranawila, Sri Lanka	W • SE Asia • 250 kW
	†TRANS WORLD R, Via Merizo, Guam	S Asia • 100 kW
12110	CHINA	
	†CHINA R INTL, Kunming	SE Asia • 50/100 kW
	CROATIA	
	†VOICE OF CROATIA, Via Germany	Australasia • 100 kW • ALT. FREQ. TO 13820 kHz
	GREECE	
	FONI TIS HELLADAS, Kavála	S • Australasia • 250 kW
		S • W Africa & S America • 250 kW
	USA	
	R FREE ASIA, Via Iranawila, Sri Lanka	S • SE Asia • 250 kW
	†RFE-RL, Via Iranawila, Sri Lanka	S • C Asia • 250 kW
	VOA, Via Jülich, Germany	W • W Asia • 100 kW
12115	ICELAND	
	†RIKISUTVARPID, Reykjavik	Atlantic & Europe • DS-1 • 10 kW • ALT. FREQ. TO 13865 kHz
		Atlantic & E North Am • DS-1 • 10 kW • ALT. FREQ. TO 13865 kHz
12120	CLANDESTINE (AFRICA)	
	†"DEJEN RADIO", Via Samara, Russia	S Sa • E Africa • ANTI-ETHIOPIA GOVT • 250 kW
	†"VO ETHIOPIAN MEDHIN", Via Russia	S Su • E Africa • ANTI-ETHIOPIA GOVT • 250 kW
	†"VOICE OF LIBERTY", Via Samara, Russia	W Su • E Africa • ANTI-ERITREA GOVT • 250 kW S W • E Africa • ANTI-ERITREA GOVT • 250 kW
	"VOICE OF OROMIYAA", Via Russia	M/Th • E Africa • ANTI-ETHIOPIA GOVT • 200/250 kW • ALT. FREQ. TO 12125 kHz
	CLANDESTINE (M EAST)	
	"ARAB RADIO", Via Samara, Russia	S • Mideast • ANTI-SYRIAN GOVT • 250 kW
	NORTHERN MARIANA IS	
	†KFBS-FAR EAST BC, Saipan Island	SE Asia • 100 kW
	USA	
	†ADVENTIST WORLD R, Via Agat, Guam	W • E Asia • 100 kW S • E Asia • 100 kW
12125	CLANDESTINE (AFRICA)	
	"VOICE OF OROMIYAA", Via Russia	M/Th • E Africa • ANTI-ETHIOPIA GOVT • 200/250 kW • ALT. FREQ. TO 12120 kHz
	UNITED KINGDOM	
	†FEBA RADIO, Via Meyerton, S Africa	C Africa & E Africa • 250 kW
		S • E Africa • 250 kW
12130	USA	
	†ADVENTIST WORLD R, Via South Africa	E Africa • 250 kW
		S • E Africa • 250 kW
	†TRANS WORLD R, Via Merizo, Guam	E Asia • 100 kW
		E Asia • 100 kW • ALT. FREQ. TO 9370 kHz
12133.5	USA	
	AFRTS, Key West, Florida	Americas • B kW • USB
12140	USA	
	†RFE-RL, Via Iranawila, Sri Lanka	W • W Asia & C Asia • 250 kW
		W Asia & S Asia • 250 kW
	†VOA, Via Iranawila, Sri Lanka	S • W Asia & S Asia • 250 kW
		W Asia & S Asia • 250 kW
12150	USA	
	†VOA, Via Iranawila, Sri Lanka	W • S Asia • 250 kW
12155	USA	
	†VOA, Via Iranawila, Sri Lanka	S • S Asia • 250 kW
12160	USA	
	†WWCR, Nashville, Tennessee	S • E North Am & Europe • 100 kW
		E North Am & Europe • 100 kW
		E North Am & Europe • 100 kW • ALT. FREQ. TO 5070 kHz
12172	USA	
	†WWRB, Manchester, Tennessee	Su-F • E North Am, Europe & N Africa • 65 kW
		S • E North Am, Europe & N Africa • 65 kW
12257	PIRATE (EUROPE)	
	"WREKIN RADIO INTL", England	Irr • Su • W Europe • 0.03 kW
12579	USA	
	AFRTS, Via Diego Garcia	S Asia • USB • ALT. FREQ. TO 4319 kHz
13362	USA	
	AFRTS, Via Guam	Pacific • USB • ALT. FREQ. TO 5765 kHz
13570	USA	
	†WINB-WORLD INTL BC, Red Lion, Pa	C America & W North Am • 50 kW
	World Time	0 1 2 3 4 5 6 7 8 9 10 11 12 13 14 15 16 17 18 19 20 21 22 23 24

ENGLISH ▬   ARABIC ⬚⬚⬚   CHINESE □□□   FRENCH ▬▬   GERMAN ▬▬   RUSSIAN ═══   SPANISH ═══   OTHER ─

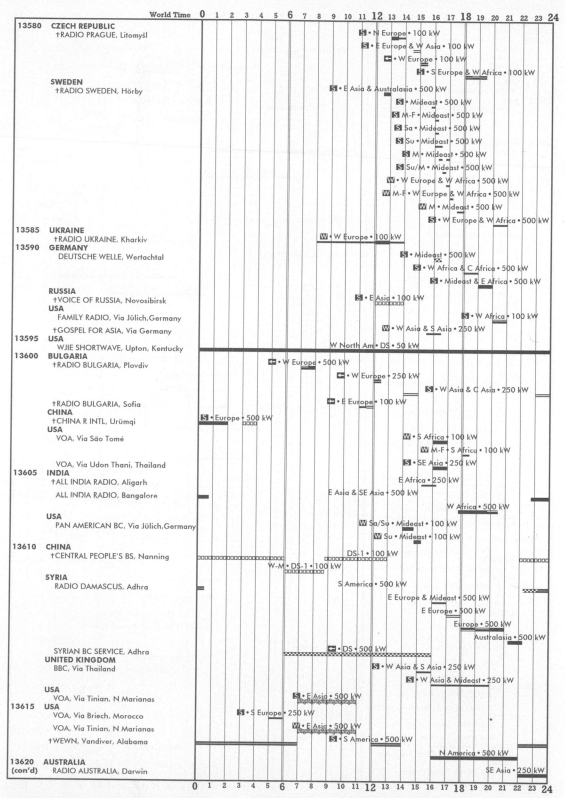

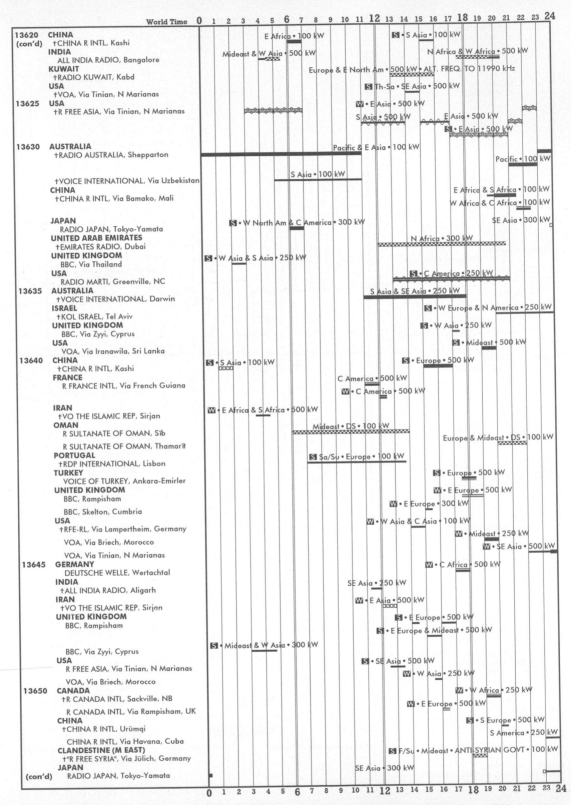

	World Time	0 1 2 3 4 5 6 7 8 9 10 11 12 13 14 15 16 17 18 19 20 21 22 23 24
13620 (con'd)	**CHINA** †CHINA R INTL, Kashi	E Africa • 100 kW / S • S Asia • 100 kW
	INDIA ALL INDIA RADIO, Bangalore	Mideast & W Asia • 500 kW / N Africa & W Africa • 500 kW
	KUWAIT †RADIO KUWAIT, Kabd	Europe & E North Am • 500 kW • ALT. FREQ. TO 11990 kHz
	USA †VOA, Via Tinian, N Marianas	S • Th-Sa • SE Asia • 500 kW
13625	**USA** †R FREE ASIA, Via Tinian, N Marianas	W • E Asia • 500 kW / S Asia • 500 kW / E Asia • 500 kW / S • E Asia • 500 kW
13630	**AUSTRALIA** †RADIO AUSTRALIA, Shepparton	Pacific & E Asia • 100 kW / Pacific • 100 kW
	†VOICE INTERNATIONAL, Via Uzbekistan	S Asia • 100 kW
	CHINA †CHINA R INTL, Via Bamako, Mali	E Africa & S Africa • 100 kW / W Africa & C Africa • 100 kW
	JAPAN RADIO JAPAN, Tokyo-Yamata	S • W North Am & C America • 300 kW / SE Asia • 300 kW
	UNITED ARAB EMIRATES †EMIRATES RADIO, Dubai	N Africa • 300 kW
	UNITED KINGDOM BBC, Via Thailand	S • W Asia & S Asia • 250 kW
	USA RADIO MARTI, Greenville, NC	S • C America • 250 kW
13635	**AUSTRALIA** †VOICE INTERNATIONAL, Darwin	S Asia & SE Asia • 250 kW
	ISRAEL †KOL ISRAEL, Tel Aviv	S • W Europe & N America • 250 kW
	UNITED KINGDOM BBC, Via Zyyi, Cyprus	S • W Asia • 250 kW
	USA VOA, Via Iranawila, Sri Lanka	S • Mideast • 500 kW
13640	**CHINA** †CHINA R INTL, Kashi	S • S Asia • 100 kW / S • Europe • 500 kW
	FRANCE R FRANCE INTL, Via French Guiana	C America • 500 kW / W • C America • 500 kW
	IRAN †VO THE ISLAMIC REP, Sirjan	W • E Africa & S Africa • 500 kW
	OMAN R SULTANATE OF OMAN, Sīb	Mideast • DS • 100 kW / Europe & Mideast • DS • 100 kW
	R SULTANATE OF OMAN, Thamarīt	
	PORTUGAL †RDP INTERNATIONAL, Lisbon	S • Sa/Su • Europe • 100 kW
	TURKEY VOICE OF TURKEY, Ankara-Emirler	S • Europe • 500 kW
	UNITED KINGDOM BBC, Rampisham	W • E Europe • 500 kW
	BBC, Skelton, Cumbria	W • E Europe • 300 kW
	USA †RFE-RL, Via Lampertheim, Germany	W • W Asia & C Asia • 100 kW
	VOA, Via Briech, Morocco	W • Mideast • 250 kW
	VOA, Via Tinian, N Marianas	W • SE Asia • 500 kW
13645	**GERMANY** DEUTSCHE WELLE, Wertachtal	W • C Africa • 500 kW
	INDIA †ALL INDIA RADIO, Aligarh	SE Asia • 250 kW
	IRAN †VO THE ISLAMIC REP, Sirjan	W • E Asia • 500 kW
	UNITED KINGDOM BBC, Rampisham	S • E Europe • 500 kW
		S • E Europe & Mideast • 500 kW
	BBC, Via Zyyi, Cyprus	S • Mideast & W Asia • 300 kW
	USA R FREE ASIA, Via Tinian, N Marianas	S • SE Asia • 500 kW
	VOA, Via Briech, Morocco	W • W Asia • 250 kW
13650	**CANADA** †R CANADA INTL, Sackville, NB	W • W Africa • 250 kW
	R CANADA INTL, Via Rampisham, UK	W • E Europe • 500 kW
	CHINA †CHINA R INTL, Urümqi	S • S Europe • 500 kW
	CHINA R INTL, Via Havana, Cuba	S America • 250 kW
	CLANDESTINE (M EAST) †"R FREE SYRIA", Via Jülich, Germany	S • F/Su • Mideast • ANTI-SYRIAN GOVT • 100 kW
(con'd)	**JAPAN** RADIO JAPAN, Tokyo-Yamata	SE Asia • 300 kW

| | World Time | 0 1 2 3 4 5 6 7 8 9 10 11 12 13 14 15 16 17 18 19 20 21 22 23 24 |

ENGLISH ▬   ARABIC ▦   CHINESE ▭▭▭   FRENCH ▬   GERMAN ▬   RUSSIAN ▬   SPANISH ▬   OTHER ▬

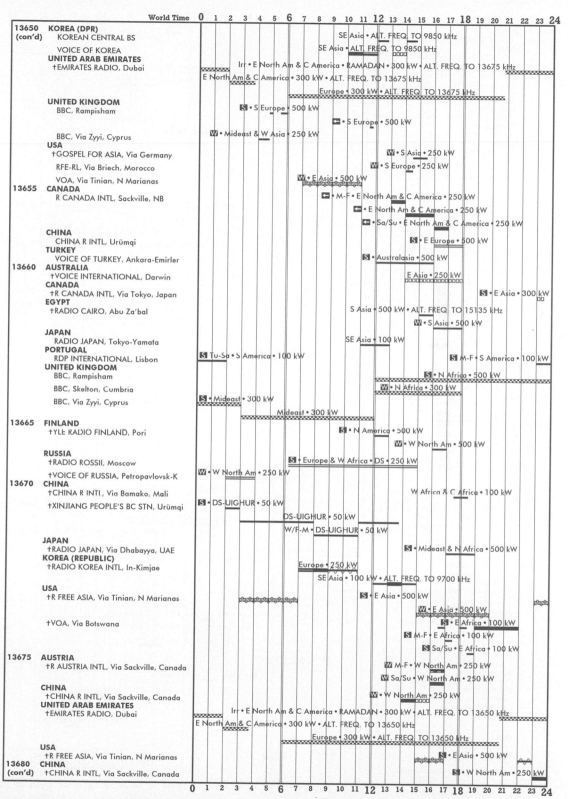

13650 (con'd)	KOREA (DPR)	KOREAN CENTRAL BS	SE Asia • ALT. FREQ. TO 9850 kHz
		VOICE OF KOREA	SE Asia • ALT. FREQ. TO 9850 kHz
	UNITED ARAB EMIRATES	†EMIRATES RADIO, Dubai	Irr • E North Am & C America • RAMADAN • 300 kW • ALT. FREQ. TO 13675 kHz
			E North Am & C America • 300 kW • ALT. FREQ. TO 13675 kHz
			Europe • 300 kW • ALT. FREQ. TO 13675 kHz
	UNITED KINGDOM	BBC, Rampisham	S • S Europe • 500 kW
			S • S Europe • 500 kW
		BBC, Via Zyyi, Cyprus	W • Mideast & W Asia • 250 kW
	USA	†GOSPEL FOR ASIA, Via Germany	W • S Asia • 250 kW
		RFE-RL, Via Briech, Morocco	W • S Europe • 250 kW
		VOA, Via Tinian, N Marianas	W • E Asia • 500 kW
13655	CANADA	R CANADA INTL, Sackville, NB	M-F • E North Am & C America • 250 kW
			E North Am & C America • 250 kW
			Sa/Su • E North Am & C America • 250 kW
	CHINA	CHINA R INTL, Urümqi	S • E Europe • 500 kW
	TURKEY	VOICE OF TURKEY, Ankara-Emirler	S • Australasia • 500 kW
13660	AUSTRALIA	†VOICE INTERNATIONAL, Darwin	E Asia • 250 kW
	CANADA	†R CANADA INTL, Via Tokyo, Japan	S • E Asia • 300 kW
	EGYPT	†RADIO CAIRO, Abu Za'bal	S Asia • 500 kW • ALT. FREQ. TO 15135 kHz
			W • S Asia • 500 kW
	JAPAN	RADIO JAPAN, Tokyo-Yamata	SE Asia • 100 kW
	PORTUGAL	RDP INTERNATIONAL, Lisbon	S Tu-Sa • S America • 100 kW
	UNITED KINGDOM	BBC, Rampisham	S M-F • S America • 100 kW
			S • N Africa • 500 kW
		BBC, Skelton, Cumbria	W • N Africa • 300 kW
		BBC, Via Zyyi, Cyprus	S • Mideast • 300 kW
13665	FINLAND	†YLE RADIO FINLAND, Pori	Mideast • 300 kW
			S • N America • 500 kW
	RUSSIA	†RADIO ROSSII, Moscow	W • W North Am • 500 kW
		†VOICE OF RUSSIA, Petropavlovsk-K	S • Europe & W Africa • DS • 250 kW
13670	CHINA	†CHINA R INTL, Via Bamako, Mali	W • W North Am • 250 kW
		†XINJIANG PEOPLE'S BC STN, Urümqi	W Africa & C Africa • 100 kW
			S • DS-UIGHUR • 50 kW
			DS-UIGHUR • 50 kW
			W/F-M • DS-UIGHUR • 50 kW
	JAPAN	†RADIO JAPAN, Via Dhabayya, UAE	S • Mideast & N Africa • 500 kW
	KOREA (REPUBLIC)	†RADIO KOREA INTL, In-Kimjae	Europe • 250 kW
			SE Asia • 100 kW • ALT. FREQ. TO 9700 kHz
	USA	†R FREE ASIA, Via Tinian, N Marianas	S • E Asia • 500 kW
		†VOA, Via Botswana	W • E Asia • 500 kW
			S • E Africa • 100 kW
			S M-F • E Africa • 100 kW
			S Sa/Su • E Africa • 100 kW
13675	AUSTRIA	†R AUSTRIA INTL, Via Sackville, Canada	W M-F • W North Am • 250 kW
			W Sa/Su • W North Am • 250 kW
	CHINA	†CHINA R INTL, Via Sackville, Canada	W • W North Am • 250 kW
	UNITED ARAB EMIRATES	†EMIRATES RADIO, Dubai	Irr • E North Am & C America • RAMADAN • 300 kW • ALT. FREQ. TO 13650 kHz
			E North Am & C America • 300 kW • ALT. FREQ. TO 13650 kHz
			Europe • 300 kW • ALT. FREQ. TO 13650 kHz
	USA	†R FREE ASIA, Via Tinian, N Marianas	S • E Asia • 500 kW
13680 (con'd)	CHINA	†CHINA R INTL, Via Sackville, Canada	S • W North Am • 250 kW

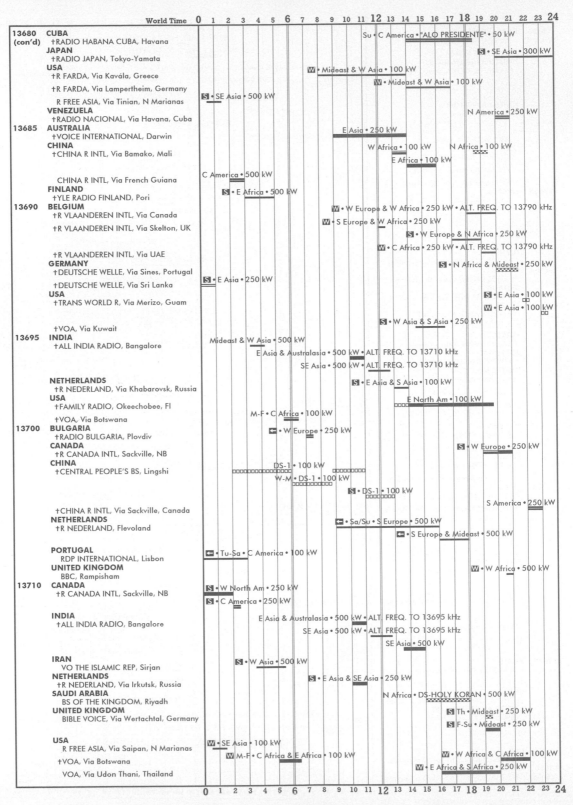

World Time   0 1 2 3 4 5 6 7 8 9 10 11 12 13 14 15 16 17 18 19 20 21 22 23 24

13680 **CUBA**
(con'd) †RADIO HABANA CUBA, Havana
         JAPAN
         †RADIO JAPAN, Tokyo-Yamata
         USA
         †R FARDA, Via Kavála, Greece
         †R FARDA, Via Lampertheim, Germany
         R FREE ASIA, Via Tinian, N Marianas
         VENEZUELA
         †RADIO NACIONAL, Via Havana, Cuba
13685 **AUSTRALIA**
         †VOICE INTERNATIONAL, Darwin
         CHINA
         †CHINA R INTL, Via Bamako, Mali

         CHINA R INTL, Via French Guiana
         FINLAND
         †YLE RADIO FINLAND, Pori
13690 **BELGIUM**
         †R VLAANDEREN INTL, Via Canada
         †R VLAANDEREN INTL, Via Skelton, UK

         †R VLAANDEREN INTL, Via UAE
         GERMANY
         †DEUTSCHE WELLE, Via Sines, Portugal
         †DEUTSCHE WELLE, Via Sri Lanka
         USA
         †TRANS WORLD R, Via Merizo, Guam

         †VOA, Via Kuwait
13695 **INDIA**
         †ALL INDIA RADIO, Bangalore

         NETHERLANDS
         †R NEDERLAND, Via Khabarovsk, Russia
         USA
         †FAMILY RADIO, Okeechobee, Fl
         †VOA, Via Botswana
13700 **BULGARIA**
         †RADIO BULGARIA, Plovdiv
         CANADA
         †R CANADA INTL, Sackville, NB
         CHINA
         †CENTRAL PEOPLE'S BS, Lingshi

         †CHINA R INTL, Via Sackville, Canada
         NETHERLANDS
         †R NEDERLAND, Flevoland

         PORTUGAL
         RDP INTERNATIONAL, Lisbon
         UNITED KINGDOM
         BBC, Rampisham
13710 **CANADA**
         †R CANADA INTL, Sackville, NB

         INDIA
         †ALL INDIA RADIO, Bangalore

         IRAN
         VO THE ISLAMIC REP, Sirjan
         NETHERLANDS
         †R NEDERLAND, Via Irkutsk, Russia
         SAUDI ARABIA
         BS OF THE KINGDOM, Riyadh
         UNITED KINGDOM
         BIBLE VOICE, Via Wertachtal, Germany

         USA
         R FREE ASIA, Via Saipan, N Marianas
         †VOA, Via Botswana
         VOA, Via Udon Thani, Thailand

Su • C America • "ALÓ PRESIDENTE" • 50 kW
S • SE Asia • 300 kW
W • Mideast & W Asia • 100 kW
W • Mideast & W Asia • 100 kW
S • SE Asia • 500 kW
N America • 250 kW
E Asia • 250 kW
W Africa • 100 kW   N Africa • 100 kW
E Africa • 100 kW
C America • 500 kW
S • E Africa • 500 kW
W • W Europe & W Africa • 250 kW • ALT. FREQ. TO 13790 kHz
W • S Europe & W Africa • 250 kW
S • W Europe & N Africa • 250 kW
W • C Africa • 250 kW • ALT. FREQ. TO 13790 kHz
S • N Africa & Mideast • 250 kW
S • E Asia • 250 kW
S • E Asia • 100 kW
W • E Asia • 100 kW
S • W Asia & S Asia • 250 kW
Mideast & W Asia • 500 kW
E Asia & Australasia • 500 kW • ALT. FREQ. TO 13710 kHz
SE Asia • 500 kW • ALT. FREQ. TO 13710 kHz
S • E Asia & S Asia • 100 kW
E North Am • 100 kW
M-F • C Africa • 100 kW
W Europe • 250 kW
S • W Europe • 250 kW
DS-1 • 100 kW
W-M • DS-1 • 100 kW
S • DS-1 • 100 kW
S America • 250 kW
Sa/Su • S Europe • 500 kW
S Europe & Mideast • 500 kW
Tu-Sa • C America • 100 kW
W • W Africa • 500 kW
S • W North Am • 250 kW
S • C America • 250 kW
E Asia & Australasia • 500 kW • ALT. FREQ. TO 13695 kHz
SE Asia • 500 kW • ALT. FREQ. TO 13695 kHz
SE Asia • 500 kW
S • W Asia • 500 kW
S • E Asia & SE Asia • 250 kW
N Africa • DS-HOLY KORAN • 500 kW
S Th • Mideast • 250 kW
S F-Su • Mideast • 250 kW
W • SE Asia • 100 kW
W M-F • C Africa & E Africa • 100 kW
W • W Africa & C Africa • 100 kW
W • E Africa & S Africa • 250 kW

0 1 2 3 4 5 6 7 8 9 10 11 12 13 14 15 16 17 18 19 20 21 22 23 24

ENGLISH ▬   ARABIC ≈≈≈   CHINESE □□□   FRENCH ══   GERMAN ▬▬   RUSSIAN ══   SPANISH ══   OTHER ──

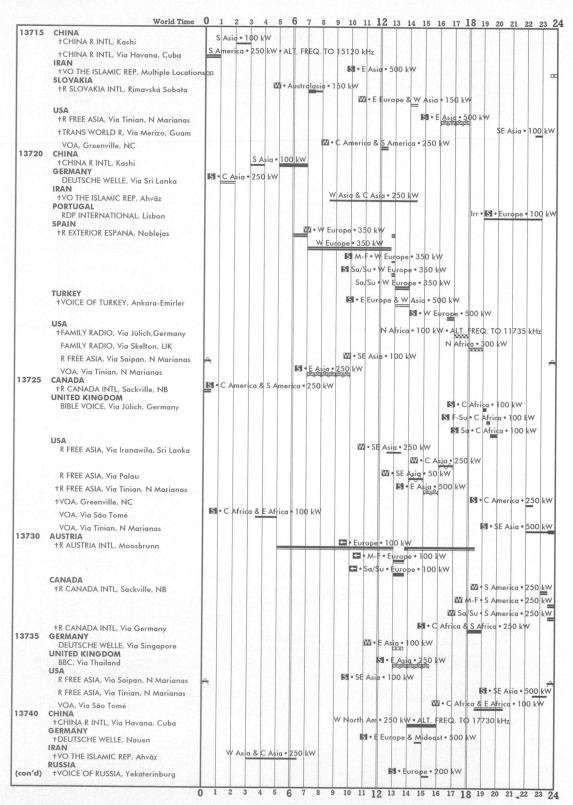

| World Time | 0 | 1 | 2 | 3 | 4 | 5 | 6 | 7 | 8 | 9 | 10 | 11 | 12 | 13 | 14 | 15 | 16 | 17 | 18 | 19 | 20 | 21 | 22 | 23 | 24 |

13715 CHINA
†CHINA R INTL, Kashi — S Asia • 100 kW
†CHINA R INTL, Via Havana, Cuba — S America • 250 kW • ALT. FREQ. TO 15120 kHz
IRAN
†VO THE ISLAMIC REP, Multiple Locations — S • E Asia • 500 kW
SLOVAKIA
†R SLOVAKIA INTL, Rimavská Sobota — W • Australasia • 150 kW
— W • E Europe & W Asia • 150 kW
USA
†R FREE ASIA, Via Tinian, N Marianas — S • E Asia • 500 kW
†TRANS WORLD R, Via Merizo, Guam — SE Asia • 100 kW
VOA, Greenville, NC — W • C America & S America • 250 kW
13720 CHINA
†CHINA R INTL, Kashi — S Asia • 100 kW
GERMANY
DEUTSCHE WELLE, Via Sri Lanka — S • C Asia • 250 kW
IRAN
†VO THE ISLAMIC REP, Ahvāz — W Asia & C Asia • 250 kW
PORTUGAL
RDP INTERNATIONAL, Lisbon — Irr • S • Europe • 100 kW
SPAIN
†R EXTERIOR ESPANA, Noblejas — W • W Europe • 350 kW
— W Europe • 350 kW
— S • M-F • W Europe • 350 kW
— S • Sa/Su • W Europe • 350 kW
— Sa/Su • W Europe • 350 kW
TURKEY
†VOICE OF TURKEY, Ankara-Emirler — S • E Europe & W Asia • 500 kW
— S • W Europe • 500 kW
USA
†FAMILY RADIO, Via Jülich, Germany — N Africa • 100 kW • ALT. FREQ. TO 11735 kHz
FAMILY RADIO, Via Skelton, UK — N Africa • 300 kW
R FREE ASIA, Via Saipan, N Marianas — W • SE Asia • 100 kW
VOA, Via Tinian, N Marianas — S • E Asia • 250 kW
13725 CANADA
†R CANADA INTL, Sackville, NB — S • C America & S America • 250 kW
UNITED KINGDOM
BIBLE VOICE, Via Jülich, Germany — S • C Africa • 100 kW
— S F-Su • C Africa • 100 kW
— S Sa • C Africa • 100 kW
USA
R FREE ASIA, Via Iranawila, Sri Lanka — W • SE Asia • 250 kW
— W • C Asia • 250 kW
R FREE ASIA, Via Palau — W • SE Asia • 50 kW
†R FREE ASIA, Via Tinian, N Marianas — S • E Asia • 500 kW
†VOA, Greenville, NC — S • C America • 250 kW
VOA, Via São Tomé — S • C Africa & E Africa • 100 kW
VOA, Via Tinian, N Marianas — S • SE Asia • 500 kW
13730 AUSTRIA
†R AUSTRIA INTL, Moosbrunn — Europe • 100 kW
— M-F • Europe • 100 kW
— Sa/Su • Europe • 100 kW
CANADA
†R CANADA INTL, Sackville, NB — W • S America • 250 kW
— W M-F • S America • 250 kW
— W Sa/Su • S America • 250 kW
†R CANADA INTL, Via Germany — S • C Africa & S Africa • 250 kW
13735 GERMANY
DEUTSCHE WELLE, Via Singapore — W • E Asia • 100 kW
UNITED KINGDOM
BBC, Via Thailand — S • E Asia • 250 kW
USA
R FREE ASIA, Via Saipan, N Marianas — S • SE Asia • 100 kW
R FREE ASIA, Via Tinian, N Marianas — S • SE Asia • 500 kW
VOA, Via São Tomé — W • C Africa & E Africa • 100 kW
13740 CHINA
†CHINA R INTL, Via Havana, Cuba — W North Am • 250 kW • ALT. FREQ. TO 17730 kHz
GERMANY
†DEUTSCHE WELLE, Nauen — S • E Europe & Mideast • 500 kW
IRAN
†VO THE ISLAMIC REP, Ahvāz — W Asia & C Asia • 250 kW
RUSSIA
(con'd) †VOICE OF RUSSIA, Yekaterinburg — S • Europe • 200 kW

| 0 | 1 | 2 | 3 | 4 | 5 | 6 | 7 | 8 | 9 | 10 | 11 | 12 | 13 | 14 | 15 | 16 | 17 | 18 | 19 | 20 | 21 | 22 | 23 | 24 |

SEASONAL ⑤ OR Ⓦ   1-HR TIMESHIFT MIDYEAR ⇦ OR ⇨   JAMMING / OR /\   EARLIEST HEARD ◁   LATEST HEARD ▷   NEW FOR 2005 †

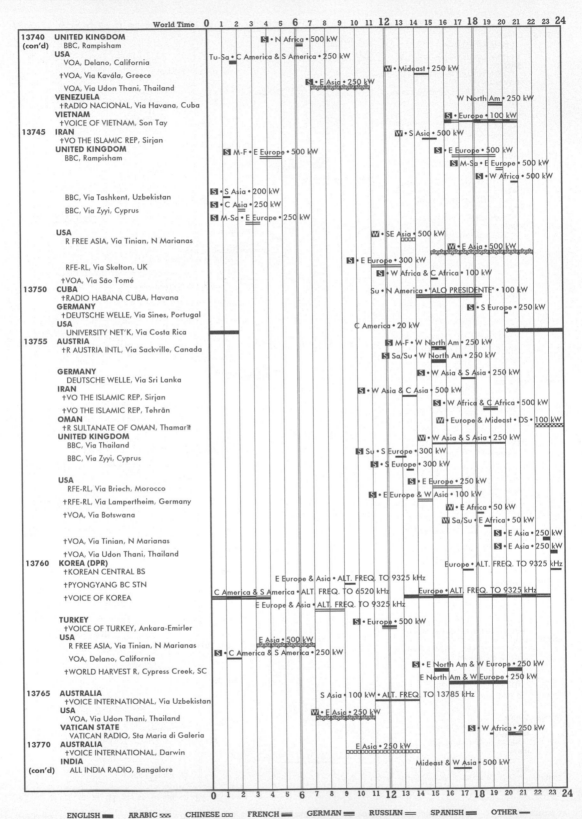

World Time 0 1 2 3 4 5 6 7 8 9 10 11 12 13 14 15 16 17 18 19 20 21 22 23 24

13740 **UNITED KINGDOM**
(con'd) BBC, Rampisham — Ⓢ • N Africa • 500 kW
USA
VOA, Delano, California — Tu-Sa • C America & S America • 250 kW
†VOA, Via Kavála, Greece — Ⓦ • Mideast • 250 kW
VOA, Via Udon Thani, Thailand — Ⓢ • E Asia • 250 kW
VENEZUELA
†RADIO NACIONAL, Via Havana, Cuba — W North Am • 250 kW
VIETNAM
†VOICE OF VIETNAM, Son Tay — Ⓢ • Europe • 100 kW
13745 **IRAN**
†VO THE ISLAMIC REP, Sirjan — Ⓦ • S Asia • 500 kW
UNITED KINGDOM
BBC, Rampisham — Ⓢ M-F • E Europe • 500 kW   Ⓢ • E Europe • 500 kW
Ⓢ M-Sa • E Europe • 500 kW
Ⓢ • W Africa • 500 kW
BBC, Via Tashkent, Uzbekistan — Ⓢ • S Asia • 200 kW
BBC, Via Zyyi, Cyprus — Ⓢ • C Asia • 250 kW
Ⓢ M-Sa • E Europe • 250 kW
USA
R FREE ASIA, Via Tinian, N Marianas — Ⓦ • SE Asia • 500 kW
Ⓦ • E Asia • 500 kW
RFE-RL, Via Skelton, UK — Ⓢ • E Europe • 300 kW
†VOA, Via São Tomé — Ⓢ • W Africa & C Africa • 100 kW
13750 **CUBA**
†RADIO HABANA CUBA, Havana — Su • N America • "ALO PRESIDENTE" • 100 kW
GERMANY
†DEUTSCHE WELLE, Via Sines, Portugal — Ⓢ • S Europe • 250 kW
USA
UNIVERSITY NET'K, Via Costa Rica — C America • 20 kW
13755 **AUSTRIA**
†R AUSTRIA INTL, Via Sackville, Canada — Ⓢ M-F • W North Am • 250 kW
Ⓢ Sa/Su • W North Am • 250 kW
GERMANY
DEUTSCHE WELLE, Via Sri Lanka — Ⓦ • W Asia & S Asia • 250 kW
IRAN
†VO THE ISLAMIC REP, Sirjan — Ⓢ • W Asia & C Asia • 500 kW
†VO THE ISLAMIC REP, Tehrān — Ⓦ • W Africa & C Africa • 500 kW
OMAN
†R SULTANATE OF OMAN, Thamarīt — Ⓦ • Europe & Mideast • DS • 100 kW
UNITED KINGDOM
BBC, Via Thailand — Ⓦ • W Asia & S Asia • 250 kW
BBC, Via Zyyi, Cyprus — Ⓢ Su • S Europe • 300 kW
Ⓢ • S Europe • 300 kW
USA
RFE-RL, Via Briech, Morocco — Ⓢ • E Europe • 250 kW
†RFE-RL, Via Lampertheim, Germany — Ⓢ • E Europe & W Asia • 100 kW
†VOA, Via Botswana — Ⓦ • E Africa • 50 kW
Ⓦ Sa/Su • E Africa • 50 kW
†VOA, Via Tinian, N Marianas — Ⓢ • E Asia • 250 kW
†VOA, Via Udon Thani, Thailand — Ⓢ • E Asia • 250 kW
13760 **KOREA (DPR)**
†KOREAN CENTRAL BS — Europe • ALT. FREQ. TO 9325 kHz
†PYONGYANG BC STN — E Europe & Asia • ALT. FREQ. TO 9325 kHz
C America & S America • ALT. FREQ. TO 6520 kHz   Europe • ALT. FREQ. TO 9325 kHz
†VOICE OF KOREA — E Europe & Asia • ALT. FREQ. TO 9325 kHz
TURKEY
†VOICE OF TURKEY, Ankara-Emirler — Ⓢ • Europe • 500 kW
USA
R FREE ASIA, Via Tinian, N Marianas — E Asia • 500 kW
VOA, Delano, California — Ⓢ • C America & S America • 250 kW
†WORLD HARVEST R, Cypress Creek, SC — Ⓢ • E North Am & W Europe • 250 kW
E North Am & W Europe • 250 kW
13765 **AUSTRALIA**
†VOICE INTERNATIONAL, Via Uzbekistan — S Asia • 100 kW • ALT. FREQ. TO 13785 kHz
USA
VOA, Via Udon Thani, Thailand — Ⓦ • E Asia • 250 kW
VATICAN STATE
VATICAN RADIO, Sta Maria di Galeria — Ⓢ • W Africa • 250 kW
13770 **AUSTRALIA**
†VOICE INTERNATIONAL, Darwin — E Asia • 250 kW
INDIA
(con'd) ALL INDIA RADIO, Bangalore — Mideast & W Asia • 500 kW

0 1 2 3 4 5 6 7 8 9 10 11 12 13 14 15 16 17 18 19 20 21 22 23 24

ENGLISH ▬   ARABIC ▨   CHINESE ▫▫▫   FRENCH ▬   GERMAN ▬   RUSSIAN ▬   SPANISH ▬   OTHER ▬

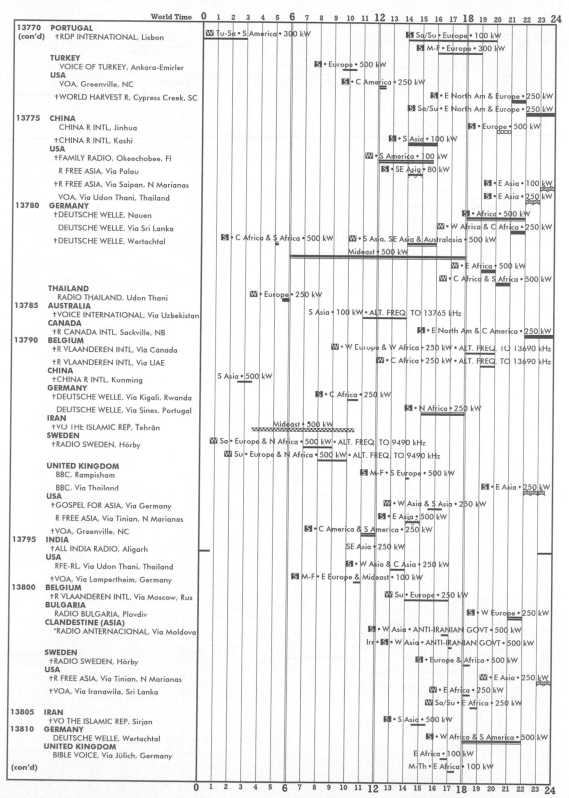

	World Time	0 1 2 3 4 5 6 7 8 9 10 11 12 13 14 15 16 17 18 19 20 21 22 23 24

13770 PORTUGAL
(con'd) †RDP INTERNATIONAL, Lisbon
- W • Tu-Sa • S America • 300 kW
- S • Sa/Su • Europe • 100 kW
- S • M-F • Europe • 300 kW

TURKEY
VOICE OF TURKEY, Ankara-Emirler
- S • Europe • 500 kW

USA
VOA, Greenville, NC
- S • C America • 250 kW

†WORLD HARVEST R, Cypress Creek, SC
- S • E North Am & Europe • 250 kW
- S • Sa/Su • E North Am & Europe • 250 kW

13775 CHINA
CHINA R INTL, Jinhua
- S • Europe • 500 kW

†CHINA R INTL, Kashi
- S • S Asia • 100 kW

USA
†FAMILY RADIO, Okeechobee, Fl
- W • S America • 100 kW

R FREE ASIA, Via Palau
- S • SE Asia • 80 kW

†R FREE ASIA, Via Saipan, N Marianas
- S • E Asia • 100 kW
- S • E Asia • 250 kW

VOA, Via Udon Thani, Thailand

13780 GERMANY
†DEUTSCHE WELLE, Nauen
- S • Africa • 500 kW

DEUTSCHE WELLE, Via Sri Lanka
- W • W Africa & C Africa • 250 kW

†DEUTSCHE WELLE, Wertachtal
- S • C Africa & S Africa • 500 kW
- W • S Asia, SE Asia & Australasia • 500 kW
- Mideast • 500 kW
- W • E Africa • 500 kW
- W • C Africa & S Africa • 500 kW

THAILAND
RADIO THAILAND, Udon Thani
- W • Europe • 250 kW

13785 AUSTRALIA
†VOICE INTERNATIONAL, Via Uzbekistan
- S Asia • 100 kW • ALT. FREQ. TO 13765 kHz

CANADA
†R CANADA INTL, Sackville, NB
- S • E North Am & C America • 250 kW

13790 BELGIUM
†R VLAANDEREN INTL, Via Canada
- W • W Europe & W Africa • 250 kW • ALT. FREQ. TO 13690 kHz

†R VLAANDEREN INTL, Via UAE
- W • C Africa • 250 kW • ALT. FREQ. TO 13690 kHz

CHINA
†CHINA R INTL, Kunming
- S Asia • 500 kW

GERMANY
†DEUTSCHE WELLE, Via Kigali, Rwanda
- S • C Africa • 250 kW

DEUTSCHE WELLE, Via Sines, Portugal
- S • N Africa • 250 kW

IRAN
†VO THE ISLAMIC REP, Tehrān
- Mideast • 500 kW

SWEDEN
†RADIO SWEDEN, Hörby
- W • Sa • Europe & N Africa • 500 kW • ALT. FREQ. TO 9490 kHz
- W • Su • Europe & N Africa • 500 kW • ALT. FREQ. TO 9490 kHz

UNITED KINGDOM
BBC, Rampisham
- S • M-F • S Europe • 500 kW

BBC, Via Thailand
- S • E Asia • 250 kW

USA
†GOSPEL FOR ASIA, Via Germany
- W • W Asia & S Asia • 250 kW

R FREE ASIA, Via Tinian, N Marianas
- S • E Asia • 500 kW

†VOA, Greenville, NC
- S • C America & S America • 250 kW

13795 INDIA
†ALL INDIA RADIO, Aligarh
- SE Asia • 250 kW

USA
RFE-RL, Via Udon Thani, Thailand
- S • W Asia & C Asia • 250 kW

†VOA, Via Lampertheim, Germany
- S • M-F • E Europe & Mideast • 100 kW

13800 BELGIUM
†R VLAANDEREN INTL, Via Moscow, Rus
- W • Su • Europe • 250 kW

BULGARIA
RADIO BULGARIA, Plovdiv
- S • W Europe • 250 kW

CLANDESTINE (ASIA)
"RADIO ANTERNACIONAL, Via Moldova
- S • W Asia • ANTI-IRANIAN GOVT • 500 kW
- Irr • S • W Asia • ANTI-IRANIAN GOVT • 500 kW

SWEDEN
†RADIO SWEDEN, Hörby
- S • Europe & Africa • 500 kW

USA
†R FREE ASIA, Via Tinian, N Marianas
- S • E Asia • 250 kW

†VOA, Via Iranawila, Sri Lanka
- W • E Africa • 250 kW
- W • Sa/Su • E Africa • 250 kW

13805 IRAN
†VO THE ISLAMIC REP, Sirjan
- S • S Asia • 500 kW

13810 GERMANY
DEUTSCHE WELLE, Wertachtal
- S • W Africa & S America • 500 kW

UNITED KINGDOM
BIBLE VOICE, Via Jülich, Germany
- E Africa • 100 kW
- M-Th • E Africa • 100 kW

(con'd)

	0 1 2 3 4 5 6 7 8 9 10 11 12 13 14 15 16 17 18 19 20 21 22 23 24

SEASONAL S OR W   1-HR TIMESHIFT MIDYEAR ⊡ OR ⊟   JAMMING / OR ∧   EARLIEST HEARD ◁   LATEST HEARD ▷   NEW FOR 2005 †

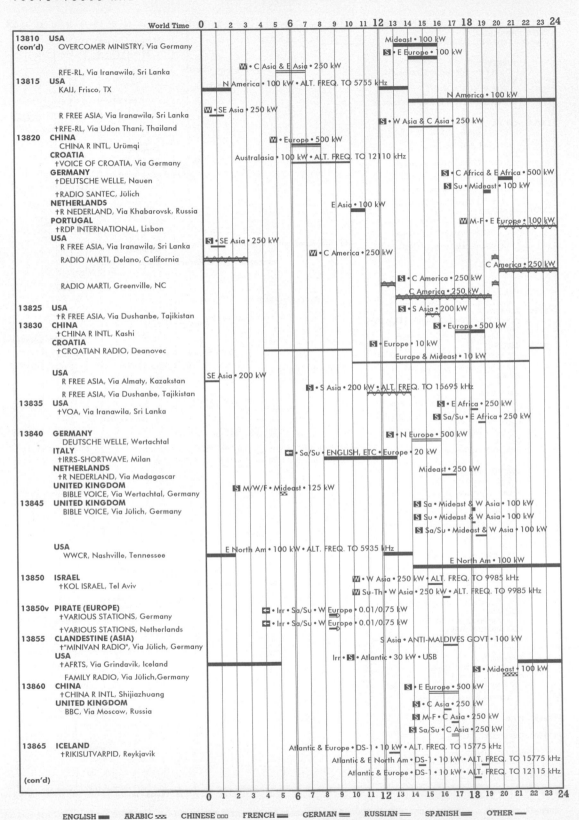

| | | World Time | 0 | 1 | 2 | 3 | 4 | 5 | 6 | 7 | 8 | 9 | 10 | 11 | 12 | 13 | 14 | 15 | 16 | 17 | 18 | 19 | 20 | 21 | 22 | 23 | 24 |

13810 USA
(con'd) OVERCOMER MINISTRY, Via Germany — Mideast • 100 kW
S • E Europe • 100 kW
W • C Asia & E Asia • 250 kW
RFE-RL, Via Iranawila, Sri Lanka

13815 USA
KAIJ, Frisco, TX — N America • 100 kW • ALT. FREQ. TO 5755 kHz
N America • 100 kW

R FREE ASIA, Via Iranawila, Sri Lanka — W • SE Asia • 250 kW
S • W Asia & C Asia • 250 kW
†RFE-RL, Via Udon Thani, Thailand

13820 CHINA
CHINA R INTL, Urümqi — W • Europe • 500 kW
CROATIA
†VOICE OF CROATIA, Via Germany — Australasia • 100 kW • ALT. FREQ. TO 12110 kHz
GERMANY
†DEUTSCHE WELLE, Nauen — S • C Africa & E Africa • 500 kW
†RADIO SANTEC, Jülich — S • Su • Mideast • 100 kW
NETHERLANDS
†R NEDERLAND, Via Khabarovsk, Russia — E Asia • 100 kW
PORTUGAL
†RDP INTERNATIONAL, Lisbon — W M-F • E Europe • 100 kW
USA
R FREE ASIA, Via Iranawila, Sri Lanka — S • SE Asia • 250 kW
RADIO MARTI, Delano, California — W • C America • 250 kW
C America • 250 kW
RADIO MARTI, Greenville, NC — S • C America • 250 kW
C America • 250 kW

13825 USA
†R FREE ASIA, Via Dushanbe, Tajikistan — S • S Asia • 200 kW
13830 CHINA
†CHINA R INTL, Kashi — S • Europe • 500 kW
CROATIA
†CROATIAN RADIO, Deanovec — S • Europe • 10 kW
Europe & Mideast • 10 kW

USA
R FREE ASIA, Via Almaty, Kazakstan — SE Asia • 200 kW
R FREE ASIA, Via Dushanbe, Tajikistan — S • S Asia • 200 kW • ALT. FREQ. TO 15695 kHz
13835 USA
†VOA, Via Iranawila, Sri Lanka — S • E Africa • 250 kW
S Sa/Su • E Africa • 250 kW

13840 GERMANY
DEUTSCHE WELLE, Wertachtal — S • N Europe • 500 kW
ITALY
†IRRS-SHORTWAVE, Milan — Sa/Su • ENGLISH, ETC • Europe • 20 kW
NETHERLANDS
†R NEDERLAND, Via Madagascar — Mideast • 250 kW
UNITED KINGDOM
BIBLE VOICE, Via Wertachtal, Germany — S M/W/F • Mideast • 125 kW
13845 UNITED KINGDOM
BIBLE VOICE, Via Jülich, Germany — S Sa • Mideast & W Asia • 100 kW
S Su • Mideast & W Asia • 100 kW
S Sa/Su • Mideast & W Asia • 100 kW

USA
WWCR, Nashville, Tennessee — E North Am • 100 kW • ALT. FREQ. TO 5935 kHz
E North Am • 100 kW

13850 ISRAEL
†KOL ISRAEL, Tel Aviv — W • W Asia • 250 kW • ALT. FREQ. TO 9985 kHz
W Su-Th • W Asia • 250 kW • ALT. FREQ. TO 9985 kHz

13850v PIRATE (EUROPE)
†VARIOUS STATIONS, Germany — • Irr • Sa/Su • W Europe • 0.01/0.75 kW
†VARIOUS STATIONS, Netherlands — • Irr • Sa/Su • W Europe • 0.01/0.75 kW
13855 CLANDESTINE (ASIA)
†"MINIVAN RADIO", Via Jülich, Germany — S Asia • ANTI-MALDIVES GOVT • 100 kW
USA
†AFRTS, Via Grindavik, Iceland — Irr • S • Atlantic • 30 kW • USB
FAMILY RADIO, Via Jülich, Germany — S • Mideast • 100 kW
13860 CHINA
†CHINA R INTL, Shijiazhuang — S • E Europe • 500 kW
UNITED KINGDOM
BBC, Via Moscow, Russia — S • C Asia • 250 kW
S M-F • C Asia • 250 kW
S Sa/Su • C Asia • 250 kW

13865 ICELAND
†RIKISUTVARPID, Reykjavik — Atlantic & Europe • DS-1 • 10 kW • ALT. FREQ. TO 15775 kHz
Atlantic & E North Am • DS-1 • 10 kW • ALT. FREQ. TO 15775 kHz
Atlantic & Europe • DS-1 • 10 kW • ALT. FREQ. TO 12115 kHz

(con'd)

| | World Time | 0 | 1 | 2 | 3 | 4 | 5 | 6 | 7 | 8 | 9 | 10 | 11 | 12 | 13 | 14 | 15 | 16 | 17 | 18 | 19 | 20 | 21 | 22 | 23 | 24 |

ENGLISH ▬　ARABIC ▨　CHINESE ▥　FRENCH ▬　GERMAN ▬　RUSSIAN ▬　SPANISH ▬　OTHER ▬

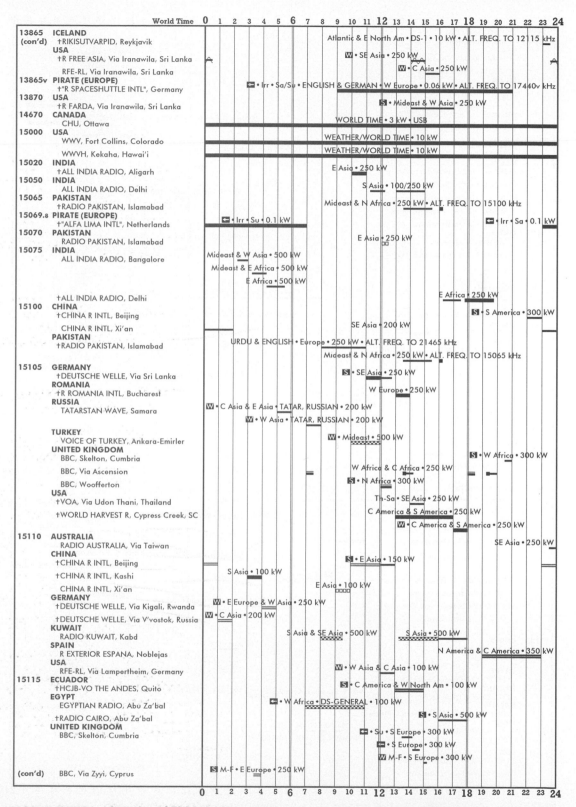

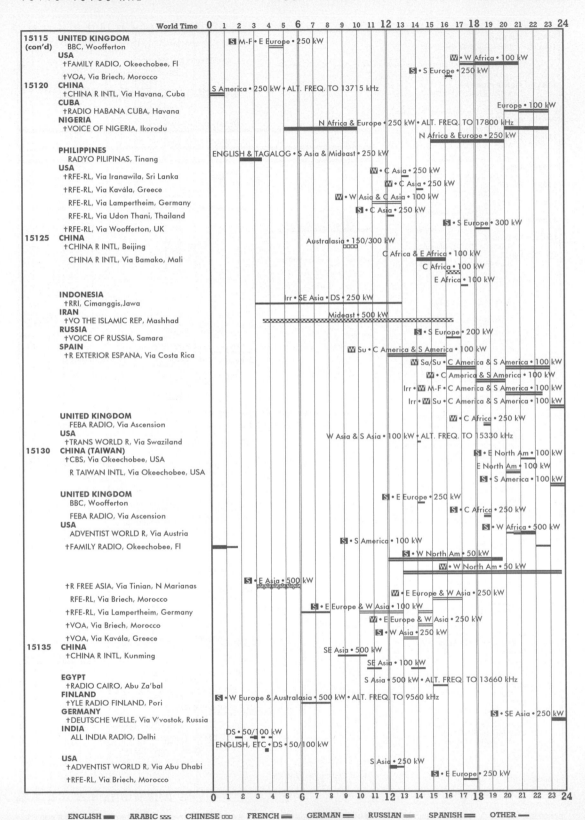

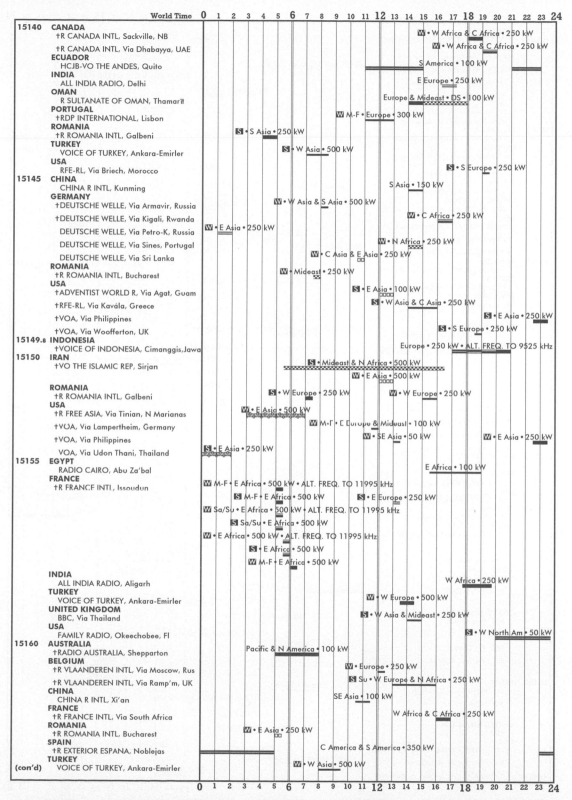

	World Time	0 1 2 3 4 5 6 7 8 9 10 11 12 13 14 15 16 17 18 19 20 21 22 23 24
15140	**CANADA**	
	†R CANADA INTL, Sackville, NB	W • W Africa & C Africa • 250 kW
	†R CANADA INTL, Via Dhabayya, UAE	W • W Africa & C Africa • 250 kW
	ECUADOR	
	HCJB-VO THE ANDES, Quito	S America • 100 kW
	INDIA	
	ALL INDIA RADIO, Delhi	E Europe • 250 kW
	OMAN	
	R SULTANATE OF OMAN, Thamarīt	Europe & Mideast • DS • 100 kW
	PORTUGAL	
	†RDP INTERNATIONAL, Lisbon	W M-F • Europe • 300 kW
	ROMANIA	
	†R ROMANIA INTL, Galbeni	S • S Asia • 250 kW
	TURKEY	
	VOICE OF TURKEY, Ankara-Emirler	S • W Asia • 500 kW
	USA	
	RFE-RL, Via Briech, Morocco	S • S Europe • 250 kW
15145	**CHINA**	
	CHINA R INTL, Kunming	S Asia • 150 kW
	GERMANY	
	†DEUTSCHE WELLE, Via Armavir, Russia	W • W Asia & S Asia • 500 kW
	†DEUTSCHE WELLE, Via Kigali, Rwanda	W • C Africa • 250 kW
	DEUTSCHE WELLE, Via Petro-K, Russia	W • E Asia • 250 kW
	DEUTSCHE WELLE, Via Sines, Portugal	W • N Africa • 250 kW
	DEUTSCHE WELLE, Via Sri Lanka	W • C Asia & E Asia • 250 kW
	ROMANIA	
	†R ROMANIA INTL, Bucharest	W • Mideast • 250 kW
	USA	
	†ADVENTIST WORLD R, Via Agat, Guam	S • E Asia • 100 kW
	†RFE-RL, Via Kavála, Greece	S • W Asia & C Asia • 250 kW
	†VOA, Via Philippines	S • E Asia • 250 kW
	†VOA, Via Woofferton, UK	S • S Europe • 250 kW
15149.8	**INDONESIA**	
	†VOICE OF INDONESIA, Cimanggis,Jawa	Europe • 250 kW • ALT. FREQ. TO 9525 kHz
15150	**IRAN**	
	†VO THE ISLAMIC REP, Sirjan	S • Mideast & N Africa • 500 kW
		W • E Asia • 500 kW
	ROMANIA	
	†R ROMANIA INTL, Galbeni	S • W Europe • 250 kW W • W Europe • 250 kW
	USA	
	†R FREE ASIA, Via Tinian, N Marianas	W • E Asia • 500 kW
	†VOA, Via Lampertheim, Germany	W M-F • C Europe & Mideast • 100 kW
	†VOA, Via Philippines	W • SE Asia • 50 kW W • E Asia • 250 kW
	VOA, Via Udon Thani, Thailand	S • E Asia • 250 kW
15155	**EGYPT**	
	RADIO CAIRO, Abu Za'bal	E Africa • 100 kW
	FRANCE	
	†R FRANCE INTL, Issoudun	W M-F • E Africa • 500 kW • ALT. FREQ. TO 11995 kHz
		S M-F • E Africa • 500 kW S • E Europe • 250 kW
		W Sa/Su • E Africa • 500 kW • ALT. FREQ. TO 11995 kHz
		S Sa/Su • E Africa • 500 kW
		W • E Africa • 500 kW • ALT. FREQ. TO 11995 kHz
		S • E Africa • 500 kW
		W M-F • E Africa • 500 kW
	INDIA	
	ALL INDIA RADIO, Aligarh	W Africa • 250 kW
	TURKEY	
	VOICE OF TURKEY, Ankara-Emirler	W • W Europe • 500 kW
	UNITED KINGDOM	
	BBC, Via Thailand	S • W Asia & Mideast • 250 kW
	USA	
	FAMILY RADIO, Okeechobee, Fl	S • W North Am • 50 kW
15160	**AUSTRALIA**	
	†RADIO AUSTRALIA, Shepparton	Pacific & N America • 100 kW
	BELGIUM	
	†R VLAANDEREN INTL, Via Moscow, Rus	W • Europe • 250 kW
	†R VLAANDEREN INTL, Via Ramp'm, UK	S Su • W Europe & N Africa • 250 kW
	CHINA	
	CHINA R INTL, Xi'an	SE Asia • 100 kW
	FRANCE	
	†R FRANCE INTL, Via South Africa	W Africa & C Africa • 250 kW
	ROMANIA	
	†R ROMANIA INTL, Bucharest	W • E Asia • 250 kW
	SPAIN	
	†R EXTERIOR ESPANA, Noblejas	C America & S America • 350 kW
	TURKEY	
(con'd)	VOICE OF TURKEY, Ankara-Emirler	W • W Asia • 500 kW

	0 1 2 3 4 5 6 7 8 9 10 11 12 13 14 15 16 17 18 19 20 21 22 23 24

SEASONAL S OR W   1-HR TIMESHIFT MIDYEAR ⇦ OR ⇨   JAMMING / OR ∧   EARLIEST HEARD ◁   LATEST HEARD ▷   NEW FOR 2005 †

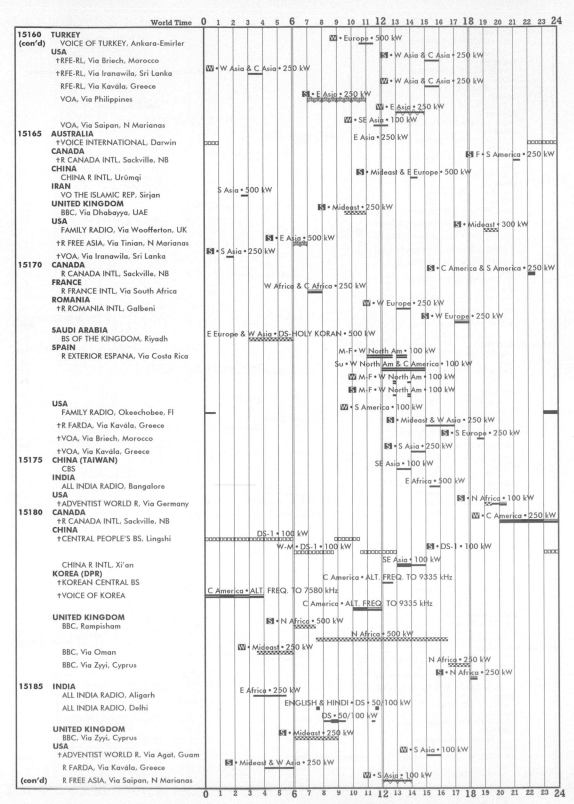

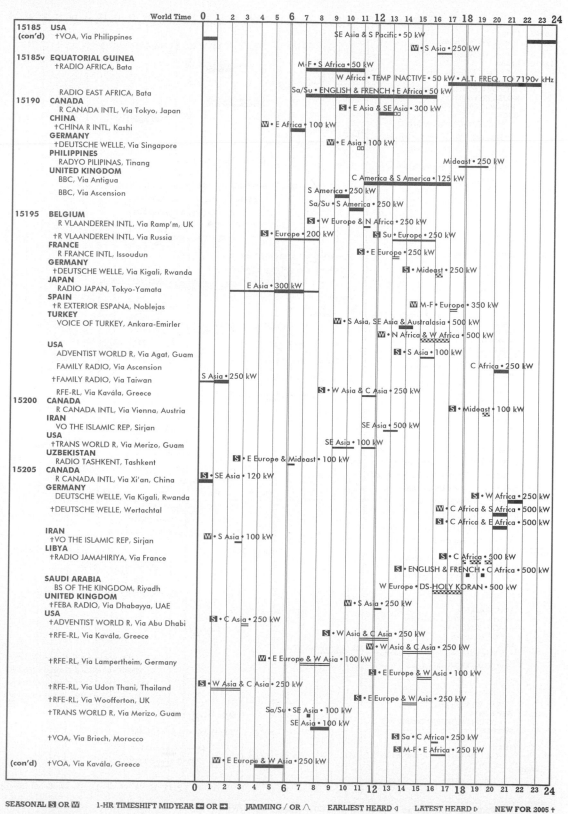

	World Time	0 1 2 3 4 5 6 7 8 9 10 11 12 13 14 15 16 17 18 19 20 21 22 23 24
15185 (con'd)	USA †VOA, Via Philippines	SE Asia & S Pacific • 50 kW — W • S Asia • 250 kW
15185v	EQUATORIAL GUINEA †RADIO AFRICA, Bata	M-F • S Africa • 50 kW — W Africa • TEMP INACTIVE • 50 kW • ALT. FREQ. TO 7190v kHz
	RADIO EAST AFRICA, Bata	Sa/Su • ENGLISH & FRENCH • E Africa • 50 kW
15190	CANADA R CANADA INTL, Via Tokyo, Japan	S • E Asia & SE Asia • 300 kW
	CHINA †CHINA R INTL, Kashi	W • E Africa • 100 kW
	GERMANY †DEUTSCHE WELLE, Via Singapore	W • E Asia • 100 kW
	PHILIPPINES RADYO PILIPINAS, Tinang	Mideast • 250 kW
	UNITED KINGDOM BBC, Via Antigua	C America & S America • 125 kW
	BBC, Via Ascension	S America • 250 kW — Sa/Su • S America • 250 kW
15195	BELGIUM R VLAANDEREN INTL, Via Ramp'm, UK	S • W Europe & N Africa • 250 kW
	†R VLAANDEREN INTL, Via Russia	S • Europe • 200 kW — S • Su • Europe • 250 kW
	FRANCE R FRANCE INTL, Issoudun	S • E Europe • 250 kW
	GERMANY †DEUTSCHE WELLE, Via Kigali, Rwanda	S • Mideast • 250 kW
	JAPAN RADIO JAPAN, Tokyo-Yamata	E Asia • 300 kW
	SPAIN †R EXTERIOR ESPANA, Noblejas	W • M-F • Europe • 350 kW
	TURKEY VOICE OF TURKEY, Ankara-Emirler	W • S Asia, SE Asia & Australasia • 500 kW — W • N Africa & W Africa • 500 kW
	USA ADVENTIST WORLD R, Via Agat, Guam	S • S Asia • 100 kW
	FAMILY RADIO, Via Ascension	C Africa • 250 kW
	†FAMILY RADIO, Via Taiwan	S Asia • 250 kW
	RFE-RL, Via Kavála, Greece	S • W Asia & C Asia • 250 kW
15200	CANADA R CANADA INTL, Via Vienna, Austria	S • Mideast • 100 kW
	IRAN VO THE ISLAMIC REP, Sirjan	SE Asia • 500 kW
	USA †TRANS WORLD R, Via Merizo, Guam	SE Asia • 100 kW
	UZBEKISTAN RADIO TASHKENT, Tashkent	S • E Europe & Mideast • 100 kW
15205	CANADA R CANADA INTL, Via Xi'an, China	S • SE Asia • 120 kW
	GERMANY DEUTSCHE WELLE, Via Kigali, Rwanda	S • W Africa • 250 kW
	†DEUTSCHE WELLE, Wertachtal	W • C Africa & S Africa • 500 kW — S • C Africa & E Africa • 500 kW
	IRAN †VO THE ISLAMIC REP, Sirjan	W • S Asia • 100 kW
	LIBYA †RADIO JAMAHIRIYA, Via France	S • C Africa • 500 kW — S • ENGLISH & FRENCH • C Africa • 500 kW
	SAUDI ARABIA BS OF THE KINGDOM, Riyadh	W Europe • DS-HOLY KORAN • 500 kW
	UNITED KINGDOM †FEBA RADIO, Via Dhabayya, UAE	W • S Asia • 250 kW
	USA †ADVENTIST WORLD R, Via Abu Dhabi	S • C Asia • 250 kW
	†RFE-RL, Via Kavála, Greece	S • W Asia & C Asia • 250 kW — W • W Asia & C Asia • 250 kW
	†RFE-RL, Via Lampertheim, Germany	W • E Europe & W Asia • 100 kW — S • E Europe & W Asia • 100 kW
	†RFE-RL, Via Udon Thani, Thailand	S • W Asia & C Asia • 250 kW
	†RFE-RL, Via Woofferton, UK	S • E Europe & W Asia • 250 kW
	†TRANS WORLD R, Via Merizo, Guam	Sa/Su • SE Asia • 100 kW — SE Asia • 100 kW
	†VOA, Via Briech, Morocco	S Sa • C Africa • 250 kW — S M-F • E Africa • 250 kW
(con'd)	†VOA, Via Kavála, Greece	W • E Europe & W Asia • 250 kW

World Time 0 1 2 3 4 5 6 7 8 9 10 11 12 13 14 15 16 17 18 19 20 21 22 23 24

SEASONAL S OR W   1-HR TIMESHIFT MIDYEAR ⬅ OR ➡   JAMMING / OR /\   EARLIEST HEARD ◁   LATEST HEARD ▷   NEW FOR 2005 †

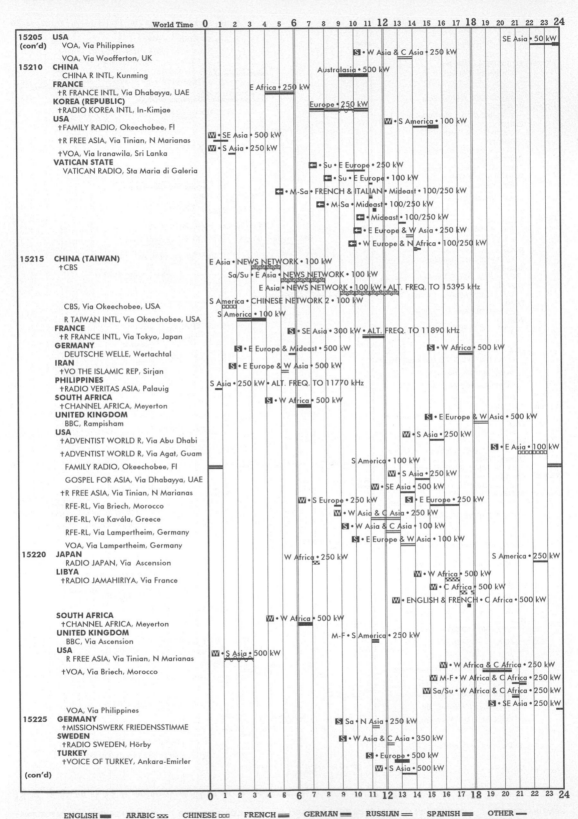

| World Time | 0 | 1 | 2 | 3 | 4 | 5 | 6 | 7 | 8 | 9 | 10 | 11 | 12 | 13 | 14 | 15 | 16 | 17 | 18 | 19 | 20 | 21 | 22 | 23 | 24 |

15205 USA
(con'd)   VOA, Via Philippines — SE Asia • 50 kW
      VOA, Via Woofferton, UK — S • W Asia & C Asia • 250 kW

15210 CHINA
    CHINA R INTL, Kunming — Australasia • 500 kW
  FRANCE
    †R FRANCE INTL, Via Dhabayya, UAE — E Africa • 250 kW
  KOREA (REPUBLIC)
    †RADIO KOREA INTL, In-Kimjae — Europe • 250 kW
  USA
    †FAMILY RADIO, Okeechobee, Fl — W • S America • 100 kW
    †R FREE ASIA, Via Tinian, N Marianas — W • SE Asia • 500 kW
    †VOA, Via Iranawila, Sri Lanka — W • S Asia • 250 kW
  VATICAN STATE
    VATICAN RADIO, Sta Maria di Galeria — • Su • E Europe • 250 kW / • Su • E Europe • 100 kW / • M-Sa • FRENCH & ITALIAN • Mideast • 100/250 kW / • M-Sa • Mideast • 100/250 kW / • Mideast • 100/250 kW / • E Europe & W Asia • 250 kW / • W Europe & N Africa • 100/250 kW

15215 CHINA (TAIWAN)
    †CBS — E Asia • NEWS NETWORK • 100 kW / Sa/Su • E Asia • NEWS NETWORK • 100 kW / E Asia • NEWS NETWORK • 100 kW • ALT. FREQ. TO 15395 kHz
    CBS, Via Okeechobee, USA — S America • CHINESE NETWORK 2 • 100 kW
    R TAIWAN INTL, Via Okeechobee, USA — S America • 100 kW
  FRANCE
    †R FRANCE INTL, Via Tokyo, Japan — S • SE Asia • 300 kW • ALT. FREQ. TO 11890 kHz
  GERMANY
    DEUTSCHE WELLE, Wertachtal — S • E Europe & Mideast • 500 kW / S • W Africa • 500 kW
  IRAN
    †VO THE ISLAMIC REP, Sirjan — S • E Europe & W Asia • 500 kW
  PHILIPPINES
    †RADIO VERITAS ASIA, Palauig — S Asia • 250 kW • ALT. FREQ. TO 11770 kHz
  SOUTH AFRICA
    †CHANNEL AFRICA, Meyerton — S • W Africa • 500 kW
  UNITED KINGDOM
    BBC, Rampisham — S • E Europe & W Asia • 500 kW
  USA
    †ADVENTIST WORLD R, Via Abu Dhabi — W • S Asia • 250 kW
    †ADVENTIST WORLD R, Via Agat, Guam — S • E Asia • 100 kW
    FAMILY RADIO, Okeechobee, Fl — S America • 100 kW
    GOSPEL FOR ASIA, Via Dhabayya, UAE — W • S Asia • 250 kW
    †R FREE ASIA, Via Tinian, N Marianas — W • SE Asia • 500 kW
    RFE-RL, Via Briech, Morocco — W • S Europe • 250 kW / S • E Europe • 250 kW
    RFE-RL, Via Kavála, Greece — W • W Asia & C Asia • 250 kW
    RFE-RL, Via Lampertheim, Germany — S • W Asia & C Asia • 100 kW
    VOA, Via Lampertheim, Germany — S • E Europe & W Asia • 100 kW

15220 JAPAN
    RADIO JAPAN, Via Ascension — W Africa • 250 kW / S America • 250 kW
  LIBYA
    †RADIO JAMAHIRIYA, Via France — W • W Africa • 500 kW / W • C Africa • 500 kW / W • ENGLISH & FRENCH • C Africa • 500 kW
  SOUTH AFRICA
    †CHANNEL AFRICA, Meyerton — W • W Africa • 500 kW
  UNITED KINGDOM
    BBC, Via Ascension — M-F • S America • 250 kW
  USA
    R FREE ASIA, Via Tinian, N Marianas — W • S Asia • 500 kW
    †VOA, Via Briech, Morocco — W • W Africa & C Africa • 250 kW / W M-F • W Africa & C Africa • 250 kW / W Sa/Su • W Africa & C Africa • 250 kW / S • SE Asia • 250 kW
    VOA, Via Philippines

15225 GERMANY
    †MISSIONSWERK FRIEDENSSTIMME — S Sa • N Asia • 250 kW
  SWEDEN
    †RADIO SWEDEN, Hörby — S • W Asia & C Asia • 350 kW
  TURKEY
    †VOICE OF TURKEY, Ankara-Emirler — S • Europe • 500 kW / W • S Asia • 500 kW

(con'd)

| 0 | 1 | 2 | 3 | 4 | 5 | 6 | 7 | 8 | 9 | 10 | 11 | 12 | 13 | 14 | 15 | 16 | 17 | 18 | 19 | 20 | 21 | 22 | 23 | 24 |

ENGLISH ▬ ARABIC ▨ CHINESE ▢▢ FRENCH ▬ GERMAN ▬ RUSSIAN ▭ SPANISH ▬ OTHER ▬

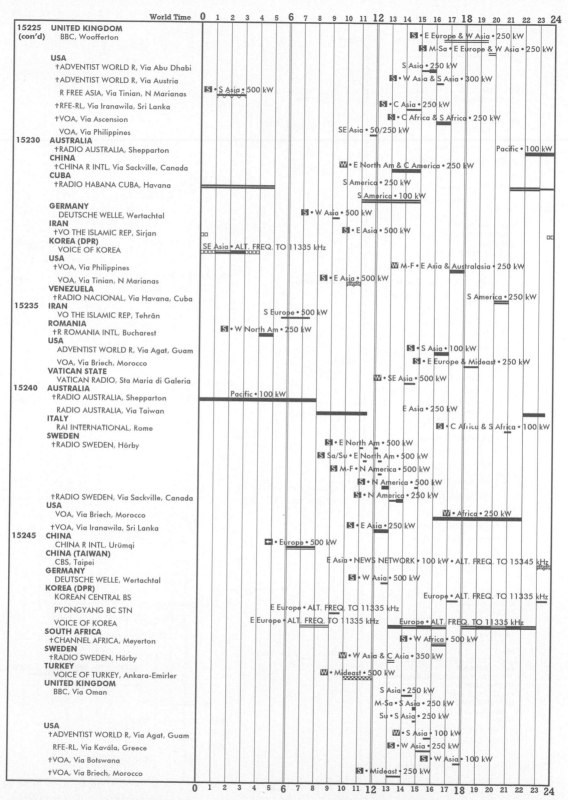

15225	UNITED KINGDOM
(con'd)	BBC, Woofferton
	USA
	†ADVENTIST WORLD R, Via Abu Dhabi
	†ADVENTIST WORLD R, Via Austria
	R FREE ASIA, Via Tinian, N Marianas
	†RFE-RL, Via Iranawila, Sri Lanka
	†VOA, Via Ascension
	VOA, Via Philippines
15230	AUSTRALIA
	†RADIO AUSTRALIA, Shepparton
	CHINA
	†CHINA R INTL, Via Sackville, Canada
	CUBA
	†RADIO HABANA CUBA, Havana
	GERMANY
	DEUTSCHE WELLE, Wertachtal
	IRAN
	†VO THE ISLAMIC REP, Sirjan
	KOREA (DPR)
	VOICE OF KOREA
	USA
	†VOA, Via Philippines
	VOA, Via Tinian, N Marianas
	VENEZUELA
	†RADIO NACIONAL, Via Havana, Cuba
15235	IRAN
	VO THE ISLAMIC REP, Tehrān
	ROMANIA
	†R ROMANIA INTL, Bucharest
	USA
	ADVENTIST WORLD R, Via Agat, Guam
	VOA, Via Briech, Morocco
	VATICAN STATE
	VATICAN RADIO, Sta Maria di Galeria
15240	AUSTRALIA
	†RADIO AUSTRALIA, Shepparton
	RADIO AUSTRALIA, Via Taiwan
	ITALY
	RAI INTERNATIONAL, Rome
	SWEDEN
	†RADIO SWEDEN, Hörby
	†RADIO SWEDEN, Via Sackville, Canada
	USA
	VOA, Via Briech, Morocco
	†VOA, Via Iranawila, Sri Lanka
15245	CHINA
	CHINA R INTL, Urümqi
	CHINA (TAIWAN)
	CBS, Taipei
	GERMANY
	DEUTSCHE WELLE, Wertachtal
	KOREA (DPR)
	KOREAN CENTRAL BS
	PYONGYANG BC STN
	VOICE OF KOREA
	SOUTH AFRICA
	†CHANNEL AFRICA, Meyerton
	SWEDEN
	†RADIO SWEDEN, Hörby
	TURKEY
	VOICE OF TURKEY, Ankara-Emirler
	UNITED KINGDOM
	BBC, Via Oman
	USA
	†ADVENTIST WORLD R, Via Agat, Guam
	RFE-RL, Via Kavála, Greece
	†VOA, Via Botswana
	†VOA, Via Briech, Morocco

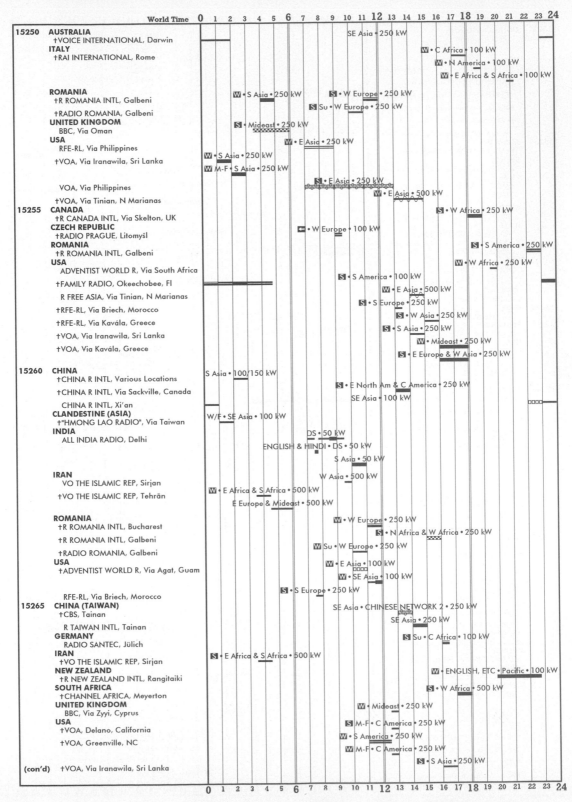

World Time 0 1 2 3 4 5 6 7 8 9 10 11 12 13 14 15 16 17 18 19 20 21 22 23 24

15250
AUSTRALIA
  †VOICE INTERNATIONAL, Darwin — SE Asia • 250 kW
ITALY
  †RAI INTERNATIONAL, Rome — W • C Africa • 100 kW / W • N America • 100 kW / W • E Africa & S Africa • 100 kW
ROMANIA
  †R ROMANIA INTL, Galbeni — W • S Asia • 250 kW / W • W Europe • 250 kW
  †RADIO ROMANIA, Galbeni — S Su • W Europe • 250 kW
UNITED KINGDOM
  BBC, Via Oman — S • Mideast • 250 kW
USA
  RFE-RL, Via Philippines — W • E Asia • 250 kW
  †VOA, Via Iranawila, Sri Lanka — W • S Asia • 250 kW / W M-F • S Asia • 250 kW
  VOA, Via Philippines — S • E Asia • 250 kW
  †VOA, Via Tinian, N Marianas — W • E Asia • 500 kW

15255 CANADA
  †R CANADA INTL, Via Skelton, UK — S • W Africa • 250 kW
CZECH REPUBLIC
  †RADIO PRAGUE, Litomyšl — W Europe • 100 kW
ROMANIA
  †R ROMANIA INTL, Galbeni — S • S America • 250 kW
USA
  ADVENTIST WORLD R, Via South Africa — W • W Africa • 250 kW
  †FAMILY RADIO, Okeechobee, Fl — S • S America • 100 kW
  R FREE ASIA, Via Tinian, N Marianas — W • E Asia • 500 kW
  †RFE-RL, Via Briech, Morocco — S • S Europe • 250 kW
  †RFE-RL, Via Kavála, Greece — W • W Asia • 250 kW
  †VOA, Via Iranawila, Sri Lanka — S • S Asia • 250 kW
  †VOA, Via Kavála, Greece — W • Mideast • 250 kW / S • E Europe & W Asia • 250 kW

15260 CHINA
  †CHINA R INTL, Various Locations — S Asia • 100/150 kW
  †CHINA R INTL, Via Sackville, Canada — S • E North Am & C America • 250 kW
  CHINA R INTL, Xi'an — SE Asia • 100 kW
CLANDESTINE (ASIA)
  †"HMONG LAO RADIO", Via Taiwan — W/F • SE Asia • 100 kW
INDIA
  ALL INDIA RADIO, Delhi — DS • 50 kW / ENGLISH & HINDI • DS • 50 kW / S Asia • 50 kW
IRAN
  VO THE ISLAMIC REP, Sirjan — W Asia • 500 kW
  †VO THE ISLAMIC REP, Tehrān — W • E Africa & S Africa • 500 kW / E Europe & Mideast • 500 kW
ROMANIA
  †R ROMANIA INTL, Bucharest — W • W Europe • 250 kW
  †R ROMANIA INTL, Galbeni — S • N Africa & W Africa • 250 kW
  †RADIO ROMANIA, Galbeni — W Su • W Europe • 250 kW
USA
  †ADVENTIST WORLD R, Via Agat, Guam — W • E Asia • 100 kW / W • SE Asia • 100 kW
  RFE-RL, Via Briech, Morocco — S • S Europe • 250 kW

15265 CHINA (TAIWAN)
  †CBS, Tainan — SE Asia • CHINESE NETWORK 2 • 250 kW
  R TAIWAN INTL, Tainan — SE Asia • 250 kW
GERMANY
  RADIO SANTEC, Jülich — S Su • C Africa • 100 kW
IRAN
  †VO THE ISLAMIC REP, Sirjan — S • E Africa & S Africa • 500 kW
NEW ZEALAND
  †R NEW ZEALAND INTL, Rangitaiki — W • ENGLISH, ETC • Pacific • 100 kW
SOUTH AFRICA
  †CHANNEL AFRICA, Meyerton — S • W Africa • 500 kW
UNITED KINGDOM
  BBC, Via Zyyi, Cyprus — W • Mideast • 250 kW
USA
  †VOA, Delano, California — S M-F • C America • 250 kW / W • S America • 250 kW
  †VOA, Greenville, NC — W M-F • C America • 250 kW

(con'd) †VOA, Via Iranawila, Sri Lanka — S • S Asia • 250 kW

0 1 2 3 4 5 6 7 8 9 10 11 12 13 14 15 16 17 18 19 20 21 22 23 24

ENGLISH ■■   ARABIC ⋙   CHINESE ⬚⬚⬚   FRENCH ▬▬   GERMAN ▭▭   RUSSIAN ═══   SPANISH ▭▭   OTHER ──

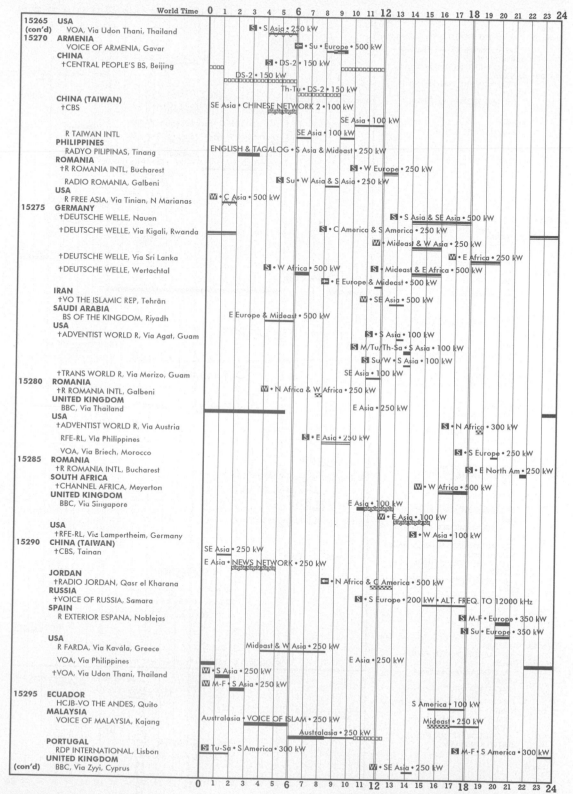

15265	**USA**	
(con'd)	VOA, Via Udon Thani, Thailand	S • S Asia • 250 kW
15270	**ARMENIA**	
	VOICE OF ARMENIA, Gavar	Su • Europe • 500 kW
	CHINA	
	†CENTRAL PEOPLE'S BS, Beijing	S • DS-2 • 150 kW
		DS-2 • 150 kW
		Th-Tu • DS-2 • 150 kW
	CHINA (TAIWAN)	
	†CBS	SE Asia • CHINESE NETWORK 2 • 100 kW
		SE Asia • 100 kW
	R TAIWAN INTL	SE Asia • 100 kW
	PHILIPPINES	
	RADYO PILIPINAS, Tinang	ENGLISH & TAGALOG • S Asia & Mideast • 250 kW
	ROMANIA	
	†R ROMANIA INTL, Bucharest	S • W Europe • 250 kW
	RADIO ROMANIA, Galbeni	S • Su • W Asia & S Asia • 250 kW
	USA	
	R FREE ASIA, Via Tinian, N Marianas	W • C Asia • 500 kW
15275	**GERMANY**	
	†DEUTSCHE WELLE, Nauen	S • S Asia & SE Asia • 500 kW
	†DEUTSCHE WELLE, Via Kigali, Rwanda	S • C America & S America • 250 kW
		W • Mideast & W Asia • 250 kW
	†DEUTSCHE WELLE, Via Sri Lanka	W • E Africa • 250 kW
	†DEUTSCHE WELLE, Wertachtal	S • W Africa • 500 kW / S • Mideast & E Africa • 500 kW
		• E Europe & Mideast • 500 kW
	IRAN	
	†VO THE ISLAMIC REP, Tehrän	W • SE Asia • 500 kW
	SAUDI ARABIA	
	BS OF THE KINGDOM, Riyadh	E Europe & Mideast • 500 kW
	USA	
	†ADVENTIST WORLD R, Via Agat, Guam	S • S Asia • 100 kW
		S • M/Tu/Th-Sa • S Asia • 100 kW
		S • Su/W • S Asia • 100 kW
	†TRANS WORLD R, Via Merizo, Guam	SE Asia • 100 kW
15280	**ROMANIA**	
	†R ROMANIA INTL, Galbeni	W • N Africa & W Africa • 250 kW
	UNITED KINGDOM	
	BBC, Via Thailand	E Asia • 250 kW
	USA	
	†ADVENTIST WORLD R, Via Austria	S • N Africa • 300 kW
	RFE-RL, Via Philippines	S • E Asia • 250 kW
	VOA, Via Briech, Morocco	S • S Europe • 250 kW
15285	**ROMANIA**	
	†R ROMANIA INTL, Bucharest	S • E North Am • 250 kW
	SOUTH AFRICA	
	†CHANNEL AFRICA, Meyerton	W • W Africa • 500 kW
	UNITED KINGDOM	
	BBC, Via Singapore	E Asia • 100 kW
		W • E Asia • 100 kW
	USA	
	†RFE-RL, Via Lampertheim, Germany	S • W Asia • 100 kW
15290	**CHINA (TAIWAN)**	
	†CBS, Tainan	SE Asia • 250 kW
		E Asia • NEWS NETWORK • 250 kW
	JORDAN	
	†RADIO JORDAN, Qasr el Kharana	• N Africa & C America • 500 kW
	RUSSIA	
	†VOICE OF RUSSIA, Samara	S • S Europe • 200 kW • ALT. FREQ. TO 12000 kHz
	SPAIN	
	R EXTERIOR ESPANA, Noblejas	S M-F • Europe • 350 kW
		S Su • Europe • 350 kW
	USA	
	R FARDA, Via Kavála, Greece	Mideast & W Asia • 250 kW
	VOA, Via Philippines	E Asia • 250 kW
	†VOA, Via Udon Thani, Thailand	W • S Asia • 250 kW
		W M-F • S Asia • 250 kW
15295	**ECUADOR**	
	HCJB-VO THE ANDES, Quito	S America • 100 kW
	MALAYSIA	
	VOICE OF MALAYSIA, Kajang	Australasia • VOICE OF ISLAM • 250 kW
		Mideast • 250 kW
		Australasia • 250 kW
	PORTUGAL	
	RDP INTERNATIONAL, Lisbon	S Tu-Sa • S America • 300 kW / S M-F • S America • 300 kW
	UNITED KINGDOM	
(con'd)	BBC, Via Zyyi, Cyprus	W • SE Asia • 250 kW

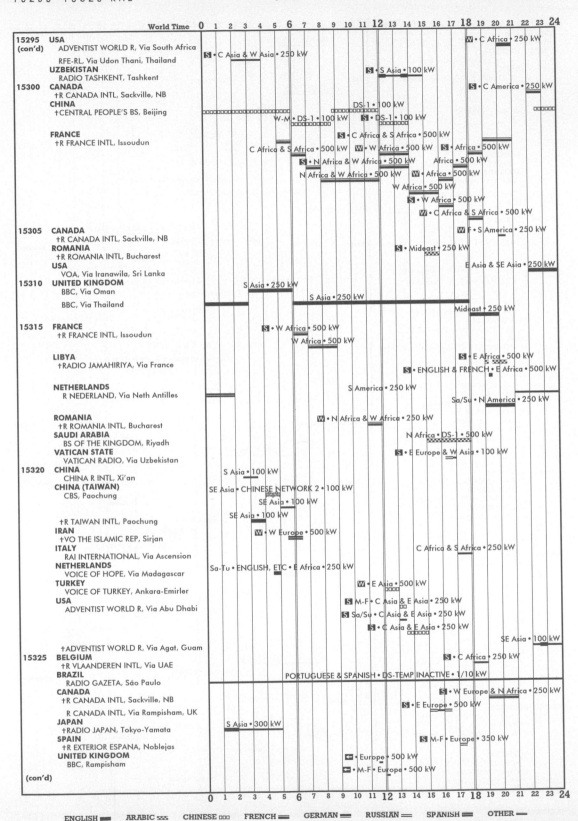

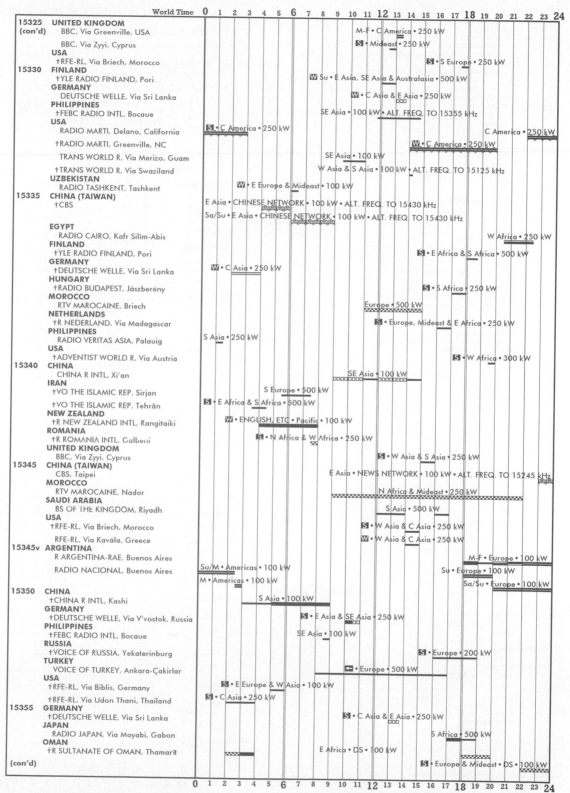

15325	**UNITED KINGDOM**	
(con'd)	BBC, Via Greenville, USA	M-F • C America • 250 kW
	BBC, Via Zyyi, Cyprus	S • Mideast • 250 kW
	USA	
15330	†RFE-RL, Via Briech, Morocco	S • S Europe • 250 kW
	FINLAND	
	†YLE RADIO FINLAND, Pori	W Su • E Asia, SE Asia & Australasia • 500 kW
	GERMANY	
	DEUTSCHE WELLE, Via Sri Lanka	W • C Asia & E Asia • 250 kW
	PHILIPPINES	
	†FEBC RADIO INTL, Bocaue	SE Asia • 100 kW • ALT. FREQ. TO 15355 kHz
	USA	
	RADIO MARTI, Delano, California	S • C America • 250 kW C America • 250 kW
	†RADIO MARTI, Greenville, NC	W • C America • 250 kW
	TRANS WORLD R, Via Merizo, Guam	SE Asia • 100 kW
	†TRANS WORLD R, Via Swaziland	W Asia & S Asia • 100 kW • ALT. FREQ. TO 15125 kHz
	UZBEKISTAN	
	RADIO TASHKENT, Tashkent	W • E Europe & Mideast • 100 kW
15335	**CHINA (TAIWAN)**	
	†CBS	E Asia • CHINESE NETWORK • 100 kW • ALT. FREQ. TO 15430 kHz
		Sa/Su • E Asia • CHINESE NETWORK • 100 kW • ALT. FREQ. TO 15430 kHz
	EGYPT	
	RADIO CAIRO, Kafr Silim-Abis	W Africa • 250 kW
	FINLAND	
	†YLE RADIO FINLAND, Pori	S • E Africa & S Africa • 500 kW
	GERMANY	
	†DEUTSCHE WELLE, Via Sri Lanka	W • C Asia • 250 kW
	HUNGARY	
	†RADIO BUDAPEST, Jászberény	S • S Africa • 250 kW
	MOROCCO	
	RTV MAROCAINE, Briech	Europe • 500 kW
	NETHERLANDS	
	†R NEDERLAND, Via Madagascar	S • Europe, Mideast & E Africa • 250 kW
	PHILIPPINES	
	RADIO VERITAS ASIA, Palauig	S Asia • 250 kW
	USA	
	†ADVENTIST WORLD R, Via Austria	S • W Africa • 300 kW
15340	**CHINA**	
	CHINA R INTL, Xi'an	SE Asia • 100 kW
	IRAN	
	†VO THE ISLAMIC REP, Sirjan	S Europe • 500 kW
	†VO THE ISLAMIC REP, Tehrān	S • E Africa & S Africa • 500 kW
	NEW ZEALAND	
	†R NEW ZEALAND INTL, Rangitaiki	W • ENGLISH, ETC • Pacific • 100 kW
	ROMANIA	
	†R ROMANIA INTL, Galbeni	S • N Africa & W Africa • 250 kW
	UNITED KINGDOM	
	BBC, Via Zyyi, Cyprus	S • W Asia & S Asia • 250 kW
15345	**CHINA (TAIWAN)**	
	CBS, Taipei	E Asia • NEWS NETWORK • 100 kW • ALT. FREQ. TO 15245 kHz
	MOROCCO	
	RTV MAROCAINE, Nador	N Africa & Mideast • 250 kW
	SAUDI ARABIA	
	BS OF THE KINGDOM, Riyadh	S Asia • 500 kW
	USA	
	†RFE-RL, Via Briech, Morocco	S • W Asia & C Asia • 250 kW
	RFE-RL, Via Kavála, Greece	W • W Asia & C Asia • 250 kW
15345v	**ARGENTINA**	
	R ARGENTINA-RAE, Buenos Aires	M-F • Europe • 100 kW
	RADIO NACIONAL, Buenos Aires	Su/M • Americas • 100 kW Su • Europe • 100 kW
		M • Americas • 100 kW Sa/Su • Europe • 100 kW
15350	**CHINA**	
	†CHINA R INTL, Kashi	S Asia • 100 kW
	GERMANY	
	†DEUTSCHE WELLE, Via V'vostok, Russia	S • E Asia & SE Asia • 250 kW
	PHILIPPINES	
	†FEBC RADIO INTL, Bocaue	SE Asia • 100 kW
	RUSSIA	
	†VOICE OF RUSSIA, Yekaterinburg	S • Europe • 200 kW
	TURKEY	
	VOICE OF TURKEY, Ankara-Çakirlar	☐ • Europe • 500 kW
	USA	
	†RFE-RL, Via Biblis, Germany	S • E Europe & W Asia • 100 kW
	†RFE-RL, Via Udon Thani, Thailand	S • C Asia • 250 kW
15355	**GERMANY**	
	†DEUTSCHE WELLE, Via Sri Lanka	S • C Asia & E Asia • 250 kW
	JAPAN	
	RADIO JAPAN, Via Moyabi, Gabon	S Africa • 500 kW
	OMAN	
	†R SULTANATE OF OMAN, Thamarīt	E Africa • DS • 100 kW
(con'd)		S • Europe & Mideast • DS • 100 kW

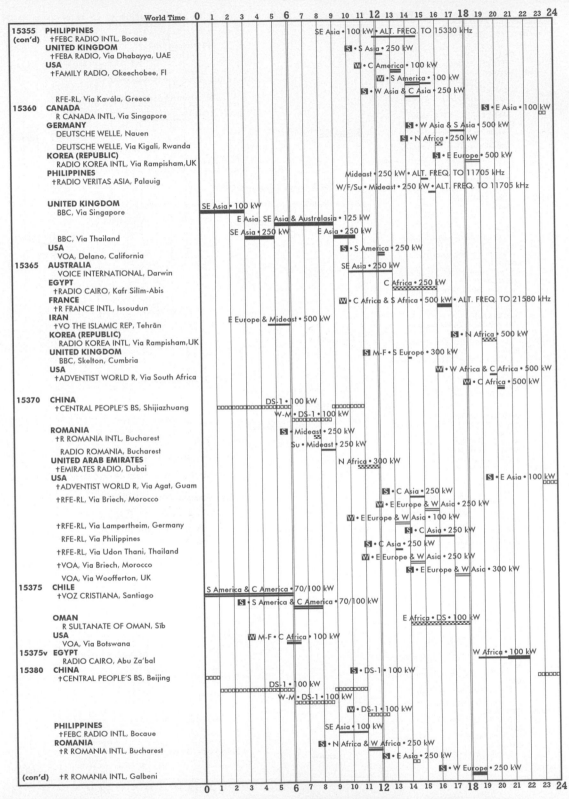

15355	**PHILIPPINES**
(con'd)	†FEBC RADIO INTL, Bocaue
	UNITED KINGDOM
	†FEBA RADIO, Via Dhabayya, UAE
	USA
	†FAMILY RADIO, Okeechobee, Fl
	RFE-RL, Via Kavála, Greece
15360	**CANADA**
	R CANADA INTL, Via Singapore
	GERMANY
	DEUTSCHE WELLE, Nauen
	DEUTSCHE WELLE, Via Kigali, Rwanda
	KOREA (REPUBLIC)
	RADIO KOREA INTL, Via Rampisham, UK
	PHILIPPINES
	†RADIO VERITAS ASIA, Palauig
	UNITED KINGDOM
	BBC, Via Singapore
	BBC, Via Thailand
	USA
	VOA, Delano, California
15365	**AUSTRALIA**
	VOICE INTERNATIONAL, Darwin
	EGYPT
	†RADIO CAIRO, Kafr Silim-Abis
	FRANCE
	†R FRANCE INTL, Issoudun
	IRAN
	†VO THE ISLAMIC REP, Tehrān
	KOREA (REPUBLIC)
	RADIO KOREA INTL, Via Rampisham, UK
	UNITED KINGDOM
	BBC, Skelton, Cumbria
	USA
	†ADVENTIST WORLD R, Via South Africa
15370	**CHINA**
	†CENTRAL PEOPLE'S BS, Shijiazhuang
	ROMANIA
	†R ROMANIA INTL, Bucharest
	RADIO ROMANIA, Bucharest
	UNITED ARAB EMIRATES
	†EMIRATES RADIO, Dubai
	USA
	†ADVENTIST WORLD R, Via Agat, Guam
	†RFE-RL, Via Briech, Morocco
	†RFE-RL, Via Lampertheim, Germany
	RFE-RL, Via Philippines
	†RFE-RL, Via Udon Thani, Thailand
	†VOA, Via Briech, Morocco
	VOA, Via Woofferton, UK
15375	**CHILE**
	†VOZ CRISTIANA, Santiago
	OMAN
	R SULTANATE OF OMAN, Sīb
	USA
	VOA, Via Botswana
15375v	**EGYPT**
	RADIO CAIRO, Abu Za'bal
15380	**CHINA**
	†CENTRAL PEOPLE'S BS, Beijing
	PHILIPPINES
	†FEBC RADIO INTL, Bocaue
	ROMANIA
	†R ROMANIA INTL, Bucharest
(con'd)	†R ROMANIA INTL, Galbeni

ENGLISH ▬ ARABIC ▧ CHINESE □□□ FRENCH ══ GERMAN ▭▭ RUSSIAN ＝＝ SPANISH ▬▬ OTHER ──

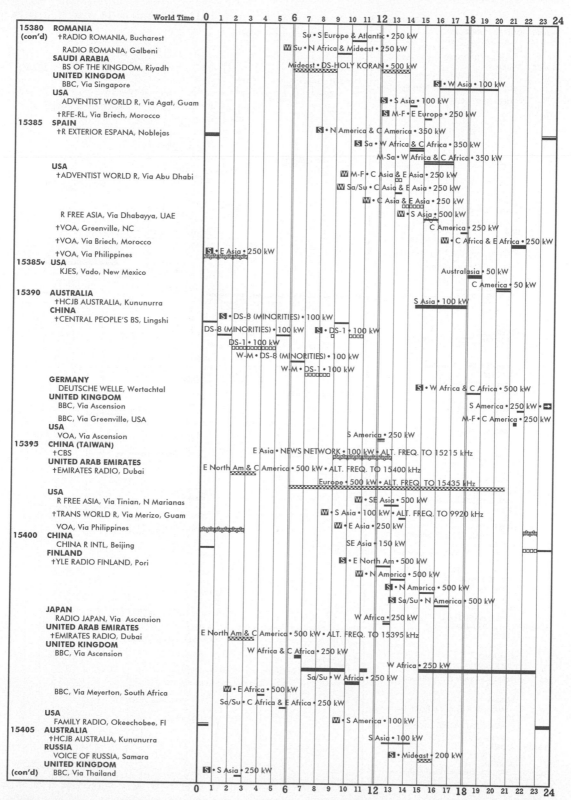

World Time 0 1 2 3 4 5 6 7 8 9 10 11 12 13 14 15 16 17 18 19 20 21 22 23 24

15380 (con'd)	ROMANIA	
	†RADIO ROMANIA, Bucharest	Su • S Europe & Atlantic • 250 kW
		W Su • N Africa & Mideast • 250 kW
	RADIO ROMANIA, Galbeni	
	SAUDI ARABIA	
	BS OF THE KINGDOM, Riyadh	Mideast • DS-HOLY KORAN • 500 kW
	UNITED KINGDOM	
	BBC, Via Singapore	S • W Asia • 100 kW
	USA	
	ADVENTIST WORLD R, Via Agat, Guam	S • S Asia • 100 kW
	†RFE-RL, Via Briech, Morocco	S M-F • E Europe • 250 kW
15385	SPAIN	
	†R EXTERIOR ESPANA, Noblejas	S • N America & C America • 350 kW
		S Sa • W Africa & C Africa • 350 kW
		M-Sa • W Africa & C Africa • 350 kW
	USA	
	†ADVENTIST WORLD R, Via Abu Dhabi	W M-F • C Asia & E Asia • 250 kW
		W Sa/Su • C Asia & E Asia • 250 kW
		W • C Asia & E Asia • 250 kW
	R FREE ASIA, Via Dhabayya, UAE	W • S Asia • 500 kW
	†VOA, Greenville, NC	C America • 250 kW
	†VOA, Via Briech, Morocco	W • C Africa & E Africa • 250 kW
	†VOA, Via Philippines	S • E Asia • 250 kW
15385v	USA	
	KJES, Vado, New Mexico	Australasia • 50 kW
		C America • 50 kW
15390	AUSTRALIA	
	†HCJB AUSTRALIA, Kununurra	S Asia • 100 kW
	CHINA	
	†CENTRAL PEOPLE'S BS, Lingshi	S • DS-8 (MINORITIES) • 100 kW
		DS-8 (MINORITIES) • 100 kW S • DS-1 • 100 kW
		DS-1 • 100 kW
		W-M • DS-8 (MINORITIES) • 100 kW
		W-M • DS-1 • 100 kW
	GERMANY	
	DEUTSCHE WELLE, Wertachtal	S • W Africa & C Africa • 500 kW
	UNITED KINGDOM	
	BBC, Via Ascension	S America • 250 kW • ➡
	BBC, Via Greenville, USA	M-F • C America • 250 kW
	USA	
	VOA, Via Ascension	S America • 250 kW
15395	CHINA (TAIWAN)	
	†CBS	E Asia • NEWS NETWORK • 100 kW • ALT. FREQ. TO 15215 kHz
	UNITED ARAB EMIRATES	
	†EMIRATES RADIO, Dubai	E North Am & C America • 500 kW • ALT. FREQ. TO 15400 kHz
		Europe • 500 kW • ALT. FREQ. TO 15435 kHz
	USA	
	R FREE ASIA, Via Tinian, N Marianas	W • SE Asia • 500 kW
	†TRANS WORLD R, Via Merizo, Guam	W • S Asia • 100 kW • ALT. FREQ. TO 9920 kHz
	VOA, Via Philippines	W • E Asia • 250 kW
15400	CHINA	
	CHINA R INTL, Beijing	SE Asia • 150 kW
	FINLAND	
	†YLE RADIO FINLAND, Pori	S • E North Am • 500 kW
		W • N America • 500 kW
		S • N America • 500 kW
		S Sa/Su • N America • 500 kW
	JAPAN	
	RADIO JAPAN, Via Ascension	W Africa • 250 kW
	UNITED ARAB EMIRATES	
	†EMIRATES RADIO, Dubai	E North Am & C America • 500 kW • ALT. FREQ. TO 15395 kHz
	UNITED KINGDOM	
	BBC, Via Ascension	W Africa & C Africa • 250 kW
		W Africa • 250 kW
		Sa/Su • W Africa • 250 kW
	BBC, Via Meyerton, South Africa	W • E Africa • 500 kW
		Sa/Su • C Africa & E Africa • 250 kW
	USA	
	FAMILY RADIO, Okeechobee, Fl	W • S America • 100 kW
15405	AUSTRALIA	
	†HCJB AUSTRALIA, Kununurra	S Asia • 100 kW
	RUSSIA	
	VOICE OF RUSSIA, Samara	S • Mideast • 200 kW
	UNITED KINGDOM	
(con'd)	BBC, Via Thailand	S • S Asia • 250 kW

0 1 2 3 4 5 6 7 8 9 10 11 12 13 14 15 16 17 18 19 20 21 22 23 24

SEASONAL ⓢ OR ⓦ   1-HR TIMESHIFT MIDYEAR ⬅ OR ➡   JAMMING / OR ⋀   EARLIEST HEARD ◁   LATEST HEARD ▷   NEW FOR 2005 †

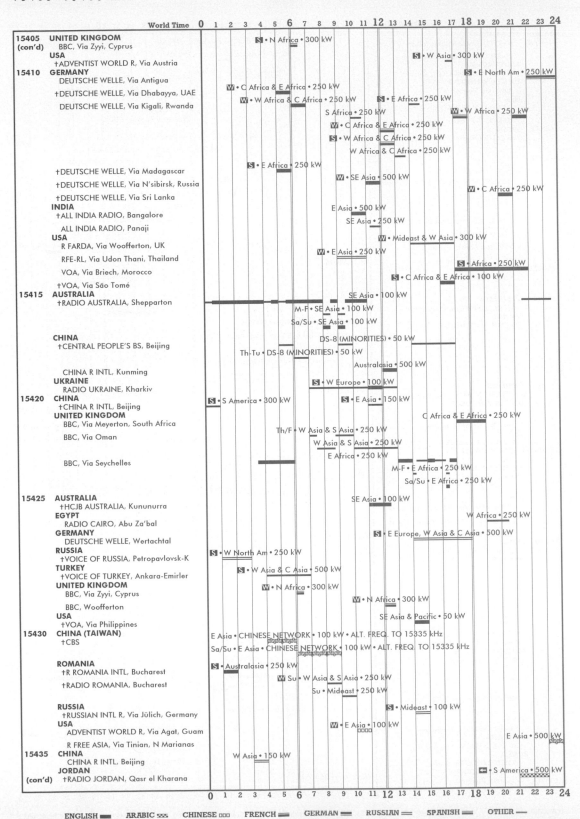

World Time 0 1 2 3 4 5 6 7 8 9 10 11 12 13 14 15 16 17 18 19 20 21 22 23 24

15405 (con'd) UNITED KINGDOM
BBC, Via Zyyi, Cyprus — [S] • N Africa • 300 kW

USA
†ADVENTIST WORLD R, Via Austria — [S] • W Asia • 300 kW

15410 GERMANY
DEUTSCHE WELLE, Via Antigua — [S] • E North Am • 250 kW
†DEUTSCHE WELLE, Via Dhabayya, UAE — [W] • C Africa & E Africa • 250 kW
DEUTSCHE WELLE, Via Kigali, Rwanda — [W] • W Africa & C Africa • 250 kW; [S] • E Africa • 250 kW; S Africa • 250 kW; [W] • W Africa • 250 kW; [W] • C Africa & E Africa • 250 kW; [S] • W Africa & C Africa • 250 kW; W Africa & C Africa • 250 kW
†DEUTSCHE WELLE, Via Madagascar — [S] • E Africa • 250 kW
†DEUTSCHE WELLE, Via N'sibirsk, Russia — [W] • SE Asia • 500 kW
†DEUTSCHE WELLE, Via Sri Lanka — [W] • C Africa • 250 kW

INDIA
†ALL INDIA RADIO, Bangalore — E Asia • 500 kW
ALL INDIA RADIO, Panaji — SE Asia • 250 kW

USA
R FARDA, Via Woofferton, UK — [W] • Mideast & W Asia • 300 kW
RFE-RL, Via Udon Thani, Thailand — [W] • E Asia • 250 kW
VOA, Via Briech, Morocco — [S] • Africa • 250 kW
†VOA, Via São Tomé — [S] • C Africa & E Africa • 100 kW

15415 AUSTRALIA
†RADIO AUSTRALIA, Shepparton — SE Asia • 100 kW; M-F • SE Asia • 100 kW; Sa/Su • SE Asia • 100 kW

CHINA
†CENTRAL PEOPLE'S BS, Beijing — DS-8 (MINORITIES) • 50 kW; Th-Tu • DS-8 (MINORITIES) • 50 kW
CHINA R INTL, Kunming — Australasia • 500 kW

UKRAINE
RADIO UKRAINE, Kharkiv — [S] • W Europe • 100 kW

15420 CHINA
†CHINA R INTL, Beijing — [S] • S America • 300 kW; [S] • E Asia • 150 kW

UNITED KINGDOM
BBC, Via Meyerton, South Africa — C Africa & E Africa • 250 kW
BBC, Via Oman — Th/F • W Asia & S Asia • 250 kW; W Asia & S Asia • 250 kW
BBC, Via Seychelles — E Africa • 250 kW; M-F • E Africa • 250 kW; Sa/Su • E Africa • 250 kW

15425 AUSTRALIA
†HCJB AUSTRALIA, Kununurra — SE Asia • 100 kW

EGYPT
RADIO CAIRO, Abu Za'bal — W Africa • 250 kW

GERMANY
DEUTSCHE WELLE, Wertachtal — [S] • E Europe, W Asia & C Asia • 500 kW

RUSSIA
†VOICE OF RUSSIA, Petropavlovsk-K — [S] • W North Am • 250 kW

TURKEY
†VOICE OF TURKEY, Ankara-Emirler — [S] • W Asia & C Asia • 500 kW

UNITED KINGDOM
BBC, Via Zyyi, Cyprus — [W] • N Africa • 300 kW
BBC, Woofferton — [W] • N Africa • 300 kW

USA
†VOA, Via Philippines — SE Asia & Pacific • 50 kW

15430 CHINA (TAIWAN)
†CBS — E Asia • CHINESE NETWORK • 100 kW • ALT. FREQ. TO 15335 kHz; Sa/Su • E Asia • CHINESE NETWORK • 100 kW • ALT. FREQ. TO 15335 kHz

ROMANIA
†R ROMANIA INTL, Bucharest — [S] • Australasia • 250 kW
†RADIO ROMANIA, Bucharest — [W] Su • W Asia & S Asia • 250 kW; Su • Mideast • 250 kW

RUSSIA
†RUSSIAN INTL R, Via Jülich, Germany — [S] • Mideast • 100 kW

USA
ADVENTIST WORLD R, Via Agat, Guam — [W] • E Asia • 100 kW
R FREE ASIA, Via Tinian, N Marianas — E Asia • 500 kW

15435 CHINA
CHINA R INTL, Beijing — W Asia • 150 kW

JORDAN (con'd)
†RADIO JORDAN, Qasr el Kharana — ← • S America • 500 kW

0 1 2 3 4 5 6 7 8 9 10 11 12 13 14 15 16 17 18 19 20 21 22 23 24

ENGLISH ARABIC CHINESE FRENCH GERMAN RUSSIAN SPANISH OTHER

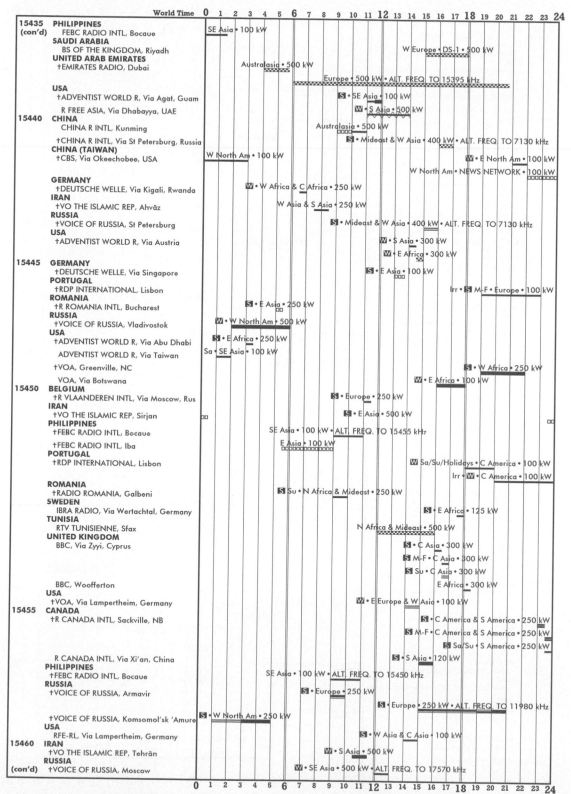

| World Time | 0 | 1 | 2 | 3 | 4 | 5 | 6 | 7 | 8 | 9 | 10 | 11 | 12 | 13 | 14 | 15 | 16 | 17 | 18 | 19 | 20 | 21 | 22 | 23 | 24 |

15435 PHILIPPINES (con'd)
  FEBC RADIO INTL, Bocaue — SE Asia • 100 kW

SAUDI ARABIA
  BS OF THE KINGDOM, Riyadh — W Europe • DS-1 • 500 kW

UNITED ARAB EMIRATES
  †EMIRATES RADIO, Dubai — Australasia • 500 kW
  Europe • 500 kW • ALT. FREQ. TO 15395 kHz

USA
  †ADVENTIST WORLD R, Via Agat, Guam — Ⓢ • SE Asia • 100 kW
  R FREE ASIA, Via Dhabayya, UAE — Ⓦ • S Asia • 500 kW

15440 CHINA
  CHINA R INTL, Kunming — Australasia • 500 kW
  †CHINA R INTL, Via St Petersburg, Russia — Ⓢ • Mideast & W Asia • 400 kW • ALT. FREQ. TO 7130 kHz

CHINA (TAIWAN)
  †CBS, Via Okeechobee, USA — W North Am • 100 kW
  Ⓦ • E North Am • 100 kW
  W North Am • NEWS NETWORK • 100 kW

GERMANY
  †DEUTSCHE WELLE, Via Kigali, Rwanda — Ⓦ • W Africa & C Africa • 250 kW

IRAN
  †VO THE ISLAMIC REP, Ahvāz — W Asia & S Asia • 250 kW

RUSSIA
  †VOICE OF RUSSIA, St Petersburg — Ⓢ • Mideast & W Asia • 400 kW • ALT. FREQ. TO 7130 kHz

USA
  †ADVENTIST WORLD R, Via Austria — Ⓦ • S Asia • 300 kW
  Ⓦ • E Africa • 300 kW

15445 GERMANY
  †DEUTSCHE WELLE, Via Singapore — Ⓢ • E Asia • 100 kW

PORTUGAL
  †RDP INTERNATIONAL, Lisbon — Irr • Ⓢ • M-F • Europe • 100 kW

ROMANIA
  †R ROMANIA INTL, Bucharest — Ⓢ • E Asia • 250 kW

RUSSIA
  †VOICE OF RUSSIA, Vladivostok — Ⓦ • W North Am • 500 kW

USA
  †ADVENTIST WORLD R, Via Abu Dhabi — Ⓢ • E Africa • 250 kW
  ADVENTIST WORLD R, Via Taiwan — Sa • SE Asia • 100 kW
  †VOA, Greenville, NC — Ⓢ • W Africa • 250 kW
  VOA, Via Botswana — Ⓦ • E Africa • 100 kW

15450 BELGIUM
  †R VLAANDEREN INTL, Via Moscow, Rus — Ⓢ • Europe • 250 kW

IRAN
  †VO THE ISLAMIC REP, Sirjan — Ⓢ • E Asia • 500 kW

PHILIPPINES
  †FEBC RADIO INTL, Bocaue — SE Asia • 100 kW • ALT. FREQ. TO 15455 kHz
  †FEBC RADIO INTL, Iba — E Asia • 100 kW

PORTUGAL
  †RDP INTERNATIONAL, Lisbon — Ⓦ Sa/Su/Holidays • C America • 100 kW
  Irr • Ⓦ • C America • 100 kW

ROMANIA
  †RADIO ROMANIA, Galbeni — Ⓢ Su • N Africa & Mideast • 250 kW

SWEDEN
  IBRA RADIO, Via Wertachtal, Germany — Ⓢ • E Africa • 125 kW

TUNISIA
  RTV TUNISIENNE, Sfax — N Africa & Mideast • 500 kW

UNITED KINGDOM
  BBC, Via Zyyi, Cyprus — Ⓢ • C Asia • 300 kW
  Ⓢ M-F • C Asia • 300 kW
  Ⓢ Su • C Asia • 300 kW
  E Africa • 300 kW

  BBC, Woofferton
USA
  †VOA, Via Lampertheim, Germany — Ⓦ • E Europe & W Asia • 100 kW

15455 CANADA
  †R CANADA INTL, Sackville, NB — Ⓢ • C America & S America • 250 kW
  Ⓢ M-F • C America & S America • 250 kW
  Ⓢ Sa/Su • S America • 250 kW
  R CANADA INTL, Via Xi'an, China — Ⓢ • S Asia • 120 kW

PHILIPPINES
  †FEBC RADIO INTL, Bocaue — SE Asia • 100 kW • ALT. FREQ. TO 15450 kHz

RUSSIA
  †VOICE OF RUSSIA, Armavir — Ⓢ • Europe • 250 kW
  Ⓢ • Europe • 250 kW • ALT. FREQ. TO 11980 kHz
  †VOICE OF RUSSIA, Komsomol'sk 'Amure — Ⓢ • W North Am • 250 kW

USA
  RFE-RL, Via Lampertheim, Germany — Ⓢ • W Asia & C Asia • 100 kW

15460 IRAN
  †VO THE ISLAMIC REP, Tehrān — Ⓦ • S Asia • 500 kW

RUSSIA (con'd)
  †VOICE OF RUSSIA, Moscow — Ⓦ • SE Asia • 500 kW • ALT. FREQ. TO 17570 kHz

| | 0 | 1 | 2 | 3 | 4 | 5 | 6 | 7 | 8 | 9 | 10 | 11 | 12 | 13 | 14 | 15 | 16 | 17 | 18 | 19 | 20 | 21 | 22 | 23 | 24 |

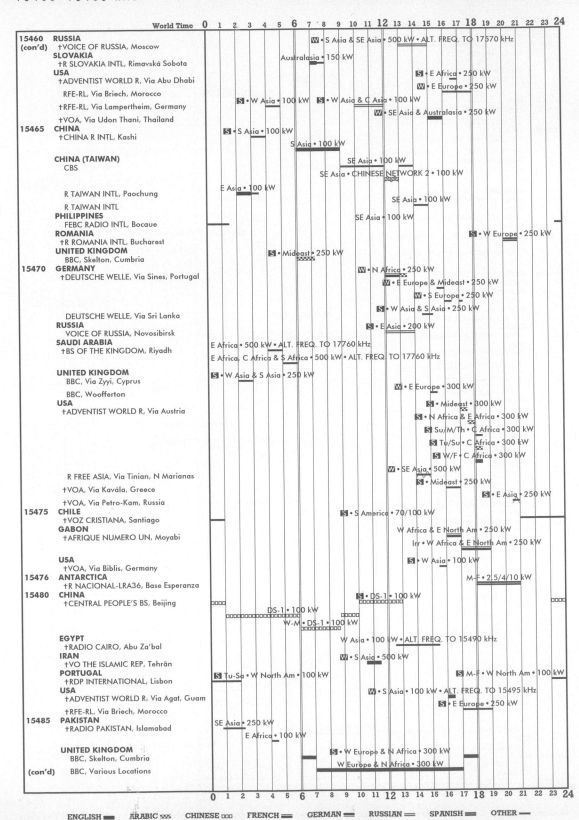

| | World Time | 0 | 1 | 2 | 3 | 4 | 5 | 6 | 7 | 8 | 9 | 10 | 11 | 12 | 13 | 14 | 15 | 16 | 17 | 18 | 19 | 20 | 21 | 22 | 23 | 24 |

15460
(con'd)   RUSSIA
          †VOICE OF RUSSIA, Moscow — W • S Asia & SE Asia • 500 kW • ALT. FREQ. TO 17570 kHz
          SLOVAKIA
          †R SLOVAKIA INTL, Rimavská Sobota — Australasia • 150 kW
          USA
          †ADVENTIST WORLD R, Via Abu Dhabi — S • E Africa • 250 kW
                                              W • E Europe • 250 kW
          RFE-RL, Via Briech, Morocco
          †RFE-RL, Via Lampertheim, Germany — S • W Asia • 100 kW   S • W Asia & C Asia • 100 kW
                                              W • SE Asia & Australasia • 250 kW
          †VOA, Via Udon Thani, Thailand
15465   CHINA
          †CHINA R INTL, Kashi — S • S Asia • 100 kW
                                 S Asia • 100 kW
          CHINA (TAIWAN)
          CBS — SE Asia • 100 kW
                SE Asia • CHINESE NETWORK 2 • 100 kW
          R TAIWAN INTL, Paochung — E Asia • 100 kW
          R TAIWAN INTL — SE Asia • 100 kW
          PHILIPPINES
          FEBC RADIO INTL, Bocaue — SE Asia • 100 kW
          ROMANIA
          †R ROMANIA INTL, Bucharest — S • W Europe • 250 kW
          UNITED KINGDOM
          BBC, Skelton, Cumbria — S • Mideast • 250 kW
15470   GERMANY
          †DEUTSCHE WELLE, Via Sines, Portugal — W • N Africa • 250 kW
                                                 W • E Europe & Mideast • 250 kW
                                                 W • S Europe • 250 kW
          DEUTSCHE WELLE, Via Sri Lanka — S • W Asia & S Asia • 250 kW
          RUSSIA
          VOICE OF RUSSIA, Novosibirsk — S • E Asia • 200 kW
          SAUDI ARABIA
          †BS OF THE KINGDOM, Riyadh — E Africa • 500 kW • ALT. FREQ. TO 17760 kHz
                                        E Africa, C Africa & S Africa • 500 kW • ALT. FREQ. TO 17760 kHz
          UNITED KINGDOM
          BBC, Via Zyyi, Cyprus — S • W Asia & S Asia • 250 kW
          BBC, Woofferton — W • E Europe • 300 kW
          USA
          †ADVENTIST WORLD R, Via Austria — S • Mideast • 300 kW
                                            S • N Africa & E Africa • 300 kW
                                            Su/M/Th • C Africa • 300 kW
                                            Tu/Su • C Africa • 300 kW
                                            W/F • C Africa • 300 kW
          R FREE ASIA, Via Tinian, N Marianas — W • SE Asia • 500 kW
          †VOA, Via Kavála, Greece — S • Mideast • 250 kW
          †VOA, Via Petro-Kam, Russia — S • E Asia • 250 kW
15475   CHILE
          †VOZ CRISTIANA, Santiago — S • S America • 70/100 kW
          GABON
          †AFRIQUE NUMERO UN, Moyabi — W Africa & E North Am • 250 kW
                                        Irr • W Africa & E North Am • 250 kW
          USA
          †VOA, Via Biblis, Germany — S • W Asia • 100 kW
15476   ANTARCTICA
          †R NACIONAL-LRA36, Base Esperanza — M-F • 2.5/4/10 kW
15480   CHINA
          †CENTRAL PEOPLE'S BS, Beijing — S • DS-1 • 100 kW
                                           DS-1 • 100 kW
                                           W-M • DS-1 • 100 kW
          EGYPT
          †RADIO CAIRO, Abu Za'bal — W Asia • 100 kW • ALT. FREQ. TO 15490 kHz
          IRAN
          †VO THE ISLAMIC REP, Tehrān — W • S Asia • 500 kW
          PORTUGAL
          †RDP INTERNATIONAL, Lisbon — S • Tu-Sa • W North Am • 100 kW   S • M-F • W North Am • 100 kW
          USA
          †ADVENTIST WORLD R, Via Agat, Guam — W • S Asia • 100 kW • ALT. FREQ. TO 15495 kHz
          †RFE-RL, Via Briech, Morocco — S • E Europe • 250 kW
15485   PAKISTAN
          †RADIO PAKISTAN, Islamabad — SE Asia • 250 kW
                                        E Africa • 100 kW
          UNITED KINGDOM
          BBC, Skelton, Cumbria — S • W Europe & N Africa • 300 kW
(con'd)   BBC, Various Locations — W Europe & N Africa • 300 kW

| | | 0 | 1 | 2 | 3 | 4 | 5 | 6 | 7 | 8 | 9 | 10 | 11 | 12 | 13 | 14 | 15 | 16 | 17 | 18 | 19 | 20 | 21 | 22 | 23 | 24 |

ENGLISH ▬   ARABIC ▨   CHINESE ▦   FRENCH ▬   GERMAN ▬   RUSSIAN ▬   SPANISH ▬   OTHER ▬

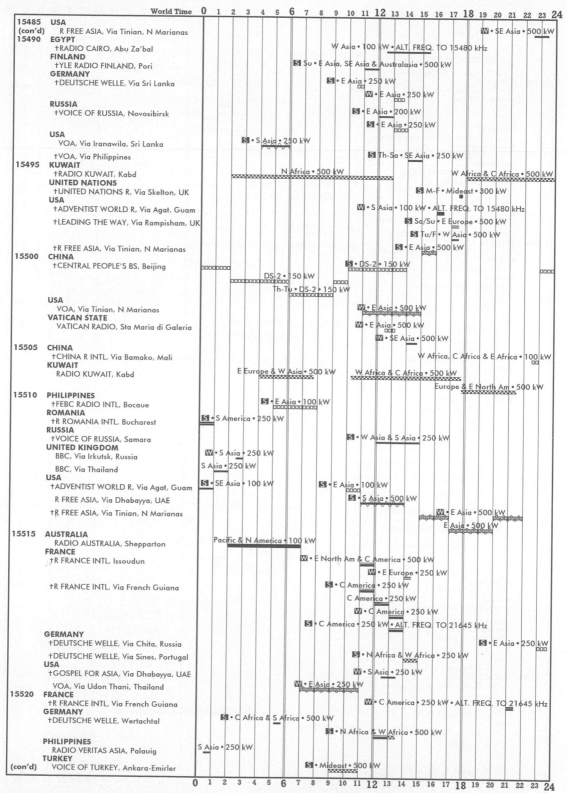

| | | World Time | 0 1 2 3 4 5 6 7 8 9 10 11 12 13 14 15 16 17 18 19 20 21 22 23 24 |

15485 USA
(con'd) R FREE ASIA, Via Tinian, N Marianas — W • SE Asia • 500 kW
15490 EGYPT
†RADIO CAIRO, Abu Za'bal — W Asia • 100 kW • ALT. FREQ. TO 15480 kHz
FINLAND
†YLE RADIO FINLAND, Pori — S Su • E Asia, SE Asia & Australasia • 500 kW
GERMANY
†DEUTSCHE WELLE, Via Sri Lanka — S • E Asia • 250 kW
— W • E Asia • 250 kW
RUSSIA
†VOICE OF RUSSIA, Novosibirsk — S • E Asia • 200 kW
— S • E Asia • 250 kW
USA
VOA, Via Iranawila, Sri Lanka — S • S Asia • 250 kW
†VOA, Via Philippines — S Th-Sa • SE Asia • 250 kW
15495 KUWAIT
†RADIO KUWAIT, Kabd — N Africa • 500 kW   W Africa & C Africa • 500 kW
UNITED NATIONS
†UNITED NATIONS R, Via Skelton, UK — S M-F • Mideast • 300 kW
USA
†ADVENTIST WORLD R, Via Agat, Guam — W • S Asia • 100 kW • ALT. FREQ. TO 15480 kHz
†LEADING THE WAY, Via Rampisham, UK — S Sa/Su • E Europe • 500 kW
— S Tu/F • W Asia • 500 kW
†R FREE ASIA, Via Tinian, N Marianas — S • E Asia • 500 kW
15500 CHINA
†CENTRAL PEOPLE'S BS, Beijing — S • DS-2 • 150 kW
DS-2 • 150 kW
Th-Tu • DS-2 • 150 kW
USA
VOA, Via Tinian, N Marianas — W • E Asia • 500 kW
VATICAN STATE
VATICAN RADIO, Sta Maria di Galeria — W • E Asia • 500 kW
— W • SE Asia • 500 kW
15505 CHINA
†CHINA R INTL, Via Bamako, Mali — W Africa, C Africa & E Africa • 100 kW
KUWAIT
RADIO KUWAIT, Kabd — E Europe & W Asia • 500 kW   W Africa & C Africa • 500 kW
— Europe & E North Am • 500 kW
15510 PHILIPPINES
†FEBC RADIO INTL, Bocaue — S • E Asia • 100 kW
ROMANIA
†R ROMANIA INTL, Bucharest — S • S America • 250 kW
RUSSIA
†VOICE OF RUSSIA, Samara — S • W Asia & S Asia • 250 kW
UNITED KINGDOM
BBC, Via Irkutsk, Russia — W • S Asia • 250 kW
BBC, Via Thailand — S Asia • 250 kW
USA
†ADVENTIST WORLD R, Via Agat, Guam — S • SE Asia • 100 kW   S • E Asia • 100 kW
R FREE ASIA, Via Dhabayya, UAE — S • S Asia • 500 kW
†R FREE ASIA, Via Tinian, N Marianas — W • E Asia • 500 kW
— E Asia • 500 kW
15515 AUSTRALIA
RADIO AUSTRALIA, Shepparton — Pacific & N America • 100 kW
FRANCE
†R FRANCE INTL, Issoudun — W • E North Am & C America • 500 kW
— W • E Europe • 250 kW
— S • C America • 250 kW
†R FRANCE INTL, Via French Guiana — C America • 250 kW
— W • C America • 250 kW
— S • C America • 250 kW • ALT. FREQ. TO 21645 kHz
GERMANY
†DEUTSCHE WELLE, Via Chita, Russia — S • E Asia • 250 kW
†DEUTSCHE WELLE, Via Sines, Portugal — S • N Africa & W Africa • 250 kW
USA
†GOSPEL FOR ASIA, Via Dhabayya, UAE — W • S Asia • 250 kW
VOA, Via Udon Thani, Thailand — W • E Asia • 250 kW
15520 FRANCE
†R FRANCE INTL, Via French Guiana — W • C America • 250 kW • ALT. FREQ. TO 21645 kHz
GERMANY
†DEUTSCHE WELLE, Wertachtal — S • C Africa & S Africa • 500 kW
— S • N Africa & W Africa • 500 kW
PHILIPPINES
RADIO VERITAS ASIA, Palauig — S Asia • 250 kW
TURKEY
(con'd) VOICE OF TURKEY, Ankara-Emirler — S • Mideast • 500 kW

| | World Time | 0 1 2 3 4 5 6 7 8 9 10 11 12 13 14 15 16 17 18 19 20 21 22 23 24 |

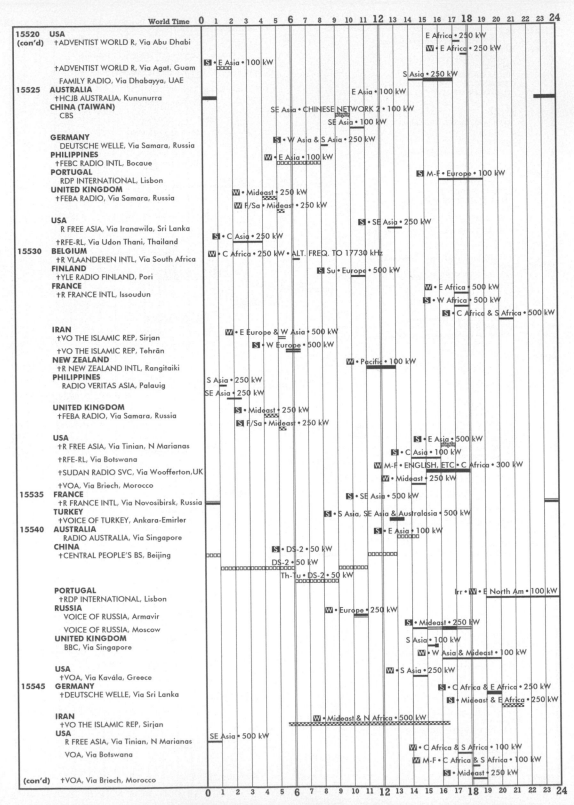

World Time	0 1 2 3 4 5 6 7 8 9 10 11 12 13 14 15 16 17 18 19 20 21 22 23 24

15520 USA
(con'd) †ADVENTIST WORLD R, Via Abu Dhabi — E Africa • 250 kW; W • E Africa • 250 kW

†ADVENTIST WORLD R, Via Agat, Guam — S • E Asia • 100 kW

FAMILY RADIO, Via Dhabayya, UAE — S Asia • 250 kW

15525 AUSTRALIA
†HCJB AUSTRALIA, Kununurra — E Asia • 100 kW

CHINA (TAIWAN)
CBS — SE Asia • CHINESE NETWORK 2 • 100 kW; SE Asia • 100 kW

GERMANY
DEUTSCHE WELLE, Via Samara, Russia — S • W Asia & S Asia • 250 kW

PHILIPPINES
†FEBC RADIO INTL, Bocaue — W • E Asia • 100 kW

PORTUGAL
RDP INTERNATIONAL, Lisbon — M-F • Europe • 100 kW

UNITED KINGDOM
†FEBA RADIO, Via Samara, Russia — W • Mideast • 250 kW; W F/Sa • Mideast • 250 kW

USA
R FREE ASIA, Via Iranawila, Sri Lanka — S • SE Asia • 250 kW

†RFE-RL, Via Udon Thani, Thailand — S • C Asia • 250 kW

15530 BELGIUM
†R VLAANDEREN INTL, Via South Africa — W • C Africa • 250 kW • ALT. FREQ. TO 17730 kHz

FINLAND
†YLE RADIO FINLAND, Pori — S • Su • Europe • 500 kW

FRANCE
†R FRANCE INTL, Issoudun — W • E Africa • 500 kW; S • W Africa • 500 kW; S • C Africa & S Africa • 500 kW

IRAN
†VO THE ISLAMIC REP, Sirjan — W • E Europe & W Asia • 500 kW

†VO THE ISLAMIC REP, Tehrān — S • W Europe • 500 kW

NEW ZEALAND
†R NEW ZEALAND INTL, Rangitaiki — W • Pacific • 100 kW

PHILIPPINES
RADIO VERITAS ASIA, Palauig — S Asia • 250 kW; SE Asia • 250 kW

UNITED KINGDOM
†FEBA RADIO, Via Samara, Russia — S • Mideast • 250 kW; S F/Sa • Mideast • 250 kW

USA
†R FREE ASIA, Via Tinian, N Marianas — S • E Asia • 500 kW

†RFE-RL, Via Botswana — S • C Asia • 100 kW

†SUDAN RADIO SVC, Via Woofferton, UK — W M-F • ENGLISH, ETC • C Africa • 300 kW

†VOA, Via Briech, Morocco — W • Mideast • 250 kW

15535 FRANCE
†R FRANCE INTL, Via Novosibirsk, Russia — S • SE Asia • 500 kW

TURKEY
†VOICE OF TURKEY, Ankara-Emirler — S • S Asia, SE Asia & Australasia • 500 kW

15540 AUSTRALIA
RADIO AUSTRALIA, Via Singapore — S • E Asia • 100 kW

CHINA
†CENTRAL PEOPLE'S BS, Beijing — S • DS-2 • 50 kW; DS-2 • 50 kW; Th-Tu • DS-2 • 50 kW

PORTUGAL
†RDP INTERNATIONAL, Lisbon — Irr • W • E North Am • 100 kW

RUSSIA
VOICE OF RUSSIA, Armavir — W • Europe • 250 kW

VOICE OF RUSSIA, Moscow — S • Mideast • 250 kW

UNITED KINGDOM
BBC, Via Singapore — S Asia • 100 kW; W • W Asia & Mideast • 100 kW

USA
†VOA, Via Kavála, Greece — W • S Asia • 250 kW

15545 GERMANY
†DEUTSCHE WELLE, Via Sri Lanka — S • C Africa & E Africa • 250 kW; S • Mideast & E Africa • 250 kW

IRAN
†VO THE ISLAMIC REP, Sirjan — W • Mideast & N Africa • 500 kW

USA
R FREE ASIA, Via Tinian, N Marianas — SE Asia • 500 kW

VOA, Via Botswana — W • C Africa & S Africa • 100 kW; W M-F • C Africa & S Africa • 100 kW; S • Mideast • 250 kW

(con'd) †VOA, Via Briech, Morocco

ENGLISH ▬   ARABIC ▨   CHINESE ▢▢▢   FRENCH ▬   GERMAN ▬   RUSSIAN ═   SPANISH ▬   OTHER —

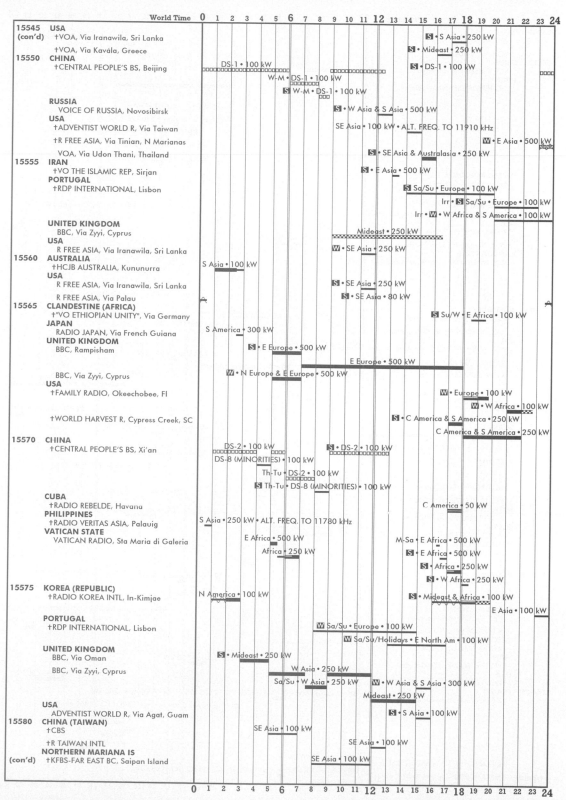

	World Time	0 1 2 3 4 5 6 7 8 9 10 11 12 13 14 15 16 17 18 19 20 21 22 23 24
15545 (con'd)	USA †VOA, Via Iranawila, Sri Lanka	S • S Asia • 250 kW
	†VOA, Via Kavála, Greece	S • Mideast • 250 kW
15550	CHINA †CENTRAL PEOPLE'S BS, Beijing	DS-1 • 100 kW ▫▫▫ S • DS-1 • 100 kW
		W-M • DS-1 • 100 kW
		S W-M • DS-1 • 100 kW
	RUSSIA VOICE OF RUSSIA, Novosibirsk	S • W Asia & S Asia • 500 kW
	USA †ADVENTIST WORLD R, Via Taiwan	SE Asia • 100 kW • ALT. FREQ. TO 11910 kHz
	†R FREE ASIA, Via Tinian, N Marianas	W • E Asia • 500 kW playtit
	VOA, Via Udon Thani, Thailand	S • SE Asia & Australasia • 250 kW
15555	IRAN †VO THE ISLAMIC REP, Sirjan	S • E Asia • 500 kW
	PORTUGAL †RDP INTERNATIONAL, Lisbon	S Sa/Su • Europe • 100 kW
		Irr • S Sa/Su • Europe • 100 kW
		Irr • W • W Africa & S America • 100 kW
	UNITED KINGDOM BBC, Via Zyyi, Cyprus	Mideast • 250 kW
	USA R FREE ASIA, Via Iranawila, Sri Lanka	W • SE Asia • 250 kW
15560	AUSTRALIA †HCJB AUSTRALIA, Kununurra	S Asia • 100 kW
	USA R FREE ASIA, Via Iranawila, Sri Lanka	S • SE Asia • 250 kW
	R FREE ASIA, Via Palau	S • SE Asia • 80 kW
15565	CLANDESTINE (AFRICA) †"VO ETHIOPIAN UNITY", Via Germany	S Su/W • E Africa • 100 kW
	JAPAN RADIO JAPAN, Via French Guiana	S America • 300 kW
	UNITED KINGDOM BBC, Rampisham	S • E Europe • 500 kW
		E Europe • 500 kW
	BBC, Via Zyyi, Cyprus	W • N Europe & E Europe • 500 kW
	USA †FAMILY RADIO, Okeechobee, Fl	W • Europe • 100 kW
		W • W Africa • 100 kW
	†WORLD HARVEST R, Cypress Creek, SC	S • C America & S America • 250 kW
		C America & S America • 250 kW
15570	CHINA †CENTRAL PEOPLE'S BS, Xi'an	DS-2 • 100 kW ▫▫▫ S • DS-2 • 100 kW
		DS-8 (MINORITIES) • 100 kW
		Th-Tu • DS-2 • 100 kW
		S Th-Tu • DS-8 (MINORITIES) • 100 kW
	CUBA †RADIO REBELDE, Havana	C America • 50 kW
	PHILIPPINES †RADIO VERITAS ASIA, Palauig	S Asia • 250 kW • ALT. FREQ. TO 11780 kHz
	VATICAN STATE VATICAN RADIO, Sta Maria di Galeria	E Africa • 500 kW M-Sa • E Africa • 500 kW
		Africa • 250 kW S • E Africa • 500 kW
		S • Africa • 250 kW
		S • W Africa • 250 kW
15575	KOREA (REPUBLIC) †RADIO KOREA INTL, In-Kimjae	N America • 100 kW S • Mideast & Africa • 100 kW
		E Asia • 100 kW
	PORTUGAL †RDP INTERNATIONAL, Lisbon	W Sa/Su • Europe • 100 kW
		W Sa/Su/Holidays • E North Am • 100 kW
	UNITED KINGDOM BBC, Via Oman	S • Mideast • 250 kW
	BBC, Via Zyyi, Cyprus	W Asia • 250 kW
		Sa/Su • W Asia • 250 kW W • W Asia & S Asia • 300 kW
		Mideast • 250 kW
	USA ADVENTIST WORLD R, Via Agat, Guam	S • S Asia • 100 kW
15580	CHINA (TAIWAN) †CBS	SE Asia • 100 kW
	†R TAIWAN INTL	SE Asia • 100 kW
(con'd)	NORTHERN MARIANA IS †KFBS-FAR EAST BC, Saipan Island	SE Asia • 100 kW

	0 1 2 3 4 5 6 7 8 9 10 11 12 13 14 15 16 17 18 19 20 21 22 23 24

SEASONAL S OR W   1-HR TIMESHIFT MIDYEAR ⇦ OR ⇨   JAMMING / OR ∧   EARLIEST HEARD ◁   LATEST HEARD ▷   NEW FOR 2005 †

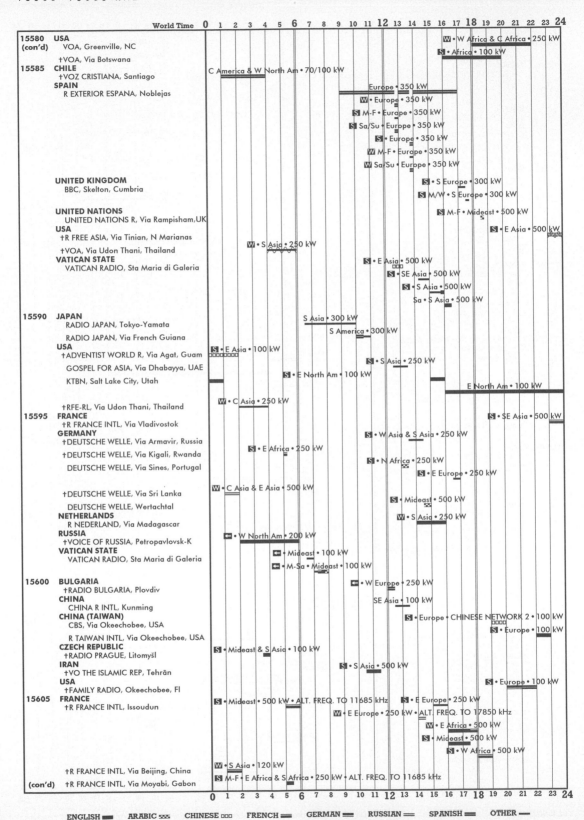

| | | World Time | 0 | 1 | 2 | 3 | 4 | 5 | 6 | 7 | 8 | 9 | 10 | 11 | 12 | 13 | 14 | 15 | 16 | 17 | 18 | 19 | 20 | 21 | 22 | 23 | 24 |

15580 **USA**
(con'd)   VOA, Greenville, NC — W • W Africa & C Africa • 250 kW
          †VOA, Via Botswana — S • Africa • 100 kW
15585 **CHILE**
          †VOZ CRISTIANA, Santiago — C America & W North Am • 70/100 kW
          SPAIN
          R EXTERIOR ESPANA, Noblejas — Europe • 350 kW
                                         W • Europe • 350 kW
                                         S M-F • Europe • 350 kW
                                         S Sa/Su • Europe • 350 kW
                                         S • Europe • 350 kW
                                         W M-F • Europe • 350 kW
                                         W Sa/Su • Europe • 350 kW
          UNITED KINGDOM
          BBC, Skelton, Cumbria — S • S Europe • 300 kW
                                   S M/W • S Europe • 300 kW
          UNITED NATIONS
          UNITED NATIONS R, Via Rampisham, UK — M-F • Mideast • 500 kW
          USA
          †R FREE ASIA, Via Tinian, N Marianas — S • E Asia • 500 kW
          †VOA, Via Udon Thani, Thailand — W • S Asia • 250 kW
          VATICAN STATE
          VATICAN RADIO, Sta Maria di Galeria — S • E Asia • 500 kW
                                                 S • SE Asia • 500 kW
                                                 S • S Asia • 500 kW
                                                 Sa • S Asia • 500 kW
15590 **JAPAN**
          RADIO JAPAN, Tokyo-Yamata — S Asia • 300 kW
          RADIO JAPAN, Via French Guiana — S America • 300 kW
          USA
          †ADVENTIST WORLD R, Via Agat, Guam — S • E Asia • 100 kW
          GOSPEL FOR ASIA, Via Dhabayya, UAE — S • S Asia • 250 kW
          KTBN, Salt Lake City, Utah — S • E North Am • 100 kW
                                        E North Am • 100 kW
          †RFE-RL, Via Udon Thani, Thailand — W • C Asia • 250 kW
15595 **FRANCE**
          †R FRANCE INTL, Via Vladivostok — S • SE Asia • 500 kW
          GERMANY
          †DEUTSCHE WELLE, Via Armavir, Russia — S • W Asia & S Asia • 250 kW
          †DEUTSCHE WELLE, Via Kigali, Rwanda — S • E Africa • 250 kW
          DEUTSCHE WELLE, Via Sines, Portugal — S • N Africa • 250 kW
                                                 S • E Europe • 250 kW
          †DEUTSCHE WELLE, Via Sri Lanka — W • C Asia & E Asia • 500 kW
          DEUTSCHE WELLE, Wertachtal — S • Mideast • 500 kW
                                        W • S Asia • 250 kW
          NETHERLANDS
          R NEDERLAND, Via Madagascar
          RUSSIA
          †VOICE OF RUSSIA, Petropavlovsk-K — • W North Am • 200 kW
          VATICAN STATE
          VATICAN RADIO, Sta Maria di Galeria — • Mideast • 100 kW
                                                 • M-Sa • Mideast • 100 kW
15600 **BULGARIA**
          †RADIO BULGARIA, Plovdiv — • W Europe • 250 kW
          CHINA
          CHINA R INTL, Kunming — SE Asia • 100 kW
          CHINA (TAIWAN)
          CBS, Via Okeechobee, USA — S • Europe • CHINESE NETWORK 2 • 100 kW
          R TAIWAN INTL, Via Okeechobee, USA — S • Europe • 100 kW
          CZECH REPUBLIC
          †RADIO PRAGUE, Litomyšl — S • Mideast & S Asia • 100 kW
          IRAN
          †VO THE ISLAMIC REP, Tehrān — S • S Asia • 500 kW
          USA
          †FAMILY RADIO, Okeechobee, Fl — S • Europe • 100 kW
15605 **FRANCE**
          †R FRANCE INTL, Issoudun — S • Mideast • 500 kW • ALT. FREQ. TO 11685 kHz
                                      W • E Europe • 250 kW • ALT. FREQ. TO 17850 kHz
                                      S • E Europe • 250 kW
                                      • E Africa • 500 kW
                                      S • Mideast • 500 kW
                                      S • W Africa • 500 kW
          †R FRANCE INTL, Via Beijing, China — W • S Asia • 120 kW
(con'd)   †R FRANCE INTL, Via Moyabi, Gabon — S M-F • E Africa & S Africa • 250 kW • ALT. FREQ. TO 11685 kHz

ENGLISH ▬ ARABIC ░ CHINESE □□□ FRENCH ══ GERMAN ▬ RUSSIAN ══ SPANISH ══ OTHER ──

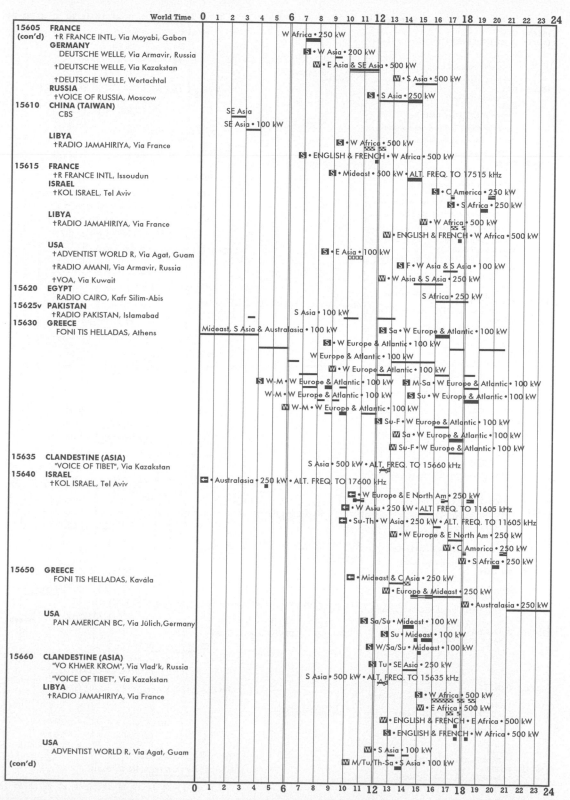

World Time	0 1 2 3 4 5 6 7 8 9 10 11 12 13 14 15 16 17 18 19 20 21 22 23 24

15605 **FRANCE**
(con'd)   †R FRANCE INTL, Via Moyabi, Gabon   W Africa • 250 kW
GERMANY
    DEUTSCHE WELLE, Via Armavir, Russia   S • W Asia • 200 kW
    †DEUTSCHE WELLE, Via Kazakstan   W • E Asia & SE Asia • 500 kW
    †DEUTSCHE WELLE, Wertachtal   W • S Asia • 500 kW
RUSSIA
    †VOICE OF RUSSIA, Moscow   S • S Asia • 250 kW
15610 **CHINA (TAIWAN)**
    CBS   SE Asia / SE Asia • 100 kW

LIBYA
    †RADIO JAMAHIRIYA, Via France   S • W Africa • 500 kW
    S • ENGLISH & FRENCH • W Africa • 500 kW

15615 **FRANCE**
    †R FRANCE INTL, Issoudun   S • Mideast • 500 kW • ALT. FREQ. TO 17515 kHz
ISRAEL
    †KOL ISRAEL, Tel Aviv   S • C America • 250 kW
    S • S Africa • 250 kW

LIBYA
    †RADIO JAMAHIRIYA, Via France   W • W Africa • 500 kW
    W • ENGLISH & FRENCH • W Africa • 500 kW

USA
    †ADVENTIST WORLD R, Via Agat, Guam   S • E Asia • 100 kW
    †RADIO AMANI, Via Armavir, Russia   S • F • W Asia & S Asia • 100 kW
    †VOA, Via Kuwait   W • W Asia & S Asia • 250 kW
15620 **EGYPT**
    RADIO CAIRO, Kafr Silim-Abis   S Africa • 250 kW
15625v **PAKISTAN**
    †RADIO PAKISTAN, Islamabad   S Asia • 100 kW
15630 **GREECE**
    FONI TIS HELLADAS, Athens   Mideast, S Asia & Australasia • 100 kW
    S Sa • W Europe & Atlantic • 100 kW
    S • W Europe & Atlantic • 100 kW
    W Europe & Atlantic • 100 kW
    W • W Europe & Atlantic • 100 kW
    S W-M • W Europe & Atlantic • 100 kW   S M-Sa • W Europe & Atlantic • 100 kW
    W-M • W Europe & Atlantic • 100 kW   S Su • W Europe & Atlantic • 100 kW
    W W-M • W Europe & Atlantic • 100 kW
    S Su-F • W Europe & Atlantic • 100 kW
    W Sa • W Europe & Atlantic • 100 kW
    W Su-F • W Europe & Atlantic • 100 kW

15635 **CLANDESTINE (ASIA)**
    "VOICE OF TIBET", Via Kazakstan   S Asia • 500 kW • ALT. FREQ. TO 15660 kHz
15640 **ISRAEL**
    †KOL ISRAEL, Tel Aviv   • Australasia • 250 kW • ALT. FREQ. TO 17600 kHz
    • W Europe & E North Am • 250 kW
    • W Asia • 250 kW • ALT. FREQ. TO 11605 kHz
    • Su-Th • W Asia • 250 kW • ALT. FREQ. TO 11605 kHz
    W • W Europe & E North Am • 250 kW
    W • C America • 250 kW
    W • S Africa • 250 kW

15650 **GREECE**
    FONI TIS HELLADAS, Kavála   • Mideast & C Asia • 250 kW
    • Europe & Mideast • 250 kW
    W • Australasia • 250 kW

USA
    PAN AMERICAN BC, Via Jülich, Germany   S Sa/Su • Mideast • 100 kW
    S Su • Mideast • 100 kW
    S W/Sa/Su • Mideast • 100 kW
15660 **CLANDESTINE (ASIA)**
    "VO KHMER KROM", Via Vlad'k, Russia   S Tu • SE Asia • 250 kW
    "VOICE OF TIBET", Via Kazakstan   S Asia • 500 kW • ALT. FREQ. TO 15635 kHz
LIBYA
    †RADIO JAMAHIRIYA, Via France   S • W Africa • 500 kW
    W • E Africa • 500 kW
    W • ENGLISH & FRENCH • E Africa • 500 kW
    S • ENGLISH & FRENCH • W Africa • 500 kW

USA
    ADVENTIST WORLD R, Via Agat, Guam   W • S Asia • 100 kW
(con'd)   W • M/Tu, Th-Sa • S Asia • 100 kW

World Time	0 1 2 3 4 5 6 7 8 9 10 11 12 13 14 15 16 17 18 19 20 21 22 23 24

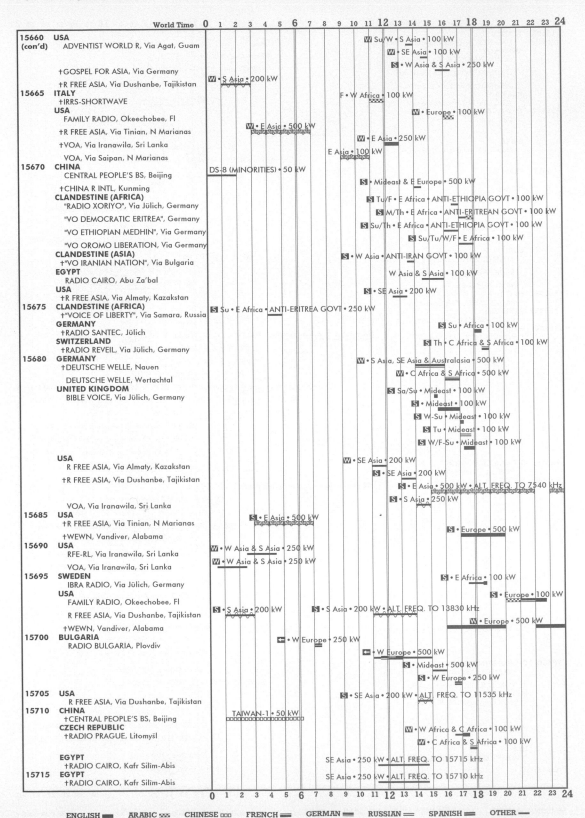

World Time	0 1 2 3 4 5 6 7 8 9 10 11 12 13 14 15 16 17 18 19 20 21 22 23 24
15660 USA	
(con'd) ADVENTIST WORLD R, Via Agat, Guam	W Su/W • S Asia • 100 kW
	W • SE Asia • 100 kW
	S • W Asia & S Asia • 250 kW
†GOSPEL FOR ASIA, Via Germany	F • W Africa • 100 kW
†R FREE ASIA, Via Dushanbe, Tajikistan	W • S Asia • 200 kW
15665 ITALY	
†IRRS-SHORTWAVE	
USA	W • Europe • 100 kW
FAMILY RADIO, Okeechobee, Fl	
†R FREE ASIA, Via Tinian, N Marianas	W • E Asia • 500 kW
†VOA, Via Iranawila, Sri Lanka	W • E Asia • 250 kW
VOA, Via Saipan, N Marianas	E Asia • 100 kW
15670 CHINA	DS-8 (MINORITIES) • 50 kW
CENTRAL PEOPLE'S BS, Beijing	
†CHINA R INTL, Kunming	S • Mideast & E Europe • 500 kW
CLANDESTINE (AFRICA)	S Tu/F • E Africa • ANTI-ETHIOPIA GOVT • 100 kW
"RADIO XORIYO", Via Jülich, Germany	
"VO DEMOCRATIC ERITREA", Germany	S M/Th • E Africa • ANTI-ERITREAN GOVT • 100 kW
"VO ETHIOPIAN MEDHIN", Via Germany	S Su/Th • E Africa • ANTI-ETHIOPIA GOVT • 100 kW
"VO OROMO LIBERATION, Via Germany	S Su/Tu/W/F • E Africa • 100 kW
CLANDESTINE (ASIA)	S • W Asia • ANTI-IRAN GOVT • 100 kW
†"VO IRANIAN NATION", Via Bulgaria	
EGYPT	W Asia & S Asia • 100 kW
RADIO CAIRO, Abu Za'bal	
USA	S • SE Asia • 200 kW
†R FREE ASIA, Via Almaty, Kazakstan	
15675 CLANDESTINE (AFRICA)	S Su • E Africa • ANTI-ERITREA GOVT • 250 kW
†"VOICE OF LIBERTY", Via Samara, Russia	
GERMANY	S Su • Africa • 100 kW
†RADIO SANTEC, Jülich	
SWITZERLAND	S Th • C Africa & S Africa • 100 kW
†RADIO REVEIL, Via Jülich, Germany	
15680 GERMANY	W • S Asia, SE Asia & Australasia • 500 kW
†DEUTSCHE WELLE, Nauen	
DEUTSCHE WELLE, Wertachtal	W • C Africa & S Africa • 500 kW
UNITED KINGDOM	S Sa/Su • Mideast • 100 kW
BIBLE VOICE, Via Jülich, Germany	S • Mideast • 100 kW
	S W-Su • Mideast • 100 kW
	S Tu • Mideast • 100 kW
	S W/F-Su • Mideast • 100 kW
USA	W • SE Asia • 200 kW
R FREE ASIA, Via Almaty, Kazakstan	
†R FREE ASIA, Via Dushanbe, Tajikistan	S • SE Asia • 200 kW
	S • E Asia • 500 kW • ALT. FREQ. TO 7540 kHz
VOA, Via Iranawila, Sri Lanka	S • S Asia • 250 kW
15685 USA	S • E Asia • 500 kW
†R FREE ASIA, Via Tinian, N Marianas	
†WEWN, Vandiver, Alabama	S • Europe • 500 kW
15690 USA	W • W Asia & S Asia • 250 kW
RFE-RL, Via Iranawila, Sri Lanka	
VOA, Via Iranawila, Sri Lanka	W • W Asia & S Asia • 250 kW
15695 SWEDEN	S • E Africa • 100 kW
IBRA RADIO, Via Jülich, Germany	
USA	S • Europe • 100 kW
FAMILY RADIO, Okeechobee, Fl	S • S Asia • 200 kW
R FREE ASIA, Via Dushanbe, Tajikistan	S • S Asia • 200 kW • ALT. FREQ. TO 13830 kHz
†WEWN, Vandiver, Alabama	W • Europe • 500 kW
15700 BULGARIA	◄ • W Europe • 250 kW
RADIO BULGARIA, Plovdiv	◄ • W Europe • 500 kW
	S • Mideast • 500 kW
	S • W Europe • 250 kW
15705 USA	S • SE Asia • 200 kW • ALT. FREQ. TO 11535 kHz
R FREE ASIA, Via Dushanbe, Tajikistan	
15710 CHINA	TAIWAN-1 • 50 kW
†CENTRAL PEOPLE'S BS, Beijing	
CZECH REPUBLIC	W • W Africa & C Africa • 100 kW
†RADIO PRAGUE, Litomyšl	W • C Africa & S Africa • 100 kW
EGYPT	SE Asia • 250 kW • ALT. FREQ. TO 15715 kHz
†RADIO CAIRO, Kafr Silim-Abis	
15715 EGYPT	SE Asia • 250 kW • ALT. FREQ. TO 15710 kHz
†RADIO CAIRO, Kafr Silim-Abis	
	0 1 2 3 4 5 6 7 8 9 10 11 12 13 14 15 16 17 18 19 20 21 22 23 24

ENGLISH ▬   ARABIC ▨▨   CHINESE □□□   FRENCH ▭▭   GERMAN ▬▬   RUSSIAN ══   SPANISH ▬▬   OTHER ──

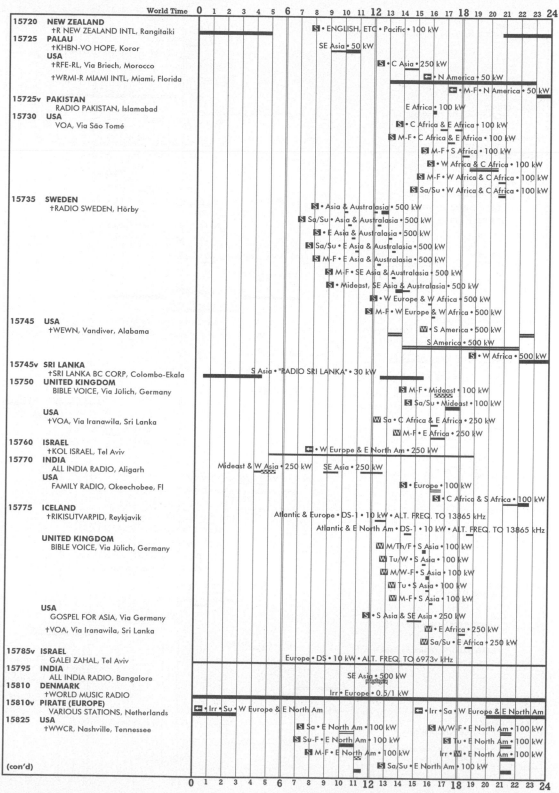

	World Time	0 1 2 3 4 5 6 7 8 9 10 11 12 13 14 15 16 17 18 19 20 21 22 23 24
15720	NEW ZEALAND	
	†R NEW ZEALAND INTL, Rangitaiki	S • ENGLISH, ETC • Pacific • 100 kW
15725	PALAU	
	†KHBN-VO HOPE, Koror	SE Asia • 50 kW
	USA	
	†RFE-RL, Via Briech, Morocco	S • C Asia • 250 kW
	†WRMI-R MIAMI INTL, Miami, Florida	• N America • 50 kW
		• M-F • N America • 50 kW
15725v	PAKISTAN	
	RADIO PAKISTAN, Islamabad	E Africa • 100 kW
15730	USA	
	VOA, Via São Tomé	S • C Africa & E Africa • 100 kW
		S M-F • C Africa & E Africa • 100 kW
		S M-F • S Africa • 100 kW
		S • W Africa & C Africa • 100 kW
		S M-F • W Africa & C Africa • 100 kW
		S Sa/Su • W Africa & C Africa • 100 kW
15735	SWEDEN	
	†RADIO SWEDEN, Hörby	S • Asia & Australasia • 500 kW
		S Sa/Su • Asia & Australasia • 500 kW
		S • E Asia & Australasia • 500 kW
		S Sa/Su • E Asia & Australasia • 500 kW
		S M-F • E Asia & Australasia • 500 kW
		S M-F • SE Asia & Australasia • 500 kW
		S • Mideast, SE Asia & Australasia • 500 kW
		S • W Europe & W Africa • 500 kW
		S M-F • W Europe & W Africa • 500 kW
15745	USA	
	†WEWN, Vandiver, Alabama	W • S America • 500 kW
		S America • 500 kW
		S • W Africa • 500 kW
15745v	SRI LANKA	
	†SRI LANKA BC CORP, Colombo-Ekala	S Asia • "RADIO SRI LANKA" • 30 kW
15750	UNITED KINGDOM	
	BIBLE VOICE, Via Jülich, Germany	S M-F • Mideast • 100 kW
		S Sa/Su • Mideast • 100 kW
	USA	
	†VOA, Via Iranawila, Sri Lanka	W Sa • C Africa & E Africa • 250 kW
		W M-F • E Africa • 250 kW
15760	ISRAEL	
	†KOL ISRAEL, Tel Aviv	• W Europe & E North Am • 250 kW
15770	INDIA	
	ALL INDIA RADIO, Aligarh	Mideast & W Asia • 250 kW SE Asia • 250 kW
	USA	
	FAMILY RADIO, Okeechobee, Fl	S • Europe • 100 kW
		S • C Africa & S Africa • 100 kW
15775	ICELAND	
	†RIKISUTVARPID, Reykjavik	Atlantic & Europe • DS-1 • 10 kW • ALT. FREQ. TO 13865 kHz
		Atlantic & E North Am • DS-1 • 10 kW • ALT. FREQ. TO 13865 kHz
	UNITED KINGDOM	
	BIBLE VOICE, Via Jülich, Germany	W M/Th/F • S Asia • 100 kW
		W Tu/W • S Asia • 100 kW
		W M/W-F • S Asia • 100 kW
		W Tu • S Asia • 100 kW
		W M-F • S Asia • 100 kW
	USA	
	GOSPEL FOR ASIA, Via Germany	S • S Asia & SE Asia • 250 kW
	†VOA, Via Iranawila, Sri Lanka	W • E Africa • 250 kW
		W Sa/Su • E Africa • 250 kW
15785v	ISRAEL	
	GALEI ZAHAL, Tel Aviv	Europe • DS • 10 kW • ALT. FREQ. TO 6973v kHz
15795	INDIA	
	ALL INDIA RADIO, Bangalore	SE Asia • 500 kW
15810	DENMARK	
	†WORLD MUSIC RADIO	Irr • Europe • 0.5/1 kW
15810v	PIRATE (EUROPE)	
	VARIOUS STATIONS, Netherlands	• Irr • Su • W Europe & E North Am • Irr • Sa • W Europe & E North Am
15825	USA	
	†WWCR, Nashville, Tennessee	S Sa • E North Am • 100 kW S M/W-F • E North Am • 100 kW
		S Su-F • E North Am • 100 kW S Tu • E North Am • 100 kW
		S M-F • E North Am • 100 kW Irr • W • E North Am • 100 kW
		S Sa/Su • E North Am • 100 kW
(con'd)		0 1 2 3 4 5 6 7 8 9 10 11 12 13 14 15 16 17 18 19 20 21 22 23 24

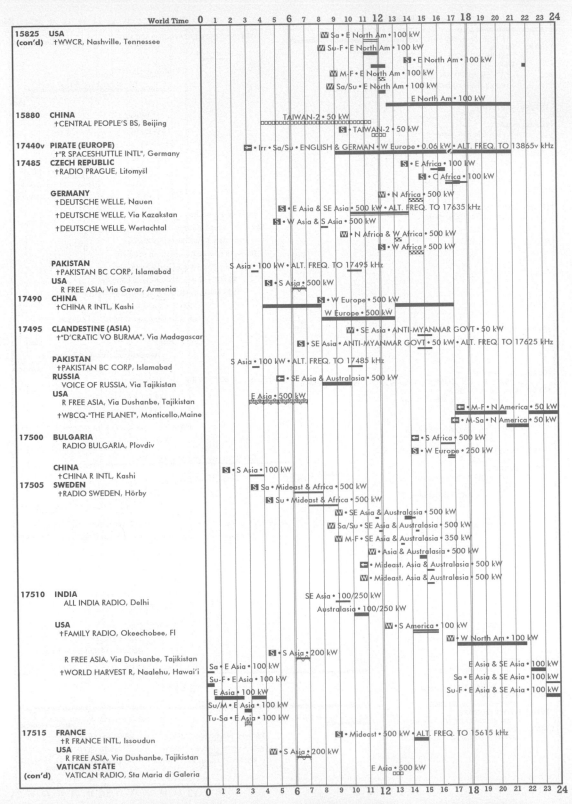

		World Time	0 1 2 3 4 5 6 7 8 9 10 11 12 13 14 15 16 17 18 19 20 21 22 23 24

15825 USA
(con'd) †WWCR, Nashville, Tennessee
- W • Sa • E North Am • 100 kW
- W • Su-F • E North Am • 100 kW
- S • E North Am • 100 kW
- W • M-F • E North Am • 100 kW
- W • Sa/Su • E North Am • 100 kW
- E North Am • 100 kW

15880 CHINA
†CENTRAL PEOPLE'S BS, Beijing
- TAIWAN-2 • 50 kW
- S • TAIWAN-2 • 50 kW

17440v PIRATE (EUROPE)
†"R SPACESHUTTLE INTL", Germany
- Irr • Sa/Su • ENGLISH & GERMAN • W Europe • 0.06 kW • ALT. FREQ. TO 13865v kHz

17485 CZECH REPUBLIC
†RADIO PRAGUE, Litomyšl
- S • E Africa • 100 kW
- S • C Africa • 100 kW

GERMANY
†DEUTSCHE WELLE, Nauen
- W • N Africa • 500 kW
†DEUTSCHE WELLE, Via Kazakstan
- S • E Asia & SE Asia • 500 kW • ALT. FREQ. TO 17635 kHz
†DEUTSCHE WELLE, Wertachtal
- S • W Asia & S Asia • 500 kW
- W • N Africa & W Africa • 500 kW
- S • W Africa • 500 kW

PAKISTAN
†PAKISTAN BC CORP, Islamabad
- S Asia • 100 kW • ALT. FREQ. TO 17495 kHz
USA
R FREE ASIA, Via Gavar, Armenia
- S • S Asia • 500 kW

17490 CHINA
†CHINA R INTL, Kashi
- S • W Europe • 500 kW
- W Europe • 500 kW

17495 CLANDESTINE (ASIA)
†"D'CRATIC VO BURMA", Via Madagascar
- W • SE Asia • ANTI-MYANMAR GOVT • 50 kW
- S • SE Asia • ANTI-MYANMAR GOVT • 50 kW • ALT. FREQ. TO 17625 kHz

PAKISTAN
†PAKISTAN BC CORP, Islamabad
- S Asia • 100 kW • ALT. FREQ. TO 17485 kHz
RUSSIA
VOICE OF RUSSIA, Via Tajikistan
- SE Asia & Australasia • 500 kW
USA
R FREE ASIA, Via Dushanbe, Tajikistan
- E Asia • 500 kW
†WBCQ-"THE PLANET", Monticello, Maine
- M-F • N America • 50 kW
- M-Sa • N America • 50 kW

17500 BULGARIA
RADIO BULGARIA, Plovdiv
- S Africa • 500 kW
- S • W Europe • 250 kW

CHINA
†CHINA R INTL, Kashi
- S • S Asia • 100 kW
17505 SWEDEN
†RADIO SWEDEN, Hörby
- S • Sa • Mideast & Africa • 500 kW
- S • Su • Mideast & Africa • 500 kW
- W • SE Asia & Australasia • 500 kW
- W • Sa/Su • SE Asia & Australasia • 500 kW
- W • M-F • SE Asia & Australasia • 350 kW
- W • Asia & Australasia • 500 kW
- Mideast, Asia & Australasia • 500 kW
- W • Mideast, Asia & Australasia • 500 kW

17510 INDIA
ALL INDIA RADIO, Delhi
- SE Asia • 100/250 kW
- Australasia • 100/250 kW

USA
†FAMILY RADIO, Okeechobee, Fl
- W • S America • 100 kW
- W • W North Am • 100 kW

R FREE ASIA, Via Dushanbe, Tajikistan
- S • S Asia • 200 kW
†WORLD HARVEST R, Naalehu, Hawai'i
- Sa • E Asia • 100 kW
- E Asia & SE Asia • 100 kW
- Su-F • E Asia • 100 kW
- Sa • E Asia & SE Asia • 100 kW
- E Asia • 100 kW
- Su-F • E Asia & SE Asia • 100 kW
- Su/M • E Asia • 100 kW
- Tu-Sa • E Asia • 100 kW

17515 FRANCE
†R FRANCE INTL, Issoudun
- S • Mideast • 500 kW • ALT. FREQ. TO 15615 kHz
USA
R FREE ASIA, Via Dushanbe, Tajikistan
- W • S Asia • 200 kW
VATICAN STATE
(con'd) VATICAN RADIO, Sta Maria di Galeria
- E Asia • 500 kW

	World Time	0 1 2 3 4 5 6 7 8 9 10 11 12 13 14 15 16 17 18 19 20 21 22 23 24

ENGLISH ▬   ARABIC ▨▨▨   CHINESE □□□   FRENCH ═══   GERMAN ▬▬   RUSSIAN ▭▭   SPANISH ══   OTHER ──

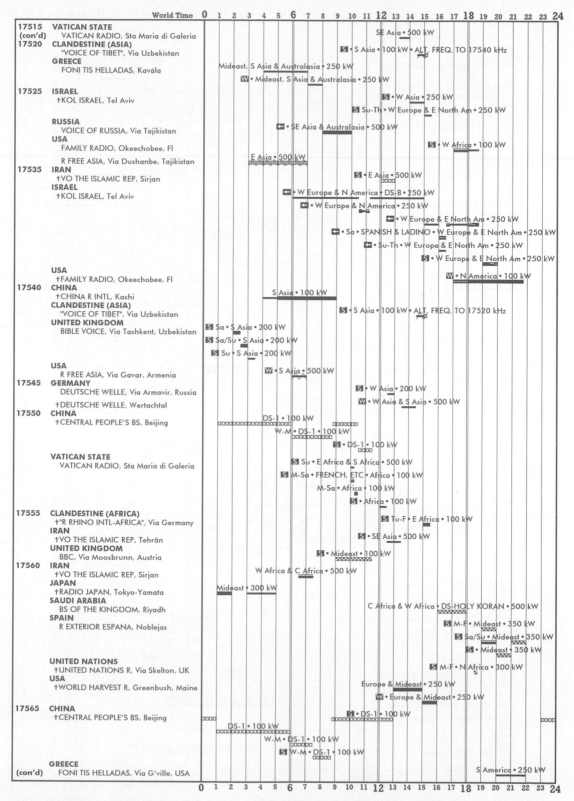

| | World Time | 0 | 1 | 2 | 3 | 4 | 5 | 6 | 7 | 8 | 9 | 10 | 11 | 12 | 13 | 14 | 15 | 16 | 17 | 18 | 19 | 20 | 21 | 22 | 23 | 24 |

17515 VATICAN STATE
(con'd)   VATICAN RADIO, Sta Maria di Galeria — SE Asia • 500 kW

17520 CLANDESTINE (ASIA)
"VOICE OF TIBET", Via Uzbekistan — ⑤ • S Asia • 100 kW • ALT. FREQ. TO 17540 kHz
GREECE
FONI TIS HELLADAS, Kavála — Mideast, S Asia & Australasia • 250 kW
Ⓦ • Mideast, S Asia & Australasia • 250 kW

17525 ISRAEL
†KOL ISRAEL, Tel Aviv — ⑤ • W Asia • 250 kW
⑤ Su-Th • W Europe & E North Am • 250 kW

RUSSIA
VOICE OF RUSSIA, Via Tajikistan — ⇦ • SE Asia & Australasia • 500 kW
USA
FAMILY RADIO, Okeechobee, Fl — ⑤ • W Africa • 100 kW
R FREE ASIA, Via Dushanbe, Tajikistan — E Asia • 500 kW

17535 IRAN
†VO THE ISLAMIC REP, Sirjan — ⑤ • E Asia • 500 kW
ISRAEL
†KOL ISRAEL, Tel Aviv — ⇦ • W Europe & N America • DS-B • 250 kW
⇦ • W Europe & N America • 250 kW
⇦ • W Europe & E North Am • 250 kW
⇦ • Sa • SPANISH & LADINO • W Europe & E North Am • 250 kW
⇦ • Su-Th • W Europe & E North Am • 250 kW
⑤ • W Europe & E North Am • 250 kW

USA
†FAMILY RADIO, Okeechobee, Fl — Ⓦ • N America • 100 kW

17540 CHINA
†CHINA R INTL, Kashi — S Asia • 100 kW
CLANDESTINE (ASIA)
"VOICE OF TIBET", Via Uzbekistan — ⑤ • S Asia • 100 kW • ALT. FREQ. TO 17520 kHz
UNITED KINGDOM
BIBLE VOICE, Via Tashkent, Uzbekistan — ⑤ Sa • S Asia • 200 kW
⑤ Sa/Su • S Asia • 200 kW
⑤ Su • S Asia • 200 kW

USA
R FREE ASIA, Via Gavar, Armenia — Ⓦ • S Asia • 500 kW

17545 GERMANY
DEUTSCHE WELLE, Via Armavir, Russia — ⑤ • W Asia • 200 kW
†DEUTSCHE WELLE, Wertachtal — Ⓦ • W Asia & S Asia • 500 kW

17550 CHINA
†CENTRAL PEOPLE'S BS, Beijing — DS-1 • 100 kW
W-M • DS-1 • 100 kW
⑤ • DS-1 • 100 kW

VATICAN STATE
VATICAN RADIO, Sta Maria di Galeria — ⑤ Su • E Africa & S Africa • 500 kW
⑤ M-Sa • FRENCH, ETC • Africa • 100 kW
M-Sa • Africa • 100 kW
⑤ • Africa • 100 kW

17555 CLANDESTINE (AFRICA)
†"R RHINO INTL-AFRICA", Via Germany — ⑤ Tu-F • E Africa • 100 kW
IRAN
†VO THE ISLAMIC REP, Tehrān — ⑤ • SE Asia • 500 kW
UNITED KINGDOM
BBC, Via Moosbrunn, Austria — ⑤ • Mideast • 100 kW

17560 IRAN
†VO THE ISLAMIC REP, Sirjan — W Africa & C Africa • 500 kW
JAPAN
†RADIO JAPAN, Tokyo-Yamata — Mideast • 300 kW
SAUDI ARABIA
BS OF THE KINGDOM, Riyadh — C Africa & W Africa • DS-HOLY KORAN • 500 kW
SPAIN
R EXTERIOR ESPANA, Noblejas — ⑤ M-F • Mideast • 350 kW
⑤ Sa/Su • Mideast • 350 kW
⑤ • Mideast • 350 kW

UNITED NATIONS
†UNITED NATIONS R, Via Skelton, UK — ⑤ M-F • N Africa • 300 kW
USA
†WORLD HARVEST R, Greenbush, Maine — Europe & Mideast • 250 kW
Ⓦ • Europe & Mideast • 250 kW

17565 CHINA
†CENTRAL PEOPLE'S BS, Beijing — ⑤ • DS-1 • 100 kW
DS-1 • 100 kW
W-M • DS-1 • 100 kW
⑤ W-M • DS-1 • 100 kW

GREECE
(con'd)   FONI TIS HELLADAS, Via G'ville, USA — S America • 250 kW

| | 0 | 1 | 2 | 3 | 4 | 5 | 6 | 7 | 8 | 9 | 10 | 11 | 12 | 13 | 14 | 15 | 16 | 17 | 18 | 19 | 20 | 21 | 22 | 23 | 24 |

SEASONAL ⑤ OR Ⓦ   1-HR TIMESHIFT MIDYEAR ⇦ OR ⇨   JAMMING / OR ∧   EARLIEST HEARD ◁   LATEST HEARD ▷   NEW FOR 2005 †

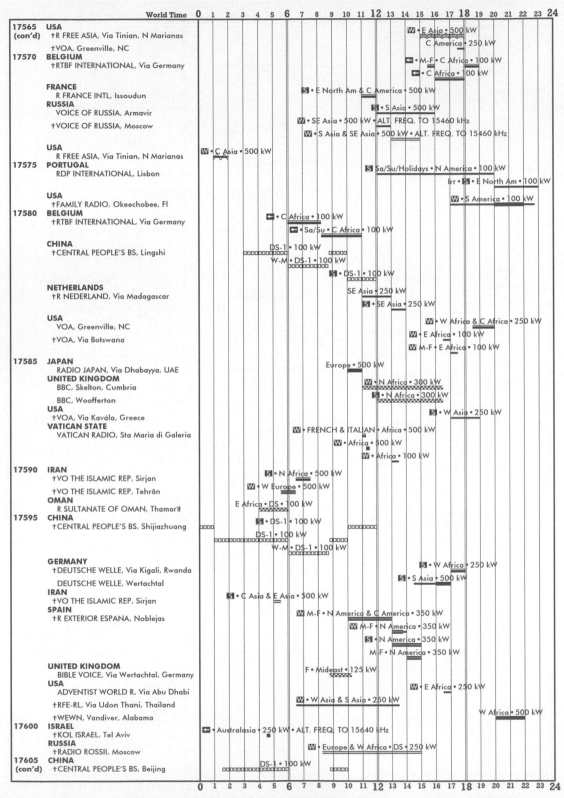

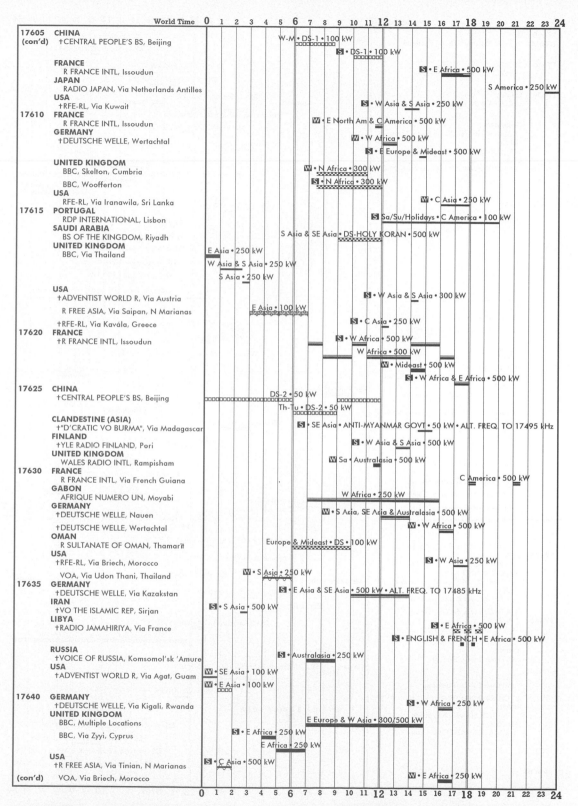

World Time   0 1 2 3 4 5 6 7 8 9 10 11 12 13 14 15 16 17 18 19 20 21 22 23 24

17605 CHINA
(con'd)   †CENTRAL PEOPLE'S BS, Beijing
     W-M • DS-1 • 100 kW
     S • DS-1 • 100 kW

FRANCE
     R FRANCE INTL, Issoudun   S • E Africa • 500 kW
JAPAN
     RADIO JAPAN, Via Netherlands Antilles   S America • 250 kW
USA
     †RFE-RL, Via Kuwait   S • W Asia & S Asia • 250 kW

17610 FRANCE
     R FRANCE INTL, Issoudun   W • E North Am & C America • 500 kW
GERMANY
     †DEUTSCHE WELLE, Wertachtal   W • W Africa • 500 kW
     S • E Europe & Mideast • 500 kW

UNITED KINGDOM
     BBC, Skelton, Cumbria   W • N Africa • 300 kW

     BBC, Woofferton   S • N Africa • 300 kW
USA
     RFE-RL, Via Iranawila, Sri Lanka   W • C Asia • 250 kW

17615 PORTUGAL
     RDP INTERNATIONAL, Lisbon   S • Sa/Su/Holidays • C America • 100 kW
SAUDI ARABIA
     BS OF THE KINGDOM, Riyadh   S Asia & SE Asia • DS-HOLY KORAN • 500 kW
UNITED KINGDOM
     BBC, Via Thailand   E Asia • 250 kW
     W Asia & S Asia • 250 kW
     S Asia • 250 kW

USA
     †"ADVENTIST WORLD R, Via Austria   S • W Asia & S Asia • 300 kW
     R FREE ASIA, Via Saipan, N Marianas   E Asia • 100 kW
     †RFE-RL, Via Kavála, Greece   S • C Asia • 250 kW

17620 FRANCE
     †R FRANCE INTL, Issoudun   S • W Africa • 500 kW
     W Africa • 500 kW
     W • Mideast • 500 kW
     S • W Africa & E Africa • 500 kW

17625 CHINA
     †CENTRAL PEOPLE'S BS, Beijing   DS-2 • 50 kW
     Th-Tu • DS-2 • 50 kW

CLANDESTINE (ASIA)
     †"D'CRATIC VO BURMA", Via Madagascar   S • SE Asia • ANTI-MYANMAR GOVT • 50 kW • ALT. FREQ. TO 17495 kHz
FINLAND
     †YLE RADIO FINLAND, Pori   S • W Asia & S Asia • 500 kW
UNITED KINGDOM
     WALES RADIO INTL, Rampisham   W • Sa • Australasia • 500 kW

17630 FRANCE
     R FRANCE INTL, Via French Guiana   C America • 500 kW
GABON
     AFRIQUE NUMERO UN, Moyabi   W Africa • 250 kW
GERMANY
     †DEUTSCHE WELLE, Nauen   W • S Asia, SE Asia & Australasia • 500 kW
     †DEUTSCHE WELLE, Wertachtal   W • W Africa • 500 kW
OMAN
     R SULTANATE OF OMAN, Thamarīt   Europe & Mideast • DS • 100 kW
USA
     †RFE-RL, Via Briech, Morocco   S • W Asia • 250 kW
     VOA, Via Udon Thani, Thailand   W • S Asia • 250 kW

17635 GERMANY
     †DEUTSCHE WELLE, Via Kazakstan   S • E Asia & SE Asia • 500 kW • ALT. FREQ. TO 17485 kHz
IRAN
     †VO THE ISLAMIC REP, Sirjan   S • S Asia • 500 kW
LIBYA
     †RADIO JAMAHIRIYA, Via France   S • E Africa • 500 kW
     S • ENGLISH & FRENCH • E Africa • 500 kW

RUSSIA
     †VOICE OF RUSSIA, Komsomol'sk 'Amure   S • Australasia • 250 kW
USA
     †ADVENTIST WORLD R, Via Agat, Guam   W • SE Asia • 100 kW
     W • E Asia • 100 kW

17640 GERMANY
     †DEUTSCHE WELLE, Via Kigali, Rwanda   S • W Africa • 250 kW
UNITED KINGDOM
     BBC, Multiple Locations   E Europe & W Asia • 300/500 kW
     BBC, Via Zyyi, Cyprus   S • E Africa • 250 kW
     E Africa • 250 kW

USA
     †R FREE ASIA, Via Tinian, N Marianas   S • C Asia • 500 kW
(con'd)   VOA, Via Briech, Morocco   W • E Africa • 250 kW

0 1 2 3 4 5 6 7 8 9 10 11 12 13 14 15 16 17 18 19 20 21 22 23 24

SEASONAL S OR W   1-HR TIMESHIFT MIDYEAR ⊟ OR ⊡   JAMMING / OR ∧   EARLIEST HEARD ◁   LATEST HEARD ▷   NEW FOR 2005 †

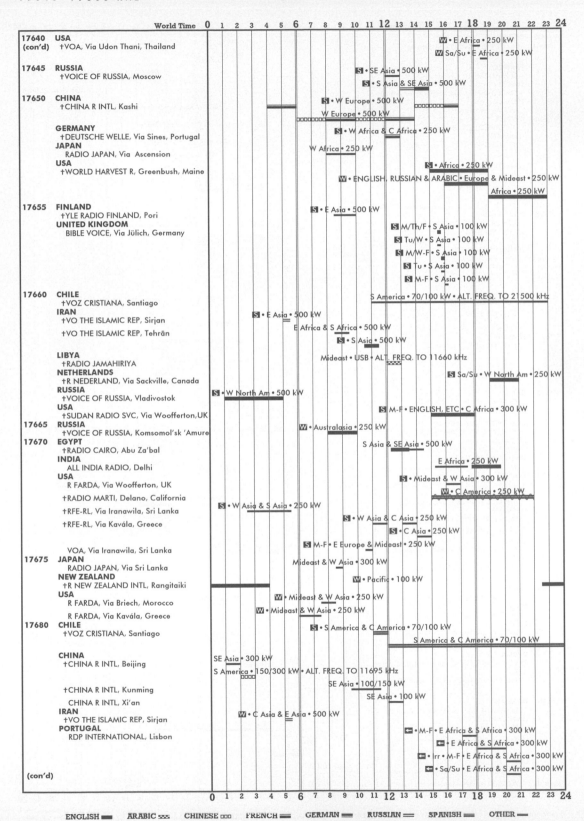

World Time 0 1 2 3 4 5 6 7 8 9 10 11 12 13 14 15 16 17 18 19 20 21 22 23 24

17640 USA
(con'd) †VOA, Via Udon Thani, Thailand
- W • E Africa • 250 kW
- W Sa/Su • E Africa • 250 kW

17645 RUSSIA
  †VOICE OF RUSSIA, Moscow
- S • SE Asia • 500 kW
- S • S Asia & SE Asia • 500 kW

17650 CHINA
  †CHINA R INTL, Kashi
- S • W Europe • 500 kW
- W Europe • 500 kW

  GERMANY
  †DEUTSCHE WELLE, Via Sines, Portugal
- S • W Africa & C Africa • 250 kW
  JAPAN
  RADIO JAPAN, Via Ascension
- W Africa • 250 kW
  USA
  †WORLD HARVEST R, Greenbush, Maine
- S • Africa • 250 kW
- W • ENGLISH, RUSSIAN & ARABIC • Europe & Mideast • 250 kW
- Africa • 250 kW

17655 FINLAND
  †YLE RADIO FINLAND, Pori
- S • E Asia • 500 kW
  UNITED KINGDOM
  BIBLE VOICE, Via Jülich, Germany
- S M/Th/F • S Asia • 100 kW
- S Tu/W • S Asia • 100 kW
- S M/W-F • S Asia • 100 kW
- S Tu • S Asia • 100 kW
- S M-F • S Asia • 100 kW

17660 CHILE
  †VOZ CRISTIANA, Santiago
- S America • 70/100 kW • ALT. FREQ. TO 21500 kHz
  IRAN
  †VO THE ISLAMIC REP, Sirjan
- S • E Asia • 500 kW
  †VO THE ISLAMIC REP, Tehrān
- E Africa & S Africa • 500 kW
- S • S Asia • 500 kW

  LIBYA
  †RADIO JAMAHIRIYA
- Mideast • USB • ALT. FREQ. TO 11660 kHz
  NETHERLANDS
  †R NEDERLAND, Via Sackville, Canada
- S Sa/Su • W North Am • 250 kW
  RUSSIA
  †VOICE OF RUSSIA, Vladivostok
- S • W North Am • 500 kW
  USA
  †SUDAN RADIO SVC, Via Woofferton, UK
- S M-F • ENGLISH, ETC • C Africa • 300 kW
17665 RUSSIA
  †VOICE OF RUSSIA, Komsomol'sk 'Amure
- W • Australasia • 250 kW
17670 EGYPT
  †RADIO CAIRO, Abu Za'bal
- S Asia & SE Asia • 500 kW
  INDIA
  ALL INDIA RADIO, Delhi
- E Africa • 250 kW
  USA
  R FARDA, Via Woofferton, UK
- S • Mideast & W Asia • 300 kW
  †RADIO MARTI, Delano, California
- W • C America • 250 kW
  †RFE-RL, Via Iranawila, Sri Lanka
- S • W Asia & S Asia • 250 kW
  †RFE-RL, Via Kavála, Greece
- S • W Asia & C Asia • 250 kW
- S • C Asia • 250 kW

  VOA, Via Iranawila, Sri Lanka
- S M-F • E Europe & Mideast • 250 kW
17675 JAPAN
  RADIO JAPAN, Via Sri Lanka
- Mideast & W Asia • 300 kW
  NEW ZEALAND
  †R NEW ZEALAND INTL, Rangitaiki
- W • Pacific • 100 kW
  USA
  R FARDA, Via Briech, Morocco
- W • Mideast & W Asia • 250 kW
  R FARDA, Via Kavála, Greece
- W • Mideast & W Asia • 250 kW
17680 CHILE
  †VOZ CRISTIANA, Santiago
- S • S America & C America • 70/100 kW
- S America & C America • 70/100 kW

  CHINA
  †CHINA R INTL, Beijing
- SE Asia • 300 kW
- S America • 150/300 kW • ALT. FREQ. TO 11695 kHz
  †CHINA R INTL, Kunming
- SE Asia • 100/150 kW
  CHINA R INTL, Xi'an
- SE Asia • 100 kW
  IRAN
  †VO THE ISLAMIC REP, Sirjan
- W • C Asia & E Asia • 500 kW
  PORTUGAL
  RDP INTERNATIONAL, Lisbon
- ← • M-F • E Africa & S Africa • 300 kW
- ← • E Africa & S Africa • 300 kW
- ← irr M-F • E Africa & S Africa • 300 kW
- ← • Sa/Su • E Africa & S Africa • 300 kW

(con'd)

0 1 2 3 4 5 6 7 8 9 10 11 12 13 14 15 16 17 18 19 20 21 22 23 24

ENGLISH ▬ ARABIC ▧ CHINESE ▨ FRENCH ▬ GERMAN ▬ RUSSIAN ▬ SPANISH ▬ OTHER ▬

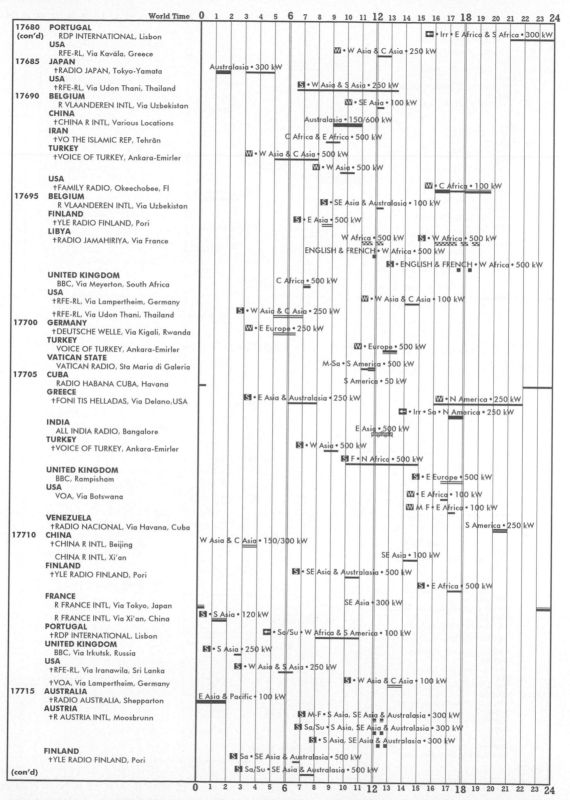

World Time   0   1   2   3   4   5   6   7   8   9   10 11 12 13 14 15 16 17 18 19 20 21 22 23 24

17680 (con'd)	PORTUGAL
	RDP INTERNATIONAL, Lisbon
	USA
	RFE-RL, Via Kavála, Greece
17685	JAPAN
	†RADIO JAPAN, Tokyo-Yamata
	USA
	†RFE-RL, Via Udon Thani, Thailand
17690	BELGIUM
	R VLAANDEREN INTL, Via Uzbekistan
	CHINA
	†CHINA R INTL, Various Locations
	IRAN
	†VO THE ISLAMIC REP, Tehrān
	TURKEY
	†VOICE OF TURKEY, Ankara-Emirler
	USA
	†FAMILY RADIO, Okeechobee, Fl
17695	BELGIUM
	R VLAANDEREN INTL, Via Uzbekistan
	FINLAND
	†YLE RADIO FINLAND, Pori
	LIBYA
	†RADIO JAMAHIRIYA, Via France
	UNITED KINGDOM
	BBC, Via Meyerton, South Africa
	USA
	†RFE-RL, Via Lampertheim, Germany
	†RFE-RL, Via Udon Thani, Thailand
17700	GERMANY
	†DEUTSCHE WELLE, Via Kigali, Rwanda
	TURKEY
	VOICE OF TURKEY, Ankara-Emirler
	VATICAN STATE
	VATICAN RADIO, Sta Maria di Galeria
17705	CUBA
	RADIO HABANA CUBA, Havana
	GREECE
	†FONI TIS HELLADAS, Via Delano, USA
	INDIA
	ALL INDIA RADIO, Bangalore
	TURKEY
	†VOICE OF TURKEY, Ankara-Emirler
	UNITED KINGDOM
	BBC, Rampisham
	USA
	VOA, Via Botswana
	VENEZUELA
	†RADIO NACIONAL, Via Havana, Cuba
17710	CHINA
	†CHINA R INTL, Beijing
	CHINA R INTL, Xi'an
	FINLAND
	†YLE RADIO FINLAND, Pori
	FRANCE
	R FRANCE INTL, Via Tokyo, Japan
	R FRANCE INTL, Via Xi'an, China
	PORTUGAL
	†RDP INTERNATIONAL, Lisbon
	UNITED KINGDOM
	BBC, Via Irkutsk, Russia
	USA
	†RFE-RL, Via Iranawila, Sri Lanka
	†VOA, Via Lampertheim, Germany
17715	AUSTRALIA
	†RADIO AUSTRALIA, Shepparton
	AUSTRIA
	†R AUSTRIA INTL, Moosbrunn
	FINLAND
	†YLE RADIO FINLAND, Pori
(con'd)	

Bar chart annotations (left to right, top to bottom):

- ⬅•Irr•E Africa & S Africa•300 kW
- W•W Asia & C Asia•250 kW
- Australasia•300 kW
- S•W Asia & S Asia•250 kW
- W•SE Asia•100 kW
- Australasia•150/600 kW
- C Africa & E Africa•500 kW
- W•W Asia & C Asia•500 kW
- W•W Asia•500 kW
- W•C Africa•100 kW
- S•SE Asia & Australasia•100 kW
- S•E Asia•500 kW
- W Africa•500 kW   S•W Africa•500 kW
- ENGLISH & FRENCH•W Africa•500 kW
- S•ENGLISH & FRENCH•W Africa•500 kW
- C Africa•500 kW
- W•W Asia & C Asia•100 kW
- S•W Asia & C Asia•250 kW
- W•E Europe•250 kW
- W•Europe•500 kW
- M-Sa•S America•500 kW
- S America•50 kW
- S•E Asia & Australasia•250 kW
- W•N America•250 kW
- ⬅•Irr•Sa•N America•250 kW
- E Asia•500 kW
- S•W Asia•500 kW
- S•F•N Africa•500 kW
- S•E Europe•500 kW
- W•E Africa•100 kW
- W M F•E Africa•100 kW
- S America•250 kW
- W Asia & C Asia•150/300 kW
- SE Asia•100 kW
- S•SE Asia & Australasia•500 kW
- S•E Africa•500 kW
- SE Asia•300 kW
- S•S Asia•120 kW
- •Sa/Su•W Africa & S America•100 kW
- S•S Asia•250 kW
- S•W Asia & S Asia•250 kW
- S•W Asia & C Asia•100 kW
- E Asia & Pacific•100 kW
- S M-F•S Asia, SE Asia & Australasia•300 kW
- S Sa/Su•S Asia, SE Asia & Australasia•300 kW
- S•S Asia, SE Asia & Australasia•300 kW
- S Sa•SE Asia & Australasia•500 kW
- S Sa/Su•SE Asia & Australasia•500 kW

World Time   0   1   2   3   4   5   6   7   8   9   10 11 12 13 14 15 16 17 18 19 20 21 22 23 24

SEASONAL S OR W   1-HR TIMESHIFT MIDYEAR ⬅ OR ➡   JAMMING / OR ∧   EARLIEST HEARD ◁   LATEST HEARD ▷   NEW FOR 2005 †

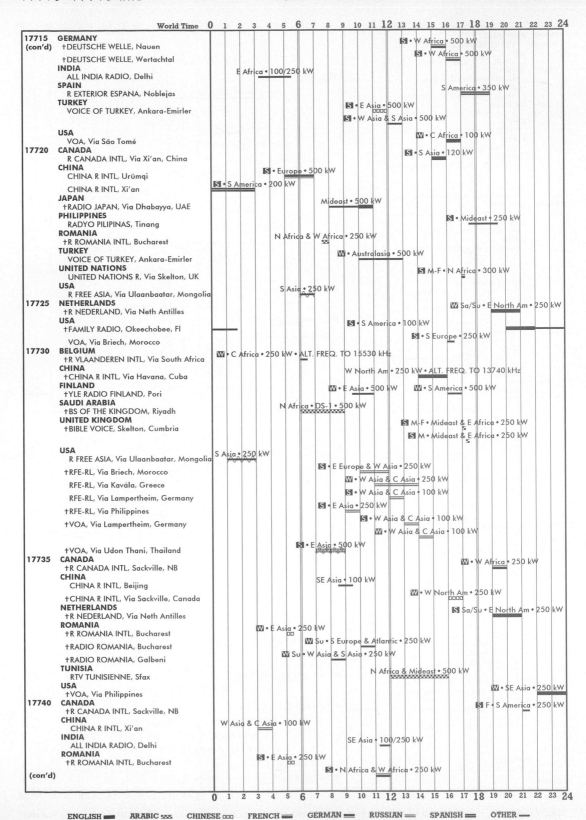

	World Time	0 1 2 3 4 5 6 7 8 9 10 11 12 13 14 15 16 17 18 19 20 21 22 23 24

17715 **GERMANY**
(con'd) †DEUTSCHE WELLE, Nauen — S • W Africa • 500 kW
         †DEUTSCHE WELLE, Wertachtal — S • W Africa • 500 kW
INDIA
   ALL INDIA RADIO, Delhi — E Africa • 100/250 kW
SPAIN
   R EXTERIOR ESPANA, Noblejas — S America • 350 kW
TURKEY
   VOICE OF TURKEY, Ankara-Emirler — S • E Asia • 500 kW
                                     S • W Asia & S Asia • 500 kW
USA
   VOA, Via São Tomé — W • C Africa • 100 kW
17720 **CANADA**
   R CANADA INTL, Via Xi'an, China — S • S Asia • 120 kW
CHINA
   CHINA R INTL, Urümqi — S • Europe • 500 kW
   CHINA R INTL, Xi'an — S • S America • 200 kW
JAPAN
   †RADIO JAPAN, Via Dhabayya, UAE — Mideast • 500 kW
PHILIPPINES
   RADYO PILIPINAS, Tinang — S • Mideast • 250 kW
ROMANIA
   †R ROMANIA INTL, Bucharest — N Africa & W Africa • 250 kW
TURKEY
   VOICE OF TURKEY, Ankara-Emirler — W • Australasia • 500 kW
UNITED NATIONS
   UNITED NATIONS R, Via Skelton, UK — S M-F • N Africa • 300 kW
USA
   R FREE ASIA, Via Ulaanbaatar, Mongolia — S Asia • 250 kW
17725 **NETHERLANDS**
   †R NEDERLAND, Via Neth Antilles — W Sa/Su • E North Am • 250 kW
USA
   †FAMILY RADIO, Okeechobee, Fl — S • S America • 100 kW
   VOA, Via Briech, Morocco — S • S Europe • 250 kW
17730 **BELGIUM**
   †R VLAANDEREN INTL, Via South Africa — W • C Africa • 250 kW • ALT. FREQ. TO 15530 kHz
CHINA
   †CHINA R INTL, Via Havana, Cuba — W North Am • 250 kW • ALT. FREQ. TO 13740 kHz
FINLAND
   †YLE RADIO FINLAND, Pori — W • E Asia • 500 kW   W • S America • 500 kW
SAUDI ARABIA
   †BS OF THE KINGDOM, Riyadh — N Africa • DS-1 • 500 kW
UNITED KINGDOM
   †BIBLE VOICE, Skelton, Cumbria — S M-F • Mideast & E Africa • 250 kW
                                    S M • Mideast & E Africa • 250 kW
USA
   R FREE ASIA, Via Ulaanbaatar, Mongolia — S Asia • 250 kW
   †RFE-RL, Via Briech, Morocco — S • E Europe & W Asia • 250 kW
   RFE-RL, Via Kavála, Greece — W • W Asia & C Asia • 250 kW
   RFE-RL, Via Lampertheim, Germany — S • W Asia & C Asia • 100 kW
   †RFE-RL, Via Philippines — S • E Asia • 250 kW
   †VOA, Via Lampertheim, Germany — S • W Asia & C Asia • 100 kW
                                    W • W Asia & C Asia • 100 kW
   †VOA, Via Udon Thani, Thailand — S • E Asia • 500 kW
17735 **CANADA**
   †R CANADA INTL, Sackville, NB — W • W Africa • 250 kW
CHINA
   CHINA R INTL, Beijing — SE Asia • 100 kW
   †CHINA R INTL, Via Sackville, Canada — W • W North Am • 250 kW
NETHERLANDS
   †R NEDERLAND, Via Neth Antilles — S Sa/Su • E North Am • 250 kW
ROMANIA
   †R ROMANIA INTL, Bucharest — W • E Asia • 250 kW
   †RADIO ROMANIA, Bucharest — W Su • S Europe & Atlantic • 250 kW
   †RADIO ROMANIA, Galbeni — W Su • W Asia & S Asia • 250 kW
TUNISIA
   RTV TUNISIENNE, Sfax — N Africa & Mideast • 500 kW
USA
   †VOA, Via Philippines — W • SE Asia • 250 kW
17740 **CANADA**
   †R CANADA INTL, Sackville, NB — S F • S America • 250 kW
CHINA
   CHINA R INTL, Xi'an — W Asia & C Asia • 100 kW
INDIA
   ALL INDIA RADIO, Delhi — SE Asia • 100/250 kW
ROMANIA
   †R ROMANIA INTL, Bucharest — S • E Asia • 250 kW
                               S • N Africa & W Africa • 250 kW
(con'd)

	0 1 2 3 4 5 6 7 8 9 10 11 12 13 14 15 16 17 18 19 20 21 22 23 24

ENGLISH ▬ ARABIC ≈≈≈ CHINESE □□□ FRENCH ▬ GERMAN ▬ RUSSIAN ═ SPANISH ═ OTHER ─

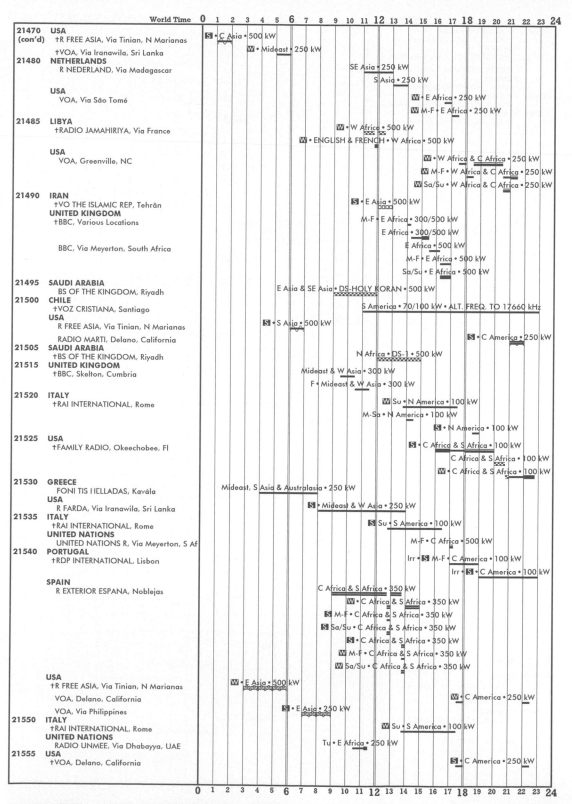

World Time 0 1 2 3 4 5 6 7 8 9 10 11 12 13 14 15 16 17 18 19 20 21 22 23 24

21470 USA
(con'd) †R FREE ASIA, Via Tinian, N Marianas — S • C Asia • 500 kW
         †VOA, Via Iranawila, Sri Lanka — W • Mideast • 250 kW
21480 NETHERLANDS
         R NEDERLAND, Via Madagascar — SE Asia • 250 kW
                                        S Asia • 250 kW
         USA
         VOA, Via São Tomé — W • E Africa • 250 kW
                             W M-F • E Africa • 250 kW
21485 LIBYA
         †RADIO JAMAHIRIYA, Via France — W • W Africa • 500 kW
                                          W • ENGLISH & FRENCH • W Africa • 500 kW
         USA
         VOA, Greenville, NC — W • W Africa & C Africa • 250 kW
                               W M-F • W Africa & C Africa • 250 kW
                               W Sa/Su • W Africa & C Africa • 250 kW
21490 IRAN
         †VO THE ISLAMIC REP, Tehrān — S • E Asia • 500 kW
         UNITED KINGDOM
         †BBC, Various Locations — M-F • E Africa • 300/500 kW
                                   E Africa • 300/500 kW
         BBC, Via Meyerton, South Africa — E Africa • 500 kW
                                           M-F • E Africa • 500 kW
                                           Sa/Su • E Africa • 500 kW
21495 SAUDI ARABIA
         BS OF THE KINGDOM, Riyadh — E Asia & SE Asia • DS-HOLY KORAN • 500 kW
21500 CHILE
         †VOZ CRISTIANA, Santiago — S America • 70/100 kW • ALT. FREQ. TO 17660 kHz
         USA
         R FREE ASIA, Via Tinian, N Marianas — S • S Asia • 500 kW
         RADIO MARTI, Delano, California — S • C America • 250 kW
21505 SAUDI ARABIA
         †BS OF THE KINGDOM, Riyadh — N Africa • DS-1 • 500 kW
21515 UNITED KINGDOM
         †BBC, Skelton, Cumbria — Mideast & W Asia • 300 kW
                                  F • Mideast & W Asia • 300 kW
21520 ITALY
         †RAI INTERNATIONAL, Rome — W Su • N America • 100 kW
                                    M-Sa • N America • 100 kW
21525 USA
         †FAMILY RADIO, Okeechobee, Fl — S • N America • 100 kW
                                        S • C Africa & S Africa • 100 kW
                                        C Africa & S Africa • 100 kW
                                        W • C Africa & S Africa • 100 kW
21530 GREECE
         FONI TIS HELLADAS, Kavála — Mideast, S Asia & Australasia • 250 kW
         USA
         R FARDA, Via Iranawila, Sri Lanka — S • Mideast & W Asia • 250 kW
21535 ITALY
         †RAI INTERNATIONAL, Rome — S Su • S America • 100 kW
         UNITED NATIONS
         UNITED NATIONS R, Via Meyerton, S Af — M-F • C Africa • 500 kW
21540 PORTUGAL
         †RDP INTERNATIONAL, Lisbon — Irr • S M-F • C America • 100 kW
                                      Irr • S • C America • 100 kW
         SPAIN
         R EXTERIOR ESPANA, Noblejas — C Africa & S Africa • 350 kW
                                       W • C Africa & S Africa • 350 kW
                                       S M-F • C Africa & S Africa • 350 kW
                                       S Sa/Su • C Africa & S Africa • 350 kW
                                       S • C Africa & S Africa • 350 kW
                                       W M-F • C Africa & S Africa • 350 kW
                                       W Sa/Su • C Africa & S Africa • 350 kW
         USA
         †R FREE ASIA, Via Tinian, N Marianas — W • E Asia • 500 kW
         VOA, Delano, California — W • C America • 250 kW
         VOA, Via Philippines — S • E Asia • 250 kW
21550 ITALY
         †RAI INTERNATIONAL, Rome — W Su • S America • 100 kW
         UNITED NATIONS
         RADIO UNMEE, Via Dhabayya, UAE — Tu • E Africa • 250 kW
21555 USA
         †VOA, Delano, California — S • C America • 250 kW

World Time 0 1 2 3 4 5 6 7 8 9 10 11 12 13 14 15 16 17 18 19 20 21 22 23 24

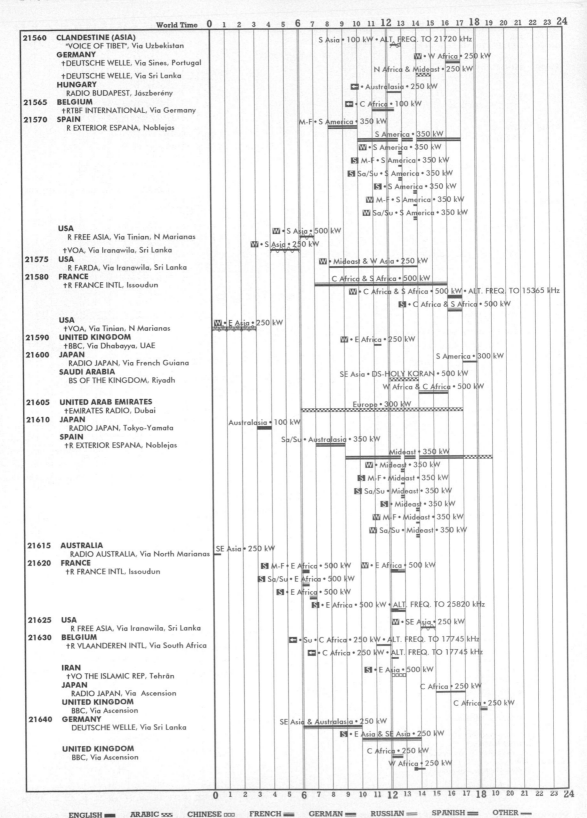

World Time 0 1 2 3 4 5 6 7 8 9 10 11 12 13 14 15 16 17 18 19 20 21 22 23 24

21560 CLANDESTINE (ASIA)
"VOICE OF TIBET", Via Uzbekistan — S Asia • 100 kW • ALT. FREQ. TO 21720 kHz
GERMANY
†DEUTSCHE WELLE, Via Sines, Portugal — W • W Africa • 250 kW
†DEUTSCHE WELLE, Via Sri Lanka — N Africa & Mideast • 250 kW
HUNGARY
RADIO BUDAPEST, Jászberény — ← • Australasia • 250 kW
21565 BELGIUM
†RTBF INTERNATIONAL, Via Germany — ← • C Africa • 100 kW
21570 SPAIN
R EXTERIOR ESPANA, Noblejas — M-F • S America • 350 kW
S America • 350 kW
W • S America • 350 kW
S M-F • S America • 350 kW
S Sa/Su • S America • 350 kW
S • S America • 350 kW
W M-F • S America • 350 kW
W Sa/Su • S America • 350 kW

USA
R FREE ASIA, Via Tinian, N Marianas — W • S Asia • 500 kW
†VOA, Via Iranawila, Sri Lanka — W • S Asia • 250 kW
21575 USA
R FARDA, Via Iranawila, Sri Lanka — W • Mideast & W Asia • 250 kW
21580 FRANCE
†R FRANCE INTL, Issoudun — C Africa & S Africa • 500 kW
W • C Africa & S Africa • 500 kW • ALT. FREQ. TO 15365 kHz
S • C Africa & S Africa • 500 kW

USA
†VOA, Via Tinian, N Marianas — W • E Asia • 250 kW
21590 UNITED KINGDOM
†BBC, Via Dhabayya, UAE — W • E Africa • 250 kW
21600 JAPAN
RADIO JAPAN, Via French Guiana — S America • 300 kW
SAUDI ARABIA
BS OF THE KINGDOM, Riyadh — SE Asia • DS-HOLY KORAN • 500 kW
W Africa & C Africa • 500 kW
21605 UNITED ARAB EMIRATES
†EMIRATES RADIO, Dubai — Europe • 300 kW
21610 JAPAN
RADIO JAPAN, Tokyo-Yamata — Australasia • 100 kW
SPAIN
†R EXTERIOR ESPANA, Noblejas — Sa/Su • Australasia • 350 kW
Mideast • 350 kW
W • Mideast • 350 kW
S M-F • Mideast • 350 kW
S Sa/Su • Mideast • 350 kW
S • Mideast • 350 kW
W M-F • Mideast • 350 kW
W Sa/Su • Mideast • 350 kW

21615 AUSTRALIA
RADIO AUSTRALIA, Via North Marianas — SE Asia • 250 kW
21620 FRANCE
†R FRANCE INTL, Issoudun — S M-F • E Africa • 500 kW   W • E Africa • 500 kW
S Sa/Su • E Africa • 500 kW
S • E Africa • 500 kW
S • E Africa • 500 kW • ALT. FREQ. TO 25820 kHz
21625 USA
R FREE ASIA, Via Iranawila, Sri Lanka — W • SE Asia • 250 kW
21630 BELGIUM
†R VLAANDEREN INTL, Via South Africa — ← • Su • C Africa • 250 kW • ALT. FREQ. TO 17745 kHz
← • C Africa • 250 kW • ALT. FREQ. TO 17745 kHz

IRAN
†VO THE ISLAMIC REP, Tehrān — S • E Asia • 500 kW
JAPAN
RADIO JAPAN, Via Ascension — C Africa • 250 kW
UNITED KINGDOM
BBC, Via Ascension — C Africa • 250 kW
21640 GERMANY
DEUTSCHE WELLE, Via Sri Lanka — SE Asia & Australasia • 250 kW
S • E Asia & SE Asia • 250 kW

UNITED KINGDOM
BBC, Via Ascension — C Africa • 250 kW
W Africa • 250 kW

0 1 2 3 4 5 6 7 8 9 10 11 12 13 14 15 16 17 18 19 20 21 22 23 24

ENGLISH ▬   ARABIC ⌇⌇⌇   CHINESE ▫▫▫   FRENCH ▬   GERMAN ▬   RUSSIAN ═   SPANISH ▬   OTHER ▬

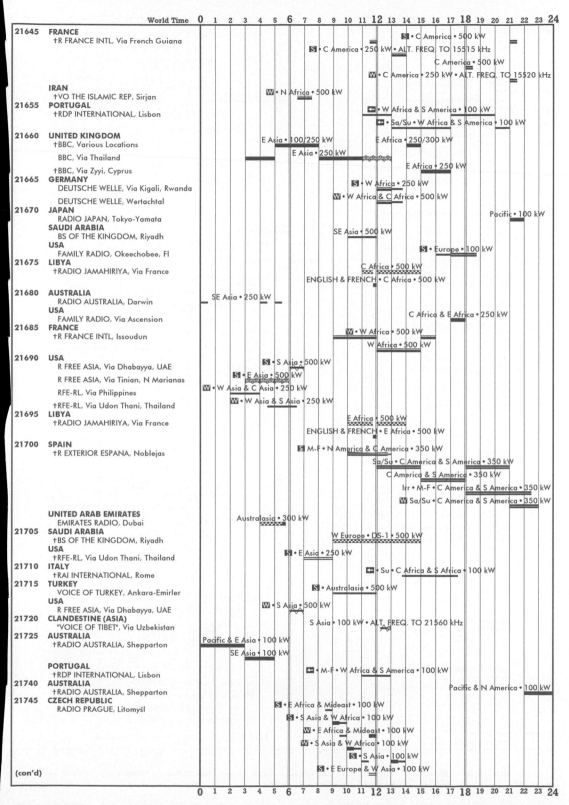

World Time		
21645	**FRANCE**	
	†R FRANCE INTL, Via French Guiana	S•C America•500 kW
		S•C America•250 kW•ALT. FREQ. TO 15515 kHz
		C America•500 kW
		W•C America•250 kW•ALT. FREQ. TO 15520 kHz
	IRAN	
	†VO THE ISLAMIC REP, Sirjan	W•N Africa•500 kW
21655	**PORTUGAL**	
	†RDP INTERNATIONAL, Lisbon	•W Africa & S America•100 kW
		•Sa/Su•W Africa & S America•100 kW
21660	**UNITED KINGDOM**	
	†BBC, Various Locations	E Asia•100/250 kW E Africa•250/300 kW
	BBC, Via Thailand	E Asia•250 kW
	†BBC, Via Zyyi, Cyprus	E Africa•250 kW
21665	**GERMANY**	
	DEUTSCHE WELLE, Via Kigali, Rwanda	S•W Africa•250 kW
	DEUTSCHE WELLE, Wertachtal	W•W Africa & C Africa•500 kW
21670	**JAPAN**	
	RADIO JAPAN, Tokyo-Yamata	Pacific•100 kW
	SAUDI ARABIA	
	BS OF THE KINGDOM, Riyadh	SE Asia•500 kW
	USA	
	FAMILY RADIO, Okeechobee, Fl	S•Europe•100 kW
21675	**LIBYA**	
	†RADIO JAMAHIRIYA, Via France	C Africa•500 kW
		ENGLISH & FRENCH•C Africa•500 kW
21680	**AUSTRALIA**	
	RADIO AUSTRALIA, Darwin	SE Asia•250 kW
	USA	
	FAMILY RADIO, Via Ascension	C Africa & E Africa•250 kW
21685	**FRANCE**	
	†R FRANCE INTL, Issoudun	W•W Africa•500 kW
		W Africa•500 kW
21690	**USA**	
	R FREE ASIA, Via Dhabayya, UAE	S•S Asia•500 kW
	R FREE ASIA, Via Tinian, N Marianas	S•E Asia•500 kW
	RFE-RL, Via Philippines	W•W Asia & C Asia•250 kW
	†RFE-RL, Via Udon Thani, Thailand	W•W Asia & S Asia•250 kW
21695	**LIBYA**	
	†RADIO JAMAHIRIYA, Via France	E Africa•500 kW
		ENGLISH & FRENCH•E Africa•500 kW
21700	**SPAIN**	
	†R EXTERIOR ESPANA, Noblejas	S•M-F•N America & C America•350 kW
		Sa/Su•C America & S America•350 kW
		C America & S America•350 kW
		Irr•M-F•C America & S America•350 kW
		W Sa/Su•C America & S America•350 kW
	UNITED ARAB EMIRATES	
	EMIRATES RADIO, Dubai	Australasia•300 kW
21705	**SAUDI ARABIA**	
	†BS OF THE KINGDOM, Riyadh	W Europe•DS-1•500 kW
	USA	
	†RFE-RL, Via Udon Thani, Thailand	S•E Asia•250 kW
21710	**ITALY**	
	†RAI INTERNATIONAL, Rome	•Su•C Africa & S Africa•100 kW
21715	**TURKEY**	
	VOICE OF TURKEY, Ankara-Emirler	S•Australasia•500 kW
	USA	
	R FREE ASIA, Via Dhabayya, UAE	W•S Asia•500 kW
21720	**CLANDESTINE (ASIA)**	
	"VOICE OF TIBET", Via Uzbekistan	S Asia•100 kW•ALT. FREQ. TO 21560 kHz
21725	**AUSTRALIA**	
	†RADIO AUSTRALIA, Shepparton	Pacific & E Asia•100 kW
		SE Asia•100 kW
	PORTUGAL	
	†RDP INTERNATIONAL, Lisbon	•M-F•W Africa & S America•100 kW
21740	**AUSTRALIA**	
	†RADIO AUSTRALIA, Shepparton	Pacific & N America•100 kW
21745	**CZECH REPUBLIC**	
	RADIO PRAGUE, Litomyšl	S•E Africa & Mideast•100 kW
		S•S Asia & W Africa•100 kW
		W•E Africa & Mideast•100 kW
		W•S Asia & W Africa•100 kW
		S•S Asia•100 kW
		S•E Europe & W Asia•100 kW
(con'd)		

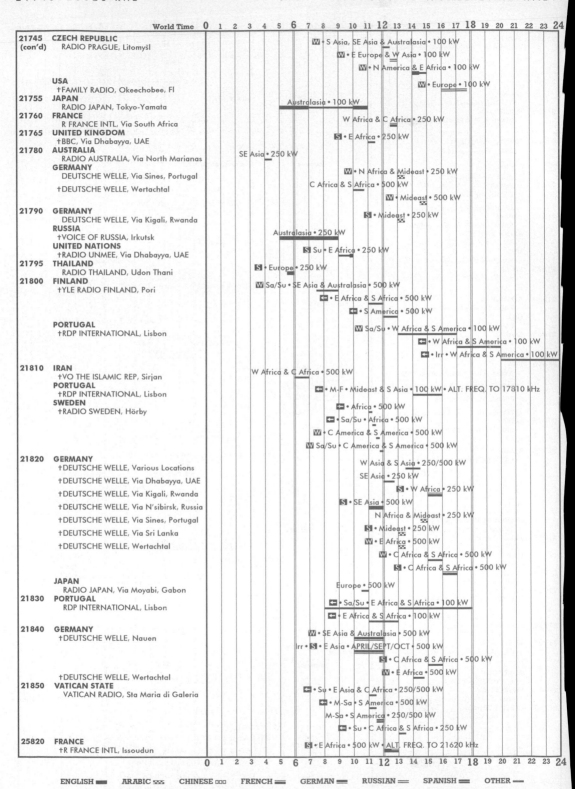

| | World Time | 0 | 1 | 2 | 3 | 4 | 5 | 6 | 7 | 8 | 9 | 10 | 11 | 12 | 13 | 14 | 15 | 16 | 17 | 18 | 19 | 20 | 21 | 22 | 23 | 24 |

21745 CZECH REPUBLIC
(con'd)   RADIO PRAGUE, Litomyšl
- W • S Asia, SE Asia & Australasia • 100 kW
- W • E Europe & W Asia • 100 kW
- W • N America & E Africa • 100 kW
- W • Europe • 100 kW

USA
   †FAMILY RADIO, Okeechobee, Fl
21755 JAPAN
   RADIO JAPAN, Tokyo-Yamata
- Australasia • 100 kW
21760 FRANCE
   R FRANCE INTL, Via South Africa
- W Africa & C Africa • 250 kW
21765 UNITED KINGDOM
   †BBC, Via Dhabayya, UAE
- S • E Africa • 250 kW
21780 AUSTRALIA
   RADIO AUSTRALIA, Via North Marianas
- SE Asia • 250 kW
GERMANY
   DEUTSCHE WELLE, Via Sines, Portugal
- W • N Africa & Mideast • 250 kW
   †DEUTSCHE WELLE, Wertachtal
- C Africa & S Africa • 500 kW
- W • Mideast • 500 kW

21790 GERMANY
   DEUTSCHE WELLE, Via Kigali, Rwanda
- S • Mideast • 250 kW
RUSSIA
   †VOICE OF RUSSIA, Irkutsk
- Australasia • 250 kW
UNITED NATIONS
   †RADIO UNMEE, Via Dhabayya, UAE
- S • Su • E Africa • 250 kW
21795 THAILAND
   RADIO THAILAND, Udon Thani
- S • Europe • 250 kW
21800 FINLAND
   †YLE RADIO FINLAND, Pori
- W Sa/Su • SE Asia & Australasia • 500 kW
- ⊡ • E Africa & S Africa • 500 kW
- ⊡ • S America • 500 kW

PORTUGAL
   †RDP INTERNATIONAL, Lisbon
- W Sa/Su • W Africa & S America • 100 kW
- ⊡ • W Africa & S America • 100 kW
- ⊡ • Irr • W Africa & S America • 100 kW

21810 IRAN
   †VO THE ISLAMIC REP, Sirjan
- W Africa & C Africa • 500 kW
PORTUGAL
   †RDP INTERNATIONAL, Lisbon
- ⊡ • M-F • Mideast & S Asia • 100 kW • ALT. FREQ. TO 17810 kHz
SWEDEN
   †RADIO SWEDEN, Hörby
- ⊡ • Africa • 500 kW
- ⊡ • Sa/Su • Africa • 500 kW
- W • C America & S America • 500 kW
- W Sa/Su • C America & S America • 500 kW

21820 GERMANY
   †DEUTSCHE WELLE, Various Locations
- W Asia & S Asia • 250/500 kW
- SE Asia • 250 kW
   †DEUTSCHE WELLE, Via Dhabayya, UAE
- S • W Africa • 250 kW
   †DEUTSCHE WELLE, Via Kigali, Rwanda
   †DEUTSCHE WELLE, Via N'sibirsk, Russia
- S • SE Asia • 500 kW
   †DEUTSCHE WELLE, Via Sines, Portugal
- N Africa & Mideast • 250 kW
   †DEUTSCHE WELLE, Via Sri Lanka
- S • Mideast • 250 kW
   †DEUTSCHE WELLE, Wertachtal
- W • E Africa • 500 kW
- W • C Africa & S Africa • 500 kW
- S • C Africa & S Africa • 500 kW

JAPAN
   RADIO JAPAN, Via Moyabi, Gabon
- Europe • 500 kW
21830 PORTUGAL
   RDP INTERNATIONAL, Lisbon
- ⊡ • Sa/Su • E Africa & S Africa • 100 kW
- ⊡ • E Africa & S Africa • 100 kW

21840 GERMANY
   †DEUTSCHE WELLE, Nauen
- W • SE Asia & Australasia • 500 kW
- Irr • S • E Asia • APRIL/SEPT/OCT • 500 kW
- S • C Africa & S Africa • 500 kW
- W • E Africa • 500 kW
   †DEUTSCHE WELLE, Wertachtal
21850 VATICAN STATE
   VATICAN RADIO, Sta Maria di Galeria
- ⊡ • Su • E Asia & C Africa • 250/500 kW
- ⊡ • M-Sa • S America • 500 kW
- M-Sa • S America • 250/500 kW
- ⊡ • Su • C Africa & S Africa • 250 kW

25820 FRANCE
   †R FRANCE INTL, Issoudun
- S • E Africa • 500 kW • ALT. FREQ. TO 21620 kHz

| | | 0 | 1 | 2 | 3 | 4 | 5 | 6 | 7 | 8 | 9 | 10 | 11 | 12 | 13 | 14 | 15 | 16 | 17 | 18 | 19 | 20 | 21 | 22 | 23 | 24 |

ENGLISH ▬ ARABIC ⁓⁓ CHINESE ▫▫▫ FRENCH ═ GERMAN ▬ RUSSIAN ═ SPANISH ▬ OTHER ▬